The 9 Competencies and 31 Component Behaviors (EPAS, 2015)	Chapter(s) Where Referenced
Competency 6—Engage with Individuals, Families, Groups, Organizations, and Communities:	1, 2, 4
a. Apply knowledge of human behavior and the social environment, person-in-environment, and other multidisciplinary theoretical frameworks to engage with clients and constituencies	1, 5, 14
b. Use empathy, reflection, and interpersonal skills to effectively engage diverse clients and constituencies	1, 4, 5, 8, 12–14
Competency 7—Assess Individuals, Families, Groups, Organizations, and Communities:	1, 2, 4, 13, 14
a. Collect and organize data, and apply critical thinking to interpret information from clients and constituencies	1–6, 8–16
b. Apply knowledge of human behavior and the social environment, person-in-environment, and other multidisciplinary theoretical frameworks in the analysis of assessment data from clients and constituencies	1, 3–9, 13–16
c. Develop mutually agreed-on intervention goals and objectives based on the critical assessment of strengths, needs, and challenges within clients and constituencies	1, 3–5, 9–16
d. Select appropriate intervention strategies based on the assessment, research knowledge, and values and preferences of clients and constituencies	1, 3–5, 9–16
Competency 8—Intervene with Individuals, Families, Groups, Organizations, and Communities:	1, 2, 4, 13–15
a. Critically choose and implement interventions to achieve practice goals and enhance capacities of clients and constituencies	1–6, 8–16
b. Apply knowledge of human behavior and the social environment, person-in-environment, and other multidisciplinary theoretical frameworks in interventions with clients and constituencies	1, 3–5, 7–9, 13, 14, 16
c. Use inter-professional collaboration as appropriate to achieve beneficial practice outcomes	1, 2, 4, 5, 7–13, 15
d. Negotiate, mediate, and advocate with and on behalf of diverse clients and constituencies	1–13, 15, 16
e. Facilitate effective transitions and endings that advance mutually agreed-on goals	1, 4, 10, 12, 15, 16
Competency 9—Evaluate Practice with Individuals, Families, Groups, Organizations, and Communities:	1, 2, 4
a. Select and use appropriate methods for evaluation of outcomes	1, 4
b. Apply knowledge of human behavior and the social environment, person-in-environment, and other multidisciplinary theoretical frameworks in the evaluation of outcomes	1, 4, 5, 13
c. Critically analyze, monitor, and evaluate intervention and program processes and outcomes	1, 4, 13, 14, 16
d. Apply evaluation findings to improve practice effectiveness at the micro, mezzo, and macro levels	1, 4

TENTH EDITION

Direct Social Work Practice: **Theory and Skills**

DEAN H. HEPWORTH
Professor Emeritus, University of Utah and Arizona State University

RONALD H. ROONEY
University of Minnesota

GLENDA DEWBERRY ROONEY
Augsburg College

KIMBERLY STROM-GOTTFRIED
University of North Carolina at Chapel Hill

CENGAGE
Learning®

Australia • Brazil • Mexico • Singapore • United Kingdom • United States

Direct Social Work Practice: Theory and Skills, **Tenth Edition**

Dean H. Hepworth, Ronald H. Rooney, Glenda Dewberry Rooney, and Kimberly Strom-Gottfried

Product Manager: Julie Martinez

Content Developer: Shannon LeMay-Finn and Michelle Clark

Product Assistant: Stephen Lagos

Marketing Manager: Jennifer Levanduski

Art and Cover Direction, Production Management, and Composition: MPS Limited

Manufacturing Planner: Judy Inouye

Photo and Text Researcher: Lumina Datamatics

Cover Image: Mabry Campbell/Moment/ Getty Images

For product information and technology assistance, contact us at **Cengage Learning Customer & Sales Support, 1-800-354-9706.**

For permission to use material from this text or product, submit all requests online at **www.cengage.com/permissions**. Further permissions questions can be e-mailed to **permissionrequest@cengage.com**.

Library of Congress Control Number: 2015941189

Student Edition:
ISBN: 978-1-305-63380-3

Loose-leaf Edition:
ISBN: 978-1-305-86629-4

Cengage Learning
20 Channel Center Street
Boston, MA 02210
USA

Cengage Learning is a leading provider of customized learning solutions with employees residing in nearly 40 different countries and sales in more than 125 countries around the world. Find your local representative at **www.cengage.com**.

Cengage Learning products are represented in Canada by Nelson Education, Ltd.

To learn more about Cengage Learning Solutions, visit **www.cengage.com**.

Purchase any of our products at your local college store or at our preferred online store **www.cengagebrain.com**.

Printed in the United States of America
Print Number: 01   Print Year: 2016

Brief Contents

Contents

Preface

When we, your authors, teach BSW and MSW students, we are often confronted with the question "What should I do if … ?" The easy (and usually correct) answer is "It depends." How a social worker responds in any given situation *depends* on a variety of factors: the setting in which he or she is working, the client, the nature of the helping relationship that has developed, the advantages and disadvantages of any given action or choice, and so on.

We wrote this book to help answer the "it depends"—to equip you with the knowledge and critical thinking to weigh the factors involved in decisions throughout the helping process, both as a student social worker and as a professional. At first, that process can seem cumbersome. It can be difficult to digest all this new information and recall it as needed during client interactions. This learning process involves becoming acquainted with the concepts in this book, understanding the pros and cons of various choices, becoming familiar with the different variables that affect practice, and using this knowledge and these skills in supervision, in work with colleagues and classmates, and in practice with clients.

As social workers ourselves, we have the utmost respect for the complexity of the work, the power that professionals hold, and the grave situations in which we are entrusted to help others. In this text, we have tried to provide you with a foundation to practice with excellence and integrity in this vital profession. We write this in a context in which many clients of color are fearful about the values and motives of authorities, whether they be police or social service workers. Skills taught in the text include ways to listen effectively, share power, and pursue social justice. An additional context is practice with clients that is trauma informed, and we consider contemporary services to LGBTQ clients, military families, and emerging immigrant populations, among others. The book also includes the context of the Affordable Care Act.

As in previous editions, the text and supporting materials explicitly integrate the related video content, allowing instructors to use the video materials for in-class or homework activities. Adjustments in design and content clearly link the text to student skill development and core competencies specified by CSWE and EPAS (2015). We describe how to construct SOAP notes to assist quality planning and recording of practice. Students and practitioners have been confused about the use of various terms to describe responses that are sensitive to client content and emotion. Sensitive to the current widespread use of the term "reflection," we now use "reflection of emotion" to describe the previous term and "paraphrasing" and "reflection of content" to add dimension to the previous global term "reflection." Additional content has been added on intimate partner violence and work with military families. Practice guidelines are now designed to be less adult-centric and include more appropriate guidance for interviewing children and adolescents. We continue to seek guidelines for practices that are responsive to diversity.

THE STRUCTURE OF THE TEXT

The book has four parts. Part 1 introduces the reader to the social work profession and direct practice and provides an overview of the helping process, including core competencies, the role of evidence-based practice, the domains and roles of social work, and the elements of ethical practice.

Part 2 presents the beginning phase of the helping process, and each chapter includes examples from the videotapes developed for the text. It addresses strategies and skills for building relationships, providing direction and focus in interviews, avoiding common communication errors, and substituting better options. Subsequent chapters in this section address problem and strengths exploration, theories and techniques for individual, family, and group assessment, and the processes involved in goal setting.

Part 3 presents the middle, or goal attainment, phase of the helping process. It describes change-oriented strategies, including updated material on task-centered, crisis intervention, cognitive restructuring, and solution-focused approaches to practice, large-systems change, advocacy, case management, family practice, and group work. Readers learn advanced communication and intervention techniques and common social worker and client barriers to change.

Part 4 deals with the final phase of the helping process, incorporating material on evaluating and terminating social work relationships in an array of circumstances.

ALTERNATIVE CHAPTER ORDER

This book has been structured around phases of practice at systems levels ranging from individual to family to group to macro practice. Some instructors prefer to teach all content about a particular mode of practice in one block. In particular, those instructors whose courses emphasize individual contacts may choose to present chapters in a different order than we have organized them (see Table 1). They may teach content in Chapters 5–9, skip ahead to Chapters 12 and 13, and then delve into Chapters 17 and 18. Similarly, family content can be grouped by using Chapters 10 and 15 together, and group content by using Chapters 11 and 16 together. We have presented the chapters in the book in the current order because we think that presentation of intervention by phases fits a systems perspective better than beginning with a choice of intervention mode.

TABLE 1 Organization of Chapters by Mode of Practice

MODE OF PRACTICE	
Across levels	Chapters 1–4, 19
Individual	Chapters 5–9, 12, 13, 17, 18
Family	Chapters 10, 15
Group	Chapters 11, 16
Macro	Chapter 14

The Empowerment Series: Relationship with the Educational Policy Statement and Accreditation Standards (EPAS), and Professional Competencies

This book is part of the Cengage Learning Empowerment Series and addresses accreditation standards established by the Council on Social Work Education (CSWE). Our intent is to facilitate programs' ability to link content provided in this textbook with expectations for student learning and accomplishment. As is true in almost all learning, students must acquire knowledge before they are expected to apply it to practice situations.

CSWE has identified nine core competencies that are critical for professional practice (CSWE, 2015). For clarity, we have alphabetized in lowercase the practice behaviors under each competency. "Helping Hands" Icons located within paragraphs clearly show the linkage between content in the textbook and specific practice behaviors and competencies. Each icon is labeled with the specific competency that relates directly to the content conveyed in the paragraph. For example, an icon might be labeled EP [Educational Policy] 1, which is the competency "Demonstrate ethical and professional behavior" (CSWE, 2015). Accredited social work programs are required to demonstrate that students have mastered all practice behaviors for competence as specified in the EPAS. (Please refer to www.cswe.org for the EPAS document.)

Corresponding to each icon, "Competency Notes" at the end of each chapter explain the relationship between chapter content and CSWE's competencies. A summary chart of the icons' locations in all chapters and their respective competency or practice behavior is placed in the front matter of the book.

A new Practice Behaviors Workbook is available to instructors and students through MindTap. This workbook includes exercises that provide students with opportunities to develop the practice behaviors in class or as part of their homework, facilitating their mastery over practical aspects of social work and minimizing the need for programs to develop additional assessments.

NEW FEATURES AND RESOURCES FOR THE 10TH EDITION

The 10th edition continues to integrate many videos, demonstrating cross-cultural practice, engagement with an adolescent, sessions from the middle of the helping process, and motivational interviewing.

Chapter 1

In this chapter we included an updated presentation of evidence-based practice, reframed the presentation of social work challenges to opportunities, revised the values section, and presented the case study more quickly in the chapter. We included a link to a George Will article commenting on an earlier version of the text.

Chapter 2

We included more details to explain the social work practice framework. A brief discussion of the micro, mezzo, and macro systems is included, and we added a comment on technology in social work. We added to the definition of clinical social work practice and direct social work practice and added more detail to the discussions of social work roles.

Chapter 3

Concepts were added pertaining to cultural competence throughout the chapter. For example, interior decorations that are sensitive to diverse populations are discussed in the section on physical conditions of the interview.

Chapter 4

This chapter features extra attention to the maintenance of professional boundaries in online contexts and the importance of professional self-awareness and self-regulation. Ethics in cases of interpersonal violence and other challenging venues have been added.

Chapter 5

The empathy scale was revised to reflect a bottom level for "no empathy demonstrated." The list of affective words was modified to make it more contemporary. Recent theory and research on empathy was included, and guidelines for self-disclosure were revised.

Chapter 6

Use of the term "reflection" was expanded to include both reflection of emotion and reflection of content, replacing the former term "paraphrasing." There is more content aimed at interviewing children and adolescents. Guidelines for interviewing include expanded attention to strengths and resources.

Chapter 7

This chapter now includes a short discussion on the importance of putting away cell phones in the section on nonverbal behaviors. Throughout the chapter we discuss self-awareness and self-correction when errors are noticed. We added double-barreled questions and cognitive bias to the list of counterproductive patterns of communication.

Chapter 8

Chapter 8 has been updated to include a more comprehensive section addressing the treatment of children and adolescents as well as a section highlighting important changes from DSM-4 to DSM-5.

Chapter 9

Chapter 9 now includes greater detail regarding the collection of data for developmental assessments as well as additional examples of assessments and documentation. In addition, the issue of elder misuse of drugs is addressed and changes from DSM-4 to DSM-5 are discussed.

Chapter 10

Chapter 10 has been reorganized and adds new content that will help social work students integrate family systems assessments into their practice. It includes expanded attention to self-awareness and practice with diverse families and a detailed articulation of a family systems framework for assessment of family strengths and adaptive capacity. The chapter closes with a description of three assessment strategies, including the use of circular questions, genograms, and standardized assessment scales.

Chapter 11

This edition features expanded examples of group types and a deeper discussion of task groups. A new section has been added to address single-session groups. Other sections have been streamlined, and contemporary issues, such as the use of devices in sessions and online contact outside of group, have been included.

Chapter 12

Chapter 12 discusses the purpose and function of goals and the process involved in goal development with voluntary clients, involuntary clients, and minors. General and specific tasks or objectives are discussed as instrumental strategies for goal attainment. Revisions include the use of video and case examples to demonstrate the process of developing goals. Each example demonstrates the link between goals and a target, and the subsequent development of general and specific tasks.

Sample contracts are provided, and methods for monitoring and measuring the progress and outcome of goals are discussed.

Chapter 13

Chapter 13 provides students with comprehensive knowledge and skills of evidence-based intervention strategies and procedures. Case and video case examples illustrate the application of each strategy. Trauma-informed care and its principles and importance in work with clients is introduced in this edition. The fit between trauma-informed care and the values and principles of social work practice is discussed. Resources intended to further knowledge and understanding of the prevalence of client trauma are presented at the end of the chapter.

Chapter 14

Chapter 14 provides a condensed foundation for understanding macro practice. Micro to macro assessment questions and problem-solving strategies are emphasized, as is the connection between micro and macro concerns. Case examples illustrate the shift from case to cause in social work practice with diverse clients and target problems. A social justice lens is adopted in this chapter as a framework for understanding social work advocacy efforts. New content in this chapter considers the social worker's role as a policy advocate, in which the macro-level change effort focuses on organization practices and policies that influence the environment experienced by clients.

Chapter 15

Chapter 15 was revised to conceptualize social work with families in the diverse settings in which social workers routinely encounter families, in addition to traditional family therapy settings and programs. Moreover, the chapter presents intervention skills that are at the heart of most contemporary evidence-based approaches to social work with families. Interventions are organized into first- and second-order change strategies, and new content was included to support skill-training interventions, as well as to emphasize the continuity between intervention strategies presented in earlier chapters and their application to social work with families.

Chapter 16

This chapter has been more closely integrated with Chapter 11. It has an expanded and reorganized section on task groups, a new section on single-session groups, and more detailed coverage of technology and groups.

Chapter 17

This chapter links to earlier coverage of empathy and includes a review of new research on empathy. It adds cultural bias as a barrier to interpretation. Many examples have been revised and adapted, including new skill development examples. The decision about when interpretation is appropriate has been clarified.

Chapter 18

Chapter 18 makes use of case examples to identify and resolve relations dynamics between the social worker and clients. A video case example demonstrates motivational interviewing as a strategy to assist clients in the change effort.

Chapter 19

This chapter has new sections on avoiding treatment dropouts, endings in short-term therapy such as crisis and single-session services, and the effects of endings on students. There is also information on practical, hybrid models of evaluation that can be adopted in an array of agency settings.

INSTRUCTOR ANCILLARIES
MindTap

MindTap for *Direct Social Work Practice: Theory and Skills* engages and empowers students to produce their best work—consistently. By seamlessly integrating course material with videos, activities, apps, and much more, MindTap creates a unique learning path that fosters increased comprehension and efficiency.

For students:

- MindTap delivers real-world relevance with activities and assignments that help students build critical thinking and analytic skills that will transfer to other courses and their professional lives.
- MindTap helps students stay organized and efficient with a single destination that reflects what's important to the instructor, along with the tools students need to master the content.
- MindTap empowers and motivates students with information that shows where they stand at all times—both individually and compared to the highest performers in class.

Additionally, for instructors, MindTap allows you to:

- Control what content students see and when they see it with a learning path that can be used as is or matched to your syllabus exactly.
- Create a unique learning path of relevant readings, multimedia, and activities that move students up the learning taxonomy from basic knowledge and comprehension to analysis, application, and critical thinking.
- Integrate your own content into the MindTap Reader using your own documents or pulling from sources like RSS feeds, YouTube videos, websites, Google Docs, and more.
- Use powerful analytics and reports that provide a snapshot of class progress, time in course, engagement, and completion.

In addition to the benefits of the platform, Mind-Tap for *Direct Social Work Practice: Theory and Skills* includes:

- Helper Studio, an interactive video case in which students respond as if they were the social worker.
- Video examples demonstrating skills and concepts presented in the text.
- Case studies to help students apply chapter content.

Online Instructor's Manual

The Instructor's Manual (IM) contains a variety of resources to aid instructors in preparing and presenting text material in a manner that meets their personal preferences and course needs. It presents chapter-by-chapter suggestions and resources to enhance and facilitate learning.

Online Test Bank

For assessment support, the updated test bank includes true/false, multiple-choice, matching, short answer, and essay questions for each chapter.

Online PowerPoint

These vibrant Microsoft® PowerPoint® lecture slides for each chapter assist you with your lecture by providing concept coverage using images, figures, and tables directly from the textbook.

ACKNOWLEDGMENTS

We want to express our thanks and admiration for Dean Hepworth, a social work educator and the first author of this text, for his inspiration and example in developing a text that would help students become more effective practitioners.

In addition, we want to thank the following colleagues for their help in providing useful comments and suggestions. We have been supported by members of our writers' groups, including Laurel Bidwell, Mike Chovanec, Elena Izaksonas, Kari Fletcher, Catherine Marrs Fuchsel, Lance Peterson, Pa Der Vang, and Nancy Rodenborg. Research assistants Aileen Aylward and Alyssa Ventimiglia Elliott conducted comprehensive literature reviews, tracked bibliographic changes, and reviewed drafts with keen eyes. We also want to thank Miriam Itzkowitz, Richard Coleman, Mary Vang Her, Michele Gricus, and Hugh Armstrong for their roles in creating new videos for the textbook. Finally, we are grateful to our students—the users of this text— and social workers in the field for their suggestions, case examples, and encouragement.

This edition could not have been completed without the support, inspiration, and challenge of our colleagues, friends, and families, including George Gottfried, Lola Dewberry, and Chris Rooney. We want to remember in this edition Louis DuBary, Glenda's brother, a social worker who spent his career as an advocate for youth both as a professional and as a volunteer.

Finally, we want to express special appreciation to Julie Martinez, Shannon LeMay-Finn, Jitendra Kumar, and the rest of the team from Cengage for their responsiveness, support, expertise, and patience.

About the Authors

Dean H. Hepworth is Professor Emeritus at the School of Social Work, Arizona State University, Tempe Arizona, and the University of Utah. Dean has extensive practice experience in individual psychotherapy and marriage and family therapy. Dean was the lead author and active in the production of the first four editions, and he is the co-author of *Improving Therapeutic Communication*. He is now retired and lives in Phoenix, Arizona.

Ronald H. Rooney is a Professor at the School of Social Work, University of Minnesota. Dr. Rooney is also the author of *Strategies for Work with Involuntary Clients*. His experience includes practice, consultation, and training in child welfare and work with involuntary clients. He has made international presentations in Canada, Great Britain, Holland, Korea, Taiwan, and Australia.

Glenda Dewberry Rooney is a Professor Emeritus, Department of Social Work, Augsburg College, Minneapolis, Minnesota. She taught undergraduate and graduate direct practice courses, ethics, research, and organization and administration. Her practice experience includes child welfare, mental health, and work with families and children. In addition to her practice experience, she has been involved with agencies concerned with children, youth, and families as a trainer and as clinical, program, and management consultant, and in community-based research projects. Active in retirement, Dr. Rooney continues as an advocate for child welfare policies and practices that strengthen and support children and families. She was one of the statewide leaders involved with the education efforts and enrollment periods of the Affordable Care Act.

Dr. Kim Strom-Gottfried is the Smith P. Theimann Jr. Distinguished Professor of Ethics and Professional Practice at the UNC–Chapel Hill School of Social Work. Dr. Strom-Gottfried teaches in the areas of direct practice, higher education, and management. Her scholarly interests involve ethics, moral courage, and social work education. She is the author of *Straight Talk about Professional Ethics*, *The Ethics of Practice with Minors*, and the forthcoming book *Cultivating Courage*. Dr. Strom-Gottfried is also the coauthor of the texts *Best of Boards* and *Teaching Social Work Values and Ethics: A Curriculum Resource*.

Craig Schwalbe, MSW, PhD, is an Associate Professor and Associate Dean for Academic Affairs at the Columbia University School of Social Work. Dr. Schwalbe began his career with more than 10 years of direct practice in child welfare and mental health agency settings. His current scholarship focuses on the development of evidence-based strategies to foster successful juvenile justice interventions on behalf of court-involved youths. He was the recipient of the William T. Grant Scholars award in 2009, which funded a study of success and failure on probation, and co-led a UNICEF-funded international development effort to design and implement juvenile diversion programs for delinquent youths in Jordan. His current scholarship promotes community-based alternatives to detention and incarceration for adolescent juvenile offenders.

Pa Der Vang, PhD, is an Assistant Professor in the St. Catherine University/St. Thomas University School of Social Work in St. Paul, Minnesota. She earned her master's and PhD in Social Work from the University of Minnesota–Twin Cities. Her area of research involves refugees and immigrants. Her area of teaching is primarily direct practice with individuals, families, and groups.

Caroline B. R. Evans is a Research Associate at the University of North Carolina at Chapel Hill. She is currently working on a federally funded youth violence prevention initiative. Her practice experience includes extensive work with the Latino/Hispanic population in a hospital setting and in various outpatient community mental health settings. She has also worked with children and adolescents involved with the juvenile court system.

Introduction

Part 1 of this book provides you with a background of concepts, values, historical perspectives, and information about systems. This information will, in turn, prepare you to learn the specific direct practice skills described in Part 2.

Chapter 1 introduces you to the social work profession; explains its context, mission, purposes, and values; and describes how systems perspectives can guide you in conceptualizing your work.

Chapter 2 elaborates on the roles played by social workers, including the distinctions made between clinical and direct social work practice, and presents a philosophy of direct practice.

Chapter 3 offers an overview of the helping process, including exploration, implementation, and termination.

Finally, Chapter 4 introduces the cardinal values and ethical concerns underlying social work.

CHAPTER 1

The Challenges and Opportunities of Social Work

Chapter Overview

This chapter presents a context for social work practice. After completing this chapter, you will be able to:

- Understand the context, mission, and purposes and opportunities of social work services.
- Identify the value perspectives that guide social workers.
- Appreciate the role of systems and ecological concepts for understanding the interaction of individuals and families with their environments.
- Describe competencies that you will be expected to achieve in your academic career.
- Reflect on our perspective on diversity that will guide how we present issues.

EPAS Competencies in Chapter 1

This chapter will provide you with the information you need to meet several Educational Policy and Accreditation Standards (EPAS) competencies—a set of nine standards or competencies centered on an educational format that prescribes attention to outcome performance (CSWE, 2014). The goal of aligning social work education to such competencies is that social workers will be self-reflective, value guided, and able to think critically while utilizing knowledge and skills. The following are the competencies we cover in this chapter:

- Competency 1: Demonstrate Ethical and Professional Behavior
- Competency 2: Engage Diversity and Difference in Practice
- Competency 3: Advance Human Rights and Social, Economic, and Environmental Justice
- Competency 4: Engage in Practice-Informed Research and Research-Informed Practice
- Competency 5: Engage in Policy Practice
- Competency 6: Engage with Individuals, Families, Groups, Organizations, and Communities
- Competency 7: Assess Individuals, Families, Groups, Organizations, and Communities
- Competency 8: Intervene with Individuals, Families, Groups, Organizations, and Communities
- Competency 9: Evaluate Practice with Individuals, Families, Groups, Organizations, and Communities

THE CONTEXT OF SOCIAL WORK

Let's start our discussion of social work by examining the context of the profession. Social work seeks to promote human and community well-being, enhance quality of life, and promote social and economic justice and the elimination of poverty (EPAS, 2015). Toward these objectives, social work practice includes both opportunities and challenges for assisting individuals, families, groups, organizations, and communities. These opportunities and challenges exist in a context that has been relatively stable over time but has also changed in the recent past. For example, many social workers continue to practice with clients at the lower levels of the social economic ladder, although those clients now have access to the Patient Care and Affordable Care Act (PCACA), commonly known as Obamacare. Meanwhile, long-lasting concerns among African Americans about whether police act more to serve them or harass them now exist in a context in which FBI Director James Comey has acknowledged a legacy of poor treatment of African Americans by police and unconscious bias, recognizing that poverty and educational gaps often bring that community and police together in dangerous circumstances (Comey, 2015). In addition, differences of opinion remain regarding same-sex marriage, while at the same time more and more states made it legal within their borders, and the Supreme Court has now established it as a right in all states. A national resolution of a debate about the proper role of immigration has still not occurred, creating challenges for social workers who provide services to people who are undocumented.

Meanwhile, social work practice continues to be provided in organizational and resource settings that are fraught with limitations. In addition, social workers work in many different settings—governmental agencies, schools, health care centers, family and child welfare agencies, mental health centers, business and industry, correctional settings, and private practices, to name a few. Social workers also work with people of all ages, races, ethnic groups, socioeconomic levels, religions, sexual orientations, and abilities. Social workers themselves variously describe their work as rewarding, frustrating, satisfying, discouraging, stressful, and, most of all, challenging (Pooler, Wolfer, & Freeman, 2014).

Clearly, the context of social work presents both challenges and opportunities. This book will assist you in developing practice skills, values, and knowledge so that you can be helpful to individuals, families, and groups in any social work setting. This chapter begins with a case example that highlights several aspects of social work practice and provides the context for concepts we will introduce in the chapter.

Many social workers practice in settings, such as schools, where they perform dual roles, protecting both the community at large and vulnerable individuals, in addition to playing other supportive roles (Trotter, 2006). No matter where they are employed, social workers are influenced by the social work value of self-determination for their clients. For this reason, in addition to exploring school attendance issues with Mrs. Ramirez and her children, Tobias addressed Mrs. Ramirez's other concerns.

EP 2, 3, 6, 7, and 8

Of course, social workers are not the only helping professionals who provide direct services to clients in need. They have a special interest, however, in helping empower members of oppressed groups (Parsons, 2002). Indeed, as a profession, social workers are committed to the pursuit of social justice for poor, disadvantaged, disenfranchised, and oppressed people (Carniol, 1992; Finn & Jacobson, 2003; Marsh, 2005; Pelton, 2001; Van Wormer, 2002). In this case, in addition to seeing his client, Mrs. Ramirez, as a parent struggling with school attendance issues, Tobias also saw her as a client experiencing challenges possibly related to issues in the United States surrounding undocumented immigrants (Cleaveland, 2010; Padilla et al., 2008). Interestingly, a law passed by the U.S. House of Representatives in 2005, but not in the Senate, would have made it a crime for service providers such as Tobias to assist undocumented immigrants. However, according to the National Association of Social Workers (NASW) Immigration Toolkit (NASW, 2006, p. 4), "the plight of refugees and immigrants must be considered on the basis of human values and needs rather than on the basis of an ideological struggle related to foreign policy." The contrast between these two positions suggests that social workers grapple with issues of social justice in their everyday practice. As a social worker, Tobias obviously could not personally resolve the uncertain situation of undocumented immigrants. However, he could work with Mrs. Ramirez and local health institutions to explore possible solutions to her problems.

Note that in this case example, Mrs. Ramirez did not seek assistance herself. Rather, she was referred by school staff because of her children's poor school attendance. She would therefore be referred to as a **legally mandated client** who receives services under the threat of a court order. Those clients who *themselves apply* for

CASE EXAMPLE

Marta Ramirez was referred to child welfare services because her two elementary-school-age children had more than seven days of unexcused absences from school during the term, the standard for educational neglect in her state. When Tobias, a child welfare social worker, met with Mrs. Ramirez, he found that the children had missed similar amounts of time when they had lived in another state. There had not been earlier investigations, however, as legal standards for educational neglect were different in the previous state. Mrs. Ramirez noted that her children had been frequently ill with "flu and asthma." She also said that the children did not feel comfortable at the school, and they felt that the teachers were mean to them because they were Hispanic. In addition, Mrs. Ramirez had sustained a work-related back injury that limited her ability to get out of bed some mornings. As an undocumented immigrant, Mrs. Ramirez was ineligible for the surgery she needed. Finally, she acknowledged experiencing depression and anxiety.

Tobias shared with Mrs. Ramirez the reason for the referral under statute and asked for her perspective on school attendance. He explained that child welfare workers are called on to assist families in having their children educated. He also asked about how things were going for Mrs. Ramirez and her family in their community. In doing so, Tobias explained his dual roles of (1) responding to the law violation by statute and (2) helping families address issues of concern to them.

Mrs. Ramirez acknowledged that her children's school attendance had been sporadic. She attributed this to their illnesses, their feeling unwelcome in the school, and her own health difficulties that inhibited her in getting the children ready for school.

Tobias asked Mrs. Ramirez if she would like to receive assistance in problem solving, both about how to get her children to school and how to help them have a better educational experience there. In addition, although health issues were not served directly by his child welfare agency, Tobias offered to explore linkages with the medical field to address Mrs. Ramirez's health and depression concerns.

---

services are referred to as **voluntary clients**. Many potential clients, including those like Mrs. Ramirez, become more voluntary if their own concerns are explicitly addressed as part of the social work assessment. Many potential clients fall between the two extremes of legally mandated and voluntary clients, as they are neither legally coerced nor seeking a service themselves (Trotter, 2006). These potential clients, who often experience nonlegal pressures from family members, teachers, and referral sources, are known as **nonvoluntary clients** (R. H. Rooney, 2009).

 With each type of client (legally mandated, voluntary, and nonvoluntary), social work assessments include three facets:

EP 7

1. Exploration of multiple concerns expressed by potential clients
2. Circumstances that might involve legally mandated intervention or concerns about health or safely
3. Other potential problems that emerge from the assessment

Such assessments also seek to reveal strengths and potential resources. For example, Mrs. Ramirez's potential strengths and resources include her determination that her children have a better life than their parents, as well as other community and spiritual support systems, both locally and in her home country of Mexico. Those potential resources must be assessed in the context of challenges, both internal and external, such as the lack of a health care safety net for undocumented immigrants and Mrs. Ramirez's own medical and psychological concerns.

THE MISSION OF SOCIAL WORK

The perspectives taken by social workers in their professional roles will influence how their clients' concerns are conceptualized and addressed. According to the NASW, "the primary mission of the social work profession is to enhance human well-being and help meet the basic human needs of all people with particular attention to the needs and empowerment of people who are vulnerable, oppressed, and living in poverty" (NASW, 2008a). The International Federation of Social Workers (IFSW) defines the purpose of social work as including the promotion of social change and the empowerment and liberation of people to enhance well-being (IFSW, 2000, p. 1). Comparisons of the mission of social work in the United States to the international definition note the shared focus on marginalized peoples and empowerment but add an emphasis on global and cultural sensitivity (Bidgood, Holosko, & Taylor, 2003).

In this book, we will delineate the core elements that lie at the heart of social work wherever it is practiced. These core elements can be classified into two dimensions: purposes of the profession and core competencies, where core competencies include characteristic knowledge, values, and practice behaviors (CSWE, 2015, p. 1). Let's now turn to the purposes of social work and the nine core competencies.

THE PURPOSES OF SOCIAL WORK

Social work practitioners help clients move toward specific objectives. The means of accomplishing those objectives, however, vary based on the unique circumstances of each client. Even so, all social workers share common goals that constitute the purpose and objectives of the profession. These goals unify the profession and help members avoid developing narrow perspectives that are limited to particular practice settings. To best serve their clients, social workers must be willing to assume responsibilities and engage in actions that expand upon the functions of specific social agencies and their designated individual roles as staff members. For example, Tobias, the child welfare social worker who met with Mrs. Ramirez, assessed her issues and concerns and went beyond the child protection mission of the child welfare setting.

EP 3

According to the Council on Social Work Education (CSWE), a key competency of the social work profession is to advance human rights and social and economic justice. **Social justice** refers to the creation of social institutions that support the welfare of individuals and groups (Center for Economic and Social Justice, n.d.). **Economic justice** refers to those aspects of social justice that relate to economic well-being, such as a livable wage, pay equity, nondiscrimination in employment, and social security.

In 2007, the columnist George Will and a group of conservative scholars charged that the NASW social work Code of Ethics, as well as the authors of a previous edition of this book, prescribed political orthodoxy in violation of freedom of speech and in opposition to critical thinking (NASW, 2007; Will, 2007). While support for social and economic justice as national priorities ebbs and flows in the U.S. political landscape, the social work profession supports these goals at all times as part of its core mission. It is not relevant to the profession whether the political majority in such times label themselves as liberal, conservative, green, independent, or otherwise. Social workers ally with those political groups that benefit the oppressed groups who form their core constituencies. Social workers therefore seek to promote social and economic justice for both Americans and immigrants with or without documentation. As such, in our case example, the prevention of conditions that limit human rights and quality of life guides Tobias to take seriously the allegation that Mrs. Ramirez and her family have not been made to feel welcome at the school. Indeed, with national priorities of raising testing scores for reading and writing, attention to the needs of those who speak English as a second language may be in conflict with the goal of increasing test scores.

The purposes outlined also suggest that Tobias might assist Mrs. Ramirez and her family in a variety of other ways to meet their needs. Those ways include the creation of policies to find solutions to the health needs of immigrants without documents. Social workers perform preventive, restorative, and remedial functions in pursuit of this purpose:

- **Prevention** involves the timely provision of services to vulnerable persons, promoting social functioning before problems develop. It includes programs and activities such as family planning, well-baby clinics, parent education, premarital and preretirement counseling, and marital enrichment programs (Pomeroy & Steiker, 2012).
- **Restoration** seeks to restore functioning that has been impaired by physical or mental difficulties. Included in this group of clients are persons with varying degrees of paralysis caused by severe spinal injury, individuals afflicted with chronic mental illness, persons with developmental disabilities, persons with deficient educational backgrounds, and individuals with many other types of disability.
- **Remediation** entails the elimination or amelioration of existing social problems. Many potential

clients in this category are similar to Mrs. Ramirez in that they are referred by others, such as the school system, family members, neighbors, or doctors, who have perceived a need.

In addition, the Educational Policy and Accreditation Standards (EPAS) affirm the commitment of social programs to the core values of the profession: service, social justice, dignity and worth of the person, importance of human relationships, integrity, competence, human rights, and scientific inquiry (CSWE, 2015; NASW, 2008a).

SOCIAL WORK VALUES

EP 1

All professions have value preferences that give purpose and direction to their practitioners. Indeed, the purpose and objectives of social work and other professions come from their respective value systems. Professional values, however, are not separate from societal values. Rather, professions espouse selected societal values. Society, in turn, sanctions the activities of professions through supportive legislation, funding, delegation of responsibility for certain societal functions, and mechanisms for ensuring that those functions are adequately discharged. Because a profession is linked to certain societal values, it tends to serve as society's conscience with respect to those particular values.

Values represent strongly held beliefs about how the world should be, about how people should normally behave, and about what the preferred conditions of life are. Broad societal values in the United States are reflected in the Declaration of Independence, the Constitution, and the laws of the land, which declare and ensure certain rights of the people. In addition, societal values are reflected in governmental entities and programs designed to safeguard the rights of people and to promote the common good. Interpretations of values and rights, however, are not always uniform. Consider, for example, the heated national debates over the right of women to have abortions; the controversy over the rights of gays and lesbians to enjoy the benefits of marriage; and conflicts between advocates of gun control and those espousing individual rights. These debates continue despite the fact that same-sex marriage has now been legalized, for example. Similarly, national concern over gun control and safety contends with concerns over constitutional protections.

The values of the social work profession also reflect strongly held beliefs about the rights of people to free choice and opportunity. They recognize the preferred conditions of life that enhance people's welfare, ways that members of the profession should view and treat people, preferred goals for people, and ways in which those goals should be reached. We next consider five values and purposes that guide social work education. These five values are italicized, and the content that follows each is our commentary.

1. *Social workers' professional relationships are built on regard for individual worth and dignity and are advanced by mutual participation, acceptance, confidentiality, honesty, and responsible handling of conflict.* This value is reflected in several parts of the NASW Code of Ethics. The code states: "Social workers' primary goal is to help people in need" (NASW, 2008a). That is, service to others is elevated above self-interest; social workers should therefore use their knowledge, values, and skills to help people in need and to address social problems. The code also states that social workers should "respect the inherent dignity and worth of the person." Every person is unique and has inherent worth; therefore, social workers' interactions with people as they pursue and utilize resources should enhance their dignity and individuality, enlarge their competence, and increase their problem-solving and coping abilities.

People who receive social work services are often overwhelmed by their circumstances and have exhausted their coping resources. Many feel stressed by a multitude of problems. In addition to helping clients reduce their stress level, social workers aid clients in many other ways: They help them view their difficulties from a fresh perspective, consider various remedial alternatives, foster awareness of strengths, mobilize both active and latent coping resources, enhance self-awareness, and teach problem-solving strategies and interpersonal skills.

Social workers perform these functions while recognizing "the central importance of human relationships" (NASW, 2008a). Social workers therefore engage clients as partners in purposeful efforts to promote, restore, maintain, and enhance the clients' well-being. This value is reflected in yet another Code of Ethics principle: "Social workers behave in a trustworthy manner." This principle suggests that social workers practice consistently with the profession's mission, values, and ethical standards, and that they promote ethical practices in the organizations with which they are affiliated (NASW, 2008a).

2. *Social workers respect the individual's right to make independent decisions and to participate actively in the helping process.* People have a right to freedom as long as they do not infringe on the rights of others. Therefore, transactions with people who are seeking and utilizing resources should enhance their independence and self-determination. Too often in the past, social workers and other helping professionals focused on "deficit, disease, and dysfunction" (Cowger, 1992). The attention currently devoted by social workers to client empowerment and strengths means that social workers assist clients in increasing their personal potential and political power such that clients can improve their life situation (Krogsrud, Miley, O'Melia, & Dubois, 2013; Parsons, 2002; Saleebey, 2006). Consistent with this value, this book incorporates an empowerment and strength-oriented perspective for working with clients. Chapter 13 focuses on skills designed to enhance empowerment and capacity for independent action.

3. *Social workers are committed to assisting clients to obtain needed resources.* The social worker's commitment to client self-determination and empowerment is hollow if clients lack access to the resources necessary to overcome their problems and achieve their goals (Hartman, 1993). Because people such as Mrs. Ramirez from our case example often know little about available resources, social workers must act as brokers by referring people to resource systems such as public legal services, health care agencies, child welfare divisions, mental health centers, centers for elderly persons, and family counseling agencies. Some individual clients or families may require goods and services from many different providers and may lack the language facility, physical or mental capacity, experience, or skills needed to avail themselves of these goods and services. Social workers then may assume the role of case managers; that is, they may not only provide direct services but also assume responsibility for connecting the client to diverse resources and ensuring that the client receives needed services in a timely fashion.

Clients sometimes need resource systems that are not available. In these cases, social workers must act as program developers by creating and organizing new resource systems. Examples of such efforts include working with citizens and public officials to arrange transportation to health care agencies for the elderly, persons with disabilities, and indigent people; developing neighborhood organizations to campaign for better educational and recreational programs; organizing tenants to assert their rights to landlords and housing authorities for improved housing and sanitation; and organizing support groups, skill development groups, and self-help groups to assist people in coping with difficult problems of living.

Social workers also frequently perform the role of facilitator or enabler to enhance access to resources. For example, they may enhance communication among family members; coordinate efforts of teachers, school counselors, and social workers in assisting troubled students; help groups provide maximal support to their members; open channels of communication between coworkers; include patients or inmates in the governance of institutions; facilitate teamwork among members of different disciplines in hospitals and mental health centers; and provide for consumer input into agency policy-making boards.

4. *Social workers strive to make social institutions more humane and responsive to human needs.* Although many social workers primarily provide direct service, they also have a responsibility to work toward improving clients' quality of life by promoting policies and legislation that enhance their clients' physical and social environments. For example, the problems of individuals, families, groups, and neighborhoods can often be prevented (or at least ameliorated) by implementing laws and policies that prohibit contamination of the physical environment and enrich both physical and social environments. Therefore, social workers should not limit themselves to remedial activities but rather should seek out causes of problems and sponsor or support efforts aimed at improving their clients' environments.

5. *Social workers engage diversity and difference in practices.* Social workers perform their services with populations that are characterized by great diversity, including the intersection of dimensions such as "age, class, culture, disability, ethnicity, gender, gender identity and expression, immigration status, political ideology, race, religion, sex and sexual orientation, religion, physical or mental ability, and national origin"

EP 2

(CSWE, 2015). NASW's Code of Ethics requires social workers to have a knowledge base about and recognize strengths of their clients' cultures and deliver services that are sensitive to those cultures (NASW, 2008a). Social workers must therefore be informed about and respectful of differences. Social workers must also continually update their knowledge about the strengths and resources associated with individuals from diverse groups to increase the sensitivity and effectiveness of the services they provide to those clients. An increasing number of social workers are themselves members of these diverse populations. They face the challenge of working effectively with both clients and agency staff from the majority culture as well as persons from their own groups.

EP 1

Turning the five values just described into reality should be the mutual responsibility of individual citizens and of society. Society should foster conditions and provide opportunities for citizens to participate in policy-making processes. Citizens, in turn, should fulfill their responsibilities to society by actively participating in those processes.

Considered individually, these five values are not unique to social work. Their unique combination, however, differentiates social work from other professions. Considered in their entirety, these values make it clear that social work's identity derives from its connection with the institution of social welfare. According to Gilbert (1977), **social welfare** represents a special helping mechanism devised to aid those who suffer from the variety of ills found in industrial society: "Whenever other major institutions, be they familial, religious, economic, or educational in nature, fall short in their helping and resource providing functions, social welfare spans the gap" (p. 402).

For example, the ideal social work practitioner is a warm, caring, open, and responsible person who safeguards the confidentiality of information disclosed by clients. Because you, the reader, have chosen to enter the field of social work, most of your personal values probably coincide with the cardinal values espoused by the majority of social work practitioners.

However, your personal values may conflict with professional values. For example, some social workers have personal and/or religious beliefs that homosexuality is an unhealthy choice, not a natural, perhaps genetic, circumstance. In EPAS Competency 2, the competent social worker is expected to understand how diversity and difference shape human experience and form human identity. Among those factors are gender identity and sexual orientation. Hence the personal value that some social workers might hold regarding sexual orientation must be superseded by the professional commitment to understanding diversity and difference.

Conflicts between the personal and/or professional values of the social worker and the personal values of a client or group sometimes arise. Not infrequently, students (and even seasoned social workers) experience conflicts over value-laden, problematic situations such as incest, infidelity, rape, child neglect or abuse, spousal abuse, and criminal behavior. Because social workers encounter these and other problems typically viewed by the public as appalling, and because personal values inevitably shape the social worker's attitudes, perceptions, feelings, and responses to clients, it is vital that social workers remain flexible and nonjudgmental in their work. It is therefore vital that you be aware of your own values, recognize how they fit with the profession's values, and assess how they may affect clients whose values differ from your own or whose behavior offends you. It is particularly important that you become aware of your own values because social workers often have opportunities and power that many clients do not possess and may therefore inadvertently impose their own values on their clients.

EPAS COMPETENCIES

In this chapter, we will introduce the nine competencies of EPAS and state them in terms of what social work graduates should be able to do when they have completed their course of study. Please don't feel apprehensive about whether you are capable of performing these competencies now. It will be your task and that of your educational program to prepare you to reach these competencies by the time you graduate. While each of these competencies will be covered in greater detail in later chapters, the following sections summarize the main points of each competency.

EPAS Competency 1

This competency requires that social workers understand the value base and ethical standards of the profession, as well as relevant laws and regulations that may affect

EP 1

social work practice at various levels. In addition, this competency requires that social workers understand frameworks of ethical decision making and how to apply principles of critical thinking to those frameworks in practice, research, and policy. Social workers must also recognize their own personal values, the distinction between personal and professional values, and how their personal experiences and reactions influence their professional judgment and behavior. For example, if Tobias from our case example had any personal values that might impede his work with Mrs. Ramirez and her children, he would take care that his professional values supersede those personal values.

Note that this competency requires that ethical and professional behavior be understood in the context of the profession's history, its mission, and the roles and responsibilities of social workers. It is understood that learning continues after graduation through lifelong learning, in which social workers are committed to continually updating their skills to ensure they are relevant and effective. According to this competency, social workers also must understand emerging forms of technology and the ethical use of technology in social work practice. Hence, social workers must use technology such as voice messages, emails, and texts mindfully and responsibly in ways that protect client confidentiality.

Social workers engage in a variety of practice behaviors to fulfill this competency. For example, they make ethical decisions by applying the standards of the NASW Code of Ethics and relevant laws and regulations and by utilizing the models for ethical decision making, ethical conduct of research, and additional codes of ethics as appropriate to context. Social workers also employ reflection and self-regulation to manage their personal values and maintain professionalism in practice situations. They demonstrate professional demeanor in their behavior, appearance, and oral, written, and electronic communication. Social workers use technology ethically and appropriately to facilitate practice outcomes. Finally, they use supervision and consultation to guide professional judgment and behavior.

EPAS Competency 2

EP 2

Social workers are guided in this competency to understand how diversity and difference characterize and shape the human experience and are critical to the formation of identity. They understand the dimensions of diversity as the intersection of multiple factors, including, but not limited to, age, class, color, culture, ethnicity, gender, gender identity and expression, immigration status, marital status, physical and mental ability, political ideology, race, religion/spirituality, sex, sexual orientation, and tribal sovereign status. For example, Tobias, the social worker in our case example, would try to understand Mrs. Ramirez from many perspectives, including her immigration status, gender, ethnicity, and other perspectives relevant to her situation. This competency guides social workers to understand that, as a consequence of difference, a person's life experiences may include oppression, poverty, marginalization, and alienation as well as privilege, power, and acclaim. Social workers also understand the forms and mechanisms of oppression and discrimination and recognize the extent to which a culture's structures and values, including social, economic, political, and cultural exclusions, may oppress, marginalize, alienate, or create privilege and power. Social workers are aware of privilege and act mindful of it.

This competency also contains the recommendation that social workers use reflection to manage their personal values. For example, early in his working with Mrs. Ramirez, Tobias wrote in his case notes that he suspected that her children were not attending school in part because she and other undocumented immigrants did not value education as much as their fellow students and families in their new community in the United States. In fact, there is evidence to suggest that Mexican immigrants value education highly (Valencia & Black, 2002). Tobias's statement might be seen as a belief, a hypothesis, or a possible bias that could have profound implications for his work with Mrs. Ramirez. If he acted on his belief that her children were not attending primarily because she and other Mexican immigrants were not motivated about education, he might not explore other community- or school-based barriers to their attendance, such as their perception that the children were not welcome. Holding members of oppressed groups personally responsible for all aspects of their condition is an unfortunate value predicated on the Horatio Alger myth that all successful people lift themselves up by their own bootstraps. This competency therefore requires sensitivity to structures that may act to oppress.

This competency also guides social workers to consider the importance of their commitment to diversity as we consider the Eurocentric assumptions that undergird many practice models (Sue & Sue, 2012). We take the position that some factors are universal.

For example, pathology occurs across cultures, although the forms may vary (Sue & Sue, 2012). On the other hand, much of social work practice relates to specific cultural manifestations of both difficulties and solutions.

We believe that cultural competence requires continual upgrading and lifelong learning over the course of a social worker's career. Just as your clinical or direct practice skills should continue to grow, so should your level of cultural competence. To do this, you will need to engage in continual education about the culture and experiences of client groups with whom you work. This also means that you must approach each client as an individual whose experience is in many ways unique. That is, clients bear unique combinations of personality characteristics, family dynamics, and experiences with acculturation and assimilation. Social workers must therefore learn as much as they can about the cultural frames that are significant for their clients before they can be open to learning the uniqueness of those clients (Dean, 2001; Johnson & Munch, 2009). Hence, when we report some cultural characteristics as commonly represented in some groups, it is shared in the sense of background information that must be assessed with each individual. For example, although *some* Asian American clients may expect the social worker to take an expert role and advise them, many will not, based on their individual experiences and personalities (Fong, 2007). Further, *Asian American* as a category can subsume great variation, including Pacific Islanders and mainland Asians, whose cultural heritages are very distinct from each other.

VIDEO CASE EXAMPLE

In the video "Working with Yan Ping," Kim Strom-Gottfried interviews Yan Ping, an exchange student from the Republic of China. Kim cannot assume that she and Yan Ping share assumptions about help seeking, so Kim carefully explores expectations and explains what she can offer as a social worker. In this way, she guards against applying stereotypic assumptions about how Yan Ping views her concerns and what is possible in seeking help. Together, Kim and Yan Ping explore goals and ways of working together, as well as whether a referral to a social worker more familiar with Yan Ping's culture could be helpful.

EPAS Competency 3

EP 3

This competency requires that social workers advance human rights and social justice and asserts that each person in society has basic human rights, such as freedom, safety, privacy, an adequate standard of living, health care, and education. This competency is also reflected in the NASW Code of Ethics: "Social workers challenge social injustice" (2008a).

To meet this competency, social workers should be aware of the global implications of oppression, be knowledgeable about theories of justice and strategies to promote human and civil rights, and strive to incorporate social justice practices into organizations, institutions, and society. Social workers should also understand the mechanisms of oppression and discrimination in society and advocate for and engage in practices that advance human rights and social and economic justice. This competency clearly specifies that advocating for human rights and social and economic justice is a professional expectation.

Following this competency, Tobias from our case example would attempt to understand the issue of children's school attendance in a broader framework of understanding why Mrs. Ramirez and her children had moved to his locality. Awareness of the economic incentive of seeking a better income as an influence on immigration would be appropriate. For example, in addition to working directly with Mrs. Ramirez, Tobias or other social workers might approach the circumstance of undocumented immigrants in their community from the standpoint of community organization and advocacy, working to promote the interests of the group rather than solely those of the individual. While this book focuses primarily on direct social work intervention, other courses and texts provide additional sources of information for pursuing this goal.

EPAS Competency 4

EP 4

This competency requires that social workers engage in practice-informed research and research-informed practice. To fulfill this competency, social workers use their practice experience to inform research, employ evidence-based interventions, evaluate their own practice, and use research findings to improve practice, policy, and social service delivery. This competency requires that social workers be knowledgeable about quantitative and qualitative research, understand scientific and ethical approaches to building knowledge, and use their practice experience to inform scientific inquiry and use research evidence to inform their practice.

Some proponents suggest that employing evidence-based intervention entails being able to explain an evidence-based approach to clients; creating a useful, realistic evaluation format; refining such intervention and evaluation formats based on knowledge of the client; understanding the relevant elements of evidence-based techniques; incorporating evidence from use of the intervention; and being critical consumers of evidence in practice situations (Pollio, 2006; Thyer, 2013). Others suggest the need to use knowledge of the context in formulating such interventions and to consider the theoretical base in selecting interventions (Adams, Matto, & Le Croy, 2009; Gitterman & Knight 2013; Payne, 2005; Walsh, 2006). More recently there have been calls to integrate attention to common factors and common elements with attention to evidence-based practice (Barth et al., 2012).

Given the range of evidence available in different fields of practice, we agree that evidence-based practice should be a highly valued source of information in the context of planning an intervention. Following this principle, in our case example, Tobias and his agency would be advised to be mindful of evidence-based interventions that assist families with the problem of low school attendance. He and his agency would be wise to become familiar with programs that promote personal relationships between school personnel and families around attendance issues, such as the evidence-based program Check & Connect (checkandconnect.umn.edu). They would also need to integrate this knowledge with information about the environmental context and relevant interventions. For example, assisting Mrs. Ramirez in getting her children ready for transportation to school might be one part of the intervention, as well as working with the school to construct a more welcoming environment for the children. Part of this context is also Mrs. Ramirez's physical and emotional health. She may be more likely to have her children ready for school if she is linked to health care providers who can assist her with her need for surgery and her depression.

EPAS Competency 5

EP 5

This competency requires that social workers engage in policy practice to advance social and economic well-being and to deliver effective social work services. One of the distinguishing features of social

work as a helping profession is the understanding that all direct practice occurs in a policy context. Hence, social workers need to know about the history of and current structures for policies and services. In pursuit of this competency, social workers analyze, formulate, and advocate for policies that advance the social well-being of their clients. They also collaborate with colleagues and clients for effective policy action. While some social workers provide direct services to clients, others act indirectly to influence the environments supporting their clients, thereby developing and maintaining the social infrastructure that assists clients in meeting their needs. Many social work programs contain one or more required courses in policy and practice as well as an advanced practice curriculum in this area. In our case example, Tobias's interaction with Mrs. Ramirez must be considered in the context of policies related to school attendance and policies related to health care access.

EPAS Competency 6

EP 6

This competency focuses on engagement with individuals, families, groups, organizations, and communities. Social workers apply their knowledge of human behavior in the social environment and the practice context to engage with clients and constituencies. They also use empathy, reflection, and interpersonal skills to effectively engage diverse clients and constituencies. In our case example, Tobias would seek to use empathy in his interactions with Mrs. Ramirez and use his interpersonal skills to help her to the greatest extent possible.

EPAS Competencies 7 and 8

EP 7 and 8

These competencies focus on engaging with, assessing, intervening with, and evaluating individuals, families, groups, organizations, and communities. These competencies get at the heart of social work intervention and reflect the knowledge and skills that this book is designed to address. In order to meet these competencies, social workers prepare for action with individuals, families, groups, organizations, and communities both substantively and emotionally. They do this by using empathy and other interpersonal skills, developing a mutually agreed-upon focus of work, and identifying desired outcomes. Utilizing these skills, Tobias in our case example would attempt to personally engage Mrs. Ramirez and her family. We recognize that the success of such engagement efforts depends in part on sensitivity to cultural norms and hence also includes attention to the competency related to diversity.

These competencies also include attention focused on assessment and refer to the knowledge and skills required to collect, organize, and interpret client data. In this context, social workers must have skills in assessing both a client's strengths and limitations. They must be able to develop mutually agreed-upon intervention goals and objectives and be able to select appropriate intervention strategies.

EPAS Competency 9

EP 9

This competency requires knowledge and skills in evaluation. To meet this competency, social workers must be able to critically analyze, monitor, and evaluate interventions. Following this competency, Tobias from our case example would establish goals with Mrs. Ramirez and regularly assess progress with her. This competency requires that social workers select appropriate means of evaluation, critically analyze efforts to evaluate and monitor programs, and apply evaluation data to improve service delivery.

LEVELS OF PRACTICE

Social workers address the competencies we have just discussed at multiple levels of practice:

- **Micro-level practice.** The population served by social workers at this level of practice includes individuals, couples, and families. Practice at the micro level is designated as **direct practice** because practitioners deliver services directly to clients in face-to-face situations. Direct practice, however, is by no means limited to such face-to-face contact.
- **Mezzo-level practice.** The second level of social work practice is defined as "interpersonal relations that are less intimate than those associated with family life; more meaningful than among organizational and institutional representatives; [including] relationships between individuals in a self-help or therapy group, among peers at school or work or among neighbors" (Sheafor, Horejsi, & Horejsi, 1994, pp. 9–10). Mezzo events are "the interface where the individual and those most immediate and important to him/her meet" (Zastrow & Kirst-Ashman, 1990, p. 11). Mezzo intervention is hence

designed to change the systems that directly affect clients, such as the family, peer group, or classroom.
- **Macro-level practice.** Still further removed from face-to-face delivery of services, macro-level social work practice involves the processes of social planning and community organization. On this level, social workers serve as professional change agents who assist community action systems composed of individuals, groups, or organizations in dealing with social problems. For example, social workers may work with citizen groups or with private, public, or governmental organizations. Activities of practitioners at this level include (1) development of and work with community groups and organizations; (2) program planning and development; and (3) implementation, administration, and evaluation of programs (Meenaghan, 1987).

Effective practice requires knowledge related to all three levels of practice. Nevertheless, schools of social work often offer "concentrations" in either micro or macro practice and require less preparation in the other levels. Concentrations are often designated around an area of direct practice in particular populations or settings, such as adult mental health, child welfare, family practice, group work, school social work, aging, and work with children and adolescents. Such concentrations may emphasize micro practice or incorporate mezzo and macro practice. Some schools have generalist practice curricula, which require students to achieve balanced preparation in all three levels of practice. Undergraduate programs and the first year of graduate programs typically feature generalist practice curricula, which aim to prepare students for working with all levels of client systems.

Macro concentrations often refer to practice in community organization, planning, management, and advocacy. Administration entails playing a leadership role in human service organizations that seek to effectively deliver services in accordance with the values and laws of society. It includes the processes involved in policy formulation and subsequent translation of that policy into operational goals, program design and implementation, funding and resource allocation, management of internal and interorganizational operation, personnel direction and supervision, organizational representation and public relations, community education, monitoring, evaluation, and innovation to improve organizational productivity (Sarri, 1987, pp. 29–30).

Direct practitioners are necessarily involved to some degree in administrative activities. In addition, many direct practitioners who hold master's degrees become supervisors or administrators later in their professional careers. Knowledge of administration, therefore, is vital to direct practitioners at the master's degree level, and courses in administration are frequently part of the required master's degree curriculum in social work. Although many direct practitioners engage in little or no macro-level practice, those who work in rural areas where practitioners are few and specialists in social planning are not available may work in concert with concerned citizens and community leaders in planning and developing resources to prevent or combat social problems.

ORIENTING FRAMEWORKS TO ACHIEVE COMPETENCIES

Practitioners and beginning students need orienting frameworks to ground their work in achieving the competencies just described. There is ever-increasing information from the social sciences, social work, and allied disciplines that point to specific interventions for specific problem situations. Successful use of such interventions represents formidable challenges because available knowledge is often fragmented. Further, because social work often takes place in agency settings with clients whose concerns cut across psychological and environmental needs, an orienting perspective is needed to address these levels of concerns and activities. As we'll see in this section, the *ecological systems model* is useful in providing an orienting perspective (Germain & Gitterman, 1996; Pincus & Minahan, 1973; Siporin, 1980).

Ecological Systems Model

EP 7

A system is a set of orderly elements that are related to make a whole. Systems theory emphasizes the interactions between these elements (Kirst-Ashman & Hull, 2012). Adaptations of the **ecological systems model**, originating in biology, make a close conceptual fit with the "person-in-environment" perspective that dominated social work until the mid-1970s. Although that perspective recognized the influence of environmental factors on human functioning, internal factors had received an inordinate emphasis in assessing human problems. In addition, a perception of the environment as constraining the individual did not sufficiently acknowledge the individual's ability to affect the environment. In social work practice, an ecological

systems model is understood as a way to examine strengths and weaknesses in transactions between persons, families, cultures, and communities as systems.

This emphasis, which resulted from the prominence and wide acceptance of Freud's theories in the 1920s and 1930s, reached its zenith in the 1940s and 1950s. With the emergence of ego psychology, systems theory, theories of family therapy, expanded awareness of the importance of ethnocultural factors, and emphasis on ecological factors in the 1960s and 1970s, increasing importance was accorded to environmental factors and to understanding the ways in which people interact with their environments. Systems models were first created in the natural sciences, and ecological theory developed from the environmental movement in biology; ecological systems theory in social work adapted concepts from both of these models.

Habitats and Niche

Two concepts of ecological theory that are especially relevant to social workers are *habitat* and *niche*. **Habitat** refers to the places where organisms live and, in the case of humans, consists of the physical and social settings within particular cultural contexts. When habitats are rich in the resources required for growth and development, people tend to thrive. When habitats are deficient in vital resources, physical, social, and emotional development and ongoing functioning may be adversely affected. For example, a substantial body of research indicates that supportive social networks of friends, relatives, neighbors, work and church associates, and pets mitigate the damaging effects of painful life stresses. By contrast, people with deficient social networks may respond to life stresses by becoming severely depressed, resorting to abuse of drugs or alcohol, engaging in violent behavior, or coping in other dysfunctional ways.

Niche refers to the statuses or roles occupied by members of the community. One of the tasks in the course of human maturation is to find one's niche in society, which is essential to achieving self-respect and a stable sense of identity. Being able to locate one's niche, however, presumes that opportunities congruent with human needs exist in society. That presumption may not be valid for members of society who lack equal opportunities because of race, ethnicity, gender, poverty, age, disability, sexual identity, or other factors.

Mutual Influence of People and Environments

An objective of social work, as noted earlier, is to promote social justice so as to expand opportunities for people to create appropriate niches for themselves. Ecological systems theory posits that individuals constantly engage in transactions with other humans and with other systems in the environment, and that these individuals and systems reciprocally influence each other.

Each system is unique, varying in its characteristics and ways of interacting; no two individuals, families, groups, or neighborhoods are the same. As a consequence, people do not merely react to environmental forces. Rather, they act on their environments, thereby shaping the responses of other people, groups, institutions, and even the physical environment. For example, people make choices about where to live, whether to upgrade or to neglect their living arrangements, and whether to initiate or support policies that combat urban decay, safeguard the quality of air and water, and provide adequate housing for the elderly poor.

Adequate assessments of human problems and plans of interventions, therefore, must consider how people and environmental systems influence one another. The importance of considering this reciprocal interaction when formulating assessments has been reflected in changing views of certain human problems over the past decade. Disability, for example, is now defined in psychosocial terms rather than in medical or economic terms. As Roth (1987) has clarified, "What is significant can be revealed only by the ecological framework in which the disabled person exists, by the interactions through which society engages a disability, by the attitudes others hold, and by the architecture, means of transportation, and social organization constructed by the able bodied" (p. 434). Disability is thus minimized by maximizing the goodness of fit between the needs of people with physical or mental limitations and the environmental resources that correspond to their special needs, such as rehabilitation programs, special physical accommodations, education, and social support systems.

The Development of Needed Resources

It is clear from the ecological systems perspective that the satisfaction of human needs and mastery of developmental tasks require adequate resources in the environment and positive transactions between people and their environments. For example, effective learning by a student requires adequate schools, competent teachers, parental support, adequate perception and intellectual ability, motivation to learn, and positive relationships between teachers and students. Any gaps in the environmental resources, limitations of

individuals who need or utilize these resources, or dysfunctional transactions between individuals and environmental systems threaten to block the fulfillment of human needs and lead to stress or impaired functioning. To reduce or remove this stress requires coping efforts aimed at gratifying the needs—that is, achieving adaptive fit between person and environment. People, however, often do not have access to adequate resources or may lack effective coping methods. Social work involves helping such people meet their needs by linking them with or developing essential resources. It can also include enhancing clients' capacities to utilize resources or cope with environmental forces.

The Diverse Systems

Assessment from an ecological systems perspective obviously requires knowledge of the diverse systems involved in interactions between people and their environments:

- Subsystems of the individual—biophysical, cognitive, emotional, behavioral, motivational
- Interpersonal systems—parent/child, marital, family, kin, friends, neighbors, cultural reference groups, spiritual belief systems, other members of social networks
- Organizations, institutions, communities
- The physical environment—housing, neighborhood environment, buildings, other artificial creations, water, weather and climate

A major advantage of the ecological systems model is its broad scope. Typical human problems involving health care, family relations, inadequate income, mental health difficulties, conflicts with law enforcement agencies, unemployment, educational difficulties, and so on can all be subsumed under this model, enabling the practitioner to analyze the complex variables involved in such problems.

Applying the Model: First Steps

Assessing the sources of problems and determining the foci of interventions are the first steps in applying the ecological systems model. Assessment tools have been developed that can engage clients in gathering information to assist in discovering the strengths, resources, and challenges of the systems surrounding individuals and families. For example, **ecomaps** such as that shown in Figure 1-1 can depict a family context (Hartman,

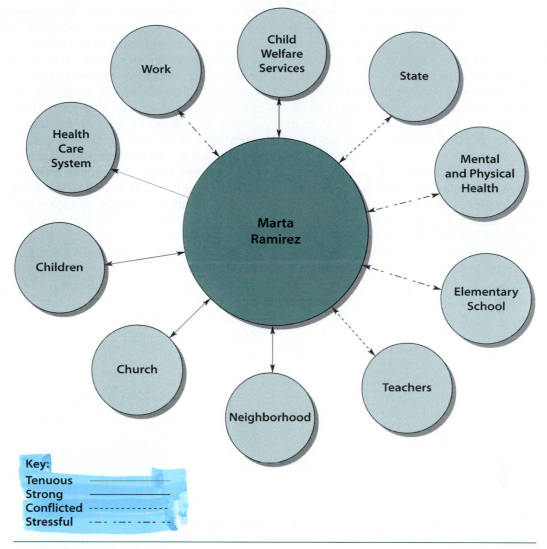

FIG 1-1 Ecomap

1994). A solid line connecting systems to individuals and families can indicate a strong relationship, a dotted line can indicate a tenuous relationship, and hatch marks can indicate a stressful relationship (Cournoyer, 2011; Mattaini, 1995). The ecomap depicted in Figure 1-1 suggests that Mrs. Ramirez experiences her relationship with her spiritual community as sustaining, whereas she considers her relationships with the school system, health care system, and work as stressful. Those relationships are influenced by her work-related injury and lack of access to health care as an undocumented person and contribute to her symptoms of depression and oversleeping. Creation of an ecomap can then form the basis of a plan for utilizing available resources, such as seeking assistance from her spiritual

community and others. New adaptations of ecomaps include *virtual ecomaps*, which can help clients assess their digital world and online resources (Gustafsson & MacEachron, 2013).

Adapting systems models to social work practice, Pincus and Minahan (1973) suggested that a **client system** includes those persons who are requesting a change, sanction it, are expected to benefit from it, and contract to receive it (Compton, Galaway, & Cournoyer, 2005). As noted previously, potential clients who request a change are described as *voluntary clients*. Also noted previously, many clients reach social workers not through their own choice but rather through referral from others. Nonvoluntary clients (or *referrals*) are persons who do not seek services on their own but who do so at the behest of other professionals and family members. Meanwhile, *contacted persons* are approached through an outreach effort (Compton & Galaway, 2005). Some referred and contacted individuals may not experience pressure from that contact. However, some individuals do experience pressure; social workers should consider them as "potential clients" and be aware of the route that brought them to the social worker and their response to that contact.

Applying the Model: Next Steps

The next step is to determine what should be done related to the pertinent systems involved in the problem situation. In this step, the social worker surveys the broad spectrum of available practice theories and interventions. To be maximally effective, interventions must be directed to all systems that are critical in a given problem system.

The **target system** refers to the focus of change efforts. With a voluntary client, it typically encompasses the concerns that brought the individual to seek services. With nonvoluntary clients, it may include illegal or dangerous behaviors that the person does not acknowledge (see Figure 1-2). As noted previously, the *client system* consists of those persons who request or are expected to benefit from services. Note that this definition includes both voluntary and nonvoluntary clients (see Figure 1-3).

When a client desires assistance with a personal problem, the target and client systems overlap. Frequently, however, clients request assistance with a problem outside themselves. In such instances, that problem could become the center of a target system. For example, Mrs. Ramirez from our case example acknowledges psychological and physical health concerns as well as concerns about how welcome her children feel in school. Meanwhile, Tobias must carry out a legally defined educational neglect assessment. These problem areas may merge as a contract is developed to address several concerns. It is important that target problems focus on a target concern rather than on the entire person as the target. Focusing on a person as the target system objectifies that individual and diminishes the respect for individuality to which each person is entitled. Hence, concerns with school attendance can be the target system rather than Mrs. Ramirez and her children.

The **action system** refers to those formal and informal resources and persons that the social worker needs to cooperate with to accomplish a purpose. It often includes family, friends, and other resources as well as more formal resources. For example, an action system for school attendance might include school attendance officers, teachers, relatives, neighbors, spiritual resources, or transportation providers, according to the plan agreed upon by Mrs. Ramirez and Tobias (see Figure 1-4).

The **agency system** is a special subset of an action system that includes the practitioners and formal service

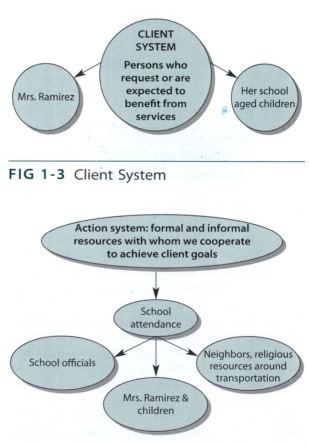

FIG 1-3 Client System

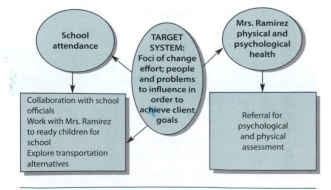

FIG 1-2 Target System

FIG 1-4 Action System

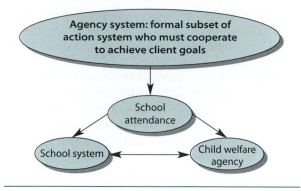

FIG 1-5 Agency System

systems involved in work on the target problems (Compton & Galaway, 2005). In Mrs. Ramirez's case, the agency system primarily includes the elementary school and the child welfare agency (see Figure 1-5).

Social systems also vary in the degree to which they are open and closed to new information or feedback. **Closed systems** have relatively rigid boundaries that prevent the input or export of information. **Open systems** have relatively permeable boundaries, permitting a freer exchange. Families may vary from being predominantly closed to new information to being excessively open. In fact, all families and human systems exhibit a tension between trying to maintain stability and boundaries in some areas while seeking and responding to change in others. Systems theorists also suggest that change in one part of a system often affects other parts of the system. For example, Mrs. Ramirez's emotional and physical health may greatly influence her capacity to prepare her children for school. Hence, facilitating a referral for her may have a significant impact on the school attendance issue.

The principle of **equifinality** suggests that the same outcome can be achieved even with different starting points. For example, your classmates have come from different places both geographically and in terms of life experience. Despite your different origins, you have all ended up in the same program of study. The principle of **multifinality** suggests that beginning from the same starting points may end in different outcomes. Just as you and your classmates are engaged in the same course of study, you are likely to end in diverse settings and locales for your own practice experience.

Nonlinear Applications of Systems Theory

Traditional systems theory suggests that systems or organizations are characterized by order, rationality,

and stability (Warren, Franklin, & Streeter, 1998). Hence, the emphasis in such stable systems is on concepts such as boundaries, homeostasis, and equilibrium. In addition to ordered circumstances, systems theory can be useful for consideration of nonlinear systems. Systems in the process of change can be very sensitive to initial events and feedback to those events. For example, a nonlinear change would be the circumstance in which an adolescent's voice changes by 1 decibel of loudness resulting in a change of 10 decibels in an adult (Warren et al., 1998). Minor incidents in the past can reverberate throughout a system. Some have suggested that this proliferation supports the notion that family systems can make significant changes as a result of a key intervention that reverberates and is reinforced in a system.

Such nonlinear circumstances emphasize the concept of multifinality—that is, the same initial conditions can lead to quite varied outcomes. Among the implications of multifinality are the possibility of considering chaos not as a lack of order but rather as an opportunity for flexibility and change.

Limitations of Systems Theories

While systems models often provide useful concepts for describing person–situation interactions, they may have limitations in suggesting specific intervention prescriptions (Whittaker & Tracy, 1989). Similarly, Wakefield (1996a, 1996b) has argued that systems concepts do not add much to domain-specific knowledge. Others claim that, however faulty or inadequate, systems theory provides useful metaphors for conceptualizing the relations between complex organizations.

Perhaps we should not place such high expectations on the theory (Gitterman, 1996). We take the view that systems theory provides useful metaphors for conceptualizing the varied levels of phenomena social workers must recognize. By themselves, those metaphors are insufficient to guide practice. Concepts such as equifinality and multifinality cannot be rigidly applied in all human and social systems.

DECIDING ON AND CARRYING OUT INTERVENTIONS

How do social workers decide on what interventions they will carry out to assist client systems in reaching their goals? Throughout our professional history, social workers have drawn selectively on theories

EP 4

to help understand circumstances and guide intervention. Psychodynamic theory was an important early source of explanations to guide social work interventions through adaptations such as the functional approach, the psychosocial approach, and the problem-solving approach (Hollis & Woods, 1981; Perlman, 1957; Taft, 1937). In each of these approaches, ego psychology was a particularly valuable source in explaining how individuals coped with their environments. While psychodynamic theory provided a broad-ranging explanatory framework, it was less useful as a source of specific interventions, and the level of abstraction required in the approach did not lend itself well to the evaluation of its effectiveness.

Concerns about the effectiveness of social work services led to an emphasis on employing methods that could be expected to be successful based on proven effectiveness (Fischer, 1973). Rather than seeking single approaches to direct practice in all circumstances, social workers were guided to find the approach that made the best fit for the particular client circumstance and problem (Fischer, 1978). Eclectic practice is designed to meet this goal, but it carries its own concerns. For example, selecting techniques employed in particular approaches should be based on knowledge of the approach the techniques come from and an assessment of the strengths and weaknesses of that approach (Coady & Lehmann, 2008; Marsh, 2004).

Berlin and Marsh (1993) suggest that there are legitimate roles for many influences on practice decision making. These include clear conceptual frameworks to guide the social worker in what to look for, commitments and values, intuitive hunches, spontaneous improvisation, empathic understanding, and empirically derived data (p. 230).

Evidence-Based Practice

Empirically derived data as a source has a prominent role in determining, together with clients, how to proceed. Empirically based practice refers to promoting models of practice based on scientific evidence (Barker, 2003). In such an approach, problems and outcomes are conceived in measurable terms, and data are gathered to monitor interventions and evaluate effectiveness. Interventions are selected based on their scientific support and effectiveness as systematically measured and evaluated (Cournoyer, 2004; Petr & Walter, 2005). The term **evidence-based practice** has been suggested as broader than empirically based practice, since external research findings are considered in

the context of fit to particular situations, which in turn are considered within the context of informed consent and client values and expectations (Petr & Walter, 2005, p. 252; Thyer & Gambrill, 2004).

Evidence-based practice began in medicine as an attempt to conscientiously identify best practices for client care, assess the quality of evidence available, and present that evidence to clients and patients so that they could share in decision making (Adams & Drake, 2006; Scheyett, 2006). More recently, two forms of evidence-based practice have become prominent.

The Process Model

The first form, the **process model**, is consistent with the medical definition of evidence-based practice cited previously and focuses on the practices of the individual practitioner. Specifically, the individual practitioner learns how to formulate a question about his or her work with a client that is answerable with data (Rubin, 2007). Based on that question, the social worker gains access to appropriate empirical literature through online journals and studies. The social worker does not need to review *all* the relevant literature from all of the available studies but may seek secondary reviews and meta-analyses of an intervention that summarize the state of knowledge about that intervention. For example, the evidence about stages of change in a child welfare context has been summarized by Littell and Girvin (2004).

In assessing studies of interventions, a hierarchy of levels has been developed to assess the reliability of an intervention measure. For example, multiple randomized studies are considered to provide potentially strong support for an intervention. With some social problems and settings such as child welfare, such studies are rare; however, studies with other adequate controls may be available (Kessler, Gira, & Poertner, 2005; Thomlison, 2005; Blome & Steib, 2004). Whatever the range of studies available, the practitioner needs to have the skills to assess the level of support for the intervention. Based on this assessment of data, the social worker can share that evidence with his or her client in order to better make an informed decision together about what to do. After making this joint decision, the practitioner and client can implement the intervention with fidelity and assess how well it works. This has been characterized as a bottom-up model because the questions raised and interventions selected are assumed to be defined by the people closest to the intervention: the practitioner and client (Rubin, 2007).

There are several assumptions about the process model as presented in this form that must be assessed. The model assumes that the practitioner is free to select an intervention and that the client is free to accept or reject it. In fact, agency-level practice has many influences that determine which interventions can be utilized (Payne, 2005). Some interventions are supported by the agency and supervisor based on policies, laws, prior training, and accepted practices. Practitioners utilizing the process model hope that such interventions are supported by a review of the research evidence.

Recognizing this issue and that the choice of intervention may not be fully in the control of the practitioner, some proponents have suggested that one solution is for teams to study evidence about particular problems and interventions and make recommendations about practices to be used by the team (Proctor, 2007). In partnership with schools of social work, agency teams can identify problems and secure administrative support while the schools provide training in evidence-based practices. Another consideration is that when clients are not entirely voluntary, practitioners and agencies may and should make evidence-based decisions, but involuntary clients may not feel empowered to reject them (Kessler et al., 2005; Scheyett, 2006). In such cases, however, clients are entitled through informed consent to know the rationale for the intervention and its evidence of effectiveness. This model also assumes that the practitioner has sufficient time to access the appropriate literature and appropriate resources. Finally, it assumes that the practitioner has the skill, training, and supervision to carry out the evidence-based intervention effectively (Rubin, 2007).

Training in Evidence-Based Approaches

Partly in response to the difficulties associated with the process model, another version of evidence-based practice refers to *training* in evidence-based practice approaches. In this approach, the emphasis is on identifying models of practice that have demonstrated efficacy for particular problems and populations, learning about them, and learning how to implement them. An advantage of this approach, according to proponents, is that it focuses not just on knowing about the intervention but on acquiring the skills necessary to carry it out effectively (Rubin, 2007). A form of this approach is the adoption of empirically supported approaches for particular conditions. This form has had more widespread use as agencies and funding bodies have encouraged its use (Barth et al., 2012). Difficulties also emerge with this form of evidence-based practice, however, as it is not readily convertible to individual circumstances and cultural variations.

Criticism of Evidence Approaches and Alternatives

Critics, however, suggest that training in the evidence-based practices approach carries its own dangers. For one, students often experience anxiety in learning how to become effective practitioners and, having learned one evidence-based practice, might be inclined to generalize it beyond its original effectiveness, thus replicating in part the problem mentioned earlier of students trained in a theory or model and carrying it out without evidence of effectiveness and without having an alternative: If your only tool is a hammer, all problems may appear to be nails (Scheyett, 2006).

Second, evidence-based practices have their own limited shelf life, with new studies supporting some methods and qualifying the support for others. Hence, the fact that you learn one evidence-based approach does not preclude and should not preclude learning others. In fact, we believe that becoming effective practitioners is a career-long proposition, not limited by the completion of your academic program.

Finally, behavioral and cognitive behavioral approaches are well represented among evidence-based practices. Some have suggested that such approaches have an advantage because their practice fits research protocols and, therefore, that other approaches have been underrepresented (Coady & Lehmann, 2008; Walsh, 2006). It becomes a challenge to other approaches to enhance their effectiveness base rather than question the value of research protocols or representativeness of the model. There is growing evidence that some emerging approaches, such as the solution-focused approach, are in fact increasing their effectiveness base (Kim, 2008).

Advocates suggest that there is room in social work education both for a process and for training in evidence-based approaches—that all students should learn how to carry out the process model of evidence-based practice and all students should become proficient in at least one evidence-based practice modality (Rubin, 2007). These proponents also suggest that such skills may require specialization in certain methods and may not be consistent with those programs that include an advanced generalist curriculum (Howard, Allen-Meares, & Ruffolo, 2007). We do not take sides on this issue, recognizing that programs that have developed advanced generalist curricula have done so mindful of the context and expectations for practitioners in their area, and that generalist practice remains the standard for BSW programs and the first year of MSW programs.

Social workers should consult practice-informed research and research-informed practice. Evidence-based practice is one such source, as it assists practitioners in identifying problems, assessing data about those problems, and consulting with clients in selecting interventions. Note that research-informed practice has long been proposed in schools of social work. However, its actual implementation in practice has often lagged behind (Fortune, 2014). Reasons for this lag include lack of time, lack of access, and lack of skill in assessing studies.

Two more recent guides have emerged to assist social workers in this quest. The **common elements approach** examines commonalities across effective interventions (Chorpita, Daleiden, & Weisz, 2005). The **common factors approach** emphasizes other factors shared by different intervention approaches, such as strength of relationship or alliance (Duncan, Miller, Wampold, & Hubble, 2010). In the common factors approach, the social worker frequently assesses the quality of the relationship. Barth and colleagues have suggested a framework for integrating these guides starting with agency values (Barth et al., 2012).

As this discussion indicates, social work has long attempted to make practice more scientific and to bring rigor to the selection of intervention approaches (Brekke, 2012). The proper relationship between science and artistry, theory and values, is an ongoing discussion in social work (Gitterman & Knight, 2013; Thyer, 2013).

Guidelines Influencing Intervention Selection

We recommend the following guidelines to assist you in deciding when and how to intervene with clients in social work practice:

1. *Social workers value maximum feasible self-determination, empowerment, and enhancing of strengths to increase the client's voice in decision making.* Manualized approaches that imply that all major decisions are in the hands of and controlled by the social worker are alien to these values. Following these values, we seek to include clients to the extent possible in access to information that would assist them in making decisions (Coady & Lehmann, 2008).

2. *Social workers assess circumstances from a systems perspective, mindful of the person in the situation, the setting, the community, and the organization.* We assess for the level of the problem and the appropriate level of interventions (Allen-Meares & Garvin, 2000). We recognize that resources are often needed at multiple levels and attempt to avoid a narrow clinical focus on the practitioner and client. Hence our use of data and perspectives to guide us must be governed in part by the multiple roles we play, including systems linkage as well as direct practice or clinical interventions (Richey & Roffman, 1999).

3. *Social workers are sensitive to diversity in considering interventions.* We avoid assumptions that interventions tested with one population will necessarily generalize to another. In so doing, we are particularly sensitive to the clients' own perspectives about what is appropriate for them (Allen-Meares & Garvin, 2000).

4. *Social workers draw on evidence-based practices at both process and intervention levels as well as common factors in determining, together with the client, how to proceed.* We expect social workers to have access to evidence about efficacious interventions for the problem at hand. Such evidence may derive from individual study, organizational priorities, or collaboration with university teams to construct guidelines for practice in critical areas. Because our code of ethics requires us to act within our level of competence and supervision, knowledge of what interventions are efficacious does not mean that we can carry out those interventions. It may be a useful goal to learn how to carry out two or more evidence-based approaches as part of your education program. The goal of this book, however, is to equip you with the basic skills to carry out practice at the beginning level. We are influenced by the process model of evidence-based practice, and we seek to give you useful tools by modeling ways that questions can be asked and that data can be consulted in making decisions with clients. Further, in our chapters on intervention models, we will be influenced by evidence-based practice models. It is not realistic at this level to attempt to teach evidence-based practice approaches such that you would be able to implement them right away. We can introduce you to them, but further training and supervision will be required.

5. *Social workers think critically about practice, checking out assumptions and examining alternatives.*

We try to avoid early social work patterns of applying theories more widely than data suggest by being open to examining alternatives (Briggs & Rzepnicki, 2004; Gambrill, 2004). One danger of following a single approach is that data that do not fit the preferences of the approach are discounted (Maguire, 2002). Conversely, this danger can also apply to selecting an approach based on its label as evidence-based, for example, without assessing fit with client and circumstances (Scheyett, 2006).

SUMMARY

This chapter introduced social work as a profession, marked by a specific context, mission, and well-established values, that includes the practice of specific competencies. As social workers and their clients operate in many different kinds and levels of environments, ecological and systems concepts are useful metaphors for conceptualizing what social workers and clients must deal with. Chapter 2 will delve more deeply into specifying direct practice and the roles that social workers play.

COMPETENCY NOTES

EP 1   Demonstrate Ethical and Professional Behavior
- Demonstrate professional demeanor in behavior, appearance, and oral, written, and electronic communication.

EP 2   Engage Diversity and Difference in Practice
- Apply and communicate your understanding of the importance of diversity and difference in shaping life experiences. This also includes presenting yourself as a learner and engaging clients and constituents as experts in their own experience.

EP 3   Advance Human Rights and Social, Economic, and Environmental Justice
- Apply your understanding of social, economic, and environmental justice to advocate for human rights at the individual and system levels, and engage in practices that advance social, economic, and environmental justice.

EP 4   Engage in Practice-Informed Research and Research-Informed Practice
- Use practice experience and theory to inform scientific inquiry and research.
- Engage in critical analysis of quantitative and qualitative research methods and research findings.
- Use and translate research findings to inform and improve practice, policy, and service delivery.

EP 5   Engage in Policy Practice
- Assess how social welfare and economic policies affect the delivery of and access to social services.
- Critically analyze and promote policies that advance human rights and social, economic, and environmental justice.

EP 6   Engage with Individuals, Families, Groups, Organizations, and Communities
- Apply knowledge of human behavior and the social environment and practice context to engage with clients and constituencies.
- Use empathy, reflection, and interpersonal skills to effectively engage diverse clients and constituencies.

EP 7   Assess Individuals, Families, Groups, Organizations, and Communities
- Collect, organize, and critically analyze and interpret information from clients and constituencies.
- Apply knowledge of human behavior and the social environment, person-in-environment, and other multidisciplinary theoretical frameworks in the analysis of assessment data from clients and constituencies.
- Develop mutually agreed-on intervention goals and objectives based on the critical assessment of strengths, needs, and challenges within clients and constituencies.
- Select appropriate intervention strategies based on the assessment, research knowledge, and values and preferences of clients and constituencies.

EP 8   Intervene with Individuals, Families, Groups, Organizations, and Communities
- Implement interventions to achieve practice goals and enhance capacities of clients and constituencies.
- Apply knowledge of human behavior and the social environment, person-in-environment, and other multidisciplinary theoretical

frameworks in interventions with clients and constituencies.

- Use interprofessional collaboration as appropriate to achieve beneficial practice outcomes.
- Negotiate, mediate, and advocate with and on behalf of clients and constituencies.
- Facilitate effective transitions and endings that advance mutually agreed-on goals.

EP 9 **Evaluate Practice with Individuals, Families, Groups, Organizations, and Communities**

- Select and use appropriate methods for evaluation of outcomes.
- Critically analyze, monitor, and evaluate intervention and program processes and outcomes.
- Apply evaluation findings to improve practice effectiveness at the micro and macro levels.

CHAPTER 2

Direct Practice: Domain, Philosophy, and Roles

with Pa Der Vang

Chapter Overview

This chapter presents a context and philosophy for direct practice, definitions of direct and clinical practice, and descriptions of the varied roles played by direct social work practitioners. After completing this chapter, you will be able to:

- Define direct and clinical practice.
- Delineate roles performed by direct practice social workers.

EPAS Competencies in Chapter 2

This chapter will give you the information needed to meet the following practice competencies:

- Competency 1: Demonstrate Ethical and Professional Behavior
- Competency 2: Engage Diversity and Difference in Practice
- Competency 3: Advance Human Rights and Social, Economic, and Environmental Justice
- Competency 4: Engage in Practice-Informed Research and Research-Informed Practice
- Competency 5: Engage in Policy Practice
- Competency 6: Engage with Individuals, Families, Groups, Organizations, and Communities

- Competency 7: Assess Individuals, Families, Groups, Organizations, and Communities
- Competency 8: Intervene with Individuals, Families, Groups, Organizations, and Communities
- Competency 9: Evaluate Practice with Individuals, Families, Groups, Organizations, and Communities

DOMAIN

Prior to 1970, social work practice was defined by methodologies or by fields of practice. Social workers were thus variously identified as *caseworkers*, *group workers*, *community organizers*, *child welfare workers*, *psychiatric social workers*, *school social workers*, *medical social workers*, and so on. The terms *direct practice* and *clinical practice* are therefore relatively new in social work nomenclature. The profession was unified in 1955 by the creation of the National Association of Social Workers (NASW) and, with the inauguration of the journal *Social Work*, the gradual transformation from more narrow views of practice to the current broader view was underway. This transformation accelerated during the 1960s and 1970s, when social unrest in the United States prompted challenges and criticisms of all institutions, including social work. Persons of color, organized groups of poor people, and other oppressed groups accused the profession of being irrelevant, given their pressing needs. These accusations were often justified; many social workers were engaged in narrowly focused and therapeutically oriented activities, such as casework and group work, that often failed to address the social problems of concern among oppressed groups (McLaughlin, 2002; Specht & Courtney, 1994). Some argue that social workers are currently more likely to espouse social justice than to prioritize strategies to achieve it. Such critics assert that the profession aims more at protecting social work roles than transforming social service delivery (Jacobson, 2001).

Casework was the predominant social work method during this period. Casework comprised activities in widely varying settings, aimed at assisting individuals, couples, or families to cope more effectively with problems that impaired their social functioning. At the same time, **group work** evolved as a practice method, with group workers practicing in settlement houses and neighborhoods, on the streets with youth gangs, in hospitals and correctional institutions, and in other settings. Although the units targeted by group workers were larger, their objectives still did not address broad social problems such as discrimination and lack of resources for oppressed groups. It was clear that urgent needs for broadly defined social services could not be met through the narrowly defined remedial (therapeutic) efforts of the casework and group work methods.

In response to the demand that social work consist of a body of knowledge or a practice philosophy that could be used in a wide variety of settings, authors such as Gordon (1965), Bartlett (1964; 1970), and Minahan and Pincus (1977) formulated a framework, or common base, for social work practice. This framework consisted of a purpose, values, sanction, knowledge, and common skills related to social work, which resulted in a broadened perspective of the profession. Because this new framework was not oriented to methods of practice, a new generic term was created to describe it: **social work practice**. The early social work practice framework identified a common knowledge base for social workers that included strategies to address client relationships, resources (Minahan & Pincus, 1977), use of the helping process (Minahan & Pincus, 1977), the importance of both direct practice and practice that influenced programs and institutions (Bartlett, 1964), and the interplay between people and society (Gordon, 1965).

Generalist Practice

The Council on Social Work Education (CSWE) responded to the evolution of the social work practice framework by adopting a curriculum policy statement stipulating that to meet accreditation standards, social work educational programs must have a curriculum containing foundation courses that embody the common knowledge base of social work practice. Both undergraduate (BSW) and graduate (MSW) programs embody such foundation courses and thus prepare students for generalist practice. BSW curricula, however, are designed primarily to prepare generalist social workers and avoid specialization in practice methods. The rationale for generalist programs is that practitioners should view problems holistically and be prepared to plan interventions aimed at multiple levels of systems related to client concerns.

A holistic approach considers multiple dimensions of human functioning, such as biological, social, and psychological factors, among others. Client goals and needs should suggest appropriate interventions, rather than letting interventions inspire the selection of compatible client goals. In other words, social workers should base their interventions on findings from the assessment rather than fitting clients into intervention models regardless of identified problems and goals. As noted in Chapter 1, client systems range from *micro systems* (individuals, couples, families, and groups) to *mezzo systems* (communities) to *macro systems* (organizations, institutions, regions, and nations). Client problems are also influenced by factors that exist in the micro, mezzo, and macro systems, including individual relationships, relationships with organizations and groups, and social norms or larger policies that affect clients' everyday lives. More recently, the strengths perspective and social justice have become enduring elements in social work practice (Gasker & Fischer, 2014; Saleebey, 2013).

Connecting client systems to resource systems that can provide needed goods and services is a paramount function of BSW programs (Minahan & Pincus, 1977). Many BSW programs, in fact, prepare students to assume the role of case manager, a role that focuses on linking clients to resources.

The foundation component of MSW programs also prepares graduate students for generalist practice. Although a few MSW programs prepare students for "advanced generalist practice," most second-year curricula in MSW programs permit students to select specializations or "concentrations" within methods of practice or within fields of practice, such as substance abuse, aging, child welfare, work with families, health care, or mental health (Lavitt, 2009; Raymond, Teare, & Atherton, 1996). MSW students thus are prepared for both generalist and specialized practice.

Similarities in orientation and differences in function between BSW and MSW social workers and the importance of having practitioners at both levels are highlighted in this chapter's case example. Note that similarities and differences exist on a continuum such that some MSW social workers perform some of the tasks otherwise ascribed to BSW practitioners and vice versa. Similarly, differences in their tasks may arise based on geographic region, field of practice, and availability of MSW-trained practitioners.

Direct Practice

Direct practice includes work with individuals, couples, families, and groups. Direct social work practitioners perform many roles in addition to delivering face-to-face service; they work in collaboration with other professionals, organizations, and institutions, and they act as advocates with landlords, agency

CASE EXAMPLE

EP 2

Arthur Harrison and Marlene Fisher were unmarried adults, each of whom had developmental disabilities. They had two sons. Mr. Harrison and Ms. Fisher came to the attention of child protection services because Roger, the older of their two sons, who also had a developmental disability, had told his teacher that his younger brother, Roy, 13, who did not have a developmental disability, and Roy's friends had sexually molested Roger. Roy admitted to the offense when interviewed, as did his friends. Roy stated that he learned the behavior from a neighbor who had been sexually abusing him since age 7.

EP 7

The family participated in an assessment conducted by Christine, a BSW social worker employed by the county's child protection agency. Roger was placed in residential care, and Roy was charged with sexual assault. Meanwhile, the neighbor boy was charged with three counts of first-degree sexual assault and was incarcerated pending a hearing. Christine then met with the parents to conduct a strengths-based and risk assessment. This assessment revealed that Mr. Harrison and Ms. Fisher had coped well with parenting on many fronts, including supporting their children in their school performance and supporting their hobbies and avocations. Some concern was raised about their capacities to protect their children from danger, however. As a result of the collaborative assessment conducted by the social worker Christine, a plan was developed with the goal of having the parents resume care for their children.

Christine acted as the case manager, coordinating the efforts of several people who were assisting Mr. Harrison and Ms. Fisher and their children in pursuit of their goal of restoration of custody. Christine played dual roles (Trotter, 2006) in this case: (1) ensuring social control designed to protect the public and vulnerable persons and (2) providing assistance to the family (a helping role). Sometimes those roles can be played simultaneously, sometimes they can be played in sequence, and sometimes only one of the two roles can be filled by the caseworker. In this instance, Christine carried out her initial assessment largely guided by her role of protecting the public and vulnerable persons.

After she came to agreement with the parents about the plan for regaining custody of their sons, Christine was more able to play a helping role. This plan included a referral to Debra, an MSW practitioner who had expertise working with children with sexual behavior difficulties. The MSW practitioner was able to work with Roy, Roger, and their parents and make a recommendation to the child welfare agency and court about when and under what conditions living together as a family would again be safe. As this example indicates, MSW practitioners frequently provide more in-depth individual and family services than fits the caseloads, responsibilities, and training of BSW practitioners. Thus, BSW and MSW practitioners can coordinate their services to better serve families.

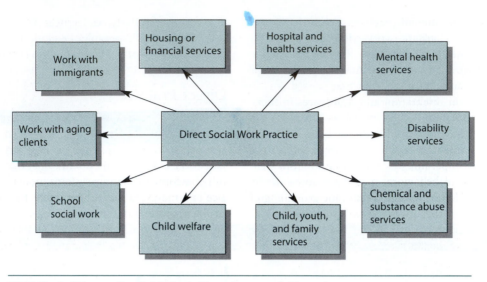

FIG 2-1 Direct Social Work Practice and Components

administrators, policy-making boards, and legislatures, among others. Direct social work practice is conducted in a variety of settings and problem areas. For example, direct practice includes services organized by the life-cycle stage of clients (children, adolescents and young adults, the elderly, etc.), by problem area (child welfare, domestic violence, health and mental health, substance abuse, antipoverty issues, work programs, etc.), by mode of intervention (work with families, work with groups, etc.), and by agency setting (school social work, disability services, etc.) (see Figure 2-1).

An Overview of Direct Practice

Direct practice encompasses a full range of roles, including acting as a caseworker or counselor. Central to assisting people with difficulties is knowledge of and skill in helping people decide how best to work on their concerns. This entails knowledge and skills in assessing human problems and in locating, developing, and utilizing appropriate resource systems. Skills in engaging clients, mutually planning relevant goals, and defining the roles of the participants are also integral parts of the helping process. Likewise, direct practitioners must possess knowledge of interventions and have skills in implementing them. Chapter 3 contains a more extensive review of the helping process, and this entire book is devoted to explicating the theory and skills related to direct practice with clients.

Direct practitioners of social work must also have a firm grasp of foundational social work knowledge and skills. Foundational knowledge includes understanding the interaction between the biological,

psychological, social, cultural, and spiritual aspects of human development and the impact on human functioning. Such foundational knowledge also includes an understanding of the helping process; the micro, mezzo, and macro systems; and a strengths perspective to assessment of client problems. Foundational social work skills include interviewing, assessing, and intervening in problematic interactions involving individuals, couples, families, and groups. Knowledge of group processes and skills in leading groups are also essential, as are skills in forming natural helping networks, functioning as a member of an interdisciplinary team, and negotiating within and between systems. The negotiating function requires skills in mediating conflicts, advocating for services, and obtaining resources, all of which embody high levels of interpersonal skills.

While this range of activities covers much of direct practice, pressures exist to emphasize the intensive individual end of the continuum through presenting billable hours (Frey & Dupper, 2005). For example, services such as advocacy and case management are often considered extra services that are rarely reimbursed by third-party payers. This may lead to the neglect of direct practice roles that emphasize the social worker's role in enhancing client relationships with resources (Frey & Dupper, 2005).

Clinical Social Work Practice

The term *clinical practice* is sometimes used interchangeably with the term *direct practice*. **Clinical social work practice** has been defined as "the provision of mental health services for the diagnosis, treatment and prevention of mental, behavioral and emotional disorders in individuals, families and groups" (Clinical Social Work Federation, 1997). The focus of clinical work is said to be "to provide mental health treatment in agencies, clinics, hospitals and as private practitioners" (Clinical Social Work Association, 2008). However, Walsh defines clinical social work practice broadly to include the resolution and prevention of psychosocial problems experienced by individuals, families, and groups, not just mental health treatment but emotional and behavioral disorders more broadly (Walsh, 2006). He further emphasizes the grounding of clinical practice in social work values, such as promoting social and economic justice and focusing on diversity and multiculturalism.

Linking clients to resources and advocating for access to resources are important aspects of practice when working with oppressed clients. These activities may contribute to improved mental health for clients struggling with poverty, lack of housing, or discrimination. Therefore, clinical interventions include therapeutic, supportive, educational, and advocacy functions (Walsh, 2006). Clinical case management therefore includes developing comprehensive assessments and monitoring client progress (including mental status), among other activities (Sherrer & O'Hare, 2008). Meanwhile, empirical clinical practice emphasizes the use of empirical information in the design and delivery of clinical services (Thyer, 2001a). In addition, with advancements in technology, clinical social work services can now be delivered online for clients seeking more accessibility (Dombo, Kays, & Weller, 2014).

As noted, clinical social work practitioners at times also provide mental health services in the performance of their duties. However, though mental health treatment may be provided to clients in many settings, such treatment is not the primary function in those settings. For example, although mental health services may be useful to some clients in a homeless shelter, environmental interventions to assist with housing are the social worker's primary function in this case.

Some have questioned whether engaging in psychotherapy is appropriate for a profession whose mission focuses on social justice (Specht & Courtney, 1994). Others have countered that a social justice mission is not necessarily inconsistent with use of psychotherapy as one tool in pursuit of this goal (Wakefield, 1996a, 1996b). According to Swenson (1998), clinical work that draws on client strengths, that is mindful of social positions and power relationships, and that attempts to counter oppression is consistent with a social justice perspective. In our opinion, these debates are moot. While clinical social workers are often called on to provide therapeutic services to persons with mental illness, clinical social workers must also utilize foundational social work practice knowledge and skills in specific practice settings, which include a social justice framework and the role of being a system broker and advocate as necessary. Many of today's practitioners in social work and other helping professions practice psychotherapy that draws on additional theory bases such as behavioral and family systems models. Clinical practice in a managed care environment focuses on specific problems, strengths, and resources; is highly structured and goal oriented; and develops tangible objectives for each session intended to achieve overall treatment goals (Franklin, 2002).

Note that the title of *clinical social worker* has special significance in some states because an advanced license is labeled as "clinical." In such states, licensing provisions are such that diagnosis and treatment of mental health difficulties requires that the provider have a clinical license or be under the supervision of a person with such a license. Achievement of such a license is based on completion of specified hours in training and supervision as well as completion of an exam. Holding such a license then becomes a required credential for social workers to be eligible for third-party reimbursement for delivering psychotherapy or counseling.

Although we recognize the significance of these licensing and reimbursement issues, as well as the attached status and prestige of the term "clinical social worker," we do not think it necessary to subsume all direct social work practice under the term *clinical practice*. We prefer to describe clinical services as a particular form of direct service that can be delivered in many fields of practice but which include the assessment and treatment of mental health issues as one function. Clinical social workers are encouraged not to ignore the varied roles they often fulfill as social workers in direct practice with individuals. Crucial interventions are performed to assist children and families in child welfare, for example, regardless of whether they are related to mental health services. Some seem to use the term *clinical practice* to connote "quality social work practice," in that one-on-one therapeutic experiences are seen as more important than case management experiences (Xenakis & Primack, 2013). In this book, we will use both terms, *direct practice* and *clinical practice*, guided by the primary functions of the settings in which micro-level services are delivered.

A PHILOSOPHY OF DIRECT PRACTICE

As a profession evolves, its knowledge base expands and practitioners gain experience in applying abstract values and knowledge to specific practice situations. Instrumental values gradually evolve as part of this transformation; as they are adopted, they become principles or guidelines to practice. Such principles express preferred beliefs about the nature and causes of human problems. They also describe perspectives about people's capacity to deal with problems, desirable goals, and valued qualities in helping relationships. Finally, those principles include beliefs about vital elements of the helping process, the roles of the practitioner and the client, characteristics of effective group leaders, and the nature of the human growth process.

Over many years, we have evolved a philosophy of practice from a synthesis of principles gained from sources too diverse to acknowledge, including our own value preferences. We thus offer as our philosophy of direct practice the principles outlined in Figure 2-2.

ROLES OF DIRECT PRACTITIONERS

During recent years, increasing attention has been devoted to the various roles that direct practitioners perform in discharging their responsibilities. We have

PHILOSOPHY OF DIRECT PRACTICE

1. The problems experienced by social work clients stem from lack of resources, knowledge, and skills (societal, systemic, and personal sources), either alone or in combination.

2. Because social work clients are often subject to poverty, racism, sexism, heterosexism, discrimination, and lack of resources, social workers negotiate systems and advocate for change to ensure that their clients obtain access to their rights, resources, and treatment with dignity. They also attempt to modify or develop resource systems to make them more responsive to client needs.

3. People are capable of making their own choices and decisions. Although controlled to some extent by their environment, they are able to direct their environment more than they realize. Social workers aim to assist in the empowerment of their clients by (1) helping them gain the ability to make decisions, (2) assisting them in accessing critical resources that affect their lives, and (3) increasing their ability to change those environmental influences that adversely affect them individually and as members of groups.

4. Because social service systems are often funded on the basis of individual dysfunctions, social workers play an educational function in sensitizing service delivery systems to more systemic problem-solving approaches that emphasize health, strengths, and natural support systems.

5. Frequently, social workers encounter clients who are reluctant to receive services through referrals; these clients are often pressured by others or are under threat of legal sanctions. While people have a right to their own values and beliefs, sometimes their behaviors violate the rights of others, and the social worker assists these clients in facing these aspects of their difficulties. Because reluctant or involuntary clients are often not seeking a helping relationship but rather wishing to escape one, negotiation is frequently required.

6. Some clients seek services because they wish to experience change through a social worker's assistance. Such clients are often helped by having an accepting relationship with the social worker involving appropriate self-disclosure, which will allow them to seek greater self-awareness and to live more fully in the reality of the moment.

7. All clients, whether voluntary or involuntary, are entitled to be treated with respect and dignity and to have their choices facilitated.

8. Client behavior is goal directed, although these goals are often not readily discernible. Clients are, however, capable of learning new skills, knowledge, and approaches to resolving their difficulties. Social workers are responsible for helping clients discover their strengths and affirming their capacity for growth and change.

9. Although clients' current problems are often influenced by past relationships and concerns, and limited focus on the past is sometimes beneficial, most difficulties can be alleviated by focusing on present choices and by mobilizing strengths and coping patterns.

FIG 2-2 Principles of a Philosophy of Direct Practice

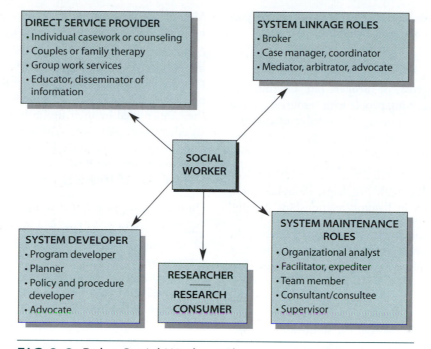

FIG 2-3 Roles Social Workers Play

already touched on some of these roles, but in this section we explore these and other roles in greater detail and refer to sections of the book where we discuss certain roles more explicitly. We have categorized the roles based in part on a schema presented by Lister (1987) (see Figure 2-3).

Direct Provision of Services

Roles subsumed under this category include those in which social workers meet face to face with clients or consumer groups in providing services.

- *Individual casework or counseling (case manager, intake worker, crisis worker):* Social workers may provide individual case management and counseling at the same time.
- *Couples and family therapy:* This may include sessions with individuals, conjoint sessions, and group sessions.
- *Group work services:* This may include support groups, therapy groups, self-help groups, task groups, and skill development groups.
- *Educator/disseminator of information:* Social workers may provide essential information in individual, conjoint, or group sessions or may make educational presentations to consumer groups or

to the public. For example, practitioners may conduct educational sessions dealing with parenting skills, marital enrichment, stress management, or various aspects of mental health or health care (Dore, 1993).

These roles are primary in the work of most direct service social workers. However, note that these roles are not mutually exclusive. Social workers may have a duty to fulfill multiple roles at the same time, regardless of their job title or area of focus. For example, a case manager will often be in the role of educator or disseminator, or a group worker may be asked to provide brief case management to address an immediate client need. Because this book is aimed at preparing social workers to provide such direct services, we will not elaborate further on these roles in this section.

System Linkage Roles

Because clients may need resources not provided by a given social agency and may lack knowledge of or the ability to utilize other available resources, social workers often perform roles in developing new resources, linking people to resources, facilitating linkages between resources, and facilitating client relationships with resources. **Resources** refer to tangible resources such as links to institutions as well as nontangible resources such as coping and cognitive resources.

Broker

To perform the role of **broker** (an intermediary who assists in connecting people with resources), social workers must have a thorough knowledge of community resources so that they can make appropriate referrals. Familiarity with the policies of resource systems and working relationships with key contact persons are essential to making successful referrals. In the earlier case example, Christine, the BSW-trained social worker, brokered services for Mr. Harrison, Ms. Fisher, and their children, including the referral to Debra, the MSW-trained sexual behaviors counselor. Note that before some people are able to avail themselves of resources, they may require the social worker's assistance in overcoming fears and misconceptions about those services. Counselors and psychotherapists, meanwhile, must be knowledgeable in theory and practice models that help clients to understand and access internal human resources such as cognitive and emotional strengths.

Social workers also may be responsible for developing simple and effective referral mechanisms and ways of monitoring whether clients actually follow through on referrals. This is the process of facilitating client relationships with resources.

Case Manager/Coordinator

Some clients lack the ability, skills, knowledge, or resources to follow through on referrals to other systems. In such instances, the social worker may serve as case manager, assuming primary responsibility for assessing the needs of a client and arranging and coordinating the delivery of essential goods and services provided by other resources. Case managers also work directly with clients and resource networks to ensure that the needed goods and services are provided in a timely manner.

It is noteworthy that in the case manager role, social workers function at the interface between the client and the environment more so than in any other role. Because of recent dramatic increases in the numbers of people needing case management services, such as homeless individuals, elderly clients, and persons with serious and persistent mental illness, numerous articles have appeared in the literature focusing on clients who need such services, issues related to case management, and various functions of case managers.

Mediator/Arbitrator

EP 9

Occasionally, breakdowns occur between clients and service providers so that clients do not receive the needed services to which they are entitled. For example, clients may be seeking a resource to which they believe they are entitled by their health insurance. In other cases, participants in workfare programs may find themselves sanctioned for failure to meet program expectations (Hage, 2004).

Service may be denied for several reasons. Perhaps clients did not adequately represent their eligibility for services, or strains that sometimes develop between clients and service providers may precipitate withdrawals of requests for services by clients or withholding of services by providers.

In such instances, practitioners may serve as mediators with the goal of eliminating obstacles to service delivery. **Mediation** is a process that "provides a neutral forum in which disputants are encouraged to find a mutually satisfactory resolution to their problems" (Chandler, 1985, p. 346). When serving as a mediator, you must carefully listen to and draw out facts and feelings from both parties to determine the cause of the breakdown. It is important not to take sides with either party until you are confident that you have accurate and complete information. When you have determined the nature of the breakdown, you can plan appropriate remedial action aimed at removing barriers, clarifying possible misunderstandings, and working through negative feelings that have impeded service delivery. The communication skills used in this process are delineated in subsequent chapters of this book.

In recent years, knowledge of mediation skills has evolved to a high level of sophistication. Today, a growing number of social workers are working independently or in tandem with attorneys to mediate conflicts between divorcing partners regarding child custody, visitation rights, and property settlements. These same skills can be used to mediate personnel disputes, labor management conflicts, and victim–offender situations (Nugent et al., 2001).

Client Advocate

EP 3

With respect to linking clients with resources, **advocacy** is the process of working with and/or on behalf of clients to obtain services and resources that would not otherwise be provided. Social workers have assumed the role of advocate for a client or group of clients since the inception of the profession. The obligation to assume this role has been reaffirmed most recently in the NASW Code of Ethics, which includes advocacy among the activities performed by social workers in pursuit of the professional mission (NASW, 2008a).

System Maintenance and Enhancement

As staff members of social agencies, social workers bear responsibility for evaluating structures, policies, and functional relationships within agencies that impair effectiveness in service delivery.

Organizational Analyst

EP 3 and 8

Discharging the role of **organizational analyst** entails pinpointing factors in agency structure, policy, and procedures that have a negative impact on service delivery. Knowledge of organizational and administrative theory is essential to performing this role effectively. For example, it is well documented that African American children are overrepresented in the child welfare system in the United States (Boyd, 2014; Font, Berger, & Slack, 2012; Marshall & Haight, 2014). This means that a greater proportion of Caucasian children are returned to their parents after child welfare assessments. The reasons for this disproportion are complex and not tied to any one factor. Engaging in the organizational assessor role, social workers in child welfare would examine the decisions made in the system. They would then try to make sure that resources such as family group decision making are especially available to families of color as that resource is promising as a way to safely preserve families.

Facilitator/Expediter

After pinpointing factors that impede service delivery, social workers have a responsibility to plan and implement ways of enhancing service delivery. This may involve providing relevant input to agency boards and administrators, recommending staff meetings to address problems, working collaboratively with other staff members to bring pressure to bear on resistant administrators, encouraging and participating in essential in-service training sessions, and other similar activities.

Team Member

In many agency and institutional settings, such as mental health, health care, rehabilitation, and education settings, practitioners function as members of clinical teams that collaborate in assessing clients' problems and delivering services (Sands, 1989; Sands, Stafford, & McClelland, 1990). Such teams commonly consist of a psychiatrist or physician, a psychologist, a social worker, a nurse, and perhaps a rehabilitation counselor, occupational therapist, educator, or recreational therapist, depending on the setting. Members of the team have varying types of expertise that are tapped in formulating assessments and planning and implementing therapeutic interventions. As team members, social workers often contribute knowledge related to family dynamics and engage in therapeutic work with family members. Social workers who are either leaders or members of a team or group use knowledge and skills in working with groups, such as group dynamics and group process.

Sometimes such teams are dominated by members from more powerful professions (Bell, 2001). Dane and Simon (1991) note that social workers in such host settings, in which the mission and decision making may be dominated by non–social workers, often experience a discrepancy between their professional mission and the values of the employing institution. They can act, however, to sensitize team members to client strengths and advocate for a more holistic approach while exercising their knowledge of resources and expertise in linking clients with resources.

Social workers also are expected to apply their knowledge of community resources in planning for the discharge of patients and facilitating their reentry into the community following periods of hospitalization. In so doing, social workers bring their systems and strengths perspectives to teams that are sometimes more deficit focused.

In addition, social workers are involved in interdisciplinary work across systems, such as schools and child welfare, which require the ability to work within several systems simultaneously (Bailey-Dempsey & Reid, 1996). As team members, social workers also often serve as case managers in coordinating discharge planning for patients (Dane & Simon, 1991; Kadushin & Kulys, 1993).

Consultant/Consultee

Consultation is a process whereby an expert enables a consultee to deliver services more effectively to a client by increasing, developing, modifying, or freeing the consultee's knowledge, skills, attitudes, or behavior with respect to the problem at hand (Kadushin, 1977). Although social workers both provide and receive consultation, there has been a trend for licensed MSW social workers to serve less as consumers of consultation and more as providers. MSW trainees must seek regular consultation services until they are licensed to practice independently. BSW social workers may provide consultation regarding the availability of specific community resources. More often, however, they are consumers of consultation when they need information about how to work effectively in problem solving that encompasses complex situations and behaviors. Social workers assume the consultee role when they need expert knowledge from supervisors, doctors and nurses, psychiatrists, psychologists, and other social workers who possess high levels of expertise related to certain types of problems (e.g., substance abuse, child maltreatment, sexual problems).

Social workers serve as consultants to members of other professions and to other social workers in need of their special expertise, including when they fill the role of supervisor. For example, they may provide consultation to school personnel who need assistance in understanding and coping with problem students; to health care providers who seek assistance in understanding a patient's family or ethnic and cultural factors; to court staff regarding matters that bear on child custody decisions and decisions about parole and probation; and in many other similar situations.

Supervisor

Relations between consultants and consultees in social work frequently occur within the supervisory relationship. **Supervisors** play a critical role in the support of quality direct practice work performed by social work practitioners. Supervisors are responsible for orienting staff to how they can learn through supervision, lines of authority, requirements, and policies of the setting (Munson, 2002). Supervisors are responsible for guiding supervisees on how to use theory in practice and in understanding the helping process. Social work supervisors frequently use case presentations by staff social workers as a key mechanism of learning during case consultation. Such presentations should be organized around questions to be answered. Supervisors provide strategies for engagement and assist staff in linking assessment with intervention plans and evaluation. Special responsibilities include helping supervisees identify when client advocacy is needed, identifying and resolving ethical conflicts, and monitoring issues of race, ethnicity, lifestyle, and vulnerability as they affect the client–social worker interaction. In addition, supervisors often take the lead in securing resources for staff and facilitating linkages with other organizations.

Researcher/Research Consumer

EP 4 and 9

Practitioners face responsibilities in both public and private settings to select interventions that can be evaluated, to evaluate the effectiveness of their interventions, and to systematically monitor the progress of their clients. Implementing these processes requires practitioners to conduct and make use of research.

As described in Chapter 1, social workers are expected to incorporate research skills into their practice. Such incorporation occurs at several levels. For example, being able to define questions in ways that help in consulting the research literature about effectiveness is one such competency. Conducting ongoing evaluation of the effectiveness of practice is another.

Some practitioners utilize single-subject (i.e., single-system) designs. This type of research design enables practitioners to obtain measures of the extent (frequency and severity) of problem behaviors before they implement interventions aimed at eliminating or reducing the problem behaviors or increasing the frequency of positive but currently insufficient behaviors (e.g., doing homework, engaging in prosocial behaviors, setting realistic and consistent limits with children, sending positive messages, abstaining from drinking). These measures provide a baseline against which the results of the interventions can be assessed by applying the same measures periodically during the course of the interventions, at termination, and at follow-up (Reid, 1994). Perhaps more frequently, practitioners use some form of Goal Attainment Scaling that calls for rating goal achievement on a scale with points designated in advance (Corcoran & Vandiver, 1996).

As noted in Chapter 1, the Council on Social Work Education (CSWE) Educational Policy and Accreditation Standards (EPAS) state that social workers engage in research-informed practice and practice-informed research. Not only are social practices informed by research, knowledge from social work practice itself must inform the research. The term *evidence-based practice* has gained popularity when referring to research-informed practice. Evidence-based practice is defined as the "incorporation of available research evidence into practice efforts" (Drisko, 2014, p. 123). The growing use and support of evidence-based practice suggests that social work practices must be informed by results derived from the scientific method, including both quantitative and qualitative designs. At the same time, findings from social work practice are used to inform research through publications of scholarly work and organizational or government reports.

A criticism of an overemphasis on evidence-based practice is the heavy reliance on the practitioner as the expert, while client experience or practice knowledge is considered less important because of a lack of empirical evidence. In addition, the bulk of evidence-based practice models rely on research that is validated and normed by the dominant culture, while alternative models of practice relevant to minority cultural groups have not gained much recognition (Eisenberg, 2008; Gonzalez, 2012).

System Development

EP 6

Direct practitioners sometimes have opportunities to improve or expand agency services based on assessment of unmet client needs, gaps in service, needs for preventive services, or research indicating that more promising results might be achieved by interventions other than those currently employed.

Program Developer

As noted earlier, practitioners often have opportunities to develop services in response to emerging needs of clients and new client populations. **Program developers** seek to fill a gap in services. Such services may include educational programs (e.g., for immigrants or pregnant teenagers), support groups (e.g., for rape victims, adult children of alcoholics, or victims of incest), culturally appropriate programs that respond to new cultural groups, and skill development programs (e.g., stress management, parenting, and assertiveness training groups).

Planner

In small communities and rural areas that lack access to community planners, direct practitioners may need to assume a planning role, usually in concert with individuals in positions with access to monetary resources and social power. In this role, the practitioner works both formally and informally with directors and managers of departments to plan programs that respond to unmet and emerging needs. Such needs could include child care programs, transportation for elderly and disabled persons, and recreational and health care programs, to name just a few. Planners have an inside perspective on factors such as financial parameters, local and national policies, expressed community needs and concerns, and agency parameters around the creation of new services and the maintenance of current services.

Policy and Procedure Developer

EP 5

Participation of direct practitioners in formulating policies and procedures typically is limited to the agencies in which they provide direct services to clients. Their degree of participation in such activities is largely determined by the style of administration within a given agency. Able administrators generally solicit and invite input from professional staff about how the agency can more effectively respond to the consumers of its services. Because social workers serve on the "front lines," they are strategically positioned to evaluate clients' needs and to assess how policies and procedures serve—or fail to serve—the best interests of clients. For these reasons, social workers should become actively involved in decision-making processes related to policies and procedures.

In rural areas and small communities, direct practitioners often participate in policy development concerned with the needs of a broad community rather than the needs of a circumscribed target group. In such instances, social workers must draw from knowledge and skills gained in courses in social welfare policy and services and community planning.

Advocate

Just as social workers may advocate for an individual client, they may also join client groups, other social workers, and allied professionals in advocating for legislation and social policies aimed at providing needed resources and enhancing social justice. Social workers may also be in the role of advocate within their agencies when a gap in or lack of services is recognized within an agency.

EP 1 and 3

SUMMARY

Direct social work practice is characterized by performance of multiple roles; these roles are often performed at the same time and are carried out at several system levels, depending on the concerns addressed. Knowledge and skills related to some of these roles are taught in segments of the curriculum that lie outside direct practice courses. To do justice in one volume to the knowledge and skills entailed in all these roles is impossible; consequently, we have limited our focus primarily to the roles involved in providing direct service.

COMPETENCY NOTES

EP 1 Demonstrate Ethical and Professional Behavior
- Demonstrate professional demeanor in behavior, appearance, and oral, written, and electronic communication.

EP 2 Engage Diversity and Difference in Practice
- Apply and communicate understanding of the importance of diversity and difference in shaping life experiences in practice at the micro, mezzo, and macro levels.

EP 3 Advance Human Rights and Social, Economic, and Environmental Justice
- Apply your understanding of social, economic, and environmental justice to advocate for human rights at the individual and system levels, and engage in practices that advance social, economic, and environmental justice.

EP 4 Engage in Practice-Informed Research and Research-Informed Practice
- Use practice experience and theory to inform scientific inquiry and research.
- Engage in critical analysis of quantitative and qualitative research methods and research findings.
- Use and translate research findings to inform and improve practice, policy, and service delivery.

EP 5 Engage in Policy Practice
- Assess how social welfare and economic policies affect the delivery of and access to social services.
- Critically analyze and promote policies that advance human rights and social, economic, and environmental justice.

EP 6 Engage with Individuals, Families, Groups, Organizations, and Communities
- Apply knowledge of human behavior and the social environment and practice context to engage with clients and constituencies.
- Use empathy, reflection, and interpersonal skills to effectively engage diverse clients and constituencies.

EP 7 Assess Individuals, Families, Groups, Organizations, and Communities
- Collect, organize, and critically analyze and interpret information from clients and constituencies.
- Apply knowledge of human behavior and the social environment, person-in-environment, and other multidisciplinary theoretical frameworks in the analysis of assessment data from clients and constituencies.
- Develop mutually agreed-on intervention goals and objectives based on the critical assessment of strengths, needs, and challenges within clients and constituencies.
- Select appropriate intervention strategies based on the assessment, research knowledge, and values and preferences of clients and constituencies.

EP 8 Intervene with Individuals, Families, Groups, Organizations, and Communities
- Implement interventions to achieve practice goals and enhance capacities of clients and constituencies.
- Apply knowledge of human behavior and the social environment, person-in-environment, and other multidisciplinary theoretical frameworks in interventions with clients and constituencies.
- Use interprofessional collaboration as appropriate to achieve beneficial practice outcomes.
- Negotiate, mediate, and advocate with and on behalf of clients and constituencies.
- Facilitate effective transitions and endings that advance mutually agreed-on goals.

EP 9 Evaluate Practice with Individuals, Families, Groups, Organizations, and Communities
- Select and use appropriate methods for evaluation of outcomes.
- Critically analyze, monitor, and evaluate intervention and program processes and outcomes.
- Apply evaluation findings to improve practice effectiveness at the micro and macro levels.

CHAPTER 3

Overview of the Helping Process

with Pa Der Vang

Chapter Overview

This chapter provides an overview of the three phases of the helping process: exploration, implementation, and termination. The helping process focuses on problem solving with social work clients in a variety of settings, including those found along a continuum of voluntarism. Hence, the process is presented with the larger systems context in mind. In addition, we present an overview of the structure and ingredients of interviews.

At the completion of your work on this chapter, you will be able to:

- Identify steps in the helping process, from exploration through implementation and termination.
- Plan the structure and environment for interviews.

EPAS Competencies in Chapter 3

This chapter will give you the information needed to meet the following practice competencies:

- Competency 1: Demonstrate Ethical and Professional Behavior
- Competency 2: Engage Diversity and Difference in Practice

- Competency 6: Engage with Individuals, Families, Groups, Organizations, and Communities
- Competency 7: Assess Individuals, Families, Groups, Organizations, and Communities
- Competency 8: Intervene with Individuals, Families, Groups, Organizations, and Communities
- Competency 9: Evaluate Practice with Individuals, Families, Groups, Organizations, and Communities

COMMON ELEMENTS AMONG DIVERSE THEORISTS AND SOCIAL WORKERS

Direct social workers working with individuals, couples, families, groups, and other systems draw on contrasting theories of human behavior, use different models of practice, implement diverse interventions, and serve widely different clients (Cameron & Keenan, 2010). Despite these varied factors, such social workers share a common goal: to assist clients in coping more effectively with problems of living and improving the quality of their lives. People are impelled by either internal or external forces to secure social work services because current solutions are not succeeding in their lives. Helping approaches differ in the extent to which they are problem versus goal focused. We take the position that it is important for direct social workers to take seriously the problems compelling clients to seek services as well as to work creatively with them toward achieving solutions that *improve* upon the initial problematic situation (McMillen, Morris, & Sherraden, 2004).

Whether a potential client perceives a need or seeks help is a critical issue in planning how services may be offered. Clients' reaction to internal or external forces plays a part in their motivation for and reaction to the prospects for contact with a social worker. Often, a need for help has been identified by external sources such as teachers, doctors, employers, or family members. Such persons might be best considered referrals because they did not apply for service (Compton, Galaway, & Cournoyer, 2005). Persons who are referred vary in the extent to which they perceive that referral as a source of pressure or simply as a source of potential assistance. Individuals who initiate contact themselves as voluntary clients, referrals, or involuntary clients are all potential clients if they can negotiate a contract addressing some of their concerns. Children are a special type of potential client as they are rarely applicants themselves but rather are usually referred by teachers or family members for concerns others have about their behavior.

In whatever way potential clients begin their contact, they face a situation in which they can potentially enhance their problem-solving ability by developing new resources or employing untapped resources to reduce tension and achieve mastery over problems. Whatever their approach to assisting clients, most direct social workers employ a process aimed at reducing client concerns. That is, social workers try to assist clients in assessing the concerns that they perceive or that their environment presses upon them, making decisions about fruitful ways to identify and prioritize those concerns. Next, the social worker and client jointly identify potential approaches to reduce those concerns and make decisions about which courses of action to pursue.

VIDEO CASE EXAMPLE

In the video "Hanging with Hailey," a school social worker, Emily, meets with Hailey, an adolescent referred to her by teachers because of their concern with Hailey's declining academic performance. Hailey is not legally required to meet with Emily, yet she amply demonstrates that she is not a voluntary client seeking service either. Indeed, it is not unusual in these circumstances for adolescents to view a referral to a social worker negatively, as a punishment for bad behavior.

The challenge for social workers such as Emily is to empathically respond to Hailey's concerns at the same time as she conducts an assessment to determine what might account for Hailey's change in behavior. Emily therefore takes time to work together with Hailey to jointly identify concerns related to Hailey's feeling lonely and isolated at school and feeling disconnected to her mother, as well as concerns about her declining grades. In order to arrive at these joint concerns, Emily must assess Hailey's depressed affect in their second session and conduct a danger assessment to determine whether Hailey is at risk of self-harm.

Intervention approaches are selected in part because of available evidence about how effective they are at reducing client concerns. Involuntary clients face situations in which some of the concerns are not their own and some of the approaches to reduce those concerns may be mandated by other parties. Yet even in these circumstances, clients have the power to make at least constrained choices regarding how they address these concerns or additional concerns beyond those that they have been mandated to address. After these strategic approaches have been identified and selected, they are implemented.

Working together, the client and the social worker then assess the success of their efforts and revise their plans as necessary. Social workers use a variety of communication skills to implement the problem-solving process, given the many different systems involved in clients' concerns.

The first portion of this chapter provides an overview of the helping process and its three distinct phases; subsequent parts of the book are organized to correspond to these phases. The latter part of this chapter focuses on the structure and processes involved in interviewing—a critical aspect of dealing with clients. Later chapters deal with the structure, processes, and skills involved in modifying the processes of families and groups.

THE HELPING PROCESS

The helping process consists of three major phases (see Figure 3-1):

- Phase I: Exploration, engagement, assessment, and planning
- Phase II: Implementation and goal attainment
- Phase III: Evaluation and termination

Each of these phases has distinct objectives, and the helping process generally proceeds successively through them. The three phases, however, are not sharply demarcated by the activities and skills employed. Indeed, the activities and skills employed in the three phases differ more in terms of their frequency and intensity than in the kind used. The processes of exploration and assessment, for example, are central during Phase I, but these processes continue in somewhat diminished significance during subsequent phases of the helping process.

Phase I: Exploration, Engagement, Assessment, and Planning

EP 6, 7, 8, and 9

Phase I of the helping process lays the groundwork for subsequent implementation of interventions and strategies aimed at resolving clients' problems and promoting problem-solving skills. It represents a key step in helping relationships of any duration and setting—from crisis intervention and discharge planning to long-term and institutional care. Processes involved and tasks to be accomplished during Phase I include the following:

1. Exploring clients' problems by eliciting comprehensive data about the person(s), the problem, and environmental factors, including forces influencing the referral for contact
2. Establishing rapport and enhancing motivation
3. Formulating a multidimensional assessment of the problem, identifying systems that play a significant

Phase I: Exploration, Engagement, Assessment, and Planning	Phase II: Implementation and Goal Attainment	Phase III: Evaluation and Termination
1. Exploring clients' problems by eliciting comprehensive data about the person(s), the problem, and environmental factors, including forces influencing the referral for contact	1. Prioritize goals into general and specific tasks	1. Assessing when client goals have been satisfactorily attained
2. Establishing rapport and enhancing motivation	2. Select and implement interventions	2. Helping the client develop strategies that maintain change and continue growth following the termination
3. Formulating a multidimensional assessment of the problem, identifying systems that play a significant role in the difficulties, and identifying relevant resources that can be tapped or must be developed	3. Plan task implementation, enhancing self-efficacy	3. Successfully terminating the helping relationship
	4. Maintain focus within sessions	
	5. Maintain continuity between sessions	
4. Mutually negotiating goals to be accomplished in remedying or alleviating problems and formulating a contract	6. Monitor progress	
	7. Identify and address barriers to change	
5. Making referrals	8. Employ appropriate self-disclosure and assertiveness to facilitate change	

FIG 3-1 Phases of the Helping Process and Constituent Activities and Processes

role in the difficulties, and identifying relevant resources that can be tapped or must be developed

4. Mutually negotiating goals to be accomplished in remedying or alleviating problems and formulating a contract
5. Making referrals

We briefly discuss each of these five processes in the following sections and refer to portions of the book that include more extensive discussions of these processes.

Exploring Clients' Problems

EP 7

Contact begins with an initial exploration of the circumstances that have led the potential client to meet with the social worker. Social workers should not assume that potential clients are applicants at this point because self-referred persons are the minority of clients served in many settings; even those who self-refer often do so at the suggestion or pressure of others (Cingolani, 1984).

Potential clients may be anxious about the prospect of seeking help and lack knowledge about what to expect. The social worker often will have information from an intake form or referral source about the circumstances that have brought the client into contact. These many possibilities can be explored by asking questions such as the following:

- "I have read your intake form. Can you tell me what brings you here, in your own words?"
- "How can we help you?"

These questions should elicit a beginning elaboration of the concern or pressures that the potential client sees as relating to his or her contact. The social worker can begin to determine to what extent the motivation for contact was initiated by the potential client and to what extent the motivation represents a response to external forces. For example, adolescents such as Hailey in the Video Case described above are often referred by teachers who are concerned about their classroom behavior or ability to learn in the classroom. The social worker should begin in such circumstances with a matter-of-fact, nonthreatening description of the circumstances that led to the referral. For example, in the Video Case described above, the social worker, Emily, might have said the following:

- "You were referred by a teacher who was concerned about some changes in your behavior. Be assured

that you have done nothing wrong. I would like to check with you to see how things are going with you and whether I might be of service."

The social worker should also give a clear, brief description of his or her own view of the purpose of this first contact and encourage an exploration of how the social worker can be helpful, such as the following:

- "We are meeting both to explore the teacher's concerns and also to hear from you about how things are going at school as you see it. My job is to find out what things you would like to see go better and to figure out with you ways that we might work together so that you get more out of school."

Skills that are employed in the exploratory process with individuals, couples, families, and groups are delineated later in this chapter and at length in subsequent chapters.

Establishing Rapport and Enhancing Motivation

Effective communication in the helping relationship is crucial. Unless the social worker succeeds in engaging the potential client, the client may be reluctant to reveal vital information and feelings and, even worse, may not return after the initial session.

EP 6

Engaging clients successfully means establishing **rapport**, which reduces the level of threat and gains the trust of clients, who recognize that the social worker intends to be helpful. One condition of rapport is that clients perceive a social worker as understanding and genuinely interested in their well-being. To create such a positive perception among clients who may differ in significant ways from the social worker (including race or ethnicity, gender, sexual orientation, and age, for example), the social worker must attend to relevant cultural factors and vary interviewing techniques accordingly. (We discuss establishing rapport in interviewing in more detail later in this chapter and throughout the book.)

Potential clients may also draw conclusions about the openness of the agency to their concerns through the intake forms that they must complete. For example, agency forms asking for the client's gender with only check boxes for male, female, or "other" may seem closed off to clients who do not identify as either male or female. The use of "other" as a selection for gender seems to marginalize clients who may not identify as male or female; therefore, an open-ended text box may be preferred when asking for gender (Charnley & Langley, 2007).

Further, when potential clients have been referred by others, these clients will need to be reassured that their wishes are important and that they do not necessarily have to work on the concerns seen by the referral source. Such clients frequently have misgivings about the helping process. They do not perceive themselves as having a problem and often attribute the source of difficulties to another person or to untoward circumstances. Such clients face social workers with several challenging tasks:

- Neutralizing negative feelings
- Attempting to help potential clients understand problems identified by others and assessing the advantages and disadvantages of dealing with those concerns
- Creating an incentive to work on acknowledged problems and identifying goals

Skillful social workers often succeed in tapping into the motivation of such involuntary clients.

In other instances, clients may freely acknowledge problems and may have incentive for change but assume a passive role, expecting social workers to magically work out their difficulties for them. Social workers must avoid taking on the impossible role that some clients would ascribe to them. Instead, they should voice a belief in clients' abilities to work as partners in searching for remedial courses of action and mobilize clients' energies in implementing the tasks essential to successful problem resolution. It is important that social workers delineate the difference between the tasks and the goal; often, clients become overwhelmed with the tasks although they agree with the goal. When using a **strengths-based approach**, it is necessary to identify not just concerns but also what things are going well in the client's life in order to highlight current coping mechanisms.

One very useful strategy is to acknowledge the client's problem and explicitly recognize the client's motivation to actively work toward its solution. Phrasing the solution as a goal will help differentiate the goal from tasks. Potential clients do not lack motivation; rather, they sometimes lack motivation to work on the problems and goals perceived by others. In addition, motivation relates to past experience, which leads clients to expect either that they will be successful or that they will fail when they attempt to reach their goals. Hence, individuals with limited expectations for success often appear to lack motivation. As a consequence, social workers must often attempt to increase motivation by helping clients discover that their actions can be effective in reaching their goals (Gold, 1990).

Motivation can also be seen in terms of stages of change. In some cases, clients are said to be in the **precontemplation stage**: they have not yet considered a problem that has been perceived by others (Di Clemente & Prochaska, 1998). For example, a student who is referred to a school social worker for lateness and perceived tiredness may not have considered this an issue for which he was personally responsible, perhaps feeling instead that he is powerless in this regard and that it is his parents' responsibility to help him get to school or to bed on time.

Frequently, clients are in the **contemplation stage**: they are aware of the issue but are not fully aware of their options, the benefits of changing, and the consequences for not doing so (Di Clemente & Prochaska, 1998). Such clients can be helped to explore those possibilities. For example, in our example of the student who has been referred to the school social worker for lateness and tardiness, the social worker can gather information from the student about his sleeping patterns and rituals involved in getting ready for school. Together they can explore what might happen if the student continues to arrive late and be tired in school and how things might be different if behavior patterns are modified to arrive at school on time and rested.

Social workers, therefore, must be able to tap into client motivation and assist those individuals who readily acknowledge a problem but are reluctant to expend the required effort or bear the discomfort involved in effecting essential change. A major task in this process is to provide information to the potential client about what to expect from the helping process. This socialization effort includes identifying the kinds of concerns with which the social worker and agency can help; client rights, including confidentiality and the circumstances in which it might be abridged; and information about what behaviors to expect from the social worker and what behaviors will be expected from the client (Trotter, 2006).

The task for clients in group situations is twofold: They must develop a rapport with and trust in the social worker, and they must also develop a rapport with and trust in the other group members. If group members vary in terms of race, ethnicity, social class, or in other ways, the **group leader** must be sensitive to such potential influences on group members' behavior. He or she must assume a facilitative role in breaking down related barriers to rapport not only between the social worker and individual group members but also among group members. Such cultural competency is an important aspect of competence; indeed, it is a core value in social work.

Developing group norms and mutual expectations assists in the creation of a group cohesiveness that helps groups become successful. In sum, establishing rapport requires that social workers demonstrate a non-judgmental attitude, respect for clients' right of self-determination, and respect for clients' worth and dignity, uniqueness and individuality, and problem-solving capacities. Finally, social workers foster rapport when they relate to clients with empathy and authenticity. Both skills are considered in later chapters of this book.

Formulating a Multidimensional Assessment of the Problem, Identifying Systems, and Identifying Relevant Resources

EP 7

Social workers must simultaneously establish rapport with their clients and explore their problems. These activities reinforce each other, as astute exploration yields both information and a sense of trust and confidence in the social worker.

As noted earlier, a social worker who demonstrates empathy is able to foster rapport and show the client that the social worker understands what he or she is expressing. This, in turn, encourages more openness on the client's part and expands his or her expression of feelings. The greater willingness to share deepens the social worker's understanding of the client's situation and the role that emotions play both in the client's difficulties and in his or her capabilities. Thus, the social worker's communication skills serve multiple functions: They not only establish rapport but they facilitate relationship building and encourage information sharing as well.

Problem exploration is a critical process because the social worker must gather comprehensive information before he or she can understand all of the dimensions of a problem and their interaction. Exploration begins by attending to the emotional states and immediate concerns manifested by the client. Gradually, the social worker broadens the exploration to encompass relevant systems (individual, interpersonal, and environmental) and explores the most critical aspects of the problem in depth. During this discovery process, the social worker is also alert to and highlights client strengths, realizing that these strengths represent a vital resource to be tapped during the goal attainment phase. Social workers can assist clients in identifying ways in which they are currently coping and exceptions when problems

do occur (Greene, Lee, & Hoffpauir, 2005). For example, the school social worker working with the tardy and tired student can help him to identify days on which he is on time and rested for school and then to trace back the environmental conditions at home that facilitated such an outcome.

Indeed, problem exploration skills are used during the entire assessment and helping process, beginning with the first contact with clients and continuing throughout the relationship. For example, during interviews, social workers weigh the significance of clients' behavior, thoughts, beliefs, emotions, and, of course, information revealed. These moment-by-moment assessments guide social workers in deciding which aspects of problems to explore in depth, when to explore emotions more deeply, and so on. In addition to this ongoing process of assessment, social workers must formulate a working assessment from which flow the goals and contract upon which Phase II of the problem-solving process is based. An adequate assessment includes analysis of the problem, the person(s), and the ecological context.

Because there are many possible areas that can be explored but limited time available to explore them, focus in assessment is critical. Retaining such a focus is promoted by conducting the assessment in layers. At the first layer, social workers must focus their attention on issues of client safety, legal mandates, and the client's wishes for service. The rationale for this threefold set of priorities is that client wishes should take precedence in circumstances in which legal mandates do not impinge on choices or in which no dangers to self or others exist.

When the social worker analyzes the problem, he or she can identify which factors are contributing to difficulties—for example, inadequate resources; decisions about a crucial aspect of one's life; difficulties in individual, interpersonal, or societal systems; or interactions between any of the preceding factors. Analysis of the problem also involves making judgments about the duration and severity of a problem as well as the extent to which the problem is susceptible to change, given the client's potential coping capacity. In considering the nature and severity of problems, social workers must weigh these factors against their own competencies and the types of services provided by the agency. If the problems call for services that are beyond the agency's function, such as prescribing medication or offering speech therapy, referral to another professional or agency may be indicated.

Analysis of the **individual system** includes assessment of the client's wants and needs, coping capacity, strengths and limitations, and motivation to work on the problem(s). In evaluating the first two dimensions, the social worker must assess such factors as flexibility, judgment, emotional characteristics, degree of responsibility, capacity to tolerate stress, ability to reason critically, cultural worldview, and interpersonal skills. These factors, which are critical in selecting appropriate and attainable goals, are discussed at length in Chapter 9.

Assessment of **ecological factors** entails consideration of the adequacy or deficiency, success or failure, and strengths or weaknesses of salient systems in the environment that bear on the client's problem. Such **ecological assessment** aims to identify systems that must be strengthened, mobilized, or developed to satisfy the client's unmet needs. Systems that often affect clients' needs include couple, family, and social support systems (e.g., kin, friends, neighbors, coworkers, peer groups, and ethnic reference groups); spiritual belief systems; child care, health care, and employment systems; various institutions; and the societal and physical environment. For example, in our earlier example, the social worker could work with the student and his parents to identify pertinent support systems, such as people who could provide transportation as well as conditions that foster a bedtime and morning routine that would help the student arrive at school on time and rested.

Cultural factors are also vital in ecological assessment because personal and social needs and the means of satisfying them vary widely from culture to culture. Moreover, the resources that can be tapped to meet clients' needs vary according to cultural contexts. Some cultures include indigenous helping persons, such as folk healers, religious leaders, and relatives from extended family units who have been invested with authority to assist members of that culture in times of crisis. These persons can often provide valuable assistance to social workers and their clients.

Assessment of the client's situational context also requires analyzing the circumstances as well as the actions and reactions of participants in the problematic interaction. Knowledge of the circumstances and specific behaviors of participants before, during, and after troubling events is crucial to understanding the forces that shape and maintain problematic behavior. Assessment, therefore, requires that social workers elicit detailed information about actual transactions between people.

Whether making assessments of individuals per se or assessments of individuals as subsets of couples, families, or groups, it is important to assess the functioning of these larger systems. These systems have unique properties, including power distribution, role definitions, rules, norms, channels of communication, and repetitive interactional patterns. Such systems also boast both strengths and problems that strongly shape the behavior of constituent members. It follows that individual difficulties tend to be related to systemic difficulties, so interventions must therefore be directed to both the system and the individual.

Assessments of systems are based on a variety of data-gathering procedures. With couples and families, social workers may or may not conduct individual interviews, depending on the evidence available about the effectiveness of family intervention with particular concerns, agency practices, and impressions gained during preliminary contacts with family members. If exploration and assessment are implemented exclusively in conjoint sessions, these processes are similar to those employed in individual interviews except that the interaction between the participants assumes major significance. Whereas information gleaned through individual interviews is limited to reports and descriptions by clients, requiring the social worker to make inferences about the actual interaction within the relevant systems, social workers can view interactions directly in conjoint interviews and group sessions. In such cases, the social worker should be alert to strengths and difficulties in communication and interaction and to the properties of the system. As a consequence, assessment focuses heavily on the styles of communication employed by individual participants, interactional patterns among members, and the impact of individual members on processes that occur in the system. These factors are weighed when selecting interventions intended to enhance functioning at these different levels of the larger systems.

Finally, a working assessment involves synthesizing all relevant information gathered as part of the exploration process. To enhance the validity of such assessments, social workers should involve clients in the process by soliciting their perceptions and assisting them in gathering data about their perceived difficulties and hopes. Social workers can share their impressions with their clients, for example, and then invite affirmation or disconfirmation of those impressions. It is also beneficial to highlight their strengths and to identify other relevant resource systems that can be tapped or need to be developed to resolve the difficulties.

Mutually Negotiating Goals and Formulating a Contract

When social workers and their clients reach agreement about the nature of the problems involved, they are

EP 7

ready to enter the process of negotiating goals. This mutual process aims to identify what needs to be changed and what related actions need to be taken to resolve or ameliorate the problematic situation. We discuss the process of goal selection briefly in this chapter and at length in Chapter 13. If agreement is not reached about the appropriateness of services or if clients choose not to continue, then services may be terminated. In some situations, then, services are finished when the assessment is completed. In the case of involuntary clients, some may continue the social work contact under pressure even if agreement is not reached about the appropriateness of services or if problems are not acknowledged.

After goals have been negotiated, participants undertake the next task: formulating a contract. The **contract**, which is also mutually negotiated, consists of a formal agreement or understanding between the social worker and the client that specifies the goals to be accomplished, relevant strategies to be implemented, roles and responsibilities of participants, practical arrangements, and other factors. When the client system is a couple, family, or group, the contract also specifies group goals that tend to accelerate group movement and to facilitate accomplishment of group goals.

Mutually formulating a contract is a vital process because it demystifies the helping process and clarifies for clients what they may realistically expect from the social worker and what is expected of them; what they will mutually be seeking to accomplish and in what ways; and what the problem-solving process entails. Contracting with voluntary clients is relatively straightforward; the contract specifies what the client desires to accomplish through social work contact. Contracting with involuntary clients contains another layer of legally mandated problems or concerns in addition to the clients' expressed wishes.

The solution-focused approach takes the position that goals are central when working with clients (De Jong & Berg, 2002). Those goals, however, may not be directly related to rectifying or eliminating the concern that initially prompted the contact. Utilizing a solution-focused approach, clients and practitioners can sometimes create or co-construct a solution that will meet the concerns of clients as well as legal requirements (De Jong & Berg, 2001). The solution may be reached without working from a problem viewpoint. For example, a child referred for setting fires might work toward a goal of becoming safe,

trustworthy, and reliable in striking matches under adult supervision. By focusing on goals as perceived by clients, an empowering momentum may be created that draws out hidden strengths and resources. We also take the position that empowering clients to discover and make best use of available resources is desirable. Sometimes, focusing on problems can be counterproductive. However, in funding and agency environments that are problem focused, both in terms of philosophy and funding streams, ignoring problem conceptions carries risk (McMillen et al., 2004).

In summary, we are influenced by solution-focused methods to support client ownership of goals and methods for seeking them (De Jong, 2001). We differ from the solution-focused method, however, in that we do not assume that all clients have within them the solutions to all of their concerns. Expert information about solutions that have worked for clients in similar situations can often prove valuable (Reid, 2000). Rather than assuming that "the client always knows" or "the social worker always knows," we take the position that the social worker's task is to facilitate a situation in which both client and worker share their information while constructing plans for problem resolution (Reid, 2000). We explore the solution-focused approach more in Chapter 13.

Making Referrals

Exploration of clients' problems often reveals that resources or services beyond those provided by the agency are needed to remedy or ameliorate presenting difficulties. This is especially true of clients who have multiple unmet needs. In such

EP 8

instances, referrals to other resources and service providers may be necessary. Unfortunately, clients may lack the knowledge or skills needed to avail themselves of these badly needed resources. Social workers may assume the role of case manager in such instances (e.g., for persons with severe and persistent mental illness, individuals with developmental and physical disabilities, foster children, and infirm elderly clients). Linking clients to other resource systems requires careful handling if clients are to follow through in seeking and obtaining essential resources.

Phase II: Implementation and Goal Attainment

After mutually formulating a contract, the social worker and client(s) enter the heart of the problem-solving

EP 8

process: the **implementation and goal attainment phase**, also known as the **action-oriented or change-oriented phase**. Problem solving is a key part of the helping process, especially in the implementation phase of the intervention stage.

Phase II involves translating the plans formulated jointly by the social worker and individual clients, couples, families, or groups into actions. In short, the participants combine their efforts in working toward the goal assigned the highest priority. This process begins with dissecting the goal into general tasks that identify general strategies to be employed in pursuit of the goal. These general tasks are then subdivided into specific tasks that designate what the client and social worker plan to do between one session and the next (Epstein & Brown, 2002; Fortune, McCallion, & Briar-Lawson, 2010; Reid, 1992; Robinson, 1930; Taft, 1937).[1] Tasks may relate to the client's personal functioning or to his or her interaction with others, or they may involve interaction with other resource systems, such as schools, hospitals, or law enforcement agencies. The processes of negotiating goals and tasks are discussed in detail in Chapter 12.

After formulating goals with clients, social workers select and implement interventions designed to assist clients in accomplishing those goals and subsidiary tasks. Interventions should relate directly to the problems that were identified and the goals that were mutually negotiated with clients and derived from accurate assessment. Helping efforts often fail when social workers employ global interventions without considering clients' views of their problems and ignore the uniqueness of each client's problems.

Enhancing Self-Efficacy

Research findings (Bandura & Locke, 2003; Dolan, Martin, & Rosenow, 2008; Lane, Daugherty, & Nyman, 1998; Washington & Moxley, 2003) have strongly indicated that the helping process is greatly enhanced when clients experience an increased sense of self-efficacy as part of this process. **Self-efficacy** refers to an expectation or belief that one can successfully accomplish tasks or perform behaviors associated with specified goals. Note that the concept overlaps with notions of individual empowerment.

The most powerful means for enhancing self-efficacy is to assist clients in actually performing certain behaviors prerequisite to accomplishing their goals.

Another potent technique is to make clients aware of their strengths and to recognize incremental progress of clients toward goal attainment.

Family and group members also represent potential resources for enhancing self-efficacy. Social workers can develop and tap these resources by assisting families and groups to accomplish tasks that involve perceiving and accrediting the strengths and progress of group and family members. We consider other sources of self-efficacy and relevant techniques in Chapter 13.

Monitoring Progress

As work toward goal attainment proceeds, it is important to monitor progress on a regular basis. The reasons for this are fourfold:

EP 9

1. *To evaluate the effectiveness of change strategies and interventions.* Social workers are increasingly required to document the efficacy of services to satisfy third-party payers within a managed care system. In addition, social workers owe it to their clients to select interventions based on the best available evidence (Thyer, 2002). If an approach or intervention is not producing desired effects, social workers should determine the reasons for this failure or consider negotiating a different approach.

2. *To guide clients' efforts toward goal attainment.* Evaluating progress toward goals enhances continuity of focus and efforts and promotes efficient use of time (Corcoran & Vandiver, 1996).

3. *To keep abreast of clients' reactions to progress or lack of progress.* When they believe they are not progressing, clients tend to become discouraged and may lose confidence in the helping process. By evaluating progress periodically, social workers will be alerted to negative client reactions that might otherwise undermine the helping process.

4. *To concentrate on goal attainment and evaluate progress.* These efforts will tend to sustain clients' motivation to work on their problems.

Methods of evaluating progress range from eliciting subjective opinions to using various types of measurement instruments. Chapters 12 and 19 include both quantitative and qualitative methods for monitoring progress and measuring change.

Barriers to Goal Accomplishment

As clients strive to accomplish goals and related tasks, their progress is rarely smooth and uneventful. Instead, clients typically encounter obstacles and experience anxiety, uncertainties, fears, and other undesirable reactions as they struggle to solve problems. Furthermore, family or group members or other significant persons may undermine the client's efforts to change by opposing such changes, by ridiculing the client for seeing a social worker, by making derisive comments about the social worker, or by otherwise making change even more difficult for the client. (For this reason, it is vital to involve significant others in the problem-solving process whenever feasible.) Because of the challenges posed by these barriers to change, social workers must be mindful of their clients' struggles and skillful in assisting them to surmount these obstacles.

Barriers to goal accomplishment are frequently encountered in work with families and groups. Such barriers include personality factors that limit participation of certain group members, problematic behaviors of group members, or processes within the group that impede progress. They also encompass impediments in the family's environment.

Still other barriers may involve organizational opposition to change within systems whose resources are essential to goal accomplishment. Denial of resources or services (e.g., health care, rehabilitation, or public assistance) by organizations or policies and procedures that unduly restrict clients' access to resources may require the social worker to assume the role of mediator or advocate.

Relational Reactions

As social workers and clients work together to solve problems, emotional reactions on the part of either party toward the other may impair the effectiveness of the working partnership and pose an obstacle to goal accomplishment. Clients, for example, may have unrealistic expectations or may misperceive the intent of the social worker. Consequently, clients may experience disappointment, discouragement, hurt, anger, rejection, longing for closeness, or many other emotional reactions that may seriously impede progress toward goals.

Couple partners, parents, and group members may also experience **relational reactions** to other members of these larger client systems, resulting in problematic interactional patterns within these systems. Not uncommonly, these reactions reflect attitudes and beliefs learned from relationships with parents or significant others. In many other instances, however, the social worker or members of clients' systems may unknowingly behave in ways that trigger unfavorable relational reactions by individuals or family or group members. In either event, it is critical to explore and resolve these harmful relational reactions. Otherwise, clients' efforts may be diverted from working toward goal accomplishment or—even worse—clients may prematurely withdraw from the helping process.

Social workers are susceptible to relational reactions as well. Social workers who relate in an authentic manner provide clients with experience that is transferable to the real world of the client's social environment. They communicate that they are human beings who are not immune to making blunders and experiencing emotions and desires as part of their relationships with clients. It is vital that social workers be aware of their reactions to clients and understand how to manage them. Otherwise, they may be working on their own problems rather than the client's issues, placing the helping process in severe jeopardy. For example, a student practitioner became aware that she was relating to a client who had difficulty in making and carrying out plans as if the client were a family member with whom the student had similar difficulties. Becoming aware of those associations through supervision made it possible to separate out the client before her from the family member. Chapter 18 offers advice to assist social workers in coping with potential relational reactions residing with the client(s), the social worker, or both.

Enhancing Clients' Self-Awareness

As clients interact in a novel relationship with a social worker and risk trying out new interpersonal behaviors in their couple, family, or group contacts, they commonly experience emotions that may be pleasing, frightening, confusing, and even overwhelming. Although managing such emotional reactions may require a temporary detour from goal attainment activities, these efforts frequently represent rich opportunities for growth in self-awareness. Self-awareness is the first step to self-realization. Many voluntary clients wish to understand themselves more fully, and they can benefit from becoming more aware of feelings that have previously been buried or denied expression.

Social workers can facilitate the process of self-discovery by employing additive empathic responses during the goal attainment phase. **Additive empathic responses** focus on deeper feelings than do **reciprocal empathic responses** (related to establishing rapport in the discussion of Phase I). Additive empathy, elaborated in Chapter 17, refers to making interpretations of what clients have shared. For example, a client comments on a close relationship another person has had with his parent and appears to resent it. Previous discussions have suggested that the client laments the lack of such a close relationship in his own life. The social worker makes a tentative connection between the client's own experience with parental relations and those the client has commented on. This technique can be appropriately applied in both individual and conjoint interviews as well as in group sessions. Additive empathy is particularly beneficial in assisting clients to get in touch with their emotions and express those feelings clearly to their significant others.

Another technique used to foster self-awareness is **confrontation**. This technique helps clients become aware of growth-defeating discrepancies in perceptions, feelings, communications, behavior, values, and attitudes, and then examine these discrepancies in relation to stated goals. Confrontation is also used in circumstances when clients act to violate laws or threaten their own safety or the safety of others. Confrontation must be offered in the context of goodwill, and it requires high skill. For example, noting a discrepancy between a goal of graduating with a degree and current attendance problems can stimulate anxiety but also lead to developing a plan to resolve the discrepancy.

Use of Self

EP 1

As helping relationships grow stronger during the implementation and goal attainment phase, social workers increasingly use themselves as tools to facilitate growth and accomplishment. Relating spontaneously and appropriately disclosing one's feelings, views, and experiences ensure that clients have an encounter with an open and authentic human being. Modeling authentic behavior encourages clients to reciprocate by risking authentic behavior themselves, thereby achieving significant growth in self-realization and in interpersonal relations. Indeed, there is research showing that clients who perceive their social workers as acting in prosocial ways, through actions such as returning telephone calls promptly, have better outcomes than clients who

perceive their social workers as less responsive (Trotter, 2006). And when group leaders model authentic behavior in groups, members may follow suit by exhibiting similar behavior.

Social workers who relate in an authentic manner also provide their clients with experience that is transferable to the clients' real-world social relationships. A contrived, detached, and sterile "professional" relationship, by contrast, lacks transferability to other relationships. Obviously, these issues should be covered in the training process for social workers.

Assertiveness is another important aspect of the social worker using himself or herself to help the client. In the social work context, assertiveness involves dealing tactfully but firmly with problematic behaviors that impinge on the helping relationship or impede progress toward goal attainment. For example, when clients' actions conflict with their goals or are potentially harmful to themselves or others, the social worker must deal with these situations. Further, social workers must sometimes relate assertively to larger client systems—for example, to focus on behavior of group members that hinders the accomplishment of goals. Using oneself to relate authentically and assertively is a major focus of Chapter 5.

Phase III: Termination

The terminal phase of the helping process involves three major aspects:

EP 8

1. Assessing when client goals have been satisfactorily attained
2. Helping the client develop strategies that maintain change and continue growth following the termination
3. Successfully terminating the helping relationship

Deciding when to terminate is relatively straightforward when time limits are specified in advance as part of the initial contact, as is done with the task-centered approach and other brief treatment strategies. Decisions about when to terminate are also simple when individual or group goals are clear-cut (e.g., to get a job, obtain a prosthetic device, arrange for nursing care, secure tutoring for a child, implement a specific group activity, or hold a public meeting).

In other instances, goals involve growth or changes that have no limits; thus, judgments must be made by the social worker and client in tandem about when a satisfactory degree of change has been achieved.

Examples of such goals include increasing self-esteem, communicating more effectively, becoming more outgoing in social situations, and resolving conflicts more effectively. In these cases, the ambiguity of termination can be reduced by developing specific, operational indicators of goal achievement. Today, however, many decisions about termination and extension involve third parties, as contracts for service and payers such as managed care may regulate the length and conditions of service (Corcoran & Vandiver, 1996).

Successfully Terminating Helping Relationships

Social workers and clients often respond positively to termination, reflecting pride and accomplishment on the part of both parties (Fortune, Pearlingi, & Rochelle, 1992). Clients who were required or otherwise pressured to see the social worker may experience a sense of relief at getting rid of the pressure or freeing themselves from the strictures of outside scrutiny. In contrast, because voluntary clients share personal problems and are accompanied through rough emotional terrain by a caring social worker, they often feel close to the social worker. Consequently, termination tends to produce mixed feelings for these types of clients. They are likely to feel strong gratitude to the social worker but are also likely to experience a sense of relief over no longer having to go through the discomfort associated with exploring problems and making changes (not to mention the relief from paying fees).

Although clients are usually optimistic about the prospects of confronting future challenges independently, they sometimes experience a sense of loss over terminating the working relationship. Moreover, uncertainty about their ability to cope independently may be mixed with their optimism.

When they have been engaged in the helping process for a lengthy period of time, clients may develop a strong attachment to a social worker, especially if the social worker has fostered dependency in their relationship. For such individuals, termination involves a painful process of letting go of a relationship that has satisfied significant emotional needs. Moreover, these clients often experience apprehension about facing the future without the reassuring strength represented by the social worker. Group members may experience similar painful reactions as they face the loss of supportive relationships with the social worker and group members as well as a valued resource that has assisted them to cope with their problems.

To effect termination with individuals or groups and minimize psychological stress requires both perceptiveness to emotional reactions and skills in helping clients to work through such reactions. The social worker must also be adept at modeling healthy endings to relationships.

Planning Change Maintenance Strategies

Social workers have voiced concern over the need to develop strategies that maintain clients' changes and continue their growth after formal social work service is terminated (Rzepnicki, 1991). These concerns have been prompted by findings that after termination many clients relapse or regress to their previous level of functioning. Consequently, more attention is now being paid to strategies for maintaining change after termination. Planning for follow-up sessions not only makes it possible to evaluate the durability of results but also facilitates the termination process by indicating the social worker's continuing interest in clients, a matter we discuss in Chapter 19. Follow-up must be conducted mindfully because in some cases, follow-up may trigger past dependency behaviors.

THE INTERVIEWING PROCESS: STRUCTURE AND SKILLS

Direct social workers employ interviewing as the primary vehicle of influence, although administrators and social planners also rely heavily on interviewing skills to accomplish their objectives. With the increasing emphasis on evidence-based practice, it becomes yet more important to develop core skills in interviewing that can be applied and revised according to varied situations. Skills in interviewing, active listening, discerning and confronting discrepancies, reframing, and reciprocal empathy are key ingredients in the generalist practice model (Adams, Matto, & Le Croy, 2009). These nonspecific factors have a considerable impact on outcomes (Cameron & Keenan, 2010; Drisko, 2004). That is, the relationship or therapeutic alliance has been shown to have considerable influence across studies (Norcross & Lambert, 2006). In fact, such relationship factors have been shown to account for up to 30 percent of variation in social work outcomes, while particular model and technique factors account for only about 15 percent (Duncan & Miller, 2000; Hubble, Duncan, & Miller, 1999).

Interviews vary according to purpose, type of setting, client characteristics, and number of participants. For example, they may involve interaction between a social worker and individuals, couples, and family units. Interviews are conducted in offices, homes, hospitals, prisons, automobiles, and other diverse settings. Interviews conducted with children differ from interviews with adults or seniors. Despite the numerous variables that affect interviews, certain factors are common to all effective interviews. This section identifies and discusses these essential factors and highlights relevant skills.

Physical Conditions

EP 6

Interviews sometimes occur in offices or other settings over which the social worker has some control. Interviews that take place in a client's home, of course, are more subject to the client's preferences. The physical climate in which an interview is conducted partly determines the attitudes, feelings, and degree of cooperation and responsiveness of people during interviews. That environment should be constructed to feel supportive and not intimidating to potential clients. Indeed, some of the first conclusions clients draw about the values and competency of a setting are likely to reflect their first encounters with staff over the telephone or in person. If these potential clients are responded to promptly, courteously, and respectfully, this treatment may go a long way toward preparing for a successful interaction with the social worker. The following conditions are conducive to productive interviews:

1. Adequate ventilation and light
2. Comfortable room temperature
3. Ample space (to avoid a sense of being confined or crowded)
4. Attractive and clean furnishings and decor
5. Chairs that adequately support the back
6. Privacy appropriate to the cultural beliefs of the client
7. Freedom from distraction
8. Open space between participants
9. Interior decorations that are sensitive to diverse client populations

The first five items obviously involve providing a pleasant and comfortable environment and need no elaboration.

Privacy is vital, of course, because people are likely to be guarded in revealing personal information and expressing feelings if other people can see or hear them. Likewise, interviewers sometimes have difficulty in concentrating or expressing themselves when others can hear them. Settings vary in the extent to which

social workers can control these conditions. For example, in some circumstances families may prefer to have trusted family members, friends, or spiritual leaders present to consider resolution of some issues (Burford & Hudson, 2009). In some settings, it may be impossible to ensure complete privacy. Even when interviewing a patient in a hospital bed, however, privacy can be maximized by closing doors, drawing curtains that separate beds, and requesting that nursing staff avoid nonessential interruptions. Privacy during home interviews may be even more difficult to arrange, but people will often take measures to reduce unnecessary intrusions or distractions if interviewers stress that privacy enhances the productivity of sessions (Allen & Tracy, 2009). Social workers in public social service settings often work in cubicle offices. To ensure privacy, they can conduct client interviews in special interview rooms.

Because interviews sometimes involve intense emotions by participants, freedom from distraction is a critical requirement. Telephone calls, text messages, knocks on the door, and external noises can impair concentration and disrupt important dialogue. Moreover, clients are unlikely to feel important and valued if social workers permit avoidable intrusions. Other sources of distraction include crying, attention seeking, and restless behavior of clients' infants or children. Small children, of course, cannot be expected to sit quietly for more than short periods of time. For this reason, the social worker should encourage parents to make arrangements for the care of children during interviews (except when it is important to observe interaction between parents and their children). Because requiring such arrangements can create a barrier to service utilization, many social workers and agencies maintain a supply of toys for such occasions.

Having a desk between an interviewer and interviewee emphasizes the authority of the social worker. For clients from some cultural groups, emphasizing the authority or position of the social worker may be a useful way to indicate that he or she occupies a formal, appropriate position. With many others, a desk between social worker and client creates a barrier that is not conducive to open communication. If safety of the social worker is an issue, then a desk barrier can be useful, unless it prevents the social worker from leaving if necessary. In some instances, an interviewer may believe that maximizing the social worker's authority through a desk barrier will promote his or her service objectives.

In most circumstances, however, social workers strive to foster a sense of equality. Hence, they arrange their desks so that they can rotate their chairs to a position where there is open space between them and their clients. Others prefer to leave their desks entirely and use other chairs in the room when interviewing.

Practitioners who interview children often find it useful to have available a small number of toys or items that children can manipulate with their hands as well as materials for drawing pictures. Such tools or devices seem to reduce tension for children in communicating with unfamiliar adults and assist them in telling their story (Krahenbuhl & Blades, 2006; Lamb & Brown, 2006; Lukas, 1993).

Structure of Interviews

Interviews in social work have a purpose and a structure. The purpose is to exchange information systematically with a view toward illuminating and solving problems, promoting growth, or planning strategies or actions aimed at improving people's quality of life. The structure of interviews varies somewhat from setting to setting, from client to client, and from one phase of the helping process to another. Indeed, skillful interviewers adapt flexibly both to different contexts and to the ebb and flow of each individual session.

Each interview is unique. Nevertheless, effective interviews conform to a general structure, share certain properties, and reflect the interviewer's use of certain basic skills. In considering these basic factors, we begin by focusing on the structure and processes involved in initial interviews.

Establishing Rapport

EP 6

Earlier in the chapter, we discussed how important it is for social workers to establish rapport with their clients. In this section, we'll examine how social workers can effectively establish rapport during initial meetings with clients, as well as why it is important to do so.

Rapport with clients fosters open and free communication, which is the hallmark of effective interviews. Achieving rapport enables clients to gain trust in the helpful intent and goodwill of the social worker, so that they will be willing to risk revealing personal and sometimes painful feelings and information. Some clients readily achieve trust and confidence in a social worker, particularly when they have the capacity to form relationships easily. Voluntary clients often ask, "Who am I and why am I in this situation?"; involuntary clients have less reason to be initially trusting and ask, "Who are you and when will you leave?" (R. H. Rooney, 2009).

Establishing rapport begins by greeting the client(s) warmly and introducing yourself. If the client system is a family, you should introduce yourself to each family member. In making introductions and addressing clients, it is important to extend the courtesy of asking clients how they prefer to be addressed; doing so conveys your respect and desire to use the title they prefer. Although some clients prefer the informality involved in using first names, social workers should be discreet in using first name introductions with all clients because of their diverse ethnic and social backgrounds. For example, some adult African Americans and members of other groups may interpret being addressed by their first names as indicating a lack of respect (Edwards, 1982; McNeely & Badami, 1984).

With many clients, social workers must surmount formidable barriers before establishing rapport. Bear in mind that the majority of clients have had little or no experience with social work agencies and enter initial interviews or group sessions with uncertainty and apprehension. Many did not seek help initially; they may view having to seek assistance with their problems as evidence of failure, weakness, or inadequacy. Moreover, revealing personal problems is embarrassing and even humiliating for some people, especially those who have difficulty confiding in others.

Cultural factors and language differences compound potential barriers to rapport even further. For example, some Asian Americans and persons of other ethnic groups who retain strong ties to cultural traditions have been conditioned not to discuss personal or family problems with outsiders. Revealing problems to others may be perceived as a reflection of personal inadequacy and as a stigma upon the entire family. The resultant fear of shame may impede the development of rapport with clients from these ethnic groups (Kumabe, Nishida, & Hepworth, 1985; Lum, 1996; Tsui & Schultz, 1985). Some African Americans, Native Americans, and Latinos may also experience difficulty in developing rapport because of distrust that derives from a history of being exploited or discriminated against by other ethnic groups (Longres, 1991; Proctor & Davis, 1994). Children may be unfamiliar with having conversational exchanges with unfamiliar adults (Lamb & Brown, 2006). For example, their exchanges with teachers may be primarily directive or a test of their knowledge. Asking them to describe events or family situations may be a new experience for them, and they may look for cues from the accompanying adult about

EP 2

how to proceed. Open-ended questions are advised to avoid providing leading questions.

Clients' difficulties in communicating openly tend to be exacerbated when their problems involve allegations of socially unacceptable behavior, such as child abuse, moral infractions, or criminal behavior. In groups, the pain is further compounded by having to expose one's difficulties to other group members, especially in early sessions when the reactions of other members represent the threat of the unknown.

EP 6

One means of fostering rapport with clients is to employ a **"warm-up" period**. This is particularly important with some ethnic minority clients for whom such openings are the cultural norm, including Native Americans, persons with strong roots in the cultures of Asia and the Pacific Basin, and Latinos. Aguilar (1972), for example, has stressed the importance of warm-up periods in work with Mexican Americans. Many Native Hawaiians and Samoans also expect to begin new contacts with outside persons by engaging in "talk story," which involves warm, informal, and light personal conversation similar to that described by Aguilar. To plunge into discussion of serious problems without a period of talk story would be regarded by members of these cultural groups as rude and intrusive. Social workers who neglect to engage in a warm-up period are likely to encounter passive resistant behavior from members of these cultural groups. A warm-up period and a generally slower tempo are also critically important with many Native American clients (Hull, 1982). Palmer and Pablo (1978) suggest that social workers who are most successful with Native Americans are low-key, nondirective individuals. Similarly, increased self-disclosure is reported by Hispanic practitioners as a useful part of developing rapport with Hispanic clients (Rosenthal-Gelman, 2004).

Warm-up periods are also important in establishing rapport with adolescents, many of whom are in a stage of emancipating themselves from adults. Consequently, they may be wary of social workers. This is especially true of individuals who are delinquent or are otherwise openly rebelling against authority. Moreover, adolescents who have had little or no experience with social workers have an extremely limited grasp of their roles. Many adolescents, at least initially, are involuntary clients and perceive social workers as adversaries, fearing that their role is to punish or to exercise power over them. The judgment of how much warm-up is necessary and how much is too much is a matter of art and experience with initially reluctant

potential clients. This is seen in the "Hanging with Hailey" video featured in the Video Case earlier in the chapter, in which Emily, the social worker, attempts to reduce Hailey's sense of strangeness and stigma about being referred for services.

With the majority of clients, a brief warm-up period is usually sufficient. When the preceding barriers do not apply, introductions and a brief discussion of a timely topic (unusual weather, a widely discussed local or national event, or a topic of known interest to the client) will adequately foster a climate conducive to exploring clients' concerns.

Most clients, in fact, expect to immediately plunge into discussion of their problems, and their anxiety level may grow if social workers delay getting to the business at hand (Ivanoff, Blythe, & Tripodi, 1994). This is particularly true with involuntary clients who did not seek the contact. With these clients, rapport often develops rapidly if social workers respond sensitively to their feelings and skillfully give direction to the process of exploration by sharing the circumstances of the referral, thereby defusing the threat sensed by such clients. Tuning in to their feelings and explaining what they can expect in terms of their role and that of the social worker go a long way toward reducing these tensions. (We'll discuss these topics in more depth in Chapter 5.)

Respect for clients is critical to establishing rapport, and we stress the importance of respecting clients' dignity and worth, uniqueness, capacities to solve problems, and other factors. An additional aspect of showing respect is demonstrating common courtesy. Being punctual, attending to the client's comfort, listening attentively, remembering the client's name, and assisting a client who has limited mobility convey the message that the social worker values the client and esteems his or her dignity and worth. Courtesy should never be taken lightly.

Verbal and nonverbal messages from social workers that convey understanding and acceptance of clients' feelings and views also facilitate the development of rapport. This does not mean agreeing with or condoning clients' views or problems but rather apprehending and affirming clients' rights to have their own views, attitudes, and feelings.

Attentiveness to feelings and empathic responses to these feelings convey understanding that clients readily discern. Empathic responses clearly convey the message, "I am with you. I understand what you are saying and experiencing." The "workhorse" of successful helping persons, empathic responding, is important not only in Phase I of the helping process but in subsequent phases as well. Mastery of this vital skill (discussed extensively in Chapter 5) requires consistent and sustained practice.

Authenticity, or genuineness, is yet another quality that facilitates rapport. Being authentic during the initial stages of the helping process means relating as a genuine person rather than assuming a contrived and sterile professional role. Authentic behavior by social workers also models openness, which encourages clients to reciprocate by lowering their defenses and relating more openly (Doster & Nesbitt, 1979).

Encounters with authentic social workers also provide clients with a relationship experience that more closely approximates relationships in the real world than do relationships with people who conceal their real selves behind a professional facade. A moderate level of authenticity or genuineness during early interviews often fosters openness. At this level, the social worker is spontaneous and relates openly by being nondefensive and congruent. In other words, the social worker's behavior and responses match her or his inner experience.

Being authentic also permits the constructive use of humor, as elaborated in Chapter 7. Relating with a moderate level of authenticity, however, precludes a high level of self-disclosure. Rather, the focus is on the client, and the social worker reveals personal information or shares personal experiences judiciously. During the change-oriented phase of the helping process, however, social workers sometimes engage in self-disclosure when they believe that doing so may facilitate client growth.

Rapport is also enhanced by avoiding certain types of responses that block communication. To avoid hindering communication, social workers must be knowledgeable about such types of responses and must eliminate them from their communication repertoires. Toward this end, Chapter 7 identifies various types of responses and interviewing patterns that inhibit communication and describes strategies for eliminating them.

Beginning social workers often fear that they will forget something, freeze up or become tongue-tied, talk endlessly to reduce their anxiety, or fail to observe something crucial in the interview that will lead to dire consequences (Epstein & Brown, 2002). Practice interviews such as those presented in subsequent chapters will assist in reducing this fear. It also helps to be aware that referred clients need to know the circumstances of the referral and clarify choices, rights, and

expectations before they are likely to establish rapport with the social worker.

Starting Where the Client Is

Social work researchers have suggested that **motivational congruence**—that is, the fit between client motivation and what the social worker attempts to provide—is a major factor in explaining more successful findings in studies of social work effectiveness (Reid & Hanrahan, 1982). Starting with client motivation aids social workers in establishing and sustaining rapport and in maintaining psychological contact with clients.

If, for example, a client appears to be in emotional distress at the beginning of the initial interview, the social worker might focus attention on the client's distress before proceeding to explore the client's problematic situation. An example of an appropriate focusing response would be, "I can sense that you are going through a difficult time. Could you tell me what this is like for you right now?" Discussion of the client's emotions and related factors tends to reduce the distress, which might otherwise impede the process of exploration. Moreover, responding sensitively to clients' emotions fosters rapport—clients begin to regard social workers as concerned, perceptive, and understanding persons.

Novice social workers sometimes have difficulty in starting where the client is because they worry that they will not present quickly and clearly the services of the agency, thus neglecting or delaying exploration of client concerns. Practice will allow them to relax and recognize that they can meet the expectations of their supervisors and others by focusing on client concerns while sharing content about the circumstances of referrals and their agency's services.

Starting where the client is has critical significance when social workers are working with involuntary clients. Because these clients are often compelled by external sources to see social workers, they frequently enter initial interviews with negative, hostile feelings. Social workers, therefore, should begin by eliciting these feelings and focusing on them until they have subsided. By responding empathically to negative feelings and conveying understanding and acceptance of them, skillful social workers often succeed in neutralizing these feelings, which enhances clients' receptivity to exploring their problem situations. For example, social workers can often reduce negative feelings by clarifying the choices available to the involuntary client. If social workers fail to deal with their clients' negativism, they are likely to encounter persistent oppositional responses. These responses are frequently labeled as resistance, opposition to change, and lack of motivation. It is useful to reframe these responses by choosing not to interpret them with deficit labels but rather replacing them with expectations that these attitudes and behaviors are normal when something an individual values is threatened (R. H. Rooney, 2009). As children and adolescents are often referred because adults are concerned about their behavior, and they may therefore be particularly resistant, the practitioner can clarify that he or she wants to hear how things are going from the child's or adolescent's viewpoint.

Language also poses a barrier with many ethnic minority and immigrant clients who may have a limited grasp of the English language, which could cause difficulty in understanding even commonplace expressions. Where there are language differences, social workers must slow down the pace of communication and be especially sensitive to nonverbal indications that clients are confused. To avoid embarrassment, some clients who speak English as a second language sometimes indicate that they understand messages when, in fact, they are perplexed.

Using Interpreters

When ethnic minority and immigrant clients have virtually no command of the English language, effective communication requires the use of an interpreter of the same ethnicity as the client, so that the social worker and client bridge both cultural value differences and language differences. To work effectively together, however, both the social worker and the interpreter must possess special skills. For their part, interpreters must be carefully selected and trained to understand the importance of the interview and their role in the process, as well as to interpret cultural nuances to the social worker. In this way, skilled interpreters assist social workers by translating far more than verbal content—they also convey nonverbal communication, cultural attitudes and beliefs, subtle expressions, emotional reactions, and expectations of clients.

To achieve rapport, of course, the social worker must also convey empathy and establish an emotional connection with the ethnic minority client. The interpreter thus "must have the capacity to act exactly as the interviewer acts—express the same feelings, use the same intonations to the extent possible in another language, and through verbal and nonverbal means

convey what the interviewer expresses on several levels" (Freed, 1988, p. 316).

The social worker should explain the interpreter's role to the client and ensure the client of neutrality and confidentiality on the part of both the social worker and the interpreter. Obviously, these factors should also be covered in the training process for interpreters. In addition, successful transcultural work through an interpreter requires that the social worker be acquainted with the history and culture of the client's and the interpreter's country of origin.

Social workers must also adapt to the slower pace of interviews when an interpreter is involved. When social workers and interpreters are skilled in collaborating in interviews, effective working relationships can evolve, and many clients experience the process as beneficial and therapeutic. As implied in this brief discussion, interviewing through an interpreter is a complex process requiring careful preparation of interviewers and interpreters.

The Exploration Process

Earlier we discussed some basics of the exploration process. Here, we'll discuss the process in more detail, relating especially to client interviews.

EP 6

When clients indicate that they are ready to discuss their problematic situations, it is appropriate to begin the process of exploring their concerns. Messages like the following are typically employed to initiate the exploration process:

- "Could you tell me about your situation?"
- "I'm interested in hearing about what brought you here."
- "Tell me about what has been going on with you so that we can think together about what you can do about your concerns."
- "How are things going with school?"

The client will generally respond by beginning to relate his or her concerns. The social worker's role at this point is to draw out the client, to respond in ways that convey understanding, and to seek elaboration of information needed to gain a clear picture of factors involved in the client's difficulties.

Some clients spontaneously provide rich information with little prompting. Others—especially referred and involuntary clients—may hesitate, struggle with their emotions, or have difficulty finding the right words to express themselves. Because referred clients may perceive that they were forced into the interview as the result of others' concerns, they may respond by recounting those external pressures. The social worker can assist in this process by sharing his or her information about the circumstances of the referral.

Furthering Responses, Paraphrasing, and Feedback

To facilitate the process of exploration, social workers employ a multitude of skills, often blending two or more in a single response. One such skill, **furthering responses**, encourages clients to continue verbalizing their concerns. Furthering responses include actions such as repeating a word expressed by a client, nodding, or in other ways encouraging continued expression. It is done to convey attention, interest, and an expectation that the client will continue verbalizing. We discuss such responses in depth in Chapter 6.

EP 6

Other responses facilitate communication (and rapport) by providing immediate feedback that assures clients that social workers have not only heard but also understood their messages. **Reflection of content** provides feedback indicating that the social worker has grasped the content of the client's message. In using reflection of content, the interviewer rephrases (with different words) what the client has expressed. **Reflection of feelings**, by contrast, shows that the social worker is aware of the emotions the client has experienced or is currently experiencing. Reflection of content and reflection of feelings, discussed in Chapter 6, are especially crucial with clients who have limited language facility, including ethnic minority, immigrant, and developmentally disabled clients. When language barriers exist, social workers should be careful not to assume that they correctly understand the client or that the client understands the social worker. Video examples of empathic responding are included in Chapter 5, and reflections of content and feelings are included in Chapter 6.

If clients are hesitant about discussing personal or family problems with outsiders, social workers need to make special efforts to grasp their intended meanings. Many such clients are not accustomed to participating in interviews and tend not to state their concerns openly. Rather, they may send covert (hidden) messages and expect social workers to discern their problems by reading between the lines. Social workers need to use **feedback** extensively to determine whether their perceptions of the clients' intended meanings are on target.

EP 1 and 2

Using feedback to ascertain that the social worker has understood the client's intended meaning, and vice versa, can avoid unnecessary misunderstandings. In addition, clients generally appreciate a social worker's efforts to reach shared understanding, and they interpret patience and persistence in seeking to understand as evidence that the social worker respects and values them. It is not the ethnic minority client's responsibility, however, to educate the social worker.[2] Conversely, what the social worker thinks he or she knows about the minority client's culture may actually be an inappropriate stereotype, because individuals and families vary on a continuum of assimilation and acculturation with majority culture norms (Congress, 1994). Based on a common Latino value, for example, the social worker might say, "Can you call on other family members for assistance?" In this way, the worker can assess a cultural generalization that may or may not have relevance for the particular individual or family.

VIDEO CASE EXAMPLE

In the video "Getting Back to Shakopee," the potential client, Valerie, is quite hesitant about sharing personal concerns with the social worker, Dorothy. This hesitation is influenced by a combination of factors, such as having been referred by her employer, suspicion that social workers remove children, and cultural differences. Only after several questions are answered to Valerie's satisfaction about who would have access to information in the interview and Dorothy's cultural knowledge does Valerie proceed to describe her personal concerns.

Exploring Expectations

Before exploring problems, it is important to determine clients' expectations, which vary considerably and are influenced by socioeconomic level, cultural background, level of sophistication, and previous

EP 6

experience with helping professionals. In fact, socialization that includes clarifying expectations about the roles of clients and social workers has been found to be associated with more successful outcomes, especially with involuntary clients (R. H. Rooney, 2009; Videka-Sherman, 1988). Video examples of clarifying to a client what information will be shared with a referral source and what information remains confidential are cited in Chapter 5.

In some instances, clients' expectations diverge markedly from what social workers can realistically provide. Unless social workers are aware of and deal successfully with such unrealistic expectations, clients may be keenly disappointed and disinclined to continue beyond the initial interview. In other instances, referred clients may have mistaken impressions about whether they can choose to work on concerns as they see them as opposed to the views of referral sources such as family members. By exploring these expectations, social workers create an opportunity to clarify the nature of the helping process and to work through clients' feelings of disappointment. Being aware of clients' expectations also helps social workers select their approaches and interventions based on their clients' needs and expectations.

Eliciting Essential Information

EP 9

During the exploration process, the social worker assesses the significance of information revealed as the client discusses problems and interacts with the social worker, group members, or significant others. Indeed, judgments about the meaning and significance of fragments of information guide social workers in deciding issues such as which aspects of a problem are salient and warrant further exploration, how ready a client is to explore certain facets of a problem more deeply, which patterned behaviors of the client or system interfere with effective functioning, and when and when not to draw out intense emotions.

The direction of problem exploration proceeds from general to specific. Clients' initial accounts of their problems are typically general in nature ("We fight over everything," "I don't seem to be able to make friends," "We just don't know how to cope with Scott. He won't do anything we ask," or "Child protection says I don't care for my children"). Clients' concerns typically have many facets, however, and accurate understanding requires careful assessment of each one. Whereas

open-ended responses may be effective in launching problem explorations, other types of responses are used to probe for the detailed information needed to identify and unravel the various factors and systems that contribute to and maintain the problem. Responses that seek concreteness are employed to elicit such detailed information. These types of responses are considered at length in Chapter 6.

Focusing in Depth

EP 8

In addition to possessing discrete skills needed to elicit detailed information, social workers must be able to maintain the focus on problems until they have elicited comprehensive information. Adequate assessment of problems is not possible until a social worker possesses sufficient information concerning the various forces (involving individual, interpersonal, and environmental systems) that interact to produce the problems. Focusing skills (discussed at length in Chapter 6, with video examples) blend the various skills identified so far with summarizing responses.

During the course of exploration, social workers should elicit information relevant to numerous questions whose answers are crucial to understanding the factors, including ecological factors, that bear on the clients' problems. These questions (discussed in Chapter 8, with video examples) serve as guideposts for social workers and provide direction to interviews.

Employing Outlines

In addition to answering questions that are relevant to virtually all interviews, social workers may need to collect information that answers questions pertinent to specific practice settings. Outlines that list essential questions to be answered for a given situation or problem can prove extremely helpful to beginning social workers. It is important, however, to maintain flexibility in the interview and to focus on the client, not the outline. Chapter 6 provides examples of outlines and suggestions for using them.

Assessing Emotional Functioning

EP 7

During the process of exploration, social workers must be keenly sensitive to clients' moment-to-moment emotional reactions and to the part that emotional patterns (e.g., inadequate anger control, depression, or widely fluctuating moods) play in their difficulties. Emotional reactions during the interview (e.g., crying, intense anxiety, anger, hurt feelings) often impede problem exploration and require detours aimed at helping clients regain their equanimity. Note that the anxiety and anger exhibited by involuntary clients may be influenced by the circumstances of the involuntary contact as much as by more enduring emotional patterns.

Emotional patterns that powerfully influence behavior in other contexts may also be problems in and of themselves that warrant careful exploration. Depression, for example, is a prevalent problem in our society but generally responds well to proper treatment. When clients exhibit symptoms of depression, the depth of the depression and risk of suicide should be carefully explored. Empathic communication is a major skill used to explore these types of emotional patterns.

Factors to be considered, instruments that assess depression and suicidal risk, and relevant skills are discussed in Chapter 9.

Exploring Cognitive Functioning

Because thought patterns, beliefs, and attitudes are powerful determinants of behavior, it is important to explore clients' opinions and interpretations of those circumstances and events deemed salient to their difficulties. Often, careful exploration reveals that misinformation, distorted meaning attributions, mistaken beliefs, and dysfunctional patterns of thought (such as rigid, dogmatic thinking) play major roles in clients' difficulties.

Messages commonly employed to explore clients' thinking include the following:

- "How did you come to that conclusion?"
- "What meaning do you make of … ?"
- "How do you explain what happened?"
- "What are your views (or beliefs) about that?"

Assessment of cognitive functioning and other relevant assessment skills are discussed further in Chapter 9.

Exploring Substance Abuse, Violence, and Sexual Abuse

Because of the prevalence and magnitude of problems associated with substance abuse (including alcohol), violence, and sexual abuse in our society, the possibility that these problems contribute to or represent the primary source of clients' difficulties should be routinely explored. Because of the significance of these problematic behaviors, we devote a major portion of Chapters 8 and 9 to their assessment.

Negotiating Goals and a Contract

EP 8

When social workers and clients believe that they have adequately explored the problems prompting the initial contact, they are ready to enter the process of planning. By this point (if not sooner), it should be apparent whether other resources or services are needed. As mentioned earlier, if other resources are needed or are more appropriate, the social worker may initiate the process of referring the client elsewhere. If the client's problems match the function of the agency and the client expresses a willingness to continue with the helping process, then it is appropriate to begin negotiating a contract. When involuntary clients are unwilling to participate further in the helping process, their options should be clarified at this point. For example, they can choose to return to court, choose not to comply and risk the legal consequences of this tactic, choose to comply minimally, or choose to work with the social worker on problems as they see them in addition to legal mandates (R. H. Rooney, 2009).

In a problem-solving approach, goals specify the end results that will be attained if the problem-solving efforts succeed. Generally, after collaborating in the exploration process, social workers and clients share common views about which results or changes are desirable or essential. In some instances, however, social workers may recognize the importance of accomplishing certain goals that clients have overlooked, and vice versa. Social workers introduce the process of **goal negotiation** by explaining the rationale for formulating those goals. If stated in explicit terms, goals will give direction to the problem-solving process and serve as progress guideposts and as outcome criteria for the helping efforts. To employ goals effectively, social workers need skills in persuading clients to participate in selecting attainable goals, in formulating general task plans for reaching these goals, and in developing specific task plans to guide the social worker's and client's efforts between sessions.

When resolving the problematic situation requires satisfying more than one goal (the usual case), social workers should assist clients in assigning priorities to those goals so that the first efforts can be directed to the most burdensome aspects of the problem. Stimulating clients to elaborate goals enhances their commitment to participate actively in the problem-solving process by ensuring that goals are of maximal relevance to them. Techniques such as the "**miracle question**" from the solution-focused approach can be employed to engage clients in elaborating their vision of goals (De Jong & Berg, 2002). For example, a client might be asked to share a vision of how the situation would look if he or she were to awaken the next day and find that, by a miracle, the problem was gone. What would he or she notice as different? These responses are useful in elaborating the elements of a goal. Even involuntary clients can often choose the order in which goals are addressed or participate in the process of making that choice. Essential elements of the goal selection process and the contracting process are discussed in depth in Chapter 12.

Ending Interviews

EP 8

Both initial interviews and the contracting process conclude with a discussion of "housekeeping" arrangements and an agreement about the next steps to be taken. During this final portion of the interview process, social workers should suggest the length and frequency of sessions, who will participate in them, the means of accomplishing goals, the duration of the helping period, fees, the date and time of the next appointment, pertinent agency policies and procedures, and other relevant matters. When social workers have completed these interview processes, or when the time allocated for the interview has elapsed, they conclude the interview. Messages appropriate for ending interviews include the following:

- "I see our time for today is nearly at an end. Let's stop here, and we'll begin next time by reviewing our experience in carrying out the tasks we discussed."
- "Our time is running out, and there are still some areas we need to explore. Let's arrange another session when we can finish our exploration and think about where you'd like to go from there."
- "We have just a few minutes left. Let's summarize what we accomplished today and what you and I are going to work on before our next session."

Goal Attainment

EP 8

During Phase II of the helping process, interviewing skills are used to help clients accomplish their goals. Much of the focus during this phase is on identifying and carrying out actions or tasks that clients must implement to accomplish their goals.

Not surprisingly, preparing clients to carry out these actions is crucial to successful implementation. Fortunately, effective strategies of preparation are available (see Chapter 13).

As clients undertake the challenging process of making changes in their lives, it is important that they maintain focus on a few high-priority goals until they have made sufficient progress to warrant shifting to other goals. Otherwise, they may jump from one concern to another, dissipating their energies without achieving significant progress. The burden, therefore, falls on the social worker to provide structure for and direction to the client. Toward this end, skills in maintaining focus during single sessions and continuity between sessions are critical.

As noted earlier, obstacles to goal attainment commonly arise during the helping process. Individual barriers typically include fears associated with change as well as behavior and thought patterns that are highly resistant to change efforts because they serve a protective function (usually at great psychological cost to the individual). With couples and families, barriers may include entrenched interactional patterns that resist change because they perpetuate power or dependence, maintain safe psychological distance, or foster independence (at the cost of intimacy). In groups, barriers may involve dysfunctional processes that persist despite repeated efforts by leaders to replace these patterns with others that are conducive to group goals and to group maturation.

Additive empathy is used with individuals, couples, and groups as a means to recognize and to resolve emotional barriers that block growth and progress. Confrontation is a high-risk skill used to assist clients in recognizing and resolving resistant patterns of thought and behavior. Because of the sophistication required to use these techniques effectively, we have devoted Chapter 17 to them and have provided relevant skill development exercises. Additional techniques for managing barriers to change (including relational reactions) are discussed in Chapter 18.

SUMMARY

This chapter examined the three phases of the helping process from a global perspective and briefly considered the structure and processes involved in interviewing. The remaining parts of the book focus in detail on the three phases of the helping process and on the interviewing skills and interventions employed during each phase.

COMPETENCY NOTES

EP 1 Demonstrate Ethical and Professional Behavior
- Use supervision and consultation to guide professional judgment and behavior.

EP 2 Engage Diversity and Difference in Practice
- Apply and communicate your understanding of the importance of diversity and difference in shaping life experiences. This also includes presenting yourself as a learner and engaging clients and constituents as experts in their own experience.
- Apply self-awareness and self-regulation to manage the influence of personal biases.

EP 6 Engage with Individuals, Families, Groups, Organizations, and Communities
- Use empathy, reflection, and interpersonal skills to effectively engage diverse clients and constituencies.

EP 7 Assess Individuals, Families, Groups, Organizations, and Communities
- Collect, organize, and critically analyze and interpret information from clients and constituencies.
- Develop mutually agreed-on intervention goals and objectives based on the critical assessment of strengths, needs, and challenges within clients and constituencies.
- Select appropriate intervention strategies based on the assessment, research knowledge, and values and preferences of clients and constituencies.

EP 8 Intervene with Individuals, Families, Groups, Organizations, and Communities
- Critically choose and implement interventions to achieve practice goals and enhance capacities of clients and constituencies.
- Apply knowledge of human behavior and the social environment, person-in-environment, and other multidisciplinary theoretical frameworks in interventions with clients and constituencies.
- Facilitate effective transitions and endings that advance mutually agreed-on goals.

EP 9 Evaluate Practice with Individuals, Families, Groups, Organizations, and Communities
- Critically analyze, monitor, and evaluate intervention and program processes and outcomes.

NOTES

1. The idea of specific phases and their accompanying tasks in structuring casework was originally developed by Jessie Taft and Virginia Robinson and the Functional School. This concept was later extended by Reid (2000) and Epstein and Brown (2002) in the task-centered approach.
2. Lila George, Research Director, Leech Lake Tribe (personal communication, 1993).

CHAPTER 4

Operationalizing the Cardinal Social Work Values

Chapter Overview

Social work practice is guided by knowledge, skills, and values. This chapter addresses the last of those three areas, introducing the cardinal values of the profession and the ethical obligations that arise from those values. Because, in practice, values can clash and ethical principles may conflict with each other, this chapter also describes some of these dilemmas and offers guidance about resolving them. As you read this chapter, you will have opportunities to place yourself in complex situations that will challenge you to analyze your personal values and to assess their compatibility with social work values.

At the completion of your work on this chapter, you will be able to:

- Understand the core social work values and how they play out in practice.

- Develop self-awareness and professional competence by examining the tensions that can occur when personal values intersect with professional values.

- Learn the role that the NASW Code of Ethics plays in guiding professional practice.

- Be familiar with four core ethical issues: self-determination, informed consent, professional boundaries, and confidentiality.

- Know the steps for resolving ethical dilemmas and the ways in which these apply to a case.

- Understand the complexities of applying ethical standards to clients who are minors.

EPAS Competencies in Chapter 4

This chapter will give you the information needed to meet the following EPAS:

- Competency 1: Demonstrate Ethical and Professional Behavior

- Competency 2: Engage Diversity and Difference in Practice

THE INTERACTION BETWEEN PERSONAL AND PROFESSIONAL VALUES

Values are "preferred conceptions," or beliefs about how things ought to be. All of us have values: our beliefs about what things are important or proper that then guide our actions and decisions. The profession of social work has values, too. They indicate what is important to social workers and guide the practice of the profession. Social workers must be attuned to their personal values and be aware of when those values mesh or clash with those espoused by the profession as a whole. They must recognize that their clients also have personal values that shape their beliefs and behaviors, and these may conflict with the social worker's own values or with those of the profession. Further, the larger society has values that are articulated through cultural norms, policies, laws, and public opinion. These, too, can diverge from social workers' beliefs, their clients' values, or the profession's values.

Self-awareness is the first step in sorting out these potential areas of conflict. The following sections describe the core values of the profession, provide opportunities to become aware of personal values, and describe the difficulties that can occur when social workers impose their own beliefs on clients.

THE CARDINAL VALUES OF SOCIAL WORK

The Code of Ethics developed by the National Association of Social Workers (NASW, 2008a) and the professional literature articulate the core values of the profession and the ethical principles that represent those values. They can be summarized as follows:

1. **Access to Resources.** All human beings deserve access to the resources they need to deal with life's problems and to develop their full potential. The value of service is embodied in this principle in that social workers are expected to elevate service to others above their own self-interest. In particular, the profession's values place a premium on working for social justice. Social workers' "change efforts are focused primarily on issues of poverty, unemployment, discrimination, and other forms of social injustice. These activities seek to promote sensitivity to and knowledge about oppression and cultural and ethnic diversity. Social workers strive to ensure access to needed information, services, and resources; equality of opportunity; and meaningful participation in decision making for all people" (NASW, 2008a, p. 5).

2. **Dignity and Worth.** The importance that social workers place on the dignity and worth of their clients is demonstrated through respect for the inherent value of the persons with whom they work and in efforts to examine prejudicial attitudes that may diminish their ability to embrace each client's individuality.

3. **Interpersonal Relationships.** Social workers view interpersonal relationships as essential for well-being and as "an important vehicle for change" (NASW, 2008a, p. 5). The value placed on human relationships affects the way social workers relate to their clients and the efforts that social workers make to improve the quality of the relationships in their clients' lives.

4. **Integrity.** The value of integrity means that professional social workers behave in a trustworthy manner. They treat their clients and colleagues in a fair and respectful fashion; they are honest and promote responsible and ethical practices in others.

5. **The Value of Competence.** The value of competence requires that social workers practice only within their areas of ability and continually develop and enhance their professional expertise. As professionals, social workers must take responsibility for assuring that their competence is not diminished by personal problems, substance abuse, or other difficulties. Similarly, they should take action to address incompetent, unethical, or impaired practice by other professionals.

What do these values mean? What difficulties can arise in putting them into practice? How can they conflict with social workers', clients', and society's values? The following sections describe these values and situations in which challenges can occur.

EP 1

Skill-building exercises at the end of the chapter will assist you in identifying and working through value conflicts.

Access to Resources

1. *All human beings deserve access to the resources they need to deal with life's problems and to develop to their fullest potential.*

A historic and defining feature of social work is the profession's focus on individual well-being in a social context. Attending to the environmental forces that "create, contribute to, and address problems in living" is a fundamental part of social work theory and practice (NASW, 2008a, p. 1).

Implementing this value means believing that people have the right to resources. It also means that, as a social worker, you are committed to helping secure those resources for your clients and to developing policies and implementing programs to fill unmet needs. Although this value seems an easy choice to embrace, certain cases can bring out conflicting beliefs and personal biases that challenge the social worker.

To enhance your awareness of situations in which you might experience such difficulties, imagine yourself in interviews with the clients in each of the following scenarios. Take note of your feelings and of possible discomfort or conflict. Next, contemplate whether your response is consistent with the social work value in question. If the client has not requested a resource but the need for one is apparent, consider what resource might be developed and how you might go about developing it.

Scenario 1

You are a practitioner in a public assistance agency that has limited special funds available to assist clients to purchase essential devices such as eyeglasses, dentures, hearing aids, and other prosthetic items. Your client, Mr. Y, lives in a large apartment complex for single persons and is disabled by a chronic psychiatric disorder. He requests special aid in purchasing new glasses. He says he accidentally dropped his old glasses and a passerby stepped on them. However, you know from talking to his landlord and his previous worker that, due to his confusion, Mr. Y regularly loses his glasses and has received emergency funds for glasses several times in the last year alone.

Scenario 2

Scenario 2 relates to one of the videos accompanying this text, as described in the following Video Case.

VIDEO CASE EXAMPLE

In the video "Working with Yanping," Yanping, a Chinese student studying in the United States, has decided she wants to major in history, while her parents insist that she study business so that she can eventually take over the family company. The American social worker values Yanping's autonomy but understands the risk her client faces in defying parental authority and tradition. The Chinese social worker values family harmony and probes Yanping's insistence on choosing a major at odds with her parents' wishes.

Scenario 3

During a routine visit to an elderly couple who are recipients of public assistance, you discover that the roof on their home leaks. The couple has had small repairs on several occasions, but the roof is old and worn out. They have gathered bids for reroofing, and the lowest bid was more than $3,500. They ask whether your agency can assist them with funding. State policies permit expenditures for such repairs under exceptional circumstances, but much red tape is involved, including securing special approval from the county director of social services, the county advisory board, and the state director of social services. It will be a hassle to try to get the funds, the effort may not be successful, and you may develop a reputation for being too assertive in using limited funds.

Scenario 4

Mr. M sustained a severe heart attack 3 months ago and took a medical leave from his job as a furniture mover. His medical report indicates that he must limit his future physical activities to light work. Mr. M has given up looking for new work and is asking you to pursue worker's compensation and other resources that would help support his family. You are concerned that although Mr. M might be entitled to these supports, they may reduce his motivation to pursue rehabilitation and work that he can reasonably do given his physical condition.

Scenario 5

A military mental health provider is treating a client with mild trauma symptoms. The client wants to be sent home from the deployment, though his/her unit needs him/her to continue in combat. Is the client genuinely traumatized or malingering? Is going home ultimately more harmful for the person's mental health than staying and fulfilling his/her commitments to the unit, the mission, and fellow personnel? Since fear is common in combat, should everyone who is traumatized be allowed to go home? How should the client's self-determination be honored when he/she knew upon enlisting what the job would entail? (Simmons & Rycraft, 2010).

The preceding scenarios depict situations in which people need resources or opportunities to develop their skills or potential or to ensure their safety and quality of life. Possible obstacles to responding positively to these needs are as follows:

- Scenario 1: A judgmental attitude toward Mr. Y, who believes he has lost his glasses
- Scenario 2: A clash of values among Yanping (the client), the social worker(s), and the client's family system

- Scenario 3: Failure to offer options for assistance because of the effort involved in securing help for the couple to pay for the needed roof or the pressure of other responsibilities
- Scenario 4: Skepticism that services will be effective in helping Mr. M, the client who has given up looking for work after his injury, and apprehension that such services may have unintended effects
- Scenario 5: Divergent priorities among the social worker, the client, and the military (which employs both the client and the social worker)

Perhaps, as you read the scenarios, you experienced similar reactions. This discomfort is not uncommon, but these responses indicate a need for expanded self-examination and additional experience to embrace the social work value in challenging situations. The next section describes some strategies for addressing these types of conflicting reactions.

Respect for Dignity and Worth and Interpersonal Relationships

2. *Social workers respect the inherent dignity and worth of the person.*
3. *Social workers recognize the central importance of human relationships.* (NASW, 2008a, p. 5)
These values mean that social workers believe that all people have intrinsic importance, whatever their past or present behaviors, beliefs, way of life, or social status, and that understanding these qualities is essential in involving clients as partners in change. These values embody several related concepts, sometimes referred to as "unconditional positive regard," "nonpossessive warmth," "acceptance," and "affirmation."

These values also recognize that respect is an essential element of the helping relationship. Before individuals will risk sharing personal problems and expressing deep emotions, they must first feel fully accepted and have trust in the goodwill and helpful intent of their service providers. This may be especially difficult when people feel ashamed or inadequate in requesting assistance. When clients are seeking services involuntarily, or when they have violated social norms by engaging in interpersonal violence, criminal behavior, or other infractions, they will be especially alert to perceived judgments or condemnation on the part of the social worker. Your role is not to judge whether clients are to blame for their problems or to determine whether they are good or bad, evil or worthy, guilty or innocent. Rather, your role is to seek to understand them, with all of their difficulties and assets, and assist them in searching for solutions to their problems.

Intertwined with acceptance and a nonjudgmental attitude is the equally important value of stating that every person is unique and that social workers should affirm the individuality of all the people they serve. People are, of course, endowed with widely differing physical and mental characteristics; moreover, their life experiences are infinitely diverse. People differ in terms of appearance, beliefs, physiological functioning, interests, talents, motivation, goals, values, emotional and behavioral patterns, and many other factors. To affirm the uniqueness of another person, you must be committed to entering that individual's world, endeavoring to understand how that person experiences life. Only by attempting to walk in his or her shoes can you gain a full appreciation of the rich and complex individuality of another person.

Affirming each person's individuality, of course, goes far beyond gaining an appreciation of that person's perspectives on life. You must be able to convey awareness of what your client is experiencing moment by moment and affirm the validity of that experience. This affirmation does not mean agreeing with or condoning all of that person's views and feelings. Part of your role as a social worker entails helping people disentangle their confusing, conflicting thoughts and feelings; align their perceptions with reality; mobilize their particular strengths; and differentiate rational reactions from irrational ones. To fulfill this role, you must retain your own separateness and individuality. Otherwise, you may overidentify with clients, thereby losing your ability to provide fresh input. Affirming the experiences of another person means validating those experiences, thus fostering that person's sense of personal identity and self-esteem.

Our opportunities for affirming individuality and sense of self-worth are lost when unexamined prejudices and stereotypes (either positive or negative) blind us to the uniqueness of each individual client. Labels—such as "thug," "sorority girl," "old lady," or "psychiatric patient"—perpetuate damaging stereotypes because they obscure the individual characteristics of the people assigned to those labels. Whether the preconceptions are positive or negative, professionals who hold them may fail to effectively engage with the person behind the label; they may overlook needs or capacities and, as a result, their assessments, goals, and interventions will be distorted.

The consequences of such practices are troubling. Imagine an elderly client whose reversible health problems (associated with inadequate nutrition or need for medication) are dismissed as merely symptomatic of advanced age. Also consider the client with developmental disabilities who is interested in learning about sexuality and contraceptives but whose social worker fails to address those issues, considering them irrelevant for members of this population. Perhaps the sorority member will fail to disclose symptoms of a learning disorder or suicidal ideation to the social worker who presumes she "has everything going for her." What about the man with schizophrenia who is more concerned about his aging parents than he is about his illness and symptom management? Clearly, avoiding assumptions and prejudices is central to effective social work practice.

Sometimes, the ability to embrace these two sets of social work values comes with increased experience and exposure to a range of clients. Veteran practitioners have learned that acceptance comes through understanding the life experience of others, not by criticizing or judging their actions. As you work with service recipients, you should try to view them as persons in distress and avoid perceiving them based on labels such as "lazy," "borderline," "irresponsible," "delinquent," "dysfunctional," or "promiscuous." As you learn more about your clients, you will find that many of them have suffered various forms of deprivation and have themselves been victims of abusive, rejecting, or exploitative behavior. Remember also that all people have abilities and assets that may not be apparent to you. Consistent respect and acceptance on your part are vital in helping them gain self-esteem and mobilize capacities that are essential to change and to well-being.

However, withholding judgment does not mean condoning or approving illegal, immoral, abusive, exploitative, or irresponsible behavior. It is often our responsibility to help people live not according to our particular values and moral codes, but according to the norms and laws of society. In doing so, social workers, without blaming, must assist clients in taking responsibility for the part they play in their difficulties. Indeed, change is possible in many instances only when individuals gain awareness of the effects of their decisions and seek to modify their behavior accordingly. The difference between "blaming" and "defining ownership of responsibilities" is that the former tends to be punitive, whereas the latter flows from the social worker's positive intentions to be helpful and to assist clients in change. As a professional, you will inevitably confront the challenge of maintaining your own values without imposing them on your clients (Doherty, 1995). A first step toward resolving this issue is addressing your own judgmental tendencies.

The values clarification exercises that follow will help you to identify your own particular areas of vulnerability. In each scenario, imagine yourself in an interview or group session with the client(s). If appropriate, you can role-play the scenario with a fellow student, changing roles so that you can benefit by playing the client's role as well. As you imagine or role-play the scenario, be aware of your feelings, attitudes, and behavior. After each scenario, contemplate or discuss the following questions:

EP 1

1. What feelings and attitudes did you experience? Were they based on what actually occurred, or did they emanate from preconceived beliefs about such situations or individuals?
2. Were you comfortable or uneasy with the client? How did your classmate perceive your attitudes toward the "client"? What cues alerted him or her to your values and reactions?
3. Did any of the scenarios disturb you more than others? What values were reflected in your feelings, attitudes, and behavior?
4. What assumptions did you make about the needs of the client(s) in each scenario?
5. What actions would you take (or what information would you seek) to move beyond stereotypes in understanding your client(s)?

Scenario 6

Your client is a 35-year-old married male who was sentenced by the court to a secure mental health facility following his arrest for peering in the windows of a women's dormitory at your college. He appears uncomfortable and blushes as you introduce yourself.

Scenario 7

You are assigned to do a home study for a family interested in adoption. When you arrive at the home for the first interview, you realize that the couple interested in the adoption consists of two male partners.

Scenario 8

You are a child protection worker and your client is a 36-year-old man whose 13-year-old stepdaughter ran away from home after he had sexual intercourse with her on several occasions during the past 2 months. In your first meeting, he states that he "doesn't know what the big deal is … it's not like we're related or anything."

Scenario 9

Your 68-year-old client has been receiving chemotherapy for terminal cancer at your hospital for the past month. Appearing drawn and dramatically more emaciated than she was last month, the client reports that she has been increasingly suffering with pain and believes her best course of action is to take an overdose of sleeping pills.

Scenario 10

You are a probation officer. The judge has ordered you to complete a presentencing investigation of a woman who was arrested for befriending elderly and disabled individuals, then stealing their monthly disability checks.

Scenario 11

You have been working for 8 weeks with a 10-year-old boy who has experienced behavioral difficulties at school. During play therapy, he demonstrates with toys the process of strangling cats and dogs.

Scenario 12

Your client, Mrs. O, was admitted to a domestic violence shelter following an attack by her husband, in which she sustained a broken collarbone and arm injuries. This occasion is the eighth time she has contacted the shelter. Each previous time she has returned home or allowed her husband to move back into the home with her.

Scenario 13

A low-income family with whom you have been working recently received a substantial check as part of a settlement with their former landlord. During a visit in which you plan to help the family budget the funds to pay their past due bills, you find the settlement money is gone—spent on a large television and gambling at a local casino.

Scenario 14

You are a Latino outreach worker. One Caucasian client has expressed appreciation for the help you have provided, yet tells you repeatedly that she is angry at her difficulty finding a job, blaming it on "all these illegals."

Scenario 15

You are working with a high school senior, the eldest girl in a large family from a strict religious background. Your client wants desperately to attend college but has been told by her parents that she is needed at home to care for her younger siblings and assist in her family's ministry.

If you experienced uneasy or negative feelings as you read or role-played any of the preceding scenarios, your reactions were not unusual. Although social workers take many situations in stride, each of us may be tripped up by a scenario that is new to us, challenges our embedded beliefs, or triggers value conflicts. It can be challenging to look beyond differences, our comfort zones, or distressing behaviors to see clients as individuals in need. However, by focusing selectively on the person rather than on the behavior, you can gradually overcome initial reactions and learn to see clients, colleagues, and others in full perspective.

How does this acceptance play out in practice? Acceptance is conveyed by listening attentively; by responding sensitively to the client's feelings; by using facial expressions, voice intonations, and gestures that convey interest and concern; and by extending courtesies and attending to the client's comfort.

EP 1

If you are unable to be open and accepting of people whose behavior runs counter to your values, your effectiveness in helping them will be diminished, because it is difficult—if not impossible—to conceal negative feelings toward others. People quickly detect insincerity; even masking your feelings may make it difficult to create a truly effective relationship. To expand your capacity for openness and acceptance, it may be helpful to view associations with others whose beliefs, backgrounds, and behaviors differ from yours as opportunities for growth and enrichment. Truly open people view differences as refreshing and stimulating and seek out these interactions. By embracing the opportunity to relate to all types of people and by seeking to understand them, you will gain a deeper appreciation of the diversity and complexity of human beings. In so doing, you will be less likely to pass judgment and will achieve personal growth in the process. It will also be helpful to talk with other professionals who have been in the field for some time. What value conflicts did they initially experience, and how do they manage conflicts now? How do they convey respect for clients, even those whose actions they disdain?

The Value of Integrity

4. *The value of integrity means that professional social workers behave in a trustworthy manner.*

As an ethical principle, integrity means that social workers act honestly, encourage ethical practices in their agencies, and take responsibility for their own ethical conduct (Reamer, 1998). In practice, it means that social workers present themselves and their credentials accurately, avoid other forms of misrepresentation (e.g., in billing practices or in presentation of research findings), and do not participate in fraud and deception. Integrity also refers to the ways that social workers treat their colleagues. Professionals are expected to treat one another with respect, avoid involving clients or others in professional disputes, and be forthright in their dealings with fellow professionals. These expectations are important not only for our individual trustworthiness, but also because each of us serves as a representative of the larger profession and we should act in ways that do not dishonor it.

This may seem to be a relatively straightforward expectation. However, challenges can arise when pressures from other colleagues or employing organizations create ethical dilemmas. In those cases, the challenge is not what is right, but rather how to do it. Following are two examples of such dilemmas involving the principle of integrity. What strategies might you pursue to resolve these dilemmas and act with honesty and professionalism?

Scenario 16

Your agency recently received a large federal grant to implement a "Return to Work" program as part of welfare reform. Although the evaluation protocol is very clear about what constitutes "work," the agency is pressuring you and your coworkers (none of whom are social workers) to count clients' volunteer efforts and other nonpaying jobs as "work" in an effort to ensure that this valuable program will continue. The agency maintains that paying jobs are difficult to find, so clients who are actively working—even in noncompensated jobs—"fit the spirit, if not the letter of the law."

Scenario 17

Your supervisor wants to assess your effectiveness in conducting family sessions. Because he fears that client behaviors will change and his findings will be distorted if clients know they are being taped, he has told you to tape these sessions without their knowledge. The supervisor feels that because he discusses your cases with you anyway, the taping without explicit client permission should be acceptable.

The Value of Competence

5. *The value of competence requires that social workers practice only within their areas of ability and continually develop and enhance their professional expertise.*

EP 1

As with the value of integrity, this principle places the burden for self-awareness and self-regulation on the social worker. An expectation of practice as a professional is that the individual will take responsibility for knowing his or her own limits and seek out the knowledge and experience needed to develop further expertise throughout the span of his or her career. This principle means that social workers will decline cases where they lack sufficient expertise, and that they will seek out opportunities for continuous self-examination and professional development. The commitment to utilizing evidence-based practices means that professionals must be lifelong learners, staying abreast of practice-related research findings, discarding ineffective or harmful practices, and tailoring interventions to the client's unique circumstances (Gambrill, 2007). Each of these elements speaks to developing and maintaining professional competence. The NASW Code of Ethics also includes cultural competence among its expectations for social workers, requiring an understanding of various groups, their strengths, the effects of oppression, and the provision of culturally sensitive services (NASW, 2008a).

EP 1

Self-regulation also requires the social worker to be alert to events or problems that affect his or her professional competence. For example, is a health or mental health problem hindering the social worker's service to clients? Are personal reactions to the client (such as anger, partiality, or sexual attraction) impairing the social worker's judgment in a particular case? Are family problems or other stressors detracting from the social worker's capacity to respond to clients' needs? **Countertransference** refers broadly to the ways that a social worker's experiences and emotional reactions influence his or her perceptions of and interactions with a client. Its correlate, **transference**, refers to the same dynamic when the client consciously or unconsciously associates the social worker with past experiences in such a way that perceptions and interactions with the social worker are affected. Later in this book you will learn more about the ways that transference and countertransference can constructively or destructively affect the helping process. It is important to be alert to such reactions and use supervisory sessions to examine and address their impact.

EP 1

Supervision is an essential element in professional development and ongoing competence. In the helping professions, a supervisor is not someone looking over the social worker's shoulder to catch and correct mistakes. More typically, supervisors can be thought of as mentors, teachers, coaches, and counselors all wrapped up into one role (Haynes, Corey, & Moulton, 2003). Successful use of supervision requires you to be honest and self-aware in seeking guidance, raising issues for discussion, sharing your challenges and successes, and being open to feedback, praise, critiques, and change. Effective supervisors will help you develop skills to look clearly at yourself so that you understand your strengths and weaknesses, preferences and prejudices, and become able to manage these for the benefit of your clients.

Developing and maintaining competence is a career-long responsibility, yet it can be challenging to uphold. Consider the following scenarios.

Scenario 18

You are a new employee at a small, financially strapped counseling center. The director of your agency just received a contract to do outreach, assessments, and case management for frail elders. Although you took a human behavior course as a social work student, you have never studied or worked with older adults, especially those at risk. The director has asked you to lead this new program and has emphasized how important the new funding is for the agency's survival.

Scenario 19

For the past few weeks, you've found yourself attracted to one of your clients, thinking about him or her often and wondering what the client is doing at different times of the day. You wonder if this attraction could affect your objectivity on the case but are reluctant to discuss the situation with your supervisor because it might affect his or her evaluation of you later this year.

Scenario 20

Your internship is at a busy metropolitan hospital. In one morning alone you encounter a woman from Somalia whose dialect you are unfamiliar with, a Muslim woman reluctant to disrobe for the physical exam, and a Korean family at odds over the placement of their teenager's newborn infant. You are called in to assist the medical team but wonder how to effectively address all of the cultural and individual differences in these cases within the pressure-packed schedule of the hospital workday.

What is competence? Do social workers ever feel totally competent? What is impairment? And how can we tell when it applies to us and our practice?

Self-evaluation requires self-knowledge and introspection. Measuring one's competence requires honest self-examination and the pursuit of input from colleagues and supervisors. Professional development requires actively seeking out opportunities to hone existing skills and develop new ones, whether through reading, continuing education, course work, or case conferences. It means knowing what we do not know and being willing to acknowledge our shortcomings. It means being aware of the learning curve in developing new skills or testing new interventions and using staff development and supervision to assure that clients are receiving high-quality services (NASW, 2008a). It also means that when we lack the skills, abilities, or capacity demanded by a client's situation that we make proper referrals, thereby elevating the client's needs above our own.

CHALLENGES IN EMBRACING THE PROFESSION'S VALUES

In this section's presentation of the social work profession's values, numerous scenarios have highlighted the potential for value conflicts. Self-awareness, openness to new persons and events, and practice experience are all crucial elements in overcoming value conflicts. But what if you have made these efforts and your values continue to conflict with others' values?

EP 1

Social workers occasionally encounter situations in which they cannot conform to the profession's values or in which a client's behaviors or goals evoke such powerful reactions that a constructive helping relationship cannot be established. Practitioners who have personal experiences with child abuse, for example, may find it difficult to accept an alleged abuser as a client. Social workers who are intensely opposed to abortions may find it difficult to engage in objective problem

IDEAS IN ACTION

EP 2

One way that social workers can assess and enhance competence is through the review of case recordings. These may be pen-and-paper process recordings of the dialogue in a client session or audio- or videotapes of individual, family, or group meetings (Murphy & Dillon, 2008). Many social workers resist recording sessions on the premise that it makes clients uncomfortable, though the greater likelihood is that the client will forget the recording is taking place; it may be that the social worker him- or herself is distressed at its presence and at having to look at his or her performance at a later point. Ethical practice, however, requires facing this discomfort for the greater good of evaluating strengths and weaknesses and, ultimately, assuring competent practice. Ali, the social worker interviewing Irwin and Angela Corning in the videos that accompany this text ("Problem Solving with the Corning Family"), received an array of insights as a result of reviewing the tapes of her sessions. Among her findings are the following:

At the outset of the first session, Irwin clearly stated his frustration with attending the meeting. His comment set the tone for our working relationship, which was strained at first. I remember thinking that exploring his frustration at that time would be a difficult conversation, and I did not want to get off to a bad start. The alternative was hardly any easier to work with. By ignoring his comment (though it was really his tone that got my attention!) I communicated to both clients that I was not willing or ready to meet them where they were emotionally. The space between us was muddled for the remainder of the session. I could sense that Irwin was getting tense. I am thankful that rather than explode or walk out, he interjected himself into the conversation to explain his brusque demeanor and negative emotions.

Because I did not address Irwin's frustration, he remained distant, and the business of the meeting was conducted with Angela. For a majority of the first session, my legs were crossed in front of me and I was turned toward Angela. At times, I crossed my arms in front of me over the notepad. You can see by my posture that I was uncomfortable with the tension in the room.

I noticed that my nerves were showing in other ways as well. Occasionally during the interview I explored the details of personal situations with the couple. As I asked these sensitive questions, my voice trailed off, so much so that it is hard to hear the entire question on the recording. In contrast, a calm and even tone would normalize these difficult inquiries and the information they elicit.

It is amazing to hear how many times I said "You know" and "So." I never realized it before, but I use these phrases as a pause in my sentences. I have been trying to pay attention to it lately and make sure that when I am working with clients all of my words help to convey a point or information. I also say "you guys" a lot, which seems too casual and potentially disrespectful.

I also noticed that as I got more anxious, I talked a lot and fumbled around. Much of the time in the first session was spent sorting through what exactly I could provide the couple. Looking at it on tape, I can see why Angela and Irwin were so frustrated and uncomfortable. I eventually gave them a plan, to provide them with contact information for affordable apartment complexes and employment placement services, but I could have been clearer in how I conveyed the information. It just got more confusing when I sought the couple's corroboration in a partnership that they knew little about. This is a point in the interview where I could have checked in with the clients to be sure that we were all on the same page.

In the second session, my hesitancy to engage Irwin persisted. At that appointment, Irwin discovered for the first time that he and Angela were carrying a $2,000 balance on their credit card account. The couple exchanged words back and forth, which I remember was a poignant moment in my work with them. As I watched the tape, I was struck by this opportunity to explore the couple's money management methods. Instead of having that discussion, I got into the activity of listing all of the other barriers that the couple would face in attaining a new apartment. My personal goal was to be prepared in the second session. I wanted to be sure to get all of the items on my list, one of which was a discussion of the barriers to attaining the couple's stated goals.

Processing the disclosure of the credit card in the moment with the couple not only would have yielded information and helped the couple to share household financial tasks more effectively, but would have also engaged the clients and may have fostered rapport between Irwin and me. Because I did not address the issue, and it was a surprise and disappointment to Irwin, he was unable to follow the thread about barriers. When I checked in with him to see if he wanted to add anything, he revealed that he was consumed with thoughts of the debt discovery over the past several minutes rather than following the discussion.

I did a good job of seeking out which areas the clients wanted to address in their goals. The clients reported that they were happy with the outcomes of our work together and that they became more comfortable with the process as the relationship grew. At the same time, we could have been more detailed in making the task lists. While I was speaking with Irwin about his objectives for employment and career advancement he indicated that in the future he would like to see himself admitted to, or already enrolled in, a masonry apprentice program. This could have been thoughtfully broken down into task steps that Irwin would have control over. Should Irwin meet his objectives, but not attain the goal because of factors out of his control, he would see documentation of his accomplishments and the efficacy of setting objectives and goals. (Unfortunately, we only had enough time to give

this goal cursory treatment at the end of the interview.)

Near the end of our time together, Irwin and Angela had made considerable gains in the realms of housing, employment, and communicating with the school and I was feeling more confident in my work with them. I was glad to have the opportunity to go over the Eco-Map with them to illustrate how much they had done to change their lives. Watching the tape, I realized that I did not emphasize their success and efforts enough. I sense that this was a missed opportunity for offering congratulations and praise.

In the final session, I evaluated the work with Irwin and Angela. At one point I ask, "I didn't seem too nosy, did I?" Watching it, I realize that the wording of the question suggests a need for validation rather than feedback. Actually, one of my focal points for career development is to learn to encourage and foster self-determination as opposed to **doing** for the client. It is important to me that the clients I work with see the relationship as collaborative, with us all on equal ground. I really wanted to know if I seemed too pushy or bossy. I can see how rephrasing my question could allow Irwin and Angela to give more honest feedback. I could have asked, "Did you feel respected in our work together?" (or "Did you feel disrespected in our work together?"). "Did I respond to your needs and concerns?"

All in all, I was glad to see the series of tapes because I saw steady improvement in my skills and comfort over time. It is good that my supervisor reviewed them, too, as she was able to identify strengths of mine that I can build on, as well as areas for change.

solving with a woman experiencing an unintended pregnancy. In such instances, it is important to acknowledge these reactions and to explore them through supervision or therapy. It may be feasible to overcome these difficulties in order to be more fully available as a helping person. If this is not possible, however, or if the situation is exceptional, the social worker and his or her supervisor should explore the possibility of transferring the case to another practitioner who can accept both the client and the goals.

In such circumstances, it is vital to clarify for clients that the reason for the transfer is not a personal rejection of them but rather recognition that they deserve the best service possible and that the particular social worker cannot provide that service. It is not usually necessary to go into detail about the social worker's challenges. A general explanation conveys goodwill and safeguards clients' well-being. When a transfer is not possible, the social worker is responsible for seeking intensive assistance to ensure that services are provided properly and that ethical and professional responsibilities are upheld. Practitioners who are consistently unable to accept clients' differences or carry out their roles in a professional manner owe it to themselves and to future clients to reflect seriously on their suitability for the social work field.

EP 1

Cross-cultural and cross-national social work poses further challenges in the application of professional values (Healy, 2007). Are values such as justice and acceptance universally recognized guidelines for behavior, or should their application become tempered by cultural norms? Some have suggested that NASW and other social work codes of ethics place too great a value on individual rights over the collective good and emphasize independence over interdependence (Jessop, 1998; Silvawe, 1995). As such, they may reflect a Western bias and give insufficient attention to the values of other cultures. This is not merely a philosophical dispute. It creates significant challenges for practitioners working with individuals or groups with vastly different values. How can social workers reconcile their responsibility to advocate for justice and equality while simultaneously demonstrating respect for cultural practices such as female circumcision, corporal punishment of children, arranged marriages, or differential rights based on social class, gender, skin tone, or sexual orientation? Cultural values shift and evolve over time, and social workers' systems change efforts may appropriately target stances that harm or disenfranchise certain groups. But how can social workers ensure that their efforts are proper and congruent with the desires of the particular cultural group and not a misguided effort born of paternalism and ethnocentrism?

Are ethics fixed guidelines that should be applied universally (a **deontological perspective**), or are they flexible, depending on the place and population to which they are applied (a **relativist** position)? Healy (2007) concludes that "social work is obligated to work for cultural change when equal rights are in jeopardy" (p. 6), labeling this position as "moderate universalism" (p. 24), where the human rights of equality and protection are promoted along with the importance of cultural diversity and community ties. Ultimately, striking this balance means that social workers, individually and collectively, must be aware of their values and those of their colleagues and clients and engage in ongoing education and conversation in reconciling these value tensions. Congruent with cultural humility

(Hunt, 2001), this approach encourages the professional to adopt a "learner" perspective in order to determine where the ethical tensions reside and how much of an impediment they are to the helping process.

ETHICS

Codes of ethics are the embodiment of a profession's values. They set forth principles and standards for behavior of members of that profession. In social work, the primary Code of Ethics is promulgated by the NASW. It addresses a range of responsibilities that social workers have as professionals—to their clients, to their colleagues, to their employers, to their profession, and to society as a whole. This section addresses four primary areas of ethical responsibility for social workers: self-determination, informed consent, maintenance of client–social worker boundaries, and confidentiality. First, however, it details how ethics are related to legal responsibilities and malpractice risks. The section concludes by summarizing the resources and processes available for resolving ethical dilemmas.

The Intersection of Laws and Ethics

The practice of social work is governed by a vast array of policies, laws, and regulations. Whether established by court cases, the U.S. Congress, state legislatures, licensure boards, or regulatory agencies, these rules affect social workers' decisions and actions.

EP 1

For example, state mandatory reporting laws require social workers to report cases in which child abuse is suspected. The Health Insurance Portability and Accountability Act (HIPAA) regulates the storage and sharing of patient records (U.S. Department of Health and Human Services, 2003). Some states' administrative rules forbid the placement of children with same-sex foster parents. Licensure board regulations may forbid social work practice by persons with felony convictions. Federal court cases may extend evidential privilege to communications with social workers (Reamer, 1999) while federal, state, or local laws may prohibit the provision of certain benefits to undocumented immigrants. Good social work practice requires social workers to be aware of the laws and regulations that govern the profession and apply to their area of practice and the populations they serve. But knowing the laws is not enough. Consider the following case.

CASE EXAMPLE

Alice is a 38-year-old woman who has presented for treatment, filled with guilt as the result of a brief extramarital affair. In her third session, she discloses that she is HIV-positive but is unwilling to tell her husband of her status because then the affair would be revealed, and she fears losing him and her two young daughters. You are concerned about the danger to her husband's health and press her to tell him or to allow you to do so. Alice responds that if you do, you will be breaking your promise of confidentiality and violating her privacy. She implies that she would sue you or report you to your licensing board and to your profession's ethics committee.

This case neatly captures the clash of ethics, laws, and regulations and illustrates the stakes for social workers who make the "wrong" decision. In a scenario such as this one, the social worker needs a clear answer from a lawyer or supervisor who will tell him or her exactly what to do. Unfortunately, matters are not that simple. Good practice requires knowledge of both the applicable ethical principles and the relevant laws. Even with this knowledge, dilemmas may persist. In this case example, the ethical principles of self-determination and confidentiality are pitted against the principle to protect others from harm, which itself is derived from a court case (Cohen & Cohen, 1999; Reamer, 1995). The particular state or setting where the case takes place may have laws or regulations that govern the social worker's actions. Finally, the threat of civil litigation for malpractice looms large, even when the social worker's actions are thoughtful, careful, ethical, and legal.

When you think about the intersection of laws and ethics, it may be helpful to think of a Venn diagram with two ovals overlapping (see Figure 4-1). In the center are areas common to both ethics and laws; within each oval are items that are exclusive to laws and ethics, respectively. Some standards contained in the NASW Code of Ethics are not addressed by laws and regulations (such as the prohibition of sexual relationships with supervisees or standards on treating colleagues with respect). Similarly, some areas of the law are not covered by the Code of Ethics. For example, it is illegal to drive while intoxicated, but the Code of Ethics lacks a standard related to that act. Where the two realms intersect, there can be areas of agreement as well as areas of discord. As the Code of Ethics notes:

Social workers' primary responsibility is to promote the well-being of clients. In general, clients' interests are primary. However, social workers' responsibility to the larger society or specific legal obligations may on limited occasions supersede the loyalty owed clients, and clients should be so advised. (NASW, 2008a, p. 7)

Also:

Instances may arise when social workers' ethical obligations conflict with agency policies or relevant laws or regulations. When such conflicts occur, social workers must make a responsible effort to resolve the conflict in a manner that is consistent with the values, principles, and standards expressed in this Code. If a reasonable resolution of the conflict does not appear possible, social workers should seek proper consultation before making a decision. (NASW, 2008a, pp. 3–4)

Processes for ethical decision making are addressed later in this chapter. For now, it is important to acknowledge that social workers must know both the law and ethical principles to practice effectively. They must also recognize that sometimes conflicts will occur between and among ethical and legal imperatives. For example, state laws may prohibit the provision of services or resources to undocumented immigrants, but ethics would expect social workers to fill basic human needs. Thoughtful examination, consultation, and skillful application of the principles will serve as guides when laws and ethics collide.

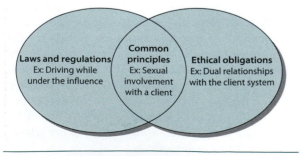

FIG 4-1 The Relationship of Law and Ethics

Key Ethical Principles

EP 1

The NASW Code of Ethics contains 155 standards, addressing a variety of ethical issues (such as conflicts of interest, competence, or confidentiality) for social workers in a range of roles (such as supervisor, teacher, direct practitioner, or administrator). In this section, we examine four key areas of immediate relevance to direct practitioners: self-determination, informed consent, professional boundaries, and confidentiality.

Self-Determination

Biestek (1957) has defined **self-determination** as "the practical recognition of the right and need of clients to freedom in making their own choices and decisions" (p. 103). Self-determination is central to the social worker's ethical responsibility to clients:

> *Social workers respect and promote the right of clients to self-determination and assist clients in their efforts to identify and clarify their goals. Social workers may limit clients' right to self-determination when, in their professional judgment, clients' actions or potential actions pose a serious, foreseeable, and imminent risk to themselves or others.* (NASW, 2008a, p. 7)

This value also embodies the beliefs that individuals have the capacity to grow and change and to develop solutions to their difficulties, as well as the right and capacity to responsibly exercise free choice. These values are magnified when practitioners adopt a strengths-oriented perspective, looking for positive qualities and undeveloped potential rather than pointing out limitations and past mistakes (Cowger, 1994; Saleebey, 1997). Such a positive perspective engenders hope and courage on the client's part and nurtures self-efficacy. These factors, in turn, enhance the client's motivation, which is indispensable to achieving a successful outcome.

The extent to which you affirm an individual's right to self-determination rests in large measure on your perceptions of the helping role and of the helping process. If you consider your major role to be that of providing solutions or dispensing advice freely, you may foster dependency, demean clients by failing to recognize and affirm their strengths, and relegate them to a position of passive cooperation (or passive resistance). However, controlling behavior is counterproductive. Not only does it discourage open communication, but, with equal importance, it denies people the opportunity to gain strength and self-respect as they actively wrestle with their difficulties. Fostering dependency generally leaves people weaker rather than stronger and is a disservice to them.

The type of relationship that affirms self-determination and supports growth is a partnership wherein the practitioner and the client (whether an individual, a couple, or a group) are joined in a mutual effort to search for solutions to problems or to promote growth. As enablers of change, social workers facilitate clients' quest to view their problems realistically, to consider various solutions and their consequences, to implement change-oriented strategies, to understand themselves and others more fully, to gain awareness of previously unrecognized strengths and opportunities for growth, and to tackle obstacles to change and growth. As helpful as these steps are, ultimately the responsibility for pursuing these options rests with the client.

Just as fostering self-determination enhances client autonomy, exhibiting **paternalism** (i.e., preventing self-determination based on a judgment of the client's own good) infringes on autonomy. Linzer (1999) refers to paternalism as "the overriding of a person's wishes or actions through coercion, deception or nondisclosure of information, or for the welfare of others" (p. 137). A similar concept is **paternalistic beneficence**, wherein the social worker implements protective interventions to enhance the client's quality of life, sometimes despite the client's objections (Abramson, 1985; Murdach, 1996).

EP 1

Under what conditions might it be acceptable for a social worker to override a client's autonomy? Paternalism may be acceptable when a client is young or judged not to have sufficient decision-making capacity, when an irreversible act such as suicide can be prevented, or when the interference with the client's decisions or actions ensures other freedoms or liberties, such as preventing a serious crime (Abramson, 1985; Reamer, 1989). Murdach suggests three gradations of beneficent actions, which vary in their level of intrusiveness depending on the degree of risk and the client's decision-making capacity. Even under these circumstances, social workers must weigh the basis for their decisions against the potential outcomes of their actions.

For example, if a psychiatric patient refuses medication, some would argue that the client lacks capacity to make such a decision, and that forcing him or her to take the medication would be "for the client's own good." Yet diagnosis or placement is not a sufficient basis for overriding a person's autonomy. For this reason, states have developed elaborate administrative and judicial processes that must be traversed before an individual can be involuntarily hospitalized or medicated (Montross, 2014).

Even when clients have reduced ability for exercising self-determination, social workers should act to ensure that they exercise their capacities to the fullest feasible extent. For example, self-determination can be extended to individuals who are terminally ill by educating them about their options and encouraging them to articulate their desires through advance directives that provide instructions to family members and health care personnel regarding which medical interventions are acceptable. Although child clients are not authorized to give consent for treatment, through the process of seeking *assent*, social workers can explain the proposed services to the child and seek his or her agreement for care.

EP 1

Operationalizing clients' rights to self-determination can sometimes pose perplexing challenges. Adding to the complexity is the reality that in certain instances, higher-order principles such as safety supersede the right to self-determination. To challenge your thinking about how you might affirm the value of self-determination in practical situations, we have provided scenarios that consist of problematic situations actually encountered by the authors or colleagues. As you read each scenario, analyze the alternative courses of action that are available and think of the laws, policies, and resources that you might consult as part of your decision making. Consider how you would work with the client to maximize self-determination, taking care also to promote the client's best interests.

Scenario 21

In your work for the state welfare department, you oversee the care of numerous nursing home residents whose services are paid for by the state. Two of your clients, both in their 90s, reside in the same facility and declared their intention of marrying each other. The couple's family members oppose the union for various reasons, and the administrator of the facility strenuously protests that "letting them do that will create a dangerous precedent. Then everyone will want to get married." Further, she has stressed that she has no private room for a couple and that if they insist on marrying, they will have to be discharged.

Scenario 22

A 15-year-old who is 4 months pregnant has contacted you several times in regard to planning for her child. During her last visit, she confided that she is habituated to heroin. You have expressed your concern that the drug may damage her unborn child, but she does not seem worried, nor does she want to give up use of the drug. You also know that she obtains money for heroin through prostitution and is living on the street.

Scenario 23

While making a visit to Mr. F, an elderly man living in a rural farmhouse, you discover that he is disheveled and thin and that the house is unclean, piled high with old newspaper and magazines, and occupied by more than a dozen cats. The homecare aides have been inattentive and untrustworthy, so Mr. F fired them, and he now reports that he is "managing fine on my own."

Scenario 24

As a rehabilitation worker, you have arranged for a young woman to receive training as a beautician in a local technical college, a vocation in which she expressed intense interest. Although initially enthusiastic, she now tells you that she wants to discontinue the program and go into nursing. According to your client, her supervisor at the college is highly critical of her work, and the other trainees tease her and talk about her behind her back. You are torn about what to do, because you know that your client tends to antagonize other people with her quick and barbed remarks. You wonder if, rather than change programs, your client needs to learn more appropriate ways of communicating and relating to her supervisor and coworkers.

Scenario 25

A middle-aged woman with cancer was so debilitated by her latest round of chemotherapy that she has decided to refuse further treatment. Her physician states that her age, general health, and stage of cancer all argue for continuing her treatments, given the likelihood of a successful outcome. Her family is upset at seeing the woman in pain and supports her decision.

Providing Informed Consent

Six principles in the NASW Code of Ethics address facets of **informed consent**. In essence, informed consent requires that social workers:

EP 1

use clear and understandable language to inform clients of the purpose of the services, risks related to the services, limits to services because of the requirements of a third-party payer, relevant costs, reasonable alternatives, clients' right to refuse or withdraw consent, and the time frame covered by the consent. Social workers should provide clients with an opportunity to ask questions. (NASW, 2008a, pp. 7–8)

The Code of Ethics also indicates that clients should be informed when their services are being provided by a student. Timely and understandable informed consent sets the stage for social work services by acquainting the client with expectations for the process. For example, a common element of informed consent involves the limits on client privacy. Social workers explicitly state that in situations involving concerns about the client's danger to self or others, the social worker reserves the right to break confidentiality to seek appropriate help. Mandatory reporting requirements (for child and elder abuse and other circumstances, such as communicable diseases) are typically also covered at this time.

In addition to respectfully educating the client about his or her rights and responsibilities, informed consent lays the groundwork for future actions the social worker might need to take. In the Case Example earlier in the chapter about the woman who refused to let her husband know about her HIV-positive status, informed consent would have alerted the client at the outset to the social worker's responsibility to protect others from harm and her duty to notify public health or other authorities about the risk created by the client's unprotected sexual activity.

Some social workers view informed consent as a formality to be disposed of at the first interview or as a legalistic form to have clients sign and then file away. In fact, informed consent should be an active and ongoing part of the helping process. Given the tension and uncertainty that can accompany a first session, clients may not realize the significance of the information you are providing. In addition, new issues may emerge that require discussion of the client's risks, benefits, and options (Strom-Gottfried, 1998b). Therefore, it makes sense to revisit the parameters of service and invite questions throughout the helping process. Having a "fact sheet" that describes relevant policies and answers commonly asked questions can also help clients by giving them something to refer to between meetings, should questions arise (Houston-Vega, Nuehring, & Daguio, 1997; Zuckerman, 2008).

To facilitate informed consent for persons with hearing, literacy, or language difficulties, social workers should utilize interpreters and multiple communication methods as appropriate. When clients are temporarily or permanently incapable of providing informed consent, "social workers should protect clients' interests by seeking permission from an appropriate third party, informing clients consistent with the client's level of understanding," and "seek to ensure that the third party acts in a manner consistent with the client's wishes and interests" (NASW, 2008a, p. 8). Even clients who are receiving services involuntarily are entitled to know the nature of the services they will be receiving and to understand their right to refuse service.

VIDEO CASE EXAMPLE

In the video "Home for the Holidays," the social worker, Kim, covers the following aspects of informed consent in the initial moments of her interview with Anna and Jackie:

- The expectation of confidentiality by the social worker and by the two clients in regard to what each shares in the session.
- The limits of confidentiality (risk to self or others).
- Should either partner see the social worker in an individual session, the information discussed or revealed there will not be held in confidence during conjoint sessions.
- The amount of time that the social worker has set aside for the session (40 minutes).
- The purpose of the first session. Kim tells the clients that this is the time for them to tell her about themselves as individuals and as a couple and to share their concerns and struggles with her.
- The nature of couples' work. Kim informs the couple that she will not take sides or act as a referee. She explains to the couple that her clinical focus is on their interactions, and that she considers her client to be their relationship rather than either person individually.
- Although the relationship will be the therapeutic focus of the work, at times the social worker will push and challenge one of the partners in particular. Kim explains that this is sometimes necessary to learn more about how the partners interact and to gain clarity about how the relationship works.

The following are other aspects of informed consent that could have been covered:

- The social worker's experience with couples, specifically her work with same-sex partners
- The social worker's preferred theoretical framework for couple's therapy
- Alternatives to pursuing couple's therapy (e.g., couple's education groups, group therapy, bibliotherapy)
- Fee schedule and terms of insurance coverage
- The clients' right to withdraw consent and to cease therapy

Preserving Professional Boundaries

EP 1

Boundaries refer to clear lines of difference that are maintained between the social worker and the client in an effort to preserve the working relationship. They are intended to help prevent conflicts of interest, making the client's interests the primary focus and avoiding situations in which the social worker's professionalism is compromised. In part, boundaries help clarify that the client–social worker relationship is not a social one. Also, even though it may involve a high degree of trust and client disclosure, the relationship is not an intimate one, such as might be experienced with a friend, partner, or family member. When clients can trust that boundaries exist and will be maintained by the social worker, they are more able to focus on the issues for which they are seeking help. They can freely share of themselves and trust that the social worker's reactions and statements—whether of support, confrontation, or empathy—are artifacts of the working relationship, not social or sexual overtures or personal reactions such as might arise when friends agree or disagree.

Sometimes social workers and other helping professionals have a difficult time with the notion of boundaries, perceiving that they establish a hierarchical relationship in which the client is deemed "less worthy" than the social worker. Some professionals may also feel that establishing such boundaries is a cold and clinical move, treating the client as an object instead of a fellow human deserving of warmth and compassion (Lazarus, 1994). Our viewpoint is that the two positions are not mutually exclusive. Social workers can have relationships with clients that are

characterized by collaborative problem solving and mutuality, and they can react to clients authentically and kindly, without blurring the boundaries of their relationship or obscuring the purpose of their work.

The NASW Code of Ethics addresses boundaries through six provisions:

EP 1

1. "Social workers should not take unfair advantage of any professional relationship or exploit others to further their personal, religious, political, or business interests" (NASW, 2008a, p. 9)
2. "Social workers should not engage in dual or multiple relationships with clients or former clients in which there is a risk of exploitation or potential harm to the client. In instances when dual or multiple relationships are unavoidable, social workers should take steps to protect clients and are responsible for setting clear, appropriate, and culturally sensitive boundaries. (Dual or multiple relationships occur when social workers relate to clients in more than one relationship, whether professional, social, or business. Dual or multiple relationships can occur simultaneously or consecutively.)" (NASW, 2008a, pp. 9–10)
3. "Social workers should not engage in physical contact with clients when there is a possibility of psychological harm to the client as a result of the contact (such as cradling or caressing clients)." (NASW, 2008a, p. 13)
4. "Social workers should under no circumstances engage in sexual activities or sexual contact with current clients, whether such contact is consensual or forced." (NASW, 2008a, p. 13)
5. "Social workers should not engage in sexual activities or sexual contact with clients' relatives or other individuals with whom clients maintain a close personal relationship when there is a risk of exploitation or potential harm to the client. Sexual activity or sexual contact with clients' relatives or other individuals with whom clients maintain a personal relationship has the potential to be harmful to the client and may make it difficult for the social worker and client to maintain appropriate professional boundaries. Social workers—not their clients, their clients' relatives, or other individuals with whom the client maintains a personal relationship—assume the full burden for setting clear, appropriate, and culturally sensitive boundaries." (NASW, 2008a, p. 13)

6. "Social workers should not engage in sexual activities or sexual contact with former clients because of the potential for harm to the client." (NASW, 2008a, p. 13)

Although these standards of practice may seem self-evident, they represent an area fraught with difficulty within social work and other helping professions. Research on ethics complaints indicates that in NASW-adjudicated cases, boundary violations accounted for more than half of all cases in which violations occurred (Strom-Gottfried, 1999a). Most social workers cannot imagine developing sexual relationships with their clients; yet this outcome is often the culmination of a "slippery slope" of boundary problems that may include excessive self-disclosure on the part of the social worker, the exchange of personal gifts, socializing or meeting for meals outside the office, and arranging for the client to perform office and household chores or other favors (Borys & Pope, 1989; Epstein, Simon, & Kay, 1992; Gabbard, 1996; Gartrell, 1992).

It is not uncommon to experience feelings of attraction, even sexual attraction, for clients. When such feelings arise, however, it is crucial to raise them with faculty or supervisors so they can be acknowledged and examined. Such discussion normalizes and neutralizes these feelings and decreases the likelihood that the social worker will act on the attraction (Pope, Sonne, & Greene, 1993). These issues will be explored further in Chapter 18 as we discuss relational reactions and their effects on the helping process.

EP 1

Other boundary issues can be both subtle and complex. For example, you may meet a neighbor in the agency waiting room or run into a consumer while doing your grocery shopping. A client may ask to "friend" you on Facebook or visit his or her "Caring Bridge" website. You may decide to buy a car and find that the salesperson is a former client. You may visit a relative in the hospital and discover that her roommate is a current or former client. Friends in need of social work services may ask to be assigned to your caseload because you already know them so well. A client may ask you to attend a "family" event, such as a graduation or wedding. You may resonate with a particular client and think what a great friend he or she could be. You may have experienced a problem similar to the client's and wish to tell the client how you handled it. You may sympathize with a particular client's job search plight and consider referring him to a friend who is currently hiring new workers.

Not all encounters with clients outside the helping relationship are unethical. Contacts with clients that are unplanned, manageable, temporary, and transparent may simply be boundary crossings rather than boundary violations (Reamer, 2001). Certain settings (such as rural practice) and types of work (such as home-based care and community-based interventions) may create special opportunities for boundary confusion (Strom-Gottfried, 2005, 2009). The possibilities for boundary complication are endless, and addressing them involves nuanced application of the standards on boundary setting and other ethical principles, such as maintaining confidentiality and avoiding conflicts of interest. Therefore, setting "clear, appropriate, and culturally sensitive boundaries" (NASW, 2008a, pp. 9–10) might mean different things in different settings.

Many social workers routinely discuss the possibility of public contact with clients during the first session, explaining, for example, that in deference to privacy, they will not acknowledge the client unless spoken to first, should they encounter the client in a grocery store or on the street. A social worker invited to "friend" a client on a social networking site (or join the client in an in-person social activity) can sensitively explain the importance of not blurring the working relationship with other kinds of contact. Buying a car (or some other product or service with variable pricing) from a client or former client could be exploitive of the client or the social worker, and could complicate the working relationship if the product or service is flawed. Such arrangements should be avoided. If they cannot be, boundary setting may mean ending the commercial relationship or the helping relationship if the two cannot be successfully merged. If neither choice is a possibility, consultation and intercession of a supervisor would be recommended to assure that neither the client nor social worker is disadvantaged by the transaction.

An invitation to a client's graduation or marriage ceremony should be processed with the client to explore the meaning of the offer. Ethical boundary setting might variously involve declining the invitation, accepting it, or attending the public portion of the event rather than the more private elements, such as a reception. The desire to disclose personal experiences with a client may be a form of authenticity (discussed further in Chapter 5) or an upsetting derailment where attention is switched from the client's experiences and needs to the social worker's. Social workers should always be mindful of what they are trying to accomplish in making a personal self-disclosure and consider alternate ways of achieving the same objective.

For example, rather than the social worker saying, "When I have that kind of conflict with my mother, I do X," he or she could simply state, "Sometimes, people in conflict with their parents find that X is helpful."

Later in this chapter, we discuss strategies for more thoroughly examining and resolving ethical dilemmas. The key in managing boundaries is to be alert to **dual relationships**, to discuss troubling situations with colleagues and supervisors, and to take care that the primacy of the helping relationship is preserved in questionable boundary situations (Brownlee, 1996; Erickson, 2001; Reamer, 2001). Consultation helps social workers determine whether dual relationships are avoidable and whether they are problematic. It is incumbent on the social worker to ensure that clients are not taken advantage of and that their services are not obscured or affected detrimentally when boundaries must be crossed.

Safeguarding Confidentiality

From a practical standpoint, **confidentiality** is a *sine qua non* of the helping process. Without the assurance of confidentiality, it is unlikely that clients would risk disclosing private aspects of their lives that, if revealed, could cause shame or damage to their reputations. This is especially true when clients' problems involve infidelity, deviant practices, illicit activities, traumatic experiences, and the like. Implied in confidentiality is an assurance that the practitioner will never reveal such personal matters to others.

EP 1

Social workers are bound by the NASW Code of Ethics to safeguard their clients' confidentiality. While numerous standards operationalize this principle, in essence, social workers are expected to respect clients' privacy, to gather information only for the purpose of providing effective services, and to disclose information only with clients' consent. Disclosure of information without clients' permission should be done only for compelling reasons, and even then there are limits on what information can be shared and with whom. These exceptions to confidentiality will be addressed later in this section.

An unjustified breach of confidentiality is a violation of justice and is tantamount to theft of a secret with which one has been entrusted (Biestek, 1957). Maintaining strict confidentiality requires a strong commitment and constant vigilance because clients sometimes reveal information that is shocking, humorous, bizarre, or titillating. To fulfill your responsibility in maintaining privacy, you must guard against disclosing information in inappropriate situations. Examples include discussing details of your work with family and friends, having gossip sessions with colleagues, dictating within the listening range of others, discussing client situations within earshot of other staff, posting pictures of clients on social media sites such as Facebook, and making remarks about cases in elevators or other public places.

The emergence of technology that permits the electronic collection, transfer, and storage of information raises new complexities for maintaining client privacy (Gelman, Pollack, & Weiner, 1999). When you leave a voice mail for a client, are you certain that only the client will receive the message? Will you agree to accept and send text messages to clients? When a colleague sends you a fax on a case, can you be sure that others will not see that information before you retrieve the document? Further complexities arise in the electronic provision of services through text messages, websites, online groups, and so on. There are many advantages to such interventions: they are commonly used methods of modern communication, they can efficiently offer reminders of appointments or tips for relapse prevention, and they can assist with symptom management and increase service access for homebound individuals and those who need access to services on a 24/7 basis (Kessler et al., 2009; Shapiro et al., 2009). However, electronic media present challenges for confidentiality, informed consent, and professional liability (Manhal-Baugus, 2001; Santhiveeran, 2009; Strom-Gottfried & Thomas, 2012).

Beyond ethical standards, the Health Insurance Portability and Accountability Act of 1996 (HIPAA) established federal standards to protect the privacy of personal health information. HIPAA regulations affect pharmacies, health care settings, and insurance plans as well as individual health and mental health providers. The rules affect identifiable client information in all forms, including paper records, electronic data and communications, and verbal communications. There are several important provisions for social workers in HIPAA (HIPAA Medical Privacy Rule, 2003; Protecting the Privacy of Patients' Health Information, 2003; U.S. Department of Health and Human Services, 2007; Zuckerman, 2008):

- Psychotherapy notes have a particular protection under HIPAA. The release of those notes requires special, separate authorization. Psychotherapy notes must be kept separately in client files and must meet other criteria in order to be considered protected.

- A general principle of the Privacy Rule is that if a person has the right to make a health care decision, then that person has a right to the **information** associated with that decision.
- Although clients should be provided access to their records, and have the opportunity to seek corrections if they identify errors or mistakes, client access to psychotherapy notes is restricted.
- Clients must be given information on the organization's privacy policies, and they must sign a form or otherwise indicate that they have received the information.
- Client records or data should be protected from nonmedical uses, such as marketing, unless the client gives specific permission otherwise.
- Clients should understand their rights to request other reasonable efforts to protect confidentiality, such as requesting to be contacted only at certain times or numbers.
- Organizations and the individuals who work in them (in clinical, clerical, administrative, and other roles) must take care to ensure that security standards are in place and that they are reinforced through staff development and agency policies.
- When state laws are more stringent than the provisions in HIPAA (when they offer greater protections for clients), those laws take precedence over HIPAA.
- HIPAA recognizes the validity of professional standards, such as those contained in the NASW Code of Ethics, and in some cases, those provisions may be more stringent than HIPAA's.
- In the case of minors, parents are generally considered the "personal representatives" for their children and as such can have access to personal health information as well as make health care decisions on behalf of their children. Some exceptions are: (1) when State law does not require parental consent for a minor to receive treatment, (2) when a court has appointed someone other than the parent as the child's guardian, and (3) if the parent agrees to a confidential relationship between the health care provider and the child.
- The health care provider does not have to disclose information to the parent of a minor if (1) the provider has reasonable belief of abuse or neglect or that the information to be provided may endanger the child, or (2) using personal judgment, the provider decides that it is not in the minor client's best interest to treat the parent as the minor's individual representative.

What Are the Limits on Confidentiality?

Although social workers are expected to safeguard the information they collect in the course of their professional duties, there are several situations in which helping professionals are allowed or are compelled to share case information. These include when the social worker is seeking supervision or consultation, when the client waives confidentiality, when the client presents a danger to self or others, when the social worker is reporting suspicions of child or elder maltreatment, and when the social worker presented with a subpoena or court order.

Supervision and Consultation

The right to confidentiality is not absolute, because case situations are frequently discussed with supervisors and consultants and may be presented at staff conferences. Disclosing information in these instances, however, is for the purpose of enhancing the provision of services, and clients will generally consent to these uses when the purpose is clarified. The client has a right to be informed that such disclosures may occur, and practitioners seeking supervision have a responsibility to conceal the identity of the client to the fullest extent possible and to reveal no more personal information than is absolutely necessary to get assistance on the case.

EP 1

Other personnel such as administrators, volunteers, clerical staff, consultants, board members, researchers, legal counsel, and outside persons who may review records for purposes of quality assurance, peer review, or accreditation may have access to files or case information. This access to information should be for the purposes of better serving the client, and these individuals should sign binding agreements not to misuse confidential information. Further, it is essential that social workers promote policies and norms that protect confidentiality and assure that case information is treated carefully and respectfully.

Client Waivers of Confidentiality

Social workers are often asked by other professionals or agencies to provide confidential information about the nature of their client's difficulties or the services provided. Sometimes, these requests can be made with such authority that the recipient is caught off guard, inadvertently acknowledging a particular person as a client or providing the information requested about the case. In these instances, it is important that such data be provided only with the written, informed consent of clients, as this releases the practitioner and agency from liability in disclosing the requested information. Even when informed consent is obtained, it is important to reveal information selectively based on the essential needs of the other party.

In some exceptional circumstances, information can be revealed without informed consent, such as a bona fide emergency in which a client's life appears to be at stake or when the social worker is legally compelled to do so, as in the reporting of child or elder abuse. In other instances, it is prudent to obtain supervisory and legal input before disclosing confidential information without the client's written consent for release of information.

A final example of the client's waiver of confidentiality occurs if the client files a malpractice claim against the social worker. Such an action would "terminate the patient or client privilege" (Dickson, 1998, p. 48), freeing the practitioner to share publicly such information as is necessary to mount a defense against the lawsuit.

Danger to Self or Others

In certain instances, the client's right to confidentiality may be less compelling than the rights of other people who could be severely harmed or damaged by actions planned by the client and confided to the practitioner. For example, if the client plans to commit kidnapping, injury, or murder, the practitioner is obligated to disclose these intentions to the intended victim and to law enforcement officials so that timely preventive action can be taken. Indeed, if practitioners fail to make appropriate disclosures under these circumstances, they may be liable to civil prosecution for negligence. The fundamental case in this area is the *Tarasoff* case (Reamer, 1994). In this case, a young man seeing a psychologist at a university health service threatened his girlfriend, Tatiana Tarasoff. The therapist notified university police; after interviewing the young man, they determined that he did not pose a danger to his girlfriend. Some weeks later the young man murdered Tarasoff, and her family filed a lawsuit alleging that she should have been warned. Ultimately, the court ruled that mental health professionals have an obligation to protect their clients' intended victims.

This court decision has led to varying interpretations in subsequent cases and in resulting state laws, but two principles have consistently resulted from it (Dickson, 1998; Houston-Vega, Nuehring, & Daguio, 1997): If the worker perceives a serious, foreseeable,

and imminent threat to an identifiable potential victim, the social worker should (1) act to warn that victim or (2) take other precautions (such as notifying police or placing the client in a secure facility) to protect others from harm.

Another application of the duty to protect personal safety involves intervening to prevent a client's suicide. Typically, lawsuits that cite a breach of confidentiality undertaken to protect suicidal clients have not been successful (VandeCreek, Knapp, & Herzog, 1988). Conversely, "liability for wrongful death can be established if appropriate and sufficient action to prevent suicide is not taken" (Houston-Vega, Nuehring, & Daguio, 1997, p. 105). Knowing when the risk is sufficient to warrant breaking a client's confidence is both a clinical decision and an ethical matter. Chapter 9 offers guidelines for determining the risk of lethality in cases of suicidal threats or client aggression.

Suspicion of Child or Elder Abuse

The rights of others also take precedence over the client's right to confidentiality in instances of child abuse or neglect. In fact, all 50 states have statutes making it mandatory for professionals to report suspected or known child abuse. Moreover, statutes governing the mandatory reporting of child abuse may contain criminal clauses related to the failure to report. States have established similar provisions for reporting the suspected abuse of the elderly or other vulnerable adults (Corey, Corey, Corey, & Callanan, 2014; Dickson, 1998; Donovan & Regehr, 2010). The mandate to report suspicions of abuse does not empower the social worker to breach confidentiality in other ways. That is, even though the social worker is a mandated reporter, he or she should still use caution in the amount of unrelated case information he or she shares with child welfare authorities. Furthermore, the requirement is to report suspicions to specific protective agencies, not to disclose information to the client's family members, teachers, or other parties.

Although afforded immunity from prosecution for reporting, practitioners must still confront the difficult challenge of preserving the helping relationship after having breached the client's confidentiality. One way of managing this tension is through informed consent. As noted earlier, clients should know at the outset of service what the "ground rules" for service are and what limits exist on what the social worker can keep private. When clients understand that the social worker must report suspected child abuse, such a report may not be as damaging to the helping relationship. Similarly, the Code of Ethics states, "Social workers should inform clients, to the extent possible, about the disclosure of confidential information and the potential consequences, when feasible before the disclosure is made" (NASW, 2008a, p. 10). With a trusting relationship, informed consent, and careful processing of the decision to file a child abuse report, feelings of betrayal can be diminished and the working alliance preserved.

Subpoenas and Privileged Communication

Yet another constraint on the client's right to confidentiality is that this right does not necessarily extend into courts of law. Unless social workers are practicing in states that recognize the concept of privileged communication, they may be compelled by courts to reveal confidential information and to produce confidential records. **Privileged communication** refers to communications made within a "legally protected relationship," which "cannot be introduced into court without the consent of the person making the communication," typically the patient or client (Dickson, 1998, p. 32). Statutes that recognize privileged communication exempt certain professions from being legally compelled to reveal content disclosed in the context of a confidential relationship.

Determining the presence and applicability of privilege can be complicated, however. As Dickson notes, "Privilege laws can vary with the profession of the individual receiving the communication, the material communicated, the purpose of the communication, whether the proceeding is criminal or civil, and whether the professional is employed by the state or is in private practice, among other factors" (1998, p. 33). At the federal level, the U.S. Supreme Court in *Jaffee v. Redmond* upheld client communications as privileged and specifically extended "that privilege to licensed social workers" (Social Workers and Psychotherapist–Patient Privilege: *Jaffee v. Redmond* Revisited, 2005).

Laws recognizing privileged communication are created for the protection of the client; thus, the privilege belongs to the client, not to the professional (Schwartz, 1989). In other words, if the practitioner were called to take the witness stand, the attorney for the client could invoke the privilege to prohibit the practitioner's testimony (Bernstein, 1977). Conversely,

the client's attorney could waive this privilege, in which case the practitioner would be obligated to disclose information as requested by the court.

Another important factor regarding privileged communication is that the client's right is not absolute (Levick, 1981). If, in a court's judgment, disclosure of confidential information would produce benefits that outweigh the injury that might be incurred by revealing that information, the presiding judge may waive the privilege. Occasionally, the privilege is waived in instances of legitimate criminal investigations because the need for information is deemed more compelling than the need to safeguard confidentiality (Schwartz, 1989). In the final analysis, courts make decisions on privilege-related issues on a case-by-case basis.

Because subpoenas, whether for records or testimony, are orders of the court, social workers cannot ignore them. Of course, subpoenas may sometimes be issued for irrelevant or immaterial information. Therefore, social workers should be wary about submitting privileged materials. Careful review of the subpoena, consultation with the client, and consultation with a supervisor and agency attorney can help you determine how to respond. The following sources provide helpful information for social workers contending with subpoenas: Austin, Moline, and Williams (1990); Barsky and Gould (2002); Bernstein and Hartsell (2005); Houston-Vega, Nuehring, and Daguio (1997); Polowy and Gilbertson (1997); Sarnoff (2004); and NASW (2008b).

Confidentiality in Various Types of Recording

Accreditation standards, funding sources, state and federal laws—all may dictate how agencies maintain record-keeping systems. Because case records can be subpoenaed and because clients and other personnel have access to them, it is essential that practitioners develop and implement policies and practices that provide maximal confidentiality. To this end, social workers should adhere to the following guidelines (Kagle & Kopels, 2008; Moline, Williams, & Austin, 1998; Reamer, 2005; Zuckerman, 2008):

1. Record no more than is essential to the services being provided. Identify observed facts and distinguish them from opinions. Use descriptive terms rather than professional jargon, and avoid using psychiatric and medical diagnoses that have not been verified.

2. Unconfirmed reports about a third party by the client; the personal judgments, opinions, or clinical hypotheses of the clinician; and sensitive information that is not relevant to treatment should be omitted from documentation.

3. Do not include verbatim or process recordings in case files.

4. Maintain and update records to assure their accuracy, relevance, timeliness, and completeness.

5. Employ private and soundproof dictation facilities.

6. Keep case records in locked files and issue keys only to those personnel who require frequent access to the files. Take similar privacy precautions to protect electronically stored data.

7. Do not remove case files from the agency except under extraordinary circumstances and with special authorization.

8. Do not leave case files on desks where others might gain access to them or keep case information on computer screens where it may be observed by others.

9. Take precautions, whenever possible, to ensure that information transmitted through texts, email, fax machines, voice mail, and other technology is secure. Be sure it is sent to the correct party and that identifying information is not conveyed.

10. Use in-service training sessions to stress confidentiality and to monitor adherence to agency policies and practices instituted to safeguard clients' confidentiality.

11. Inform clients of the agency's authority to gather information, the conditions under which that information may be disclosed, the principal uses of the information, and the effects, if any, of limiting what is shared with the agency.

EP 1

Beyond written records, special precautions are needed for recordings of client interactions. As noted earlier, social workers sometimes record live interviews or group sessions so that they can analyze interactional patterns or group process at a later time, or scrutinize their own performance with a view toward improving their skills and techniques. Recording is also used extensively for instructional sessions between students and practicum instructors and as evidence in investigations, for example about child abuse. Yet another use of recordings is to provide first-hand feedback to clients by having them listen to or view their actual behavior in live sessions.

Before recording sessions for any of these purposes, social workers should obtain written consent from clients on a form that explicitly specifies how the recording will be used, who will listen to or view the recording, and when it will be erased. A recording should never be made without the client's knowledge and consent. Clients vary widely in their receptivity to having sessions recorded; if they indicate reluctance, their wishes should be respected. The chances of gaining their consent are enhanced by discussing the matter openly and honestly, taking care to explain the right to decline. If approached properly, the majority of clients will consent to recording.

Social workers who record sessions assume a heavy burden of responsibility in safeguarding confidentiality because live sessions can prove extremely revealing. Recordings should be guarded to ensure that copies cannot be made and that unauthorized persons do not have access to them. When they have served their designated purpose, they should be promptly erased. Failure to heed these guidelines may constitute a breach of professional ethics.

Beyond protecting files or recordings from misuse, the NASW Code of Ethics also addresses clients' rights with respect to records, stating that "social workers should provide clients with reasonable access" to their records (NASW, 2008a, p. 12). It further notes that the social worker should provide "assistance in interpreting the records and consultation with the client" (p. 12) in situations where the social worker is concerned about misunderstandings or harm arising from seeing the records. Access to records should be limited "only in exceptional circumstances when there is compelling evidence that such access would cause serious harm to the client" (p. 12). In our opinion, the trend toward greater client access to records has enhanced the rights of clients by avoiding misuse of records and has compelled practitioners to be more prudent, rigorous, and circumspect in keeping case records.

The Ethics of Practice with Minors

A particular challenge in social work practice is interpreting ethical standards as they apply to clients under the age of 18 (Strom-Gottfried, 2008). Although minor clients have the right to confidentiality, informed consent, self-determination, and the protection of other ethical principles, their rights

EP 1

are limited by laws and policies, by differences in maturity and decision-making capacity, and by their very dependence on adults as their caretakers. As such, parents may retain the right to review a child's treatment record and to be kept informed of issues the child raises in therapy. A 15-year-old teen parent has the right to make decisions about her baby's health care that she cannot legally make about her own. Child welfare experts and other authorities are empowered to decide where to place children and when to move them based on their appraisal of the best interests of the child. A 10-year-old may resist medication or treatment but lacks the ability to withhold consent in light of his age and cognitive capacities. As such, his parents or guardians can compel him to comply, even against his expressed wishes.

Minors' rights are also affected by the particular service setting and by their presenting problems. For example, a youth seeking substance abuse services would have privacy protections under federal regulations that assure confidentiality (42-CFR) even if his parents insisted on service information (Strom-Gottfried, 2008). Similarly, a minor in need of prenatal care or treatment for sexually transmitted diseases could offer her own consent for services and be assured of confidentiality. Emergency services may be provided for a minor if delaying for parental consent could jeopardize the minor's well-being. School districts that accept "abstinence only" funding for health care will limit the information that social workers and nurses can share with students about contraception and HIV prevention.

As you can see, practice with minors is a complex tangle of legal, developmental, ethical, and social issues (Konrad, 2013). Unsnarling this web requires a thorough understanding of child development and the physical, emotional, and cognitive capacities that emerge over the first two decades of the life span. It also requires an understanding of ethical standards, so that the worker appreciates the areas in which tensions might arise between legal and developmental limits to a minor's rights and the expectations of the profession for honoring clients' prerogatives, irrespective of age. Professionals in child-serving settings should be familiar with the policies and practices that govern services for their clientele. Through supervision, staff consultation, and careful decision making, social workers must consider various factors on a case-by-case basis in order to ensure that minors' rights are maximized, even amid constraints on those rights.

VIDEO CASE EXAMPLE

In the "Hanging with Hailey" videos, several issues relating to ethical service to mature minors arise:

- In light of Hailey's age and the policies at the school, the social worker (Emily) was not required to get parental permission for service; Hailey could consent to her own treatment.

- Emily carefully describes the parameters of confidentiality during the first session. During this segment, Hailey interjects, "I guess, but I still don't know why I'm here." Although Emily is careful to acknowledge the statement, she continues with her explanation and makes sure Hailey understands the limits of privacy.

- Perhaps because of Hailey's age, Emily fails to include possible abuse as a reason for breaking confidentiality; thorough informed consent would have also included letting Hailey know that if her safety were at risk, Emily would need to divulge that information.

- In the second session, when Hailey describes smoking "weed" and having suicidal ideations, Emily continues her assessment and concludes that the situation is not serious enough to necessitate informing Hailey's mother. This assessment has both clinical and ethical dimensions, weighing risk, the client's capacity for decision making, agency policies, parental rights, client self-determination, and safety. Changes in any of these factors might shift the balance, leading a worker to notify parents or guardians of risky behaviors, or to work with the client to do so.

UNDERSTANDING AND RESOLVING ETHICAL DILEMMAS

Social workers sometimes experience quandaries in deciding which of two values or ethical principles should take precedence when a conflict exists. In the foregoing discussions of self-determination and confidentiality, for example, we cited examples of how the rights of clients and ethical obligations of social workers are sometimes superseded by higher-order values (e.g., the right to life, safety, and well-being). Thus, clients' right to confidentiality takes second place when they confide that they have physically or sexually abused a child or when they reveal imminent and serious plans for harmful acts that would jeopardize the health or safety of other people. Dilemmas can also arise if you find that certain policies or practices of your employing agency seem detrimental to clients. You may be conflicted about your ethical obligations to advocate for changes because doing so may jeopardize your employment or pose a threat to your relationships with certain staff members.

EP 1

Situations such as these present social workers with agonizingly difficult choices. Reamer (1989) has developed general guidelines that can assist social workers in making these decisions. Here we present our versions of some of these guidelines and illustrate instances of their application:

1. *The right to life, health, well-being, and the necessities of life takes precedence over rights to confidentiality and opportunities for additive "goods" such as wealth, education, and recreation.* We have previously alluded to the application of this principle in instances of child or elder abuse or threats of harm to another person. In such circumstances, the rights of both children and adults to health and well-being take precedence over clients' rights to confidentiality.

2. *An individual's basic right to well-being takes precedence over another person's right to privacy, freedom, or self-determination.* As stated in the language of the courts (which have consistently upheld this principle), "The protective privilege ends where the public peril begins" (Reamer, 1994, p. 31). For example, the rights and needs of infants and children to receive medical treatments supersede parents' rights to withhold medical treatment because of their religious beliefs.

3. *A person's right to self-determination takes precedence over his or her right to basic well-being.* This principle maintains that people are entitled to act in ways that may appear contrary to their best interests, provided they are competent to make an informed and voluntary decision with consideration of relevant knowledge, and as long as the consequences of their decisions do not threaten the well-being of others. For example, if an adult chooses to live under a highway overpass,

we may find that lifestyle unwise or unhealthy, but we have no power to constrain that choice. This principle affirms the cherished value of freedom to choose and protects the rights of people to make mistakes and to fail. As noted earlier, this principle must yield when an individual's decision might result either in death or in severe and impeding damage to his or her physical or mental health.

4. *A person's rights to well-being may override laws, policies, and arrangements of organizations.* Ordinarily, social workers are obligated to comply with the laws, policies, and procedures of social work agencies, other organizations, and voluntary associations. When a policy is unjust or otherwise harms the well-being of clients or social workers, however, violation of the laws, policies, or procedures may be justified. Examples of this principle include policies or practices that discriminate against or exploit certain persons or groups. An agency, for example, cannot screen clients to select only those who are healthiest or most affluent (a practice known as "creaming" or "cherry-picking") and then refuse services to individuals in dire conditions. In situations such as these, the well-being of affected groups takes precedence over compliance with the laws, policies, and arrangements at issue.

Ethical social work includes advocacy for changes in laws and policies that are discriminatory, unfair, or unethical. For example, in regard to the ethical challenges posed by managed care, Sunley (1997) suggests engaging in both "case advocacy" and "cause advocacy" to help both individual clients and groups of clients who may be disadvantaged by particular policies or practices. Resources such as Brager and Holloway (1983), Corey, Corey, Corey, and Callanan (2014), and Frey (1990) provide helpful guidance for acting as an effective agent of change within troubled systems.

Steps in Ethical Decision Making

Although Reamer's guidelines serve as a valuable resource in resolving value dilemmas, applying them to the myriad situations that social workers encounter inevitably involves uncertainties and ambiguities, a reality that practitioners must accept. What should you do when you find yourself confronted with an ethical dilemma? Ethical decision-making models are as yet untested for their capacity to yield high-quality outcomes. Nevertheless, a list of recommended steps can be used to ensure thoughtful and thorough examination of options (Corey, Corey, Corey, & Callanan, 2014; Reamer, 2006; Strom-Gottfried, 2008, 2015):

1. Identify the problem or dilemma, gathering as much information about the situation from as many perspectives as possible, including that of the client.
2. Determine the core principles and the competing issues.
3. Review the relevant codes of ethics.
4. Review the applicable laws and regulations.
5. Consult with colleagues, supervisors, or legal experts.
6. Consider the possible and probable courses of action and examine the consequences of various options.
7. Decide on a particular course of action, weighing the information you have and the impact of your other choices.
8. Develop a strategy for effectively implementing your decision.
9. Evaluate the process and results to determine whether the intended outcome was achieved, and consider modifications for future decisions.

These procedures need not be followed in the order listed. For example, consultation can prove useful in revealing options, identifying pros and cons, and rehearsing strategies for implementing the decision. Laws, ethical standards, and values can be examined after options are developed. Even decisions that must be made on the spot with little planning or consultation can be evaluated using this model, so that critical thinking is brought to bear for future dilemmas and actions. The key is to go beyond mere intuition or reactionary decision making to mindful, informed, critically examined choices.

Beyond these steps, you should be sure to document carefully the input and considerations taken into account at each phase of the decision-making process. This documentation may be in the client's formal record, your informal notes, or in the notes from supervisory sessions.

Applying the Ethical Decision-Making Model

To apply this model, let's use the case of Alice from earlier in the chapter. As you may recall, Alice is a 38-year-old woman who refuses to notify her husband of her HIV-positive (HIV+) status for fear of revealing her extramarital affair.

The dilemma for the social worker in the case arises from Alice's disclosure about her HIV+ status and her refusal to tell her husband, which places him at risk for infection. The social worker has a loyalty to Alice's needs and wishes but also a responsibility to prevent her from harming another person (her husband). If the social worker reveals the truth, he or she may save the husband's health (and ultimately his life), but in so doing is violating Alice's trust and right to privacy and potentially putting the marriage at risk by exposing the affair. On the other hand, maintaining the secret, although protecting Alice's privacy, could put the unwitting husband at significant risk for contracting a life-limiting or life-ending disease. The social worker may also worry about legal liability for actions or inaction in the case. In fact, either party who is disgruntled or damaged in the case could seek to hold the social worker accountable: Alice for the breach of privacy, or the husband for negligence in failing to protect him from harm.

Several provisions in the NASW Code of Ethics (2008a) speak to this dilemma:

Social workers should protect the confidentiality of all information obtained in the course of professional service, except for compelling professional reasons. The general expectation that social workers will keep information confidential does

EP 1

not apply when disclosure is necessary to prevent serious, foreseeable, and imminent harm to a client or other identifiable person or when laws or regulations require disclosure without a client's consent. In all instances, social workers should disclose the least amount of confidential information necessary to achieve the desired purpose; only information that is directly relevant to the purpose for which the disclosure is made should be revealed. (1.07c)

Social workers should inform clients, to the extent possible, about the disclosure of confidential information and the potential consequences, when feasible before the disclosure is made. This applies whether social workers disclose confidential information on the basis of a legal requirement or client consent. (1.07d)

Social workers should discuss with clients and other interested parties the nature of confidentiality and limitations of clients' right to confidentiality.

Social workers should review with clients the circumstances where confidential information may be requested and where disclosure of confidential information may be legally required. This discussion should occur as soon as possible in the social worker–client relationship and as needed throughout the course of the relationship. (1.07e)

Embedded in these provisions are important ethical concepts: respect for client self-determination, the importance of informed consent, and the significance of discretion around private information. It would be helpful to know how the social worker handled informed consent with Alice at the outset of services. Did Alice understand the social worker's responsibilities should she prove to be a danger to herself or someone else? If so, the question of notifying her husband should not come as a surprise or betrayal, but rather as a natural consequence of the conditions of service and the established limits of confidentiality.

Beyond ethical standards, social workers must be familiar with the laws, regulations, practices, and policies that apply in their jurisdictions and practice settings. The disclosure of HIV+ status is one example where laws and policies vary widely across states. Some states explicitly shield health professionals from liability for making disclosures to protect the health of another, as long as they do so following established procedures. Other states view partner notification as a public health responsibility and require professionals to alert health departments in cases such as Alice's so that health authorities can undertake necessary disclosures. Preferably, the agency where Alice sought services was already apprised of the laws and had incorporated them into policies and informed consent procedures for all clients prior to the outset of service. The social worker should also consider how Alice knows she is HIV+ and the partner notification policies in the jurisdiction where she was diagnosed. Depending on where and how she was diagnosed, Alice's condition may have already been processed by medical personnel to initiate notification of her husband, her paramour, and any other individuals who may be at risk by contact with her.

Supervisory guidance is essential in this case. Alice's social worker needs help thinking through the implications (for Alice, Alice's husband, the social worker herself, the helping relationship, and the agency).

EP 1

The social worker should use supervision to help identify her alternatives and the various pros and cons involved, anticipate reactions and prepare to address them, and think through ways to improve her practices in the future. Beyond talking with her supervisor, the social worker may seek consultation from legal and medical experts to address specific questions about her choices, her legal liability, or best practices in working with clients with infectious diseases. In these conversations, the social worker should protect the identity of her client, focusing on the issues that gave rise to her dilemma rather than details of this particular client's case.

Options for Action

As a result of these discussions, the social worker may identify at least six options that can be employed singly or in combination:

1. Honor Alice's wishes and keep the secret.
2. Work with Alice to institute safe-sex practices and other control procedures to limit her husband's exposure to her disease.
3. Encourage Alice to tell her husband about her HIV+ status by educating her about the implications of her silence.
4. Offer to assist Alice in telling her husband and processing the information.
5. Offer Alice the chance to tell her husband and let her know that if she does not, the social worker will.
6. Make a report (anonymously or not) to the public health authorities about the risk to Alice's husband.

Regardless of what option the social worker pursues, she should make sure that Alice understands the nature of her disease, is getting proper care, and is taking precautionary steps to protect others from contracting HIV. This is congruent with the ethics of putting the client's needs first and has the pragmatic effect of mitigating damage resulting from Alice's secrecy about her illness.

To Tell or Not to Tell

The question, however, remains: to tell or not to tell? The options that ultimately involve alerting Alice's husband will protect his health and well-being, clearly an advantage of these choices. These options comply with ethical standards, principles, and policies that require social workers to protect others from significant, foreseeable harm. Alerting the husband will probably make the social worker feel more comfortable if she is worried about her complicity and her liability should she keep Alice's secret and he contracts HIV as a result.

The downsides of telling include violating Alice's expressed desire for privacy, rupturing the trust that is central to the helping relationship, and possibly putting Alice's marriage at risk if the secret of her affair is revealed. Alice may make good on a threat to file a regulatory board complaint or lawsuit against the worker or agency for breach of confidentiality. The options in which the social worker encourages Alice to tell may take time to employ, but they have the advantage of empowering her to take control of the situation and face her dilemma head on. Her ability to rely on the social worker is essential in this process. The social worker can help her look at the long-term effects of deception in contrast to the short-term effects of revealing her condition and how she contracted HIV. The social worker can help Alice anticipate and plan for that very difficult conversation with her husband and family and can be a support to her after the fact, whatever the husband's reactions are. All of the advantages of working *with* the client on this challenging problem are lost if the social worker decides to abruptly override Alice's wishes and notify the husband.

Honoring Alice's demands for secrecy without considering the husband's needs and interests fits with the principle of client self-determination but may be at odds with laws and policies about protecting the safety of others. It may also be at odds with Alice's own best interests. Social workers must often navigate between clients' wishes and the steps needed to adequately address their problems. Alice's desire to avoid telling her husband in the short run will not spare anyone pain or harm in the long run. In fact, her insistence on silence now may keep her stuck while her health and family relationships suffer. The social worker who can empathize with her and help her forthrightly address her fears and problems will be carrying out both ethical and professional responsibilities. Should this process fail, the social worker may resort to notification against Alice's will. Given the greater expertise and experience of public health authorities in the area of notifications, the social worker should refer the case to them for assistance.

EP 1

Self-awareness and self-evaluation are important elements of competent, ethical, and professional practice. Throughout this process, Alice's social worker should examine her own motivations, decisions, and actions. Fear of liability, revulsion about Alice's behavior, or other factors might lead the social worker to act precipitously or thoughtlessly. In doing so, she may make a decision that is more in her own interest than her client's.

Supervision is also an important element in self-evaluation. An adept and involved supervisor can help the social worker walk through the decision-making process, identify positive and problematic outcomes, and work on areas for improvement and skill development. Did the decision adequately resolve the dilemma? If it created unplanned or problematic results, what can be done to remedy them? For example, if the social worker's efforts to get Alice to inform her husband of her illness result in Alice's withdrawal from treatment, evaluation will help the social worker determine next steps as well as assess her past actions.

SUMMARY

This chapter introduced the ethics and values that support the social work profession and highlighted the ways these values may create conflicts in professional practice. It provided guidelines for supporting self-determination, respecting confidentiality, obtaining informed consent, maintaining boundaries, and resolving ethical dilemmas. The chapter suggested steps to aid in resolving ethical dilemmas and applied these steps to a case in which self-determination and client confidentiality conflicted with another's safety. Throughout, the chapter considered the importance of self-understanding and self-regulation so that social workers learn to be intentional in their statements and actions and assure that clients' needs and the working relationship are given precedence. In the following chapters we will move toward putting these insights into action as you learn beginning skills for effective communication with and on behalf of clients.

COMPETENCY NOTES

EP 1   Demonstrate Ethical and Professional Behavior

● **Practice personal reflection and self-correction to assure continual professional development**. Social workers must be attuned to their intentions, feelings, and values so that these are used constructively and purposefully in helping relationships. Self-awareness and self-regulation are essential for enacting this practice behavior.

• **Attend to professional roles and boundaries**. Boundaries assure that the helping relationship and the client's interests are accorded the highest priority in social work practice. Social workers are careful not to mix roles (friend/worker). They are alert to actions that may create conflicts of interest or otherwise blur boundaries with clients (physical contact, nonprofessional communications, friending on Facebook, etc.).

• **Demonstrate professional demeanor in behavior, appearance, and oral, written, and electronic communication**. Social workers strive for recognition on par with other professionals such as nurses, lawyers, and psychologists. Professionalism involves adopting the roles, values, and norms of a particular discipline and consistently upholding high standards of conduct.

• **Use supervision and consultation to guide professional judgment and behavior**. Social work practice is complex. Even experienced professionals require the expertise, feedback, and wisdom of supervisors and consultants. Through supportive conversation, practitioners can look at themselves and their cases to improve service, increase competence, and grow professionally.

• **Recognize and manage personal values in a way that allows professional values to guide practice**. Our choices in life are guided by our values. In accepting the role as a professional social worker, the individual must also consider the values of the profession, society, and the clients served. Self-awareness and wise supervision are essential to ensure that personal values, experiences, and emotions do not negatively impinge on the helping process.

• **Make ethical decisions by applying standards of the National Association of Social Workers Code of Ethics, relevant laws and regulations, models for ethical decision making, ethical conduct of research, and additional codes of ethics as appropriate to context**. Knowing the ethical standards for social work is a key step in making sound decisions and avoiding errors of omission and commission. This chapter introduces a model to guide readers in weighing considerations and standards in resolving dilemmas.

• **Understand frameworks of ethical decision making and how to apply principles of critical thinking to those frameworks**. Ethical dilemmas arise out of competing goods. The choice of which path to take is rarely clear cut. Helping professionals must be able to weigh a variety of factors to decide which decision is best in a given situation. Using a thoughtful, stepwise process helps practitioners to weigh the various alternatives in ethical dilemmas; examine policies, principles, and standards involved; and select sound choices.

EP 2   **Engage Diversity and Difference in Practice**

• **Apply and communicate understanding of the importance of diversity and difference in shaping life experiences in practice at the micro, mezzo and macro levels**. When social workers fail to appreciate the characteristics of persons who are different (in race, gender, age, ability, sexual orientation, etc.) they may damage the helping process with inappropriate judgments or other damaging reactions.

SKILL DEVELOPMENT EXERCISES
in Operationalizing Cardinal Values

To assist you in developing skills in operationalizing the cardinal values of social work in specific practice situations, we have provided a number of exercises with modeled responses. As you read each one, note which values are germane to the situation. To refresh your memory, the values are as follows:

1. **Access to Resources:** Social workers value service to others and a commitment to social justice in helping clients get deserved and needed resources.
2. **Dignity and Worth:** Social workers value the inherent dignity and worth of others.
3. **Interpersonal Relationships:** Social workers value the primacy of human relationships.
4. **Integrity:** Social workers behave with integrity.
5. **Competence:** Social workers are responsible for practicing with competence.

Next, assume you are the client's service provider and formulate a response that implements the relevant social work value. After completing each exercise, compare your response with the modeled response that follows the exercises. Bearing in mind that the modeled response is only one of many possible acceptable responses, analyze it and compare it with your own. Also, remember that *vocal tone* is an essential component of effective, congruent communications. Imagine the modeled responses that follow spoken with different verbal and emotional tones: sensitivity, tentativeness, anger, impatience, pity, kindness, and conceit. Which feel genuine to you? Which will help achieve your objectives with the client? Which are congruent with professional values of respect and support for client dignity? By carefully completing these exercises, you will improve your competence in putting values into action in the varied and challenging situations encountered in direct social work practice.

Client Statements

1. *Group member [in first group session]:* Before I really open up and talk about myself, I need to be sure what I say isn't spread around to other people. *[Turning to social worker.]* How can I be sure that won't happen?

2. *Adolescent in correctional institution [after social worker introduces him/herself]:* So you want to help me, huh? I'll tell you how you can help. You can get me out of this effing place—that's how!

3. *Female client, age 21 [to mental health practitioner]:* Yeah, I know that kicking the habit was a victory of sorts. But I look at my life and I wonder what's there to live for. I've turned my family against me. I've sold my body to more rotten guys than I can count—just to get a fix. I've had three STDs. What do I have to offer anyone? I feel like my life has been one big pile of crap.

4. *Teenage male [in a group session in a correctional setting]: [Takes off shoes and sprawls in his chair. His feet give off a foul odor; other members hold noses and make derisive comments. He responds defensively.]* Hey, get off my back, you creeps. What's the big deal about taking off my shoes?

5. *Female [initial interview in family counseling center]:* Before I talk about my marital problems, I need to let you know I'm a Seventh Day Adventist. Do you know anything about my church? I'm asking because a lot of our problems involve my religion.

6. *Female client [sixth interview]:* Maybe it sounds crazy, but I've been thinking this last week that you're not really interested in me as a person. I have the feeling I'm just someone for you to analyze or to write about.

7. *Teenage female [caught with contraband in her possession by a supervisor-counselor in a residential treatment center]:* Please don't report this. I've been doing better lately, and I've learned my lesson. You won't need to worry about me. I won't mess with drugs anymore.

8. *Client [observing social worker taking notes during initial interview]:* I'm dying to know what you're writing down about me. Maybe you think I'm a nut. Can I take a copy of your notes with me when we're done?

9. *Male parolee, age 27, who has a reputation as a con artist [in a mandatory weekly visit to his parole officer]:* Man, you've really got it made. Your office is really fine. But then you deserve what you've got. You've probably got a terrific wife and kids, too. Is that their picture over there?

10. *Female client, age 34 [in third interview]:* I'm really wound up right now. I've got this tight feeling I get in my chest when I'm nervous. *[Pause.]* Well, I guess I'll have to tell you if I expect to get anything out of this. *[Hesitant]* You know the problems I'm having at home … ? Well, Jack doesn't know this, but I'm attracted to other women. *[Blushes.]* I've tried—I've really tried, but Jack doesn't turn me on. I can't even tolerate sex unless I'm thinking about other women. Jack thinks something's wrong with him, but it's not his fault. *[Chin quivers.]*

11. *Black male probationer [to white therapist]:* You're so damn smug. You say you want to help me, but I don't buy that crap. You don't know the first thing about black people. Man, I grew up where it's an accomplishment just to survive. What do you know about life in my world?

Modeled Social Worker Responses

1. "Ginny raises a good point that concerns all of you. So that you can feel more comfortable about sharing personal feelings and experiences with the group, we need an understanding that each of you will keep what is shared in the strictest confidence. What are your thoughts about Ginny's concern?"

2. "I guess that's what I'd want if I were in your situation. As a matter of fact, that's what I want for

you, too. But we both know the review board won't release you until they feel you're prepared to make it on the outside. I can't get you out, but with your cooperation I can help you to make changes that will get you ready for release."

3. "It seems that despite all you have accomplished, the past still haunts you. You've done a lot that you feel bad about, but you've also done a lot to get and stay clean. How can we keep your regrets about the past from sabotaging the path you're on now?"

4. "I think we need to look as a group at how we can give Jim some helpful feedback rather than making fun of him. Let's talk about what just happened. Maybe you could begin, Jim, by sharing with the group what you're feeling just now."

5. "I have to confess I know only a little bit about your religion, which may make you wonder if I can appreciate your problems. I'll do my best to understand if you're willing to help me with that. The most important thing, though, is your comfort about it. How do you feel about sharing your problems with me under these circumstances?"

6. "That sounds painful—that I'm not personally concerned with you as an individual. I'd like to explore that, because that's not at all how I feel about you. Let's talk a bit about how I've come across and how you've reached that conclusion."

7. "I'm sorry you're still involved with drugs, Joy, because of the difficulties it's caused you. I don't like to see you get into trouble but I have no choice. I have to report this. If I didn't, I'd be breaking a rule myself by not reporting you. That wouldn't help you in the long run. Frankly, I'm going to keep worrying about you until I'm satisfied you're really sticking to the rules."

8. "It's not nutty at all to wonder what I'm thinking and writing. I'm writing down what we talk about. What you tell me is important, and notes help to refresh my memory. You're welcome to look at them if you like. Actually, I would be interested in hearing a little more about your concerns regarding what I might think of you."

9. "As a matter of fact it is, and I think they're pretty terrific. But we're here to talk about you, Rex. I'd like to hear how your job interview went."

10. "Keeping this secret has been taking a toll on you. I'm grateful that you brought it up so that we can work on it together. It took some real courage on your part, and I respect you for that."

11. "I'd be phony if I said I understood all about being black and living in your neighborhood … and I'm sorry if it seems I'm being smug. I am interested in you, and I'd like to understand more about your life."

SKILL DEVELOPMENT EXERCISES
in Managing Ethical Dilemmas

The following cases will give you practice in applying ethics concepts and ethical decision making to specific practice situations. These cases include some of the most difficult ones that we and our colleagues have encountered in practice. Note that the appropriate response or course of action is rarely cut and dried. After reading each case, answer the following questions:

1. What conflicting principles and feelings are in play in the case?
2. What are the pros and cons of the various courses of action?
3. What guidelines are applicable in resolving this dilemma?
4. What resources could you consult to help you decide on an ethical course of action?

Ethics Case 1

A classmate has told you that she is Googling clients from her field agency as well as looking them up on Facebook. She states that the information is public, so there is no confidentiality involved, and the more she learns about them the better she can help them. In your own placement, workers send Snapchat messages to each other of the wacky ways clients dress and behave. They say it builds camaraderie in the team and is harmless since the photos and comments go away after only a few seconds.

Ethics Case 2

You are forming a youth group in a state correctional facility. From past experience, you know that members sometimes make references in the group to previous offenses that they have committed without being apprehended. You also know that they may talk about indiscretions or misdemeanors they (or others) may have committed or plan to commit within the institution, such as smoking marijuana, engaging in sexual encounters, receiving contraband from visitors, or stealing supplies or property from peers or staff. Are you required to share all of the information you learn in the group? How can you encourage trust and sharing if there are limits to confidentiality?

Ethics Case 3

In conducting an intake interview with a young woman in a family agency, you observe that both of her young children are withdrawn and listless. Throughout the interview, the client seems defensive and suspicious and appears ambivalent about having come for the interview. At one point, she states that she feels overwhelmed with her parenting responsibilities and is having difficulty in coping with her children. She also alludes to her fear that she may hurt them but then abruptly changes the subject. As you encourage her to return to the discussion of her problems with the children, your client says that she has changed her mind about wanting help, takes her children in hand, and hastily leaves the office.

Ethics Case 4

You have seen a husband and wife and their 15-year-old daughter twice regarding relationship problems between the parents and the daughter. The parents are both angry and fed up with their daughter, stating that they never had such problems with their other children and that she just needs to "shape up." Today your received a text from the girl that she is pregnant and knows her parents "will explode" if they find out, and she needs to see you without her parents present to talk about her plans.

Ethics Case 5

You have been working in a mental health agency with a middle-aged male who has a history, when angered, of becoming violent and physically abusive. He has been under extreme psychological pressure lately because of increased expectations at work. In an interview today, he is extremely angry, clenching his fists as he tells you that his boss is giving him a very hard time, singling him out for criticism, and threatening that he will lose his job. "If that happens," he says, "they'll be sorry."

Ethics Case 6

A murder was reported tonight on the evening news. You recognize the victim as a woman who had numerous brief stays at the domestic violence agency where you work. You suspect that her boyfriend was the perpetrator and wonder if you should contact the police with this information.

Ethics Case 7

You are working with a 17-year-old to stay on track for graduation. Today he acknowledged that he was sleeping in class because he sometimes sneaks out of his house after his father is asleep to go "hang out" with his girlfriend. You do not know who she is, but you know that she is under 16.

Exploring, Assessing, and Planning

Part 2 of this book deals with processes and skills involved in the first phase of the helping process. These processes and skills are also demonstrated in video clips included with MindTap. Chapter 5 begins this exploration by setting the context and developing skills for building effective working relationships with clients, one of the two major objectives of initial interviews. Chapter 6 shifts the focus to skills required to explore clients' difficulties and recognize and enhance strengths.

Chapter 7 identifies verbal and nonverbal patterns of communication that impede the development of effective working relationships and suggests positive alternatives.

Chapters 8 and 9 focus specifically on the process of assessment. Chapter 8 deals with explaining the process, sources of information, delineation of clients' problems, and questions to be addressed during the process. Chapter 9 highlights the many dimensions of ecological assessment, delineating the intrapersonal, interpersonal, cultural, and environmental systems and noting how they reciprocally interact to produce and maintain problems.

Chapter 10 narrows the focus to family systems. It discusses various types of family structures and considers the dimensions of family systems that must be addressed in assessing family functioning, including the cultural context of families.

In Chapter 11, the focus changes to groups. Here the discussion hones in on purposes of groups, selection of group members, arrangements to be made, and ways to begin group process. It then points out various factors to be considered in assessing the functioning of groups.

Part 2 concludes with Chapter 12, which deals with negotiating goals and contracts with both voluntary and involuntary clients. Included in this chapter are theory, skills, and guidelines that address these processes, which lay the foundation for the process of goal attainment.

CHAPTER 5

Building Blocks of Communication: Conveying Empathy and Authenticity

Chapter Overview

Social workers practice in a variety of environments, influenced by both professional and organizational demands (Cameron & Keenan, 2010). Part of the context of social work is an emphasis on exploring the use of evidence-based knowledge where possible to influence intervention. Whatever intervention and theory are selected, however, underlying common factors account for as much as 70 percent of the success of interventions (Barth et al., 2012; Drisko, 2004; Norcross & Lambert, 2006). Research on treatment outcomes describes four factors that are associated with much of the positive change in client outcomes (Adams et al., 2008; Miller et al., 2013):

- Client or extra-therapeutic factors (40 percent)
- Relationship factors (30 percent)
- Placebo, hope, and expectancy factors (15 percent)
- Model/technique factors (15 percent)

Consequently, nearly half of the outcome relies on fundamental skills and abilities that social workers need to learn, apart from the type of treatment offered.

Of course, social work relationships themselves develop in a context too. This chapter will help you develop direct practice skills and apply them in a context to help your clients. Interviews follow a structure that reflects predictable elements of contact between a potential client, a social worker, and the setting that the social worker represents. In other words, interviews have beginnings that focus on settling into roles, reviewing legal and ethical limits and boundaries, and attempting to establish rapport. From this point, the social worker engages the client in assessing what has brought the client into contact with the setting or agency. Based on this joint exploration, the social worker and the client then discuss creating a contract or agreement about what they will attempt to do together to address the client's concerns and developing goals to guide the social worker's practice in the case. If contact will last beyond one session, the session ends with the development of tasks or concrete plans about what the social worker and the client will do prior to the next session to advance their common work. This interview structure is held together with practice skills that are designed to help the social worker connect with clients by communicating empathically, assertively, and authentically.

As a result of reading this chapter and learning and applying skills, you will be able to:

- Develop an empathic response.
- Explain client rights and limits to confidentiality.
- Explain social worker and client roles.

- Act assertively.
- Self-disclose appropriately.
- Identify surface feelings and deeper feelings.
- Increase your ability to convey accurate empathy.
- Convey positive feedback.
- Make a firm request.
- Confront in an empathic context.

EPAS Competencies in Chapter 5

This chapter will give you the information needed to meet the following practice competencies:

- Competency 1: Demonstrate Ethical and Professional Behavior
- Competency 6: Engage with Individuals, Families, Groups, Organizations, and Communities
- Competency 7: Assess Individuals, Families, Groups, Organizations, and Communities

ROLES OF THE PARTICIPANTS

Clients often have an unclear idea about what to expect from contact with a social worker, and those ideas may differ from the social worker's expectations as well (Kadushin & Kadushin, 1997). This is most evident when the client has been referred or mandated for service. Clarifying expectations becomes a key intervention in work with clients who have not chosen to see a social worker (Rooney et al., 2009; Trotter, 2006).

The following guidelines will assist you in achieving positive results in role clarification.

Determine Your Client's Expectations

The varied expectations that clients bring to initial sessions include lectures, magical solutions, advice giving, changing other family members, and so on. With clients who are members of ethnic minority groups or inexperienced with professional helping relationships, sensitively exploring expectations and modifying the social worker's role when necessary are especially critical.

Clients sometimes explicitly state their expectations without prompting from a social worker. For example, after reciting the difficulties created by her son, a mother declared, "We were hoping you could talk with him and help him understand how much he is hurting us."

Notice that the mother's "hope" involved a request for specific action by the social worker. When clients express their expectations spontaneously in this way, you have the opportunity to deal with unrealistic goals. Frequently, however, clients do not openly express their expectations, and you will need to elicit them.

It is important not to probe too far into expectations until you have established rapport, however, because the client's request often turns out to be a most intimate revelation. For this reason, seeking disclosure too soon may put a client on the defensive. The social worker should therefore try to weave exploration of the client's expectations into the natural flow of the session sometime after the client has had ample opportunity to report his or her difficulties and to discern the sensitive understanding and goodwill of the social worker.

If voluntary clients have not spontaneously revealed their requests and the timing appears right, you can elicit their requests by asking a question similar to one of the following:

- "How do you hope (or wish) I (or the agency) can assist (or help) you?"
- "When you thought about coming here, what were your ideas about the kind of help you wanted?"

For potential clients who were referred or mandated to receive service, social workers often find it necessary to describe the parameters of what accepting an offer of service might entail because potential clients did not seek the service.

VIDEO CASE EXAMPLE

In the video "Getting Back to Shakopee," Dorothy, a social worker in a private child and family service agency, finds that Valerie, a Native American client referred by her employer for job performance issues, has many concerns about confidentiality that need to be addressed before she will consider whether she will accept an offer of service.

It can be useful in circumstances like these, where the client did not seek service, to elicit client concerns in the following way:

1. *"We have explored the reasons why you were referred/ required to seek our service. But I would like to know*

what you hope to gain from this process." In this way, the social worker signals from the beginning that he or she is working with the potential client, not acting as the agent of the referring source.

2. *Briefly explain the nature of the helping process and define the client–social worker relationship as partners seeking a solution to the client's difficulties.* Clients often hope that social workers will give them advice that they can implement immediately, thereby quickly remedying their problems. They will give up these unrealistic expectations with less disappointment in favor of a more realistic understanding if you clarify how you can actually be of help and why it would be less useful to approach their problems with this kind of "magic potion" strategy. It is important to convey your intention to help clients find the best possible solution and to clarify that offering advice prematurely would likely be a disservice to them. In the absence of such an explanation, clients may conclude that you are unwilling to meet their expectations because you are not concerned about them. Taking the time to explore expectations and to clarify how you can be of assistance goes a long way in preventing clients from drawing unwarranted negative conclusions that may result in premature termination of the contact.

Note that we are not arguing against the value of giving advice to clients. Rather, our point is that to be effective, advice must be based on adequate knowledge of the dynamics of a problem and of the participants involved. This level of understanding is unlikely to be achieved in an initial session.

You can help many clients modify their unrealistic expectations as well as clarify your respective roles by delivering a message similar to the following:

- "I can sense the urgency you feel in wanting to solve your problems. I wish I could give advice that would lead to an easy solution. You've probably already had plenty of advice, because most people offer advice freely. It has been my experience, though, that what works for one person (couple or family) may not work at all for another."

- "As I see it, our task is to work together in considering a number of options so that you can decide which solution best fits you and your situation. In the long run, that's what will work best for you. But finding the right solution takes some time and a lot of thought."

The preceding role clarification embodies the following essential elements mentioned earlier: (1) acknowledging and empathizing with the client's unrealistic expectation and sense of urgency; (2) expressing the social worker's helpful intent; (3) explaining why the client's unrealistic expectation cannot be fulfilled; and (4) as part of the social worker's expertise, clarifying the helping process and defining a working partnership that places responsibility on the client for actively participating and ultimately making choices as to the courses of action to be taken.

When couples seek help for relationship problems, they commonly view the partner as the source of difficulties and have the unrealistic expectation that the couple's counselor will influence the partner to shape up. Because this expectation is so pervasive, we often elicit partners' expectations early in the initial session (individual or conjoint) and clarify the social worker's helping role, thereby setting the stage for more productive use of the exploration to follow. Clarifying the helping process early in the session tends to diminish the partners' tendency toward mutual blaming and competition. Moreover, partners are less likely to respond defensively when the social worker refuses to be drawn into the "blame game" and focuses instead on assisting each person to become aware of his or her part in the difficulties.

VIDEO CASE EXAMPLE

The following excerpt from the video "Home for the Holidays Part 1" demonstrates how social workers can establish ground rules:

Social worker: Let me suggest some ground rules for how couples sessions may be useful to you. I want this to be a safe place, so anything said here will be private unless something is shared that would seriously harm someone else, such as possible suicide or transmission of AIDS. I won't take sides in your concerns but will act more like a referee to help you express them.

Implied in the preceding video excerpt is another aspect of the client's role: to be open in sharing feelings, thoughts, and events. With clients seeking psychotherapy or counseling, it is important to elicit those feelings. We recognize that many social workers work with clients who do not seek this kind of help. They may be seeking help with concrete resources or problem solving that does not involve a commitment to therapy. With that proviso, for those clients seeking therapy or counseling assistance, you will need to express your intent that the client communicate openly. To focus on this aspect of the client's role, consider making the following points:

Social worker: For you to get the help you are seeking, I want to encourage you to be as open as you can be with me. That means not holding back troubling feelings, thoughts, or events that are important. I can understand you and your difficulties only if you're open and honest. Only you know what you think and feel; I can know only as much as you share with me. Sometimes it's painful to share certain thoughts and feelings, but often those are the very feelings that trouble us the most. If you do hold back, remind yourself that you may be letting yourself down. If you're finding it difficult to share certain things, let me know. Discussing what's happening inside you—why it's difficult—may make it easier to discuss those painful things. I'll be open and honest with you, too. If you have any questions or would like to know more about me, please ask. I'll be frank with you. I may not answer every question, but I'll explain why if I don't.

Some social workers do not have ongoing contact with clients beyond one session. The guidelines for communication provided later in the chapter will be relevant to their situation.

Emphasize Client Responsibility

For those who have ongoing contact, it is important to emphasize that clients can speed their progress by working on their difficulties between appointments. Some clients mistakenly believe that change will result largely from what occurs in sessions. In actuality, the content of sessions is far less significant than how clients apply the information gained from them. The following message clarifies this aspect of a client's responsibility:

Social worker: We'll want to make progress toward your goals as rapidly as possible. One way you can speed your progress is by working hard between our sessions. That means carrying out tasks you've agreed to, applying what we talk about in your daily life, and making mental notes or actually writing down thoughts, feelings, and events that relate to your problems so we can consider them in your next session. Actually, what you do between sessions is more important in accomplishing your goals than the session itself. We'll be together only a brief time each week. The rest of the week you have opportunities to apply what we talk about and plan together.

Yet another aspect of the client's role involves keeping appointments. This factor is obvious, but discussing it emphasizes clients' responsibilities and prepares them to cope constructively with obstacles that may cause them to fail or to cancel appointments. The following message clarifies this aspect of the client's role:

Social worker: As we work together, it will be critical for you to keep your appointments. Unforeseen things such as illness happen occasionally, of course, and we can change appointments if such problems arise. At other times, however, you may find yourself feeling discouraged or doubting whether coming here really helps. You may also feel upset over something I've said or done and find yourself not wanting to see me. I won't knowingly say or do anything to offend you, but you may have some troubling feelings toward me anyway. The important thing is that you not miss your appointment, because when you're discouraged or upset, we need to talk about it. I know that may not be easy, but it will help you to work out your problematic feelings. If you miss your appointment, you may find it even harder to return.

Conversely, when clients are referred, social workers should not assume that potential clients plan to return for another session.

VIDEO CASE EXAMPLE

For example, in the video "Getting Back to Shakopee," the social worker, Dorothy, suggests near the end of the session: "If you decide to come back for another session, next time we would break down all of the concerns you are facing and try to address them one at a time, starting with the ones you consider most important."

Emphasize Difficulties Inherent in Process

A final task for the social worker is to emphasize that difficulties are inherent in the process of making changes. Clarifying this reality further prepares clients for the mixed feelings that they will inevitably experience. When these difficulties are highlighted early in the helping process, clients can conceive of such feelings and experiences as natural obstacles that must be surmounted rather than yield to them or feel defeated. An explanation about these predictable difficulties similar to the following clarifies the vicissitudes of the change process:

Social worker: We've talked about goals you want to achieve. Accomplishing them won't be easy. Making changes is seldom possible without a difficult and sometimes painful struggle. People usually have ups and downs as they seek to make changes. If you understand this, you won't be disappointed. I don't want to discourage you. I am optimistic about the prospects of you attaining your goals.

Over the years, numerous clients have reported retrospectively that they appreciated receiving these kinds of explanations during the initial session. When the going became rough and they began to waver in pursuing their goals, they recalled that such discouragement was natural and, rather than discontinuing the contact, mustered up the determination to persevere.

Clarify Your Own Role

In addition to clarifying the client's role, it is vital to clarify your own role (Trotter, 2006). Part of this means stressing that you will be a partner in helping clients understand their difficulties more fully. Because you have an outside vantage point, you may be able to help them see their difficulties from a new perspective and to consider solutions that they may have overlooked. We recommend that you clarify further that, although you will be an active partner in considering possible remedial actions, the final decisions rest with the clients themselves. You will help them to weigh alternatives, but your desire is to see clients develop their strengths and exercise their capacities for independent action to the fullest extent possible. In addition, emphasize that you plan to assist clients in focusing on their strengths and any incremental growth they achieve. Stress that although you will actively perform this function in the initial stage of the helping process, at the same time, you will be encouraging your clients to learn to recognize their own strengths and grow independently.

VIDEO CASE EXAMPLE

In the video "Serving the Squeaky Wheel," the social worker, Ron Rooney, is replacing another social worker who has been abruptly transferred. The client, Molly, has a serious and persistent mental illness. Much of the session is devoted to beginning to develop trust that has been jeopardized by the loss of the previous social worker. Such circumstances are not ideal but occur frequently enough that it is important to have models for dealing with them. The social worker describes his role as helping Molly make a plan in which she will be supported to live safely in a community of her choosing.

Another aspect of the helping role that you should clarify for clients is your intention to assist them in anticipating obstacles they will encounter in striving to attain their goals and your willingness to help them formulate strategies to surmount these obstacles. Clarifying this facet of your role further reinforces the reality that change is difficult but you will be with and behind your clients at all times, offering support and direction. You might share that each family faces its own unique situation and has its own set of values, noting that it will be your job to get to know these values and situations from the clients' point of view. Only then will you attempt to help the clients plan what makes sense for them to do.

Some special hurdles must be overcome to develop productive working relationships between social workers and clients in mandated settings, because the mandated client did not seek the contact and often perceives it as being contrary to his or her interests. In the following dialogue, notice how the social worker begins to develop expectations about a collaborative relationship.

Client: I didn't like the earlier workers because they came into my house telling me what I can and can't do. One thing I don't like is someone telling me what I can do with my kids and what I can't.
Social worker: It sounds like you had a negative experience with earlier workers.

Client: Yeah, I did. I did not like it at all because they were telling me what I should do.

Social worker: I'm going to take a different approach with you because I don't feel that I know it all; you know best about the situation occurring in your own family and in your own life. I will want you to tell me about the problems you are concerned about and how we can best resolve those together.

Client: Okay.

Social worker: My job will be to develop a case plan with you. I won't be the one to say, "This is what you need to do." I want you to have input in that decision and to say, "Well, I feel I can do this." I will be willing to share ideas with you as we decide what to work on and how to do it. I will need to include any court-mandated requirements, such as our need to be meeting together, in the agreement. However, I want you to have a lot of say in determining what we work on and how.

The social worker interprets the client's comment about previous workers as pertinent to exploring what their own working relationship might be like. She describes her own role and clarifies what the client can do in a clear and tangible way to work on goals important to her.

Children as Participants

Guidelines for interviewing often make assumptions that best fit adult participants (Petr, 2003). In situations in which the client is a child, role explanations needs to convey accurately what the child can expect from the social worker and what will be expected of him or her. For example, a school social worker might say something like the following:

Social worker: My name is Julie and I am the school social worker. That means that I talk to kids who may have problems at school or at home and I help them think about ways to solve their problems. I'd like to talk to you about what you're feeling and thinking. Sometimes the principal will be part of our talks when it comes to discussing discipline issues, but my role is to help you learn to better solve your problems. While you're here, please play with the items on my desk like my squishy balls and paperclips if that will make you feel more comfortable. Kids can feel nervous around new adults, and that might make you feel better.

COMMUNICATING ABOUT INFORMED CONSENT, CONFIDENTIALITY, AND AGENCY POLICIES

EP 1

The encounter between the social worker and the client exists within a context of limits, possibilities, and rights. In this regard, the social worker must share the rights and limits to communication discussed in Chapter 4: discuss confidentiality and its limits, obtain informed consent, and share agency policies and legal limits.

VIDEO CASE EXAMPLE

In the video "Getting Back to Shakopee," the social worker, Dorothy, and her Native American client, Valerie, discuss limits to confidentiality for the first several minutes of the video. Valerie is concerned about what material from the session will get back to the supervisor who referred her for service. In addition, she has concerns about Dorothy's mandated reporter responsibilities related to child welfare because her teenaged daughter supervises younger children in the summer. This video demonstrates how discussion of confidentiality issues can be vital with clients who are referred by others in less than voluntary circumstances.

Dorothy, the social worker in the Video Case, might have shared the limits, possibilities, and rights regarding confidentiality in the following fashion:

Social worker: What you say to me is private in most circumstances. I will share what we have discussed with my supervisor. In certain circumstances, however, I might have to share what we have discussed with others. For example, if you threaten to seriously harm another person, I would have a duty to warn, which would mean that I could not keep that information private. For example, if your children were in danger, I am a **mandated reporter**, and I would have to share that information. Similarly, if you were to seriously consider harming yourself, I would have to share that information. If a judge were to subpoena my records, he or she could gain access to a general summary of what we have done together. Do you have any questions about this?

It is important that this section of the initial interview be presented in language that the client readily understands so that the discussion embodies the spirit of informed consent. The exact content of this discussion will vary with the setting in which you work. It is important that you carry out this duty in a genuine fashion rather than presenting it as a ritualistic sharing of written forms that has the appearance of obtaining informed consent but ignores its intent. In hurried agency practice, sometimes this principle is violated. Discuss with your supervisor what information needs to be shared with clients and how that is done in ways that are useful to those clients.

With children as clients, such explanations of privacy and confidentiality need to be conveyed in a way that the child can understand. For example, some social workers use a green–yellow–red light approach, explaining to children that much of what they discuss will be a green light: private between them. However, if the child shares something that may cause a danger to himself/herself or others, that would be a red light, and the social worker would need to share it with others.

FACILITATIVE CONDITIONS

Social workers use communication skills to help develop a productive working relationship with clients. This chapter focuses on two of the three skills embodied in what have been called the **facilitative conditions** (or **core conditions**) in helping relationships. These conditions or skills were originally denoted by Carl Rogers (1957) as *empathy, unconditional positive regard,* and *congruence.* Other terms have since evolved, and we will refer to the conditions as *empathy, respect* (or *nonpossessive warmth*), and *authenticity* or *genuineness.* Because we addressed respect at length in Chapter 4, we limit our focus here to empathy and authenticity.

Facilitative conditions are often thought to be the foundation-level skills that undergird many treatment models and help create a positive client–social worker relationship (Hill & Nakayama, 2000; Mason, 2009). Research has especially supported the correlation of empathy with positive social work outcomes (Bohart & Greenburg, 1997). In addition, a study by a social worker (Nugent, 1992) found that these facilitative

conditions were effective in fostering positive helping relationships. For example, there is a particularly close relationship between techniques designed to enhance empathy that come from the Rogerian nondirective approach and motivational interviewing (Mason, 2009). Efforts in the latter are often intended to facilitate client change, particularly related to problematical behavior. Although social workers are often engaged in activities designed to influence such behavior, they are not always aimed at changing behavior and are guided by professional values supporting self-determination. Hence, these chapters will present techniques designed to enhance empathy as valuable in their own right. In some instances, social workers will also attempt to influence behavior. Given the agreed-upon contribution of a positive relationship to outcomes, techniques for encouraging a positive relationship are important (Miller et al., 2013).

These facilitative skills are particularly useful in treatment situations with voluntary clients. However, we will also describe ways that the facilitative conditions can serve as building blocks in both involuntary relationships and other situations that do not have therapy as the primary focus (Bennett, Legon, & Zilberfein, 1989).

EMPATHIC COMMUNICATION

Empathic communication involves the ability of the social worker to perceive accurately and sensitively the inner feelings of the client and to communicate his or her understanding of those feelings in language attuned to the client's experiencing of the moment. The first dimension of empathy, **empathic recognition**, means demonstrating through accurate reflection of feelings that the social worker comprehends the client's inner experiencing. Such affective sharing also requires a self–other awareness such that the social worker can both experience what the client is conveying and also separate himself or herself from those feelings (Gerdes & Segal, 2013). Failure to separate can contribute to **compassion fatigue**, which can make the social worker less effective (Conrad & Kellar-Guenther, 2006). Such compassion fatigue can occur, for example, when a social worker has prolonged contact with clients with trauma. Fortunately, there are personal and organizational responses that can mitigate compassion fatigue. We will return to compassion fatigue in Chapter 18.

For social workers, it is not enough to grasp what the client is feeling and experiencing and reflect that understanding back. Social workers are also called on by our code of ethics to take **empathic action** (Gerdes & Segal, 2009). That is, beyond reflecting the conflict and pain clients may be experiencing, we are called on to consider ways they might alleviate their situation. Similarly, on a macro level, it is not enough for social workers to notice and document a deleterious condition plaguing a neighborhood. Social workers are called on to utilize **social empathy** to act with others to address social and economic justice concerns.

Empathic communication plays a vital role in nurturing and sustaining the helping relationship and in providing the vehicle through which the social worker becomes emotionally significant and influential in the client's life. In mandated circumstances in which involuntary clients are not seeking a helping relationship, conveying empathic understanding reduces the level of threat perceived by the client and mitigates his or her defensiveness, conveys interest and helpful intent, and creates an atmosphere conducive to behavior change.

In responding to clients' feelings, social workers must avoid being misled by the conventional facades used to conceal emotions. As a consequence, the empathic communicator responds to the feelings that underlie such flippant messages as "Oh, no, it doesn't really matter" or "I don't care what he does!" These messages often mask disappointment or hurt, as do messages such as "I don't need anyone" when the client is experiencing painful loneliness, or "I don't let anyone hurt me" when the client is finding rejection hard to bear. To enter the client's private world of practical experience, the social worker must also avoid making personal interpretations and judgments of the client's private logic and feelings that, in superficial contacts, might appear weak, foolish, or undesirable.

Being empathically attuned involves not only grasping the client's immediately evident feelings, but also, in a mutually shared, exploratory process, identifying the client's underlying emotions and discovering the meaning and personal significance of the client's feelings and behavior. In getting in touch with these camouflaged feelings and meanings, the social worker must tune in not only to verbal messages but also to more subtle cues, including facial expressions, tone of voice, tempo of speech, and postural cues and gestures that amplify and sometimes contradict verbal meanings. Such nonverbal cues as blushing, crying, pausing, stammering, changing voice intonation, clenching jaws

or fists, pursing the lips, lowering the head, or shifting the posture often reveal the presence of distressing feelings and thoughts.

For example, it is not uncommon for adolescents to be relatively silent during initial interviews while at the same time nonverbally conveying a variety of emotions. It is also common for adolescents (and others!) to use their cell phones to text or check social media during interviews. Often, such initial contact is the result of a referral to the social worker, so that the adolescent feels he or she is in a strange situation with an unknown adult. Rather than assume that such cell phone behavior means that the adolescent is "resisting change," it is more useful to normalize the situation by explaining the context of contact, how he or she was referred, and to ask for the adolescent's view of the situation. The social worker may also suggest some ground rules that will assist them in focusing, such as not using such devices during the session. The social worker may also provide other activities that permit an outlet for nervous energy, such as bending pipe cleaners. Asking the client what he or she thinks or feels may elicit a shrug. However, asking what others might say, such as "What would your friends say are your strengths?" may make communication easier (Greene, Lee, & Hoffpauir, 2005).

A person who experiences feelings in common with another person and is similarly affected by whatever the other person is experiencing usually responds sympathetically rather than empathically. **Sympathetic responding**, which depends on achieving emotional and intellectual accord, involves supporting and condoning the other person's feelings (e.g., "I'd feel the same way if I were in your position" or "I think you're right"). In contrast, empathic responding involves understanding the other person's feelings and circumstances without taking that person's side (e.g., "I sense you're feeling …" or "You seem to be saying …").

Being empathic entails more than just recognizing clients' feelings. Social workers must also respond verbally and nonverbally in ways that affirm their understanding of clients' inner experiencing. It is not unusual for a person to experience empathic feelings for another individual without conveying those feelings in any way to the second party. Exhibiting high-level empathy requires skill in verbally and nonverbally demonstrating understanding. A common mistake made by social workers is to tell clients, "I understand how you feel." Rather than producing a sense of being understood, such a response often creates doubts in the client's mind about the social worker's perceptiveness, because any specific demonstration of understanding is lacking. Indeed, use of this response may mean that the social worker has not explored the client's feelings sufficiently to fully grasp the significance of the problematic situation. Social workers attempt to share emotion and get on the inside without losing awareness of who they are.

Later in this chapter, we present theory and exercises for developing skill in empathic responding. Initially, we provide a list of affective words and phrases intended to expand your vocabulary so that you can meet the challenge of responding to the wide range of emotions experienced by clients. We also provide exercises to help you to refine your ability to perceive the feelings of others—a prerequisite to the mastery of empathic communication. To assist you in discerning levels of empathy, we include a rating scale for empathic responding, accompanied by examples of social worker responses and exercises. These exercises will help you gain mastery of empathic communication at an effective working level.

DEVELOPING PERCEPTIVENESS TO FEELINGS

Feelings or emotions exert a powerful influence on behavior and often play a central role in the problems of clients. Applicants or voluntary clients often enter into the helping relationship with openness, hoping to explore both their concerns and their related feelings. Conversely, involuntary clients experience strong feelings but have not actively sought out a helping relationship for dealing with them (Cingolani, 1984). Hence, use of the skills sometimes takes a slightly different course with these clients, as one of the social worker's goals is to express empathy with the *situation* the involuntary client experiences and the feelings related to those situations and experiences.

To respond to the broad spectrum of emotions and feeling states presented by clients, the social worker must be fully aware of the diversity of human emotions. They also need to take a "not knowing" position of learning what emotional expression means for the particular client in front of them. Further, the social worker needs a rich vocabulary of words and expressions that not only reflect clients' feelings accurately

but also capture the intensity of those feelings. For example, dozens of descriptive feeling words may be used to express anger, including *furious*, *aggravated*, *provoked*, *put out*, *irritated*, and *impatient*—all of which express different shades and intensities of this feeling.

When used judiciously, such words serve to give sharp and exact focus to clients' feelings. Possessing and utilizing a rich vocabulary of affective words and phrases that accurately reflect these feelings is a skill that often is not developed by even experienced social workers. It is important to realize that high-level empathic responding takes place in two phases: (1) a thinking process and (2) a responding process. A deficient vocabulary for describing feelings limits social workers' ability to conceptualize and hence to reflect the full intensity and range of feelings experienced by clients.

It has been our experience that beginning social workers typically have a limited range of feeling words from which to draw in conveying empathy. Although many words may be used to capture feelings, learners often limit themselves to, and use to excess, a few terms, such as *upset* or *frustrated*, losing much of the richness of client messages in the process. Meanwhile, it is not uncommon in current usage for younger clients (and social workers) to use the word *awesome* to mean a range of things, making it hard to determine what the word means other than something positive.

The accompanying lists illustrate the wide range of expressions social workers can use when responding to clients' feelings. Note, however, that using feeling words in a discriminating fashion is not merely important in empathic responding but is indispensable in relating authentically as well. Becoming a competent professional requires passing through a maturing process whereby you develop not only the capacity to deeply share the inner experiencing of others but also a way to express your own personal feelings constructively.

Note that particular word usages can vary over time, in different regions, and with different populations. In addition to the accompanying lists, it can be useful as a class to take each significant emotion and brainstorm the words that carry the same meaning in the regions and populations you work with. Similarly, some of the expressions in the accompanying lists may be alien to some of the people you work with. Select those that are compatible with your clients.

AFFECTIVE WORDS AND PHRASES

COMPETENCE/STRENGTH

convinced you can	confident
sense of mastery	powerful
potent	courageous
resolute	determined
strong	influential
brave	impressive
forceful	inspired
successful	secure
in charge	in control
well equipped	committed
sense of	daring
accomplishment	
undaunted	effective
sure	sense of conviction
trust in yourself	self-reliant
sharp	able
adequate	firm
capable	on top of it
can cope	important
up to it	ready
equal to it	skillful

HAPPINESS/SATISFACTION

elated	superb
ecstatic	on cloud nine
on top of the world	organized
fantastic	splendid
exhilarated	jubilant
terrific	euphoric
delighted	marvelous
excited	enthusiastic
thrilled	great
super	in high spirits
joyful	cheerful
elevated	happy
light-hearted	wonderful
glowing	jolly
neat	glad
fine	pleased
good	contented
hopeful	mellow
satisfied	gratified
fulfilled	tranquil
serene	calm
at ease	awesome

CARING/LOVE

adore	loving
infatuated	enamored
cherish	idolize
worship	attached to
devoted to	tenderness toward
affection for	hold dear
prize	caring
fond of	regard
respect	admire
concern for	taken with
turned on	trust
close	esteem
hit it off	value
warm toward	friendly
like	positive toward
accept	enchanted by

DEPRESSION/DISCOURAGEMENT

anguished	in despair
dreadful	miserable
dejected	disheartened
rotten	awful
horrible	terrible
hopeless	gloomy
dismal	bleak
depressed	despondent
grieved	grim
broken hearted	forlorn
distressed	downcast
sorrowful	demoralized
pessimistic	tearful
weepy	down in the dumps
deflated	blue
lost	melancholy
in the doldrums	lousy
kaput	unhappy
down	low
bad	blah
disappointed	sad
below par	unnerved

INADEQUACY/HELPLESSNESS

worthless	depleted
good for nothing	washed up
powerless	helpless
impotent	crippled
inferior	emasculated
useless	finished
like a failure	impaired
inadequate	whipped
defeated	stupid
incompetent	puny
inept	clumsy
overwhelmed	ineffective
like a klutz	lacking
awkward	deficient
unable	incapable
small	insignificant
like a wimp	unimportant
over the hill	incomplete
immobilized	like a puppet
at the mercy of	inhibited
insecure	lacking confidence
unsure of self	uncertain
weak	inefficient
unfit	feeble

ANXIETY/TENSION

terrified	frightened
intimidated	horrified
desperate	panicky
terror-stricken	paralyzed
frantic	stunned
shocked	threatened
afraid	scared
stage fright	dread
vulnerable	fearful
apprehensive	jumpy
shaky	distrustful
butterflies	awkward
defensive	uptight
tied in knots	rattled
tense	fidgety
jittery	on edge
nervous	anxious
unsure	hesitant
timid	shy
worried	uneasy
bashful	embarrassed
ill at ease	doubtful
uncomfortable	self-conscious
insecure	alarmed
restless	

CONFUSION/TROUBLEDNESS	
bewildered	puzzled
tormented by	baffled
perplexed	overwhelmed
trapped	confounded
in a dilemma	befuddled
in a quandary	at loose ends
going around in	mixed-up
circles	
disorganized	in a fog
troubled	adrift
lost	disconcerted
frustrated	floored
flustered	in a bind
torn	ambivalent
disturbed	conflicted
stumped	feeling pulled apart
mixed feelings	uncertain
about	
unsure	uncomfortable
bothered	uneasy
undecided	overwhelmed

REJECTION/OFFENSIVE	
crushed	destroyed
ruined	pained
wounded	devastated
tortured	cast off
betrayed	discarded
knifed in the back	hurt
belittled	abused
depreciated	criticized
censured	discredited
disparaged	laughed at
maligned	mistreated
ridiculed	devalued
scorned	mocked
scoffed at	used
exploited	debased
slammed	slandered
impugned	cheapened
mistreated	put down
slighted	neglected
overlooked	minimized
let down	disappointed
unappreciated	taken for granted
taken lightly	underestimated
degraded	discounted
shot down	disrespected

ANGER/RESENTMENT	
furious	enraged
livid	seething
could chew nails	fighting mad
burned up	hateful
bitter	galled
vengeful	resentful
indignant	irritated
hostile	pissed off
have hackles up	had it with
upset with	bent out of shape
agitated	annoyed
got dander up	bristle
dismayed	uptight
disgusted	bugged
turned off	put out
miffed	ruffled
irked	perturbed
ticked off	teed off
chagrined	griped
cross	impatient
infuriated	violent

LONELINESS	
all alone in the	isolated
universe	
abandoned	totally alone
forsaken	forlorn
lonely	alienated
estranged	rejected
remote	alone
apart from others	shut out
left out	excluded
lonesome	distant
aloof	cut off

GUILT/EMBARRASSMENT	
sick at heart	unforgivable
humiliated	disgraced
degraded	horrible
mortified	exposed
branded	could crawl in a hole
like two cents	ashamed
guilty	remorseful
crummy	really rotten
lost face	demeaned
foolish	ridiculous
silly	stupid
egg on face	regretful
wrong	embarrassed
at fault	in error
responsible for	goofed
lament	blew it

Using the Lists of Affective Words and Phrases

The lists of affective words and phrases may be used with the exercises at the end of the chapter and in the *Practice Behaviors Workbook* to formulate responses that capture the nature of feelings expressed by clients. Note that potential clients referred by others and involuntary clients may be more likely to initially experience the emotions of anger, resentment, guilt, embarrassment, rejection, confusion, tension, inadequacy, helplessness, depression, and discouragement. Similarly, many potential clients may have had little experience or valuing of expressing emotions verbally. In Chapter 7, we will explore barriers to effective communication. One of those barriers can be the social worker's inability to achieve empathy with involuntary clients, as the social worker may believe that they have brought on these negative feelings as a result of their own irresponsible actions. That is, some social workers feel that perhaps involuntary clients deserve these feelings because they have not fully accepted responsibility for their part in the difficulties they have experienced. As noted in Chapter 4, the social work value of acceptance of worth suggests that we can empathize with feelings of despair and powerlessness even if clients have not yet taken responsibility for the consequences of their actions. In fact, involuntary and referred clients often express anger and frustration about even being in an introductory session with a social worker.

VIDEO CASE EXAMPLE

You may note how this occurs in the video "Serving the Squeaky Wheel." Notice how the social worker attempts to reflect this anger and frustration and reframe it more constructively toward action they could take together to alleviate those feelings.

After you have initially practiced responding to messages in which clients convey feelings, check the lists to determine whether some other words and phrases might more accurately capture the client's feelings. Also, scan the lists to see whether the client's message involves feelings in addition to those you identified. The lists may similarly assist you in checking out the accuracy of your reflective responses as you review taped sessions.

Acquisition of a broader emotional vocabulary is a step toward expressing greater empathy for clients. It allows you to more effectively convey your understanding and compassion for what they are experiencing. Because many clients want to change their situations as well as their feelings about it, conveying empathy is the first step toward helping them work on those concerns. The lists of affective words and phrases are offered for the purpose of helping you communicate more empathically with your clients. However, issues may arise if you try to use unfamiliar slang or vernacular, thus defeating the purpose of empathizing. Making an effort to clarify words that describe what the client is feeling often conveys your genuine interest.

Although the lists of affective words and phrases presented in this chapter are not exhaustive, they encompass many of the feelings and emotions frequently encountered in the helping process. Feeling words are subsumed under 11 categories, running the gamut of emotions from intense anguish and pain (e.g., *grieved*, *terrified*, *bewildered*, *enraged*, and *powerless*) to positive feeling states (e.g., *joy*, *elation*, *ecstasy*, *bliss*, and *pride in accomplishment*). Given our emphasis on clients' strengths, we have taken care to include a grouping of terms to assist social workers in capturing clients' feelings related to growth, strength, and competence.

Feeling words in each category are roughly graduated by intensity, with words conveying strong intensity grouped toward the beginning of each category and words of moderate to mild intensity appearing toward the end. In responding to client messages, the social worker should choose feeling words that accurately match the intensity of the feelings the client is experiencing.

To illustrate, consider that you are working with an African American client in a drug aftercare program who has returned to work as a meter reader. He reports that when he knocked on the door in a largely white suburb intending to read the meter, the elderly white woman would not let him in, despite his wearing his picture identification name tag on his uniform: "I was so low down and depressed. What can you do? I am doing my thing to keep straight, and I can't even do my job because I'm black." Such a response appropriately calls for an intense response by the social worker: "Sounds like you felt as if you were not accepted to do your job because of this woman's fear of black people. And yet you did not let that carry you back to drug use—you kept straight, and were not stopped by other people's perceptions."

In addition to using words that accurately reflect the intensity of the client's feelings, it is important to respond with a tone of voice and nonverbal gestures and expressions that similarly reflect the intensity of feelings conveyed by the verbal response. The proper intensity of affect may also be conveyed by using appropriate qualifying words—for example, "It sounds like you feel (somewhat) (quite) (very) (extremely) discouraged by your low performance on the entrance test."

Clients' messages may also contain multiple feelings. Consider the following client message: "I don't know what to do about my teenage daughter. I know that she's on drugs, but she shuts me out and won't talk to me. All she wants is to be out with her friends, to be left alone. There are times when I think she really dislikes me." Feeling words that would capture the various facets of this message include *confused, bewildered, alarmed, troubled, overwhelmed, lost, desperate, worried, frightened, alienated, rejected,* and *hurt.* A response that included all of these feeling words would be extremely lengthy and overwhelming to the client. However, a well-rounded empathic response should embody at least several of the surface feelings, such as *worried* and *confused,* and be delivered with appropriate timing. The social worker might also bring deeper-level feelings into focus, as explained in the following paragraphs.

Notice in the preceding client message that many feelings were implied but not explicitly stated. Some of these emotions would likely be just beyond the client's level of awareness but could easily be recognized if they were drawn to the client's attention. For example, the client might emphatically confirm a social worker response that sensitively identifies the hurt, rejection, and even anger inherent in the client's message. Without the social worker's assistance, the client might not develop full awareness of those deeper-level feelings.

In responding to client messages, you must be able to distinguish between readily apparent feelings and probable deeper feelings. In the early phase of the helping process, the social worker's objectives of developing a working relationship and creating a climate of understanding are best accomplished by using a reciprocal level of empathy—that is, by focusing on the client's immediately evident feelings. As the client perceives your genuine effort and commitment to understand his or her situation, that experience of being "empathically received" gradually creates a low-threat environment that obviates the need for self-protection.

Note that clients from oppressed groups, such as the African American client in the earlier example, may rightly feel better understood by the social worker yet continue to feel disillusioned by an alien environment. It is important to acknowledge those feelings about the environment. Trust may be gained by actions taken outside the session that indicate that the social worker is trustworthy and has the client's best interest at heart, as well as by verbal conveyance of empathy during the session. Similarly, Ivanoff, Blythe, and Tripodi suggest that too much emphasis on empathy can feel manipulative to involuntary clients (1994). With voluntary clients, the resultant climate of trust sets the stage for self-exploration, a prerequisite to self-understanding, which in turn facilitates behavior change. This positive ambience prepares the way for the use of "additive" or "expanded" levels of empathy to reach for underlying

feelings as well as to uncover hidden meanings and goals of behavior.

Conversely, attempting to explore underlying feelings during the early phase of the helping process is counterproductive. Uncovering feelings beyond the client's awareness before a working relationship is firmly established tends to mobilize opposition and may precipitate premature termination of the contact. Involuntary clients in a negotiated relationship may never desire such uncovering of deeper feelings and may find exploration of them to be intrusive (Ivanoff, Blythe, & Tripodi, 1994, p. 21).

Exercises in Identifying Surface and Underlying Feelings

In the following exercise, identify both the apparent surface feelings and the probable underlying feelings embodied in each of the four client statements below. Remember that most of the feelings in the statements are merely implied, as people often do not use feeling words. To complete the exercise, (1) read each statement carefully and (2) write down the apparent feelings and probable deeper feelings involved. (3) Scan the lists of affective words and phrases to see whether you might improve your response. After you have responded to all four statements, (4) check the feeling words and phrases you identified with those given at the end of the chapter. If the feelings you identified were similar in meaning to those identified in the answers at the end of the chapter (see page 137), consider your responses to be accurate. If they were not, review the client statements for clues about the client's feelings that you overlooked.

Client Statements

1. **Elderly client:** I know my children have busy lives. It is hard for them to have time to call me.

   Apparent feelings:
   Probable deeper feelings:

2. **Lesbian client referring to partner who has recently come out to her family:** When I was at your brother's wedding, and they wanted to take family pictures, nobody wanted me in the pictures. In fact nobody wanted to talk to me.

   Apparent feelings:
   Probable deeper feelings:

3. ***Tearful female client who is a mother:*** When I was a teenager, I thought that when I was married and had my own children, I would never yell at them like my mother yelled at me. Yet here I am doing the same things with Sonny.

   Apparent feelings:

   Probable deeper feelings:

4. ***African American client in child welfare system:*** The system is against people like me. People think that we drink, beat our kids, lay up on welfare, and take drugs.

   Apparent feelings:

   Probable deeper feelings:

Exercises at the end of this chapter for formulating reciprocal empathic responses will also assist you in increasing your perceptiveness to feelings.

ACCURATELY CONVEYING EMPATHY

EP 6

Empathic responding is a fundamental yet complex skill that requires systematic practice and extensive effort to achieve competency. Skill in empathic communication has no limit or ceiling; rather, this skill is always in the process of "becoming." In listening to their taped sessions, even highly skilled professionals discover feelings they overlooked. Many social workers, however, do not fully utilize empathic responding. They fail to grasp the versatility of this skill and its potency in influencing clients and fostering growth in moment-by-moment transactions.

In fact, some social workers dismiss the need for training in empathic responding, mistakenly believing themselves to already be empathic in their contacts with clients. Few people are inherently helpful in the sense of relating naturally with high levels of empathy or any of the other core conditions. Although people achieve varying degrees of empathy, respect, and genuineness through their life experiences, attaining high levels of these skills requires rigorous training. Research scales that operationalize empathy conditions have been developed and validated in extensive research studies (Duan & Hill, 1996; Truax & Carkhuff, 1967). These scales, which specify levels of empathy along a

continuum ranging from high- to low-level skills, represented a major breakthrough not only in operationalizing essential social worker skills but also in establishing a relationship between these skills and successful outcomes in practice. The empathic communication scale has been employed to help students distinguish between high- and low-level empathic responses and has been used by peers and instructors in group training to assess levels of students' responses. Students then receive guidance in reformulating responses to bring them to higher levels.

The Carkhuff (1969) empathy scale, which consists of nine levels, has been widely used in training and research. Although we have found nine-point scales valuable as training aids, they have proven somewhat confusing to students, who often have difficulty in making such fine distinctions between levels. For this reason, we have adapted the nine-level scale described by Hammond, Hepworth, and Smith (1977) by collapsing it to the five-level scale presented here.

Empathic Communication Scale

Level 0: Lack of Empathic Responding

We created this level because we have observed that some contact lacks empathy or is in fact anti-empathic. There can be circumstances where the norm in the setting and/or the skill and the beliefs of the social worker are such that it is not assumed to be the purview of the helping professional to convey empathy or understanding. Indeed, it can be the practice to actively challenge client perceptions if those are considered invalid or antisocial. We do not condone such expression and organizational norms and consider them to be counterproductive. Our disapproval of such expression does not mean it does not exist, however. We discuss it here so that you will be aware of it and, if you witness it, reflect on what alternatives to such communication exist.

Unfortunately, Level 0 responses occur with some frequency in settings in which clients are involuntary, stigmatized, or considered deviant. Such responses may provoke client anger but pose few consequences for the social worker unless there are norms that clients must be treated respectfully in all circumstances. We share these responses here not for the purpose of modeling them but rather to alert you that if you see them occurring or find yourself participating in them, they signal problems with the social worker or the setting. Such responses could just be the product of a social worker having a bad day, but they may represent a standard of practice that passes unnoticed. Consider the following example of a mother in the child welfare system who has recently completed a drug treatment program.

Client: I want to go into an aftercare treatment program near my home that is culturally sensitive and allows me to keep my job.

Level 0 response: You should not be thinking about what is convenient for *you* but rather what might ultimately benefit your child by your being a safe parent for her. Your thinking here is symptomatic of the problem of why your child is in custody, and your chances of regaining custody are limited.

This response does not convey empathy. It is actively judgmental and inappropriately confrontational. It is possible that the social worker might have valid reasons for wishing the client to consider a variety of options. However, making the judgmental statement only makes the circumstances worse and makes it unlikely that the client will consider the social worker's opinion. Social workers' frustration with clients who endanger others is understandable. Statements like the one above, however, greatly hinder further efforts to work with them in a collaborative fashion.

Level 1: Low Level of Empathic Responding

At Level 1, the social worker communicates limited awareness or understanding of the client's feelings; the social worker's responses are irrelevant and often abrasive, hindering rather than facilitating communication. Operating from a personal frame of reference, the social worker changes the subject, argues, gives advice prematurely, lectures, or uses other ineffective styles that block communication, often diverting clients from their problems and fragmenting the helping process. Furthermore, the social worker's nonverbal responses are not appropriate to the mood and content of the client's statement.

When social workers relate at this low level, clients often become confused or defensive. They may react by discussing superficialities, arguing, disagreeing, changing the subject, or withdrawing into silence. Thus, the client's energies are diverted from exploration and/or work on problems.

In the previous example, if the social worker were to respond to the client seeking a culturally sensitive treatment option near her home with "I see that you want to find a program near your home," that would be a Level 1 response. This response is minimally facilitative but at least avoids the judgmental statements of the previous example.

Here is another example to consider, with a number of Level 1 responses.

African American male client [to child welfare worker]: I don't trust you people. You do everything you can to keep me from getting back my son. I have done everything I am supposed to do, and you people always come up with something else.

Level 1 Responses:
- *"Just carry out the case plan and you are likely to succeed."* (Giving advice)
- *"Just think what would have happened if you had devoted more energy in the last year to carrying out your case plan: You would have been further along."* (Persuading with logical argument; negatively evaluating client's actions)
- *"How did you get along with your last social worker?"* (Changing the subject)
- *"Don't you think it will all work out in time?"* (Leading question, untimely reassurance)
- *"Why, that's kind of an exaggeration. If you just work along with me, before you know it things will be better."* (Reassuring, consoling, giving advice)

VIDEO CASE EXAMPLE

You can see two versions of the same situation in the video "Domestic Violence and the Probation Officer." In the first version, note the client's reaction to the social worker's Level 0 response. Note how the situation looks different when the social worker employs higher levels of empathy in the second version of the situation.

The preceding examples illustrate ineffective styles of communication used at this low level. Notice that messages reflect the social worker's own formulations concerning the client's problem; they do not capture the client's inner experiencing. Such responses stymie clients, blocking their flow of thought and producing negative feelings toward the social worker.

Level 2: Moderately Low Level of Empathic Responding

At Level 2, the social worker responds to the client's surface message but erroneously omits feelings or factual aspects of the message. The social worker may also inappropriately qualify feelings (e.g., "somewhat," "a little bit," "kind of") or may inaccurately interpret feelings (e.g., "angry" for "hurt," "tense" for "scared"). Responses may also emanate from the social worker's own conceptual formulations, which may be diagnostically accurate but not empathically attuned to the client's expressions. Although Level 2 responses are only partially accurate, they do convey an effort to understand and, for this reason, do not completely block the client's communication or work on problems.

Consider the following Level 2 responses to the earlier example of the African American male client expressing his feelings about the child welfare system.

Level 2 Responses:

- *"You'll just have to be patient. I can see you're upset."* The word *upset* defines the client's feelings only vaguely, whereas feeling words such as *angry*, *furious*, and *discounted* more accurately reflect the client's inner experiencing.
- *"You feel angry because your case plan has not been more successful to date. Maybe you are expecting too much too soon; there is a lot of time yet."* The listener begins to accurately capture the client's feelings but then moves to an evaluative interpretation ("you expect too much too soon") and inappropriate reassurance.
- *"You aren't pleased with your progress so far?"* This response focuses on external, factual circumstances to the exclusion of the client's feelings or perceptions regarding the event in question.
- *"You feel like things aren't going too well."* This response contains no reference to the client's immediately apparent feelings. Beginning social workers often use the lead-in phrase "You feel like …" without noticing that, in employing it, they have not captured the client's feelings.
- *"You're disappointed because you haven't gotten your son back?"* This response, although partially accurate, fails to capture the client's anger and distrust of the system, wondering whether any of his efforts are likely to succeed.
- *"I can see you are angry and disappointed because your efforts haven't been more successful so far, but I think you may be expecting the system to work too quickly."* Although the message has a strong beginning, the empathic nature of the response is negated by the listener's explanation of the reason for the client's difficulties. This response represents

a form of taking sides—that is, justifying the actions of the child welfare system by suggesting that too much is expected of it.

VIDEO CASE EXAMPLE

In the video "Getting Back to Shakopee," the social worker, Dorothy, listens as her client provides an account of her uncomfortable relations with her coworkers. She summarizes and adds a Level 2 empathic comment: "So just that I understand what you are talking about, you were working on your own project and Mary came over and added hers to yours and asked you to finish it for her? What did that do for you?" The empathy is implied in the social worker's question, but it could have been more explicit. For example, Dorothy might have asked, "Did you feel disrespected by how she acted toward you?"

The preceding responses illustrate many of the common errors made by social workers in responding empathically to client messages. Although some part of the messages may be accurate or helpful, all the responses in some way ignore or subtract from what the client is experiencing.

Level 3: Interchangeable or Reciprocal Level of Empathic Responding

The social worker's verbal and nonverbal responses at Level 3 convey understanding and are essentially interchangeable with the client's obvious expressions, accurately reflecting factual aspects of the client's messages and surface feelings or state of being. Reciprocal responses do not appreciably add affect or reach beyond the surface feelings, nor do they subtract from the feeling and tone expressed.

Acknowledging the factual content of the client's message, although desirable, is not required; if included, this aspect of the message must be accurate. Level 3 responses facilitate further exploratory and problem-focused responses by the client. The beginning social worker does well in achieving skill in reciprocal empathic responding, which is an effective working level. Consider the following examples of Level 3 responses.

Level 3 Responses:

- *"You're really angry about the slow progress in your case and are wondering whether your efforts are likely to succeed."*
- *"I can tell you feel very let down and are asking yourself, 'Will I ever get my son back?'"*

VIDEO CASE EXAMPLE

The video "Serving the Squeaky Wheel" contains a lengthy exchange in which the client, Molly, expresses her suspicion about what is written about her in the social worker's case records. The social worker responds, "I am hearing that it is a real sore point with you about what I write and think and what goes into the records about you." This is a Level 3 response that deals directly with her concern.

Level 3 responses such as these express accurately the immediately apparent emotions in the client's message. The content of the responses is also accurate, but deeper feelings and meanings are not added. The second response above also illustrates a technique for conveying empathy that involves changing the reflection from the third to the first person, and speaking as if the social worker were the client.

Level 4: Moderately High Level of Empathic Responding

Responses at Level 4 are somewhat additive, accurately identifying the client's implicit underlying feelings and/or aspects of the problem. The social worker's response illuminates subtle or veiled facets of the client's message, enabling the client to get in touch with somewhat deeper feelings and unexplored meanings and purposes of behavior. Level 4 responses thus are aimed at enhancing self-awareness. Consider the following example of a Level 4 response.

Level 4 Response:

- *"You feel very frustrated with the lack of progress in getting your son back. You wonder whether there is any hope in working with a new worker and this system, which you feel hasn't been helping you."*

VIDEO CASE EXAMPLE

In the video "Serving the Squeaky Wheel," the client, Molly, says that other people's conceptions of mental illness do not include her. The social worker responds, "Let me see if I understand what you are saying: Some people may think because you have a car and you speak up for yourself, that you are a very competent person who doesn't need any resources [Client: "There you go."] and if you ask for them [Client: "I am screwing the system."] that you are trying to take things that you are not entitled to. But your view is that you can have a car and speak up for yourself and still have other needs." This Level 4 response not only conveys immediately apparent feelings and content but also is noticeably additive in reflecting the client's deeper feelings. In this case, the client's immediate response—finishing the practitioner's sentences—indicates that the empathic response is perceived as accurate.

Level 5: High Level of Empathic Responding

Reflecting each emotional nuance and using voice and intensity of expressions finely attuned to the client's moment-by-moment experiencing, the social worker accurately responds to the full range and intensity of both surface and underlying feelings and meanings at Level 5. The social worker may connect current feelings and experiencing to previously expressed experiences or feelings, or may accurately identify implicit patterns, themes, or purposes. Responses may also identify implicit goals embodied in the client's message, which point out a promising direction for personal growth and pave the way for action. Responding empathically at this high level facilitates the client's exploration of feelings and problems in much greater breadth and depth than responding at lower levels. Conveying this level of empathy occurs rarely with inexperienced interviewers and only somewhat more often with highly experienced interviewers. It should be noted that conveying higher levels of empathy can also be a factor of the setting and expectations as well as social worker skill. The opportunity to respond at higher levels of empathy is more likely to occur near the end of an interview and with clients who have become more voluntary. As you consult your notes, with notations of key words, you can sometimes convey an empathic summary near the end of a session that captures themes and emotions, both expressed and implied. Consider the following example of a Level 5 response.

Level 5 Response:

An example of a Level 5 response can be found in the following video case.

VIDEO CASE EXAMPLE

In the video "Serving the Squeaky Wheel," Molly, a client with serious and persistent mental illness, acts, as she puts it, as a "greasy wheel," always advocating for herself and acting assertively, as she has been trained to do in many education programs. And yet those skills act as a "two- or three-edged sword" in that sometimes she is punished for this assertiveness. Reflecting these themes and Molly's language, the social worker, Ron Rooney, says, "You just seem to be courageous in fighting battles, and you have learned some skills in assertiveness, and as you say, that can be a two-edged or three-edged sword. Sometimes your assertiveness gets you what you want and sometimes your assertiveness causes some people to look at you as the squeaky wheel that has squeaked too much."

Exercises in Discriminating Levels of Empathic Responding

The following exercises ask you to rate responses for their level of empathy and are designed to assist you in refining your ability to determine the helpfulness of responses. These exercises will prepare you for subsequent practice in formulating your own empathic messages. Three client statements are given, followed by several possible responses. Using the empathic scale, rate each response from Level 0 to Level 5. Rating messages will be less difficult if, using the list of affective words and phrases, you first identify the feelings contained in the client's message. After you have rated each response, compare your rating with those given at the end of the chapter (see page 137). Referring to the rating scale, analyze the responses you rated inaccurately, trying to pinpoint the reason for the authors' ratings. Additional exercises are available in the *Practice Behaviors Workbook*.

Client Statement

1. *Single woman, age 80 [to social worker concerning her request to move to an independent living complex provided for ambulatory older persons]:* Goodness, the more I think of moving, the more scared I get. I have neighbors here who look after me, and I won't know a soul there. I'm afraid I'll be all alone.

Possible Responses

1. "It's pretty scary to you, leaving your neighbors and familiar surroundings. But there will be a lot of friendly people there and things to do. Besides, they fix one hot meal for you every day."
2. "Don't worry, you'll make friends in no time, and you'll wish you'd moved sooner."
3. "Did you sign those application papers I left with you a few days ago?"
4. "Just thinking about moving worries you because you'll be leaving your own neighborhood and friends. Even though your life would be much easier, you're unsure you'll be better off in other ways."
5. "So I gather in some ways you'd rather stay right where you are rather than gamble on a change."
6. "Lots of other people in the new apartments were just as scared as you before they moved, but I don't know a single one who's sorry now."
7. "It sounds as though you have some pretty mixed feelings about moving. Part of you wants to go because you could live more comfortably, but another part of you is afraid you'll feel alone and lost and wants to cling to people you know care about you."
8. "Are you saying we just ought to forget the whole thing?"

Client Statement

2. *Male, age 16 [in weekly visit to social work probation officer]:* I don't see the sense in having to come here every (expletive) week. I haven't been in any trouble now since I went to court a month ago. You should know by now you can trust me.

Possible Responses

1. "A month isn't very long, you know. And how can I be sure you're staying out of trouble?"
2. "I gather you'd rather not have to see me. I can understand that, but the judge ordered it and

you'd be in trouble with him if you didn't meet the conditions of your probation."

3. "Has it been a month since you went to court? I didn't think that it had been that long."
4. "You'd prefer not coming here and feel you've earned my trust."
5. "Having to come here each week irritates you, and I gather you may be disappointed that I am encouraging you to follow the judge's order."
6. "Look, you got yourself into this mess so don't complain to me if you don't like it. Maybe you'd like to talk the judge into changing his mind."
7. "It irritates you to have to come here each week. You'd like to get me off your back."
8. "You're confused about why you have to come here and wish you didn't have to."

Client Statement

3. *Group member [in hesitant, quiet voice]:* It's really hard for me to say what I want to say in this group. When I do start to talk, I get tongue-tied, and my heart starts beating faster and faster. I feel like some of you are critical of me.

Possible Responses (By Group Members or Group Leader)

1. "Yeah, I feel that same way sometimes, too."
2. "It is frightening to you to try to share your feelings with the group. Sounds like you find yourself at a loss for words and wonder what others are thinking of you."
3. "I know you're timid, but I think it's important that you make more of an effort to talk in the group, just like you're doing now. It's actually one of the responsibilities of being a group member."
4. "You get scared when you try to talk in the group."
5. "I sense that you're probably feeling pretty tense and tied up inside right now as you talk about the fear you've had in expressing yourself."
6. "Although you've been frightened of exposing yourself, I gather there's a part of you that wants to overcome that fear and become more actively involved with the rest of the group."
7. "What makes you think we're critical of you? You come across as a bit self-conscious, but that's no big deal."
8. "You remind me of the way I felt the first time I was in a group. I was so scared, I just looked at the floor most of the time."

9. "I wonder if we've done anything that came across as being critical of you."

Client Statement

4. *A homeless client who has been referred to a housing program [when asked by the social worker about what led to his losing his job]:* Budget cuts, layoffs, and I did not have seniority.

Possible Responses

1. "How did you feel about that?"
2. "So several things, including budget cuts, layoffs, and low seniority, contributed to your losing your job and contributed to your homelessness."
3. "How long have you been homeless?"
4. "Don't you think you have some responsibility for losing your job?"

RESPONDING WITH RECIPROCAL EMPATHY

EP 6

Reciprocal or interchangeable empathic responding (Level 3) is a basic skill used throughout the helping process to acknowledge client messages and to encourage exploration of problems. In the initial phase, empathic responding serves a vital purpose in individual, conjoint, and group sessions: It facilitates the development of a working relationship and fosters the climate of understanding necessary to promote communication and self-disclosure. In this way, it sets the stage for deeper exploration of feelings during subsequent phases of the helping process.

Note that the benefits of making additive empathic responses at Levels 4 and 5 are not contingent on the frequency of their usage. In fact, making one such response in a first or second interview may be helpful and appropriate. More frequent attempts presume a depth of relationship that has not yet developed. Additive empathic responses often exceed the level of feelings and meanings expressed by clients during early sessions and are thus reserved, in large part, for later phases of the helping process.

Because reciprocal responding is an essential skill used frequently to meet the objectives of the first phase of the helping process, we recommend that you first aim to achieve beginning mastery of responding at Level 3. Extended practice of this skill should significantly increase your effectiveness in establishing viable helping relationships, interviewing, and gathering data. The remainder of this chapter provides guidelines and practice exercises that will help you in mastering reciprocal responding. Although responding at additive levels represents an extension of the skill of reciprocal responding, it is an advanced skill that can be used in a variety of ways to achieve specific objectives. For this reason, it has been grouped with other change-oriented or "action" skills presented in Part 3 of the book.

Constructing Reciprocal Responses

To reach Level 3 on the empathic scale, you must be able to formulate responses that accurately capture the content and the surface feelings in the client message. It is also important to frame the message so that you do not merely restate the client's message.

The following paradigm, which identifies the elements of an empathic or reflective message, has proven useful for conceptualizing and mastering the skill of empathic responding:

You feel _____ about _____ because _____.
                                          Accurately
                                          identifies or
                                          describes
                                          feelings

The response focuses exclusively on the client's message and does not reflect the social worker's conceptualizations.

The following excerpt from a session involving a social worker and a 17-year-old female illustrates the use of the preceding paradigm in constructing an empathic response.

Client: I can't talk to my father without feeling scared and crying. I'd like to be able to express myself and to disagree with him, but I just can't.

Social worker: It sounds as though you just feel panicky when you try to talk to your father. You feel down on yourself, because at this point you can't say what you want without falling apart.

This message conveys a reflection with a twist, which we will explore more in the following chapter (Miller & Rollnick, 2002). That is, it reflects the client's current feeling but implies that it could change at another point when she acquires more confidence and skill (Greene,

Lee, & Hoffpauir, 2005). Many times, client messages contain conflicting or contrasting emotions, such as the following: "I like taking drugs, but sometimes I worry about what they might do to me." In such cases, each contrasting feeling should be highlighted:

- *You feel _____, yet you also feel _____.*
- *I sense that you feel torn because while you find taking drugs enjoyable, you have nagging thoughts that they might be harmful to you.*

Note that such highlighting of opposing feelings is a key technique for assisting clients in assessing their readiness for change in the motivational interviewing method (Miller & Rollnick, 2002).

Remember that to respond empathically at a reciprocal level, you must use language that your clients will readily understand. Abstract, intellectualized language and professional jargon create barriers to communication and should be avoided. It is also important to vary the language you use in responding. Many professionals tend to respond with stereotyped, repetitive speech patterns, commonly using a limited variety of leads to begin their empathic responses. Such leads as "You feel …" and "I hear you saying …" repeated over and over not only distract the client but also seem phony and contrived. This kind of stereotyped responding draws more attention to the social worker's technique than to his or her message. One of the many advantages to audio or video recording your own work is that these habitual responses—often so instinctive that you don't notice them—will become readily apparent to you.

Below you will find a list of varied introductory phrases that will help you expand your repertoire of possible responses. We encourage you to read the list aloud several times and to review it frequently while practicing the empathic communication training exercises in this chapter and in Chapter 17, which covers additive empathic responding. The reciprocal empathic response format ("You feel _____ because _____") is merely a training tool to assist you in focusing on the affect and content of client messages. The leads list below will help you respond more naturally.

Leads for Empathic Responses

Could it be that …	You're feeling …
I wonder if …	I'm not sure if I'm with
What I guess I'm hearing is …	you but …
	You appear to be feeling …

Correct me if I'm wrong, but I'm sensing …
Perhaps you're feeling …
Sometimes you think …
Maybe this is a long shot, but …
I'm not certain I understand; you're feeling …
As I hear it, you …
Is that the way you feel?
The message I'm getting is that …
Let me see if I'm with you; you …
If I'm hearing you correctly …
So, you're feeling …
You feel …
It sounds as though you are saying …
I hear you saying …
So, from where you sit …
I sense that you're feeling …
Your message seems to be …
I gather you're feeling …
If I'm catching what you say …
What you're saying comes across to me as …
It appears you feel …
Maybe you feel …
Do you feel …
I'm not sure that I'm with you; do you mean …
It seems that you …
Is that what you mean?
What I think I'm hearing is …
I get the impression that …
As I get it, you felt that …
To me it's almost like you are saying …
So, as you see it …
I'm picking up that you …
I wonder if you're saying …
So, it seems to you …
Right now you're feeling …
You must have felt …
Listening to you, it seems as if …
You convey a sense of …
As I think about what you say, it occurs to me you're feeling …
From what you say …
I gather you're feeling …

Exercises designed to help you to develop Level 3 reciprocal empathic responses appear at the end of the chapter and in the *Practice Behaviors Workbook*. Included in the exercises are a variety of client statements taken from actual work with individuals, groups, couples, and families in diverse settings. In addition to the skill development exercises, we recommend that you record the number of empathic responses you employ in sessions over several weeks to determine the extent to which you are applying this skill. We also suggest that either you or a knowledgeable associate rate your responses and determine the mean level of empathic responding for each session. If you find (as most beginning social workers do) that you are underutilizing empathic responses or responding at low levels, you may wish to set a goal to improve your skill.

Employing Empathic Responding

In early sessions with the client, empathic responding should be used frequently as a method of developing rapport with the client. Responses should be couched in a tentative manner to allow for inaccuracies in the social worker's perception. Checking out the accuracy of responses with appropriate lead-in phrases such as "Let me see if I understand …" or "Did I hear you right?" is helpful in communicating a desire to understand and a willingness to correct misperceptions.

In initially using empathic responses, learners are often leery of the flood of emotions that sometimes occurs as the client, experiencing none of the usual barriers to communication, releases feelings that may have been pent up for months or years. It is important to understand that empathic responses have not "caused" such feelings but rather have facilitated their expression, thus clearing the way for the client to explore and to consider such feelings more rationally and objectively.

You may worry, as do many beginning social workers, about whether you will "damage" the client or disrupt the helping relationship if your empathic responses do not always accurately reflect the client's feelings. Perhaps even more important than accuracy, however, is the commitment to understand conveyed by your genuine efforts to perceive the client's experience. If you consistently demonstrate your goodwill and intent to help through attentive verbal and nonverbal responding, an occasional lack of understanding or faulty timing will not damage the client–social worker relationship. In fact, your efforts to clarify the client's message will usually enhance rather than detract from the helping process, particularly if you respond to corrective feedback in an open, nondefensive, and empathic manner.

Multiple Uses of Empathic Communication

Earlier in the chapter, we referred to the versatility of empathic communication. In this section, we delineate a number of ways in which you can employ reciprocal empathic responding.

Establishing Relationships with Clients in Initial Sessions

As discussed previously, the use of empathic responding actively demonstrates the social worker's keen awareness of clients' feelings and creates an atmosphere in which clients feel safe enough to risk exploring their personal thoughts and feelings.

Although empathic communication is important in bridging cultural gaps, at times it can be used to excess. We must be careful with generalizations to ethnic groups because there is variation within each group related to individual differences, family experiences, education, and interaction with other groups (Dean, 2001). Classification systems tend to stereotype members of ethnic groups and in fact create distance (Johnson & Munch, 2009). Social workers have to be prepared to be learners, operating from a "not knowing" stance, which may, however, be influenced by hypotheses that they explore rather than act on as realities. With this caveat, some members of Asian American and Native American groups may tend to be lower in emotional expressiveness than members of other client groups, and they may react with discomfort and confusion if a social worker relies too heavily on empathic communication. Nevertheless, it is important to "read between the lines" and to sensitively respond to troubling emotions that these clients do not usually express directly. Like other clients, they are likely to appreciate a social worker's sensitive awareness to the painful emotions associated with their difficulties.

This can lead to assuming a more directive, active, and structured stance in situations such as crises where immediate action is required. This can also apply to some Asian American clients. As Tsui and Schultz (1985) have clarified, "A purely empathetic, passive, nondirective approach serves only to confuse and alienate the [Asian] client" (p. 568). The same can be said of many Native American clients, based on their levels of acculturation and experience with other groups. We recommend that you respond to each client independently and avoid judging his or her level of emotional responsiveness.

VIDEO CASE EXAMPLE

In the video "Getting Back to Shakopee," the social worker, Dorothy, is working with a Native American client, Valerie, who appears guarded and apprehensive about contact with a social worker after referral by her employer. Valerie appears worried that seeing a social worker might lead to a child welfare investigation. Her guarded stance appears to be associated with a belief, based on her experience, that social workers are more likely to remove children than act as her agent toward her own goals. In this case, these beliefs are not so much cultural beliefs as "folk wisdom" about the experience of her group with public child welfare. Dorothy makes many efforts to establish empathic and cultural linkages. A turning point appears to occur when Valerie discovers that Dorothy knows about an upcoming powwow and plans to attend. Taking a not knowing, learner stance leads Dorothy to find out about the particular employment, stress, sobriety, and family responsibility pressures that Valerie experiences.

Staying in Touch with Clients

Reciprocal empathic responding operationalizes the social work principle of "starting where the client is" and keeps social workers attuned to their clients' current feelings. Although they inevitably employ many other skills and techniques, social workers constantly return to empathic responding to keep in touch with their clients. In that sense, empathic communication is a fundamental intervention and a prerequisite to the use of other interventions.

Gendlin (1974) used the analogy of driving a car to illuminate the vital role of empathy in keeping in touch with clients. Driving involves much more than watching the road. A driver does many things, including steering, braking, signaling, and watching signs. One may glance at the scenery, visit with others, and think private thoughts, but watching the road must be accorded the highest priority. When visibility becomes limited or hazards appear, all other activities must cease, and the driver must attend exclusively to observing the road and potentially dangerous conditions.

Just as some drivers fail to pay proper attention to their surroundings and become involved in accidents, so some social workers also fail to attend sufficiently to cultural differences and changes in clients' moods and reactions, mistakenly assuming they know their clients' frame of mind. As a consequence, social workers may fail to discern important feelings, and their clients may perceive them as disinterested or insensitive and subsequently disengage from the helping process. Indeed, it is often true with beginners that so much of their own processing is focused on preparing the next thing they will say that they often miss what the client says. It takes time and experience to stay focused on what the client is expressing and trust that you will be able to respond adequately. Part of this is reframing your expectations of yourself. Instead of aspiring to be the social worker who can quickly assess and resolve client concerns, you can aspire to be a social worker who is able to accurately reflect what clients are saying and feeling and, in that process, be useful to them as they consider how to deal with their concerns.

Accurately Assessing Client Problems

EP 7

The levels of empathy offered by social workers are likely to correlate with their clients' levels of self-exploration. That is, high-level empathic responding should increase clients' exploration of self and problems. As the social worker moves "with" clients by frequently using empathic responses in initial sessions, clients will begin to lay out their problems and to reveal events and relevant data. Figuratively speaking, clients then take social workers where they need to go by providing information crucial to making an accurate assessment. Such an approach contrasts sharply with sessions that emphasize history taking and in which social workers, following their own agendas rather than the clients', spend unnecessary time asking hit-or-miss questions and gathering extraneous information.

Responding to Clients' Nonverbal Messages

Through their facial expressions, gestures, and body postures, clients often hint at feelings that they do not express verbally. In the course of a session, for instance, a client may become pensive, or may show puzzlement,

pain, or discomfort. In such instances, the social worker may convey understanding of the client's feeling state and verbalize the feeling explicitly through a reflective response that attends to the emotion suggested in the client's nonverbal expressions. For instance, in response to a client who has been sitting dejectedly with her head down for several minutes after having reported some bad grades, a social worker might say, "At this moment you seem to be feeling pretty down." In group or conjoint sessions, the social worker might reflect the nonverbal messages of several, or all, of the members. For example, the social worker might say, "We seem kind of antsy today, and we're having a hard time staying on our topic. Am I reading you correctly?"

Children are likely to communicate more nonverbally than verbally with unfamiliar adults such as social workers. A child interacting with a toy, making limited eye contact, and giving one-word replies to questions about how things are going at home may be communicating some things about how uncomfortable or unfamiliar he or she is with the process. Rather than forcing the child to explain what is happening in words, using play therapy techniques can permit children to tell a story, through actions, of what is occurring to them (Lukas, 1993).

Empathic responses that accurately tune into clients' nonverbal experiencing will usually prompt clients to begin exploring feelings they have been experiencing.

Making Confrontations More Palatable

Confrontation is employed in the change-oriented phase to expand clients' awareness and to motivate them to action. It is most appropriate when clients are contemplating actions that are unlawful or that are dangerous to themselves or others. Confrontation is also appropriate·when such actions conflict with the goals and values a client has chosen for himself or herself.

EP 6

CASE EXAMPLE

A social worker working with a child who was having difficulties at school made a home visit. The child was particularly interested in a toy piano, playing little melodies on it. The social worker, attempting to tune in to the child client, sat beside him and played a little melody and sang a little

song, "How was your day?" The child sat for a moment then repeated the melody, singing "Pretty good." The social worker responded with a variation of the melody, "What was good about it?" and the child responded.

Of course, even well-timed confrontations may meet with varying degrees of receptiveness. Both concerns for the client's welfare and prudence dictate that the social worker determine the impact of a potential confrontation on the client and implement a process for making such an intervention more palatable. This may be accomplished by employing empathic responses attuned to the client's reaction immediately following a confrontation. As social workers listen attentively and sensitively to their clients' expressions, the clients' defensiveness may abate. Indeed, clients often begin to process new information and think through and test the validity of their ideas, embracing those that fit and rejecting others that seem inapplicable. Guidelines for this important skill are presented in Chapter 17.

Blending confrontation and empathic responses is a particularly potent technique for managing group processes when the social worker must deal with a controversial issue or distractive behavior that is interfering with the work of the group.

Handling Obstacles Presented by Clients

Client opposition to what is happening in a session is sometimes healthy. What is often interpreted as unconscious resistance may, in fact, be a negative reaction to poor interviewing and intervention techniques used by the social worker or to client confusion, misunderstanding, or even inertia. For these reasons, it is important to carefully monitor clients' reactions and to deal directly and sensitively with their related feelings. Clients' verbal or nonverbal actions may comment indirectly on what is occurring in the helping process. For instance, a client may look at her cell phone and ask how long the session will last, shift her body position away from the social worker, begin tapping her foot, or stare out the window. When it appears that the client is disengaging from the session in this way, an empathic response that reflects the client's verbal and/or nonverbal message may effectively initiate discussion of what is occurring.

Social workers sometimes practice with highly verbal clients who talk rapidly and jump quickly from one topic to another. Overly verbal clients present a particular challenge to beginning social workers, who must often overcome the misconception that interrupting clients is rude. Because of this misconception, novice interviewers sometimes spend most of an initial session listening passively to highly verbal clients without providing any form or direction to the helping process.

They may also allow clients to talk incessantly because they mistakenly view this as constructive work on problems. Quite the contrary, excess verbosity often keeps the session on a superficial level and interferes with problem identification and exploration. It may also indicate a more serious affective mental health problem.

It is important that social workers provide structure and direction to each session, thereby conveying an expectation that specific topics will be considered in depth. Much more will be said about this in later chapters. For now, we simply underscore the necessity of using empathic responses with highly verbal clients as a preliminary strategy to slow the process and to provide some depth to the discussion. For example, a social worker might interject or intervene with "I'd like to interrupt to check whether I'm understanding what you mean. As I get it, you're feeling …" or "Before you talk about that topic, I would like to make sure I'm with you. You seem to be saying …" or "Could we hold off discussing that for just a minute? I'd like to be sure I understand what you mean. Would you expand on the point you were just making?"

Managing Anger and Patterns of Violence

During individual or group sessions, clients (especially those who were not self-referred and may be involuntary clients) often experience surges of intense and conflicting feelings, such as anger, hurt, or disappointment. In such instances, empathic responding is a key tool for assisting clients to work through those feelings. As empathic responses facilitate expanded expression of these feelings, clients engage in a process of venting, clarifying, and experiencing different feelings. Over time, they may achieve a mellowing of emotions and a more rational and thoughtful state of being.

When it is employed to focus sharply on clients' feelings, empathic responding efficiently manages and modifies strong emotions that represent obstacles to progress. As the social worker successfully handles such moments and clients experience increased self-awareness and cathartic benefits, the helping relationship is strengthened.

Empathic responding is particularly helpful in dealing with hostile clients and is indispensable when clients become angry with the social worker, as illustrated in the following client statement: "What you're doing to help me with my problems doesn't seem to be doing me any good. I don't know why I keep coming." At such moments, the social worker must resist the temptation to react defensively, because such a response will further antagonize the client and exacerbate the situation. Responding by challenging the client's perception, for instance, would damage the helping relationship. The social worker's responses should represent a genuine effort to understand the client's experiencing and feelings and to engage the client in fully exploring those feelings.

Involuntary clients sometimes become frustrated with the seemingly slow pace of progress toward goals and may feel that policies and individuals in the system are acting to thwart them. Empathizing with this anger is necessary before the social worker and client can collaborate productively and figure out how to make the system work toward client goals (Rooney & Chovanec, 2004).

Keeping this idea in mind, consider the impact of the following reciprocal empathic response: "You're very disappointed that things aren't better and are irritated with me, feeling that I should have been more helpful to you." This response accurately and nondefensively acknowledges the client's frustration with the situation and with the social worker. By itself, however, it would not be sufficient to calm the client's ire and to free the client to consider the problem more fully and rationally.

Carefully following the client's feelings and remaining sensitively attuned to the client's experience by employing empathic responses for several minutes usually helps both the social worker and the client to understand more clearly the strong feelings that prompted the client's outburst and to adequately assess the source of those feelings. Attending to the emotions expressed does not mean that the content is discounted. The social worker might, for example, follow the empathic response above by saying, "I'd like to explore more fully with you which parts of our work have not felt worthwhile."

When faced with angry clients in group and conjoint sessions, it is critical that the social worker empathically not only reflect the negative feelings and positions of the clients who are displaying the anger but also reach for and reflect the feelings or observations of members who may be experiencing the situation differently. Utilizing empathic responses in this manner assists the social worker in gathering information that will elucidate the problem, helping angry members air and examine their feelings, and bringing out other points of view for the group's consideration. In addition, employing empathic responding at such moments encourages a more rational discussion of the issues involved in the problem and thus sets the stage for possible problem solving. For example, a group leader might emphasize with members' frustration at having chosen to be part of an involuntary group such as one addressing alternatives to violence rather than risking prosecution. Having made a limited choice to be part of the group, members can then be encouraged to take part in establishing content areas that they would like to have covered in the group.

The principles just discussed also apply to clients who are prone to violent behavior. Such clients often come to the attention of social workers because they have abused their children and/or partners. People who engage in violence often do so because they have underlying feelings of helplessness and frustration and because they lack skills and experience in coping with troubling situations in more constructive ways. Some have short fuses and weak emotional controls, and many come from backgrounds in which they vicariously learned violence as a mechanism of coping. Using empathy to defuse their intense anger and to tune into the exceptions when they have been more successful in managing it can be an important first step in working with such clients (Lee, Uken, & Sebold, 2004). Other clients may have difficulties with anger and express this emotion only when under the influence of alcohol or other substances. Helping them experience and ventilate anger when sober and in control is a major approach employed to assist such clients to learn constructive ways of coping with anger (Potter-Efron & Potter-Efron, 1992).

VIDEO CASE EXAMPLE

Several parts of the "Serving the Squeaky Wheel" video deal with the client, Molly, expressing anger and frustration, and the practitioner, Ron Rooney, attempting to respond empathically to that anger. In particular, Molly is frustrated with an abrupt replacement of her previous caseworker and insists that Ron prove his identity as a social worker. Note how this challenge is met. At other points, Molly scales her level of trust at below zero and attributes this to a history of distrust of social workers.

Utilizing Empathic Responses to Facilitate Group Discussions

EP 6

Social workers may facilitate discussion of specific issues in conjoint or group sessions by first identifying a particular topic and then using empathic responses to reflect the observations of various group members in relation to that topic. The social worker may also actively seek responses from members who have not contributed and then employ empathic responses (or paraphrases) to acknowledge their observations. Utilized frequently in this manner, empathic responding encourages (and reinforces) clients' participation in group discussions.

Teaching Clients to Respond Empathically

Clients often experience difficulties in their relationships because their styles of communication include many barriers that prevent them from accurately hearing messages or conveying understanding to others. An important task for the social worker involves teaching clients to respond empathically. This task is accomplished in part by modeling, which is generally recognized as a potent technique for promoting client change and growth. People who distort or ignore others' messages (e.g., in marital, family, and other close relationships) may benefit vicariously by observing the social worker listen effectively and respond empathically. Moreover, clients who are hard to reach or who have difficulties in expressing themselves may gradually learn to recognize their own emotions and to express themselves more fully as a result of the social worker's empathic responding.

Teaching empathic communication skills to clients also can entail assuming an educational role. Several approaches to assisting partners who are having serious conflicts rely on teaching both parties to gain and express empathy for each other. Social workers' roles as educators require them to intervene actively at opportune moments to enable their clients to respond empathically, particularly when they have ignored, discounted, or attacked the contributions of others in a session. With respect to this role, we suggest that social workers consider taking the following actions:

1. Teach clients the paradigm for empathic responding introduced in this chapter. If appropriate, ask them to engage briefly in a paired practice exercise similar to the one recommended for beginning social workers at the end of the chapter. Utilizing topics neutral to the relationship, have each person carefully listen to the other party for several minutes, and then reverse roles. Afterward, evaluate with participants the impact of the exercise on them.

2. Introduce clients to the list of affective words and phrases and to the Leads for Empathic Responses list provided in this chapter. If appropriate, you may wish to have clients assume tasks during the week to broaden their feeling vocabulary similar to the tasks recommended for beginning social workers.

3. Intervene in sessions when clients ignore or fail to validate messages—a situation that occurs frequently during direct social work with couples, families, and groups. At those moments, interrupt the process in a facilitative fashion to ask the sender to repeat the message and the receiver to paraphrase or capture the essence of the former's message with fresh words, as illustrated in the following example.

16-year-old daughter: I don't like going to school. The teachers are zoned out most of the time, have no control over the class, and most of the kids laugh and make fun of me.

Mother: But you've got to go. If you'd just buckle down and study, school wouldn't be half so hard for you. I think …

Social worker [interrupting and speaking to mother]: I can see that you have some real concerns about Janet's not going to school, but for a moment, I'm going to ask you to show that you heard what she said to you by repeating it back to her.

Mother [looking at social worker]: She said she doesn't like school.

Social worker: That's close, but turn and talk to Janet. See if you can identify what she's feeling.

Mother [turning to daughter]: I guess it's pretty hard for you to go to school. And you don't like your teachers and you feel shut out and ridiculed by the kids.

Janet [tearfully]: Yeah, that's it … it's really hard.

Notice that the mother did not respond empathically to her daughter's feelings until the social worker intervened and coached her. This example illustrates the importance of persevering in teaching clients to "hear" the messages of others, a point we cannot overemphasize. People often have considerable trouble mastering listening skills because habitual responses are difficult to discard. This is true even when clients are highly motivated to communicate more effectively and when social workers actively intervene to assist them.

4. Give positive feedback when you observe clients listening to each other or, as in the preceding example, when they respond to your coaching. In the example, the social worker might have praised the mother as follows: "I liked the way you responded, because your message accurately reflected what your daughter was experiencing. I think she felt you really understood what she was trying to say." It is also helpful to ask participants to discuss what they experienced during the exchange and to highlight positive feelings and observations.

AUTHENTICITY

Although many theorists agree that empathy and respect are vital to developing effective working relationships, they do not agree about the amount of openness or self-disclosure practitioners should offer. **Self-disclosure** refers to the conscious and intentional revealing of information about oneself through both verbal expressions and nonverbal behaviors (e.g., smiling, grimacing, or shaking one's head in disbelief). Decisions about whether or when to self-disclose must be guided by a perception of benefit to the client, not the social worker's need to share. As one client said, "My case worker wanted to tell me all about his weekend and his girlfriend and so on. And I said, 'TMI: too much information. I don't need to know this, and I don't want to know this.' I don't want to share this kind of information with him and don't want to know it from him." Clearly, this client did not perceive the benefit of this kind of personal sharing. Deal (1999) reports that although beginning social workers frequently report engaging in self-disclosure, they seem less clear about the conditions under which it is appropriate to do so.

With respect to empirical evidence, numerous research studies cited by Truax and Mitchell (1971) and Gurman (1977) indicated that empathy, respect, and genuineness are correlated with positive outcomes. Critical analyses of these studies and conflicting findings from other research studies, however, have led experts to question these early findings and to conclude that "a more complex association exists between outcome and therapist 'skills' than originally

hypothesized" (Parloff, Waskow, & Wolfe, 1978, p. 251). Research needs to distinguish between intellectual empathy and empathic emotions and between therapist and client experience of empathy (Duan & Hill, 1996). That is, conveying understanding of the client's perception of the situation (intellectual empathy) is not the same as conveying feeling the same emotions (empathic empathy). Both are useful, but they may have independent effects.

Nevertheless, authenticity (also called genuineness) and the other facilitative conditions are still viewed as central to the helping process. **Authenticity** is defined as the sharing of self by relating in a natural, sincere, spontaneous, open, and genuine manner. Being authentic, or genuine, involves relating personally so that expressions are spontaneous rather than contrived. In addition, it means that social workers' verbalizations are congruent with their actual feelings and thoughts. Authentic social workers relate as real people, expressing their feelings and assuming responsibility for them rather than denying the feelings or blaming the client for causing them. Authenticity also involves being nondefensive and human enough to admit one's errors to clients. Realizing that they expect clients to lower their defenses and to relate openly (thereby increasing their vulnerability), social workers themselves must model humanness and openness and avoid hiding behind a mask of "professionalism."

Relating authentically does not mean that social workers indiscriminately disclose their feelings. Indeed, authentic expressions can be abrasive and destructive. Social workers should thus relate authentically only when doing so is likely to further therapeutic objectives. This qualification provides considerable latitude and is merely intended to constrain social workers from (1) relating abrasively (even though they may be expressing genuine feelings) and (2) meeting their own needs by focusing on their personal experiences and feelings rather than those of the client.

With respect to the first constraint, social workers should avoid misconstruing authenticity as granting free license to act as they wish, especially in expressing hostility. The second constraint reiterates the importance of social workers responding to clients' needs rather than their own. Moreover, when social workers share their feelings or experiences for a therapeutic purpose, they should immediately shift the focus back to the client. Keep in mind that the purpose of relating authentically—whether with individuals, families, or groups—is to facilitate growth of clients, not to demonstrate one's own honesty or authenticity.

Types of Self-Disclosure

Viewed from a therapeutic perspective, self-disclosure encourages clients to reciprocate with trust and openness. Lee (2014) has identified two types of self-disclosure: self-involving statements and personal self-disclosing. **Self-involving statements** include messages that express the social worker's personal reaction to the client during the course of a session. The following are examples of self-involving statements:

- *"I'm impressed with the progress you've made this past week. You applied what we discussed last week and have made another step toward learning to control angry feelings."*
- *"I want to share my reaction to what you just said. I feel sad for you because you are very hard on yourself."*
- *"You know, as I think about the losses you've experienced this past year, I am impressed with how well you have coped."*

Personal self-disclosure messages, by contrast, center on struggles or problems the social worker is currently experiencing or has experienced that are similar to the client's problems. The following are examples of this type of self-disclosure:

- [To couple] *"As you talk about your problems with your children, it reminds me of similar difficulties I had with mine when they were that same age."* [The social worker goes on to relate his experience.]
- [To individual client] *"I hear that some of your concerns relate to being a first-generation college student without family role models for this kind of coping. I can relate to that, having also been a first-generation college student."* [The social worker goes on to relate events in which she experienced similar concerns.]

Research findings comparing the effects of different types of self-disclosure have been mixed (Farber, 2006). Given the inconclusive findings, social workers should use personal self-disclosure judiciously. They should also recognize cultural variations that may suggest that some relatively low-level self-disclosure may be necessary early in the helping process. Rosenthal-Gelman (2004) has reported in a study that Hispanic practitioners are more likely to engage in some self-disclosure at the beginning of contact with Hispanic clients, honoring the cultural norm of establishing a more personal contact. Similarly, Gonzalez and Acevedo (2012) suggest that a Latin value of "personalismo" values making a personal connection beyond establishing professional competency and credentials. Logic suggests that self-disclosures of current problems may undermine the confidence of clients, who may well wonder how social workers can presume to help others when they haven't successfully resolved their own problems. Moreover, focusing on the social worker's problems diverts attention from the client, who may conclude that the social worker prefers to focus on his or her own problems. Self-involving disclosures, by contrast, appear to be of low risk and are relevant to the helping process.

> ## VIDEO CASE EXAMPLE
>
> As noted in the video "Getting Back to Shakopee," self-disclosure of cultural experiences by the social worker, Dorothy, appears essential in beginning to develop trust and rapport with her client, Valerie.

Timing and Intensity of Self-Disclosure

Yet another aspect of self-disclosure focuses on the timing and level of intensity of the social worker's sharing, ranging from superficial to highly personal statements. Social workers should avoid sharing personal feelings and experiences until they have established rapport and trust with their clients and the clients have, in turn, demonstrated readiness to engage on a more personal level. The danger in premature self-disclosure is that such responses can threaten clients and lead to emotional retreat at the very time when it is vital to reduce threat and defensiveness.

The danger is especially great with clients from cultures in which relating on an intense personal basis might be less common. Tsui and Schultz (1985) have suggested that self-disclosure by social workers may facilitate the development of rapport with some Asian clients. The logic of this recommendation is that given the generally low level of emotional expressiveness in some Asian families, the social worker is, in effect, acting as a role model for the client, thereby showing the client how the appropriate expression of emotion facilitates the treatment process (Tsui & Schultz, 1985). Members of Asian

American families, of course, are not homogenous, as their members differ in terms of their level of acculturation and familiarity with values such as self-disclosure. Hence, assessing their cultural experience can be part of determining whether self-disclosure might be useful. Lee (2014) suggests that social workers take care in such self-disclosure to avoid imposing or implying cultural stereotypes of good coping. That is, it is important to honor the client's perspective and values even when it is not consistent with the worker's own experience.

As clients experience trust, social workers can appropriately relate with increased openness and spontaneity, assuming that their authentic responses are relevant to their clients' needs and do not shift the focus from the client for more than brief periods. Even when trust is strong, social workers should exercise only moderate self-disclosure—beyond a certain level, even authentic responses no longer facilitate the helping process (Truax & Carkhuff, 1964).

A Paradigm for Responding Authentically

Beginning social workers (and clients) may learn the skill of relating authentically more readily if they have a paradigm for formulating effective messages. This paradigm includes the four elements of an authentic message:

(1) "I"( )	About	Because
(2) Specific feeling or wants	(3) Neutral description of event	(4) Impact of situation on sender or others

The following example (Larsen, 1980), involving a social work student intern's response to a message from an institutionalized youth, illustrates the use of this paradigm. The student describes the situation: "Don and I had a hard time together last week. I entered the living unit only to find that he was angry with me for some reason, and he proceeded to abuse me verbally all night long. This week, Don approached me to apologize."

Don: I'm really sorry about what happened the other night. I didn't mean to dis you.

Student social worker: Well, you know, Don, I'm sorry it happened, too. I was hurt and puzzled that night because I didn't understand where all your anger was coming from. You wouldn't talk to me about it, so I felt frustrated, and I didn't quite know what to do or make of it. One of my real fears that night was that this was going to get in the way of our getting to know each other. I really didn't want to see that happen.

Note that the student uses all of the elements of the paradigm: identifying specific feelings (hurt, puzzlement, frustration, fear); describing the events that occurred in a neutral, nonblaming manner; and identifying the impact she feared these events might have on the client–social worker relationship.

As you consider the paradigm, note that we are not recommending that you use it in a mechanistic and undeviating "I-feel-this-way-about …" response pattern. Rather, we suggest that you learn and combine the elements of the paradigm in a variety of ways as you practice constructing authentic messages. Later, as you incorporate authentic relating into your natural conversational repertoire, you will no longer need to refer to the paradigm.

Note that this paradigm is also applicable in teaching clients to respond authentically. We suggest that you present the paradigm to clients and guide them through several practice messages, assisting them to include all elements of the paradigm in their responses. For example:

Specific "I" Feelings	Description of Event	Impact
I get frustrated	when you keep reading the paper while I'm speaking	because I feel very unimportant to you.

It is important to stress with clients the need to use conversational language when they express authentic messages. Also emphasize, however, that they should talk about their own feelings and opinions rather than slip into accusatory forms of communication.

Guidelines for Responding Authentically

As you practice authentic responding and teach clients to respond authentically in their encounters with others, we suggest you keep in mind the following guidelines related to the four elements of an authentic message. Please note that we do not want to imply that helping clients respond more authentically is a goal in many forms of service in which clients are not seeking therapy.

1. *Personalize messages by using the pronoun "I."* When attempting to respond authentically, both social workers and clients commonly make the mistake of starting their statements with "You." This introduction tends to focus a response on the other person rather than on the sender's experiencing. In contrast, beginning messages with "I" encourages senders to own responsibility for their feelings and to personalize their statements.

   Efforts by social workers to use "I" statements when responding can profoundly affect the quality of group processes, increasing both the specificity of communications and the frequency with which their clients use "I" statements. As a general rule, groups (including couples and families) are likely to follow a social worker's communication style.

   Just as groups tend to follow suit when social workers frequently use "I" messages, they may also imitate counterproductive behaviors of the social worker. That includes communicating in broad generalities, focusing on issues external to the individual, or relating to the group in an interrogative or confrontational manner.

   Social workers must be careful to model the skills they wish clients to acquire. They should master relating authentically to the extent that they automatically personalize their messages and constructively share their inner experiencing with clients. To facilitate personalizing messages, social workers can negotiate an agreement with individuals or groups specifying that clients will endeavor to incorporate the use of "I" statements in their conversational repertoires. Thereafter, it is critical to intervene consistently to assist clients to personalize their messages when they have not done so.

2. *Share feelings that lie at varying depths.* Social workers must reach for those feelings that underlie their immediate experiencing. Doing so is particularly vital when social workers experience strong negative feelings (e.g., dislike, anger, repulsion, disgust, boredom) toward a client, because an examination of the deeper aspects of feelings often discloses more positive feelings toward the client. Social workers need to be in tune with their feelings, positive and negative, and learn when and how sharing such emotions appropriately can be useful to clients. Expressing these feelings preserves the client's self-esteem, whereas expressing superficial negative feelings often poses a threat to the client, creating defensiveness and anger.

   For example, in experiencing feelings of anger (and perhaps disappointment) toward a client who is chronically late for appointments, the social worker may first connect his feelings of anger to feeling inconvenienced. In reaching for his deeper feelings, however, the social worker may discover that the annoyance derives from a concern that the client may not find the sessions useful. At an even deeper level may lie hurt in not being more important to the client. Further introspection may also uncover a concern that the client is exhibiting similar behavior in other areas of life that could adversely affect his or her relationships with others. The fact is that the social worker does not know why the client is late for appointments, and overt exploration of the obstacles can lead the social worker and client into a more productive discussion on how to resolve the issue. The social worker may discover multiple (and sometimes conflicting) feelings that may be beneficially shared with the client, as illustrated in the following message:

Social worker [to client]: I would like to check some things out with you. You apologized for being late for the session, and I appreciate that. However, this has occurred before, so I wanted to check out with you how things are going for you about our sessions. You lead a busy life, balancing many commitments. I am not sure what part these sessions are playing for you in addressing the issues you brought in. I would also like to know what you're feeling just now about what I said.

Like prospective social workers, clients are prone to focus on one aspect of their experiencing to the exclusion of deeper and more complex emotions. Clients often have difficulty, in fact, in pinpointing any feelings they are experiencing. In either case, social workers should persevere to help clients broaden their awareness of their emotions and to express them openly, as illustrated in the following exchange:

Social worker: When you told your wife you didn't want to take her to a movie, and she said you never want to do anything with her—what feelings did you experience?

Husband: I was mad. I do want to do things, just not maybe going to a movie.

Social worker: Can you get in touch with what you were feeling? You told me a little bit about what you thought, but what's happening inside? Try to use feeling words to describe what you're experiencing.

Husband: OK. I felt taken for granted, unappreciated.

Social worker: So you experienced not feeling fully valued. What was under that feeling of being devalued?

Husband: Uh, I'd say again that I am doing the best I can. Maybe I am not the most exciting guy to be around.

Social worker: I would like to check out something with you. Right now, as you're talking about this, it seems you're experiencing a real sense of disappointment in the relationship and perhaps some sadness about not being able to do what your wife would want.

Husband: Yeah, sometimes I get down and depressed and think that there is not anything I can do to satisfy her.

Social worker: I'm glad that you can recognize that sense of despair you're feeling. I also appreciate your hanging in there with me for a minute to get in touch with some of your feelings. You seem to be a person whose feelings run deep, and sometimes expressing them may come hard for you. I'm wondering how you view yourself in relation to being in touch with your feelings.

In the preceding excerpt, the social worker engaged in extensive coaching to assist the client in discovering his underlying feelings. Deeper than the feelings of frustration and being devalued that the client identified lay the more basic emotions related to feeling hurt and being unimportant to his wife. By providing other spontaneous "training sessions," the social worker can help this client to identify his feelings more readily, to find the feeling words to express them, and to begin formulating "I" statements.

3. *Describe the situation or targeted behavior in neutral or descriptive terms.* In their messages, clients often omit references or make only vague references to the situations that prompted their responses. Moreover, they may convey their messages in a blaming manner, engendering defensiveness that overshadows other aspects of their self-disclosure. In either event, self-disclosure is minimal, and respondents do not receive information that could otherwise be of considerable value. Consider, for example, the low yield of information in the following messages:

- *"You're a nice person."*
- *"You should be more conscientious."*
- *"You're progressing well in your work."*
- *"You have a bad attitude."*

All of these messages lack supporting information that respondents need to identify specific aspects of their behavior that are competent and warrant recognition or are substandard. Social workers should assist parents, spouses, or others to provide higher-yield feedback by including behavioral references. Examples of such messages follow (they involve a parent talking to a 6-year-old girl):

- *"I've really appreciated all that you've done tonight by yourself. You put away your toys, washed your hands before dinner, and you came to dinner without my having to ask. I'm so pleased."*
- *"I'm very disappointed with your behavior right now. You didn't change your clothes when you came home from school; you didn't feed the dog; and you haven't started your homework."*

Note in the last example that the parent sent an "I" message and owned the feelings of disappointment rather than attacking the child for being undependable.

When responding authentically, social workers should carefully describe specific events that prompted their responses, particularly when they wish to draw clients' attention to some aspect of their behavior or to a situation of which they may not be fully aware. The following social worker's message illustrates this point:

Social worker: I need to share something with you that concerns me. Just a moment ago, I gave you feedback regarding the positive way I thought you handled a situation with your partner. *[Refers to specific behaviors manifested by client.]* When I did that, you seemed to discount my response by *[mentions specific behaviors].* Actually, this is not the first time I have seen this happen. It appears to me that it is difficult for you to give yourself credit for the positive things you do and the progress you are making.

Social workers constantly need to assess the specificity of their responses to ensure that they give clients the benefit of behaviorally specific feedback and provide positive modeling experiences for them. It is also vital to coach clients in giving specific feedback whenever they make sweeping generalizations and do not document the relationship between their responses and specific situations.

4. *Identify the specific impact of the problem situation or behavior on others.* Authentic messages often stop short of identifying the specific effects of the situation on the sender or on others, even though such information would be very appropriate and helpful. This element of an "I" message also increases the likelihood that the receiver will adjust or make changes, particularly if the sender demonstrates that the receiver's behavior is having a tangible effect on him or her.

Consider a social worker's authentic response to a male member of an adult group:

Social worker: Sometimes I sense some impatience on your part to move on to other topics. *[Describes situation that just occurred, documenting specific messages and behavior.]* At times I find myself torn between responding to your urging us to "get on with it" or staying with a discussion that seems beneficial to the group. It may be that others in the group are experiencing similar mixed feelings and some of the pressure I feel.

Here the social worker first clarifies the tangible effects of the client's behavior on himself and then suggests that others may experience the behavior similarly. Given the social worker's approach, others in the group may be willing to give feedback as well. The client is then free to draw his own conclusions about the cause-and-effect relationship between his behaviors and the reactions of others and to decide whether he wishes to alter his way of relating in the group.

Social workers can identify how specific client behaviors negatively impact not only the social worker but also the clients themselves (e.g., "I'm concerned about *[specific behavior]* because it keeps you from achieving your goal"). Further, they may document how a client's behavior affects others (e.g., his wife) or the relationship between the client and another person (e.g., "It appears that your behavior creates distance between you and your son").

People often have difficulty in identifying the impact of others' behavior on themselves. For example, a mother's message to her child, "I want you to play someplace else," establishes no reason for the request, nor does it specify the

negative impact of the behavior on her. If the mother responds in an authentic manner, however, she clearly identifies the tangible effect of her child's behavior: "I'm having a hard time getting through the hallway because I keep stumbling over toys and having to go around you. I've almost fallen several times, and others might, too. I'm worried that someone might get hurt, so I'm asking you to move your toys to your room."

The preceding illustration underscores the point that when clients clarify how a situation affects them, their requests do not appear arbitrary and are more persuasive; hence, others are likely to make appropriate accommodations. We suspect that an important reason why many clients have not changed certain self-defeating behaviors before entering the helping process is that others have previously attacked or pressured them to change rather than authentically and unabrasively imparting information that highlights how the clients' behavior strikes them. Others may have also attempted to prescribe behavioral changes that appear to be self-serving (e.g., "Come on, stop that sulking") instead of relating their feelings (e.g., "I'm concerned that you're down and unhappy; I'd like to help but I'm not sure how"). Such statements do not strike a responsive chord in clients, who may equate making changes with putting themselves under the control of others (by following their directives), thereby losing their freedom to make their own decisions.

In the following exchange, note how the social worker assists Carolyn, a group member, to personalize her statements and to clarify her reaction to the behavior of another member who has remained consistently silent throughout the first two sessions:

Carolyn: We've talked about needing to add new guidelines for the group as we go along. I think we ought to have a guideline that everyone should talk in the group. *[Observe that Carolyn has not personalized her message but has proposed a solution to meet a need she has not identified.]*

Social worker [to Carolyn]: The group may want to consider this guideline, but for a minute, can you get in touch with what you're experiencing and put it in the form of an "I" statement?

Carolyn: Well, all right. Janet hasn't talked at all for two solid weeks, and it's beginning to really irritate me.

Social worker: I'm wondering what else you may be experiencing besides irritation? *[Assists Carolyn to identify her feelings besides mild anger.]*

Carolyn: I guess I'm a little uneasy because I don't know where Janet stands. Maybe I'm afraid she's sitting in judgment of us—I mean, me. And I guess I feel cheated because I'd like to get to know her better, and right now I feel shut out by her.

Social worker: That response helps us to begin to get to the heart of the matter. Would you now express yourself directly to Janet? Tell her what you are experiencing and, particularly, how her silence is affecting you.

Carolyn [to Janet]: I did wonder what you thought about me since I really opened up last week. And I do want to get to know you better. But, underneath all this, I'm concerned about you. You seem unhappy and alone, and that makes me uncomfortable—I don't like to think of your feeling that way. Frankly, I'd like to know how you feel about being in this group, and if you're uneasy about it, as you seem to be, I'd like to help you feel better somehow.

In the preceding example, the social worker assisted Carolyn to experience a broader range of feelings and to identify her reaction to Janet's silence. In response to the social worker's intervention, Carolyn also expressed more positive feelings than were evident in her initial message—a not infrequent occurrence when social workers encourage people to explore deeper-level emotions.

Engaging one member in identifying specific reactions to the behavior of others provides a learning experience for the entire group, and members often expand their conversational repertoires to incorporate such facilitative responding. In fact, the extent to which social workers assist clients to acquire specific skills is correlated with the extent to which clients acquire those same skills.

Cues for Authentic Responding

The impetus for social workers to respond authentically may emanate from (1) clients' messages that request self-disclosure or (2) social workers' decisions to share perceptions and reactions they believe will be helpful. Next, we consider authentic responding that emanates from these two sources.

Authentic Responding Stimulated by Clients' Messages

Requests from Clients for Personal Information. Clients often confront students and social workers with questions aimed at soliciting personal information, such as "How old are you?," "Do you have any children?," "What is your religion?," "Are you married?," and "Are you a student?" It is natural for clients to be curious and to ask questions about a social worker in whom they are confiding, especially when their well-being and future are at stake.

Self-disclosing responses may or may not be appropriate, depending on the social worker's assessment of the client's motivation for asking a particular question. When questions appear to be prompted by an attempt to be sociable, such responses are often very appropriate. For example, it is appropriate for clients to want to know whether you are likely to be helpful to them and hence whether talking to you is a good use of their time and energy. They often want to know "Are you any good at what you do?" Their way of assessing this may take the form of asking about your personal experience with the topic at hand, whether it be drug use or raising children. Consider the following exchange from an initial session involving a 23-year-old student social worker and a 43-year-old woman who requested help in dealing with her marital problems:

Client: Are you married?

Student social worker: No, I am not. Is it important to you to work with a married helper?

Client: Oh, I don't know. I just wondered.

Given the context of an older adult with a much younger student, the client's question was likely motivated by a concern that the student might lack life experience essential to understanding her marital difficulties or the competence needed to assist her in resolving them. In this instance, immediate authentic disclosure by the student was inappropriate because it did not facilitate exploration of the feelings underlying the client's inquiry.

Conversely, such an exchange may yield information vital to the helping process if the social worker avoids premature self-disclosure. It is sometimes very difficult to distinguish whether clients' questions are motivated by a natural desire for information or by hidden concerns or feelings. As a rule of thumb, when you have questions about clients' motivation for making personal inquiries, precede disclosures of views or feelings with either open-ended or empathic responses. Responding in this manner significantly increases the probability that clients will reveal their underlying concerns. Notice what happens when the social worker utilizes an empathic response before responding authentically:

Student social worker: When you say you wondered whether I was married, please help me understand how knowing that could be helpful to you.

Client: Well, I guess I was thinking that someone who is married could understand my situation. I hope it doesn't offend you.

Student social worker: Not at all, in fact I appreciate your frankness. It's natural that you want to know whether your social worker might be able to help you. I know there's a lot at stake for you. Tell me more about your concerns.

Here the student responded to the probable concern of the client and struck pay dirt. Such astuteness tends to foster confidence in clients and greatly facilitates the establishment of a partnership. The fact that the student "leans into" the situation by inviting further exploration rather than skirting the issue may also be read by the client as an indicator of the student's own confidence in his or her ability to help. After fully exploring the client's concerns, the student can respond with an authentic response identifying personal qualifications:

Student social worker: I do want you to know that I believe I can be helpful to you. I have worked with other clients whose difficulties were similar to your own. I also consult with my supervisor regularly. Of course, the final judgment of my competence will rest with you. It will be important for us to discuss any feelings you may still have at the end of the interview as you make a decision about returning for future sessions.

Questions That Solicit the Social Worker's Perceptions. Clients may also pose questions that solicit the social worker's opinions, views, or feelings. Typical questions include "How do I compare to your other clients?," "Do you think I need help?," "Am I crazy?," and "Do you think there's any hope for me?" Such questions can pose a challenge for social workers, who must consider the motivation behind the question and judge whether to disclose their views or feelings immediately or to employ either an empathic or open-ended response.

When social workers do disclose their perceptions, however, their responses must be congruent with their inner experiencing. In response to the question "Do

you think there's any hope for me?," the social worker may congruently respond with a message that blends elements of empathy and authenticity:

Social worker: Your question tells me you're probably afraid that you're beyond help. Although you do have some difficult problems, I'm optimistic that if we work hard together, things can improve. You've shown a number of strengths that should help you make changes.

It is not necessary to answer all questions from clients in the service of authenticity. If you feel uncomfortable about answering a personal question or deem it inadvisable to do so, you should feel free to decline answering. When doing so, it is important to explain your reason for not answering directly, again utilizing an authentic response. If a teenage client, for example, asks whether the social worker had sexual relations before she married, the social worker may respond as follows:

Social worker: I would rather not reveal that information to you, because it is a very private part of my life. Asking me took some risk on your part. I have an idea that your question probably has to do with a struggle you're having, although I could be wrong. I would appreciate your sharing your thoughts about what sparked your question.

The social worker should then utilize empathic responding and open-ended questions to explore the client's reaction and motivation for asking her question.

Authentic Responding Initiated by Social Workers

Authentic responding initiated by social workers may take several forms, which are considered next.

Disclosing Past Experiences. As previously indicated, self-disclosure should be brief, relevant to the client's concerns, well timed, and used sparingly. In relating to a particular client's struggle, a social worker might indicate, "I remember I felt very much like that when I was struggling with …" In so doing, he or she must be careful to check out whether the client considers this experience comparable. A fundamental guideline that applies to such situations is that social workers should be certain they are focusing on themselves to meet the therapeutic needs of their clients.

Sharing Perceptions, Ideas, Reactions, and Formulations. A key role of the social worker in the change-oriented phase of the helping process is to act as a "candid feedback system" by revealing personal thoughts and perceptions relevant to client problems (Hammond et al., 1977). Such responding is intended to further the change process in one or more of the following ways:

1. To heighten clients' awareness of dynamics that may play an important part in problems
2. To offer a different perspective regarding issues and events
3. To aid clients in conceptualizing the purposes of their behavior and feelings
4. To enlighten clients on how they affect others (including the social worker)
5. To bring clients' attention to cognitive and behavioral patterns (both functional and dysfunctional) that operate at either an individual or a group level
6. To share the social worker's here-and-now affective and physical reactions to clients' behavior or to processes that occur in the helping relationship
7. To share positive feedback concerning clients' strengths and growth

After responding authentically to achieve any of these purposes, it is vital to invite clients to express their own views and draw their own conclusions. Sharing perceptions with clients does involve some risk. In particular, clients may misinterpret the social worker's motives and feel criticized, put down, or rebuked. Clarifying the social worker's helpful intent before responding diminishes this risk somewhat. Nevertheless, it is critical to watch for clients' reactions that may indicate a response has struck an exposed nerve.

To avoid damaging the relationship (or to repair it), the social worker should be empathically attuned to the client's reaction to candid feedback, shifting the focus back to the client to determine the impact of the self-disclosure. If the client appears to have been emotionally wounded by the social worker's authentic response, the social worker can use empathic skills to elicit troubled feelings and to guide subsequent responses aimed at restoring the relationship's equilibrium. Expressions of concern and clarification of the goodwill intended by the social worker are also usually facilitative:

Social worker: I can see that what I shared with you hit you pretty hard—and that you're feeling put down right now. *[Client nods but avoids eye contact.]* I feel bad about that, because the last thing I'd want is to hurt you. Please tell me what you're feeling.

Openly (and Tactfully) Sharing Reactions When Put on the Spot. Clients sometimes create situations that put social workers under considerable pressure to respond to messages that bear directly on the relationship, such as when they accuse a social worker of being uninterested, unfeeling, irritated, displeased, critical, inappropriate, or incompetent. Clients may also ask pointed questions (sometimes before the relationship has been firmly established) that require immediate responses.

The first statement of one female client in an initial interview, for example, was "I'm gay. Does that make any difference to you?" This is likely to be a very important question for this client, determining whether she will feel comfortable and accepted in discussing her concerns. The client is entitled to expect that the social worker will be supportive and understanding and that, whatever his or her personal beliefs, the social worker will assist the client in meeting her goals or refer her to someone who is better able to do so.

Experiencing Discomfort in Sessions. Sometimes intense discomfort may indicate that something in the session is going awry and needs to be addressed. It is important to reflect on your discomfort, seeking to identify events that seem to be causing or exacerbating it (e.g., "I'm feeling very uneasy because I don't know how to respond when my client says things like 'You seem to be too busy to see me' or 'I'm not sure I'm worth your trouble'"). After privately exploring the reason for the discomfort, the social worker might respond as follows:

Social worker: I'd like to share some impressions about several things you've said in the last two sessions. *[Identifies client's statements.]* I sense you're feeling pretty unimportant—as though you don't count for much—and that perhaps you're imposing on me just by being here. I want you to know that I'm pleased you had the courage to seek help in the face of all the opposition from your family. It's also important to me that you know that I want to be helpful to you. I am concerned, however, that you feel you're imposing on me. Could you share more what contributes to that feeling for you?

Notice how the social worker specifically identifies the self-defeating thoughts and feelings and blends elements of empathy and authenticity in the response.

Other situations that put social workers on the spot include clients' angry attacks, as we discuss later in this chapter. Social workers must learn to respond authentically in such scenarios. Consider a situation in which an adolescent attacks a social worker in an initial interview, protesting, "I don't want to be here. You social workers are all assholes." In such instances, social workers should share their reactions, as illustrated in the following response:

Social worker: It sounds as though you're really angry about having to see me and that your previous experiences with social workers haven't been good. I respect your feelings and don't want to pressure you to work with me. I want you to know that I am interested in you and that I would like to know what you are facing.

Intertwining empathic and authentic responses in this manner often defuses clients' anger and encourages them to think more rationally about a situation.

Sharing Feelings When Clients' Behavior Is Unreasonable or Distressing. Although social workers should be able to take most client behaviors in stride, sometimes they may experience justifiable feelings of frustration, anger, or even hurt. In one case, a client acquired a social worker's home phone number from another source and began calling frequently about daily crisis situations, although discussions of these events could easily have waited until the next session. In another instance, an intoxicated client called the social worker in the middle of the night "just to talk." In yet another case, an adolescent client let the air out of a social worker's automobile tires.

In such situations, social workers should share their feelings with clients—*if they believe they can do so constructively.* In the following case example, note that the student social worker interweaves authentic and empathic responses in confronting a Latino youth in a correctional institution who had maintained he was innocent of hiding drugs that staff had found in his room. Believing the youth's story, the student went to bat for him, only to find out later that the client had lied. Somewhat uneasy at her first real confrontation, the student tries to formulate an authentic response. In an interesting twist, the youth helps her to be "upfront" with him:

Student social worker: There's something I wanted to talk to you about, Randy … [*Stops to search for the right words.*]

Randy: Well, come out with it, then. Just lay it on me.
Student social worker: Well, remember last week when you got that incident report? You know, I really believed you were innocent. I was ready to go to the hearing and tell staff I was sure you were innocent and that the charge should be dropped. I guess I'm feeling kind of bad because when I talked to you, you told me you were innocent, and, well, that's not exactly the way it turned out.
Randy: You mean I lied to you. Go ahead and say it.
Student social worker: Well, yes, I guess I felt kind of hurt because I was hoping that maybe you had more trust in me than that.
Randy: Well, Susan, let me tell you something. Where I come from, that's not lying—that's what we call survival. Personally, I don't consider myself a liar. I just do what I need to do to get by. That's an old trick, but it just didn't work.
Student social worker: I hear you, Randy. I guess you're saying we're from two different worlds, and maybe we both define the same thing in different ways. I guess that with me being Anglo, you can't really expect me to understand what life has been like for you.

Several minutes later in the session, after the student has further explored the client's feelings, the following interchange occurs:

Student social worker: Randy, I want you to know a couple of things. The first thing is that when social workers work with clients, they must honor what they call confidentiality, so I can't share what we talk about without your permission in most cases. An exception to this relates to rule or law violations. I can't keep that confidential. The second thing is that I don't expect you to share everything with me. I know there are certain things you don't want to tell me, so rather than lying about something that I ask you about, maybe you can just tell me you don't want to tell me. Would you consider that?
Randy: Yeah, that's okay. [*Pause.*] Listen, Susan, I don't want you to go around thinking I'm a liar now. I'll tell you this, and you can take it for what it's worth, but this is the truth. That's the first time I've ever lied to you. But you may not believe that.
Student social worker: I do believe you, Randy. [*He seems a little relieved and there is a silence.*]
Randy: Well, Susan, that's a deal, then. I won't lie to you again, but if there's something I don't want to say, I'll tell you I don't want to say it.

Student social worker: Sounds good to me. *[Both start walking away.]* You know, Randy, I really want to see you get through this program and get out as fast as you can. I know it's hard starting over because of the incident with the drugs, but I think we can get you through. *[This seemed to have more impact on Randy than anything the social worker had said to him in a long time. The pleasure was visible on his face, and he broke into a big smile.]*

Noteworthy in this exchange is that the social worker relied almost exclusively on the skills of authenticity and empathy to bring the incident to a positive conclusion. Ignoring her feelings would have impaired the student's ability to relate facilitatively to the client and would have been destructive to the relationship. In contrast, focusing on the situation proved beneficial for both.

Sharing Feelings When Clients Give Positive Feedback. Social workers sometimes have difficulty responding receptively to clients' positive feedback about their own attributes and/or performance. We suggest that social workers model the same receptivity to positive feedback that they ask clients to demonstrate in their own lives, as illustrated in the following exchange:

Client: I don't know what I would have done without you. I'm just not sure I would have made it if you hadn't been there when I needed you. You've made such a difference in my life.

Social worker: I'm touched by your gratitude and pleased you are feeling so much more capable of coping with your situation. I want you to know, too, that even though I was there to help, your efforts have been the deciding factor in your growth.

Positive Feedback: A Form of Authentic Responding

Because positive feedback plays such a vital role in the change process, we have allocated a separate section in our attempt to do justice to this topic. Social workers often employ (or should employ) this skill in supplying information to clients about positive attributes or specific areas in which they demonstrate strengths, effective coping mechanisms, and incremental growth. In so doing, social workers enhance their clients' motivation to change and foster hope for the future.

Many opportune moments occur in the helping process when social workers experience warm or positive feelings toward clients because of the latter's actions or progress. When appropriate, social workers should share such feelings spontaneously with clients, as illustrated in the following messages:

- "You have what I consider exceptional ability to pay attention to your own behavior and to analyze the part you play in relationships. I think this strength will serve you well in solving the problems you have identified."
- "I've been touched several times in the group when I've noticed that, despite your grief over the loss of your husband, you've reached out to other members who needed support."
- *[To newly formed group]:* "In contrast to our first session, I've noticed that this week we haven't had trouble getting down to business and staying on task. I've been pleased as I've watched you develop group guidelines for the past 20 minutes with minimal assistance from me. I had the thought, 'This group is really moving.'"

The first two messages acknowledge strengths of individuals. The third lauds a behavioral change the social worker has observed in a group process. Both types of messages sharply focus clients' attention on specific behaviors that facilitate the change process, ultimately increasing the frequency of such behaviors. When sent consistently, positive messages also have the long-range effect of helping people who have low self-esteem to develop a more positive self-image. When positive feedback is employed to document the cause-and-effect relationship between their efforts and positive outcomes, individuals also experience a sense of satisfaction, accomplishment, and control over their situation.

Positive feedback can have the additional effect of increasing clients' confidence in their own coping ability. We have occasionally had experiences with clients who were on the verge of falling apart when they came to a session but left feeling able to manage their problems for a while longer. We attribute their increased ability to function in part to authentic responses that documented and highlighted areas in which they were coping and successfully managing problems.

Taped sessions of students and social workers often reveal relatively few authentic responses that underscore clients' strengths or incremental growth. This lack of positive feedback is unfortunate because, in our experience, clients' rates of change often correlate with the extent to which social workers focus on these two vital areas. If social workers consistently focus on their clients' assets and the subtle positive changes that often occur in early sessions, clients will typically invest more effort in the change process. As the rate of change accelerates, social workers can in turn focus more extensively on clients' successes, identifying and reinforcing their strengths and functional coping behaviors.

Social workers face several challenges in accrediting clients' strengths and growth, including improving their own ability to recognize and express fleeting positive feelings when clients manifest strengths or progress. Social workers must also learn to document events so that they can provide information about specific positive behaviors. Another challenge and responsibility is to teach clients to give positive feedback to one another.

To increase your ability to discern client strengths, we recommend that you and your clients construct a profile of their resources. This task may be completed with individuals, couples, families, or groups, and preferably occurs early in the helping process. In individual sessions, the social worker should ask the client to identify and list all the strengths she or he can think of. The social worker also shares observations of the client's strengths, adding them to the list, which is kept for ongoing review to add further strengths as they are discovered.

With families, couples, or groups, social workers may follow a similar procedure in assessing the strengths of individual members, but they should ask other group members to share their perceptions of strengths with each member. The social worker might also ask couples, families, or groups to identify the strengths and incremental growth of the group periodically throughout the helping process. After clients have identified their personal strengths or the strengths of the group, the social worker should elicit observations regarding their reactions to the experience. Often clients may mutually conclude that they have many more strengths than they had realized. The social worker should also explore any discomfort experienced by clients as they identify strengths, with the goal of having them acknowledge more comfortably their positive attributes and personal resources.

We further suggest that you carefully observe processes early on in sessions. Note the subtle manifestations of strengths and positive behavioral changes, systematically recording these in your progress records. Record not only the strengths and incremental growth of clients, but also whether you (or group members) focused on those changes. Keep in mind that changes often occur very subtly within a single session. For instance, clients may begin to discuss problems more openly during a later part of a session, tentatively commit to work on problems they had refused to tackle earlier, show growing trust in the social worker by confiding high-risk information about themselves, or own responsibility for the first time regarding their part in their problems. Groups and families may likewise experience growth within short periods of time. It is vital to keep your antenna finely tuned to such changes so that you do not overlook clients' progress.

RELATING ASSERTIVELY TO CLIENTS

Another aspect of relating authentically entails relating assertively to clients when a situation warrants such behavior. There are myriad reasons for relating assertively. To inspire confidence and to influence clients to follow their lead, social workers must relate in a manner that projects competence. This is especially important in the initial phase of the helping process. Clients often covertly test or check out social workers to determine whether they can understand their problems and appear competent to help them.

In conjoint or group sessions, clients may question whether the social worker is strong enough to protect them from destructive interactional processes that may occur in sessions. Indeed, family or group members generally will not fully share, risk, or commit to the helping process until they have answered this question affirmatively through consistent observation of assertive actions by the social worker.

If social workers are relaxed and demonstrate through decisive behavior that they are fully capable of handling clients' problems and providing the necessary protection and structure to control potentially chaotic or volatile processes, clients will typically relax, muster hope, and begin to work on problems. If the social worker fails to curtail dysfunctional processes that render clients vulnerable, clients will have justifiable doubts about whether they should be willing to place themselves in jeopardy and, consequently, may disengage from the helping process.

In this section, we identify guidelines that can help you to intervene assertively with clients.

Making Requests and Giving Directives

To assist clients to relate more easily and work constructively to solve their problems, social workers frequently must make requests of them. Some of these requests may involve relating in new ways during sessions. For example, social workers may ask clients to do any of the following:

1. Speak directly to each other rather than through the social worker.
2. Give feedback to others in the session.
3. Respond by checking out the meanings of others' messages, take a listening stance, or personalize messages.
4. Change the arrangement of chairs.
5. Role-play.
6. Make requests of others.
7. Take responsibility for responding in specified ways during sessions.
8. Agree to carry out defined tasks during the week.
9. Identify strengths or incremental growth for themselves or others in the group or family.

When making requests, it is important to express them firmly and decisively and to deliver them with assertive nonverbal behavior. Social workers often err by couching their requests too tentatively.

Many times, social workers' requests of clients are actually *directives*. In essence, directives are declarative statements that place the burden on clients to object if they are uncomfortable, as the following message illustrates:

Social worker: Before you answer that question, please turn your chair toward your wife. *[Social worker leans over and helps client to adjust chair. Social worker speaks to wife.]* Will you please turn your chair also, so that you can speak directly to your husband? Thank you. It's important that you be in full contact with each other while we talk.

If the social worker had given these clients a choice (e.g., "Would you like to change your chairs?"), they might not have responded affirmatively. We suggest that when you want clients to behave differently in sessions, you simply state what you would like them to do in a polite fashion. If clients verbally object to directives or display nonverbal behavior that may indicate that they have reservations about complying with a request, it is vital to respond empathically and to explore the

basis of their opposition. Such exploration often resolves fears or misgivings, freeing clients to engage in requested behavior.

Maintaining Focus and Managing Interruptions

Maintaining focus is a vital task that takes considerable skill and assertiveness on the social worker's part. It is often essential to intervene verbally to focus or refocus processes when interruptions or distractions occur. Sometimes, social workers may also respond assertively on a nonverbal level to prevent members from interrupting important processes that may need to be brought to positive conclusion, as illustrated in the following excerpt from a family session:

Kim, age 14 [in tears, talking angrily to her mother]: You hardly ever listen. At home, you just always yell at us and go to your bedroom.

Mother, Rachel: I thought I was doing better than that …

Father, Don [interrupting his wife to speak to social worker]: I think it's hard for my wife because …

Social worker [holds up hand to father in a "halt" position, while continuing to maintain eye contact with mother and daughter; speaks to Don]: Excuse me, Don. Let's allow Rachel to finish what she was saying.

Interrupting Problematic Processes

Unseasoned social workers often permit problematic processes to continue for long periods either because they lack knowledge of how to intervene or because they think they should wait until clients have completed a series of exchanges. In such instances, social workers fail to fulfill one of their major responsibilities— that is, to *guide and direct* processes and to influence participants to interact in more facilitative ways. Remember that clients often seek help because they cannot manage their problematic interactional processes. Thus, permitting them to engage at length in their usual patterns of arguing, cajoling, threatening, blaming, criticizing, and labeling each other merely exacerbates their problems. The social worker should intervene in such circumstances, teaching the clients more facilitative behaviors and guiding them to implement such behaviors in subsequent interactions.

If you decide to interrupt ongoing processes, do so decisively so that clients will listen to you or heed your directive. If you intervene unassertively, your potential to influence clients (particularly aggressive clients) will suffer, because being able to interrupt a discussion successfully demonstrates your power or influence in the relationship. If you permit clients to ignore or to circumvent your interventions to arrest problematic processes, you yield control and assume a "one-down" position in terms of the relationship to the client.

With respect to interrupting or intervening in processes, we advocate using assertive—not aggressive—behavior. You must be sensitive to the vested interests of clients, because even though you may regard certain processes as unproductive or destructive, clients may not. The timing of interruptions is therefore vital. If it is not critical to draw clients' attention to what is happening immediately, you can wait for a natural pause. If such a pause does not occur shortly, you should interrupt. You should *not* delay interrupting destructive interactional processes, however, as illustrated in the following excerpt:

Wife *[to social worker]:* I feel the children need to mind me, but every time I ask them to do something, he *[husband]* says they don't have to do it. I think we're just ruining our kids, and it's mostly his fault.

Husband: Oh—well—that shows how dumb you are.

Social worker: I'm going to interrupt you because judging each other is not likely to help us resolve these issues. Let's slow down and process what is happening about child discipline between you.

In this exchange, the social worker intervenes to refocus the discussion after just two dysfunctional responses on the clients' part. If participants do not disengage immediately, the social worker will need to use body movements that interfere with communication pathways or, in extreme instances, an exclamation such as "Time out!" to interrupt behavior. When social workers have demonstrated their intent to intervene quickly and decisively, clients will usually comply immediately when asked to disengage.

"Leaning Into" Clients' Anger

We cannot overstate the importance of openly addressing clients' anger and complaints. It is not unusual to feel defensive and threatened when such anger arises. Many social workers, especially those who are working with involuntary clients who are alleged to have harmed others, are inclined to retaliate, conveying the message, "You have no right to your anger. You have brought this on yourself. Do it my way or suffer the consequences." Responding assertively to a person's anger does not mean that you become a doormat, accepting that anger passively and submissively. Unless social workers can handle themselves assertively and competently in the face of such anger, they will lose the respect of most clients and thus their ability to help them. Further, clients may use their anger to influence and intimidate social workers just as they have done with others.

To help you respond assertively in managing clients' anger, we offer the following suggestions:

- Respond empathically to reflect clients' anger and, if possible, other underlying feelings (e.g., "I sense you're angry at me for _____ and perhaps disappointed about _____").
- Continue to explore the situation and the feelings of participants until you understand the nature of the events that inspired the angry feelings. During this exploration, you may find that the anger toward you dissipates and that clients begin to focus on themselves, assuming appropriate responsibility for their part in the situation at hand. The "real problem," as often happens, may not directly involve you.
- As you explore clients' anger, authentically express your feelings and reactions if it appears appropriate (e.g., "I didn't know you felt that way." "I want to hear how I might have contributed to this situation." "There may be some adjustments I'll want to make in my style of relating." "I'm pleased that you shared your feelings with me.").
- Apply a problem-solving approach, if appropriate, so that all concerned make adjustments to avoid similar occurrences or situations in the future.
- If a particular client expresses anger frequently and in a dysfunctional manner, you may also focus on the client's style of expressing anger, identify problems that this communicative approach may cause him or her in relationships with others, and negotiate a goal of modifying this response pattern.
- In addition to empathizing with client anger, you can model assertive setting of personal limits and boundaries. For example, you might say, "I think that I have a good idea about how you're feeling about this situation and what you would like to have be different about it. But I can't readily talk with you when you're so upset. Do you have a way of calming yourself down, or should we plan to

meet again when you feel more in control of your emotions?" Alternatively, you might say, "I have pledged to do my part to listen to and respond to the issues you have raised. I am not willing to continue to be verbally abused, however."

Saying No and Setting Limits

Many tasks that social workers perform on behalf of their clients are quite appropriate. For example, negotiating for clients and conferring with other parties and potential resources to supplement and facilitate client action are tasks that are rightly handled by social workers (Epstein, 1992). In contracting with clients, however, social workers must occasionally decline requests or set limits. This step is sometimes difficult for beginning social workers to take, as they typically want to demonstrate their willingness to help others. Commitment to helping others is a desirable quality, but it must be tempered with judgment as to when acceding to clients' requests is in the best interests of both social worker and client.

Some clients may have had past experiences that led them to believe that social workers will do most of the work required out of sessions. However, clients are often more likely to experience empowerment by increasing the scope of their actions than by having social workers perform tasks on their behalf that they can learn to do for themselves. Consequently, if social workers unthinkingly agree to take on responsibilities that clients can perform now or could perform in the future, they may reinforce passive client behavior.

Setting limits has special implications when social workers work with involuntary clients. Cingolani (1984) has noted that social workers engage in negotiated relationships with such clients. In **negotiated relationships**, social workers assume the roles of compromiser, mediator, and enforcer in addition to the more comfortable role of counselor. For example, when an involuntary client requests a "break" related to performance of a court order, the social worker must be clear about the client's choices and consequences of making those choices. He or she must also clarify what the client should expect from the social worker.

Rory [*member of domestic violence group*]: I don't think that it is fair that you report that I didn't meet for eight group sessions. I could not get off work for some of those sessions. I did all I could do.

Social worker: You did attend seven of the sessions, Rory, and made efforts to attend others. However,

the contract you signed, which was presented in court, stated that you must complete eight sessions to be certified as completing the group. I do not have the power to change that court order. Should you decide to comply with the court order, I am willing to speak with your employer to urge him to work with you to arrange your schedule so that you can meet the court order.

In his response, the social worker made it clear that he would not evade the court order. At the same time, he assured Rory that if he chose to comply with the court order, the social worker would be willing to act as a mediator to assist him with difficulties in scheduling with the employer.

Being tactfully assertive is no easier for social workers with excessive needs to please others than it is for other persons. These social workers have difficulty declining requests or setting limits when doing so is in the best interests of clients. To remedy this, such social workers may benefit by setting tasks for themselves related to increasing their assertiveness. Participating in an assertiveness training group and delving into the popular literature on assertiveness may be highly beneficial as well. Dietz and Thompson (2004) have suggested that social work has given too much emphasis to distance between clients and social workers for fear of abuse of power. In so doing, these authors suggest that social workers may abrogate possibilities of special help that powerless clients may need. We suggest that you consult with your supervisor about requests that pose special questions. In some cases, this can lead to problem solving around where else a client might be assisted to find a resource, rather than dwelling only on whether it is appropriate to get that resource from the social worker. The following are a few of the many situations in which you may need to decline clients' requests:

1. When clients invite you to participate with them socially or through social media such as Facebook or Twitter
2. When clients ask you to grant them preferential status (e.g., set lower fees than are specified by policy)
3. When clients request physical intimacy
4. When clients ask you to intercede in a situation they should handle themselves
5. When clients request a special appointment after having broken a regular appointment for an invalid reason

6. When clients ask to borrow money
7. When clients request that you conceal information about violations of probation, parole, or institutional policy
8. When spouses request that you withhold information from their partners
9. When clients disclose plans to commit crimes or acts of violence against others
10. When clients ask you to report false information to an employer or other party

In addition to declining requests, you may need to set limits with clients in situations such as the following:

1. When clients make excessive phone calls or text messages to you at home or in the office
2. When clients cancel appointments without giving advance notice
3. When clients express emotions in abusive or violent ways
4. When clients habitually seek to go beyond designated ending points of sessions
5. When clients consistently fail to abide by contracts (e.g., not paying fees or missing numerous appointments)
6. When clients make sexual overtures toward you or other staff members
7. When clients come to sessions while intoxicated or under the influence of drugs

Part of maturing professionally means learning to decline requests, set limits, and feel comfortable in doing so. As you gain experience, you will realize that you help clients as much by ensuring that they have reasonable expectations as you do by providing a concrete action for them. Modeled responses for refusing requests and for saying no to clients are found in the answers to the exercises below designed to assist social workers to relate authentically and assertively.

Of course, social workers must also assert themselves effectively with other social workers and with members of other professions. Lacking experience and sometimes confidence, beginning social workers tend to be in awe of physicians, lawyers, psychologists, and more experienced social workers. Consequently, they may relate passively or may acquiesce in plans or demands that appear unsound or unreasonable. Although it is critical to remain open to the ideas of other professionals, beginning social workers should nevertheless risk expressing their own views and asserting their own rights. Otherwise, they may know more about a given client than other professionals but fail to contribute valuable information in joint case planning.

Beginning social workers should also set limits and assert their rights by refusing to accept unreasonable referrals and inappropriate assignments. Likewise, assertiveness may be required when other professionals deny resources to which clients are entitled, refer to clients with demeaning labels, or engage in unethical conduct. In fact, being assertive is critical when you act as a client advocate, a role discussed at length in Chapter 14.

SUMMARY

This chapter should help you communicate with clients and other persons on behalf of clients with appropriate empathy, authenticity, assertiveness, and self-disclosure. Chapter 6 will build on these skills by developing your abilities in listening, focusing, and exploring. First, however, you should practice your new skills by completing the exercises in this chapter.

COMPETENCY NOTES

EP 1 Demonstrate Ethical and Professional Behavior
- Use reflection and self-regulation to manage personal values and maintain professionalism in practice situations.

EP 6 Engage with Individuals, Families, Groups, Organizations, and Communities
- Engage with individuals by using empathy, reflection, and interpersonal skills to effectively engage diverse clients and constituencies.

EP 7 Assess Individuals, Families, Groups, Organizations, and Communities
- Collect and organize data, and apply critical thinking to interpret information from clients and constituencies.

SKILL DEVELOPMENT EXERCISES
in Empathic Communication

The following exercises, which include a wide variety of actual client messages, will assist you in gaining mastery of reciprocal empathic responding (Level 3). Read each client statement and compose on paper an empathic response that captures the client's surface feelings. You may wish to use the paradigm, "You feel _____ about (or because) _____," in organizing your response before phrasing it in typical conversational language. Strive to make your responses fresh, varied, and spontaneous. To expand your repertoire of responses, we encourage you to use the lists of affective words and phrases in the chapter (see pages 100–101).

After formulating your responses, compare them with the modeled responses provided at the end of the exercises. Analyze the differences, paying particular attention to the various forms of responding and the elements that enhance the effectiveness of your own responses and the modeled responses.

Because this exercise includes 20 different client statements, we recommend that you not attempt to complete the entire exercise in one sitting but rather work through it in several sessions. Consistent practice and careful scrutiny of your responses are essential in gaining mastery of this vital skill.

Client Statements

1. **Father of developmentally disabled child, age 14** [who is becoming difficult to manage]: We just don't know what to do with Henry. We've always wanted to take care of him, but we've reached the point where we're not sure it's doing any good for him or for us. Henry has grown so strong—we just can't restrain him anymore. He hit my wife last week when she wouldn't take him to the store late at night—I was out of town—and she's still bruised. She's afraid of him now, and I have to admit I'm getting that way, too.

2. **Latino** [living in urban barrio]: Our children do better in school if they teach Spanish, not just English. We're afraid our children are behind because they don't understand English so good. And we don't know how to help them. Our people have been trying to get a bilingual program, but the school board pays no attention to us.

3. **Female client, age 31:** Since my husband left town with another woman, I get lonely and depressed a lot of the time. I find myself wondering whether something is wrong with me or whether men just can't be trusted.

4. **Mother** [to child welfare protective services worker on doorstep during initial home visit]: Who'd want to make trouble for me by accusing me of not taking care of my kids? [Tearfully.] Maybe I'm not the best mother in the world, but I try. There

are a lot of kids around here that aren't cared for as well as mine.

5. **Male ninth-grade student** [to school social worker]: I feel like I'm a real zero. In sports I'm no good. When they choose sides, I'm always the last one chosen. A couple of times they've actually got into a fight over who doesn't have to choose me.

6. **Member of abused women's group:** That last month I was living in mortal fear of Art. He'd get that hateful look in his eyes, and I'd know he was going to let me have it. The last time I was afraid he was going to kill me—and he might have, if his brother hadn't dropped in. I'm afraid to go back to him. But what do I do? I can't stay here much longer!

7. **Male, age 34** [to marital therapist]: Just once I'd like to show my wife I can accomplish something without her prodding me. That's why I haven't told her I'm coming to see you. If she knew it, she'd try to take charge and call all the shots.

8. **African American man** [in a group session]: All I want is to be accepted as a person. When I get hired, I want it to be for what I'm capable of doing—not just because of my skin color. That's as phony and degrading as not being hired because of my skin color. I just want to be accepted for who I am.

9. **Client in a state prison** [to rehabilitation worker]: They treat you like an animal in here—herd you around like a damn cow. I know I've got to do my time, but sometimes I feel like I can't stand it any longer—like something's building up in me that's going to explode.

10. **Client** [to mental health worker]: I don't have any pleasant memories of my childhood. It seems like just so much empty space. I can remember my father watching television and staring at me with a blank look—as though I didn't exist.

11. **Patient in hospital** [to medical social worker]: I know Dr. Brown is a skilled surgeon, and he tells me not to worry—that there's very little risk in this surgery. I know I should feel reassured, but to tell you the truth, I'm just plain panic-stricken.

12. **Female member, age 29** [in marital therapy group]: I'd like to know what it's like with the rest of you. Hugh and I get into nasty fights because I feel he doesn't help me when I really need help. He tells me there's no way he's going to do women's work! That really irritates me. I start feeling like I'm just supposed to be his slave.

13. **Male college student, age 21:** Francine says she's going to call me, but she never does—I have to do

all the texting, or I probably wouldn't hear from her at all. It seems so one-sided. If I didn't need her so much I'd ask her what kind of game she's playing. I wonder if she isn't pretty selfish.

14. **White student, age 14** *[to school social worker]*: To be really honest, I don't like the black kids in our school. They pretty much stay to themselves, and they aren't friendly to whites. I don't know what to expect or how to act around them. I'm antsy when they're around and—well, to be honest—I'm scared I'll do something they won't like, and they'll jump me.

15. **Single female, age 27** *[to mental health worker]*: I've been taking this class on the joys of womanhood. Last time the subject was how to catch a man. I can see I've been doing a lot of things wrong. But I won't lower myself to playing games with men. If that's what it takes, I guess I'll always be single.

16. **Married male, age 29** *[to marital therapist]*: Sexually, I'm unfulfilled in my marriage. At times I've had thoughts of trying sex with men. That idea kind of intrigues me. My wife and I can talk about sex all right, but it doesn't get better.

17. **Married female, age 32** *[to family social worker]*: I love my husband and children, and I don't know what I'd do without them. Yet on days like last Thursday, I feel I could just climb the walls. I want to run away from all of them and never come back.

18. **Blind female** *[to other blind group members]*: You know, it really offends me when people praise me or make a fuss over me for doing something routine that anyone else could do. It makes me feel like I'm on exhibition. I want to be recognized for being competent—not for being blind.

19. **Male teacher** *[to mental health social worker]*: I have this thing about not being able to accept compliments. A friend told me about how much of a positive impact I've had on several students over the years. I couldn't accept that and feel good. My thought was, "You must be mistaken. I've never had that kind of effect on anyone."

20. **Lesbian, age 26** *[to private social worker]*: The girls at the office were talking about lesbians the other day and about how repulsive the very thought of lesbianism was to them. How do you think I felt?

Modeled Social Worker Responses

1. "So you're really in a difficult situation. You've wanted to keep Henry at home, but in light of his recent aggression and his increasing strength, you're becoming really frightened and wonder if

other arrangements wouldn't be better for both you and him."

2. "I can see you're worried about how your children are doing in school and believe they need a bilingual program."

3. "It's been a real blow—your husband leaving you for another woman—and you've just felt so alone. And you find yourself dwelling on the painful question, 'Is something wrong with me, or is it that you just can't trust men?'"

4. "This is very upsetting for you. You seem to be saying that it's not fair being turned in when you believe you take care of your children. Please understand I'm not accusing you of neglecting your children. But I do have to investigate complaints. It may be that I'll be able to turn in a positive report. I hope so. But I do need to talk with you further. May I come in?"

5. "It's humiliating to you to feel so left out and be the last guy chosen."

6. "It sounds as though you lived in terror that last month and literally feared for your life. You were wise to remove yourself when you did. A number of other women in the group have had similar experiences and are facing the same dilemma about what to do now. As group members, each of us can be helpful to other group members in thinking through what's the best course of action. In the meantime, you have a safe place to stay and some time to plan."

7. "Sounds like you get pretty annoyed, thinking about your wife's prodding and trying to take charge. It seems important right now that you prove to her and to yourself you can do something on your own."

8. "I gather you're fed up with having people relate to you because of your race instead of being accepted as an individual—as yourself."

9. "If I understand you, you feel degraded by the way you're treated—as though you're less than a human being. And that really gets to you."

10. "From what you say, I get a picture of you just feeling so all alone as you were growing up—as though you didn't feel very important to anyone, especially your father."

11. "So intellectually, you tell yourself not to worry, that you're in good hands. Still, on another level you have to admit you're terrified of that operation. *[Brief pause.]* Your fear is pretty natural, though. Most people who are honest with themselves experience fear."

12. "So the two of you get into some real struggles over differences in your views about what is

reasonable of you to expect from Hugh. You seem to be saying you very much resent his refusal to pitch in—that it's not fair to have to carry the burden alone. Hugh, I'd be interested in hearing your views. Then we can hear how other members deal with this kind of situation."

13. "Sounds like part of you is saying that you have a right to expect more from Francine—that you don't feel good about always having to be the one to take the initiative. You also seem to feel you'd like to confront her with what she's doing, but you're uneasy about doing that because you don't want to risk losing her."

14. "So, you're uncomfortable around your black classmates and just don't know how to read them. I gather you kind of walk on eggshells when they're around for fear you'll blow it."

15. "There is a lot of conflicting advice around these days about how men and women should relate to one another, and it is hard to figure out what to believe. You know you don't want to play games, yet that is what the class is telling you to do if you don't want to be single."

16. "Things don't get better despite your talks, and you get pretty discouraged. Sometimes you find yourself wondering if you'd get sexual fulfillment with men, and that appeals to you in some ways."

17. "So even though you care deeply for your family, there are days when you just feel so overwhelmed you'd like to buy a one-way ticket out of all the responsibility."

18. "Are you saying that you feel singled out and demeaned when people flatter you for doing things anyone could do? It bothers you, and you wish people would recognize you for being competent?"

19. "In a way, you seem to be saying that you don't feel comfortable with compliments because you feel you don't really deserve them. It's like you feel you don't do anything worthy of a compliment."

20. "You must have felt extremely uncomfortable believing that they would condemn you if they knew. It must have been most painful for you."

SKILL DEVELOPMENT EXERCISES
in Responding Authentically and Assertively

The following exercises will assist you in gaining skill in responding authentically and assertively. Read each client statement, and then formulate a written response as though you were the social worker in the situation presented. Compare your written responses with the modeled responses that follow, keeping in mind that these models represent just a few of the many possible responses that would be appropriate.

You will find additional exercises that require authentic and assertive responding in Chapter 17 (in the confrontation exercises) and in Chapter 18 (in the exercises concerned with managing relational reactions and resistance).

Client Statements

1. *Marital partner* [in third conjoint marital therapy session]: It must be really nice being a marriage counselor—knowing just what to do and not having problems like ours.

2. *Female client, age 23* [in first session]: Some of my problems are related to my church's stand on birth control. Tell me, are you a Catholic?

3. *Client* [fifth session]: You look like you're having trouble staying awake. [Social worker is drowsy from having taken an antihistamine for an allergy.]

4. *Adult group member* [to social worker in second session; group members have been struggling to determine the agenda for the session]: I wish you'd tell us what we should talk about. Isn't that your job? We're just getting nowhere.

5. *Male client* [sixth session]: Say, my wife and I are having a fundraiser next Wednesday. We'd like to have you and your wife come.

6. *Client* [calls 3 hours before scheduled appointment]: I've had the flu the past couple of days, but I feel like I'm getting over it. Do you think I should come today?

7. *Client* [scheduled time for ending appointment has arrived, and social worker has already moved to end session; in previous sessions, client has tended to stay beyond designated ending time]: What we were talking about reminded me of something I wanted to discuss today but forgot. I'd like to discuss it briefly, if you don't mind.

8. *Client* [has just completed behavioral rehearsal involving talking with employer and played role beyond expectations of social worker].

9. *Female client* [tenth interview]: I've really felt irritated with you during the week. When I brought up taking the correspondence course in art, all you could talk about was how some correspondence courses are rip-offs and that I could take courses at a college for less money. I knew that, but I've

checked into this correspondence course, and it's well worth the money. You put me down, and I've resented it.

10. *Client [seventh session]:* You seem uptight today. Is something bothering you? *[Social worker has been under strain associated with recent death of a parent and assisting surviving parent, who has been distraught.]*

11. *Client [eighth session]:* I really feel as if we have connected through these sessions. I would like to stay in touch with you when we are done, through Facebook or Twitter.

Modeled Social Worker Responses

1. *[Smiling.]* "Well, I must admit it's helpful. But I want you to know that marriage is not easy for marriage counselors either. We have our rough spots, too. I have to work like everyone else to keep my marriage alive and growing."

2. "I gather you're wondering what my stand is and whether I can understand and accept your feelings. I've worked with many Catholics and have been able to understand their problems. Would it trouble you if I weren't Catholic?"

3. "You're very observant. I have been sleepy these past few minutes, and I apologize for that. I had to take an antihistamine before lunch, and a side effect of the drug is I can get drowsy. My sleepiness has nothing to do with you. If I move around a little, the drowsiness passes."

4. "I can sense your frustration and your desire to firm up an agenda. If I made the decision, though, it might not fit for many of you and I'd be taking over the group's power to make its own decisions. Perhaps it would be helpful if the group followed the decision-by-consensus approach we discussed in our first session."

5. "Thank you for the invitation. I'm flattered that you'd ask me. I appreciate your asking, but I must decline your invitation. If I were to socialize with you while you're seeing me professionally, it would conflict with my role, and I couldn't be as helpful to you. I hope you can understand my not accepting."

6. "I appreciate your calling to let me know. I think it would be better to change our appointment until you're sure you've recovered. Quite frankly, I don't want to risk being exposed to the flu, which I hope you can understand. I have a time open on the day after tomorrow. I'll set it aside for you, if you'd like, in the event you're fully recovered by then."

7. "I'm sorry I don't have the time to discuss the matter today. Let's save it for next week, and I'll make a note that you wanted to explore this issue. We'll have to stop here today because I'm scheduled for another appointment."

8. "I want to share with you how impressed I was with how you asserted yourself and came across so positively. If you'd been with your boss, he'd have been impressed, too."

9. "I'm glad you shared those feelings with me. I can see I owe you an apology. You're right, I didn't explore whether you'd checked into the program, and I made some incorrect assumptions. I guess I was overly concerned about your not being ripped off because I know others who have been by taking correspondence courses. But I can see I made a mistake because you had already looked into the course."

10. "Thank you for asking. Yes, I have been under some strain this past week. My mother died suddenly, which was a shock, and my father is taking it very hard. It's created a lot of pressure for me, but I think I can keep it from spilling over into our session. If I'm not able to focus on you, I will stop the session. Or if you don't feel that I'm fully with you, please let me know. I don't want to short-change you."

11. "I appreciate how positively you are feeling about our sessions together. I greatly admire how far you have come and wonder if your asking about maintaining a connection is in part about wanting that progress to continue. We will want to plan for how you can receive assistance should the need arise after we end our sessions. I have great confidence in your ability to continue deal with concerns and get help again if needed. You can also send letters or emails to this agency, and they will forward them to me."

Answers to Exercise in Identifying Surface and Underlying Feelings

1. *Apparent feelings:* unimportant, neglected, disappointed, hurt. *Probable deeper feelings:* rejected, abandoned, forsaken, deprived, lonely, depressed.

2. *Apparent feelings:* unloved, insecure, confused, embarrassed, left out or excluded. *Probable deeper feelings:* hurt, resentful, unvalued, rejected, taken for granted, degraded, doubting own desirability.

3. *Apparent feelings:* chagrined, disappointed in self, discouraged, letting children down, perplexed.

Probable deeper feelings: guilty, inadequate, crummy, sense of failure, out of control, fear of damaging children.

4. *Apparent feelings:* frustrated, angry, bitter. *Probable deeper feelings:* depressed, discouraged, hopeless.

Answers to Exercises to Discriminate Levels of Empathic Responding

CLIENT STATEMENT

Client 1	
Response	*Level*
1.	2
2.	1
3.	1
4.	3
5.	2
6.	2
7.	4
8.	1

CLIENT STATEMENT

Client 2		Client 3	
Response	*Level*	*Response*	*Level*
1.	0	1.	1
2.	3	2.	4
3.	1	3.	2
4.	2	4.	2
5.	4	5.	2
6.	0	6.	4
7.	3	7.	0
8.	2	8.	1

Client 4	
Response	*Level*
1.	1
2.	2
3.	1
4.	0

Verbal Following, Exploring, and Focusing Skills

Chapter Overview

Chapter 6 introduces verbal following skills and their uses in exploring client concerns and focusing. This chapter includes skills for accurately following and reflecting what clients are expressing and feeling about their situation. It also introduces skills for helping clients to consider taking action about concerns for which they have mixed feelings. These skills are the building blocks for social workers' efforts to communicate empathically with clients. In addition to being helpful in work with clients in micro practice, such skills are useful at the mezzo level in work on behalf of clients, through advocacy, and in work with colleagues and other professionals. This chapter also includes references to videos accompanying the text.

As a result of reading this chapter, you will be able to:

- Construct reflective responses that respond to content and emotions, including both simple reflections and double-sided reflections.
- Construct furthering responses, and know when to use them.
- Construct open-ended questions, and know when to use them.
- Construct closed-ended questions, and know when to use them.
- Construct responses to seek concreteness.
- Construct responses to provide and maintain focus.
- Construct summarizing responses, and know when to provide them.

EPAS Competencies in Chapter 6

This chapter will give you the information needed to meet the following practice competencies:

- Competency 2: Engage Diversity and Difference in Practice
- Competency 6: Engage with Individuals, Families, Groups, Organizations, and Communities
- Competency 7: Assess Individuals, Families, Groups, Organizations, and Communities

MAINTAINING PSYCHOLOGICAL CONTACT WITH CLIENTS AND EXPLORING THEIR PROBLEMS

Verbal following involves the use and sometimes blending of discrete skills that enable social workers to maintain psychological contact with clients on a moment-by-moment basis and to convey accurate understanding of their messages. Moreover, verbal following behavior takes into account two performance variables that are essential to satisfaction and continuance on the part of the client:

EP 6

1. **Stimulus-response congruence:** The extent to which social workers' responses provide feedback to clients that their messages are accurately received.
2. **Content relevance:** The extent to which the content of social workers' responses is perceived by clients as relevant to their substantive concerns.

Skills in following have been related to client continuance (Rosen, 1972). Further, incongruent responses to clients have been more associated with discontinuance (Duehn & Proctor, 1977). Continued use of questions and other responses that are not associated with previous client messages and that do not relate to the client's substantive concerns contribute to consistent client dissatisfaction. One study of the outcome of working with persons with drinking problems found that two-thirds of the variance of outcomes after six months was predicted by the degree of empathy demonstrated by the counselors (Miller, 1980). Effective use of attending behaviors and demonstrated empathy should enhance motivational congruence (the fit between client motivation and social worker goals), a factor that is associated with better outcomes in social work effectiveness studies (Reid & Hanrahan, 1982). Employing responses that directly relate to client messages and concerns thus enhances client satisfaction, fosters continuance, and greatly contributes to the establishment of a viable working relationship. Studies of practice by social work students of the skills taught in this book have shown that while most of the practice skills of second-year students were not significantly more advanced than those of first-year students, the second-year students were better able to focus on tasks and goals, an objective of this chapter, compared with first-year students (Deal & Brintzenhofeszok, 2004).

Clients do not always perceive social worker questions about concerns as helpful. While noting the differences within Asian and Pacific Islander groups, including those with immigrant and resident status, Fong (2007) notes that some Asian clients (as well as members of other groups) may express emotional conflicts in a physical form. In such cases, the social worker must be respectful of the client's experience with the physical concern as well as explain the rationale for asking questions about factors such as family background that are not directly related to the physical complaint (Cormier & Nurius, 2003). The linkage of these issues to their current symptoms is not clear to many clients. Some Asian clients conceive of mental distress as the result of a physiological disorder or character flaws. This issue must be dealt with sensitively before any useful therapeutic work can occur (Fong, 2007). Similarly, clients who are members of historically oppressed groups may perceive questions as interrogations not designed to help them with their own concerns but rather as ways to explore whether they have broken the law or endangered their children. That is, they may not readily assume that the social worker is acting as their agent or advocate but rather as an agent of the state or majority community and hence a potential danger to their family (Sue, 2006).

VIDEO CASE EXAMPLE

In the video "Getting Back to Shakopee," the potential client, Valerie, has been referred to an employee assistance program by her employer. She asks many questions about who will gain access to the information shared in their sessions. These questions reflect a concern that her answers about child care and adult supervision could result in a child welfare investigation.

In addition to enabling social workers to maintain close psychological contact with clients, verbal following skills serve two other important functions in the helping process. First, they yield rich personal information, allowing social workers to explore clients' problems in depth. Second, they enable social workers to focus selectively on components of the clients' experiences and on dynamics in the helping process that facilitate positive client change.

EP 2

The following pages introduce a variety of skills for verbally following and exploring clients' problems. Some of these skills are easily mastered. Others require more effort to acquire. The exercises in the body of the chapter will assist you in acquiring proficiency in these important skills. Although empathic responding is the most vital skill for verbally following clients' messages, we have not included it in this chapter because it was discussed in detail in Chapter 5. Later, we discuss the blending of empathic responses with other verbal following skills to bolster your ability to focus on and fully explore relevant client problems.

VERBAL FOLLOWING SKILLS

EP 6

The discrete skills highlighted in this chapter include seven types of responses:

1. Furthering responses
2. Reflection responses
3. Closed-ended responses
4. Open-ended responses
5. Seeking concreteness
6. Providing and maintaining focus
7. Summarizing

We will discuss each of these skills in turn.

FURTHERING RESPONSES

Furthering responses indicate social workers are listening attentively and encourage the client to verbalize. There are two types of furthering responses: *minimal prompts* and *accent responses.*

Minimal Prompts

Minimal prompts signal the social worker's attentiveness and encourage the client to continue verbalizing. They can be either nonverbal or verbal.

Nonverbal minimal prompts consist of nodding the head, using facial expressions, or employing gestures that convey receptivity, interest, and commitment to understanding. They implicitly convey the message, "I am with you; please continue."

Verbal minimal prompts consist of brief messages that convey interest and encourage or request expanded verbalizations along the lines of the client's previous expressions. These messages include "Yes," "I see," "But?," "Mm-mmm," "Tell me more," "And then what happened?," "And?," "Please go on," "Tell me more, please," and other similar brief messages that affirm the appropriateness of what the client has been saying and prompt him or her to continue.

Accent Responses

Accent responses (Hackney & Cormier, 2005) involve repeating, in a questioning tone of voice or with emphasis, a word or a short phrase. Suppose a client says, "I've really had it with the way my supervisor at work is treating me." The social worker might reply, "Had it?" This short response is intended to prompt further elaboration by the client.

REFLECTION RESPONSES

Reflections are used to respond to both content messages and affect. There are several forms of reflection. We will discuss simple, complex, and double-sided reflections, as well as reflections with a twist.

Reflections of Content

Reflections of content emphasize the cognitive aspects of client messages, such as situations, ideas, objects, or persons (Hackney & Cormier, 2005).[1] Reflecting a content message in response to a client's thoughts does not mean that you agree with or condone those thoughts. The following are four examples of reflections of content:

Example 1

Senior client: I don't want to get into a living situation in which I will not be able to make choices on my own.

Social worker: So independence is a very important issue for you.

Example 2

Client: I went to the doctor today for a final checkup, and she said that I was doing fine.

Social worker: She gave you a clean bill of health, then.

Example 3

Native American client: The idea of a promotion makes me feel good; I could earn more money.

Social worker: So advancement would show that you are being recognized for the quality of your work.

Example 4

Managed care utilization reviewer: We don't think that your patient's condition justifies the level of service that you recommend.

Social worker: So you feel that my documentation does not justify the need that I have recommended according to the approval guidelines you are working from.

VIDEO CASE EXAMPLE

In the video "Elder Grief Assessment," the social worker asks a recently widowed senior client what she would like to see occur at the end of their work together. The client replies: "I would like to feel better myself, the house looking better, the yard looking better, I would like to go grocery shopping when I want to, get to the doctor without calling someone." The social worker, Kathy, paraphrases the content by saying, "You would like to remain independent."

Note that in Example 4, reflection of content is used as part of the communication with a person whose opinion is important because it relates to delivering client services—the health insurance care manager (Strom-Gottfried, 1998a). When employed sparingly, reflection of content may be interspersed with other facilitative responses to prompt client expression. Used to excess, however, such reflection produces a mimicking effect. Reflection is helpful when social workers want to bring focus to an idea or a situation for client consideration.

Exercises in Reflection of Content

In the following exercises, read each client/colleague statement and formulate written responses that reflect the content of the statement. Modeled responses for these exercises appear at the end of the chapter (see page 166).

Client/Colleague Statements

1. ***Client:*** I can't talk to people. I just completely freeze up in a group.
2. ***Wife:*** I think that in the last few weeks I've been able to listen much more often to my husband and children.
3. ***Senior client:*** It wasn't so difficult to adjust to this place because the people who run it are helpful

and friendly and I am able to make contacts easily—I've always been a people person.
4. ***Mother*** *[speaking about daughter]:* When it comes right down to it, I think I'm to blame for a lot of her problems.
5. ***Member of treatment team:*** I just don't see how putting more services into this family makes sense. The mother is not motivated, and the kids are better off away from her. This family has been messed up forever.

Reflections of Affect

Reflections of affect focus attention on the affective part of the communication (Cormier, Nurius, & Osborn, 2009). In reflections of affect, social workers relate with responses that accurately capture clients' affect and help them reflect on and sort through their feelings. Sometimes social workers may choose to direct the discussion away from feelings for therapeutic purposes. For instance, a social worker might believe that a chronically depressed client who habitually expresses discouragement and disillusionment would benefit by focusing less on feelings and more on actions to alleviate the distress. When the social worker chooses to deemphasize feelings, paraphrases that reflect content are helpful and appropriate.

Forms of Reflections

Simple reflections, which identify the emotions expressed by the client, are a heritage from nondirective, client-centered counseling. That is, they simply identify the emotion. They do not take a stand or attempt to help the client deal with the emotion. They do not go beyond what the client has said or directly implied (Moyers et al., 2003).

VIDEO CASE EXAMPLE

In the video "How Can I Help?," social worker Peter Dimock works with Julie, a client who is recovering from drug use and is involved with the child welfare system. When Julie shares her frustration about all the things she has to do on her case plan, Peter responds with a simple reflection that stays close to her message of being overwhelmed.

Julie: "Well it's just really hard getting around with baby and I just, you know, I've got a lot of stuff that I'm supposed to be doing for my case plan and I just am having a really hard time getting to all the places on time."

Peter: "Well you've been pretty stressed, it sounds like. Having to do all these things and get around and make it to all of your appointments, it's pretty overwhelming."

Complex reflections go beyond what the client has directly stated or implied, adding substantial meaning or emphasis to convey a more complex picture. These reflections may *add content* that focuses on meanings or feelings that the client did not directly express (Moyers et al., 2003). For example, when a teenaged client said, "My mother really expects a lot from me," a social worker made a response that added implied content by saying, "She has high expectations for you; she thinks that you have a lot of ability." *Verbalizing an unspoken emotion* is a form of reflection that names an emotion that the client has implied but not stated. When a teenaged client reflects on what it feels like to be new to her school by saying, "I'm new here. I don't know anyone. I just try to stick to myself and stay out of trouble," the social worker could verbalize, "That sounds to me as if it could be a little lonely," to tune in to the unspoken emotion of sadness.

A **reframe** is another form of adding content. Here, the social worker puts the client's response in a different light beyond what the client had considered (Moyers et al., 2003). For example, when a client reported on earlier drug treatment experience, he emphasized failure, saying, "I have gone through treatment three or four times. Maybe one of these times, I will get it right." The social worker chose not to agree with the failure message but rather reframed to say, "It sounds as if you have persisted, trying treatment again after earlier disappointments; you haven't given up on yourself."

Sometimes, the reflection can use a metaphor or simile to paint a picture of what the client has stated. For example, when a client commented about his job, "I just do the same thing every day, nothing ever changes or ever gets better, always the same," the social worker responded, "It sounds like a rat in a maze" (Moyers et al., 2003). Sometimes the reflection might focus on *amplification*, either strengthening or weakening the intensity of client expression (Moyers et al., 2003). For example, a client shared, "I am disappointed with how

long this has taken," and the social worker chose to emphasize the strength of the implied feeling by saying, "You are really frustrated and exhausted by all the time you have put into this with little to show for it." On the other hand, when a client expressed doubts about her abilities, saying, "I never get anything right," the social worker chose to agree but weaken its intensity, "Sometimes you doubt whether you can succeed."

Sometimes clients express indecision and conflict between several alternatives. In such circumstances, it is possible to present a **double-sided reflection** that captures both sides of the dilemma that is fostering ambivalence about acting (Miller & Rollnick, 2002). For example, a teen parent had expressed that she wanted to succeed both in school and as a parent and one day become a probation officer or social worker. On the other hand, in their discussion she had reported frequent instances of verbal and physical altercations at school and gang involvement. She described members of the gang as members of her family. In a double-sided reflection, the social worker tried to identify the conflicting factors that make consistent decision making difficult. The social worker responded, "Rhonda, it sounds as if part of you is doing your best to succeed in school and act as a responsible parent and plan for the future. Another part of you is conflicted about wanting to be true to your friends and, as you describe them, family members, who are members of the gang."

VIDEO CASE EXAMPLE

At a later point in the video "How Can I Help?," Julie is commenting on how she is torn about returning to school to get a GED, seeing both advantages and disadvantages. She says, "I don't know, I guess it would be a good accomplishment, but I just, I don't know, I just don't think, I don't just think I can do it, like, it's just hard. I don't know." The social worker, Peter, reflects the two sides of her feelings by saying, "So it's important to you on one hand, and then on the other hand, you don't feel confident in your ability to do it. Is that true?"

Reflections with a twist are reflections in which the social worker agrees in essence with the dilemma expressed by the client but changes the emphasis, perhaps to indicate that the dilemma is not unsolvable but rather that the client has not at this time solved it

(Miller & Rollnick, 2013). For example, in the previous situation with Rhonda, the social worker might add, "It sounds, Rhonda, as if at this point in time you don't feel that you can make a decision about what you are going to do about interacting with your friends in the gang."

These variations on reflections come from the **motivational interviewing (MI) approach** (Miller & Rollnick, 2013). They are useful in circumstances in which clients or potential clients are considering taking an action but have not decided on what to do. Rather than labeling such behavior as resistance, MI considers ambivalence as an important and useful step in deciding whether to address a situation. From the stages of change approach, such circumstances are described as being in a state of either **precontemplation**, in which a person has not decided whether an issue exists or whether they wish to address it, or **contemplation**, in which they are aware of an issue but have not decided whether to take action (De Clemente & Velasquez, 2002). These circumstances occur frequently in social work practice, but not always. Hence, the skills are presented here as important and useful adjuncts to reflection skills that can be applied when, in the course of exploration, potential ambivalence about considering an issue or taking action on it emerges. The spirit of MI is consistent with social work values of self-determination at this point in presenting the role of the helper as addressing ambivalence and helping the client consider whether he or she wishes to take action, without exerting pressure on that decision (Miller & Rollnick, 2013).

Exercises with Reflections of Affect

In the following exercises, read each client/colleague statement and formulate written responses that reflect the affective state of clients. Modeled responses for these exercises appear at the end of the chapter (see pages 166–167).

Client/Colleague Statements

1. *Client:* Whenever I get into an argument with my mother, I always end up losing. I guess I'm still afraid of her.
2. *Mother [participating in a welfare-to-work program]:* I don't know how they can expect me to be a good mother and make school appointments, supervise my kids, and put in all these work hours.
3. *Terminally ill cancer patient:* Some days I am really angry because I'm only 46 years old and

there are so many more things I wanted to do. Other days, I feel kind of defeated, like this is what I get for smoking two packs of cigarettes a day for 25 years.

4. *Elementary school student:* Kids pick on me at school. They are mean. If they try to hurt me, then I try to hurt them back.
5. *Husband:* I just can't decide what to do. If I go ahead with the divorce, I'll probably lose custody of the kids—and I won't be able to see them very much. If I don't, though, I'll have to put up with the same old thing. I don't think my wife is going to change.

CLOSED- AND OPEN-ENDED RESPONSES

Generally used to elicit specific information, **closed-ended questions** define a topic and restrict the client's response to a few words or a simple yes or no answer. Typical examples of closed-ended questions follow:

EP 7

- *"When did you obtain your divorce?"*
- *"Do you have any sexual difficulties in your marriage?"*
- *"When did you last have a physical examination?"*
- *"Is your health insurance Medicare?"*

Although closed-ended questions restrict the client and elicit limited information, in many instances these responses are both appropriate and helpful. Later in this chapter, we discuss how and when to use this type of response effectively.

In contrast to closed-ended responses, which circumscribe client messages, **open-ended questions** and statements invite expanded expression and leave the client free to express what seems most relevant and important. For example:

Social worker: You've mentioned your daughter. Tell me how she enters into your problem.
Client: I don't know what to do. Sometimes I think she is just pushing me so that she can go live with her father. When I ask her to help around the house, she won't, and says that she doesn't owe me anything. When I try to insist on her helping, it just ends up in an ugly scene without anything being accomplished. It makes me feel so helpless.

In this example, the social worker's open-ended question prompted the client to expand on the details of the problems with her daughter, including a description of her daughter's behavior, her own efforts to cope, and her present sense of defeat. The information contained in the message is typical of the richness of data obtained through open-ended responding.

In circumstances like the example of a conversation with a managed care utilization reviewer noted earlier, the social worker can use an open-ended question to attempt to explore common ground that can lead to a mutually beneficial resolution:

Social worker [to managed care utilization reviewer]: Can you clarify for me how appropriate coverage is determined for situations such as the one I have described?

Some open-ended responses are unstructured, leaving the topic to the client's choosing (e.g., "Tell me what you would like to discuss today" or "What else can you tell me about the problems that you're experiencing?"). Other open-ended responses are structured such that the social worker defines the topic to be discussed but leaves the client free to respond in any way that he or she wishes (e.g., "You've mentioned feeling ashamed about the incident that occurred between you and your son. I'd be interested in hearing more about that."). Still other open-ended responses fall along a continuum between structured and unstructured, giving the client leeway to answer with a few words or to elaborate with more information (e.g., "How willing are you to do this?").

Social workers may formulate open-ended responses either by asking a question or by giving a polite command. Suppose a terminally ill cancer patient said, "The doctor thinks I could live about six or seven months now. It could be less; it could be more. It's just an educated guess, he told me." The social worker could respond by asking, "How are you feeling about that prognosis?" Polite commands have the same effect as direct questions in requesting information but are less forceful and involve greater finesse. Similar in nature are **embedded questions** that do not take the form of a question but embody a request for information. Examples of embedded questions include "I'm curious about …," "I'm wondering if …," and "I'm interested in knowing.…"

Open-ended questions often start with "What" or "How." "Why" questions are often unproductive because they may ask for reasons, motives, or causes that are obvious, obscure, or unknown to the client. Asking how ("How did that happen?") rather than why ("Why did that happen?") often elicits far richer information regarding client behavior and patterns.

Exercises in Identifying Closed- and Open-Ended Responses

The following exercises will assist you in differentiating between closed- and open-ended messages. Identify each statement with either a C for a closed-ended question or an O for an open-ended question. Turn to the end of the chapter (page 167) to check your answers.

1. "Did your mother ask you to see me because of the problem you had with the principal?"
2. "When John says that to you, what do you experience inside?"
3. "You said you're feeling fed up and you're just not sure that pursuing a reconciliation is worth your trouble. Could you elaborate?"
4. "When is your court date?"

Now read the following client statements and respond by writing open-ended responses to them. Avoid using *why* questions. Examples of open-ended responses to these messages appear at the end of the chapter (see page 167).

Client Statements

1. **Client:** Whenever I'm in a group with Ralph, I find myself saying something that will let him know that I am smart, too.
2. **Client:** I have always had my parents call for me about appointments and other things I might mess up.
3. **Teenager** [speaking of a previous probation counselor]: He sure let me down. And I really

trusted him. He knows a lot about me because I spilled my guts.

4. **Group nursing home administrator:** I think that we are going to have to move Gladys to another, more suitable kind of living arrangement. We aren't able to provide the kind of care that she needs.

The next sections of this chapter explain how you can blend open-ended and reflective responses to keep a discussion focused on a specific topic. In preparation for that, respond to the next two client messages by formulating a reflection followed by an open-ended question that encourages the client to elaborate on the same topic.

5. **Unwed teenage girl seeking abortion** [brought in by her mother, who wishes to discuss birth alternatives]: I feel like you are all tied up with my mother, trying to talk me out of what I have decided to do.

6. **Client:** Life is such a hassle, and it doesn't seem to have any meaning or make sense. I just don't know whether I want to try figuring it out any longer.

The difference between closed-ended and open-ended responses may seem obvious to you, particularly if you completed the preceding exercises. It has been our experience, however, that social workers have difficulty in actual sessions in determining whether their responses are open-ended or closed-ended, in observing the differential effect of these two types of responses in yielding rich and relevant data, and in deciding which of the two types of responses is appropriate at a given moment. We recommend, therefore, that as you converse with your associates, you practice drawing them out by employing open-ended responses and noting how they respond. We also recommend that you use the form provided at the end of the chapter (see page 167) to assess both the frequency and the appropriateness of your closed- and open-ended responses in several taped client sessions.

Discriminant Use of Closed- and Open-Ended Responses

Beginning social workers typically ask an excessive number of closed-ended questions, many of which block communication or are inefficient or irrelevant to the helping process. When this occurs, the session tends to take on the flavor of an interrogation, with the social worker bombarding the client with questions and taking responsibility for maintaining verbalization. Notice what happens in the following excerpt from a recording of a social worker interviewing an institutionalized youth:

Social worker: I met your mother yesterday. Did she come all the way from Colorado to see you?

Client: Yeah.

Social worker: It seems to me that she must really care about you to take the bus and make the trip up here to see you. Don't you think so?

Client: I suppose so.

Social worker: Did the visit with her go all right?

Client: Fine. We had a good time.

Social worker: You had said you were going to talk to her about a possible home visit. Did you do that?

Client: Yes.

When closed-ended responses are used to elicit information in lieu of open-ended responses, as in the preceding example, many more discrete interchanges will occur. However, the client's responses will be brief and the information yield will be markedly lower.

Open-ended responses often elicit the same data as closed-ended questions but draw out much more information and elaboration of the problem from the client. The following two examples contrast open-ended and closed-ended responses that address the same topic with a given client. To appreciate the differences in the richness of information yielded by these contrasting responses, compare the likely client responses elicited by such questions to the closed-ended questions used in the previous section.

Example 1

Closed-ended: "Did she come all the way from Colorado to see you?"

Open-ended: "Tell me about your visit with your mother."

Example 2

Closed-ended: "Did you talk with her about a possible home visit?"

Open-ended: "How did your mother respond when you talked about a possible home visit?"

Because open-ended responses elicit more information than closed-ended ones, frequent use of the former technique increases the efficiency of data gathering.

In fact, the richness of information revealed by the client is directly proportional to the frequency with which open-ended responses are employed. Frequent use of open-ended responses also fosters a smoothly flowing session; consistently asking closed-ended questions, by contrast, may result in a fragmented, discontinuous process.

Closed-ended questions are used chiefly to elicit essential factual information. Skillful social workers use closed-ended questions sparingly, because clients usually reveal extensive factual information spontaneously as they unfold their stories, aided by the social worker's open-ended and furthering responses. Although they are typically employed little during the first part of a session, closed questions are used more extensively later to elicit data that clients may have omitted, such as names and ages of children, place of employment, date of marriage, medical facts, and data regarding family of origin.

In obtaining these kinds of factual data, the social worker can unobtrusively weave into the discussion closed-ended questions that directly pertain to the topic. For example, a client may relate certain marital problems that have existed for many years, and the social worker might ask parenthetically, "And you've been married for how many years?" Similarly, a parent may explain that a child began to have irregular attendance at school when the parent started to work 6 months ago, to which the social worker might respond, "I see. Incidentally, what type of work do you do?" It is vital, of course, to shift the focus back to the problem. If necessary, the social worker can easily maintain focus by using an open-ended response to pick up the thread of the discussion. For example, the social worker might comment, "You mentioned that Ernie began missing school when you started to work. I'd like to hear more about what was happening in your family at that time."

Because open-ended responses generally yield rich information, they are used throughout initial sessions. They are used most heavily, however, in the first portion of sessions to open up lines of communication and to invite clients to reveal problematic aspects of their lives. The following open-ended polite command is a typical opening message: "Could you tell me what you wish to discuss, and we can think about it together." Such responses convey interest in clients as well as respect for clients' abilities to relate their problems in their own way; as a consequence, they also contribute to the development of a working relationship.

As clients disclose certain problem areas, open-ended responses are extensively employed to elicit additional relevant information. Clients, for example, may reveal difficulties at work or in relationships with other family members. Open-ended responses like the following will elicit clarifying information:

- *"Tell me more about your problems at work."*
- *"I'd like to hear more about the circumstances when you were mugged coming home with the groceries."*

Open-ended responses can be used to enhance communication with collaterals, colleagues, and other professionals as well. For example, Strom-Gottfried (1998a) suggests using effective communication skills in negotiation and communication between care providers and utilization reviewers. When a client has not been approved for a kind of service that the social worker has recommended, the social worker can attempt to join with the reviewer in identifying goals that both parties would embrace and request information in an open-ended fashion:

I appreciate your concern that she gets the best available services and that her condition does not get worse. We are concerned with safety, as we know you are. Could you tell me more about how this protocol can help us assure her safety? (Strom-Gottfried, 1998a, p. 398)

It may sometimes be necessary to employ closed-ended questions extensively to draw out information if the client is unresponsive and withholds information or has limited conceptual and mental abilities. However, in the former case, it is vital to explore the client's immediate feelings about being in the session, which often are negative and impede verbal expression. Focusing on and resolving negative feelings (discussed at length in Chapter 17) may pave the way to using open-ended responses to good advantage.

When you incorporate open-ended responses into your repertoire, you will experience a dramatic positive change in your interviewing style and confidence level. To assist you to develop skill in blending and balancing open-ended and closed-ended responses, we have provided a recording form to help you examine your own interviewing style (see Figure 6-1). Using this form, analyze several recorded individual, conjoint, or group sessions over a period of time to determine changes you are making in employing these two types of responses. The recording form will assist you in determining the extent to which you have used open- and closed-ended responses.

SOCIAL WORKER'S RESPONSES	OPEN-ENDED RESPONSES	CLOSED-ENDED RESPONSES
1.		
2.		
3.		
4.		
5.		
6.		
7.		

Directions: Record your discrete open- and closed-ended responses and place a check in the appropriate column. Agency time constraints will dictate how often you can practice it.

FIG 6-1 Recording Form for Open- and Closed-Ended Responding Seeking Concreteness

In addition, you may wish to review your work for the following purposes:

1. To determine when relevant data are missing and whether the information might have been more appropriately obtained through an open- or closed-ended response
2. To determine when your use of closed-ended questions was irrelevant or ineffective, or distracted from the data-gathering process
3. To practice formulating open-ended responses you might use instead of closed-ended responses, to increase client participation and elicit richer data

SEEKING CONCRETENESS

Many of us are inclined to think and talk in generalities and to use words that lack precision when speaking of our experiences ("How was your weekend?" "It was awesome.") To communicate one's feelings and experiences so that they are fully understood, however, a person must be able to respond concretely—that is, with specificity. **Responding concretely** means using words that describe in explicit terms specific experiences, behaviors, and feelings. As an example, in the following

message, an intern supervisor provides feedback in vague and general terms: "I thought you had a good interview." Alternatively, he might have described his experience in more precise language: "During your interview, I was impressed with the way you blended open-ended with closed-ended questions in a relaxed fashion."

You should consider seeking concreteness when the client uses language that suggests to you that you may not understand their terms in the way they intend. This can be particularly true when interviewing children or adolescents whose colloquial expressions may not be entirely clear to the interviewer. Similarly, nonnative speakers may be conveying ideas that do not readily translate into the language you are speaking. In summary, seeking concreteness can be useful to:

1. Check out perceptions
2. Clarify the meaning of vague or unfamiliar terms
3. Explore the basis of conclusions drawn by clients
4. Assist clients in personalizing their statements
5. Elicit specific feelings
6. Focus on the here and now rather than on the distant past
7. Elicit details related to clients' experiences

8. Elicit details related to interactional behavior
9. Clarify details of timelines, expectations

To test your comprehension of the concept of concreteness, assess which of the following messages give descriptive information concerning what a client experiences:

1. "I have had a couple of accidents that would not have happened if I had full control of my hands. The results weren't that serious, but they could be."
2. "I'm uneasy right now because I don't know what to expect from counseling, and I'm afraid you might think that I really don't need it."
3. "You are a good girl, Susie."
4. "People don't seem to care whether other people have problems."
5. "My last social worker did not answer my calls."
6. "I really wonder if I'll be able to keep from crying and to find the words to tell my husband that it's all over—that I want a divorce."
7. "You did a good job."

You could probably readily identify which messages contained language that increased the specificity of the information conveyed by the client.

In developing competency as a social worker, one of your challenges is to consistently recognize clients' messages expressed in abstract and general terms and to assist them to reveal highly specific information related to feelings and experiences. Such information will assist you to make accurate assessments and, in turn, to plan interventions accordingly. A second challenge is to help clients learn how to respond more concretely in their relationships with others—a task you will not be able to accomplish unless you can model the dimension of concreteness yourself. A third challenge is to describe your own experience in language that is precise and descriptive. It is not enough to recognize concrete messages; in addition, you must familiarize yourself with and practice responding concretely to the extent that it becomes a natural style of speaking and relating to others.

The remainder of our discussion on the skill of seeking concreteness is devoted to assisting you in meeting these three challenges.

Types of Responses That Facilitate Specificity of Expression by Clients

Social workers who fail to move beyond general and abstract messages often have little grasp of the specificity and meaning of a client's problem. Eliciting highly specific information that minimizes errors or misinterpretations, however, represents a formidable challenge. People typically present impressions, views, conclusions, and opinions that, despite efforts to be objective, are inevitably biased and distorted to some extent. As previously mentioned, it is common for many of us to speak in generalities and to respond with imprecise language. As a consequence, those messages may be understood differently by different people.

To help you conceptualize the various ways you may assist clients to respond more concretely, the following sections examine different facets of responses that seek concreteness. In addition to discussing these aspects, this section includes 10 skill development exercises designed to bring your comprehension of concreteness from the general and abstract to the specific and concrete.

Checking Out Perceptions

Responses that help social workers clarify and "check out" whether they have accurately heard clients' messages (e.g., "Do you mean …" or "Are you saying …") are vital in building rapport with clients and in communicating the desire to understand their problems. Such responses also minimize misperceptions or projections in the helping process. Clients benefit from social workers' efforts to understand, because clarifying responses assist clients in sharpening and reformulating their thinking about their own feelings and other concerns, thereby encouraging self-awareness and growth.

Sometimes, perception checking becomes necessary because clients' messages are incomplete, ambiguous, or complex. Occasionally, social workers may encounter clients who repeatedly communicate in highly abstract or metaphorical styles, or clients whose thinking is scattered and whose messages just do not "track" or make sense. In such instances, social workers must spend considerable time sorting through clients' messages and clarifying perceptions.

At other times, the need for clarification arises not because the client has conveyed confusing, faulty, or incomplete messages, but rather because the social worker has not fully attended to the client's message or comprehended its meaning. Fully attending throughout each moment of a session requires intense concentration. Of course, it is impossible to fully focus on and comprehend the essence of every message delivered in group and family meetings, where myriad transactions occur and competing communications bid for the social worker's attention.

It is important that you develop skill in using clarifying responses to elicit ongoing feedback regarding your perceptions and to acknowledge freely your need for clarification when you are confused or uncertain. Rather than reflecting personal or professional inadequacy, your efforts to accurately grasp the client's meaning and feelings will most likely be perceived as signs of your genuineness and your commitment to understand.

To check your perceptions, try asking simple questions that seek clarification or try combining your request for clarification with a paraphrase or empathic response that reflects your perception of the client's message (e.g., "I think you were saying ___. Is that right?"). Examples of clarifying messages include the following:

- "You seem to be really irritated, not only because he didn't respond when you asked him to help but because he seemed to be deliberately trying to hurt you. Is that accurate?"
- "I'm not sure I'm following you. Let me see if I understand the order of events you described …"
- "Would you expand on what you're saying so I can be sure I understand what you mean?"
- "Could you go over that again and perhaps give an illustration that might help me understand?"
- "I'm confused. Let me try to restate what I think you're saying."
- "As a group, you seem to be divided in your approach to this matter. I'd like to summarize what I'm hearing, and I would then appreciate some input regarding whether I understand the various positions that have been expressed."

VIDEO CASE EXAMPLE

In the video "Serving the Squeaky Wheel," the social worker, Ron Rooney, asks Molly, a client with a diagnosed serious and persistent mental illness (SPMI) the following question to verify his perception: "So you feel that other people's ideas about what mental illness means are not the same as yours?"

In addition to clarifying their own perceptions, social workers need to assist clients in conjoint or group sessions to clarify their perceptions of the messages of others who are present. This may be accomplished in any of the following ways:

- By modeling clarifying responses, which occur naturally as social workers seek to check out their own perceptions of clients' messages.
- By directing clients to ask for clarification. Consider, for example, the following response by a social worker in a conjoint session:

[To the mother of the daughter who had just spoken]: "You had a confused look on your face, and I'm not sure that you understood your daughter's point. Would you repeat back to her what you heard and then ask her if you understood correctly?"

- By teaching clients how to clarify perceptions and by reinforcing their efforts to "check out" the messages of others, as illustrated in the following responses:

[To group]: "One of the reasons families have communication problems is that members don't hear accurately what others are trying to say and, therefore, often respond or react on the basis of incorrect or inadequate information. I would like to encourage all of you to frequently use what I call 'checking out' responses, such as 'I'm not sure what you meant. Were you saying …?' to clarify statements of others. As we go along, I'll point out instances in which I notice any of you using this kind of response."

[To family]: "I'm wondering if you all noticed Jim 'checking out' what his dad said. As you may recall, we talked about the importance of these kinds of responses earlier.

[To father]: I'm wondering, Bob, what you experienced when Jim did that?"

Clarifying the Meaning of Vague or Unfamiliar Terms

In expressing themselves, clients often employ terms that have multiple meanings or use terms in idiosyncratic ways. For example, in the message "The kids in this school are mean," the word *mean* may have different meanings to the social worker and the client. If the social worker does not identify what this term means to a particular client, he or she cannot be certain whether the client is referring to behavior that is violent, unfriendly, threatening, or something else. The precise meaning can be clarified by employing one of the following responses:

- "Tell me about the way that some kids are mean in this school."
- "I'm not sure I know what is happening when you say that some kids act in a mean way. Could you clarify that for me?"
- "Can you give me an example of something mean that has happened at this school?"

Many other words also lack precision, so it is important to avoid assuming that the client means the same thing you mean when you use a given term. For example, "codependent," "irresponsible," "selfish," and "careless" conjure up meanings that vary according to the reference points of different persons. Exact meanings are best determined by asking for clarification or for examples of events in which the behavior alluded to actually occurred.

Exploring the Basis of Conclusions Drawn by Clients

Clients often present views or conclusions as though they are established facts. For example, the messages "I'm losing my mind" and "My partner doesn't love me anymore" include views or conclusions that the client has drawn. To accurately assess the client's difficulties, the social worker must elicit the information on which these views or conclusions are based. This information helps the social worker assess the thinking patterns of the client, which are powerful determinants of emotions and behavior. For example, a person who believes he or she is no longer loved will behave as though this belief represents reality. The social worker's role, of course, is to reveal distortions and to challenge erroneous conclusions in a facilitative manner.

The following responses would elicit clarification of the information that serves as the basis of the views and conclusions embodied in the messages cited earlier:

- "How have you concluded that you're losing your mind?"
- "What leads you to believe your partner no longer loves you?"

Note that entire groups may hold in common fixed beliefs that may not be helpful to them in attempting to better their situations. In such instances, the social worker faces the challenging task of assisting members to reflect upon and to analyze their views. For example, the social worker may need to help group members assess conclusions or distortions like the following:

- "We can't do anything about our problems. We are helpless and others are in control of our lives."
- "People in authority are out to get us."
- "Someone else is responsible for our problems."
- "They (members of another race, religion, group, etc.) are no good."

In Chapter 13, we discuss the social worker's role in challenging distortions and erroneous conclusions and identify relevant techniques that may be used for this purpose.

Assisting Clients in Personalizing Their Statements

The relative concreteness of a specific client message is related in part to the focus or subject of that message. Client messages fall into several different classes of topic focus (Cormier, Nurius, & Osborn, 2009), each of which emphasizes different information and leads into very different areas of discussion:

- Focus on self, indicated by the subject *I* (e.g., "I'm disappointed that I wasn't able to keep the appointment.")
- Focus on others, indicated by subjects such as *they, people, someone,* or names of specific persons (e.g., "They haven't fulfilled their part of the bargain.")
- Focus on the group or mutual relationship between self and others, indicated by the subject *we* (e.g., "We would like to do that.")
- Focus on content, indicated by such subjects as events, institutions, situations, ideas (e.g., "School wasn't easy for me.")

People are more prone to focus on others or on content, or to speak of themselves as a part of a group, rather than to personalize their statements by using "I" or other self-referent pronouns. This tendency is illustrated in the following messages: "Things just don't seem to be going right for me," "They don't like me," and "It's not easy for people to talk about their problems." In the last example, the client means that it is not easy for *her* to talk about *her* problems, yet she uses the term *people,* thereby generalizing the problem and obscuring her personal struggle.

In assisting clients in personalizing statements, social workers have a three-part task:

1. Social workers must model, teach, and coach clients to use self-referent pronouns (*I, me*) in talking about their concerns and their own emotional response to those concerns. For example, in response to a vague client message that focuses on content rather than self ("Everything at home seems to be deteriorating"), the social worker might gently ask the client to reframe the message by starting the response with "I" and giving specific information about what she is experiencing. It is also helpful to teach clients the difference between messages that focus on self ("I think …" "I feel …," "I want …") and messages that are *other-related* ("It …," "Someone …")

2. Social workers must teach the difference between self-referent messages and subject-related messages (those dealing with objects, things, ideas, or situations). Although teaching clients to use self-referent pronouns when talking about their concerns is a substantive task, clients derive major benefits from it. Indeed, not owning or taking responsibility for feelings and speaking about problems in generalities and abstractions are among the most prevalent causes of problems in communicating.

3. Social workers must focus frequently on the client and use the client's name or the pronoun *you*. Beginning social workers are apt to respond passively to client talk about other people, distant situations, the group at large, various escapades, or other events or content that give little information about self and the relationship between self and situations or people. A more active response is to request that the client be more specific about his or her concerns in the present situation related to the issues raised. In the following illustration, the social worker's response focuses on the situation rather than on the client:

Client: My kids want to shut me up in a nursing home.
Social worker: What makes you think that?

In contrast, the following message personalizes the client's concern and explicitly identifies the feelings she is experiencing:

Social worker: You worry that your children might be considering a nursing home for you. You want to be part of any decision about what would be a safe environment for you.

A social worker may employ various techniques to assist clients in personalizing messages. In the preceding example, the social worker used an empathic response. In this instance, this skill is invaluable to the social worker in helping the client to focus on self. Recall that personalizing feelings is an inherent aspect of the paradigm for responding empathetically ("You feel _____ about _____ because _____"). Thus, clients can make statements that omit self-referent pronouns, and by utilizing empathic responding, social workers may assist clients to "own" their feelings.

Eliciting Specific Feelings

Even when clients personalize their messages and express their feelings, social workers often need to elicit additional information to clarify what they are experiencing, because certain "feeling words" denote general feeling states rather than specific feelings. For example, in the message, "I'm really upset that I didn't get a raise," the word *upset* helps to clarify the client's general frame of mind but fails to specify the precise feeling. In this instance, *upset* may refer to feeling disappointed, discouraged, unappreciated, devalued, angry, resentful, or even incompetent or inadequate because of failing to receive a raise. Until the social worker has elicited additional information, he or she cannot be sure of how the client actually experiences being "upset."

Other feeling words that lack specificity include *frustrated, uneasy, uncomfortable, troubled,* and *bothered.* When clients employ such words, you can pinpoint their feelings by using responses such as the following:

- "How do you mean, 'upset'?"
- "I'd like to understand more about that feeling. Could you clarify what you mean by 'frustrated'?"
- "Can you say more about in what way you feel 'bothered'?"

Focusing on the Here and Now

Another aspect of concreteness takes the form of responses that shift the focus from the past to the present, the here and now. Messages that relate to the immediate present are high in concreteness, whereas those that center on the past are low in concreteness. Many of us are prone to dwell on past feelings and events.

Unfortunately, precious opportunities for promoting growth and understanding may slip through the fingers of social workers who fail to focus on emotions and experiences that unfold in the immediacy of the interview. Focusing on feelings as they occur will enable you to observe reactions and behavior firsthand, eliminating any bias and error caused by reporting feelings and experiences after the fact. Furthermore, the helpfulness of your feedback is greatly enhanced when this feedback relates to the client's immediate experience.

The following exchange demonstrates how to achieve concreteness in such situations:

Client [*choking up*]: When she told me it was all over, that she was in love with another man—well, I just felt—it's happened again. I felt totally alone, like there just wasn't anyone.

Social worker: That must have been terribly painful. [*Client nods; tears well up.*] I wonder if you're not having the same feeling just now—at this moment. [*Client nods in agreement.*]

Not only do such instances provide direct access to the client's inner experience, but they also may produce lasting benefits as the client shares deep and painful emotions in the context of a warm, accepting, and supportive relationship. Here-and-now experiencing that involves emotions toward the social worker (e.g., anger, hurt, disappointment, affectional desires, fears) is known as **relational immediacy**. Skills pertinent to relational immediacy warrant separate consideration and are dealt with in Chapter 18.

Focusing on here-and-now experiencing with groups, couples, and families is a particularly potent technique for assisting members of these systems to clear the air of pent-up feelings. Moreover, interventions that focus on the immediacy of feelings bring buried issues to the surface, paving the way for the social worker to assist members of these systems to clearly identify and explore their difficulties and (if appropriate) to engage in problem solving.

Eliciting Details Related to Clients' Experiences

As previously mentioned, one reason why concrete responses are essential is that clients often offer up vague statements regarding their experiences—for example, "Some people in this group don't want to change bad enough to put forth any effort." Compare this with the following concrete statement, in which the client assumes ownership of the problem and fills in details that clarify its nature:

Client: I'm concerned because I want to do something to work on my problems in this group, but when I do try to talk about them, you, John, make some sarcastic remark. It seems that then several of you [*gives names*] just laugh about it and someone changes the subject. I really feel ignored then and just go off into my own world.

Aside from assisting clients to personalize their messages and to "own" their feelings and problems, social workers must ask questions that elicit illuminating information concerning the client's experiencing, such as that illustrated in the preceding message. Questions that start with "how" or "what" are often helpful in assisting the client to give concrete data. For example, to the client message, "Some people in this group don't want to change bad enough to put forth any effort," the social worker might respond, "What have you seen happening in the group that leads you to this conclusion?"

Eliciting Details Related to Interactional Behavior

Concrete responses are also vital in accurately assessing **interactional behavior**. Such responses pinpoint what actually occurs in interactional sequences—that is, what circumstances preceded the events, what the participants said and did, what specific thoughts and feelings the client experienced, and what consequences followed the event. In other words, the social worker elicits details of what happened, rather than settling for clients' views and conclusions. The following is an example of a concrete response to a client message:

High school student: My teacher really lost it yesterday. She totally dissed me, and I hadn't done one thing to deserve it.

Social worker: That must have been aggravating. Can you describe for me the sequence of events—what led up to this situation, and what each of you said and did? To understand better what went wrong, I'd like to get the details as though I had been there and observed what happened.

In such cases, it is important to keep clients on topic by continuing to assist them to relate the events in question, using responses such as "Then what happened?," "What did you do next?," or "Then who said what?" If dysfunctional patterns become evident after exploring numerous events, social workers have a responsibility to share their observations with clients, to assist them to evaluate the effects of the patterned behavior, and to assess their motivation to change it.

Specificity of Expression by Social Workers

Seeking concreteness applies to the communication of both clients and social workers. In this role, you will frequently explain, clarify, and give feedback to clients. As a social worker who has recently begun a formal professional educational program, you may be prone to speak with the vagueness and generality that characterize much of the communication of the lay public. When such vagueness occurs, clients and others may understandably misinterpret, draw erroneous conclusions, or experience confusion about the meaning of your messages.

Consider the lack of specificity in the following messages actually delivered by social workers:

- *"You seem to have a lot of pent-up hostility."*
- *"You really handled yourself well in the group today."*
- *"I think a lot of your difficulties stem from your self-image."*

Vague terms such as *hostility, handled yourself well,* and *self-image* may leave the client in a quandary as to what the social worker actually means. Moreover, in this style of communication, conclusions are presented without supporting information. As a result, the client must accept them at face value, reject them as invalid, or speculate on the basis of the conclusions. Fortunately, some people are sufficiently perceptive, inquisitive, and assertive to request greater specificity—but many others are not.

Contrast the preceding messages with how the social worker responds to the same situations with messages that have a high degree of specificity:

- "I've noticed that you've become easily angered and frustrated several times as we've talked about ways you might work out child custody arrangements with your wife. This appears to be a very painful area for you."
- "I noticed that you responded several times in the group tonight, and I thought you offered some very helpful insight to Marjorie when you said _____. I also noticed you seemed to be more at ease than in previous sessions."

- "We've talked about your tendency to feel inferior to other members of your family and to discount your own feelings and opinions in your contacts with them. I think that observation applies to the problem you're having with your sister that you just described. You've said you didn't want to go on the trip with her and her husband because they fight all the time, yet you feel you have to go because she is putting pressure on you. As in other instances, you appear to be drawing the conclusion that how you feel about the matter isn't important."

When social workers speak with specificity, clarify meanings, personalize statements, and document the sources of their conclusions, clients are much less likely to misinterpret or project their own feelings or thoughts. Clients like to be clear about what is expected of them and how they are perceived, as well as how and why social workers think and feel as they do about matters discussed in their sessions. Clients also learn vicariously to speak with greater specificity as social workers model sending concrete messages.

Both beginning and experienced social workers face the additional challenge of avoiding inappropriate use of jargon. Unfortunately, jargon has pervaded professional discourse and runs rampant in social work literature and case records. Its use confuses, rather than clarifies, meanings for clients. The careless use of jargon with colleagues also fosters stereotypical thinking and is therefore antithetical to the cardinal value of individualizing the client. Furthermore, labels tend to conjure up images of clients that vary from one social worker to another, thereby injecting a significant source of error into communication. Consider the lack of specificity in the following messages that are rich in jargon:

- "Mrs. N manifests strong passive-aggressive tendencies."
- "Sean displayed adequate impulse control in the group and tested the leader's authority in a positive manner."
- "Hal needs assistance in gaining greater self-control."
- "The client shows some borderline characteristics."
- "The group members were able to respond to appropriate limits."
- "Ruth appears to be emotionally immature for an eighth-grader."

To accurately convey information about clients to your colleagues, you must explicitly describe their behavior and document the sources of your conclusions. For example, with the vague message, "Ruth appears to be emotionally immature for an eighth-grader," consider how much more accurately another social worker would perceive your client if you conveyed information in the form of a concrete response: "The teacher says Ruth is quiet and stays to herself in school. She doesn't answer any questions in class unless directly called upon, and she often doesn't complete her assignments. She spends considerable time day-dreaming or playing with objects." By describing behavior in this way, you avoid biasing your colleague's perceptions of clients by conveying either vague impressions or erroneous conclusions.

It has been our experience that mastery of the skill of communicating with specificity is gained only through extended and determined effort. The task becomes more complicated if you are not aware that your communication is vague. We recommend that you carefully and consistently monitor your recorded sessions and your everyday conversations with a view toward identifying instances in which you did or did not communicate with specificity. This kind of monitoring will enable you to set relevant goals for yourself and to chart your progress. We also recommend that you enlist your practicum instructor to provide feedback about your performance level on this vital skill.

Exercises in Seeking Concreteness

In the following exercises, read each client statement and then formulate a written response that will elicit concrete data regarding the client's problems. You may wish to combine your responses with either an empathic response or a paraphrase. Review the eight guidelines for seeking concreteness as you complete the exercise to help you develop effective responses and conceptualize the various dimensions of this skill. After you have finished the exercises, compare your responses with the modeled responses at the end of the chapter (see page 167).

Client Statements

1. **Adolescent** [*speaking of his recent recommitment to a correctional institution*]: It really seems weird to be back here.
2. **Client:** You can't depend on friends; they'll stab you in the back every time.

3. **Client:** He's got a terrible temper—that's the way he is, and he'll never change.
4. **Client:** My supervisor is so insensitive, you can't believe it. All she thinks about are reports and deadlines.
5. **Client:** I was upset after I left your office last week. I felt you really didn't understand what I was saying and didn't care how I felt.
6. **Client:** My dad's 58 years old now, but I swear he still hasn't grown up. He always has a chip on his shoulder.
7. **Senior client:** My rheumatoid arthritis has affected my hands a lot. It gets to be kind of tricky when I'm handling pots and pans in the kitchen.
8. **Client:** I just have this uneasy feeling about going to the doctor. I guess I've really got a hang-up about it.
9. **African American student** [*to African American social worker*]: You ask why I don't talk to my teacher about why I'm late for school. I'll tell you why. Because she's white, that's why. She's got it in for us black students, and there's just no point talking to her. That's just the way it is.
10. **Client:** John doesn't give a damn about me. I could die, and he wouldn't lose a wink of sleep.

PROVIDING AND MAINTAINING FOCUSING

Skills in focusing are critical to your practice for several reasons. Because your time with clients is limited, it is critical to make the best use of each session by honing in on key topics. You are also responsible for guiding the helping process and avoiding EP 6 wandering. Unlike normal social relations, helping relationships should be characterized by purposeful focus and continuity. As social workers, we perform a valuable role by assisting clients to focus on their problems in greater depth and to maintain focus until they accomplish desired changes.

In addition, families and groups sometimes experience interactional difficulties that prevent them from focusing effectively on their problems. To enhance family and group functioning, social workers must be able to refocus the discussion whenever dysfunctional interactional processes cause families and groups to prematurely drift away from the topic at hand.

To assist you in learning how to focus effectively, we consider the three functions of focusing skills:

1. Selecting topics for exploration
2. Exploring topics in depth
3. Managing obstacles to focusing

Knowledge of these functions will enable you to focus sharply on relevant topics and elicit sufficient data to formulate an accurate problem assessment—a prerequisite for competent practice.

Selecting Topics for Exploration

Areas relevant for exploration vary from situation to situation. However, clients who have contact with social workers in the same setting, such as in nursing homes, group homes, or child welfare agencies, may share many common concerns.

 Before meeting with clients whose concerns differ from client populations with which you are familiar, you can prepare yourself to conduct an effective exploration by developing (in consultation with your practicum instructor or field supervisor) a list of relevant and promising problem areas to be explored. This preparation will help you avoid a mistake commonly made by some beginning social workers—namely, focusing on areas irrelevant to clients' problems and eliciting reams of information of questionable utility.

EP 7

In your initial interview with an institutionalized youth, for example, you could more effectively select questions and responses if you knew in advance that you might explore the following areas:

1. Client's own perceptions of the concerns at hand
2. Client's perceived strengths and resources
3. Reasons for being institutionalized and brief history of past problems related to legal authority and to use of drugs and alcohol
4. Details regarding the client's relationships with individual family members, both as concerns and sources of support
5. Brief family history
6. School adjustment, including information about grades, problem subjects, areas of interest, and relationships with various teachers
7. Adjustment to institutional life, including relationships with peers and supervisors
8. Peer relationships outside the institution

9. Life goals and short-term goals
10. Reaction to previous experiences with helpers
11. Attitude toward engaging in a working relationship to address concerns

Because the institutionalized youth is an involuntary client, part of this exploration would include the youth's understanding of which parts of his or her work are nonnegotiable requirements and which parts could be negotiated or free choices (R. H. Rooney, 2009).

Similarly, if you plan to interview a self-referred middle-aged woman whose major complaint is depression, the following topical areas could assist you in conducting an initial interview:

1. Concerns as she sees them, including the nature of depressive symptoms such as sleep patterns and appetite changes
2. Client's perceived strengths and resources
3. Hopes and vision for a better future without depression
4. Health status, date of last physical examination, and medications being taken
5. Onset and duration of depression, previous depressive or manic episodes
6. Life events associated with onset of depression (especially losses)
7. Exceptions when depression has not occurred or occurred less frequently
8. Possible suicidal thoughts, intentions, or plans
9. Problematic thought patterns (e.g., self-devaluation, self-recrimination, guilt, worthlessness, helplessness, hopelessness)
10. Previous coping efforts, previous treatment
11. Quality of interpersonal relationships (e.g., interpersonal skills and deficiencies, conflicts and supports in marital and parent–child relationships)
12. Reactions of significant others to her depression
13. Support systems (adequacy and availability)
14. Daily activities
15. Sense of mastery versus feelings of inadequacy
16. Family history of depression or manic behavior

Because she is self-referred, this client is likely to be more voluntary than the institutionalized youth. You should therefore pay more attention to identifying the specific concerns that have led her to seek help at this point in time.

As noted previously, problem areas vary, and outlines of probable topical areas likewise vary accordingly. Thus, a list of areas for exploration in an initial session with a couple seeking marriage counseling or with a group of alcoholics will include a number of items that differ from those in the first list (the areas identified for the institutionalized youth). Note that questions should tap into hopes, resources, exceptions, and skills as much as concerns and problems.

In using an outline, you should avoid following it rigidly or using it as a crutch; otherwise, you could potentially destroy the spontaneity of sessions and block clients from relating their stories in their own way. Instead, encourage your clients to discuss their problems freely while you play a facilitative role in exploring in greater depth any problems that emerge. In particular, you must use outlines flexibly—reordering the sequence of topics; modifying, adding, or deleting topics; or abandoning the outline altogether if using it hinders communication. You need to be alert to pacing related to appropriate depth and breadth, given the time available.

Of course, you cannot always anticipate fruitful topical areas. After all, although clients from the same population may share many commonalities, their problems inevitably have unique aspects. For this reason, it is important to review tapes of sessions with your practicum instructor or a field supervisor for the purpose of identifying other topical areas you should explore in future sessions.

Exploring Topics in Depth

A major facet of focusing is centering discussions on relevant topics to assure that exploration moves from generality and superficiality to greater depth and meaning. Social workers must have the skills needed to explore problems thoroughly, because their success in the helping process depends on their ability to obtain clear and accurate definitions of problems.

Selectively attending to specific topics is challenging for beginning social workers, who often wander in individual or group sessions, repeatedly skipping across the surface of vital areas of content and feelings, eliciting largely superficial and sometimes distorted information. This tendency is illustrated in the following excerpt from a first session with an adolescent in a school setting:

Social worker: Tell me about your family.
Client: My father is ill and my mother is dead, so we live with my sister.
Social worker: How are things with you and your sister?
Client: Good. We get along fine. She treats me pretty good.

Social worker: How about your father?
Client: We get along pretty well. We have our problems, but most of the time things are okay. I don't really see him very much.
Social worker: Tell me about school. How are you getting along here?
Client: Well, I don't like it very well, but my grades are good enough to get me by.
Social worker: I notice you're new to our school this year. How did you do in the last school you attended?

By focusing superficially on the topics of family and school, this social worker misses opportunities to explore potential problem areas in the depth necessary to illuminate the client's situation. Not surprisingly, this exploration yielded little information of value, in large part because the social worker failed to employ responses that focused in depth on topical areas. In the next sections, we further delineate the skills that will considerably enhance a social worker's ability to maintain focus on specific areas.

Open-Ended Responses

As we discussed earlier, social workers may employ open-ended responses throughout individual, conjoint, and group sessions to focus unobtrusively on desired topics. Earlier we noted that some open-ended responses leave clients free to choose their own topics, whereas others focus on a topic but encourage clients to respond freely to that topic. The following examples, taken from an initial session with a mother of eight children who has depression, illustrate how social workers can employ open-ended responses to define topical areas that may yield a rich trove of information vital to grasping the dynamics of the client's problems.

- *"What have you thought that you might like to accomplish in our work together?"*
- *"You've discussed many topics in the last few minutes. Could you pick the most important one and tell me more about it?"*
- *"You've mentioned that your oldest son doesn't come home after school as he did before and help you with the younger children. I would like to hear more about that."*
- *"Several times as you've mentioned your concern that your husband may leave you, your voice has trembled. I wonder if you could share what you are feeling."*

- *"You've indicated that your partner doesn't help you enough with the children. You also seem to be saying that you feel overwhelmed and inadequate in managing the children by yourself. Tell me what happens as you try to manage your children."*
- *"You indicate that you have more problems with your 14-year-old daughter than with the other children. Tell me more about Janet and your problems with her."*

In the preceding examples, the social worker's open-ended questions and responses progressively moved the exploration from the general to the specific. Note also that each response or question defined a new topic for exploration. To encourage in-depth exploration of the topics defined in this way, the social worker must blend open-ended questions with other facilitative verbal following responses that focus on and elicit expanded client expressions. After having defined a topical area by employing an open-ended response, for instance, the social worker might deepen the exploration by weaving other open-ended responses into the discussion. If the open-ended responses shift the focus to another area, however, the exploration suffers a setback. Note in the following exchange how the social worker's second open-ended response shifts the focus away from the client's message, which involves expression of intense feelings:

Social worker: You've said you're worried about retiring. I'd appreciate you sharing more about your concern. *[Open-ended response.]*

Client: I can't imagine not going to work every day. I feel at loose ends already, and I haven't even quit work. I'm afraid I just won't know what to do with myself.

Social worker: How do you imagine spending your time after retiring? *[Open-ended response.]*

Even though open-ended responses may draw out new information about clients' problems, they may not facilitate the helping process if they prematurely lead the client in a different direction. If social workers utilize open-ended or other types of responses that frequently change the topic, they will obtain information that is disjointed and fragmented. As a result, assessments will suffer from large gaps in the social worker's knowledge concerning clients' problems. As social workers formulate open-ended responses, they must be acutely aware of the direction that responses will take.

Seeking Concreteness

Earlier we discussed and illustrated the various facets of seeking concreteness. Because seeking concreteness enables social workers to move from the general to the specific and to explore topics in depth, it is a key focusing technique. We illustrate this ability in an excerpt from a session involving a client with a serious and persistent mental illness:

Client: I just don't have energy to do anything. This medicine really knocks me out.

Social worker: It sounds as if the side effects of your medication are of concern. Can you tell me specifically what those side effects have been?

By focusing in depth on topical areas, social workers are able to discern—and to assist clients in discerning—problematic thoughts, behavior, and interaction. Subsequent sections consider how social workers can effectively focus on topical areas in exploratory sessions by blending concreteness with other focusing skills. In actuality, the majority of responses that social workers typically employ to establish and maintain focus are blends of various types of discrete responses.

Empathic Responding

As noted earlier, empathic responding serves a critical function by enabling social workers to focus in depth on troubling feelings, as illustrated in the next example:

Client: I can't imagine not going to work every day. I feel at loose ends already, and I haven't even quit work. I'm afraid I just won't know what to do with myself.

Social worker: You seem to be saying, "Even now, I'm apprehensive about retiring. I'm giving up something that has been very important to me, and I don't seem to have anything to replace it." I gather that feeling at loose ends, as you do, you worry that when you retire, you'll feel useless.

Client: I guess that's a large part of my problem. Sometimes I feel useless now. I just didn't take time over the years to develop any hobbies or to pursue any interests. I guess I don't think that I can do anything else.

Social worker: It sounds as if part of you feels hopeless about the future, as if you have done everything you can do. And yet I wonder if another part of you might think that it isn't too late to look into some new interests.

Client: I do dread moping around home with time on my hands. I can just see it now. My wife will want to keep me busy doing things around the house for her all the time. I've never liked to do that kind of thing. I suppose it is never too late to look into other interests. I have always wanted to write some things for fun, not just for work. You know, the memory goes at my age, but I have thought about just writing down some of the family stories.

Note how the client's problem continued to unfold as the social worker utilized empathic responding, revealing rich information in the process. The social worker also raises the possibility of new solutions, not just dwelling in the feelings of uselessness.

Blending Open-Ended, Empathic, and Concrete Responses to Maintain Focus

After employing open-ended responses to focus on a selected topic, social workers should use other responses to maintain focus on that topic. In the following excerpt, observe how the social worker employs both open-ended and empathic responses to explore problems in depth, thereby enabling the client to move to the heart of her struggle. Notice also the richness of the client's responses elicited by the blended messages.

Social worker: As you were speaking about your son, I sensed some pain and reluctance on your part to talk about him. I'd like to understand more about what you're feeling. Could you share with me how it is for you to be talking about him? *[Blended empathic and open-ended response that seeks concreteness.]*

Client: I guess I haven't felt too good about coming this morning. I almost called and canceled. I feel I should be able to handle these problems with Jim [son] myself. Coming here is like having to admit I'm no longer capable of coping with him.

Social worker: So you've had reservations about coming [reflection]—you feel you're admitting defeat and that perhaps you've failed or that you're inadequate—and that hurts. *[Empathic response.]*

Client: Well, yes, although I know that I need some help. It's just hard to admit it, I think. My biggest problem in this regard, however, is my husband. He feels much more strongly than I do that we should manage this problem ourselves, and he really disapproves of my coming in.

Social worker: So even though it's painful for you, you're convinced you need some assistance with Jim, but you're torn about coming here because of your husband's attitude. I'd be interested in hearing more about that. *[Blended empathic and open-ended response.]*

In the preceding example, the social worker initiated discussion of the client's here-and-now experiences through a blended open-ended and empathic response, following it with other empathic and blended responses to explore the client's feelings further. With the last response, the social worker narrowed the focus to a potential obstacle to the helping process (the husband's attitude toward therapy), which could also be explored in a similar manner.

Open-ended and empathic responses may also be blended to facilitate and encourage discussion from group members about a defined topic. For instance, after using an open-ended response to solicit group feedback regarding a specified topic ("I'm wondering how you feel about ..."), the social worker can employ empathic or other facilitative responses to acknowledge the contribution of members who respond to the invitation to comment. By utilizing open-ended responses, the social worker can also successively reach for comments of individual members who have not contributed ("What do you think about ..., Ray?").

In the next example, the social worker blends empathic and concrete responses to facilitate in-depth exploration. Notice how these blended responses bring out specific behavioral descriptions of the problem. The empathic messages convey the social worker's sensitive awareness and concern for the client's distress. The open-ended and concrete responses focus on details of a recent event and yield valuable clues that the client's rejections by women may be associated with insensitive and inappropriate social behavior. Awareness of this behavior is a prelude to formulating relevant goals. Goals formulated in this way are highly relevant to the client.

Single male client, age 20: There has to be something wrong with me, or women wouldn't treat me like a leper. Sometimes I feel like I'm doomed to be alone the rest of my life. I'm not even sure why I came to see you. I think I'm beyond help.

Social worker: You sound like you've given up on yourself—as though you're utterly hopeless. At the same time, it seems like part of you still clings to hope and wants to try. *[Empathic response.]*

Client: What else can I do? I can't go on like this, but I don't know how many more times I can get knocked down and get back up.

Social worker: I sense you feel deeply hurt and discouraged at those times. Could you give me a recent example of when you felt you were being knocked down? *[Blended empathic and concrete response.]*

Client: Well, a guy I work with got me a blind date for a dance. I took her, and it was a total disaster. I figured that she would at least let me take her home. After we got to the dance, she ignored me the whole night and danced with other guys. Then, to add insult to injury, she went home with one of them and didn't even have the decency to tell me. There I was, wondering what had happened to her.

Social worker: Besides feeling rejected, you must have been very mad. When did you first feel you weren't hitting it off with her? *[Blended empathic and concrete response.]*

Client: I guess it was when she lit up a cigarette while we were driving to the dance. I kidded her about how she was asking for lung cancer.

Social worker: I see. What was it about her reaction, then, that led you to believe you might not be in her good graces? *[Concrete response.]*

Client: Well, she didn't say anything. She just smoked her cigarette. I guess I really knew then that she was upset at me.

Social worker: As you look back at it now, what do you think you might have said to repair things at that point? *[Stimulating reflection about problem solving.]*

In the next example, observe how the social worker blends empathic and concrete responses to elicit details of interaction in an initial conjoint session. Such blending is a potent technique for eliciting specific and abundant information that bears directly on clients' problems. Responses that seek concreteness elicit details. In contrast, empathic responses enable social workers to stay attuned to clients' moment-by-moment experiencing, thereby focusing on feelings that may present obstacles to the exploration.

Social worker: You mentioned having difficulties communicating. I'd like you to give me an example of a time when you felt you weren't communicating effectively, and let's go through it step by step to see if we can understand more clearly what is happening.

Wife: Well, weekends are an example. Usually I want to go out and do something fun with the kids, but John just wants to stay home. He starts criticizing me for wanting to go, go, go.

Social worker: Could you give me a specific example? *[Seeking concreteness.]*

Wife: Okay. Last Saturday I wanted all of us to go out to eat and then to a movie, but John wanted to stay home and watch TV.

Social worker: Before we get into what John did, let's stay with you for a moment. There you are, really wanting to go to a movie—tell me exactly what you did. *[Seeking concreteness.]*

Wife: I think I said, "John, let's take the kids out to dinner and a movie."

Social worker: Okay. That's what you said. How did you say it? *[Seeking concreteness.]*

Wife: I expected him to say no, so I might not have said it the way I just did.

Social worker: Turn to John, and say it the way you may have said it then. *[Seeking concreteness.]*

Wife: Okay. *[Turning to husband.]* Couldn't we go out to a movie?

Social worker: There seems to be some doubt in your voice as to whether John wants to go out. *[Focusing observation.]*

Wife [interrupting]: I knew he wouldn't want to.

Social worker: So you assumed he wouldn't want to go. It's as though you already knew the answer. *[To husband]:* Does the way your wife asked the question check out with the way you remembered it? *[Husband nods.]*

Social worker: After your wife asked you about going to the movie, what did you do? *[Seeking concreteness.]*

Husband: I said, nope! I wanted to stay home and relax Saturday, and I felt we could do things at home.

Social worker: So your answer was short. Apparently you didn't give her information about why you didn't want to go but just said no. Is that right? *[Focusing observation.]*

Husband: That's right. I didn't think she wanted to go anyway—the way she asked.

Social worker: What were you experiencing when you said no? *[Seeking concreteness.]*

Husband: I guess I was just really tired. I have a lot of pressures from work, and I just need some time to relax. She doesn't understand that.

Social worker: You're saying, then, "I just needed some time to get away from it all," but I take it you had your doubts as to whether she could appreciate your feelings. *[Husband nods.]* *[Turning to wife.]*

Now, after your husband said no, what did you do? *[Blended empathic and concrete response.]*

Wife: I think that I started talking to him about the way he just sits around the house.

Social worker: I sense that you felt hurt and somewhat discounted because John didn't respond the way you would have liked. *[Empathic response.]*

Wife *[nods]*: I didn't think he even cared what I wanted to do.

Social worker: Is it fair to conclude, then, that the way in which you handled your feelings was to criticize John rather than to say, "This is what is happening to me?" *[Wife nods.] [Seeking concreteness.]*

Social worker *[to husband]*: Back, then, to our example. What did you do when your wife criticized you? *[Seeking concreteness.]*

Husband: I guess I criticized her back. I told her she needed to stay home once in a while and get some work done.

In this series of exchanges, the social worker asked questions that enabled the couple to describe the sequence of their interaction in a way that elicited key details and provided insight into unspoken assumptions and messages.

Managing Obstacles to Focusing

EP 6

Occasionally you may find that your efforts to focus selectively and to explore topical areas in depth do not yield pertinent information. Although you have a responsibility in such instances to assess the effectiveness of your own interviewing style, you should also analyze clients' styles of communicating to determine to what extent their behaviors are interfering with your focusing efforts. Many clients seek help because they have—but are not aware of—patterns of communicating or behaviors that create difficulties in relationships. In addition, involuntary clients who do not yet perceive the relationship as helping may be inclined to avoid focusing. The following list highlights common types of client communications that may challenge your efforts to focus in individual, family, and group sessions:

- Responding with "I don't know"
- Changing the subject or avoiding sensitive areas
- Rambling from topic to topic
- Intellectualizing or using abstract or general terms
- Diverting focus from the present to the past

- Responding to questions with questions
- Interrupting excessively
- Failing to express opinions when asked
- Producing excessive verbal output
- Using humor or sarcasm to evade topics or issues
- Verbally dominating the discussion

You can easily see how individuals who did not seek help from a social worker and want to avoid focusing might use these kinds of methods to protect their privacy. With such involuntary clients, such behaviors are likely to indicate a low level of trust and a skepticism that contact with a social worker can be helpful. You can counter repetitive behaviors and communications that divert the focus from exploring problems by tactfully drawing them to clients' attention and by assisting clients in adopting behaviors that are compatible with their goals for work together. In groups, social workers must assist group members to modify behaviors that repeatedly disrupt effective focusing and communication; otherwise, the groups will not move to the phase of group development in which most of the work related to solving problems is accomplished. Children as clients often respond at first contact in a limited, passive, nonexpressive style. This might be interpreted as noncommunicative behavior. In fact, such behavior is often what children expect to be appropriate in interactions with strange authority figures (Evans, 2004; Hersen & Thomas, 2007; Lamb & Brown, 2006; Powell, Thomson, & Dietze, 1997).

VIDEO CASE EXAMPLE

In the video "Hanging with Hailey," the adolescent client, Hailey, is apprehensive about having to see a social worker and insists that she has done nothing wrong. The social worker, Emily, clarifies that Hailey can choose whether she wants to see a social worker, that she has not done anything wrong, but that teachers who knew her to be a good student have become concerned that something might have changed in her life to affect her school performance. By emphasizing her choice, Emily is able to allow Hailey to relax enough to share some of what is going on in her life currently.

Social workers may use many different techniques for managing and modifying client obstacles. These techniques include asking clients to communicate or behave differently; teaching, modeling for, and coaching clients to assume more effective communication styles; reinforcing facilitative responses; and selectively attending to functional behaviors.

Intervening to Help Clients Focus or Refocus in Group or Conjoint Sessions

Communications that occur in group or conjoint sessions are not only complex but may also be distractive or irrelevant. Consequently, the social worker's task of assisting members to explore the defined topics fully, rather than meander from subject to subject, is a challenging one. Related techniques that social workers can employ include highlighting or clarifying issues and bringing clients' attention to a comment or matter that has been overlooked. In such instances, the objective is not necessarily to explore the topic (although an exploration may subsequently occur) but rather to stress or elucidate important content. The social worker focuses clients' attention on communications or events that occurred earlier in the session or immediately preceded the social worker's focusing response. This technique is used in the following messages:

- *[To son in session with parents]:* "Ray, you made an important point a moment ago that I'm not sure your parents heard. Would you please repeat your comment?"
- *[To individual]:* "I would like to return to a remark made several moments ago when you said _____. I didn't want to interrupt then. I think perhaps the remark was important enough that we should return to it now."
- *[To family]:* "Something happened just a minute ago as we were talking. *[Describes event.]* We were involved in another discussion then, but I made a mental note of it because of how deeply it seemed to affect all of you at the time. I think we should consider what happened for just a moment."
- *[To group member]:* "John, as you were talking a moment ago, I wasn't sure what you meant by _____. Could you clarify that for me and for others in the group?"
- *[To group]:* "A few minutes ago, we were engrossed in a discussion about _____, yet we have moved away from that discussion to one that doesn't really seem to relate to our purpose for being here. I'm concerned about leaving the other

subject hanging because you were working hard to find some solutions and appeared to be close to a breakthrough."

Because of the complexity of communications in group and family sessions, some inefficiency in the focusing process is inescapable. Nevertheless, the social worker can sharpen the group's efforts to focus and encourage more efficient use of its time by teaching effective focusing behavior. We suggest that social workers actually explain the focusing role of the group and identify desirable focusing behaviors, such as attending, active listening, and asking open-ended questions. During this discussion, it is important to emphasize that by utilizing these skills, members will facilitate exploration of problems.

Social workers can encourage greater use of these skills by giving positive feedback to group or family members when they have adequately focused on a problem, thus reinforcing their efforts. Indeed, given the difficulties in encouraging some clients to speak even minimally, some social workers can be so relieved to have a verbal client that they neglect the focusing skills that make the session most valuable and useful to the client. Although group members usually experience some difficulty in learning how to focus, they should be able to delve deeply into problems by the third or fourth session, given sufficient guidance and education by social workers. Such efforts by social workers tend to accelerate movement of groups toward maturity, a phase in which members achieve maximum therapeutic benefits. A characteristic of a group in this phase, in fact, is that members explore issues in considerable depth rather than skim the surface of many topics.

SUMMARIZING RESPONSES

The technique of **summarization** embodies four distinct yet related facets:

1. Highlighting key aspects of discussions of specific problems, strengths, and resources before changing the focus of the discussion
2. Making connections between relevant aspects of lengthy client messages
3. Reviewing major focal points of a session and tasks that clients plan to work on before the next session
4. Recapitulating the highlights of a previous session and reviewing clients' progress on tasks during the week for the purpose of providing focus and continuity between sessions

Although employed at different times and in different ways, each of these facets of summarization serves the common purpose of tying together functionally related elements that occur at different points in the helping process. They are considered in detail in the following sections.

Highlighting Key Aspects of Problems, Strengths, and Resources

During the phase of an initial session in which problems and resources are explored in moderate depth, summarization can be effectively employed to tie together and highlight essential aspects before proceeding to explore additional concerns and strengths. For example, the social worker might describe how the problem appears to be produced by the interplay of several factors, including external pressures, overt behavioral patterns, unfulfilled needs and wants, and covert thoughts and feelings. Connecting these key elements assists clients in gaining a more accurate and complete perspective of their circumstances.

Employed in this fashion, summarization involves fitting pieces of the problem together to form a coherent whole. Those concerns can also be matched with a summary of values and current and potential resources and strengths identified. Seeing the situation in a fresh and more accurate perspective often proves beneficial because it expands clients' awareness and can generate hope and enthusiasm for tackling an issue that has hitherto seemed insurmountable.

Summarization that highlights problems and resources is generally employed at a natural point in the session when the social worker believes that relevant aspects have been adequately explored and clients appear satisfied in having had the opportunity to express their concerns. The following example illustrates this type of summarization. In this case, the client, an 80-year-old widow, has been referred to a Services to Seniors program for exploration of alternative living arrangements because of her failing health, isolation, and recent falls. As the social worker and client have worked together to explore alternative living arrangements, the pair has identified several characteristics that would be important for the client in an improved living situation. Highlighting the salient factors, the social worker summarizes the results to this point:

Social worker: It sounds as if you are looking for a situation in which there is social interaction, but your privacy is also important to you. You want

to maintain your independence. You also want to have someone available to help in emergencies and some assistance with cooking and cleaning.

Summarizing responses of this type serve as a prelude to the process of formulating goals, as goals flow naturally from problem formulations. Moreover, highlighting various dimensions of the problem facilitates the subsequent identifications of subgoals and tasks that must be accomplished to achieve the overall goal. In the preceding example, to explore an improved living situation, the social worker would help the client analyze the specific form of privacy (whether living alone or with someone else) and the type of social interaction (how much and what kind of contact with others) she desires.

Summarizing salient aspects of problems and resources is also a valuable technique in sessions with groups, couples, and families. It enables the social worker to stop at timely moments and highlight the difficulties experienced by each participant. In a family session with a pregnant adolescent and her mother, for example, the social worker might make the following statements:

- *[To pregnant adolescent]:* "You feel as if deciding what to do about this baby is your decision—it's your body, and you have decided that an abortion is the best solution for you. You know that you have the legal right to make this decision and want to be supported in making it. You see your mother as a potential resource and know that your mother wants to help. You value your independence in decision making and know that she can't tell you what decision to make."

- *[To mother]:* "As you spoke, you seemed saddened and very anxious about this decision your daughter is making. You are saying, 'I care about my daughter, but I don't think she is mature enough to make this decision on her own.' As you have noted, women in your family have had a hard time conceiving, and you wish that she would consider other options besides abortion. So you feel a responsibility to your daughter, but also to this unborn baby and the family history of conceiving children."

Such responses synthesize in concise and neutral language the needs, concerns, and problems of each participant for all other members of the session to hear. This type of summarization underscores the fact that all participants are struggling with and have responsibility for problems that are occurring, thus counteracting the tendency of families to view one person as the exclusive cause of family problems.

Summarizing Lengthy Messages

Clients' messages range from one word or one sentence to lengthy and sometimes rambling monologues. Although the meaning and significance of brief messages are often readily discernible, lengthy messages challenge the social worker to encapsulate and tie together diverse and complex elements. Linking the elements together often highlights and expands the significance and meaning of the client's message. For this reason, such messages represent one form of additive empathy, a skill discussed in Chapter 17.

Because lengthy client messages typically include emotions, thoughts, and descriptive content, you will need to determine how these dimensions relate to the focal point of the discussion. To illustrate, consider the following message of a mildly brain-damaged and socially withdrawn 16-year-old female—an only child who is extremely dependent on her overprotective but subtly rejecting mother:

Client: Mother tells me she loves me, but I find that hard to believe. Nothing I do ever pleases her; she yells at me when I refuse to wash my hair alone. But I can't do it right without her help. "When are you going to grow up?" she'll say. And she goes out with her friends and leaves me alone in that old house. She knows how scared I get when I have to stay home alone. But she says, "Nancy, I can't just babysit you all the time. I've got to do something for myself. Why don't you make some friends or watch TV or play your guitar? You've just got to quit pitying yourself all the time." Does that sound like someone who loves you? I get so mad at her when she yells at me; it's all I can do to keep from killing her.

Embodied in the client's message are the following elements:

1. Wanting to be loved by her mother yet feeling insecure and rejected at times
2. Feeling inadequate about performing certain tasks, such as washing her hair
3. Feeling extremely dependent on her mother for certain services and companionship
4. Feeling afraid when her mother leaves her alone
5. Feeling hurt (implied) and resentful when her mother criticizes her or leaves her alone
6. Feeling intense anger and wanting to lash out when her mother yells at her

The following summarizing response ties these elements together:

Social worker: So you find your feelings toward your mother pulling you in different directions. You want her to love you, but you feel unloved and resent it when she criticizes you or leaves you alone. And you feel really torn because you depend on her in so many ways. Yet at times, you feel so angry you want to hurt her back for yelling at you. You'd like to have a smoother relationship without the strain.

Occasionally, client messages may ramble to the extent that they contain numerous unrelated elements that cannot all be tied together. In such instances, your task is to extract and focus on those elements of the message that are most relevant to the thrust of the session at that point. When employed in this manner, summarization provides focus and direction to the session and averts aimless wandering. With clients whose thinking is loose or who ramble to avoid having to focus on unpleasant matters, you may need to interrupt to assure some semblance of focus and continuity. Otherwise, the interview will be disjointed and unproductive. Skills in maintaining focus and continuity are discussed in more depth in Chapter 13.

Reviewing Focal Points of a Session

During the course of an individual, conjoint, or group session, it is common to focus on more than one problem and to discuss numerous factors associated with each problem. Toward the end of the first or second session, depending on the length of the initial exploration, summarization is employed to review key concerns that have been discussed and to highlight themes and patterns related to these problems. Summarizing themes, patterns, and resources expands each client's awareness of concerns and tunes them in to promising avenues for addressing those concerns, awareness of opportunities, and potential resources. Through summarizing responses, social workers can not only review themes, patterns, and resources that have emerged in their sessions but also test clients' readiness to consider goals aimed at modifying these problematic patterns.

VIDEO CASE EXAMPLE

In the video "Getting Back to Shakopee," Dorothy, the social worker, summarizes: "You have had a lot of stress at work with a poor performance review and anxiety that your coworkers are being rude to you over the possibility that you might get promoted. At home, you are dealing with your mother, who is living with you; your son and his girlfriend not working outside of the home and their baby; your daughter who helps take care of the little ones. All of the work of keeping up the household comes back to you. You are not eating, not sleeping very well, and have lost interest in some things you used to like to do. You have also been considered for promotion at work in the past and care deeply for those family members living with and relying on you."

In conjoint interviews or group sessions, summarization can also be used effectively to highlight and to tie together key elements and dynamics embodied in transactions, as illustrated in the following video case.

VIDEO CASE EXAMPLE

In the video "Home for the Holidays, Part 1," lesbian partners who come to family treatment are in conflict about how open to be about their relationship to their families. Jackie comes from a family in which there is open communication. She is frustrated with the reticence to deal openly with feelings that is reflected in Anna's family. Kim, the social worker, makes the following summarizing statement: "Often when we are forming new families and new couples, we are torn between the families we come from and the new family we are creating. This can play out in logistical decisions about the holidays."

Providing Focus and Continuity

Social workers can also use summarization at the beginning of an individual, group, or conjoint session to review work that clients have accomplished in the last session(s) and to set the stage for work in the present session. At the same time, the social worker may decide to identify a promising topic for discussion or to refresh clients' minds concerning work they wish to accomplish in that session. In addition, summarization can be employed periodically to synthesize salient points at the conclusion of a discussion or used at the end of the session to review the major focal points. In so doing, the social worker will need to place what was accomplished in the session within the broad perspective of the clients' goals. The social worker tries to consider how the salient content and movement manifested in each session fit into the larger whole. Only then are the social worker and clients likely to maintain a sense of direction and avoid needless delays caused by wandering and detours—problems that commonly occur when continuity within or between sessions is weak.

Used as a "wrap-up" when the allotted time for a session is nearly gone, summarization assists the social worker to draw a session to a natural conclusion. In addition to highlighting and linking together the key points of the session, the social worker reviews clients' plans for performing tasks before the next session. When the session ends with such a summarization, all participants should be clear about where they have been and where they are going in relation to the goals toward which their mutual efforts are directed.

Analyzing Your Verbal Following Skills

After taking frequency counts over a period of time of some of the major verbal following skills (accent responses, reflections, responses that seek concreteness, open- and closed-ended responses, and so on), you are ready to assess the extent to which you employ, blend, and balance these skills in relation to each other. On the form for recording verbal following (Figure 6-2), categorize each of your responses from a recorded session. As you analyze your relative use and blending of responses alone or with your practicum instructor, determine whether certain types of responses were used either too frequently or too sparingly. Think of steps you might take to correct any imbalances in your utilization of skills for future sessions.

CLIENT MESSAGE	OPEN-ENDED RESPONSES	CLOSED-ENDED RESPONSES	EMPATHIC RESPONSES	LEVEL OF EMPATHY	CONCRETE RESPONSES	SUMMARIZING RESPONSES	OTHER TYPES OF RESPONSES
1.							
2.							
3.							
4.							
5.							
6.							
7.							

Directions: Categorize each of your responses from a recorded session. Where responses involve more than one category (blended responses), record them as a single response, but also check each category embodied in the response. Excluding the responses checked as "Other Type of Responses," analyze whether certain types of responses were utilized too frequently or too sparingly. Define tasks for yourself to correct imbalances in future sessions. Retain a copy of the form so that you can monitor your progress in mastering verbal following skills over an extended period of time.

FIG 6-2 Recording Form for Verbal Following Skills

SUMMARY

This chapter has helped you learn how to explore, reflect, and appropriately use closed- and open-ended responses as means to better focusing, following, and summarizing in your social work practice. These skills may be applied both with clients and with other persons and colleagues on behalf of clients. In Chapter 7, we will explore some common difficulties experienced by beginning social workers and some ways to overcome them.

COMPETENCY NOTES

EP 2   Engage Diversity and Difference in Practice
- Apply and communicate understanding of the importance of diversity and difference in shaping life experiences in practice at the micro, mezzo, and macro levels.
- Present oneself as a learner, and engage clients and constituencies as experts on their own experiences.
- Apply self-awareness and self-regulation to manage the influence of personal biases and values in working with diverse clients and constituencies.

EP 6   Engage with Individuals, Families, Groups, Organizations, and Communities
- Apply knowledge of human behavior and the social environment, person-in-environment, and other multidisciplinary theoretical frameworks to engage with clients and constituencies.
- Use empathy, reflection, and interpersonal skills to effectively engage diverse clients and constituencies.

EP 7   Assess Individuals, Families, Groups, Organizations, and Communities
- Collect and organize data, and apply critical thinking to interpret information from clients and constituencies.

MODELED SOCIAL WORKER
Responses to Exercises in Reflection of Content

1. "You just get so uptight in a group you don't function."
2. "So you've made some real progress in tuning in to your husband and children."

3. "So people's helpfulness here and your own skills in meeting people have helped your adjustment here."
4. "So you see yourself as having contributed to many of her problems."
5. "It sounds as if your experience causes you to doubt whether more services would be helpful. Could you tell me about your conclusion that the mother is not motivated?"

MODELED SOCIAL WORKER
Responses to Exercises with Reflection of Affect

1. "Because your fears really block you when you argue with your mother, you seem to feel anxious and frustrated." [simple reflection]
2. "So you feel caught by competing parenting and work responsibilities; if you meet all your work hours, you are concerned about how it affects your parenting. If you do what you think you should as a parent, it can conflict with work requirements." [double-sided reflection]
3. "So sometimes you feel cheated by life, and at other times that your illness is a consequence for your smoking history." [double-sided reflection]
4. "So it sounds as if it has not been easy for you to relax and have friends in this school; when they have acted in a way that feels mean to you, you have felt a need to act to protect yourself." [simple reflection]
5. "You're really torn and wonder if not seeing the children very often is too high a price to pay for a divorce. On the other hand, you fear that if you stay with her, there won't be any improvement. Right now you don't see a way out of this dilemma." [reflection with a twist]

ANSWERS TO EXERCISES IN
Identifying Closed- and Open-Ended Responses

Statement	Response
1	C
2	O
3	O
4	C

MODELED SOCIAL WORKER

Responses to Exercises in Identifying Closed- and Open-Ended Responses

1. "Could you tell me more about your wanting to impress Ralph?"
2. "What are you afraid you'd do wrong?"
3. "Given your experience with that probation officer, how would you like your relationship with me to be?"
4. "So you feel that your facility cannot provide what Gladys needs. Can you describe the kind of care you believe she needs?"
5. "So you don't trust that I want to try to help you make what you feel will be the best decision. Can you tell me what I have done that has caused you to think that your mother and I are allies?"
6. "You sound as if you are at a pretty hopeless point right now. When you say you don't know if you want to keep trying to figure it out, can you tell me more about what you are thinking about doing?"

MODELED SOCIAL WORKER

Responses to Exercises in Seeking Concreteness

1. "Can you tell me how it feels weird to you?"
2. "I gather you feel that your friends have let you down in the past. Could you give me a recent example in which this has happened?"
3. "Could you tell me more about what happens when he loses his temper with you?" or "You sound like you don't have much hope that he'll ever get control of his temper. How have you concluded he will never change?" *[A social worker might explore each aspect of the message separately.]*
4. "Could you give me some examples of how she is insensitive to you?"
5. "Sounds like you've been feeling hurt and disappointed over my reaction last week. I can sense you're struggling with those same feelings right now."
6. "It sounds as if you feel that your dad's way of communicating with you is unusual for someone his age. Could you recall some recent examples of times you've had difficulties with how he communicates with you?"
7. "It sounds as if the arthritis pain is aggravating and blocking what you normally do. When you say that handling the pots and pans is kind of tricky, can you tell me about recent examples of what has happened when you are cooking?"
8. "Think of going to the doctor just now. Let your feelings flow naturally. *[Pause.]* What goes on inside you—your thoughts and feelings?"
9. "So you see it as pretty hopeless. You feel pretty strongly about Ms. Wright. I'd be interested in hearing what's happened that has led you to the conclusion she's got it in for black students."
10. "So you feel as if you're nothing in his eyes. I'm wondering how you've reached that conclusion?"

NOTE

1. In previous editions we referred to reflections of content responses as *paraphrases* if they were being used to provide fresh words to restate the client's content message concisely.

Eliminating Counterproductive Communication Patterns and Substituting Positive Alternatives

with Pa Der Vang

Chapter Overview

Chapter 7 explores communication difficulties that often arise in the practice of beginning (and many experienced) social workers and suggests some positive alternatives to these defective patterns. By becoming alert to these difficulties, beginning social workers can focus their attention on communicating in a constructive fashion. In addition to applications in direct practice, the chapter provides numerous communication examples related to both mezzo and macro practice. As with the previous chapters, additional video examples are included in the accompanying CourseMate for *Direct Social Work Practice* at www.cengagebrain.com.

As a result of reading this chapter and practicing with classmates, you will be able to:

- Identify when you have experienced an error or counterproductive pattern in your verbal and nonverbal behavior.

- Identify more constructive alternatives in those instances.

EPAS Competencies in Chapter 7

This chapter will give you the information needed to meet the following practice competencies:

- Competency 1: Demonstrate Ethical and Professional Behavior

- Competency 2: Engage Diversity and Difference in Practice

- Competency 6: Engage with Individuals, Families, Groups, Organizations, and Communities

- Competency 7: Assess Individuals, Families, Groups, Organizations, and Communities

- Competency 9: Evaluate Practice with Individuals, Families, Groups, Organizations, and Communities

IMPACTS OF COUNTERPRODUCTIVE COMMUNICATION PATTERNS

EP 1 and 6

All social workers, even experienced ones, experience counterproductive communication patterns. We all want to experience error-free learning. In fact, though, each of the authors who developed videos for this text made communication errors in their videos (some of which we will share with you). We trust, however, that each of us improves by examining our practice. Competence includes being able to recognize our errors, taking ownership of those errors, and working toward improvement. In this chapter, we will help you become aware of potential communication errors and will explore ways to deal with those errors by replacing them with more productive patterns. In some cases, this means referring back to content in earlier chapters.

Previous research provides direction for identifying communication errors and suggests that improvements can occur. A study of beginning student practice, based on an analysis of 674 role-play videos completed by 396 BSW and 276 MSW students, revealed patterns of frequent errors, which we will review in the following sections (Ragg, Okagbue-Reaves, & Piers, 2007). Nugent and Halvorson (1995) demonstrated how differently worded active listening responses may lead to different short-term client affective outcomes. At the end of your work on this chapter, it is our hope that you will both be aware of things you need to work on *and* feel increasingly confident in your abilities to replace those errors with more productive responses.

IDENTIFYING AND IMPROVING NONVERBAL BARRIERS TO EFFECTIVE COMMUNICATION

EP 1

Nonverbal behaviors strongly influence interactions between people, and social workers' nonverbal interview behavior contributes significantly to ratings of their effectiveness. Nonverbal cues, which serve to confirm or deny messages conveyed verbally, are in large part beyond the conscious awareness of participants. There may be incongruence between what the social worker intends to communicate and the resulting impact of his or her behavior. Or there may be "leakage"—the transmission of information about feelings and responses that the sender did not intend to communicate to the receiver. Facial expressions—a blush, a furrowed brow, or a look of shock or dismay, for example—convey much more about the social worker's attitude toward the client or the client's message than what is said aloud. In fact, if there is a discrepancy between the social worker's verbal and nonverbal communication, the client is more likely to discredit the verbal message. Over time, people learn through myriad transactions with others that nonverbal cues more accurately indicate feelings than do spoken words. Note that, as a social worker, you are more likely to attend to these errors if you have opportunities to view your practice in videos.

Physical Attending

Beginning social workers are often relatively unaware of their nonverbal behaviors, and they may not have learned to consciously use these behaviors to advantage in conveying caring, understanding, and respect. Therefore, mastering **physical attending**—a basic skill critical to the helping process—is one of the social worker's first learning tasks. Physical attentiveness to another person is communicated by receptive behaviors, such as facing the client squarely, leaning forward, maintaining eye contact, and remaining relaxed.

Attending also requires social workers to be fully present—that is, to keep in moment-to-moment contact with the client through disciplined attention. Attending in a fully present (though perhaps not relaxed) fashion is expected of beginning social workers, despite their typical anxiety about what to do next, how to help, and how to avoid harming clients. Such skill is more likely to evolve with greater experience after novice social workers have engaged in considerable observation of expert social workers, role-playing, initial interviews with clients, and viewing of their own practice.

Cultural Nuances of Nonverbal Cues

EP 2

To consciously use nonverbal behaviors to full advantage in transcultural relationships, social workers must be aware that some members of different cultural groups ascribe different meanings to certain nonverbal behaviors. Eye-to-eye contact, for example, is expected behavior among members of mainstream American culture. In fact, people who avoid eye-to-eye contact may be viewed as untrustworthy or evasive. Conversely, members of some Native American tribes regard direct gazing as an intrusion on privacy. It is important to observe and investigate the norms for gazing before using eye-to-eye contact with members of some tribes (Gross, 1995).[1]

Yet it is hazardous to make generalizations across ethnic groups. For example, one study reported that Filipino students were more similar to Caucasians students than to Chinese students in relation to many attitudes, perceptions, and beliefs. Meanwhile, the same study showed that women were more similar to one another across ethnic groups than they were to men within their own group (Agbayani-Siewart, 2004). These examples suggest that although it is important to understand a client's culture or group identity, it is also important to acknowledge in-group differences.

With this proviso in mind, social workers should consider the possibility of differences in cultural assumptions about helping professionals as authorities who can solve problems by providing advice. For instance, in some cultures, clients might not be forthcoming unless they are spoken to by the social worker. The social worker in turn may mistakenly perceive the client's behavior as passive or reticent. Consequently, "long gaps of silence may occur as the client waits patiently for the social worker to structure the interview, take charge, and thus provide the solution" (Tsui & Schultz, 1985, p. 565). Such gaps in communication engender anxiety in both parties that may undermine the development of rapport and defeat the helping process. Further, failure to correctly interpret the client's nonverbal behavior may lead the social worker to conclude erroneously that the client has flat affect (i.e., limited emotionality). Given these potential hazards, social workers should strive to understand the client's cultural frame of reference. Clarifying roles and expectations should also be emphasized. Consider being more active with some Asian clients, including placing greater emphasis on clarifying role expectations.

Other Nonverbal Behaviors

EP 1

Barriers that prevent the social worker from staying in psychological contact with the client can be caused by preoccupation with peripheral curiosities or evaluations about the client or by inner pressures to find immediate solutions to the client's problems. In fact, many beginning social workers

have prior experience in positions where their job was to quickly assess a situation and provide a rapid solution. Such skills are to be valued but not overly generalized such that you short-circuit exploration of client concerns and prematurely move to solutions. It is important to spend an adequate amount of time on engagement and assessment before moving into intervention planning. Likewise, reduced focus on the client can result from being preoccupied with oneself while practicing new skills. In addition, extraneous noise, a ringing or buzzing phone, an inadequate interviewing room, a pile of paperwork on your lap, or a lack of privacy can interfere with the social worker's being psychologically present.

Clients need to perceive that the social worker is concerned about their situation. Social workers must be aware of several behaviors that may convey a lack of concern for the client. For example, staring vacantly, looking out the window, frequently glancing at the clock, yawning, and fidgeting suggest a lack of attention; trembling hands or rigid posture may communicate hurriedness or anxiety. These and a host of other behavioral cues that convey messages such as inattention or lack of interest are readily perceived by most clients, many of whom are highly sensitive to criticism or rejection in any form. Social workers must also pay attention to societal preoccupation with checking cell phones for messages, as social workers are not immune to this habit. Doing so in a client's presence could readily convey inattention and disrespect. Voluntary clients with sufficient resources and self-esteem are not likely to accept social worker behavior that they consider disrespectful, nor should they. This leaves the social worker with just those involuntary clients with fewer choices, fewer resources, and lower self-esteem, who may believe that they have little recourse other than accepting such behavior.

VIDEO CASE EXAMPLE

The "Work with Probation Officer" video contains an example of disrespectful nonverbal and verbal behavior, approximating Level 0 empathy as described in Chapter 5. Such examples are unfortunately not uncommon in settings dealing with persons who are alleged to have engaged in deviant behavior such as violence against a partner, in which clients have low power and the social worker is under time pressure to complete an assessment. Note the social worker in this video calling the client's attention to time pressures and judging how little the client had accomplished in previous anger management training. Fortunately, you can also link to an improved example with the same social worker and client that revisits the same scenario from a much more respectful perspective. In the *Practice Behaviors Workbook,* you will have an opportunity to make a list of the counterproductive social worker behaviors you see in the first example and the corrections demonstrated in the second.

Taking Inventory of Nonverbal Patterns of Responding

EP 9

To assist you in taking inventory of your own styles of responding to clients, Table 7-1 identifies recommended and not recommended nonverbal behaviors. You will probably find that you have a mixed repertoire of nonverbal responses, some of which have the potential to enhance helping relationships and foster client progress. Other, less desirable behaviors of the beginning social worker may include nervousness that may block your clients from freely disclosing information and otherwise limit the flow of the helping process. You thus have a threefold task: (1) to assess your

TABLE 7-1 Inventory of Practitioner's Nonverbal Communication

RECOMMENDED	NOT RECOMMENDED
Facial Expressions	
Direct eye contact (except when culturally proscribed)	Avoidance of eye contact
Warmth and concern reflected in facial expression	Staring or fixating on person or object
Eyes at same level as client's	Lifting eyebrow critically
Appropriately varied and animated facial expressions	Eye level higher or lower than client's
Mouth relaxed; occasional smiles	Nodding head excessively
	Yawning
	Frozen or rigid facial expressions
	Inappropriate slight smile
	Pursing or biting lips
Posture	
Arms and hands moderately expressive; appropriate gestures	Rigid body position; arms tightly folded
Body leaning slightly forward; attentive but relaxed	Body turned at an angle to client
	Fidgeting with hands
	Squirming or rocking in chair
	Leaning back or placing feet on desk
	Hand or fingers over mouth
	Pointing finger for emphasis
Voice	
Clearly audible but not loud	Mumbling or speaking inaudibly
Warmth in tone of voice	Monotonic voice
Voice modulated to reflect nuances of feeling and emotional tone of client messages	Halting speech
Moderate speech tempo	Frequent grammatical errors
	Prolonged silences
	Excessively animated speech
	Slow, rapid, or staccato speech
	Nervous laughter
	Consistent clearing of throat
	Speaking loudly
Physical Proximity	
Three to five feet between chairs	Excessive closeness or distance
	Talking across desk or other barrier

repetitive nonverbal behaviors; (2) to eliminate nonverbal styles that hinder effective communication; and (3) to sustain and perhaps increase desirable nonverbal behaviors. As noted earlier, it is helpful to make a video recording of your practice to determine your behavior.

At the end of this chapter, you will find a checklist intended for use in training or supervision to obtain feedback on nonverbal aspects of attending. Given the opportunity to review a videotape of your performance in actual or simulated interviews and/or to receive behaviorally specific feedback from supervisors and peers, you should be able to adequately master physical aspects of attending in a relatively brief time.

A review of your taped performance may reveal that you are already demonstrating many of the desirable physical attending behaviors listed in Table 7-1. You may also possess personal nonverbal mannerisms that are particularly helpful in establishing relationships with others, such as a friendly grin or a relaxed, easy manner. As you take inventory of your nonverbal behaviors, solicit feedback from others regarding these behaviors. Try to note your behaviors when you are and are not at ease with clients. When appropriate, increase the frequency of recommended behaviors that you have identified. In particular, try to cultivate the quality of conveying acceptance and understanding.

As you review videotapes of your sessions, pay particular attention to your nonverbal responses at those moments when you experienced pressure or tension; this assessment will assist you in determining whether your responses were counterproductive. All beginning interviewers experience moments of discomfort in their first contacts with clients, and nonverbal behaviors serve as an index of their comfort level. To enhance your self-awareness of your own behavioral patterns, develop a list of the verbal and nonverbal behaviors you display when you are under pressure. When you review your videotaped sessions, you may notice that under pressure you respond with humor, fidget, change voice inflection, assume a rigid body posture, or manifest other nervous mannerisms. Making an effort to become aware of and to eliminate obvious signs of anxiety is an important step in achieving mastery of your nonverbal responding.

VIDEO CASE EXAMPLE

In the video "Serving the Squeaky Wheel," the social worker, Ron Rooney, was surprised by questions about his credentials when he became, in the role-play, the new case manager for a client with serious and persistent mental illness. Notice how he responded at first defensively, expressing sarcasm and disgruntlement, before he recovered to consider how the client was in fact acting to protect herself from possible exploitation. As a social worker, it is a good rule to assume that the client is not deliberately trying to embarrass you or make you uncomfortable. By listening better, you are often able to uncover other intentions for behaviors that may have inadvertently pushed your buttons. If you discover that the client may indeed have been attempting to provoke you, reflection about what may have contributed to this behavior can be useful. In this particular situation, the client, Cali, described feeling treated disrespectfully by her previous social worker, who had not told her that she would be terminating. Reflecting how you are feeling and linking it to themes the client has shared can be useful. For example, the social worker might have said, "It sounds, Cali, as if you feel like you weren't treated well by your previous social worker in her not coming to closure with you prior to making a transfer to me. Is that right? If so, I've been feeling a little under fire from you in your questioning my credentials. I'm wondering if I'm feeling at all like you have felt in sensing disrespect? Am I off base here?"

ELIMINATING VERBAL BARRIERS TO COMMUNICATION

Many types of ineffective verbal responses inhibit clients from exploring problems and sharing freely with the social worker. To understand why, we refer to **reactance theory**, which suggests that clients will act to protect valued freedoms (Brehm & Brehm, 1981; Wright, Greenberg, & Brehm, 2004). Such freedoms can include the freedom to have one's own opinions and the inclination to action. When such valued freedoms are threatened, clients will often withdraw, argue, or move to a superficial topic.

The following list identifies common verbal barriers that usually have an immediate negative effect on communications, thereby inhibiting clients from revealing pertinent information and working on problems.

EP 1

In each case, we will explore positive alternatives to these barriers.

1. Reassuring, sympathizing, consoling, or excusing
2. Advising and giving suggestions or solutions prematurely
3. Using sarcasm or employing humor that is distracting or makes light of clients' problems
4. Judging, criticizing, or placing blame
5. Trying to convince the client about the right point of view through logical arguments, lecturing, instructing, or arguing
6. Analyzing, diagnosing, or making glib or dogmatic interpretations
7. Threatening, warning, or counterattacking

The first three behaviors are mistakes that beginning social workers commonly make across a variety of populations and settings, often reflecting their nervousness and an abounding desire to be immediately helpful. Numbers 4–7 are also common but are more likely to occur when the social worker is working with "captive clients"—a situation in which there is a power differential and the client cannot readily escape. An underlying theme of these behaviors can be the social worker and the agency reflecting a sense of superiority over people whose behavior or problem solving has been harmful to themselves or others.

Reassuring, Sympathizing, Consoling, or Excusing

- *"You'll feel better tomorrow."*
- *"Don't worry, things will work out."*
- *"You probably didn't do anything to aggravate the situation."*
- *"I really feel sorry for you."*

A pattern found in 90 percent of the taped interviews completed by beginning students was that they would reassure clients that their responses were normal and that they were not responsible for the difficulty they were concerned about (Ragg, Okagbue-Reaves, & Piers, 2007). When used selectively and with justification, well-timed reassurance can engender much needed hope and support. By glibly reassuring clients that "things will work out," "everybody has problems," or "things aren't as bleak as they seem," however, social workers avoid exploring clients' feelings of despair, anger, hopelessness, or helplessness. Situations faced by clients are often grim, with no immediate relief at hand.

Social workers must undertake to explore those distressing feelings and to assist clients in acknowledging painful realities rather than glossing over clients' feelings. It is important for the social worker to develop awareness of their own reactions to clients' strong feelings. Beginning social workers need to convey that they hear and understand their clients' difficulties as they experience them. They will also want to convey hope while exploring prospects for change—albeit at the appropriate time in the dialogue.

Reassuring clients prematurely or without a genuine basis for hope often serves the purposes of social workers more than the purposes of clients and, in fact, may represent efforts by social workers to dissuade clients from revealing their troubling feelings. That is, reassurance may serve to restore the comfort level and equilibrium of social workers rather than to help clients. Instead of fostering hope, these glib statements convey a lack of understanding of clients' feelings and raise doubts about the authenticity of social workers. Clients, in turn, may react with thoughts such as "It's easy for you to say that, but you don't know how very frightened I really am," or "You're just saying that so I'll feel better." In addition, responses that excuse clients (e.g., "You're not to blame") or sympathize with their position (e.g., "I can see exactly why you feel that way; I think I would probably have done the same thing") often have the effect of unwittingly reinforcing inappropriate behavior or reducing clients' anxiety and motivation to work on problems.

In place of inappropriate reassurance, more positive and useful responses can come from reflecting that you heard and understood what the client was conveying and, in some cases, positive reframing, which does not discount concerns but places them in a different light.

VIDEO CASE EXAMPLE

In the video "Getting Back to Shakopee," the client, Valerie, begins to describe her concerns about a possible drug relapse. Rather than discount those concerns, the social worker, Dorothy, asks a question about how Valerie has been managing to cope with the desire to relapse. Instead of saying, "You will feel better tomorrow," a more constructive response would be, "I hear that this has been a very discouraging day for you. You have gotten through some difficult situations in the past.

What are some of the ways you have coped with such bad days before?" Similarly, rather than saying, "You probably did not do anything to aggravate the situation," it might be better to reflect, "That sounds like a complicated, disappointing situation. You are sorry that what you tried was not successful." Additional examples of consoling, sympathizing responses and more positive alternatives are contained in the *Practice Behaviors Workbook*.

Advising and Giving Suggestions or Solutions Prematurely

- *"I suggest that you move to a new place because you have had so many difficulties here."*
- *"I think you need to try a new approach with your daughter. Let me suggest that ...."*
- *"I think it would be best for you to try using timeout."*
- *"Because your partner isn't supportive, why don't you try to create some new relationships with other people?"*

Another frequent pattern found in the Ragg, Okagbue-Reaves, and Piers (2007) study was that in 90 percent of the videos of beginning social workers, they would appear at points to turn off from listening to the client and seem to be engaging in an internal dialogue related to formulating a solution to concerns raised. Such patterns may have been fostered in previous work positions and exchanges with friends where the pattern was to move quickly to problem-solving solutions without grasping the larger situation. We do not mean to discount the social worker's capacity to think about a problem and possible solutions. Rather, we want to stress the importance of waiting until the social worker has fully grasped the situation and empathized with the client before moving into a mutual examination of alternatives.

Little is known about the actual provision of advice in terms of its frequency or the circumstances in which it occurs (Brehm & Brehm, 1981). Clients often seek advice, and appropriately timed advice can be an important helping tool. Conversely, untimely advice may elicit opposition. Even when clients solicit advice in early phases of the helping process, they often react negatively when they receive it because the recommended solutions, which are invariably based on superficial information, often do not address their real needs. Further,

because clients are frequently burdened and preoccupied with little-understood conflicts, feelings, and pressures, they are not ready to take action on their problems at this point. For these reasons, after offering premature advice, social workers may observe clients replying with responses such as "Yes, but I've already tried that," "That won't work," or "I could try that" with little enthusiasm demonstrated for actually doing so. In fact, these responses can serve as feedback clues that you may have slipped into the habit of giving premature advice.

Although many clients seek advice from social workers because they see the social workers as expert problem solvers, those social workers can (wrongly) seek to expedite problem solving by quickly comparing the current situation to other similar ones encountered in the past and recommending a solution that has worked for other clients or themselves. In such cases, social workers may feel pressure to provide quick answers or solutions for clients who unrealistically expect magical answers and instant relief from problems that have plagued them for long periods of time. Beginning social workers may also experience inner pressure to dispense solutions to clients' problems, mistakenly believing that their new role demands that they, like physicians or advice columnists, prescribe a treatment regimen. They thus run the risk of giving advice before they have conducted a thorough exploration of clients' problems. In reality, instead of dispensing wisdom, a major role of social workers is to create and shape processes with clients in which they engage in mutual discovery of problems and solutions—work that will take time and concentrated effort.

Beginning social workers who are working with nonvoluntary clients may feel justified in "strongly suggesting" their opinions because of the poor choices or problem solving they may presume landed these clients in their current predicament. As suggested in Chapter 4, social work practice does not have a place for judging clients: We may have to evaluate clients' performance and capabilities in certain circumstances, but that is not the same as judging them as people. Assisting clients through modeling and reinforcement of prosocial behavior is not the same as judging clients and imposing social workers' own opinions (Trotter, 2006).

The timing and form of recommendations are all-important in the helping process. Advice should be offered sparingly, and only after thoroughly exploring the problem and the client's ideas about possible solutions. At that point, the social worker may serve as a consultant, tentatively sharing ideas about solutions to supplement those developed by the client, and assisting the client in weighing the pros and cons of different alternatives. Clients who try to pressure social workers to dispense knowledge prematurely are merely depriving themselves of the opportunity to develop effective solutions to these problems. In such circumstances, social workers should stress clients' roles in helping to discover and tailor solutions to fit their unique problems.

EP 1 and 7

Clients may expect to receive early advice if social workers have not appropriately clarified roles and expectations about how mutual participation in generating possible solutions will further the client's own growth and self-confidence. Assuming a position of superiority and quickly providing solutions for problems without encouraging clients to think through the possible courses of action fosters dependency and stifles creative thinking. Freely dispensing advice also minimizes or ignores clients' strengths and potentials, and many clients tend to respond with inner resentment to such high-handed treatment. In addition, clients who have not been actively involved in planning their own courses of action may lack motivation to implement the social worker's advice. Moreover, when advice does not remedy a problem—as it often doesn't—clients may blame social workers and disown any responsibility for an unfavorable outcome.

Rather than say, "I suggest that you move to a new place because you have had so many difficulties here," a more productive response would be to say, "You have had a lot of difficulties in your current place. What have you considered doing about your living situation?" Based on that response, you could assist the client either in considering ways to improve that situation or in looking for alternative living arrangements.

Instead of saying, "I think you need to try a new approach with your daughter. Let me suggest that …," you might say, "It sounds as if what you have tried with your daughter has not worked as you had hoped. What other solutions have you considered?" Based on the client's response, you can ask if he or she would like to consider some other possibilities. Additional examples of reframing premature advice situations are presented in the *Practice Behaviors Workbook*.

Humor can be helpful, bringing relief and sometimes perspective to work that might otherwise be tense and tedious. Pollio (1995) has suggested ways to determine appropriate use of humor. Are you the social worker capable of telling something that is humorous? Do others, including clients, think so? Does the comment fit the situation? Is something needed to unstick or free up a situation in a way that humor might help? What do you know about the client's sense of humor? Similarly, van Wormer and Boes (1997) have described ways that humor permits social workers to continue to operate in the face of trauma. Using plays on words or noting a sense of the preposterous or incongruous can help social workers and clients face difficult situations. Humor can also allow clients to express emotions in safe, less emotionally charged ways (Dewayne, 1978). Kane (1995) describes the way humor in group work can facilitate work with persons with HIV. Caplan (1995) has also described how in group work, facilitation of humor can create a necessary safety and comfort level in work with men who batter. Teens have been described as using irony, sarcasm, mocking, and parody as ways of coping with difficult situations (Cameron et al., 2010). Similarly, humor can be used in ways to diffuse conflict (Norrick & Spitz, 2008).

Excessive or untimely use of humor, however, can be distracting, keeping the content of the session on a superficial level and interfering with mutual objectives. Sarcasm often emanates from unrecognized hostility that tends to provoke counter-hostility in clients. Similarly, making a comment such as "you really win the prize for worst week" when a client recounts a series of crises and unfortunate incidents runs the risk of conveying that the difficulties are not taken seriously. A better response would be to empathize with the difficulties of the week and compliment the client on persisting to cope despite them.

EP 1 and 6

Rather than saying, "Did you get up on the wrong side of the bed?," a more descriptive response that does not run the risk of diminishing the client's experience would be to say, "It sounds as if today was difficult from the time you got up."

Using Sarcasm or Employing Humor Inappropriately

- *"Did you get up on the wrong side of the bed?"*
- *"It seems to me that we've been through all this before."*
- *"You really fell for that line."*

Judging, Criticizing, or Placing Blame

- *"You're wrong about that."*
- *"Running away from home was a bad mistake."*
- *"One of your problems is that you're not willing to consider another point of view."*
- *"You're not thinking straight."*

Clients do not feel supported when they perceive the social worker as critical, moralistic, and defensive rather than warm and respectful (Coady & Marziali, 1994; Eaton, Abeles, & Gutfreund, 1993; Safran & Muran, 2000). Responses that evaluate and show disapproval can be detrimental to clients and to the helping process. Clients usually respond defensively and sometimes counterattack when they perceive criticism from social workers; some may simply cut off any meaningful communication with social workers. When they are intimidated by a social worker's greater expertise, some clients also accept negative evaluations as accurate reflections of their poor judgment or lack of worth or value. In making such negative judgments about clients, social workers violate the basic social work values of nonjudgmental attitude and acceptance.

Such responses are unlikely to be tolerated by voluntary clients with adequate self-esteem or enough power in the situation to have alternatives. Such clients are likely to "fire" you, speak to your supervisor, or put you on notice if you act in such seemingly disrespectful ways. Others may shut down, perceiving you as having some power over them.

Involuntary clients often face what they believe to be dangerous consequences for not getting along with the social worker. Hence, some clients with substantial self-control and self-esteem may put up with such browbeating without comment. Others may respond in kind with attacks of their own that then appear in case records as evidence of client resistance.

Your own judging in the situation is not useful and is often counterproductive. On the other hand, it could be useful in some circumstances to help the client reflect about actions that might be a danger to him- or herself or others, or about violations of the law. In such circumstances, asking about the client's awareness of consequences and alternatives can be useful. For example, the social worker might ask, "How do you look now at the consequences of running away from home?" or "How would this appear from your partner's point of view?" The social worker might also provide a double-sided reflection, as described in Chapter 6.

Trying to Convince Clients about the Right Point of View through Logic, Lecturing, Instructing, or Arguing

- "Let's look at the facts about drugs."
- "You have to take some responsibility for your life, you know."

- "Running away from home will only get you in more difficulty."
- "That attitude won't get you anywhere."

Clients sometimes consider courses of action that social workers view as unsafe, illegal, or contrary to the clients' goals. However, attempting to convince clients through lecturing, instructing, and similar behavior often provokes a kind of boomerang effect—that is, clients are not only unconvinced of the merits of the social worker's argument but may also be more inclined to hold onto their beliefs than before. As noted earlier, according to reactance theory, clients will attempt to defend their valued freedoms when these privileges are threatened (Brehm & Brehm, 1981). For some clients (especially adolescents, for whom independent thinking is associated with a particular developmental stage), deferring to or agreeing with social workers is tantamount to giving up their individuality or freedom. The challenge when working with such clients is to learn how to listen to and respect their perspective at the same time as you make sure that they are aware of alternatives and consequences. Compare the two ways of handling the same situation described in the following.

Teen parent client: I have decided to drop out of high school for now and get my cosmetology license.

Social worker: Don't you know that dropping out of high school is going to hurt you and your children, both now and in the future? Are you willing to sacrifice hundreds of thousands of dollars less that you would earn over your lifetime for you and your children just to buy a few little knick-knacks now?

Teen parent client: But this is my life! My babies need things now! You don't know what it is like scraping by! You can't tell me what to do! You are not my mom! I know what is best for me and my children!

Rather than escalate into what has been called the **confrontation-denial cycle** (Murphy & Baxter, 1997), a better alternative is to respond to the teen parent client with an effort to understand her perspective, before exploring alternatives and consequences.

Teen parent client: I have decided to drop out of high school for now and get my cosmetology license.

Social worker: So you have been going to high school for a while now with some success, and now you are considering that going in a different direction and getting your cosmetology license may work better for you. Tell me about that.

Teen parent client: Well, it is true that I have been working hard in high school. But I need more money now, not just far off in the future. My babies and I don't have enough to get by.

Social worker: And you feel that getting a cosmetology license will help you do that.

Teen parent client: I do. I still want to finish high school and get my diploma. I know that I will earn more for my kids and myself with a diploma than if I don't finish. If I get my cosmetology degree, it will take a little longer to get my high school diploma, but I think I am up to it.

Social worker: So your longer-term plan is still to get your high school diploma but just to delay it. You think that getting your cosmetology degree will help you and your kids get by better now. Are there any drawbacks to withdrawing from high school at this time?

Teen parent client: Only if I get distracted and don't return. I could kind of get out of the habit of going to school and I might be around people who haven't finished school.

Social worker: Those are things to consider. How might you be sure that your withdrawal from high school was only temporary?

In the first example above, the social worker attempts to vigorously persuade the client about the course of action he or she deems wisest. Such efforts, while well meaning, often create power struggles, thereby perpetuating dynamics that have previously occurred in clients' personal relationships. By confronting before attempting to understand the client's perception, social workers ignore their clients' feelings and views, focusing instead on the social worker's "being right"; this tactic may engender feelings of resentment, alienation, or hostility in clients. Such efforts are both unethical and ineffective. Persuasion in the sense of helping clients to obtain accurate information with which to make informed decisions can be an ethical intervention. When clients contemplate actions that run contrary to their own goals, or will endanger themselves or others, then an effort to persuade can be an ethical intervention. Such efforts should not focus on the one "pet" solution of the social worker, however, but rather should assist the client in examining the advantages and disadvantages of several options, including those with which the social worker may disagree (R. H. Rooney, 2009). Hence, the effort is not to convince but rather to assist clients in making informed decisions. By not being confrontational with the client in the second example, the social worker is able to support the client's right to make decisions for herself and to do so considering alternatives and consequences.

Analyzing, Diagnosing, or Making Glib or Dogmatic Interpretations

- *"You're behaving that way because you're angry with your partner."*
- *"Your attitude may have kept you from giving their ideas a fair hearing."*
- *"You're acting in a passive-aggressive way."*
- *"You're really hostile today."*

When used sparingly and timed appropriately, interpretation of the dynamics of behavior can be a potent change-oriented skill (see Chapter 17). However, even accurate interpretations that focus on purposes or meanings of behavior substantially beyond clients' levels of conscious awareness tend to inspire client opposition and are doomed to failure.

When stated dogmatically ("I know what's wrong with you," or "how you feel," or "what your real motives are"), interpretations also present a threat to clients, causing them to feel exposed or trapped. When a glib interpretation is thrust upon them, clients often expend their energies in disconfirming the interpretation, explaining themselves, making angry rebuttals, or passively acquiescing rather than working on the problem at hand.

Using social work jargon such as *fixation*, *resistance*, *reinforcement*, *repression*, *passivity*, *neuroticism*, and a host of other terms to describe the behavior of clients in their presence is also destructive to the helping process. Indeed, it may confuse or bewilder clients and provoke opposition to change. These terms also oversimplify complex phenomena and psychic mechanisms and stereotype clients, thereby obliterating their uniqueness. In addition, these sweeping generalizations provide no operational definitions of clients' problems, nor do they suggest avenues for behavior modification. If clients accept social workers' restricted definitions of their problems, they may define themselves in the same terms as those used by social workers (e.g., "I am a passive person" or "I have a schizoid personality"). This type of stereotypic labeling often causes clients to view themselves as "sick" and their situations as hopeless, providing them with a ready excuse for not working on their problems.

It is important to help clients identify their feelings and behaviors as a means toward increasing client self-awareness and coping. Introducing terminology to describe behavior and feelings should be done as a suggestion, while inviting the client to correct the social worker if he or she is incorrect: "Correct me if I'm wrong, but it seems like you are uncomfortable with what we're talking about because I'm guessing that it makes you feel vulnerable."

VIDEO CASE EXAMPLE

Use of diagnostic labels is a reality in some direct practice settings. It is used as a way of identifying treatable conditions, applying evidence-based forms of treatment, and also as a requirement for health insurance coverage of treatment. In the video "Getting Back to Shakopee," follow the discussion between the client, Valerie, and her social worker, Dorothy, about the meaning of the term *depression*. Valerie is worried about being labeled as "depressed." They go on to talk about how the concept of depression can be useful in part to explain some of her experience, to possibly lead to useful medication, and to fit agency and health insurance guidelines.

Threatening, Warning, or Counterattacking

- "You'd better … or else!"
- "If you don't …, you'll be sorry."
- "If you know what's good for you, you'll …"

Sometimes, clients consider actions that would endanger themselves or others or are illegal. In such instances, alerting clients to the potential consequences of those actions is an ethical and appropriate intervention. Conversely, making threats of the sort above often produces a kind of oppositional behavior that exacerbates an already strained situation.

EP 1

Even the most well-intentioned social workers may occasionally bristle or respond defensively under the pressure of verbal abuse, accusatory or blaming responses, or challenges to their integrity, competence, motives, or authority. For example, a social worker was scheduled to offer services to a veteran who was entering hospice care. The veteran exploded with a series of expletives and insults to the effect that he had no need of such services. Rather than choose to inform the client of proper respect and boundaries, the social worker asked if she could come at another time to explain the possible services so that the client could be sure about whether they might be helpful. He calmed down and averred that coming at another time would be fine.

Whatever the dynamics behind clients' provocative behavior, responding defensively is counterproductive, as it may duplicate the destructive pattern of responses that clients have typically elicited and experienced from others. To achieve competence, therefore, you must learn to master your own natural defensive reactions and evolve effective ways of dealing with negative feelings, putting the client's needs before your own.

Empathic communication produces a cathartic release of negative feelings, defusing a strained situation and permitting a more rational emotional exploration of factors that underlie clients' feelings. For example, replying to a client, "You have difficult decisions to make and are caught between alternatives that you don't consider very attractive; I wish you well in making a decision that you can live with in the future," can convey support and respect for the right to choose.

The negative effects of certain types of responses are not always immediately apparent because clients may not overtly demonstrate negative reactions at the time or because the dampening effect on the helping process cannot be observed in a single transaction. To assess the effect of responses, then, the social worker must determine the frequency with which he or she issues the dampening responses and evaluate the overall impact of those responses on the helping process. Frequent use of some types of responses by the social worker indicates the presence of counterproductive patterns of communication such as the following (note that this list is a continuation of the list of problematic social worker behaviors on page 173):

8. Stacking questions and using double-barreled questions
9. Asking leading questions
10. Interrupting inappropriately or excessively
11. Dominating the interaction
12. Keeping discussion focused on safe topics
13. Responding infrequently
14. Parroting or overusing certain phrases or clichés
15. Dwelling on the remote past
16. Going on fishing expeditions (tangential exploration)
17. Failing to be aware of cognitive bias

Individual responses that fall within these patterns may or may not be ineffective when used occasionally. When they are employed extensively in lieu of using varied response patterns, however, they inhibit the natural flow of a session and limit the richness of information revealed. The sections that follow expand on each of these verbal barriers and detrimental social worker responses.

Stacking Questions and Using Double-Barreled Questions

In exploring problems, social workers should use facilitative questions that assist clients in revealing detailed information about specific problem areas. Asking multiple questions at the same time, or **stacking questions**, diffuses the focus and confuses clients. Consider the vast amount of ground covered in the following messages:

- "When you don't feel you have control of situations, what goes on inside of you? What do you think about? What do you do?"
- "Have you thought about where you are going to live? Is that one of your biggest concerns, or is there another that takes priority?"
- "How satisfied are you with the housing situation and your case worker?"

Stacking questions is a problem frequently encountered by beginning social workers, who may feel an urgent need to help clients by providing many options all at one time. Adequately answering even one of the foregoing questions would require a client to give an extended response. Rather than focus on one question, however, clients often respond superficially and nonspecifically to the social worker's multiple inquiries, omitting important information in the process. Stacked questions thus have "low yield" and are unproductive and inefficient in gathering relevant information. Slowing down and asking one question at a time is preferable. If you have asked stacked questions (and all social workers have at many points), and the client hesitates in response, you can correct for the problem by repeating your preferred question.

Asking Leading Questions

Leading questions have hidden agendas designed to induce clients to agree with a particular view or to adopt a solution that social workers deem to be in clients' best interests. For example:

- "Do you think you've really tried to get along with your partner?"
- "You don't really mean that, do you?"
- "Aren't you too young to move out on your own?"
- "Don't you think that arguing with your mother will provoke her to come down on you as she has done in the past?"

In actuality, these types of questions often obscure legitimate concerns that social workers should discuss with clients. Social workers may conceal their feelings and opinions about such matters, however, and present them obliquely in the form of solutions (e.g., "Don't you think you ought to …") in the hope that leading questions will guide clients to desired conclusions. It is an error, however, to assume that clients will not see through such maneuvers. Indeed, clients often discern the social worker's motives and inwardly resist having views or directives imposed on them under the guise of leading questions. Nevertheless, to avoid conflict or controversy with social workers, they may express feeble agreement or simply divert the discussion to another topic.

By contrast, when social workers authentically assume responsibility for concerns they wish clients to consider, they enhance the likelihood that clients will respond receptively to their questions. In addition, they can raise questions that are not slanted to imply the "correct" answer from the social worker's viewpoint. For example, "How have you attempted to reach agreement with your partner?" does not contain the hint about the "right" answer found in the first question given. Similarly, the last question could be rephrased as follows: "I am not clear how you see arguing with your mother is likely to be more successful than it has proved to be in the past."

Interrupting Inappropriately or Excessively

Beginning social workers often worry excessively about covering all items on their own and their agency's agenda ("What will I tell my supervisor?"). To maintain focus on relevant problem areas, social workers must sometimes interrupt clients. To be effective, however, these interruptions must be purposeful, well timed, and smoothly executed. Interruptions may damage the helping process when they are abrupt or divert clients from exploring pertinent problem areas. For example, interrupting to challenge a client's account of events or to confirm an irrelevant detail can break the flow and put the client on the defensive. Frequent untimely interruptions tend to annoy clients, stifle spontaneous expression, and hinder exploration of problems.

Identifying and prioritizing key questions in advance with an outline can assist in avoiding this pattern. Appropriate interruptions can occur if you want to convey that you have heard what a client has to say. For example, some clients seem like a broken record, repeating certain stories and accusations about bad things that have occurred to them. A more useful response is to provide an empathic summary. For example, "Let me interrupt, Mrs. Jones, to see if I am getting what you are saying. You are not opposed to having home health care. In fact you welcome it. However, timing has been a problem for you. Too often aides have come early in the day when you were not yet up for the day, is that correct?" Such an empathic summary can free some clients from needing to repeat the story and to move on to consider what feasible options to their dilemma there might be.

Dominating the Interaction

Social workers should guide discussions. They should not dominate the interaction by talking too much or by asking too many closed-ended questions. Other domineering behaviors by social workers include repeatedly offering advice, pressuring clients to improve, presenting lengthy arguments to convince clients, interrupting frequently, offering excessive or inappropriate self-disclosure, and so on. Some social workers are also prone to behave as though they are all-knowing, failing to convey respect for clients' points of view or capacities to solve problems. Such dogmatic and authoritarian behavior discourages clients from expressing themselves and fosters a one-up, one-down relationship in which clients feel at a great disadvantage and resent the social worker's supercilious demeanor.

Social workers should monitor the relative distribution of participation by all participants (including themselves) involved in individual, family, or group sessions. Although clients naturally vary in their levels of verbal participation and assertiveness, all group members should have equal opportunity to share information, concerns, and views in the helping process. Social workers have a responsibility to ensure that this opportunity is available to them.

VIDEO CASE EXAMPLE

As a general guideline, clients should consume more "speaking time" than social workers in the helping process, although during initial sessions with some Asian American clients and others with whom there are language differences, social workers must be more direct than they are with others, as discussed earlier. For example, in the video "Working with Yan Ping," the social worker, Kim Strom-Gottfried, is quite active in clarifying roles and expectations, frequently reflecting to make sure they are on the same page.

Sometimes social workers defeat practice objectives in group or conjoint sessions by dominating the interaction through such behaviors as speaking for members, focusing more on some members than on others, or giving speeches. Even social workers who are not particularly verbal may dominate sessions that include reserved or nonassertive clients, as a means of alleviating their own discomfort with silence and passivity. Although it is natural to be more active with reticent or withdrawn clients than with those who are more verbal, social workers must avoid seeming overbearing.

Using facilitative responses that draw clients out is an effective method of minimizing silence and passivity. When a review of one of your taped sessions reveals that you have monopolized the interaction, it is important that you explore the reasons for your behavior. Identify the specific responses that were authoritarian or domineering and the events that preceded those responses. Also examine the clients' style of relating for clues regarding your own reactions, and analyze the feelings you were experiencing at the time. Based on your review and assessment of your performance, you should then plan a strategy for modifying your own style of relating by substituting facilitative responses for ineffective ones. You may also need to focus on and explore the passive or nonassertive behavior of clients with the objective of contracting with them to increase their participation in the helping process.

Keeping Discussions Focused on Safe Topics

Keeping discussions focused on safe topics that exclude feelings and minimize client disclosures is inimical to the helping process. Social chitchat about the weather, news, hobbies, mutual interests or acquaintances, and the like tends to foster a social rather than a therapeutic relationship. In contrast to the lighter and more diffuse communication characteristic of a social relationship, helpful, growth-producing relationships feature sharp focus and high specificity. Another frequent pattern found in the Ragg, Okagbue-Reaves, and Piers (2007) study was that beginning practitioners would attempt to defuse expressions of high emotion such as anger, dismay, or sadness rather than reflect them, as indicated in the following example:

Parent: I have had about all I can take from these kids sometimes. They are so angry and disrespectful that it is all I can do to keep from blowing up at them.
Social worker: Kids nowadays can be difficult.

A more appropriate response would be:

Social worker: You sometimes feel so frustrated when your kids act disrespectfully that you want to do something about it, and it is hard to keep the lid on.

In general, such "safe" social interaction in the helping process should be avoided. Two exceptions to this rule exist, however:

- Discussion of "safe" topics may be utilized to help children or adolescents lower their defenses and risk increasing openness, thereby assisting social workers to cultivate a quasi-friend role with such clients.
- A brief discussion of conventional topics may be appropriate and helpful as part of the getting-acquainted or warm-up period of initial sessions or during early portions of subsequent sessions. A warm-up period is particularly important when you are engaging clients from ethnic groups for which such informal openings are the cultural norm, as discussed in Chapter 3.

Even when you try to avoid inappropriate social interaction, however, some clients may resist your attempts to move the discussion to a topic that is relevant to the problems they are experiencing and to the purposes of the helping process. Techniques for managing such situations are found in Chapter 18. For now, simply note that it is appropriate for the social worker to bring up the agreed-upon agenda within a few minutes of the beginning of the session.

Responding Infrequently

Monitoring the frequency of your responses in individual, conjoint, or group sessions is an important task. As a social worker, you have an ethical responsibility to utilize fully the limited contact time you have with clients in pursuing your practice objectives and promoting your clients' general well-being. Relatively inactive social workers, however, are likely to ignore fruitful moments that could be explored to promote clients' growth, and they may allow the focus of a session to stray to inappropriate or unproductive content. To be maximally helpful, social workers must structure the helping process by developing contracts with clients that specify the respective responsibilities of both sets of participants. For their part, they engage clients in identifying and exploring problems, formulating goals, and delineating tasks to alleviate clients' difficulties.

Inactive social workers can contribute to counterproductive processes and failures in problem solving. One deleterious effect, for example, is that clients lose confidence in social workers when they fail to intervene in situations that are destructive to the client or to others. In particular, clients' confidence is eroded if social workers fail to intervene when clients communicate destructively in conjoint or group sessions.

EP 1

Although social workers' activity per se is important, the quality of their moment-by-moment responses is critical. Social workers significantly diminish their effectiveness by neglecting to utilize or by underutilizing facilitative responses.

Self-assessment of your sessions and discussions with your supervisor can be helpful in determining whether you are modeling an appropriate level of interaction with the client. For example, some beginning social workers may welcome highly verbal clients. However, overly talkative clients may come to dominate the session. While catharsis can be useful, usually such clients are coming in because there is an issue they wish to address. The client would be better served by refocusing the discussion and coming back to the concern that brought the client in.

Parroting or Overusing Certain Phrases or Clichés

Parroting a message irritates clients, who may issue a sharp rebuke to the social worker: "Well, yes, I just said that." Rather than merely repeating clients' words,

EP 1

social workers should use fresh language that captures the essence of clients' messages and places them in sharper perspective. In addition, social workers should refrain from punctuating their communications with superfluous phrases. The distracting effect of such phrases can be observed in the following message:

Social worker: You know, a lot of people wouldn't come in for help. It tells me, you know, that you realize that you have a problem, you know, and want to work on it. Do you know what I mean?

Frequent use of such phrases as "you know," "Okay?" ("Let's work on this task, okay?"), "and stuff" ("We went to town, and stuff"), or "that's neat" can annoy some clients (and social workers, for that matter). If used in excess, the same may be said of some of the faddish clichés that have permeated today's language—for example, "awesome," "sweet," "cool," "tight," or "dude."

VIDEO CASE EXAMPLE

In the video "Work with the Corning Family," the social worker, Ali, frequently uses the term "you guys" to refer to her husband and wife clients. We don't know how they respond to this plural term and whether they respond to it positively or negatively. What alternative terms could be used to refer to these clients?

Another mistake social workers sometimes make is trying to "over-relate" to youthful clients by using adolescent jargon to excess. Adolescents tend to perceive such communication as phony and the social worker as inauthentic, which hinders the development of a working relationship. It can be part of the learning process, however, to discover the meaning of terms unfamiliar to the social worker, so that in some cases you can translate concepts using terms you have learned from the client.

Dwelling on the Remote Past

Social workers' verbal responses may focus on the past, the present, or the future. Helping professionals differ regarding the amount of emphasis they believe should be accorded to gathering historical facts about clients.

Focusing largely on the present is vital, however, because clients can change only their present circumstances, behaviors, and feelings. Permitting individuals, groups, couples, or families to dwell on the past may reinforce diversionary tactics they have employed to avoid dealing with painful aspects of their present difficulties and with the need for change.

Messages about the past may reveal feelings the client is currently experiencing related to the past. For example:

Client *[with trembling voice]:* He used to make me so angry.
Social worker: There was a time when he really infuriated you. As you think about the past, even now it seems to stir up some of the anger and hurt you felt.

As in this excerpt, changing a client's statement from past to present tense often yields rich information about clients' present feelings and problems. The same may be said of bringing future-oriented statements of clients to the present (e.g., "How do you feel now about the future event you're describing?"). As you see, it is not only possible but often productive to shift the focus to the present experiencing of clients, even when historical facts are being elicited, in an effort to illuminate client problems.

Going on Fishing Expeditions (Tangential Exploration)

Another counterproductive interviewing strategy is pursuing content that is only tangentially related to client concerns, issues of client and family safety, or legal mandates. Such content may relate to pet theories of social workers or agencies and be puzzling to clients. Confusion may arise if the connection between these theories and the concerns that have brought clients into contact with the social worker is not clear. A wise precaution, therefore, would be to avoid taking clients into tangential areas if you cannot readily justify the rationale for that exploration. If the social worker feels that the exploration of new areas is relevant, then an explanation of its purpose is warranted. For example, if a social worker were concerned that a client's social interactions are largely through the Internet and texting and proposed to the client that excessive use of social media is unhealthy, it would be better not to impose such a judgment but rather to remain focused on the client's satisfaction with his or her social interactions.

Failing to Be Aware of Cognitive Bias

Cognitive bias refers to seeking out information that confirms our understanding, preferences, or perceptions while ignoring information that contradicts these biases. Cognitive biases may have both positive and negative influences on client interactions. For example, social workers may influence clients to make decisions that confirm the social worker's bias about how humans should function in the world. A social worker who is biased toward individualism, for example, may attempt to counsel a client from a collectivist culture to make decisions that align with individualistic lifestyles. Or social workers may screen out negative assessments of themselves while paying attention only to positive assessments, even when the negative assessments may contribute to growth. These types of biases influence how we as social workers interact with clients and require substantial self-awareness to change and address. It is therefore important for social workers to recognize how personal experiences and cognition shape our understanding of the world and the manner in which we engage with clients.

GAUGING THE EFFECTIVENESS OF YOUR RESPONSES

The preceding discussion should assist you in identifying ineffective patterns of communication you may have been employing. Because most learners ask too many closed-ended questions, change the subject frequently, and recommend solutions before completing a thorough exploration of clients' problems, you should particularly watch for these patterns. In addition, you will need to monitor your interviewing style for idiosyncratic counterproductive patterns of responding.

The *Practice Behaviors Workbook* contains exercises designed to assist students in recognizing and eliminating ineffective responses. Because identifying ineffective styles of interviewing requires selective focusing on the frequency and patterning of responses, you will also find it helpful to analyze extended segments of taped sessions using the form "Assessing Verbal Barriers to Communication," found near the end of this chapter.

As noted earlier, one way of gauging the effectiveness of your responses is to carefully observe clients' reactions immediately following your responses. Because multiple clients are involved in group and family sessions, you will often receive varied verbal

and nonverbal cues regarding the relative effectiveness of your responses when engaging clients in these systems. As you assess your messages, keep in mind that a response is probably helpful if clients react in one of the following ways:

- They continue to explore the problem or stay on the topic.
- They express pent-up emotions related to the problematic situation.
- They engage in deeper self-exploration and self-experiencing.
- They volunteer more personally relevant material spontaneously.
- They affirm the validity of your response either verbally or nonverbally.

In contrast, a response may be too confrontational, poorly timed, or off target if clients react in one of the following ways:

- They reject your response either verbally or nonverbally.
- They change the subject.
- They ignore the message.
- They appear mixed up or confused.
- They become more superficial, more impersonal, more emotionally detached, or more defensive.
- They argue or express anger rather than examine the relevance of the feelings involved.

In analyzing social worker–client interactions, keep in mind that the participants mutually influence each other. Thus, a response by either person in an individual interview affects the expressions of the other person.

Although social workers may demonstrate ineffective patterns of communication in individual interviews, these are even more likely to occur in groups or in conjoint sessions with spouses or family members. In fact, orchestrating an effective conjoint interview or group meeting often presents a stiff challenge because of clients' use of ineffective communications, which may provoke intense anger, defensiveness, and confusion among family or group members. Establishing mutually accepted ground rules for communication can be useful in such settings.

In summary, your task is twofold: You must monitor, analyze, and eliminate your own ineffective responses while simultaneously observing, managing, and modifying ineffective responses by your clients.

That's a rather tall order. Although modifying dysfunctional communications among clients requires advanced skill, you can eliminate your own barriers to effective communication in a relatively short time.

You will make even faster progress if you also eliminate ineffective styles of responding and test out your new communication skills in your private life. Unfortunately, many social workers compartmentalize and limit their helping skills to their work with clients but continue to use ineffective communication styles with their professional colleagues, friends, and families. Social workers who have not fully integrated the helping skills into their private lives typically do not relate as effectively to their clients as do social workers who have fully implemented and assimilated those skills as a part of their general style of relating. We are convinced that to adequately master these essential skills and to fully tap into their potential for assisting clients, social workers must promote their own interpersonal competence and personality integration, thereby modeling for their clients a self-actualized or fully functioning person. Pursuing this personal goal prepares social workers for one of their major roles: teaching new skills of communicating and relating to their clients.

THE CHALLENGE OF LEARNING NEW SKILLS

Because of the unique nature of the helping process, establishing and maintaining a therapeutic relationship requires highly disciplined efforts on the social worker's part. Moment by moment, transaction by transaction, the social worker must sharply focus on the needs and problems of his or her clients. The success of each transaction is measured in terms of the social worker's adroitness in consciously applying specific skills to move the process toward the therapeutic objectives.

Interestingly, one of the major threats to learning new skills comes from students' fear that in relinquishing their old styles of relating, they are giving up an intangible, irreplaceable part of themselves. Similarly, students who have previously engaged in social work practice may experience fear related to the fact that they have developed methods or styles of relating that have influenced and "moved" clients in the past; abandoning these response patterns may mean surrendering a hard-won feeling of competency. These fears are often exacerbated when instruction and supervision in the classroom and practicum primarily strive to eliminate errors and ineffective interventions and responses rather than to develop new skills or enhance positive responses or interventions with clients. In such circumstances, students may receive considerable feedback about their errors but inadequate input regarding their effective responses or styles of relating. Consequently, they may feel vulnerable and stripped of their defenses (just as clients do) and experience more keenly the loss of something familiar.

As a beginning social worker, you must learn to openly and nondefensively receive constructive feedback about your styles of relating or intervening that have not been helpful in the past. Effective supervisors should not dwell exclusively on shortcomings but rather be equally focused on identifying your expanding skills (Rooney & De Jong, 2011). If they do not do so, then you should take the lead in eliciting positive feedback from educators and peers about your growing strengths. Remember that supervision time is limited and that the responsibility for utilizing that time effectively and for acquiring competency necessarily rests equally with you and your practicum instructor. It is also vital that you take steps to monitor your own growth systematically by reviewing audio and video recordings, by counting your desirable and undesirable responses in client sessions, and by comparing your responses with the guidelines for constructing effective messages found in this book. Perhaps the single most important requirement for you in furthering your competency is to assume responsibility for advancing your own skill level by consistently monitoring your responses and practicing proven skills.

Most of the skills delineated in this book are not easy to master. In fact, competent social workers will spend years perfecting their ability to sensitively and fully attune themselves to the inner experiences of their clients; in furthering their capacity to share their own experiencing in an authentic, helpful manner; and in developing a keen sense of timing in employing these and other skills.

In the months ahead, as you forge new patterns of responding and test your newly developed skills, you will inevitably experience growing pains—that is, a sense of disequilibrium as you struggle to respond in new ways and, at the same time, to relate warmly, naturally, and attentively to your clients. Sometimes, you may feel that your responses are mechanistic and experience a keen sense of transparency: "The client will know that I'm not being real." If you work intensively to master specific skills, however, your awkwardness will gradually diminish, and you will eventually incorporate these skills naturally into your repertoire.

ASSESSING VERBAL BARRIERS TO COMMUNICATION

Directions: In reviewing each 15-minute sample of recorded interviews, tally your use of ineffective responses by placing marks in appropriate cells.

15-Minute Recorded Samples	1	2	3	4
1. Reassuring, sympathizing, consoling, or excusing				
2. Advising and giving suggestions or solutions prematurely				
3. Using sarcasm or employing humor that is distracting or makes light of clients' problems				
4. Judging, criticizing, or placing blame				
5. Trying to convince the client about the right point of view through logical arguments, lecturing, instructing, or arguing				
6. Analyzing, diagnosing, or making glib or dogmatic interpretations				
7. Threatening, warning, or counterattacking				
8. Stacking questions and using double barreled questions				
9. Asking leading questions				
10. Interrupting inappropriately or excessively				
11. Dominating the interaction				
12. Keeping discussion focused on safe topics				
13. Responding infrequently				
14. Parroting or overusing certain phrases or clichés				
15. Dwelling on the remote past				
16. Going on fishing expeditions (tangential exploration)				
17. Failing to be aware of cognitive bias				
Other responses that impede communication. List:				

ASSESSING PHYSICAL ATTENDING BEHAVIORS

	Comments
1. Direct eye contact 0 1 2 3 4	
2. Warmth and concern reflected in facial expression 0 1 2 3 4	
3. Eyes at same level as client's 0 1 2 3 4	
4. Appropriately varied and animated facial expressions 0 1 2 3 4	
5. Arms and hands moderately expressive; appropriate gestures 0 1 2 3 4	
6. Body leaning slightly forward; attentive but relaxed 0 1 2 3 4	
7. Voice clearly audible but not loud 0 1 2 3 4	
8. Warmth in tone of voice 0 1 2 3 4	
9. Voice modulated to reflect nuances of feeling and emotional tone of client messages 0 1 2 3 4	
10. Moderate speech tempo 0 1 2 3 4	
11. Absence of distracting behaviors (fidgeting, yawning, gazing out window, looking at watch) 0 1 2 3 4	
12. Other 0 1 2 3 4	

Rating Scale:
0 = Poor, needs marked improvement
1 = Weak, needs substantial improvement
2 = Minimally acceptable, room for growth
3 = Generally high level with a few lapses
4 = Consistently high level

SUMMARY

This chapter outlined a series of nonverbal and verbal barriers to effective communication that are often experienced by beginning social workers. As you become alert to these potential obstacles and more skilled in applying more productive alternatives, you will become more confident in your progress. Chapter 8 asks you to apply your communication skills to one of the most important tasks you will face: conducting a multisystemic assessment.

COMPETENCY NOTES

EP 1   Demonstrate Ethical and Professional Behavior
- Demonstrate professional demeanor in behavior, appearance, and oral, written, and electronic communication.

EP 2   Engage Diversity and Difference in Practice
- Apply and communicate understanding of the importance of diversity and difference in shaping life experiences in practice at the micro, mezzo, and macro levels.
- Present oneself as a learner, and engage clients and constituencies as experts on their own experiences.
- Apply self-awareness and self-regulation to manage the influence of personal biases and values in working with diverse clients and constituencies.

EP 6   Engage with Individuals, Families, Groups, Organizations, and Communities
- Apply knowledge of human behavior and the social environment, person-in-environment, and other multidisciplinary theoretical frameworks to engage with clients and constituencies.
- Use empathy, reflection, and interpersonal skills to effectively engage diverse clients and constituencies.

EP 7   Assess Individuals, Families, Groups, Organizations, and Communities
- Collect and organize data, and apply critical thinking to interpret information from clients and constituencies.

EP 9   Evaluate Practice with Individuals, Families, Groups, Organizations, and Communities
- Select and use appropriate methods for evaluation of outcomes.

NOTE

1. It is important not to set up artificial dichotomies that do not represent actual behaviors. Emma Gross (1995) argues, for example, that too frequently writers have inappropriately generalized across Native American cultures.

CHAPTER 8

Assessment: Exploring and Understanding Problems and Strengths

with Caroline B. R. Evans

Chapter Overview

Assessment involves gathering information and formulating it into a coherent picture of the client and his or her circumstances. Assessments also involve social workers' inferences about the nature and causes of clients' difficulties and therefore serve as the basis for ongoing client–social worker interactions, including goal setting, intervention implementation, and progress evaluation. This chapter focuses on the fundamentals of assessment and the strategies used in assessing clients' problems and strengths. All of the skills introduced in the preceding chapters are used to create an accurate assessment. Therefore, you should read this chapter with these prior skills in mind and refer back to them as needed. Chapter 9 describes the characteristics taken into account when examining and portraying an individual's functioning and his or her relations with others and with the surrounding environment. Together, Chapters 8 and 9 cover the individual's interpersonal functioning and his or her related social systems and environments.

As a result of reading this chapter, you will be able to:

- Understand that assessments involve both gathering information and synthesizing it into a working hypothesis.
- Identify the distinctions between *assessment* and *diagnosis*.
- Explain what the DSM-5 is and how it is organized.
- Explain how to capture client strengths and resources in assessment.
- Recognize the elements of culturally competent assessments and the risks of ethnocentric assessments.
- Identify the roles that knowledge and theories play in framing assessments.
- Identify the sources of data that may inform social workers' assessments.
- Identify questions to bear in mind while conducting an assessment.
- Recall the various elements of problem analysis.

EPAS Competencies in Chapter 8

This chapter will give you the information needed to meet the following practice competencies:

- Competency 2: Engage Diversity and Difference in Practice
- Competency 4: Engage in Practice-Informed Research and Research-Informed Practice
- Competency 7: Assess Individuals, Families, Groups, Organizations, and Communities

THE MULTIDIMENSIONALITY OF ASSESSMENT

Human problems—even those that appear to be simple at first glance—often involve a complex interplay of many factors. Rarely do sources of problems reside solely within an individual or within that individual's environment. Rather, **reciprocal interaction** occurs between a person and the external world. The person acts upon and responds to the external world, and the quality of those actions affects the external world's reactions (and vice versa). For example, a parent may complain about having poor communication with an adolescent, attributing the difficulty to the fact that the teenager is sullen and refuses to talk about most things. The adolescent, in turn, may complain that it is pointless to talk with the parent because the latter consistently pries, lectures, or criticizes. Each participant's complaint about the other may be accurate, but each unwittingly behaves in ways that have produced and now maintain their dysfunctional interaction. Thus, the behavior of neither person is the sole cause of the breakdown in communication in a simple cause-and-effect (linear) fashion. Rather, their reciprocal interaction produces the difficulty; the behavior of each is both cause and effect, depending on one's vantage point.

The multidimensionality of human problems is also a consequence of the fact that human beings are social creatures who depend both on other human beings and on complex social institutions to meet their needs. Meeting basic needs such as food, housing, clothing, and medical care requires adequate economic means and the availability of goods and services. Meeting educational, social, and recreational needs requires interacting with social institutions. Meeting needs to feel close to and loved by others, to have companionship, to experience a sense of belonging, and to experience sexual gratification requires satisfactory social relationships within one's intimate relationships, family, social network, and community. Likewise, the extent to which people experience self-esteem depends on certain individual psychological factors and the quality of feedback from other people. In conducting an assessment, a social worker needs extensive knowledge about the client and the numerous systems (economic, legal, educational, medical, religious, social, and interpersonal) that impinge upon the client system.

Assessing the functioning of an individual entails evaluating various aspects of that person's functioning. For example, the social worker may need to consider dynamic interactions among the individual's biophysical, cognitive, emotional, cultural, behavioral, and motivational subsystems and the relationships of those interactions to the client's problems. When the client system is a couple or family, assessment entails paying attention to communications and patterns of interaction as well as to each individual member of the system. Not every system and subsystem plays a significant role in the problems experienced by a client. However, overlooking relevant systems will result in an assessment that is incomplete at best and irrelevant or erroneous at worst. Interventions based on poor assessments, therefore, may be ineffective, misdirected, or even harmful.

In summary, the client's needs and the helping agency's purpose and resources will influence your choices and priorities during the assessment. You must be sure to attend to the client's immediate concern, or presenting problem; identify any legal or safety concerns that may alter your priorities; be attuned to the strengths and resources that appear in the case; and consider all of the sources of information you may draw upon to arrive at your assessment. You must also recognize the many facets to be taken into account in a multidimensional assessment, as well as the reciprocal nature of interactions, which requires an assessment that goes beyond mere cause and effect. Finally, you must be alert to your own history, values, biases, and behaviors that might inject subjectivity into your interactions with clients and into the resulting assessment.

DEFINING ASSESSMENT: PROCESS AND PRODUCT

EP 7

The word **assessment** can be defined in several ways. For example, it refers to a process occurring between a social worker and client in which information is gathered, analyzed, and synthesized to provide a concise picture of the client and his or her needs and strengths. In settings in which social work is the primary profession, the social worker often makes the assessment independently or consults with colleagues or a member of another discipline. Typically, formal assessments may be completed in one or two sessions. Assessments also represent opportunities to determine whether the agency and the particular social worker are best suited to address the client's needs. The social worker may identify the client's eligibility for services (based, for example, on the client's needs, insurance coverage, or enrollment criteria) and make a referral to other resources if either the program or the social worker is not appropriate to meet the person's needs.

In settings in which social work is not the only or not the primary profession (**secondary** or **host settings**), the social worker may be a member of a clinical team (e.g., in mental health, school, medical, and correctional settings), and the process of assessment may be a joint effort of a psychiatrist, social worker, psychologist, nurse, teacher, speech therapist, or members of other disciplines. In such settings, the social worker typically compiles a social history and contributes knowledge related to interpersonal and family dynamics. The assessment process may take longer because of the time required for all of the team members to complete their individual assessments and to reach collective agreement during a group meeting.

Assessment: Focus and Timing

Although some data are common to all interviews, the focus of a particular interview and assessment formulation will vary according to the social worker's task, mission, theoretical framework, or other factors. For example, a social worker who is investigating an allegation of child endangerment will ask questions and draw conclusions related to the level of risk or potential for violence in the case. A social worker whose expertise lies in cognitive behavioral theory will structure the assessment to address the effects of misconceptions or cognitive distortions on the client's feelings and actions. A clinician in a correctional setting will use different concepts and standards to categorize offenders and to determine risks and needs (Beyer & Balster, 2001). This does not mean that in any of those cases, the social worker addresses *only* those topics, but rather that the interview and findings will be narrowed by the social worker's mission, theory, setting, and clinical focus.

Social workers engage in the process of assessment from the beginning of their contact with the client until the relationship's termination, which may occur weeks, months, or even years later. Thus, assessment is a fluid and dynamic process that involves receiving, analyzing, and synthesizing new information as it emerges during the entire course of a given case. In the first session, the social worker generally elicits abundant information; he or she must then assess the information's meaning and significance as the client–social worker interaction unfolds. This moment-by-moment assessment guides

the social worker in deciding which information is salient and merits deeper exploration, and which is less relevant to understanding the individual and the presenting problem. After gathering sufficient information to illuminate the situation, the social worker analyzes it and, in collaboration with the client, integrates the data into a tentative formulation of the problem. Many potential clients do not proceed with the social worker beyond this point. If their concerns can be best handled through a referral to other resources, if they do not meet eligibility criteria, or if they choose not to continue the relationship, contact often stops here.

Should the social worker and the client continue the contact, assessment continues, although it is not a central focus of the work. Clients often disclose new information as the problem-solving process progresses, casting the original evaluation in a new light. Sometimes this new insight emerges as the natural result of coming to know the client better. In other cases, individuals may withhold vital information until they are certain that the social worker is trustworthy and capable. As a result, preliminary assessments often turn out to be inaccurate and must be discarded or drastically revised.

Note that the term *assessment* also refers to the written products that result from the process of understanding the client. As a product, assessment involves an actual formulation or statement at a given time regarding the nature of a client's problems, resources, and other related factors. A formal assessment requires analysis and synthesis of relevant data into a working definition of the problem. It identifies associated factors and clarifies how they interact to produce and maintain the problem. Because assessments must constantly be updated and revised, it is helpful to think of an assessment as *a complex working hypothesis based on the most current data available.*

EP 7

Written assessments range from comprehensive biopsychosocial reports to brief analyses about very specific topics, such as the client's mental status, substance use, capacity for self-care, or suicidal risk. An assessment may summarize progress on a case or provide a comprehensive overview of the client (to facilitate his or her transfer to another resource or termination of the case). The scope and focus of the written product and of the assessment itself will vary depending on three factors: the *role* of the social worker, the *setting* in which the social worker works, and the *needs* presented by the client. For example, a school social worker's assessment of an elementary school student may focus on the history and pattern of disruptive behaviors in the classroom, as well as on the classroom environment itself. A social worker in a family services agency seeing the same child may focus more broadly on the child's developmental history and his or her family's dynamics, as well as on the troubling classroom behavior. A worker evaluating the child's eligibility to be paired with an adult mentor would look at family income, the child's existing social systems, and other information to determine his or her capacity to benefit from the match.

Priorities in Assessments

EP 7

Although a social worker's assessment will be guided by the setting in which the assessment is conducted, certain priorities in assessment influence all social work settings. Without prioritization, social workers run the risk of conducting unbalanced, inefficient, or misdirected evaluations. Initially, three questions should be assessed in all situations:

1. *What does the client see as his or her primary concerns or goals?* Sometimes referred to as "starting where the client is," this question highlights social work's emphasis on self-determination and commitment to assisting individuals (where legal, ethical, and possible) to reach their own goals. Practically speaking, sharing concerns helps relieve clients of some of the burdens and apprehensions that brought them to the interview and may also identify their hopes and goals for service.
2. *What (if any) current or impending legal mandates must the client and social worker consider?* If clients are mandated to receive services or face other legal concerns, this factor may shape the nature of the assessment and the way that clients present themselves. Therefore, it is important to "address this issue" at the outset. For example, an adult protection worker must assess the risk of abuse, neglect, or other danger to an older client, regardless of whether the client shares those concerns.
3. *What (if any) potentially serious health or safety concerns might require the social worker's and client's attention?* Social workers must be alert to health problems and other conditions that may place clients at risk. These complications may be central to the client's presenting problem, or they may indicate a danger that requires immediate

intervention by the social worker. An assessment focused on a client's employability following incarceration may need to take a different direction if the client reports self-destructive thoughts, hazardous living conditions, substance use, untreated injuries, predatory roommates, or other issues of more immediate concern. Although the profession places high value on self-determination, social workers must act—even if it means overruling the client's wishes—in situations that present "serious, foreseeable, and imminent harm" (NASW, 2008a, p. 7).

After addressing these three fundamental questions, the social worker goes on to explore the client's functioning, interactions with his or her environment, problems and challenges, strengths and resources, developmental needs and life transitions, and key systems related to the case. Often these elements are referred to as a **basic social history** or **personal history** (Wiger, 2009). The remainder of this chapter and Chapter 9 further delineate how each of these areas is assessed (see Figure 8-1).

ASSESSMENT AND DIAGNOSIS

It is important at this point to clarify the difference between diagnoses and assessments. **Diagnoses** are labels or terms that may be applied to an individual or his or her situation. A diagnosis provides a shorthand categorization based on specifically defined criteria. It can reflect a medical condition (e.g., "end-stage renal disease," "type 2 diabetes"), mental disorder (e.g., "depression," "agoraphobia"), or other classification (e.g., "emotionally and behaviorally disturbed," "gifted and talented," "learning disabled"). Diagnostic labels serve many purposes. For example, they provide a language through which professionals and patients can communicate about a commonly understood constellation of symptoms. The use of accepted diagnostic terminology facilitates research on problems, identification of appropriate treatments or medications, and linkages among people with similar problems. For example, diagnosing a set of troubling behaviors as "bipolar disorder" helps the client, his or her physician, and the social worker to identify necessary medication and therapeutic services. The diagnosis may comfort the individual by helping "put a name to" the experiences he or she has been having. It may also help the client and family members to learn

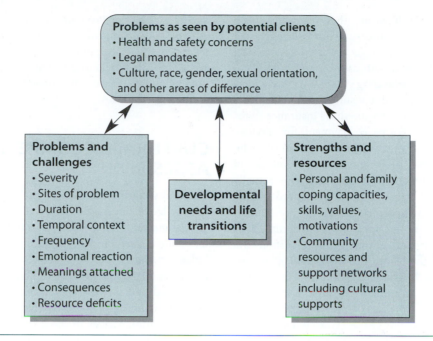

FIG 8-1 Overview: Areas for Attention in Assessing Strengths and Problems

more about the condition, locate support groups, and stay abreast of developments in understanding the disorder.

However, there is a negative side to diagnoses. Although such labels provide an expedient way of describing complex problems, they never tell the whole story. Diagnoses can become self-fulfilling prophecies, wherein clients, their families, and their helpers begin to define the client only in terms of the diagnostic label. This distinction is captured in the difference between saying "Joe is schizophrenic," "Joe has schizophrenia," or "Joe is a person with schizophrenia." Although diagnostic labels hold a lot of power, they can sometimes be bestowed in error (the result of misdiagnosis or diagnostic categories that change over time), and they may obscure important information about the client's difficulties and capacities. Referring to a client as "developmentally delayed," for example, may speak only to that individual's score on an IQ test—not to his or her level of daily functioning, interests, goals, joys, and challenges.

At this point, assessment steps in. Assessments describe the symptoms that support a particular diagnosis, but they go further to help us understand the client's history and background, the effect of the symptoms on the individual, the available support and resources to manage the problem, and so on. In other words, diagnoses may result from assessments, but they tell only part of the story.

The Diagnostic and Statistical Manual (DSM-5)

The Diagnostic and Statistical Manual, Fifth Edition (DSM-5) is an important tool for understanding and formulating mental and emotional disorders (American Psychiatric Association, 2013b). It is linked to *The International Statistical Classification of Diseases and Related Health Problems*, 10th Revision *(ICD-10)*, a commonly used system to codify health and mental health disorders, symptoms, social circumstances, and causes of injury or illnesses (Quan et al., 2005). Diagnostic systems such as the *DSM-5* have come under fire for a number of reasons, including excessive focus on individual pathologies rather than strengths and societal and environmental factors. Critics suggest that the manual is bound by time and culture, throwing the validity of the categorizations into dispute. Some find the use of the *DSM* to be particularly incongruent with social work, in light of the history and focus of the profession (Kirk & Kutchins, 1992). The latest revision, *DSM-5*, was released in May 2013. Certain changes from the *DSM-IV-TR* (the previous

EP 4

edition of the *DSM*) illustrate that diagnosis is an imperfect and evolving process. Thus, although the *DSM* provides useful language for common understanding, it must be used with caution and humility.

Criticisms notwithstanding, the *DSM-5* is widely used by professionals and consumers; the diagnoses and assessments are often required for insurance reimbursement and other forms of payment for services, and many social workers work with individuals who have received mental health diagnoses, regardless of whether the social worker or someone else actually gave the diagnosis. You will need specialized knowledge and training in order to be thoroughly familiar with the *DSM* system and apply it to the complexities of human behavior and emotions. This section will acquaint you with the features of the classification system and serve as a reference point for discussions in Chapter 9 about prominent cognitive and affective diagnoses.

The multiaxial system of the *DSM-IV-TR* has been replaced with the nonaxial system of the *DSM-5*, though the two use similar coding and reporting procedures. Disorders are assigned a three- to five-digit code, with digits after the decimal point specifying the severity and course of the disorder. Thus, for example, 296.21 would represent major depressive disorder, single episode, mild (American Psychiatric Association, 2013a). New to the *DSM-5* is the inclusion of the *ICD-10* code in parenthesis following each *DSM-5* diagnostic code. For each disorder, the manual uses a standardized format to present relevant information. The sections contain:

- Diagnostic criteria
- Subtypes/specifiers
- Recording procedures
- Diagnostic features
- Associated features supporting diagnosis
- Prevalence
- Development and course
- Risk and prognostic factors
- Specific culture, gender, and age features
- Functional consequences of the specific diagnosis
- Differential diagnosis
- Comorbidity

The manual attempts to be strictly descriptive of the conditions it covers. It does not use a specific theoretical framework, recommend appropriate treatments, or address the causation (or etiology) of a disorder, except in unique circumstances. Resources such

as *The Synopsis of Psychiatry* (Sadock, Sadock, & Ruiz, 2014), *DSM-5 Clinical Cases* (Barnhill, 2014), and the *DSM-5* itself (American Psychiatric Association, 2013b) are helpful materials to prepare for regular use of the manual and to develop the clinical acumen for making and using diagnoses.

CULTURALLY COMPETENT ASSESSMENT

EP 2

Culturally competent assessment requires knowledge of cultural norms, acculturation, and language differences; the ability to differentiate between individual and culturally linked attributes; the initiative to seek out needed information so that evaluations are not biased and services are culturally appropriate; and an understanding of the ways that cultural differences may reveal themselves in the assessment process.

Cultures vary widely in their prescribed patterns of child rearing, communication, family member roles, mate selection, and care of the aged—to name just a few areas of differentiation. For example, to whom in a Latino family would you properly address concerns about a child's truancy? What are normative dating patterns in the gay and lesbian communities? At what age is it proper to allow a child to babysit for younger siblings? What are appropriate expectations for independence for a young adult with Down syndrome? How might Laotian parents view their child's educational aspirations?

Knowledge of your client's cultural norms is indispensable when his or her cultural background differs markedly from your own. Without such knowledge, you may make serious errors in assessing both individual and interpersonal systems, because patterns that are functional in one cultural context may prove problematic in another, and vice versa. Errors in assessment can lead to culturally insensitive interventions that may aggravate rather than diminish clients' problems. The necessary knowledge about cultural norms is not easy to obtain, however. It requires a baseline understanding of areas of difference and histories and risks of oppression experienced by different groups, self-examination for biases and prejudices, and ongoing conversation with clients and other key informants (Gilbert, 2003; Johnson & Munch, 2009; Smith, 2004).

Even in homogeneous cultural subgroups, wide variations also exist among individuals. As a consequence,

IDEAS IN ACTION

Some noteworthy changes have been made from the *DSM-IV-TR* to the *DSM-5*:

- Following a federal statute in the United States (Rosa's Law, Public Law 111-256), the term *mental retardation* from *DSM-IV-TR* has been replaced with the term *intellectual disability*.
- The *DSM-IV-TR* disorders of autistic disorder, Asperger's disorder, childhood disintegrative disorder, and pervasive developmental disorder not otherwise specified have been combined into the *DSM-5* diagnosis of autism spectrum disorder.
- The *DSM-5* includes more specific diagnostic criteria for diagnosing attention-deficit/hyperactivity disorder.
- The category Communication Disorders has been updated in the *DSM-5* and includes language disorder, speech sound disorder, and childhood onset fluency disorder (an updated name for stuttering from *DSM-IV-TR*; American Psychiatric Association, 2013b).
- Changes were made to the diagnosis of schizophrenia spectrum and other psychotic disorders.
- Several new depressive disorders were added. For example, to address the overdiagnosis of bipolar disorder in children, a new disorder, disruptive mood dysregulation disorder, was added to the *DSM-5*, to be applied to children up to age 18 who display persistent irritability and recurrent episodes of out-of-control behavior.

- Premenstrual dysphoric disorder was added, and the diagnosis of dysthymia from *DSM-IV-TR* is now categorized as persistent depressive disorder.
- In the *DSM-IV-TR*, there was an exclusion criterion for major depression if the symptoms appeared less than 2 months after the death of a loved one; this "bereavement exclusion" was removed from *DSM-5* (American Psychiatric Association, 2013b).
- Obsessive compulsive disorder (OCD) and posttraumatic stress disorder (PTSD) were removed from the Anxiety Disorder section. OCD now has its own section in *DSM-5*, and PTSD falls under the Trauma and Stressor-Related Disorders section.
- Another new diagnostic criterion, gender dysphoria, was added to the *DSM-5*. This new addition focuses on "gender incongruence" instead of cross-gender identification.
- Disruptive, Impulse-Control, and Conduct Disorders is another new section in *DSM-5* that combines Disorders First Diagnosed in Infancy, Childhood, or Adolescence (e.g., conduct disorder, oppositional defiant disorder) with Impulse Control Disorders (e.g., intermittent explosive disorder, kleptomania).
- The Substance Related and Addictive Disorders section has been expanded to include gambling disorder (American Psychiatric Association, 2013b).

being knowledgeable about a given group is necessary but not sufficient for understanding the behavior of individual members of the group. It is important to remember that cross-cultural and cross-racial work must be tailored to each individual client (Miller & Garran, 2008). Knowing about Laotian parents is not the same as knowing about the particular Laotian parents you are serving. The task confronting practitioners, therefore, is to differentiate between behavior that is culturally mediated and behavior that is a product of individual personality and life experience. This journey is guided by your fundamental knowledge of different cultures and your interest in your particular clients.

The Person-in-Environment

In assessment, it is important to consider the degree to which the client experiences a **goodness of fit** with the culture in which he or she is situated. Many people are actually members of multiple cultures, so their functioning must be considered in relationship to both their predominant cultural identity and the majority culture. An older lesbian may feel alienated or accepted depending on how the culture around her views her age, gender, and sexual orientation. This goodness of fit is a consideration when examining any person in the context of his or her environment. Individuals from the same ethnic group may vary widely in the degree of their acculturation or their comfort with biculturalism, depending on several factors—for example, the number of generations that have passed since their original emigration, the degree of socialization to the majority culture, and interactions with the majority culture. Several factors influence the goodness of fit between cultures, including the degree of commonality between the two cultures with regard to norms, values, beliefs, and perceptions; the individual's degree of bilingualism; and the level of similarity in physical appearance from the majority culture, such as skin color, facial features, and body type (De Anda, 1984).

Cross-cultural contact also occurs between minority professionals and clients from the majority culture. Although the minority practitioner is usually more familiar with the majority culture than the majority practitioner is with minority cultures, clients may challenge the credibility of minority professionals and/or evaluate them less favorably compared to those from the majority (Louis, Lalonde, & Esses, 2010). The client may assign credibility to a social worker because of his or her education, position, role, age, gender, and other factors emphasized in the client's culture—that is, because of factors over which a professional has little control.

EMPHASIZING STRENGTHS IN ASSESSMENTS

Assessments often focus on the problems and difficulties for which clients seek help. Sometimes eligibility requirements from funding sources (e.g., insurance companies) require the client to have particular challenges or diagnoses to qualify for or continue to receive services (Frager, 2000), which puts pressure on the social worker to focus on the client's deficits. However, it is equally important for the social worker to assess client strengths.

To emphasize strengths and empowerment in the assessment process, Cowger (1994) makes three suggestions to social workers:

EP 7

1. Give preeminence to the *client's* understanding of the facts.
2. Discover what the client wants.
3. Assess personal and environmental strengths on multiple levels.

Cowger (1994) has developed a two-dimensional matrix framework for assessment that can assist social

FIG 8-2 Framework for Assessment

Source: Adapted from Saleebey, Dennis, *The Strengths Perspective in Social Work Practice*, 2nd edition, © 1997. Printed and electronically reproduced by permission of Pearson Education, Inc., Upper Saddle River, New Jersey.

workers in attending to both needs and strengths. On the vertical axis, potential strengths and resources are depicted at one end and potential deficits, challenges, and obstacles are shown at the other end. The horizontal axis ranges from environmental (family and community) to individual factors. This framework prods us to move beyond the frequent preoccupation with personal deficits (*quadrant 4*), to include personal strengths and environmental strengths and obstacles. Figure 8-2 illustrates this framework and highlights two facts: A useful assessment is not limited to either deficits or strengths, and both the environmental and personal dimensions are important. Use of all four quadrants provides information that can help in pursuing the client's goals, while remaining mindful of obstacles and challenges.

VIDEO CASE EXAMPLE

The following outline applies Cowger's matrix to the case of Jackie and Anna, featured in the video "Home for the Holidays Part I."

Strengths or Resources

Quadrant 1: Environmental Factors   EP 7

• Anna and Jackie are both in contact with, and value, their immediate and extended family. Anna's hesitancy to discuss the couple's relationship, in spite of the conflict it causes, demonstrates her desire to remain connected to her family of origin.

- Anna and Jackie are both employed. Anna owns her own business.

Quadrant 2: Personal Factors

- Anna and Jackie's intimate relationship and friendship are sources of strength and joy for both of them. Their willingness to attend conjoint sessions and create assignments at the end of the first meeting attests to their appreciation of their partnership.
- Jackie has a bold personality and is not afraid to stand up for herself, demanding the respect she deserves.
- Anna is thoughtful and deliberate. She considers all of the consequences of her actions.

Deficit, Obstacle, or Challenge

Quadrant 3: Environmental Factors

- Anna's parents are uncomfortable talking about their daughter's intimate relationship with another woman.
- Anna's work schedule is busy, and her days are full. She is often drained when she comes home and lacks the energy to connect with Jackie.

Quadrant 4: Personal Factors

- Anna is prone to social withdrawal. She avoids conflict with her parents and Jackie.
- Jackie appears impatient to Anna. Her communication style comes off as "pushy."

EP 7

The following list emphasizes strengths that are often overlooked or taken for granted during assessment. Cultivating your sensitivity to these strengths will help you be attuned to others as they emerge.

1. Facing problems and seeking help rather than denying or otherwise avoiding confronting them
2. Taking a risk by sharing problems with the social worker—a stranger
3. Persevering under difficult circumstances
4. Being resourceful and creative in making the most of limited resources

5. Seeking to further knowledge, education, and skills
6. Expressing caring feelings to family members and friends
7. Asserting one's rights rather than submitting to injustice
8. Being responsible in work or financial obligations
9. Seeking to understand the needs and feelings of others
10. Having the capacity for introspection or for examining situations by considering different perspectives
11. Demonstrating the capacity for self-control
12. Functioning effectively in stressful situations
13. Demonstrating the ability to consider alternative courses of actions and the needs of others when solving problems

THE ROLE OF KNOWLEDGE IN ASSESSMENTS

EP 4

"What you see depends on what you look for." This saying captures the roles that knowledge and theory play in shaping the questions that are asked in assessment and the resulting hypotheses. Competent, evidence-based practice requires that assessments be informed by problem-specific knowledge (O'Hare, 2015). As a result, you would consider the nature of the problem presented by the client at intake (e.g., explosive anger, hoarding, parent–child conflict, truancy) and refer to available research to identify the factors that contribute to, sustain, and ameliorate those problems. This knowledge would help you to know the relevant data to be collected during assessment and the formulations that result.

For example, the literature might suggest that truancy is caused by a poor fit between the student's needs and the classroom environment or the teacher's attitude and methods. Or it might stem from chaos at home in which children are not awakened for school, prepared for the day, or even expected to attend. Poor school attendance may come from poor performance as a result of vision or hearing problems, attention deficits, or learning disabilities. It may also arise from shame on the child's part about hygiene, dress, worthiness, bullying, or other negative peer experiences. Regardless of the factors involved, there is rarely a strictly linear, cause-and-effect explanation for truancy. Instead, the influence of some factors (e.g., poor vision or hearing) leads to behaviors (acting out or truancy) that distance the child from peers, irritate the teacher, and lead to a withdrawal by the student that puts him or her even further behind, and in turn more likely to act out or withdraw further—a reciprocal interaction. Your understanding of the research and theories on human behavior will help focus the assessment on those elements that are involved in a particular client's difficulties.

The demand for evidence-based assessments may make it appear that you have to do a research paper or literature review for every client. Although this would be too onerous, do not underestimate the importance of thorough research; poorly directed assessments and interventions also come with high costs, ranging from client discouragement and wasted professional and agency resources to perhaps even harm, if the resulting services are negligent. To the extent that you and your organization specialize in particular problems or populations, the knowledge gained from research done for any one case can be called on for similar cases. And with increased access to electronic resources and reference guides that summarize the best available evidence in a variety of areas, it has become much easier to find and evaluate existing knowledge (O'Hare, 2015).[1]

THE ROLE OF THEORY IN ASSESSMENTS

As with available knowledge, theories shape assessments. Some theories have a selective influence as concepts associated with that theory are adopted for more general use. For example, multidimensional assessments make use of concepts drawn from the fields of ego psychology, such as reality testing, judgment, and coping mechanisms, and concepts prominent in object relations theory, such as attachment and interpersonal relationship patterns. Most assessments address patterns in thought, behaviors, and actions, interpersonal relationships, affect, and role transitions, although they may not be targeted toward the provision of interpersonal therapy (IPT), which uses those concepts in a particular fashion. In addition, assessments typically utilize concepts such as risk and resilience, and empowerment and strengths, even if the assessment is not wholly organized around those frameworks.

Some theoretical orientations play a greater role in the structure of the assessment and the conclusions that are drawn. For example, **brief, solution-focused therapy** is one model that is encountered in a variety of settings. This model is based on a number of assumptions—for example, making small changes can

lead to larger changes, focusing on the present can help the client tap into unused capacities and generate creative alternatives, and paying attention to solutions is more relevant than focusing on problems. Although solution-building questions may be used with other frameworks, an assessment guided by this practice model will utilize:

- *Seeking exceptions:* Questions that determine when the problem does not exist or does not occur. The answer may refer to different sites, times, or contexts. Exploration then asks the client to elaborate on what is different in those incidents and what other factors might cause the problem to be absent.

- *Scaling the problem:* This involves asking the client to estimate the severity of the problem on a scale of 1 (very minor) to 10 (very severe). The response can help in tracking changes over time, open up the opportunity to ask what accounts for the current level of difficulty or relief, and determine what it might take to move from the current level to a lower point on the scale.

- *Scaling motivation:* Similar to scaling problems or concerns, this involves asking clients to estimate the degree to which they feel hopeful about resolution, or perhaps the degree to which they have given up hope. How would they rate their commitment to working on the problem on a scale of 1 to 10?

- *The miracle question:* This helps the practitioner determine the client's priorities and operationalize the areas for change. Essentially, the social worker asks, "If, while you were asleep, a miracle occurred and your problem were solved, how would things be different when you woke up?" This question can be adapted for use with children by asking: "If you had a magic wand, what changes would you make?" This technique helps the client envision the positive results of the change process and elicits important information for structuring specific behavioral interventions (Jordan & Franklin, 2003).

As with other assessment tools, the key to successful use of these techniques lies in the sensitivity and timing with which they are employed. For example, asking the miracle question prematurely may lead the client to believe that you are not listening or are minimizing his or her distress. Typically, these questions may be prefaced by statements acknowledging the client's concern—for example, "I know your son's misbehavior has been troubling to you, but I wonder if there are times when he does follow your directions?" Sensitivity is also demonstrated through inflection or tone of voice, eye contact, and other nonverbal methods of attending that assure the client of your attention and regard.

EP 7

Other theoretical orientations with demonstrable efficacy will shape the entire assessment. For example, cognitive theories suggest that thoughts mediate emotions and actions (Beck 1995; Wright, Basco, & Thase, 2006). Therefore, assessments derived from these theories focus on the nature of the client's thoughts and schemas (cognitive patterns), causal attributions, the basis for the client's beliefs, and antecedent thoughts in problematic situations (Walsh, 2006). Behavioral theories suggest that actions and emotions are created, maintained, "and extinguished through principles of learning" (Walsh, 2006, p. 107). As such, the assessment focuses on the conditions surrounding troubling behaviors, the conditions that reinforce the behavior, and the consequences and secondary gains that might result. Questions to address this sequence include:

EP 7

- *When do you experience the behavior?*
- *Where do you experience the behavior?*
- *How long does the behavior usually last?*
- *What happens immediately after the behavior occurs?*
- *What bodily reactions do you experience with the behavior?*
- *What do the people around you usually do when the behavior is happening?*
- *What happened after the behavior that was pleasant?* (Bertolino & O'Hanlon, 2002; Cormier, Nurius, & Osborn, 2009; Walsh, 2006)

The intent of these questions is to create a hypothesis about what triggers and reinforces the behavior in order to construct a plan involving new reinforcement patterns and a system for measuring change.

Caveats about Using Knowledge and Theories

Naturally, there are cautions about the degree to which existing knowledge or theories influence assessment. Although they are helpful in predicting and explaining client behaviors and in structuring assessments and interventions, when applied too rigidly, theories may oversimplify the problem and objectify the individual client (Walsh, 2006). Adhering to a single preferred framework may obscure other relevant factors in the case, blind the practitioner to limits in existing theory or knowledge, and inhibit him or her from pursuing promising new knowledge and interventions. Critical thinking and proper training are required so that professionals can effectively evaluate and apply frameworks to enhance client services (O'Hare, 2015).

SOURCES OF INFORMATION FOR ASSESSMENTS

Where do social workers get the information on which they base their assessments? Numerous sources can be used individually or in combination. The following are the most common:

1. Background sheets or other intake forms that clients complete
2. Interviews with clients (e.g., accounts of problems, history, views, thoughts, events, and the like)
3. Direct observation of nonverbal behavior
4. Direct observation of interaction between partners, family members, and group members
5. Collateral information from relatives, friends, physicians, teachers, employers, and other professionals
6. Tests or assessment instruments
7. Personal experiences of the practitioner based on direct interaction with clients

EP 7

The information obtained from client interviews is usually the primary source of assessment information. The skills described in Chapters 5 and 6 for structuring and conducting effective interviews will help in establishing a trusting relationship and acquiring the information needed for assessment. It is important to respect clients' feelings and reports, to use empathy to convey understanding, to probe for depth, and to check with the client to ensure that your understanding is accurate. Interviews with child clients may be enhanced or facilitated by the use of instruments (McConaughy & Achenbach, 1994; Schaffer, 1992) and by play, drawing, and other techniques. As with other information sources, verbal reports often need to be augmented because faulty recall, biases, mistrust, and limited self-awareness may result in a skewed or inaccurate picture (Konrad, 2013; Webb, 2003).

Direct observation of nonverbal behavior adds information about emotional states and reactions such as anger, hurt, embarrassment, and fear. To use these sources of data, the social worker must be attentive to nonverbal cues, such as tone of voice, tears, clenched fists, vocal tremors, quivering hands, a tightened jaw, pursed lips, variations of expression, and gestures; he or she must link these behaviors to the topic or theme during which they arise. The social worker may share these observations in the moment ("Your whole body deflated when you were telling me what she said") or note them to be included with other data ("The client's voice softened and he had tears in his eyes when talking about his wife's illness").

Observations of interactions between spouses or partners, family members, and group members are also often enlightening. Social workers may be surprised at the differences in people's reports of their relationships and the behaviors they actually demonstrate in those relationships. A social worker may observe a father interacting with his daughter, impatiently telling her "I know you can do better"; in an earlier session, however, the father may have described his behavior to her as "encouraging." Direct observation may reveal that his words are encouraging whereas his tone and gestures are not.

Observation can occur in natural settings (e.g., a child in the classroom, adults in a waiting room, or a family as they answer a worker's question in session). Home visits are a particularly helpful forum for observation. One major benefit of in-home, family-based services is the opportunity to observe the family's lived experiences firsthand rather than rely on second-hand accounts (Strom-Gottfried, 2009). Observing clients' living conditions typically reveals resources and challenges that would otherwise not come to light.

Enactment

Social workers can also employ **enactment** to observe interactions firsthand rather than rely on verbal reports. With this technique, clients reenact an event during a session. The social worker might explain: "To understand what produced the difficulties in the situation you just described, I'd like you to recreate it here in our session. By seeing what both of you do and say, and how you do it, I can get an accurate picture of what typically happens. I'd like you to replay the situation exactly as it happened. Use the same words, gestures, and tone of voice as you did originally. Now, where were you when it happened, and how did it

start?" To counteract the temptation to create a favorable impression, the social worker can ask each participant afterward about the extent to which the behaviors demonstrated in the enactment corresponded with the behaviors that occurred in actual situations.

Enactment can also be used in contrived situations to see how people interact in situations that involve decision making, planning, role negotiation, child discipline, or similar activities. Social workers will need to exercise their creativity in designing situations or creating role-plays that will generate and clarify the types of interaction they wish to observe. Another form of enactment involves the use of **symbolic interactions**—for example, through the use of dolls, games, or other forms of expressive or play therapy (Jordan & Hickerson, 2003).

Remember, however, that direct observation is subject to perceptual errors by the observer. Take care when drawing conclusions from your observations. Scrutinize how congruent your conclusions are with the information acquired from other sources. Despite the flaws, information from various forms of direct observation adds significantly to that gained from verbal reports.

Client Self-Monitoring

Client self-monitoring is a potent source of information (Wright et al., 2006). It produces a rich and quantifiable body of data and empowers the client by turning him or her into a collaborator in the assessment process. In self-monitoring, clients track

EP 2

symptoms on logs or in journals, write descriptions, and record feelings, behaviors, and thoughts associated with particular times, events, symptoms, or difficulties. The first step in self-monitoring is to recognize the occurrence of the event (e.g., signs that lead to anxiety attacks, temper tantrums by children, episodes of drinking or gambling). Using self-anchored rating scales (Jordan & Franklin, 2003) or simple counting measures, clients and/or those around them can keep a record of the frequency or intensity of a behavior. How often was Joe late for school? How would Joan rate the severity of her anxiety in the morning, at noon, and in the evening? Which nights did Carlos have particular difficulty sleeping? Did this difficulty relate to events during the day, medications, stresses, or anything he ate or drank?

A major advantage of self-monitoring is that the process itself requires the monitor to focus attention on patterns. As a result, clients gain insights into their situations and the circumstances surrounding their successes or setbacks. As they discuss their recorded observations, they may "spontaneously operationalize goals and suggest ideas for change" (Kopp, 1989, p. 278). The process of recording also assists in evaluation, because progress can be tracked more precisely by examining data that show a reduction of problematic behaviors or feelings and an increase in desirable characteristics.

Collateral Contacts

EP 7

Another source for assessment data is **collateral contacts**—that is, information provided by relatives, friends, teachers, physicians, child care providers, and others who possess essential insights about relevant aspects of clients' lives. Collateral sources are of particular importance when, because of developmental capacity or functioning, the client's ability to generate information may be limited or distorted. For example, parents, guardians, and other caregivers are often the primary source of information about a child's history, functioning, resources, and challenges. Similarly, assessments of individuals with memory impairment or cognitive limitations will be enhanced by the data that collaterals (family members, caregivers, or friends) can provide.

Social workers must exercise discretion when deciding that such information is needed and in obtaining it. Clients can assist in this effort by suggesting which collateral contacts might provide useful information. Their written consent (through agency release of information forms) is required prior to making contact with these sources.

In weighing the validity of information obtained from collateral sources, it is important to consider the nature of their relationship with the client and the ways in which that might influence these contacts' perspectives. For example, members of the immediate family may be emotionally involved or exhausted by the individual's difficulties and unconsciously skew their reports accordingly. For example, studies indicate that older clients may overrate their functional capacity while families underrate it, and nurses' evaluations fall somewhere in the middle (Gallo, 2005). Individuals who have something to gain or to lose from pending case decisions (e.g., custody of a child, residential placement) may be less credible as collaterals than individuals who do not have a conflict of interest or are further removed from case situations. Conversely, individuals who have limited contact with the client (such as other service providers) may have narrow or otherwise distorted views of the client's situation. As with other sources of information, input from collateral contacts must be viewed critically and weighed against other information in the case.

Assessment Instruments

Another possible source of information consists of various **assessment instruments**, including psychological tests, screening instruments, and assessment tools. Some of these tests are administered by professionals, such as psychologists or educators, who have undergone special training in the administration and scoring of assessment tools. In these cases, social workers might receive reports of the testing and incorporate the findings into their psychosocial assessments or treatment plans. Examples of these instruments include intelligence tests, such as the Wechsler Adult Intelligence Scale, 4th Edition (WAIS-IV) or the Wechsler Intelligence Scale for Children, 5th Edition (WISC-V) (Lukas, 1993; Wechsler, 2008, 2014), and instruments to assess health and mental health problems, such as the Millon Clinical Multiaxial Inventory-IV (MCMI-IV; Millon, Grossman, & Millon, 2015), the Minnesota Multiphasic Personality Inventory-2-RF (MMPI-2-RF; Ben-Porath & Tellegen, 2008), or the Patient Health Questionnaire (PHQ-9; Kroenke, Spitzer, & Williams, 2001).

Instruments such as the Burns Depression Checklist (Burns, 1996), the Beck Depression Inventory (BDI-II; Beck, Steer, & Brown, 1996), the Zung Self-Rating Depression Scale (Zung, 1965), and the Beck Scale for Suicidal Ideation (Beck, Kovacs, & Weissman, 1979) have well-established validity and reliability, can be effectively administered and scored by clinicians from a variety of professions, and can assist practitioners in evaluating the seriousness of a client's condition. These measures examine the presence of depressive symptoms, such as fatigue, appetite and sleep changes, impaired concentration, suicidal ideation, and guilt.

VIDEO CASE EXAMPLE

In the video "Elder Assessment," the social worker administers a scale like the one described above to assess the client, Josephine's, symptoms and finds a substantial basis for concern about depression.

EP 7

Other instruments to measure alcohol or drug impairment may be administered by the social worker, self-administered by the client, or computer administered (Abbott & Wood, 2000). Commonly used tools include the Michigan Alcoholism Screening Test (MAST; Pokorny, Miller, & Kaplan, 1972; Selzer, 1971) and the Drug Abuse Screening Test (DAST; Gavin, Ross, & Skinner, 1989).

Some instruments use mnemonic devices to structure assessment questions. For example, the CRAFFT utilizes six questions to assess problematic alcohol use in adolescents (Knight et al., 2002), and the CAGE (Project Cork, n.d.) consists of four items in which an affirmative answer to any single question is highly correlated with alcohol dependence:

1. Have you ever felt you should **Cut** down on your drinking?
2. Have people **Annoyed** you by criticizing your drinking?
3. Have you ever felt bad or **Guilty** about your drinking?
4. Have you had an **Eye opener** first thing in the morning to steady your nerves or get rid of a hangover?   (www.projectcork.org/clinical_tools/html/_CAGE.html)

EP 7

Other tools may be helpful for identifying clients' strengths and needs when used within the context of an assessment interview (Burns, Lawlor, & Craig, 2004; Van Hook, Berkman, & Dunkle, 1996). Examples include the Older Americans Resources and Services Questionnaire (OARS), which provides information about the client's functioning across a variety of domains, including economic and social resources and **activities of daily living** (common activities carried out during the day, such as meal preparation or brushing one's teeth; George & Fillenbaum, 1990). Other tools can be applied to a range of client populations to measure variables such as social functioning, caregiver burden, well-being, mental health, and social networks, and still others may be used in the evaluation of specific syndromes, such as posttraumatic stress disorder, conduct disorders, or anxiety (O'Hare, 2015; Parks & Novielli, 2000).

Tests and screening instruments are useful and expedient methods of quantifying data and behaviors. They are also essential components in evidence-based practice, in that they "enhance the reliability and validity of the assessment and provide a baseline for monitoring and evaluation" (O'Hare, 2015, p. 7). As a consequence, scales and measures play an important role in case planning and intervention selection. To use these tools effectively, however, practitioners must be well grounded in test theory and in the characteristics of specific tests. Many instruments, for example, have biases, low reliability, and poor validity; some are ill suited for certain populations and thus should be used with extreme caution. To avoid the danger of misusing these tools, social workers should thoroughly understand any instruments they are using or recommending, and seek consultation in the interpretation of tests administered by other professionals. Sources such as Bloom, Fischer, and Orme (2009) and Fischer and Corcoran (2013) can acquaint social workers with an array of available instruments and their proper use.

Social Worker's Personal Experience

EP 2

A final source of information for assessment is the social worker's personal experience based on direct interaction with the client. You will react in different ways to different people, and these insights may prove useful in understanding how others respond to the client. For example, you may view certain individuals as withdrawn, personable, dependent, caring, manipulative, seductive, assertive, overbearing, or determined. These impressions should be considered in light of other information you are gathering about the client and his or her circumstances. For instance, a client who reports that others take him for granted and place unreasonable demands on him may appear to you to be meek and reluctant to make his needs known, even in stating what he wants from counseling. These observations may provide you with clues about the nature of his complaint that others take advantage of him.

Some cautions are warranted in using this method. Clients may not behave with the social worker as they do with other people. Apprehension, involuntariness, and the desire to make a good impression may all skew a person's presentation of himself or herself. Also, initial impressions can be misleading and must be confirmed by other sources of information or additional contact with the person. All human perceptions are subjective and may be influenced by our own interpersonal patterns and perceptions. Your reactions to clients will be affected by your own life experiences. Before drawing even tentative conclusions, scrutinize your reactions to identify possible biases, distortions, or actions on your part that may have contributed to the behavior you are observing. For example, confrontational statements by the social worker may spur a defensive response from the client. Perhaps the response reveals more about the incident than the client's typical way of relating. Social constructions and personal experience may lead us to identify another's acts and statements as either "stubborn" or "determined," "arrogant" or "confident," "submissive" or "cooperative." Self-awareness is indispensable to drawing valid conclusions from your interactions with others.

Assessments that draw from multiple sources of data can provide a thorough, accurate, and helpful representation of the individual's history, strengths, and challenges. However, workers must be attuned to the advantages and disadvantages inherent in different types of input and weigh those carefully in creating a comprehensive picture of the client system.

QUESTIONS TO ANSWER IN PROBLEM ASSESSMENT

As noted in earlier chapters, good practice requires you to use a variety of communication methods to encourage the client to tell his or her story. Therefore, the following questions are not intended to be *asked* in the assessment, but instead are meant to be used as a guide or checklist to ensure that you have not overlooked a significant factor in your assessment of the problem.

EP 2

1. What are the clients' concerns and problem(s) as they and other concerned parties perceive them?
2. Are any current or impending legal mandates relevant to the situation?
3. Do any serious health or safety concerns need immediate attention?
4. What are specific indications of the problem? How is it manifesting itself? What are the consequences?
5. Who else (persons or systems) is involved in the problem(s)?
6. What unmet needs and/or wants are involved?
7. How do developmental stages or life transitions affect the problem(s)?
8. How do ethnocultural, societal, and social class factors bear on the problem(s)?
9. How severe is the problem, and how does it affect the participants?

10. What meanings do clients ascribe to problem(s)?
11. Where, when, and how often do the problematic behaviors occur?
12. How long has the problem gone on? Why is the client seeking help now?
13. Have other risk factors (e.g., alcohol or substance abuse, physical or sexual abuse) affected the functioning of the client or family members?
14. What are the client's emotional reactions to the problem(s)?
15. How has the client attempted to cope with the problem(s), and what are the required skills to resolve the problem?
16. What are the client's skills, strengths, and resources?
17. What support systems exist or need to be created for the client?
18. What external resources does the client need?

Questions 1–3 should serve as preliminary inquiries so that the social worker learns about the client's past and knows where to guide the direction of the interview. The remaining questions pertain to further specification of problems and help identify possible patterns for reciprocal interaction. They do not imply that a problem focus takes priority over exploration of strengths and resources, which is also covered by some of the questions. As suggested in the strengths matrix depicted in Figure 8-2, assessment of abilities, resources, and limitations or challenges is required for a full assessment. Data on problems (both when they occur and when they do not) help complete that picture.

Getting Started

After opening social amenities and an explanation of the direction and length of the interview, you should begin by exploring the client's presenting problem. Sometimes this question is a simple, open-ended inquiry: "Mrs. Smith, what brings you in to see me today?" or "I'm glad you came in. How can I help you?" Questions such as these allow the client an opportunity to express his or her concerns and help give direction to the questions that will follow.

EP 2

At this point, the social worker must be attentive to other factors that may alter the direction of the interview, at least at the outset. If the client's request for service is nonvoluntary, and particularly if it results from a legal mandate (e.g., a probation requirement or the consequence of a child maltreatment complaint), then the nature of the mandate, referring information, and the client's perception of the referral will frame the early part of the first interview.

A further consideration at the first interview is whether any danger exists that the client might harm him- or herself or others. Some referrals—for example, in emergency services—clearly involve the risk for harm, which should be discussed and evaluated at the outset. In other instances, the risk may be more subtle. For example, a client may open an interview by saying, "I'm at the end of my rope ... I can't take it any longer." The social worker should respond to this opening by probing further: "Can you tell me more ...?" or "When you say you can't take it, what do you mean by that?" If further information raises the social worker's concerns about the danger for suicidal or aggressive behavior, more specific questioning should follow, geared toward assessing the lethality of the situation.

Whatever the client's presenting problem, if shared information gives rise to safety concerns, the social worker must redirect the interview to focus on the degree of danger. If the threats to safety are minor or manageable, the practitioner may resume the interview's focus on the presenting problem that brought the person in for service. However, if the mini-assessment reveals serious or imminent risk to the client or others, the focus of the session must be on ensuring safety rather than continuing the more general assessment.

Chapter 9 describes the process for conducting a suicide lethality assessment. The American Psychiatric Association (2003), Morrison (1995), Roberts, Monferrari, and Yeager (2008), and others offer additional guidelines for interviewing about self-harm and assessing the degree of risk in various situations. Such texts can be useful resources for learning more about the topic.

Identifying the Problem, Its Expressions, and Other Critical Concerns

Your initial contacts with clients will concentrate on identifying the **presenting problem**, uncovering the sources of this problem, and engaging the client in planning appropriate remedial measures. People typically seek help because they have exhausted their coping efforts and/or lack resources required for satisfactory living. They may have found that, despite their most earnest attempts, their coping efforts were insufficient or seemed to only aggravate the problem, and

therefore be forthright in problem exploration. When clients are referred or coerced into seeking services, empathy, motivational interviewing skills, and negotiation will be essential in finding common ground on the needs that the social worker might help address. Culturally derived attitudes toward seeking help may also affect a person's capacity for and comfort with problem exploration. For example, conceptions about fate, destiny, self-reliance, and other beliefs affect the meaning given to problems and the ways that people are expected to respond to them. In many groups, pursuing help through formal services is a sign of desperation or a cause of shame. Your capacity to start where the client is will be crucial to your success in trying to unpack their reasons for seeking your help.

When asked to describe their problems or concerns, people often respond in generalities. The description typically involves a deficiency of something needed (e.g., health care, adequate income or housing, companionship, harmonious family relationships, self-esteem) or an excess of something that is not desired (e.g., fear, guilt, temper outbursts, marital or parent–child conflict, or addiction). In either event, the presenting problem often results in feelings of disequilibrium, tension, and apprehension. The emotions themselves are often a prominent part of the problem configuration, which is one reason why empathic communication is such a vital skill during the interview process.

When working with children and adolescents, it is helpful to first meet with the caregiver and child together to discuss your role, confidentiality, and the general presenting problem. It is then important to meet alone with the caregiver to obtain a more in-depth understanding of the presenting problem; caregivers might not feel comfortable talking openly in front of the child, and it is therefore necessary to meet with caregivers alone. Finally, the social worker should then meet alone with the child/adolescent to assess his or her view of the presenting problem. Caregivers and children/adolescents might have differing opinions and views about the nature of the presenting problem and might be more likely to express their honest views alone with the social worker. Throughout work with minors, it is vital that the social worker continually check in with caregivers about the client's behavior and any changes at home; this allows for an accurate and comprehensive ongoing assessment of the child/adolescent.

This understanding of the presenting problem is significant because it reflects the client's immediate perceptions of the problem and is the impetus for seeking help. It is distinct from the **problem for work** (e.g., the problem that the social worker and client ultimately focus on in therapy). The problem(s) that bring the client and the social worker together initially may not, in fact, end up being the focus of goals and interventions later in the relationship. The problem for work may differ from the original or presenting problem for a number of reasons. As the helping process progresses, the development of greater information, insights, and trust may reveal factors that change the focus of work and goals for service. This does not mean, however, that you should disregard the problems that brought people to you in the first place. The assessment process will reveal to you and the client whether the problem for work differs from the one that brought him or her to your service.

The presenting problem is also important because it suggests areas to be explored in assessment. If the difficulty described by parents involves their adolescent's truancy and rebellious behavior, for example, the exploration will include the family, school, and peer systems. As the exploration proceeds, it may also prove useful to explore the parental system if difficulty in the marital relationship appears to be negatively affecting the parent–child relationship. If learning difficulties appear to contribute to the truancy, the cognitive and perceptual subsystems of the adolescent may need to be assessed as part of the problem. The presenting problem thus identifies systems that are constituent parts of the predicament and suggests the resources needed to ameliorate it.

The Interaction of Other People or Systems

The presenting problem and the exploration that follows usually identify key individuals, groups, or organizations that are part of the client's difficulties. An accurate assessment must consider all of these elements and determine how they interact. Furthermore, an effective plan of intervention should take these same elements into account, even though it is not always feasible to involve everyone who is a participant in a given problematic situation.

To understand more fully how the client and other involved systems interact to produce and maintain the problem, you must elicit specific information about the functioning and interaction of these various systems. It is important to note that in order to discuss the client with any system external to the therapy office, a release

of information must be signed by the client. If the client is a minor, the child's caregiver must sign a release of information.

People commonly interact with the following systems:

1. The family and extended family or kinship network
2. The social network (friends, neighbors, coworkers, associates, club members, and cultural groups)
3. Public institutions (educational, recreational, law enforcement and protection, mental health, social service, health care, employment, economic security, legal and judicial, and various governmental agencies)
4. Personal service providers (doctor, dentist, barber or hairdresser, bartender, auto mechanic, landlord, banker)
5. The faith community (religious leaders, lay ministers, fellow worshipers)

Understanding how the interaction of these elements plays out in your client's particular situation requires detailed information about the behavior of all participants, including what they say and do before, during, and after problematic events. For example, certain circumstances or behaviors may typically precede problematic behavior. A family member may say or do something that precipitates an angry, defensive, or hurt reaction by another. Pressure from the landlord about past due rent may result in tension and impatience between family members. A child's outburst in the classroom may follow certain stimuli, such as teasing by a classmate. Events that precede problematic behavior are referred to as **antecedents**. Antecedents often give valuable clues about the behavior of one participant that may provoke or offend another participant, thereby triggering a negative reaction, followed by a counter negative reaction, thus setting the reciprocal interaction in motion. In addition to finding out about the circumstances preceding troubling episodes, it is important to learn about the consequences or outcomes associated with problematic behaviors. These results may shed light on factors that perpetuate or reinforce the client's difficulties.

Analyzing the antecedents of problematic behavior, describing the behavior in specific terms, and assessing the consequences or effects of the behavior provide a powerful means of detecting patterns and targeting interventions. This straightforward approach to analyzing the functional significance of behavior is termed the

ABC model (A = antecedent, B = behavior, C = consequence; Ellis, 2001). Although it is far less simple than it may seem, the ABC model provides a coherent and practical approach to understanding problems, the systems involved, and the roles they play.

Assessing Needs and Wants

As we noted earlier, problems commonly involve unmet needs and desires that result from a poor fit between these needs and the resources available. Determining unmet needs, then, is the first step in identifying which resources must be tapped or developed. If resources are available but clients have been unable to avail themselves of those resources, it is important to determine the barriers to utilization. Some people, for example, may suffer from loneliness not because of an absence of support systems but because their interpersonal behavior alienates others and leaves them isolated. Or their loneliness may stem from shame or other feelings that keep them from asking for assistance from family or friends. Still other clients may *appear* to have emotional support available from family or others, but closer exploration may reveal that these potential resources are unresponsive to clients' needs. Reasons for the unresponsiveness typically involve reciprocal unsatisfactory transactions between the participants. The task in such instances is to assess the nature of the negative transactions and to attempt to modify them to the benefit of the participants so that resources can be unblocked to address the client's wishes.

Human needs include the universal necessities (adequate nutrition, safety, clothing, housing, and health care). They are critical and must be at least partially met for human beings to survive and maintain sound physical and mental well-being. As we use the term, *wants* consist of strong desires that motivate behavior and that, when fulfilled, enhance satisfaction and well-being. Although fulfillment of wants is not essential to survival, some desires develop a compelling nature, rivaling needs in their intensity. For illustrative purposes, we provide the following list of examples of typical wants involved in presenting problems.

Typical Wants Involved in Presenting Problems

- To have less family conflict
- To feel valued by one's spouse or partner
- To be self-supporting
- To achieve greater companionship in marriage or relationship

- To gain more self-confidence
- To have more freedom
- To control one's temper
- To overcome depression
- To have more friends
- To be included in decision making
- To get discharged from an institution
- To make a difficult decision
- To master fear or anxiety
- To cope with children more effectively

In determining clients' unmet needs and wants, it is essential to consider the developmental stage of the individual, couple, or family. For example, the psychological needs of an adolescent—for acceptance by peers, sufficient freedom to develop increasing independence, and development of a stable identity (including a sexual identity)—differ markedly from the typical needs of older persons—for health care, adequate income, social relationships, and meaningful activities. As with individuals, families go through developmental phases that include both tasks to be mastered and needs that must be met if the family is to provide a climate conducive to the development and well-being of its members.

Although clients' presenting problems often reveal obvious needs and wants (e.g., "Our unemployment benefits have expired and we have no income"), sometimes the social worker must infer what is lacking. Presenting problems may reveal only what is troubling the person on the surface, and careful exploration and empathic "tuning in" are required to identify unmet needs and wants. A couple, for example, may initially complain that they disagree over virtually everything and fight constantly. From this information, one could safely conclude that the pair wants a more harmonious relationship. Exploring their feelings on a deeper level, however, may reveal that their ongoing disputes are actually a manifestation of unmet needs of both partners for trust, caring, appreciation, or increased companionship.

The process of translating complaints and problems into needs and wants is often helpful to clients, who may have dwelled on difficulties or blamed others and not thought in terms of their own specific needs and wants. The presenting problem of one client was that her husband was married to his job and spent little time with her. The social worker responded, "I gather, then, you're feeling left out of his life and want to feel important to him and valued by him." The woman replied, "You know, I hadn't thought of it that way, but that's exactly what I've been feeling." The practitioner then encouraged her to express this need directly to her husband, which she did. He listened attentively and responded with genuine concern. The occasion was the first time she had expressed her needs directly. Previously, her messages had been sighs, silence, or complaints, and her husband's usual response had been defensive withdrawal.

Identifying needs and wants also serves as a prelude to the process of negotiating goals. Expressing goals in terms that address needs and wants enhances clients' motivation to work toward goal attainment, as the payoff for goal-oriented efforts is readily apparent to them. Even though some desires may seem unachievable in light of the individual's capacities or the opportunities in the social environment, these aspirations are still worthy of discussion. Goal setting is addressed in detail in Chapter 12.

Stresses Associated with Life Transitions

EP 2

In addition to developmental stages that typically correspond to age ranges, individuals and families commonly must adapt to other major transitions that are less age specific. Your assessment should take into account whether the person's difficulties are related to such a transition and, if so, which aspects of the transition are sources of concern. Some transitions (e.g., geographical moves and immigrations, divorce, and untimely widowhood) can occur during virtually any stage of development. Many of these transitions can be traumatic, and the adaptations required may temporarily overwhelm the coping capacities of individuals or families. Transitions that are involuntary (a home is destroyed by fire) or abrupt (job relocation) and separations (from a person, homeland, or familiar role) are highly stressful for most persons and often temporarily impair social functioning of individuals and/or their loved ones.

The person's history, concurrent strengths and resources, and past successful coping can all affect the adaptation to these transitions. The environment plays a crucial role as well. People with strong support networks (e.g., close relationships with family, kin, friends, and neighbors) generally have less difficulty in adapting to traumatic changes than do those who lack strong support systems. Assessments and interventions related to transitional periods, therefore, should consider the availability or lack of essential support systems.

The following are major transitions encountered in adulthood:

Common Role and Developmental Transitions

Work, career choices	Retirement
Health impairment	Separation or divorce
Parenthood	Institutionalization
Post-parenthood years	Single parenthood
Geographic moves and migrations	Death of a spouse or partner
Marriage or partnership commitment	Military deployments

Many of these major transitions would also affect children or adolescents. However, there are additional transitions that affect this younger age group:

Changing grades, especially transitioning to middle school or high school	The loss of a friendship either through death or argument
The birth of a sibling	Death of a parent or caregiver
Illness of a parent or caregiver	Personal illness
Loss of social status at school through bullying or peer victimization	Questions surrounding sexual identity
Breaking up with a dating partner	Addition of a new stepparent to a divorced family

In addition to these transitions, other milestones affect specialized groups. For example, gay and lesbian persons have difficult decisions to make about to whom and under what conditions they will reveal their sexual identities (Cain, 1991a, 1991b). A child whose parents are divorcing may experience a loss of friends and change of school along with the disruption of his or her family structure. Life events such as graduations, weddings, and holidays may be more emotionally charged and take on greater complexity when there has been divorce or death in the family of origin. The parents and siblings of individuals with severe illnesses or disabilities may experience repeated "losses" if typical milestones such as sleepovers, graduations, dating, proms, marriage, and parenthood are not available to their loved ones. Retirement may not represent a time of release and relaxation if it is accompanied by poverty, poor health, or new responsibilities such as caring for ill family members or raising grandchildren (Gibson, 1999). Military deployments and returns may be easier for service members than for reservists, in that the former typically have formal and informal supports on base, whereas reservists may deploy from decentralized communities.

Clearly, life transitions can be differentially affected by individual circumstances, culture, socioeconomic status, and other factors. Social workers must be sensitive to these differences and take care not to make assumptions about the importance or unimportance of a transitional event or developmental milestone.

Cultural, Societal, and Social Class Factors

EP 2

As we noted earlier, ethnocultural factors influence what kinds of problems people experience, how they feel about requesting assistance, how they communicate, how they perceive the role of the professional, and how they view various approaches to solving problems. It is therefore vital that you be knowledgeable about these factors and competent in responding to them. Your assessment of clients' life situations, needs, and strengths must be viewed through the lens of cultural competence (Rooney & Bibus, 1996). What does this mean in practice? Some examples follow:

- A person immigrating from another country may display psychological distress that is directly related to the migration or refugee experience. Beyond this consideration, a social worker who understands the ramifications of immigration would need to be sensitive to the complications that may arise for refugees or others whose immigration was made under forced or dire circumstances (Mayadas, Ramanathan, & Suarez, 1998–1999) or whose presence in the United States is illegal or unwelcome.

- An interview with an older person experiencing isolation should take into account that hearing difficulties, death or illness of peers, housing and economic status, local crime, and other factors may impede the client's ability to partake in social activities.

- Racial and ethnic stereotypes may lead to differences in the way that minority youth and majority youth are perceived when accused of juvenile crimes. Similarly, detrimental experiences with authority figures and institutional racism may affect the way that these youths interact with the social worker (Miller & Garran, 2008).

- A young woman is persistently late for appointments, which her social worker interprets as a sign of resistance and poor organizational skills. In fact, the young woman must make child care arrangements and take three buses to reach the mental health clinic. Rather than indicating shortcomings, her arrival at appointments (even late) is a sign of persistence and precise organization in light of scarce resources.

As discussed throughout the book, professionals must possess cultural sensitivity and the capacity to take many perspectives when viewing clients' situations and drawing conclusions about them. Chapter 9 further addresses these skills as they apply to individual and environmental factors.

Severity of the Problem

In general, assessment of the severity of the problem helps you to determine patterns when the concern is more or less acute and discover the features associated with those changes in severity. Another reason to focus on severity is to evaluate whether clients have the capacity to continue functioning in the community or whether hospitalization or other strong supportive or protective measures are needed. When functioning is temporarily impaired by extreme anxiety and loss of emotional control, such as when people experience acute posttraumatic stress disorder, short-term hospitalization may be required. The intensity of the situation will necessarily influence your appraisal of the client's stress, the frequency of sessions, and the speed at which you need to mobilize support systems.

Meanings That Clients Ascribe to Problems

The next element of assessment involves understanding and describing the client's perceptions and definitions of the problem. The meanings people place on events (**meaning attributions**) are as important as the events themselves because they influ-

EP 2

ence the way people respond to their difficulties. For example, a father might attribute his son's suicide attempt to his grounding the boy earlier in the week. A job loss might mean shame and failure to one person and a routine and unavoidable part of economic downturn for another. Determining these views is an important feature of assessment. Exploratory questions such as the following may help elicit the client's meaning attributions:

- *"What do you make of his behavior?"*
- *"What were the reasons for your parents' disciplining you?"*
- *"What conclusions have you drawn about why your landlord evicted you?"*
- *"What are your views as to why you didn't get a promotion?"*

Discovering meaning attributions is also vital because these beliefs about cause and effect may represent powerful barriers to change. The following examples demonstrate distorted attributions (Hurvitz, 1975):

1. *Pseudoscientific explanations:* "My family has the gene for lung cancer. I know I'll get it, and there's nothing we can do about it."
2. *Psychological labeling:* "Mother is senile; she can't be given a choice in this matter."
3. *Fixed beliefs about others:* "My mother-in-law will never think I am good enough for her son."
4. *Unchangeable factors:* "I've never been an affectionate person. It's just not in my character."
5. *Reference to "fixed" religious or philosophical principles, natural laws, or social forces:* "Sure, I already have as many children as I want. But I don't really have a choice. It's God's will."
6. *Assertion based on presumed laws of human nature:* "All children tell lies at that age. It's just natural. I did when I was a kid."

Fortunately, many attributions are not permanent: people are capable of cognitive flexibility and are open—even eager—to examine their role in problematic situations and want to modify their behavior. When obstacles such as those listed are encountered, however, it is vital to explore and resolve them before attempting to negotiate change-oriented goals or to implement interventions. When working with children and adolescents, it is vital to assess the meaning that both the client and his or her caregiver ascribe to the problematic behavior and to investigate any potential distorted thought attributions held by the child or caregiver. Although the child is the identified client, the caregiver's view of the problem will significantly affect the child and his or her success in therapy.

Sites of Problematic Behaviors

Determining *where* problematic behavior occurs may provide clues about which factors trigger it. For example, children may throw tantrums in certain locations but not in others. As a result of repeated experiences, they soon learn to discriminate where certain behaviors are tolerated and where they are not. Adults may experience anxiety attacks in certain environmental contexts but not in others. Some older individuals become more confused in community settings than at home. Determining where problematic behavior occurs will assist you in identifying patterns that warrant further exploration and in pinpointing factors associated with the behavior in question.

Identifying where problematic behavior *does not* occur is also valuable because it provides clues about the features that might help in alleviating the problem and identify situations in which the client experiences relief from difficulties. For example, a child may act out in certain classes at school but not in all of them. What is happening in the incident-free classes that might explain the absence of symptoms or difficulties there? How can it be replicated in other classes? A client in residential treatment may gain temporary respite from overwhelming anxiety by visiting a cherished aunt on weekends. In other instances, clients may gain permanent relief from intolerable stress by changing employment, discontinuing college, or moving out of relationships when tension or other unpleasant feeling states are experienced exclusively in these contexts.

Temporal Context of Problematic Behaviors

Determining *when* problematic behaviors occur also offers valuable clues about factors at play in problems. The onset of a depressive episode, for example, may coincide with the time of year when a loved one died or when a divorce occurred. Family problems may occur when one parent returns from work or travel, at bedtime for the children, at mealtimes, when visitations are beginning or ending, or when children are (or should be) getting ready for school. Similarly, couples may experience severe conflict when one partner is working the midnight shift, after participation by either partner in activities that exclude the other, or when one or both drink at parties. These clues can shed light on the patterns of clients' difficulties, indicate areas for further exploration, and lead to helpful interventions.

Frequency of Problematic Behaviors

The frequency of problematic behavior provides an index to both the pervasiveness of a problem and its effects on the participants. As with the site and timing of symptoms, information on frequency helps you to assess the context in which problems arise and the pattern they follow in the client's life. Services for clients who experience their problems on a more or less ongoing basis may need to be more intensive than for clients whose symptoms are intermittent. Determining the frequency of problematic behaviors thus helps to clarify the degree of difficulty and the extent to which it impairs the daily functioning of individuals and their families. Assessing the frequency of problematic behaviors also provides a baseline against which to measure behaviors targeted for change. Making subsequent comparisons of the frequency of the targeted behaviors enables you to evaluate the efficacy of your interventions.

Duration of the Problem

Another important dimension vital to assessing problems relates to the history of the problem—namely, *how long* it has existed. Knowing when the problem developed and under what circumstances assists in further evaluating the degree of the problem, unraveling psychosocial factors associated with the problem, determining the source of motivation to seek assistance, and planning appropriate interventions. Often significant changes in life situations, including even seemingly positive ones, may disrupt a person's equilibrium to the extent that he or she cannot adapt to changes. An unplanned pregnancy, loss of employment, job promotion, severe illness, birth of a first child, promotion, move to a new city, death of a loved one, divorce, retirement, severe disappointment— these and many other life events may cause severe stress. Careful exploration of the duration of problems often discloses the antecedents to current difficulties.

Events that immediately precede decisions to seek help are particularly informative. Sometimes referred to as **precipitating events**, these antecedents often yield valuable clues about critical stresses that might otherwise be overlooked. Clients often report that their problems have existed longer than a year. Why they chose to ask for help at a particular time is not readily apparent, but uncovering this information may cast their problems in a somewhat different light. For example, a parent who complained about his teenage daughter's longstanding rebelliousness did not seek assistance until he became aware (1 week before calling the agency) that she was engaging in an intimate relationship with a

man 6 years her senior. The precipitating event is significant to the call for help and would not have been disclosed had the practitioner not sought to answer the critical question of why they were seeking help at this particular time.

In some instances, people may not be fully aware of their reasons for initiating the contact, and it may be necessary to explore what events or emotional experiences occurred shortly before their decision to seek help. Determining the duration of problems is also vital in assessing clients' levels of functioning and in planning appropriate interventions. This exploration may reveal that a person's adjustment has been marginal for many years and that the immediate problem is simply an exacerbation of long-term multiple problems. In other instances, the onset of a problem may be acute, and clients may have functioned at an adequate or high level for many years. In the first instance, modest goals and long-term intermittent service may be indicated; in the second instance, short-term crisis intervention may suffice to restore them to their previous level of functioning.

When working with children or adolescents, it is vital to obtain information from both child and caregiver about where, when, how often, and for how long the problematic behaviors occur. It is also important to consult with other adults in the child's life (teacher, coach, school social worker or counselor, pediatrician) who might have additional information not available to the caregiver.

Other Issues Affecting Client Functioning

EP 7

Numerous other circumstances and conditions can affect the problem that the client is presenting and his or her capacity to address it. For this reason, it is often wise to explore specifically the use of alcohol or other substances, exposure to abuse or violence, the presence of health problems, depression or other mental health problems, and use of prescription medication.

Questions to probe into these areas should be a standard element of the initial interview. As such, they can be asked in a straightforward and nonjudgmental fashion. For example, opening questions might include the following:

- *"Now, I'd like to know about some of your habits. First, in an average month, on how many days do you have at least one drink of alcohol?"*

- *"Have you ever used street drugs of any sort?"*
- *"Have you had any major illnesses in the past?"*
- *"Are you currently experiencing any health problems?"*
- *"What medications do you take?"*
- *"How do these medications work for you?"*
- *"Have you been in situations recently or in the past where you were harmed by someone or where you witnessed others being hurt?"*

The answers you receive to these questions will determine which follow-up questions you ask. In some circumstances, you may ask for more specific information—for example, to determine the degree of impairment due to drug and alcohol use or whether the client is able to afford medications and is taking them as prescribed. At a minimum, you will want to learn how the person views these issues in light of the presenting problem. For example, you might ask these follow-up questions:

- *"How has the difficulty sleeping affected your ability to care for your kids?"*
- *"What role do you see your alcohol use playing in this relationship conflict?"*
- *"Did the change of medication occur at the same time these other difficulties began?"*
- *"I wonder if the run-in with the bullies has anything to do with your skipping school lately?"*

Depending on the setting and purpose of the interview and on the information gathered, the social worker may focus the interview specifically on the client's medical history, abuse, substance use, or mental health. Further information on these assessments is included in Chapter 9.

When working with adolescent clients, it is useful to ask the caregiver these questions when the child is out of the room to assess the caregiver's knowledge of his or her adolescent's risky behavior. However, it is vital to also ask the adolescent these questions without the caregiver present. Clearly explaining the guidelines of confidentiality is a must to make adolescent clients feel comfortable and to ensure they understand when you would have to alert the caregiver about troubling behavior. If you are concerned that the adolescent is at risk of harming him- or herself or someone else, or is being harmed by someone, confidentiality must be broken. For example, smoking cigarettes or drinking beer occasionally would not likely necessitate alerting the caregiver, but something that puts the adolescent at serious risk, such as consistent binge drinking or having sex with an underage girlfriend, would necessitate inclusion of the caregiver.

Emotional Reactions

EP 7

When people encounter problems in daily living, they typically experience emotional reactions to those problems. It is important to explore and assess these reactions for three major reasons. First, people often gain relief simply by expressing troubling emotions. Common reactions to problem situations are worry, agitation, resentment, hurt, fear, and feeling overwhelmed, helpless, or hopeless. Being able to express painful emotions in the presence of an understanding and concerned person is a source of great comfort. Releasing pent-up feelings can bring relief from a heavy burden.

Second, because emotions strongly influence behavior, the emotional reactions of some people impel them to behave in ways that exacerbate or contribute to their difficulties. In some instances, people create new difficulties as a result of emotionally reactive behavior. Burdened by financial concerns, an individual may become impatient and verbally abusive, behaving in ways that frighten, offend, or alienate employers, customers, or family members. An adult experiencing unremitting grief may cut himself or herself off from loved ones who "cannot stand" to see him or her cry. Powerful emotional reactions may thus be an integral part of the overall problem configuration.

Third, intense reactions often become primary problems, overshadowing the antecedent problematic situation. For example, some people experience powerful emotions associated with their life problems. A mother may become depressed over an unwed daughter's pregnancy; a man may react with anxiety to unemployment or retirement; and culturally dislocated persons may become angry following relocation, even though they may have fled intolerable conditions in their homeland. Other individuals may react to problematic events by experiencing feelings of helplessness or panic that cause virtual paralysis. In these instances, interventions must address the overwhelming emotional reactions as well as the situations that triggered them.

Coping Efforts and Needed Skills

"What have you tried to address this problem?" "How has it worked?" The coping methods that people employ give valuable clues about their levels of stress

EP 7

and of functioning. Exploration may reveal that a person has few coping skills but rather relies on rigid patterns that are unhelpful or cause further problems. Some people follow avoidance patterns—for example, dealing with trouble at home by immersing themselves in tasks or work, withdrawing, or numbing with drugs or alcohol. People may cope with interpersonal conflict through controlling behavior, or by passivity and submissiveness. Others demonstrate flexible and effective coping patterns but collapse under unusually high levels of stress.

There are also cultural variations in how people approach problem solving. Some people are most comfortable with an individually focused, analytical-cognitive approach while others may reach out to social networks, family supports, and group problem solving. Cultures typically exert pressure on individuals to follow familiar solutions for a given problem, and deviating from cultural expectations for coping or problem solving may add to the client's distress. It is helpful to know the source of people's coping mechanisms, their efficacy in the past, and the person's comfort with trying new strategies if old ways have failed.

Another important insight from exploring coping efforts emerges when you are discussing mechanisms and skills that have worked in the past but no longer do. In such instances, it is important to explore carefully what has changed. For example, a person may have been able to cope with the demands of one supervisor but not with a new one who is more critical and aloof or who is of a different generation, race, or gender than the client. A parent may have skillfully raised an infant but be stymied by a toddler. Socially inhibited individuals may be comfortable conversing with those they already know but need to learn skills in approaching others, introducing themselves, and engaging in conversation. A person's typical ability to cope may also be affected by changes in functioning: a severely depressed individual, for example, may overestimate his impairment and underestimate his resources and abilities.

By exploring the different circumstances, meaning attributions, and emotional reactions, you should be able to identify subtle differences that account for the varied effectiveness of your clients' coping patterns in different contexts. This part of assessment is also essential before exploring treatment goals or service options. Offering premature advice or interventions may be rejected by a client who says, "I did that already and it didn't work." Without understanding what the client

has tried and when, how and how much it helped, it is risky to jump to conclusions about what assistance is needed now.

Support Systems

An essential part of understanding individuals involves understanding the systems with which they interact. This can include **formal systems**, such as schools, medical clinics, mentors, or home health aides, and **natural or informal systems**, such as neighbors, family, or friends. These systems are also important parts of problem and strengths assessments. Formal support systems may be part of the problem (the school that cannot provide adequate educational resources to help a child with disabilities or the child welfare service plan that is too demanding for the client to manage along with part-time work and adequate child care). Natural support systems may also be part of the problem configuration (the family member whose criticism fuels a client's despair or the peer network that encourages theft and drug use). On the flip side, formal and informal networks can be part of coping and client strengths ("I can always go to my caseworker when I'm feeling overwhelmed"; "My neighbor watches my kids when I get called into work"; "Our church helped us with food and companionship when my mother was sick").

EP 7

Chapter 9 offers an extensive examination of the roles support systems play in affecting intrapersonal and interpersonal functioning and the strategies social workers can use in identifying them. It also addresses environmental (home, neighborhood) and other factors that may be linked to needed supports.

Resources Needed

When people request services, you must determine (1) whether the services requested match the function of the agency and (2) whether the staff possesses the skills required to provide high-quality service. If not, a referral is needed to assure that the individual receives the highest-quality service to match the needs presented. Referrals may also be required to complement services within your agency or to obtain a specialized assessment that will be factored into your services (e.g., "Are the multiple medications that Mrs. Jones is taking causing her recent cognitive problems?"; "Are there neurological causes for John's outbursts?"). In such instances, the practitioner performs a broker or case manager role, which requires knowledge of community resources (or at least knowledge of how to obtain relevant information). Fortunately, many communities have online resource information centers that can help clients and professionals locate needed services. Remember that irrespective of the presenting problem, people can benefit from help in a variety of areas—from financial assistance, transportation, and health care to child or elder care, recreation, and job training. Problem exploration will help identify possible needs.

In certain instances, in addition to the public and private resources available in your community, you should consider two other major resources that may be less visible forms of assistance. The first is self-help groups, in which members look to themselves for mutual aid and social support. In particular, the Internet has expanded the reach of such groups across geographic distances on a round-the-clock basis (Fingeld, 2000). The second resource is natural support systems, including relatives, friends, neighbors, coworkers, and close associates from school, social groups, or one's faith community.

In instances of cultural dislocation, natural support systems may be limited to the family, and practitioners may need to mobilize other potential resources in the community (Hulewat, 1996). Assisting refugees poses a particular challenge because a cultural reference group may not be available in some communities. A language barrier may create another obstacle, and practitioners may need to search for interpreters and other interested parties who can assist these families in locating housing, gaining employment, learning the language, adapting to a new culture, and developing social support systems.

In still other instances, people's environments may be virtually devoid of natural support systems. Consequently, environmental changes may be necessary to accomplish a better fit between needs and resources, a topic we consider at greater length in the following chapter.

ASSESSING CHILDREN AND OLDER ADULTS

EP 2

Social workers are often employed in settings serving children and older adults. Assessment with these populations utilizes many of the skills and concepts noted elsewhere in this chapter and in earlier sections. However, older clients and child clients also present unique requirements because of

their respective life stages and circumstances. This section is intended to acquaint you with some of the considerations that will shape assessments with these populations.

Because children and older adults often present for service in relation to systems of which they are already a part (e.g., hospitals, schools, families, assisted living facilities), your assessment may be bound by those systems. This can present a challenge for creating an integrated assessment, as several caregivers, agencies, and professionals may hold pieces of the puzzle while none possesses the mandate or capacity to put all of the pieces together.

Similarly, children and older adults typically appear for service because someone else has identified a concern. These referral sources may include parents or guardians, caregivers, teachers, neighbors, or health care providers. This factor does not automatically mean that the client will be resistant but rather indicates that he or she may disagree about the presence or nature of the problem or be unmotivated to address it.

Data Sources and Interviewing Techniques

In working with children and older adults, particularly the frail elderly, you may need to rely more than usual on certain data sources (e.g., collateral contacts or observations) and less than usual on other sources (e.g., the client's verbal reports). A trusting relationship with the client's primary caregivers will be vital to your access to the client and will dramatically affect the rapport you achieve with him or her. Depending on the child's level of development or the older adult's capacities, he or she may have difficulty helping you construct the problem analysis or identify strengths or coping methods. It is important to include caregivers in the ongoing treatment of children (Konrad, 2013). Other data sources, such as interviews with collateral contacts (e.g., teachers, family members, service providers, institutional caregivers), may be essential in completing a satisfactory assessment, although, as noted earlier, these can be open to various distortions. Obtaining information from various sources is particularly important when it comes to making an accurate diagnosis; having information from multiple sources can help avoid an inaccurate diagnosis (Konrad, 2013).

Child assessments may also require new skills, such as the use of drawings, board games, dolls, or puppets as sources

EP 2

of information for the assessment (Hamama & Ronen, 2009; Konrad, 2013; Webb, 2003). The way the child approaches these activities can be as telling as the information he or she reveals (Webb, 2003). For example, are the child's interests and skills age appropriate? What mood is reflected in the child's play, and is it frequently encountered in children of that age and situation? Do themes in the child's play relate to possible areas of distress? How often do those themes recur? How does the child relate to you and to adversity (the end of play, losing, or a "wrong move" in a game)? How well can the child focus on the task? In this context, play is not a random activity meant for the child's distraction or enjoyment. Instead, you must use it purposefully and be attentive to the implications of various facets of the experience. Your impressions of the significance and meaning of the play activities should be evaluated on the basis of other sources of information.

A **developmental assessment** may be particularly relevant for understanding the child's history and current situation. With this type of assessment, a parent or other caregiver provides information about the circumstances of the child's delivery, birth, and infancy; achievement of developmental milestones (e.g., language and motor development); family description and atmosphere (e.g., ages of family members, who lives in the home, financial situation, family relationship dynamics); interests (e.g., hobbies, friends); significant life transitions (e.g., separations from caregivers, loss of loved ones to death); presenting problem including history of the problem; and school history (Jordan & Hickerson, 2003; Konrad, 2013; Levy & Frank, 2011). This information helps form impressions about the child's experiences and life events, especially as they may relate to his or her current functioning. As with other forms of assessment, you must organize and interpret what you discover from all sources so as to paint a meaningful picture of the child's history, strengths, and needs; this assessment will then serve as the basis of your goals and interventions. Knowledge of child development is useful to help gauge whether the child is in the developmentally appropriate range (Konrad, 2013). It is also useful to have parents construct a **genogram** (a visual picture of a client's family, usually in the form of a family tree) of members of the immediate and extended family, identifying information about each person in order to obtain a comprehensive understanding of the family situation (Konrad, 2013; Webb, 2003).

Screening instruments intended specifically for child clients or problems associated with childhood may also be useful. Some involve the child as a participant-respondent while others are completed by the parent or guardian in reference to the child. The Denver Developmental Screening Test (DDST-II; Frankenburg et al., 1992) is used with children up to age 6 to determine whether development is in the normal range and to offer early identification of neurological and other problems. The kit utilizes props such as a tennis ball, a doll, a zippered bag, and a pencil for drawing to test personal and social functioning (self-care, getting along with others), fine motor skills (eye–hand coordination, manipulation of small objects), language (hearing and understanding), and gross motor skills (sitting, walking, jumping).

Comprehensive, competent assessments for geriatric clients also involve items that go beyond the typical multidimensional assessment. For example, functional assessments would address the client's ability to perform various tasks, typically activities of daily living (ADLs)—those things required for independent living such as dressing, hygiene, feeding, and mobility. **Instrumental ADLs (IADLs)** involve measuring the client's ability to perform more intricate tasks such as managing money, taking medicine properly, completing housework, shopping, and preparing meals (Gallo, 2005). Because some of the IADL skills may be traditionally performed by one gender or another, you should ascertain the client's baseline functioning in these areas before concluding that there are deficits or declines in IADLs. For example, driving is a complex skill, an area of significant risk, and a powerful symbol of independence, and the potential loss of this freedom often evokes strong emotions in the elderly population; thus, assessment of driving capacity is a specialized and important aspect of functioning (Gallo, 2005).

EP 2

Aging is not synonymous with decline and death. However, the inevitability of decline and death are often on the minds of older clients and are thus worthy of exploration. Assessments in these areas might include reminiscence and discussion of spirituality and beliefs, all of which examine how the older client derives purpose and meaning in his or her life (Richardson & Barusch, 2006). Clients may have significant concerns about incapacitation and death and find that they have few outlets with which to share those thoughts. Too often, family, friends, and helping professionals shut down such conversations as "morbid" or "signs of giving up." Social workers can effectively open up these conversations with questions such as:

EP 7

1. How would you describe your philosophy of life? How satisfactory is this philosophy to you now?
2. How do you express your spirituality? What kinds of practices enhance your spirituality?
3. How do you understand hope? What do you hope for?
4. What helps you the most when you feel afraid or need special help?
5. What is especially meaningful to you now? For what do you live? What is most important to you now?
6. How has being sick made any difference for you in what or how you believe?
7. What do death, being sick, suffering, pain, and so on mean to you?
8. How do you handle feelings such as anger, doubt, resentment, guilt, bitterness, and depression? How does your spirituality influence how you respond to such feelings? Do you want to receive spiritual support to deal with such feelings or thoughts about them?
9. Where do you get the love, courage, strength, hope, and peace that you need? (Dudley, Smith, & Millison, 1995)

These questions may be appropriate for clients at the end of life and in other situations where traumatic experiences or existential crises are part of the presenting problem.

Physical examinations and health histories also take on particular importance in the assessment of older clients. These assessments must take into account the impact of limitations in vision and hearing, restricted mobility and reaction times, pain management, and medication and disease interactions. Sexual functioning is another element of assessments that is commonly overlooked in older clients. Specialized and comprehensive evaluations require interdisciplinary teams with expertise in geriatric care. Assessing physical health is particularly important when working with older clients, as poor physical health is a significant risk factor for depression in this population. About 80% of older adults have at least one chronic health condition, and 50% have two or more (Centers for Disease

Control and Prevention, 2012). Further, 15% of Americans over age 65 and 50% of nursing home residents suffer from depression (Geriatric Mental Health Foundation, n.d.; National Alliance on Mental Illness, 2009). Older persons may also be socially isolated and thus lack a sense of community belonging, which can serve to exacerbate symptoms of depression (Windle, Francis, & Coomber, 2011). One way to combat depression in the older adults is through social engagement and community connection (see Fiske, Wetherell, & Gatz, 2009 for a review). Social workers can help connect older clients to support groups or other community resources that might foster a feeling of connection and community.

As with other populations, standardized tools are effective in evaluating the needs and functioning of older adults. Examples include the Determination of Need Assessment (DONA; Paveza et al., 1989), the Instrumental Activities of Daily Living Screen (Gallo, 2005), and the Katz Index of Activities of Daily Living (Katz et al., 1963). Tests like the Direct Assessment of Functioning Scale (DAFS; Lowenstein et al., 1989) and the Physical Performance Test (Reuben & Siu, 1990; Rozzini et al., 1993) require clients to demonstrate or simulate basic tasks such as climbing stairs, lifting a book and placing it on a shelf, writing, making a phone call, brushing teeth, telling time, and eating. Other tests focus on the presence and severity of dementia, querying caregivers about the frequency with which the client shouts, laughs, or makes accusations inappropriately, wanders aimlessly, smokes carelessly, leaves the stove on, appears disheveled, is disoriented in familiar surroundings, and so on (Gallo, 2005).

For both very young and very old clients, direct observation of functioning may yield more reliable results than either self-reports or information from collateral sources. This may mean classroom visits, home visits, and other efforts to view the client in his or her natural setting. Specialized expertise is required to ensure that assessments are properly conducted and interpreted for these and other especially vulnerable populations.

Maltreatment

Older adults and children are both at particular risk for maltreatment at the hands of caregivers. Therefore, it is important for all professionals to understand the principles for detecting abuse or neglect and their responsibilities for reporting it. For both minors and older adults, mistreatment can be categorized into four areas: neglect, physical abuse, sexual abuse, and emotional or verbal abuse. For older persons, additional categories include self-neglect and financial exploitation (Bergeron & Gray, 2003; Donovan & Regehr, 2010). The specific definitions of various forms of abuse vary by jurisdiction (Rathbone-McCuan, 2008; Wells, 2008). Sometimes abusive individuals or their victims will forthrightly report abuse to the social worker. More commonly it is covered by fear, confusion, and shame, and thus the professional must be alert to signs of abuse, such as:

- *Physical injuries:* Burns, bruises, cuts, or broken bones for which there is no satisfactory or credible explanation; injuries to the head and face
- *Lack of physical care:* Malnourishment, poor hygiene, unmet medical or dental needs
- *Unusual behaviors:* Sudden changes, withdrawal, aggression, sexualized behavior, self-harm, guarded or fearful behavior at the mention of or in the presence of caregiver
- *Financial irregularities:* For the older client, missing money or valuables, unpaid bills, coerced spending (Donovan & Regehr, 2010; Mayo Clinic, 2007)

Social workers (including student workers) are mandated to report suspicions of child abuse to designated child protective agencies; most jurisdictions also compel workers to report elder abuse, although it may be voluntary in other regions. All professionals should know the steps required in their setting and state for making an abuse report. It is often helpful for social workers to first discuss the case with a supervisor prior to making a report (Webb, 2003). Referring the case to agencies that have the mandate and expertise to investigate maltreatment is the best way to assure that proper legal and biopsychosocial interventions are brought to bear in the case.

SUMMARY

This chapter introduced the knowledge and skills entailed in multidimensional assessment. A psychiatric diagnosis may be part of, but is not the same as, a social work assessment. The discussion in this chapter emphasized strengths and resources in assessments. A framework for prioritizing what must be done in assessment was presented, along with the components of problem exploration and their application to specific

populations. In Chapter 9, we will consider the assessment of intrapersonal and environmental systems and the terms and concepts used to describe their functioning, as well as the processes for writing effective assessments.

COMPETENCY NOTES

EP 2   Engage Diversity and Difference in Practice
- **Apply self-awareness and self-regulation to manage the influence of personal biases and values in working with diverse clients and constituencies.** In doing assessments, social workers gather and synthesize information to create a working hypothesis of the client's problems, strengths, and needs. Professionals must be alert to the ways that personal biases can affect the interpretation of case information or the way that data are configured in creating a service plan.
- **Apply and communicate understanding of the importance of diversity and difference in shaping life experiences in practice at the micro, mezzo and macro levels.** This chapter emphasizes the concept of cultural humility, wherein the worker's attitude and demeanor invite the client to teach about his/her lived experience. While professionals continually endeavor to learn more about populations that differ from their own culture of origin, that knowledge provides a backdrop for understanding a person in the context of his or her personal history.
- **Present oneself as a learner, and engage clients and constituencies as experts in their own experiences.** Each of us is the expert on our own life. During assessment, social workers strive to see the world through the eyes of the client, understanding that person's experiences, wishes, attributes, challenges, and needs as he/she sees them.

EP 4   Engage in Practice-Informed Research and Research-Informed Practice
- **Use and translate research evidence to inform and improve practice, policy, and service delivery.** When research shapes classification systems, such as the *DSM-5*, or instruments such as assessment measures, social workers must understand the scientific bases and limitations of these tools.

EP 7   **Assess Individuals, Families, Groups, Organizations, and Communities**

- **Apply knowledge of human behavior and the social environment, person-in-environment, and other multidisciplinary theoretical frameworks in the analysis of assessment data from clients and constituencies.** The scope and depth of assessments are guided by the worker role, agency setting, and client needs in any given case. Social workers must understand how those factors interact in particular types of assessments, such as those to determine risk of abuse, suicide lethality, or medical conditions.

- **Collect and organize data and apply critical thinking to interpret information from clients and constituencies.** In the *process* of assessment, social workers synthesize data about the client's problem and various aspects of personal functioning. The resulting *product* is typically a written document that summarizes pertinent information and offers the worker's assessment about the factors creating, sustaining, and mitigating the client's difficulties. Social workers view problems as arising from the reciprocal interaction between the person and his/her environment. Assessments seek to specify what factors are interacting and the ways they influence each other, so that problematic patterns can be broken.

- **Develop mutually agreed-on intervention goals and objectives based on the critical assessment of strengths, needs, and challenges within clients and constituencies.** Although people seek social work services in times of difficulty, they possess abilities, resources, and experiences that serve as the foundation for change. Social workers identify these in order to get a comprehensive picture of the client and create sound case plans.

SKILL DEVELOPMENT EXERCISES

in Exploring Strengths and Problems

On April 16, 2007, 23-year-old Seung-Hui Cho killed 32 people on the campus of Virginia Tech University before turning the gun on himself. In the months leading up to the murders, Cho had numerous encounters with mental health professionals. He had been declared an "imminent danger to self or others as a result of mental illness" on a temporary detention order from a Virginia District Court. Two students had filed complaints against him for bizarre phone calls and emails he had sent. Another student, his former roommate, called campus police stating that Cho could be suicidal. A poetry professor at the school recalled that he was "menacing" in class, and other students stopped attending after he began photographing them. This professor later removed Cho from her class and worked with him one on one. She also reported that the content of his poems and other writings was disturbing and seemed to have an underlying threat.

A South Korean national, Cho moved with his family to the United States at the age of 8. As a youngster, he was diagnosed with depression and selective mutism, a condition associated with social anxiety, and received therapy and special education services as a result. He was a successful elementary school student, but by middle school he was apparently subject to mockery from fellow students because of his speech abnormalities, his accent, and his isolation.

Imagine that you worked in a setting where Seung-Hui Cho presented for service at age 10, 15, or 22, and address the following questions:

1. What sources of information would you use to better understand your client, his problems, and his strengths?
2. What cross-cultural concerns should you be aware of in this case?
3. What questions would you ask as part of problem analysis?
4. What transitional and developmental issues might be of particular interest?
5. What role would your client's diagnoses play in your assessment?
6. What environmental and interpersonal interactions are relevant in this case?
7. What consultation would be helpful to you in completing this assessment?

NOTE

1. See the U.S. Department of Health and Human Services Substance Abuse and Mental Health Services Administration (www.samhsa.gov), the North Carolina Evidence Based Practice Center (www.ncebp-center.org), the National Institute of Mental Health (www.nimh.nih.gov), the Cochrane Collaboration (www.cochrane.org), and the Campbell Collaboration (http://www.campbellcollaboration.org) for toolkits and other resources for evidence-based practice in an array of problem areas.

Assessment: Intrapersonal, Interpersonal, and Environmental Factors

with Caroline B. R. Evans

Chapter Overview

Chapter 9 reviews three key aspects of a comprehensive assessment: the client's personal functioning (physical, emotional, behavioral, and cognitive), the client's environment, and the transactions between the two. The chapter introduces these areas for examination and helps you develop an understanding of the difficulties and the assets to consider in all of these systems. It also discusses how culture and worker–client differences can affect these factors.

As a result of reading this chapter, you will:

- Understand how assessments capture the reciprocal nature of client systems.

- Learn the elements of intrapersonal functioning, including physical, emotional, cognitive, and behavioral.

- Be able to assess the spiritual and environmental factors affecting the client system.

- Know the questions to ask to assess substance use, including commonly abused drugs.

- Learn the diagnostic criteria for common thought and affective disorders.

- Recognize the elements of a mental status exam and a social history.

- Understand how to evaluate suicide risk and risk for violence.

- Know the do's and don'ts for writing assessments and examine examples of assessments.

EPAS Competencies in Chapter 9

This chapter will give you the information needed to meet the following practice competencies:

- Competency 1: Demonstrate Ethical and Professional Behavior

- Competency 2: Engage Diversity and Difference in Practice

- Competency 7: Assess Individuals, Families, Groups, Organizations, and Communities

THE INTERACTION OF MULTIPLE SYSTEMS IN HUMAN PROBLEMS

Problems, strengths, and resources encountered in direct social work practice result from interactions among intrapersonal (e.g., internal thoughts, perceptions, or reactions), interpersonal (e.g., communication and interactions between two or

EP 7

INTRAPERSONAL SYSTEMS

Biophysical Functioning

Physical characteristics and presentation

Physical health

Use and abuse of medications, alcohol, and drugs

Alcohol use and abuse

Use and abuse of other substances

Dual diagnosis: comorbid addictive and mental disorders

Cognitive/Perceptual Functioning

Intellectual functioning

Judgment

Reality testing

Coherence

Cognitive flexibility

Values

Misconceptions

Self-concept

Assessing thought disorders

Affective Functioning

Emotional control

Range of emotions

Appropriateness of affect

Assessing affective disorders

Bipolar disorder

Major depressive disorder

Suicidal risk

Depression and suicidal risk with children, adolescents, and older adults

Behavioral Functioning

Excesses

Risk of violence

Deficiencies

Motivation

FIG 9-1 Overview: Areas for Attention in Assessing Intrapersonal Functioning

more people), and environmental systems (e.g., work, home, school, community). Difficulties are rarely confined to one of these systems. A functional imbalance in one system typically contributes to an imbalance in others. For example, individual difficulties (e.g., illness, feelings of worthlessness, or depression) invariably influence how one relates to other people (e.g., withdrawn, irritable, demanding). Interpersonal difficulties (e.g., job strain or parent–child discord) likewise affect individual functioning (e.g., stress or difficulty concentrating). Similarly, environmental deficits (e.g., inadequate housing, hostile working conditions, or social isolation) affect individual and interpersonal functioning (e.g., stress, anger, relationships).

The reciprocal effects among the three major systems (intrapersonal, interpersonal, and environmental) are not limited to the negative effects of functional imbalance and system deficits. Assets, strengths, and resources also have reciprocal *positive* effects. A supportive environment may partially compensate for intrapersonal difficulties; similarly, strong interpersonal relationships may provide positive experiences that more than offset an otherwise impoverished environment. Figure 9-1 depicts the range of elements to be considered in assessing individual and interpersonal functioning.

INTRAPERSONAL SYSTEMS

A comprehensive assessment of the individual considers a variety of elements, including biophysical, cognitive/perceptual, affective (emotional), behavioral, and motivational factors, and examines the ways that these affect interactions with people

EP 7

and institutions in the individual's environment. Keeping this in mind, the social worker's assessment and written products may focus more sharply on some of these areas than others, depending on the nature of the client's difficulties, the reason for the assessment, and the setting in which the assessment is taking place. It is important to remember, however, that an assessment is just a "snapshot" of the client system's functioning at any point in time. As we noted in Chapter 8, the social worker's beliefs and actions, and the client's feelings about seeking help, may distort the assessment. For all of these reasons, care and respect are required when collecting and synthesizing assessment information into a working hypothesis for intervention.

ASSESSING BIOPHYSICAL FUNCTIONING

Biophysical functioning encompasses physical characteristics, health factors, and genetic factors, as well as the use and abuse of drugs and alcohol.

Physical Characteristics and Presentation

People's physical characteristics and appearance may be either assets or liabilities. In many cultures, physical attractiveness is highly valued, and unattractive people may be disadvantaged in terms of their social desirability, employment opportunities, or marriageability. Social workers should take care to observe distinguishing physical characteristics that may affect social functioning. Particular attributes that merit attention include body build, dental health, posture, facial features, gait, and any physical anomalies that may create positive or negative perceptions about the client, affect his or her self-image, or pose a social liability.

EP 7

How people present themselves is worthy of note. Individuals who walk slowly, display stooped posture, talk slowly and without animation, lack spontaneity, and show minimal changes in facial expression may be depressed, in pain, or overmedicated. Dress and grooming often reveal much about a person's morale, values, and standard of living. The standard for assessing appearance is generally whether the dress is appropriate for the setting. Is the client barefoot in near-freezing weather or wearing a helmet and overcoat in the summer sun? Is the client dressed seductively, in pajamas, or "overdressed" for an appointment with the social worker? While attending to these questions, social workers should take care in the conclusions they reach. The determination of "appropriateness" is greatly influenced by the interviewer's cultural background and values (Westermeyer, 1993). A "disheveled" appearance may indicate poverty, carelessness, grunge, or "rock star" fashion. Being clothed in bright colors may indicate mania or simply an affiliation with a cultural group that favors that particular form of dress (Morrison, 1995). As with other elements of assessment, your description of what you observe ("collared shirt, dress pants, clean-shaven") should be separate from your assessment of it ("well-groomed and appropriately dressed").

Other important factors associated with appearance include hand tremors, facial tics, rigid or constantly shifting posture, and tense muscles of the face, hands, or arms. Sometimes these characteristics reflect the presence of an illness, physical problem, or overmedication. They may also indicate a high degree of tension or anxiety, warranting exploration by the social worker. During the assessment, an effective social worker will determine whether the anxiety displayed is normative for the given situation or whether it is excessive and might reveal an area for further discussion.

Physical Health

Ill health can contribute to depression, sexual difficulties, irritability, low energy, restlessness, anxiety, poor concentration, and a host of other problems. It is therefore important for social workers to routinely consider their clients' state of health during the intake session. Social workers should determine if clients are under medical care and when they last had a medical examination; they should rule out medical sources of difficulties by referring clients for physical evaluations, when appropriate, before attributing problems solely to psychosocial factors. Social workers should also be cautious and avoid drawing premature conclusions about the sources of problems when there is even a remote possibility that medical factors may be involved.

Assessing the health of clients is especially important with groups known to underutilize medical care. Some clients may have a greater than average need for health care because of their specific conditions, whereas others may simply have more difficulty accessing basic care. Assessments should determine whether the individual's access to care is limited by affordability, availability, or acceptability (Julia, 1996).

Whether care is *affordable* depends on whether the client has health insurance coverage and whether he or she can pay for the services not covered by insurance. Even those who do have coverage may be unable or reluctant to pursue care, given the cost of

EP 7

medications, deductibles, and copayments not covered by insurance. Concerns about costs may lead clients to delay basic care until the situation worsens to a dangerous level or to the point where even more expensive interventions are required. Individuals with extensive or chronic health problems (e.g., AIDS, cancer, traumatic brain injury) may find that hospitalization and drug costs outstrip both their insurance coverage and their income regardless of their wealth and resources.

Availability refers not only to the location of health care services but also the hours they are available, the transportation needed to reach them, and the adequacy of the facilities and personnel to meet the client's needs (Mokuau & Fong, 1994). If the nearest after-hours health care resource is a hospital emergency room, it may be the facility of choice for a desperate mother, even if the health concern (e.g., a child's ear infection) might be better addressed in another setting.

Acceptability refers to the extent to which the health services are compatible with the client's cultural values and traditions. Chapter 8 discussed the importance of understanding how culture may affect a person's interpretation of his or her problems. An important task in intrapersonal assessment involves determining clients' views about the causes of illness, physical aberrations, disabling conditions, and mental symptoms, because their expectations regarding diagnoses and treatment may differ sharply from those presented by Western health care professionals (Yamamoto et al., 1993) and their rejection of these formulations may be misinterpreted as noncompliance or resistance (Al-Krenawi, 1998). For these reasons, all practitioners should be knowledgeable about the significance of caregivers, folk healers, and shamans for clients from an array of cultural groups (Canda, 1983).

Beyond differences in beliefs, differences arise related to people's comfort in accepting care. New immigrants may have limited knowledge of Western medical care and of the complex health care provider systems in the United States, and they may be reticent to seek care because of concerns about their documentation and fears of deportation (Congress, 1994). The use of indigenous healers or bilingual and bicultural staff can enhance the acceptability of health care to these individuals.

A health assessment may also entail gathering information about illnesses in the client's family.[1] A **genogram** may be helpful in capturing this information. This tool, which is similar to a family tree, graphically depicts relationships within the family, dates of births and deaths, illnesses, and other significant life events. It reveals patterns across generations of which even the client may not have been aware (Rempel, Neufeld, & Kushner, 2007). You may also find out about family history simply by asking. For example, "Has anyone else in your family ever had an eating disorder?," "Is there a history of substance abuse in your family?," or "How have other relatives died?" This information helps in assessing the client's understanding of and experience with a problem. It may also identify the need for a referral for specialized information and counseling related to genetically linked disorders (Waltman, 1996).

Assessing Use and Abuse of Medications, Alcohol, and Drugs

An accurate understanding of a client's biophysical functioning must include information on his or her use of both legal and illicit drugs. First, it is important to determine which prescribed and over-the-counter medications the client is taking, whether he or she is taking them as instructed, and whether they are having the intended effect. Another reason for evaluating drug use is that even beneficial drugs can produce side effects that affect the functioning of various biopsychosocial systems.[2] An array of common reactions such as drowsiness, changes in sexual functioning, muscle rigidity, disorientation, apathy, and stomach pains may result from inappropriate combinations of prescription drugs or as side effects of single medications (Denison, 2003). Finally, questioning in this area is important because the client may report a variety of conditions, from confusion to sleeplessness, which may necessitate a referral for evaluation and medication.

EP 7

Alcohol is another form of legal drug, but its abuse can severely impair health, disrupt or destroy family life, and create serious community problems. Alcohol use disorders afflict about 16.6 million adults over the age of 18 and over half a million adolescents ages 12 through 17 (Substance Abuse and Mental Health Services Administration [SAMHSA], 2013). Alcoholism can occur in any culture, although it may be more prevalent in some than in others. Alcohol use and alcoholism are also associated with high incidences of suicide and violent behavior, including homicide, child abuse, and partner violence (National Council on Alcoholism and Drug Dependence, n.d.; World Health Organization, n.d.).

Like alcohol abuse, the misuse of illicit drugs may have detrimental consequences for both the user and his or her family, and drug abuse brings further problems due to its connotation as a banned or illegal substance. For example, users may engage in dangerous or illegal activities (such as prostitution or theft) to support their habits. In addition, variations in the purity of the drugs used or the methods of administration (e.g., sharing needles) may expose users to risks beyond those associated with the drug itself. The following sections introduce the areas for concern related to alcohol and drug abuse and the strategies for effectively assessing use and dependence.

Alcohol Use and Abuse

Understanding a person's alcohol use is essential for a number of reasons. Clearly, problematic use may be related to other problems in work, school, and family functioning. Even moderate use may be a sign of escape or self-medication and lead to impaired judgment and risky behavior, such as driving while intoxicated.

Alcoholism, or alcohol dependency, can be distinguished from heavy drinking in that it causes distress and disruption in the life of the person with alcohol dependency, as well as in the lives of members of that person's social and support systems (Goodwin & Gabrielli, 1997). Alcoholism is marked by a preoccupation with making sure that the amount of alcohol necessary for intoxication remains accessible at all times. As a result, individuals may affiliate with other heavy drinkers in an attempt to escape observation. As alcoholism advances, the signs tend to become more concealed, as the user hides bottles or other "evidence," drinks alone, and covers up drinking binges. Feelings of guilt and anxiety over the behavior begin to appear, which usually leads to more drinking in an effort to escape the negative feelings, which in turn leads to an intensification of the negative feelings.

Females who abuse alcohol present a somewhat different profile. They are more likely to abuse prescription drugs as well, to consume substances in isolation, and to have had the onset of abuse after a traumatic event such as incest or racial or domestic violence (Nelson-Zlupko, Kauffman, & Dore, 1995; Weiss-Ogden, 2014). Women are less likely than men to enter and complete treatment programs because obstacles to treatment often include social stigma associated with alcoholism and a lack of available transportation and child care while in treatment (Greenfield et al., 2007; Yaffe, Jenson, & Howard, 1995).

Another serious problem associated with alcohol abuse involves adverse effects on offspring produced by the mother's alcohol consumption during pregnancy. The potential effects range from full-blown fetal alcohol syndrome (FAS) to fetal alcohol effects (FAE). Because of these risks, social workers should routinely question women about their use of alcohol during pregnancy, gathering a history of consumption of beer, wine, and liquor (focusing on frequency, quantity, and variability). Questions for substance abuse assessment are included in Table 9-1.

Use and Abuse of Other Substances

EP 7

People abuse many types of drugs. Because immediate medical care may be essential in instances of acute drug intoxication, and because abusers often attempt to conceal their use of drugs, it is important that practitioners recognize the signs of abuse of commonly used drugs. Table 9-2 categorizes the most commonly abused drugs and their indications. In addition to those signs of abuse of specific drugs, common general indications include the following:

- Changes in attendance at work or school
- Decrease in normal capabilities (e.g., work performance, efficiency, habits)
- Poor physical appearance, neglect of dress and personal hygiene
- Use of sunglasses to conceal dilated or constricted pupils and to compensate for inability to adjust to sunlight
- Unusual efforts to cover arms to hide needle marks
- Association with known drug users
- Involvement in illegal or dangerous activities to obtain drugs

In assessing the possibility of drug abuse, it is important to elicit information not only from the suspected user (who may not be a reliable reporter for a number of reasons), but also from people who are familiar with the habits and lifestyle of the individual. Likewise, the social worker should assess problems of alcohol and drug abuse from a systems perspective and identify reciprocal interactions between the individual's use and the (conscious and unconscious) actions of his or her family, social contacts, and others.

Although illicit drug use is minimal among older adults compared to younger age groups, rates among adults ages 50 to 64 are on the rise and increased from 2.7% in 2002 to 6.0% in 2013 (SAMHSA, 2014). Older adults are at a particularly high risk for misuse of prescription drugs, which can lead to abuse (Simoni-Wastilla & Yang, 2006). Assessing elder misuse and abuse of drugs is especially important given that older adults often take multiple medications. Although these medications serve to treat disease, alleviate symptoms, and improve and extend quality of life, multiple medication use is a risk factor for medication adherence problems (Steinman & Hanlon, 2010) that could potentially lead to misuse and abuse of these medications. It is therefore vital to obtain an accurate account of the medications that elderly patients are taking, not only from the patient but also from his or her health care provider. There are often discrepancies between the medications older patients take and what medications providers have recorded on patients' medication lists (Kaboli et al., 2004). Further, patients might take unprescribed medications, miss doses, take incorrect combinations, or

TABLE 9-1 Interviewing for Substance Abuse Potential

THE FIRST SIX QUESTIONS WILL HELP GUIDE THE DIRECTION OF YOUR INTERVIEW, THE QUESTIONS YOU ASK, AND YOUR FURTHER ASSESSMENT

1. Do you—or did you ever—smoke cigarettes? For how long? How many per day?
2. Do you drink alcohol?
3. What do you drink? (Beer, wine, liquor?)
4. Do you take any prescription medications regularly? If yes, which ones? What dosage? How do they make you feel?
5. Do you use any over-the-counter medications regularly? If yes, which ones? What dosage? How do they make you feel?
6. Have you ever used any other drugs (e.g., marijuana, cocaine, heroin)?
7. When was the last time you consumed alcohol and/or used drugs?
8. How much did you have to drink/use?
9. When was the last time before that?
10. How much did you have?
11. Do you always drink/use approximately the same amount? If not, is the amount increasing or decreasing?
12. (If it is increasing) Does that concern you?
13. Do most of your friends drink/use?
14. Do (or did) your parents drink/use?
15. Have you ever been concerned that you might have a drinking/drug problem?
16. Has anyone else ever suggested to you that you have (or had) a drinking/drug problem?
17. How does drinking/using help you?
18. Do other people report that you become different or change when you have been drinking/using (for example, more careless, angry, or out of control)?
19. Do you drink/use to "get away from your troubles"?
20. (If so) What troubles are you trying to get away from?
21. Are you aware of any way in which drinking/using is interfering with your work?
22. Are you having any difficulties or conflict with your spouse or partner because of drinking/using?
23. Are you having financial difficulties? Are they related in any way to your drinking/using?
24. Have you ever tried to stop drinking/using? How?

Source: From *Where to Start and What to Ask: An Assessment Handbook* by Susan Lukas. Copyright © 1993 by Susan Lukas. Used by permission of W. W. Norton & Company, Inc.

consume incorrect dosages; the risk for these errors increases with patient age (Bedell et al., 2000). Having the older client sign a release of information will allow the social worker to consult directly with the prescriber, obtain an accurate list of medications and dosages, and talk with caregivers who are responsible for monitoring and dispensing medications.

Dual Diagnosis: Addictive and Mental Disorders

Because alcohol and other drug abuse problems can co-occur with a variety of health and mental health problems (known as **comorbidity**), accurate assessment is important for proper treatment planning. As Lehman (1996) suggests, several combinations of factors must be taken into account:

- The type and extent of the substance use disorder
- The type of mental disorders and the related severity and duration
- The presence of related medical problems
- Comorbid disability or other social problems resulting from use, such as correctional system involvement, poverty, or homelessness

TABLE 9-2 Commonly Abused Drugs and Their Indications

TYPE OF DRUG	TYPICAL INDICATIONS	COMMERCIAL/STREET NAME
1. Central nervous system depressants (alcohol, sedative-hypnotics, benzo-diazepines, barbitu-rates, flunitraze-pam, GHB)	Intoxicated behavior with/without odor, staggering or stumbling, "nodding off" at work, slurred speech, dilated pupils, disorientation, difficulty concentrating, potential memory loss	(benzodiazepines) *Ativan, Halcion, Librium, Valium, Xanax*: candy, downers, sleeping pills, tranks (barbiturates) *Amytal, Nembutal, Seconal, Phe-nobarbital*: barbs, reds, red birds, phennies, tooies, yellows, yellow jackets (flunitrazepam) *Rohypnol*: forget-me pill, Mexican Valium, R2, Roche, roofies, roofinol, rope, rophies (GHB) *Gamma-hydroxybutyrate*: G, Georgia Home Boy, grievous bodily harm, liquid ecstasy, soap, scoop, liquid X
2. Central nervous system stimulants (amphetamines, methamphetamine, MDMA, methyl-phenidate, nicotine)	Excessively active, increased alertness, euphoric, irritable, argumentative, nervous, long periods without eating or sleeping, weight loss, decreased inhibition, irregular heart beat	(amphetamines) *Biphetamine, Dexedrine*: bennies, black beauties, crosses, hearts, LA turnaround, speed, truck drivers, uppers (methamphetamine) *Desoxyn*: chalk, crank, crystal, fire, glass, go fast, ice, meth, speed (MDMA) Adam, clarity, ecstasy, Eve, lover's speed, peace, STP, X, XTC (methylphenidate) *Ritalin*: JIF, MPH, R-ball, Skippy, the smart drug, vitamin R (nicotine) cigarettes, cigars, smokeless tobacco, snuff, spit tobacco, bidis, chew
3. Cocaine and crack (also CNS)	Energetic, euphoric, fixed and dilated pupils, reduced appetite, relatively quick or slow heart beat (euphoria quickly replaced by anxiety, panic attacks, irri-tability and/or depression, sometimes accompanied by hallucinations and paranoid delusions), erratic and violent behavior	*Cocaine hydrochloride*: blow, bump, C, candy, Charlie, coke, crack, flake, rock, snow, toot
4. Opiates (codeine, fentanyl, opium, heroin, morphine, other opioid pain killers)	Euphoric, clouded thinking, scars from injecting drugs, fixed and constricted pupils, frequent scratching, loss of appetite (but frequently eat sweets); may have sniffles, red and watering eyes, nausea and vomiting, constipation, and cough until another "fix"; lethargic, drowsy, and alternate between dozing and awakening ("nodding")	(codeine) *Empirin with Codeine, Fiorinal with Codeine, Robitussin A-C, Tylenol with Codeine*: Captain Cody, Cody, schoolboy; (with glutethi-mide) doors and fours, loads, pancakes and syrup (fentanyl) *Actiq, Duragesic, Sublimaze*: Apache, China girl, China white, dance fever, friend, goodfella, jackpot, murder 8, TNT, Tango and Cash (opium) *laudanum, paregoric*: big O, black stuff, block, gum, hop (heroin) *diacetylmorphine*: brown sugar, china white, dope, H, horse, junk, skag, skunk, smack, white horse (morphine) *Roxanol, Duramorph*: M, Miss Emma, monkey, white stuff (other opioid pain killers) *Tylox, OxyContin, Percodan, Percocet*: oxy 80s, oxycotton, oxycet, hillbilly heroin, percs; *Demerol, meperidine hydro-chloride*: demmies, pain killer; *Dilaudid*: juice, dillies; *Vicodin, Lortab, Lorcet; Darvon, Darvocet*

TABLE 9-2 Continued

TYPE OF DRUG	TYPICAL INDICATIONS	COMMERCIAL/STREET NAME
5. Cannabinoid (marijuana, hashish)	In early stages, may be euphoric or anxious and appear animated, speaking rapidly and loudly with bursts of laughter; this is often followed by drowsiness/relaxation; pupils may be bloodshot; may have distorted perceptions such as increased sense of taste or smell; reduced short-term memory; lowered coordination, difficulty with balance, and slowed reaction time; increased appetite and heart rate	(marijuana) blunt, bud, dope, ganja, grass, herb, joints, Mary Jane, pot, reefer, sinsemilla, skunk, smoke, trees, weed (hashish) boom, gangster, hash, hemp
6. Hallucinogens (LSD, mescaline psilocybin, DMT, ayahuasca)	Behavior and mood vary widely: may sit or recline quietly in trancelike stare or appear fearful or even terrified; dilated pupils in some cases; may experience nausea, chills, flushes, dizziness, irregular breathing, extreme lability, sweating, or trembling of hands; may experience changes in sense of sight, hearing, touch, smell, and time manifested as hallucinations; sedation, confusion, and problems sleeping or moving	(LSD) *lysergic acid diethylamide:* acid, blotter, blue, heaven, cubes, microdot, yellow sunshine (mescaline) buttons, cactus, mesc, peyote (psilocybin) little smoke, magic mushroom, purple passion, shrooms (DMT) Dimitri (ayahuasca) aya, yage, hoasca
7. Dissociative drugs (ketamine, PCP, Salvia divinorum, DXM)	Feelings of being separate from one's body and environment; impaired motor function/anxiety; memory loss; respiratory problems; potential hallucinations	(ketamine) cat, Valium, K, Special K, vitamin K (PCP) *phencyclidine:* angel dust, boat, hog, love boat, peace pill (Salvia divinorum) magic mint, maria pastora, Sally-D, shepherdess's herb, diviner's sage (DXM) *dextromethorphan:* Robotripping, Robo, Triple C
8. Inhalants and volatile hydrocarbons (chloroform, nail polish remover, metallic paints, carbon tetrachloride, amyl nitrate, butyl, isobutyl, nitrous oxide, lighter fluid, fluoride-based sprays)	Varies by chemical: Reduced inhibitions, euphoria, dizziness, slurred speech, unsteady gait, giddiness, drowsiness, nystagmus (constant involuntary eye movement), weight loss, depression, memory impairment, confusion, nausea	solvents (paint thinners, gasoline, glues) gases (butane, propane, aerosol propellants, nitrous oxide) nitrites (isoamyl, isobutyl, cyclohexyl): laughing gas, poppers, snappers, whippets
9. Anabolic and androgenic steroids	Increased muscle strength and reduced body mass, acne, aggression, changes to libido and mood, competitiveness, combativeness, yellowing of the skin and whites of the eyes, fluid retention	*Anadrol, Oxandrin, Durabolin, Depo-Testosterone, Equipoise:* roids, juice, gym candy, pumpers

Source: National Institute on Drug Abuse. (2015). *Commonly Abused Drugs Charts.* Retrieved from http://www.drugabuse.gov/drugs-abuse/commonly-abused-drugs-charts-0.

Depending on the combination of factors that affect them, clients may have difficulty seeking out and adhering to treatment programs. Furthermore, an understanding of the reciprocal interaction of these factors may affect the social workers' assessment and resulting intervention. For example, some psychiatric problems (e.g., paranoia or depression) may emerge as a result of substance use. Social problems such as joblessness or incarceration may limit the client's access to needed treatment for substance abuse, and substance use may limit job and housing opportunities. Problems such as personality disorders may impede the development of trusting and effective treatment relationships needed to treat drug addiction.

Using Interviewing Skills to Assess Substance Use

Social workers are often involved with substance users before they have actually acknowledged they have a problem or sought help for it (Barber, 1995). It may be difficult to be nonjudgmental when the user denies that illicit or licit substances are a problem and attempts to conceal the abuse by blaming others, lying, arguing, distorting, attempting to intimidate, diverting the interview focus, or verbally attacking the social worker. Despite these aversive behaviors, the social worker needs to express empathy and sensitivity to the client's feelings, recognizing that such behaviors are often a subterfuge behind which lie embarrassment, hopelessness, shame, ambivalence, and anger.

When asking about alcohol use, be forthright in explaining why you are pursuing that line of questioning. Vague, wordy, or indirect questions tend to support the client's evasions and yield unproductive responses. The questions listed in Table 9-1 should be asked in a direct and compassionate manner. They address the extent and effects of the client's substance use, and the impact on his or her environment.

ASSESSING COGNITIVE/ PERCEPTUAL FUNCTIONING

EP 2

How individuals perceive the world is important because people's perceptions of others, themselves, and events largely determine how they feel and respond to life experiences in general and to their problematic situations in particular. Recall

from Chapter 8 that the meanings or interpretations of events—rather than the events themselves—motivate human beings to behave as they do. Every person's world of experience is unique. Perceptions of identical events or circumstances vary widely according to the complex interaction of belief systems, values, attitude, state of mind, and self-concept, all of which in turn are highly idiosyncratic.

It follows, then, that to understand and to influence human behavior you must first be knowledgeable about how people think. Our thought patterns are influenced by *intellectual functioning*, *judgment*, *reality testing*, *coherence*, *cognitive flexibility*, *values*, *beliefs*, *self-concept*, and the dynamic interaction among cognitions, emotions, and behaviors that influence social functioning. In the following sections, we briefly consider each of these factors and demonstrate their use in a mental status assessment (see Figure 9-2, p. 235).

Intellectual Functioning

EP 7

Understanding the client's intellectual capacity is essential for a variety of reasons. Your assessment of intellectual functioning will allow you to adjust your verbal expressions to a level that the client can readily comprehend, and it will help you in assessing strengths and difficulties, negotiating goals, and planning tasks commensurate with the client's capacities. In most instances, a rough estimate of level of intellectual functioning will suffice. In making this assessment, you may want to consider the client's ability to grasp abstract ideas, to express himself or herself, and to analyze or think logically. Additional criteria include level of educational achievement and vocabulary employed, although these factors must be considered in relation to the person's previous educational opportunities, primary language, or learning difficulties because normal or high intellectual capacity may be masked by these and other factors.

When communicating with clients who have marked intellectual limitations, use simple and easily understood words and avoid abstract explanations. To avoid embarrassment, many people will pretend that they understand when, in fact, they do not. Therefore, you should make keen observations and actively seek feedback to determine whether the client has grasped your intended meaning. You can also assist the client by using multiple, concrete examples to convey complex ideas.

When a client's presentation is inconsistent with his or her known intellectual achievement, it may reveal an area for further investigation. For example, have the client's capacities been affected by illness, medications, a head injury, or the use of substances? Or has scholarly achievement (social promotion in school, grade inflation) masked intellectual limitations?

Judgment

Some people who have adequate or even keen intellect may nevertheless encounter severe difficulties in life because they suffer deficiencies in judgment. Examples of problems in judgment include consistently living beyond one's means, becoming involved in "get rich quick" schemes without carefully exploring the possible ramifications, quitting jobs impulsively, leaving small children unattended, moving in with a partner without adequate knowledge of that person, failing to safeguard or maintain personal property, and squandering resources.

Deficiencies in judgment generally come to light when you explore problems and the patterns surrounding them. You may find that a person acts with little forethought, fails to consider the probable consequences of his or her actions, or engages in wishful thinking that things will somehow magically work out. Dysfunctional coping patterns may lead predictably to unfavorable outcomes. Because individuals with poor judgment often fail to learn from their past mistakes, they appear to be driven by intense impulses that overpower consideration of the consequences of their actions. Impulse-driven clients may lash out at authority figures, write bad checks, misuse credit cards, or take other actions that provide immediate gratification but ultimately lead to adverse consequences such as the loss of a job or an arrest.

Reality Testing

Reality testing is a critical index to a person's mental health. Strong functioning on this dimension means meeting the following criteria:

1. Being properly oriented to time, place, person, and situation
2. Reaching appropriate conclusions about cause-and-effect relationships
3. Perceiving external events and discerning the intentions of others with reasonable accuracy
4. Differentiating one's own thoughts and feelings from those of others

Clients who are markedly disoriented may be severely mentally disturbed, under the influence of drugs, or suffering from a pathological brain syndrome. Disorientation is usually easily identifiable, but when doubt exists, questions about the date, day of the week, current events that are common knowledge, and recent events in the client's life will usually clarify the matter. Clients who are disoriented typically respond inappropriately, sometimes giving bizarre or unrealistic answers. For example, in responding to a question about his daily activities, a reclusive man reported that he cannot shower because he has to be on call at all times to consult with the White House about foreign policy.

Some clients who do not have thought disorders may still have poor reality testing, choosing to blame circumstances and events rather than take personal responsibility for their actions. For example, one man who stole an automobile externalized responsibility for his behavior by blaming the owner for leaving the keys in the car. Some clients blame their employers for losing their jobs, even though they habitually missed work for invalid reasons. Still others attribute their difficulties to fate, claiming that it decreed them to be losers. Whatever the sources of these problems with reality testing, they serve as impediments to motivation and meaningful change. Conversely, when people take appropriate responsibility for their actions, that ownership should be considered an area of strength.

Perceptual patterns that involve distortions of external events are fairly common but may cause difficulties, particularly in interpersonal relationships. **Mild distortions** may be associated with stereotypical perceptions (e.g., "All social workers are liberals" or "The only interest men have in women is sexual"). **Moderate distortions** often involve marked misinterpretations of the motives of others and may severely impair interpersonal relationships (e.g., "My boss told me I was doing a good job and that there is an opportunity to be promoted to a job in another department; he's only saying that to get rid of me" or "My wife says she wants to take an evening class, but I know what she really wants is to meet other men"). In instances of **extreme distortions**, individuals may have **delusions** or false beliefs—for example, that others plan to harm them when they do not. On rare occasions, people suffering from delusions may take violent actions to protect themselves from their imagined persecutors.

Dysfunctions in reality testing of psychotic proportions occur when clients hear voices or other sounds (**auditory hallucinations**) or see things that are not there (**visual hallucinations**). These individuals lack the capacity to distinguish between thoughts and beliefs that emanate from themselves and those that originate from external sources. As a consequence, they may present a danger to themselves or others when acting in response to such commands or visions. Social workers must be able to recognize such severe cognitive dysfunction and respond with referrals for medication, protection, and/or hospitalization.

Coherence

Social workers occasionally encounter individuals who demonstrate major thought disorders, which are characterized by rambling and incoherent speech. For example, successive thoughts may be highly fragmented and disconnected from one another, a phenomenon referred to as **looseness of association** or **derailment** in the thought processes. As Morrison puts it, the practitioner "can understand the sequence of the words, but the direction they take seems to be governed not by logic but by rhymes, puns or other rules that might be apparent to the patient but mean nothing to you" (1995, p. 113). Another form of derailment is **flight of ideas**, in which the client's response seems to "take off" based on a particular word or thought, unrelated to logical progression or the original point of the communication.

These difficulties in coherence may be indicative of head injury, mania, or thought disorders such as schizophrenia. Incoherence, of course, may also be produced by acute drug intoxication, so practitioners should be careful to rule out this possibility.

Cognitive Flexibility

People who are receptive to new ideas and able to analyze many facets of problematic situations are highly adaptable and capable of successful problem solving. Individuals with **cognitive flexibility** generally seek to grow, to understand the part they play in their difficulties, and to understand others; these individuals can also ask for assistance without perceiving such a request to be an admission of weakness or failure. Many people, however, are rigid and unyielding in their beliefs, and their inflexibility poses a major obstacle to progress in the helping process.

A common pattern of cognitive inflexibility is thinking in absolute terms (e.g., a person is good or evil, a success or a failure, responsible or irresponsible—there are no in-betweens). People who think this way are prone to criticize others who fail to measure up to their stringent standards. Because they can be difficult to live with, many of these individuals appear at social agencies because of relationship problems, workplace conflict, or parent–child disputes. Improvement often requires helping them examine the destructive impact of their rigidity, broaden their perspectives of themselves and others, and "loosen up" in general.

Negative cognitive sets also include biases and stereotypes that impede relationship building or cooperation with members of certain groups (e.g., authority figures, ethnic groups, and the opposite sex) or individuals. Severely depressed clients often have another form of "tunnel vision," viewing themselves as helpless or worthless and the future as dismal and hopeless. When they are lost in the depths of illness, these individuals may selectively attend to their own negative attributes, have difficulty feeling good about themselves, and struggle with being open to other options.

Values

EP 2

Values are an integral part of the cognitive/perceptual subsystem because they strongly influence human behavior and often play a key role in the problems presented for work. For this reason, you should seek to identify your clients' values, assess the role those values play in their difficulties, and consider ways in which clients' values can be deployed to create incentives for change. Your ethical responsibility to respect the client's right to maintain his or her values and to make choices consistent with them requires you to become aware of those values. Because values result from our cultural conditioning, understanding the client's cultural reference group is important, particularly if it differs from your own. Understanding the individual *within* his or her culture is also critical, however, because people adopt values on a continuum, with considerable diversity occurring among people within any given race, faith, culture, or community (Gross, 1995).

VIDEO CASE EXAMPLE

Value conflicts are often at the heart of clients' difficulties. For example, in the video "Working with Yanping," the client, a Chinese college student named Yanping, is torn between loyalty to her parents, who want her to study business, and her desire to follow her own interests and study history. Such value conflicts are often central to difficulties between people in other contexts as well. For example, parents and children may disagree about dress, behavior, or responsibilities. Partners may hold different beliefs about how chores should be divided, how finances should be handled, or how they should relate to each person's family of origin.

Examples of questions that will clarify values include:

- *"You say you believe your parents are old-fashioned about sex. What are your beliefs?"*
- *"If you could be married to an ideal partner, what would that person be like?"*
- *[To a couple]: "What are your beliefs about how couples should make decisions?"*
- *"So you feel you're not succeeding in life. To you, what does being successful involve?"*

Being aware of values also helps you in using those values to create incentives for changing dysfunctional behavior—for example, when clients express strong values yet behave in direct opposition to those values. **Cognitive dissonance** may result when people discover inconsistencies between their values and behaviors. Examining these contradictions can help reveal whether this tension is problematic or self-defeating. For example, consider an individual coming to terms with his homosexuality within a religious faith that condemns his sexual orientation. Tension, confusion, and distress can result as this client and others attempt to reconcile disparate beliefs. The social worker may help by identifying and labeling the cognitive dissonance and working with the client to reconcile the differences or create options so that they are no longer mutually exclusive. The techniques associated with motivational interviewing, which we discuss later in the chapter, are helpful in gently calling attention to incongruent values and actions.

Beliefs

Cognitive theory holds that beliefs are important mediators of both emotions and actions (Wright, Basco, & Thase, 2006). It makes sense, then, that mistaken beliefs can be related to problems in functioning. Sometimes, beliefs are not misconceptions but rather are unhelpful, though accurate, conceptions. Examples

of common destructive beliefs and contrasting functional beliefs include: "The world is a dog-eat-dog place; no one really cares about anyone except themselves" versus "There are all kinds of people in the world, including those who are ruthless and those who are caring; I need to seek out the latter and strive to be a caring person myself"; or "All people in authority use their power to exploit and control others" versus "People in authority vary widely—some exploit and control others, while others are benevolent; I must reserve judgment, or I will indiscriminately resent all authority figures."

It is important to identify misconceptions and their sources so as to create a comprehensive assessment. Depending on how central these beliefs are to the client's problems, the goals for work that follow may involve modifying key misconceptions, thereby paving the way to behavioral change. As with other areas, client strengths may derive from the *absence* of misconceptions and from the ability to accurately, constructively, or positively perceive and construe events and motivations.

Self-Concept

Convictions, beliefs, and ideas about the self (that is, one's **self-concept**) have been generally recognized as crucial determinants of human behavior. Thus, there are strengths in having good self-esteem and in being realistically aware of one's positive attributes, accomplishments, and potential as well as one's limitations and deficiencies. A healthy person can accept limitations as a natural part of human fallibility without being overly distressed or discouraged. People with high self-esteem, in fact, can joke about their weaknesses and mistakes.

Many people, however, are tormented with feelings of worthlessness, inadequacy, and helplessness. These and similarly self-critical feelings pervade their functioning in diverse negative ways, including the following:

- Underachieving in life because of imagined deficiencies
- Passing up opportunities because of fears of failing
- Avoiding social relationships because of expectations of being rejected
- Permitting oneself to be taken for granted and exploited by others
- Excessive drinking or drug use to fortify oneself because of feelings of inadequacy

IDEAS IN ACTION

Cognitive or Thought Disorders

EP 7

As you assess cognitive functioning, you may note signs and symptoms of thought disorders and developmental delays. Three particular disorders to be alert to are intellectual disability, schizophrenia, and major neurocognitive disorder (*DSM-5*; American Psychiatric Association, 2013a).

Intellectual disability is typically diagnosed in infancy or childhood. It is defined as lower-than-average intelligence and "deficits in general mental abilities and impairment in everyday adaptive functioning, in comparison to an individual's age-, gender-, and socioculturally matched peers" (American Psychiatric Association, 2013a, p. 37). General intellectual functioning is appraised using standardized tests, and other measurement instruments may be used to assess the client's adaptive functioning, or ability to meet common life demands. Four levels of intellectual disability are distinguished: mild, moderate, severe, and profound.

Schizophrenia is a psychotic disorder that causes marked impairment in social, educational, and occupational functioning. Its onset typically occurs during adolescence or young adulthood, and development of the disorder may be abrupt or gradual. It is signified by a combination of positive and negative symptoms. In this context, these terms do not refer to whether something is good or bad but rather to the presence or absence of normal functioning. For example, **positive symptoms** of schizophrenia include delusions (i.e., fixed beliefs that cannot be altered even in the presence of conflicting evidence), hallucinations (i.e., perception experiences of sound, sight, touch, or taste in the absence of external stimuli), disorganized thinking and/or speech, and grossly disorganized behavior (e.g., switching rapidly between topics) or abnormal motor behavior (e.g., catatonia, agitation) (American Psychiatric Association, 2013a). **Negative symptoms** include flattened affect, restricted speech, and **avolition**, or limited initiation of goal-directed behavior.

Major neurocognitive disorder (NCD), formerly referred to as *dementia* in *DSM-IV-TR* (American Psychiatric Association, 2013a), is a broader term than dementia, and individuals with a major decline in a single domain can be diagnosed with NCD. Major NCD is characterized by "evidence of significant cognitive decline from previous level of performance in one or more cognitive domains (complex attention, executive function, learning and memory, language, perceptual-motor, or social cognition)" (American Psychiatric Association, 2013a, p. 602). These deficits must be of sufficient severity to affect one's daily functioning to warrant a diagnosis of NCD (Corcoran & Walsh, 2010).

Treatment of individuals with these diagnoses is specialized and varied but may include use of medication as well as vocational, residential, and case management services. Understanding the features of these and other cognitive or thought disorders will assist you in better understanding clients, in planning appropriate treatment, and in considering how your role on cases meshes with that of other service providers.

- Devaluing or discrediting worthwhile achievements
- Failing to defend one's rights

Often clients will spontaneously discuss how they view themselves, or their description of patterns of difficulty may convey a damaged self-concept. An open-ended query, such as "Tell me how you see yourself," will often elicit rich information. Because many people have not actually given much thought to the matter, they may hesitate or appear perplexed. An additional query, such as "What comes into your head when you think about the sort of person you are?" is usually all that is needed to prompt the client to respond.

ASSESSING AFFECTIVE FUNCTIONING

Emotions are affected by cognitions and powerfully influence behavior. People who seek help often do so because they have experienced strong emotions or a sense that their emotions are out of control. Some individuals, for example, are emotionally volatile and

EP 7

engage in aggressive behavior while in the heat of anger. Others are emotionally unstable, struggling to stay afloat in a turbulent sea of feelings. Some people become emotionally distraught as the result of stress associated with the death of a loved one, divorce, severe disappointment, or another blow to self-esteem. Still others are pulled in different directions by opposing feelings and seek help to resolve their emotional dilemmas. To assist you in assessing emotional functioning, the following sections examine vital aspects of this dimension and the related terms and concepts. Figure 9-2 (p. 235) demonstrates the use of these concepts in a mental status exam.

Emotional Control

People vary widely in the degree of control they exercise over their emotions, ranging from emotional constriction to emotional excesses. Individuals who are experiencing **emotional constriction** may appear unexpressive and withholding in relationships. Because they are out of touch with their emotions, they do not appear to permit themselves to feel joy, hurt, enthusiasm, vulnerability, and other emotions that might otherwise invest life with zest and meaning. These individuals may be comfortable intellectualizing but retreat from expressing or discussing feelings. They often favorably impress others with their intellectual styles but sometimes have difficulties maintaining close relationships because their emotional detachment thwarts them from fulfilling the needs of others for intimacy and emotional stimulation.

A person with **emotional excesses**, on the other hand, may have "a short fuse," losing control and reacting intensely to even mild provocations. This behavior may involve rages and escalate to interpersonal violence. Excesses can also include other emotions such as irritability, crying, panic, despondency, helplessness, or giddiness. The key to assessing whether the emotional response is excessive is determining whether the response is appropriate and proportionate to the situation.

EP 2

Your assessment may stem from your personal observation of the client, feedback from collateral contacts, or the client's own report of his or her response to a situation. As always, your appraisal of the appropriateness of the response must factor in the client's social and cultural context and the nature of his or her relationship with you. Both may lead you to misjudge the client's normal emotional response and what is considered "appropriate" emotional regulation.

Cultures vary widely in their approved patterns of emotional expression. Nevertheless, emotional health in any culture shares one criterion: It means having control over emotions to the extent that one is not overwhelmed by them. Emotionally healthy persons also enjoy the freedom of experiencing and expressing emotions appropriately. Likewise, strengths include the ability to bear painful emotions without denying or masking feelings or being incapacitated by them. Emotionally healthy persons are able to discern the emotional states of others, empathize, and discuss painful emotions openly without feeling unduly distressed—recognizing, of course, that a certain amount of discomfort is natural. Finally, the ability to mutually share deeply personal feelings in intimate relationships is also considered an asset.

Range of Emotions

Another aspect of emotional functioning involves the ability to experience and to express a wide range of emotions that befits the vast array of situations that humans encounter. Some individuals' emotional expression is confined to a limited range, which can cause interpersonal difficulties. For example, if one partner has difficulty expressing tender emotions, the other partner may feel rejected, insecure, or deprived of deserved affection.

Some individuals are unable to feel joy or to express many pleasurable emotions, a dysfunction referred to as **anhedonia**. Still others have been conditioned to block out their angry feelings, blame themselves, or placate others when friction develops in relationships. Because of this blocking of natural emotions, they may experience extreme tension or physiological symptoms such as asthma, colitis, and headaches when they face situations that normally would engender anger or sadness. Finally, some people, to protect themselves from unbearable emotions, develop psychic mechanisms early in life that block them from experiencing rejection, loneliness, and hurt. Often this blockage is reflected by a compensatory facade of toughness and indifference, combined with verbal expressions such as "I don't need anyone" and "No one can hurt me." Whatever its source, a blocked or limited range of emotions may affect the client's difficulties and thus represent a goal for work.

Emotionally healthy people experience the full gamut of human emotions within normal limits of intensity and duration. The capacity to experience joy, grief, exhilaration, disappointment, and the rest of the full spectrum of emotions is, therefore, an area of strength.

Appropriateness of Affect

Direct observation of clients' **affect** (emotionality) usually reveals valuable information about their emotional functioning. Some anxiety or mild apprehension is natural in initial sessions as contrasted to intense apprehension and tension at one extreme or complete relaxation or giddiness at the other. Healthy functioning involves spontaneously experiencing and expressing emotion appropriate to the context and the material being discussed. The ability to laugh, to cry, and to express hurt, discouragement, anger, and pleasure when these feelings match the mood and content of the session constitutes an area of strength. Such spontaneity indicates that clients are in touch with their emotions and can express them appropriately.

Inordinate apprehension—often demonstrated by muscle tension, constant fidgeting or shifts in posture, hand wringing, lip-biting, and similar behaviors— usually indicates that a person is fearful, suspicious, or exceptionally uncomfortable in unfamiliar interpersonal situations. Such extreme tension may be expected in involuntary situations. In other cases, it may be characteristic of a client's demeanor in other contexts.

Clients who appear completely relaxed and express themselves freely in a circumstance that would normally evoke apprehension or anxiety may reflect a denial of a problem and or a lack of motivation to engage in the problem-solving process. Further, a charming demeanor may reflect the client's skill in projecting a favorable image when it is advantageous to do so. In some situations, such as in sales, promotional, or political work, this kind of charm may be an asset; in other circumstances, it may be a coping style developed to conceal the individual's insecurity, self-centeredness, and manipulation or exploitation of others.

Emotional blunting is what the term suggests: a muffled or apathetic response to material that would typically evoke a stronger response (e.g., happiness, despair, anger). For example, emotionally blunted clients may discuss, in a detached and matter-of-fact manner, traumatic life events or conditions such as the murder of one parent by another, deprivation, or physical and/or sexual abuse. Emotional blunting can be indicative of a severe mental disorder, a sign of drug misuse, a side effect of medications, or an indication of past trauma, so it always warrants special attention.

Inappropriate affect can also appear in other forms, such as laughing when discussing a painful event (gallows laughter) or smiling constantly regardless of what is being discussed. Elation or euphoria that is incongruent with the individual's life situation, combined with constant and rapid shifts from one topic to another (flight of ideas), irritability, expansive ideas, and constant motion, also suggests mania.

In transcultural work, appropriateness of affect must be considered in light of cultural differences. According to Lum (1996), minority clients may feel uncomfortable with nonminority social workers but mask their emotions as a protective measure, or they may control painful emotions according to culturally prescribed norms. Measures to assure appropriate interpretation of affect include understanding the features of the client's culture, consulting others who are familiar with the culture or the client, and evaluating the client's current presentation with his or her demeanor in the past.

Suicidal Risk

Not all individuals with depressive symptoms are suicidal and not all suicidal individuals are depressed. Nevertheless, whenever clients exhibit depressive symptoms or hopelessness, it is critical to evaluate suicidal risk so that precautionary measures can be taken when indicated. With adults, the following factors are associated with high risk of suicide:

- Feelings of despair and hopelessness
- Previous suicide attempts
- Concrete, available, and lethal plans to commit suicide (when, where, and how)
- Family history of suicide
- Perseveration about suicide
- Lack of support systems and other forms of isolation
- Feelings of worthlessness
- Belief that others would be better off if the client were dead
- Advanced age (especially for white males)
- Substance abuse

When a client indicates, directly or indirectly, that he or she may be considering suicide, it is essential that you address those concerns through careful and direct questioning. You may begin by stating, "You sound pretty hopeless right now; I wonder if you might also be thinking of harming yourself?" or "When you say 'They'll be sorry' when you're gone, I wonder if that means you're thinking of committing suicide?" An affirmative answer to these probes should be followed with a frank and calm discussion of the client's thoughts about suicide. Has the client considered how he or she might do it?

EP 7

When? What means would be used? Are those means accessible? In asking these questions, you are trying to determine not only the lethality of the client's plans but also the specificity. If a client has a well-thought-out plan in mind, the risk of suicide is significantly greater. An understanding of the client's history, especially with regard to the risk factors mentioned and previous suicide attempts, will also help you decide the degree of danger and the level of intervention required. Standardized scales can also be used to evaluate suicidal risk.

When the client's responses indicate a potentially lethal attempt, it is appropriate to mobilize client support systems and arrange for psychiatric evaluation and/or hospitalization if needed. Such steps provide a measure of security for the client who may feel unable to control his or her impulses or who may become overwhelmed with despair.

Depression and Suicidal Risk with Children and Adolescents

Children and adolescents may experience depression just as adults do, and suicide can be a risk with these groups (Morrison & Anders, 1999). In the United States, more than 4,000 youths ages 10 to 24 die by suicide each year, accounting for 11.7% of all deaths

IDEAS IN ACTION

Affective Disorders

EP 7

The *DSM-5* (American Psychiatric Association, 2013a) contains extensive information on the criteria for diagnosing bipolar and related disorders and depressive disorders. Treatment of these diagnoses generally includes medication (often with concurrent cognitive or interpersonal psychotherapy). Understanding these diagnoses is important for treatment planning and detection of suicidal ideation and other serious risk factors (Corcoran & Walsh, 2010).

Bipolar Disorder

The dominant feature of **bipolar disorder** is the presence of manic episodes (mania) with intervening periods of depression. Among the symptoms of mania are "A distinct period of abnormally and persistently elevated, expansive or irritable mood" (American Psychiatric Association, 2013a, p. 124) and at least three of the following:

- Inflated self-esteem or grandiosity
- Decreased need for sleep
- More talkative than usual or pressure to keep talking
- Flight of ideas or subjective experience that thoughts are racing
- Distractibility (i.e., attention too easily drawn to unimportant or irrelevant external stimuli), as reported or observed
- Increase in goal-directed activity (either socially, at work or school, or sexually) or

psychomotor agitation (i.e., purposeless non-goal-directed activity)

- Excessive involvement in pleasurable activities with a high potential for painful consequences, such as unrestrained buying sprees, sexual indiscretions, or unwise business investments

Full-blown **manic episodes** require that symptoms be sufficiently severe to cause marked impairment in job performance or relationships, or to necessitate hospitalization to protect patients or others from harm.

If exploration seems to indicate a client has the disorder, immediate psychiatric consultation is needed for two reasons: (1) to determine whether hospitalization is needed and (2) to determine the need for medication. Bipolar disorder is biogenetic, and various compounds containing lithium carbonate may produce remarkable results in stabilizing and maintaining affected individuals. Close medical supervision is required, however, because commonly used medications for this disorder have a relatively narrow margin of safety.

Major Depressive Disorder

Major depressive disorder, in which affected individuals experience recurrent episodes of depressed mood, is far more common than bipolar disorder. Major depression differs from the "blues" in that painful emotions (**dysphoria**) and the absence of pleasure in previously enjoyable activities (**anhedonia**) are present. The painful emotions are commonly related to anxiety, mental anguish, an extreme sense of guilt (often over what appear to be relatively minor offenses), and restlessness (agitation).

To be assigned a diagnosis of major depressive disorder, a person must have evidenced depressed mood and loss of interest or pleasure as well as at least five of the following nine symptoms for at least 2 weeks (American Psychiatric Association, 2013a, pp. 160–161):

- Depressed mood for most of the day, nearly every day
- Markedly diminished interest or pleasure in all or almost all activities
- Significant weight loss or weight gain when not dieting or decrease or increase in appetite
- Insomnia or hypersomnia
- Psychomotor agitation or retardation nearly every day
- Fatigue or loss of energy

- Feelings of worthlessness or excessive or inappropriate guilt
- Diminished ability to think or concentrate or indecisiveness
- Recurrent thoughts of death or suicidal ideation or attempts

As noted in Chapter 8, a number of scales are available to assess the presence and degree of depression. When assessment reveals that clients are moderately or severely depressed, psychiatric consultation is indicated to determine the need for medication and/or hospitalization. Antidepressant medications have proven to be effective in accelerating recovery from depression and work synergistically with cognitive or interpersonal psychotherapy.

In assessing depression, it is important to identify which factors precipitated the depressive episode. An important loss or series of losses may lead to depression associated with bereavement.

in this age group (CDC, 2004). In fact, in the United States, suicide is the third leading cause of death for children ages 10 to 14 as well as for young people ages 15 to 34 (CDC, 2015). The World Health Organization (WHO), reporting global statistics, notes that each year 800,000 people take their own lives and that suicide is the second leading cause of death for those between the ages of 15 and 29 (WHO, 2014).

VIDEO CASE EXAMPLE

In Session 2 of the video "Hanging with Hailey," Emily, the social worker, takes note of changes in Hailey's demeanor, her isolation, and her misery as a result of rejection by peers. As a result, Emily inquires about Hailey's coping and then directly asks, "Do you ever think about wanting to hurt yourself?" Although she determines that Hailey's risk is currently only at the level of ideation, she puts a plan in place should her suicidal thoughts and symptoms increase.

Clearly, it is important to recognize the symptoms of depression in adolescents and the behavioral

manifestations that may be reported by peers, siblings, parents, or teachers. The symptoms of depression in adolescents are similar to those in adults mentioned above, though irritability and somatic complaints may be more prominent with children and teens (American Psychiatric Association, 2013a; Dulcan, 2009).

EP 7

Childhood depression does not differ markedly from depression in adolescence; the behaviors manifested and the intensity of feelings are similar once developmental differences are taken into consideration (Birmaher et al., 2004; Morrison & Anders, 1999; Wenar, 1994). One major difference between childhood and adolescent depression appears when comparing prevalence rates between the sexes. The prevalence of depression is approximately the same in boys and girls in middle childhood, but beginning in adolescence, twice as many females as males experience depression (Hankin et al., 1998; Negriff & Susman, 2011). Also, adolescent girls diagnosed with depression report more feelings of anxiety, inadequacy, and low self-esteem in middle childhood, whereas adolescent boys report more aggressive and antisocial feelings (Behnke et al., 2011; Leadbeater et al., 1999; Wenar, 1994).

Because parents, teachers, coaches, and friends often do not realize that the child or adolescent is depressed, it is important to alert them to the following potentially troublesome symptoms (American Association of Suicidology, 2004; Gold, 1986):

- Deterioration in personal habits
- Decline in school achievement
- Marked increase in sadness, moodiness, and sudden tearful reactions
- Loss of appetite
- Use of drugs or alcohol
- Talk of death or dying (even in a joking manner)
- Withdrawal from friends and family
- Making final arrangements, such as giving away valued possessions
- Sudden or unexplained departure from past behaviors (from shy to thrill-seeking or from outgoing to sullen and withdrawn)

EP 2

Specific subgroups may experience additional, unique risk factors related to their particular gender, race or ethnicity, or sexual orientation and the ways that these interact with the environments around them (Macgowan, 2004). Given the tumultuous nature of adolescence, it may be difficult to distinguish warning signs of depression from normative actions and behavior. Cautious practice would suggest taking any changes such as those listed above seriously rather than minimizing them or writing them off as "typical teen behavior." Regardless of whether these changes are indicative of depression and suicide risk, changes in behavior and patterns such as these indicate that something is going on that is worthy of adult attention, as well as professional consultation and evaluation.

Suicidal risk is highest when the adolescent, in addition to exhibiting the aforementioned symptoms of severe depression, also expresses feelings of hopelessness, has recently experienced a death of a loved one, has severe conflict with parents, has lost a close relationship with a key peer or a love interest, and lacks a support system. Brent and colleagues indicate that "interpersonal conflict, especially with parents, is one of the most commonly reported precipitants for completed and attempted suicides" (1993, p. 185). Other studies have indicated that moderate to heavy drinking or drug abuse is implicated in as many as 50% of adolescent suicides and seriously increases risk for depression, suicidal ideation, and suicide attempts (Hallfors et al., 2004; Rowan, 2001).

While completed suicides and suicide attempts are more common among adolescents (with adolescent males completing more suicides and adolescent females attempting more suicides), the number of younger children completing and attempting suicide is increasing, and suicide is the third leading cause of death for children ages 10 to 14 (CDC, 2015). Therefore, it is important to be cognizant of depressed behavior and signs of suicidal ideation in children as well as adolescents. Warning signs of suicidal ideation in younger children are similar to those discussed for adolescents, albeit translated to the appropriate developmental level. When faced with a young client who is considering suicide, social workers should use the same lethality assessment questions discussed earlier for work with adults. In addition, assessment tools geared toward evaluating suicide risk in children and adolescents are available, such as the Suicidal Ideation Questionnaire (SIQ; Reynolds, 1988) and the Suicidal Ideation Questionnaire JR (SIQ-JR; Reynolds, 1987), SAD-PERSONS (Juhnke, 1996), the Diagnostic Predictive Scales (DPS; Lucas et al., 2001), and the Columbia Suicide Screen (CSS; Shaffer et al., 2004).

Depression and Suicidal Risk with Older Adults

In addition to the signs just noted for depression and suicidal ideation in adults, adolescents, and children, older adults warrant particular attention in screening for these conditions. Although older adults comprise only 12% of the U.S. population,

EP 7

they account for the majority of suicide deaths (American Association for Marriage and Family Therapy, 2015). For example, in 2013, the highest suicide rate (19.1%) was among people ages 45 to 64, and the second highest (18.6%) was among those 85 and older (American Foundation for Suicide Prevention, 2015). Certain ethnic groups and genders are at particular risk for suicide—white males accounted for 70% of all suicides in 2013 (American Foundation for Suicide Prevention, 2015)—and suicides have been increasing among middle-aged adults (Phillips, Robin, Nugent, & Idler, 2010). Particular risk factors for older persons include isolation, ill health, hopelessness, and functional and social losses. Further, older clients may be reluctant to appear for mental health services, and psychiatric conditions may be overlooked by primary care providers and loved ones, or minimized as typical features of aging. Commonly used instruments to assess depression, such as the Geriatric Depression Scale, may provide insufficient screening for suicidal ideation (Heisel, Flett, Duberstein, & Lyness, 2005). The assessment of suicidality in elder clients requires particular discernment to distinguish between suicidal intent and the awareness of mortality or preparedness for death, which may be hallmarks of that developmental phase (Heisel & Flett, 2006).

VIDEO CASE EXAMPLE

In the video "Elder Assessment," the social worker, Kathy, inquires about the recent death of the client, Josephine's, husband. Noting signs of grief and depression, Kathy probes further about past coping, patterns of sleeping, eating habits, weight loss, substance use, energy level, hobbies and interests, social contacts, and mood. She also asks the client to walk her through a typical day. Ultimately, she explains and administers a brief depression inventory and provides a booklet about grief. In the follow-up session, Kathy educates Josephine about the phases of grief and describes the results of the depression evaluation, with a typical score at 5 and Josephine's score at 12 ("off the chart"). Josephine's history and her responses to questions about hopelessness and whether life is worth living indicate that she is not at suicidal risk at the time of the interview. As a result of the assessment, Kathy recommends consideration of medication, a physician consultation regarding insomnia, and grief counseling from a widow-to-widow program or from a professional.

Zivin and Kales (2008) point out that the approach clinicians take to explain depression and antidepressants to patients can have a significant impact on their adherence to a medication regime. However, they also state that doctors often lack the time or training to give effective explanations. Although antidepressants can be effective in treating depression in older adults, 40% to 75% do not take their antidepressants as directed or at all (Zivin & Kales, 2008). Older adults who present as treatment resistant may instead simply be noncompliant with their antidepressants. Elders may intentionally not take their medications out of fear of becoming dependent, over concerns that the

medicine will prevent them from feeling natural sadness, or because they do not recognize their depression as a medical condition. Other seniors may forget to take their antidepressants or misunderstand dosage instructions, especially if they have cognitive impairment and no caregiver to assist them with medications. Some seniors are reluctant to take their antidepressants because they fear they will interact negatively with other medications.

Other risk factors for medication noncompliance include taking three or more other medications, having co-occurring diagnoses of depression and anxiety, being dependent on substances, having a caregiver who does not believe depression is a medical condition, lacking social support, and being unable to pay for medications. Although spirituality can often aid older adults in dealing with mental health issues, at times faith can have a negative effect on depression. Some older adults may feel that they do not need medical treatment because God can heal them, and others might interpret their depression as a punishment from God (Zivin & Kales, 2008).[3]

ASSESSING BEHAVIORAL FUNCTIONING

In direct social work practice, change efforts frequently target behavioral patterns that impair the client's social functioning. As you assess behavior, it is important to keep in mind that one person's behavior does not influence another person's behavior in simple linear fashion. Rather, a circular process takes place, in which the behavior of all participants reciprocally affects and shapes the behavior of other participants.

Because behavioral change is commonly the focus of social work interventions, you must be skillful in discerning and assessing both dysfunctional and functional patterns of behavior. In individual sessions, you can directly observe clients' social and communication patterns as well as some personal habits and traits. In conjoint interviews and group sessions, you can observe these behavioral patterns as well as the effects that these actions have on others. Figure 9-2 (p. 235) demonstrates the use of these concepts in a mental status exam.

In assessing behavior, it is helpful to think of problems as consisting of *excesses* or *deficiencies*. For excess-related problems, interventions aim to diminish or eliminate the behaviors, such as temper outbursts,

One specialized form of assessment is the **mental status exam**. This exam is intended to capture and describe features of the client's mental state. The terminology developed in conjunction with these instruments has greatly facilitated communication among professions for both clinical and research purposes. Certain features on the mental status exam are associated with particular conditions, such as intoxication, dementia, depression, or psychosis.

The mental status exam typically consists of the following items, which are described elsewhere in this chapter and in other sources (Gallo et al., 2000; Lukas, 1993):

Appearance

How does the client look and act?

Stated age, dress, and clothing

Psychomotor movements, tics, facial expressions

Reality Testing

Judgment

Dangerous, impulsive behaviors

Insight

- To what extent the client understands his or her problem
- How the client describes the problem

Speech

Volume: low, inaudible

Rate of speech: rapid, slow

Amount: poverty of speech

Emotions

Mood: how the client feels most of the time

- Anxious, depressed, overwhelmed, scared, tense, restless, euthymic, euphoric

Affect: how the client appears to be feeling at this time

- Variability (labile)
- Intensity (blunted, flat)

Thought

Content: What the client thinks about

- Delusions: unreal belief, distortion
  - Delusions of grandeur: unusual or exaggerated power
  - Delusions of persecution: unreal belief that someone is after the client
  - Delusions of control: someone else is controlling the client's thoughts or actions
  - Somatic delusions: unreal physical concerns
- Other thought issues
  - Obsessions: unrelenting, unwanted thoughts
  - Compulsions: repeated behaviors, often linked to an obsession
  - Phobias: obsessive thoughts that arouse intense fears
  - Thought broadcasting: belief that others can read the client's mind

- Ideas of reference: insignificant or unrelated events that have a secret meaning to the client
- Homicidal ideation: desire or intent to hurt others
- Suicidal ideation: range from thought, desire, intent, or plan to die
- Process: how the client thinks
  - Circumstantiality: lack of goal direction
  - Perseveration: repeated phrase, repeated topic
  - Loose associations: move between topics without connections
  - Tangentiality: barely talking about the topic
  - Flight of ideas: rapid speech that is unconnected

Sensory Perceptions

Illusions

- Misperception of normal sensory events

Hallucinations

- Experience of one of the senses: olfactory (smell), auditory (hearing), visual (sight), gustatory (taste), tactile (touch)

Mental Capacities

Orientation times four: oriented to time, person, place, and situation

General intellect: average or low intelligence

Memory: remote (past presidents), recent (what the client ate yesterday for breakfast), and immediate (remember three items)

Concentration: Distraction during interview, count backward by 3s

Attitude Toward Interviewer

How the client behaves toward the interviewer: suspicious, arrogant, cooperative, afraid, reserved, entertaining, able to trust and open up, forthcoming

Sample Mini Mental Status Report

Mr. Stewart presents as unshaven, thin, with unkempt hair, and older than his stated age. No abnormal body movements or tics are noted. Mr. Stewart is alert and oriented times four. His thought content and processes appear normal (although there are no specific questions to address delusions, hallucinations, or intellect). He describes his mood as euthymic, and his affect is guarded. Although he is inquisitive about the clinician's notes and he provides only brief answers, Mr. Stewart is cooperative. His judgment is impaired, as seen by his driving while intoxicated and missing work. Mr. Stewart's insight appears limited, as he has come for evaluation to appease his wife and does not see his drinking as heavy or problematic. He denies thoughts or plans of suicide or homicide.

FIG 9-2 Mental Status Exams

too much talking, arguing, competition, and consumptive excesses (e.g., food, alcohol, sex, gambling, or shopping). For behavioral deficiencies, when assessment reveals the absence of needed skills, interventions aim to help clients acquire the skills and behaviors to function more effectively. For example, a client's behavioral repertoire may not include skills in expressing feelings directly, engaging in social conversation, listening to others, solving problems, managing finances, planning nutritious meals, being a responsive sexual partner, or handling conflict. Sometimes problems can result from a combination of behavioral excesses and deficiencies.

In addition to identifying dysfunctional behavioral patterns, it is important to be aware of those behaviors that are effective and represent strengths. In assessing behavior, it is vital to specify actual problem behaviors. For example, rather than assess a person's behavior as "abrasive," a social worker might describe the behaviors leading to that conclusion: "the client constantly interrupts his fellow workers, insults them by telling them they are misinformed, and boasts about his own knowledge and achievements." It will be easier for you and the client to focus your change efforts when detrimental behavior is specified and operationalized.

An adequate assessment of behavior, of course, goes beyond merely identifying functional and dysfunctional behaviors. You must also determine the antecedents of behaviors; when, where, and how frequently they occur; and the consequences of the behaviors. Further, you should explore thoughts that precede, accompany, and follow the behavior, as well as the nature of and intensity of emotions associated with the behavior.

Risk of Aggression

EP 7

A particular behavioral concern is the risk of aggression. Aggression can take many forms, from making threats and bullying to assaults and gun violence. It may be directed at the social worker or at others in the client's environment, such as siblings, classmates, dating partners, parents, or bosses. A wide variety of tools have been developed in an attempt to assess and predict the potential for violent behavior (Borum, Bartel, & Forth, 2003; Quinsey et al., 2006).[4] Although there is significant variability in the definition and measurement of risk factors among these tools, Andrade (2009) highlights several risk factors

that have been consistently related to violent behavior. The most consistently predictive of these factors is past violent behavior or criminal behavior. Additional risk factors include early age of first criminal offense, substance abuse, gender (violence by men generally exceeds that by women), and psychopathy. Andrade (2009) also mentions research into several dynamic risk factors such as impulsiveness, anger, psychosis, interpersonal problems, and antisocial attitudes but notes that no predictive conclusions can yet be drawn. For youth violence, Borum and Verhaagen (2006) list a variety of risk factors, including prior history of violence, early initiation of violence, school achievement problems, abuse, maltreatment and neglect, substance use problems, impulsivity, negative peer relationships, and community crime and violence. Social workers concerned about the risk of aggression should assess for the following:

- *Personal history:* Child abuse or neglect; early exposure to violence in the family; problems at school, including threats, fights, or assaults on teachers; antisocial behavior; learning disabilities, ADHD, low IQ, head injury, or other physical problems
- *Interpersonal relationships and social supports:* Client's attitude toward people in general; how the client interacts with the practitioner; if the client has close friendships; how the client relates to members of the opposite sex; recent changes in relationships; difficulties with social interaction
- *Psychological factors:* Active substance use or abuse; manic phase of bipolar disorder; acute psychosis in paranoid schizophrenia; antisocial, borderline, or paranoid personality disorder; low empathy, impulsivity, intermittent explosive disorder, and inability to delay gratification
- *Physical conditions:* Intoxication; temporal lobe epilepsy; dementia, delirium; history of head trauma
- *History of violence:* How long has the client been getting into fights? How often? How badly has the client ever hurt someone? Does the client have a criminal record? Past hospitalization because of violent behavior?
- *Current threats and plans of violence:* Is the client currently angry at anyone? Is there anyone the client would like to hurt or kill? Where is this person now? Does the client have access to a weapon? How would the client carry out the threat? Where?

● *Current crisis and situation:* Current mood and behavior of the client; memory difficulty; poor concentration; poor coordination; exaggerated preoccupation with sexual thoughts and fantasies; nonadherence to medication; recent release from incarceration (Adapted from Houston-Vega, Nuehring, & Daguio, 1997, pp. 97–101)

ASSESSING MOTIVATION

As introduced in Chapter 8, evaluating and enhancing client motivation are integral parts of the assessment process. When working with family members or groups, social workers are likely to encounter a range of motivation levels within a single client system. Clients who do not believe that they can influence their environments may demonstrate a kind of **learned help-lessness**, a passive resignation that their lives are out of their hands. Others may be at different phases in their readiness to change. Prochaska and DiClemente (1986) suggest a five-stage model for change: *precontemplation, contemplation, determination, action,* and *maintenance*. The **precontemplation stage** is characterized by a lack of awareness of the need for change. In the **contemplation stage**, the client recognizes his or her problem and the consequences that result. In the **determination stage**, the client is committed to action and works with the clinician to develop a plan for change. The **action stage** implements the changes identified, and the **maintenance stage** takes steps to avoid problem recurrence.

To assess motivation, the social worker needs to understand the client, his or her perception of the environment, and the process by which he or she has decided to seek help. Motivation, of course, is a dynamic force that is strongly influenced by ongoing interaction with the environment, including interaction with the social worker. **Motivational interviewing (MI)** is a specialized, person-centered method for addressing ambivalence and enhancing motivation to move toward healthy change (Moyers & Rollnick, 2002). "Motivational interviewing is a conversation style for strengthening a person's own motivation and commitment to change" (Miller & Rollnick, 2013, p. 12). Motivational interviewing also employs specific attitudes and techniques to reduce and defuse resistance. Motivation is enhanced by developing and highlighting discrepancies, for example, within a client's statements or between the client's current situation and the one he or she aspires to (Wagner & Conners, 2008).

ASSESSING ENVIRONMENTAL SYSTEMS

EP 7

After evaluating the history and pattern of the presenting problem and various facets of individual functioning, the social worker must assess the client in the context of his or her environment (see Figure 9-3). This assessment focuses on the transactions between the two, or the **goodness of fit** between the person and his or her environment. Problem-solving efforts may be directed toward assisting people to adapt to their environments (e.g., training them in interpersonal skills), altering environments to more adequately meet the needs of clients (e.g., enhancing both the attractiveness of a nursing home and the quality of its activities), or a combination of the two (e.g., enhancing the interpersonal skills of a withdrawn, chronically ill person as well as moving that person to a more stimulating environment). This part of assessment, then, goes beyond the evaluation of resources described in Chapter 8 to take a holistic view of the client's environment and examines the adequacy of various aspects of the environment to meet the client's needs. The concepts of affordability, availability, and accessibility (introduced earlier in this chapter in regard to health care) provide a useful framework for examining transactions with other facets of the environment and targeting the nature of strengths and barriers in those transactions.

Environmental Systems
  Physical environment
    Adequacy
    Health
    Safety
  Social support systems
    Missing
    Affirming
    Harmful
  Spirituality and affiliation with a faith community
    Spirituality
    Religion
    Cognitive, affective, and behavioral dimensions
      of faith

FIG 9-3 Areas for Attention in Assessing Person-in-Environment Fit

In assessing environments, you should give the highest priority to those aspects that are most salient to the client's individual situation. The adequacy of the environment depends on the client's life stage, physical and mental health, interests, aspirations, and other resources. For example, a family may not be concerned about living in a highly polluted area unless one of the children suffers from asthma that is exacerbated by the physical environment. Another family may not worry about the availability of day treatment programs for an adult child with developmental disabilities until a crisis (e.g., death of a parent or need to return to work) forces them to look outside the family for accessible, affordable services.

You should tailor your assessments of clients' environments to their varied life situations, weighing the individual's unique needs against the availability of essential resources and opportunities within their environments. In addition to noting the limitations or problems posed by inadequate physical or social environments, it is important to acknowledge the strengths at play in the person's life—the importance of a stable, accessible, affordable residence or the value of a support system that mobilizes in times of trouble.

The following list describes basic environmental needs; you can use this list in evaluating the adequacy of your client's environments.

1. A physical environment that is adequate, is stable, and fosters health and safety (this includes housing as well as surroundings that are free of toxins and other health risks)
2. Adequate social support systems (e.g., family, relatives, friends, neighbors, organized groups)
3. Affiliation with a meaningful and responsive faith community
4. Access to timely, appropriate, affordable health care (including vaccinations, physicians, dentists, medications, and nursing homes)
5. Access to safe, reliable, affordable child and elder care services
6. Access to recreational facilities
7. Transportation—to work, socialize, utilize resources, and exercise rights as a citizen
8. Adequate housing that provides ample space, sanitation, privacy, and safety from hazards and pollution (both air and noise)
9. Responsive police and fire protection and a reasonable degree of security
10. Safe and healthful work conditions
11. Sufficient financial resources to purchase essential resources (e.g., food, clothing, housing)
12. Adequate nutritional intake
13. Predictable living arrangements with caring others (especially for children)
14. Opportunities for education and self-fulfillment
15. Access to legal assistance
16. Employment opportunities

We will address the first three areas—physical environment, social support systems, and faith community—in depth, in light of their particular importance for client functioning. This discussion may also help you to generalize some of the complexities of environmental assessment to the other 13 areas.

Physical Environment

Physical environment refers to the stability and adequacy of one's physical surroundings and whether the environment fosters or jeopardizes the client's health and safety. A safe environment is free of threats such as personal or property crimes. Assessing health and safety factors includes considering sanitation, space, and heat. Extended families may be crammed into small homes or apartments without adequate beds and bedding, homes may not be designed for running water or indoor toilets, or access to water may be broken or shut off. Inadequate heat or air conditioning can exacerbate existing health conditions and lead to danger during periods of extreme weather. Further, families may take steps to heat their residences in ways that can create further health dangers (such as with ovens or makeshift fires). Sanitation may be compromised by insect or rodent infestations or by owner or landlord negligence in conforming to building standards and maintaining plumbing. The home may be located in an area with exposure to toxic materials or poor air quality.

For an older client, an assessment of the physical environment should also consider whether the person's living situation meets his or her health and safety needs (Gallo et al., 2005; Rauch, 1993). If an older adult lives alone, does the home have adequate resources for the individual to meet his or her functional needs? Can the client use bathroom and kitchen appliances to conduct his or her daily activities? Does clutter contribute to the client's confusion or risk (e.g., not being able to find bills or stumbling over stacked newspapers)? Is the home a safe environment, or do some aspects of the building (e.g., stairs or loose carpeting) pose a danger to less mobile clients? If the client resides in an institution, are there mementos of home and personal items that bring comfort to the individual? Tools such as the

Instrumental Activities of Daily Living Screen (Gallo, 2005) and Direct Assessment of Functioning Scale (DAFS; Lowenstein et al., 1989) can assess functional ability, screen for and address risk factors, and evaluate changes in functioning.

Social Support Systems

Social systems constitute the second item on the list of needed resources. **Social support systems** fill a variety of needs to improve the client's quality of life. To assist you in identifying pertinent social systems, Figure 9-4 depicts interrelationships between individuals and families and other systems (Hartman, 1994). Systems that are central in a person's life appear in the center of the diagram. These systems typically play key roles both as sources of difficulties and as resources that may be tapped or modified in problem solving. Moving from the center to the periphery in the areas encompassed by the concentric circles are systems that are progressively distant from individuals and their families. There are exceptions, of course, such as when an individual feels

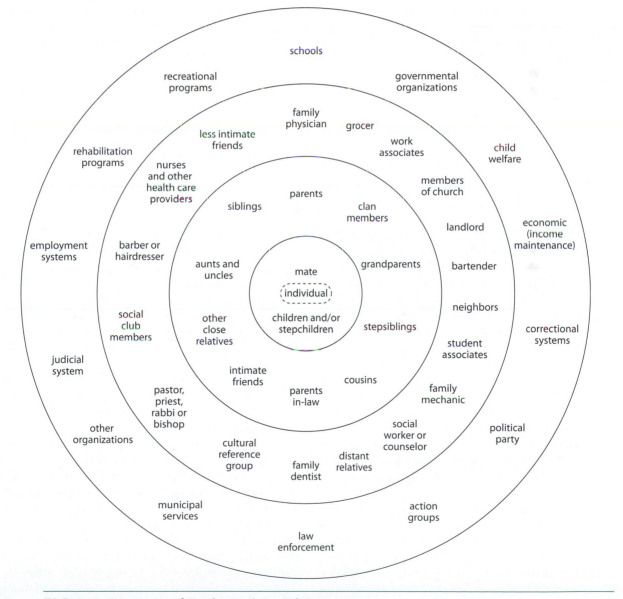

FIG 9-4 Diagram of Ecological Social Systems

closer to an intimate friend or a pastor than to family members. Moreover, if clients' situations require frequent contacts with institutions or organizations (e.g., child protective services, income maintenance programs, judicial systems), those institutions will no longer occupy a peripheral position because of how dramatically they affect individuals and families at such times. The intensity of affiliation with extended family or kinship networks may vary by cultural group and reflect the effects of migration and cultural dislocation (Mwanza, 1990; Sotomayor, 1991; Taylor et al., 2013). Reciprocal interactions thus change across time, and diagrams depicting these interactions should be viewed as snapshots that remain accurate only within limited time frames.

EP 7

The challenge in diagramming a client's social networks is to include the salient boundaries of the client's situation and to specify how the systems interact, fail to interact, or are needed to interact in response to the client's needs. One useful tool is the ecomap, introduced in Chapter 1. Ecomaps identify and organize relevant environmental factors outside of the individual or family context. These tools are useful in clarifying the supports and stresses in the client's environment and revealing patterns such as social isolation, conflicts, or unresponsive social systems. They also show the direction in which resources flow, for example, if the client gives but does not receive support.

The ecomap can be completed by the social worker following discussion with the client or in tandem with the client (Strom-Gottfried, 1999b). The client systems (individual, couple, or family) are in the middle circle of the ecomap, and the systems relevant to their lives appear in the surrounding circles. The nature of positive interactions, negative interactions, or needed resources can be depicted by using colored lines to connect the individual or other family members to pertinent systems, with different colors representing positive, negative, or needed connections and interactions with those systems. Different types of lines—single, double, broken, wavy, dotted, or cross-hatched—can also be used to characterize the relationships and the flow of resources among the systems.

Social support systems are increasingly recognized as playing a crucial role in determining the level of social functioning. Theorists have long recognized the critical importance of a nurturing environment to healthy development of infants and children, but it is now clear that adults also have vital needs that can be met only through affiliation with supportive systems. Consequently, the lack of adequate social support systems is considered an area of vulnerability and may represent a source of distress, whereas adequate social support systems reduce the effects of stressful situations and facilitate successful adaptation. Knowing what the social support systems are and what roles they play with clients is essential for assessment and may even be the focus of interventions that tap into the potential of dormant social support systems or mobilize new ones. What benefits accrue from involvement with social support systems?

1. Attachment, provided by close relationships that give a sense of security and sense of belonging
2. Social integration, provided by memberships in a network of people who share interests and values
3. The opportunity to nurture others, which provides incentive to endure in the face of adversity
4. Physical care when persons are unable to care for themselves because of illness, incapacity, or severe disability
5. Validation of personal worth (which promotes self-esteem), provided by family and colleagues
6. A sense of reliable alliance, provided primarily by kin
7. Guidance, child care, financial aid, and other assistance in coping with difficulties as well as crises

Within some cultures and geographic regions, the extended family may provide an extensive network of support and assistance in crisis situations. There may also be cultural variations in the person to whom one turns to for assistance with life problems. In many American Indian tribal groups, for example, members actively seek counsel from elders (Red Horse et al., 2000), while Southeast Asian immigrants may seek assistance from clan leaders, shamans, or herbalists, depending on the nature of the difficulty. Similar examples of specialized supports abound in other cultures and communities.

EP 2

To this point, we have highlighted the positive aspects of social support systems. It is also important to note that some social support systems may foster and sustain problems in functioning. For example, overprotective parents may stunt the development of competence, autonomy, and personal responsibility in their children. Street gangs and other antisocial peer groups may foster violence and criminality, even as they provide a sense of belonging and affiliation. Friends may ridicule or sabotage a person's aspirations, thereby undermining that individual's confidence and capacity for success. Family members may rally to support a person during joyous events (e.g., graduation, childbirth) but not be available in times of need or sadness.

You should be aware of the various social networks at play in a client's life and assess the roles that those social support systems play in the person's difficulties or in his or her ability to overcome hardships. Sometimes, a negative support system can be counteracted by the development of prosocial or positive networks. At other times, the system itself may be the focus of intervention as you strive to make the members aware of their roles in the client's problems and progress.

SPIRITUALITY AND AFFILIATION WITH A FAITH COMMUNITY

EP 7

The issue of one's spirituality and its expression actually transcends the categories of individual functioning and environmental systems. Spirituality can shape beliefs and provide strength during times of adversity, and the link to a faith community can be a tangible source of assistance and social support.

Canda (1997) differentiates between spirituality and religion, suggesting that **spirituality** is the totality of the human experience that cannot be broken into individual components, whereas **religion** is the socially sanctioned institution based on those spiritual practices and beliefs. Sherwood (1998) also distinguishes between spirituality and religion, with the former reflecting the "human search for transcendence, meaning and connectedness beyond the self" and religion referring to a "more formal embodiment of spirituality into relatively specific belief systems, organizations and structures" (p. 80). A **spiritual assessment**, then, may help the social worker better understand the client's belief system and resources.

Questions such as "What are your sources of strength and hope?," "How do you express your spirituality?," "Do you identify with a particular religion or faith?," and "Is your religious faith helpful to you?" can begin to elicit information about the client's spiritual and/or religious beliefs. A variety of guides for gathering information about clients' spiritual beliefs and religious affiliations are available (Holloway & Moss, 2010; Murray-Swank & Pargament, 2011; Nelson-Becker, Nakashima, & Canda, 2007).

At times, religious issues may be central to the clients' presenting problems. For example, parents may disagree about the spiritual upbringing of their children; couples may be at odds over the proper roles of women and men; or families may be in conflict about behaviors proscribed by certain religions, such as premarital sex, contraceptive use, alcohol use, divorce, or homosexuality (Meystedt, 1984).

Spirituality involves three relevant areas: cognitive (the meaning given to past, current, and personal events), affective (one's inner life and sense of connectedness to a larger reality), and behavioral (the way in which beliefs are affirmed, such as through group worship or individual prayer) (Thibault, Ellor, & Netting, 1991). Thus, spiritual beliefs may affect the client's response to adversity, the coping methods employed, the sources of support available (e.g., the faith community may form a helpful social network), and the array of appropriate interventions available. Particularly when clients have experienced disaster or unimaginable traumas, the exploration of suffering, good and evil, shame and guilt, and forgiveness can be a central part of the change process. Social workers must be aware of their own spiritual journeys and understand the appropriate handling of spiritual content, depending on the setting, focus, and client population involved (Ellor, Netting, & Thibault, 1999). Social workers are also advised to involve clergy or leaders of other faiths to work jointly in addressing the personal and spiritual crises faced by clients (Grame et al., 1999).

WRITTEN ASSESSMENTS

EP 1

The assessment phase is a critical part of the helping process. It provides the foundation on which goals and interventions are based. It is also an ongoing part of the helping process, as appraisals are reconsidered and revised based on new information and understanding. As a written product, assessments may be done at intake, following a period of interviews and evaluations, and at the time of transfer or termination (a summary assessment). Assessments may be brief and targeted (such as an assessment for referral), or longer, as with a social history, a detailed report for the court or another entity, or a comprehensive biopsychosocial assessment. Whichever form it takes, several standards must be followed to craft a sound document that clearly conveys accurate information and credible depictions of the client (Kagle & Kopels, 2013).

1. *Remember your purpose and audience.* These will help you decide what should be included and

EP 7

maintain that focus. Know the standards and expectations that apply in your work setting, and understand the needs of those who will review your document.

2. *Be precise, accurate, and legible.* It is important that any data you include be accurate. Erroneous information can take on a life of its own if what you write is taken as fact by others. If you are unclear on a point, or if you have gathered conflicting information, note that in your report.

Document your sources of information and specify the basis for any conclusions and the criteria on which a decision was based (for example, to refer the client to another agency, to recommend a custody placement, or to conclude that suicidal risk was slight).

Present essential information in a coherent manner. An assessment is intended to be a synthesis of information from a variety of sources, including observation, documents, collateral contacts, and client interviews. Organizing that material so that it paints a comprehensive picture of the client's situation, strengths, and challenges at that particular moment is not easy. Avoid going off on tangents or piling up excessive details that derail the clarity of your document. Keep details that illustrate your point, document your actions, or substantiate your conclusions.

3. *Avoid the use of labels, subjective terminology, and jargon.* In assessing the social functioning of individuals, social workers often make global judgments—for example, "Mr. A's job performance is marginal." Such a sweeping statement has limited usefulness because it fails to specify how the client's functioning is inferior and it emphasizes deficits. Instead of using labels ("Alice is a kleptomaniac"), use the client's own reports or substantiate your conclusion ("Alice reports a three-year history of shoplifting on a weekly basis" or "Alice has been arrested five times for theft and appears unable to resist the compulsion to steal small items"). Be factual and descriptive rather than relying on labels and subjective terms.

Various resources are available to help in honing your skills and expanding your assessment vocabulary (e.g., Kagle & Kopels, 2013; Norris, 1999; Wiger, 2009; Zuckerman, 2008).

BIOPSYCHOSOCIAL ASSESSMENTS

Assessments are often referred to as **biopsychosocial assessments** or **evaluations**. The term **biopsychosocial** refers to the notion that when social workers (or other mental health professionals such as psychologists or psychiatrists) assess clients, they evaluate the biological, psychological, and social domains and how these domains both influence and are influenced by disease, disorder, or illness. Assessing biology includes obtaining information about the clients' physical health, psychological functioning, biochemical functioning, nutritional choices, and genetic heritage; assessing the psychological domain includes evaluating emotional well-being, affective presentation, cognitive functioning, general behavior, spiritual preferences, and personality; assessment of the social domain includes examining interpersonal relationships and interactions, environment, culture, family, work, and faith community (Peterson, Goodie, & Andrasik, 2015).

Typically, biopsychosocial assessments include the following (Ross, 2000):

- Identifying information (e.g., name, age, referral source, brief overview of the presenting problem)
- A history of the present circumstances (i.e., the presenting problem, symptoms)
- The past psychiatric and medical history of the client and the client's family (e.g., injuries, operations, medical conditions, medication, ongoing medical treatment)
- The client's social history (e.g., overview of client's childhood, family structure, living situation, employment and employment history, educational history, hobbies, daily routine, religious or spiritual preferences, friends, past trauma, substance use)
- A mental status exam (see Figure 9-2, p. 235) and *DSM-5* diagnosis
- A **formulation** (e.g., a statement that summarizes and synthesizes the most important aspects of the case to create a story of the client and his or her past and presenting problems)

For children and adolescents, a brief overview of developmental milestones may be included, addressing the age at which he/she began crawling, walking, talking, toilet training, and so on.

The assessments in Figures 9-5, 9-6, and 9-7 demonstrate how the concepts described in Chapters 8 and 9 are incorporated into different written documents,

Identifying Information

Dan is a 10-year-old male of Caucasian descent who presented at the community mental health center with his mother and father following a serious car accident that occurred 3 months ago. His pediatrician referred Dan after his parents mentioned that since the car accident, Dan has been having nightmares about the car accident and has experienced difficulty sleeping, a decreased appetite, refusal to ride in the car, and apparent preoccupation with thoughts of the accident.

History of Presenting Problem

Dan and his parents were in a serious car accident about 3 months before their intake appointment. The parents report that prior to this accident, Dan was a "normal kid" who enjoyed playing soccer with his friends, did well in school, completed household chores without complaining, was on a regular sleep schedule, and had a healthy appetite. Following the accident, they report, Dan has been having nightmares about the accident a few times a week, does not want to be alone, insists on sleeping on his parents' floor (although he often does not fall asleep until after midnight), eats very little, has stopped playing soccer, is very irritable and argumentative with his parents and siblings, is very tearful, and has difficulty concentrating at school and on his homework, resulting in lower grades. Dan's parents also report that Dan now hates riding in the car and will avoid the car at all costs. They state that if he has to ride in the car, he often cries and will scream at whoever is driving to slow down and be careful. Dan states that since the accident, "I can't stop thinking about it." He reports constantly worrying about his parents because they both have to drive to work and he is terrified of one of them being in an accident. Dan states that he finds it difficult to play with his friends and have a good time because he is always thinking about the accident; as a result, Dan reports that he has been feeling very alone and lonely since the accident.

Past Psychiatric and Medical History

Dan's parents deny any previous mental health problems and state that prior to the accident, Dan was happy and healthy. In terms of family psychiatric history, Dan's mother reports that she has been treated for depression and anxiety in the past but notes no other family psychiatric history. Dan has never been hospitalized for any medical issues, is not taking any medications, and has never had any serious injuries or operations. The parents deny any significant family medical history.

Social History

Dan currently resides with his mother (age 40), father (age 41), older sister (17), and older brother (14). Dan's mother was a stay-at-home mom but recently returned to work as a secretary for a law firm because of family financial stress. Dan's father works as a landscaper during the week and tries to pick up odd jobs such as painting or construction on the weekends. Dan's sister is a senior in high school, and his brother is in the eighth grade. Dan's parents report that the family has no religious affiliation. Both sets of grandparents live nearby, and Dan is especially close with his paternal grandfather. Dan's father reports that he has two brothers in the area, and Dan's mother states that her sister lives out of state. The parents describe the family as close knit and supportive.

Dan's mother reports that when she was pregnant with Dan, it was a normal pregnancy and delivery. Dan hit all developmental milestones at the appropriate times: he crawled at about 10 months of age, walked at 14 months, began talking at 18 months, and was out of diapers by the time he was two and a half.

Dan is currently in fourth grade at the local elementary school. Prior to the accident, Dan and his parents report that he got almost all A's; however, those grades have now slipped to B's, C's, and some D's. Dan used to enjoy playing with his friends but states that now he mostly watches TV because he prefers to stay at home so he can be near his parents and he does not have the energy or desire to be with his friends. Dan also used to belong to a club soccer team but has refused to attend practice since the accident. Dan's parents state that Dan has always been popular among his peers but has really distanced himself from his friends since the accident. Dan and his parents deny any past trauma and any substance use.

Mental Status Exam

Dan presents as alert and oriented times four (he is oriented to time, person, place, and situation). He looks his stated age of 10 and was dressed appropriately in jeans and a sweatshirt and was well groomed and clean. Dan made minimal eye contact and fidgeted almost constantly as he sat in his chair, either shaking one or both legs or twisting his sweatshirt in his hands. His rate of speech was normal, but he spoke in a very quiet voice. Dan was a bit shy at first, but after a while began talking at greater length and depth about his experience with the car accident. Dan has good insight into his problems and was able to clearly identify how his life has changed following the accident. He reports feeling sad, down, and without energy. He also reports worrying all the time that another car accident will occur. Dan's downcast eyes, flat affect, and quiet and monotone voice match his reported mood. Dan denies auditory and visual hallucinations, self-harming behaviors, suicidal ideation, past and present suicide attempts, and homicidal ideation.

DSM-5 Diagnosis

Based on Dan's reported symptoms of traumatic nightmares, recurrent and intrusive memories of the car accident, constant trauma-related thoughts and feelings, constantly being reminded of the trauma when riding in a car, diminished interest in activities that he previously enjoyed, inability to experience positive emotions, sleep disturbances, difficulty concentrating, and irritability, Dan is diagnosed with Post-Traumatic Stress Disorder (PTSD; 309.81).

Formulation

Dan is a 10-year-old male of Caucasian descent who presented with his parents following a serious car accident. Dan and his parents report that following the car accident Dan has consistently displayed a number of concerning symptoms (e.g., constant thoughts about the accident, refusal to ride in the car, traumatic nightmares, sleep disturbance, difficulty concentrating), all of which are consistent with a diagnosis of PTSD. Dan comes from a very supportive and nurturing family and has a close bond with both of his parents and his paternal grandfather. He is a well-liked child, and both he and his parents report that he has many friends. However, since the accident, Dan has distanced himself from his friends, is often quiet and withdrawn at home, and does not engage with the family as much as he used to. This social isolation has likely exacerbated Dan's PTSD symptoms and contributes to his feelings of loneliness. Further, Dan's mother recently began working outside the home and thus has not been home as much as Dan is used to; this is another change that might be affecting his emotions.

FIG 9-5 Example of a Biopsychosocial Assessment

Client's name: _____ *Wu Yanping*_____ Date: _____*4/15/15*_____

1. Presenting Problem
   Client was self-referred. Presented to university counseling service for assistance with stress related to vocational decision making. She is in the final month of study in the United States from home campus in China and fears that desire to study U.S. history is at odds with her parents' wishes and values.
   Client is an only child and has no precedents among friends or family for defying parents' wishes in this manner.

2. Signs and Symptoms (*DSM-5* based) Resulting in Impairment(s)
   Experiencing mild changes in appetite, sleep, and concentration. More acute since phone discussion with her father 3 weeks ago, although not affecting performance at this time.

3. History of Presenting Problem
   Events, precipitating factors, or incidents leading to need for services:
   Client's anxiety and distress about her decision have become more acute as the date for returning to China approaches (approximately 4 weeks from now), and this has prompted her to seek treatment.
   Client discovered her interest in history in the last several months upon initiating study in the U.S. Her parents own a business and expect that she will major in business and take over their company. When client broached the topic of her preferences in a phone conversation 3 weeks ago, her father was dismissive of her plans. She has not spoken with him since, although they typically have more frequent calls.

   Frequency/duration/severity/cycling of symptoms:
   No specific data gathered in this area.

4. Current Family and Significant Relationships
   Family history:
   Little information was gathered in this area. Yanping is an only child. Her parents own a small business (type unknown) in Shanghai. She has extended family (cousins, aunts, uncles, grandparents) living in China. None of her family members have traveled outside of China.
   Yanping has enjoyed a close and caring relationship with her parents. In recent weeks, this has become strained following a phone dispute with her father when Yanping broached the topic of her new interest in history. She has not spoken with them since, reportedly because of her discomfort and concern that the topic may come up again.

   Strengths/support:
   History of family support, connectedness, parental aspirations for the client.

   Stressors/problems:
   Dispute over major may violate family and cultural norms.

   Recent changes:
   Distancing from parents in light of father's derisiveness in phone call and mother's presumed alliance with father.

   Changes desired:
   Client wishes parents would endorse her choice of studies.

   Comment on family circumstances:
   This writer is concerned about a high risk of family's rejection and fracture if client pursues her interests despite parental opposition.

5. Childhood/Adolescent History
   Client reports that she has never before objected to or defied her parents' wishes. Relationship prior to this conflict has been close and caring. No other developmental or historical information was explored.

6. Social Relationships
   Client has close relationship with her roommate on campus and with classmates, friends, and relatives in China.

FIG 9-6 Example of a Social History

Strengths/support:

Client has the capacity to make and keep friends and to seek their counsel. She has been able to make friends as a visiting student in the United States, although language and cultural differences may impede their ability to help her with certain issues. Yanping will soon return home and have greater access to her support system in China.

Stressors/problems:

Client is distanced from many of her Chinese supports due to her geographic and cultural differences at this time. The issues with which she is struggling are common among her friends, but there are no precedents for doing what she wants to do, so they can be of little help to her other than saying, "You must do what your parents wish."

Recent changes:

None reported

Changes desired:

Yanping wishes to receive more guidance and support to deal with her current problem.

7. Cultural/Ethnic

   Client is from mainland China and speaks Mandarin, with English and other Chinese dialects as secondary languages. Features of Chinese culture such as parental investment and desire for successful offspring are significant in this case. The client is struggling with values of obedience and deference to her parents as well as derisive societal attitudes toward her possible educational/vocational interests in history and teaching.

   Strengths/support:

   Client understands cultural elements affecting her dilemma. Although she wishes to reconcile her beliefs with those of her family and society, she appears firm in her desire to follow her own interests if compromise cannot be achieved.

   Stressors/problems:

   The client's wishes are at odds with parental, cultural, and societal values in her homeland.

   Beliefs/practices to incorporate into treatment:

   Address possibility of parental rejection as a result of values and culture clash. Test client's awareness of risks and commitment to her educational plan.

8. Spirituality/Religion
   Not addressed
   Strengths/support: *NA*
   Stressors/problems: *NA*
   Beliefs/practices to incorporate into therapy: *NA at this time*
   Recent changes: *NA*
   Changes desired: *NA*

9. Legal
   There are no known legal considerations in this case.
   Status/impact/stressors: *NA*

10. Education
    Client is currently a student visiting the United States who will return to China in 4 weeks for the remaining year of her under-graduate education. She wishes to study U.S. history, with the possible objective of becoming a teacher. Her parents want her to major in business and run the family company. They dismiss history as "useless" and teaching as a "low status" position and will not support the client's wishes.

    Strengths:

    Client is a good student and reports that she has been able to maintain good grades this term despite language differences, dislocation from family and supports in China, and recent stress over vocational aims.

FIG 9-6 Continued

Weaknesses:

Dispute over educational goals pits parents' interests against client's and has significant cultural, economic, and social complications.

11. Employment/Vocational
     See section above on education.
     Strengths/support: *NA*
     Stressors/problems: *NA*

12. Military
     Not applicable
     Current impact: *NA*

13. Leisure/Recreational
     Not explored
     Strengths/support: *NA*
     Recent changes: *NA*
     Changes desired: *NA*

14. Physical Health
     Client appears to be in good health, although experiencing stress, anxiety, and mild sleep, appetite, and concentration disturbance dating back 3 weeks and becoming more significant over time.

15. Chemical Use History
     Not explored.

16. Current/Prior Treatment History
     Client has not sought treatment for this issue. Other past and current services are unknown.
     Benefits of previous treatment: *NA*
     Setbacks of previous treatment: *NA*

Kim Strom-Gottfried, Ph.D., LISW   Clinician Signature

April 16, 2015   Date Completed

(This form was adapted and completed based on an example from Wiger, 2009.)

FIG 9-6 Continued

---

based on the needs and norms of the setting in which they were conducted. The second and third assessments are based on clients introduced in the videos that accompany this text.

CASE NOTES

EP 1

In addition to more comprehensive assessments, direct practitioners record information in client charts based on each meeting or contact with the client and after other significant contacts about the case, such as the receipt of test results or information from a collateral contact. Record-keeping policies are often specific to the setting. For example, in schools, social work notes would be kept separate from the child's educational record; in some settings, notes are dictated, and in others they are handwritten. Well-crafted **case notes** "provide accountability, corroborate the delivery of appropriate services and support clinical decisions" (Cameron & Turtle-Song, 2002, p. 1).

Although there are many different practices in record keeping, one commonly used practice is worthy of attention. **SOAP notes** include **S**ubjective observations, **O**bjective data, **A**ssessments, and **P**lans (Kettenbach, 2003; a variation on this, DAP, combines subjective and objective information under one heading, data). SOAP notes refer back to the most recent assessment, problem list, and treatment plan.

Date of Assessment: 11/15/15

Background

Josephine is a Caucasian female, estimated to be in her late 70s, who lost her husband to a heart attack 6 months ago. The heart attack was unexpected and hence his death was sudden. Josephine met with Kathy, a social worker from Family Services, on two occasions (9/2/15 and 9/9/15) to share background and assessment information and to formulate goals and objectives to direct her adjustment to living alone.

Mental Status Exam

On both occasions, the interviews were held in Josephine's home. She was dressed in a housecoat for the first meeting, a blouse and slacks for the second. Her hair was styled and neat. She appeared her stated age, was alert and aware of her surroundings, yet acted somewhat disengaged and uninterested, particularly in the first interview. She was physically still for most of the time that the worker spent with her, looking down at the table the two were seated at. Occasionally, Josephine moved her hand back and forth over the table and also changed her position in her chair intermittently.

Josephine showed no deficit in memory or concentration. She was responsive to the questions asked and demonstrated recollection of remote and recent events. Her self-report of memory functioning, offered during a depression screening administered by the worker, does not indicate deficits. Josephine showed evidence of sound judgment, agreeing that engaging in new activities and adopting healthy eating habits would improve her mood and health. Additionally, when asked what she would do in case of a fire in her kitchen, she responded, "Call 911." She was oriented to time, place, person, and situation and had no deficit in reality testing.

Josephine's speech was quiet and at times somber. She was brief and direct in her answers to the worker's questions. These speech characteristics match Josephine's mood and affect. She reported feeling depleted of energy, experiencing a lack of interest in activities, and having trouble sleeping. Her lack of energy has led to her neglecting her doctor's dietary recommendations. Josephine presented with a depressed affect that varied appropriately to the conversation and, at times, brightened. She scored in the high range on a depression inventory.

Josephine followed the worker's questions. Her thoughts focused on improving her mood and diet and arranging for services to allow her to remain in her home. Josephine appeared overwhelmed at times, although she reported understanding what the worker was saying.

Josephine showed no evidence of cognitive distortions or hallucinations. She was cooperative in the interviews and showed flexibility of thought by agreeing to consider the suggested interventions. Josephine reported feeling that there was hope in her future, that in the past she had found redemptive aspects of persevering through challenging times, and that her children represent her purpose in life.

Biophysical Considerations

Health

Josephine was diagnosed with high blood pressure and was prescribed two medications for this condition. She was also prescribed a third medicine to help lower her cholesterol. Her doctor told her "a couple of years ago" that she is "borderline diabetic." Josephine acknowledged that she could do more to care for this condition by preparing healthier meals. Josephine reported that she no longer drives, making her dependent on her daughter to go to the grocery store. Additionally, she stated, "I don't feel like cooking. I just grab what there is." She has lost 10 pounds in the past 6 months.

Josephine is also dependent on others for transportation to her doctor, whom she has seen for 20 years, for her monthly visits. Josephine reported some hearing loss. She is able to read and reports that she does quite a bit, with the use of glasses.

Josephine reported trouble getting to sleep at night, but she has been sleeping a few hours each afternoon. She does not have a prescription to help her sleep, although sometimes she takes an over-the-counter sleep aid.

Josephine mentioned that she used to walk regularly for exercise but has not been doing any exercise lately as she lacks the motivation, stating, "I don't have any energy." She reported no recent falls or accidents.

Josephine does not report using alcohol. She stopped smoking cigarettes 5 years ago.

She rates her overall health as "fair," which is poorer than her self-assessment of a year ago, which was "good."

Social Factors

Josephine is the lone survivor in her family of origin. Her two brothers passed away soon after World War II, and her sister died a few years ago. She mentioned that this fact, compounded with the death of her husband, amplifies her sense of isolation, stating "I'm the only one left."

Josephine was married to her husband for several decades; they met on a blind date. She has three adult children, a daughter who lives close by and another daughter and son who live out of state. She is now dependent on her daughter for transportation because her husband did the driving when he was alive. This is an uncomfortable situation, as Josephine reports feeling that she is imposing on her daughter but does not have an alternative to get to appointments and shop for groceries.

Josephine and her husband both retired after age 65. Josephine worked in retail, her husband in insurance. After retirement, the couple traveled and visited with their grandchildren. Since her husband's death, Josephine reported, she has not been involved in normal social activities because of her lack of energy and motivation. Her neighbor has visited once and offered to drive her to church, which Josephine declined but will consider this option in the future.

FIG 9-7 Example of Biopsychosocial Assessment: Older Adult

Legal/Financial

Josephine reported that she owns her house and paid for her husband's funeral. She receives Social Security, although she will receive less than she used to as a result of recalculations after her husband's death. She characterized her income as just "adequate."

Josephine is unable to care for the house by herself. Her husband was responsible for the yard work, and she states she is not strong enough to complete it alone. She reported lacking the energy to do laundry and housework and is considering the possibility of receiving assistance with household chores.

Josephine reported that she would like to remain at home until she can no longer live alone. She is open to the idea of moving in the future.

Mood

Josephine repeatedly referred to her lack of interest, motivation, and energy caused by her grieving for her husband. She noted that her past coping methods involved connecting with people close to her. With the loss of her husband, she has lost her confidant. Josephine has not received counseling or therapy in the past.

Josephine correlated her mood to her lack of activities, reporting that she does not go out often, attends to her appearance less than she used to, and does not complete household chores.

Josephine scored high on a depression inventory. The worker recommended passing on these results to her physician and speaking to him about antidepressant medication.

Josephine does not report loss of hope or purpose. She stated, "I do think there is hope," and "My life has a purpose … I have wonderful children." She did not relate any suicidal ideation or thoughts of hurting herself. In her second interview, Josephine was asked to respond to a battery of questions designed to assess spirituality. Her answers were genuinely positive and life-affirming. Notably, she indicated that the most important thing in her life at present is "to feel better."

Conclusion

The recent sudden death of Josephine's husband has resulted in financial changes, increased role demands, social withdrawal, and changes in nutrition, sleep patterns, and emotional functioning. Symptoms of grief and depression both contribute to these problems and affect Josephine's ability to reach out for assistance or participate in church and other previously valued activities. She has a clean, safe, and stable home environment and numerous relationships of long duration with family, friends, and her physician. She is interested in better understanding her situation, consulting her physician, and receiving services to assist with transportation, grief, home care, meals, and other issues.

FIG 9-7 Continued

The "subjective" section in SOAP notes includes information shared by the client or significant others, such as recent events, emotions, changes in health or well-being, and changes in attitude, functioning, or mental status. Information in this section is typically paraphrased and presented as, for example, "The client reports …", "The patient's mother states …", "She indicates …", or "Patient's husband complains of …" Direct client quotes should be kept to a minimum (Cameron & Turtle-Song, 2002).

The "objective" section in SOAP notes should be factual, precise, and descriptive, based on your observations or written material, and presented in quantifiable terms—factors that "can be seen, heard, smelled, counted or measured" (Cameron & Turtle-Song, 2002, p. 2). In such notes, the advice for writing proper assessments applies: avoid conclusions, judgments, and jargon, and substitute descriptions that would lead to such conclusions with more objective commentary. Rather than saying, "The client was resistant," an objective statement might read, "The client arrived 20 minutes late, sat with her coat on and her arms folded, and did not make eye contact with this writer."

The "assessment" section of SOAP notes is the place to include diagnoses, judgments, and clinical impressions, based on both the subjective and objective data that precede the assessment. "Carol is struggling to maintain her sobriety in light of pressure from her friends and stress at school." The last section, "plan," addresses following appointments, next steps, referrals needed, and actions expected of both the client and the worker: "Carol will attend at least one AA meeting per day, review her relapse triggers and self-care plan."

Each SOAP entry should begin with the date and end with the social worker's name, credentials, and signature. Entries should be completed as soon as possible after the actual contact to ensure they are accurate and up to date.

SUMMARY

This chapter discussed assessment of physical, cognitive/perceptual, emotional, and behavioral functioning, as well as motivation and environmental factors. Although each of these factors was presented as a discrete entity, these factors are neither independent nor static. Rather, the various functions and factors interact dynamically over time and, from the initial contact, the practitioner is a part of that dynamic interaction. Each factor is therefore subject to change, and the social worker's task is not only to assess the dynamic interplay of these multiple factors but also to instigate changes that are feasible and consonant with clients' goals.

Assessment involves synthesizing relevant factors into a working hypothesis about the nature of problems and their contributory causes. You need not be concerned in every case with assessing all of the dimensions identified thus far. Indeed, an assessment should be a concise statement that embodies only the most pertinent factors.

This chapter's scope was limited to intrapersonal and environmental dimensions. It excluded conjoint, family, and group systems, not because they are unimportant components of people's social environments but rather because they generally are the hub of people's social environments. To work effectively with interpersonal systems, however, requires an extensive body of knowledge about these systems. Therefore, we devote the next two chapters to assessing couple and family systems and therapeutic groups.

COMPETENCY NOTES

EP 1   Demonstrate Ethical and Professional Behavior
- **Demonstrate professional demeanor in behavior, appearance, and oral, written, and electronic communication.** A common feature of social work practice is the development of written assessments and case notes. These are part of a client's permanent record and thus must be accurate, clear, and thorough, synthesizing various sources of data to provide a comprehensive portrayal of the case.

EP 2   Engage Diversity and Difference in Practice
- **Apply and communicate understanding of the importance of diversity and difference in shaping life experiences in practice at the micro, mezzo, and macro levels.** Assessments require the interpretation of clients' statements, emotions, experiences, and behaviors. When workers approach assessments from an ethnocentric perspective, their interpretations can be flawed. Cultural knowledge and sensitivity are essential in accurately conveying another's life story.

EP 7   Assess Individuals, Families, Groups, Organizations, and Communities
- **Collect and organize data, and apply critical thinking to interpret information from clients and constituencies.** Social

work assessments involve collecting information from a variety of sources to help understand the reciprocal interaction of factors contributing to the presenting problem.

- **Understand methods of assessment with diverse clients and constituencies to advance practice effectiveness.** Social workers use many frameworks to understand client functioning and change processes. In individual assessment, the *Diagnostic and Statistical Manual* (*DSM-5*) is used to classify mental disorders by enumerating symptoms, patterns of onset, and other features of conditions (such as bipolar disorder, depression, or neurocognitive disorders).

- **Apply knowledge of human behavior and the social environment, person-in-environment, and other multidisciplinary theoretical frameworks in the analysis of assessment data from clients and constituencies.** Social work assessments are based on the interaction between individuals and their environment (social, physical, financial, etc.). Direct practitioners must use the assessment process to identify the "goodness of fit" in these interactions and suggest steps to reinforce strengths and bolster areas of weaknesses.

- **Recognize the implications of the larger practice context in the assessment process and value the importance of interprofessional collaboration in this process.** Assess client strengths and limitations. Individuals and their environments present both assets and liabilities. A strong assessment takes these features into account and determines the ways in which these factors interact to create or sustain the client's current difficulties. Interventions then build on strengths and resources and strive to address weaknesses, in coordination with other needed professional services.

- **Develop mutually agreed-on intervention goals and objectives based on the critical assessment of strengths, needs, and challenges within clients and constituencies.** Sound, thorough assessments set the foundation for service plans and interventions, as they identify patterns of behaviors or emotions, reciprocal interactions, past change and coping strategies, and significant areas of risk.

SKILL DEVELOPMENT EXERCISES

in Assessment

Review the opening session in the video "Work with the Corning Family," and address the following questions:

1. What words would you use to describe the clients across the following variables?

   a. Appearance (posture, attire, psychomotor functioning)
   b. Cognitive functioning (memory, concentration, judgment, reality testing, coherence, cognitive flexibility, misconceptions, sensory perceptions)
   c. Affective functioning (predominant mood, variability, range and intensity of affect)
   d. Values and self-concept
   e. Attitude toward the interviewer

2. Are there any areas in which you lack information? How would you go about getting the information in a subsequent session?

3. To what extent might the nature of the interview and the worker's style and characteristics have affected the clients' presentation of themselves in the session?

4. Now compare your findings with those of a classmate. How much congruence is there in your assessments? What might account for areas of difference?

5. How do your descriptions compare with the assessment of the Cornings on this text's website?

6. What conclusions can you draw about the skills, values, and knowledge needed to write effective, accurate assessments?

NOTES

1. Bernhardt and Rauch (1993) offer an informative guide for social workers interested in learning more about the genetic basis for illnesses and about conducting genetic family histories.

2. See Bentley and Walsh (2006) and the National Mental Health Association (www.nmha.org) for further information on psychotropic medications, their effects, and side effects.

3. Article summary by Kate Brockett, MSW.

4. Other resources that can assist with assessment of aggression and potential violence, include the following:

   • Hare, R. D. (2003). *The Hare psychopathy checklist revised* (2nd ed.). Toronto: Multi-Health Systems.
   • Feldhaus, K. M., Koziol-McLain, J., Amsbury, H. L., Norton, I. M., Lowenstein, S. R., & Abbott, J. T. (1997). Accuracy of 3 brief screening questions for detecting partner violence in the emergency department. *Journal of the American Medical Association, 277*, 1357–1361.
   • The SAVRY Version 2 (Borum et al., 2003) is a 30-item instrument using the structured professional judgment (SPJ) approach to assess violence risk in adolescents ages 12 to 18 years who have been detained or referred for an assessment of violence risk. The Early Assessment Risk List for Boys (EARL-20B) Version 2 (Augimeri, Koegl, Webster, & Levene, 2001) and the Early Assessment Risk List for Girls (EARL-21G) Version 1 (Levene et al., 2001) are SPJ risk assessment devices for use with children under 12 years of age with disruptive behavior problems. The purpose of these instruments is to increase general understanding of early childhood risk factors for violence and antisociality, provide a structure for developing risk assessment schemas for individual children, and assist with risk management planning.
   • Levene, K. S., Augimeri, L. K., Pepler, D., Walsh, M., Webster, C. D., & Koegl, C. J. (2001). Early Assessment Risk List for Girls: EARL-21G, Version 1, consultation edition. Toronto: Earlscourt Child and Family Centre.
   • The Adolescent and Child Urgent Threat Evaluation (Copeland & Ashley, 2005) is a 27-item assessment tool designed to measure risk of near future harm to self or others (within hours to days) in youth ages 8 to 18 in a variety of settings, including inpatient and outpatient clinics, schools, emergency rooms, and juvenile justice facilities.
   • Copeland, R., & Ashley, D. (2005). *Adolescent and child urgent threat evaluation: Professional manual.* Lutz, FL: Psychological Assessment Resources.

CHAPTER 10

Assessing Family Functioning in Diverse Family and Cultural Contexts

with Craig Schwalbe

Chapter Overview

Social workers encounter families in many service settings. For example, social workers in child welfare and child protective services agencies are concerned with reducing violent and neglectful family patterns that contribute to child maltreatment and neglect (Wodarski, Holosko, & Feit, 2015). Social workers who serve adult clients with severe cognitive impairments associated with traumatic brain injuries and dementia are concerned with the support that family caregivers can provide to their affected members (Albert et al., 2002; McGovern, 2015). Psychiatric social workers often implement psychoeducational interventions to families to increase support for psychiatric patients and reduce relapse (Singer, Biegel, & Conway, 2012). Forensic social workers and probation officers concern themselves with the quality of family support to reduce reoffending (Maschi, Bradley, & Ward, 2009). And finally, some social workers serve families using evidence-based family therapy models that have been in development in the United States and around the world since the 1950s (Nichols, 2012). Because social workers encounter families in these and many other service settings, social workers need frameworks for understanding transactions between family functioning and the expression of presenting problems by individual clients.

This chapter focuses on the dimensions used to assess families. It presents a framework for understanding how family functioning can exacerbate the presenting problems of individuals and how families can provide resources for client coping. It also provides a basis for understanding how the family itself can be treated as a unit of analysis, approaching problems of individual members within a context of family dynamics that themselves can become the target of change. Finally, the chapter provides a framework for family assessment that is consistent with family-based evidence-based practices. Throughout the chapter, families will be understood in the multitude of ways in which family membership can be defined. The chapter avoids using a normative template for family structure but strives to discuss family dynamics from the vantage point of the cultures within which family formation and family development occur.

As a result of reading this chapter, you will be able to:

- Take a broad view of how families are defined and how family functioning is understood.

- Understand the role of self-awareness in family assessment and how cultural values influence beliefs and values about family membership and family functioning.

- Describe the dimensions of family structure, including homeostasis, boundaries, power and decision making, roles, rules, life cycle, and sociopolitical environment.

- Discuss family adaptive capacity, including stress and resilience.

- Describe the role of culture, human rights, and social justice in the definition and expression of family system characteristics.

- Develop specialized assessment skills and strategies to observe patterns of interaction that underlie family system structure.

EPAS Competencies in Chapter 10

This chapter will give you the information needed to meet the following practice competencies:

- Competency 2: Engage Diversity and Difference in Practice

- Competency 3: Advance Human Rights and Social, Economic, and Environmental Justice

- Competency 7: Assess Individuals, Families, Groups, Organizations, and Communities

DEFINING FAMILY AND FAMILY FUNCTIONS

EP 2

Families are defined within a sociocultural milieu that prescribes acceptable ways in which family membership is determined, roles are allocated among family members, and the functions and obligations ascribed to families are carried out. In some respects, the institution called the family defies definition. Throughout time, the definition of family, or what constitutes an "accepted" or an "acceptable" family, has been contested and debated (Bengtson, 2001). In the United States, the 20th century was marked by the development of the two-generation "nuclear family" as the preferred standard for family structure. However, it should be noted that the nuclear family was a recent innovation in the history of family formation and that romantic notions of the "traditional family," corresponding with anxiety over its decline, understate the diversity of family forms that have existed throughout history and around the world. For example, the "Black" family in the United States has often been inclusive

of multiple generations, while families around the world are often viewed through a tribal or kinship lens (Williams & Stockton, 1973). Single-parent families, along with families headed by same-sex couples, are additional family models that characterize the contemporary family landscape. In view of the diversity of family forms, how families define their members is best articulated by the family members themselves.

However, debates about the accepted definition of family are not without consequences for all clients served by social workers. When families do not conform to prevailing cultural norms about proper family definitions, the conflict that results can burden families with significant strain, exacerbating stress and affecting family member functioning. Pregnancy in unmarried adolescent females is a provocative example. In some communities, pregnancy before marriage can result in consequences that systematically exclude girls from community life and even result in threats to physical safety, whereas in other communities pregnancy brings status along with its hardships, and marriage is delayed until other life goals have been realized (Edin & Kafalas, 2005). Therefore, understanding the transactions between client definitions of family and the cultural milieu in which families form can be critical to the social work assessment process.

Underlying the definition of family is a shared understanding of two elements of family structure: how family membership is composed, and the various functions that the family serves as an enduring institution in society. Following are some of the varying ways in which family membership is achieved:

- Marriage, which may be an arranged marriage
- Remarriage, recoupling after a separation, or blended family
- Birth, adoption, foster care, or legal custody
- Informal relationship, biological and nonbiological kin, friends, social networks within communities and/or cultural groups
- Nannies or other surrogates in the family

Variability in families and choices can mean that households consist of single parents or two parents of opposite or same sex, any of which may be multigenerational (Carter & McGoldrick, 2005; Crosson-Tower, 2004; Fredriksen-Goldsen & Scharlach, 2001; Sue, 2006). Multigenerational families can include parents and their children and grandparents or other kin. Also, there are generational families that consist of two generations, specifically grandparents and their grandchildren (Burnette, 1999; Goyer, 2006; Jimenez, 2002). Clearly, family configurations can be as diverse as family membership. The more critical concern, and thus the focus of practice, is the extent to which the family has the capacity to perform the essential functions that contribute to the development and well-being of its members.

Family functions refer to the ways that families have organized to solve problems of evolutionary survival. As characterized by Constable and Lee (2004), the family is "the basic informal welfare system in any society" (p. 9). In essence, the family performs certain functions and has responsibilities, such as attending to the social and educational needs, health and well-being, and mutual care of its members, that are unlike those of any other social system (Hartman, 1981; Meyer, 1990; Okun, 1996; Sue, 2006). It is largely through the family that character is formed, attachments are developed, vital roles are learned, and members are socialized for participation in their culture or subculture and in the larger society. Summarized in Table 10-1, family

functions meet the survival needs of family members in terms of biological survival, social status, emotional health, and economic resources.

It should be clear from the foregoing discussion that how families are defined in terms of structure and function has strong cultural determinants, often defined in terms of client worldviews. Client worldviews are culturally influenced beliefs about how individuals relate to the micro, mezzo, and macro dimensions of the social world, how individuals relate to the natural world, and individuals' understanding of spirituality (Sue, 2006). Worldviews about family structure and function are the basis for how family members understand many if not all of the presenting problems that bring families into contact with social workers. For example, beliefs about the proper relationship between family members across generations can lead some families to punish children who speak assertively to adults while other families will encourage youthful assertiveness. An explanation of client worldviews provides opportunities for social workers to learn about how family members understand their own families as well as opportunities for empathic listening—for example, when families express pride about their families ("We are from a good family, do not judge us"); guilt about family shortcomings ("I could not meet her/his sexual needs"); confusion about changing family roles ("How are we going to take care of Papa?"); or resignation about the need for help ("We need help raising our children").

TABLE 10-1 Family Functions

FUNCTIONS	EXPLANATION
1. Procreation	Families ensure the evolutionary survival of the human species.
2. Provide for physical needs	Families obtain and distribute resources that are instrumental for physical health and economic survival.
3. Provide secure attachment bonds	Families provide members with a sense of psychological security and safety.
4. Primary socialization of children	Families teach and reinforce social norms and rules necessary for successful performance in the social world.
5. Regulate sexuality	Family structure establishes boundaries that limit sexual relationships among its members (e.g., incest).
6. Satisfy emotional needs	Families provide members with affection, companionship, and a sense of belonging.

Source: Bengtson, 2001; Horowitz, 2005; Williams and Stockton, 1973.

SELF-AWARENESS IN FAMILY ASSESSMENT

Given the diversity of families that social workers encounter, and the myriad ways that families organize to perform tasks related to the functions described above, it perhaps goes without saying that social workers who encounter families in their EP 2 practice will be faced with frequent and significant challenges to their own deeply held worldviews. Indeed, all social work encounters with families can be described as a meeting, or mingling, of worldviews about families. Sometimes the family worldviews that are generally shared by social workers and clients act in harmony and reinforce normative definitions of family structure and functions. At other times, worldview differences between the family and the social worker can become a contest of worldviews, with the social worker representing community values about families that may or may not be shared by the client. Taken to the extreme, worldview differences can lead to oppressive social work practices. Therefore, it is critical that social workers be aware of potential worldview differences and act deliberately to understand them.

There is reason to be concerned about oppressive practices in social work with families. Beginning in the 1980s, feminist scholars began to criticize the burgeoning family therapy movement for reinforcing patriarchal family structures (Goldner, 1985). Often, mothers were directly and indirectly blamed for the presenting problems of their children, including children who later developed schizophrenia and children who came to identify as nonheterosexual. Moreover, the relative silence of prevailing family systems theories and theorists about the social construction of normative family system structures, such as the nuclear family, provided indirect support to patriarchal family arrangements. Thanks to feminist scholarship and critical scholarship in allied disciplines, social work with families today is generally understood within a broader conception of normative family structure and functioning, and social workers have a more highly developed sense of how their roles interact with client worldviews about how families are defined.

To achieve this understanding, social workers need to grapple with their own assumptions about what constitutes a "healthy" and "functional" family. In doing so, social workers, through supervision, study, and reflection, need to understand their own worldview beliefs about families, including answers to deeply personal questions such as "How should families be organized?," "What is the best way for families to raise children?," and "What are the proper roles of elders, parents, and children in a family?" Furthermore, social workers need to assess client views about families, their perspectives about family structure, and their beliefs about how families work. When social workers encounter clients whose family worldviews differ in meaningful ways from their own, they need to redouble their efforts to understand the strengths of client worldviews and perspectives on family structure and the opportunities those differences provide to promote growth and problem solving.

It is also critical to recognize that social workers, being called on to form authentic relationships with clients, are not necessarily required to accept client family worldviews at face value, nor are they required to change their own family worldviews when they conflict with those of their clients. In both extreme and subtle ways, culturally sanctioned family structure and family function practices can be oppressive, warranting social work interventions based on empowerment principles and advocacy. For example, genital mutilation is used in some cultures to regulate the sexual behavior of girls and women, as is extreme punishment as an honor-saving practice when unmarried girls violate community norms prohibiting sexual behavior with unmarried peers (Katiuzhinsky & Okech, 2014). When confronted by stark family worldview differences that suggest oppressive or abusive cultural practices, social workers are advised to consult a variety of frameworks, including professional codes of ethics, legal codes, public policy, and the social work agency's values and mission, as well as human rights frameworks.

It should be noted that important family worldview differences between clients and social workers are usually less dramatic than the examples provided above, but the implications for social work practice are nevertheless important. The most difficult challenges for social workers and their clients arise when family worldview differences have unclear impacts on family members or on society. Family worldview values related to the use of corporal punishment as a child-rearing tool are illustrative. The prevailing view of most who write about parenting practices mirrors the thrust of evidence-based programs such as **parent management training (PMT)**, emphasizing the reinforcement of positive child behaviors, minimizing the use of punishing parenting practices including corporal punishment, and resorting to "time-outs" when corrective parenting interventions are needed (Kazdin, 2005). However, evidence suggests that the use of "time-outs" may not be compatible with family worldviews across all cultures, particularly those that value family and community membership over and above individual development (Hoagwood et al., 2006). In such cultures, "time-outs" can be experienced as a highly abusive banishment, whereas a spanking provides a negative consequence for misbehavior without the implied separation from the family group.

THE FAMILY SYSTEMS FRAMEWORK

Family assessment in social work is conducted within a systems framework. The systems framework shows how families organize to achieve their goals and perform their functions as described above.

EP 7

TABLE 10-2 Dimensions of a Family Systems Framework Assessment

> Homeostasis
>
> Boundaries and Boundary Maintenance
>
> Family Decision Making, Hierarchy, and Power
>
> Family Roles
>
> Communication Styles of Family Members
>
> Family Life Cycle
>
> Family Rules
>
> Social Environment
>
> Family Adaptive Capacity (Stressors and Strengths)

Table 10-2 presents the elements of the **family systems framework** discussed in this chapter. Examining the table, it should be clear that the family systems framework defines properties and characteristics of families rather than of any particular individual within the family. This points to an important difference between the assessment of individual clients and the assessment of families. Unlike assessments of individuals, family assessment focuses social work attention on the family as a unit, with transactions among individuals providing clues about the properties of the family system. The language of family assessment also includes words that emphasize the collective rather than individuals. Whereas individual family members may be described by their moods and actions, a family assessment describes families according to their roles, rules, boundaries, and subsystems.

The shift from individual to collective has important implications for family interventions, as we will discuss in Chapter 15. In essence, assessing presenting problems in terms of family functioning deemphasizes individual pathology and blame and often diffuses responsibility for participating in solutions among multiple family members simultaneously.

When assessing families using the framework presented here, it is important to bear in mind that a family assessment does not ordinarily occur in isolation from an assessment of the presenting problem, as described in Chapters 8 and 9. Presenting problems assessed within the family systems framework also need to be understood in the context of their onset, severity, and frequency (Chapter 8) and the particular needs and conditions of individual family members, including mental health function, physical health, and social functioning (Chapter 9).

Homeostasis

Homeostasis is a systems concept that describes the tendency of a system to maintain or preserve equilibrium or balance. In essence, homeostasis is a conservative property of family systems that strives to maintain the status quo. When faced with a disruption, a system tends to try to regulate and maintain system cohesion. For example, it may try to maintain the status quo in response to family transitions in the life cycle or stressors associated with acculturation or environmental events. As systems, families develop mechanisms that serve to maintain balance in their structure and operations. They may restrict the interactional repertoires of members to a limited range of familiar behaviors and develop mechanisms for restoring equilibrium whenever it is threatened, in much the same way that the thermostat of a heating system governs the temperature of a home.

Homeostasis operates through a pattern of feedback loops to reinforce the status quo and to preserve the family structure. **Feedback loops** are cycles of interactions, or expected interactions, that are used to exert influence over families and family members. Ordinarily, feedback loops preserve one or more aspects of family system structure, such as family boundaries, roles, rules, and hierarchy. Feedback loops occur when children seek a rule change and are pushed back by their parents; when, in nuclear family arrangements, elders seek to have influence over parents and parents act to set boundaries to minimize elder influence; and when adult couples negotiate changes to family responsibilities. Sometimes feedback loops are quite dramatic, involving aversive, coercive, forceful, and loud communication strategies (e.g., yelling, threats of violence), whereas other times feedback loops are subtle, quiet, subversive, and difficult to detect (e.g., not following through on agreements).

It should be noted that all family systems are characterized by feedback loops that preserve the status quo. This property of family system structure explains what social workers throughout generations have come to understand: that changes to family system structure are often slow and difficult to achieve. Thus, the force of homeostasis can be a major frustration to social workers and family members who are striving to resolve presenting problems in areas that implicate the family system. Yet it is also important to recognize that homeostasis, and the associated feedback loops that preserve it, is an important source of family strength. It is because of the force of homeostasis that families can provide a stable and predictable environment for development and decision making. It is because of homeostasis that the family is recognized by outsiders as a distinct social system and that it is not easily changed.

Just as feedback loops operate internally to sustain the status quo of internal family functioning, feedback loops also regulate family relationships with external environments. Families themselves receive feedback from their external environments that send messages, such as "You are a good family" or "You are not a good family." Often these messages reflect the community's values, representing its views about human rights, justice, and shared obligations, while at other times these messages can be a conduit for injustice and oppression. In many instances, social workers embody community feedback loops as they represent community standards about child rearing in the case of child protective services and about proper education in the case of school social work.

Although the focus of our discussion about homeostasis has emphasized the conservative nature of family systems, this should not be taken to suggest that homeostasis, or the tendency of families to maintain the status quo, is the opposite of flexibility or adaptation. This is a naïve understanding of homeostasis. In fact, families are in a constant state of adaptation to forces in the external environment, as well as to changes among members in the internal family structure. Under most circumstances, and for most families, the tendency of family systems toward homeostasis helps families adapt in ways that preserve the integrity of the family as a distinct unit. Under such circumstances, feedback loops help to guide change and adaptation in the face of sometimes overwhelming challenges and obstacles.

Boundaries and Boundary Maintenance

Boundaries, a central concept in family systems theories, can be likened to abstract dividers that function (1) between and among other systems or subsystems within the family and (2) between the family and the environment. In essence, boundaries are invisible lines that identify people as insiders and as outsiders. They can be detected or observed by behaviors and communication patterns, both blatant and subtle, that signify who belongs within an identifiable family or subsystem within a family.

External Family Boundaries

Because family systems are part of larger systems, families necessarily engage in diverse transactions with the environment. Boundaries change over time as the family system as a whole and its members experience various developmental levels. For example, when a child begins school, the boundaries of the family system expand to permit interactions with the educational system.

At the same time, families can widely differ in the degree to which they are flexible and accepting of transactions with other systems. In operational terms, **flexibility** means the extent to which outsiders are permitted or invited to enter and become part of the family system and whether members are allowed to invest emotionally and engage in relationships outside the family. Flexibility also means the extent to which information and materials are exchanged with the environment. A family system with rigid, inflexible boundaries is characterized by strict regulation that limits its transactions with the external environment and that restricts incoming and outgoing people, objects, information, and ideas. Rigid boundaries can serve important functions for the family by preserving territoriality, protecting the family from undesired intrusions, and safeguarding privacy, among others. But rigid boundaries can also limit family members' access to social support and opportunities in the external environment.

When assessing the boundary patterns of families related to outside influences, it is essential that you consider the family's unique style, cultural preferences, strengths, and needs. Families may have more flexible boundaries with extended family members, perhaps including well-defined obligations and responsibilities to one another. Conversely, those boundaries may appear more or less flexible when external influences intrude upon family traditions and values and are seen as a source of conflict or disruption to the family system. For example, the behavior of a youth that results in the entry into the family of a juvenile probation officer can be disruptive, but the family system out of necessity can reluctantly accommodate this intrusion. At still other times, the family may change to accommodate new inputs over the course of the life cycle or during transitions.

Internal Boundaries and Family Subsystems

All families develop networks and relationships between coexisting **subsystems** that can be formed on the basis of gender, interest, generation, or functions that must be performed for the family's survival (Minuchin, 1974). Members of a family may simultaneously belong to numerous subsystems, entering into separate and reciprocal relationships with other members of the nuclear family, depending on the subsystems they share in common (e.g., parents, mother/daughter, brother/sister, father/son), or with the extended family (e.g., grandmother/granddaughter, uncle/nephew, mother/son-in-law). Each subsystem can be thought of as a natural coalition between participating members. Of course, many of the coalitions or alliances are situation-related and temporary in nature. For example, a teenager may be able to enlist his or her mother's support in asking his or her father's permission for a special privilege. A grandmother living in a home may voice disagreement with her daughter and son-in-law regarding their discipline of children, thus temporarily forming a coalition with the children. Such passing alliances are characteristic of temporary subsystems.

Other subsystems or coalitions, especially partner/spouse, parental, and sibling subsystems, are more enduring in nature. According to Minuchin (1974), the formation of stable, well-defined coalitions between members of these vital subsystems is critical to the well-being and health of the family. Unless there is a strong and enduring coalition between parents, for example, conflict will reverberate throughout a family, and children may be co-opted into one faction or another as parents struggle for power and control. In general, the boundaries of these subsystems must be clear and defined well enough to allow members sufficient differentiation to carry out functions without undue interference (Minuchin, 1974). At the same time, they must be permeable enough to allow contact and exchange of resources between members of the subsystem.

Minuchin points out that the clarity of the subsystem boundaries has far more significance in determining family functioning than the composition of the subsystem. For example, a parental subsystem that consists of a grandmother and an adult parent/child may function perfectly adequately. The relative integrity of the boundaries of spouse/partner, parental, and sibling subsystems is determined by family rules. A parent clearly defines the role of the parental subsystem, for example, by telling the oldest child not to interfere in the conversation when a younger child is being disciplined. The message, or "rule," then, is that an older child is not a co-parent. A parent, however, may delegate caretaking of younger child to an older child in the parent's absence. In this instance, the boundaries of the parental and sibling subsystems are clearly delineated.

Enmeshment and Disengagement

The clarity of boundaries within a family is a useful parameter for evaluating family functioning. Minuchin (1974) conceives of all families as falling somewhere along a continuum of extremes in boundary functioning, where the opposite poles are **disengagement** (diffused boundaries) or **enmeshment** (inappropriately rigid boundaries). Family closeness in an enmeshed family system is defined as everyone thinking and feeling alike and relationships that require a major sacrifice of autonomy, in which members are discouraged from developing their own identity and independent explorations or behaviors.

Enmeshment and disengagement are not necessarily indicative of dysfunctional relationships, because in some cultural, racial, or socioeconomic groups, these concepts may have little or no relevance. According to Minuchin (1974), every family experiences some enmeshment or disengagement between its subsystems as the family passes through various developmental phases. During a family's early developmental years, for example, a caretaker and a young child, out of necessity, are an enmeshed subsystem. A cultural variant, however, is that a child's relationship can involve several caretakers with close ties. Sharing the parental bed until a certain age or sleeping in the same room with parents has been at the center of legal and child development debates in the United States. However, it is a common practice in other cultures (Fontes, 2005). In the United States, many middle-class mothers prefer this arrangement as well; however, the risk of co-sleeping with a young child is a prominent concern of the medical profession.

By Western standards, it is expected that adolescents will gradually disengage from the parent–child subsystem as they move toward young adulthood and perhaps prepare to leave home. Of course, this too is subject to cultural preferences. For example, in certain cultures, adolescents marry but live with one of the adolescents' families. In other cultures, young adults live with their families until they are married. Therefore, fluid roles, bonding patterns, and rules as framed in Western society may not signal that a relationship is enmeshed or that a member is disengaged.

Family Decision Making, Hierarchy, and Power

Decision-making authority and power constitute an important dimension of family system structure. Indeed, all social systems have some form of hierarchy and differentiation of power that is suited to their functions. In families, power is ascribed to certain members and subsystems to enable the system to achieve its goals, described above as *family functions*. Power arrangements and family decision-making authority should create an environment in which primary attachments can flourish, in which the economic needs of the group can be met, in which social status can be preserved, and in which the emotional and developmental needs of all members can be nurtured. For most families, power alignments and decision-making structures serve as a source of strength. For some, power alignments and decision-making structures interfere with successful family functioning and serve to exacerbate presenting problems.

Formal family decision-making authority ordinarily rests with the **executive subsystem**. The executive subsystem has the right and obligation to provide overall direction to a family, to allocate resources, to manage boundaries, to protect the integrity of the family system in its external relations, and to assign roles to individual members. Membership of the executive subsystem has strong cultural determinants, usually being restricted to the parents of children in nuclear families or differentiated to include elders in multigenerational families. The membership and functioning of executive subsystems are also negotiated within individual families depending on the idiosyncratic circumstances that each family faces. For example, families that include divorced parents negotiate executive decision making and leadership, often with the aid of mediators and the courts; blended families must figure out how to form new decision-making patterns within preexisting patterns of family relations; and families with limited or strained resources often incorporate children in the decision-making process, as can be seen in single-parent families with one or more "parentified" children. Regardless of composition, executive subsystems exist to provide leadership to the family system.

The composition and functioning of the executive subsystem can be observed in the way that power and authority are wielded within the family and in relation to its external environment. Power is displayed in different forms within families, and it is important to recognize the multiple expressions that power takes. **Executive power** is the concentration of formal decision-making authority into the position of a broadly recognized leader or set of leaders. Family members can usually tell who is "in charge" of a family. These are members of the executive subsystem.

Alternatively, power can be distributed to family members based on tasks. Such **task-specific power** is evident when members of the family make decisions about which other members conform or follow. Power also exists covertly in families. Such **covert power** is held by family members who, for example, enter into coalitions to challenge or circumvent executive power or task-specific power. It also can be expressed by family members who employ their own strengths and agency to influence family decision making.

Of course, power, or the ability of one or more persons to affect the behavior and worldviews of others, is rarely distributed according to explicit rules, and herein lies the complexity of understanding how decision-making power and leadership exist within families. Although power and leadership may formally reside with the executive subsystem, shifts in power can depend on the specific circumstances faced by families. Crises, chronic stress, and external forces can elevate the influence of children on the decisions of the parental subsystem, amplifying their role in the family's power structure. Developmental changes over the life course also influence the distribution of power in a family system, as can be seen when members of an executive subsystem succumb to the effects of chronic health problems and when parental authority is challenged by adolescents. As noted above, power may be held both overtly and covertly. For example, one individual may be formally acknowledged as the central figure in the family and thus have more power in family decision making, as in families that conform to patriarchal traditions. Even so, other, less visible members or subsystems can have significant covert power in the family. For example, an individual can hold power because of a disability or chronic condition; another can gain power because of his or her level of literacy, including literacy with technology, or attainment of a level of education or income.

The distribution of power and the exercise of leadership within a family are not value free. How families organize decision-making authority, or how they wish to organize power, often expresses deeply held values that may or may not be culturally sanctioned. For this reason, it is important to understand family power and decision making within the frameworks of social justice and human rights (Mcdowell, Libal, & Brown, 2012). Whereas human rights conventions and treaties embody a strong presumption of family privacy to guard against government intrusion and government-sanctioned oppression (Convention on the Rights of the Child, September 2, 1990), there is an increasing recognition that the exercise of power within families can systematically oppress its members. This is particularly evident when patriarchal families organize in such a way so as to limit educational opportunities for girls, limit access to paid employment for adult women, or sanction intimate partner violence or abuse. Family-level oppression can also be expressed as ageism, whereby family elders are exploited either intentionally or unintentionally because of their diminished capacity to care for themselves.

The Universal Declaration of Human Rights protects the rights of individuals to physical safety, access to education, participation in the labor market, and ownership of public property, among others (Universal Declaration of Human Rights, December 10, 1948). Moreover, the codes of ethics for the National Association of Social Workers (NASW) in the United States and the International Federation of Social Workers (IFSW) embody principles of distributive justice, emphasizing that all individuals have a right to social, economic, political, and emotional resources according to their needs. How power and decision-making authority are organized within a family should maximize social justice and human rights.

In your assessment of family power and decision making, you must determine not only how power is distributed but also who, if anyone, is formally designated as the leader and to what extent covert power is exercised by individual members. It is equally important to assess the extent to which family rules allows the family system to reallocate power so that members can adjust their roles to meet changing circumstances. Finally, you must assess whether family members are satisfied with the distribution or shifts in power. Topical areas in which you can develop questions to guide your assessment include the following:

- How power has been distributed in the family in the past and whether changing conditions of the family are threatening the established power base (McGoldrick, 1998; Okun, Fried, & Okun, 1999)
- Whether the distribution of power is gender specific out of necessity for the family to survive in a hostile environment (Okun, Fried, & Okun, 1999)
- To what extent power is covertly held by members who have aligned to form a power bloc, and to what extent covert power accrues to individual members who are manifesting extreme symptoms
- The extent to which the family system allows power to be flexibly reallocated and permits roles to be adjusted to meet the demands of changing circumstances
- How members view the distribution of power in the family (even though the distribution is unequal, family members may be satisfied with the arrangement)
- The role of a family's culture in determining the distribution of power (Congress & Kung, 2005)

All families have a structure in which power is allocated in some manner. Like family rules, power in the family system has purpose. Unless power dynamics and the distribution of power have a significant role in family problems, it is inappropriate to attempt to make adjustments in this area. You should, however, assess the functionality of covert and overt power, keeping in mind that power in families can shift on a situational basis, and power can be distributed among many members on some level and at different times.

Family Roles

Roles are generally understood patterns of behavior that are accepted by family members as part of their individual identities. Usually, roles can be identified by their labels, which denote both formal roles that are socially sanctioned (e.g., grandparent, mother, father, brother, sister) and idiosyncratic roles that evolve over time within a specific family context (e.g., comedian, scapegoat, caregiver). Role theory, when applied to the family system, suggests that each person in a family fulfills many roles that are integrated into the family's structure and that represent certain expected, permitted, or forbidden behaviors (Biddle, 1986). Family roles are not independent of each other. Rather, role behavior involves two or more persons engaging in reciprocal transactions. Roles within the family system may be assigned on the basis of legal or chronological status or cultural and societal scripts. In many families, role assignments are based on gender. At the same time, as with power and decision making, roles may be flexible and diffused throughout the family system.

In sorting out roles in the family system, individual role behavior may be *enacted*, *prescribed*, or *perceived* (Longres, 1995). In an **enacted role**, a mother, for example, engages in the actual behavior—such as caretaking—relative to her status or position. A **prescribed role** is influenced by the expectations that others hold with regard to a social position. For example, despite the changes in families, in a family's interaction with a bank officer, a male is almost always presumed to be the head of a household or the primary decision maker in the family. A **perceived role** involves the expectations of self relative to one's social position. For example, an employed female may conclude that she can manage multiple responsibilities.

Roles are both learned and accrued. The role of parent, for example, is accrued, but it is also learned from others and through experience. Similarly, the various roles that exist between couples in a relationship are learned based on interactions over time. Satisfaction with the respective role behavior indicates a level of harmony in interpersonal family relationships. Janzen and Harris (1997) refer to harmonized interpersonal roles as independent–dependent relationships. In addition, roles may be complementary or symmetrical. The role relationship between a parent and a child, for example, is a **complementary relationship** (or an independent–dependent role relationship) in which the needs of both are satisfied. In contrast, in a **symmetrical relationship**, both parties function as equals—for example, the division of household or child-rearing responsibilities or decision making are shared instead of based on gender roles.

Roles for the most part are not static; rather, they can evolve as a result of family interactions and negotiations. As a consequence, they often defy traditional stereotypical role behaviors. In actuality, role relationships in most families operate along a continuum and may be characterized as complementary or symmetrical or quid pro quo as a result of negotiation.

Life transitions and conflict often demand changes, flexibility, and modifications in role behavior. A family may experience **role transition** difficulties in making the necessary adjustments when, for example, an older relative comes to live in their home. The aging parent may experience difficulties in adjusting to becoming dependent on adult children. For example, older people who are no longer able to drive can feel that they are a burden and even resent the loss of their independence. Another significant change for some parents is adjusting to the void when children leave the home.

Conflict in the family may occur when individuals become dissatisfied with their roles, when there is disagreement about roles, or when individuals holding certain or multiple roles become overburdened. **Interrole conflict** can occur when an individual is faced with excessive, competing, and multiple role obligations, especially when two or more roles are incompatible—for example, wife/partner, mother, daughter, employee. Fulfilling the responsibilities associated with these enacted and perceived roles can cause an individual to experience conflict in juggling multiple role demands (G. D. Rooney, 1997).

Understanding the roles and role behavior within the family, including the way in which roles are defined as well as role conflict, is important in the assessment of the family role dimension. In the assessment, you will want to determine what role assignment in the family is based on—for example, age or gender rather than such factors as abilities, need, and interest. As you assess the role behavior in any family, you will probably note a number of individual and family strengths, such as how well members flexibly adapt to changing roles and their role-performance behavior. Because each culture or family form may have its own definitions of roles, social workers must also determine and assess the goodness of fit with the needs of family members. Assessment then must consider whether members are satisfied with their respective roles and, if a member is dissatisfied, whether the family is amenable to modifying or changing determined roles.

Communication Styles of Family Members

One pattern that cuts across many cultural groups is that of discouraging the open expression of feelings. Although Western culture emphasizes the value that openness and honesty are best, the reality is that most people have considerable difficulty asserting themselves or confronting others, particularly in ways that are facilitative. In all instances, you must first determine whether the family's communication patterns and styles negatively affect members' relationships, and further whether change is desirable, including weighing the cultural implications.

Another aspect of communication that transcends culture, and that may be generational, is the multiple ways in which people communicate with each other. Youth, for example, use particular words, phrases, and abbreviations in their communications. In addition, today's youth are more likely to rely on text messaging or social networks as primary means of interacting with each other. These modes of communication may not conform to some conventional communication rules (such as using formal, complete sentences). These modes of communication can therefore be problematic in families, especially when used between adults and younger family members.

Whether family communication patterns are culturally influenced or otherwise determined, they may be faulty, causing significant problems for family members. In assessing the impact of a family's communication style, you must be aware of the complexities of communication and be prepared to assess the functionality of members' communication styles and the extent to which there is congruence and clarity in how members communicate with each other.

VIDEO CASE EXAMPLE

In the video "Home for the Holidays 1," Jackie and Anna scheduled the session at Jackie's request. Both women are Caucasian and appear to be close in age (25 to 35 years old). Jackie, a chef, owns the restaurant where she works. The couple have been together for 5 years and have lived together for the past year. They initiated couples' therapy because of disagreements about their holiday plans. They both would like to spend the time together. Jackie, however, feels pulled to visit her family during the holidays because they live in another state and she has not seen them in a while. Anna states that she does not feel completely comfortable at the home of Jackie's parents. She perceives them as distant and avoiding meaningful contact because of their discomfort with their relationship. In fact, when they attended a family wedding, Anna was not invited to stand with the family when pictures were taken.

Jackie recently came out to her parents as a lesbian. When she disclosed to them that she was moving in with her significant other, Anna, her parents were quiet and took up other activities. This withdrawal behavior is normalized in Jackie's family. She explained that in her family, "there is little outward expression and we don't make a big deal about everything." Nonetheless, Jackie does recognize her parents' discomfort with her sexuality. Anna acknowledged a difference between their family styles, remarking that in her family, "there were no secrets" and "everyone's state of affairs was open for discussion." Anna would like Jackie to broach the subject of her sexuality with her parents a second time to "strengthen the connection between Jackie and her parents, to hasten Jackie's parents' acceptance of our relationship."

When asked to explore the meaning that this conversation would hold for her, Jackie expressed feeling pushed by the request and that it felt like an ultimatum. For Jackie, there was too much at stake for her to risk another conversation with her parents at this time. In her mind, the worst case scenario would be that her parents would shut her out. Hearing Jackie's interpretation of the request as an ultimatum and the pressure that Jackie was feeling, Anna clarified and softened her position. To Anna, the conversation "would help Jackie open up more." Anna also stated that, as is the case in her family of origin, "Jackie does not communicate at home."

Concerning their plans for the holiday, Anna agreed to go to Jackie's house. The two made plans to cook a meal together for the family and to give gifts from both of them as a sign of unity. Jackie agreed to consider plans to hold hands with Anna at dinner; she requested time to discuss this at the next session. Their overall goal was to improve their communication with each other.

Congruence and Clarity of Communication

Family members convey messages through both verbal and nonverbal channels and qualify those messages through other verbal and nonverbal messages. A task for social workers is to assess the **congruency**—that is, whether there is correspondence between the various verbal and nonverbal elements—of messages.

VIDEO CASE EXAMPLE

Congruence may also be related to a goal to which not all family members agree. For example, in the video "Home for the Holidays 1," the dialogue between Jackie and Anna in their session with Kim, the social worker, illustrates the concepts of congruence in communication. As you watch the video, consider how you would describe the congruency of Anna's messages. For example, Anna would like Jackie to broach the subject of her sexuality with her parents. The content of her message is clear, but Jackie and Anna's goals are dissimilar, which causes tension in their relationship.

According to Satir (1967) and other communication theorists, messages may be qualified at any one of three communication levels:

- **Verbal level:** When people explain the intent of their messages verbally, they are speaking at a meta-communication level. Meta-communication happens when people discuss the content and topics of communication. Note that implied messages are also a form of meta-communication. For example, the implied message in Anna's insistence that Jackie talk to her parents is, *If you really cared about my feelings, you would stand up to your parents about our relationship.* Contradictory communications occur when two or more opposing messages are sent in sequence via the same verbal channel. For example, Anna expresses two contradictory messages to Jackie regarding Jackie's discomfort in talking to her parents about her sexuality: *You should follow my advice* and *You need to make your own decisions.*

- **Nonverbal level:** People reinforce or contradict their verbal messages nonverbally, through gestures, facial expressions, tone of voice, posture, eye contact, and so on. For example, although Jackie's parents invite the couple for the holidays, their nonverbal message (not including Anna in family photos) contradicts or modifies their verbal message.

- **Contextual level:** The situation in which communication occurs can reinforce or disqualify a speaker's verbal and nonverbal communications. For example, Jackie feels punished by what she perceives as a "right now" ultimatum from Anna, but as Jackie turns to Anna, her facial expression and tone are softer. The contextual level at which Anna sends the message to Jackie qualifies her verbal expression.

Functional communicators identify discrepancies between levels of communication and seek clarification when a person's words and expressions are incongruent. Vital to assessment, then, is the task of ascertaining the extent to which there is congruence between the verbal, nonverbal, and contextual levels of messages on the part of individuals in the family system.

In addition to considering the congruence of communications, it is important to assess the **clarity** of messages. The term **mystification** (Laing, 1965) describes how some families befuddle or mask communications and obscure the nature and source of disagreements and conflicts in their relationships. Mystification of communications can be accomplished by myriad kinds of maneuvers, including disqualifying another person's experience, addressing responses to

no one in particular even though the intent of the speaker is to convey a message to a certain person, using evasive responses that effectively obscure knowledge of the speaker, or utilizing sarcastic responses that have multiple meanings. Some couples also use their children or pets to convey messages to each other.

VIDEO CASE EXAMPLE

Family rules, interactions, and communication patterns often accompany couples and play out in their relationship with each other. For example, in the video "Home for the Holidays 1," Anna states, "In my family there are no secrets, everyone's state of affairs is open for discussion." Jackie, on the other hand, wishes to maintain homeostasis in her family by adhering to the family rule of "We don't make a big deal about everything." Clearly, Jackie and Anna have had prior conversations about their relationship and the response from Jackie's parents. They are in different stages of coming out. In their sequence of interactions, Anna appears to perceive Jackie and her family as the problem in their relationship. For example, Anna pushes Jackie to talk to her parents again, which in her mind is a premium in their relationship. Jackie is understandably reluctant to have this conversation with her parents, so the repetitive, patterned interactional cycle between the couple continues.

Barriers to Communication

In Chapter 7, we identified a number of barriers to communication that, when utilized by social workers, block client communications and hamper the therapeutic progress. Likewise, family members use these and similar responses in their communications with each other, thereby preventing meaningful exchanges and creating tension in relationships. Table 10-3 highlights communication barriers that prevent genuine dialogue in relationships.

The assessment of communication barriers also includes nonverbal behaviors, such as clients glaring, turning away from a family member, fidgeting, shifting posture, pointing a finger, rolling their eyes, or exhibiting other facial expressions that show disgust or disdain. As noted earlier, nonverbal behaviors present obstacles to communication when there are

TABLE 10-3 Communication Barriers

- Prematurely shifting the subject or avoiding topics
- Asking excessive questions, dominating interactions
- Sympathizing, excusing, or giving reassurance or advice
- Mind reading, diagnosing, interpreting, or overgeneralizing
- Dwelling on negative historical events in a relationship
- Making negative evaluations, blaming, name-calling, or criticizing
- Directing, threatening, admonishing
- Using caustic humor, excessive kidding, or teasing
- Focusing conversations on oneself

discrepancies between verbal and nonverbal levels of communication.

All families have communication barriers within their conversational repertoires. Members of some families, however, monitor their own communications and adjust their manner when their response has an adverse impact on another person. As you observe the communication styles of families, it is important to assess three issues:

- The presence of patterned negative communications
- The pervasiveness of such negative patterns
- The relative ability of individual members of the system to modify their communication styles

In addition to assessing these factors, it is vital to ascertain the various combinations of communication styles that occur repetitively as family members relate and react to one another. For example, one individual may frequently dominate, criticize, attack, or accuse the other, whereas the other may defend, apologize, placate, or agree. In an exchange in which one member continues to attack or accuse another member, the other tends to continue to defend his or her position, thus manifesting a **fault–defend pattern of communication**. Attacks or accusations generally take the form of "You never …," in which case the other defends himself or herself by providing examples that contradict the accusation. In such situations, even though the topic of conflict or the content of the discussion may change, the manner in which couples or family members relate to each other and orchestrate their scenario remains unchanged. Furthermore, the same types of

exchanges tend to occur across many other areas of the family's interaction. The thematic configurations that occur in families' or couples' communication tend to be limited, but they reinforce tensions in the relationships. Your task as a social worker is to assess the thematic communication pattern, including the context in which the fault–defend sequence occurs.

Receiver Skills

A critical dimension of communication is the degree of receptivity or openness of family members to the inner thoughts and feelings of other members in the system. Receptivity is manifested by the use of certain *receiver skills*, which we will discuss shortly. Again, a caution: These skills are in keeping with Western traditions, and therefore the assessment should include the extent to which these skills are consistent with the preferences of the family systems with which you interact.

You may observe response patterns in some families that convey understanding and demonstrate respect for other members' messages. In other families, messages can be met with response patterns such as ridicule, negative evaluations, or depreciation of character. In still other families, members may engage in **dual monologues**—that is, members communicate simultaneously, which to the casual observer might appear to be a free-for-all. Family members may also use words, sayings, or gestures specific to their family or reference group.

In general, facilitative **receiver skills** invite, welcome, and acknowledge the views and perceptions of others. For example, free-for-all conversations invite, even encourage, responses, but perhaps not in the way that may be most familiar to you. In such situations, family members feel free to express agreement or disagreement, even though doing so may sometimes spark conflict. Facilitative responses that convey understanding and acceptance include the following:

- Physical attending (direct eye contact, receptive body posture, hand gestures, attentive facial expressions)
- "Listening" or paraphrasing responses by family members that restate in fresh words the essence of a speaker's message (e.g., "Man, you said …," or as a youth might say, "I feel you …")
- Responses by receivers of messages that elicit clarification of messages (e.g., "Tell me again, I'm not sure what you meant" or "Am I right in assuming you meant …?")
- Brief responses that prompt further elaboration by the speaker (e.g., "Oh," "I see," "Tell me more")

Sender Skills

Another facet of assessing communication styles and skills is assessing family members' **sender skills**—that is, the extent to which family members can share their inner thoughts and feelings with others in the system. Becvar and Becvar (2000b) refer to such sender skills as the ability of family members to express themselves clearly as feeling, thinking, acting, valuable, and separate individuals and to take responsibility for their thoughts, feelings, and actions. **"I" messages** are messages phrased in the first person that openly and congruently reveal either pleasant or unpleasant feelings, thoughts, or reactions experienced by the speaker ("I feel …," "I think …," "I want …"). For the social worker, an essential task is to assess the extent to which the climate in the family allows family members to be candid, open, and congruent in their communications.

A positive communication climate stands in sharp contrast to situations in which family communications are indirect, vague, and guarded and individuals fail to take responsibility for their feelings, thoughts, or participation in events. Instead of "I" messages, family members are likely to use "you" messages that obscure or deny their responsibility or that attribute responsibility for the feelings to others (e.g., "You've got me so rattled, I forgot"). Such messages are barriers to communication and are often replete with injunctions concerning another's behavior (e.g., "you should" or "you ought") or negatively evaluate the message of the sender (e.g., "You shouldn't feel that way").

In assessing communication styles of families, you must gauge the extent to which individual members have the skills to utilize the facilitative responses identified in the preceding list. So that you and the family understand their communication style, part of the assessment can include asking them to keep track of the extent to which individual members (and the group as a whole) utilize facilitative communication skills. A simple grid with the relevant indicators can be developed, and responses can be rated as a plus or minus by other family members.

Also critical to assessing family communication styles is the extent to which messages contribute to the development of self-confidence and consistently validate a person's worth and potential. In contrast, consider whether the patterns and repertoires that you observe consist of constant negative messages (e.g., putdowns, attacks, or criticism) or otherwise humiliate or invalidate the experience of others in the family. It is also advisable to keep in mind that a family experience with internal and external stressors may, in fact, challenge even previously effective communication skills.

Family Life Cycle

The **family life cycle** encompasses the developmental stages through which families as a whole must pass. Based on the seminal work of Duvall (1977) and other theorists, Carter and McGoldrick (1988) developed a conceptual framework of the life cycle of the middle-class American family. This model, which focuses on the entire three- or four-generational system as it moves through time, includes both predictable development events (e.g., birth, marriage, retirement) and unpredictable events that may disrupt the life-cycle process (e.g., untimely death, birth of a developmentally delayed child, divorce, chronic illness, war). Carter and McGoldrick (1988, 2005) identified six stages of family development, all of which address nodal events related to the comings and goings of family members over time:

1. Unattached young adult
2. New couple
3. Family with young children
4. Family with adolescents
5. Family that is launching children
6. Family in later life

To master these stages, families must successfully complete certain tasks. The unattached young adult, for example, must differentiate from the family of origin and become a "self" before joining with another person to form a new family system. The new couple and the families of origin must renegotiate their relationships with one another. The family with young children must find the delicate balance between over- and underparenting. In all of these stages, problems are most likely to appear when an interruption or dislocation in the unfolding family life cycle occurs, signaling that the family is "stuck" and having difficulty moving through the transition to its next phase.

Variations in the life cycle are, of course, highly likely to occur in today's world. Families can change, readjust, and cope with stressful transitions that occur within the life cycle (McKenry & Price, 2000). In the modern life cycle of families, as Meyer (1990) notes, the ground rules have changed as far as the timing and sequence of events are concerned. In much of our society, education, work, love, marriage or a committed relationship, childbirth, and retirement are now out of synch. Older adults return to school; adult children live with their parents; and childbirth is no longer within the exclusive realm of the traditional family form. Because of various changes, one life-cycle phase may not necessarily progress in a linear fashion. In this world, life events are not preordained. Instead, they are more likely to be atomistic, mixed-and-matched responses to self-definition and opportunity (Meyer, 1990, p. 12).

Variations also occur in the family life cycle among cultures. Every culture marks off stages of living, each with its appropriate expectations, defining what it means to be a man or woman, to be young, to grow up and leave home, to get married and have children, and to grow old and die. Exploring the meaning of the life cycle with diverse families is particularly critical to determine important milestones from their perspective. Cultural variants that have a negative connotation in Western society include the legal versus the culturally derived age for marriage, family responsibilities, and roles for children. Families from other countries, therefore, may experience adverse reactions to practices that were common in their country of origin. Because culture plays an important role in family progression and life-cycle expectations, it cannot be avoided as an essential dimension in the assessment of family functioning at a particular development stage in the life cycle.

Family Rules

Family rules, which underlie all aspects of family system structure, prescribe the rights, duties, and range of appropriate behaviors of members within a family. They govern how boundaries are established and maintained, the distribution of family roles, the execution of power and decision making, how families adapt in the face of family life-cycle changes, and, in short, strive to maintain family system homeostasis. As with all dimensions of family system structure, family rules have strong cultural determinants. In general, family rules can be explored across two dimensions: explicit/implicit rules and flexible/rigid rules.

Explicit and Implicit Rules

Explicit rules are those rules that family members readily recognize and can articulate. These include expectations for behavior that parents impose on children, both **prescribed behavior** (e.g., complete your chores) and **proscribed behavior** (e.g., don't hit your

brother), as well as negotiated agreements among members of the executive subsystem (e.g., who manages money) and across subsystems (e.g., elders are expected to spoil their grandchildren). Explicit rules are important because they express family values. These rules represent family efforts to meet important goals and obligations and to respond to demands imposed on the family from both internal and external forces. Very often, explicit rules are the subject of family fights and contests.

Implicit rules are different. In general, implicit rules are hidden from family members' awareness, similar to the way in which elements of an individual's personality may be hidden in the subconscious. Being hidden, implicit rules can be difficult to detect without careful observation of behavior that tends to reveal their content. But once revealed, implicit rules showcase their importance. Implicit rules govern how family members unwittingly collaborate to maintain the status quo in the family system structure. Whereas explicit rules are often the topic of a family feud, implicit rules govern how family feuds are fought and resolved. Whereas explicit rules dictate how order is maintained, implicit rules dictate how rule changes are negotiated. And whereas explicit rules establish expected behavioral repertoires, implicit rules explain why family members do not always conform to expectations.

Family rules, both explicit and implicit, can be detected by the real or expected consequences suffered when rules are violated, what we earlier defined as *feedback loops*. Usually, feedback loops are thought of as an escalation of some aversive behavior, such as raising voices, imposing punishments, and, in extreme cases, using violence. It should be recognized that feedback loops are not limited to aversive behavior, and that all family members are involved in the regulation of family rules through the use of feedback loops. Feedback loops related to the preservation of explicit and implicit rules can be observed by answers to questions like "What happens when [a given rule is violated]?," or "What would happen if [a given rule were violated]?" In some family systems, for example, explicit and implicit rules are developed to manage the anxiety of fragile family members, being governed by expectations about the threat of decompensation in the face of stress. In such cases, the expectation of decompensation is the feedback mechanism that promotes adherence to a set of explicit and implicit rules.

Herein lies a key property of family rules: Explicit rules are often conditional, depending on circumstances, and the salience of conditions on feed-back loops depends on the simultaneous expression of implicit rules. Consider a parent who sometimes imposes consequences for a curfew violation but sometimes does not, depending on the level of stress and strain experienced within the family. Implicit rules involving the regulation of stress are often revealed after careful examination of such instances.

Flexible and Rigid Rules

The explicit and implicit rules found in a family system may be either flexible or rigid, depending on context and time. In tense conflicted situations, family members may monitor what they say and how they behave, such as "Be careful what you say around Mom." However, at other times, speaking freely is acceptable. Flexible rules enable the family system to respond to family stressors as well as to the developmental needs of individual members. As you observe families, you will want to assess the extent to which rules provide members with opportunities to explore solutions that utilize individual and collective family capacities. For example, an open discussion of member differences can facilitate an understanding of acceptable behavior. Similarly, openly discussing touchy subjects can be instrumental in bringing the family together in stressful times.

Rules that permit the system to respond flexibly are usually optimal. Examples of flexible rules that facilitate an open climate in the family include the following:

- Everyone's ideas and feedback are important.
- Family members don't always have to agree or like the same things.
- It is okay to talk about any feelings, including disappointments, fear, anger, or achievements.
- Family members should work out their disagreements with other family members.
- It is okay to admit mistakes; others in the family will understand and support you.

As you observe family processes, keep in mind that all families have flexible rules as well as rigid rules. The latter can undermine positive family dynamics, but flexible rules allow the family to work out disagreements and to encourage participation because everyone's ideas are important. Of course, variations in both types of rules can of course occur depending on the age and cognitive ability of family members.

Many family rules change over the course of the family life cycle. The developmental stage of minors, for example, often means that they press for redefinition or modification of family rules that are appropriate to their age. An individual may also pursue interests and choose values that are alien to those embraced by the family. Rules that govern the behavior of minors are by necessity modified when they become adults. Elders, however, accustomed to a certain set of rules vis-à-vis their status, may be disinclined to accept modifications. Further, it is often difficult for elders to cope with situations in which they feel acted upon by rules set forth by their adult children, professionals, or institutions. These dynamics cause "disequilibrium within the family system, a sense of loss, and perhaps a feeling of strangeness until new transactional patterns are in place to restore family balance" (Goldenberg & Goldenberg, 1991, p. 40).

In addition to assessing the stresses on rules caused by developmental changes and internal events (inner forces), it is important that you also assess the extent to which a family's rules allow the system to respond flexibly to dynamic societal stresses (outer forces), such as job loss, concerns about neighborhood safety, family relocation, natural disaster, or family uprooting experienced by immigrants or refugees.

Families may also construct rigid rules that function as protective factors to minimize real or potential risks, such as telling minors to avoid certain people, places, or situations. For immigrants or refugee families, further complicating dynamics are the vast contrasts between their rules and those of Western culture. Immigration and the related cultural transition require significant life changes over a short period of time, including material, economic, and educational changes; changes in roles; and the loss of extended family, support systems, and familiar environments (Green, 1999). These families may adopt a mix of rules from their new and old cultures.

Responding successfully to inner and outer stresses requires constant transformation of the rules and behaviors of family members to accommodate ongoing changes while maintaining family continuity. Families often seek help because of an accumulation of events that have strained the coping ability of the entire family or of individual members. Even when these changes are for the better, they may overwhelm the coping mechanisms and resilience of individual members or an entire family system.

Social Environment

EP 2, 3, and 7

A key dimension of family system structure is the depth and nature of its involvement in the social environment. Like all social systems, families require inputs of energy and resources from external environments for their survival; without such transactions with the environment, families suffer from **entropy**, or the tendency of systems to wither over time. But often, relations of families with their external environments can be a source of stress and strain, threatening family functioning and even survival. Most often, the social environments that families inhabit provide both strain and facilitative support.

The **social environment** of families can be described as a set of broad social sectors that catalog the various ways that all families engage with the outside world. These include the economic sector and the labor market, educational institutions, public health and mental health systems, public safety and corrections institutions, nongovernmental organizations and religious institutions, familial networks, and informal support networks, among others. Within each, families may experience advantages conferred through rich formal and informal networks of relationships, but also may suffer disadvantages by virtue of sparse social networks. Moreover, family social status itself confers advantages as well as disadvantages. Within each social sector listed above, prejudice and discrimination linked to minority group identity, socioeconomic status, and gender present serious challenges for families. Workplace discrimination, mass incarceration, and interreligious conflict are just a few of the problems associated with prejudice and discrimination that social workers will encounter in their work with families.

Family mobility and migration illustrate the importance of the social environment in overall family functioning (Sluzki, 2008). Family relocation can threaten family functioning even as it provides a sense of relief at escaping from threatening home country environments or excitement as people are drawn to new opportunities and challenges. It threatens family functioning first through the depletion of social resources immediately available to help families achieve their goals, as described above (e.g., meeting the attachment, economic, social status, and emotional health needs of family members). Simple problems like access to friendship networks and alternative child care arrangements can strain families who remain isolated from social support resources in their new communities.

Relocation can also strain families through the cultural conflicts that can attend movement across regional and international boundaries. In the United States, refugee and immigrant families frequently experience cultural tensions in the roles of children and adolescents in relation to their parents and family elders, as well as between parents and elders. In the face of resource challenges and cultural conflicts, successful families sustain their functioning through active engagement in their new social environment, collecting local social capital to enable them to access local resources and institutions while also sustaining their engagement with social support networks from their original homes (Smokowski & Bacallao, 2011).

How families manage their engagement with the social environment brings the interrelationship of family system structures (e.g., boundaries, rules, roles, power, and decision making) into strong focus. When navigating their external environments, families are managing boundaries, reinforcing rules, and exercising role differentiation, all at the same time. Who within a family is responsible for participation in the labor market? How do mothers, fathers, and siblings react when one if the children is facing disciplinary problems at school? Where can family members go for health care services that respect their cultural heritage? How do family rules and norms facilitate or impede access to formal and informal networks that may be available to support coping? Answers to these questions and others illustrate both how families are embedded within the social environment and how family system structure dynamics are operating to manage the transaction between the family and its environment.

Family Adaptive Capacity

The **adaptive capacity** of any given family refers to the extent to which the family can achieve its functioning goals, given the demands of family and social life. As the family faces demands from its environment and challenges from its members, its capacity to adapt is a central property of the ability to maintain itself as a cohesive unit. The concept of adaptive capacity brings to light two additional concepts that are relevant to family life: family stressors and family strengths and resilience.

Family Stressors

McKenry and Price (2000, p. 6) describe a *stressor* as "anything that provokes change or some aspect of change, such as boundaries, structures, goals, roles or values" within the family system, resulting in a

EP 7

state of family disequilibrium. Said another way, a **family stressor** is something that threatens existing family structures and patterns or that interferes with a family's capacity to achieve its goals. For example, a job loss can strain a family's capacity to assure the economic viability of the family unit; a family member's refusal to continue playing an accepted role in the family (e.g., negotiator) can strain family functioning by altering the family's usual pattern of activity; and a social worker's entry into a family can strain family definitions as to who is and is not a member of the family's executive subsystem.

The source of stress within the family system can be internal—the result of family dynamics, roles and relationships, communication patterns, or life cycle transitions or separations. The source of stress can also be external, including the neighborhood in which the family lives, inequality, racial or economic discrimination, or public policy—any one of which can marginalize families. It is quite possible to encounter reciprocal pressures between internal and external stressors; for example, stressful internal dynamics within a family system may be the result of economic pressures.

Family stressors can be classified in several ways. First, stressors can be classified based on their relationship to the family life cycle. From this perspective, stressors are considered to be **normative**—disruptive events (e.g., marriage) that are predictable based on expected patterns of growth and development of family members but that nevertheless provoke a change in prevailing family routines—or **nonnormative**—disruptive events (e.g., an accident) that are unexpected and not necessarily associated with the family life cycle. Classification of family stressors into normative and nonnormative categories showcases how life-cycle transitions can strain families and force adaptations that are often resisted as family systems strive toward homeostasis.

However, classifying stressors into normative/nonnormative categories misses the central features of stressors that may be routinely experienced, and thus may be "normative," but that are not directly the result of the family life cycle. For example, systematic exclusion from the labor market because of discrimination, or strained relations between families and key social institutions such as schools or child welfare systems, are not easily described through the normative/nonnormative classification.

Alternatively, stressors can be classified according to their frequency and duration, for example by using a three-category typology that describes stress as acute, episodic, or chronic. **Acute stressors** are usually single occurrence events. They may be relatively minor yet disruptive health problems that force family system adjustments (e.g., a sick child who cannot attend day care or school) or large events that permanently change family system structure (e.g., marriage, birth of a child, divorce, death). **Episodic stressors** are those stressors that have an ending but that are repeated periodically. Some serious mental health conditions, such as major depressive disorder, can be episodic in nature, requiring families to adapt during the period of illness. Finally, **chronic stress** persists over a long period of time. Poverty and economic insecurity, for example, are often associated with diminished family cohesion and marital discord, along with coercive and aggressive parenting and unstable housing. Moreover, poverty can determine where a family lives, the condition of the housing where they reside, their access to resources such as a full-service grocery store, the safety of their neighborhood, and the quality of education that their children receive. Furthermore, poverty is strongly associated with out-of-home care for children living in urban areas (Barth, Wildfire, & Green, 2006; Roberts, 2002; Rodenborg, 2004).

Stressors can also be characterized in terms of magnitude and number. **Stressful life events** are generally considered major disruptions that in some cases may be traumatic, whereas **daily hassles** are the pressures and responsibilities that family members must face on a daily basis. Although the impact on family functioning of serious stressful life events such as job loss, death of a close associate, and violence may seem evident, daily hassles like the burden of household chores, monitoring children in a violent neighborhood, minor health problems, problematic relations at work, concern for job security, and countless others can also have a negative impact on family functioning.

This points to the final way that stressors can be described: Stressors can be characterized in terms of number. A consistent finding in research on risk and resilience is that for most people, exposure to a single risk factor does not strongly predict negative impacts. However, as exposure to hardships increase in number, a property called **cumulative risk**, the likelihood of a host of negative outcomes increases exponentially (Fraser, 2004).

Thus, family stress—the events and challenges that threaten family homeostasis—can be described in a variety of ways. However described, families seen by social workers often face significant levels of stress that threaten families' capacity to achieve their goals and to perform critical family functions. In assessing families, it is therefore useful to pay attention to the sources of family stress and to determine whether and how stressors pose a risk to family functioning. How families cope with and adapt to stressors may depend on their resources, strengths, or resilience, bolstered by family networks, social supports, spirituality, and relational caregiving. It is also important to recognize that not all stress leads to debilitating family problems, and not all families succumb to stress, as will be made clear in the next section.

Family Strengths and Resilience

Resilience is the capability of individuals and families to sustain their functioning and to thrive when threatened by risk and adversity. It is the answer to the question "Why do some families succeed even when they suffer significant adversity?" Although resilience as a concept has been developed and operationalized by developmental psychologists, psychiatrists, and social workers at the individual level (Fraser, 2004), a small number of scholars have extended resilience to the study of families. For example, important contributions to our understanding of resilient family functioning and family strengths have been made in the United States through the study of African American families (Bell-Tolliver, Burgess, & Brock, 2009) and families involved in the child welfare system (Lietz, 2006, 2007).

The strengths perspective and the concept of resilience are closely related. The strengths perspective is based on the empowering notion that all people can change and grow, and, when applied at the family system level, that all families have available to them strengths that can be enlisted in the service of growth and change. In essence, a strengths assessment highlights what is working in families and balances it with the presenting concern. Assessing and accrediting the strengths inherent in the family system require the deliberate and disciplined effort of all involved. On your part, a strengths orientation requires you to have a respectful and positive way of thinking about people that is evident in your attitude and relationship with the family. However, note that a strengths perspective, although assessing strengths, does not do so to the exclusion of paying attention to problems or risks. In other words, it is not either/or, but rather a balance of assessing both problems and strengths.

Research on family resilience has used primarily qualitative methods, resulting in a limited list of so-called **resilience factors**. These factors provide families

with resources for problem solving and patterned ways of approaching challenges that promote growth and successful adaptation. In no way do resilience factors keep problems from happening. However, by including resilience factors in an assessment of family system functioning, social workers and families can have a full appreciation of the myriad ways that families attempt to cope with difficult problems.

A current synthesis of research on family resilience suggests the following potential strengths or resilience factors to include in family assessments (Bell-Tolliver, Burgess, & Brock, 2009; Lietz, 2006, 2007):

1. Social support, from the community as well as from kinship bonds. Families who have active and vital social support networks have ready access to coping resources.
2. Internal cohesion and commitment. Families are able to adapt to adversity when family members have a strong sense of dedication to each other and when their patterns of communication lend themselves to mutual understanding of family members' thoughts, ideas, and feelings regarding adversity.
3. Creativity and flexibility. Families that strive for creative solutions to problems, including especially demonstrating flexibility in role assignments, enable families to find solutions to stressful situations.
4. Appraisal, insight, and meaning. When families strive to understand their difficulties and to find affirmative meaning in them, they have an increasing ability to sustain their problem-solving efforts under stress. Very often appraisal and insight are linked to family spirituality and belief systems.
5. Initiative and achievement. Families who are action oriented tend to approach problem solving using positive coping strategies such as cognitive coping, problem solving, and constructive emotional regulation strategies.
6. Boundary setting. Families with a strong sense of family structure will seek to shield its members from unhelpful, unhealthy, and destructive influences.

As you are perhaps aware, assessing strengths in families is not easy. One difficulty with a strengths-based perspective is that helping professionals and the agencies in which they work, as well as funding resources and policymakers, have deeply entrenched views about the pathology of families who experience problems. Some agencies and practitioners purport to embrace a strengths perspective; however, family strengths seem to be an abstract idea, as their assessment tools will attest. Students have commented that families themselves are not always comfortable with a strengths focus. Having been socialized to focus on their problems in exchange for receiving services, they can be reluctant and indeed suspicious when you talk about strengths. Further, family members may not recognize that their capacity to cope with adversity, their support and celebration of each other, and their talents and aspirations are strengths. Regardless of the circumstances that may make it difficult for you to assess strengths, you are responsible for your choice of action. Once the conversation about family strengths takes place, you can ask family members to highlight other family strengths.

ASSESSMENT SKILLS AND STRATEGIES

Social workers assess family system structure in a variety of ways. For example, they may observe patterns of interaction as they unfold over the course of an interview. Of course, the interview process itself will be a primary source of data about family boundaries, hierarchy, rules, roles, and strengths. Finally, a host of standardized scales have been developed to describe family functioning. In the sections that follow, we will describe specialized family assessment strategies, including the use of direct observation, interviewing with circular questioning, genograms, and selected standardized scales. To illustrate these strategies in practice, we will use an assessment with the Diaz family as a case example.

Problems occur in a person or family and situational context. In this case example, the problems occurred in part because of Mr. Diaz's living situation, his access to alternative living environments, and the availability of a continuum of care that could include in-home supports. Mr. Diaz's income and health insurance coverage are external factors that can influence the alternative care arrangements that are available to the family. External factors should always be accorded prominence in the assessment to avoid the assumption that problems are caused solely by factors internal to the family system. In this case, both internal and external factors impinged upon and disrupted family functioning. When families experience a disruption, like those faced by the Diaz family, dynamics in the family tend to be directed toward maintaining homeostasis and restoring equilibrium.

Observing Patterns of Interaction

In order to assess family system structure, social workers first assess the sequences of interaction that occur between members. All families play out scenarios or a series of transactions in which they manifest redundancies in behavior and communication. Learning about these repetitive patterns of verbal communication, nonverbal communication, and behavior among family members provides clues about the presence and strength of family system boundaries, decision-making authority and power, roles, rules, and adaptive capacity. In their assessments of family system structure, social workers use interviewing skills, asking questions to reveal repeated sequences of interactions

CASE EXAMPLE

Carlos Diaz, 66, lives with his 16-year-old son John in a subsidized apartment on the second floor of a three-story building. Mr. Diaz is diabetic, is visually impaired but not legally blind, and has a history of heavy alcohol use, although he has abstained from alcohol for the last 7 years. Mr. Diaz's companion of 18 years, Ann Mercy, recently died of a massive stroke. She had provided emotional support, given Mr. Diaz his insulin injections, and managed the household. Mr. Diaz has difficulty walking, has fallen several times in the past year, and is now hesitant to leave his apartment. In addition to John, Mr. Diaz has eight children from an earlier marriage who live in nearby suburbs, though only one, Maria, calls him regularly. Mr. Diaz's physician considers his current living arrangement to be dangerous because of the need for Mr. Diaz to climb stairs. The physician is also concerned about his capacity to administer his own insulin. A medical social worker convenes a family meeting with Mr. Diaz, his son John, his daughter Maria, and his stepdaughter Anita.

surrounding a presenting problem, and also observe family interactions that occur in the presence of the social worker.

To illustrate how this works, consider the following script from the first minutes of a session with the Diaz family. The medical social worker involved with this family has convened a family group conference to consider health and safely alternatives for Mr. Diaz (Carlos), who is being considered. In this example, Mr. Diaz, daughter Maria, son John, and stepdaughter Anita demonstrate sequential verbal and nonverbal behaviors that have a powerful impact on the family system.

Anita *[to social worker]:* Carlos can't maintain himself or John. John runs wild, with no appropriate adult supervision, and Carlos can't take care of himself now that Mother has died. *[Anita looks earnestly at the social worker but signals a relational distance between herself and Mr. Diaz by using his first name. In response, Mr. Diaz sits stoically, arms folded, glowering straight ahead.]*

Maria *[to social worker]:* Dad is having trouble with John and hasn't taken care of himself all these years with Ann Mercy doing the cooking and cleaning and injecting his insulin. *[To Mr. Diaz]:* Dad, I respect you and want to help you in any way that I can, but things just can't continue like they are *[attempting to reason with her father].*

Mr. Diaz *[to social worker]:* These children "no tienen respeto." They don't give me the respect they should give the father as the head of the family. They want to put me in a nursing home and take John away from me *[appealing to the social work to notice the unfair, disrespectful way that he is being treated].*

Anita: Maybe that would be for the best, since you can't take care of yourself or John *[triumphant facial expression, resembling a smile].*

Maria *[showing frustration, explains to social worker]:* Dad is used to having his own way and we do respect him, at least I do, but he won't listen to how some things have to change.

Mr. Diaz: Maria, you have been a good daughter, and I am surprised at your behavior. I would think that you would be the loyal one and stick by your father if anyone would.

John: Dad, you know I stick by you. And I can help with some things, too. I want to stay with you. We have been getting along okay, and I want to be a good son and take care of you *[asserting his loyalty and*

attempting to maintain equilibrium by supporting the father].

Anita: John, you have been running in the streets, in trouble with the law, taking money from your father. You are no help to him, and he can't be a good parent to you *[reasserting her point of view].*

Maria: John, I know you want to help, and you are close to your dad. But you have made a lot of problems for him, and I, too, wonder if you can take care of him or he can take care of you.

In the preceding example, the Diaz family members play out a discordant yet repetitive thematic interaction that, with slight variation, can be observed over and over in their transactions. Families may discuss an endless variety of topics or content issues, but their processes often have a limited number of familiar behaviors. It is as though the family is involved in a screenplay, and once the curtain is raised, all members participate in the scenario according to the family script. It is important to understand that family scripts rarely have beginnings or endings; that is, anyone may initiate the scenario by enacting his or her "lines." The rest of the family members almost invariably follow their habitual styles of relating, editing their individual scripts slightly to fit different versions of the scene being acted out by the family. In sequenced interaction scenes, the subjects discussed will vary, but the roles taken by individual family members and the styles of communicating and behaving that perpetuate the scenario tend to fluctuate very little. Notice the sequenced interactions that occurred in this family:

1. Anita speaks forthrightly about her concerns about John and Mr. Diaz's capacity for parenting him because of Mr. Diaz's medical condition. Responding nonverbally *[folding his arms and glowering]*, Mr. Diaz declines to openly respond *[a patterned behavior when his authority is questioned or when there is disagreement].*

2. Maria affirms some of Anita's concerns but also speaks directly to her father *[affirming her respect for him as father and head of the family].*

3. Mr. Diaz asserts that his children "no tienen respeto" and that their motivation is to put him away *[maintaining his authority].*

4. Anita does not deny that a nursing home might be the best solution *[reasserting her position that he cannot care for himself].*

5. Maria reasserts her respect for her father, yet notes that some things must change.

6. Mr. Diaz addresses Maria and questions whether she is, in fact, showing proper respect for him as her father.

7. John joins the fray and tries to identify himself as a good son with "respeto," which adds another dimension to the transactions.

8. Anita puts John in his place by doubting whether he has acted as a good son or whether Mr. Diaz can be a good parent to him.

9. Maria supports John's desire to be a good son but agrees that there are persistent problems with Mr. Diaz and his care of John.

10. Six of Mr. Diaz's eight children are not active participants in the meeting. Indeed, background information suggests that Maria may be most actively involved among the sibling subsystem.

These patterned behaviors are suggestive of family system structure. First, it is clear that the family is contemplating a significant life-cycle change in which Mr. Diaz's traditional position of authority is threatened by a looming family decision regarding placement in a nursing home. He employs both the overt power of his position (invoking the authority of the head of the family) and covert power (splitting Maria away from Anita by expressing "surprise" at her behavior) to resist this family system change. Second, overt family rules regarding respect for elders continue to be invoked, and active feedback loops are in place to preserve this important rule. Feedback loops include Mr. Diaz's complaints about his children's lack of respect as well as Maria's affirmation of the importance of respect. Third, subsystem boundaries are revealed in the manner in which Maria and Anita echo each other's concerns about both Mr. Diaz and John, while John is excluded from this sibling subsystem. Additional subsystem boundaries are suggested in the way that Maria and John both seek emotional closeness with Mr. Diaz while Anita and Mr. Diaz remain emotionally distant. Fourth, a mediating role is suggested by Maria's attempt to acknowledge Anita's expressed concerns while attempting to reason with her father.

Interviewing Skills and Circular Questioning

Following on these observations of family system functioning, the social worker who interviews the Diaz family may use a variety of interviewing strategies to selectively confirm aspects of family system structure that are relevant to the resolution of the presenting problem. For example, it may be useful to learn more about the rules governing power and decision making in the Diaz family. Also, the social worker will likely be interested in the roles and positions of nonparticipating family members as well. Moreover, the social worker will want to take a strengths perspective with the family, striving to identify family resilience factors that may provide resources for problem solving. In this case, Anita's active involvement and coalition with Maria, despite being a stepdaughter, suggests a source of cohesion and commitment that may exist within the family despite the lack of involvement from other children in the family.

Social workers have available a variety of interviewing strategies to assess family system structure. Interviewing skills presented in Chapter 6, including verbal following, exploring, and focusing skills, will of course provide the basis for most if not all assessment strategies that social workers employ. In general, it is important that the social worker listen carefully to all family members who participate in family meetings. Thus, reflective listening and summarizing will be two skills that are especially featured in family meetings. Moreover, the complexity of a family meeting, given the multiple people present, will usually require that the social worker manage the interview process carefully, liberally seeking concreteness and using focusing skills to ensure that the conversation stays on track.

Circular questioning is a specialized interviewing strategy that is often employed to elicit information about the repetitive transactions that take place among family members (Benson, Schindler-Zimmerman, & Martin, 1991; Patrika & Tseliou, 2015). As the name implies, circular questions suggest the concept of circular causality, in which an antecedent produces an outcome or effect only insofar as the antecedent itself is embedded in a cyclical or repetitive chain of events. Moreover, any given sequence of events occurs within a multilayered context of actions and inactions by others, which serve to support, dampen, or alter the sequence. Circular questions treat family members as "perceivers" of family life, eliciting information from them about the interrelatedness of family members and relationships that are often external to the perceiver. The nature of circular questions will become clear through our description of three types of circular questions below.

First are circular questions that elicit member perceptions about the presenting problem. A question as simple as "What is the problem as you understand it?" can initiate a circular dialogue when it leads to a discussion of similarities and differences among family members. Importantly, a social worker employing circular questions usually adopts a neutral stance, avoiding the temptation to judge the truth or validity of family member perspectives except as these themes emerge through contrasts highlighted in the perspectives of others. The following is an exchange that took place between the social worker and the Diaz family:

Social worker: Mr. Diaz, I understand you to be saying that you do not want to go to an assisted living facility and you want to continue to take care of John. Is that correct?

Mr. Diaz: Yes, I don't want to go to one of those places. You have no freedom. You go there to die.

Social worker: Thank you, Mr. Diaz. Later, I would like to talk with you about how assisted living facilities help people manage health problems like diabetes, and about how many, many people who live in these kinds of places are quite happy. But now, I would like to stay focused on how you and members of your family are understanding the problem. What is going on here? What is the problem as you see it?

Mr. Diaz: My children want to take over. This is plain.

Social worker: I notice that John did not want to take over. He said that he wants to keep living with you.

Mr. Diaz: Yes. John is a good boy. He has some trouble some time. But he is a good boy.

Social worker: John, how does your dad's definition of the problem—that the children are trying to take over—compare with your older sisters' definition of the problem?

John: He wants to be in charge, and they want him to give up his apartment and move.

Social worker [to everyone]: It seems that members of this family are operating from two different problems: first, that the children are seeking to take control of Mr. Diaz's affairs, and second, that Mr. Diaz needs significant support to care for his health and for John, and that he may not be able to do these two things well while living alone in his apartment.

Among the skills that stand out in this vignette, it should be noticed that the social worker invited family members to provide their perceptions of what other family members might think or believe about the presenting problem. This is a signal characteristic of circular questioning, that family members external to the exchange can be recruited to provide their observations. Circular questions can also be used speculatively or as a simulation by invoking the perspectives of members who are not present in the interaction. For example, consider the following interaction, which took place approximately 5 minutes later, after further discussion of the presenting problem:

Social worker: Maria, let's imagine that your older brother is having a conversation with the doctor about your father's health care needs. What would he tell the doctor?

Maria: My brother is not helpful at all in this. He keeps his distance and tries not to get involved. I don't know what he would say.

Social worker: The purpose of my question is not to figure out exactly what he thinks. Only he can do that. But questions like this help me to understand family dynamics. What do you imagine that he would say to the doctor?

Maria: I'm not saying that he would ever meet with the doctor, but if he were forced, he would say that we should leave dad alone.

Mr. Diaz: He is a good boy with many responsibilities. He is successful in his life. He can't be bothered by this.

Maria: But Dad, he is not helping. He has never helped.

Social worker [interjecting]: Maria, let's extend the pretend question one step further. Say that the doctor expressed concerns about your father's health and ability to care for himself. What would your brother say then?

Anita [interjecting]: What does he have to do with this? He's not even here.

Social worker: Anita, I would like to learn more about your perspective as well, and will turn to you in a moment. For now, it is important to let Maria share hers. Maria, what might your brother say?

Maria: He would tell the doctor that my dad is proud and would never agree to move into assisted living, no matter how bad it got.

Social worker: Anita, I want to ask for your impressions of something I've noticed. It appears that the men of this family are all supporting independence for Mr. Diaz. On the other hand, it is the women of the family, you, Maria, and especially your mother, who have focused their energy on making sure that Mr. Diaz's health care needs are taken care of. What is your perspective?

Anita: This has always been the case. My mother went out of her way to make sure that Carlos was taken care of.

Social worker: Mr. Diaz, what is your perspective?

Mr. Diaz: Women should take care of things like this. This is the natural way of things. But it should be done with proper respect.

Social worker: So Maria and Anita are fulfilling their roles.

As mentioned, the social worker uses circular questions not to identify the truth of any of a competing number of problem definitions but rather to showcase family system functioning. In the example above, several features of the Diaz family system structure are suggested, including the nature of subsystem coalitions and strong values about gender roles. Additionally, it is interesting to note how the family is struggling to reorganize itself to account for the loss of Mr. Diaz's partner, Ann Mercy. Such family system functioning came to light because the social worker observed patterns of responses by family members as they reported their perspectives and reflected together about similarities and differences.

Second are questions to establish sequences of events related to a presenting problem. Beginning at a point in time, the social worker will ask variations of the question "What happened next?" repetitively to obtain a concrete version of how a series of events unfolded. For the Diaz family, the social worker might have established a sequence of events when members of the family first discussed with Mr. Diaz the possibility of moving into an assisted living apartment. Although the initial sequence may appear linear, a social worker who employs circular questioning will seek to understand how all members of the family relate to the event sequence. This will include members who are directly involved in the sequence as well as members who are silent or who are not apparently involved. As with problem definitions, information about the positions and reactions of family members are often elicited from peripheral actors. For example, the social worker might inquire about John's presence and behavior while the discussion of an assisted living placement took place and might ask John to describe his perceptions of the discussion as it happened.

Finally, social workers can use rating and ranking questions to highlight differences and similarities. In the context of family assessment, ranking and rating questions are often used to compare members on key family system dynamics such as boundaries, roles, rules, and power. Rating and ranking questions may be used to highlight subsystem boundaries (e.g., Who is the most involved in the family? Who is least involved? On a scale of 1 to 10, how strongly does Maria agree with Anita?); role differences (e.g., Who is the funniest person in the family? Who gets things done?); or repetitive feedback loops (e.g., Who is first to express respect for father? Who is most likely to challenge father?). Again, as discussed above, social workers generally adopt a neutral stance when seeking circular explanations for a family presenting problem, and often the questions are framed to allow peripheral actors to provide perspectives on family system structure.

Genograms

As discussed in Chapter 9, the genogram is an interviewing tool commonly employed in social work interventions with families (McGoldrick, Gerson, & Petry, 2008). In essence, a **genogram** is a pictorial representation of a family, resembling a family tree, which helps social workers and family members understand family traditions and family system structure across generations and over time. In therapeutic applications, genograms help family members understand how problems in living can be passed from generation to generation, identify problematic relationships that contribute to emotional and behavioral health problems, and point to family-based strategies to resolve presenting problems (Nichols, 2012). However, genograms can also be useful in nonclinical applications such as might be found in child welfare, health, educational, and forensic settings, among others. In these settings, genograms help the social worker and client quickly understand sources of stress that can exacerbate presenting problems and sources of support and resilient functioning that can serve as resources for problem solving.

Figure 10-1 presents a simplified genogram for a fictitious nuclear family. It shows three generations, including elders, adult children, and grandchildren. By convention, circles are usually used to identify females, boxes for males, and solid lines to denote birth and marriage relationships among members. Dashed lines are usually used to denote close relationships among unmarried partners. Deaths are indicated by an *X*, adoption is denoted as a line with an *A* above, and divorces are denoted using hash marks. Key dates (e.g., births, deaths, and marriages) are often included.

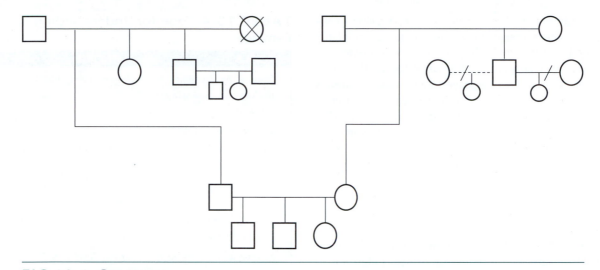

FIG 10-1 Genogram

A genogram such as the one shown in Figure 10-1 can be used as the basis for an in-depth assessment of family functioning and family system structure. Were a genogram to be completed for the Diaz family, it could be used to assess family resources, decision-making patterns, and patterns in family life-cycle adaptations. Certainly, the life-cycle changes being faced by the Diaz family are complex, and it may be useful to identify how family traditions bear on their decisions. For example, where other family members have successfully navigated the transition to some form of supported living arrangements in the past, social workers may see potential sources of support and evidence of family resilience. Moreover, a genogram could help to identify additional family members who can participate in the decision-making process.

However, the utility of genograms for other reasons should not be overlooked. For example, genograms can be a powerful tool to enhance engagement. As a genogram interview proceeds, the process of elaborating on family membership, relationships, and events often begs for family storytelling. Stories have a way of drawing attention and enhancing involvement in a way that a simple statement of facts does not. In some ways, people are wired to explain the world through stories (Dawes, 1999). Family storytelling can help family members become active participants in the social work process.

The genogram interview usually begins with a blank piece of paper and a pen, though some computer-based applications have also been developed. First, basic information about as many family members and their structural relationships as possible are arrayed on the paper, as in Figure 10-1. Often, experts recommend that genograms represent at least three generations of a family system so as to identify repetitive patterns (McGoldrick, Gerson, & Petry, 2008; Nichols, 2012). Next, the interview turns to questions related to family structure and process, depending on the purpose of the intervention and the needs of the assessment. For example, interview questions could include:

1. Circular questions about family relationships (e.g., "Who is closest to Mr. Diaz?" "Who in this family fights the most?" "What does [name] think the fights are about?")
2. Educational attainment (e.g., "Who are the college graduates in this family?")
3. Drugs and alcohol, trauma, mental health and health (e.g., "Which family members do you think have problems with alcoholism?" "Which of these have been successfully sober?")
4. Criminal/juvenile justice involvement (e.g., "Has anyone in your family spent time in prison or had trouble with the law?")
5. Resilience factors (e.g., "Who in this family has overcome this kind of problem before?")

The questions presented here are a limited set of examples. The specific questions you choose should be based on your assessment of what types of family patterns, what sets of relationships, and what historic events may be implicated in the presenting problem, either as sources of strain or as sources of resilient functioning.

Among the chief challenges when using genograms is the matter of time. Genograms can be highly detailed, and the storytelling involved can be time consuming, well beyond what is available to the social worker and family. Moreover, many social workers themselves feel drawn to family stories as a matter of curiosity and interest. Both factors, the time involved in storytelling and social worker curiosity, place an extra burden on social workers to manage time and to maintain a strong focus on the purpose of the interview. In some settings, genograms may be developed over a series of several meetings with the family. But these settings are the exception rather than the rule in contemporary social work practice. Thus, most social workers who employ genograms need to discipline their curiosity and exercise informed judgment to focus genogram interviews on factors that are most likely to reveal information relevant to the presenting problem and its resolution.

That said, it is not the case that genograms must be weighty, problem-saturated dialogues. Indeed, the genogram interview can be playful even as it elaborates on important family system structure characteristics. For example, the conventional symbols used to denote family members and relationships are not fixed, and a creative social worker might include silly drawings of pets, when these are mentioned by family members, or other pictorial devices imagined by the social worker or by family members themselves to represent events or family patterns. When straying from genogram conventions, the social worker should bear in mind that such additions should serve a specific purpose, such as engagement, that is linked to advancing the problem-solving effort.

Standardized Scales

In addition to the standardized assessment scales outlined in Chapters 8 and 9, the following instruments, summarized in Table 10-4, may be used as sources for understanding the family situation.

- The *Clinical Assessment Package for Assessing Risks and Strengths (CASPARS),* developed by Gilgun (1994, 2001), for families receiving mental health and child welfare services, responds to related concerns. Specifically, CASPARS measures both risks and protective factors related to family relationships, peer relationships, and sexuality.
- The *Culturalgram* (Congress, 1994) is a useful tool for assessing family dimensions in the context of

TABLE 10-4 Tools for Understanding Families

TOOLS	AUTHOR(S)
Clinical Assessment Package for Assessing Risks and Strengths (CASPARS)	Gilgun (1994, 2001)
Culturalgram	Congress (1994)
Ecomap	Hartman & Laird (1983)
Family Assessment Wheel	Mailick & Vigilante (1997)
Integrative Model by Level of Need	Kilpatrick & Cleveland (1993)
Multisystems Approach	Boyd-Franklin & Bry (2000)
Social Support Network Map	Tracy & Whittaker (1990)

culture, because "the systems view limits important cultural considerations" (Green, 1999, p. 8).

- The *ecomap* enables you to focus on the social context of families and interactions between the family and the larger society (Hartman & Laird, 1983).
- The *Family Assessment Wheel* allows you to examine the sociopolitical and cultural context of the family experience (Mailick & Vigilante, 1997).
- The *Integrative Model by Level of Need*, developed by Kilpatrick and Cleveland (1993), recognizes five levels of family need and functioning. The model is discussed and illustrated in Kilpatrick and Holland (2006). A Level 1 family's needs, for example, are related to basic survival, such as food, shelter, and medical care. Assessments of families at this level would therefore focus on their needs, strengths, and basic resources needed. In contrast, a Level 3 family has succeeded in satisfying its basic needs, so the assessment would focus on relationships, boundaries, alliances, and communication skills (Kilpatrick & Holland, 2006).
- The *Multisystems Approach* developed by Boyd-Franklin and Bry (2000) is derived from structural behavioral family therapy but is also applicable to social work practice with families. This approach recognizes that assessment and intervention goals involve families, as well as the systems external to the family that affect and serve as resources to families.

- The *Social Support Network Map* examines the structure and quality of the family's interconnected relationships and social supports (Tracy & Whittaker, 1990).

Hirayama, Hirayama, and Cetingok (1993) suggest both the ecomap and the genogram as useful tools in assisting refugees to understand patterns of social relationships and communication shifts associated with the tensions of immigrant and refugee relocation.

In addition to Gilgun's assessment package (1994, 2001), with its focus on strengths, other strengths-based measures for families and children include the *Family Functioning Style Scale (FSSS)* and the *Family Resources Scale (FRS)*. Both allow you to include strengths in your assessment of families and to consider a range of family functioning (i.e., capabilities). *ROPES*, a similar instrument cited in Jordan and Franklin (2003), considers family resources, options, possibilities, exceptions, and solutions (hence the instrument's name).

Often social workers are called upon to assess risks in families—for instance, in cases involving child neglect and abuse, probation, and family violence. **Risk assessments** are standardized structured actuarial tools that specify indicators in which a certain score predicts the probability of a behavior or condition. Risks can be either enduring or transient. Assessment tools, however, tend to emphasize enduring risks for which an intervention is warranted. Even in cases involving enduring risks, you should strive to conduct a balanced assessment, including micro-, mezzo-, and macro-level strengths, protective factors, and resilience. In this way, risks are not overly emphasized at the expense of strengths, and contributing environmental factors are acknowledged.

Because it can be difficult to find the right tool for a family or its problem, multiple screening inventory tools may be more appropriate for assessing family strengths and stressors (Hudson & McMurtry, 1997). Jordan and Franklin (2011) is a resource for further study on family assessment tools; see also Fontes (2005) and Dubowitz and DePanfilis (2000).

SUMMARY

The specialized family assessment skills and strategies presented in this chapter will help you to understand clients and their families within the context of a family systems framework. As can be seen by the review presented in this chapter, many of the presenting problems your clients will encounter are directly and indirectly influenced by family system arrangements and characteristics. When conducting family assessments, it is imperative that you identify those aspects of family system functioning that are most influential on the presenting problem, and that you also identify those aspects of family system functioning that represent sources of strength. Moreover, it is critical that you maintain a constant awareness of the role of culture in the definition of proper or normative family functioning. Fortunately, the assessment tools described in the chapter—including direct observation, interviewing with circular questioning, genograms, and standardized scales—can help you with these tasks.

COMPETENCY NOTES

EP 2   Engage Diversity and Difference in Practice

- Apply and communicate understanding of the importance of diversity and difference in shaping life experiences in practice at the micro, mezzo, and macro levels.
- Present oneself as a learner, and engage clients and constituencies as experts on their own experiences.
- Apply self-awareness and self-regulation to manage the influence of personal biases and values in working with diverse clients and constituencies.

EP 3   Advance Human Rights and Social, Economic, and Environmental Justice

- Apply an understanding of social, economic, and environmental justice to advocate for human rights at the individual and system levels.

EP 7   Assess Individuals, Families, Groups, Organizations, and Communities

- Collect and organize data, and apply critical thinking to interpret information from clients and constituencies.
- Apply knowledge of human behavior and the social environment, person-in-environment, and other multidisciplinary theoretical frameworks in the analysis of assessment data from clients and constituencies.

SKILL DEVELOPMENT EXERCISES

in Assessing Families

To develop your skills in assessing families, take some time to answer the following questions about your own family and experiences:

1. What are the preferred communication styles in your family?
2. Describe the different forms of power in your family, and identify who the holders are. Specify how the power in your family, in whatever form, is culturally constructed.
3. Describe how boundary maintenance, internal and external, operates in your family.
4. How are decisions made in your family, and who is involved in the process?
5. Reflecting on marginalized families that you have worked with, write a brief response to the assertion in this chapter that oppression is a normative experience for some families.

6. Review the guidelines for effective decision making, and assess your own family's adherence to these guidelines. If appropriate, identify cultural variants.
7. Put yourself in the position of a teen mother who is meeting with a social worker for the first time. What would you like to be the starting point in your initial contact?
8. Develop a set of questions or indicators that you could use to assess family strengths.
9. Think of ways in which client strengths may have a minor or major role in your experience with agencies, funding resources, and policy makers. How would you articulate the strengths perspective to any one or all of these organizations?
10. As you observe the interactions between Jackie and Anna in the video "Home for the Holidays 1," identify the barriers to communication using Table 10-3.

CHAPTER 11

Forming and Assessing Social Work Groups

Chapter Overview

Social workers frequently practice with groups. Groups instill hope and encouragement, universalize experiences, break down isolation, and allow members to experience altruism and the satisfaction of helping others (Pack-Brown, Whittington-Clark, & Parker, 1998). In groups, clients grapple with existential questions, learn coping skills for life experiences, and experience healing through cohesion and mutuality. These powerful features are common to an array of well-designed and well-executed treatment groups (K. E. Reid, 2002). Groups can provide a powerful mechanism for change, whether they are used as the only intervention or in conjunction with individual counseling, family work, or other treatments.

Social workers plan and lead groups in a variety of settings and with an array of populations. Whichever type of group the social worker leads, he or she must (1) create a group that can effectively serve the purpose for which it was designed, (2) accurately assess individual and group dynamics, and (3) intervene effectively to modify processes that are affecting the group's achievement of its goals. The success or failure of a group frequently rests on the groundwork that takes place before the group even meets. The social worker must thoughtfully and skillfully visualize a group and determine its purpose,

structure, and composition. Without careful forethought in creating group structure and atmosphere, all assessment and intervention efforts will be jeopardized by the lack of a firm foundation.

This chapter describes essential processes in developing the purpose of the group, forming and structuring the group, and conducting appropriate assessments with a variety of group types. It provides a framework that will enable you to effectively form groups and accurately assess group processes, laying the foundation for effective group interventions, the subject of Chapter 16. In both group work chapters, you will see references to the HEART (Healthy Eating, Attitudes, Relationships and Thoughts) group for teenage girls who are overweight. In these chapters, you will meet the members and read transcripts that demonstrate how the group progresses through the phases of development and the joys and struggles that accompany them.

After reading this chapter, you will be able to:

- Describe the distinctions between treatment groups and task groups, as well as different group subtypes.

- Describe the steps in planning groups.

- Describe the steps in recruiting and screening group members.

- Develop individual and group goals.

- Identify individual and group patterns in behaviors and communications.

- Understand the ethical considerations in group work.

- Apply group concepts to the HEART group.

- Describe the function of technology-mediated and single-session groups.

EPAS Competencies in Chapter 11

This chapter will give you the information needed to meet the following competencies:

- Competency 1: Demonstrate Ethical and Professional Behavior

- Competency 2: Engage Diversity and Difference in Practice

- Competency 4: Engage in Practice-Informed Research and Research-Informed Practice

- Competency 6: Engage with Individuals, Families, Groups, Organizations, and Communities

- Competency 7: Assess Individuals, Families, Groups, Organizations, and Communities

- Competency 8: Intervene with Individuals, Families, Groups, Organizations, and Communities

CLASSIFICATION OF GROUPS

Barker (2003) defines **group work** as occurring when "small numbers of people who share similar interests or common problems convene regularly and engage in activities designed to achieve certain objectives" (p. 404). Thus, social work practice with groups is goal directed.

Social workers are typically associated with two types of groups: treatment groups and task groups. In **treatment groups**, the focus is on helping individuals to make changes by seeking to enhance their socioemotional well-being through the development of social skills, education, and therapy. In such groups, communications are open, and members are encouraged to interact actively.

In **task groups**, the focus may be on the group as a whole as the unit of change or the group as a mechanism for influencing the individual members. Communications are more structured, focusing on discussion of a particular issue or agenda item. Examples of task

groups include committees, governing boards, treatment teams, and task forces that seek to complete a project or develop a product.

Member roles in treatment groups evolve as a result of interaction; in task groups, they may be assigned or elected (e.g., facilitator, minutes taker) or associated with the member's professional role (e.g., the psychiatrist in a treatment team). Procedures in treatment groups may be flexible or formal, depending on the group; task groups usually follow formal agendas and rules.

In addition, treatment groups and task groups differ with respect to participant self-disclosure, confidentiality, and evaluation. In treatment groups, self-disclosure is expected to be high, proceedings are kept within the group, and group

EP 6 and 7

success is based on individual members' success in meeting the treatment goals. In task groups, self-disclosure is low, proceedings may be private or open to the public, and the success of the group is based on members accomplishing a task, fulfilling a particular charge, or producing a result.

Traditionally, task and treatment groups have involved face-to-face meetings of group members, and the preponderance of groups today fit that model. However, with technological advances, groups can be convened electronically in synchronous (real-time) or asynchronous (anytime) formats (Meier, 2006). Such groups can meet through written Internet postings and discussion forums, as well as teleconference or videoconference formats. Technology-mediated groups pose unique advantages and challenges in service delivery, which will be noted throughout this chapter and Chapter 16.

Treatment Group Subtypes

Toseland and Rivas (2009) further refine their classification of treatment groups by describing subtypes that are characterized by their unique purposes:

1. **Support groups** help members cope with life stresses by revitalizing coping skills so that members can more effectively adapt to life events (e.g., schoolchildren meeting to discuss the effect of divorce, people with cancer discussing the effects of the disease and how to cope with it, bereaved people meeting to discuss loss and grief) (Magen & Glajchen, 1999).

2. **Educational groups** have the primary purpose of helping members learn about themselves and

their society (e.g., an adolescent sexuality group, a diabetes management group, a heart attack recovery group, a psychoeducational group for relatives of people with major mental illnesses).

3. **Growth groups** stress self-improvement, offering members opportunities to expand their capabilities and self-awareness and make personal changes (e.g., a personal development group or a communication enhancement group for couples). Growth groups contrast with other types of groups in that they focus on promoting socioemotional health rather than alleviating socioemotional deficits.

4. **Therapy groups** help members change their behavior, cope with or ameliorate their personal problems, or rehabilitate themselves after a social or health trauma (e.g., a drug addiction group, a PTSD group, an anger management group, a dialectical behavior therapy group for persons diagnosed with personality disorders). Although support and growth are also emphasized, therapy groups primarily focus on remediation and rehabilitation.

5. **Socialization groups** facilitate transitions through developmental stages, from one role or environment to another, through improved interpersonal relationships or social skills. Such groups often employ program activities, structured exercises, role-plays, and the like (e.g., a social club for formerly institutionalized persons, a social skills group for children who have difficulty making friends, a current events group for residents in an assisted living facility).

EP 6

Whatever the subtype, treatment groups take place in a variety of public and private settings serving both voluntary and involuntary clients. As noted above, some "meet" virtually in electronic and online groups (Carr, 2004; Fingeld, 2000; Schopler, Galinsky, & Abell, 1997). Social workers also find that groups are useful for supporting people who may traditionally have been marginalized by society, such as people of color, lesbian/gay/bisexual/transgender (LGBT) individuals, older adults, and those with stigmatizing illnesses (Salmon & Graziano, 2004; Saulnier, 1997; Schopler, Galinsky, Davis, & Despard, 1996). Involuntary clients, such as perpetrators of domestic violence and adolescents in correctional settings, may also benefit from the mutuality found in groups (Goodman, 1997; Rooney & Chovanec, 2004; Thomas & Caplan, 1997). Groups can also be used to foster

intergroup understanding and conflict reduction—for example, between clashing neighbors or racial and ethnic groups (Bargal, 2004).

Some group types overlap as they are designed to meet multiple purposes. For example, Bradshaw (1996) describes groups for persons with schizophrenia that simultaneously provide therapy, have a major educational component, and offer support. Groups to assist people who are caregivers for loved ones provide support as well as education and resource exchanges. A men's cooking group at a community center is intended to educate members, prepare them with skills, and provide socialization for participants, all of whom are widowed or newly divorced (Northen & Kurland, 2001). A group of teens convened after the shootings at Columbine High School helped to facilitate intergenerational communication and allowed youth the opportunity to articulate their fears and needs, in contrast to safety measures instituted by authorities without their input (Malekoff, 2006). Such groups offer the opportunity for social reform in the midst of individual change.

Self-Help Groups

In **self-help groups**, members have central shared concerns, such as coping with addiction, illness, or obesity. These groups are distinguished from treatment and task groups by the fact that they are led by nonprofessionals who are managing the same issues as members of the group, even though a social worker or other professional may have aided in the development, sponsorship, or coordination of the group.

Self-help groups emphasize interpersonal support and the creation of an environment in which individuals may retake charge of their lives. These groups offer resources and support for such shared problems as addictions, aggressive behavior, mental illness, disabilities, the death of a child, gambling, weight control, family violence, and AIDS, among others. It is the social worker's task to offer support and consultation to such groups without taking them over. For example, in a self-help group for Temporary Aid for Needy Families (TANF) recipients, the social service provider's role was to initiate the group, assist a member to become the group facilitator, and evaluate the group's effectiveness. Other members took active roles on tasks such as advertising, recruitment, supportive contact between meetings, and outreach to inform agencies of the group (Anderson-Butcher, Khairallah, & Race-Bigelow, 2004).

Task Group Subtypes

EP 6 and 7

Social workers in direct practice commonly participate in task groups as members or facilitators. Task groups are generally organized into three different subtypes (Toseland & Rivas, 2009):

1. *Groups that are created to meet client needs:* These include **treatment teams** that meet regularly to review cases or assure quality of care. In **case conferences**, all of the professionals working with a particular client or family may come together to share assessment findings or develop an interdisciplinary care plan. These meetings may be a one-time occurrence or they may meet regularly to coordinate services. **Staff development teams** may be responsible for doing needs assessments and planning, delivering, and evaluating educational sessions to assure that employees have the knowledge and skills to properly assist clientele. These responsibilities may also be delegated to supervisory teams or similar groups. In some facilities, **resident councils** composed of clients engage in self-governance when issues arise within the residence, and they also represent the needs of residents to administrative or other decision-making bodies.

2. *Groups that are intended to meet organizational needs:* In contrast to the groups in subtype 1, these task groups are generally responsible for the governance and well-being of an institution, not the clientele. For example all nonprofit organizations have **boards of directors**, **trustees**, or **governors**, which have fiduciary responsibility (legal and financial accountability) for the operation of the agency. Public human service agencies often have advisory boards. These groups may not have decision-making power, but they may be chartered to review services, statistics, incidents, and other activities and issue recommendations about the agency. All organizations utilize another form of task groups, **committees**, to get work done. Committees may be standing (established and ongoing) or ad hoc (time-limited). Examples of standing committees include a grievance committee, the management team, a fundraising team, government relations, and so on. Examples of ad hoc committees include search committees to fill vacant positions, planning groups for special events, or groups to prepare for accreditation, mergers, or other infrequent but significant occasions. **Focus groups** may be convened to help organizations understand service needs, evaluate programs, or gather feedback on proposed changes. These groups typically meet once and are highly structured to achieve the intended purpose.

3. *Groups that address community needs:* In this context, "community" refers broadly to the needs of a geographic community or a community of interest or affiliation. Social workers may be members or facilitators of such groups. For example, social workers might facilitate a meeting of citizens to respond to hate crimes, community violence, or environmental disasters. Social workers may be members of multiagency coalitions, convened to lobby for improved funding, examine service gaps, or coordinate programs. Social workers who are members of professional organizations, such as the National Association of Social Workers (NASW), may be on committees to change licensing laws, revise practice standards, or advocate for improved reimbursement for services.

Although group types may differ, several underlying principles are common to all forms of group work practice. We will begin with the evidence base supporting group work, then consider common features of creating and assessing treatment groups, and finally proceed to task groups.

THE EVIDENCE BASE FOR GROUPS

EP 4

Although the evidence base for the efficacy of groups is growing, there are particular challenges to conducting research with treatment groups, including problems maintaining equivalent control conditions, monitoring specific process events that affect outcomes, ensuring that the treatment plan is implemented as intended, and isolating the multiple parts that interact to create change (Chen, Kakkad, & Balzano, 2008; Garvin, 2011). Meta-analyses of research on group outcomes (Burlingame, Fuhriman, & Mosier, 2003; Burlingame, MacKenzie, & Strauss, 2004) have found that group treatment results in reliable positive improvement in comparison with controls, but that examination of what might explain differences in client outcomes in groups is still lacking. These analyses note that patient characteristics, such as personality and initial level of problems, robustly predict process and outcome, but other factors, such as group structure, leader characteristics, and the formal change theories of groups, need to be more closely examined to determine their impact on outcomes.

Utilizing the best existing evidence, the American Group Psychotherapy Association has compiled a comprehensive set of practice guidelines for group work, covering topics from creating successful therapy groups to preparation and pregroup training, group development and process, ethical practice and reducing adverse outcomes, and group termination (Bernard et al., 2007).

Throughout this chapter and Chapter 16, we incorporate research findings supporting particular types of groups and group strategies. Until research-supported group treatments evolve more fully, group leaders will need to take responsibility for implementing evidence-based practices. Macgowan (2008) offers several recommendations to assist with this task:

- Utilize critical thinking in examining anticipated change processes and pathways and build on introductory knowledge of research and group work in building the evidence base.
- Specify and measure variables such as problems and goals, the change theory of the group, individual member characteristics, group structural elements, group process, and leader characteristics.
- Make research questions for assessing groups "Member-relevant, Answerable, Practical (MAP)" (p. 21) and identify a specific challenge, intervention, and outcome to be studied.

Similarly, the clinician can utilize a "local clinical scientist" approach to employ scientific thinking when constructing and leading groups, thereby obtaining practice-based evidence to identify salient processes and outcomes for future refinement.

FORMATION OF TREATMENT GROUPS

The success or failure of a treatment group rests to a large extent on the thoughtful creation of the group and the careful selection and preparation of members for the group experience. In this section, you will learn the steps needed to foster a positive group outcome. Table 11-1 lists these steps.

Identifying the Need for the Group

The decision to offer services through groups can arise from a number of origins. Some agencies adopt

TABLE 11-1 Considerations in Forming and Starting Treatment Groups

Identify the Need for the Group

Establish the Group Purpose

Decide on Leadership

Determine Group Composition

Choose an Open or Closed Group

Determine Group Size and Location

Set the Frequency and Duration of Meetings

Conduct Preliminary Interviews

Determine the Group Structure

Formulate Preliminary Group Guidelines

group-based services as their primary modality because of ideological or practice considerations or as a strategy to meet efficiency or cost-containment targets. Sometimes practitioners or agencies determine that groups are needed based on the patterns of problems being presented and the evidence that group modalities are the most effective means for addressing these problems. Sometimes group work is indicated when existing groups require social work interventions—for example, in school or community settings where factional conflicts are threatening the safety of the learning environment. Social workers may construct groups based on needs assessments sparked by observations of individual clients whose needs could be addressed through mutual aid with others facing the same challenges (Toseland & Rivas, 2009). As a result, workers might contact colleagues in their own or other agencies to substantiate the need, begin recruitment, or advertise the group.

Establishing the Group Purpose

Clarifying the overall purpose of a group is vital because the group's objectives influence all the processes that follow, including recruiting and selecting members, deciding on the group's duration, identifying its size and content, and determining meeting location and time. Kurland and Salmon (1998) describe several common problems to avoid in developing an appropriate group purpose:

1. Group purposes are promoted without adequate consideration of service users' needs. That is, the purpose may make sense to the prospective leaders or the agency, but not to the potential clients.

For example, clients may be assembled because they share a status, such as having a serious and persistent illness and living independently. From the viewpoint of these potential clients, a group that relates to a commonly perceived need such as recreation or socializing may be more attractive than grouping by status.

2. The purpose of the group is confused with the content. For example, the group's purpose is described in terms of what the members will do in the group—their activities—rather than the outcome toward which those activities are directed.

3. The purpose of the group is stated too generally so that it is vague and meaningless to potential members and provides little direction to prospective leaders.

4. Leaders are reluctant to share their perceptions about the purpose, leaving members to wonder why they are there.

5. The group is formed with a "public" purpose that conflicts with its actual hidden purpose. For example, prospective members may not know the basis on which they were contacted to become part of a group. Potential clients may be invited to join on the basis of the fact that they overuse prescription drugs, yet this commonality is not shared with them.

6. Group purposes may be misunderstood as static rather than dynamic (adjusting to the evolving desires and needs of the members).

General group purposes may include overarching goals such as the following:

- To provide a forum for single parents of young children to meet for socialization and education about child development
- To participate in decision making that affects the quality of life in a nursing home by establishing a governing council for residents
- "To teach young probationers how to protect their physical safety and avoid rearrest by adopting pro-social thinking and actions" (Goodman, Getzel, & Ford, 1996, p. 375)
- "To enhance the development of personal and racial identity as well as professional advancement" of African American women (Pack-Brown, Whittington-Clark, & Parker, 1998, p. xi)

The overall purpose of a planned group should be established by the social worker in consultation with agency administrators and consumers prior to forming the group; the goals subsequently negotiated by the group should reflect the perspectives of those three stakeholders. If the agency's goals differ from the social worker's goals, those involved must negotiate a general group purpose that is agreeable to both parties. Failing to do so may lead to ambiguity in the group, send mixed messages, and triangulate its members.

The Client's Perspective

The potential member of a group wants some questions answered: "Why should I join this group? What is in it for me? What will it do for me? Will it help me?" (Kurland & Salmon, 1998, pp. 7–8). The answers to these questions will determine whether individuals join a group and, later, whether they continue attending. The potential member who is mandated or pressured to attend also wants to know the answers to these questions, even if the consequences of failure to join or attend are more punishing for this individual than they would be for the voluntary client.

EP 7

At the point of entry into a group, the service user's goals may differ considerably from those of either the agency or the social worker. Schopler and Galinsky (1974) note that the client's goals may be influenced by many internal or external forces, such as the expectations of others and the client's personal comfort, motivation, and past experiences in group settings. During group formation, the social worker must carefully explore clients' expectations of the group, help them to develop individual and collective goals that are realistically achievable, and negotiate between individual, group, and agency purposes.

For example, several members of the HEART group for overweight teen girls joined because their relatives insisted they do so. As such, the leader should acknowledge members' goals of avoiding conflict or coercion from family members as a condition for participation in the group. Alongside these goals, members may have individual goals, such as controlling unhealthy eating behaviors, seeking advice and support from others in similar situations, improving self-esteem, addressing interpersonal difficulties with parents and peers, reducing symptoms of depression and anxiety, and learning weight loss techniques pertaining to diet and exercise. Even entirely voluntary groups operate best when the leaders' and the members' purposes are compatible or when the purposes of the two diverge but the social worker goes along with the group's purpose. Conversely, when the social worker insists on goals that are incompatible with members' needs and wishes, the groups may dissolve prematurely or become preoccupied with conflict.

Deciding on Leadership

Once the group's purpose is established, group planners must consider whether individual or co-leadership will be necessary to assist the group in meeting its aims. Many types of groups benefit from co-leadership. Having two leaders can provide additional eyes and ears for the group, with one leader specifically attending to content and the other taking note of the process and **meta-messages** (underlying messages) by group members. Co-leaders bring different perspectives, backgrounds, and personalities to the group process, which can appeal to a wider array of members than a single leader might. They can also use their interactions to model effective communication and problem solving (Jacobs, Masson, & Harvill, 1998). In addition, two leaders can keep a watchful eye on each other, providing feedback and noting patterns where individual facilitators' needs and motives may impede effective management of the group (Corey et al., 2004).

Sometimes co-leadership is necessary for practical reasons. With two leaders, one can check on a member who has left the room or has been asked to take a time-out, while the other continues working with the group. Co-leadership can provide continuity if illness or another emergency on the part of one leader might otherwise result in cancellation of a session. With some populations, two leaders may help send a message of authority in an otherwise disruptive group; they may also provide a sense of physical safety and protection from liability by their very presence (Carrell, 2000). In some groups, such as those for men accused of partner violence, mixed-gender co-leaders can provide "deliberate and strategic modeling of alternative forms of male-female interactions" (Nosko & Wallace, 1997, p. 5).

Of course, co-leadership is sometimes impractical because of the costs involved and the time needed to coordinate roles, plan the group sessions, and debrief together. In managing the cost concern, some agencies utilize volunteers or "program graduates"—consumers who have had group training and can bring personal experiences to the group process.

Co-leaders who work together on a regular basis may find increased efficiencies as they formulate a common "curriculum" for the group and develop comfort and rapport with each other. Such coordination is essential to avoid disruptive rivalries or to prevent members from pitting the co-leaders against each other (Northen & Kurland, 2001). As Levine and Dang (1979) note, "co-therapists constitute an inner group that must work through its own process while facilitating the progress of the larger group" (p. 175). Nosko and Wallace (1997) suggest three ground rules for effective co-leadership: "establish a common theoretical orientation; agree on the identification and handling of problems; and agree on what constitutes the appropriate quantity and quality of each leader's participation" (p. 7). Because characteristics such as gender and race affect personal interactions and are reflected in power dynamics and status expectations, co-leaders must deliberately share all group functions and roles (such as confrontation and support). In doing so, they model equality, undo damaging expectations that members may hold, and help the group adopt norms of fairness and flexibility outside of members' stereotyped notions.

Determining Group Composition

Composition refers to the selection of members for the group. On occasion, composition may be predetermined—for example, when the group consists of all residents in a group home, all patients preparing for discharge, or all motorists mandated to attend due to charges of driving while intoxicated. In rural areas or other settings, the leader may work with a naturally formed group that has already developed around a common problem, rather than create and recruit a new group (Gumpert & Saltman, 1998).

When the leader is responsible for deciding the group's composition, the overriding factor in selecting members is whether a candidate is interested in group services, motivated to make changes, and likely to be a productive group member. Another key factor is the likelihood of that person being compatible with other members in the group. Social workers usually consider gender, age, intellectual ability, education, personality, and other features when composing group membership, weighing the relative metrics of homogeneity versus heterogeneity among members. Significant homogeneity in personal characteristics and purpose for joining the group is necessary to facilitate communication and group cohesion. Without such commonality, members will have little basis for interacting with one another. Toseland and Rivas (2009), for example, identify levels

EP 2, 6, and 7

of education, cultural background, degree of expertise relative to the group task, and communication ability as characteristics vital to creating group homogeneity.

Sometimes, the group's purpose will influence the decision for similarity among certain characteristics. For example, there are advantages to creating single-gender groups when the issues differ by gender or when mixed groups might inhibit member comfort or participation. Characteristics such as age, development, or the nature of the problem might also require homogeneity among members. For example, in composing a group for parents who have lost children, those members whose loved ones were very young when they died might have different needs and issues than those whose offspring were adults when they passed away. In cognitive behavioral groups for troubled youth, similarity in age and socioemotional development is essential to avoid dominance by older members who are more mature (Rose, 1998).

Conversely, some diversity among members with respect to coping skills, life experience, and levels of expertise fosters learning and introduces members to differing viewpoints, problem-solving skills, and ways of communicating. To attain the desired outcomes of support, learning, and mutual aid, a treatment group, for example, might include members from different cultures, social classes, occupations, or geographic areas. Multicultural diversity in group membership can bring a variety of perspectives and resources to the group's efforts (Anderson, 2007). Heterogeneity is also vital in task group membership so that the group has sufficient resources to fulfill its responsibilities and efficiently divide the labor when dealing with complex tasks (Toseland & Rivas, 2009). The challenge in any type of group is to attain a workable balance between differences and similarities of members, given the group's purpose.

Corey and Corey (2006) caution against including members in voluntary groups whose behavior or pathology is extreme, inasmuch as some people reduce the available energy of the group for productive work and interfere significantly in the development of group cohesion. This is particularly true of individuals who have a need to monopolize and dominate, hostile or aggressive people with a need to act out, and people who are extremely self-centered and seek a group as an audience. Others who are generally less likely to benefit from most groups are people who are in a state of extreme crisis, who are suicidal, who are highly suspicious, or who are lacking in ego strength and prone to fragmented and bizarre behavior (Milgram & Rubin, 1992).

A decision to include or exclude a prospective member has a lot to do with the purposes of the group. For example, a person with alcoholism might be excluded from a personal growth group but appropriately included in a homogeneous group of individuals who wrestle with various types of addictions. Oppositional behavior may be a common denominator in some groups, such as those formed to address domestic violence and delinquency (Milgram & Rubin, 1992). In such cases, this behavior would not be a criterion for exclusion but rather a central problem for work. An older woman raising her grandchildren might find little benefit in a parenting group where the focus is on education for first-time parents. This does not mean that the grandparent is not in need of group assistance, but rather that it is important for her needs to be congruent with the group purpose and composition. Turner (2011) describes the decision making involved in creating a "Young Women's Group" in which the membership "was open not only to biological females but also to anyone who identified along the feminine spectrum in some way, whether in body, gender identity, or both" (p. 249). The co-facilitators decided that the composition decisions were congruent with the group's focus on discussions of gender and sexuality, and they also broadened the group's purpose to accommodate the membership's needs.

Garvin (1987) warns against including in a treatment group a member who is very different from the others, for the danger is that this person "will be perceived as undesirable or, in sociological terms, deviant by the other members" (p. 65). Differences in socioeconomic status, age, race, problem history, or cognitive abilities may lead to the individual's discomfort and difficulty in affiliating with the group. It may also produce member behaviors that isolate or scapegoat the person. "Outliers" should be avoided, both for the satisfaction of the individual and for the health of the group. When group composition could potentially lead to the isolation of a member, Garvin recommends enrolling another member who "is either similar to the person in question or who is somewhere in the 'middle,' thus creating a continuum of member characteristics" (p. 65) and assisting in establishing the members' affiliation and comfort.

Choosing an Open or Closed Group

Groups may have either an **open format**, in which the group remains open to enrolling new members, or a **closed format**, in which   EP 6 and 7

no new members are added once the group gets under way. Typically, groups that are open or closed in terms of admitting new members are also open or closed in regard to their duration. Alcoholics Anonymous and Weight Watchers are examples of open-ended and open membership groups. An ongoing symptom management group in an inpatient psychiatric setting would be open, as the census of the unit fluctuates daily with admissions and discharges. A 10-week medication management group, an eight-session grief group, and a semester-long social skills group would be examples of closed membership, closed-ended groups.

Open-ended groups are generally used for helping clients cope with transitions and crises, providing support, acting as a means for assessment, and facilitating outreach (Schopler & Galinsky, 1981). Having open-ended groups ensures that a group is immediately available at a time of crisis. An open format itself presents different models (Henry, 1988; Reid, 1991), including the **drop-in** (or **drop-out**) **model** in which members are self-selecting, entry criteria are very broad, and members attend whenever they wish for an indefinite period. In the **replacement model**, the leader immediately identifies someone to fill a group vacancy. In the **re-formed model**, group members contract to attend for a set period of time, during which no new members are added but original members may drop out. At the end of the contract period, a new group is formed consisting of some old and some new members.

The choice of format depends on the purpose of the group, the setting, and the population served. An open format provides the opportunity for new members to bring fresh perspectives to the group and offers immediate support for those in need, who come when they need to and stay as long as they choose. At the same time, the instability of this format discourages members from developing the trust and confidence to openly share and explore their problems—a strong feature of the closed-ended group. Frequent changes of membership may also disrupt the work of the open-ended group, although the developmental patterns in such groups vary according to how many new members enter and the frequency of turnover (Galinsky & Schopler, 1989). Leaders of open-ended groups need to be attuned to clients being at different places in the group process and be able to work with core members to carry forward the particular group's traditions (Schopler & Galinsky, 1981).

Advantages associated with a closed group include higher group morale, greater predictability for role behaviors, and an increased sense of cooperation among members. Disadvantages are that the group may not be open to members when potential participants are ready to make use of it and that, if too many members drop out, the group process will be drastically affected by the high rate of attrition.

Single-session groups are intended to meet only once with a given membership. Some single-session groups are designed for only one meeting, as with a group designed to educate college students about high-risk drinking (Fried & Dunn, 2012) or a critical incident debriefing group to assist people affected by a traumatic event such as a workplace shooting (Reynolds & Jones, 1996). Other single-session groups meet routinely, for example, weekly on an acute care hospital unit, but the membership fluctuates at each session based on the census of the unit at a given time, resulting in diminished continuity of experience for group members.

Determining Group Size and Location

The size of the group depends in large part on its purpose, the age of clients, the type of problems to be explored, and the needs of members. Seven to 10 members is usually an optimal number for a group with an emphasis on close relationships (Reid, 2002). Bertcher and Maple (1985) suggest that the group should be small enough to allow it to achieve its purpose yet large enough to ensure that members have a satisfying experience. As such, educational and task groups may accommodate more members than would therapy and support groups, where cohesion is central to the group progress.

The location of group meetings should be selected with image and convenience in mind. **Image** refers to the impression that the site makes on members—the message it conveys that may attract them to the group or make them uncomfortable in attending. For example, a parenting group held at a school building may not be attractive to potential members if their own experiences with education or with the particular school system have been unfavorable. A parenting group that meets at a local YMCA/YWCA or community center may be perceived as comfortable to members who are used to going there for their children's sports or other neighborhood events.

Convenience refers to the accessibility of the site for those people whom the group chooses to attract. For example, is the site readily accessible to a public transportation line for those who do not own automobiles? Is it safe, with plenty of parking, and easy to find for those who may be uncomfortable venturing out at night? Social workers who are familiar with a community might make note of the "participation patterns" of residents, as these may reveal neutral locations for meetings (Gumpert & Saltman, 1998).

Leaders may have little choice over the meeting location if the sponsoring agency's site must be used. Those planning groups should take the image and accessibility of the location into account, however, when recruiting prospective members or when diagnosing problems related to group membership.

Setting the Frequency and Duration of Meetings

Closed groups benefit from having a termination date at the outset, which encourages productive work. Regarding the possible life span of a group, Corey and Corey (2006) note: "The duration varies from group to group, depending on the type of group and the population. The group should be long enough to allow for cohesion and productive work yet not so long that the group seems to drag on interminably" (p. 92). For a time-limited therapy group, Reid (1991) recommends approximately 20 sessions, stating that this length provides adequate time for cohesiveness and a sense of trust to develop. Others might suggest that a 20-session limit is not feasible, that attrition and other obligations may erode participation, and that ending ahead of the planned time may lead to an unwarranted sense of failure. Shorter durations, during which attendance can be assured, may leave clients "wanting more" but with a sense of accomplishment and goal achievement at the group's conclusion. In general, short-term groups vary between 1 and 12 sessions, with the shorter-duration groups being targeted at crisis situations, anxiety alleviation, and educational programs (Northen & Kurland, 2001).

Conducting Preliminary Interviews

EP 7

Before convening a treatment group, social workers often meet individually with potential group members for the purpose of screening participants, establishing rapport, exploring relevant concerns, formulating initial contracts with those motivated to join the group, and clarifying limits and options for involuntary members. Individual interviews are essential to providing effective group composition; they ensure that the members are selected according to predetermined criteria and possess the behavioral or personality attributes needed for them to make effective use of the group experience.

There are several advantages to having pregroup meetings with potential members:

- When creating a group of involuntary clients, interviews allow the opportunity to clarify participants' options and identify acknowledged as well as attributed problems.
- In rural areas, preliminary interviews provide an opportunity to notify potential members that others they know might attend; in doing so, the group leader can address any concerns that this group composition provokes.
- With groups drawn from populations who may be uncomfortable or unfamiliar with group treatment, a pregroup orientation can acquaint prospective members with the treatment process, help them understand what to expect, reduce apprehension, and learn how best to participate (Pack-Brown, Whittington-Clark, & Parker, 1998; Subramanian, Hernandez, & Martinez, 1995).
- Interviews help leaders obtain valuable information to guide interventions in early sessions, aiding in the efficiency and effectiveness of services.
- Preliminary interviews enable social workers to enter the initial group sessions with a previously established relationship with each member—a distinct advantage given that leaders must attend to multiple communication processes at both individual and group levels.
- Previous knowledge facilitates the leader's understanding of the members' behaviors and allows the leader to focus more fully on group processes and the task of assisting members to develop relationships with one another. For example, the leaders in one bereavement support group knew from initial interviews that two members' losses had been due to murder. This information alerted them to these members' unique concerns and needs and fostered a connection between the two participants who shared a common experience.
- Establishing rapport with the leader is also beneficial for members in that it enables them to feel more at ease and to open up more readily in the first meeting.

Social workers should focus on the following in preliminary interviews:

1. *Orient potential members to proposed goals and purposes of the group, its content and structure, the leader's philosophy and style in managing*

group processes, and the roles of the leader and group members. This is also a good time to identify expectations, such as attendance, confidentiality, the appropriateness of relating to members outside the group, and so on (Yalom, 2005). With involuntary groups, you must distinguish between non-negotiable rules and policies, such as attendance expectations and general themes to be discussed, and negotiable norms and procedures, such as arrangements for breaks, food, and selection of particular topics and their order.

In preliminary meetings, you should also elicit each client's reactions and suggestions on ways that the group might better meet his or her unique needs. Orientation should also address details such as the time and place of meetings, length of sessions, and the like. In addition, the social worker may wish to emphasize commonalities that the client may share with other persons considering group membership, such as problems, interests, concerns, or objectives.

2. *Elicit information on the individual's prior group experiences*, including the nature of the client's relationship with the leader and other members, his or her style of relating in the previous group, the goals that he or she accomplished, and the personal growth that was achieved. Social workers should anticipate the possibility of negative reactions, acknowledge them, and emphasize ways that this group experience can be more fulfilling and beneficial.

3. *Elicit, explore, and clarify the clients' problems*, and identify those that are appropriate for the proposed group. In some instances, either because clients are reluctant to participate in the group or because their problems appear to be more appropriately handled through other treatment modalities or community agencies, you may need to refer them to other resources.

4. *Explore the service user's hopes, aspirations, and expectations* regarding the proposed group (e.g., "What would you like to be different in your life as a result of your attending this group?").

5. *Identify specific goals that the person wishes to accomplish*, discuss whether these goals can be attained through the proposed group, and determine the client's views as to whether the group is an appropriate vehicle for resolving his or her problems. Sharing examples of goals that prior members have chosen, in addition to mandated goals, may make the group more attractive to the reluctant member.

6. *Mutually develop a profile of the client's strengths and attributes*, and determine the ways he/she will contribute to the group and capacities that the client might like to enhance through work in the group.

7. *Identify and explore potential obstacles or reservations* about participating in the group, including shyness or discomfort in group situations, opposition from significant others about entering the group, a heavy schedule that might preclude attending all group meetings, or problems with transportation or child care. In addition to exploring these barriers to group membership, the social worker and client may generate possible alternatives or determine whether the obstacles are so difficult to overcome that participation is unwise at this time.

8. *Ensure that screening for the group is a two-way process.* Potential members should have the opportunity to interview the group leader and determine whether the group is appropriate for their problems and interests and whether the relationship with the leader will likely facilitate a successful outcome.

Determining the Group Structure

In addition to determining the group's purpose, goals, composition, duration, and other elements, leaders must attend to the **group structure**, or how the time in the group will be used to most effectively meet the needs of participants. The result should be a clearly conceptualized format that provides the means for evaluating group and individual progress. The structure should also be flexible enough to accommodate differing group processes and the unique needs of members as they emerge. To ensure its continued functionality, review the format periodically throughout the life of the group.

The following activities will assist you and your members to focus your energies so as to achieve therapeutic objectives effectively and efficiently:

EP 6 and 7

1. Define group and individual goals in behavioral terms, and rank them according to priority.

2. Develop an overall plan that organizes the work to be done within the number of sessions allocated by the group to achieve its goals. The leader (or co-leaders) should have done preliminary work on this plan while designing the group.

3. Specify behavioral tasks (homework) to be accomplished outside the group each week that will assist individuals to make the desired changes.

TABLE 11-2 Example of a Group Format

15 MINUTES	1 HOUR	15 MINUTES
Checking in Reviewing and monitoring tasks	Focusing on relevant content (presentation and discussion) Mutual problem solving Formulating tasks Plan for the week	Summarizing plan for the week Evaluating group session

4. Achieve agreement among members concerning the weekly format and agenda—that is, how time will be allocated each week to achieve the group's goals. For instance, a group might allocate its weekly 1.5 hours to the format shown in Table 11-2.

Points 1 and 2 above can be facilitated by research on effective groups, existing group curricula, or best practices in services to particular populations. For example, building on the success of groups with gay and lesbian adolescents and with middle-aged persons in the coming-out process, Getzel (1998) notes that life review and socialization groups may serve as a promising resource for older LGBT persons. Others suggest that groups can be effective in addressing health issues, supporting treatment compliance, and reducing treatment dropouts. These goals are met as members share feelings about their illnesses and medications, offer mutual aid, empathize with one another's experiences and side effects, break through isolation and grief, and generate strategies for self-care (Miller & Mason, 2001). Professionals who are aware of successful activities and protocols can incorporate them into the proposed structure for group sessions.

The group leader is responsible for developing the preliminary structure and presenting it, and the rationale, to the group. Although input and mutuality are important, group members are typically ill equipped, due to their own distress or lack of group experience, to give meaningful input in creating group structure. They may, however, respond with concerns or preferences about the format offered and may be better able to offer feedback on structure as the group evolves.

Formulating Preliminary Group Guidelines

Developing consensus about group guidelines (e.g., staying on task, adhering to confidentiality) is a vital aspect of contracting in the initial phase of the group. In formulating guidelines with the group, the social worker takes the first step in shaping the group's evolving processes to create a "working group" capable of achieving specific objectives.

There are three common reasons why attempts to formulate guidelines fail. First, the social worker may establish parameters *for* the group, merely informing members of behavioral expectations to which they are expected to adhere. Although nonnegotiable requirements such as attendance are often part of involuntary groups, overemphasis on such control may convey the message, "This is my group, and this is how I expect you to behave in it." Such a message may negate later actions by the social worker to encourage members to assume responsibility for the group. Without consensus among members concerning desirable group guidelines, power struggles and disagreements may ensue. Further, members may not feel bound by what they consider the "leader's rules" and may deliberately test them, creating a counterproductive scenario.

Second, the social worker may discuss group guidelines only superficially and neglect either to identify or to obtain the group's commitment to them. This is unfortunate, because the extent to which members understand what these parameters mean will influence the extent to which they conform to them.

Third, just because the group adopts viable guidelines for behavior does not mean that members will subsequently follow them. Establishing group ground rules or mutual expectations merely sets guideposts against which members may measure their current behavior. For negotiated behaviors to become normative, leaders must consistently intervene to assist members in adhering to guidelines and in considering discrepancies between contracted and actual behaviors.

Because formulating guidelines is a critical process that substantially influences the success of a group, we offer the following suggestions to assist you in this aspect of group process:

EP 8

1. If there are nonnegotiable expectations (e.g., confidentiality, no smoking policies, or rules forbidding contact between members outside sessions), you

should present the rules, explain their rationale, and encourage discussion of them (Behroozi, 1992).

2. Introduce the group to the concept of **decision by consensus** on all negotiable items, and solicit agreement concerning adoption of this method for making decisions *prior* to formulating group guidelines.

3. Ask group members to share their vision of the kind of group they would like to have by responding to the following statement: "I would like this group to be a place where I could...." Reach for responses from all members. Once this has been achieved, summarize the collective thinking of the group. Offer your own views of supportive group structure that assists members to work on individual problems or to achieve group objectives.

4. Ask members to identify guidelines for behavior in the group that will assist them to achieve the kind of group structure and atmosphere they desire. You may wish to brainstorm possible guidelines at this point, adding your suggestions. Then, through group consensus, choose those that seem most appropriate.

The 10 items in sections that follow identify pertinent topics for treatment group guidelines, although each guideline's applicability depends on the specific focus of the group.

Help-Giving/Help-Seeking Roles

Groups can benefit from clarification of the *help-giving* and *help-seeking* roles that members play. The **help-seeking role** incorporates such behaviors as making direct requests for input or advice, authentically sharing one's feelings, being open to feedback, and demonstrating willingness to test new approaches to problems. The **help-giving role** involves such behaviors as listening attentively, refraining from criticism, clarifying perceptions, summarizing, maintaining focus on the problem, and pinpointing strengths and incremental growth.

The leader should give special attention to the issue of advice in the help-giving role and emphasize the necessity of carefully exploring fellow members' personal problems before attempting to solve them. Otherwise, groups tend to move quickly to giving advice and offering evaluative suggestions about what a member "ought" or "ought not" to do. You can further help the group to appropriately adopt the two roles by highlighting instances in which members have performed well in either of these helping roles.

New Members

Procedures for adding and orienting new members may need to be established. In some cases, the group leader may reserve the prerogative of selecting members. In other instances, the leader may permit the group to choose new members, with the understanding that those choices should be based on certain criteria and that the group should achieve consensus regarding potential members. In either case, procedures for adding new members and the importance of the group's role in orienting those entrants should be clarified. As mentioned earlier, adding new members in an open-ended group should occur in a planned way, considering the stage of development of the group.

Individual Contacts with the Social Worker

Whether you encourage or discourage individual contacts with members outside the group depends on the purpose of the group and the anticipated consequences or benefits of such contacts. In some cases, individual contacts serve to promote group objectives. For example, in a correctional setting, planned meetings with an adolescent between sessions may provide opportunities to focus on behaviors in the group, support strengths, and develop an individual contract with the youth to modify his or her actions. In the case of couples' groups, however, individual contacts initiated by one partner may be a bid to form an alliance with the social worker against the other partner (or may be perceived as such by the partner who did not initiate the contact). If you have questions regarding the advisability of having individual contacts outside the group, you should thoroughly discuss these with a supervisor and address guidelines for contact with group members.

Member Contacts Outside the Group

Contacts by members outside the group can be constructive or harmful to individuals and the group's purpose, and thus the practice literature contains differing views on this topic. Shulman (2009) explains that group sessions are but one activity in clients' lives and that therefore it is unreasonable to expect members to follow rules that extend outside the temporal and special boundaries of the group. Shulman (2009) also notes that the nature and benefit of collaborative support is limited if members are forbidden to make contact outside of session.

Toseland and Rivas (2009) list possible drawbacks to contact between members outside the group, including diversions from the group's goal, the effect of coalitions on the other members' interactions in the group, and arguments stemming from the dissolution of an alliance or friendship formed outside the group. With the advent of online search engines and social networking, members may research each other and threaten boundaries and comfort by uncovering information and connections the individual has not shared in the group. Online relationships can give rise to problematic alliances or become an avenue for dealing with concerns that should be brought to the group.

Yalom (2005) acknowledges both therapeutic benefits and pitfalls of contacts outside the group. His analysis reveals that outside group contact should be disclosed to the entire group, as clandestine contacts risk harming group unity. Sexual relationships between members is discouraged, as the connection between partners will surpass the connection that either feels for the remaining group members (Yalom, 2005). Particularly in time-limited groups, it is feasible and appropriate for members to limit outside contact for the duration of the group, unless there are therapeutic reasons for supporting such communications.

Care for Space and Cleanup

Making group decisions regarding care of the room (e.g., food, furniture, trash) and cleanup (before having to contend with a messy room) encourages members to assume responsibility for the group space. Otherwise, resentments may fester and subgroups destructive to group cohesiveness may form when some members feel responsible for cleanup and others do not.

Use of Recording Devices and Phones

Given the subtlety of current recording technology and the risks posed by inappropriate video or audio recording, this is an important topic for members and leaders alike. Members should be reminded of confidentiality expectations and be encouraged to prohibit recording as part of their ground rules. If there is a therapeutic or professional purpose for recording the group, the social worker should always ask for the group's permission before doing so (NASW, 2008a). Before asking for such a decision, the social worker should provide information concerning how the recording will be used outside the session, how it will be kept, and when it will be destroyed. Members' reservations regarding recording the session should be thoroughly aired, and the group's wishes should be respected.

A related issue involves the use of cell phones, pagers, and other handheld devices. In addition to recording and photo capabilities, these gadgets are distracting to the members checking them and to the other people around them. Groups must discuss and construct norms about the use of electronic equipment: Must all items be turned off during meetings? Can they be on but not checked if they go off? What should members do if urgent calls are expected?

Eating, Drinking, and Swearing

Opinions vary among group leaders concerning these activities in groups. Some groups and leaders believe that they distract from group process; others regard them as comforting and thus beneficial to group operation. Some groups may intentionally provide meals as an incentive to encourage group attendance (Wood, 2007). You may wish to elicit members' views about these activities and develop guidelines with the group that meet member needs, conform to organization or building policies, and facilitate group progress.

A related issue is the use of profanity in the group. Some social workers believe that group members should be allowed to use whatever language they choose in expressing themselves. However, profanity may be offensive to some participants, and the group may wish to develop guidelines concerning this matter.

Attendance

Discussing the problems that irregular attendance can pose for a group before the fact and soliciting commitments from members to attend regularly can do much to solidify group attendance in future group sessions. Involuntary groups often have attendance policies that permit a limited number of absences and late arrivals. Late arrivals and early departures by group members can typically be minimized if the group develops norms about this behavior in advance and if the leader starts and ends meetings promptly. Exceptions may be needed, of course, to accommodate crises affecting the schedules of members or to extend the session to complete an urgent item of business if the group concurs. However, individual and group exceptions to time norms should be rare.

Programming

Programming refers to the content of group sessions and the activities or exercises that are used to meet group goals. "In addition to discussion, content from games, play, structured exercises, role-playing, art, drama, guided imagery, cooking, hobbies, and other forms of creative self-expression are used to build group bonds and enhance the potential of the group to achieve group tasks and individual and social change" (Garvin & Galinsky, 2008, Programming section, para. 1). Domestic violence or substance abuse groups may use psychoeducational programming, children's groups may use activities or field trips (Rose, 1998; Ross, 1997), and cognitive behavioral groups may use role-plays and mnemonic devices to remind members of options for problem solving (Goodman, Getzel, & Ford, 1996). It is essential that the activities selected relate directly to the group's purpose. Any such activities should be prefaced and concluded by discussions and debriefing that tie the activities to the group's goals and evaluate the effectiveness of the experience.

With increased attention to evidence-based practices, **manualized curricula** have been developed that detail the sequence, content, and activities for various types of groups. These programmed approaches offer several advantages. They help to focus treatment, advance systematized practices, and support research on interventions. However, those who oppose manual-based practice are concerned that they promote paternalistic, one-size-fits-all approaches instead of the organic, empowerment-based changes that arise from members' and workers' dynamic interactions (Wood, 2007). A further concern is that they may be misused by workers who adopt curricula without supervision or sufficient appreciation for group dynamics and in the absence of group facilitation skills. Clearly, there is a balance between "intuitive practice at one pole and standardized practice at the other" (Galinsky, Terzian, & Fraser, 2006, p. 13). Knowledgeable workers can integrate tested programming ideas with practice wisdom and emerging group needs to achieve group and individual purposes.

Touching

The sensitive nature of some group topics may lead to expressions of emotion, such as crying or angry outbursts. It is important to have group guidelines that provide physical safety for members (e.g., "no hitting"). It is also important to set a climate of emotional safety, to sanction the appropriate expression of feelings. Some group guidelines prohibit members from touching one another with hugs or other signs of physical comfort. Sometimes these rules are included to protect members from unwanted or uncomfortable advances. Other groups maintain that touch is a "feeling stopper" when one is tearful and insist that group members can

display their empathy in other ways—through words or through eye contact and attention to the other, for example. Whatever the group's policy, it is important to explain the expectation and the rationale and to address member concerns rather than impose the guideline unilaterally.

Guidelines are helpful only to the extent that they expedite the development of the group and further the achievement of the group's goals. They should be reviewed periodically to assess their functionality in relationship to the group's stage of development. Outdated guidelines should be discarded or reformulated. When the group's behavior is incompatible with the group guidelines, the leader should describe what is happening in the group (or request that members do so) and, after thoroughly reviewing the situation, ask the group to consider whether the guideline in question is still viable. If used judiciously, this strategy not only helps the group to reassess its guidelines but also places responsibility for monitoring adherence to those guidelines with the group, where it belongs. Leaders who unwittingly assume the role of "enforcer" place themselves in an untenable position because group members tend to struggle against what they perceive as authoritarian control on the leader's part.

ASSESSING GROUP PROCESSES

EP 6 and 7

In group assessment, social workers must attend to processes that occur at both the individual and the group levels, including emerging themes or patterns, in an effort to enhance the functioning of individuals and the group as a whole. This section describes the procedures for accurately assessing the processes for both individuals and groups, and Table 11-3 summarizes the variables you should consider. A systems framework facilitates the identification and impact of such patterns. Instruments may also help in the identification and quantification of group processes and outcomes. For example, Macgowan (1997) has developed a group work engagement measure (GEM) that combines measures of attendance, satisfaction, perceived group helpfulness, group cohesion, and interaction to assess group members' level of engagement. Another assessment tool is the CORE-R Battery (Burlingame et al., 2006), which includes measures for selection, process, and outcome to help group leaders assess the effectiveness of their groups.

TABLE 11-3 Areas for Assessment in Groups

Individuals' Patterned Behaviors
Roles of Group Members
Individuals' Cognitions and Behaviors
The Group's Patterned Behaviors
Group Alliances
Group Norms
Group Cohesion

A Systems Framework for Assessing Groups

Like families, groups are social systems characterized by repetitive patterns. All social systems share an important principle—namely, that persons who compose a given system gradually limit their behaviors to a relatively narrow range of patterned responses as they interact with others within that system. Groups thus evolve implicit rules or norms that govern behaviors, shape patterns, and regulate internal operations.

A systems framework helps leaders to assess group processes; they can attend to the repetitive interactions of members, infer rules that govern those interactions, and weigh the functionality of those rules and patterns. For example, a group may develop a habit in which one person's complaints receive a great deal of attention while others' concerns are dismissed. The "rules" leading to such a pattern may be "If the group doesn't attend to Joe, he might drop out or become angry" or "Joe is hurting more than anyone else" or "Joe's issues resonate with those of others, so he deserves the additional attention, whereas the other concerns that are raised aren't shared concerns and don't deserve group time." This pattern may result in the disenfranchisement of the members who feel marginalized, or it may lead to relief that some members can recede while the spotlight is on Joe. More constructively, the other members may concur that Joe's issues are symptomatic of the group and thus be glad that he is bringing them to the surface for discussion.

Conceptualizing and organizing group processes into response patterns enables leaders to make systematic, ongoing, and relevant assessments. This knowledge can help "make sense" of seemingly random and chaotic interactions and bring comfort to group leaders, who may otherwise feel that they are floundering in sessions. In addition to identifying patterned behaviors, leaders must concurrently attend to individual and group

behaviors. Observing processes at both levels is difficult, however, and group facilitators sometimes become discouraged when they realize they attended more to individual dynamics than to group dynamics (or the converse), resulting in vague or incomplete assessment formulations. Recognizing this dilemma, we discuss strategies for accurately assessing both individual and group patterns in the remainder of this chapter.

Assessing Individuals' Patterned Behaviors

Some of the patterned behaviors that group members display are **functional**—that is, they enhance the well-being of individual members and the quality of group relationships. Other patterned behaviors are **dysfunctional**—that is, they erode the capacities of members and are destructive to relationships and group cohesion. Sometimes, people join groups specifically because some of their patterned behaviors are producing distress in their interpersonal relationships, although they may not be aware of the patterned nature of their behavior or of the impact it has on their ability to achieve their goals. A major role of leaders in groups, then, is to help members become aware of their patterned behavioral responses, determine the effects of these responses on themselves and others, and choose whether to change such responses. To carry out this role, leaders must formulate a profile of the recurring responses of each member, utilizing the concepts of *content* and *process*. **Content** refers to verbal statements and related topics that members discuss, whereas **process** involves the ways members relate or behave as they interact in the group and discuss content. Consider the following description of a member's behavior in two initial group sessions.

It is at the process level that leaders discover many of the patterned behavioral responses of individuals. The preceding case example revealed June's possible patterned or **thematic behaviors**. For example, we might infer that June is jockeying to establish an exclusive relationship with the leader and bidding for an informal position of co-leader in the group. Or perhaps she is uncomfortable with her peers and finds the leader to be a safe ally who will not reject her. Viewed alone, none of June's discrete behaviors provides sufficient information to justify drawing a conclusion about a possible response pattern. Viewed collectively, however, the repetitive responses warrant inferring that a pattern does, in fact, exist, and may create difficulty for June in the group and in other aspects of her life.

CASE EXAMPLE

From The Heart Group

In the first group meeting, June moved her chair close to the leader's chair. June complimented the leader when giving her introduction to the group and made a point to verbalize her agreement with several of the leader's statements. In subsequent meetings, June again sat next to the leader and offered advice to other group members, referring to opinions she thought were jointly held by her and the leader. Later, June tried to initiate a conversation with the leader concerning what she regarded as negative behavior of another group member in front of that member and the rest of the group.

Identifying Roles of Group Members

EP 7

In identifying patterned responses of individuals, leaders also need to attend to the various roles that members assume in the group. For example, members may assume **leadership roles** that are **formal** (explicitly sanctioned by the group) or **informal** (emerging as a result of group needs). Further, a group may have several members who serve different functions or who head rival subgroups.

Some members may assume **task-related** or **instrumental roles** that facilitate the group's efforts to define problems, implement solutions, or carry out tasks. These members may propose goals or actions, suggest procedures, request pertinent facts, clarify issues, or offer an alternative or conclusion for the group to consider. Other members may adopt **maintenance roles** that are oriented to altering, maintaining, and strengthening the group's functioning. Members who take on such roles may offer compromises, encourage and support the contributions of others, comment on the emotional climate of the meeting, or suggest group standards.

Some members may emerge as spokespersons around concerns of the group or enact other **expressive roles**. Rather than interpret those behaviors as a negative influence, you may consider whether that member is representing concerns held by others in the group or identifying issues that are lingering below the surface in group sessions. In short, that person may be acting as an informal group leader who can be joined in seeking to make the group succeed (Breton, 1985). Still other members may assume **self-serving roles**, seeking to meet their own needs at the expense of the group. Such members may attack the group or its values, stubbornly resist the group's wishes, continually disagree with or interrupt others, assert authority or superiority, display lack of involvement, pursue extraneous subjects, or find various ways to call attention to themselves.

Members may also carry labels assigned by other members, such as "clown," "critic," "uncommitted," "lazy," "dumb," "silent one," "rebel," "overreactor," or "good mother." Such labeling stereotypes members, making it difficult for them to relinquish the set of expected behaviors or to change their way of relating to the group. Hartford (1971) elaborates:

> For instance, the person who has become the clown may not be able to make a serious and substantial contribution to the group because, regardless of what he says, everyone laughs. If one person has established a high status as the initiator, others may not be able to initiate for fear of threatening his position. If one has established himself in a dependency role in a pair or subgroup, he may not be able to function freely until he gets cues from his subgroup partner. (p. 218)

One or more members may also be assigned the role of **scapegoat**, bearing the burden of responsibility for the group's problems and the brunt of teasing or negative responses from other members. Such individuals may attract this marginalized role because they are socially awkward and repeatedly make blunders in their attempts to elicit positive responses from others (Balgopal & Vassil, 1983; Klein, 1970). Or they may assume this role because they fail to recognize nonverbal cues that facilitate interaction in the group and thus behave without regard to the subtle nuances that govern the behavior of other members (Balgopal & Vassil, 1983; Beck, 1974). Individuals may also unknowingly perpetuate the scapegoat role they have assumed in their nuclear family, workplace, school, or social system. Although group scapegoats demonstrate repetitive dysfunctional behaviors that attract the hostility or mockery of the group, the presence of the role signals a group phenomenon (and pattern) whose maintenance requires the tacit cooperation of all members.

Individuals may also assume the role of an **isolate**—being ignored by the group, not reaching out to others, or doing so but being rejected. The isolate differs from the scapegoat in that the latter gets attention, even if it is negative, whereas the former is simply disregarded.

Some members, of course, assume roles that strengthen relationships and enhance group functioning. Reinforcing these positive behaviors both encourages the individual who demonstrates them and helps other members to emulate them. It is important to identify all of the roles that members assume because those roles profoundly affect the group's capacity to respond to the individual needs of members and its ability to fulfill the treatment objectives. Identifying roles is also vital because members tend to play out in treatment or task groups the same roles that they assume in other social contexts. Members need to understand the impact of functional and dysfunctional roles on themselves and others.

Assessing Individuals' Cognitions and Behaviors

During assessment, group leaders need to develop accurate cognitive and behavioral profiles of each individual, taking note of the functional and dysfunctional

EP 7

responses that members displayed in initial sessions. Examples of functional behaviors might include "expresses her/himself clearly, cooperates with and supports others, responds openly and positively to constructive feedback, and works within guidelines established by the group." A profile of dysfunctional behaviors could include items such as "verbally dominates group 'air time,' gives advice prematurely, and talks about tangential topics or sidetracks the group in other ways."

Patterned cognitions are a form of internal dialogue. To use an analogy, it is as though events in a person's life trigger a recording in his or her mind that automatically repeats the same messages over and over, coloring the person's perceptions of events and determining his or her reality. Examples of destructive cognitive patterns in group members include "I'm a failure," "No one wants to hear what I have to say," "This group is stupid," or "Other people are better than I am." Constructive patterns might include "I can help other people because of what I've experienced," "I deserve support," or "My opinions matter."

Patterned cognitions and behavior are inextricably related and reciprocally reinforce each other. The following case example of a group member's problem

---

CASE EXAMPLE

From The Heart Group

Amber, a 17-year-old high school student, joined a therapy group for teenage girls who are overweight. She reported experiencing low self-esteem, especially with regard to her body. She stated that she lacked confidence when interacting with boys and while changing clothes for gym and softball practice. Amber also discussed difficulties shopping with her friends, stating, "I can't fit into any of the clothes there, and I really want to because they're really cute clothes and it kind of makes me feel out of the loop with my friends."

In contrast to these moments of insecurity, Amber informed the group that there were times when she felt good about herself. Because of her skill at softball, she experienced a boost in confidence when playing on the team. Additionally, Amber stated that she received positive attention from her peers, particularly boys, at dance parties.

"You know, at parties and things, whenever rap songs come on about fat girls and booties everyone looks to me and I get to dance in front of everybody… I feel good when the attention is on me."

Amber's cognitions relate to her desire for acceptance by her peers. Although she recognizes positive aspects of herself and has been successful in putting her skills to use, she continues to seek approval from others, although on their terms. Her thoughts can be summarized as "I'm not good enough as I am" and "People will like me if I act how they want me to." In group, Amber discovered that these thoughts contribute to her feelings of low self-esteem, and she explored other ways of thinking. She stated, "They call me bootylicious sometimes. I like that because it makes me stand out from them, but maybe I'd appreciate another nickname that didn't have to do with my body."

illustrates the link between cognitions and behavior and the insidious effect that negative cognitions may have on a client's life.

These patterns can be tracked through client self-reports or by peer observation within the group. The data may be captured in charts, logs, diaries or journals, self-anchored rating scales or observations (which can be naturalistic), role-plays and simulations, or analysis of video recordings of group process (Toseland & Rivas, 2009). By assessing and identifying these patterns, the facilitator can address them in sessions, note and reinforce growth, and manage cognitions or behaviors that create problems for the member or group process.

Table 11-4 is a record of the HEART young women's support group that illustrates how leaders can develop profiles of each member. For example, a glance at Table 11-4 suggests that Liz is vulnerable to becoming an isolate in the group.

Assessing the Group's Patterned Behaviors

Beyond attending to the ritualized behaviors of individual members, group workers must be alert to the patterns of the group as a whole. To heighten your awareness of functional and dysfunctional patterned group behaviors, we provide contrasting examples in Table 11-5.

The functional behaviors in the table are characteristic of a mature therapeutic group, though constructive group behaviors may also emerge in the initial stages of development. Incidental positive behaviors that are commonly revealed early in the life of a group include the following:

- The group responds positively the first time a member takes a risk by revealing a personal problem.
- Members of the group are supportive toward other members or demonstrate investment in the group.
- The group works harmoniously for a period of time.
- Members effectively make a decision together.
- Members adhere to specific group guidelines, such as maintaining focus on work to be accomplished.
- The group responsibly confronts a member who is dominating interaction or interfering in some way with the group accomplishing its task.
- Members pitch in to clean up after a group session.

The group may also display transitory negative behaviors in initial sessions, which is to be expected in the early phases of group development. Facilitators must be alert to the continued or intensifying destructive patterns, particularly in regard to power and decision making. Groups are sometimes torn apart because unresolved power issues prevent the group from meeting the needs of some members (Smokowski, Rose, & Bacallao, 2001).

When social workers assess groups, they need to identify the current capacity of members to share power and resources and to implement problem-solving steps that ensure "win-win" solutions. Leaders must help the group make each member count if the group is to advance through stages of development into maturity. They can accelerate the group's progress through these stages by assuming a facilitative role in teaching and modeling effective decision making and by assisting the group to adopt explicit guidelines for making decisions in the initial sessions.

Assessing Group Alliances

As members of new groups find other members with compatible attitudes, interests, and responses, they develop patterns of affiliation and relationship with these members. Subgroup formations may include pairs, triads, and foursomes. Larger subgroups may develop subdivisions influencing "who addresses whom, who sits together, who comes and leaves together, and even who may meet or talk together outside of the group" (Hartford, 1971, p. 204).

The subgroupings that invariably develop do not necessarily impair group functioning. Members may derive strength and support from subgroups, in turn enhancing their participation and investment in the larger group. Indeed, it is through the process of establishing subgroups or natural coalitions that group members achieve true intimacy. Problems may arise, however, when members develop exclusive subgroups (cliques) that disallow intimate relationships with other group members or inhibit members from supporting the goals of the larger group. Subgroups that meet online or in person outside of group sessions can have a particularly pernicious effect on the functioning of the group as a whole. Competing factions can often impede or destroy a group.

Leaders must be skilled in identifying subdivisions and assessing their impact on the group. This

TABLE 11-4 Examples of Profiles of HEART Group Members

NAME	DESCRIPTIVE ATTRIBUTES	FUNCTIONAL PATTERNS	DYSFUNCTIONAL PATTERNS
Amelia	15 years old Lives with both parents and one sister Artistic; plays tennis	Participates often in the group Asks pertinent questions of other members Offers to take on maintenance tasks for the group Volunteers ideas for a warm-up exercise for the group	Challenges the leader's motivation and ability to facilitate the group Hesitates to focus on self
Liz	16 years old Lives with both parents Only child Reports intense depression and anxiety	Expresses feelings clearly Attentive Expresses desire to change	Withdrawn, speaks infrequently in the group
Maggie	16 years old Lives with both parents Only child Student body president	Expresses ambivalence about attending group Participates often and made positive contributions to the group Took a risk by sharing personal concerns about relating to peers	Sometimes off topic, pursued extraneous lines of questioning Confronts bluntly Experiences difficulty talking about self
Amber	17 years old Lives with parents and grandmother Only child Plays first base on varsity softball team	Joins in discussions, and supports others appropriately Recognizes concerns and strengths with regard to self-esteem Acknowledges the possibility for change	Teased another member Makes some distracting comments
June	16 years old Lives with mother Brother diagnosed with diabetes Participates in several activities: library club, band, and volunteers at the animal shelter and convalescent center	Initiates group discussion of several topics Outgoing and spontaneous Adds energy to group	At times interrupts others in the group Dominates "air time" Attempts to ally herself with the facilitator
Jen	15 years old Lives with both parents Recently moved, is new at her school Used to play volleyball, holds part-time job in a fast food restaurant	Attentive in group Discusses hurtful messages she receives from her parents Acknowledges change as a result of her participation in group	Speaks infrequently Expresses hopelessness about change

EP 8

may involve constructing a sociogram of group alignments. Credited to Moreno and Jennings (Jennings, 1950), a **sociogram** graphically depicts patterned affiliations and relationships between group members by using symbols for people and interactions. Figure 11-1 illustrates a sociogram that captures the predominant connections, attractions, and repulsions among members of the HEART group during the fifth session in which the teens discussed the challenges of fitting in with current fashions and peers.

TABLE 11-5 Examples of Group Behaviors

FUNCTIONAL GROUP BEHAVIOR	PROBLEMATIC GROUP BEHAVIOR
• Members openly communicate personal feelings and attitudes and anticipate that other members will be helpful.	• Members talk on a superficial level and are cautious about revealing their feelings and opinions.
• Members listen carefully to one another and give all ideas a fair hearing.	• Members are critical and evaluative of each other; they rarely acknowledge or listen to contributions from others.
• Decisions are reached through group consensus after considering everyone's views and feelings.	• Dominant members count out other members in decision making; members make decisions prematurely without identifying or weighing possible alternatives.
• Members make efforts to incorporate the views of dissenters rather than to dominate or override these views.	
• Members recognize and give feedback regarding strengths and growth of other members.	• Members are critical of differences in others, viewing them as a threat.
• Members take turns speaking.	• Members compete for the chance to speak, often interrupting one another.
• Members use "I" messages to speak for themselves, readily owning their own feelings and positions on matters.	• Members do not personalize their messages but rather use indirect forms of communication to express their feelings and positions.
• Members adhere to the guidelines established in initial sessions.	• Members display disruptive behaviors incompatible with group guidelines.
• Members assume responsibility for the group's functioning and success.	• Members resist talking about the here and now or addressing personal or group problems.
• The group shows its commitment by staying on task, assuming group assignments, and working out problems that impair group functioning.	• Members focus on others rather than on themselves.
• Members are sensitive to the needs and feelings of others and readily give emotional support.	• Members show little awareness of the needs and feelings of others; emotional investment in others is limited.

Sociograms are representations of group alliances *at a given point* because alliances inevitably shift and change, particularly in the early stages of group development. Charting the transitory bonds that occur early in group life can prove valuable to leaders in deciding where and when to intervene to modify, enhance, or stabilize relationships between members.

Assessing Group Norms

EP 6 and 7

Norms are regulatory mechanisms that give groups a measure of stability and predictability by letting members know what they can expect from the group and from one another. Norms may define the *specific* behaviors that are appropriate or permissible for individuals or they may define the *range* of behaviors that are acceptable in the group. Norms represent the internalization of the group guidelines discussed earlier in this chapter.

Groups develop formal and informal sanctions to reduce behaviors that are considered deviant and to return the system to its prior equilibrium. For example, an implicit group norm may be that other group members may not challenge the opinions of the informal leader. If a new group member treads on this norm by disputing the informal leader, other members may side with the informal leader against the "upstart," pressuring him or her to back away. As in this example, people often learn about the norms of particular groups by observing situations in which norms have been violated. Toseland and Rivas (2009) note that group members watch the behavior of other members as they

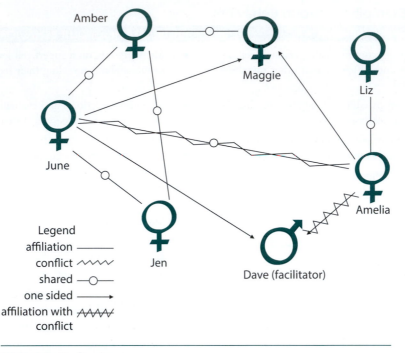

FIG 11-1 Sociogram

reward some behaviors and punish others. Once members realize that sanctions are applied to certain behaviors, they usually attempt to adapt their behavior to avoid disapproval or punishment.

The extent to which members adhere to norms varies. Some norms are flexible or weakly held, and the psychological "costs" of violation are low or nonexistent. In the HEART group, speaking out of order or speaking while another person is speaking is understood as undesirable yet often goes unchecked by the members during their sessions together. In other instances, the group's investment in norms is significant and group reaction is severe when members violate them. The members of the HEART group vigilantly uphold their shared agreement to be respectful in session. Members who put others on the spot or criticize brusquely are immediately called out for that behavior.

The status of members—that is, the evaluation or ranking of each member's position in the group relative to the others—also determines the extent to which members adhere to norms. Toseland, Jones, and Gellis (2006) observe that low-status members are the least likely to conform to group norms because they have little to lose by deviating. Such behavior is less likely if the member has hopes of gaining a higher status. Medium-status group members tend to conform to group norms so that they can retain their status and

perhaps gain a higher status. High-status members generally conform to valued group norms when they are establishing their position. At the same time, because of their elevated position, high-status members have more freedom to deviate from accepted norms.

All groups develop norms, and once certain norms are adopted, they influence the group's response to situations and determine the extent to which the group offers its members therapeutic experiences. A major role for the leader, then, is to identify evolving group norms and influence them in ways that create a positive climate for cohesion and change. Discerning norms is often difficult, however, because they are subtly embedded in the group process and can be inferred only from the behavior occurring in the group. Leaders may be able to identify norms by asking themselves key questions such as the following:

1. What subjects can and cannot be talked about in the group?
2. What kinds of emotional expressions are allowed in the group?
3. What is the group's pattern with regard to working on problems or staying on task?
4. Do group members consider it their own responsibility or the leader's responsibility to make the group's experience successful?

5. What is the group's stance toward the leader?
6. What is the group's attitude toward feedback?
7. How does the group view the contributions of individual members? What kind of labels and roles does the group assign to them?

These questions also enable the leader to improve his or her observations of redundant or patterned behaviors exhibited by members. This is a vital point, because *patterned behaviors are always undergirded by supporting norms.*

Another strategy for identifying norms is to explain the concept of norms to group members and to ask them to identify the guiding "rules" that influence their behavior in the group. This strategy forces members to bring to a conscious level the group norms that are developing and to make choices in favor of those that advance the group's goals. It is also an important topic for the leader who is joining an existing group to consider.

Table 11-6 provides examples of both constructive and problematic norms.

Assessing Group Cohesion

 In the initial phases of the group's life, leaders must also assess and foster the development of **cohesion** in groups. Defined as the degree to which members are attracted to one another, cohesion is correlated, under certain conditions, with productivity, participation in and out of the group, self-disclosure, risk taking, attendance, and other vital concerns (Rose, 1989; Stokes, 1983). Cohesion in groups positively affects members' satisfaction and personal adjustment. Greater cohesiveness leads to increased self-esteem, more willingness to listen to others, freer expression of feeling, better reality testing, higher self-confidence, and more effective use of other members' evaluations in enhancing a member's own development (Toseland & Rivas, 2009; Yalom, 2005).

EP 6 and 7

Cohesion is inextricably linked to the development of norms in a beginning group. Norms that may potentially interfere with both group formation and cohesion include irregular attendance, tardiness, subgroups, changing membership, interpersonal aggression, excessive dependence on the leader, dominance by a few members, and general passivity in the interaction (Rose, 1989). Research on negative group experiences indicates that the individuals who are damaged by the group may be those very members who are too timid to help contribute to group rules and thus have little investment in the norms that have been negotiated between the leader and more vocal members (Smokowski, Rose, & Bacallao, 2001). These detrimental norms require the attention of both the leader and the group members, because failure to address them discourages group development and jeopardizes the group itself.

SINGLE-SESSION GROUPS

Groups whose membership is the same for only a single session are common in settings where the census of potential members fluctuates frequently, such as medical and psychiatric units in hospitals, inpatient substance abuse treatment settings, shelters, and other residential facilities. This form of group is increasingly popular in

TABLE 11-6 Examples of Group Norms

CONSTRUCTIVE	PROBLEMATIC
• Take a risk by spontaneously revealing personal content about yourself.	• Ignore attendance and time commitments.
• Treat the leader with respect and seriously consider the leader's input.	• Keep the discussion centered on superficial topics; avoid taking risks or self-disclosing.
• Focus on working out personal problems.	• Play the game "Let's get the leader." Harass, criticize, or complain about the leader whenever the opportunity arises.
• Allow members equal opportunity to participate in group discussions or to become the focus of the group.	• Let aggressive members dominate the group.
• Communicate directly with other group members.	• Avoid emotionally charged or delicate subjects.
• Talk about obstacles that get in the way of achieving the group's goals.	• Direct comments to the leader.

light of reduced lengths of stay in treatment and the busy pace of life that may make it difficult for potential members to commit to attending ongoing groups. While single-session groups may sacrifice the cohesion and reflection that can be characteristic of closed multisession groups, they have demonstrated effectiveness in education and in assisting members to resolve immediate challenges, restore equilibrium, and mobilize coping skills (Fried & Dunn, 2012). Some authors conceptualize single-session groups as services or workshops rather than therapeutic interventions (Ruffalo, Nitzberg, & Schoof, 2011), and others view them as a variant of open membership groups (Turner, 2011).

The steps outlined above for establishing treatment groups apply to single-session groups. Based on a comprehensive literature review by Keast (2012), the author created a toolkit to assist clinicians in single-session group formation:

1. To determine the need and purpose for the group, planners should consult with potential referral sources and coworkers from multiple disciplines. Brief surveys at admission or reviews of intake data may also reveal the need for or interest in group services.

2. Co-leadership is recommended in single-session groups to allow continuity of leadership, with at least one facilitator attending from one group to the next. Co-leaders may divide responsibilities: one may present educational content, the other facilitate discussion, or one may lead discussion and the other help to generalize the topics to individual member needs.

3. Regardless of the demographics of the population from which the group is drawn, leaders should still consider individuals' appropriateness for the group based on the purpose and the prospective members' needs and capacities. Depending on the purpose of the group, there may be greater tolerance for significant heterogeneity in the membership. For instance, Block (1985) suggests that although an inpatient group might be composed of individuals at different stages of cancer treatment, if all share a similar concern or crisis, the differences in experience with the disease may not matter. However, when there is not enough commonality to bind the group, even a single-session experience can be off-putting and frustrating for more advanced members. In addition, composition and programming may be complicated when some group members attend repeatedly while others cycle in and out. It can be a challenge to address the needs of those attending for the first time and those who have participated for several sessions.

4. When the membership of a single-session group is affiliated with residency in a particular program, the facility may dictate the size and location of the group. For example, all the parents of children on an oncology unit would be eligible to attend a coping with cancer group, and the group would meet in an activity area or conference room at the hospital. In "freestanding" single-session groups— for example, to deal with crises, provide education about mood disorders (Ruffalo, Nitzberg, & Schoof, 2011), or prevent binge drinking (Fried & Dunn, 2012)—membership would be set at a workable number, drawn from a broader geographical area beyond an individual institution or unit, and the meeting location would be accessible and neutral, as suggested earlier in this chapter.

5. The studies reviewed by Keast (2012) suggest that single-session groups should be longer than typical treatment groups, as the membership may be larger and time is needed, within one session, to create trust and facilitate sharing. As such, groups might meet for 90 to 120 minutes (Feigin et al., 1998; Ruffalo, Nitzberg, & Schoof, 2011).

6. Although extensive preliminary interviews are not feasible for single-session groups, facilitators may get acquainted with potential members through case staffing or their other therapeutic or supervisory roles in the residence or unit. This may provide the opportunity to educate clients or family members/caregivers about group offerings and determine what pressing issues the group might help to address. The format for single-session groups may be educational or didactic, but in either case, facilitators need to be prepared to do on-the-spot assessments to make sure material is responsive to the needs of the individuals gathered for the session (Turner, 2011).

A further element to assess is whether group attendance is mandatory. As noted throughout this text, voluntariness and reactance have powerful implications for clients' quality and level of participation in services. Single-session groups may not afford the time to work through these issues, so facilitators must plan for this in structuring each session.

7. Facilitators in single-session groups may cultivate trust from the outset of the meeting by inviting members to share about their needs and expectations for the group. A common practice is for

facilitators to offer preliminary goals and guidelines and invite comment or additions by the members to clarify expectations and expedite contracting.

FORMATION OF TASK GROUPS

We move now from consideration of treatment groups to task groups. Although many of the issues in assessing treatment groups also apply to task groups, there are distinctions in their purposes, composition, and format. These unique characteristics and common themes are highlighted in the following sections.

Task Group Purpose

As described earlier in this chapter, task groups are organized to meet client, organizational, and community needs (Toseland & Rivas, 2009). All of these groups focus on generating products, planning activities, developing policies, and making decisions rather than on enhancing the personal growth of members (Ephross & Vassil, 1988). Important early steps in forming and assessing task groups are planning for the group and structuring initial sessions to address the purpose of the group.

Task Group Membership and Planning

EP 6 and 7

Membership in task groups may be dictated by the needs of the group or the task to be accomplished, or it may be constrained by organizational structure, bylaws, or regulations (Toseland & Rivas, 2009). For example:

- Agency rules may stipulate that all committees have two consumer members.
- An association board may select members based on expertise, philanthropic capacity, passion for the cause, and geographic representation.
- A committee to assist with accreditation at a school of social work might include representatives of students, alumni, community leaders, field instructors, faculty, and staff.
- Members of a treatment team may include all professionals involved in the case, or all individuals whose knowledge is needed to evaluate the case (e.g., speech therapist, teacher, social worker, behavior specialist).

Depending on the values of the organization and the culture of the team, clients and their family members may be routinely involved (or excluded) as members of the team.

Task group composition may be voluntary, by appointment, or by election, but it should always be responsive to the group's purpose and goals. For example:

- A treatment conference may have the purpose of coordinating the efforts of members of a team involved in serving a particular client or family.
- An ad hoc committee may be recruited to work on a fundraising event for an agency.
- A board of directors is appointed or elected to provide guidance and accountability to an organization.
- A community crime prevention panel may consist of volunteers from the neighborhood who want to work for increased services and police presence in the area.

The initiation of a task group and the determination of its purpose may come from many sources. For example, nonprofit agencies are required to have boards of directors as part of their nonprofit status, a staff member might propose a resident council in a halfway house, the director of an agency might initiate a committee to develop better agency communications, or residents of a housing development might suggest a social action group to deal with neighborhood violence.

Members of any task group should have the interest, information, skills, and power needed to accomplish the purpose of the group. The specific purpose of the group suggests sources for its membership. For example, a group formed to study how managed care affects service delivery might include consumers, providers, and representatives from insurance groups and regulatory agencies. A group formed to plan a new teen pregnancy program might include teen parents, health care providers, teachers, public health researchers, and child welfare workers.

Membership should be large enough and sufficiently diverse to represent the major constituencies affected by the problem being targeted, and participants should possess adequate skills and knowledge for addressing the group's purposes. As with treatment groups, organizers should ensure that no individual is an isolate. For example, a special education advisory committee should not consist of a group of professionals plus a token parent. When consumers or those whose personal experience is valuable to the task group's purpose are included, multiple representatives should be recruited for the group and, if possible, should serve as representatives of other consumers. For example, in a committee on mental health reform, multiple consumers and parents might be involved, and some should represent groups, such as the National Alliance for the Mentally Ill. Taking these steps will help enhance the comfort, power, and legitimacy of group members. Task groups that are too large make it difficult for members to have meaningful involvement; a board that has 45 members sends the message that individual viewpoints and attendance do not matter. Conversely, task groups that are too small may have insufficient membership to complete their responsibilities and may have insufficient diversity in viewpoints and expertise.

Quality planning in this stage is reflected by accurately and clearly communicating the group's purposes and expectations to prospective members. The level of clarity achieved has important implications for whether those prospective members decide to attend and, later, how well they perform the functions of the group. How often will the group meet? How much time, outside of meetings, will be required of members? Are members expected to make financial donations to the organization? How long are the terms of service?

As with treatment groups, task groups may be open or closed in time and in membership. Formal boards or committees generally are ongoing but have structures that provide for the rotation of membership in and out of the group, allowing for "staggered" terms to assure continuity. Other groups may be time limited and relatively closed in membership (e.g., a task force to review an incident in which a resident was injured, a committee to plan an agency's anniversary celebration, a search committee for a new employee). Other groups may be ongoing but have closed membership (e.g., an ethics committee that hears different cases each month as brought to them by members of the hospital staff).

Beginning the Task Group

The agenda for a beginning session of a task group is similar to that for a treatment group. It includes facilitating introductions, clarifying the purpose of the group, discussing ground rules, helping members feel a part of the group, setting goals, and anticipating obstacles (Toseland & Rivas, 2009). An opening statement, including the host agency's function and mission as it relates to the group purpose, should be shared so that members will understand why they have been called together. Members can then be assisted to find commonalities in their concerns and experiences and to identify shared goals for group participation. Some members may know one another from previous roles and have positive or negative preconceptions from that past. "Ice breakers" and other introductory activities can be used to facilitate communication and identify experiences and resources that members bring to the group (Dossick & Shea, 1995; Gibbs, 1995).

Developing group rules and concurrence on decision making (e.g., majority rule, consensus) then follows. A common rule involves adherence to confidentiality, as premature or distorted release of information might hinder the work and destroy the cohesion of the group. Other rules in task groups usually include expectations about attendance and preparation, processes for recusing oneself on items that may involve conflicts of interest, and structural issues such as timing of meetings, submission of agenda items, and effective communications (Levi, 2007). On boards of directors, a subcommittee may be responsible for recruiting and orienting new members, and the "ground rules" are specified in bylaws and board policies. New members may also be paired with veteran members who can help them prepare for and participate fully in meetings from the outset of their service (Thomas & Strom-Gottfried, 2011).

Task groups then proceed to goal setting. Such goals always include those mandated by the purpose of the group, such as revising agency policies, planning a conference, reviewing audit reports, implementing new regulations, or coordinating care. In addition, the group may generate its own goals—for example, generating a list of best practices in achieving its purpose or tailoring its response to the group's purpose based on the specific talents and assets available in the group.

As with treatment groups, task group members may take on or be assigned formal (e.g., secretary, chairperson, treasurer) and informal (e.g., timekeeper, devil's advocate, instrumental leader, expressive leader) roles. Whether these roles are constructive depends on how they are enacted and the extent to which they help the group fulfill its purpose. As with other types of groups, assessing the behaviors of individual members and the group as a whole will help identify functional and dysfunctional patterns. Many of the attributes listed in Tables 11-5 and 11-6 apply to task groups as well as to treatment groups.

Other parallels with treatment groups include the evolution of subgroups, norms, cohesion, and the role of members' status in group dynamics. As with treatment groups, these phenomena can play either destructive or positive roles in the group's development. For example, a faction within a task group may form a voting bloc that inhibits the full participation of all members or hijacks the democratic decision making of the group. Members' roles and statuses outside the group may play out in their behaviors and relationships in the group. The agency director may be accustomed to deferential treatment and expect that from fellow group members, even though in that setting they are intended to be equals. Professionals may be dismissive of (or overly solicitous of) the input of consumer representatives on a committee. Counterproductive norms may include "Attendance is optional," "My opinion doesn't matter," "We never get anything done," or "No one comes prepared." Constructive norms about attendance, respect, full participation, and honesty can help the group effectively and efficiently achieve its purpose. Although developing cohesion is less crucial in task groups, the presence of socioemotional ties between members will help develop the meaning, commitment, and participation members give to the group process.

CULTURAL CONSIDERATIONS IN FORMING AND ASSESSING TASK OR TREATMENT GROUPS

EP 2

Cultural considerations emerge in many forms in practice with groups. Awareness of culture is necessary when constructing a group to address a particular problem or assist a particular population. Also, it is important when recruiting and screening potential members, when you are assessing individual and group functioning, and when you are employing interventions during different stages of the group process. Zastrow (2011) argues that a leader of a diverse group needs "(1) to be aware of personal stereotypes and preconceptions about diverse groups, (2) to have knowledge about the diverse groups that he or she is working with and the special needs of those groups, and (3) to be aware of which intervention techniques are apt to be effective with those groups and which are not" (p. 225). Other authors recommend multilingual materials and group leaders, attention to in-group cultural differences, and group activities that utilize culturally specific or culturally adapted curricula and foster storytelling and creative expression (Greif & Ephross, 2011; Whaley & Davis, 2007).

Davis, Galinsky, and Schopler (1995) recommend a specific framework when working with multicultural

groups: Recognize, Anticipate, and Problem-solve. The RAP framework encourages group leaders to recognize and respect racial, ethnic, and cultural differences among group members; anticipate and respond preventively to potential sources of racial/ethnic or cultural tension; and problem-solve using conflict resolution approaches so that the issues and needs of all parties are understood. In its Treatment Improvement Protocol for substance abuse groups, the Substance Abuse and Mental Health Services Administration (SAMHSA) (2005) offers the following suggestions for facilitating diverse groups:

- Understand personal biases and prejudices about specific cultural groups.
- Pay special attention to issues of diversity when forming groups because the feelings of belonging to an ethnic group can be intensified where there are several individuals to "feel different" from, not just the therapist.
- Pay attention to cultural traditions and how they play out in group processes to ensure that these traditions do not interfere with the purpose or progress of the group.
- Be aware of how cultural practices affect compliance with treatment requirements as well as communication among group members.
- Explore each member's self-identification with an ethnic group (do not assume group membership) because individuals may self-identify in ways other than appearance would indicate.
- Be open to learning about different cultures, customs, and beliefs held by members of the group.
- The greater the mix of ethnicities within a group, the more likely biases will surface and mediation by the facilitator will be required.
- Before placing a client in a group, the facilitator must assess the influence of culture, family structure, language, identity processes, health beliefs and attitudes, political issues, and the stigma associated with minority status.
- From the start of a multicultural group, members should feel that race or other cultural issues are permitted topics for discussion.
- The behavior of a minority group member might be significantly influenced by cultural norms about sharing personal material with strangers, speaking up before others, offering answers, or advising other members.

Assessment of group interactions must occur in light of knowledge about each member's culture and his or her individual characteristics within that culture. An instrument proposed by Drankus (2010) offers helpful insight into the nuances of culture and the acculturation continuum from one's "heritage culture" to the dominant culture. It examines three indicators of acculturation: language, cultural behavior, and cultural knowledge. Although designed to be administered to individuals, the findings would be helpful in group composition, programming, and facilitation as they identify often hidden areas of commonality and difference.

Finally, as with individual practice, group workers must be careful not to discredit behavior they do not understand, behavior that may arise from the member's upbringing, or attempts to cope with the current environment and the stress and strain of adaptation (Chau, 1993; Mason, Benjamin, & Lewis, 1996; Pack-Brown, Whittington-Clark, & Parker, 1998). Some individuals are unwilling to participate in groups. Whether this is a cultural or personal characteristic, labeling it as simple resistance is a disservice to the client and will be an impediment to finding interventions that *do* fit for the individual.

"The group therapist thus needs to assess how leader-member, member-member, and member-group alliances may be affected by the presence of cultural diversity in the group" (Chen, Kakkad, & Balzano, 2008, p. 1269). Group planners and facilitators can adopt a stance of cultural humility, creating a respectful partnership with clients in order to learn about and learn from the client's lived experience. In groups with pluralistic membership, workers can also teach group members this stance of "reflexive attentiveness" (Hunt, 2001, p. 4) and the concept of cultural humility to assist them in developing norms of mutual acceptance and curiosity.

Of course, culture in groups can manifest in ways beyond race and ethnicity. Sexual orientation, gender, and religious, generational, and geographic differences are but a few of the identities that may affect client participation and group cohesion. For example, in applying group work concepts to practice in rural areas, Gumpert and Saltman (1998) identified several challenges that warrant leaders' attention:

- Cultural factors such as distrust of confidentiality assurances, strong values of self-reliance, and suspicion of outsiders
- Geographic factors such as distance, weather and travel conditions, and difficulty finding a convenient location
- Demographic factors such as insufficient numbers of individuals with similar difficulties, resource

problems such as the lack of public transportation, insufficient child care, and too few potential group leaders

When working with groups for traditionally marginalized persons, workers may adopt an empowerment-based approach drawn from feminist theory and liberation theology as resources for empowerment-focused social group work (Lewis, 1991). For example, Cox (1991) has described how female welfare recipients have begun to advocate for themselves with social services and other agencies through participation in empowerment-oriented groups. A feminist orientation to group therapy for women survivors of sexual trauma capitalizes on women's relational abilities to address feelings of mistrust, and to repair and develop socialization and emotional regulation skills (Fallot & Harris, 2002; Rittenhouse, 1997).

ETHICS IN PRACTICE WITH TASK OR TREATMENT GROUPS

EP 1

The values and ethical standards introduced in Chapter 4 apply to social work practice with systems of all sizes. However, the nature of in-person and online groups presents particular challenges for interpreting and applying ethical standards. In this chapter, we will focus on five specific areas: informed consent, confidentiality, self-determination, competence, and nondiscrimination.

Informed Consent, Confidentiality, and Self-Determination

Informed consent involves explaining in clear and understandable language the potential risks and anticipated benefits of service, the limits of confidentiality, the consequences of service refusal, and other policies and considerations that will shape the course of treatment. This should be done as early as feasible in the helping process so that the client can agree to (or decline) those conditions before service commences. Sometimes informed consent is a verbal agreement that is documented in the case record, but more commonly it takes the form of a written document that is acknowledged by both the social worker and the client. In task groups, the ground rules and mutual expectations should be documented in meeting minutes.

A common tension in informed consent is the perception by professionals that if they provide a thorough

CASE EXAMPLE

Informed Consent in the HEART Group

First Session

Dave (facilitator): Good evening, everyone, and thank you for joining this group. I am glad to see you all again, and I want to start this session by saying a few words about housekeeping, things about how I'd like the group to go, or what I'd like to see us get out of the group, and also talk about confidentiality requirements for this setting.

So to begin, I hope that we can create a safe space for you all to talk about any concerns that you have about symptoms of depression or anxiety and concerns you have about being overweight and about behaviors that might contribute to that for you. I would like for us to decide how we are going to accomplish that as a group; it's a process that we call consensus decision making. So, together we'll come up with the rules for how we're going to operate for the next 12 weeks that will determine how business is conducted, how each member takes time, and how we support each other and interact to make this group work. As a consideration for everybody and as required by law, everything that happens in the group has to stay in the group. You are allowed to talk about what you say in group outside, but we're not allowed to talk about anybody else's business outside of the group. I'd like to see, just by the nods of your heads, that this is something that you understand and agree with. One exception to that rule is that if I find that someone appears to be in danger either from somebody else or in danger of harming themselves, then I have a duty to report that, to keep everybody safe. And I would like to know that everybody understands and is comfortable with that. *[Group nods.]* Okay, terrific.

As a way to start, then, I'd like to ask you to introduce yourselves to the group. I'm okay to take a volunteer if somebody wants to volunteer to go first, otherwise I'll need to choose somebody. Would anybody like to lead and introduce themselves to the rest of the group?

Amelia: I'll start.
Dave: Terrific, Amelia. Go ahead.
Amelia: Okay. Can I actually ask a question?
Dave: Of course.
Amelia: When you say you have to tell people if you're going to hurt yourself, what if you've already hurt yourself—is that an issue that you would have to tell?
Dave: I would want to know if you currently feel like you're not safe physically. If you're in harm's way, however that may happen, I have to take steps to keep you safe, even if that means breaking our confidentiality agreement.
June: So if I say, Maggie told me, "Oh you can eat wraps in this certain place and they're good for you," I shouldn't tell that to anybody?
Dave: You shouldn't tell anybody that Maggie told you that.
June: Okay. I can say that wraps are good.
Dave: You can say that. I'm particularly focused on personal information about members of the group. So information about eating and exercise and dieting you can share; just don't say who said it.
Amelia: So, like, what's said in group stays in group, right?
Dave: Yes, that's it.

accounting of risks, benefits, and limitations, clients will balk at agreeing to those terms, or they will agree but be overly guarded in what they share with the social worker. From the consumer's perspective, though, it is vital to understand from the outset what the "rules of the game" will be, to avoid surprises and to support self-determination. Therefore, it is important to alert group members to the limits of confidentiality before they unknowingly divulge such events. People in time-limited services or programs with a particular focus may be notified at the beginning that the program only addresses certain issues or utilizes a particular type of intervention. For example, in the HEART group for teen girls with obesity, the social worker described how the group might fit with (or differ from) the members' expectations: "We won't be doing exercises together or focusing on good eating habits, though sometimes you might trade ideas about those things. Mostly, we'll talk about what it is like for you, what some of the struggles are in losing weight, and how you can help each other understand and overcome those barriers."

In groups, an important part of informed consent involves articulating the expectations and limits of confidentiality. The social worker must explain his or her commitment to members' privacy, along with the legal and ethical limits to that commitment. The worker must also involve the group in discussing confidentiality, what it means, and how the commitment to each other's privacy will be reinforced. The following case example illustrates some of these ideas.

EP 1

Although group workers endeavor to extract and enforce agreements about privacy, informed consent requires facilitators to acknowledge that they cannot control the actions of other members of the group. As the NASW Code of Ethics (2008a) states:

When social workers provide counseling services to families, couples, or groups, social workers should seek agreement among the parties involved concerning each individual's right to confidentiality and obligation to preserve the confidentiality of information shared by others. Social workers should inform participants in family, couples, or group counseling that social workers cannot guarantee that all participants will honor such agreements. (1.07f)

Social workers should inform clients involved in family, couples, marital, or group counseling of the social worker's, employer's, and agency's policy concerning the social worker's disclosure of confidential information among the parties involved in the counseling. (1.07g)

This can lead to ethical dilemmas as group facilitators try to balance standards for self-determination, confidentiality, safety, and informed consent.

These already complex issues can be exacerbated in online and other electronically facilitated groups. Facilitators must take steps to confirm the identity of participants and reduce risks posed by severely distressed members, minors, or participants who

CASE EXAMPLE

Such a dilemma emerged for Dave facilitating the HEART group when the group was talking about the challenges of peer acceptance and Amber talked about "hooking up" with boys who would later reject her. The group, all older teens but still legal minors, had not discussed the bounds of confidentiality or their parents' and guardians' rights to information. The resulting dilemma for Dave was whether to alert Amber and the others to the possibility that he might need to divulge such risky behavior. In the moment, he decided to let the group focus on the problem Amber was raising, although he shared his dilemma with his supervisor after the session. From that consultation, he decided that he needed to discuss with the group their parents' expectations and how their questions about the group might be handled. He reiterated his intention to alert adult caregivers if he felt members in the group were in danger and engaged the girls in a discussion about what kinds of things parents had a right to know, including binging and purging behavior, risky sexual activity, and drug and alcohol use.

The girls clearly expected privacy when they shared about things they had done in the past (cutting behavior, casual sex, sneaking food) and when they shared about things that "normal teens do, but parents might not like," such as drinking. However, they agreed that it was their responsibility to be honest about their thoughts and actions and Dave's responsibility to assure their safety if he felt they were doing or planning on doing something that could bring immediate harm.

In individual contacts with the girls' parents and caregivers, Dave reaffirmed the boundaries of confidentiality and sought their consent. For example, "As June's mom, you have a right to look at her records and learn about her treatment, but it is our experience that group members need to trust that we'll support their privacy, if they are to bring up the things they are experiencing and feeling most deeply. I'll certainly alert you, or expect June to tell you, if she is putting herself or someone else at risk, but I hope you'll trust me to make that call, knowing that she will share a great deal of personal information that she may want me to keep private. Will that be okay with you?"

misrepresent themselves and their problems. Some steps to address this include posting agency policies and informed consent procedures on the website so that prospective group members can review them in advance of applying for the group. During the recruitment phase, facilitators are urged to contact prospective members in person to assess suitability for the group and determine how and where the individual will be accessing the group (Meier, 2006). This conversation also provides the opportunity to address another ethical concern: upholding the integrity of written communications and protecting others' privacy. Preliminary discussions with group members should address whether their computer is secure from use by others, their capacity for privacy during group phone calls, and expectations about confidentiality. All members of technology-mediated groups should sign and discuss informed consent statements indicating that they understand the expectations and limits of confidentiality (ASWB, 2015).

Competence

While ethical practice demands that all group leaders must be competent in both the issues under discussion in the group and group processes themselves, social workers facilitating electronic groups must also be familiar with the challenges of the particular medium (Northen, 2006). For example, this means being skilled in interpreting phone-only communications, mastering expression in instant messaging and online formats (Meier, 2006), and understanding the complexities that can arise in this novel and evolving form of service. Beyond the specialized competence required for technology-enhanced groups, the general standards of professional competence in group work demand that workers:

- Avoid using techniques with which they are unfamiliar
- Understand group processes, dynamics, and skills, even if using manualized curricula (Galinsky, Terzian, & Fraser, 2006)
- Respect group members and avoid creating conditions in which members are bullied, coerced, or manipulated
- Provide supportive and respectful confrontations when they are required
- Put the needs of group members ahead of their own (Corey, Corey, & Callanan, 2007)
- Help members to differentiate their personal needs from collective, community needs

- "Operationalize values of democracy and self-determination in task group process" (Congress & Lynn, 1997, p. 72).

Nondiscrimination

A final set of ethical dilemmas for group leaders arises in balancing group composition considerations with values and ethics that emphasize nondiscrimination (Fluhr, 2004). For example, in creating the HEART group, a decision was made to limit membership to girls ages 15 to 17, with the rationale that developmental differences would be too great if older or younger members were allowed, and that a mixed-sex group would impede the members' comfort and depth of sharing about crucial issues such as body image, peer relationships, dating, and so on. These are appropriate decisions, driven by the purpose and nature of the group. However, composition decisions naturally exclude certain people on the basis of gender, age, problem profile, and other characteristics. Is this unethical? Such decisions are legitimate if they are made for appropriate clinical reasons, taking into account the need for, purpose of, and goals of the group. Consternation about exclusion can be addressed by creating parallel groups to address unmet needs or excluded populations (overweight teen boys, for example). Of course, competent professionals must always be mindful of their own prejudices and ensure that they are not veiling biases with an indefensible rationale.

SUMMARY

This chapter presented guidelines for assessing and beginning treatment groups and task groups. We addressed considerations in structuring the group, such as format (open or closed), size, frequency, duration, and composition. We used a systems framework to examine the intersection of individual needs and behaviors with those of the group as a whole. We discussed common concerns for members at the outset of a group and the strategies for introducing and assessing group guidelines, norms, and values. In Chapter 12, we turn to considerations of how to build on the social worker's assessment knowledge to construct workable contracts with individuals. We will return to consideration of groups in Chapter 16 to identify the skills needed to intervene at various stages of group development.

COMPETENCY NOTES

EP 1 **Demonstrate Ethical and Professional Behavior**
- **Make ethical decisions by applying the standards of the NASW Code of Ethics, relevant laws and regulations, models for ethical decision making and ethical conduct of research, and additional codes of ethics as appropriate to context.** The NASW Code offers guidance about practitioner competence, exceptions to confidentiality and self-determination, and informed consent in group treatment.

EP 2 **Engage Diversity and Difference in Practice**
- **Apply and communicate understanding of the importance of diversity and difference in shaping life experiences in practice at the micro, mezzo, and macro levels.** Members of task and treatment groups reflect diversity in age, ethnic and racial backgrounds, professions, SES, experiences, sexual orientation, political affiliation, and other factors. These differences often emerge in the process of groups as members interact with the leader and each other. Group workers must possess sophisticated understanding of such differences and the ways they can enhance or derail the group process.

EP 4 **Engage in Practice-Informed Research and Research-Informed Practice**
- **Use and translate research evidence to inform and improve practice, policy, and service delivery.** Because of all of the variables at play, it can be particularly difficult to systematically evaluate the effectiveness of group interventions. Nevertheless, research exists to support the use of group work for various conditions and populations. Research also indicates the worker attributes that can lead to success or failure in groups.

EP 6 **Engage with Individuals, Families, Groups, Organizations, and Communities**
- **Apply knowledge of human behavior and the social environment, person-in-environment, and other multidisciplinary theoretical frameworks to engage with clients and constituencies.** Group interventions use a distinct set of considerations and concepts. Forming and facilitating groups involves decisions about leadership, homogeneity or heterogeneity in membership, group structure, the use of curricula, the development of norms, power, cohesion, addressing counterproductive patterns, and a variety of other concepts unique to the group format.

EP 7 **Assess Individuals, Families, Groups, Organizations, and Communities**
- **Collect and organize data, and apply critical thinking to interpret information from clients and constituencies.** Social workers often meet with prospective group members prior to forming the group to understand their needs, interests, experiences, and readiness for the group process. During the life of the group, clients' interactions with the facilitator and with other members will reveal, verbally and nonverbally, much about themselves and how they approach the world.
- **Apply knowledge of human behavior and the social environment, person-in-environment, and other multidisciplinary theoretical frameworks in the analysis of assessment data from clients and constituencies.** The assessment of individual readiness for group membership and the identification of constructive or problematic patterns in individual and group behaviors depend on fundamental knowledge of human functioning, systems, and other concepts.
- **Develop mutually agreed-on intervention goals and objectives based on the critical assessment of strengths, needs and challenges within clients and constituencies.** Before and during groups, social workers must be attuned to the needs, resources, and abilities that members will bring to the task or treatment group process. Group goals and objectives should be shared when members are recruited for task or treatment groups, then negotiated and amended as new issues and individual needs or interests emerge throughout the group process.

EP 8 **Intervene with Individuals, Families, Groups, Organizations, and Communities**
- **Critically choose and implement interventions to achieve practice goals and enhance capacities with clients and constituencies.** Task and treatment groups provide a

powerful medium for change. Social workers facilitating these groups help participants engage in mutual aid, problem solving, and planning to address shared problems.

SKILLS DEVELOPMENT EXERCISES
in Planning Groups

Imagine that you are planning a group to address one of the following populations or problems:

1. People charged with domestic violence
2. Middle school students with diabetes
3. Teenage fathers
4. Families of people with schizophrenia
5. Elementary school children who have been exposed to family or community violence
6. Parents and community members who wish to change a school policy on suspensions
7. Elderly residents recently admitted to a nursing home
8. Seventh- and eighth-grade "outcasts" who have no friends
9. Teens who want to start a Gay–Straight Alliance in their high school
10. Premarital couples
11. Widowers
12. People concerned about bullying in a school

Using the guidelines in this chapter, determine:

a. The name you will give the group
b. The type of group
c. A one-sentence statement of purpose
d. The size of the group
e. The length, structure, and format
f. The location where you will meet
g. Important factors in group composition
h. How you will recruit and screen members

CHAPTER 12

Developing Goals and Formulating a Contract

Goals and contracts are products that flow from the assessment process. This chapter elaborates on elements of Phase I of the helping process by focusing on the knowledge and skills related to the development of goals and the social worker–client agreement to work together. (Note that the phases of the helping process are illustrated on the inside back cover of this text.) First, we will discuss the purpose and function of goals, with special emphasis on developing goals with voluntary clients, involuntary clients, and minors. The remainder of the chapter is devoted to formulating the contract or service agreement and to methods for monitoring and measuring progress.

As a result of reading this chapter, you will be able to:

- Better understand the purpose and function of goals.
- Articulate the relationship between goals and the target concern.
- Develop specific, feasible, and measurable goals.
- Monitor and measure progress toward goal attainment.
- Formulate a contract or service agreement.

EPAS Competencies in Chapter 12

This chapter will give you the information needed to meet the following practice competencies:

- Competency 1: Demonstrate Ethical and Professional Behavior
- Competency 2: Engage Diversity and Difference in Practice
- Competency 7: Assess Individuals, Families, Groups, Organizations, and Communities
- Competency 9: Evaluate Practice with Individuals, Families, Groups, Organizations, and Communities

GOALS

Goals are central to achieving outcomes and working in systematic, process-oriented approaches such as the helping process discussed in this text. Goals are also prominent in the task-centered and crisis intervention models, cognitive restructuring (a cognitive behavioral procedure), solution-focused brief treatment, and case management. These change-oriented approaches (discussed in greater depth in Chapter 13) share a common process for the development of a **goal statement**—the

EP 7

agreement that becomes the focus of the work to be completed by the social worker and client. Whether an approach emphasizes developing a goal or a solution, ultimately the intent is to address a client's priority concern, condition, want, or need, or in the case of involuntary clients, to meet the requirements of a legal mandate.

The Purpose and Function of Goals

While the stated goal is the desired end product, attainment of a goal is a process. It may be useful to imagine the process as being similar to going on a road trip. A map details your progress from Point A to Point B, from your point of origin to your desired destination. During the trip, you may develop short-term goals—for example, reaching a certain point within a certain time period. The mileage signs along the road and your arrival at a certain location chart your progress. Using the analogy with an individual client, Point A, the starting point, is their **priority concern**. Point B, goal attainment, is the desired outcome. In essence, a goal guides the ongoing process of reaching a final destination point. Once goals are established, **tasks** or **objectives** represent the incremental action steps taken toward the desired outcome and within a designated time frame. In much the same way that you would make use of mileage markers to chart the progress of a trip, the client's completion of tasks or objectives may be envisioned as representing observable points of progress of the change effort.

In your work with clients, having goals facilitates clients' reaching a destination point in which a specific condition, need, status, or functioning has changed. In your agency, you may have become familiar with **SMART goals**. SMART goals function in much the same way as in the above analogy, ensuring that clients can travel successfully from Point A to Point B. SMART goals are **s**pecific, **m**easurable, **a**ction-oriented, **r**ealistic, and **t**imely, providing focus and direction to the work to be completed by the social worker and client.

In addition to facilitating the movement between Point A and Point B, setting goals also:

- Ensures that you and the client are in agreement, where possible, about outcomes to be achieved
- Provides direction, focus, and continuity to the helping process and prevents wandering off course
- Facilitates the development and selection of appropriate strategies and interventions

- Assists you and the client in monitoring progress
- Establishes the criteria for evaluating the effectiveness of a specific intervention and of the helping process

Linking Goals to Target Concerns

Goals evolve from concerns or problems presented by clients. As you listen to clients tell their stories during the assessment interview, you are obtaining useful information for developing preliminary goals. In the case of involuntary clients, goals are prescribed in a mandate or court order. In either case, goals function best when they are linked to a specific concern or problem and have clear performance standards (Corwin, 2002; Huxtable, 2004; O'Hare, 2009; Ribner & Knei-Paz, 2002; Varlas, 2005). The link between goals and target concerns is illustrated in the following case example and the assessment summary of Margaret in Table 12-1.

Older persons like Margaret and her friends often have complex social, psychological, biological, and support needs. These needs do not diminish their desire or their capacity to make decisions about their lives. For the most part, although their physical capacity may be limited in certain domains, they are capable of caring for themselves, albeit with varying levels of support. Most older persons also retain an interest in being socially active. For example, it was important to Margaret to participate in the activities at the senior center. These activities met her psychological and social needs of feeling connected, especially because she lived alone. At the same time, attention to her biological needs was important as her diminished physical capacity limited her ability to routinely prepare nutritious meals. In spite of their needs, it is not uncommon for elderly persons to want to be involved in decisions about the type of help that they receive and to guard against having their lives drastically changed. For many, as it was for Margaret, it can be a trade-off between accepting help and remaining in charge of their lives.

There will be times when achieving a goal will require accessing the resources of another agency. For example, if Margaret decided to remain in her home, other agencies such as home health services and perhaps home-delivered meals would provide most of the essential supports that she requires to be able to do so. It is also quite possible that informal arrangements with neighbors or community organizations could augment the formal services. As the social work case

CASE EXAMPLE

Margaret is an 85-year-old widow who lives alone but is involved with a community-based multiservice senior center. Her four adult children live in other states. She is involved in activities offered by the center, including senior aerobics classes. She considers herself to be generally in good health. Because Margaret lives alone, regular contact with the senior center is an important part of her daily life. During the assessment interview, she talked about feeling unsafe in her home because she lacks a sustained level of energy to complete many of the activities of daily living. For example, she tires easily when doing housework, and at times she has had difficulty getting in and out of the bathtub. Margaret prefers to remain in her own home because she is afraid that she will lose the level of independence that she now enjoys. She had considered home health services, but after hearing the complaints of friends, some of whom were conflicted about the benefit, she too is ambivalent about this resource. In fact, some her friends have emphasized that the scheduled visits of helpers limited their freedom. She laughed as she recounted the complaint of one friend, "You have to get up and out of bed on a schedule, and there are times when you just don't want people in your house." After a lengthy discussion with the social worker, Margaret identified her primary goal as living in a safe environment, preferably in her own home. However, she is open to considering other options, such as home health care or moving to an assisted living facility. Her second goal is to maintain her independence. Maintaining independence was defined as being able to make decisions about her life, continuing to be involved with social activities, and being able to do what she can for herself.

TABLE 12-1 Linkage between Assessment, Target Concerns, and Goals

ASSESSMENT SUMMARY	TARGET CONCERNS	GOALS
Margaret, age 85, feels unable to remain in her home because of concerns for her safety. Central to her safety concerns is her recognition that her ability to complete activities of daily living has diminished. She also wants to maintain her independence.	Margaret is concerned about her ability to continue to live safely in her own home.	To live in a safe environment. To maintain her independence.

manager, your role would involve assessing Margaret's needs and identifying, coordinating, monitoring, and evaluating the various formal and informal service providers.

Distinguishing Program Objectives and Client Goals

The goals of a particular organization are often found in its organizational mission statement. Indeed, you may have been attracted to work at a particular agency because of its mission. Program objectives flow from mission statements and inform how organizational resources are utilized to target a specific need or population or respond to a particular social problem. In some cases, program objectives are directly related to outcomes sought by funders or a purchase of service agreement (POS). (In a POS, a governmental agency funds particular services to be provided by a nonprofit community agency.) Statements may focus on micro (individual), mezzo (family/group), or macro (system/environmental) level issues. For example, one organization may define its mission and programs as responding to the micro-level needs of gay, lesbian, bisexual, and transgender youth in a safe and supporting environment, whereas another may direct its resources to address mezzo-level issues such as reducing the number of homeless families with children by assisting them to find affordable housing. A macro-level program objective might be to end poverty by advocating for legislation that would increase the earned income of a segment of the population.

Within agencies, client goals and program objectives are often used interchangeably to articulate expected outcomes for service recipients. In some instances, an organization may use a standardized evidence-based template to assess competencies or functioning upon which the goals of a treatment regime are established. To distinguish agency program objectives from individual client goals, it may be useful to think of **program objectives** as general statements regarding the outcomes that are expected for all service recipients who are involved with an agency's program. To avoid the one-size-fits-all approach, you should selectively include program objectives in the case goal or treatment plan as they pertain to and fit with the unique situation of each client, much as how priority concerns and goals are linked (Gardner, 2000).

Factors Influencing Goal Development

EP 2

During your discussion with clients about goals, a number of factors and considerations can influence the process. Let's take a look at each of these factors, which are summarized in Table 12-2.

Client Participation

Goal pursuits begin with a client identifying a concern, need, or want; in the instance of nonvoluntary or involuntary clients, responding to a goal that is promoted or assigned by someone other than the client is the starting point. In either case, you should not expect the process of developing goals to be a neatly defined, linear process. During the assessment interview, you may hear about a number of concerns for which the client is seeking a solution. Attending to individual stories takes time, but this is time well spent. As you listen, summarize and clarify what the client has said so that you and the client have an opportunity to explore options before reaching a decision about a priority goal. There are two types of experts in the goal development decision-making process: the client and you, the social worker, in a mutual

partnership of problem solving. Your respective roles in this process are outlined here:

Social worker: As the social worker, your professional expertise, knowledge, and skills facilitate the process by assisting clients to specify, prioritize, and define goals in measurable language. Also, as goals are discussed, you can help clients to assess feasibility, identify potential barriers, and become aware of resources and strengths related to goal attainment. Skills that you will utilize to elicit goal-directed information include the communication and facilitative skills discussed in Chapter 6.

Client: The client is the foremost expert in articulating what he or she would like to be different. Social work principles in support of clients' active involvement in goal decisions include empowerment, social justice, and the axiom "starting where the client is" (Finn & Jacobson, 2003; Marsh, 2002; Meyer, 2001; Smith & Marsh, 2002). Finn and Jacobson (2003) emphasize the social justice aspect of clients' involvement, stressing that "clients have a right to their reality, and to have their reality be a part of their service provisions" (pp. 128–129).

Your sensitivity to and empathy for the reality of clients in goal decisions can be especially important in cross-cultural interactions. Without client participation, goals may be developed that are counterproductive to his or her needs or interests, cause stress, and potentially reinforce a sense of marginalization that mirrors the experience of oppression and inequality (Clifford & Burke, 2005; Dietz, 2000; Guadalupe & Lum, 2005; Pollack, 2004; G. D. Rooney, 2009; Vera & Speight, 2003; Weinberg, 2006). Although, your professional expertise is a vital resource, it is important that you acknowledge and respect clients' appraisals of life experiences to create an atmosphere of a mutual problem-solving partnership.

Irrespective of whether a client is voluntary or involuntary, participation in goal decisions is essential. Clients, whether voluntary or involuntary, are motivated by a process in which they are self-involved and, further, one in which they perceive the process as being just (Greenberg & Tyler, 1987). In contrast, the absence of active participation can influence commitment, self-definition, and self-efficacy (Bandura, 1997; Boehm & Staples, 2004; Gendolla, 2004; Meyer, 2001; Wright, Greenberg, & Brehm, 2004) and ultimately the helping process.

TABLE 12-2 Factors Influencing Goal Development

Client Participation

Involuntary Status

Values and Beliefs

Resources and Supports

Environmental Conditions

Involuntary Status

Involuntary status can mean that clients may be hesitant to cooperate in a process in which they may perceive themselves as having limited power and control with regard to goal decisions. Perhaps the most volatile issues stem from client suspicion, mistrust, and reactance to prescriptive goals that are constructed around their deficits (Lum, 2004; R. H. Rooney, 2009; Sue, 2006). When you invite involuntary clients to participate in goal decisions, their response may be highly charged and emotion focused, with a presentation of self based on their perception of your authority. Furthermore, social distance (caused by perceptions of race, class, and/or cultural differences) between you and the client, as well as your privileged status as a professional, may further exaggerate relational dynamics. Consider the contextual nature of a client's behavioral response. A significant number of the clients with whom you will have contact are involuntary, the majority of them members of a minority group who are disproportionately represented among the involuntary client population. As such, they share certain attributes—for example, tensions related to external control versus personal control, marginal status, constrained self-determination, and the perception of a real or imagined lack of power (G. D. Rooney, 2009).

These dynamics can present as issues more or less depending on the individual. Nonetheless, without your attention to the context of the potential dynamics when they are present, the potential for you to develop and maintain a working relationship can be diminished. In much the same way that you listen to the narrative of voluntary clients and encourage their participation, you begin by inviting involuntary clients to tell their story so that they feel heard, understood, and involved. In doing so, you gain an understanding of their perception of the problem, values, and beliefs. Moreover, supporting their self-efficacy and using facilitative skills can be an effective means of building trust and engaging the participation of involuntary clients (Miller & Rollnick, 2002).

Values and Beliefs

Goals are by their nature intended to facilitate change; however, exploring the client's values and beliefs is fundamental to guiding the process of goal development. Paying attention to and respecting the values and beliefs of each client is consistent with the principles of valuing the unique reality of persons and their situation. For example, individuals from impoverished or minority cultural communities may present behaviors, lifestyles, and values that are often different from conventional behavioral norms (Dunlap, Golub, & Johnson, 2006; Smith, 2006). The strengths perspective and respecting diversity notwithstanding, there may be a tendency to perceive different values and beliefs as problematic and to consider the holders of those values and beliefs as outsiders. Although you may feel challenged by the influence that different beliefs and values can have on particular goals, you should be mindful of the fact that failure to consider client views and goal aspirations can disrupt the goal development process and may lead to ethical conflicts. To illustrate this point, consider the following case example.

As you can observe in this case example, there is the potential for an ethical conflict, specifically the tension between the teen's autonomy and desired goal and the case manager's unintentional paternalism. Should the case manager insist that the teen pursue college rather than her own desired educational goal? In the interest of fairness, the case manager had a good relationship with the teen. During the time they worked together, the case manager recognized the teen's abilities and strengths that would support her pursuit of a college degree. Any one of us, in a similar situation, might be inclined to act in much the same manner, specifically urging a goal beyond what an individual wishes to pursue at a particular point in time.

CASE EXAMPLE

A social work case manager who was responsible for the coordination of the educational goals for a teen mother pressured the teen to make use of the available resources for college-bound students. Conversely, the teen's goal was to complete high school and attend a training school to become a hairstylist. She reasoned that college might be in her future, but she lived in a neighborhood where few people ever completed high school. If someone finished high school, doing so was akin to attaining a college degree and was celebrated. The teen believed that becoming a hairstylist, like others in the community that she knew, would enable her to support herself and her child.

In truth, however, clients tend to make choices and express values that are consistent with their circumstances and worldview, as well as their perception of the resources available to them (Dunlap, Golub, & Johnson, 2006; Orme, 2002; Pollack, 2004; Weinberg, 2006). Of course, the potential exists for clients to make different choices in the future. Empowerment can include coaxing and nudging clients toward aspirations beyond where they are currently, but ultimately, it is their perspective that should guide the goal decision. Although, you should respect and support self-determination, you may look for opportunities to provide clients with information or to suggest more ambitious goals than they envision (such as a client who aspires to become a certified nursing assistant [CNA] but does not explore the possibility of becoming a nurse). It can be possible to both respect a current choice and make sure that the client has the necessary information for exploring another choice in the future should he or she desire to do so.

Sue (2006, p. 135) issues a cautionary note about goals, asserting that the process in and of itself is value laden and that "there are certain values reflected in the goal setting process" that may be counter to the experience and beliefs of clients, including their cultural, racial, or socioeconomic reference group. For example, according to Sue (2006), developing goals is based on several assumptions. Perhaps the most common assumption is that the client has the ability to set a self-goal based on the notions of autonomous action and self-determination as valued by Western society. In fact, this may not be the case for clients from cultural or racial groups in which individual aspirations and esteem are derived from and interdependent with the cultural group or the family. Consequently, exploring the extent to which these cultural distinctions are pertinent to the clients with whom you are working is important.

Developing goals also assumes that all clients, including minors, are familiar with, understand, believe in, and value setting goals. In some instances, you may find that people coping with ongoing stressors may have adapted to their circumstances and therefore are skeptical about whether setting goals will alter their situation. Sue (2006) also emphasizes that the ideal of setting goals in essence profiles individuals whom he refers to with the acronym YAVIS—**y**oung, **a**rticulate, **v**erbal, **i**ntelligent, and **s**uccessful, and most often voluntary in their contact with helping professionals. This profile can result in discrimination against those who are less capable or less socially connected. Examples include persons from different cultural or racial backgrounds, people who speak a second language or regional dialect, people of low socioeconomic status, and persons with diminished cognitive capacity (James & Gilliland, 2005; Sue, 2006). These examples, however, do not mean that clients are incapable of developing goals. Irrespective of an individual client's level of sophistication, circumstances, or cognitive capacity, most are able to articulate wants and needs that can become the basis for the development of goals.

Resources and Supports

Personal motivation, skills, and strengths are among the eminent resources that facilitate the development and pursuit of goals. Individuals are, however, dependent on, and interdependent in, their relations with others. Examples include social networks; educational, virtual, cultural, interest, or faith communities; natural helpers; and families. As you and the client engage in the goal development process, an essential question is: *What resources and supports are needed and available that can enhance the capacity of the client to pursue a desired outcome?* For example, say a client's goal involves obtaining a job suitable to his or her skill level. In today's environment, most employment opportunities are posted online. The resource-related question then is: *Does the client have a computer, and if not, what available resources within the client's social network or the community can make it possible for the client to access employment information?*

Families and supportive kinship networks are among the strengths and resources to be considered in making decisions about goals, as their participation and support may enhance goal attainment. Family members can provide emotional and concrete support during stressful times, which can make a difference in accomplishing a goal. Although you should not assume that family resources are uniformly available, the extent to which the family, cultural, or social networks can be involved should be explored. Specifically, whether the family or other supportive networks are to be involved is a point of discussion, but the decision to include them should be made by the client. In this way, you are respecting the client's preference, be it based on culture, family form, or status.

Decisions concerning minors in most instances will require the involvement and support of family, as well as other individuals or systems with whom the minor has contact. For example, a goal related to school performance requires that a minor's parents and teachers be involved. Conversely, when an overwhelmed parent challenged by the behavior of a minor demands a goal that their offspring be "fixed," extra effort on your part may be required to include and encourage the parent's participation.

There is evidence that the positive support of family or significant others can facilitate goal setting and goal attainment. For example, Ritter and Dozier (2000) found that although a court mandate to complete a drug treatment program was powerful, family support and involvement was equally important in preventing a relapse. Other studies have shown that family involvement and participation provided a cultural frame of reference that was essential to developing goals and ensuring goal attainment with certain clients, including minors (Albright & Weissberg, 2010; Durlak et al., 2011; Gardner, 2000; Hodge & Nadir, 2008; Lum, 2007; Potocky-Tripodi, 2002; Sarkisian & Gerstel, 2004; Saulnier, 2002; Sue, 2006; Wong, 2007).

Increasingly, family involvement is recognized as an asset by social welfare organizations that work with families and children in goal development and attainment. Family group conference (also referred to as family decision making), a child welfare strategy, acknowledges the importance of including the family to develop goals that ensure the safety and well-being of minors (Altman & Gohagen, 2009; Waites et al., 2004).

Although the involvement of family members can be a resource, family support may not be definite or infinite. For example, goal pursuits favored by an individual can be inconsistent with the norms of his or her culture or perspectives on autonomous behavior, including the act of seeking outside help (Williams, 2006; Wong, 2007).

VIDEO CASE EXAMPLE

An example of a cultural conflict can be observed in the video "Working with Yanping." In that video, Yanping, a graduate student from China who is studying in the United States, is experiencing distress because her parents oppose her educational goal of studying history, preferring instead that she study business so that she can take over the family business. Kim, the social worker, must balance Yanping's self-goals with knowledge of the conflict that pursuing such goals might create in her culture.

Of course culture may not be the only reason that family support is unavailable or limited. A family's willingness can depend on the nature of prior and existing relationships. Families can be hesitant to support a client's behavioral change goal, for example, if their doing so might challenge other family members to also make adjustments in their behavior. In some cases, families may provide little or no support because they are burdened by their own needs, stressors, and limited resources. In addition, there are times when a family's goodwill has been exhausted by a member's need for support and, in consequence, the family will invoke a quid pro quo arrangement. In essence, they will support a goal only if certain changes or conditions are met.

Environmental Conditions

As clients cope with difficult situations, it is essential that you understand them as individuals and their situation in the context of the environment. Attributes such as age, race, gender, class, sexual orientation, and structural inequality are factors that can influence the capacity to attain goals irrespective of client motivation. Of course, like other clients with whom you have contact, diverse individuals and families experience tensions that can be characterized as interpersonal or interfamilial in nature. But it is not uncommon that their concerns will also include stressors resulting from a lack of resources and constant stressful adverse environmental interactions. Consideration must also be given to the stress associated with client involvement with multiple external systems, each of which may have different goals for the client.

In many instances, structural inequality and limited resources makes it impractical for diverse groups to survive and thrive. Helping a low-income couple to obtain affordable or subsidized housing, for example, may be constrained by the regional availability of affordable housing and federal subsidy housing funds. Discrimination in housing, employment, and institutional lending patterns is illegal, yet subtle forms still exist, posing barriers to people who are different by virtue of income, sexual orientation, culture, or race, including those with a disability and veterans (Demby, 2013; Fernandez, 2007).

Many of the problems experienced by minority and low-income adults and children include current or historical trauma and other daily living conditions that can have debilitating psychological effects, which can hinder the goal development process (Dietz, 2000; Guadalupe & Lum, 2005; Ko et al., 2008; Sue, 2006). To this point, Grote et al. (2007) found that it was not uncommon for people disadvantaged by poverty, race, or ethnic minority status to experience depression at a higher level than the general population. As such, even though they want relief and have future-oriented aspirations, some may be unable to marshal the energy required to engage in making decisions about goals. Therefore, it is important to recognize person–environment interactions insofar as they affect and influence the capacity of people to make decisions about their lives. In addition, it is important to realize that in such situations, the goal development process may require additional support and time.

By now you have an understanding of the purpose and function of goals, as well as factors that can influence them. To further your learning about goals requires knowledge of the types of goals, the criteria for selecting them, and skills in negotiation. These topics are discussed in the following sections.

Types of Goals

EP 7

Systems or subsystems that will be the focus for change will determine the type of goal to be developed. With individuals, this focus typically involves intrapersonal subsystems as well as their interaction with the social and physical environment. Goals may initially be expressed in broad terms. Examples include change in *cognitive functioning* (e.g., increase positive self-talk), *emotional functioning* (e.g., manage anger), or a *behavioral change* (e.g., listen to others without interrupting).

In some instances, change may require combining *overt* and *covert* goals. An **overt goal** requires action, whereas a **covert goal** involves changing thoughts or feeling. To illustrate, consider the scenario in which an individual is faced with eviction for failure to pay his or her rent on time. An overt *behavioral goal* would be to increase the frequency of paying the rent on time. The behavioral goal may be combined with one that requires a covert cognitive goal if the reason for the lateness is forgetting when the rent payment is due. Assuming that the individual has the funds to make timely rent payments, an overt behavioral goal would involve marking the due dates on a calendar.

Goals may be further categorized by both type and function. Specifically, goals may be shared or reciprocal depending on the systems or subsystems involved. When the target system is a couple, family, or group, goals typically involve changes on the part of all the relevant participants in the system. In these larger systems,

shared goals are held in common and agreed upon by members of the system. For example, after brainstorming ways in which group members could assist each other, members may agree to use positive and supportive messages when interacting with one another. The distinguishing feature of shared goals is that all participants agree to act or behave in certain way.

Reciprocal goals have some elements of a shared goal in that they are also developed in conjunction with all parties involved. With reciprocal goals, all involved agree upon exchanges of different behavior and to act or respond to each other in a different manner. In some instances, a reciprocal goal may be a precursor to developing other goals. For example, in a parent–child conflict situation, both have expressed a desire to improve their communication with each other. Specifically, when they talk, they interrupt each other, and neither feels that the other listened. A reciprocal goal for them would be that each agrees to listen to the other without interrupting. Reciprocal goals tend to be *quid pro quo* in nature; that is, each person agrees to modify his or her personal behavior contingent upon the other person's making a corresponding behavioral change. For example, "I will listen to you without interrupting if when I am speaking, you will also listen to me."

GUIDELINES FOR SELECTING AND DEFINING GOALS

Because goals guide the work to be completed between you and the client, it is important that a goal be selected and defined with care. In discussing the process of selecting and defining goals, we make a point of distinguishing between voluntary and involuntary clients because the dynamics of status affect each situation.

With voluntary clients, the psychological authority attributed to you as the social worker is generally positive. Therefore, their perception of your goodwill positively influences the collaborative nature of your relationship as you select and define goals.

In contrast, the dynamics of the psychological contract inherent in the explicit authority of your position means that the interaction between you and involuntary clients has a decidedly different texture. Perhaps the most volatile issue relates to the fact that, for involuntary clients, goals have been predetermined. In involuntary situations, the client's perception of the relationship is most often one in which compliance and authority, rather than collaboration, are the most

TABLE 12-3 Guidelines for Selecting and Defining Goals

Goals must relate to the desired results sought by voluntary clients.

Goals for involuntary clients should include motivational congruence.

Goals should be defined in explicit and measurable terms.

Goals must be feasible.

Goals should be commensurate with the knowledge and skills of the practitioner.

Goal should be stated in positive terms that emphasize growth.

Avoid agreeing to goals about which you have major reservations.

Goals should be consistent with function of the agency.

salient factors (De Jong & Berg, 2001; R. H. Rooney, 2009). Therefore, involuntary clients may react to engaging in a process in which they feel that their options are limited.

The guidelines highlighted in Table 12-3 and discussed in the following sections are intended to assist you in advancing your proficiency in selecting and defining goals for both voluntary and involuntary clients.

Goals Must Relate to the Desired Results Sought by Voluntary Clients

Our discussion of goals sought by voluntary clients begins with Angela and Irwin Corning. To observe the process of selecting and defining goals, you can view segments 2–4 of the video titled "Problem Solving with the Corning Family." The case is summarized in the following video case example.

VIDEO CASE EXAMPLE

Angela and Irwin Corning and their three children, Agnes (age 10), Henri (age 8), and Katrina (18 months), are homeless. Currently they are residing in a transitional housing facility. Irwin lost his job 8 months ago when the county agency that he worked for as a maintenance and cleaning specialist awarded the cleaning contract to a private contractor. Angela is employed in the evenings as a maid at a hotel. Prior to becoming homeless, the family had a comfortable living, owned their home, and were pleased with the neighborhood's diversity and their children's school. When Irwin became unemployed, the couple was unable to pay their bills or maintain their mortgage payments. For a time, they lived with Angela's sister's family. Angela and Irwin are concerned about the impact of their stressful situation on the two older children. To make matters worse, the school reports that Agnes and Henri are having difficulty at school. Both parents feel that the school situation will change once the family is stable. The social worker at the transitional housing facility referred them to a family service agency for help in finding housing and employment for Irwin. Their preference is to purchase another home, but they realize that at this point they will need to move into an apartment until their financial situation has improved.

In the session with Angela and Irwin Corning, two goals emerged: finding housing for the family and employment for Irwin. Even so, despite the stated goals and the desire for change, the process was not smooth. In many cases during the process of goal selecting and defining, expressions of emotions, anxieties, and values or beliefs heretofore unspoken can emerge. However, these dynamics do not necessarily mean that the client is less motivated. For example, in observing the Corning couple, you will have noticed that despite the identification of two goals and the couple's declared readiness to move ahead, the process of deciding what to do was circular, back and forth, and at times emotional. Both Angela and Irwin expressed feelings related to their frustration and, at times, their ambivalence about the process. At times, they also questioned whether their contact with the social worker would be helpful.

Although your experience with clients to clarify goals may not completely resemble the social worker's experience with Angela and Irwin Corning, their behavior is not atypical. For voluntary clients to be motivated and emotionally invested, they must be confident that as a result of working with you their concerns will be addressed and resolved. For example, although Angela was attentive and for the most part engaged, she was nevertheless uncertain, inquiring of the social worker, "What is it that you do, and how can you help?" Apparent in his demonstrative nonverbal behaviors such as sighing and shifting in his chair, Irwin appears to be uncomfortable and less convinced about the usefulness of the process of developing goals. Eventually, his discomfort is verbalized in his blunt complaint, "Spending time talking was a waste of time." Furthermore, his sense of self had been challenged by his emotional experience of job loss. In particular, he was having difficulty reconciling his situation with his belief that "a man should provide for his family." His perception of the personal and environmental circumstances related to his job loss further complicate the progression toward selecting and defining goals. For Irwin, the process was suspect, given his belief that neither he nor the social worker had the ability to control the circumstance that led to his becoming unemployed.

Like Irwin and Angela, a majority of clients with whom you have contact will be nonvoluntary with respect to their situation, even though they voluntarily sought help. As a result, their emotions may still be vested in their situation, so much so that they continue to recount their difficulties and their anxieties. Notice, for example, that Irwin continued to talk about his unemployment status and his belief about the potential environmental barriers to finding a permanent job.

In instances in which the process of selecting and defining goals becomes overwhelming, it is important for you to maintain focus. Doing so does not mean that you ignore the emotional expressions of clients but rather that you acknowledge their feelings as a natural part of the process. Being in touch with a feeling may call for you to use facilitative skills like seeking concreteness and empathy. Moving ahead, it can be useful for you to restate the target concern using communication skills such as clarification, paraphrasing, and summarizing as appropriate, so that you and the client are able to select and define goals.

"What is my role in helping clients to identify and define goals?" is a question often asked by beginning social workers. You should not assume that your role is passive but rather that you are a partner. Although clients may be more or less clear about their goals, many will appreciate your guidance as they sort out and prioritize the changes they wish to make. You should, however, balance sharing your professional expertise and responsibility by focusing on their primary concerns. Eventually, Angela and Irwin became clear about their goal wants and needs, yet at a certain time, Ali, the social worker, shared her ideas. Even so,

she stressed that her input would be guided by the extent to which they solicited her advice. Ultimately, two goals were selected and prioritized, but not without a number of back-and-forth deliberations.

Goals for Involuntary Clients Should Include Motivational Congruence

Unlike the goals for Angela and Irwin, who were voluntary and motivated to seek help by the weight of their circumstances, goals for involuntary clients have been articulated and defined by another party, most often the court. Even so, a mandate should not preempt or negate the assessment or goal negotiation process. At the same time, involuntary clients may have a high level of interest in complying with the mandate, primarily to remove the pressure they feel rather than because they agree with the values and direction of the mandated goal. Your conversation with clients about mandated goals should include how to meet the goals as well as an exploration of goals that the clients may have themselves.

Strategies for work with involuntary clients were first developed by R. H. Rooney (1992) based on his work with involuntary minors in schools and parents involved with child protection. These facilitative strategies, highlighted in Table 12-4, are applied to the process of selecting and defining goals with involuntary clients.

Prior to reading about the strategies, you might imagine and reflect on your feelings in a scenario in which you are enrolled in a required class. You learn that the instructor has established the highest-level performance goal for you. At this point, the course content is unfamiliar, and you might question the instructor's authority to select and define a goal when you were neither asked about your situation or performance preference nor invited to participate in the decision process. In consequence, you might become anxious, angry, or discouraged and experience a crisis of confidence. Alternatively, you might decide to accept the

TABLE 12-4 Strategies for Developing Goals with Involuntary Clients

Motivational Congruence
Agreeable Mandate
Let's Make a Deal
Getting Rid of the Mandate

performance expectation as a challenge and by doing so avoid the punishment of a lower grade. In either case, you would probably feel resentment because the instructor's decision lacked consideration of your abilities, resources, or desired level of goal attainment. Assuming that the option to enroll in another class was not available, consider the following questions:

- How would you react to the instructor?
- What pressures might you feel?
- If you accepted the established performance expectation as a challenge, how would you know what the indicators were for the highest level of performance?
- Will you be able to negotiate with the instructor?
- What could the instructor do or say that would motivate you to achieve the imposed goal?

Intensity, as described in motivation theory, raises a point that is pertinent to you as the involuntary student, and to the involuntary client. Specifically, when given a goal directive, will people "automatically mobilize maximal effort" if their doing so has "direct implications for their self-esteem, self-direction and personal interest" (Gendolla, 2004, p. 2005)? As you reflect upon this statement and the questions posed in the involuntary student scenario, think about your role in assisting the involuntary client to accomplish imposed goals.

The advantage of the strategies for developing goals with involuntary clients listed in Table 12-4 is that the focus is on a specific change while engaging the client in the instrumental behavioral change required by the mandate.

Motivational Congruence

People are motivated to work on problems that are important to them. **Motivational congruence** means that as a social worker you work on target goals that are personally meaningful to the client and that also satisfy the requirements of the mandate (R. H. Rooney, 2009). Goals are more likely to succeed and result in longer-lasting change when they are meaningful to the client than when motivation and commitment are focused on escaping a sanction or gaining a reward. The principle of "starting where the client is" is equally important with involuntary clients. Goal selection and definition should include their view of the problem in addition to the problem description in the mandate. According to De Jong and Berg (2001), congruence is possible when mandated clients are able to "take control by describing the mandated situation

themselves" (p. 364). When given the opportunity, involuntary clients will express their opinion of problems or situations that resulted in the mandate. In this way, self-definition and their involvement in the process can be a motivating factor by virtue of the fact that their view is solicited and heard.

People who are involuntary may describe their circumstances and the situation in details that includes expressions of anger, frustration, fear, and even outrage. In child welfare, a parent can be sensitive to goals established as a result of a risk assessment relative to indicators of child well-being, potential harm, and acceptable norms of parenting. The mandated goal, particularly its implied definition (characterizing the parent as irresponsible), is serious; however, it can be inconsistent with the parent's self-perception and perspective on the problem. Mandates and risk assessments are not structured in a way that aids our understanding of the circumstances of a particular behavior or act. Instead, the focus of the court's mandate is on the harm to the child and a consequent goal that requires corrective action. For example, a mother who left her children home alone for a period of time to go to a party is a legitimate concern of child welfare, child protective service, and the court. Nonetheless, the court is neither interested in, nor privy to, the circumstances, only that the well-being of the children has been compromised. However, your understanding of the circumstances can aid you in negotiating and defining the goal. Two central questions in this case are relevant with respect to achieving motivational congruence:

- What are the concerns of the court in the situation?
- Is the mother also concerned about leaving her children at home unsupervised?

Motivational congruence, as illustrated in Figure 12-1, is possible when the target goal of the court and the parent are compatible. In this regard, the relationship becomes more collaborative, as there is agreement between the mother, the court, and you as social worker about the safety and supervision of the children when she is not at home. In this case, the congruence between the concerns of the parties involved can lead to the development of goals with which both the court and the mother are satisfied. More importantly, the mother is involved and the opportunity for her autonomy and self-efficacy has improved, which in turn can influence her motivation.

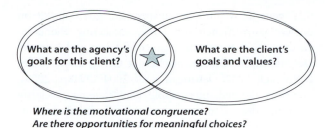

FIG 12-1 Motivational Congruence

Now that you have learned about the motivational congruence and strategies that are intended to facilitate the development of goals, think about which one would been instrumental in the scenario in which you were the involuntary student.

Agreeable Mandate

It is likely that hearing the mother's perspective on the circumstances in which the behavior occurred (leaving her children unsupervised) will provide additional information about the problem. The court, however, has reached a conclusion based on a report of neglect. Without the opportunity to tell her story, the mother is likely to resent the court's assessment of her as a parent and the fact that the decision lacked an understanding of her circumstances. For her, it is a question of fairness in both the process and the outcome (Greenberg & Tyler, 1987).

The **agreeable mandate** strategy entails a search for common ground that bridges the differing views of the involuntary client and the court (De Jong & Berg, 2001; R. H. Rooney, 2009). Pursuing the agreeable mandate may also involve reframing the definition of the problem in such a way that it adequately addresses the concerns identified in the mandate or referral source while simultaneously responding to the concerns of the client. Reframing is a useful technique for reducing reactance, facilitating a workable agreement, and increasing the client's motivation. This strategy may be combined with motivational congruence.

Let's consider an example of a participant in a treatment group for men who batter. The participant may reject the descriptive language used by the professional group leader, such as "perpetrator," and feel pressured to admit that his behavior is a starting point for developing a behavioral change goal. Instead, the participant may agree to a goal of improving his relationship with his spouse where the focus is on

how this can be accomplished. When a client has intense feelings about his or her behavior, self-reflection can be an intermediate step to goal selection. For example, if the man disagrees that he has a problem handling his anger, which leads him to become violet, you might ask him to consider a goal in which he would examine how his behavior affects those around him.

Let's Make a Deal

Negotiating goals with involuntary clients can include a bargaining strategy, or "Let's make a deal." Essentially, the private concerns of the involuntary client are combined with the problem that precipitated the mandate or referral (R. H. Rooney, 2009). To illustrate, let's return to the scenario in which the mother left her children alone while she went to a party in the neighborhood. While she was away, there was a small fire in the apartment, and the older child called the fire department. When the firefighters discovered that the children were home alone, a call was made to the child protection services agency. Subsequently, the children were moved to a temporary shelter. In meeting with a child protection agency staff member, the mother, as you might imagine, was scared and angry, stating, "They had no right to take my kids. It is hard to always be stuck at home and not have time for myself." The problem from the perspective of child protection services is that the children were left unsupervised and further, the occurrence of the fire placed the unsupervised children in danger. In this case, the "deal" could be that you would address the mother's need for self-time if she agrees to work on resolving the issue of supervision and safety for the children. The value of this strategy is derived from your willingness to offer a payoff that meaningfully addresses the mother's expressed concern. Although you can't offer her the option of not complying regarding the court's mandate, you can make the mandated situation more agreeable by addressing her concern about her lack of self-time. In this way, you are attending to her concern and you are creating an incentive for the mother to be involved in developing problem-solving goals related to the mandate.

Getting Rid of the Mandate

With some involuntary clients, none of the preceding strategies may be viable. In such situations, the only recourse left is to appeal to the client's desire to be free of the restraints imposed by a mandate or referral source.

TABLE 12-5 Goal Planning with Involuntary Clients

Client Concerns	Goals	General Tasks/ Specific Tasks
Lack of social time	Self-time	Provide supervision
Legally Mandated Problem/Concerns	**Goals**	**General Tasks/ Specific Tasks**
Children were home alone/Fire	Child safety	

This strategy appeals to the client's motivation, specifically, *getting rid of the mandate or outside pressure* (Jordan & Franklin, 2003; R. H. Rooney, 2009). Take the case of the unsupervised children: The mother is angry and feels misunderstood. She rejected the conclusion that she neglected her parental responsibility by leaving the children unsupervised. Rather, she considered it a one-time event precipitated by her "feeling I am going to lose my mind being cooped up in the house with these kids all the time." She also asserted that needing self-time did not mean that she did not care for her children: "I love my kids, they are all that I have, and I am all that they have." She is clear that her primary motivation is to "get you people out of my hair" and to escape what she considers the adversarial and invasive presence of child protection services and the court in her life. Using her desire to be rid of the oversight of the court as a motivator, the focus of a goal of having the children returned is clarified. In effect, her desire to be rid of the oversight points to the necessary incremental actions for accomplishing the goal. In essence, all parties involved share a goal—specifically, the return of the children to the home, albeit when certain requirements are met. Table 12-5 illustrates a goal summary that considers the concerns of the client and the requirements of a court mandate.

Goals Should Be Defined in Explicit and Measurable Terms

Thus far, we have discussed the process of selecting and defining goals with people who are voluntary clients as well as specific strategies that can facilitate the process of developing and defining goals with involuntary clients. Irrespective of the client's status, once a goal is identified, it must be defined in explicit and measurable terms. Goal setting and motivation theories emphasize that general, vague, or unspecified goals result in unclear performance standards, subjecting clients to an experience in which their confidence and capacity are challenged (Bloom, Fischer, & Orme, 2009; Miller & Rollnick, 2002; Oettingen et al., 2004; O'Hare, 2009). Explicitly defined, measurable goal statements clarify what the desired outcomes are, under what circumstances they are to be achieved, and by whom. Additionally, explicitly defined, measurable goal statements specify monitoring and measurement procedures (O'Hare, 2009). In determining whether a goal is measurable, it may be useful to pose an evaluative question, such as "What are the indicators that will inform you and the client when the goal has been accomplished?" The following are some examples of defined, explicit, and measurable goals:

- "The mother will provide supervision for the children each time that she goes out for the evening."
- "Mr. Diaz will be able to administer his daily insulin injection under the supervision of a home health nurse."
- "Participants in the social skills group will learn listening skills and use the skills learned in the classroom."

Each of these examples specifies who is involved, what is expected, and under what circumstances the goal is to be achieved. In each of the examples, you can see the importance of goals that are specifically defined and whose progress can be monitored and measured. At times, it will be useful for you to develop or use existing tools to aid you in monitoring and measuring progress. For example, you might establish a pregroup baseline of listening skills for each of the social skills of group participants and chart their progress over time. At the end of the group, you would compare their pregroup and postgroup skill levels to determine whether, and to what level, their listening skills had improved.

Appropriately stated, specific, and measurable goals may specify both overt and covert behavioral changes. An overt goal for a participant in a social skills group might be to "increase the number of times that a participant doesn't interrupt when the teacher or another student is talking." The achievement of this goal can be observed and measured by others including the teacher, as well as by the social worker. A covert, self-monitoring goal might be to "increase positive thoughts about the teacher," with goal progress charted and tracked over a period of time. Be aware, however, that measures of covert behavior are subject to error as a result of inconsistent self-monitoring and the effects of self-monitoring on the target behavior. Also, individuals may forget to record their thoughts and, after a time, the task may become too tedious for them to sustain.

Regardless of the tools that you use, documentation in case progress notes and/or SOAP (subjective, objective, assessment, and planning) is essential for maintaining focus and for recording, monitoring, and measuring progress. For example, having established a baseline and an overt behavioral goal for a participant in the social skills groups, you would chart the number of times that the participant did not interrupt the

teacher or other students during class. Progress toward this goal would be recorded in the case progress notes and eventually be reviewed in the termination phase in evaluating outcomes.

Although agencies typically have their own forms for recording progress, an example is illustrated in Figure 12-2. Note that both strengths and obstacles are recorded, as well as tasks for both the client and the staff. The form may also be adapted to specify action steps or objectives rather than tasks, depending on the words used in your agency. The form serves the important function of tracking progress relative to the status of a goal, indicating whether it has been completed or partially completed. This information is also

Client/Family:	Staff:		
Statement of Concern:			
Goal Statement:		Goal #__	
General Tasks:			
Identify Strengths/Resources:		Identify Potential Barriers/Obstacles:	
Tasks/Steps–Participant:		Tasks/Steps–Staff:	

Date:	Progress Notes:	Staff

Goal Status Summary: C__ PC__ NC__ (Need summary explanation)

FIG 12-2 Case Progress Notes
Source: © Glenda Dewberry Rooney. Used with kind permission of the author.

available to other staff or team members. Many experienced social workers provide clients with a folder that summarizes the priority problem or concern and the goal statement, related tasks, and progress notes, which helps motivate clients as they are encouraged by their progress. Providing clients with a copy of the agreed-upon goals can lessen perceived power differences and help maintain a collaborative relationship.

Partializing Goals

Even goals formulated with a high level of specificity are often complex and involve multiple actions that must be completed in a logical sequence. Because of this complexity, clients may feel overwhelmed and intimidated when facing the prospect of tackling goal implementation. For these reasons, it is important that goals are **partialized** into manageable parts. Partializing is not a new technique in social work practice. Indeed, partializing has long been a basic tenet of social work practice theory (Perlman, 1957). It is consistent with the social work commitment to empowerment, especially in facilitating clients' ability to make decisions and to achieve desired outcomes. Clients are better able to develop discrete corrective or problem-solving actions (general and specific tasks), giving them a sense of efficacy in support of goal attainment.

Goals and General Tasks

Rarely are clients able to go immediately from 0 to 60 in their efforts to achieve goals. Further, clients may be unclear about what needs to be done in order to achieve a goal. Consequently, **general tasks** are developed as instrumental strategies to further partialized goals (Reid, 1992). General tasks serve as the basis for the subsequent development of **objectives**, **steps**, or **specific tasks**. Whether phrased as specific tasks or objectives, the essential function of both is that they indicate the particular action steps to be taken to achieve goals. For example, attaining your degree in social work is a goal, whereas general tasks related to obtaining your degree may be to obtain financial assistance, attend classes on a regular basis, and complete required assignments, as well other necessities such as arranging for child care and transportation. These are general tasks because it is unlikely that they could be completed without your engaging in multiple smaller actions or specific tasks.[1] Keep in mind that a general task can entail multiple objectives, action steps, or specific tasks. For instance, arranging for child care is a general task that would involve specific tasks or action steps such as locating a child care provider.

Table 12-6 distinguishes between goals and general tasks. Included in the table are goals that involve both overt and covert behaviors. Notice that explicit goals refer to specific behaviors or environmental changes that suggest the nature of the corresponding intervention.

General tasks may also be categorized broadly as either *discrete* or *ongoing* (or continuous). **Discrete general tasks** consist of one-time actions or changes that resolve or ameliorate problems. Examples include obtaining a needed resource (e.g., housing or medical care), making a major decision (e.g., deciding to adopt a child), or making a change in one's environment (e.g., moving into an assisted living complex). **Ongoing general tasks** involve actions that are continuous and repetitive and rely on incremental progress toward the ultimate or global goal. For example, registration

TABLE 12-6 Goals and General Tasks

GOALS	GENERAL TASKS
1. Pursue a social work degree.	1. Submit applications for admission.
2. Provide appropriate supervision for the children each time the mother goes out for the evening.	2. Arrange for child care.
3. Live in a safe environment.	3. Visit assisted living facilities.
4. Lose 20 pounds.	4. Join a health club.
5. Learn to plan and prepare nutritious meals.	5. Prepare meals that include foods from the five food groups.
6. Improve listening skills in the classroom.	6. Listen without interrupting others in the classroom.
7. Minimize conflict with peers during recess.	7. Learn conflict resolution skills.
8. Express anger in a constructive manner.	8. Learn alternative ways of expressing anger.
9. Attend school on time on a regular basis.	9. Make preparations for getting to school on time.

for classes is a discrete task, attending classes on a regular basis is an ongoing, incremental task toward obtaining a degree (ultimate goal).

In defining explicit goals and ongoing general tasks, a part of the process involves identifying the level of desired change. With goals that involve ongoing behavior, growth is potentially infinite, so it is desirable to determine the extent of the change or the scope of the solution sought by the client or mandate—for example, "The children will be supervised when the mother goes out for the evening." The advantage of determining a specific level of change is that you and the client mutually agree to the ends sought by the latter. As another example, consider a social skills group where the goal is to increase listening skills in the classroom. With this global group goal, each student will have a different skill or behavior baseline and will undoubtedly aspire to a different level of goal attainment. Your role is to assist each participant to develop a goal that is consistent with his or her expected and desired level of goal attainment. In using a baseline for each group participant, social workers and clients are able to specify, monitor, and measure individual progress.

Goals Must Be Feasible

People prefer goals that are feasible and desirable based on their assessment of their capacity for goal attainment (Bandura, 1997; Markland et al., 2005; Oettingen et al., 2004). Similarly, motivated by self-direction, clients are capable of accomplishing the goals that they set for themselves. Thus, it is important that you affirm their sense of self by exploring the feasibility of selected goals. Pursing unachievable goals sets up clients for failure and for becoming discouraged ("*Why bother?*"), disillusionment ("*The situation is hopeless*"), or a sense of defeat ("*Nothing ever changes*").

You may encounter clients who have goals that are more difficult to attain than they had originally imagined, as well as some who have grandiose or impractical aspirations. Also, there may be clients who pay scant attention to personal or environmental limitations. Faced with this dilemma, your ethical obligation is to engage the client in a discussion about feasibility. Ethical persuasion, which affirms the client and preserves his or her dignity, can be useful at this point. In essence, **ethical persuasion** involves a conversation of mutual respect between you and the client in which alternative goals are explored and advantages and disadvantages of a goal decision are reviewed. However,

caution should be exercised. You should not assume a paternalistic or beneficent expert role or, in the case of the involuntary client, emphasize the authority vested in you by a mandate. Affirming and supporting a client's goal when feasibility is in question can be a balancing act. Important self-reflection questions related to discussing the feasibility of goals with clients may include the following:

- How can I affirm clients' goals and reinforce and support their motivation without participating in a potential situation in which they could become discouraged?
- How can I assist clients to partialize goals and to develop incremental tasks or objectives so that their goals can be realistically achieved?
- What are realistic and measurable expectations as to what can feasibly be achieved within a given time period?

Focusing on feasibility is critical as goal attainment requires more than a force of will, even in the best of circumstances, as illustrated in the following video case.

VIDEO CASE EXAMPLE

In the video "Problem Solving with the Corning Family," Angela and Irwin Corning identified a goal of owning a home. Given their financial situation and the 6-month period in which they were required to move from the transitional housing facility, home ownership as a primary goal was impossible. Ali, the social worker, did not dismiss the goal. Instead, she affirmed the legitimacy of the goal as a possibility for the future. Afterward, she directed their attention to more immediate, feasible, measurable, and attainable goals, specifically, finding a three-bedroom apartment and a job for Irwin. Even so, the feasibility of the two goals needed to be considered. For instance, given current limited income, how much rent could they afford, and would this amount be sufficient for a three-bedroom apartment? This discussion was in fact beneficial. After the session, Angela visited several apartment complexes they considered to be desirable, but they were somewhat discouraged about the rent and had to adjust their expectations.

The Feasibility of Involuntary Clients' Mandated Case Plans

Sometimes, the feasibility of goals set for involuntary clients can be especially difficult to navigate and manage. Mandated goal plans are often written in general or vague terms, and feasibility can be hindered by unrealistic expectations about what can be accomplished within a given time period. Several factors contribute to the feasibility of mandated case plans.

At times, case plan goals seem to include "everything but the kitchen sink"—including everything possible to fix the client without prioritizing the goals or assessing their feasibility. Also, because goals can require multiple changes, a client can be required to be simultaneously involved with multiple service providers. To add to the stressors that a client can experience, each of the service providers may have program objectives and expected outcomes to be met. For example, one frustrated client who was mandated to seek drug treatment and individual counseling, submit to weekly urine analysis (UAs), attend parenting classes, and find employment demanded, "How am I supposed to find a job, take care of and spend time with my kids, when I'm running around seeing all of you people?" Further, she asked, "When I find a job, nobody is going to let me miss a lot of work. How am I gonna tell my supervisor that I have to leave work to go pee in a cup? The judge said I had 6 months to complete my case plan!"

The "cookie cutter" case plans consist of program objectives and requirements that are applied uniformly to all individuals or families. There is an assumption that the client population has the same or similar needs and therefore program objectives need not be selectively applied to the unique situation of each individual client. Alternatively, in the example of the client who was court-ordered to a parenting class, a focus on the specific skills she was to learn within a certain time period would probably have had greater appeal and been less stressful for her. For the sake of example, let's specify a goal for attending the parenting classes: the preparation of nutritious meals for her children, for which she lacked the needed knowledge. Specific goals are illustrated in the following sample goal statement.

Upon completion of the parenting class, the client:

1. Will have learned about the major food groups
2. Will be able to prepare meals using foods from three of the five food groups during the next week

Selectively developing goals that respond to the uniqueness of the client situation does not preclude meeting mandates or program objectives. Instead, a specific goal focus clarifies the change that is specifically required for a particular client.

Assessing the feasibility of both kitchen sink and cookie cutter goals is especially important because they can add to the tension and distress that a client experiences. For example, resources that a client needs may be limited or unavailable; however, they have a limited time period to attain goals or face sanctions by the court. Given this scenario, some clients may resign themselves to failure and drop out, even when their doing so has serious consequences. For some, their confidence and motivation can be greatly diminished, while others can perceive the requirement as unjust. Goal attainment that requires extraordinary effort and for which feasibility is uncertain can cause undue hardship for the client (Wright, Greenberg, & Brehm, 2004).

In addition to the previous feasibility questions, there are other questions that you might consider with regard to mandated case plan goals:

- Can the required goals be attained within the time limits?
- When the client expresses frustration, is this viewed as a lack of motivation or opposition?
- What is the level of progress that would satisfy the court mandate?
- Does the client have the resources or knowledge to achieve the goal?
- Are there interpersonal, intrapersonal, or environmental barriers to goal attainment?
- What opportunities and challenges are there in the client's relationships (for example, the receptiveness and capacity of significant others to change)?

In working with mandated case plans, social workers can feel caught between their responsibility and ethical duty to the client and their obligation to the authority of the court or the referring agency. Moreover, a mandate has an expectation of compliance for both the social worker and the client. Also, if your work is funded by an agency purchase of service or performance contract, there can be program objectives, expectations, and requirements for the client that guide your work. Nonetheless, it is your ethical responsibility to increase the likelihood that a client with your help is able to achieve program requirements or mandated goals. In managing the expectations and pressures, you can assume responsibility for helping the client to partialize and prioritize the various goal requirements.

Prioritizing and partializing mandated goals would involve developing a definitive plan that focuses on the requirements of greatest significance (e.g., child safety). It may also require that you act as a mediator between the client and the county or state staff person who has responsibility for oversight of the case and reporting to the court. Part of your role may also include advocacy on behalf of the client, requesting that the court consider any constraints or barriers to goal achievement, reporting the progress that has been made, and seeking the court's permission to prioritize any remaining goals. For example, your report could inform the court, "The parent has completed the drug treatment program, and her urine analyses (UAs) have been clear for 6 months." In this way, the court is advised that progress has occurred but also that additional time is needed for the parent to find a job commensurate with her skills. Your advocacy on the parent's behalf enables the client to have a reasonable opportunity to develop and demonstrate the competencies needed to resolve the other requirements of the mandate.

Goals Should Be Commensurate with the Knowledge and Skills of the Practitioner

EP 1

Certain goals and problems—for example, child sexual abuse—require a high level of training and expertise beyond that of a beginning social worker. It is your legal and ethical responsibility to the client and to the profession that you engage in practice within the scope of you knowledge, ability, and skill level (Reamer, 2001). Practice beyond your scope can result in harm to the client and further pose a liability for you and your agency. The National Association of Social Workers (NASW) Code of Ethics and the Association of Social Work Boards (ASWB) provide clear direction with regard to engaging in practice beyond your scope of practice and competence.

Secondary Supervision

In instances where you may lack the competence or agency supervision for dealing with a situation, you may be able to contract for **secondary supervision**. This type of supervision can provide you with access to a qualified professional, making it possible for you to contract for goals beyond your scope under the professional's guidance (Caspi & Reid, 2002; Reamer, 1998; Strom-Gottfried, 2007). Contracting for secondary supervision, however, is generally restricted to a

specific case. Also, whereas secondary supervision or consultation provides you with guidance in regard to a particular area of practice expertise, ultimately it is the agency supervisor who is responsible for the ongoing oversight of your work and to whom you are accountable (NASW & ASWB, 2013; Strom-Gottfried, 2007). For this reason, secondary supervision will generally require the approval of your supervisor. In all circumstances, it is essential that all parties involved take precautions to protect client confidentiality (Loewenberg, Dolgoff, & Harrington, 2005; Panos et al., 2004; Reamer, 1998). Of course, using secondary supervision assumes that this resource is available in your particular geographic area.

When Secondary Supervision Is Not an Option

When secondary supervision is not an option, you proceed to work with a client with the approval and guidance of your supervisor, under specific restricted conditions:

1. You should explain to clients the limitations of your competence with regard to their goal. Advising clients of your practice limitations allows them to decide on an informed basis whether to continue their contact with you.
2. You must evaluate whether developing goals in an area where you lack expertise places the clients or others at risk.

Each of the options discussed offers considerations to be carefully evaluated against the potential risks to the client and to your agency. Also, you should be aware of whether undertaking an alternative arrangement and engaging in practice beyond your scope (as defined by legal regulation in your state or province) poses a risk to you (Reamer, 1998; Strom-Gottfried, 2007). In general, it is ethical and legal to engage in practice that is commensurate with your scope and competence and to refer clients who require service beyond your competence or that of your agency to a qualified professional (Reamer, 1998).

Goals Should Be Stated in Positive Terms That Emphasize Growth

Goals should emphasize growth, highlighting the benefits or gains to the client as a result of their attainment. In formulating goal statements, stipulating negative behaviors that must be eliminated tends to draw attention to what clients must give up,

EP 7

thereby emphasizing deficits in their behavior. Consider this goal statement: "Veronica's interactions with her peers need improvement so that she can participate in the spring festival." Two issues are relevant in the statement. First, "interaction with peers" and "improvement" are undefined. Second, the focus is on the negative aspects of her behavior and punishment. Rewriting this goal in positive terms—"Veronica will learn conflict resolution skills so that she avoids getting into a shouting match with her peers"—emphasizes the specific behavior to be changed as well as the expectations for the circumstances in which she will utilize the skills that she has learned.

Consider a protective services case plan for a single father who has recently been released from prison and has regained custody of his children. Shortly after his release, a teacher reported that the oldest child had bruises on his arm. An investigation of the report found evidence for the use of excessive discipline. The case plan read: "Parent will demonstrate understanding of his inability to manage stress and anger, and the resulting tendency to use punishment, resulting in physical abuse of the child." Although the father's point of contact was involuntary, he did want help. He recognized that, as a result of being in prison for 10 years, he lacked some parenting skills. The image of him reflected in the goal statement as an angry, abusive, and uncaring parent caused him to feel discouraged. Furthermore, the portrayal was inconsistent with his self-image and undermined his sense of self as "trying to do the right thing." His reaction is not uncommon. In fact, people tend to counter negative evaluations of their behavior or situation initially with disbelief, which can lead to their becoming hostile, despondent, or feeling

threatened. Also, when goals are vague, a lack of understanding of what is expected can increase a client's level of psychological stress and anxiety. In working with this particular client to complete the case plan, it would be important for you to reinforce the positive elements of his behavior. Psychologically, positive goals that have clear performance standards enhance motivation and mitigate conscious or unconscious opposition to change (Bloom, Fischer, & Orme, 2009; Miller & Rollnick, 2002). Table 12-6 highlights contrasting examples of negative and positive goal statements.

Avoid Agreeing to Goals about Which You Have Major Reservations

You may legitimately have reservations about certain client goals. For example, goals that are overly ambitious, cause harm, or have an adverse impact on the client can cause you to be concerned. Your reservation might be caused by your uncertainty about the benefits of a client's goal. For instance, an adolescent wishing to become pregnant (believing that she can be a better parent than her own) thinks that living on her own with a child will allow her to get away from a stressful family situation. Another instance in which your reservation would be appropriate involves a situation in which a parent might insist on a goal regarding a child's behavior, despite your emphasis on the entire family's involvement. Further, your concern is warranted if a client's goal is at odds with the agency's focus or values.

Increasingly, some professionals are asserting their right to serve or not serve clients because of their religious or moral beliefs, despite ethical codes that emphasize self-determination and the primacy of

TABLE 12-7 Negative and Positive Goal Statements

NEGATIVE	POSITIVE
Understand his inability to manage stress and anger when he disciplines the children	Learn alternative ways to discipline the children
Never leave the children home alone	Arrange for care of the children when you plan to be away for the evening
Prevent the formation of coalitions and nonparticipatory behaviors by group members	Unite the efforts of the group in working collectively, encouraging each member to participate
Discontinue the frequency of drinking binges	Increase periods of sobriety each day
Refrain from running away from home	Discuss curfew with parents as an alternative option to running away from home
Reduce incidents of abusive behavior	Walk away from situations when you are angry, to avoid hitting your wife

client's rights. There are also instances in which social workers may be faced with a tension between ethical and legal responsibility. For example, confidential information provided by a client for whom you are ethically responsible and have a fiduciary obligation may be in conflict with state and federal laws.

Professional Values and Goal Tensions

EP 1

Reservations can include clients' goals that are incompatible with your values. Values, of course, are highly individualized. You may work with a client with whom you do not share common ground with respect to values. How do you reconcile differences, should you find yourself in a situation where your values have the potential to intrude upon your fiduciary obligation to the client? What is an appropriate course of action?

When you are faced with situations that tax your ability to work with some people, you can rely on the ethical principles that frame the professional nature of the client–social worker relationship. Specifically, this means that ethically your personal values should not dictate how you work with clients. Doing so may require you to pause and take stock so that you can become aware of the tension and evaluate your thinking. This may also be a time when you should seek supervision. Continuing to work with clients in circumstances where you disagree with their goals can become an issue of the client's rights to effective treatment if your feelings intrude upon the helping process.

Referrals as a Resource

In some cases, ethical practice demands that you refer the client to another professional or agency, providing an honest and nonjudgmental explanation to the client and obtaining the client's consent. Often, students will assert their inability to work with a particular client with certain attributes. A reflective exploration might include such questions as "How do I know in advance of meeting the person and hearing his concerns that I am unable to work with him?" or "Have I labeled the individual based on her attributes before I fully understand what her goals are?" These self-reflection questions may in fact clarify your reservations and make a referral unnecessary. In instances where you have determined that a referral is preferable but unavailable, you should explain to clients up front the kind of help you can and cannot provide in assisting them to achieve their goals. For example, "I can help you with your goal of retaining custody of your son by submitting a report to the family court judge outlining your progress. But, on the basis of the information that you shared with me, I am unable to help you prove that the child's father is irresponsible."

There will be times, nonetheless, in which you are involved with a case and have strong reservations about or disagree with a client's goals. The tension between self-determination and your reservations poses an ethical dilemma for which you will need to seek supervision or consultation (Strom-Gottfried, 2007). Tensions can also occur when the evidence-based practices that an agency has implemented are incompatible with what an individual client wants or needs. For example, Furman (2009) comments that evidence-based practice protocols may tend to focus on outcomes and efficiency rather than on exploration of clients' goals or on the guiding principles of the social worker profession. In either case, in those instances in which you have determined that a referral is in the best interest of the client, it is important to explain the reason for referring the client to another professional and to obtain the client's consent.

Ethical and Legal Tensions

In practice, there will be times at which you may decline to assist a client with a particular goal for legal and ethical reasons. For example, goals that involve a threat of harm to the client or others are neither ethical nor legal. You may also face situations in which ethical and legal choices are in conflict. Responding to the legal choice may, in your opinion, be unjust and undermine your ethical obligation to the client (Kutchins, 1991; Reamer, 2005). The feasibility of goals can also be influenced by both legal and ethical concerns. The social worker in the following case example was confronted with such a situation.

Here, the mother had two goals. Her priority goal was to arrange for her family to come to the United States. Second, she hoped that they would eventually become citizens. The priority goals and whether they were attainable had both legal and ethical implications for the social worker. In addition, a conflict of cultural norms added to the tension.

The social worker in this case faced several difficult choices. Specifically, these choices involved her responsibility to the mother, the mother's right to autonomy and confidentiality, and compliance with the law. Observing the ethical obligations had legal implications. Although somewhat intimidated by the mother's reaction, the social worker explained the legal consequences for the family of providing false information

CASE EXAMPLE

A mother who had been a victim of political torture in Liberia escaped to a neighboring country with her children and her mother. After living in a refugee camp for 2 years, the woman, under the Liberian Immigration Act, obtained a permit that allowed her to come to the United States. She was in the process of completing the paperwork so that her children and her mother could immigrate to the United States as well. This process required DNA reports for the children as well as their birth records, which the mother was able to provide for two of the children. When asked by the Legal Aid attorney whether the third and youngest child was indeed her child, the mother replied yes. Actually, the family had found the child abandoned and had taken her in as a member of the family. Although not biologically related, in the culture of Liberia the child was considered to be the mother's child and therefore a member of the family. The social worker assisting the mother knew the status of this child and felt uncomfortable with the information that the mother had provided to the attorney. When the attorney left the room, the social worker expressed her concern and the mother became upset, telling the social worker to "remove herself from the case if she could not be more supportive."

to the attorney and to Immigration and Customs Enforcement (ICE). The social worker then explained that, because she was aware that the kinship information about the youngest child was false, being a party to the deception had legal implications for her as the social worker. She further explained that, while she was sensitive to the Liberian culture's definition of "family," she would not be able to continue working with the mother unless she agreed to tell the truth. In an effort to resolve the matter, she proposed helping the mother explain the cultural nature of the child's status to the attorney and on the immigration forms.

In a review of this case during a consultation session, some staff believed this to be primarily a legal issue because the child did not meet the legal requirement of being a biological family member. Others, including the social worker presenting the case, viewed the situation differently. For them, it was within the ethical role of the social worker to assist the Legal Aid Attorney to understand the mother's culture, within which this child was considered to be a member of this family. Knowledge of a client's culture in the provision of services is also an ethical principle, and social workers are expected to use their knowledge to explain the functions of behavior within a cultural context (NSAW Code of Ethics, Standard 1.05). You might think that this case example represents an exceptional situation, but as social workers have increasing contact with clients from diverse cultural backgrounds, they are more and more likely to encounter situations that require them to act as cultural interpreters and advocates.

Goals Should Be Consistent with the Functions of the Agency

Explorations of clients' problems, wants, and desired changes may be incompatible with the agency's mission, function, and program objectives. For example, although a family services agency provides a range of services, they might not offer vocational

EP 7

counseling. Likewise, hospitals in general do not offer family counseling, except in specific situations (e.g., grief and loss) and then only on a short-term basis. Should client needs not match or exceed agency function, it is appropriate for you to assist them in obtaining the needed services by making a referral to an appropriate agency. To facilitate the referral, it is often useful to make the call to the potential referral agency while the client is with you. Afterward, a follow-up phone call from you to the client confirms that the client has been connected to the referral agency and is satisfied with the referral.

APPLYING GOAL SELECTION AND DEVELOPMENT GUIDELINES WITH MINORS

As you read this section, you may wish to review the previously discussed guidelines for selecting, defining, and developing goals, as well as the goal strategies for involuntary clients. The strategies for involuntary clients may be especially relevant. For the

EP 2 and 7

most part, the instances in which minors have contact with professionals are the result of family involvement, a school referral, juvenile authorities or the court, or a crisis. In other cases, parents seek help for a child's problematic behavior or to facilitate the achievement of a goal they have set for the minor. Rarely are minors in contact with professionals of their own accord.

To elaborate on this point, consider a situation in which a minor has been removed from his biological home with the goal of ensuring his health and safely. In response to his removal, the minor emphasized the desire "to go home." Minors may not always understand or trust the helping motives of adults, even when they are vulnerable. In this situation, as well as others where a minor may feel acted upon, the challenge is to reconcile the minor's goals with the systems involved.

Keep in mind that decisions about goals are influenced by the minor's developmental age, cognitive and moral ability, and capacity to give consent. Although a minor may be more or less clear about goals, even the youngest minor is able to articulate wishes, wants, needs, or hopes. The following discussion points are pertinent to developing goals with minors.

Eliciting Minors' Understanding of the Goal and Point of View of the Problem and Using This Information to Assist Them to Develop Goals

As an illustration of this point, we begin with a scenario involving an experienced social worker who has worked primarily with school-based groups involving minors. The social worker emphasizes that "starting where the client is" is an absolute with this population. Further, she notes, "Because their contact with you is required, it is essential that you talk with them so that you gain a sense of their perceptions and perspectives." To this point, recall that client participation was one of the dynamics discussed earlier as influencing goals. According to this social worker, engaging minors in the telling of their story is critical.

Listening to the minor's narrative is a starting point in establishing an atmosphere in which goals or solutions can be developed (Davis, 2005; Fontes, 2005; McKenzie, 2005; Morgan, 2000; Smith & Nylund, 1997; White & Morgan, 2006). Davis (2005) notes that "telling stories is a natural ways for minors to communicate," and their doing so inspires them to be "confident about their own perceptions." A narrative-oriented approach where open-ended questions are encouraged allows minors of all ages to tell their story based on their experience and

perception of the world in which they interact. For example, in the following case example, make note of the various reasons the boys give for their behavior. In this case example, the social worker leads a discussion on the development of goals in a school-based group. The school's overall goal for the participants, and hence the reason for referral to the group, was "appropriate classroom behavior." Once demonstrated, the participants would be able to return to the classroom. At this point, the goal of appropriate behavior is vague and would need to be defined in explicit, measurable language.

In recounting the experience of this and other similar groups, the social worker commented that school-based groups are often windows into the family and community life of group participants, which can be especially challenging, and traumatic. She emphasized that she hears about parts of the students' lives outside the classroom that have little to do with the purpose of the group, but in fact these external influences do matter. Specifically, what happens to kids (or their families) often explains their behavior in the classroom. For example, the reason given by one boy for his behavior in the classroom ("I was telling my friend about the gunshots around my house last night") revealed the adverse conditions of the neighborhood in which his family lives. Of course, the sharing of this event in the mind of a minor of this age is perhaps exciting, but you can also observe his anxiety and fear of the experience. Later, when asked to share what he wanted, he responded, "I want my family to be safe." Obviously, this goal had little to do with the teacher's behavioral goal, yet his concern influenced his classroom behavior. Thus, you should be aware that disruptive behavior by minors can be a way in which they act out or cope with very real ongoing stress or trauma. Schools have structure and establish behavioral expectations so that they can meet their educational objectives. Huffine (2006) notes, however, that "blaming youth for their behaviors may be easier than addressing the social ills" that can influence that behavior (p. 15).

Three questions are relevant to the comment of the group participant who stated, "The teacher does not like _____ kids." Is this an attempt to legitimize his behavior in the classroom? Perhaps. However, before reaching this conclusion, you should be mindful of the fact that the cognitions, perceptions, and feelings of young minors influence their self-definition and self-evaluation relative to the outside world. Second, what are the relational dynamics between the boy and the teacher? Another question for you to consider is, *What are the boy's life experiences that have led him*

CASE EXAMPLE

The group is a year-long, school-based social skills group for elementary-school-age boys, led by the experienced social worker mentioned above. The boys were involuntary, having been sent to the group by their teachers for inappropriate classroom behavior. Because they were involuntary, encouraging the boys to talk and participate was time consuming and challenging. As a beginning point, the social worker asked them about their feelings about being in the group because she believed that allowing them to express their feelings was critical. Minors, depending on their age, cognitive capacity, and emotional intelligence, may not readily express their feelings unless they are asked. Given the opportunity, some referred to the group as "stupid," but the group was "better than being in the classroom." Others were resentful, embarrassed, or anxious about being in a group for "problem kids." When asked what would make their participation more comfortable, "Getting something for coming to the group"—specifically, was there an incentive for their participation?—was a unanimous response. Ultimately, the greater incentive indicated by the participants was returning to the classroom.

As a means to understanding the specifics of their classroom behavior, and so that goals could be developed, the social worker asked each participant to explain his understanding of why he was required to participate in the group. Some of the responses were as follows:

"The teacher does not like me."
"The teacher is always mad about something."
"Because I sometimes play and joke with my friends in class."
"The teacher does not like _____ kids" [snickering among group members], followed by a side comment, "Shut up, boy."
"I was telling my friend about the gunshots around my house last night."

The language associated with goals, as well as the purpose, function, and type of goal, can be meaningless to the majority of elementary-school-age minors. But by focusing on their perception of the reason for their referral to the group, the social worker facilitated the potential for selecting a goal. She also queried each participant about his specific behavior in the classroom. Also, the social worker neither judged nor dismissed the comment that "the teacher does not like me." In following up to this statement, the social worker asked, "What do you think would make the teacher like you?" to which the student replied, "If I paid attention in class." Others in the group responded to her open-ended questions—for example, "What could you do differently?"—which led them to develop a behavioral change goal. For all of the participants, the specific behavior change goals were further clarified using their desire to return to the classroom as a motivator.

to conclude that this teacher (and perhaps others) doesn't like kids with certain physical attributes?

Is the Minor Voluntary or Involuntary?

Voluntary or involuntary status can, as is the case with adult clients, make a difference in the dynamics of goal development with minors. Minors who are involuntary either because of a referral or mandate (which they may perceive as being one and the same) may be hesitant to participate and set goals (Erford, 2003). The minor's feelings should be recognized as valid relative to their self-definition, especially within their peer or reference group. Even when minors are voluntary, an adolescent or teen may feel that seeking help portrays them as being less than adequate in the context of their peer relationships (Lindsey, Korr, Broitman, Bone,

Green, & Leaf, 2006; Teyber, 2006). For youth of color and those who identify as lesbian, gay, bisexual, or transgender—peer contexts in which rejection and isolation are present in their lives—feelings of inadequacy can be particularly stressful.

Definition and Specifications of the Behavior to Be Changed

Like adults, minors will respond to clearly defined and measurable goals, objectives, or tasks. Criteria for developing clear goals with minors cited by Corwin (2002) and Huxtable (2004) are:

1. Emphasize the change in behavior that is expected (*Waiting your turn to speak*).

2. Define the conditions in which the behavior change is observed (*In the classroom*).
3. Clarify the expected level of goal performance within a specific timeline (*Listen without interrupting while others are talking*).

The example that follows illustrates further how the process works:

- Goal 1: By the end of the first midyear school term, Veronica will use the conflict resolution skills she has learned when she is likely to become involved in a shouting match with a peer.
- Goal 2: In a situation in which she is unable to use her skills, Veronica will walk away from a conflict situation without talking back or name calling.

Goals should always be tailored to individual needs; therefore, the participation of the minor is important as he or she can have insights about potential barriers to goal achievement. For example, Veronica developed a third goal because she was concerned about whether she could immediately act on the second goal. In particular, how she felt about herself and the perception of her peers seemed like potential barriers. Thus, she developed an affirming self-talk behavioral goal to use when she is faced with a conflict situation.

With minors, you will find it worthwhile to partialize goals and tasks or objectives so that they are more manageable and progress is observable. In addition to having goals that are clearly defined, specific, feasible, and measurable, a number of other factors have particular relevance to this population. Goals with minors tend to work best when they provide:

- A sense of self-direction, particularly with adolescents who tend to react to being told what to do and how to act
- Incentives that are linked to goals—in particular, something that they want for themselves
- A sense of their ability to achieve goals
- Involvement in establishing evaluative measures
- Regular feedback about performance that honors their progress
- Praise for their efforts as well as goal attainment
- The opportunity to talk about how they accomplished a goal and their level of satisfaction with their performance
- Opportunities for them to measure their progress and praise themselves
- Strengths and protective factors—for example, the support of family or significant others in their lives

Huxtable (2004) and Morgan (2000) suggest using visual aids, metaphors, stories, and games to facilitate goal development and encourage the use of creative metaphors to facilitate motivation. In appealing to a minor to develop a goal, Huxtable likened a goal to "a race to the finish line," because the minor involved was interested in racecars. Moreover, the goal selection and development process is optimal when the language used is familiar and relevant to the minor rather than when it uses professional or institutional jargon. For example, "inappropriate behavior in the classroom" is less explicit than "making noises or gestures while others are talking."

In settings in which behavioral contracts are used (residential settings or juvenile detention centers, for example), minors may not be involved in establishing their goals. These contracts generally specify goals, the action required, expected outcomes, contingency rewards, and consequences (Ellis & Sowers, 2001). However, you can help minors meet behavioral expectations by engaging them in devising ways to achieve the goals.

The reactions of minors to developing goals tend to be situation specific. For example, young minors in abuse situations can be subject to feelings of vulnerability, self-blame, anxiety, and fear (Fontes, 2005; McKenzie, 2005). Minors develop scripts about themselves, the social environment in which their relationships are formed (including with peers), and their styles of problem solving. At almost any stage of development, consideration must be given to the power differences between you and the minor as you discuss goals. Younger minors can be sensitive to power, have a tendency to want to please, and are especially conscious of how they are evaluated by others.

Older minors, particularly adolescents, may be capable of making goal decisions, but they tend to be fiercely protective of their identity, independence, and autonomous locus of control. In goal discussions, be aware of the characteristic behavior associated with the developmental stage. To counter these dynamics, it can be important to explore and appeal to the future orientation of adolescents in conversations regarding the choices that they make. Also important are understanding and empathizing with the biological, social, and psychological stressors experienced at this stage of development. The ways in which these stressors can influence behavior are illustrated in the following case.

In reading the staff's reports on Bettina and Bettina's story, you get two different perspectives. In both accounts, you can observe McCarter's (2008) emphasis that during this developmental stage, it is

CASE EXAMPLE

According to the case record summary about Bettina, age 17, she was removed from her home along with her siblings when she was 6 years of age. Each child was placed in a separate foster home. Bettina, the oldest child in the sibling group, has experienced multiple placements, and at age 16 she was on the run and pregnant. She is currently living with her child in a group home for pregnant or parenting teen mothers. She has lived in the home for the past year.

Multiple notes in the case record describe her as alternatively defiant/contrite, courteous/rude, uncooperative/cooperative, and motivated/unmotivated, depending on the day and her mood. Because of her behavior, staff have routinely initiated sanctions, and some believe that she should be placed in a more restrictive environment. Bettina's response to sanctions is unpredictable. At times she may comply; at other times, she becomes explosive. The following is Bettina's story from her own point of view. Bettina's multiple adolescent/teen development issues are highlighted in the brackets:

I don't like people telling me what to do *[independence, separating from adults]*. I know my own mind *[individuation, locus of control]*! Everyone is always watching me *[sensitivity to control and opinions of others]*, the mistakes that I make, like I care

what they think. You know what I'm saying? They never say, "Bettina, you are doing a good job caring for your baby." But you can be sure that they are just sitting around waiting and watching for me to mess up so they can come down on me. Sometimes I get confused and scared *[stress]*, but then my worker says, "Bettina you can do it!" Then we talk about stuff *[exploring range of future possibilities]* like what I want to do when I leave this place. Eventually, I want to live in my own place with my baby.

The other day I was angry and walking around cursing because I had missed an appointment with my worker. She and I had an appointment, but I had a chance to take my baby to see his Daddy. Besides, the baby could also see his Daddy's mother, who has been real helpful to me. I want my baby to have contact with his father's family *[goal need]*. I could tell that my worker was unhappy, having driven across town for the appointment with me. I hate it when I mess up with my worker, but I did not know what else to do. I had a chance to take the baby to see his Daddy and his Daddy's mother, so I left. But as soon as she opened the door, I started cursing, in case she was angry *[reactive to potential of punishment]*. She let me go on for a while and then she asked me, "What is going on in your head right now?" and I just started crying *[sensitivity to feelings/empathy, listening to presentation of self and expression of feelings]*.

important to meet the minor "where they are" and to understand that where they are and what their mood is can change frequently. In spite of her developmental turmoil, it is apparent that Bettina had two goals. One was to live on her own with her child. The other was for the child to have contact with the father and his family. Like most teens, nonetheless, she was inclined to respond to the immediacy of the moment, even though she had a vision about the future.

Bettina's behavior is not unusual, although not all teens are as dramatic, nor are they as conflicted in their interactions with adults. A majority will, however, object and react to a negative assessment of their behavior by an adult authority.

As Bettina attempted to attend to the developmental task of individuation, she was functionally independent in that she could care for herself, but she was not emotionally independent. In the absence of parents,

staff members in the home were essentially parental surrogates upon whom she depended for approval and support, even though these same staff members were often the targets of her frustration.

The social worker believed that by empathizing and supporting Bettina's sense of self-direction and desire for independence, the two of them would be able to turn the situation around. Understandably, the staff had tired of her disruptive behavior. The social worker made a facilitative "Let's make a deal" with Bettina, linking it to her desire to eventually leave the group home to live on her own. Specifically, if Bettina agreed to follow the rules of the home, the social worker would arrange for Bettina to go visit her child's father and the father's mother on a weekly basis. In addition, she reiterated her expectation that Bettina respect her time by keeping agreed-on appointments. Of the previously cited considerations for developing goals with minors, the following were pertinent in Bettina's case:

- The social worker specified the expected behavioral change—specifically, that Bettina follow the rules of the group home.
- In supporting Bettina's goal to live on her own with her child, the social worker affirmed her sense of self-direction. This was particularly helpful because adolescents tend to react to being told what to do and how to act.
- Using an incentive for behavioral change, the social worker agreed to arrange weekly visits with the child's father and his mother.
- The incentive also tapped into the supportive resources available to Bettina, specifically that of the father's family.

Resourceful solutions can be especially useful with minors, particularly those solutions that allow them to save face and feel empowered and involved. You might question this quid pro quo goal arrangement and instead insist on a behavioral change—specifically, that Bettina follow the group home rules and reduce her disruptive behavior. You may also be inclined to pressure Bettina to reduce her disruptive behavior, pointing out the consequences of her failing to do so. Given her developmental stage and what she values (independence), her response would likely be negative, in which case behavioral change would be improbable and cause additional stress. The need for her autonomous sense of self may in fact outweighs the consequences of her noncompliant behavior.

In working with minors, it can be useful to be guided by the notion of utilitarian ethics. Ask yourself, "What is the reason for the behavior? What is the overall outcome that I am seeking?" In Bettina's case, the social worker's action facilitated the development of problem-solving goals.

THE PROCESS OF NEGOTIATING GOALS

EP 7

Returning to the ideas of goals providing a road map that details progress toward a destination, you may find that it is necessary to engage in a process in which you establish a priority goal, assess readiness and commitment to reach the goal, and consider the potential barriers and obstacles that might impede progress toward achieving it. In this

TABLE 12-8 Process of Negotiating Goals

> Determine clients' readiness for goal negotiation (for both voluntary and involuntary clients).
>
> Explain the purpose and function of goals.
>
> Jointly select appropriate goals.
>
> Define goals explicitly and specify level of change.
>
> Determine potential barriers to goal attainment and discuss benefits and risks.
>
> Assist clients in making a clear choice about committing themselves to specific goals.
>
> Rank goals according to client priorities.

section, we discuss steps that will help you and clients ensure that their intended progress is not disrupted. Table 12-8 summarizes the steps involved in the negotiation of goals with both voluntary and involuntary clients. The steps may be implemented sequentially, or the sequence may be adapted to the unique circumstances of each case. For example, a client may not be prepared to negotiate goals because he or she does not fully understand the function and purpose of goals. In cases like this, an explanation would take precedence over determining readiness. If, however, the client confirms his or her readiness, you would proceed to the next step of assessing readiness to move forward.

Determine Clients' Readiness for Goal Negotiation

Generally, at this stage in the process, voluntary clients are ready to get on with the business of resolving their concerns. Determining whether they are prepared to identify specific goals may begin with a summary of their priority concerns, as explored in the following video case.

VIDEO CASE EXAMPLE

In the video "Problem Solving with the Corning Family," the social worker, Ali, summarized what appeared to be the priority concern of Angela and Irwin Corning, "We've talked about your concerns about living in transitional housing," she noted. To confirm their readiness, she asked, "I wonder if you are prepared at this point to focus on moving from transitional housing as a goal, or would you like me to provide some ideas about resources?" Angela and

Irwin affirmed that their desire to move from transitional housing was their priority goal. On the other hand, had either one of them responded, "I think so," or "Maybe," this would have been a signal that they were not quite ready to settle on this goal.

Determining readiness is essential because clients can be at different starting points and have varying levels of confidence, perhaps being unsure about their real or imagined capacity to change or to change circumstances. In either case, these are issues to be explored.

Readiness of Involuntary Clients

Determining an involuntary client's readiness for negotiating goals is essential in light of the potential relational dynamics between the client and the social worker. Indeed, educating such clients about the *purpose* and *function* of goals may be the first step in creating an atmosphere in which a discussion about what is required by a mandate can occur. This discussion may significantly change the tone of the interaction between you and the client. Points to be considered in facilitating goal readiness are illustrated in the following statements:

- **The Mandate:** "The court has identified a problem that needs to be resolved." Review the mandate and specify what is expected: "The court requires that you participate in a parent training group and that you have an assessment of your parenting skills after you complete the program."
- **Specificity:** "The court expects that the parent training sessions will help you learn to set limits with your children and learn other methods of discipline." Explaining the intent of goals provides specificity and indicates that the client is able to retain some control over his or her life. Specificity would also include alerting the client to any requirements related to attendance, being on time, and remaining in the parenting sessions for the entire duration.
- **Level of freedom:** "You do, however, have a choice. You can choose among the various parenting programs on an approved list."
- **Client's viewpoint:** "Your view of the problem as well as concerns that you may have are also important." For goals to be relevant to clients and their situations, contextual meaning is important. "It would be useful for me to hear from you how you came to be involved in the court system."
- **Involving client in setting goals:** "I'd like for you to suggest ways in which you could meet the requirements of the court."
- **Measuring progress:** "We have identified the skills that you are to learn. I will keep a record of your progress and will include this information in my reports to the court." This statement clarifies for the client the focus of the mandate and the importance of demonstrating progress to prevent further action by the court.

What is accomplished by a review of the mandate as well as the other information in the statements above? Essentially, the social worker specified the change required by the court. In soliciting the client's point of view, the social worker gave the client the opportunity to explain his or her understanding of the situation. In this way, the social worker could respond to the client's viewpoint and explore goals important to the client in addition to those contained in the mandate. Allowing the client to choose from available parenting programs gives the client a choice by which he or she can feel motivated and empowered, ultimately ensuring participation.

Another instrumental step by the social worker was providing the client with a clear indication of how their progress will be measured, which may help to defuse the client's anxiety. When indicated, clients should also be informed of other requirements of a particular referral, and this information should be included in the goal plan. For example, the parent attending parenting classes should be aware of the stipulation that participants attend a certain number of classes and participate actively. These requirements, as well as the timelines imposed by the court, need to be included in the client's goal statement. When clients understand what is expected of them, it is generally possible to move on to assessing client readiness to participate in the goal negotiation process.

During the process of negotiating and prioritizing goals, as an incentive, you can inquire if the client also has concerns that are important to him or her. For example, "As you know, the court would like to see specific changes in your parenting. In addition to the changes ordered by the court, would you also like to discuss changes that you would like to make on your own?" A review of Table 12-5 will refresh your memory about working with involuntary clients to develop self-goals as well as goals that respond to a court mandate.

Explain the Purpose and Function of Goals

Many elements of the helping process are educational. *Goals* and *objectives* are terms used within the professional community, but clients are apt to simply express what they want to be different or what they would like to do. When goals are discussed, clients may have questions. For example, a minor might ask, "What do I need a goal for?" Involuntary clients often ask, "What do I have to do?" A social worker who works with older persons noted that they are more likely to respond when the focus is on an action plan rather than on a goal. In general, when clients understand the purpose and function of goals, they are more likely to appreciate their significance.

In educating clients about goals, you can use the analogy of the road map discussed earlier. For the most part, a brief explanation is all that is required. Even so, explaining the purpose and function of goals may be a particularly critical step with clients for whom the Western structure of formal helping systems is unfamiliar (Potocky-Tripodi, 2002). Additional time may be necessary, and asking them to describe or name the process in language that is familiar to them may be helpful.

Jointly Select Appropriate Goals

Voluntary clients are generally capable of identifying most or all of the goals and general tasks that they believe will resolve their problems. Because of your external vantage point, there may be instances when goals occur to you that clients may have overlooked or omitted. Consequently, you can make suggestions about goals for the client's consideration, explaining your reasoning and making reference to their priority concern. Assuming that you do not have reservations about their goals, it is important that you stress that the final goal decision is theirs to make.

VIDEO CASE EXAMPLE

In the video "Problem Solving with the Corning Family," the social worker, Ali, said to the couple, "I have some ideas and resources that may helpful, but it is important for me to hear what you think." Similarly, she asked the couple which of their two goals (Irwin finding a job and the family finding a place to live) was a higher priority for them. Eliciting such information ensures that both you and your clients are trying to accomplish the same goals.

Define Goals Explicitly and Specify Level of Change

After jointly deciding on specific goals and clarifying expectations, the next step is to determine the level of change desired by the client or required by the mandate.

As a client verbalizes his or her goals, you may need to seek clarification. Paraphrasing or suggested rewording of a goal can help clarify meaning and specificity. In paraphrasing, be cautious about taking liberties with what clients have said, and obtain approval of any revisions by reading them what you have written. Suppose that Mrs. Lenora Johnson, an elderly African American client who has been referred for depression, stated, "I'd like to not feel blue." You would write what Mrs. Johnson said and then seek clarification by asking her to describe "feeling blue" so that you understand what that means to her. Specificity at this point will enable you and Mrs. Johnson to develop precise indicators to monitor and measure change.

Once goals are explicitly defined, specifying what clients expect to be different and the desired level of change is an important next step. To be more specific, it is important to engage clients in a discussion about their expectations for what would be different when their goals are achieved. The following questions are examples of clarifying expectations:

Ali, the social worker: "What would it be like for you and your children when you move from transitional to permanent housing?"

Irwin Corning: "There are too many people under one roof [in transitional housing]. The place is noisy; you have to go to bed at a certain time. We could establish our own routine and the children would be able to play outside instead of being cooped up in a building. It would just be less stressful."

Social worker: "When you complete the parent training program, what do you imagine to be different about your interactions with your children?"

Parent: "Oh, I don't know, maybe I would learn how to be less stressed out. Sometimes, I ignore what my kids are doing and then they get on my nerves and then I blow up. Maybe I will learn how to do things with them and be more relaxed. I think that my kids would like this."

Social worker: "When you said that you would like to not feel blue, tell me what it would be like for you to not have this feeling?"

Mrs. Johnson: "I think that I would have more energy, visit my grandchildren, and when they ask,

'How are you doing Grandma?' I could truthfully tell them that I feel good."

Notice each question asked of the clients was intended to clarify their goal expectations.

If clients have difficulty defining a goal, you can prompt them by referring to needs and wants they identified during the exploration and assessment process and suggest that they consider the related changes. To illustrate prompting, we return to the case of Margaret, the elderly woman discussed in the case example at the beginning of this chapter. Although she recognized her need for a different living environment (one in which she felt safe), she nonetheless wanted to maintain a level of independence.

Social worker: When you talk about wanting to have a level of independence, what does that look like for you?

Margaret: For me, I want the help that I need with the housework, taking a bath, or perhaps preparing meals. Other things like going to events at the senior center and shopping for my own groceries are things that I would want to do on my own.

The social worker's question effectively summarized some of the key issues related to Margaret's goal of maintaining her independence. With respect to determining the desired level of change, you can use messages similar to the following:

Social worker: You said that you want a better relationship with your wife and that you are tired of being hauled off by the police. What is the specific change that you can make that will improve your relationship with your wife and avoid contact with the police?

Client: I would just walk away when she is in my face instead of smacking her. I would wait until both of us aren't so mad at each other so we could talk.

Specifying a desired level of change is a facet of defining goals explicitly. The goal and the level of change should be congruent with the client situation. With goals that involve ongoing behavior, growth is potentially infinite.

Determine Potential Barriers to Goal Attainment and Discuss Benefits and Risks

The importance of goal feasibility was discussed at length earlier in the chapter. Exploring potential barriers to achieving goals moves to another level and includes feasibility. In essence, you are anticipating and identifying in advance events or circumstances that could undermine goal achievement. The following dialogue between the social worker and a client is an example of a discussion about potential barriers:

Social worker: You said that when your wife is in your face, you plan to walk away and to avoid hitting her. I believe that you are committed to this goal because you want to improve your relationship with your wife. Let's imagine that the two of you are angry, which as I understand has usually ended up with your hitting her. Can you think of what might get in the way of your plan to walk away?

Client: Well, at first it might be hard, especially if she keeps yapping at me or follows me out the door, screaming her fool head off, embarrassing me in front of everybody. I guess if this happens, I'll just keep on walking, because I don't want to deal with the police.

Social worker: So, for you a big motivator is not having to deal with the police. Is it also possible that your behavior could also improve your relationship with your wife?

Client: Well now, that's a big payoff, isn't it?

Identifying barriers to goal attainment can improve the likelihood of a positive goal outcome. A discussion of the risks and benefits of goal attainment can function in a similar manner. In addition, clarifying benefits can enhance a client's commitment and sustain his or her effort. For example, a benefit described by the client in the above domestic violence scenario was, "My kids won't be afraid of me anymore," as well as improving his relationship with his wife. Nonetheless, enthusiasm for relief about the benefits of achieving goals may result in a client's superficial attention to risks or negative consequences, as illustrated in the following:

Social worker: You have mentioned two benefits of changing your behavior. One of them was that your kids would not be afraid of you, the other was that you would improve your relationship with your wife. What do you see as possible risks for you when you change your behavior?

Prudent practice requires that you discuss with clients the potential benefits and risks involved in goal attainment. Reviewing potential obstacles and risks is intended to help clients think in advance about events or situations that might influence their ability to attain their goals. Risks can of course become a very real barrier, even though a client is motivated to behave differently. A further discussion between you and the client can include planning for alternative responses to barriers and risks and may result in determining that a goal is not feasible. It may also be that a short-term goal can be developed as instrumental to attaining a longer-term goal. Should this be the case, you and the client would revise either the goal or the behavior. You should also be aware that changes in behavior can result in ambivalent feelings that have both positive and negative consequences, even though the benefit of a change is clear. For the most part, clients will likely perceive the benefits resulting from goal attainment as outweighing the risks and therefore be ready to work with you toward accomplishing a priority goal.

Assist Clients in Making a Clear Choice about Committing Themselves to Specific Goals

After exploring the potential barriers, benefits, and risks of pursuing a goal, the next step is to work with the client to make a commitment to the goals that he or she has chosen. A simple but effective means to gauge commitment to a specific goal, recommended by De Jong and Berg (2007), is to have clients rate their level of commitment on a scale from 1 to 10, where 1 represents "extremely uncertain or uncommitted" and 10 represents "optimistic, eager to start, and totally committed." A level of commitment in the range of 6 to 8 is usually sufficient to move to the contracting process.

On occasion, clients can be hesitant about making a commitment, in which case you should explore the basis for their misgivings or reservations rather than attempting to convince the client to sign on to a specific goal. While respecting a client's feelings, you can explore the extent to which a concern is causing a problem. For example, despite the fact that an adolescent has stated he is tired of being suspended from school, he is hesitant to commit to a behavioral change goal that would in effect increase his number of days in school without being suspended. You might ask him an inductive question, specifically whether multiple school suspensions are related to his behavior. As a next step, you might ask whether his concern is a sufficient reason for committing to a goal of avoiding being suspended.

For some involuntary clients, commitment to mandated goals may be low. Encountering a lack of or a low level of commitment can be very frustrating, given the pressure placed on you and the client by the court. Seeking client commitment can increase the pressure that a client feels, especially if the client perceives your authority as being linked with that of the court.

Facilitating the involuntary client to commit to a goal may need to occur in incremental stages. For example, while you empathize with the clients' feelings and the accompanying pressure of a mandate, you can point out the choices or freedom that clients have in deciding how they go about responding to the goal requirement. For example, the parent who was required to attend parenting classes was given the option of choosing the location and schedule of a parenting class. Also, recall the earlier discussion of strategies for facilitating goal selection with involuntary clients. In many cases, involuntary clients may want help, but not in the way or for the reason that help is offered. As illustrated in the following example, a discussion that highlights the benefits and opportunity for growth as a result of working on a mandated goal can also be productive. The discussion takes place between a social worker and a parent who has been mandated by the court to attend parenting classes. The parent's commitment to the court's goal level falls in the lowest range because of her beliefs, feelings, and her reaction to being judged as an inadequate parent, all of which contribute to her ambivalence about participating in parenting classes. The social worker affirms and respects her feelings, yet emphasizes the potential benefits of the classes to the client.

Social worker: I respect your opinion that you do not need parenting skills. I also understand your feelings about the court telling you how to parent with your kids. You said that your mother is a parent, that your grandmother is a parent, and that you learned from them. But there seems to be a problem in the way that you discipline your children. For example, hitting a child with a belt that leaves multiple visible marks on the body is a problem. Your mother and grandmother may have used this method, but for you, it is a concern that has to be resolved.

Parent: Yeah, but being spanked didn't hurt me or my brothers and sisters, we all turned out okay! None of us are doing drugs or are in prison!

Social worker: I understand that you believe that spanking is okay, and that you feel that you and your brothers and sisters weren't harmed. Most of us learn from our parents. When we talked about your frustrations as a single parent, you said that you are stressed out a great deal of the time. Is this the time when you are most likely to hit one of the children?

Parent: Yeah, that's right; the kids do get on my nerves a lot. I feel bad after I hit one of them, then the crying starts, which doesn't help my nerves. So tell me, how is attending a parenting class going to help me?

Social worker: Are you willing to consider that by attending the parenting class you might gain skills in setting limits with your children without hitting them, and also relieve some of the stress that you feel in dealing with them?

Parent: Well, I guess so, if I can learn something that I can use and feel less stressed out.

In this dialogue, encouraging the parent to commit to the mandated goal required a great deal of work on the part of the social worker. She did not challenge her beliefs about parenting but focused on the possible benefit of stress relief in dealing with her children, which the woman valued. However, should the parent remain hesitant or fail to commit to the court's goal, the social worker is obligated to inform her of the potential consequences to ensure that, in fact, she is making an informed choice. Involuntary status does not diminish the right of self-determination, yet it is your ethical responsibility to make these clients aware of the risks associated with their choices and help them work through their concerns.

Rank Goals According to Client Priorities

Following the identification of and client commitment to specific goals, it can be helpful to rank those goals in order of their priority. The purpose of identifying high-priority goals is to ensure that beginning change efforts are directed toward the goals of utmost importance to clients. Depending on the nature of the goals, the client's developmental stage, the resources available to the client, and the time required, settling on no more than three goals is advisable. In cases with multiple mandated goals, you can help the client to prioritize so that they are more manageable, emphasizing those that have a greater consequence. Participating in a drug treatment program, for example, may have priority. When working with larger systems, you might create a list of goals for both the clients and the systems involved and rank them for the client and the system. Where there are differences, your role is to assist all parties to negotiate and rank the priority of goals.

As a lead-in to the ranking process, when the client is voluntary, the following is an example of a summarizing message:

Social worker: So far, we have talked about several concerns and goals. Among the goals that you identified were moving from transitional housing and finding a full-time permanent job for Irwin. You also mentioned that you want your children to have a quiet place to study in the current housing situation. Now that you've settled on these goals, which one is the most important for you at this time? We'll get to all of the goals in time, but we want to start with the one that is most important.

With involuntary clients, you might use a message like this:

Social worker: While we have reached an agreement about which goals are most important to you, we also need to give priority to the goal established by the court. As you have said, you want the court out of your life. Your court order states that you need to enroll in a parenting class immediately, so this has to be a priority. You also said that you feel alone and tired out by the demands of caring for four children and want to have time for yourself. You also mentioned wanting to return to school. Are you able to say which of these goals, in addition to the one required by the court, you would like to work on first?

It is up to you as a professional to help clients focus their effort by sorting out what is a priority for them so that they do not feel overwhelmed and become frustrated. When goals involve a system or more than one person, different members may naturally accord different priorities to goals. In such cases, it is important that you take the lead in helping those involved to prioritize the goals.

MONITORING PROGRESS AND EVALUATION

Monitoring and evaluating progress and the status of goals are essential components of the helping process. Once goals have been developed, agreed upon, and explicitly defined, jointly deciding with the client how progress is to be tracked and recorded is the logical next step. Measurement involves the

EP 9

Name: _____

Statement of Problem/Condition to Be Changed: _____

_____

Goal
Statement: _____

General
Tasks: _____

_____

Potential
Barriers: _____   _____   _____   _____

Benefits: _____   _____   _____   _____

Specific Tasks (steps to be taken to achieve goal):

	Completion Date	Review Date	Outcome Code
1. _____	_____	_____	_____
2. _____	_____	_____	_____
3. _____	_____	_____	_____

Outcome Codes

Tasks and Goal Status [ ] C (completed) [ ] P (partially completed) [ ] NC (not completed)

FIG 12-3 Sample Goal and Task Form

precise definition of the problem and what is to be changed, and it clarifies the observations to be made that indicate progress toward the identified goal (Bloom, Fischer, & Orme, 2009; Fischer & Corcoran, 2007). Monitoring and evaluation are planned ongoing processes that occur at various stages. Irrespective of the frequency of the review, it should be done on a regular basis to avoid surprises. In other words, an ongoing review of the status of goals and related tasks or action steps is necessary in order to determine their effectiveness relative to changing the target concern. In this way, both you and the clients are informed about their progress (or lack thereof). A lack of progress should be examined, as it may indicate that a goal plan is not producing the intended results. An example of a tool that can be used is shown in Figure 12-3. This goal and task form is developed jointly by you and the client and allows each of you to track the intermediate and overall progress toward the goal. It enables you and your client to evaluate tasks or action steps as instrumental strategies to goal attainment as well as evaluate the status of the goal. Progress toward goals should be systematically recorded in the case record.

Methods of Monitoring and Evaluating Progress

This section provides an overview of both quantitative and qualitative methods that may be used to measure progress and to evaluate outcomes. Regardless of the method used, the following components are considered fundamental to this process:

- Identifying the specific problem or behavior to be changed
- Specifying measurable and feasible goals
- Matching goal and measurement procedures
- Maintaining a systematic record of relevant information
- Evaluating intermediate and final outcomes

The first two factors were discussed earlier in this chapter. To refresh your memory, an identified target concern cannot be readily measured unless it has been defined. For example, *inappropriate classroom behavior* provides a global understanding about a concern. However, a definition of the specific behavior such as *interrupting while others are talking* is explicit. Definition of the target concern is the basis upon which specific measurable goals can be developed and subsequently observed and measured. A target concern that has been explicitly defined in measurable indicators informs you of the appropriate measurement and evaluation methods to be used.

Involving Clients in Monitoring and Evaluating Progress

Client involvement, an integral part of the goal negotiation and development process, is equally important at the measurement stage. Also, as in goal planning, client participation may mean that procedures to be used are culturally relevant and consistent with the client's values and beliefs (Potocky-Tripodi, 2002; Sue, 2006). In involving clients, it is important that you explain the way in which evaluative information is to be obtained so that they understand and are receptive to the methods that will be used.

Lum (2004), Jayaratne (1994), and O'Hare (2009) are among those who support involving clients in the process of monitoring and measuring their progress. In essence, these authors are expressing views that are consistent with the empowerment and collaborative nature of the social worker–client relationship emphasized throughout this book. Also, including clients' perspective is believed to create a balance of power held by the social worker and clients and lessens the impact of systematic methods that "cast clients' viewpoints as being less scientific" (Kagle, 1994, p. 98).

Feedback from clients regarding their progress and satisfaction with the services and rationale for their inclusion as partners in monitoring and evaluating progress is summarized as follows:

1. By eliciting clients' views of their progress or by comparing their latest rates of the target behavior with the baseline, you maintain focus on goals and enhance the continuity of change efforts.
2. Clients gain perspective in determining where they stand in relation not only to their ultimate goals but also to their pretreatment levels.
3. Observing incremental progress toward goals tends to sustain motivation and to enhance confidence in the helping process and in the social worker.
4. Eliciting clients' feelings and views about their progress can alert you to and allow you to address feelings or behaviors that can impede future progress and lead to premature termination.

5. Clients can provide feedback on the efficacy of a goal or intervention strategy and whether an approach has yielded expected results within a reasonable period of time.
6. Indications of marked progress toward goal attainment alert you to when clients might be ready to shift their focus to another goal or begin planning for termination if all goals have been achieved.

Overall, the methods for monitoring, assessing, and evaluating progress should be consistent with the agreement negotiated in the contract or treatment plan. Progress toward goals should be monitored every two to three sessions at a minimum.

Quantitative Measurements

Quantitative evaluation embodies the use of procedures that measure the frequency and/or severity of target problems. Measurements taken before implementing change-oriented interventions are termed **baseline measures** because they provide a baseline against which measures of progress and measures at termination and follow-up can be compared. These comparisons thus provide quantitative data that make it possible to evaluate the efficacy of work with clients. The **single-subject design** is one example that can be used in a variety of settings, including mental health, family, and private practice. The method can be adapted so that you can integrate evaluation as a key element in your practice. In most cases, the simple Single Subject ABA can be used.[2] Using this design is perhaps the most practical way in which you can track and evaluate progress over a period of time.

Measuring Overt Behaviors

Baseline measures can analyze either overt or covert behaviors. Overt behaviors are observable and, as such, lend themselves to frequency counts. For example, group members who have negotiated a shared goal of increasing the frequency of positive messages sent to one another would keep a tally of the number of such messages conveyed during group sessions. The session averages would then serve as a baseline against which progress could be measured. Similar baselines can be determined for target behaviors such as increasing the number of times that a student raised her hand before speaking in class. Such measures quantify behaviors and make it possible to ascertain ultimate outcomes of change efforts. In addition, clients can observe even small incremental changes.

Baselines obtained through self-monitoring, however, are not true measurements of behavior under "no treatment" conditions, because self-monitoring itself often produces therapeutic effects. For example, monitoring the rate of a desired behavior (i.e., raising one's hand before speaking) may, in itself, act to increase the frequency of that behavior. Similarly, measuring the rate of negative behavior may influence a client to reduce its frequency.

The effects of self-monitoring on the target behavior are termed **reactive effects**. When viewed by a researcher, reactive effects represent a source of contamination that confounds the effects of the interventions being tested. From your viewpoint, however, self-monitoring may be employed *as an intervention* precisely because reactive effects tend to increase or decrease certain target behaviors. Although desired changes that result from self-monitoring may be either positive or negative behaviors, emphasizing positive behaviors is preferable because doing so focuses on strengths related to goals. It is advisable to use multiple measures or observations, of which self-monitoring is one source. The teacher in the classroom situation would be a source of information with respect to the frequency of a student's raising his hand prior to speaking in class. Another measure could involve the number of times the student was referred to the "time-out" room for disruptive behavior in the classroom.

When baseline measures focus on current overt behaviors, repeated frequency counts across specified time intervals are typically used. The time intervals selected should be those during which the highest incidence of behavioral excesses occur or the times in which desired positive behaviors are demonstrated. Focusing on the latter is preferable as it highlights a positive gain. It is also important to obtain measures under relatively consistent conditions. Otherwise, the measure may not be an accurate representation of the actual behavior you are attempting to measure (Bloom, Fischer, & Orme, 2009).

Retrospective Estimates of Baseline Behaviors

Baseline measurements are obtained before change-oriented interventions are implemented, either by having clients make retrospective estimates of the incidence of behaviors targeted for change or by obtaining data before the next session. Examples include paying rent on time, preparing nutritious meals, or being on time for school. Although it is less accurate, the former method often is preferable because change-oriented efforts need not be deferred pending the gathering of baseline data. This is a key advantage because acute problems or a crisis may demand immediate attention, and delaying the intervention for even one week may not be advisable. However, delaying interventions for one week while gathering baseline data in general does not create undue difficulty, and the resulting data are likely to be far more reliable than clients' estimates.

When determining the baseline of target behavior by retrospective estimates, it is common practice to ask the client to estimate the incidence of the behavior across a specified time interval, which may range from a few minutes to one day depending on the usual frequency of the target behaviors. Time intervals selected for frequent behaviors, such as nervous mannerisms (tapping a pencil on a desk), should be relatively short (e.g., 15-minute intervals). For relatively infrequent behaviors, such as speaking up in social situations, intervals may involve several hours or days.

Self-Anchored Scales

Baseline data can also be obtained for covert behaviors, such as thoughts, feelings, or an emotional state of "feeling blue." Individuals can make frequency counts of targeted thoughts or rate degrees of emotional states. To illustrate, we return to the case of Mrs. Johnson. To track her feeling "blue," for example, a scale would be developed that represented varying levels of her internal states, ranging from the total absence of her feeling or thoughts at one end to their maximal intensity at the other.

When goals involve altering feelings, such as anger, depression, loneliness, or anxiety, it is desirable to construct **self-anchoring scales** that denote various levels of an internal state. To "anchor" such scales, ask a client to imagine experiencing the extreme degrees of the given internal state and to describe what they experience. You can then use these descriptions to define at least the extremes and the midpoint of the scale. Developing scales in this manner quantifies internal states in a unique manner for each client. In constructing self-anchoring scales, it is important to avoid mixing different types of internal states: Even though emotions such as "happy" and "sad" appear to belong on the same continuum, they are qualitatively different, and mixing them will result in confusion. Figure 12-4 depicts a seven-point anchored scale.

Clients can use self-anchoring scales to record the extent of troubling internal states across specified time intervals (e.g., 3 times daily for 7 days) in much the same way that they take frequency counts of overt behaviors. In both instances, clients keep tallies of the

1	2	3	4	5	6	7
Least anxious (calm, relaxed, serene)		Moderately anxious (tense, uptight, but still functioning with effort)			Most anxious (muscles taut, cannot concentrate or sit still, could "climb the wall")	

FIG 12-4 Example of a Self-Anchored Scale

target behaviors. A minimum of 10 separate measures is generally necessary to discern patterns among data, but urgent needs for intervention sometimes require that you settle for fewer readings. For example, the client, Mrs. Johnson, would complete the scale to record the varying levels and circumstances in which she was "feeling blue" and when she did not experience these feelings. The self-anchored scale and the incremental numeric changes can be augmented by the descriptive information based on Mrs. Johnson's narrative. For example, in reviewing her range of feeling blue from most to least, the discussion between you and her would focus on the events or situations that appeared to have triggered her feelings, plus or minus in each range.

Guidelines for Obtaining Baseline Measures

When you are using baseline measures, it is vital to maximize the reliability and validity of your measurements (Berlin & Marsh, 1993; Bloom, Fischer, & Orme, 2009). Otherwise, your baseline measures and subsequent comparisons with those measures will be flawed and will lead to inappropriate conclusions. Adhering to the following guidelines will assist you in maximizing the reliability and validity of the data collected:

1. *Define the target of measurement in clear and operational terms.* Reliability is enhanced when the behavior (overt or covert) targeted for change is specifically defined. For example, measurements of compliments given to a partner are more reliable than general measurements of positive communications because the client must make fewer inferences when measuring the former than when counting instances of the latter.
2. *Be sure your measures relate directly and specifically to the goals targeted for change.* Otherwise,

the validity of your measurements, both at the baseline and at subsequent points, will be highly suspect. For example, when a client's goal is increasing social skills, indicators of social skills should be used as measurement targets. Likewise, if a parent is to attend parenting classes to learn parenting skills, measures should be devised that directly specify observable behavioral changes. Similarly, measures of violent behavior and alcohol abuse should correspond to the frequency of angry outbursts (or control of anger in provocative situations) and consumption of alcohol (or periods of abstinence), respectively.

3. *Use multiple measures and instruments when necessary.* Clients typically present with more than one problem, and individual problems may involve several dimensions. For example, flat affect, fatigue, irritability, and anxiety are all frequent indicators of depression. Clients may also present with goals related to increasing self-confidence or improving their social skills, which would require the use of multiple measures and instruments to track.
4. *Measures should be obtained under relatively consistent conditions.* Otherwise, changes may reflect differences in conditions or environmental stimuli rather than variations in goal-related behaviors. For example, if a child's difficulty is that she does not talk while she is at preschool, measuring changes in this behavior while the child is at home, in church, or in other settings may be informative, but it is not as helpful as the indications of change at preschool, where the behavior primarily occurs.
5. *Baseline measures are not relevant when clients present with discrete goals.* Evaluating the efficacy of helping efforts in such instances is clear-cut because either a client has accomplished a goal or not. For example, with a goal of getting a job, the job seeker is either successful or not successful. By contrast, progress toward ongoing goals is incremental and not subject to fixed limits, as in the case of completing a job application. Employing baseline measures and periodic measures, therefore, effectively enables both you and the client to monitor incremental changes. Consider the following baseline measure for an ongoing goal: "Justin will sit in his seat during English class." If Justin's baseline has indicated that he is out of his seat (off task) 25 times per week then improvement to 15 times per week would be significant.

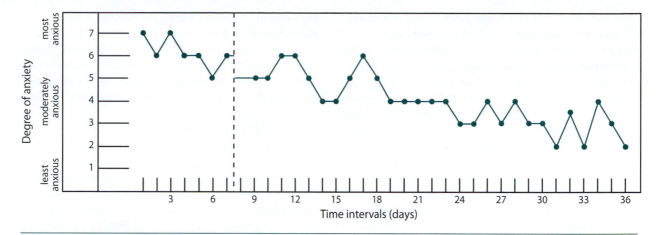

FIG 12-5 Example of a Graph Recording the Extent of Anxiety during Baseline and Intervention Periods

Measuring with Self-Administered Scales

Self-administered scales are also useful for obtaining evaluative data. Many psychological scales are available, but the WALMYR assessment scales (Hudson, 1992; Hudson & McMurtry, 1997) are especially useful for social workers. The scales tap into many of the dimensions relevant to social work practice. The ease of administration, scoring, and interpretation, as well as acceptable reliability and validity, are among the advantages of these scales.

Self-administered scales may also be used to quantify target problems. Although they are somewhat subjective and less precise than behavioral counts, they are particularly useful in measuring covert behavioral states (e.g., anxiety, depression, self-esteem, clinical stress) and clients' perceptions of their interpersonal relationships. Like tools to measure overt behaviors, selected scales can be administered before implementing treatment, at periodic intervals thereafter to monitor progress, and at termination and follow-up to assess outcomes. Unlike behavioral self-monitoring (e.g., counting behaviors or thoughts), subjective self-reporting through self-administered instruments is less likely to produce reactive effects (Applegate, 1992).

After obtaining baseline measures of targets of change, the next step is to transfer the data to a graph on which the horizontal axis denotes time intervals (days or weeks) and the vertical axis denotes the frequency or severity of target behaviors. Simple to construct, such a graph makes it possible to observe the progress of clients and the efficacy of interventions. Figure 12-5 depicts the incidence of anxiety before

and during the implementation of change using such a graph.

In Figure 12-5, note that the baseline period was 7 days and the time interval selected for self-monitoring was 1 day. Interventions to reduce anxiety were implemented over a period of 4 weeks. As illustrated in the graph, the client experienced some ups and downs (as usually occurs), but marked progress could nevertheless be observed.

In monitoring progress by taking repeated measures, it is critical to use the same procedures and instruments used in obtaining the baseline measures. Otherwise, meaningful comparisons cannot be made. It is also important to adhere to the guidelines for measurement listed in the preceding section. Repeated measurement of the same behavior at equal intervals enables practitioners not only to assess progress but also to determine variability in clients' behavior and to assess the effects of changes in the clients' life situation. For example, by charting measures of depression and increased social skills from week to week, it becomes possible to discern either positive or negative changes that correspond to concurrent stressful or positive life events. In this way, graphs of measured changes enable clients both to view evidence of their progress and to gain awareness of how particular life or environmental events contribute to their emotional states or behaviors.

Monitoring Progress with Quantitative Measurements

Monitoring progress has several other advantages. Measures establish indicators, and monitoring tells both the client and you when goals have been accomplished, when the court mandate has been satisfied, and when the relationship can be terminated. For example, when observable behaviors related to parenting skills—such as preparing three to four nutritious meals per week selecting from the five major food groups—have improved to the degree that they conform to explicit indicators, termination is justified. Similarly, termination is indicated when measurements of depression have changed to the range of nonclinical depression. Results of monitoring can also substantiate progress, justify continued coverage by third-party payers, and be used in reports to the court in the case of mandated clients. For clients, monitoring provides evidence of change, assuring them that they are not destined to remain forever involved with the social worker or agency. A final and critical advantage of monitoring is that if interventions are not achieving measurable results after a reasonable period, you can explore the reasons for this lack of progress and negotiate a different goal plan or intervention.

Receptivity of Clients to Measurement

You may feel hesitant to ask clients to engage in self-monitoring or to complete self-report instruments because of your concern that they will resist or react in a negative manner. To the contrary, research studies by Applegate (1992) and Campbell (1988, 1990) indicate that such concerns are not justified. These researchers found that clients generally were receptive to formal evaluation procedures. In fact, Campbell found that clients preferred being involved in the evaluation of their progress. In addition, clients preferred "the use of some type of systematic data collection over the reliance on social worker's opinion as the sole mean of evaluating practice effectiveness" (Campbell, 1988, p. 22). Finally, practitioners were able to accurately assess clients' feelings about different types of evaluation procedures (Campbell, 1990).

Qualitative Measurements

Qualitative measure methods are viable options for monitoring progress and evaluating outcomes. Qualitative methods differ from quantitative methods in their philosophical, theoretical, and stylistic orientation (Jordan & Franklin, 1995, 2003; Shamai, 2003). The various types of qualitative measures are consistent with narrative and social constructivism approaches. Qualitative evaluation measures have advantages for monitoring progress, depending on the information

that you are seeking. They can provide a more complete picture of the contextual conditions and dimensions in which change occurred (Holbrook, 1995; Shamai, 2003). Qualitative methods may be especially useful with minors in that they focus on subjective experiences and personal stories (Andrews & Ben-Arieh, 1999; Morgan, 2000).

In qualitative measures, the process of data collection is more open-ended and allows clients to express their reality and experience, frame of reference, or cultural realities. For example, the findings of a study that examined the use of hospice care by African Americans revealed a difference in values that were barriers to hospice utilization (Reese et al., 1999). In essence, the client is the key informant or expert (Crabtree & Miller, 1992; Jordan & Franklin, 1995, 2003). Gilgun (1994) asserts that because qualitative measures focus on client perception, they are good fit with the social work value of self-determination.

In evaluating progress or outcomes using qualitative methods, descriptive information change can be expressed in graphs, pictures, diagrams, or narratives. For example, in the structural approach to family therapy, symbols are used to create a visual map of family relationships and interaction patterns. Narratives provided by the family members at the points of change (even change that is incremental) highlight the dynamics or events associated with the change.

The aim of qualitative information is to ensure credibility, dependability, and confirmability (Jordan & Franklin, 2003; Rubin & Babbie, 2005; Weiss, 1998). Like quantitative methods, qualitative measures require systematic observation and may involve multiple points of triangulated observations. For example, triangulation would include client self-reports, your observations, and descriptive information from other relevant systems. The triangulation of data replication establishes the credibility of information and guards against bias.

A qualitative method that may be used to measure and monitor change is referred to as an *informative event* or *critical incidence*. The method has some similarity to the *logical analysis effects* (Davis & Reid, 1988) in that both informative events and critical incidence established a linkage between context, intervention, and change.

Informative Events or Critical Incidences

An **informative event**, also referred to as a **critical incidence**, is a qualitative method that seeks to determine whether intended or unintended gains can be attributed to a particular event or action. These events or actions are also referred to as *therapeutic effects*, *turning points*, or *logical analysis effects* in that they are a significant link to goal attainment, thereby changing the status of the target problem (Davis & Reid, 1988; Shamai, 2003). For example, in Bettina's case from the case example earlier in the chapter, the

social worker arranged for Bettina to visit her child's father and the father's mother once a week. The pertinent evaluation question is: Did this arrangement influence her behavioral change?

An advantage of informative event or critical incidence reports is that individuals are able to put their feelings and thoughts into words. For example, a group of mothers acknowledged that a session in which they

CASE EXAMPLE

In Figure 12-6a, significant credit card debt was identified as a major stressor for the Strong family. Paying off their debt was identified as their priority goal, which prompted a referral by the social worker to a consumer credit counselor. After the family had worked with the credit counselor, they and the social worker charted the change. In Figure 12-6b, the tenuous relationship initially reported by the family had changed to a strong resource relationship as they completed tasks related to their goal. Of course, this change occurred incrementally. Over time, it might be useful to insert one or more lines to credit card debt on the ecomap to demonstrate the progression of change.

Overall, the aim of qualitative methods in monitoring progress and assessing outcomes is to understand people's experience and the meaning that this experience holds for them (Witkin, 1993). For the Strong family, a benefit of their desired level of change was that paying off their credit card debt would enable them to begin saving to buy a home. In completing the ecomap with the family, the social worker obtained descriptive information about their desire to buy a home once they were able to manage their debt. Using qualitative methods in this case, the family's narrative provided insight into the interaction or combination of factors that contributed to their desired change.

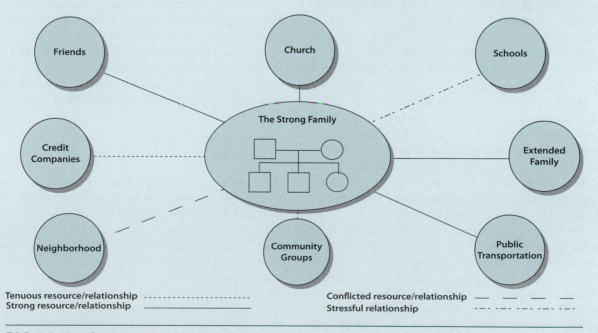

Tenuous resource/relationship ----------
Strong resource/relationship _____
Conflicted resource/relationship — — — —
Stressful relationship —··—··—··—··—

FIG 12-6a Preintervention Ecomap

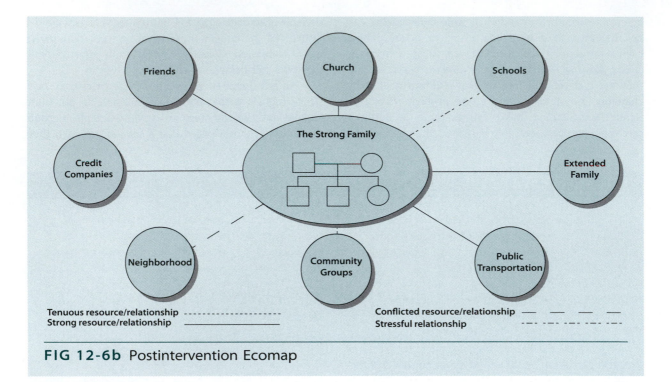

Friends   Church   Schools

The Strong Family

Credit Companies   Extended Family

Neighborhood   Community Groups   Public Transportation

Tenuous resource/relationship - - - - - - - - - - - -
Strong resource/relationship _____

Conflicted resource/relationship — — — —
Stressful relationship -·- -·- -·- -·-

FIG 12-6b Postintervention Ecomap

reflected upon and discussed their grief and sadness about the removal of their children from their homes marked a change (critical incident) in their ability to move toward reunification with their child or children. Previously, many of the mothers had stored-up feelings of anxiety, fear, and even ambivalence about reuniting with their children. For a majority of the mothers, the discussion was a therapeutic and a critical turning point because they were able to voice and subsequently release their feelings, helping them focus on the return of their children to their care. Morgan (2000, p. 91) suggests that significant turning points should be celebrated. For example, a certificate highlights such a turning point by naming the problem and the alternative story that emerged. For example, certificates for the mothers in the previous group would mark their movement from self-doubt to confidence and from guilt or shame to freedom from these feelings.

Tracking and monitoring progress need not be an ordeal, as you can use existing tools. For example, consider the ecomap, an assessment tool that we have discussed in other chapters that examines the relationship between a family and other social systems, identifying areas of tension or conflict as well as potential resources. For evaluation purposes, the ecomap may also be used pre- and postintervention to graphically track change in the tension or conflict lines that were identified as target problems.

Numbers (i.e., quantitative data) represent descriptive information that is informative about change or the reduction of symptoms; thus, statistical data fulfill an important function. Statistical data, however, cannot provide the contextual narratives associated with qualitative data. The most salient characteristic of qualitative evaluation methods is that they add "a human texture to statistical data," thereby "increasing our understanding of progress" (Shamai, 2003).

Combining Methods for Measuring and Evaluating

There are times when the depth of information you need is best obtained by combining qualitative and quantitative methods (Padgett, 2004; Rubin & Babbie, 2005; Weiss, 1998). For example, tracking the outcomes of a specific goal (such as learning new parenting skills) can be measured by using a quantitative pre/post design. In combining this method with qualitative indicators, you would be interested in determining at what point the new skill level occurred. For example, when did the parents' interactions with their children improve (turning point)? Likewise, frequency counts, such as the number of times that a student raised his or her hand before speaking in class, provide you with quantitative observations. You might also want to know whether the behavioral change was attributed to positive responses from the teacher related to the student's behavior, which provides you with qualitative information.

Obviously, each method will provide you with different information: quantitative measures provide statistical data, and qualitative methods enrich the data with descriptive information. With young minors, monitoring and measuring progress can be facilitated by using pictures, stories, and conversation-related feelings (Morgan, 2000). These methods can easily be combined with quantitative methods such as pre/post designs, rating or behavioral scales, graphs, or grids.

Your practice setting may have methods for monitoring progress and measuring outcomes—for example, goal attainment scales. In some organizations such as schools and residential facilities, standardized behavioral contracts stipulate how progress will be evaluated. Standardized tools or protocols, however, may place members of socioeconomic, cultural, and sexual minority groups at greater risk of appearing more "deviant or troubled" (Kagle, 1994, p. 96).

Increasingly, health and behavioral health organizations are relying on evidence-based practices or protocols to inform treatment decisions, beginning with an assessment, selecting an intervention, and evaluating outcomes (O'Hare, 2005; Roberts & Yeager, 2006). Evidence-based practices are available for certain problems and related goals, such as health, mental health, and specific behavioral problems (O'Hare, 2009; Roberts & Yeager, 2006; Thomlison & Corcoran, 2008). Be aware, however, that following the treatment procedures detailed in a manual that requires strict adherence is not the same as measuring effectiveness and monitoring progress.

Evidence-based practices and procedures have limitations with respect to people of color. While evidence of their effectiveness was obtained by using a large representative sample during their development, these samples have in general not included significant numbers of people of color. Thus, the appropriateness of evidence-based practices for communities of color has yet to be determined (Aisenberg, 2008; Conner & Grote, 2008; Furman, 2009).

Further notable limitations with regard to using standardized tools and evidence-based practices are that little attention is paid to barriers and obstacles to goal attainment. Moreover, the extent to which the resources recognize and make use of the social work principles such as an individual's strengths, resources, or situational factors is unclear. A question for you is whether a standardized or evidence-based resource is applicable to your clients and their problems. Above all, you should have the requisite skills for utilizing these resources and make use of supervision or consultation.

Overall, any procedure that you use to monitor and evaluate progress should be implemented in a systematic manner. An additional criterion is the extent to which the methods selected to measure outcomes are compatible and consistent with the goal. For example, a goal of avoiding eviction is tracked differently than a goal of "not feeling blue."

Evaluating Your Practice

Monitoring progress and measuring change are central to your ethical practice as a social worker. The process not only informs you and the client about the effectiveness of a strategy but also provides you with evaluative information about your own practice.

EP 1

Evaluative questions can be posed on a case-by-case basis and can also focus on aggregate information obtained by a review of all of your cases. As you gain additional knowledge and learn new skills, you can monitor and measure your skill level along a continuum. For example, you can determine if your skill level enabled you to serve the client better. Feedback from the clients with whom you are working is also integral to your self-evaluation. For example, you might ask diverse clients whether their experience with you was culturally sensitive, what could be improved, and what elements of your work together proved to be the most helpful.

Evaluating your practice need not be intimidating. Many of the quantitative and qualitative methods can be used to provide you with evaluative information. Regardless of the method you choose, you should be able to answer questions such as:

- Is the client making progress toward a goal?
- Is what I am doing with the client working, and if not, what changes do I need to make?
- Do I need to consult with a supervisor?
- Is my practice consistent with the ethical standards and principles of the profession of social work?

What you learn from the self-evaluation process is critical to maintaining a standard and for improving your practice.

CONTRACTS

EP 7

Goals focus the work that you and the client are to complete. **Contracts** are tools that detail the agreement between you and the client. Depending on the practice setting, contracts may also be referred to as **service agreements**, **behavioral contracts**, or **case** or **treatment plans**. A contract, and hence your work with an involuntary client, is generally influenced by a court order or referral source. Contracts should not be confused with legal mandates or case plans, although elements of both may be included as you develop an agreement between you and the client to work together. The legal mandate or case plan details the concern on which the contract is based and the expected outcome. It can also include concerns and goals that are important to the client. Program objectives may also be included in contracts or agreements. For example, the Behavioral Treatment Agreement found at the end of this chapter (see Figure 12-10) includes both goals for individual change and requirements that address program objectives.

There are instances in which intermediate or short-term behavioral and treatment plans related to a specific incident or behavior may be developed. For example, a **child safety plan** specifies that a parent call a relative when his or her frustration reaches a point at which the potential for hitting the child exists. This agreement identifies both the circumstances in which a behavior could occur and a resource for the parent. An example of the wording in the plan might be: "When I am frustrated and feeling overwhelmed with _____ (child's name), I will call my mother and talk it out with her." A short-term safety plan might also be reached with a client in an emotional crisis where the client agrees to refrain from harmful behavior ("I will pay attention to the psychological cues that tell me that I am at risk for harming myself"). Further, the agreement could include the condition that the client makes an appointment with a professional. The safety plan is signed by the social worker and the client.

Other types of short-term agreements include the contingency (quid pro quo) contract and good-faith contract. Used in cognitive behavioral family therapy, a **contingency contract** identifies a desired behavior change on the part of all parties involved. Its fulfillment is contingent on each individual's behavior in response to the other parties' behavior (Nichols & Schwartz, 2004). In a **good-faith contract**, the parties involved agree to change their behavior independently of one another. This type of contract may be used in a social-behavioral skills group or a behavioral parenting training group.

The Rationale for Contracts

Contracting is the final discrete activity of Phase I of the helping process; it identifies the work to be accomplished through the change-oriented strategies by which goals will be attained. Key ingredients summarize the purpose and focus of your work with clients as well as ensure mutual accountability. In some practice settings, the contract or agreement clarifies the role of the client and social worker as well as establishes the conditions under which assistance is provided.

Developing a contract or service agreement with clients may require an explanation of the purpose and rationale for the contract. Explanations may be particularly important for clients who are hesitant to sign a document without fully understanding its purpose. Involuntary clients may be suspicious or distrustful, perceiving the contract as further infringing on their freedom or that they are committing to a change with which they disagree. For minors, the concept of a contract may be a totally alien one regardless of their age and developmental stage. For this reason, you might frame the explanation as an agreement that describes expectations. In settings in which a minor's choice of whether to work with you is limited, specifying the required change and your role in supporting the minor to achieve goals, as well as clarifying rewards and benefits, can be especially important.

Formal and Informal Contracts

Contracts or service agreements can be developed with varying degrees of formality. Public agencies often require written service agreements in the form of case plans or behavioral contracts signed by clients. **Written contracts** provide space for entering the particular concerns or problems of a client situation and for listing the expected intervention outcomes. Safety plans are almost always written, and they are a ready resource for clients in a crisis. Under normal circumstances, you and the client both sign the contract, giving it much the same weight as a legal document. Some private agencies prefer **service agreements** to contracts, believing that contracts are more formal and administrative in nature.

Students often ask whether written or oral contracts are preferable. For some social workers, the rationale for using a written contract is that it provides a tangible reference to the commitments between themselves and their clients. In this way, the potential for a misunderstanding is minimized. In addition, the written contract assures accountability of services to supervisor and funders. Other social workers prefer **oral contracts** that include the same provisions but lack the formality, sterility, and finality of a written contract. If contracts or agreements are oral, questions may arise later with regard to informed consent. A third option is to utilize a partially oral and partially written contract. The latter includes the basics—for example, the target concern or problem, goal, role expectations, time limits, and provisions for revision. With minors, either oral or written contracts, or some combination of the two, may be appropriate.

Whether the contract is oral or written, at a minimum, clients should have a clear understanding of what is to be accomplished as a result of your work together. Contracts that are specific and clearly articulated ensure that clients are informed; otherwise, clients may believe they are justified in filing suit for malpractice if they do not achieve their goals (Houston-Vega, Nuehring, & Daguio, 1997; Reamer, 1998).

Contracts or agreements with either a written or oral description, as well as any changes, are documented in the case record. This documentation is consistent with the requirements of record keeping and informed consent (Reamer, 1998; Strom-Gottfried, 2007).

Developing Contracts

Generally, contracts should include certain elements, which are outlined in the Agreement for Service found at the end of this chapter (see Figure 12-7). In making use of this resource, you can adjust the various elements to fit the needs of your practice setting and the particulars of your work with clients. Keep in mind, however, that certain elements are essential. The following is a brief discussion of each element.

Goals to Be Accomplished

First and foremost, the goals to be accomplished in relation to the target concern are ranked by priority, as goals provide the focus for working over the course of ongoing sessions. At the same time, goals are fluid. They can be expanded or modified as situations change and new information that has a bearing on the initial goals emerges. Of course, there must be a valid reason for changing goals. Although the continuous shifting of target concerns and goals during the contracting process would be unusual, a client may signal that he or she is not ready to proceed. At this point, you would return to the process of identifying goals.

Roles of Participants

In Chapter 5, the process of socialization related to the client and social worker's roles was discussed. These roles may need to be revisited during the contracting process. Role clarification may be especially pertinent with involuntary clients who have a mandated case or treatment plan, in which case your role and that of the client are specified in writing. Whether the client is voluntary or involuntary, the identification of roles affirms the mutual accountability and commitment of all parties, including that of the agency involved.

Socialization about the purpose of contract roles may be required and especially important with certain clients. For example, involuntary clients may feel particularly vulnerable, and a contract may increase their feelings of being pressured or controlled. Also, Potocky-Tripodi (2002) points out that some immigrants or refugees may experience fear and apprehension about contracts, depending on their past experiences. In light of the client's past experiences, the contract may be "perceived as an instrument of authoritarian coercion" (p. 167).

Minors may also feel vulnerable. With this group, the socialization process may require you to review what is expected of them and how you will assist them. For example, "I have written down that I will help you return to the classroom" or "Your role is to attend group sessions and to learn different ways of behaving in the classroom." In all instances, taking the time to explain the function and purpose of contracts and the client's role will facilitate an individual's remaining active in the helping process.

Interventions or Techniques to Be Employed

This aspect of the contract involves specifying the interventions and techniques that will be implemented in order to accomplish the stated goals. During initial contracting, it is often possible to identify interventions only on a somewhat global level. For example, group or family sessions may involve a combination of strategies. In some instances, depending on the identified goals, you and the client can discuss intervention strategies with greater specificity—for example, decreasing the occurrence of irrational thoughts, beliefs, and fears (cognitive restructuring) and developing skills (e.g., using tasks or solution to accomplish goals). In cases where you are the case manager, you would also indicate the various coordinated services to be involved in the case (e.g., home delivered meals, home health services). Implementing an intervention strategy requires a discussion with the client in which you provide an overview of the intervention and your rationale to elicit clients' reactions and to gain their consent.

Time Frame, Frequency, and Length of Sessions

Specifying the time frame, frequency, and length of sessions is an integral part of the contract. Most people tend to intensify their efforts to accomplish a given goal or task when a deadline exists. Just consider the last-minute cramming that students do before an examination! A time frame stated in the contract counters the human tendency to procrastinate.

Yet another argument that supports the development of a definite time frame is that most of the gains that are achieved occur early in the change process. In working with families, Nichols and Schwartz (2004) note that treatment has historically been established as brief and within a limited time period based on the rationale that change occurs quickly if it occurs at all. Moreover, whatever the intended length, most contact with clients turns out to be relatively brief, the median duration being between five and six sessions (Corwin, 2002; Reid & Shyne, 1969).

On the whole, clients respond favorably to services that are offered when they need them the most and when they experience relief from their problems. This is not to say that clients will not seek help for concrete or daily living concerns that they may have. Clients may value time-limited contracts because they make a distinction between talking and actual change, and within this particular time frame the focus is on a specific concern.

Questions have been raised about the brevity of time limits. Are time-limited contracts, for example, effective with racial and ethnic minority groups? Some theorists believe that time limits are inconsistent with perspectives of time held by some minority groups (Chazin, Kaplan, & Terio, 2000; Devore & Schlesinger, 1999; Green, 1999; Logan, Freeman, & McRoy, 1990). Other theorists cite outcome studies that emphasize time-limited contracts as preferable with racial and ethnic minority clients because they focus on immediate, concrete concerns. Devore and Schlesinger (1999), Ramos and Garvin (2003), and James (2008) note that in stressful situations, persons of color respond best to a present- and action-oriented approach. Corwin (2002), citing the work of Koss and Shiang (1994) and Sue and Sue (1990), points out the advantages of time-limited, brief treatment by noting that

these approaches are "congruent with how many minority clients understand and utilize mental health and social services" (p. 10). Of course, it would be presumptuous to assert hard-and-fast rules about a relationship between time limits and minority status. As highlighted in the previous discussion, brief contact with a specific focus appears to be a preference with a majority of clients, irrespective of their status or background.

A second question relates to whether time limits are appropriate to all client populations and situations. Certainly, time-limited contracts may be inappropriate in some instances. For example, as an outpatient mental health case manager, your responsibility can be ongoing and time limits impractical. Nonetheless, you may find that time-limited contracts can be used with circumscribed problems of living or concrete needs defined as goals. In these instances, time-limited contracts can be effective when they are divided into multiple short-term contracts related to specific problems or episodes. A brief contract may, for example, involve a safety agreement, finding housing, or taking medication.

Decisions about specified time frames may be imposed on the work to be completed between you and clients. Managed care demands (specifically the brevity of the period in which outcomes are expected to be achieved) have dramatically influenced practice in both the private and the public sectors of social welfare services. In addition, agency resources, purchase of service (POS) contracts, funders, public policy, or the courts may stipulate a time frame and the duration of contact. In child welfare, for example, under the 1997 Adoption and Safe Family Act, parents are required to meet their case plan goals within a definitive time period. Time pressures resulted in tensions for many parents. For some, this pressure was a decisive factor in the eventual reunion with their children. Neither was there sufficient information given as to whether services were available or could be accessed within the required time frame. Nonetheless, these time limits would be included in the contract. Within the contract, you can help clients with the ticking of the clock by helping them focus their efforts on responding to the most pressing concerns.

The helping process, as presented in this text, relies on the time frame being brief. The time period used is one that is commonly associated with the task-centered social work model, where specific target concerns and goals are identified. The action-oriented emphasis in the social work model and other brief treatment models can foster a conductive mindset that will facilitate change. Moreover, the expectation of a change in the target concern within a specific time period can have a positive influence on self-direction and motivation.

Research done in various settings and with various groups, including minors, supports the efficacy of 6 to 12 sessions conducted over a time span of 2 to 4 months. The flexibility inherent in this time frame, however, means that you can negotiate with the client regarding the specific number of sessions to be undertaken (Nichols & Swartz, 2004).

Frequency and Duration of Sessions

In most agencies, weekly sessions are the norm, although more frequent sessions may be required in cases that need intensive support and monitoring. For example, child welfare/child protective services, job-training programs, outpatient drug treatment, services for the frail elderly, school truancy, or homeless youth programs can require daily contact. Provisions can also be made in contracts for spacing sessions farther apart during the termination phase of the helping process.

There are few solid guidelines as to the amount of time needed for sessions. Agencies generally have guidelines for the billable hour, which tends to be 50 minutes. Conversely, if your setting is a public agency (i.e., child and family or protective services), time spent is only a part of what you do. For instance, you can spend considerable time arranging for and monitoring visitations between parents and children, conducting home visits, doing crisis problem solving, and teaching parenting skills. The duration of sessions is also influenced by the client. Because some children, adolescents, and older clients have difficulty tolerating long sessions, shorter and more frequent sessions are more practical. Frequency and duration of sessions are also influenced by settings requirements (e.g., school, hospital, correctional facility). For example, in a hospital setting, your contact may last 15 or 20 minutes, depending on the condition of the patient and the goals to be achieved. Also, your contact is limited to the time that the person is an inpatient. For school-based groups, the duration and length of sessions may require a structured time frame and may be influenced by concerns teachers have about out-of-classroom time.

Means of Monitoring Progress

Early discussions between you and the client have focused on the specific methods for monitoring and measuring progress. At this stage of the contracting process, a brief review may be all that is needed. For example, when baseline measures on target problems have been obtained, you would explain that the same measuring device would be used at specified intervals to note change. Clients can also be asked to rate their progress on a scale of 1 to 10, where 1 represents no progress and 10 represents the highest level. Comparing ratings from one session to the next and over a period of time provides a rough estimate of progress.

In addition, when a narrative progress review is a part of each session, it can serve the function of monitoring progress. For example, the Goal and Task Form in Figure 12-3 enables you and the client to review completed tasks and the status of goals. With minors to whom visual methods are particularly appealing, you may opt to use scales, calibrated drawings, or a thermometer with a scale from 1 to 10 where a colored marker indicates progress.

The frequency of monitoring may be negotiated with the client. Whichever method of monitoring is chosen, devoting some time at least every other session to review progress is advisable. Of course, you can be flexible, but no more than three sessions should pass between discussions of progress.

Stipulations for Renegotiating the Contract

Contracting within a brief time frame assumes that when goals are met, a change or significant reduction in the target problem will occur. Contracting continues during the entire helping process. Renegotiating a contract with clients can occur when their circumstances change or new facts emerge and the process evolves. For this reason, it is important to clarify for clients that conditions in the contract are subject to renegotiation at any time. Above all, the contract should be continually reviewed and updated to ensure its relevance and fit. When contracting with involuntary clients, any circumstances that would cause a unilateral change in the contract (e.g., evidence of new legal violations) should be specified.

Housekeeping Items

Talking with clients about such issues as provisions for canceling or changing scheduled sessions and financial arrangements is necessary but can be awkward and mundane. Perhaps discussing fees may be the most awkward for you, and uncomfortable for the client. Your discomfort is understandable, given that your basic instinct as a social worker is to help people.

Agreement for Professional Services

Name(s) of Client(s) _____ **Name** _____

Address _____ **City** _____ **State** _____ **ZIP Code** _____

Outline for the agreement to work collaboratively in achieving goals, and joint planning in carrying out activities for the achieving goals.

I. **Problem(s) or/Concern(s):** Defined and Specified

II. **Prioritized Goals & General Tasks:**

Goals _____ General Tasks _____

_____ _____

III. Conditions under which goals might change or be revised or others added.

IV. **Time Limits Applicable to Case:** Time frame that may influence the rate at which goals may need to be accomplished or where significant progress toward goals may need to be documented.

V. **Sessions:** Meeting times, frequency and durations, location, beginning and ending dates, and the total number of sessions.

VI. **Who is involved:** Individual, couple or family, group, or a combination?

VII. **Fees:** For service, and method and arrangement of payment.

VIII. **Evaluation:** How progress will be monitored and measured, including client participation, evaluating progress each session by reviewing the goal plan, and the steps taken to achieve goals and final evaluation at termination.

IX. **Reports and Records:** Confidentiality of records and consent of Release of Information. Specifies who will receive reports about progress (e.g., court, third-party payer, referral source).

X. **Requirements of Mandated Reporting:**

XI. **Agreement:** Affirmation of the review of the terms of the agreement, and that an understanding that the agreement can be renegotiated at any time.

Signature (Client/Family/Group Member)

Name _____ Name _____ Date _____

XII. **Social Worker:**

a. I agree to work collaboratively with _____ to achieve the goals outlined in this service agreement and others that we may subsequently agree upon.

b. I agree to adhere to the conduct that _____ agency expects of its staff and to abide by the regulatory laws and ethical codes that govern my professional conduct.

c. I have provided a copy of agency information about the rights of clients, available agency services, and information about the agency.

d. I have read the above terms of the service agreement, and pledge to do my best to assist the client(s) to achieve the goals listed and others that we may subsequently agree upon.

Professional's Signature: _____

Date: _____

FIG 12-7 Agreement for Professional Services

the back door
MAKING CHANGE

Name: _____   Date: _____

File #: _____

❏ Housing   ❏ Planning   ❏ Drugs/Alcohol
❏ Employment   ❏ Volunteering   ❏ Problem Solving
❏ Education   ❏ Finances   ❏ Identification
❏ Personal   ❏ Leadership   ❏ Legal
                                              ❏ Other

CONTRACT STEP: _____ Step #: _____

WHAT I WANT TO WORK ON TODAY (i.e., WHERE I AM TODAY IN MY LIFE):
_____

_____

WHAT RESULT(S) I WOULD LIKE TO SEE (i.e., WHERE I WOULD LIKE TO BE):
_____

_____

WHAT I NEED TO MAKE IT WORK:
_____

_____

MY STEPS:
1. _____

2. _____

3. _____

4. _____

Contractor: _____   Paid by: _____

The following principles and questions reflect how *the back door* hopes to work. Please take time to think about how they worked for you in THIS contract step.

1. Principle: INTEGRITY/DIGNITY
   How did contracting this step contribute positively to your self-esteem?

2. Principle: LIFE IS SUCH THAT THINGS DO NOT ALWAYS WORK
   In attempting the above step, how did you find this to be so?

3. Principle: ACCEPTANCE WITHOUT JUDGMENT OR PREJUDICE
   How did contracting this step allow you to experience positive input from another person?

4. Principle: FORGIVENESS: EVERY DAY IS A NEW DAY
   How did contracting this step give you the freedom to learn from the past and try again?

5. Principle: PEOPLE WHO LISTEN TO EACH OTHER LEARN FROM EACH OTHER
   How did planning/working on this step help you to understand another person's point of view?

6. Principle: ALL ACTIONS/CHOICES AFFECT OTHER PEOPLE
   Did your working on this step have any effect on other people in your life?

FIG 12-8 Sample Contract The Back Door, Making Change

Source: Used by permission of *the back door* © 2000.

Sample Treatment Plan

Areas of Concern	Short-Term Goals/Objectives	Long-Term Goals	Treatment Plan

FIG 12-9 Sample Treatment Plan

Source: Adapted from Springer, D. W. (2002). Treatment planning with adolescents. In A. R. Roberts & J. J. Green (Eds.), *Social Worker's Desk Reference.* New York: Oxford University Press.

Even so, most private agencies have policies that require payment for services, and the majority of clients expect to pay, albeit on a sliding-scale fee arrangement. In addition, private insurance providers often have copayment requirements for services.

Financial arrangements, where required, are a fundamental part of the professional agreement between you and the client. A component of a social worker's competency is being able to effectively discuss financial arrangements, openly and without apology, when payment for services is expected. When clients fail to pay fees according to the contract, you should explore the matter with them promptly. Avoidance and procrastination just make matters worse and may result in you developing negative feelings toward the client. Moreover, a failure to pay fees may derive from the client's passive, negative feelings toward the professional, financial strains, or irresponsibility in meeting obligations, any of which merits immediate attention.

There are situations with exceptions to a discussion of fees. Examples in which fees are not prominent include purchase of service agreement contracts with your agency or if the service is funded by a grant. This would also include services provided to minors in school settings. When the client is a minor in an agency setting, any discussion of fees is a conversation between you and the minor's parent or legal guardian.

Having an agreement about schedules and keeping appointments is also advisable. In making home visits, nothing is more frustrating than showing up at an agreed-upon time only to find that the client or family is not at home or is unprepared for the visit. You should have the same expectations of yourself as you have of the client. Whether contact with a client is in your office or in their home, clients should be able to rely on your being available and attentive to their concerns. Of course, there are legitimate reasons that you or a client can have for changing or canceling an appointment. Discussing the "what ifs" in advance clarifies expectations about keeping appointments and prevents misunderstandings.

Sample Contracts

To assist you in developing contracts, we have included sample contracts at the end of this chapter. Each example includes most of the components discussed in preceding sections, although some are emphasized more than others. The first contract, Agreement for Professional Services (Figure 12-7), includes elements of ethical guidelines for work with clients and for managing malpractice risks articulated in the work of

Behavioral Treatment Agreement

Name _____ Client # _____ Date _____ Therapist _____

1. **Progress**

Summary _____

_____

2. **New Treatment Goals**
    1. Increased awareness of individual cues that trigger getting angry
    2. Increased awareness of no abusive alternative ways of expressing anger
    3. Increased use of support networks
    4. Accepting responsibility for past abusive behavior

3. **Plan**

Attend 18 educational themes/complete 9 tasks

4. **Outcomes**
    1. Side effects of treatment discussed ❐ yes ❐ no
    2. Outcomes of treatment discussed ❐ yes ❐ no
    3. Treatment options discussed ❐ yes ❐ no
    4. Cost of treatment explained to client ❐ yes ❐ no
    5. Client and staff rights form provided to client ❐ yes ❐ no
    6. Is client considering:

        Chemotherapy ❐ yes ❐ no

        Hospitalization ❐ yes ❐ no

        Other medical treatment ❐ yes ❐ no

If the answer is yes to any of the above, the physician or consulting psychiatrist shall inform the client of the treatment alternatives, the effects of the medical procedures, and the possible side effects.

All clinical services shall be provided according to the individual treatment plan.

5. **Expected Duration of Treatment**

18 weeks/dependent on task completion. You need to begin completing the required tasks within the first 4 weeks of the program.

6. **Frequency of Treatment**

Weekly

7. **Collateral Resources and Referrals**

_____

I understand the terms of this treatment agreement as well as my responsibilities in implementing the same. I have received a copy of this treatment plan.

Client _____   Date _____

Therapist _____   Date _____

Clinical Director _____   Date _____

FIG 12-10 Behavioral Treatment Agreement

Source: Used by permission. © MHO.

```
┌─────────────────────────────────────────────────────────────────────┐
│                        Sample Behavioral Contract                     │
│                                                                       │
│  Name _____                │
│                                                                       │
│                                                                       │
│  Date _____                │
│                                                                       │
│                                                                       │
│  Responsibilities (activities, counseling sessions, behaviors to      │
│  avoid):                                                              │
│                                                                       │
│  Privileges (outlines privileges associated with meeting              │
│  responsibilities):                                                   │
│                                                                       │
│  Bonuses (meeting requirements for a certain time period):           │
│                                                                       │
│  Sanctions (circumstances in which privileges are lost, and possible  │
│  action if requirements are                                           │
│  not met):                                                            │
│                                                                       │
│  Monitoring (identifies who is responsible for monitoring whether     │
│  requirements are met):                                               │
│                                                                       │
│  Client's Signature _____                 │
│                                                                       │
│  Social Worker's Signature _____               │
│                                                                       │
└─────────────────────────────────────────────────────────────────────┘
```

FIG 12-11 Sample Behavioral Contract
Source: Adapted from Ellis & Sowers (2001).

Houston-Vega, Nuehring, and Daguio (1997). Before using any of the contracts or agreements, you should clear them with your agency supervisor.

The Agreement for Professional Services is presented in outline form. The agreement for the social worker is much more detailed, committed to observing ethical standards of practice.

The second contract (Figure 12-8) was developed to be used with participants of the agency called "the back door" (DeLine, 2000). This agency is committed to helping homeless and runaway youth get off the streets. The contract outlines the program objective and the services the agency provides. In addition, the role of youth clients is amplified because the focus is exclusively on how they will use the agency's services to alter their situation. The intent of the contract is to identify priorities and the most manageable tasks.

The remaining examples illustrate a treatment plan (Figure 12-9) and two behavioral contracts (Figures 12-10 and 12-11). Figure 12-10 is used by a county mental health center for men in a domestic violence program. Note that program requirements and objectives are a part of each client's treatment plan. Figure 12-11 is an example of a behavioral contract used in a juvenile facility, adapted from Ellis and Sowers (2001).

SUMMARY

This chapter focused on the purpose and function of goals and the process involved in goal development with voluntary clients, involuntary clients, and minors. General and specific tasks or objectives were discussed as instrumental strategies for goal attainment. Methods for monitoring and measuring the progress and outcome of goals were also discussed.

The contract examples provided in this chapter are intended as guides that can be adapted to particular situations or settings. Settings and client situations or status may dictate the inclusion of some elements over others. Also, including or omitting certain information in a contract can depend on the developmental age and stage of minors or a client situation.

COMPETENCY NOTES

EP 1   Demonstrate Ethical and Professional Behavior

- Make ethical decisions by applying standards of the National Association of Social Worker Code of Ethics, relevant laws and regulations, models of ethical decision making, ethical conduct of research, and additional codes of ethics as appropriate in context. In instances in which competing interests pose difficulties for you and clients, the ethical standards and principles of the social work profession should guide your behavior and actions.

● Demonstrate professional demeanor in behavior, appearance, and oral, written, and electronic communication.

As an element of ethical practice, social workers monitor and evaluate their effectiveness with clients and make adjustments as indicated.

EP 2   Engage in Diversity and Differences in Practice
● Apply and communicate understanding of the importance of diversity and differences in shaping life experiences in practice at the micro and macro levels.

In developing goals, it is important to consider factors that influence the clients capacity to achieve a goal. When working with minors, consideration is given to age and stage of development and cognitive capacity.

EP 7   Assess Individuals, Families, Groups, Organizations, and Communities
● Develop mutually agreed-on intervention goals and objectives based on the critical assessment of strengths, needs, and challenges within clients and constituencies.

In working with clients in preparation for problem solving, goals are the means by which desired outcomes are achieved. Social workers understand and consider personal and environmental factors that can interact with and influence goal selection. The process of developing goals can be different depending on whether the client is voluntary, involuntary or a minor.

Agreement on goals involves as process in which goals are defined and negotiated and expected outcomes are clarified and included in the contract for the work between the social worker and the client.

EP 9   Evaluate Practice with Individuals, Families, Groups, Organizations, and Communities
● Critically analyze, monitor, and evaluate intervention and program processes outcomes.

Once goals are identified and agree upon, both the social worker and the client monitor and evaluate progress toward goal attainment.

Measuring and evaluating progress ensures that goal progress is linked to the identified target concern and provides essential information about the focus and direction of the intervention.

SKILL DEVELOPMENT EXERCISES
in Developing Goals

To advance your skills in developing goals, complete the following exercises.

1. Develop a goal for yourself. Assess the feasibility of your goal, potential barriers, and risks and benefits. Also determine which of the measurement and evaluation procedures discussed in the chapter you would use to observe goal attainment.
2. Using the same goal that you developed for yourself, rate your level of readiness. Now develop general and specific tasks or objectives that will help you meet your goal.
3. Reread the case of Bettina, the adolescent in the group home. What is your reaction to the ongoing staff pattern of punishment? Based on what you have read about involuntary clients, her developmental stage, and motivation theory, how would you work with Bettina to develop goals?
4. Review motivational congruence as a strategy for working with involuntary clients. What are ways in which you could make use of this strategy?
5. What values that you hold have the potential to create tension between what you believe and the goals that a client might want to pursue? Other than using a referral resource, which may or may not be an option, how would you deal with the differences between you and the client?

NOTES

1. In addition to the procedures for measurement and monitoring discussed in this book, we recommend Jordan and Franklin (2003), Bloom, Fischer, and Orme (2009), Fischer and Corcoran (2007), and Thyer (2001b) for more in-depth information on standardized instruments and methods to evaluate practice.
2. For those interested in further study on single-subject research, informative resources are Bloom, Fischer, and Orme (2009), Fischer and Corcoran (2007), and Thyer (2001b). These informative resources describe a wide variety of methods that may be used to evaluate practice.

The Change-Oriented Phase

After formulating a contract, service agreement, or treatment plan, the social worker and the client begin Phase II of the helping process, the goal attainment or change-oriented phase. In Phase II, social workers and clients plan and implement strategies to accomplish goals related to the identified problem or concern. Implementing these strategies involves utilizing interventions and techniques specified in the contract or service agreement and contracting to use other strategies as indicated by changing circumstances. Before considering these factors further, a preview of Part 3 is in order.

Chapter 13 begins with a discussion of planning goal attainment strategies and includes five primary brief, time-limited practice, empirically grounded approaches for work with individuals, families, and groups. Chapter 14 focuses on macro practice; its coverage is enriched by case examples from social workers addressing environmental or institutional barriers in which macro-level interventions were indicated.

In Chapter 15, we discuss social work interventions with families, building on family assessment discussed in Chapter 10. Similarly, Chapter 16 presents group interventions, which builds on the discussion of group formation and assessment in Chapter 11. Techniques to expand self-awareness and to pave the way to change (additive empathy, interpretation, and confrontation) are considered in Chapter 17. Chapter 18 identifies barriers that can impede the change effort and discusses skills for addressing and resolving issues that can occur between the social worker and the client.

CHAPTER 13

Planning and Implementing Change-Oriented Strategies

Chapter Overview

Thus far, you have gained the knowledge and skills needed to complete a multidimensional assessment, develop goals, formulate a contract or treatment plan, and select methods for monitoring and measuring progress. The step beyond this point requires that you plan and select an intervention associated with Phase II of the helping process. The content of this chapter includes a discussion of four change-oriented approaches and micro-level case management, a strategic method involving the coordination of services to address clients' needs. We conclude this chapter with an overview of trauma-informed care.

After reading this chapter, you will be able to:

- Select a change strategy to facilitate goal attainment.

- Explain the importance of matching the strategy to the problem, utilizing a person-in-situation and person-in-environment framework.

- Utilize empirically supported change strategies with clients, including with diverse groups and minors.

- Describe the major tenets and procedures of four change-oriented strategies and the functions of case management.

- Understand the principles of trauma-informed care.

EPAS Competencies in Chapter 13

This chapter will give you the information needed to meet the following practice competencies:

- Competency 1: Demonstrate Ethical and Professional Behavior

- Competency 2: Engage Diversity and Difference in Practice

- Competency 4: Engage in Practice-Informed Research and Research-Informed Practice

- Competency 7: Assess Individuals, Families, Groups, Organizations, and Communities

- Competency 8: Intervene with Individuals, Families, Groups, Organizations, and Communities

CHANGE-ORIENTED APPROACHES

The change-oriented approaches presented in this chapter may be used in your work with individuals, families, and groups. Their aim is to facilitate the attainment of goals or respond to a mandate in the case of involuntary clients. Each of the approaches is supported by research and uses empirically grounded techniques or procedures that have demonstrated their effectiveness with clients of different ages, backgrounds, and needs. The approaches are organized around the systematic interpersonal and structural elements of the helping process and follow the distinct phases of engagement, assessment, goal planning, intervention, and termination. They adhere to the principles of social work practice, which emphasize mobilizing individuals, families, and groups toward positive action. Each supports collaboration with clients, utilizing their strengths and increasing self-efficacy, all of which are critical aspects of empowerment. The approaches are:

- The task-centered model
- The crisis intervention model
- The cognitive restructuring technique
- The solution-focused brief treatment model
- Case management practice

The change approaches are process oriented and problem solving in nature; thus, they are well suited to the helping process discussed so far. In addition, they are consistent with systematic **generalist–eclectic practice** as articulated by Coady and Lehmann (2008, p. 5). The essentials of generalist–eclectic practice are:

- A person and environment focus that is informed by ecological theory
- An emphasis on establishing a positive helping relationship and empowerment as well as a holistic multilevel assessment, including a focus on diversity, oppression, and strengths
- A problem-solving model that provides structure and guidelines for work with clients
- Flexibility in the use of problem-solving methods that allows a choice among a range of theories and techniques based on their compatibility with each client's situation

PLANNING GOAL ATTAINMENT STRATEGIES

EP 7

In planning goal attainment strategies, it is important to choose an intervention that makes sense to both you and the client and is also relevant to the client's situation. The operative word is *matching*. That is, in selecting the intervention, you should ideally address the following questions (Cournoyer, 1991):

- Is the approach appropriate for addressing the problem and the service goals?

- What empirical or conceptual evidence supports the effectiveness of the approach?
- Is the approach compatible with the basic values and ethics of social work?
- Am I sufficiently knowledgeable and skilled enough in this approach to use it with others?

Is the Approach Appropriate for Addressing the Problem and the Service Goals?

During Phase I, you collected information that provided a picture of the client as a person and his or her problem, situation, strengths, and goals. The method selected to address these, however, requires an understanding of context, circumstances, and the nature of the problem and timing. The essential questions to be answered are: *What is the problem?* and *What are the client's goals and values?* To achieve a desired goal, the change strategy must be directed to the problem specified by the client or a mandate, as well as to the systems or environmental issues that are implicated in the problem. A school truancy problem, for example, will, by necessity, involve the family, the educational system, and perhaps the juvenile justice system.

Other factors that guide your consideration include developmental age and stage and the family life cycle, the latter of which can become exaggerated as a result of stressful transitions (Carter & McGoldrick, 2005; Halpern & Tramontin, 2007; James, 2008; Spoth et al., 2003). With respect to life cycle and human development, culture and race are requisite factors to be considered. For instance, not all cultural or racial groups mark life cycle or human development according to the normative Western expectations (Garcia Coll, Akerman, & Cicchetti, 2000; Garcia Coll et al., 1996; Ogbu, 1997, 1994). The following questions can help guide you in planning and eventually deciding on an approach:

- Does the approach acknowledge and allow for the integration of environmental factors—for example, the experience of minority or socioeconomic status and oppression—as contributing to a problem, so as not to add a sense of being marginalized?
- Are modifications to the approach indicated so that it is responsive to diverse individuals, families, and minors?
- Is the approach flexible enough that it respects and can be adapted to specific cultural beliefs, values, and a different worldview?

• Does the approach address the sociopolitical climate as a factor in creating and sustaining the client's problem?

These questions are, of course, by no means exhaustive. The intent is to prompt you to critically examine the appropriateness of a particular approach. In addition, in considering the third question, Green (1999, pp. 50–51) reminds us that "help-seeking behavior" is embedded in a cultural context as well as the experience of minority status. Exploring the client's cultural context can include attention to gender relations and position in the family and in the community. In some ethnic cultural and racial communities, the act of asking for help, whether formally or informally, can be frowned upon. Narratives or suspicions about change strategies, real or imagined, may be well formed in diverse communities, some of which may be based on historical and sometimes oppressive experiences. These dynamics can be so prominent that problems or feelings may be minimized or ignored for fear of being perceived as vulnerable or giving the appearance of a cultural anomaly (Kung, 2003; Mau & Jepsen, 1990; Nadler, 1996; Potocky-Tripodi, 2002; Sue, 2006).

EP 2

As you plan and select a change strategy, we encourage you to allow diverse clients to consider the cost–benefit tradeoff of seeking help, essentially determining the extent to which the approach allows the client to retain a sense of self or cultural identity and/or poses a threat to the client's cultural values and beliefs (Potocky-Tripodi, 2002; Sue, 2006; Williams, 2006). As Potocky-Tripodi (2002) explains, for example, immigrants or refugees with little or no prior experience with formal helping systems may perceive a change approach as a threat, especially if past experiences involved forceful or repressive tactics. Some clients may experience tensions with change strategies that require them to move from the familiar to the unfamiliar in such matters as child rearing and customs such as arranged marriages.

At this point, you may wonder how to go about selecting a change strategy that is consistent with the needs and interests of diverse clients. *Discovery* and *cultural humility* are two concepts that will help you understand clients and ultimately select a change strategy that is in harmony with those clients' values and beliefs. The spirit of discovery guides you to elicit clients' view of the problem at hand; the related symbolic, cultural, and social nuances of their concerns; and their ideas about an approach as a remedy to their difficulties (Green, 1999). Cultural humility encourages you to place yourself in a student role in which you are open to the clients as a teacher. Together, you and the clients are partners in understanding and clarifying the relevance of the change effort to their problem (Tervalon & Murray-Garcia, 1998).

Regarding whether the approach addresses the sociopolitical climate as a factor in creating and sustaining the client's problem, social workers must keep in mind that minority and poor families, many of whose contact with professional helpers is involuntary, often face insurmountable odds in their everyday lives, some of which are the results of limited resources, pressures to conform to dominant societal norms, marginalized status, inequity, and constrained self-determination. Societal presumptions about people, their competence, or their lifestyles are oppressive forces that create toxic environments for persons who are different, and which they contend with on a daily basis.

In most instances, overt acts of discrimination and bigotry have diminished as a result of laws. Laws, however, cannot command positive interpersonal and social behavior, especially covert interactions. **Covert interactions** are those subtle acts characterized as **microaggressions**, in which people are treated differently based on their race, ethnicity, sexual orientation, ability, or socioeconomic status (Sue et al., 2007). Conditions and circumstances that affect cognitive, physical, and psychological functioning are extraordinary stressors; therefore, a change strategy should acknowledge the existence of such ever-present stressors. At the same time, it is important to recognize that despite the circumstances, diverse individuals, families, and groups have strengths and resilience, including the fact that over time, they have coped with adversity (Connolly, 2006; Guadalupe & Lum, 2005; Sousa, Ribeiro, & Rodrigues, 2006).

Finally, note that in some instances, the approach that you use may be determined by your practice setting. In either case, in planning and selecting an approach, when you are uncertain, supervisory consultation can be useful to help you clarify or affirm your decision.

What Empirical or Conceptual Evidence Supports the Effectiveness of the Approach?

An effective intervention approach is one that has the most promise for achieving goals identified by the client or the mandate. In evaluating an approach, you are looking for evidence of its effectiveness: with whom

EP 4

did it work, under what circumstances, and what were the results? Furthermore, the evidence should specify the approach's effectiveness with respect to client problem or status, developmental stage, and cognitive ability, as well as its compatibility with diverse cultural values and beliefs.

As you are exposed to novel or emerging strategies, it is important that you evaluate the evidence of the effectiveness of each approach. Ethical standards require social workers to use approaches with clients that respect their dignity and rights and that do not cause harm. Therefore, untested interventions, as well as those that are coercive, confrontational, or dangerous, should not be utilized.

Is the Approach Compatible with Basic Values and Ethics of Social Work?

EP 1

Professional social work ethics and values provide a foundation upon which knowledge and skills are used. Two specific ethical standards are applicable in your decision making related to planning and selecting an intervention approach: safeguarding the client's right to self-determination and informed consent.

Does the Approach Safeguard the Client's Right to Self-Determination?

Promoting self-determination upholds a client's right to make decisions about his or her life. In essence, in your work with clients, they should feel empowered to fully participate in decisions that will resolve or change their situation. You might ask, *"What if the client has limitations—for example, in language, cognitive, mental, or physical capacity—that can hamper his or her ability to make decisions?"* Multiple factors are involved in this question, including the nature of the decision, age and stage of development, and the capacity to understand the consequences of a decision (Strom-Gottfried, 2007). Although some clients have limitations and may be unable to make decisions about certain aspects of their lives, the clients' limitations are not the sum total of who they are, nor does this mean that they lack the ability to process task-specific information. For example, you may recommend a change approach, followed by an explanation: *"If we select this approach to resolve your concern, it would mean that together we take steps that we believe would best change your situation."* In essence, the focus should be on the client's capacity rather than limitations. Above all, you

are cautioned to refrain from acting in a paternalistic or beneficent manner in order to achieve *your* perception of the client's best interest.

Your ethical obligation to respect a client's right to be self-directed may be a challenge with certain client populations. For example, some involuntary clients and clients who have experienced a situation in which they were victimized may be reluctant to accept the notion of self-determination, believing instead that they lack influence, knowledge, or power to effect change. In a crisis situation, respecting self-determination can become overshadowed by a strong desire to help, so much so that the client's rights and the outcome sought may be unintentionally overlooked (Fullerton & Ursano, 2005; Sommers-Flanagan, 2007). In either scenario, actively encouraging self-direction with such clients and emphasizing the ways in which they can exercise their rights and regain control over their situation should be discussed.

Note that the principle of self-determination is taken for granted in Western society. As such, the principle should be examined in a community and sociocultural context. The ideals of autonomy, self-direction, and independence can be values that are in sharp contrast to the beliefs of particular cultures. For instance, the freedom and success of the individual among Muslims is understood in terms of group or community success (Hodge & Nadir, 2008). Indeed, for some cultural groups, family, which can include a spiritual leader, relatives, or an entire community, may have a prominent role in intervention decisions (Hodge 2005; Palmer & Kaufman, 2003).

We acknowledge that the work setting in which you are employed may determine the approach utilized with a certain client population and therefore may limit decision making about an intervention approach. In other settings, professionals acting as proxies can presume that a particular client or client population lacks the capacity for self-direction. Best interest, in many instances, has become a means to sacrifice self-determination, in which social workers act in a paternalistic manner. Fostering self-determination in such settings may present a challenge for you as a social worker. Whatever the circumstances might be, the defining question for which you may need to seek supervision is, *What is the justification for ignoring a client's rights in making decisions about an intervention strategy?*

Self-Determination and Minors. When it comes to minors, the right to self-determination is complicated. In most states, minors are presumed to have limited decision-making capacity; therefore, parents or legal guardians act as their proxies (Strom-Gottfried, 2008). Developmental stage, reasoning, and cognitive capacity are also significant factors that influence a minor's capacity for decision making and self-direction. Minors who are immigrants may be unfamiliar with the ideals of self-determination, and being asked to make a decision may be outside of their realm of cultural expectations (Congress & Lynn, 1994). Nonetheless, you should not assume that a minor is unable to make choices. In general, most minors are able to express how they feel and what they want. Your task is to provide the opportunity for them to participate in intervention planning, which includes your explaining the benefits and potential risks using words that they understand (Green et al., 2003; Strom-Gottfried, 2008).

Does the Approach Safeguard the Client's Right to Informed Consent?

Ensuring that clients understand and consent to an approach is essential to ethical and collaborative practice and is supportive of the principle of self-determination. So that clients are fully informed, you should explain the approach in language that is easily understood, presenting information about the benefits, risks, and evidence of the approach's effectiveness with their problem. This same information should be provided to involuntary clients, even though they may lack the freedom to withhold consent or to refuse a goal or service plan. They can, however, be given information about their options and the consequences of their choices.

Following the conversation in which you explain the suitability of an approach for addressing the problem or service goals, you should be guided by the client's responses to the following questions:

1. Does the client understand the proposed approach?
2. Is the client in agreement with the proposed approach?
3. Does the client have concerns about the procedures and effectiveness of an intervention, strengths, and limitation related to his or her particular problem?
4. Is the client satisfied with the manner in which his or her progress would be monitored and measured?

A client's responses to these questions provide assurance that the client understands, is able to make an informed decision, and is subsequently able to give or withhold consent.

Informed Consent and Minors. The ability to give consent is informed by developmental stage, and cognitive and reasoning ability (Strom-Gottfried, 2008). In particular, informed consent presumes that clients (for verbal agreement) not only understand a proposed approach but also are able to weigh potential outcomes. A caveat for minors is that parents or legal guardians are presumed to act in the minor clients' best interest and therefore they (instead of the minors) consent to the intervention approach (Berman-Rossi & Rossi, 1990; Strom-Gottfried, 2008). Although minors are unable to give consent, they can nonetheless be provided with information about the approach and asked whether they assent; that is, they can give an "affirmative agreement" (Strom-Gottfried, 2008, p. 62). Also, as a means to involve minors, you can select appropriate questions to ask from the previous list. For example, do the minors have questions or reservations, are they concerned about the efficacy of the approach, and are they satisfied with how their progress will be monitored and measured?

Am I Sufficiently Knowledgeable and Skilled Enough in This Approach to Use It with Others?

First and foremost, you are ethically obligated to have the requisite knowledge, skills, training, and competence to use an approach to resolve a particular client problem (NASW, 1999, 1.04b). The complexities of clients' problems often necessitate having the knowledge and competence to blend strategies and techniques of multiple approaches. In many respects, techniques can transcend models. An addendum to the question of sufficient knowledge and skills in an approach is, *Are you competent enough to make use of the techniques of another approach with the one that you have selected?* For example, let's assume that the intervention approach that you are using is the task-centered model. You might blend the strategic solution-focused miracle or scaling questions to clarify a goal. Posing the miracle question in the initial crisis stage would, however, be ill advised because a solution would have precedence over attending to the client's emotional state (James, 2008). Nor is it advisable to use the miracle question solely as an intervention strategy. Coady and Lehmann (2008) refer to this type of blending generalist practice as **technical eclecticism**. In sum, in deciding to blend tactics or techniques, an essential question is whether you have

EP 1

the requisite knowledge, skills, and level of competence to engage in eclectic practice.

In working with minors, you may find that blending tactics is advisable. Very young children, for example, typically lack the cognitive capacity to think abstractly. Therefore, it can be useful if you are skilled in techniques such as play imagery or storytelling (Morgan, 2000; Nader & Mello, 2008). School-age minors, especially those in middle childhood, are influenced by self-evaluation, the evaluation of others, and their own sense of mastery (Hutchison, 2008). Hence, the use of tasks consistent with the task-centered or the solution-focused questions can be combined to support and reinforce their sense of self-efficacy.

A word of caution is in order. Eclectic practice does not mean that you select a little bit of this and that from various intervention approaches irrespective of your skill level. Ethically, in combining one approach with techniques from another, you must consider whether this is appropriate for the problem or situation at the time. In specific circumstances and with specific populations, selecting and utilizing an approach may in fact require that you have knowledge of and integrate non-Western traditional healing systems (Al-Krenawi & Graham, 2000; Hodge & Nadir, 2008; Sue, 2006). This knowledge can inform you as to whether adaptations or modifications of an approach are needed.

In general, it is advisable to use only those approaches in which you have the requisite knowledge and skills to implement them in a manner that is appropriate to the client situation and is consistent with ethical standards (NASW, 1999, 1.04a). In instances where you lack the requisite skills or competence, you should seek ongoing supervision or consultation or refer the client to a professional with the applicable skills (Strom-Gottfried, 2007).

MODELS AND TECHNIQUES OF PRACTICE

EP 8

Having described guidelines for planning and selecting a change approach, we now turn our attention to the major tenets and theoretical frameworks of the task-centered model, the basic model of crisis intervention, the cognitive behavioral technique of cognitive restructuring, the solution-focused brief treatment, and case management.[1]

THE TASK-CENTERED MODEL

The **task-centered model** is a social work practice model developed by William Reid and Laura Epstein. The model's contribution to social work practice is its specific focus on problems of concern identified by the client and its emphasis on tasks and the collaborative responsibilities between the client and the social worker. The model emerged when the prevailing view of the resistant client and open-ended models were the norm in social work and allied disciplines. Kelly (2008) credits the development of the model as strengthening the empirical orientation to social work practice.

Tenets of the Task-Centered Approach

The direction of the task-centered approach with regard to goal attainment is both systematic and efficient. Termination is considered to begin at the initial point of contact, facilitated by specific goals and the development and completion of tasks. The model is aimed at reducing problems in living within a brief, time-limited period.

Central themes of the task-centered approach are that clients are capable of solving their own problems and that it is important to work on problems that are identified by the client. Clients' identification of priority concerns and the collaborative relationship are understood to be empowering aspects of the model. The approach addresses an array of problems, including interpersonal conflicts, difficulties in social relations or role performance, reactive emotional distress, inadequate resources, and difficulties with organizations (Epstein, 1992; Ramos & Tolson, 2008; Reid, 1992; Reid & Epstein, 1972).

Theoretical Framework of the Task-Centered Model

Research by Reid and Shyne (1969) led to the development of the task-centered model as an action-oriented model in which problem-solving activities occurred within a limited time frame. The research demonstrated that a brief, focused contact

EP 4

and the conscious use of time limits were as effective as intervention strategies that required a longer time period. The results of Reid and Shyne's research were consistent with the findings of other studies that supported the efficacy of time-limited treatment (Hoyt, 2000; Wells & Gianetti, 1990).

The development of the model was further influenced by Studt's (1968) conceptualization of the efficacy of utilizing tasks and the structured procedures of Perlman's (1957) problem-solving model. Similar to the problem-solving model introduced by Perlman (1957), the task-centered model focused social work practice on the challenging problems in daily living and psychosocial factors that were observed to be common among a majority of social work constituents (Epstein, 1992; Reid, 1992). The use of tasks is supported by Bandura's (1997) research related to self-efficacy, ultimately enhancing the client's sense that through his or her efforts, he or she can be a successful agent in solving problems (Reid, 1992).

The task-centered system is designed to be eclectic. Reid (1992) emphasizes, however, that combining the procedures of the model with another (technical eclecticism) requires utilizing compatible research-based theories and intervention techniques. With this in mind, you can make use of various theories that are relevant to the client situation (Ramos & Tolson, 2008; Reid, 1992). For example, cognitive restructuring can inform task strategies when feelings, anxieties, and fears are influenced by beliefs or irrational thought patterns (Reid, 1992). Still, Reid (1992) and Berlin (2001) caution that you should first determine that the client's emotional state is consistent with cognitive theory rather than stressors caused by environmental factors, conditions, or a crisis situation. The task-centered model, however, allows for the advent of a crisis, in which techniques from the crisis intervention approach may be used.

Evidence Base and Use of the Task-Centered Model

EP 4

The task-centered model has been adapted to various settings in which social workers practice, and its use has been empirically established with different client populations, including families, organizations, and communities (Parihar, 1984; Pomeroy, Rubin, & Walker, 1995; Ramarkrishnan, Balgopal, & Pettys, 1994, 2008; Reid, 1987, 1997; Reid & Fortune, 2002; Tolson, Reid, & Garvin, 1994). Adaptations of the task-centered approach have been tested in most settings where social workers practice, including mental health, health care, and family practice (Alley & Brown, 2002; Epstein & Brown, 2002; Fortune, 1985; Fortune, McCallion, & Briar-Larson, 2010; Reid, 1987, 1992, 1997, 2000). Additional evidence of the model's

utilization and effectiveness include case management with minors and families, with elderly individuals in long-term care (Lee, Magnanano, & Smith, 2008; Naleppa & Reid, 2000, 2003; Pazaratz, 2000; Tolson, Reid, & Garvin, 1994), in supervision and staff development (Caspi & Reid, 2002), and with groups (Garvin, 1987; Larsen & Mitchell, 1980; Lo, 2005; Pomeroy, Rubin, & Walker, 1995). Building on the basic thrust of the model—specifically, eliciting the clients' view of the mandated problem and involving the client in task development and implementation strategies—R. H. Rooney (2009) and Trotter (2006) demonstrated the model's applicability and effectiveness with involuntary clients. Both Rooney and Trotter found that the approach, when combined with other strategies, reduced reactance and engaged the client.

Utilization of the Task-Centered Model with Minors

Examples of the model's application with minors include improving school performance, changing or modifying behavior in residential facilities, and reducing sibling conflict (Bailey-Dempsey & Reid, 1996; Caspi, 2008; Pazaratz, 2000, 2006; Reid & Bailey-Dempsey, 1995; Reid et al., 1980). Using the task-centered model as a guiding framework, R. H. Rooney (1981, 1992) expanded the application of the task-centered approach to include social work practice with involuntary clients in child welfare and with minors in school settings.

Application of the Task-Centered Model with Diverse Groups

According to Ramos and Tolson, the task-centered model has been used in agencies in which the client base consists of clients who are from "poor, racial and ethnocultural minority groups" (2008, p. 286). The model is thought to be sensitive to the experience of diverse individuals and families because of the emphasis on the right of clients to identify concerns, including clients who are involuntary. The use of tasks is believed to empower clients who are marginalized, lack power, and are oppressed (Boyd-Franklin, 1989; Ramos & Garvin, 2003). The model also responds to issues considered by Sue (2006) to be barriers to multicultural clinical practice because of its explicit acceptance of the client's view of the problem and a here-and-now action orientation rather than insightful talking. In their evaluation of various models of practice, Devore and Schlesinger (1999) concluded that the basic principles of the task-centered system are a "major thrust" in ethnically sensitive practice (p. 121). Because the model accommodates different worldviews, it has been translated into several languages in different practice settings (Ramos & Tolson, 2008; Rooney, 2010; Chou & Rooney, 2010).

PROCEDURES OF THE TASK-CENTERED MODEL

EP 8

Figure 13-1 presents an overview of the procedures of the task-centered model. The initial phase begins with the client identifying and prioritizing a target problem. It is recommended that priority concerns and goals be limited to a maximum of three. Goals are agreed upon, and general and specific tasks to achieve goal attainment are developed. In keeping with the model's action orientation and brevity, termination begins with the first session. Specifically, you and the client agree to work together for a particular number of sessions (e.g., 6 to 8 weeks), although there is potential for you and the client to extend contact or negotiate a new contract for a different problem. During the period of contact, progress toward the identified goal is monitored and reviewed in each session as the client moves toward termination. Let's explore aspects of developing general and specific tasks and monitoring progress in more detail.

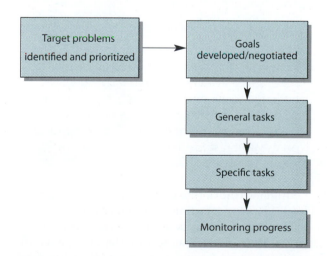

FIG 13-1 Overview of the Task-Centered Model

Developing General Tasks

As illustrated in Figure 13-1, when you and the client have identified a target problem and related goals, you are ready to develop general tasks. General tasks consist of discrete actions to be undertaken by the client and, in some instances, by you the social worker. Each general task has specific tasks that direct the incremental action steps to achieve goals.

VIDEO CASE EXAMPLE

The video "Problem Solving with the Corning Family" illustrates how goals and related general and specific tasks are developed. At this point, you will want to review all of the five video segments. A review of the family's situation is summarized here.

Target Problem

Angela and Irwin Corning, an interracial couple and their three children, are living in a transitional housing facility. Irwin lost his job 8 months ago when the county agency where he worked as a maintenance specialist hired a private contractor to reduce its labor costs. The couple's preference is to purchase another home, but their current financial situation does not permit them to do so. Consequently, the family will need to move into an apartment.

Goals

1. Move from transitional housing facility into an apartment.
2. Find employment for Irwin.

Irwin has found temporary employment that may lead to a permanent position. Now that he is employed, however, the family is no longer eligible to remain in transitional housing. They have 6 weeks to move from the facility; thus, the priority goal is finding an apartment, preferably one with three bedrooms. Irwin, in the meantime, will continue to look for more permanent employment.

To accomplish their goals, the following general tasks were developed:

General Tasks for the Couple

1. Meet with the transitional housing case manager to obtain information about affordable three-bedroom apartments.

2. Plan to visit apartments located in the general area where they want to live.
3. Identify schools in the area for the children.
4. Develop a budget.
5. Explore permanent employment for Irwin.

General Tasks for the Social Worker

In the examples provided, it is apparent that general tasks involve actions to be undertaken by one or both of the Corning spouses. In some situations, general tasks can also require actions by the social worker, either on the client's behalf or jointly with the client. In the Corning case, Ali, the social worker, agreed to a general task of providing resource information about employment opportunities as well. At the same, Irwin's general task involved pursuing employment opportunities on his own. Thus, both Ali's and Irwin's actions are jointly focused on tasks related to the job search.

Initially, general tasks may be disconnected and may not follow a logical sequence. Therefore, tasks will need to be prioritized by you and the client. For Angela and Irwin, it was important for the social worker to clarify which of the general tasks were the most significant. They agreed to the general task of moving from the transitional housing facility as a priority.

It is important to settle on tasks for which the benefit is obvious and which have a good chance of being successful. Success with one task encourages clients' confidence in their ability to tackle another task. For example, locating and visiting apartments were tasks that seemed to be more easily completed, but finding a permanent job for Irwin might prove to be more difficult. A benefit that Angela and Irwin identified in selecting the move as a priority goal, and the related general task, was the couple's belief that it would provide a more stable environment for their children.

Developing Specific Tasks

General tasks can prove to be overwhelming for some clients. The key to the task-centered system is developing general *and specific* tasks. The latter direct the actions that the client or you as the social worker will attempt between one session and the next.

VIDEO CASE EXAMPLE

The following are specific tasks related to one of the Cornings' goals and previously outlined general tasks:

- **Goal:** Move from the transitional housing facility into an apartment within the next 6 weeks.
- **General Task:** Contact the transitional housing assistance coordinator to obtain information about available and affordable three-bedroom apartments.
- **Specific Tasks:**
  1. Schedule a meeting with the housing coordinator to learn about housing options within the next week.
  2. Plan to visit apartments located in the general area where they would like to live.

Specific tasks may need to be further partialized into subtasks. Meeting with the housing coordinator more than likely is a specific one-time action step. Visiting apartments, however, may require additional actions or subtasks, such as arranging for child care, depending on the time of the visits and transportation.

Partializing goals into general tasks and ultimately into specific tasks and subtasks can consume a substantial amount of time. The same is true of the preparation for accomplishing one or more specific tasks at a time. When multiple tasks are developed, it is important to identify and plan the implementation of at least one task before ending a session. In fact, many clients are eager to get started and welcome homework assignments. Note that Angela Corning asked what the couple could do before the next session. Although mutually identifying tasks and planning for implementation in each session is time intensive, the time spent from one session to the next can sharpen the focus on the action steps that facilitate progress.

Although the Corning couple were ready to carryout identified tasks, sometimes preliminary steps may be required to help clients to move forward. The following three facilitative factors can be of assistance in this regard:

1. *Assessing client readiness to engage in an agreed-upon task.* A client's readiness to implement a

task can be gauged by asking the client to rate his or her readiness using a scale of 1 to 10, in which a rating of 1 represents a lack of readiness and 10 indicates that the client is ready to go (De Jong & Berg, 2001). Should clients indicate that their readiness is on the low end of the scale—for example, in the 1 to 3 range—you should explore the reason for the low rating, as doing so can uncover vital information concerning potential obstacles. However, even when clients have indicated a level of readiness to move ahead, implementing a task can cause a certain amount of tension and anxiety. It is neither realistic nor desirable to expect clients to be altogether comfortable with tasks, despite the fact that they were involved in them. Nonverbal behavior on the part of a client can also indicate a level of readiness in the lower range that can signal an obstacle or apprehension about undertaking a task. When you observe such behavior, you should explore the context and content so that the behavior does not become a barrier.

In those instances in which the client's level of readiness is low, you may be tempted to assign tasks. For the most part, however, individuals of all ages, irrespective of status, are unlikely to be motivated by and become reactive to assigned tasks (Brehm & Brehm, 1981; Miller & Rollnick, 2002). Reactance theory suggests that individuals are inclined to act to protect themselves, especially when a choice is imposed, and further when the choice is inconsistent with a desired direction.

VIDEO CASE EXAMPLE

Note that in the video "Problem Solving with the Corning Family," although Irwin expressed a high level of readiness, he was nonetheless apprehensive about his job search. Had his apprehension involved an inordinate level of anxiety, his feelings would need to be clarified, as anxiety can be a major deterrent to further action. Nonverbal behaviors are also visible in the video. For example, Irwin seemed uncomfortable, at times annoyed, and had very little to say unless prompted by Angela. He became animated, however, when Ali asked about his willingness to develop goal-related tasks, stating, "I am ready to do something. Instead of sitting here talking, I could be out looking for a job or a place for my family to live. So, let's get on with it."

2. *Brainstorming alternative tasks.* Essential tasks are often readily apparent; however, in instances in which tasks are less apparent, you and the client can brainstorm to identify a range of alternatives. Brainstorming alternative tasks involves a process in which you and the client mutually focus on generating a broad range of possible task options from which the individual, family, or group may choose. Note that when you suggest tasks during the brainstorming process, it is critical to check with the client to ensure that he or she agrees with and is committed to the tasks. Most clients will be generally receptive to your suggestions. Reid (1978, 2000) found that there was little difference in the rate at which clients accomplished tasks suggested by the social worker when compared to those they proposed themselves. Brainstorming can be particularly useful with minors to encourage their ownership of possible actions.

3. *Establishing a reward or an incentive.* Given the varied circumstances in which clients may be hesitant to engage in tasks, it may necessary to identify an immediate reward to support motivation. Rewards and incentives are particularly relevant when a change in behavior or cognition is associated with the choice of pain over pleasure, such as engaging in activities that may be perceived as unattractive (e.g., studying, cleaning house) instead of engaging in self-time. Possible rewards can be identified with the client; however, to be effective, the reward should be realistic. Rewards can be helpful in encouraging minors to complete tasks, in particular when doing something else is more attractive. An incentive can be especially beneficial for minors when the intent of a task is a behavioral change. You may also work with parents or other significant adults in the minor's life to establish a complementary reward.

When using an incentive or reward to motivate, it is important to observe and record incremental change, followed by an immediate reward; otherwise, the client may become discouraged or give up, believing instead that he or she is unable meet expectations. The following guidelines can help you best utilize incentives or rewards and encourage the completion of a task, especially among minors:

- Specify the time frame and the conditions under which the task is to be performed (e.g., every 2 hours, twice daily, each Wednesday, once a day for 5 days), so that the client understands the specifics of what is being asked of him or her.

- In collaboration with the client, identify the reward to be earned as well as establish a method for tracking the progress of task completion.
- When possible, identify relationship rewards (for example, going to the mall or spending time with friends or other significant individuals).
- Provide a bonus for consistent achievements of tasks over an extended period of time.
- Encourage task completion by providing consistent and positive feedback. For minors, using visuals, such as graphs to record and track progress on tasks, can be a motivator.

Task Implementation Sequence

After agreeing on one or more tasks, the next step is to assist clients in planning and preparing to implement each task. When skillfully executed, these processes enhance client motivation for undertaking tasks and substantially increase the likelihood of a successful outcome. The **task implementation sequence (TIS)**, as described by Reid (1975, 2000), involves a sequence of discrete steps. The steps (summarized in Table 13-1) involve the major elements generally associated with successful change efforts. Research suggests that clients were more successful in accomplishing tasks when TIS was implemented than when it was not (Reid, 1975, 2000), even though being faithful to the sequence may initially seem tedious. Although Reid recommends that the TIS be applied systematically, the sequence is flexible and permits adaptations or modifications that are appropriate to the circumstances of each client situation.

Merely agreeing to carry out a task doesn't guarantee that a client has the knowledge, resources, courage, interpersonal skills, or emotional readiness to successfully implement a task. Consequently, each step in the TIS is intended to increase the potential for a successful outcome: obstacles are examined and resolved in advance, and behavior involved in the task is rehearsed. It may also be useful to revisit incentives or rewards associated with task completion.

In the following sections, we discuss the steps of the TIS in greater detail.

Step 1: Enhance the Client's Commitment to Carry Out Tasks

Step 1 in the TIS is intended to ensure the client's commitment to carry out tasks. This step involves clarifying the significance of tasks for reaching the goal and identifying the potential benefits. To encourage follow-through with tasks, it is important that clients perceive that the gains of completing a task outweigh the costs (including anxiety and fear) associated with risking a new behavior or dealing with a changed problem or situation. Because change is difficult, exploring apprehension, discomfort, and uncertainty is especially critical when a client's motivation to carry out a given task is questionable.

It is advisable to begin implementing Step 1 of the TIS by asking clients to identify benefits they will gain by successfully accomplishing the task. In many instances, the potential gains and benefits of carrying out the task are obvious, and it would be pointless to dwell on this step.

TABLE 13-1 Task Implementation Sequence (TIS)

1. Enhance the client's commitment to carry out tasks.
2. Plan the details of carrying out tasks.
3. Analyze and resolve barriers and obstacles.
4. Rehearse or practice behaviors involved in tasks.
5. Summarize the task plan.

VIDEO CASE EXAMPLE

Note that in the video "Problem Solving with the Corning Family," for Irwin Corning, the benefit and subsequent gain of completing the task of seeking permanent employment, the result of which is economic stability for the family, is clear. Ali, the social worker, therefore does not need to focus extensively on this step of the TIS.

Step 2: Plan the Details of Carrying Out Tasks

Step 2 of the TIS is intended to prepare clients for all of the actions involved in a task. When a task involves both cognitive and behavioral subtasks, it is beneficial to help the client to be psychologically prepared before carrying out an overt action. For example, you can coach clients to reflect on past successes or focus on their supportive resources such as spirituality or faith.

By including cognitive (covert) strategies in this step, you are assisting clients to cope with their ambivalence or apprehension with regard to implementing actions. Of course, planning behavioral tasks that involve overt actions requires considering real-life details as well, such as transportation, child care, access to technology, financial resources, and the like.

VIDEO CASE EXAMPLE

The video "Problem Solving with the Corning Family" touches on several factors related to Step 2 of the TIS. For example, in one of the sessions, Irwin talked about himself as a low-skilled laborer, which he believed meant that he had fewer opportunities. Although the details of the job search had been discussed, addressing Irwin's cognitive appraisal of his situation would be important. In addition, the Corning couple discussed practical details about carrying out tasks, such as whether to take their three children as they looked for an apartment. If visits occurred early in the day, the two older children would be at school. In the evenings, unless the couple could arrange for child care, all three children would accompany them. Because the couple relied on public transportation, they would need bus fare for a family of five, and multiple bus rides might be required. Angela identified her sister as a child care resource. Discussing the details and discrete actions associated with completing tasks, and planning for the inevitable in advance, effectively increased the opportunity for the couple to be successful.

The Practitioner's Role in Task Planning. The details of a task may involve certain actions for which the social worker assumes responsibility. Clients may wonder about your role. (Angela Corning, for example, asked Ali, the social worker, "What kinds of things can you do for us? I'm not clear about how you can help us.") In planning the details of tasks, a social worker's tasks can be developed when he or she has ready access to resources or information that will facilitate client work. In the Corning case, for example, Ali agreed to obtain information about the couple's eligibility for temporary financial assistance to help with their move from the transitional housing facility. On the other hand, when it is advantageous for a client to complete a task on his or her own, a review of the actions involved would be helpful.

During the performance of tasks, there may be occasions on which it will be useful for you to accompany the client or make use of his or her support system. For example, if the task involved applying for financial assistance, which for some people can be intimidating, supporting task performance can involve assisting the client in completing the application or having a support person to talk to while they are waiting to be interviewed.

Conditions for Task Completion. When the time frame for completing tasks lacks specificity or is vague or abstract, clients and social workers can procrastinate, leaving little time to effectively implement the planned action. Think about a group project assignment in which your classmates agree to meet within the next week. Without specifying when and where the meeting is to take place, each person can have a different idea about what next week means. Therefore, for the sake of clarity, the details of tasks should specify when, as well as the conditions or circumstances of the action that is to occur.

For example, consider a scenario in which an elementary school student constantly disturbs his peers and speaks out in class without raising his hand. The condition for the task behavior is attentive listening (condition) while the teacher is speaking during the 1-hour math class (circumstance) for a certain time period. Although problematic behavior occurs in other classes, the task is focused in the math class within a specified time period. Of course, the overall task is movement toward the eventual change behavior in all classes. Focusing on the behavior in the math class, however, partializes the task behavior, as it would be unrealistic to expect an immediate behavior change.

Because tasks connected to *ongoing* goals are incremental, it is important that you and the client begin with a structured first task that is easy and within the individual's capacity to achieve. In the classroom situation, for example, the student's task of raising his hand for 5 straight days may be difficult to achieve. Alternatively, raising his hand in math class for 2 out of 5 days may, with positive feedback from the teacher, increase the likelihood of eventually engaging in the task directed toward the goal of behavioral change.

Step 3: Analyze and Resolve Barriers and Obstacles

In Step 3 of the TIS, you and the client deliberately anticipate and subsequently prepare for obstacles that can affect or stall task accomplishment. Returning to the student's classroom behavior as an example, as the social worker involved, it would be useful for you and the student to discuss obstacles to goal completion, such as social, physical, or psychological barriers. For the student, his behavior was reinforced because of the attention he gained from his peers and social standing within the peer group. Therefore, change for the student involved not only mastery of a new behavior but also a loss of his esteemed position within his peer group.

It is also prudent to inquire about the practical and economic resources needed for completing the tasks (Eamon & Zhang, 2006). A caveat should be observed, however: A simple action of making a phone call may prove difficult for a client, depending on his or her on level of confidence, cognitive capacity, or social ability. Fears and cognitions can be a formidable barrier to accomplishing a task.

VIDEO CASE EXAMPLE

For Irwin Corning, telephone calls to inquire about available jobs or looking online for job postings seem to be relatively easy and simple tasks. However, his fears and cognitions were a more difficult obstacle. For example, although Irwin was eager to find employment, he felt vulnerable because "being laid off" amounted to a failure, based on his belief that "a man ought to provide for his family."

When tasks are complex, obstacles likewise tend to be complex, and clients may have difficulty identifying obstacles. Tasks that involve changes in patterns of interpersonal relationships tend to be multifaceted and require developing subtasks as a prerequisite. For example, many intrapersonal tasks require the mastery of certain interpersonal skills.

Clients' capacity to resolve barriers and obstacles varies depending on the nature and complexity of the task. Some clients overlook or underestimate potential barriers and obstacles, resulting in a delay to take on tasks, needless difficulties, and in certain cases outright failure in accomplishing a task. In such instances, explaining that obstacles and barriers are common is helpful. You might take the lead in brainstorming with clients to identify and resolve obstacles that can influence the planned course of action. Returning to the example of the elementary school student, the

student and social worker would brainstorm different *what if* scenarios that could hinder the student's ability to raise his hand before speaking in class, thereby resulting in his becoming frustrated and returning to his old behavior. For example, what if he raised his hand and the teacher did not call on him? What would he do if he became discouraged? Discussing different scenarios with the student can identify potential obstacles and responses in advance (for example, "I would wait my turn," or "I could keep my hand up, even if the teacher called on another student first," or "If I felt discouraged, I might talk to the teacher after class"). Equipping the student with possible responses reinforces his motivation to engage in task behavior.

Psychological barriers to task performance leading to goal attainment are often encountered regardless of the nature of the task. Think of your cognitive appraisal of a situation in which you experienced intense emotions—for example, when you applied for a job, were required to appear in court, or had to express your feelings in a difficult situation. Now think about how the experience was intimidating or caused you anxiety. How did your appraisal of the situation affect the quality and intensity of your emotions and influence you thoughts and feeling in the situation?

VIDEO CASE EXAMPLE

Whether real or perceived, thoughts, feelings, and beliefs about self or stereotypic perceptions of others can become major obstacles to task completion. In the video "Problem Solving with the Corning Family," Irwin Corning's discomfort about losing his job dominates his thinking and self-perception—in particular, his belief about his role as the head of the household. At one point he asserts, "Nothing is comfortable about this situation." In examining the cognitive content of his message, there are several layers in his reasoning. Understandably, he is experiencing intense emotions as a displaced worker. His appraisal of the economic climate is realistic, as is his belief about the available employment opportunities for an African American male. But Irwin's perception that the company prefers hiring undocumented workers as a reason for his becoming unemployed lacks concrete evidence.

What can you do when you encounter situations in which cognitions and intense emotions have the potential to derail a client's plan of action? To begin, you and the client can develop a subsidiary task of neutralizing his or her emotions by exploring and clarifying the emotional content and empathizing with the client's apprehension. It may also be important to examine the problematic emotions, helping the client to identify the cognitive source and to align his or her thoughts and feelings with reality.

In general, the time and effort invested in overcoming and resolving barriers and obstacles are likely to pay dividends, resulting in a higher rate of success in accomplishing tasks. Consider the economy of this process, as failure to complete tasks can have an effect on an individual's sense of self-efficacy and can extend the time involved in successful problem solving.

Step 4: Rehearse or Practice Behaviors Involved in Tasks

Certain tasks involve skills that people may lack or behaviors with which they have had little or no experience. Step 4 of the TIS is aimed at assisting such clients to gain experience and mastery in performing skills or behaviors essential to task accomplishment. Bandura (1977) builds a strong case for mastery. Specifically, he emphasizes that the degree of an individual's positive expectation of his or her ability to perform will determine how much effort will be expended and the length of time an individual will persist when faced with obstacles or aversive circumstances. It follows, then, that a major goal in the TIS is to enhance clients' sense of self-efficacy so as to increase their potential for successful task completion. Successful experience, even in simulated situations, encourages a client's belief that he or she has the ability to be successful in performing a task.

Confirming research studies indicate that a sense of self-efficacy can be transferred to other situations, including those that a client previously avoided (Bandura, 1977). According to Bandura, people receive information about self-efficacy from four sources:

- **Performance accomplishments:** Major methods of increasing self-efficacy through performance accomplishment include assisting people to master essential behaviors through modeling, behavior rehearsal, and guided practice (discussed later in this chapter).
- **Vicarious experience:** Insight may be gained by observing others demonstrate certain behaviors or observing the performance of a behavior without experiencing adverse consequences. Efficacy expectations can be bolstered by a client's observing you, the social worker, or others who model the desired behaviors. Observing others, however, is clearly not as powerful as the sense of self-efficacy that results when the client successfully engages in a behavior on his or her own.
- **Verbal persuasion:** Talking to clients about their capacity to perform can be somewhat effective and also raise outcome expectations. But talking to clients about expectations or attempting to persuade them about their competence does not in fact enhance self-efficacy. To be effective, the appraisal of a client's capabilities has to be based on his or her perceptions and assumptions about competence and sense of self.
- **Emotional arousal:** Self-efficacy can be influenced by emotions, which in turn affect how people perform. Individuals who are extremely anxious or fearful about performing a new behavior are unlikely to have sufficient confidence to do so. In such instances, verbal persuasion directed toward reducing anxieties or fears is generally ineffective. Specifically, emotions such as fear are undependable source of self-efficacy in that they can overshadow the actual evidence of an individual's capacity. Perceived self-competence, however, can reduce emotional arousal rather than the converse.

Of the four sources, performance accomplishment is thought to be the most influential because it is based on the client's personal mastery experience.

Increasing Self-Efficacy Using Behavioral Rehearsal, Modeling, and Role-Play. **Behavioral rehearsal** used in an actual session is intended to reduce anxieties and help clients practice new behaviors or coping patterns. Indications for using this technique include situations in which a client feels threatened, feels inadequately prepared to face a situation, or is anxious or overwhelmed by the prospects of engaging in a given task.

Role-playing is the most common form of behavioral rehearsal to encourage mastery because the client is able to rehearse a desired behavior or outcome. In a simulated situation, a client can build on his or her existing skills, as well as identify potential barriers or obstacles. Modeling behavior through role-play, in effect, allows for the vicarious learning of a behavior before actually having to do so in a real-life, potentially difficult situation. The advantage of role-play is illustrated in the following video case.

VIDEO CASE EXAMPLE

In the video "Working with Yanping," Yanping, a student from China, has decided to change her major from business to history. Her parents have expressed their displeasure with her decision, indicating that they consider the status of a history degree as low and the financial rewards of the degree as limited. Yanping's decision is further complicated by her parents' expectation that she will return to China prepared to eventually take over the family business. Therefore, a history degree has little value to the family. At the point of contact with Kim, the social worker, Yanping's anxiety is due to her parents' disappointment and distress regarding her study decision. As the time for her return to China draws near, Yanping's anxiety has increased in anticipation of having further conversations with her parents.

In the first segment of the video, observe that Kim, the social worker, attempts to understand the cultural meaning and implications of Yanping's decision, her parents' reaction, as well her prior coping efforts. Kim also inquires whether Yanping has talked with or observed others in a similar situation (*vicarious experience*). Together, they brainstorm options regarding possible ways that Yanping can have a conversation with her parents. This case is difficult for Kim as a social worker because she is versed in the individual autonomy norms of Western society and the guiding principle of self-determination. Consequently, Kim feels that she is not sufficiently prepared to understand and be sensitive to the serious consequences for Yanping should she disregard cultural expectations.

In the second segment of the video, Kim refers Yanping to Jilan, a colleague from China, in the hopes that Jilan can help Yanping navigate the cultural expectations and perhaps resolve her dilemma. In the following session, Jilan and Yanping role-play a scenario between Yanping and her father in preparation for an eventual face-to-face conversation (*behavioral rehearsal*). As the two take turns, either as Yanping or her father, Yanping has the opportunity to rehearse responses to anticipated questions from her father and to observe Jilan's responses to her father's questions (*behavioral modeling*). Note that during the role-play, Yanping is more relaxed and more willing to approach her father. In fact, during the course of the role-play, a new idea occurs to her: she will also study business history, which she believes will appeal to her father as being advantageous to the family business.

Behavioral rehearsal need not be restricted to a session between you and the client. It can include overt behavior like making a phone call or covert behavior like self-talk, including expressing aloud defeating feelings or thoughts. These defeating feelings and thoughts can then be restructured into more encouraging language. It is often productive for clients to rehearse on their own by pretending to be involved in real-life encounters.

Modeling and behavioral rehearsal can also be integrated into family or group sessions in which members can model effective and realistic responses or coping for each other in contemplation of engaging in a particular task. As a rule of thumb, in implementing family or group role-plays, the intent is to tap into members' resources in a help-giving role.

If modeling or rehearsal proves ineffective, in the interim you can help clients to develop coping efforts rather than achieve mastery. Coping emphasizes the struggles that a person might expect to experience in completing the task behavior or activity. Emphasizing coping rather than mastery is intended to lessen anxiety and, hence, the threat of having to perform without making a mistake.

Guided Practice. Closely related to behavioral rehearsal, **guided practice** is another technique to aid task accomplishment. It differs from behavioral rehearsal in that it is in vivo rather than a simulated situation. It involves your observing the client as he or she engages in a task related to a target behavior. Afterward, you provide immediate feedback and also coach the client as he or she attempts to gain mastery toward task completion. For example, in a family session, as you observe problematic behaviors or interactions firsthand, you would provide feedback and coach members to master problem-solving or conflict resolution skills. Such an on-the-spot intervention enables you to clarify what is occurring as well as coach clients in engaging in more productive behavior.

Step 5: Summarize the Task Plan

Summarizing the task plan is the final step of the TIS. The summary, which takes place at the conclusion of a session, consists of a review of the actions or behaviors that a client has agreed to do in order to accomplish a task. In reviewing task agreements, you and the client confirm that you both have a clear understanding of what tasks are to be undertaken, in what sequence, and under what conditions, or whether further discussion or clarification is needed. Confirmation of the plan might proceed with your describing the tasks that you or the client will complete:

Social worker: I have agreed to contact the employment information specialist by our meeting next week.

Client: I will make three phone calls to potential employers who have posted job listing online.

Alternatively, the client would be asked to review and summarize his or her plans:

Social worker: What are your plans for searching for a job by our next session?

Individual clients may find it beneficial for you to provide them with a session-by-session written summary of goals and related tasks. You might also encourage clients to write their own summary as well. In either case, both you and the client should have copies. In keeping with the ethical obligation of documentation, this information is included in the case record or SOAP notes. Furthermore, documentation is essential to monitoring and evaluating during the duration and termination of the contact.

Failure to Complete Tasks

In actual practice, the process of developing of tasks may not be as smooth as you and the client would prefer, despite the fact that barriers or obstacles have been anticipated and resolved and all other possible impediments have been addressed. In the best scenarios, focus and continuity can be derailed for a variety of reasons, which are summarized in Figure 13-2. Reasons for low task performance are classified into two categories: *reasons related to the specific task* and *reasons related to the target problem*.

Reasons Related to the Specific Task

Occasionally, unforeseen circumstances or unanticipated obstacles may influence a client's ability to

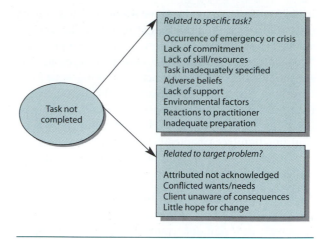

Related to specific task?

Occurrence of emergency or crisis
Lack of commitment
Lack of skill/resources
Task inadequately specified
Adverse beliefs
Lack of support
Environmental factors
Reactions to practitioner
Inadequate preparation

Task not completed

Related to target problem?

Attributed not acknowledged
Conflicted wants/needs
Client unaware of consequences
Little hope for change

FIG 13-2 Reasons for Low Task Performance

complete a task between sessions. When this happens, the obstacles that blocked the task completion should be identified and resolved. By mutual agreement, a previously identified task can be continued to the next session. The caveat, of course, is that both you and the client are in agreement that the task is still valid. If this is not the case, it is important to shift the focus to more relevant tasks.

Occurrence of an Emergency or Crisis. Certain overwhelming situations may dictate taking a brief detour from set tasks. Consequently, a client's forward momentum can be slowed, making it difficult for him or her to complete a task. Should this prove to be the case, it is appropriate for you to empathetically respond to the emotional state of the client. It may also be necessary to focus on the more urgent difficulty and to develop a goal and tasks related to the unexpected situation. If possible, an agreement should be reached about the timing for resuming work on tasks that were designated for completion prior to the crisis. If in the course of your work with the client you observe that his or her life appears to reverberate from crisis to crisis, the two of you can discuss whether it would be beneficial to remain focused on the initial tasks and see them through to completion.

Lack of Commitment. Lack of commitment has been documented as a statistically significant predictor of whether a client will engage in task performance (Reid, 1977, 1997, 2000). However, hesitation or a lack of commitment should not be confused with a lack of readiness. In the former, the willingness to change is absent. In the latter, the client is willing but is blocked from acting by other barriers. One frequent cause for a lack of commitment to undertake tasks is a covert unwillingness to own one's part of a problem. "I would raise my hand if the teacher called on me," is an example of paying lip service to carrying out a task. Unwilling clients may use excuses to blame others for their behavior and instead passively wait for others to initiate corrective actions. The technique of ethical confrontation (see Chapter 17) can be used to help clients recognize their responsibility for maintaining the status quo.

Lack of Skills/Resources. In planning tasks, it is important to ensure that clients have the necessary resources and skill for completing the agreed-upon action. For example, if the task is obtaining a job, it would be prudent to assess whether the client has adequate interviewing skills. It would be equally important to determine, for example, whether the client has the funds for transportation to the interview.

Tasks Inadequately Specified. The final step of the TIS (summarizing) provides an opportunity for you and the client to clarify and reaffirm tasks. Even so, there can be occasions when, in spite of the review, a client may end a session without fully understanding what he or she has agreed to do. As is the case in developing goals, tasks should be specific, be stated in positive terms, and indicate what action is expected within a specified time frame.

Adverse Beliefs. A client may agree to a task but may not fully disclose information about conflicting values or beliefs. For example, a parent who believes that children are to obey is likely to be hesitant to utilize reward systems, believing instead that parents should not bargain with their children. Being sensitive to and respecting different beliefs is important. By listening to the parent, the two of you could renegotiate a task that is consistent with the parent's belief as a solution.

Lack of Support. When a problem involves others or another system, the relevant individuals should be involved in supporting task accomplishment. For example, a teacher should be encouraged to call on the student we described earlier when he raises his hand or give him an indication that she will do so in time.

Environmental Factors. Support for completing tasks can also be related to family or environmental factors. For example, finding a subsidized apartment can depend on the availability of such housing. These are difficult situations in which a ready a solution may not be apparent, and you and the client will need to explore interim options. It can also be useful for you and the client to look for others in his or her network to provide support.

Reactions to the Practitioner. Negative reactions to the social worker, both verbal and nonverbal, can affect a client's ability to complete tasks. The range of possible reactions may be difficult to anticipate in a given situation. For example, clients may react to what they perceive as the social worker's arbitrary assignment of tasks. Another situation that can cause a client to react is highlighted in the following example: "She keeps telling me that she is going to make a referral to the child care resource center, but week after week, she has failed to so." Without the social worker's completing a task on behalf of the client, the client was unable to complete her work.

Inadequate Preparation. In developing tasks or planning the details involved, the skills, behavior, or time needed for the successful completion of specific tasks may have been overestimated or underestimated. Actually, it is better for clients not to attempt a task than for them to make an attempt and fail because they are unprepared. If the issue is related to timing, the time frame for completing a task can be extended. Should a lack of confidence be an issue, you can coach the individual by using behavioral rehearsal or modeling to increase his or her confidence.

Reasons Related to the Target Problem

Attributed Not Acknowledged Problems. Low task performance can occur when a client has not accepted that a problem exists and therefore is unlikely to engage in a change action. For example, "I don't have a drug problem. Sometimes I do a little meth [methamphetamine] with my buds [buddies], but that don't mean that I'm a drug head" (attributed problem). In these instances, you can begin by acknowledging this view of the situation, respecting the client's reactions, and exploring incentives that might encourage him or her to complete tasks. Persistent inaction certainly speaks louder than words, and the benefits of continuing to work with the client should be carefully weighed.

Conflicting Wants/Needs. Certainly, what can initially appear to be a lack of commitment may actually be that a client is faced with a competing or a more pressing concern. The initial task remains important; however, another issue, either new or existing, demands the client's attention. The situation need not be a crisis. It may simply mean that even though a client had prioritized a goal and developed a related task, there are other issues competing for his or her attention. Flexibility is called for in such instances until the competing concern is resolved.

Client Unaware of Consequences. A failure to perform a task may stem from a lack of understanding about the consequences of failure. For example, the consequences of failing to complete a chemical dependency treatment program and providing clean urinalysis samples should be explained.

Little Hope for Change. In spite of the fact that a client has agreed to undertake a certain task, he or she may feel that completing the task may have little or no impact on a problem or situation. This is an opportunity for you to help the client by calling attention to his or her past successes. For example, addressing these issues with Irwin Corning, you might say to him, "I understand that you are feeling some anxiety about getting a job, and I can't guarantee that you will. But remember how you felt about talking to the housing authority about rental assistance. You were able to do so, and you obtained a housing voucher." Crediting clients with past successes is particularly useful to boost confidence when a client's perception of his or her ability to effect change is uncertain.

Even when preparation has been adequate and potential obstacles and barriers have been reviewed, the successful outcomes of task efforts are not guaranteed. The preceding discussion highlighted valid reasons for low task performance. The intended message of the discussion was simple: The majority of clients with whom you work want relief from their difficulties and are motivated to take action. Nonetheless, their ability to do so can be hampered by their beliefs and other factors. To avoid or minimize the potential of a client's becoming discouraged, you should not interpret low task performance as a failure but rather as an indication of the need for additional exploration or task planning.

Monitoring Progress

EP 9

In the task-centered model, tasks are the instrumental action steps taken by the client and in some instances the social worker. Tasks are intended to alter or remediate the target concern and achieve a desired outcome. The continuous review of tasks maintains continuity and focus and monitors progress. The following procedures for the systematic review of progress are specific to the task-centered approach:

1. Once tasks have been identified and agreed upon, devote time in each session to a review of progress. In this process, both client and social worker can document which tasks have been completed and the extent to which the target problem has changed.
2. During the review process, if tasks have not been completed or have not had the intended effect on the target problem, explore barriers and obstacles and the reasons for low task performance. When necessary, renegotiate tasks or develop new tasks.

In reviewing task accomplishments, it is critical to discuss with the client details about the conditions, actions, or behaviors that facilitated completion of the task. Even when tasks have been only partially completed, it is important to connect the progress made to the client's efforts. In doing so, you are highlighting and reinforcing the client's strengths and sense of competence.

In general, the ongoing in-session review of progress provides immediate feedback of gains as well as alerting you and the client to whether adjustments need to be made. Afterward, you and the client move forward by mutually planning other tasks that will facilitate progress, albeit incremental in some instances, toward the final goal. Ultimately, the completion of tasks related to the target concern is an indicator of progress toward goal attainment and the eventual move toward termination.

Strengths and Limitations of the Task-Centered Model

The task-centered model is the first empirically based social work model of a planned, short-term, problem-solving approach based on the principles and values of the social work profession (Kelly, 2008; Reid & Epstein, 1972). The model honors self-determination, strengths, and empowerment by allowing clients to define the problem, develop goals and tasks, and participate in monitoring progress. To increase clients' self-efficacy and opportunity for mastery, obstacles to task completion and goal attainment are identified and resolved. The review of obstacles and barriers is a distinct strength of the approach. Similarly, when tasks are not completed, the reasons for low task performance are reviewed and new tasks, if indicated, are developed.

As noted earlier, the efficacy of the model has been supported by empirical evidence in multiple settings and for a range of voluntary and involuntary client problems, including minors (Ramos & Tolson, 2008; Reid, 1992; Tolson, Reid, & Garvin, 1994). The model's effectiveness has also been demonstrated in worldwide practice settings (Ramos & Garvin, 2003; Ramos & Tolson, 2008; Reid, 1996, 1997, 2000). The emphasis on taking action on problems acknowledged by clients is believed to be appealing to racial and ethnic minorities (Boyd-Franklin, 1989; Devore & Schlesinger, 1999; Lum, 2004; Sue, 2006). Key aspects of the model, namely the use of tasks, have become foundational elements of a number of other intervention approaches (Hoyt, 2000; Ramos & Tolson, 2008).

Opinions are mixed about the efficacy of the model with certain populations and in certain situations. Critiques of the central tenets of the model—in particular, time limits and the systematic structure—have led some observers to conclude that a sustained therapeutic relationship with clients is unlikely to evolve (Ramos & Tolson, 2008). Given the utilization and effectiveness of the model with a range of client problems and settings, there is limited evidence to support this claim.

THE CRISIS INTERVENTION MODEL

EP 8

The crisis intervention model discussed in this text is the **equilibrium model**, which is based on basic crisis theory. Knowledge of how to intervene with clients who are experiencing a crisis is considered essential for skilled practice (Knox & Roberts, 2008; Walsh, 2010). Depending on the nature of the crisis and the systems involved, it may be necessary for you to intervene at the micro, mezzo, and macro levels (Gelman & Mirabito, 2005). While multiple disciplines including social work have played an important role in developing crisis theory, social workers have been responsible for advancing practice methods and skills and for formulating strategies for responding to crises (Bell, 1995; Fast, 2003; Komar, 1994; Lukton, 1982; Parad & Parad, 1990).

Tenets of the Crisis Intervention Equilibrium Model

The equilibrium model is a basic approach to crisis intervention. The model is action oriented, with the central intent being to reduce the intensity of a client's emotional, mental, physical, and behavioral reactions to a crisis and to restore client functioning to the precrisis state. Promptness of response, a key aspect of the model, is considered critical to prevent deterioration in functioning. It is during the acute period that people are most likely to be receptive to an intervention. The procedures of the model involve assessing the nature of the crisis, identifying priority concerns, and developing limited goals.

Assessment in the crisis situation, as outlined by James (2008), involves determining the following:

- The severity of the crisis
- The client's current emotional status and level of mobility/immobility
- Alternatives, coping mechanisms, support systems, and other available resources
- The client's level of lethality (specifically whether the client is a danger to self or others)

James (2008; James & Gilliland, 2013) and Roberts (2005) cite the **triage assessment system** developed by Meyer, Williams, Ottens, and Schmidt (1991) as a "fast" and efficient way to assess and "obtain a real time estimate of what is occurring with a client" in a crisis situation (pp. 43–48). This assessment system provides a framework for social workers to assess the client's affective, behavioral, and emotional functioning; assess the severity of the situation; and plan the appropriate intervention strategy. Where possible, you use the three domains to establish a baseline that can subsequently be compared to the triage assessment system results to determine the functioning level prior to and after the crisis (James, 2008).

Definition of Crisis

A **crisis**, as defined by James (2008, p. 3), is "a perception of an event or situation as an intolerable difficulty that exceeds the resources or coping mechanism of the person." Prolonged crisis-related stressors have the potential to severely affect cognitive, behavioral, and physical functioning.

In your work with clients, you have no doubt assisted them to deal with crisis situations. These situations may have ranged from job loss to death, a medical diagnosis, eviction, divorce, domestic violence, child abuse or neglect, crime, relocation, or even a natural disaster. Similarly, revealing one's sexual orientation to an unsupportive family (often a high-anxiety event) can result in an unmanageable crisis, accompanied by additional stressors for which relief is uncertain.

Uncertainty can also become a stressor for refugees, immigrants, and migrants, who may simultaneously experience demands related to their transition and the related sense of loss as a result of leaving their homeland, familiar networks, and culture. (However, note that despite the stress of having to adjust to the norms, values, and language of another country, migrants tend to perceive their relocation as an opportunity, unless the transition was not of their choosing.)

It is important to note that segments of the population experience cumulative events or circumstances that result in a perpetual state of crisis (Ell, 1995). Consider, for example, the hypervigilance of unauthorized immigrants related to fear of deportation and family disruption, or the very real threats experienced by gay and lesbian individuals as a result of hate crimes, brutal beatings, and even murder. Intense anxiety related to threats and potential harm is pervasive in many among minorities who live in impoverished urban communities. Residents in these communities face ongoing violence, including institutionalized violence such as negative encounters with the police, poverty-related stressors, and inadequate services or resources, resulting in perpetual disequilibrium. Studies have shown that the continuous exposure to violence can also have an enduring effect on minors, resulting in depression, delinquency, or acting-out behavior (Lindsey, Korr, Broitman, Bone, Green, & Leaf, 2006; Maschi, 2006; Maschi, Perez, & Tyson, 2010; Voisin, 2007; Zeira, Astor, & Benbenishty, 2003). Emotional and psychosocial crises resulting from the experience of combat by military personnel, specifically posttraumatic stress disorder (PTSD), can pose a lifetime risk for these individuals (Halpern & Tramontin, 2007; James, 2008). Stress-related symptoms may also be observed in professionals who work in highly stressful, emotionally charged situations (Bell, 2003; Curry, 2007; Knight, 2006). In addition, crises can occur in the lives of some people on a regular basis.

VIDEO CASE EXAMPLE

In the video "Working with the Cornings," Irwin Corning's job loss set in motion a series of stressful events that were significant threats to the family's stability. While the family was experiencing a situational crisis, the continuation of stressful events could eventually reach a level of emotional and behavioral distress that exceeded the family's coping capacity.

Crisis Reactions and Stages

A **crisis reaction** is described as any event or situation that upsets the client's normal psychic balance to the extent that his or her sense of equilibrium is severely diminished (James, 2008; Roberts, 2005). Crisis intervention theory posits that people's crisis reactions typically go through several stages, although theorists differ as to whether three or four stages are involved. The following description is a synthesis of models and stages identified by various authors (Caplan, 1964; James & Gilliland, 2001, 2013; Okun, 2002; Roberts, 2005):

- **Stage 1:** The initial tension is accompanied by shock and perhaps even denial of the crisis-provoking event.
- **Stage 2:** To reduce the tension, the client attempts to utilize his or her usual emergency problem-solving skills. If these skills fail to result in a lessening of tension, the stress level will become heightened.
- **Stage 3:** The client experiences severe tension, feels confused, overwhelmed, helpless, angry, or perhaps acutely depressed. The length of this phase varies according to the nature of the hazardous event, the strengths and coping capacities of the client, and the degree of responsiveness from social support systems.

Patterns of behavior associated with these stages may be characterized as disorganization, recovery, and reorganization (Lum, 2004; Parad & Parad, 1990, 2006; Roberts, 1990, 2005).

Crisis situations inevitably have a subjective element because people's perceptions and coping capacities vary widely. Keep in mind, therefore, that a crisis that is severely stressful and overwhelming for some people may be manageable for others. Variations in reaction can depend in part on the point at which the social worker has contact with the client.

In reacting to a crisis, the potential exists for clients to cope in ways that are either adaptive or maladaptive. You should be aware, however, that prolonged stress may have exceeded clients' coping capacity and usual problem solving to such an extent that they are unable to effectively handle the stressors. Achieving equilibrium for some clients may depend on the extent to which their strengths, resilience, and social supports are mobilized. In some instances, the crisis may even evoke a positive change opportunity. Specifically, a client's reaction may be to seek help and succeed, thereby using the opportunity for his or her benefit (James, 2008). For others, the level of tension can become elevated, in which case the client's coping patterns reach a level of danger. Danger is evident when restoring equilibrium is not immediately possible because the client is unable to function.

Duration of Contact and Focus

Typically, crisis work is time limited, spanning 4 to 8 weeks, although some clients or situations may require prolonged contact. Your contact with a client during the acute crisis period may be daily for a period of time, and may take place in an office, a shelter, a hospital, or in the home. Interventions range from a single-session telephone intervention to comprehensive services with an individual, group, family, or an entire community (Fast, 2003; Gibar, 1992; James & Gilliland, 2001; West, Mercer, & Altheimer, 1993). The active, intense, time-limited, focused, and action-oriented nature of the crisis intervention approach is believed to help people return to a level of precrisis functioning (James & Gilliland, 2013; Roberts, 2005; Walsh, 2010). Ultimately, the level of distress, whether the crisis is acute or chronic, and client characteristics (perception of the crisis, ego strengths, and situation-specific resources such as social supports) will dictate the time required. Follow-up as an additional contact—included as a step in the Seven-Step Crisis Intervention Model (Roberts, 2005; Roberts & Ottens, 2006) and the Hybrid Model (James & Gilliland, 2013)—may be incorporated in the basic equilibrium model discussed in this chapter.

The guiding principles of time-limited crisis intervention are as follows:

- The focus of crisis intervention is on the here and now. Hence, no attempt is made to deal with either precrisis personality dysfunction or intrapsychic conflict, although attention to these symptoms may be required.
- Goals are limited to alleviating distress and assisting clients to regain equilibrium.
- Tasks are identified, and task performance is intended to help clients achieve a new state of equilibrium.

In crisis situations, the level of incapacity presented by the client may require you to have a more active and directive role than you might have in other interventions. Even though you may direct and define tasks, you should encourage clients to participate to the extent that they are capable of doing so. Although clients' ability to actively participate and perform tasks may be limited during periods of severe emotional distress, their capacity to do so generally increases as the distress level diminishes.

Intervening with Minors

Minors are more vulnerable and at greater risk when a crisis or traumatic event occurs (Halpern & Tramontin, 2007; James, 2008). Understanding the nature of the crisis and the minor's response to it is the first intervention step (Terr, 1991). Two distinct crisis categories can be used to distinguish the minor's reaction to a crisis (James, 2008, p. 163): **Type I** involves a single, distinct crisis experience in which symptoms and signs are manifested; for example, the minor can display fully detailed etched-in memories, misperceptions, cognitive reappraisals, and reasons for the crisis event (James, 2008). **Type II**, in contrast, is the result of long-standing, repeated trauma whose cumulative effects result in the minor's psyche developing defensive coping strategies, anxiety, depression, or acting-out behavior (James, 2008; Lindsey et al., 2006; Maschi, 2006; Voisin, 2007).

For minors, a crisis event has the potential to disrupt biological, social, and cognitive development, and age can make a significant difference in how minors respond. The Type I category seems to fit best with the basic equilibrium crisis intervention approach, in which the focus is on restoring the precrisis state of their caregivers in order to help minors. The stages of crisis and the reaction may differ with minors. They may, for example, need additional help in understanding their reaction to the crisis and in developing problem-solving skills. The **triage system** assessment can be especially important in determining the minor's cognitions and behaviors as a result of the crisis. Cognitively, a crisis event can increase minors' sense of vulnerability and their perceived lack of power. Behavioral interventions to a crisis event may involve the minor's coping by role-playing, for example, an all-powerful action figure of their choosing (Knox & Roberts, 2008).

Korol, Green, and Grace (1999) developed the **Interactive Trauma/Grief-Focused Model (IT-GFT)**, which emphasizes a developmental ecological framework as another approach to crisis work with minors. The premise of this framework is that the developmental stage and the environment within which the minor operates are interrelated. Four attributes based on research address the effects of a crisis experienced by a minor and guide the intervention (Halpern & Tramontin, 2007; Nader & Mello, 2008):

- **Characteristics of the stressors:** These include the perception of threat related to the event, physical proximity to the event, duration, and intensity.
- **Characteristics of the minor:** Developmental stage, gender, and vulnerability play a significant role in how a minor experiences a threat, as do psychological or behavioral problems that existed prior to the threat.
- **The minor's efforts to cope:** Generally, a minor with good communications skills, a sense of self, internal locus of control, and average intelligence are indicators of a positive outcome.
- **Characteristics of the postdisaster environment:** The minor's reaction is strengthened by social supports from significant others and resources, which can reduce stress and act as protective factors.

Eclectic in nature, the model utilizes theories relevant to the situation, including psychodynamic and cognitive behavioral approaches, as well as a minor's narrative, emotions, cognitions, and memories, to aid in recovery and precrisis functioning.

The basic crisis intervention equilibrium model, consistent with generalist practice, is appropriate for minors who have experienced a Type I crisis event. Adaptations from the IT/G-FT, in particular the developmental ecological framework emphasis and the attribute proposed by Korol and colleagues (1999), can be useful in intervening with minors.

Benefits of a Crisis

Much of the literature has tended to focus on the adverse reactions or effects that a crisis has on people. Not surprisingly, then, intervention strategies, while incorporating strengths, coping, and social support, have sought to restore functioning to the precrisis level. However, some theorists and researchers suggest that negative events may actually promote growth in the aftermath of a crisis (Caplan, 1964; Dziegielewski & Powers, 2005; Halpern & Tramontin, 2007; James, 2008; Joseph, Williams, & Yule, 1993; McMillen & Fisher, 1998; McMillen, Smith, & Fisher, 1997; McMillen, Zuravin, & Rideout, 1995). Note, however, that these findings are specific to adult populations.

Building on prior research and the notion of benefits advanced by Caplan (1964), McMillen and Fisher

(1998) explored the perceived harm and benefit to individuals who have experienced a crisis event. People involved in the study reported experiencing benefits such as increased self-efficacy, spirituality, faith in people, and community closeness. The McMillen and Fisher study results are significant for two reasons:

- The deficit approach to psychosocial consequences appears to influence how human services professionals view clients and how clients view the experience. Specifically, professionals may tend to focus on the trauma alone, whereas clients may view the situation or event through multiple lenses.
- By understanding the benefits that accrue from crises, professionals can construct interventions that recognize and strengthen the benefits and increase successful outcomes.

These findings emphasize the subjective nature of the crisis experience as a key element to be included in crisis intervention work. Understanding clients' reactions to a crisis, their perception of harm or vulnerability, and their affective, emotional, and behavioral functioning will help you plan and intervene appropriately. Otherwise, your intervention strategy may have little or no value to the client's situation.

Theoretical Framework of Crisis Intervention

Caplan (1964), Parad (1965), and Golan (1981) were early and significant contributors to basic crisis intervention theory, delineating the nature of crises, stages, and intervention strategies for crisis resolution within a brief time period. Parad and

EP 4

Caplan (1960) and Lukton (1982) further developed a practice theory and practice skills for social workers. Early crisis intervention theory spanned the life course to include grief and loss reactions, role transitions, traumatic events, and maturational or biopsychosocial crisis at various developmental stages (Lindemann, 1944, 1956; Rapoport, 1967). Early theories of crisis intervention strategies tended to reflect the psychoanalytic paradigm. For example, in Erikson's (1963) psychosocial stages of human development, a crisis was thought to develop if the individual failed to master the requisite developmental tasks in each stage.

Over time, additional theories have emerged based on a belief that basic crisis theory as a single framework was incapable of fully explaining the human response to trauma (James, 2008; Knox & Roberts, 2008). A prominent issue is that the theory paid little or no attention to environmental and situational crises and subsequent reactions. Consequently, other crisis theories have emerged—in particular, ego psychology, cognitive behavioral, chaos, ecological systems, and life cycle theories—which distinguish the types of crises and define an underlying contextual theoretical framework in which a crisis can occur (James, 2008; Lantz & Walsh, 2007; Okun, 2002; Potocky-Tripodi, 2002; Walsh, 2010).

Evidence Base and Use of Crisis Intervention

EP 4

Crisis intervention as a systemic strategy is recognized and widely used throughout the world in response to a range of client, professional, and community crisis situations and in a variety of settings, including schools, hospitals, and residential treatment facilities (James & Gilliland, 2013; Roberts, 2005; Roberts & Ottens, 2005).

The prevalence of crises has resulted in teams of professionals being trained to respond to crisis situations and events. In addition, beginning with the Memphis Police Department in 1988, municipal and state police departments have established **Crisis Intervention Teams (CITs).** Published reviews of CITs emphasize the effectiveness of the approach in improving interactions between police and persons who are mentally ill, reducing the use of force (Compton, Bahora, Watson, & Oliva, 2008; Compton et al., 2011) and in response to domestic violence (Corcoran, Stephenson, Perryman, & Allen, 2001)

Research has demonstrated the effectiveness of the crisis intervention approach in reducing disruptive classroom behavior (Gibson & Holden, 2008; Grskovic & Goetze, 2005) and as an alternative to seclusion, punishment, and restraints in residential treatment facilities (Colton, 2008; Day, 2002; Day, Bullard, & Nunno, 2008). Positive results were confirmed in studies in which the approach was used in intensive in-home family-based services, the results of which were reductions in child abuse and neglect and out-of-home placements (Corcoran, 2000; Roberts & Everly, 2006), as well as in stabilizing persons with mental illness and medication adherence (Everly, Lating, & Mitchell, 2005; Haynes et al., 2008; Joy, Adams, & Rice, 2006). Informal evidence and anecdotal case information also indicate client satisfaction with the efficacy of the

approach; however, the longevity of resulting change has not been established (Dziegielewski & Powers, 2005; Roberts & Everly, 2006; Walsh, 2010).

Application of Crisis Intervention with Diverse Groups

An advantage of crisis intervention is that the strategy is believed to be applicable to different populations (Knox & Roberts, 2008). Lum (2004), in addressing the multicultural sensitivity of the approach, asserts that crisis intervention as a generalist practice approach has "universal application to people of color" (p. 272) because people of color "often experience personal and environmental crisis" and in many instances have "exhausted community and family resources" prior to seeking professional help (p. 273). In some communities of color, patterns of help-seeking behavior and historically based anxieties can result in delayed contact, and as a result a crisis situation can reach a chronic state prior to contact. Also, influenced by culture, different communities may respond and cope differently to a traumatic event (Halpern & Tramontin, 2007).

However, note that crisis intervention embodies ideals specific to Western norms and that are unfamiliar to the majority of the world (James, 2008). Crisis intervention, like other practice models, calls for multicultural helping that includes the social worker's sensitivity to differences and worldviews, self-knowledge, and awareness of his or her bias. A crisis can be culturally universal or culture specific. In this regard, it is important to understand the meaning of the crisis to the client and his or her preference for resolution (James, 2008; Roberts, 2005; Sommers-Flanagan, 2007; Stone & Conley, 2004; Sue, 2006). Chazin, Kaplan, and Terio (2000) further note that crisis-related deficits, rather than strengths and resources, can be particularly counterproductive with diverse groups. Also, in crisis situations with diverse clients, attention should be given to such pertinent issues as inequality, faith, and social justice (Freud, 1999; Silove, 2000; Stone & Conley, 2004; Walsh, 2010).

Although research and literature related to the crisis intervention modality with regard to culture, gender, and racial groups is limited, practice literature and research have advanced the knowledge base. Examples include Congress (2000) and Potocky-Tripodi (2002), with a focus on culturally diverse and immigrant families, and Cornelius et al. (2003) and Ligon (1997) with a focus on African Americans. Halpern and Tramontin (2007) amplify how culturally based perceptions influence expectations in certain Asian communities—in particular, crisis reactions—that can differ from those in Western societies. In working with immigrants and refugees, Potocky-Tripodi (2002) suggests that, while crisis intervention strategies are appropriate, ideally the approach should be implemented as a preventive measure prior to the resettlement stage. Congress (2000, 2002) identifies common precipitants of crisis among immigrants and refugees—namely, intergenerational conflicts, changes in roles, unemployment, and interactions with formal institutions—for which crisis strategies are appropriate.

Ligon (1997) departs somewhat from the basic equilibrium crisis model and instead relies on cultural and ecological systems perspectives integrated with empowerment. Using this framework, Ligon demonstrated the merit of these perspectives with populations of color and clients with serious health or mental health concerns. Poindexter (1997) makes the point that for HIV-infected clients, the diagnosis may involve a series of crises beginning with their learning of the disease as a precipitating event. As the condition progresses, multiple crises—social, situational, and developmental—can occur simultaneously. Poindexter's work, along with that of Ell (1995), Ligon (1997), and

Potocky-Tripodi (2002), is significant in that it helps us to move beyond certain assumptions about the episodic nature of crises and to understand the evolving stages of certain crisis situations.

Procedures of Crisis Intervention

The procedures of the six-step basic crisis intervention model, initially developed by Gilliland (1982), provide a framework for systematically intervening in a crisis situation. These steps, illustrated in Figure 13-3, guide the application of the approach and are consistent with the eclectic problem-solving approach. Figure 13-3 also specifies the fundamental skills needed and the actions required of you in a crisis situation. In the following sections, we apply the steps of the approach to a case example involving Lia, a pregnant teen.

EP 8

Step 1: Define the Problem

The first step in the six-step model of crisis intervention is to define the problem.

As a social worker in a crisis situation, you must determine the unique meaning of the crisis and the

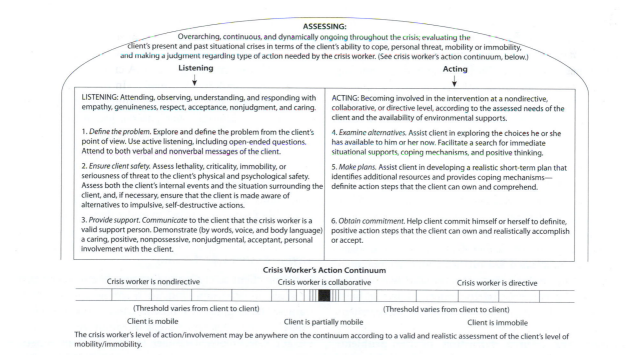

ASSESSING:
Overarching, continuous, and dynamically ongoing throughout the crisis; evaluating the client's present and past situational crises in terms of the client's ability to cope, personal threat, mobility or immobility, and making a judgment regarding type of action needed by the crisis worker. (See crisis worker's action continuum, below.)

Listening → **Acting** →

LISTENING: Attending, observing, understanding, and responding with empathy, genuineness, respect, acceptance, nonjudgment, and caring.

1. *Define the problem.* Explore and define the problem from the client's point of view. Use active listening, including open-ended questions. Attend to both verbal and nonverbal messages of the client.

2. *Ensure client safety.* Assess lethality, criticality, immobility, or seriousness of threat to the client's physical and psychological safety. Assess both the client's internal events and the situation surrounding the client, and, if necessary, ensure that the client is made aware of alternatives to impulsive, self-destructive actions.

3. *Provide support.* Communicate to the client that the crisis worker is a valid support person. Demonstrate (by words, voice, and body language) a caring, positive, nonpossessive, nonjudgmental, acceptant, personal involvement with the client.

ACTING: Becoming involved in the intervention at a nondirective, collaborative, or directive level, according to the assessed needs of the client and the availability of environmental supports.

4. *Examine alternatives.* Assist client in exploring the choices he or she has available to him or her now. Facilitate a search for immediate situational supports, coping mechanisms, and positive thinking.

5. *Make plans.* Assist client in developing a realistic short-term plan that identifies additional resources and provides coping mechanisms—definite action steps that the client can own and comprehend.

6. *Obtain commitment.* Help client commit himself or herself to definite, positive action steps that the client can own and realistically accomplish or accept.

Crisis Worker's Action Continuum

Crisis worker is nondirective	Crisis worker is collaborative	Crisis worker is directive
(Threshold varies from client to client)		(Threshold varies from client to client)
Client is mobile	Client is partially mobile	Client is immobile

The crisis worker's level of action/involvement may be anywhere on the continuum according to a valid and realistic assessment of the client's level of mobility/immobility.

FIG 13-3 The Six-Step Model of Crisis Intervention

Source: From James, "Crisis Intervention Strategies," 6e. © 2008 Wadsworth, a part of Cengage Learning, Inc. Reproduced by permission, www.cengage.com.

CASE EXAMPLE

For Lia, age 17, the problem was being unmarried and pregnant. During the school year, she participated in a school-based teen social group for female students. On the day of the referral, Lia became so emotionally distraught that the group leader asked the group to take a break so that she and Lia could talk. During the conversation, Lia told the leader that she was pregnant and that she was in trouble with her family as a result. The group leader referred her to a social worker at the community-based health and mental health center, located within walking distance of the school. Lia calmed down after the group leader explained that the social worker would be able to see Lia immediately. As Lia explained her situation to the social worker, she again became emotional and distressed.

severity of the situation to the client. Having clients talk about the meaning and significance of the crisis provides you with essential information about how clients define their problem and can be a cathartic process for clients as well. In the case of Lia, culturally held beliefs and expectations were critical reference points in the social worker's understanding of Lia's reaction. The social worker's initial tasks in this session were twofold:

1. **Assess and alleviate Lia's emotional distress:** During the interview, Lia cried, had trouble breathing, and expressed concern about whether the social worker could understand her situation. The social worker used a breathing technique to help her calm down. By listening and responding empathically, the social worker encouraged Lia to talk about her feelings to reduce her emotional distress. Eventually, the social worker was able to gain an understanding of the magnitude of Lia's distress in relationship to her problem within her culture. During the conversation, Lia stated that she had thought about suicide. Furthermore, she had shared her thoughts in a conversation with her 12-year-old brother. The social worker therefore made an immediate referral to the center's mental health services for further evaluation. As the social worker questioned Lia further about her potential for self-harm, Lia's responses revealed two hopeful signs: her concern for the safety of her unborn child and her desire to continue her involvement with the teen group.

2. **Elicit the client's definition of the problem:** According to Lia, the problem began when her family became aware of her pregnancy, which was further complicated by the fact that she had ignored the cultural norms of her community and was told by her family that in being pregnant and unmarried, she had brought shame to the family. The crisis escalated when, upon learning that Lia was pregnant, her father dismissed her from the family, refused to talk to her, and forbade other family members from doing so. The fact that Lia faced social ostracism and loss of face and would be disconnected from her family and members of the clan increased her distress.

Clearly, being pregnant and unmarried was worrisome to Lia, but she believed that she could manage her situation and had some ideas about how to do so. Her family's definition of the problem, however, was grounded in the context of cultural norms and expectations. Unwed pregnancy requires considerable adaptation in most cultures but may pose an extreme threat for a client who is a first-generation child of an immigrant family. Although her parents had made significant adjustments to their new culture, Lia's pregnancy was a situation for which the parents did not have a point of reference. Therefore, in this context, being unwed and pregnant, as defined by Lia's family and community and their reactions, became a multilayered crisis, all of which contributed to the significance of the crisis and her level of distress.

Step 2: Ensure Client Safety

Ensuring client safety is the first and foremost concern in crisis intervention and an ongoing consideration (James, 2008; James & Gilliland, 2001; Roberts, 2005). Safety involves deliberate steps to minimize the physical and psychological danger to the client or others. The social worker requested, and Lia agreed to complete, a depression scale. The results confirmed the necessity of making the referral to the center's mental health services for further evaluation.

Because Lia had indicated that she had thoughts of self-harm, the social worker developed a safety plan contract with her. Together Lia and the social worker identified resources, including a crisis hotline that Lia would call when her feelings reached a level at which she considered harming herself. As an additional precaution, the social worker reminded Lia of her desire to keep her unborn child safe.

The results of the assessment of Lia's affective, cognitive, and behavioral domains were in the moderate range, which also confirmed the need for Lia to be seen by a mental health professional. In focusing on Lia's strengths, the social worker shared her observation of Lia's coping and resilient behaviors—namely, that she often volunteered for the closing shift at work and afterward walked to her sister's home to spend the night because she was unable to go home. Also, Lia's concern for her unborn child and desire to continue with the group were indications of her future-oriented thinking. An additional safety concern related to Lia's working late and walking alone to her sister's home, so she and the social worker explored other options.

In assessing the three domains, the social worker was able to evaluate the extent of Lia's adaptive and coping capacities. She also learned about family resources that could be tapped to alleviate some of her distress, as well as options to ensure her safety.

Step 3: Provide Support

In this step, the social worker's objective was to identify and mobilize Lia's social support systems network, which is essential for intervening in a crisis situation. Social supports may include friends, relatives, and in some cases institutional programs that care about the client and can provide comfort and compassion (James & Gilliland, 2001).

As Lia and the social worker explored potential support resources, several were identified: her sister, an aunt, and certain clan members who were sympathetic to her situation. These individuals, and the social worker, were also included in the safety plan. A school-based group for pregnant and parenting teens was identified as a new support resource. In a supportive role, the social worker walked with her to the appointment with the professional who would complete the mental status evaluation and also introduced Lia to the nurse practitioner in the healthy baby program at the center.

Step 4: Examine Alternatives

In this step, both the social worker and Lia explored courses of action appropriate to her situation.

Of course, some choices that they considered were better and more realistic than others, so together Lia and the social worker selected and prioritized available options. Ideally, alternatives are considered to the extent to which they are:

- Situational supports, involving people who care about what happens to the client
- Coping mechanisms that represent actions, behaviors, or environmental resources that the client may use to get past the crisis situation
- Positive and constructive thinking patterns that effectively alter how a client views the problem, thereby lessening his or her level of stress and anxiety

Lia had actually thought of alternatives, yet initially she was too immobilized emotionally to act on them. For example, in response to the threat from her father to change the locks on the doors, forcing her out of the home, she had considered moving in with her sister or an aunt (*situational supports*) until her child was born. Afterward, she would be 18 years of age and able to live independently. Instead of acting on this option, however, she planned to wait until her parents were asleep or at work and appeal to her siblings (*coping mechanism*) to let her in the house. In the past, her siblings had opened the door for her when she had stayed out late with her boyfriend. Relying on this choice was a short-term solution at best and posed a greater risk for both Lia and her siblings.

A more viable option suggested by the social worker involved Lia's moving into a housing complex for pregnant teens, located near the high school and her job (*highlighting constructive thinking and action*). Program services offered in the housing complex included transportation to prenatal visits, group counseling, independent living skills classes, and assistance in finding permanent housing. Although she was initially reluctant, Lia agreed to consider this option. Social workers who understand the client's point of view may be better able to plan alternatives and encourage clients to consider other options. For example, Lia's qualms about the pregnant teen housing program reflected her desire to remain with, or at least near, her family and community.

Of course, there were additional alternatives to consider in stabilizing this crisis situation. You should be aware, however, that multiple options can be overwhelming for clients. Furthermore, the alternatives that you and the client consider should be realistic for the situation (James, 2008). In Lia's case, two options were discussed: moving in with her aunt on a short-term basis and moving to a housing facility for pregnant teens. Lia chose the housing program because of the supportive services that were available. She and the social worker, however, also discussed ways in which she could have some contact with her family.

Step 5: Make Plans

Planning and contracting flow from the previous steps and involve the same planning and action steps that were discussed in Chapter 12. In this step, Lia and the social worker agreed on specific action steps or tasks. General and specific tasks will vary, of course, according to the nature of the crisis situation and the unique characteristics of each individual and/or family.

In developing and negotiating tasks, the social worker solicited Lia's views on what she believed would help her to function at a level of precrisis equilibrium. In planning, Lia's safety was identified as a priority, and related tasks were developed. Other tasks were related to her eventual move to the pregnant teen housing facility.

Lia's estrangement from her parents continued to be a central source of her distress. The social worker asked Lia to consider writing a letter of apology to her parents and also whether such a gesture was culturally appropriate. Lia was unsure, and she proposed an interim task of talking to her aunt about the letter.

There are times during this step when your interaction with a client requires you to be directive. For example, the idea of writing a letter to her family was the social worker's idea. James and Gilliland (2001), however, caution against "benevolently imposing" a plan on clients. Instead, you should strive to find a balance between being directive and respecting the client's autonomy by encouraging and reinforcing feasible independent actions. As it turned out, Lia thought the idea was a good one, yet she was unsure about the impact that the letter might have, hence the decision to talk with her aunt before writing the letter.

Step 6: Obtain Commitment

In the sixth and final step, Lia and the social worker committed to collaboratively engage in specific, intentional, and positive tasks designed to restore her to a level of precrisis functioning.

After a week, Lia informed the social worker that she was ready to move forward and develop tasks related to the plan to move into the housing facility for pregnant teens. In the meantime, she proposed living with her sister or her aunt, perhaps dividing her time between the two. The following is a summary of the agreed-upon tasks:

Lia's Tasks

- Call the 24-hour crisis line or other supports when she is feeling overwhelmed.
- Talk to her sister or aunt about moving in with one of them.
- Visit the pregnant teen housing facility.
- Explore ways to have contact with family members.
- Continue to attend the school-based teen group.

Social Worker's Tasks

- Provide Lia with information on the pregnant teen facility program prior to her visit.
- Accompany Lia on her visit to the housing program.
- Obtain information about financial support for Lia and her unborn child.

When Lia began her relationship with the social worker, she was in a highly emotional state. In assessing Lia's cognitive, behavioral, and emotional functioning, the social worker was able to evaluate the extent of Lia's adaptive and coping capacities. She also learned about family resources that could be tapped to alleviate some of her distress, as well as options to ensure her safety. Subsequent tasks were developed that were intended to move Lia beyond the crisis of her pregnancy. You will note that not all of her concerns were resolved. Nonetheless, the tasks developed were instrumental in assisting her to regain a level of equilibrium.

Anticipatory Guidance

In addition to completing the six steps of the model, you may also find anticipatory guidance to be a complementary technique. This technique involves assisting clients to anticipate future crisis situations and to plan coping strategies that will prepare them to face future stressors. Similar to identifying obstacles and barriers in the task-centered model, anticipatory guidance involves a discussion of scenarios of potential or future stressors. Used in Lia's case, the social worker and Lia discussed ways in which she could cope in the event that, despite her best efforts, she remained estranged from her family. They might also explore stressors related to the eventual but normative stress of the birth of her baby and living in a group setting with other pregnant teens. In their discussion, the social worker helped Lia to focus on her problem-solving, coping, and adaptation skills (strengths) in her current situation. For example, Lia had proposed living with her aunt or sister as a temporary solution to her home situation, which showed her aptitude for problem solving and adaptation capacities.

In using anticipatory guidance, it is important that you do not convey an expectation that people will always be able to independently manage future crisis situations. Even though you have reassured them of their skills and helped them to anticipate future scenarios, you should clarify that you or other professionals are available if they need future help.

Strengths and Limitations of the Strategy

The crisis intervention equilibrium/disequilibrium model is a structured, time-limited model consisting of a series of steps informed by basic crisis theory. As noted, the initial intervention phase has three strategic objectives: (1) relieve the client's emotional distress; (2) complete an assessment of the client's cognitive, behavioral, and emotional functioning; and (3) plan the strategy of intervention, focusing on relevant tasks the client is able to perform. The goal of the intervention is to restore the client to a precrisis level of functioning. Promising research and practice have demonstrated the effectiveness of crisis strategies with diverse populations to include an understanding that the definition of a crisis is influenced by culture. Strengths of the model are that perceptions of a crisis vary based on associated threats, client cognitions, ego strengths, coping capacity, and problem-solving skills.

The basic model retains the assumption of a crisis as an episodic, time-limited event. As such, crisis professionals aim to relieve emotional distress and develop a plan of action so that an individual or family's precrisis level of functioning is restored. Ell (1995) questions the assumption of time-limited crisis as well as the notion of homeostasis—specifically, whether the goal of restoring equilibrium is always possible. For instance, ongoing difficulties in the daily lives of people who are exposed to a chronic and constant state of vulnerability in their environments can mean that the focus on time-limited crisis episodes is neither feasible nor realistic. The efficacy of crisis intervention strategies nevertheless is not entirely diminished by Ell's observations.

However, these observations do suggest significant factors that can impact cognitive, affective, and behavioral functioning as a result of the cumulative effects of ongoing distress for a prolonged period of time.

Understanding basic crisis theory provides you with a framework for working with both adults and minors. The model is consistent with generalist practice and utilizes the practice values, knowledge, and skills with which you are already familiar.

COGNITIVE RESTRUCTURING

Cognitive restructuring is a therapeutic process derived from cognitive behavioral therapy (CBT). Also referred to as *cognitive replacement*, cognitive restructuring is "considered to be the cornerstone of cognitive behavioral approaches" (Cormier & Nurius, 2003, p. 435). Intervention techniques in CBT are designed to help clients modify their beliefs, faulty thought patterns or perceptions, and destructive verbalizations, thereby leading to changes in behavior. An assumption of cognitive restructuring is that people often manifest cognitive distortions, which in turn affects their emotions and actions. Distortions are irrational thoughts derived from negative schemas that lead to unrealistic interpretations of people, events, or circumstances. Frequently, although a client may be aware of his or her thinking, he or she may still lack the emotional strength to alter the schematic thought patterns.

Theoretical Framework

To fully appreciate the foundation of cognitive restructuring, it is important to understand the theories on which the procedures of the technique are based. CBT attempts to alter the client's interpretation of self and his or her environment, and the

EP 4

manner in which he or she creates interpretations. The theory considers the behavior of clients to originate from their processing of both internal and external information. According to cognitive theorists, most social and behavioral problems or dysfunctions are directly related to the misconceptions that people hold about themselves, other people, and various life situations (J. Beck, 1995; Dobson & Dozios, 2001). An understanding of the reciprocal relationship of cognition, affect, and behavior is considered central in using this approach.

The early and historic work of Ellis (1962), Beck (1976), and others led to cognitive theories and techniques that can be applied directly and systematically to problems of cognitive dysfunction. Ellis's (1962) seminal work, *Reason and Emotion in Psychotherapy*, explicated the theory underlying **rational-emotive therapy (RET)**. Perhaps the most significant contribution is *The Cognitive Therapy of Depression*, which is widely recognized as the definitive work on treatment of depression (Beck, Rush, Shaw, & Emery, 1979).

The classical conditioning work of Pavlov (1927) and the operant conditioning studies of Skinner (1974) are prominent in the theoretical framework of CBT (Cobb, 2008). Learning as a primary focus is influenced by Bandura's (1986) social learning theory. According to the theory, thoughts and emotions are best understood in the context of behaviors associated with cognition or cognitive processes, and the extent to which individuals adapt and respond to different stimuli and make self-judgments. Increasingly, cognitive behavioral approaches include social constructionists' perspectives of the specific realities of different clients and unique behaviors relative to their culture, beliefs, and worldview (Berlin, 2001; Cobb, 2008; Cormier & Nurius, 2003).

In the 1960s, behavioral theory and methods were introduced by Edwin Thomas at the University of Michigan (Gambrill, 1995). Berlin's (2001) *Clinical Social Work Practice: A Cognitive-Integrative Approach* is a significant contribution to adaptation of CBT to social work practice.

Tenets of Cognitive Behavioral Therapy and Cognitive Restructuring

In general, the goal of cognitive behavioral intervention strategies is to increase the client's cognitive and behavioral skills so as to enhance his or her functioning. **Restructuring** is a cognitive procedural technique that aims to change a client's thoughts, feelings, or overt behaviors that contribute to and maintain problem behavior. To be effective in using cognitive restructuring as an intervention strategy, you must be skilled in assessing cognitive functioning and in applying appropriate interventions.

CBT is based on the assumption that people construct their own reality. It is within the realm of processing information that people assess and make judgments that fit into their cognitive schemas. The basic tenets of CBT are as follows:

- **Thinking** is a primary determinant of behavior and involves statements that people say to or

about themselves. This inner dialogue, rather than unconscious forces, is critical to understanding behavior. To fully grasp this first tenet, you must clearly differentiate thinking from feeling, as confusing feelings with thoughts tends to create problematic communications. This confusion can be observed in messages such as "I feel our relationship is on the rocks," or "I feel that the teacher does not like me." Here, the use of the word *feel* does not actually identify feelings, but rather it embodies the client's *thoughts* or *beliefs*. *Thoughts* per se are devoid of feelings, although they are often accompanied by and generate feelings or emotions. *Feelings* consist of emotions, such as sadness, joy, or disappointment.

- **Cognitions** affect behavior, which is manifested in behavioral responses. Behavioral responses are a function of the cognitive processes of attention, retention, production, and motivation, as well as of rewarding or unrewarding consequences (Bandura, 1986). Cognitions that lead to cognitive distortions or faulty thinking can be monitored and changed.

- **Behavioral change** involves assisting clients to make constructive change by focusing on their misconceptions and the extent to which they produce or contribute to their problems. The thrust is that a change in behavior can be accomplished by changing the way clients think.

In identifying distortions and faulty thoughts and behaviors, a basic assumption is that the client can learn new patterns of thinking. You should, of course, temper this assumption by recognizing that other factors influence a client's self-perception and the manner in which the client thinks and process information. Specifically, cognitions are not necessarily faulty, given the realities of culture, unequal sociopolitical structures, and social interactions in which class, race, gender, and sexual orientation are major contextual life issues. The realities of people's lives and beliefs have a significant impact on thinking and cognitions; therefore, the relationship between cognition, culture, and context should not be minimized or overlooked (Berlin, 2001; Hays, 2009; Pollack, 2004).

Cognitive Distortions

Beck (1967), in separating thinking from cognition, identified automatic thoughts and cognitive distortions as factors for which cognitive restructuring is indicated.

The processing of information for most of us is automatic, as our minds attempt to navigate and narrate our interactions and environment. Problems occur when thoughts are consistently distorted because of a client's ingrained beliefs and faulty reasoning. While cognitive distortions are irrational, they make logical sense to the client. Moreover, distortions maintain negative thinking and reinforce negative emotions. The most common types of distortions and negative thinking patterns conceptualized by Beck (1976) have been summarized in the literature (Cormier, Nurius, & Osborn, 2009; Leahy & Holland, 2000; Walsh, 2006) and are as follows:

- **All-or-nothing thinking** involves seeing things as all-or-nothing scenarios, and in most instances seeing the glass as half empty. *"I wanted to do well on the exam, and now that I didn't, I will never get into graduate school." "If I don't smoke stuff [dope] with my friends they won't ever hang with me." "Unless we know the background of these clients, we won't be able to help them."* In these statements, you may see the similarities between this thinking and catastrophizing and overgeneralizing.
- **Blaming** occurs when a client perceives others as the source of negative feelings or emotions and can therefore avoid taking responsibility. *"I feel so stressed out because a driver cut in front of me on the way home." "Her snippy attitude about going shopping with me put me in a bad mood."*
- **Catastrophizing** is the belief that if a particular event or situation occurs, the results would be unbearable, effectively influencing your sense of self-worth. *"I need to study all the time, because if I don't get the highest grade possible on the exam, I will lose my financial aid and return home a failure."*
- **Discounting positives** is the tendency to disqualify or minimize the good things that you or others do and instead treat a positive as a negative. *"My friends said that I looked great in an outfit from the secondhand store, but really, they were just being nice and feel sorry for me because I don't have money."* Similarly, say you are reviewing evaluations after making a presentation and you focus on the following, *"Of the 40 people at the presentation, two said that I was boring,"* instead of focusing on the 38 positive responses.
- **Emotional reasoning** guides your interpretation based on how you feel rather than on reality.

Interpretations and beliefs are facts bolstered by negative emotions, which are assumed to reflect reality. *"If I feel stuck [stupid] in social situations, then that's really who I am."*

- **Inability to disconfirm** functions very much like a barricade in that you are unable to accept any information that is inconsistent with your beliefs or negative thoughts. For example, if a relative with whom you frequently argue is unwilling to keep your kids because of an appointment, your mental response may be *That's not the real reason; the relative never liked me or my kids,"* in effect discounting the numerous other occasions on which the relative did care for your children.
- **Judgment focus** leads to a perception of self and others or an assessment of events as good or bad, excellent or awful, rather than describing, accepting, or attempting to understand what is happening or considering alternatives. *"I know that when I go to a party people won't talk to me."* In some instances, you may establish arbitrary standards by which you measure yourself, only to find that you are unable to perform at this level. *"I won't do well in the class no matter how hard I try"* is an example of a self-defeating judgment statement, as is *"Everyone in the class gets good grades, but not me."* A judgment in contrast to one that is self-defeating is an assumption that a presentation was good because *"a lot of people came."*
- **Jumping to conclusions** assumes the negative when there may be limited supporting evidence. Assumptions may also take the form of mind reading and fortune telling based on a prediction of a negative outcome. *"If I don't watch the children, she will be upset with me, a risk that I am unwilling to take."*
- **Mind reading** assumes that you know what people will think, do, or respond. *"There's no point in my asking my daughter to visit me more often. She will just see it as my attempt to get attention or embarrass her. If I bring up the topic, she and I will end up in an argument; besides, she is busy with her own family."*
- **Negative (mental) filtering** results in mentally singling out bad events and ignoring the positives. *"As I was standing in the hallway at work, this kid bumped into me, you know, they are all like that. I was so angry. Then he turned around and apologized, but I pretended not to hear him. He should have apologized sooner."* In some instances, negative filters are linked to thoughts that are overgeneralized to people or events.

- **Overgeneralizations**, or **globalization**, involve perceiving isolated events and using them to reach broad conclusions. *"Today, when I raised my hand in class, the instructor called on another student. He never calls on me."* **Labeling** is another form of overgeneralizing in which a negative label is attached to self or others based on a single incident. *"I am not a very good student, so the instructor does not value my opinion." "He is a lousy instructor, otherwise he would help everyone [me]."*

- **Personalizing** assumes that you had a role in or that you are responsible for a negative situation, assuming that the results were in your control. *"We were close friends and then she was called to active duty and we lost contact. I wonder if I did something that caused her to forget about me."* Personalizing, when applied to others, is very much like blaming. *"She could have written to me while she was away." "The party that I planned in the park was a failure because it rained and people left early."*

- **Regret orientation** is generally focused on the past. *"If I had worked harder, I could have gotten a better grade." "I had a chance for a better job if I had been willing to relocate to a different city."*

- **"Should" statements** are about self-failure or judgments about others relative to how things should be. *"I should be able to take the bus on my own when I work late." "My sister ought to be willing to care for my child when I am working late."* Judging statements about others generally result in feelings of resentment and anger. *"My sister has a husband, so she doesn't really understand how hard it is for me to manage as a single parent."*

- **Unfair comparisons** measure self against others believed to have desirable attributes. *"She is prettier than I am." "Everybody in the class is smarter than me." "My college roommate is a CEO already; I'm nothing compared to him."* Unfair comparisons can also lead to "I could or should be" or "I shouldn't be" statements when comparing self to others; for example, *"My college roommate is a CEO already; I could have a job like that."*

- **What ifs** refer to the tendency for people to continually question themselves about the potential for events or the catastrophe that might happen. *"I would go to the doctor to examine the mole on my back, but what if I am really sick?" "What if I tell my relative that I can't watch the kids tonight and she gets upset with me and she refuses to talk to me ever again?"*

Cognitive Schemas

In each of the examples above, you are able to see how distorted and negative thoughts fit within a client's cognitive schemas. **Cognitive schemas**, either positive or negative, are the memory patterns that a client uses to organize information (Berlin, 2001; Cormier & Nurius, 2003; Cormier, Nurius, & Osborne, 2009; McQuaide & Ehrenreich, 1997). Whether they originate from a strengths or deficit orientation, cognitive schemas are shortcuts in thinking. Because such schemas are ingrained beliefs, it is often difficult for people to hear or process new or different information or an alternative explanation, the result of which is cognitive dissonance. When cognitive dissonance occurs, clients can experience a high level of stress, so much so that they may completely shut down.

The activation of a negative cognitive schema can result from external or internal events that are adaptive or maladaptive. It is the latter that is the focus of your work with clients. Consider the influence of the negative image when the youth bumped into the woman in the hallway. Her automatic thought was, "They're all like that." Even though the youth apologized, the woman's memory pattern (her global thinking about "they") was already operating in full force. Consequently, she was unable to process the youth's apology as new information and unable to alter her cognition of the event. Of course, this event could have been triggered by a negative past experience or could simply be the result of her ingrained biased thinking. If we were to examine this same situation from an internal vantage point, context would involve assessing her mood at the time of the incident and the extent to which it influenced her cognition and behavior.

In either case, it is important that you first determine the context and the type of situation that triggers and maintains problematic behavior (Berlin, 2001; Cormier & Nurius, 2003). Further, where negative filtering about self and others has emotional content, blaming statements may be related to the mood of the client at a particular point in time. By the same token, negative thoughts may be grounded in the client's reality, however irrational the thoughts may appear to be. Hence you would assess whether external and internal stimuli that led to cognitive errors, are actual distortions or a client's misunderstanding of his or her experiences. Keep in mind that negative thoughts and schemas do not represent the whole person. People generally are able to go about their daily lives until such time that an external or internal event ignites a particular thought pattern upon which their reality is constructed.

EP 2

You should also be mindful that marginalized and oppressed people and involuntary clients are often perceived as negative thinkers with distorted realities. When faced with a client's narrative in this regard, we may tend to think of them as overgeneralizing, blaming others for their misfortune, or jumping to conclusions. Yet if the narrative is derived from ongoing and sustained adverse events or inequality, can we conclude, without further examination, that thoughts are based on distortions or discrepancies? Also, a culture different from your own may be challenging, especially if cultural practices and traditions are inconsistent with what you believe to be true. As difficult as it may be for us to acknowledge truths that may be different from our own experiences, ultimately the focus should be on what is meaningful to the client rather than what is considered an acceptable pattern of thinking and behaving.

Empirical Evidence and Uses of Cognitive Restructuring

EP 4

Cognitive restructuring procedures are particularly relevant for treating problems associated with low self-esteem; distorted perceptions in interpersonal relations; unrealistic expectations of self, others, and life in general; irrational fears, panic, anxiety, and depression; control of anger and other impulses; and lack of assertiveness (Cormier & Nurius, 2003; Walsh, 2006). Selected studies have demonstrated the range of cognitive restructuring components in treating anger (Dahlen & Deffenbacher, 2000), impulse control associated with child abuse and gambling (Sharpe & Tarrier, 1992), and substance abuse and relapse (Bakker et al., 1997; Steigerwald & Stone, 1999). Results of studies have also shown cognitive restructuring to be effective in the treatment of posttraumatic stress disorder (Foa et al., 2005), social phobias and anxiety (Feeny, 2004), spousal caregiver support groups (Gendron et al., 1996), and in crisis or trauma situations (Glancy & Saini, 2005; Jaycox, Zoellner, & Foa, 2002). The procedures of cognitive restructuring are often blended with other interventions (e.g., modeling, behavioral rehearsal, imagery, and psychoeducation) because combinations of interventions are believed to be more potent than single interventions in producing change (Corcoran, 2002).

Using Cognitive Restructuring with Minors

In comparison to adult populations, there are fewer studies that show evidence of the effectiveness of cognitive restructuring with minors. However, when combined with other strategies—for example, narrative and enactive performance-based procedures—cognitive restructuring can be effective with younger minors. The work of Graham (1998) found that distorted thinking can affect the social and interpersonal skills of minors. Studies conducted by Rheingold, Herbert, and Franklin (2003) and Guadiano and Herbert (2006) showed that cognitive restructuring can increase self-efficacy and reduce social anxiety in adolescents. Findings of a pilot study highlighted the feasibility of cognitive restructuring in reducing the symptoms of posttraumatic stress disorder in minors (Rosenberg et al., 2011).

Giacola et al. (1999), Liau, Barriga, and Gibbs (1998), and Rudolph and Clark (2001) emphasize assessing the context in which the minor's behavior occurs. To this point, several studies found contextual variations among minors with respect to cognitive distortions. Young minors exhibiting depressive and aggressive symptoms, for example, may exaggerate accounts of true negatives, raising the question as to whether cognitions were distorted or were expressions of the minor's actual reality (Rudolph & Clark, 2001). With older minors, in particular those who are engaged in antisocial behaviors, distorted thinking may be used as self-serving explanations for behavior (Liau, Barriga, & Gibbs, 1998). Giacola et al. (1999) suggest that, unfortunately, the context of distortions and negative self-talk exhibited by minors may not be fully explored by professionals. Instead, their behavior is often interpreted or diagnosed as oppositional defiant behavior or attention deficit or conduct disorder. In their further exploration of context, however, Giacola and colleagues found that the negative thought patterns and self-talk of minors were linked to harsh punishment and excessive criticism in their home life. Collectively, these studies highlight the need to help minors distinguish between feelings and cognitions in view of their circumstances and symptoms.

Studies specific to anger control in minors include Seay et al. (2003), Sukhodolsky, Kassinore, and Gorman (2004), and Tate (2001). Tate, however, emphasized peer influence and positive cognitive restructuring in schools rather than strategies to control and rehabilitate and maintain adult-imposed order.

Sukhodolsky and colleagues found the procedure to be more effective with older adolescents than with younger children, especially when the former did not have a prior history of violent behavior. Seay et al. reported improvement in anger control when specific behavior was targeted, accompanied by practicing different responses. Bailey (2001) cited the importance of family and school involvement and discussed cognitive restructuring as effective when age-appropriate strategies were used. Use of the technique as an intervention with minors included the reduction of HIV risk behavior among African American adolescents (St. Lawrence et al., 1995). Another study provided evidence of effectiveness in changing the thought processes of African American adolescents who had been abused as children (Lesure-Lester, 2002).

Applying Cognitive Restructuring with Diverse Groups

The worldview and social psychological processes that shape minority perceptions and resulting thoughts or experiences may be different from those of the majority culture. Specifically, differences in reality, history, and context can influence cognitive development and processes. For example, Shih and Sanchez (2005) examined the role of identity among youth who have multiple identities with respect to cognition that shaped how the youth viewed the world and the extent in which they adjusted to the reality of rejection and discrimination. In sum, the findings of multiple studies reinforce the importance of examining the context of distortions or negative thought patterns before concluding that a client's cognitions and thought patterns are irrational.

At the practice level, cognitive restructuring is widely used in correctional institutions in which the majority of inmates are members of minority groups. Based on the belief that change is needed in the criminal mindset, cognitive procedures are intended to reduce recidivism. The assumption is that the inmates' patterned way of thinking essentially short-circuits their ability to think logically and use reason to make decisions. As a therapeutic intervention, the goal is to alter criminal thought processes by restructuring or replacing them with more acceptable patterns of behavior. Pollack (2004), in critiquing cognitive procedures, stresses that the procedures tend to overlook or deemphasize the influence of environmental and structural inequities. Potocky-Tripodi (2002), however, suggests that under specific circumstances, cognitive restructuring as "supportive" counseling may help immigrants and refugees with their maladaptive thoughts and increase their coping skills in intercultural situations.

Hays (1995), as cited in Cormier and Nurius (2003), critiques cognitive restructuring with multicultural groups and observes that this "approach supports the status quo of mainstream society" (p. 437). With this in mind, you should be aware that cognition and thoughts expressed by different individuals and groups can be considered highly irregular behavior when measured by majority culture. In using the technique, modifications may be required so that it is responsive and does not oppress or punish differences.

Culturally compatible adaptations and modifications of cognitive procedures are illustrated in studies with Chinese Americans (Chen & Davenport, 2005), Latino clients (Organista, Dwyer, & Azocar, 1993), Native Americans (Renfrey, 1992), and Muslims (Hodge & Nadir, 2008). Still, you should observe that preferences, such as spirituality, beliefs, and self-perceptions that give purpose and direction to what people think and feel, are constructed by culture and within the context of the environment (Bandura, 1988; Berlin, 2001; Bronfenbrenner, 1989). For example, Renfrey (1992) combined Native American religious ceremonies with cognitive procedures, and Hodge and Nadir (2008) advocate for adaptations to achieve congruence between individual self-statements that are consistent with the beliefs of Muslims.

Although there is a need for further study of the cognitive development and processes of diverse groups, there are studies that demonstrate the efficacy of cognitive restructuring with different racial and cultural groups. Selected examples include interventions with African American women smokers (Ahijevych & Wewers, 1993) and low-income African American woman in group treatment (Kohn et al., 2002), and in addressing race-related stressors among Asian American Pacific Islanders in the military (Loo, Ueda, & Morton, 2007). Work by Kuehlwein (1992), Ussher (1990), and Wolfe (1992) reported positive results with gay and lesbian clients. The technique used as a component of treatment with women effectively helped them gain a sense of power in confronting cultural messages of ideal physical attributes (Brown, 1994; Srebnik & Saltzberg, 1994).

On the whole, research on the efficacy of cognitive restructuring with diverse groups is limited. The studies discussed here have demonstrated that adaptations in language, culture, and specific group circumstances can result in cognitive restructuring being an effective intervention strategy with diverse groups.

Procedures of Cognitive Restructuring

EP 8

The primary goal of cognitive restructuring is to alter clients' thoughts and feelings and their accompanying self-statements or behaviors. Cognitive restructuring is particularly useful in assisting clients to gain awareness of self-defeating thoughts and misconceptions that impair their personal functioning and to replace them with beliefs and behaviors that are aligned with reality.

Several discrete procedural steps are involved in cognitive restructuring. Although different authors vary slightly in how the steps are defined, the similarities between the various models are far greater than the differences. These steps, summarized in Table 13-2, are adapted from the steps identified by Goldfried (1977) and Cormier and Nurius (2003). In this section, we illustrate each step through a case example of a military veteran who has returned home after serving two tours of duty in Iraq.

1. Assist Clients in Accepting That Their Self-Statements, Assumptions, and Beliefs Largely Determine Their Emotional Reactions to Life's Events

The power difference between you and clients is likely to become heightened when you present a goal of changing how they perceive themselves or their

TABLE 13-2 Steps in Cognitive Restructuring

1. Assist clients in accepting that their self-statements, assumptions, and beliefs determine their emotional reactions to life's events. (Tool: explanation and treatment rationale)

2. Assist clients in identifying dysfunctional self-statements, beliefs, and thought patterns that underlie their problem. (Tool: self-monitoring)

3. Assist clients in identifying situations that engender dysfunctional cognitions.

4. Assist clients in replacing dysfunctional cognitions with functional self-statements.

5. Assist clients in identifying rewards and incentives for successful coping efforts.

world. Mistrust and suspicion may be particularly acute with minors, members of a racial or ethnic minority, and clients who are involuntary. Thus, in the first step, it is important to provide clients with an explanation and your rationale for selecting cognitive restructuring as an intervention procedure, as illustrated in the following dialogue:

Social worker: I understand from what you have said so far that you want to be with friends in social situations, but you become anxious before and during the times you are actually with friends. So that you may achieve your goal, we first need to determine what happens that causes you to feel anxious. This will help you become aware of the thoughts you experience in the situation. Specifically, we need to review what you say to yourself *before*, *during*, and *after* you are with your friends, because thoughts occur automatically, and often we may not be fully aware of them. Becoming aware of your thoughts, assumptions, and beliefs is an important first step in replacing them with others that will help you achieve your goal.

To guide you in assisting clients to understand cognitive restructuring, it may be advisable to use self as an example to explain the technique, as demonstrated in the following dialogue. The social worker draws upon his own experience to show how ways of thinking and responding mediate cognitions, emotions, and thoughts:

Social worker: What you think determines in large measure what you feel and do. For example, I'm planning a trip to a country, despite the fact that my knowledge of that country and its language and culture is limited. When I shared my plan with a friend, he told me that my idea was stupid and questioned whether my decision was wise. Instead, the friend thought that I should travel to a more familiar place. I could have made various meanings or self-statements related to my friend's message, each of which would have resulted in different feelings and actions. Consider the potential responses that I might have made to my friend's comment:

- Response 1: *He's probably right; he's a bright guy, and I respect his judgment. Why didn't I think of taking a trip to a place where I would be more comfortable? He thinks that I am stupid.*

CASE EXAMPLE

Erik is a military veteran whose goal is to reduce his anxiety so that he is comfortable in social situations. Having completed two tours of duty in Iraq, he is grateful to have returned home without a serious physical injury. Erik explained that "trouble" began shortly after he returned home, when friends invited him to social gatherings. Urged by his family, he initially accepted the invitations and looked forward to the various events. Eventually, however, his doing so caused him to become anxious, which intensified between the time he accepted an invitation and when he actually went. Erik described himself as never being much of a talker. When people talked to him, they mostly wanted him to describe his tours of duty, and he generally declined to do so, preferring instead to have a normal conversation. Because of his anxiety, Erik declined future invitations, believing that he did not fit in, even though he wanted the social contact. Erik's future goal is to return to school to obtain a degree, but his anxiety level has prevented him from moving forward.

If I think that my friend is right, then my feelings and statements are negative and I consider changing my plan.

● Response 2: *Who does he think he is, calling me stupid? He's the one who's stupid. What a jerk!*

If I think this way about my friend, I am likely to become angry and defensive, leading to an argument between the two of us about which one of us is right.

● Response 3: *It's apparent that my friend and I have different ideas about travel. He's entitled to his opinion, although I don't agree with him and I feel good about my plan. I don't like his referring to my choice as stupid, though. There's no point in getting bent out of shape over it, but I think I'll let him know how I feel about what he said to me.*

If I think the thoughts in the third example, I'm less likely to experience negative feelings about myself. I'll feel good about my decision despite the differences of opinion, and I'll ignore my friend's insensitive remarks.

In using a self example, the social worker highlights for his client, Erik, how thoughts and beliefs can cause difficulties and the manner in which cognitive restructuring facilitates the development of other thoughts that are realistic and consistent with his goal. Further, the social worker suggests that other responses could be appropriate, but the three examples suffice to make his point. The social worker then points out that the task at hand is to help Erik to master his anxiety and to understand how his self-statement of not fitting in influences his feelings and behavior.

This example shows how the rationale for cognitive restructuring can be presented to a client in a simple, straightforward manner. A majority of clients, given an explanation, will agree to proceed. However, a client's commitment to the procedure is necessary because beliefs are not easily changed.

2. Assist Clients in Identifying Dysfunctional Self-Statements, Beliefs, and Patterns of Thoughts That Underlie Their Problem

Once the client accepts that thoughts and beliefs mediate emotional reactions, your next task is to help the client identify the associated thoughts and beliefs relevant to his or her difficulties. This step requires a detailed exploration of events related to problematic situations and antecedents, with particular emphasis on cognitions pertinent to the distressing emotions.

To begin the process, you would focus on problematic events that occurred during the preceding week or on events surrounding a problem the client has targeted for change. For example, for Erik, the targeted change is increasing his comfort level in social situations. As the client recalls events, you are listening for specific details regarding overt behaviors, cognitions (i.e., self-statements and images), and emotional reactions. Focusing on the cognitive and emotional aspects related to the event clarifies the connection between what a client perceives and his or her emotions and thoughts. From this point on, the aim is to identify self-statements and beliefs related to an event and to increase the client's awareness of the way in which automatic thoughts and beliefs are powerful determinants of behavior.

As the client continues to explore his or her thought patterns, you will be able to identify thoughts and feelings that occur before, during, and after events. To elicit self-statements, ask the client to recreate the situation as it unfolded, recalling exactly what he or she thought, felt, and did. For example, the social worker asked Erik to describe his thoughts and feelings when he was in a social situation. Should the reflection prove to be too difficult, as an alternative, the social worker could ask Erik to close his eyes and run a movie of his thoughts and feelings prior to, during, and after he accepted an invitation.

As the social worker listened to Erik describe his thoughts, the cognitive sets that predisposed him to experience anxiety and to behave in predictable ways were identified. To illustrate, consider Erik's inner dialogue or self-statements *prior* to going to a social event:

- "If I go, I'll be unsure of what to say because I don't talk much."
- "When people talk to me about Iraq, I feel uncomfortable, and they probably think that something is wrong with me. So it's better to not go."

Erik's self-statements increased his anxiety and influenced his expectation that he did not fit in. As the social worker listened to Erik's self-debate as he recreated the social situation, he also made note of his nonverbal behavior. His physical posture, for example, spoke volumes. Previously, Erik sat tall and erect, but as he talked he begin to slouch in the chair. So in addition to his self-defeating thoughts, which dominated his cognition, it would be useful to explore whether his nonverbal behavior also contributed to his presentation of self in the situation.

Exploration of self-statements during events often reveals that thoughts maintain self-defeating feelings and behaviors and drastically reduce personal effectiveness. For example, Erik tended to dwell on the perceived negative reactions of others. As a result, he was unable to fully tune in to conversations or to verbally express himself in a way that created favorable impressions. In other words, he found it difficult to be fully present and involved because of his self-consciousness and anxiety about exposing his imagined personal inadequacies.

To illustrate the impact of his thoughts, let's consider his self-statements *during* the time he attended a social event:

- "Well, here I am, nothing is different. I'm not talking and people are not talking to me and I feel left out of conversations."

- "I wish I had something interesting to say. But they aren't interested in me. I'm just the boy who went off to war, and I don't want to talk about my experience. Right now my life is not about much and not very interesting."
- "Even if I talked more or people talked to me, I don't add anything to the conversation, so going to events has become unimportant to me."

Because Erik's interactions with people were not what he had hoped for, he continued to be preoccupied with self-defeating thoughts. If he doesn't talk about his military experience, for instance, he concludes that he has little or nothing to offer and behaves accordingly; therefore, his thoughts about not fitting in and being unworthy are reinforced. In consequence, the potential of having a positive experience of engaging with others is blocked.

A client's thoughts and feelings after an event can have an impact on his or her subsequent behaviors. In listening to clients tell what occurred and their conclusions, you can further highlight the mediating function of cognitions. Consider Erik's thoughts and feelings as he described his experience *after* he attended a social event:

- "I'm finished; I might as well quit trying. I just can't talk to people, no use in kidding myself."
- "People didn't really try to include me. It's clear that they aren't interested in me. If I don't go to the next party, I'm sure that no one would notice or care."
- "This situation is so uncomfortable. I won't go to future parties. I don't enjoy myself, and I'm sure they don't enjoy being around me."

The following are general inquiries that can be developed into questions to help clients to assess the rationality of beliefs and self-statements:

- Ask how a client has reached certain conclusions.
- Elicit evidence that supports the client's perceptions or beliefs.
- Explore the logic of beliefs that have magnified the feared consequences of certain actions.

To assist Erik in assessing the rationality of his conclusions, for example, the social worker asked him the following question:

Social worker: So when you went to the party, what happened that made you think that people were not interested in you and didn't want you around?

As illustrated in the following example, a client may be unable to immediately acknowledge irrational beliefs:

Erik: Well, there was a girl there I've known most of my life, but by the way she looked at me I could tell she didn't want to talk to me.

Clients can tenaciously cling to misconceptions and argue persuasively about the validity of a belief to prove a point. For example, Erik's perception about the young woman's behavior was a confirmation that he did not fit in. As the social worker, you must therefore be prepared to challenge or "dispute" the validity of irrational beliefs by emphasizing the costs or disadvantages associated with counterproductive beliefs. To illustrate how disputing or challenging an irrational belief works, the social worker's response prompted Erik to consider the association between his thoughts and his goal:

Social worker: Okay, if you continue to think that you don't fit in and you continue to decline invitations, how will achieve your goal of becoming comfortable in social situations?

Clusters of misconceptions are commonly associated with problematic behavior, and they also tend to have a common theme. For Erik, a central theme or a slight derivative of his self-statements and expectations was that he is unwelcome and unworthy in social situations. Consequently, Erik's thoughts and beliefs automatically supported his conclusions, contributing to his expectations of self and unrealistic expectations of others. It is possible to observe such thought patterns by exploring accompanying thought clusters, examples of which are illustrated in Table 13-3. By identifying clusters or patterns of misconceptions, you can direct your efforts to the theme common to all of them rather than dealing with each misconception separately.

3. Assist Clients in Identifying Situations That Engender Dysfunctional Cognitions

Identifying the places where cognitions cause stress, the key persons involved, and situations in which the client feels demeaned helps you and the client to develop and tailor tasks and coping strategies to specific situations.

Self-monitoring between sessions is a concrete way for a client to monitor and recognize cognitions related to difficulties around problematic events. Such recognition increases self-awareness of the pervasive nature of thoughts and the need to actively cope. Self-monitoring thus expands self-awareness and paves the way for later change efforts.

To facilitate self-monitoring, the social worker asked Erik to keep daily logs to record information, as illustrated in Figure 13-4. In the log, Erik recorded his feelings, beliefs, and self-statements in a social situation. The log may also reveal other factors that influence his feelings about social situations—for example, his comfort level in instances in which he is the only person with military experience.

Daily self-monitoring is a valuable tool because it focuses a client's efforts between sessions, clarifies the connections between cognitions and feelings, and appraises information regarding the prevalence and intensity of thoughts, images, and feelings. In Erik's case, keeping a daily log helped him to logically examine his thoughts. The social worker then discussed the log with Erik in their next session:

Social worker [to Erik]: After completing a week of logs, did you discover anything about yourself

TABLE 13-3 Beliefs and Self-Expectations

BELIEFS	SELF-EXPECTATIONS
Beliefs about oneself	I am usually not very good at anything that I do. My accomplishments aren't that significant, anyone could have done it.
Beliefs about others' perceptions and expectations of oneself	My partner dismisses my opinion, because I am not very smart. When I compare myself with others, I never quite measure up.
Expectations of oneself	At work, I feel I must perform better than others in my unit. I should be able to do lots of things and perform at a high level.
Expectations of others	My daughter should understand how I feel without my having to tell her. She should want to visit me.

Date: Tuesday, September 6, 2015

Situation or Event	Feelings (Rate intensity from 1 to 10)	Beliefs or Self-Statements (Rate rationality from 1 to 10)
1. I went to a party.	I'm feeling uncomfortable (7)	No one will talk to me (6)
2. No one said anything to me; I didn't say anything.	I'm anxious (7); reluctant to join in (8); I don't fit in (7)	I should talk (9); but people will ignore me and I'm embarrassed (2); it's not worth the hassle (3)

FIG 13-4 Daily Log for Erik

and the way that you think and behave when you go to a party?

Erik: Yeah, I could see the times when I felt uncomfortable and most anxious.

To prevent a person from becoming overwhelmed by the task of keeping a log, you might suggest that recordings be limited to no more than three. As an alternative, or in addition, self-monitoring can also include images drawn by the client. As other counterproductive thought patterns emerge during sessions, the focus of self-monitoring can be shifted as necessary.

As you and the client review completed log sheets and identify problematic feelings and cognitions, it is important to note recurring situations or themes. A recurring theme for Erik, for example, was his concern about a lack of fit between himself and others at the social events.

4. Assist Clients in Replacing Dysfunctional Cognitions with Functional Self-Statements

As clients become aware of their dysfunctional thoughts, beliefs, and images, the goal is to help them recognize the connection to negative emotional reactions. Having done so, an additional goal is to help them cope as an intermediary step to learning new behavioral responses. Coping strategies typically involve self-statements that are both realistic and instrumental in diminishing or eliminating negative emotional reactions and self-defeating behaviors. Although functional self-statements are intended to foster courage and facilitate active coping efforts, it is

important to not ignore the struggle as a client shifts from habitual and ingrained patterns of thinking to adopting new behavioral patterns. In recognition of the difficulty and anxiety that a client may experience, coping self-statements are intended to support the transition to risking new behavior.

First, to introduce Erik to positive self-statements, the social worker explains the rationale for developing new self-statements:

Social worker: Now that you've identified key self-defeating beliefs and thoughts, let's focus on how you can replace them with positive statements. It will take a lot of hard work on your part, but as you practice, you'll find that they will become more and more natural, allowing you to rely less on old ways of thinking.

Because mastery is unlikely to be immediate, after an explanation, the social worker modeled coping self-statements that Erik could use as substitutes for his thoughts and beliefs. In the exercise, the social worker assumed the role of Erik, using his words and thoughts as he coped with the target situation.

Social worker as Erik: "I know a part of me wants to avoid social situations because I feel anxious about fitting in, but it's not going to get any better if I continue to decline invitations. I don't have to talk a lot. If I listen to the others and get my mind off myself, I could become more involved in conversations."

Notice how the social worker modeled Erik's struggle and the idea of coping rather than mastery of new self-statements. Modeling coping self-statements should reflect the client's actual experience, whereas mastery of self-statements does not. Moreover, the former conveys empathy for and understanding of a client's struggle, which can inspire greater confidence in the process. As an alternative coping self-statement, the social worker proposed the following:

Social worker: "Yes, you might think, 'I can't expect them to include me in their conversations. It would be great if this happened, but if not, I'll be responsible for including myself, because doing so is better than withdrawing and feeling left out.'"

After modeling coping self-statements, it is appropriate to encourage the client to practice the behavior.

To enhance the effectiveness of guided practice, you could suggest that clients close their eyes and picture themselves in the exact situation they will be in *before* engaging in the targeted behavior. When they report they have succeeded in capturing the situation, ask them to think aloud the thoughts they typically experience when contemplating the targeted behavior. Then ask clients to substitute coping thoughts, coaching them as needed. Give positive feedback and encouragement when they produce reinforcing self-statements independently, even though they may continue to struggle with conflicting thoughts. You may also expect clients to express doubt and uncertainly about their ability to eventually master new patterns of thinking. If they do, explain that it is natural for people to experience misgivings as they experiment with new ways of thinking. Continue to practice and coach them until they feel relatively comfortable in their ability to develop new self-statements.

When the client has demonstrated his or her confidence in using coping self-statements before entering a targeted situation, you can shift to self-statements *during* the time the client is actually in the target situation, as demonstrated by the social worker's modeling coping self-statements:

Social worker as Erik: "Okay, I'm feeling anxious. That's to be expected. I can still pay attention and show interest in the conversation. I communicate by nodding my head, laughing if someone tells a funny story. As I begin to feel more comfortable, I can join in by asking questions if I want to know more. This is another way to show interest, especially if I have some take on the subject people are discussing. I think that my opinions are worth as much as others. Go ahead, take a chance and join in the conversation and maybe look at people as I talk."

Following the modeling exercise, the social worker asked Erik to describe his feelings about what had happened so far. Inquiring about Erik's feelings is important; if the modeling results in his becoming anxious, uncomfortable, or skeptical, the social worker should deal with these feeling before proceeding further. Again, it may be worthwhile for you to model and eventually have the client rehearse reinforcing statements. Here are some examples:

Social worker as Erik: "Well, I did it. I stuck it out and even said a couple of things. That's a step in the right direction." "No one ignored me when I joined the conversation. It wasn't so bad after all, even though I was a little nervous at first."

To further assist clients in utilizing positive statements, it is beneficial to negotiate using such statements as tasks between sessions. Between-session tasks foster autonomy and independent action. Even so, don't pressure the client, because undue pressure may be perceived as threatening or discouraging. You may use the readiness scale (discussed earlier in this chapter) as a gauge.

Continued self-monitoring is essential as clients implement Step 4 of the cognitive restructuring process, using the daily log format illustrated in Figure 13-4 as a tool. As Erik makes progress, for example, a fourth column could be added titled "Rational or Positive Coping Self-Statements." By having clients fill in a column such as this, the exercise can facilitate the development of reinforcing statements, eventually replacing self-defeating ones.

Another technique that can help clients replace their automatic problematic self-statements is encouraging them, upon their first awareness of such thoughts, to nip them in the bud. For example, you might use the image of a flashing yellow traffic signal, alerting clients of the need to replace problematic thoughts. Substituting positive self-statements for self-defeating ones is the heart of cognitive restructuring. Because thoughts tend to be automatic, deeply embedded, and persistent, it is important to explain that Step 4 may extend over a time span in which a satisfactory degree of mastery is gradual; however, it is possible to achieve over time.

5. Assist Clients in Identifying Rewards and Incentives for Successful Coping Efforts

For clients who dwell on their failures and shortcomings and rarely, if ever, give themselves positive feedback, Step 5 in cognitive restructuring is especially important. When clients have mastered new statements and behaviors, you should reinforce their accomplishment by coaching to observe and credit success, as indicated in the following dialogue:

Social worker: So you joined a conversation. That's exciting, given where you started. What are your thoughts on how you would like to celebrate?

Erik: Well, actually it was okay. I made an effort to talk with the girl I knew, and we had a brief conversation.

Social worker: That's a good thing! I also want you to think about rewarding statements that you can make to yourself. I'm going to pretend that I am you. I'll say aloud a self-statement you might think about: "I wasn't sure that I was up to it but I did it!" Now what would you do for yourself?

For some people, rewarding self-statements can be difficult and feel awkward or self-conscious. When a person is hesitant, empathic understanding and encouragement on your part will usually prompt them to try this exercise. Some clients, like Erik, may tend to focus on the overall outcome. For example, the conversation with the young woman was positive, and he felt less anxious as a result. In any case, it is important that you review and credit a client's progress so that the learned behavior can be attempted in other or future situations.

Strengths, Limitations, and Cautions of the Approach

Cognitive restructuring is an effective procedure that is intended to address a range of problems related to a client's cognitions and thought patterns. Research studies have shown the procedure to be particularly useful in altering perceptions, distorted beliefs, and thought patterns that result in negative or self-defeating behaviors. As a systematic process and problem-solving procedure, cognitive restructuring is compatible with crisis intervention, the task-centered system, and solution-focused treatment. In assisting clients to change, however, social workers must not mistakenly assume that clients will be able to perform new behaviors solely as a result of changes in their cognitions or beliefs. In reality, they may lack cognitive and social skills and require instruction and practice before they can effectively perform new behaviors. Cognitive restructuring is intended to remove cognitive barriers to change and foster a willingness to risk new behaviors, but it does not always equip clients with the skills required to perform those new behaviors.

Attempts to reshape thought patterns and perceptions to reflect a different pattern—in contrast to their actual experience—may be perceived as a threat, especially with diverse and involuntary clients. Furthermore, as noted by Vodde and Gallant (2002), simply changing one's story does not ensure a certain outcome, given the presence of very real external factors such as oppression or rejection. Thus, without an acknowledgment of these factors, diverse clients may perceive cognitive restructuring as blaming or just another form of social control

and ideological domination. Of course, some minority group members have mastered a dual frame of reference that is selectively congruent with dominant views and beliefs. Thus, for these clients, cognitive restructuring can be a useful intervention procedure.

Finally, although cognitive theorists attribute most dysfunctional emotional and behavioral patterns to mistaken beliefs, dysfunctional emotions and beliefs are by no means the only causes. Dysfunctions may be produced by numerous biophysical problems, including brain injury, neurological disorders, thyroid imbalance, blood sugar imbalance, circulatory disorders associated with aging, ingestion of toxic substances, malnutrition, and other forms of chemical imbalance. Consequently, these possibilities should be considered before undertaking cognitive restructuring.

SOLUTION-FOCUSED BRIEF TREATMENT MODEL

Solution-focused brief treatment is a postmodern, constructivist approach with a unique focus on resolving client's concerns (De Jong & Berg, 2008; Murray & Murray, 2004). The approach was developed by EP 8 Steve de Shazer and Insoo Kim Berg and their associates at the Brief Family Therapy Center in Milwaukee, Wisconsin (Nichols & Schwartz, 2004; Trepper et al., 2006). Influenced by the views of Milton Erickson, de Shazer and Berg embraced his assumption that people were constrained by the social construction of their problems. Thus, a goal of the approach is to release a client's unconscious resources, thereby shifting from a problem-oriented perspective to one that is more solution based. In this regard, the approach integrates aspects of cognitive restructuring. As the social worker, you have an active role in first "helping clients to question self-defeating constructions" and then assisting them to construct "new and more productive perspectives" (Nichols & Schwartz, 2004, p. 101). Work with clients is facilitated by having them identify and prioritize solutions. Like the task-centered system, the solution-focused approach is based on the premise that change can occur over a brief period of time.

Tenets of the Solution-Focused Brief Treatment Model

The solution-focused approach has emerged over the past 20 years as a strategy for working with adults, minors, and families, including clients who are involuntary. The approach emphasizes identifying solutions rather than resolving problems. A series of interview questions used during the phases of the approach are instrumental in the development of solutions (De Jong & Berg, 1998, 2008). The solution-focused approach draws on people's strengths and capacities, with the intent of empowering them to create solutions. Although clients may begin with a problem statement, a key belief of the approach is that the analysis of a problem does not necessarily predict a client's ability to problem-solve (Corcoran, 2008). Furthermore, solutions and problems are not necessarily connected. Therefore, the thrust of your work with clients encourages solution talk rather than assessing how problems developed or are perpetuated (Koob, 2003; Nichols & Schwartz, 2004).

Oriented toward the future rather than the past, the solution-focused treatment approach asserts that clients have a right to determine their desired outcomes. Change is believed to occur in a relatively brief time period, especially when people are empowered as experts and are encouraged to use their expertise to construct solutions. As the social worker, your role is to listen, absorb information that a person provides, and subsequently guide them toward solutions utilizing the "language of change" (De Jong & Berg, 2002, p. 49). Lee (2003) believes that these principles are motivating factors that strengthen the efficacy of the solution-focused approach in cross-cultural practice.

The manner in which clients are categorized is unique to solution-focused treatment. Three types of individuals are identified: *customers*, *complainants*, and *visitors* (Corcoran, 2008; De Jong & Berg, 2008; Jordan & Franklin, 2003). **Customers** are individuals who willingly make a commitment to change. Therefore, the series of questions and the tasks to be completed are directed to them. Those individuals who identify a concern but do not see themselves as part of the problem or solution are referred to as **complainants**. A person who is willing to be minimally or peripherally involved but is not invested in the change effort is designated a **visitor**. These distinctions allow you to identify where potential clients stand relative to their commitment to change and their ownership of concerns. Distinguishing the various types enables you to focus on the concern and solution identified by the customer. There may be instances, however, when it is advisable to engage the complainant or visitor, if only to ensure that he or she does not interfere with the customer's change efforts.

Theoretical Framework

The solution-focused approach borrows from the social constructivists' perspective that people use language to create their reality (de Shazer & Berg, 1993). In the solution-focused approach, reality is constructed by culture and context, as well as perceptions and life experiences; thus, an absolute truth does not exist (Murray & Murray, 2004). For example, professionals have tended to impose truths about normative functioning or development that may have little relation to the reality of a client's situation (Freud, 1999; Nichols & Schwartz, 2004). Therefore, it is more important for you to understand the way in which a client constructs the meaning of his or her experiences and relationships. The approach also draws from assumptions of CBT—specifically, that cognitions influence a person's language and behavior.

EP 4

Empirical Evidence and Uses of Solution-Focused Strategies

Empirical evidence was at one point considered to be less than robust. There is, however, substantial evidence of the effectiveness of the approach in practice settings and with different populations (Corcoran, 2008; Corcoran & Pillai, 2009; Kim, 2008). Solution-focused brief treatment has been utilized in a variety of settings and with diverse populations, including persons with mental illness and involuntary clients (Berg & Kelly, 2000; Corcoran, 2008; De Jong & Berg, 2001; Greene et al., 2006; Hopson & Kim, 2005; Hsu, 2009; Tohn & Oshlag, 1996; Trepper et al., 2006). Ingersoll-Dayton, Schroepfer, and Pryce (1999) found that a focus on positive attributes of nursing home residents with dementia, rather than on their behavioral problems, changed interactions between the residents and the staff. The efficacy of the approach has also been demonstrated in couples' therapy and premarital counseling (McCollum & Trepper, 2001; Murray & Murray, 2004; Nelson & Kelley, 2001). Research on specific strategies of the model—for example, using exception-based solutions—found strategies of the model were successful in changing domestic violence behavior (Corcoran & Franklin, 1998; Lee, Greene, & Rheinscheld, 1999; McQuaide, 1999).

EP 4

Utilization with Minors

There is increasing evidence on the utilization and effectiveness of solution-focused strategies with minors (Kelly, Kim, & Franklin, 2008). In public school settings, study results show that successful, specific solution-focused therapy explores feelings, develops behavioral goals, and encourages positive behaviors (Corcoran & Stephenson, 2000; Franklin & Streeter, 2004; Kim & Franklin, 2009; Newsome, 2004; Springer, Lynch, & Rubin, 2000; Teall, 2000). Similarly, positive outcomes were reported for improving client social skills and managing school-related behavioral problems (Cook & Kaffenberger, 2003; Gingerich & Eisengard, 2000; Gingerich & Wabeke, 2001). Multiple studies involving adolescents have shown positive results. These studies include high-risk juvenile offenders, students referred for academic and behavioral problems or drug use, and pregnant and parenting teens (Corcoran, 1997, 1998; Froeschle, Smith, & Ricard, 2007; Harris & Franklin, 2003; Kelly, Kim, & Franklin, 2008; Selekman, 2005).

Application of Solution-Focused Approach with Diverse Groups

Critiques of the solution-focused approach point to a lack of attention to the diversity of clients (Corcoran, 2008). Demer, Hemesath, and Russell (1998) praise the approach for its explicit attention to competence and strengths, but they believe that it fails to address gender-related power differences. For example, they might argue that despite a change in the narrative of men and women in abusive relationships, the change lacked sufficient attention to actual power differences. Proponents of the approach, however, assert that the solution-focused approach is responsive to diverse groups because its basic thrust recognizes the expertness of the narrative and language of the client. Further, they assert that because professionals respect and honor the distinct cultural background of clients, the basic tenets of the approach are consistent with competent multicultural practice with clients in social service agencies (De Jong & Berg, 2002; Pichot & Dolan, 2003; Trepper et al., 2006). The results of previously cited research studies with adolescents, the majority of whom were members of diverse groups and also involuntary clients, are promising.

Solution-Focused Procedures and Techniques

EP 8

The stages of solution building as outlined by De Jong and Berg (2003, p. 17) proceed as follows:

- **Description of the problem:** Clients are invited to give an account of their concern or problem. However, as a practitioner, you refrain from eliciting details about antecedents, severity, or the cause of their concern. While listening to clients' description of the problem, you are looking for ways in which you can guide them toward a solution.
- **Developing well-formed goals:** In this stage, your work involves encouraging the client to think about what will be different once the problem no longer exists. This information facilitates the development of a client's goal.
- **Exploring exceptions:** Questions asked of the client in this stage are focused on those times in his or her life when the problem was not an issue or was less of a concern. These questions are followed by questions relating to what could happen that would decrease the concern and make exceptions possible.
- **End-of-session feedback:** The aim of this stage is to compliment and reinforce what a client has already done to solve the problem. Feedback is based on the information that the client provided about goals and exceptions. Also, clients are asked what they should do more or less of in order to accomplish a goal.
- **Evaluating progress:** Monitoring progress is ongoing and is specific to evaluating the client's level of satisfaction with reaching a solution. The scaling question facilitates this process. After a client has rated his or her satisfaction level, you work with him or her to identify what needs to occur so that the problem is resolved. In later sessions, a central question posed to the client is: "What's better?" When the client's primary concern is resolved in a satisfactory manner, contact with you is terminated.

Throughout your work with clients, you make use of a series of questions that follow the phases of helping—specifically, engagement, assessment, goal setting, intervention, and termination. Four questions typically guide the engagement, the formation of goals, and the solution-building process. The various types of interview questions are listed in Table 13-4; they are intended to move clients toward goals and to think of solutions.

Scaling questions, using a scale of 1 to 10, solicit a client's level of willingness and confidence in moving toward developing a solution and are subsequently used to observe progress. These questions may also be instrumental in preventing the client from returning to describing problematic behaviors and in developing

TABLE 13-4 Types of Solution-Focused Questions

Scaling Questions
Coping Questions
Exception Questions
Miracle Questions

specific behavioral indicators along a continuum of change (Corcoran, 2008; Trepper et al., 2006).

Coping questions are intended to highlight and reinforce a client's resources and strengths. For example, how has the client managed the current difficulty, or what resources has he or she used previously when dealing with the issue? Coping questions credit the client's prior efforts to manage a difficulty and reenergize his or her strengths and capacities.

Exception questions are considered the core of the intervention (Corcoran, 2008). Designed to diminish the problem focus, these questions assist a client to describe life when the current difficulty did not exist (Bertolino & O'Hanlon, 2002; De Jong & Berg, 2002, 2008; Shoham, Rorhbaugh, & Patterson, 1995; Trepper et al., 2006). The exception question also advances the client's ability to externalize or separate self from the problem by highlighting strengths and resources (Corcoran, 2008).

Miracle questions draw the client's attention to what would be different once a desired outcome is achieved (Corcoran, 2008; Koob, 2003; Lipchik, 2002).

VIDEO CASE EXAMPLE

In the video "Working with the Cornings," a *coping question* to Irwin and Angela Corning might be: "In view of the chaos that you described in the transitional housing facility, how were you able to find the time to be actively involved with your children?" An example of an *exception question* to the couple might be: "What was it like when you owned your home and lived in a neighborhood of your own choosing?" At one point in the video, Irwin declares, "A man should provide for his family." To separate his sense of self from his job loss and highlight his strengths, you could emphasize that he had done so previously before he lost his job due to circumstances beyond his control. In essence,

you would be helping Irwin to *reframe* and address his negative self-talk.

An example of a *miracle question* to the couple might be: "How do you imagine that you will feel when the family moves from the housing facility to an apartment?"

Typical interview questions that facilitate a client's capacity to think about the future and to identify solutions include the following questions adapted from De Jong and Berg (2008), Lipchik (2002), and de Shazer and Berg (1993):

- How can I help?
- What's better?
- How will you know when your problem is solved?
- What will be different when the problem is solved?
- What signs will indicate to you that you don't have to see me any longer?
- Can you describe what will be different in terms of your behavior, thoughts, or feelings?
- What signs will indicate to you that others involved in this situation are behaving, thinking, or feeling differently?

Questions will vary, of course, depending on the stage of the intervention, as highlighted in the following examples adapted from De Jong and Berg (2008):

- "How can I help?" is typically asked in the engagement session.
- "What do you want to be different?" is intended to facilitate the development of a well-formed goal. Goals sought by the client are framed on the basis of exceptions; specifically, clients are asked about the absence of the problem (the exception), and it is on this basis that the work toward a solution is formed.

For clients who are involuntary, De Jong and Berg (2008, p. 372) recommend beginning the interview with questions that encourage the client's participation by allowing the client to provide his or her view of the situation. Examples are:

- "Whose idea was it that you needed to come here?"
- "What is your understanding of why you are here?"

- "What makes the (pressuring person or mandating authority) believe that you needed to see me?"
- "What is the difference between your point of view and that of the person who required that you come here?"

These questions are followed by, for example, "What could be different?" and, as appropriate, coping or scaling questions and the miracle question.

In subsequent sessions, from one session to the next, interview questions are focused on:

- What is better?
- What could the client continue to do more or less of?

Again, the flow and sequence of the questions will vary, influenced by the content of the conversation with each client. For example, if a client reports that little or no change has occurred, you would inquire about how he or she is coping. If indicated, you might ask a scaling question to gauge the level of stress. For instance, you would have the client rate his or her current level of concern and also what would be different or better at the next level. "Would you rate what will be different in terms of your behavior, thoughts, or feelings when you move to the next level?"

Before and during the termination phase, the focus of your questions would emphasize signs of what can be and is different. Specifically, you would ask, "What signs will indicate to you that others involved in this situation are behaving, thinking, or feeling differently?" *Compliments, bridging, amplification,* and *tasks* are techniques that are integrated into the process of asking questions. **Compliments** provide feedback about a client's efforts and reinforce strengths and successes. **Bridging** is also a part of the feedback, clarifying goals, exceptions, or strengths. **Amplification** questions encourage clients to elaborate on the "What's different?" question. The question may also be used as a link to a compliment or to link tasks to the miracle question. Used in another way, amplification can inform goals and tasks related to the miracle question. Tasks that you suggest can be either *formula* or *predictive* in nature, and they may be completed during or after a session. For example, a postsession formula task for a couple experiencing relationship conflict would be to imagine how their relationship would be if the miracle occurred. In using a prediction task, you would direct the couple to predict the status of their conflict, for better or for worse, tomorrow (de Shazer, 1988). In essence, the predictive task invites the couple to think about what would be different in their relationship.

The following case example demonstrates the procedures and techniques of the solution-focused approach.

In the session with Antonio, you will have noticed that the social worker's use of various solution-focused questions and techniques flowed from the information that Antonio provided. In critiquing the overall session, the social worker pointed out that she moved too quickly to encourage a solution. For example, when she asked, "What's would it take …?," Antonio seemed to become bored or perhaps discouraged. But at the point in which Antonio provided concrete, specific behavioral actions that he could do to make the miracle happen, he and the social worker were able to move toward developing a well-formed goal (De Jong & Berg, 2008).

Strengths and Limitations of the Approach

The solution-focused approach involves practical procedures and questions that can be readily learned and applied in many practice situations. For example, a miracle question can amplify a client's goal and encourage an investment in a future vision. The particular emphasis on clients' strengths and attributes is also a significant contribution in that this focus promotes a positive image of clients and their capacities. The strategic focus on change affirms that gains, albeit small, can occur over a brief period of time.

As the approach has matured, a promising body of empirical evidence has shown its efficacy with diverse populations and with the variety of problems presented by clients (Corcoran, 2008; Corcoran & Pillai, 2009; Kim, 2008; Trepper et al., 2006). Previously discussed studies have also demonstrated the effectiveness of using certain questions with specific populations, especially minors (Corcoran & Stephenson, 2000; Franklin & Streeter, 2004; Springer, Lynch, & Rubin, 2000).

Particular aspects of the procedures of the solution-focused approach have been criticized. Both critics and proponents have questioned whether the approach is, in fact, collaborative—in particular, the assignment of tasks by the practitioner based on the assumption that assigned tasks help the client to focus on solutions (Lipchik, 1997; O'Hanlon, 1996; Wylie, 1990). To the latter point, research conducted with solution-focused family therapists revealed discrepancies between clients'

CASE EXAMPLE

Antonio, age 16, is a resident in a treatment facility for juvenile offenders. Since the previous session with the social worker, he has transitioned from the lockdown area in the facility to a less restrictive area, referred to as the "freedom house." Case notes indicate that Antonio had made significant changes in his aggressive, antisocial behavior, hence the move to another level in the facility. Prior to his admission to the facility, Antonio lived with his mother, stepfather, and siblings. The parents are now divorced. For the most part, he has had a good relationship with his family, especially with his mother. This is the third of eight sessions with the social worker. As Antonio enters the room, he takes a seat on the couch and leans back. In previous meetings, he and the social worker engaged in small talk, but today he is unusually quiet. The session begins with the social worker asking him, "What has happened that's better?" In reply, Antonio informs the social worker that he is moving to freedom house after the session. Afterwards, he becomes silent and slumps down on the couch. The social worker waits for him to speak. After about 5 minutes of silence, he presents a new concern.

Social worker: Wow, Antonio, you are moving to "freedom house." *[reinforce/compliment]*

Antonio: Yep, now I can wear my own clothes, be in a room by myself, and go home on weekends. Soon, I will be able to get out of this place!

Social worker: How did this happen? *[amplify]*

Antonio: Well, I stopped messing up, you know, acting all bad and stuff and fighting. You helped me a lot with my attitude.

Social worker: Thank you. But you did the work on your own and now you are moving to another level. That's great! *[complimenting/bridging]* Now that you've reached this level, what will it take for you to remain in freedom house and eventually go home? *[do more of]*

Antonio: Like I said, I can keep a check on my attitude. Right now, everything here is going okay. But I am not talking to my mother right now!

Social worker: You and your mother usually talk every day. What's different?

Antonio: Well, you see, whenever my mom has a new boyfriend or dude, whatever, me and my brothers and sisters make up a name for him as a joke, and my mother always laughs too, you know. This new dude is Clarence, so I called him Claudius, and she got all bent; told me that I needed to respect him and some s…, whatever!

Social worker: Is this a different reaction from your mother? *[What's different?]*

Antonio: Yeah, like she was really mad. I was surprised.

Social worker: You said that there were times when your mother laughed when you joked about Clarence. What was different about this time? *[exception]*

Antonio: Well, at other times, it was just me and my sister and brothers, no one else was around.

Social worker: What else was different?

Antonio: I didn't change my voice and mimic the way he talks.

Social worker: So you noticed that your mother did not get mad at you when you did not mimic Clarence? *[amplify]* Could you do this more often?

Antonio: Yeah, I guess so.

Social worker: Is it possible that she's more serious with this guy than others? *[amplify, to encourage evaluation of his perception]*

Antonio: Nooo … Man, she told me that she met this dude a month ago and then she brought him here to meet me when she visited. After a month! So she told me to say hello, so I said hello, and then I called him Claudius and she said that I was being disrespectful, and they left. The next day she called wanting us to do something together, and I'm like … whatever.

Social worker: So you have used funny names to deal with the men your mother has been involved with since she and your stepfather divorced. Using funny names and joking around worked for you until now, and your mother also laughed with you. *[coping]*

Antonio: Pretty much. But the way they acted, I think that they really like each other.

Social worker: So, you think that this relationship is different. What will it take for you to talk to your mother? *[encouraging a solution]*

Antonio: Mmm, I don't know, I don't really care that much right now. I kind of need a break from her anyway. I'm feeling super stressed out.

Social worker: You are feeling super stressed, okay. Have there been other times when you felt this way that caused you to want to take a break from your mother? *[exception]*

Antonio: Yeah, when she was late for my birthday party that the staff had for me.

Social worker: What did you do?

Antonio: Nothing, 'cause when she arrived, we were okay.

Social worker: Can I ask you a 1-to-10 question? Would you compare the two situations and rate your level of stress with your mother, then and now? *[scaling question]*

Antonio: Yeeaahh (said sarcastically).

Social worker: That wasn't super convincing Antonio, thanks (laughs). I asked because it's a good way to let me know where you're at now, since, unfortunately, I'm not a mind reader.

Antonio: (Laughs) Alright, go ahead …

Social worker: Where is your stress level about the party and now: If you tell me a 10, this means that your stress is very high, and a 1 means that you are being calm as a cucumber. *[scaling question]*

Antonio: Ahh, like a 3 for the party, because I got over it as soon as she arrived. Now, maybe a 5.

Social worker: Okay, so like right in the middle? You're not super stressed about your mom, but she is still on your mind.

Antonio: Yeah, for now anyway.

Social worker: What would it take for you to feel less stressed about your relationship with your mother? *[bridging, encouraging his ideas about a solution]* (At this point, the social worker noted that Antonio seemed bored with the conversation, so she shifted to a miracle question).

Social worker: Antonio, I sense that you are ready to move on, am I correct?

Antonio: Sort of. I'm not sure what to do. I want to get along with my mother, but just not right now!

Social worker: I understand, because the two of you have worked hard to have a good relationship, but right now things aren't going well. During this stressful time, you have not returned to some of your old acting-out behavior. This is good. Also, your mother, despite her frustration, has continued to visit you. *[complementing, acknowledging client and relationship strengths]*

Social worker: Let's try something different.

Antonio: Like what?

Social worker: I am going to ask you a question. It's called the miracle question.

Antonio: The what (rolling his eyes)?

Social worker: The question is: What if you imagined being less stressed out with your mother? *[moving toward a goal]*

Antonio: Oh, I can answer that! She would dump this new dude, but I don't really have a say in this, do I?

Social worker: That's a good point. Let me ask the question a different way. What if tomorrow, you woke up and were talking to your mother, what would be different?

Antonio: Wow, you're asking a lot, but I'll give it a shot. I think that if I didn't joke about him, she and I would get along better. I could have a conversation with her without her getting all bent.

Social worker: Okay, well, that sounds like good insight, which I know you are pretty good at. Is this something that you would like to work on in our next session? *[goal formulation]*

Antonio: Yeah, okay.

Social worker: Next time, we can work on signs that will tell you that things are better between you and your mother, and whether you are coping better with the situation. As we end the session, let's summarize what we accomplished today.

experiences and the observations made by therapists related to outcomes (Metcalf et al., 1996). Storm (1991) and Lipchik (1997) concluded that the primary focus on solutions was disconcerting for some clients.

Specifically, clients reported that the positive thrust of the approach prevented them from discussing real concerns, and instead they felt persuaded to explore solutions. Further, they perceived the avoidance of talking about a problem to have limited value (Efran & Schenker, 1993). Similarly, the limited attention to behaviors instead of feelings ignores the connection between feelings and cognitions (Lipchik, 2002). These critiques, in many respects, ignore the fact that when clients seek help, they have been socialized to talk about and describe problems in great detail in exchange for services. For this reason, it is important that you explain the basic intent of the process and procedures of solution-focused approach, and perhaps give clients time to talk about their concerns.

Other critics have suggested that the simplicity and practicality of some of the solution-focused questions and techniques may lead in some cases to a "cookbook" that ignores the relational dynamics between the social worker and the client. In particular, Lipchik (1997) emphasizes collaboration between the professional and the client as a key factor that keeps the "axles turning" and also influences the "speed and success of solution construction, which depend on the therapist's ability to stay connected with the client's reality throughout the course of therapy" (p. 329). Critiques related to the client–social worker relationship are not specific to the solution-focused approach. Such discussions about whether a relationship with clients can be fully developed have been ongoing since the emergence of brief treatment approaches.

Professionals who work in environments that are frequently, if not always, problem or pathology focused may experience limited support for using the solution-focused approach (Trotter, 1999). For example, clients who are involved in the legal system are typically required to demonstrate that problems have been resolved or that assessed dangers have been reduced. Of course, the same can be true for any problem-solving approach in these systems, as strengths and empowerment often tend to be ignored. Nonetheless, some professionals suggest that encouraging solutions, rather than focusing on the problem, results in an attempt to remedy a situation that may not be fully understood.

The research literature regarding involuntary clients has shown success in using the solution-focused approach with this often neglected and marginalized client group (Berg & Kelly, 2000; Corcoran, 1997, 1998; De Jong & Berg, 1998, 2001; Tohn & Oshlag, 1996). Work with this population is believed to be enhanced by combining solution-focused procedures with other techniques such as motivational interviewing (De Jong & Berg, 2001; Lewis & Osborn, 2004; Miller & Rollnick, 2002; Tohn & Oshlag, 1996).

The solution-focused approach supports the construction of the client's reality and is considered to be essential to interactions with diverse groups. In this regard, the expertise of the social worker is minimized, as is the opportunity to rely on basic stereotypes and generalizations. On this basis, well-informed goals are more likely to be relevant to the client. Even so, the assignment of tasks by the social worker would appear to be more directive than collaborative.

Aspects of this approach—in particular, the commitment to empowerment and a focus on clients' competence, strengths, and capacities—are values that are consistent with social work's commitment to self-determination. However, having faith in and wishing to support client capacities should not lead us to assume that clients have within them the solutions to all difficulties. In fact, some clients may lack sufficient cognitive skills and resources or face sociopolitical barriers that affect their ability to actually achieve their miracle. As Chapters 8 and 9 discussed, practice need not focus exclusively on either problems and deficits or strengths and resources. Rather, an appraisal of each, including risks and protective factors, is important in developing a realistic view of a situation and the systems involved (McMillen, Morris, & Sherraden, 2004).

CASE MANAGEMENT

Case management entails work that interfaces between the client and his or her environment. As a method, case management has moved to the forefront of direct social work practice in recognition of the fact that people with unmet needs are often unable to negotiate the complex and often uncoordinated health and human services delivery systems. As defined by Rothman, case management "is designed to coordinate the provision of services from multiple sources for the benefit of the individual client" (2002, p. 267).

EP 8

Although the profession of social work does not have an exclusive claim to case management, the method's facilitative and coordinating functions can be traced to charity organization societies. The intent of coordinating services was twofold: to address the multiple problems that individuals and families experienced and to preserve public resources (National Association of Social Workers, 1992). Over time, the momentum for case management has grown, beginning in the 1960s with deinstitutionalization initiatives to relocate and maintain people in their community.

To a large extent, the growth of case management has been driven by federal and state-funded programs, the majority of which mandate the coordination and integration of services. Medicaid, for example, requires case management to help beneficiaries gain access to needed medical, social, educational, and other services.

Most recently, **targeted case management**, an amendment to the Budget Reduction Act of 2005, was added as a provision of Medicaid case management services. Under this provision, certain beneficiary groups, such as clients with an identified chronic health or mental health problem or developmental disabilities and minors in foster care, are considered to be primary recipients of targeted case management services. Also included in the Medicaid provisions are individuals or groups who reside in a particular geographic region and clients whose needs have been identified by the health and human services organization in their respective states (Binder, 2008). In the current human services state and federal reimbursement environment, case management is integral to services in health and mental health settings, long-term care facilities, homeless shelters, schools, adult and juvenile probation situations, and child welfare.

Tenets of Case Management

As a direct practice method, case management is not in and of itself a change-oriented intervention strategy. The method does, however, involve the procedural elements similar to the intervention approaches discussed earlier in this chapter. Referred to in health or institutional settings as *care planning, care coordination,* or *patient-centered care*, case management is viable and often vital to persons in need of comprehensive services.

A critical function of case management is linking individuals or families to a range of services based on their assessed needs. In essence, people are able to gain access to health, mental health, and social welfare service providers that otherwise might be difficult for them to navigate on their own. The coordination of services by the case manager is intended to reduce duplication, fragmentation, and ultimately the frustration of the client. In some settings, evaluating the costs of services is a critical component of case management. The Affordable Care Act (ACA) and the resulting expansion of Medicaid provide greater opportunities in this regard. Specifically, the care coordination and integration goals of the Act are consistent with the overall intent and function of case management (Andrews et al., 2013; Darnell, 2013).

As a problem-solving method, case management is theoretically open (Epstein & Brown, 2002). As such, the method can make use of theories and intervention tactics or techniques that are appropriate to clients' situations. For example, the protocols of the task-centered model have been integrated with case management services in addressing the needs of older persons in long-term care (Naleppa & Reid, 2003), youth in residential treatment centers (Pazaratz, 2006), and in improving school performance (Colvin et al., 2008). Solution-focused techniques have been central to case management services for persons with mental disabilities (Greene et al., 2006; Hagen & Mitchell, 2001; Rapp, 2002) and in the treatment of drug use and abuse (Hall et al., 2002). Intensive case management that made use of cognitive behavioral treatment methods was effective in assisting women to move from welfare to work (Lee, 2005) and in assisting low-income depressed older adults (Arean, Alexopoulos, & Chu, 2008). Similar results were observed when case managers used cognitive behavioral intervention techniques to reduce risky behaviors among HIV-positive drug injectors (Robles et al., 2004). The *Social Work Desk Reference* (Roberts, 2009) contains a number of chapters on case management in regard to specific populations, including immigrant and refugee children and families. With respect to the latter, case management in particular is recommended for immigrant children and families (Fong et al., 2008; Potocky-Tripodi, 2002).

Standards of Case Management Practice

Both the National Association of Social Workers (NASW) (1992) and the Case Management Society of America (CMSA) (2010) have developed practice standards to include the educational and licensing requirements for case managers. In 2008, the two organizations joined together to develop advisory standards for case managers' caseloads.

Core elements of the standards for practice of NASW (1992) and the CMSA (2010) are based on a set of beliefs and professional values considered to be essential to case management practice:

- Utilizing a comprehensive assessment to determine the biopsychosocial functioning and care needs of clients, including their strengths and resources
- A client-centric, shared decision-making collaborative relationship between the client and the case

manager, in which the client and, where appropriate, family members are involved in all phases of the case management process

- Planning and implementing services that address and are responsive to the unique needs of the client or family
- Adhering to professional values and principles, including self-determination, privacy, confidentiality, informed consent, and empowerment
- The primacy of the obligation to the client, which may involve advocacy, mediation, and negotiation to ensure access to services
- Monitoring progress and the evaluation of the achievement of targeted outcomes
- Utilizing the best evidence available to inform case management practice with specific populations, conditions, and needs

In promoting these standards, the aim of both organizations was to establish uniformity in case management functions and practices across disciplines and organizational settings.

The CMSA articulates an explicit standard with regard to cultural competence. Within these standards, there is an expectation that the case manager is informed, utilizes relevant client cultural information, and is sensitive to cultural contexts, including verbal and nonverbal communication styles. An expectation of culturally competent practice is similarly set forth in the NASW practice and policy statements (2007, 2009a) and also in the federal guidelines of the U.S. Department of Health and Human Services, Office of Minority Health (2001).

Empirical Evidence of Case Management

EP 4

Although case management is a widely used practice method, some researchers assert that evidence of its effectiveness cannot be generalized (DePalma, 2001; Major, 2004; Orwin et al., 1994; Simons, Shepherd, & Murro, 2008). There are studies, nevertheless, whose findings support the method's efficacy with clients and families and for specific conditions or problems. In health, substance abuse, and mental health settings, case management significantly improved the outcomes for HIV-infected clients, improved the retention of substance abuse users in treatment, and served as a prevention and intervention strategy for homeless youth, adults, and families (Chinman, Rosenheck, & Lam, 2000; Gardner et al.,

2005; Havens et al., 2007; Helvic & Alexey, 1992; Herman et al., 2007; Kasprow & Rosenheck, 2007; Mercier & Racine, 2005; Susser et al., 1997; Young & Grella, 1998). Clinically oriented studies summarized by Hoagwood and colleagues (2001) show that case management was effective in reducing the number of inpatient psychiatric hospitalizations for young children, the length of stay for youths in substance abuse treatment programs, and the number of placement disruptions for youths in foster care.

Case management is also reported to have advanced the effectiveness of a school-based approach to minimize the impact of a chronic illness on school performance, social skills, and quality of life (Keehner Engelke, Guttu, Warren, & Swanson, 2008). As an innovative approach that combines specific social work practice methods, case management is cited as an effective method in the treatment of substance abuse with individuals lived in rural communities (Hall et al., 2002).

The integration of the strengths perspective was cited by Rapp (1993) as critical to case management practice. Implementing strengths-based case management calls for a focus on people's assets, resilience, and capacity for self-direction (Brun & Rapp, 2001). Several strengths-based case management studies have demonstrated promising results. Positive outcomes were reported for people in substance abuse treatment, including their retention and their relationship with their case managers (Brun & Rapp, 2001; Rapp, 2002; Siegal et al., 1995, 1996, 1998).

Case Management Functions

EP 8

Although case management processes may vary with respect to settings and organizational priorities and goals, there is a consensus that case management always includes the functions or phases summarized in Table 13-5.

Although the phases and tasks of case management are for the most part self-explanatory, for some, elaboration and a brief rationale are indicated. Outreach and case finding, for example, may be particularly important for vulnerable populations such as homeless, frail elderly, and disabled persons, many of whom are likely to be eligible for health and supportive social services but who may be reluctant to seek formal help. Although the phases are procedural in nature, the practice standards are consistent with the ethical principles of social work practice—in particular, the

TABLE 13-5 Case Management Functions

PHASES	TASKS
Access and Outreach	Outreach or case finding identifies people who are likely to need case management services.
Intake and Screening	Preliminary to an assessment, screening is an initial step in determining eligibility for services. A preliminary plan may be developed at this stage.
Multidimensional Assessment	Information is collected about the client's physical, mental, social, and psychological functioning and the physical environment, including strengths and resources. This multidimensional assessment guides the development of the case plan.
Goal Setting	Goals and objectives are developed based on assessed needs, in collaboration with the client. The goal plan and objectives are based on the client's perception of needs and may be structured as long or short term.
Planning Interventions and Linking to Resources	Planning the intervention and linking clients to resources are interdependent functions. Both formal and informal resources and the appropriate service providers are identified. The specific services, as well as the frequency and duration of contact with the service provider, are specified.
Monitoring the Progress and Adequacy of Services	Monitoring progress and the extent to which service providers continue to meet the needs identified in the case plan is a vital and ongoing process. Three sources of information are indicated: regular contact with service providers to determine if services are responsive, monitoring progress toward the stated goals, and the client's observations regarding the level of progress and satisfaction with the providers.
Reassessment at Fixed Intervals	It is particularly important to be sensitive to changes in clients' needs and to adjust or modify the plan as indicated. Reassessments can be formal or informal and are completed at fixed intervals. The information gathered can also determine the level of change since the initial assessment.
Outcome Evaluation/ Termination	Outcome evaluation, in brief situations in which goals have been achieved, leads to termination. In longer-term situations, reassessment and evaluation of outcomes are ongoing.

Source: Case Management Society of America, 2010; Holt, 2002; National Association of Social Workers, 1992; Rothman, 2002.

emphasis on self-determination and collaboration with service recipients as key informants in the assessment and goal-setting process and the implementation of the case plan.

Although the case manager is ultimately responsible for overseeing the implemented plan, the individual or family is also involved in the evaluation of the adequacy of the service. You will also note that monitoring progress and reassessment depend on the goals and time frame of the case plan. For example, long-term plans may require an infinite amount of services, in which case the reassessment intervals are ongoing. In these instances, reassessment is critical, and assessing progress may require the use of pre/post baseline or standardized instruments. In contrast, with brief case management services (e.g., locating housing, securing medical care, attaining the capacity to live independently), satisfactory progress and goal attainment should lead to termination.

Case Managers

Case managers are fundamental to the case management tasks. Whether your title in an organization is case manager, plan coordinator, or care coordinator, you are the human interaction between clients and various systems. You may work as part of a team in some settings; in others, you may be solely responsible for providing case management services. The type of setting will also determine whether your involvement as a case manager is brief or time limited, targeted, ongoing, or open-ended.

In practice, your role and your responsibilities relative to the phases and tasks can be as varied as the settings in which you are employed. For example, with a patient due to be discharged from a hospital, your contact with the client would most likely occur at the assessment phase and proceed forward from this point. Similarly, screening and intake can be abbreviated when a targeted population has been designated in a Purchase of Service (POS) agreement. Conversely, as a case manager in a shelter for homeless youth, outreach or case finding would be a first step. In yet another scenario, you are the authorized professional who is solely responsible for completing the comprehensive assessment, developing an individualized service plan, and negotiating and coordinating services.

The phases of case management and the point of contact notwithstanding, and irrespective of your case manager role, it is important to keep in mind that case management begins with an assessed *need* rather than a *service*. No two clients will have or express needs, problems, or goal preferences in the same way. For this reason, the implemented case or care plan is tailored to the unique needs of the people involved. Specifically, each person or family should be able to expect that his or her case plan is responsive to a specific identified need, rather than the service priorities of an agency. Figure 13-5

Name:	Angela and Irwin Corning			
Children:	Agnes, age 10 Henri, age 8 Katrina, age 18 months			
Case Manager	Ali Smith			
SUMMARY OF ASSESSED NEEDS				
Housing √	Health care √	Debt Counseling √	Tutors √	Employment √
Financial Assistance √	Preschool √			
COORDINATED REFERRALS				
Goals	Providers	Sessions/Duration	Monitoring	Reassessment
Obtain affordable Housing	Clarion Housing Program	1–3 months	Weekly	Every month
Permanent Full-time Employment (Irwin)	Employment Resource Center	8 weeks	Weekly	Monthly
Credit card debt reduction	Consumer Credit Counseling	4 Weeks	On going	1 month
Obtain rental deposit and 1 month's rental	County Temporary Housing Assistance Office	1–2 Sessions	2–3 days	N/A
Family Physicals Childhood Inoculations	Community Health Center	1 year	Ongoing	
Grade Level Assistance (Agnes & Henri)	After School Tutorial Program	1 year	Ongoing	Monthly
Social and Educational Activities	Head Start	1 year	Ongoing	Monthly
Outcome Evaluation & Reassessment:	**Monthly**			

FIG 13-5 Case Management Plan

shows a sample case management plan. The video case involving the Corning family is used to illustrate a case management plan.

VIDEO CASE EXAMPLE

In the video "Working with the Cornings," implementation of Angela and Irwin Corning's case plan required that Ali, the social work case manager, be both facilitative and active. Effectively responding to the goals of the plan required that Ali facilitate the concurrent efforts of public and private organizations and other professional disciplines. In collaboration with Angela and Irwin, decisions were made about the number of sessions with each provider. For example, the couple anticipated that applying for and obtaining approval for temporary rental assistance would require no more than two to three appointments. Conversely, the family's access to and utilization of health care providers were established over a longer period of time. In linking the Corning family with the mix of providers, Ali, as case manager, was actively involved; it would have been insufficient for her to simply identify and refer Angela and Irwin to providers and subsequently expect them to follow through. Making the connections to service is a central task. Afterwards, it was Ali's responsibility to oversee the plan on an ongoing basis.

Clearly, implementing a case plan requires a great deal of up-front work. Essential activities include determining the eligibility criteria of each provider, the provider's ability to meet the plan's goals, and the case review and monitoring process. Once you are satisfied that there is a *fit* between the client's needs and the service provisions of each provider, service agreements are developed with each. Similar to the service agreement or contract with clients (refer to Chapter 12), the case management plan specifies the work to be completed.

As a case manager, the *broker* role is vital to facilitating interagency coordination and cooperation. In this capacity, you need to have a working knowledge of, and an effective relationship with, a range of service providers, including available informal resources. The broker role, specifically connecting to critical resources,

is evident in the response to the array of needs in the Corning family case. As a case manager, helping people gain access to available resources may require *negotiating* with the various service providers. Where indicated, *advocacy* at the systems level may be necessary to ensure that clients have access to resources to which they are entitled. In addition to the broker role, in any one case, mediating between a client and various systems is required. For instance, the role of *mediator* between the school and the Corning parents would have been indicated had the school been reluctant to support the goal of enhancing the performance of the Corning children by providing tutorial assistance. Furthermore, had the school lacked this resource, it would have been important for Ali to explore or develop an alternative resource.

Strengths and Limitations

Case management is a problem-solving practice method that is designed to link the needs of clients to a range of service providers. Based on assessed needs, services are individualized in recognition of the unique capabilities, goals, and circumstances of each service recipient. Although the assessment is integral to case management, it is only one part of the core functions that make up the entire process. Other core tasks involve developing and implementing the case plan and monitoring progress. Hence, it is important that a case manager be skilled in all aspects of the problem-solving process.

The utilization of case management has grown over time, in part as a response to federal funding requirements that emphasize improved access to services and the coordination and integration of the services that clients receive. Utilization of this method can also be attributed to goals of the Affordable Care Act—specifically, greater continuity and coordination in care and a reduction of duplication in service delivery systems. Standards and principles of case management developed by the NASW and the CMSA have contributed to the uniformity of case management functions and the role of the case manager across settings.

As evidenced by the previous discussion which summarized results of research studies, case management, either as a stand-alone practice method or when integrated with another treatment approach, has demonstrated its effectiveness in addressing a range of needs and problems with specific populations. Several of the summarized studies demonstrated the benefit of this integration.

An assumption of case management is that the resources or service providers that a client needs are always available in adequate quality and quantity. In reality, gaps in services exist. In some instances, the service may be available but the provider may be overwhelmed with demands. Herein lies a challenge for the case manager, particularly in an age in which funding for services are reduced.

On the whole, case management is intended to meet the multiple needs of a client in a coordinated, comprehensive manner. The phases and associated tasks allow for the development of a case plan unique to the client. The greater benefit of case management is the fact that services are identified based on assessed needs, which eliminates clients' having to navigate complex helping systems on their own.

TRAUMA-INFORMED CARE: AN OVERVIEW OF CONCEPTS, PRINCIPLES, AND RESOURCES

This final section of Chapter 13 is intended to increase your understanding of trauma and to acquaint you with the core principles and elements of trauma-informed care and services.

Defining Trauma

While trauma is broadly defined, we have chosen the definition articulated by the Substance Abuse Mental Health Services Administration (SAMHSA), which refers to **trauma** as a "single event, multiple events or a set of circumstances that is experienced by an individual as physically and emotionally harmful or threatening and that has lasting adverse effects on the individual's social, emotional and spiritual well-being" (SAMHSA, 2012, p. 2).

There are three main types of trauma. Type I refers to trauma in which the individual retains complete memory of the experience. Type II trauma involves repetitive and prolonged exposure to a traumatic event or experience, resulting in intense psychological and physical reactions. Type III trauma involves multiple pervasive violent events, often taking place in childhood and continuing into adulthood (Solomon & Heide, 1999). Clients who experience Type III trauma often suffer severe, persistent psychological effects requiring different treatment strategies.

Trauma in clients with a diagnosis of serious and persistent mental health problems (Felitti et al., 1998):

- Is interpersonal and intentional in nature: prolonged, repeated, and serious
- Involves emotional, sexual, or physical abuse, serious neglect, witnessing violence, repeated abandonment, or a sudden and traumatic event
- Occurs in childhood or adolescence and may extend over a client's life span

The Effects of Trauma

The effects of trauma over the life span are biological, psychological, social, and spiritual in nature. Their impact is associated with changes in brain neurobiology; social, emotional, and cognitive impairment; and the adoption of health risk behaviors as coping mechanisms (Mueser et al., 1998; Mueser & Taub, 2008).

An individual's response to trauma depends on his or her age and stage of development at the time of the traumatic event, the severity of the traumatic event, the violence and level of force involved, and whether the event occurred multiple times. The nature of the relationship to the person who caused the traumatic event also has consequences for the survivor. A survivor's response can also depend on whether he or she is believed when the trauma experience is disclosed, as well as the help that is received.

Gender differences are observed in the rates, impact, and response to trauma. Adult and adolescent females, for example, experience more trauma in the form of sexual or physical abuse and psychological distress when compared to males (Shin Tang & Freyd, 2012; Tolin & Foa, 2006). Sexual abuse is associated with posttraumatic stress disorder (PTSD) and self-harm, health risks behaviors, and depression and anxiety (Chamberlain & Moore, 2002; Mueser & Taub, 2008; Smith, Chamberlain, & Leve, 2006). The trauma experience of males is more often related to being involved in or a witness to violence, resulting in antisocial behaviors and posttraumatic stress.

Posttraumatic stress disorders were also found to be higher among racial and ethnic minorities, and these groups also had a higher lifetime risk of developing PTSD. Participants in the study reported a prevalence of high exposure to or the experience of trauma; however, they were less likely to seek or receive treatment for PTSD (Roberts et al., 2011).

The Adverse Childhood Exposure (ACE) study advanced our knowledge of the longevity of exposure or the experience of trauma by identifying adverse childhood experiences and exposure (Felitti et al., 1998). Results of this study confirmed that 60% of

Americans ages 18 to 50 had experienced at least one type of trauma, and more that 20% had experienced three or more traumatic events in their lifetime. This study was the first and largest investigation that linked the physical effects of trauma and identified the association between childhood maltreatment and household dysfunction and later-life health and well-being. Certain experiences were linked to major risks factors— for example, smoking, suicide attempts, alcoholism, substance use and abuse, including illicit drug use, and chronic disease.

The psychological and emotional effects of trauma are spiritual and relational in nature, resulting in behavioral and relationship problems (Breslau et al., 2004; Thompson & Massat, 2005). Behavioral effects include reactions and symptoms that persist into adulthood, including a decreased ability to concentrate, disturbed sleep patterns, and disruptive behavior when an individual is in a situation that reminds him or her of the traumatic experience.

Childhood trauma is associated with changes in brain neurobiology; social, emotional, and cognitive impairment; and the adoption of health risk behaviors as a coping mechanism (National Childhood Trauma Network, 2004; Terr, 1991). In the aftermath of trauma exposure or experience, children and youth exhibit posttraumatic stress symptoms and behaviors, behavioral disorders, and a greater risk of engaging in antisocial and risky behaviors (Becker & McClosky, 2002; Chamberlain & Moore, 2002; Cicchetti & Rogosch, 2002; D'Andrea et al., 2012; Dube et al., 2001; Herrera & McClosky, 2001; Hillis et al., 2004; Kessler & Walters, 1998; Terr, 1991).

Prevalence of Trauma: What Is Known

Until recently, trauma and trauma symptoms and reactions were thought to be confined to combat exposure and the experience of a large-scale disaster (Bowman & Chu, 2000; Kessler et al., 1995). Counter to the earlier assumptions about the experience or exposure to trauma in specific populations, trauma literature and research studies have documented the high incidence and prevalence of trauma in the general population, including among youth and young adults (Dube et al., 2001; Finkelhor et al., 2009; Kessler et al., 1995; Kessler & Walters, 1998; Kim & Cicchetti, 2004). Trauma histories were observed among women in maternity care (Seng et al., 2009) and among urban and immigrant youth and minority child populations (Breslau et al., 2004; de Arellano et al., 2008; Jaycox et al., 2002). Trauma

history has also been documented among females and males in prison populations (Grella, Lovinger, & Warda, 2013; Haugebrook et al., 2010; Maschi, Violn, & Morgen, 2013; Zgoba et al., 2012).

Trauma experience among children and youth has led to involvement in the juvenile justice system and residential treatment facilities (Brosky & Lolly, 2004; Ford & Blaustein, 2013; Ford, Chapman, & Cruise, 2012; Hummer, Robst, Dollard, & Armstrong, 2010; Kerig et al., 2009; Simpkins & Katz, 2004) and adolescent pregnancy (Hillis et al., 2004). Trauma or a trauma-causing event are linked to lower school achievement and to behavioral and relationship problems (Breslau et al., 2004; Dube et al., 2001; Keller-Dupree, 2013; Thompson & Massat, 2005).

Parental trauma or exposure to a trauma-causing event or condition has resulted in involvement with child protective services (Blakey & Hatcher, 2013; Marcenko, Lynn, & Courtney, 2011). While homelessness is a traumatic circumstance in and of itself, a history of trauma is evident among home less clients and families (Hooper, Bassuk, & Olivet, 2010).

Trauma-Informed Care

Trauma-informed care refers to a person-centered and strengths-based service delivery approach in recognition of the prevalence of trauma among clients across settings and human services systems. **EP 7 and 8**
Trauma-informed care understands and is responsive to the impact of trauma and emphasizes the "physical, psychological and emotional safety of providers and survivors, and creates opportunities to rebuild a sense of control and empowerment" in their lives (Hooper, Bassuk, & Olivet, 2010, p. 82). A trauma-informed system of care requires a significant shift in an organization's culture, structure, programs, policies, and practices. Particular attention is paid to practices that inadvertently cause distress for the trauma survivor. At the most basic level, helping should not cause harm.

In general, a **trauma-informed approach** refers to the delivery of services and includes an understanding and awareness of the impact and consequences of trauma exposure and of a history across settings and populations. Trauma is viewed through an ecological and cultural lens—specifically, the importance of context and the client perception and processing of traumatic events. Essential organizational and professional characteristics recognized by SAMHSA (2012, p. 4) as integral to a trauma-informed approach and trauma-informed care are that the treatment:

- Realizes the prevalence of trauma and understands the potential for recovery
- Recognizes the signs and symptoms of trauma in clients and how trauma affects all clients involved with the service delivery system, including its own workforce
- Responds by integrating the knowledge about trauma into practice, policies, and procedures
- Actively avoids practice and polices that can result in retraumatization

It is the perspective of SAMHSA that in working with trauma survivors, it is critical to promote the linkage to recovery and resilience for those clients and families impacted by trauma. Consistent with SAMHSA's definition of recovery, services and supports that are trauma-informed build on the best evidence available and consumer and family engagement, empowerment, and collaboration. Trauma-specific interventions support and recognize:

- The survivors' need to be respected, informed, connected, and hopeful regarding their own recovery
- The interrelation between trauma and symptoms of trauma such as substance abuse, eating disorders, depression, and anxiety
- The need to work in a collaborative way with survivors, family and friends of the survivor, and other human services agencies in a manner that will empower survivors and consumers

Six Key Principles of a Trauma-Informed Approach and Trauma-Informed Care

Although a trauma-informed approach can be initiated and implemented in a range of service delivery systems, SAMHSA (2014) has established six principles rather than a set of prescriptive practices and procedures for trauma-informed care because settings, client populations, and practices can vary. SAMHSA's perspective on a trauma-informed approach reflects adherence to the following key principles (SAMHSA, 2012):

- **Safety:** Trauma survivors and the staff involved in service delivery feel emotional, physical, and psychological safety; and interpersonal interactions promote a sense of safety.

- **Trustworthiness and transparency:** Organizational decisions and operations are clear to clients receiving services, the goal of which is to build and maintain trust among all involved. Trust and transparency are maximized through task clarity, consistency, and interpersonal boundaries.
- **Peer support and mutual help:** These are considered integral to the organizational and service delivery approach and are understood as vehicles for building trust, establishing safety, and empowerment.
- **Collaboration and mutuality:** There is a true partnership and leveling of power differences between staff and clients and among direct care staff and administration, as well as a recognition that healing happens in relationships and in the meaningful sharing of power and decision making rather than through exclusive reliance on the professional's specific skills or services.
- **Empowerment, voice, and choice:** Throughout the organization and among clients, resilience and strengths are recognized, built upon, and validated as new skills are developed. The organization allows clients, staff, and family members to experience choice and recognizes that every person's experience is unique and requires an individualized approach. There is a belief in resilience and in the ability of individuals, organizations, and communities to heal and promote recovery from trauma, building on what clients, staff, and communities have to offer rather than responding to perceived deficits.
- **Cultural, historical, and gender issues:** Cultural, historical, and gender issues are addressed in a manner that actively moves past cultural stereotypes and biases, offers gender-responsive services, leverages the healing value to traditional cultural connections, and recognizes and addresses historical trauma.

SAMHSA's principles of a trauma-informed approach and care are intended to specifically address the consequences of trauma in the client and to promote healing.

The Need for a Trauma-Informed Service Approach

The recognition and collective understanding of the prevalence and effects of trauma have resulted in a paradigm shift—in particular, the need for social services and mental behavioral and mental health providers and professionals to be trauma informed. Although trauma is thought to be subjective and defined by the individual, sensitivity to the potential of a trauma history is encouraged regardless of the client's presenting problem (Huckshorn & Lebel, 2013). Even so, the treatment approach should be person centered; specifically, it cannot be assumed that a one-size-fits-all approach is appropriate.

In support of the development of trauma-informed service delivery across settings and systems, the National Center for Trauma-Informed Care (NCTIC) was created in 2005 and funded by SAMHSA. The NCTIC provides education, outreach, consultation, resources, and technical assistance to assist organizations to address and respond to the needs of clients with trauma histories (NCTIC/SAMHSA, 2014).

Implementing a trauma-informed approach consistent with the tenets of trauma-informed care and SAMHSA's principles is a conscious, intentional, and ongoing process. In the best circumstance of helping, trauma survivors can be problematic, but this is more so in settings that are non-trauma-informed—specifically, in instances in which the treatment provided does not address trauma nor respond adequately to the needs of trauma survivors.

Research studies point to the need for an approach beyond social services and mental health settings to include health, educational systems, and child welfare and juvenile systems (Ford & Blaustein, 2012; Keller-Dupree, 2013; Ko et al., 2008). Recommendations for and examples of implementing trauma-informed care include Ford and Blaustein (2012), Harris and Fallot (2001), Hooper, Bassuk, and Olivet (2010), and Hummer et al. (2010).

Evidence of the Approach

EP 4 and 8

Trauma-informed care is considered evidence-based practice particularly for clients who have histories of trauma. This is the gold standard of care. Policies and practice recognize and acknowledge the histories that shape clients lives. Trauma histories are recognized as part of the treatment process rather than denying they exist. In the absence of trauma-informed policies and practices, survivors of trauma are unlikely to heal and recover. In essence, the trauma-informed approach can:

- Validate a part of people and a history that often has been dismissed or denied

- Create a safe place where people come for help, restoration, and motivation to continue
- Increase the effectiveness of services designed to empower clients in transition periods
- Provide opportunity to plant seeds of hope, demonstrate that someone in this world cares about them, and show clients that they matter

At the very least, the services provided should not harm clients, and at best should leave survivors better off than when they first sought help.

Evidence-based studies that demonstrate the effectiveness of trauma-informed care continue to evolve. Presently, CBT and trauma-focused CBT (T-F-CBT) are the most widely used interventions and are regarded as the most promising (Beehler, Birman, & Campbell, 2012; Black et al., 2012; Brown, Pearlman, & Goodman, 2004; Dorsey, Briggs, & Woods, 2011; Getz, 2012; Hinton et al., 2011; Stambaugh et al., 2007) and include cultural adaptations (Bernal, 2006; Cohen et al., 2000; Jaycox et al., 2002; Katoaka et al., 2003; Lau, 2006).

Implications for Social Work Practice

In reality, social workers have always worked with vulnerable clients, many of whom have experienced trauma and who have conditions that meet criteria in the *Diagnostic and Statistical Manual for Mental Disorders* (2013). The growing knowledge about trauma effects leads the profession toward practice that is consistent with trauma-informed care despite the fact that the work setting may not be trauma informed. The consequences of trauma are complex, and as such, traditional treatment plans and goals are limited in their capacity to respond to the needs of trauma survivors. Trauma-informed practice is ideally individualized and flexible and validates the survivor's solution for recovery and healing.

The trauma assessment may be incorporated with the biopsychosocial as discussed in Chapters 8 and 9. Exploring whether a current difficulty is related to a traumatic event is an important part of the assessment process. For example, certain behaviors that are considered to be maladaptive may in fact be a means of coping. Various trauma screening tools exist that can confirm the presence of and extent of trauma. However, professionals are encouraged to avoid hiding behind a mound of papers in order to determine the problem rather than listening to the client and the meaning that their difficulties has for them.

In some instances, persons with a trauma history may be reluctant to disclose because of psychological barriers—for example, embarrassment, shame, or fear—focusing instead on more pressing needs or problems. The foundation of a trauma-informed assessment is "What happened to you?" rather than "What is wrong with you?" The former is facilitative and nonjudgmental, establishes rapport, and fosters trust by creating a safe environment.

Historically, social workers have worked in a range of settings, organizations, and systems, while engaging in practice that adheres to the values and principles of the profession. Concepts and principles associated with trauma-informed care—for example, client participation, empowerment, recognition and utilization of strengths, resilience, the capacity for change and growth, and respecting the dignity and worth of clients—are in harmony with the ethics and value base of the profession. For this reason, trauma-informed care is not a radical shift for social work practice.

Trauma-Informed Resources

The following is a brief list of trauma-informed resources:

- SAMHSA provides a range of resources that can be ordered or downloaded free of charge at www.samhsa.hhs.gov.
- Check out the following treatment improvement protocols:

  - *Trauma-Informed Care in Behavioral Health Services.* (TIP Series 57). HHS Publication No. (SMA) 13-4801. Rockville, MD: Substance Abuse and Mental Health Services Administration, 2014.
  - *Improving Cultural Competence.* (TIP Series 59). HHS Publication No. (SMA) 14-4845. Rockville, MD: Substance Abuse and Mental Health Services Administration, 2014.

- The National Center for Trauma Informed Care (NCTIC) offers trauma-informed care and alternatives to seclusion and restraint at www.samhas.gov/nctic.
- National Child Traumatic Stress Network (NCTSN): www.nctsn.com
- National Native Children's Trauma Center: http//iers.umt.edu/National_Native_ Children-Trauma Center

- Culturally Sensitive Trauma-Informed Care Health Care Toolbox: www.healthcaretoolbox.org/index.php/cultural-considerations
- Child Welfare Information Gateway: www.child-trauma.com

SUMMARY

This chapter discussed four intervention approaches, processes and procedures of cognitive restructuring, and case management practice. Examples of questions that may be used in the selection of an intervention strategy were presented, along with factors to be considered in the process, such as evaluating the extent to which an approach has demonstrated its effectiveness, with whom, under what circumstances, and with what types of problems. The theoretical framework and empirical support for each of the approaches was summarized, including its use with diverse populations, age groups, and settings. The final section of the chapter introduced the concepts and principles of trauma-informed care and their implications for social work practice.

COMPETENCY NOTES

EP 1 Demonstrate Ethical and Professional Behavior
- Make ethical decisions by applying the standards of the NASW Code of Ethics, relevant laws and regulation, models for ethical decision making, ethical conduct of research, and additional codes of ethics as appropriate to context.

  Selecting and implementing an intervention strategy, social workers observe the principles, values and ethics of the profession.
  In selecting a strategy, social workers are obligated to have the knowledge and skills necessary to implement the strategy.

EP 2 Engage Diversity and Difference in Practice
- Apply and communicate understanding of the importance of diversity and differences in shaping life experiences in practice at the micro, mezzo, and macro levels.

  Selecting an intervention strategy understand and are guided by the context of people's lives, differences, perceptions, experiences, abilities, and the client's cultural frame of reference.

Social workers understand and appraise difference and determine if a particular strategy has certain limitations with certain groups, and whether the approach should be modified so that it fits with the needs, values, and beliefs of a client.

People interact and react within the context of their environment. The social environment shapes their perceptions, cognitions, experiences, and sense of self.

EP 4   Engage in Practice-Informed Research and Research-Informed Practice

- Use and translate research evidence to inform and improve practice, policy, and service delivery.

Selecting and planning an intervention strategy requires that social workers have knowledge of the strategy utilization and evidence of effectiveness with the problems and goals of different clients and in different settings. Understanding the conceptual and theoretical framework upon which an intervention is based is essential to the effective implementation of the strategy and ethical practice.

EP 7   Assess Individuals, Families, Groups, Organizations, and Communities

- Collect, organize, critically analyze, and interpret information from clients and constituencies.

Selecting and intervention strategy is guided by questions that clarify whether the strategy is appropriate to the presenting problem, meets the needs of diverse groups and is consistent with professional ethics.

- Apply knowledge of human behavior and the social environment, person-in-environment, and other multidisciplinary theoretical frameworks in the analysis of assessment data for clients and constituencies.

Understand differences and use this knowledge to guide practice competence with in planning interventions with diverse clients.

- Select appropriate intervention strategies based on the assessment, research

knowledge, and values and preferences of clients and constituencies.

Selecting an intervention strategy requires an understanding of the basic tenets of the strategy and its effectiveness to ensure that the strategy is capable of resolving the client's problem and achieves a desire goal.

Social worker's also evaluate also evaluate whether they have the requisite knowledge and skills to successfully implement the strategy.

EP 8   Intervene with Individuals, Families, Groups, Organizations, and Communities

- Implement interventions to achieve practice goals and enhance capacities of clients and constituencies.

Intervention approaches have procedures and techniques that are implemented in a systematic manners to enhance client's capacity, and to assist them to resolve problems and achieve goals.

An approach should have demonstrated evidence of effectiveness with a client's problem.

SKILL DEVELOPMENT EXERCISES

in Planning and Implementing Change-Oriented Strategies

1. Using the Corning case, select the task-centered and solution-focused approach as a change-oriented strategy and assess the merits of each approach in this case. In what way could you combine aspects of both approaches in this case?
2. A mother who has been sanctioned for failing to comply with the welfare-to-work rule tells you that her caseworker is "out to get her." What additional information or factors would you consider to determine how to respond to the client's statement?
3. You are the social worker for a minor in a residential treatment program. How would you determine if the minor is able to give consent for his treatment plan?
4. Review Lipchik's (2002) solution-focused questions and answer the questions based on a current concern that you have. Also, indicate how you would use scaling, coping, exceptions, and the miracle question.

5. Using the same situation that you have identified, develop a goal and general and specific tasks in the task-centered approach. Indicate how you would measure goal attainment.

6. Choose one of the cognitive distortion statements that you may have used. What strategies would you use to modify your thinking?

7. Review what you have learned about trauma and the principles of trauma-informed care. Reflect on how you might change the way in which you complete an assessment of clients.

NOTE

1. For additional information on brief treatment models, see Corwin (2002), Roberts and Greene (2002), and Walsh (2006, 2010).

Developing Resources, Advocacy, and Organizing as Intervention Strategies

Chapter Overview

Chapter 14 transitions from direct practice assessment and intervention to macro-level intervention strategies. In this chapter, you will become familiar with assessing macro-level problems and utilizing change efforts directed toward systems that benefit individuals as members of groups and communities. The chapter concludes with a discussion of general guidelines for evaluating outcomes.

As a result of reading this chapter, you will acquire knowledge that will enable you to:

- Understand the micro and macro practice relationship.
- Become familiar with macro intervention strategies.
- Use assessment questions and other available sources of data to guide intervention decisions.
- Understand the role of a change agent.
- Apply social work ethical principles and standards.
- Evaluate macro practice activities.

EPAS Competencies in Chapter 14

This chapter provides information that you will need to meet the following practice competencies:

- Competency 1: Demonstrate Ethical and Professional Behavior
- Competency 2: Engage Diversity and Difference in Practice
- Competency 3: Advance Human Rights and Social, Economic, and Environmental Justice
- Competency 4: Engage in Practice-Informed Research and Research-Informed Practice
- Competency 5: Engage in Policy Practice
- Competency 7: Assess Individuals, Families, Groups, Organizations, and Communities
- Competency 8: Intervene with Individuals, Families, Groups, Organizations, and Communities
- Competency 9: Evaluate Practice with Individuals, Families, Groups, Organizations, and Communities

SOCIAL WORK'S COMMITMENT

Brueggemann (2006) and Schneider and Lester (2001) link macro practice to the historical commitment of the social work profession to the ideal of improving the human condition through social reform, social justice, and equality. These longstanding ideals are practice principles reflected in the National Association of Social Workers (NASW) Code of Ethics and the Council of Social Work Education (CSWE) Educational Policy Accreditation Standards (EPAS) for the professional educational preparation of social workers.

Global standards that frame the core purpose of international social work also emphasize social action, political action, and advocacy "to facilitate the inclusion of marginalized, socially excluded, dispossessed, and vulnerable at-risk groups of people" (Global Standards for Social Work Education and Training, 2004, p. 3). Fundamental among the principles of international social work are respect for diverse beliefs, traditions, and cultures as well as regard for human rights and social justice. Similarly, these principles are articulated in the NASW Standards for Cultural Competence in Social Work Practice (NASW, 2001).

The ethical standards and educational policy statements of the national professional organizations regarding economic and social justice and equality are hardly the exclusive domains of social work as a profession. Other professionals and organizations that act as change agents and address some or all of the same concerns include clergy, physicians, environmentalists, political activists, community planners, citizens and civic groups, and faith communities. However, social work—unlike any other profession—accepted as its mandate a focus on the person-in-the-environment, social justice, oppression, and equality as organizing principles and values. In addition, the principles of social work dictate intolerance for systems that create and maintain social conditions that result in personal problems.

Urging the profession to go further in its social justice agenda, Hodge (2007) points to the need for the profession to advocate for a Universal Declaration of Human Rights, in particular for religious freedom, and to work toward ending religious persecution on a national and global level. Like Hodge, McKinnon (2008) advocates for expanding justice to include the ecological focus of the profession, specifically the challenges of the physical environment and its impact on people.

DEFINING MACRO PRACTICE

By definition, **macro practice** involves professionally guided interventions in which the targets are social problems and conditions. As summarized by Brueggemann (2006), macro social work is the "practice of helping people solve social problems and make social change at the community, organizational, societal and global levels" (p. 7). A distinctive feature of macro-level interventions is the belief that seeing the whole picture and intervening can ultimately change and improve the lives of people (Burghardt, 2011; Parsons, Jorgensen, & Hernandez, 1988, 1994; Long, Tice, & Morrison, 2006). In the course of examining the whole picture, you are able to determine the impact of an issue on human behavior (Alexander, 2010; McKinnon, 2008; Saleebey, 2004).

The profession's emphasis on the relationship between people and their environment can be traced to the belief system that guided the work of the **settlement house movement**. Settlement house workers promoted the person and environment transaction in which improving social conditions and changing the social and economic environment through advocacy, community organizing, empowerment, and social action would ultimately improve the functioning of the individual and the community. Reminiscent of this movement, Breton (2006) asserts "there is a dialectical relationship between social change and personal change" (p. 34).

LINKING MICRO AND MACRO PRACTICE

The micro-to-macro continuum is a natural extension of helping individual clients deal with the social problems, conditions, or policies that affect their lives. Understanding this continuum is consistent with the social justice agenda of the profession and helps you to be aware of issues beyond the individual, family, or group (Hasenfeld & Garrow, 2012; Rothman & Mizrahi, 2014). It is not unusual for you as a direct service practitioner to have observed patterns in the frequency of certain problems and conditions throughout your caseload. Your work with individuals and families places you in an opportune position to make the connection between micro concerns that may require macro strategies to remedy. There may be days in which you feel that with each individual client or family, you are working at the edge of a much larger problem, one person or one family at a time. You may, however, question

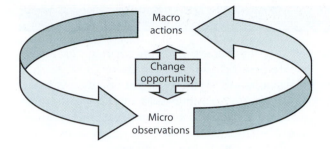

FIG 14-1 Linking Micro and Macro Practice

your ability to act, given your role in your organization. Nonetheless, your observations of the experience of individual clients, as illustrated in Figure 14-1, can be the basis of the critical linkage between micro and macro practice.

Figure 14-1 illustrates how micro-level observations can inform social workers of common problems and conditions that are experienced by individuals, groups, and communities. For example, let's say that you have observed the frequency of a certain presenting problem among the clients with whom you have regular contact. As an initial inquiry as to whether your observation is in fact valid or emblematic of a large system change opportunity, you might ask yourself: *To what extent are the individual problems pervasive among the larger group experience to which the individual belongs?* The question provides you with a snapshot of the whole picture and information that would inform a macro-level assessment of a problem (Breton, 2006; Burghardt, 2011; White & Epston, 1990). In essence, the question bridges micro and macro practice by moving the focus beyond an individual's problem. To further inform your inquiry, you would assess and document the individual and external factors associated with the problem—for example, substantive social and economic conditions that create, perpetuate, and sustain individual client problems (Parson, Jorgenson, & Hernandez, 1994; Vodde & Gallant, 2002; White & Epston, 1990).

Because of the dual, interlocking connection between the public and the private, there are times when a two-prong approach (specifically a combination of micro and macro) is required (Austin, Coombs, & Barr, 2005; Long, Tice, & Morrison, 2006; Vodde & Gallant, 2002). White and Epston (1990) emphasize broad societal concerns and social conditions that create and sustain problems experienced by individuals; according to these authors, the social worker has a duty to assist clients to externalize problems and

conditions beyond the individual level. This linkage is illustrated in the case example on page 426.

In addressing the macro-level issues related to access to employment opportunities, the health and human services agency staff achieved the county's goal—specifically, the payment of child support by fathers. In effect, the actions of the staff bridged micro and macro practice strategies by addressing the external social conditions that influenced individual problems (Vodde & Gallant, 2002; White & Epston, 1990; Parsons, Jorgenson, & Hernandez, 1994). The presentation to the county board provided the board with context to the problem. Context provides details about individual problems and examines issues and problems that are common to groups. A systems-level solution reframes the problem as a group problem rather than an individual one.

As you read this chapter, you will appreciate that knowledge and skills you learned in earlier chapters are also compatible with macro practice. For example, you will use both structural and interpersonal skills in macro practice as in micro practice. Structural skills include assessing, documenting, developing and planning measurable strategic goals, and monitoring and evaluating outcomes. On an interpersonal level, you will use oral and written communication skills and facilitative and relationship-building skills such as empathy, authenticity, genuineness, and self-awareness.

MACRO PRACTICE INTERVENTION STRATEGIES

Change at the macro level is often focused on collective, large-scale interventions (Burghardt, 2011; Netting, Kettner, McMurtry, & Thomas, 2012). Many different interventions are used to alter conditions, improve environments, and respond EP 8 to needs found within organizations, groups, or communities. A full discussion of the various macro-level strategies is beyond the scope of this text. Instead, we will use case examples and focus our discussion on the following selected general strategies:

- Developing and mobilizing resources
- Engaging in advocacy and social action
- Engaging in community organization

Developing resources and advocacy, for example, were illustrated in the example of the county board's response to fathers' nonpayment of child support.

CASE EXAMPLE

During a weekly review of cases, health and human services agency staff located in a small semirural community recognized that a majority of their cases involved fathers who failed to pay child support. This failure, in turn, negatively impacted families who were struggling with limited financial resources. In addition, nonpayment of child support was frequently reported as a source of relationship tension between the custodial and noncustodial parents. Members of the county board were adamant about pursuing the fathers for payment of their debts because the families affected by this problem were a financial drain on county resources.

Focus groups involving fathers were convened to explore the issues related to the nonpayment of child support. Dominant themes that emerged from the group discussion included unemployment or underemployment and the lack of low-skill-level employment opportunities in the county. Limited regional transportation to and from the county to jobs in the metro area posed additional employment challenges. County staff used the results from the focus group sessions to develop and mobilize resources for a job skills program to help the fathers refresh existing or gain new employable skills. Staff appeals and engaging the community at large resulted in community members' providing transportation and donating cars that allowed the fathers to pursue jobs outside of the county.

On a policy level, staff made presentations to the county board and the courts in an effort to help the members understand the issues faced by the nonpaying fathers. Ultimately, staff persuaded the county board and the courts to support a less punitive approach toward the fathers—for example, postponing jail sentences related to failure to pay child support. Undoubtedly, some fathers were shirking their parental responsibility. Nevertheless, by making an appeal to the county board and by taking action that empowered those fathers who had the desire but not the means to provide for their children, staff reframed the problem and the problem arena, influenced public policy, and developed resources.

This example further demonstrated that staff can take the lead as change agents in organizations to promote effective service responses to individual problems at the systems level. When the staff engaged in the macro change effort, the intervention approach was systematic and involved three overlapping focal points: the problem, the population, and the "change arena" as conceptualized by Netting et al. (2004). The ultimate beneficiaries of the effort were the individual families involved as well as the community at large.

Theories and Perspectives

Before discussing each strategy, we address the theories and perspective that inform macro-level change.

- **Systems theory** is relevant to working with groups and communities because such entities are subsystems that interact with and are influenced by larger systems in the social environment. An important consideration is the extent to which these subsystems are marginalized or have a relationship that promotes and sustains growth and development. For example, do groups and communities have equitable access to resources and have power over the decisions that affect their functioning?

- **Conflict theory** is compatible with systems theory, in particular because tensions between subsystems and larger systems may revolve around issues of power, either the lack thereof or attempts by marginalized subsystems to gain power.

- **Human agency theory** refers to the capacity of groups and communities to be active participants in collective action to increase their power to address inequality and injustice. Perspectives include empowerment, strengths, and social justice, each of which is amplified in human agency theory.

- **Social justice**, as articulated in the Council of Social Work Educational Policy Standards, includes economic and social justice. Social justice is broadly understood to include equality and fairness in access to and distribution of resources (distributive justice) and access to opportunity. Procedural justice relates to people's participation in the decisions that influence their lives—for example, decisions about the distribution of resources.

Empowerment and Strengths

EP 2

Empowerment and strengths perspectives are critical to any change effort. All people at various times in their lives experience limited power. However, social work constituents are more likely to involve groups and entire communities who lack power because of their status in the larger social environment. Indeed, the powerless are more likely to have government agencies and public policies exert significant authority in their lives. The **empowerment perspective** assumes that power and powerlessness are inextricably linked to the experience of inequality. Understanding human agency theory at the individual and collective levels is essential to empowerment in that both recognize the shared competence of groups or communities to act to prevent problems and to interact with the systems in the social environment to change their situation (Burghardt, 2013; Gutierrez, GlenMaye, & Delois, 1995; Long, Tice, & Morrison, 2006; Weil, 1996).

When working with certain vulnerable groups who may have a limited sense of individual and group efficacy, you may tend to think of empowerment as giving them power. Even in these circumstances, empowerment means that you recognize, tap into, and mobilize people's power by working in collaboration with them to develop their awareness of their collective ability to alter or improve their situation (Burkhardt, 2013; Carter, 2000; White & Epston, 1990). In essence, empowerment is a process in which your work includes mobilizing the efforts of those affected to improve or change their situations (Cowger & Snively, 2002; Gutierrez, 2001; Gutierrez & Ortega, 1991). If you are involved in creating more favorable conditions for a group or community—for example, in developing resources or advocacy—you should be careful that your actions are not disempowering to those you are attempting to help. To this end, it is vital that you observe and respect their values and beliefs and that your actions are consistent with the ethical principles of the profession. In your entry into a community or group, valuing the community or group's definitions of problems is vital to establishing a collaborative problem-solving relationship (Burhardt, 2013; Gutierrez, 1994; Gutierrez & Lewis, 1999; Long, Tice, & Morrison, 2006; Saleebey, 2004; Van Voorhis & Hostetter, 2006).

Assessing and utilizing the collective **strengths** and engaging participants in a change effort essentially avoids a trickle down approach in which you as a professional identify a concern and the solution. As social workers, we respond to the needs and interests identified by groups or communities in ways that build on their strengths and that will assist them to realize their hopes, dreams, and aspirations. Recognizing strengths at the macro level means seeing people as resourceful and resilient, being respectful of their stories, and working in collaboration with them to achieve a range of human and community capital goals based on their viewpoints.

Combined strengths and empowerment are critical to communities and groups developing, owning, and governing their self-efficacy. In this way, the shape and influence of the change effort are directed by active community leadership (Van Voorhis & Hostetter, 2006; Weil, 1996).

Selecting a Strategy

EP 7

The decision about which strategy to use depends on the contextual nature and assessment of the target concern and the related goal. In some instances, a particular strategy may be sufficient to achieve a desired outcome. At other times, however, a particular strategy—for example, advocacy as a means to address an issue—may lead to another strategy, such as organizing a group or community in the change effort, as indicated in the following case example.

General Assessment Questions

EP 7

Assessment is an ongoing process, and each of the strategies discussed consists of specific questions to help you obtain more precise information. However, as you prepare to further your understanding of a concern and subsequently engage in a change effort, the following general assessment questions and discussion can guide your inquiry.

What Is the Nature of the Condition or Problem for Change?

Identifying, assessing, and documenting long-term trends, the nature and extent of the problem or condition, and the ways in which a group or community is affected is an essential first step. Although you may have observed the prevalence of a problem or condition among your clients, it is important to gather information that clarifies who is affected, in what way, the resulting consequences, and whether and how the issues have been addressed. Gathering information

CASE EXAMPLE

A social worker at a senior center attempted to advocate on behalf of older clients regarding a decision by a metropolitan transit authority to relocate a bus stop to an isolated and less accessible area. The change caused undue hardship for the largely poor, elderly, and minority residents, the majority of whom were dependent on public transportation. Advocacy efforts by the social worker, which included documenting the impact on the community and a request for reconsideration of the decision, were unsuccessful. The transit authority's position was that there had been very little community response to an email that had been sent to residents in the area about the route change. Dissatisfied with the decision, the social worker then appealed to local merchants, religious leaders, and health care providers to join an organized coalition of community residents to present the situation to city, county, and state elected officials. The coalition was successful in reversing the transit authority's plan for the bus shelter.

from clients—in particular, their view of the problem or condition—is included in the assessment process. For example, how does a group or community experience the problem, and how do they think things would be different if the problem or condition did not exist? Both questions are pertinent to empowerment because people know what needs to happen to change their circumstances.

Who or What Is Responsible for the Problem or Condition?

Assessing who or what is responsible for the problem is perhaps the most difficult to document because the answer often involves multiple factors, including values and public policy. In particular, understanding how values frame almost all public and private discussions about remedies to social problems and the distribution of resources is critical to the assessment process. For example, Lens (2005), noting that every "social problem has its own value constellation," emphasized the contrast between a theme of compassion in policy discussions—for example, universal health and welfare-to-work requirements—and an emphasis on independence and personal responsibility. Of course, responsibility assumes that all citizens have equal standing, resources, and opportunity. An inherent notion of the availability and distribution of resources, and social problems and policies intended to address them, is that of personal responsibility as opposed to society's responsibility to ensure equality and the well-being of all citizens. On balance, the question of *who* in particular is responsible appears to have overshadowed the questions of *what* is responsible, and in

consequence, societal obligation to resolve social problems and conditions is diminished. Perhaps a confirming conclusion about who or what is responsible for a problem is not possible.

Nonetheless, asking these questions, assessing established fact, and reaching a conclusion based on the information gathered helps you to understand the issues involved and to use this information to inform the intervention (Kirst-Ashman, 2014). The way you identify and frame the problem, who is affected, and how provides context and documentation that have the potential to make a difference in how people respond, despite their values.

To illustrate, consider the issue of poverty. A *what* question might focus on the multiplicity of beliefs about why people are poor, the political ideology of poverty, the role of the economy in poverty, and the role of wage structure (such as the minimum wage) in poverty, each of which frames the discussion around factors that create, sustain, and perpetuate poverty. A *who* question considers poverty from the notion of personal responsibility and is framed by beliefs and values that emphasize work. However, what such a *who* question doesn't consider is that many poor people are employed, often in one or more minimum wage jobs without employee benefits, yet the earnings from such jobs are insufficient to lift them out of poverty. In essence, these individuals, referred to as the "diligent working and still poor" (Spriggs, 2007, p. A6), by all accounts exemplify motivation, human agency, personal responsibility, and individual industry. Systems-level thinking allows you to examine the interrelated aspects of poverty and to frame the issue as a social problem rather than an individual problem; specifically, poor people do not *make* themselves poor, nor do they choose to be or remain poor.

What Are the Social Justice Concerns Related to the Problem or Condition?

EP 3

An assessment of social justice includes an examination of the nexus between the problems that people have, the conditions in which they live, and the extent to which social policies remedy or have an adverse impact on individuals, groups, and communities. Using social justice as a framework to assess social problems and conditions contributes to an understanding of the debilitating effects of inequality and oppression that influence people's ability to reach their potential. Social justice further illuminates how problems are defined, as well as issues of human and civil rights, and raises questions of whether people at the lower stratification level have equal access to resources and to opportunities that promote well-being, dignity, and worth or whether stigma and marginal status determine who they are and what they can become.

Social justice also leads to an inquiry about public policy and societal responses to social problems and conditions, especially the power endowed in social welfare organizations as agents of change. For example, to a large extent, social welfare services continue to be directed primarily toward individual change (Breton, 2006; Brueggemann, 2006; Long, Tice, & Morrison, 2006). Over the past several decades, this focus has been reinforced by the emphasis on personal responsibility at the expense of equality and justice. In many instances, personal responsibility has been selectively applied in public policy. For the most part, the emphasis pertains to particular segments of the population, mainly the poor and disenfranchised. Furthermore, as noted by Breton (2006), the funding entities upon which social welfare organizations depend are rarely interested in collective social action that promote system-level change. Instead, adherence to the notion of individual change or responsibility tends to emphasize goals and values that for the most part are acceptable to society. What is acceptable to society can, of course, shift because of conflicting political and societal ideologies. For example, the emphasis on individual autonomy and effort stands in contrast to views about societal responsibility, a collective ideological viewpoint that emphasizes that social conditions and problems

are beyond the individual's ability to resolve and, as such, calls for a more comprehensive policy response (Breton, 2006; Segal, 2010).

More than 50 years ago, in 1964, recognizing the need for a more comprehensive approach to improve the lives of all Americans, President Lyndon Johnson gave a speech at the University of Michigan that set in motion an unprecedented bold vision for the "**Great Society**" and the "War on Poverty," resulting in legislative initiatives that, in effect, became a social justice agenda for America (Caro, 2012). Johnson's bottom-to-top approach sought to equalize opportunities for citizens whose birth, age, race, or gender consigned them to lives in which inequality and oppression diminished opportunities that sustained social problems or impoverished conditions.

Implicit in Johnson's vision and subsequent legislative initiatives were questions about the who and what: Who is affected by policy decisions or the lack thereof, and in what way are these people affected? Do social policies have a disparate impact on, ignore, or place at a disadvantage certain segments of the population in particular? In response, the passage of the Economic Opportunity Act (1964) led to the creation of the Office of Economic Opportunity, which was responsible for the administration of the War on Poverty programs. These programs provided, for example, equal access to quality elementary, secondary, and higher education; food and nutrition assistance; health care; housing; job training and employment; and community action programs. Empowerment and human agency and capacity were cornerstones of the community action program, which was intended to mobilize urban, rural, and migrant communities to act as their own agents. Each of the War on Poverty initiatives was a major thrust toward the vision of the Great Society—creating a safety net, providing opportunities, advancing equality, reducing poverty, discrimination, and economic hardship, and promoting social justice.

For a period of time, the Great Society initiatives were front and center of a justice agenda. Over time, many of the initiatives were changed or dismantled, influenced by a shift in public support and a variety of economic and political realities. Even so, a majority of these programs, which provide opportunities for disadvantaged segments of the population, currently exist in some form, including those related to education, nutrition, health care, and housing (Bailey & Danziger, 2013; Bradley & Taylor, 2013). In many respects, President Johnson's vision and the ensuing legislative initiatives embodied the beliefs associated with the settlement house movement, specifically confronting the problems people faced at a systems level.

Different Perspectives of Social Justice

Segal (2007) proposes that many of the shortcomings and injustices in social policies can be understood with respect to the social distance between those in need and those who make policy. This distance, according to Segal, contributes to a lack of social empathy, the results of which frame how social problems are conceptualized, and the underpinnings of which are influenced by the historical and ongoing debate regarding the role of the government as a problem solver. Thus, social distance has a decisive role in the provision of government assistance, which often consists of mandates and procedural requirements that are restrictive and punitive due to a lack of understanding about the context and complexities of a problem, who is affected by the problem, and how. To this point, consider the beliefs about the motivation to work, welfare dependency, out-of-wedlock pregnancy, and family dissolution that resulted in a public policy remedy that curtailed support for children in single-parent families. Notably absent in the policy decision was an understanding of, and consideration for, the contextual, economic, and structural barriers these families experienced. These factors led to expectations that were difficult for the families to achieve (Anderson, Halter, & Gryzlak, 2004; Banerjee, 2002; Ozawa & Yoon, 2005).

Thus, as a social worker, you should be aware of the way in which distance influences public policy, as well as the difference between how the term *social justice* is understood and articulated by the social work profession and how it is understood and articulated by policy makers. Specifically, promoting economic and social equality and defending the rights of disenfranchised and oppressed people are not universal viewpoints. The tensions between power and the lack thereof can result in conflict, particularly when the less powerful attempt to gain power, which is often framed as a negative and misunderstood by the public. Also, as Barusch (2002) explains, social justice can be defined differently depending on the philosophical and ideological orientation of public opinion. For example, presented with the idea that the mandate and compliance requirement for welfare recipients is unjust, libertarian values, according to Barusch (2002), would perhaps stress the "distribution of benefits on the basis of production." Conversely, liberals tend to be utilitarian in their thinking (e.g., the greatest good for the greatest number of people) and therefore place emphasis on "economic liberty and political equality for all" (p. 15). Viewpoints, however, can vary depending on the issue. Therefore, finding common ground on particular issues is possible, and political labels should not prevent you from exploring opportunities for involving certain individuals or building coalitions. Recognition of this fact might lead you to explore how opinions about a particular issue were influenced.

As a social worker in contact with clients who are affected by social problems and conditions and by policy decisions, you have access to a wealth of information that can be used to inform policy makers about the realities of clients' lives. Presenting information about a particular problem to the public and to policy makers is a means by which you can lessen the distance between them and those who are affected by a social problem or a policy, as well as advance social justice. Also, consider that people's thinking is complex and their perspectives can range from liberal to moderate to centrist to conservative, depending on the issue at hand. Understanding the basis of different perspectives is essential. An understanding of the ideological, political, and value context in which social problems and policies are framed can inform your assessment of the forces that may promote, resist, or inhibit change.

The general assessment questions presented earlier are by no means exhaustive; rather, they are intended as guides and as a frame of reference you can use for understanding social problems and conditions, and whether the policy decisions intended to alter social problems and conditions adversely affect or have a disparate impact on groups and communities. Using general assessment questions in an initial inquiry provides data that can be used to inform policy makers about the context of social problems or conditions. In this way, we meet the obligation of the profession to advance clients' collective well-being.

Note that Breton (2006) asserts that social workers need not become revolutionaries in order to effect change. Justice work demands, however, that we as social workers articulate the consequences of social problems and conditions as well as evaluate and monitor the impact of policies on those problems or conditions. Acting on behalf of or with client groups and taking an active role in documenting problems, social workers can be instrumental in lessening the distance between policy makers and people and in that sense promote social justice.

Ultimately, the assessment information you gather helps you to develop a plan of action and potentially build a coalition that includes the people affected by the problem to address it. Answers also provide an opportunity for you as a social worker to give voice to the powerless and to frame issues to increase the likelihood that the public becomes invested in the problem, irrespective of their values (Linhorst, 2002).

In the next section of the chapter, each of the selected macro-level intervention strategies is discussed.

DEVELOPING AND MOBILIZING RESOURCES

EP 8

Regular, meaningful contact with individuals, families, and groups places you in a strategic position to identify the needs of people living in impoverished conditions as well as to assist people in becoming aware of resources for which they may be eligible. Within the context of this work, resource development includes educating policy makers, civic groups, and administrators of social welfare organizations about social conditions for which responsive resources are needed. In augmenting or developing resources for groups and communities, some specific needs of individuals may also be met. However, as noted by Vosler (1990), resource needs often go unnoticed, perhaps in large part due to the structure of social welfare services in which the primary focus tends to be on individual treatment. Because of the emphasis on individual change, the need for aggregate information about whole groups or populations may not be as obvious.

Resources for addressing concrete needs may vary depending on the community. For example, rural communities may have fewer formal resources, and those that exist are often strained beyond capacity. Also, we have a tendency to construct an idealized image of the rustic rural community, in which informal networks exist and seamlessly meet all needs—in essence, neighbor helping neighbor. Although this image has merit, informal networks cannot make up for a shortage of affordable housing, transportation, and job opportunities, or inadequate health, mental health, and social services. During the enrollment periods for the Affordable Care Act, for example, the lack of social services in some rural areas meant that residents had to travel great distances to obtain help from staff who were trained as educators and navigators.

Resource development must also take into account that rural communities are increasingly becoming less racially homogeneous, which may indicate a need for new and different resources. Similarly, the assumption of affluence in suburban communities may impede the development of resources, the results of which often mean that low-income individuals in these communities are invisible, remain isolated, and lack access to a range of adequate services.

Whether the population of interest is urban, rural, or suburban, conditions may exist for which resource development is needed to help individuals, families, or groups secure essential services. Developing or supplementing resources is indicated when it is apparent that a significant number of people within given ecological boundaries (e.g., neighborhoods, communities, institutions) or populations who share certain characteristics have needs for which matching resources are unavailable. Moreover, in a world characterized by relentless change—whether in the physical environment, technology, or politics—social workers are constantly confronted with unmet needs and the pressure to organize resources. The roles of enabler, broker, and mediator, as supported by the principles of empowerment, may be particularly important for social workers involved in developing resources. For example, when a large affluent metropolitan church had an interest in providing resources for the largely low-income community in which the church was located, the leadership asked a social worker to help them determine the needs of the community by gathering information, with the social worker acting as the go-between for the community and the church. In essence, the church wanted to ensure that the resources to be provided were identified *by* the community rather than *for* the community.

In some instances, resource needs are obvious. For example, working families in all economic strata need affordable child care, and some need financial assistance to meet a portion or all of the costs of daily living. Individuals or families may need assistance in acquiring or paying for health insurance and preventative care. However, resource needs vary according to specific concerns, and they can differ substantially between and within groups, communities, and populations. For example, the resource needs of aging gay and lesbian individuals in rural areas tend to be different from the needs of their urban peers. In some instances, existing resources may be inadequate for the level of need, in which case resources may need to be supplemented or expanded. In some scenarios, you may find that certain values and beliefs about people and stigma may result in reinforcing oppression and a denial of access to needed resources. These and other factors will continue to shape the ways that social services are designed and delivered.

Both demand and normative resource needs are likely to change because of our changing demographic landscape—a landscape in which the number of older people is growing faster than the young—and the increasing immigrant population. In the beginning of the year 2011, the first group of the post–World War II generation referred to as the "Baby Boomers" in the United States turned 65 years of age. Aging, specifically the number of people over the age of 65, is a global trend. An aging population will have a profound effect on the types of resources that are needed, ranging from ways to keep this population healthy and ensure economic and family stability to the ways in which business is conducted. Aging needs will vary, of course, and will be influenced by such factors as income, health status, geographic residence, gender, sexual orientation, and race.

Data from the 2010 U.S. Census Survey also provides a portrait of a changing and more diverse population, adding to the diversity that already exists in this country. Increasingly, immigrants—who will account for a larger percentage of population growth in the United States—can be expected to have a range of resource needs. Latino immigrants, for instance, need access to health care, education, and information about resources (Ayòn, 2014). Also, more immigrants are likely to follow job opportunities in suburban and rural communities, resulting in a change in the homogeneity of these communities, in terms of both people and resource needs.

Determining and Documenting Needs

Whether the goal is to develop resources, deliver useful services, or influence a social policy, a starting point is a **needs assessment**, in which you gain an understanding of and document the nature and the extent of resource needs. In general, you assess who needs what and why. One step is to determine whether the resource is intended to respond to a normative need or a demand need (Rubin & Babbie, 2005). **Normative needs** refers to a gap or discrepancy between a need considered to be a norm and the resources that exist to respond to that need. For example, green space for children to play is considered a developmental normative need and is available in most communities. However, in other communities, the resource of green space does not exist.

Therefore, when the two communities are compared, there is a gap in what is considered to be a normal need. **Demand needs** relate to the needs of a particular group or community to address deprivation, the absence of a resource, or a particular concern (for example, the lack of affordable housing for low-income families, in which the need is greater that the supply).

Understanding the different types of needs can help you to construct a comprehensive picture of needs and to develop a response. Specific assessment questions that may clarify the need for resource development and guide the data to be gathered include:

- What are the resource needs of a particular group?
- How would a group or community describe their resource needs?
- Are there unmet needs, gaps, or underutilized existing resources?
- How prevalent are the needs across the population and in various subgroups?
- Are there barriers to the utilization of existing resources?
- Are the current resources an effective response?

Numerous data collection tools are available for understanding and documenting resource needs. **Mapping** utilizes geographic information systems to track problems of interest (Hillier, 2007). Ferguson (2007), for example, used mapping to access geographic data about homeless youth in an area of Los Angeles, which led to the development of a new resource and intervention strategy that focused on service-related needs, employment training, and mental health resources.

EP 4

Qualitative methods involve inviting client groups to identify their resource needs, such as through focus groups, group interviews, standardized self-administered questionnaires, or community forums with key informants or a targeted group (Ayòn, 2014; Bergold & Thomas, 2012; DePoy, Hartman, & Haslett, 1999; Dobbie & Richards-Schuster, 2008; Reese et al., 1999).

Whichever method you use, as noted earlier, you should focus on discovering unmet or undeclared needs. Noting that all groups and communities have resource capabilities, the overall intent of the needs assessment is to assist them in determining whether there is a need for action to address a resource need (Homan, 2008; Lewis, Lewis, Packard, & Souflee, 2001). An example of how this worked is the Homeless

Against Homelessness Project, in which homeless individuals worked with a social worker to determine the resource needs of other homeless individuals. The social worker and the group combined facets of the participatory action research framework with a needs assessment. **Participatory action research** involves the governance, composition, and active participation of stakeholders throughout the project (Depoy, Hartman, & Haslett, 1999). In this case, the active stakeholders were the homeless individuals who actually designed the project and conducted needs assessment interviews. As key informants, they were essential to the development of interview questions that were relevant to the population and that could easily be administered on the street. The findings from this project were presented to the county commission on homelessness.

Similarly, Minkler and Wallerstein (2008) engaged communities in identifying community health needs. Minkler (2012), in writing about this experience, emphasized the collaborative aspects and cultural relevance of participatory research as instrumental in developing a resource agenda for building healthy communities.

Butler and Hope (1999) conducted group interviews with older lesbian women living in metropolitan and rural communities in order to better understand their current and future resource needs. Similarly, Ayòn (2014) held focus groups to identify the resource needs of Latino immigrant families. Dialogue groups proved to be an effective method to understand and subsequently educate service providers about the particular issues and concerns of older gays and lesbians in a community (Anetzberger et al., 2004). Observing the low participation of ethnic and racial minorities in using hospice services as a resource, Reese et al. (1999) relied on a group of African American ministers as key informants to identify cultural and institutional barriers that prevented African Americans from using hospice care.

These examples represent ways in which you can identify and document resource needs in the aggregate. You should also be aware of the wealth of information available in your agency's case records. For example, a review of agency case records can inform you as to whether resource needs identified by a significant number of clients at intake remained a concern at termination. Whichever method you use to document resource needs, the results may lead to advocacy for social action involving a coalition of agencies and other professionals in order to influence a desired outcome. Be aware also that the methods are not limited to documenting resource needs. They may be used as informative resources for each of the forthcoming intervention strategies to be discussed.

Developing Resources with Diverse Groups

EP 2

You need not be apprehensive about documenting needs of and for diverse groups so that a resource can be developed. You should be aware, however, that a group may identify resource needs that are different from your own ideas and that differences may be observed within groups (Green, 1999; Sue, 2006). For example, the needs of immigrants or refugees may depend on their length of stay, extent of acculturation, and income level; each of these factors may ultimately influence the types and appropriateness of resources. Therefore, whether you are looking to develop resources in response to the needs of older or newly arrived immigrant groups, it is critical for you to be sensitive to and familiarize yourself with cultural nuances, values, norms, and social and political structures. Beyond your efforts to assess and document a resource need, entry into a situation that is unfamiliar to you requires interpersonal skills such as respectful preparation and engagement, building trust and relationship resources, and facilitating empowerment. In addition, unfamiliar situations call for you to engage in self-reflection so that you are aware of your bias and any predetermined notions you might have of a particular group.

Most of the previously discussed questions and data collection methods can be used to identify and document the resource needs of a diverse group. Mapping, for example, can show you whether a group is clustered in a particular geographic area. From this point, you can assess the resources available to a community and whether there are resource gaps. Relying on the group or community as key informants and cultural interpreters and positioning yourself as a learner, you gain an understanding of the community or group resource needs (Green, 1999; Tervalon & Murray-Garcia, 1998).

Mobilizing Community Resources

Mobilizing existing community resources can address concrete needs, but available resources can vary depending on the community and the situation. In some instances, a resource may exist but people lack

EP 8

information about the resource. Person-to-person contact can be instrumental in providing information and increasing access to available resources. However, there are certain situations that arouse an emotional and altruistic response in people, irrespective of where they live (Homan, 2008). Nowhere has this been more evident than in the community volunteer responses in the aftermath of national and global disastrous events.

Homan (2008), citing the Pew Partnership for Civic Change (2001), asserts that *people* are the most valuable community resource, and that a majority are willing to become and remain involved when asked. The results of the report showed that 90% of Americans "believe that working with others is the way to solve community problems." Primary factors were "knowing what to do," "having a linkage to the community," and "having a strong cultural or ethnic identity." In mobilizing community resources, Homan suggests four steps for eliciting and encouraging people's involvement (p. 188):

1. Contact people.
2. Give them a reason to join.
3. Ask them to join.
4. Maintain their involvement.

The implementation of the Affordable Care Act (ACA) (2010) and the subsequent open enrollment periods resulted in the need to educate the uninsured about its provisions. Much of this work was accomplished by statewide and nationally coordinated partnerships of community-based advocacy groups, nonprofit organizations, and a range of citizen volunteers. Social workers were involved as educators and navigators, specifically assisting people to select an insurance plan suitable to their needs (Andrews et al., 2013; Darnell, 2013). However, the definitive success of informing and educating people depended on volunteers recruited through social media, book clubs, client groups, fraternal and civic groups, and faith and professional communities. Volunteers held public media events and distributed information in neighborhoods, in social services agencies, and at community and health care centers. The volunteer recruitment communications appeal, which began with "We need your help," effectively engaged volunteers as active stakeholders in informing the public about provisions in the ACA. Direct appeals such as this one have the potential to engage the altruistic instincts and basic values of potential volunteers, many of whom desire equality

and dignity for the disenfranchised but are unaware of how to achieve it.

As you develop, tap into, and mobilize existing resources, the capacity of the community should be considered; the appeal need not be on a large-scale basis like the mobilization effort associated with the ACA. The capacity to help others in times of need can be found in most communities. Community-level resources can be inspired when people become aware of a particular situation for which help is needed. McRoy (2003), for example, worked collaboratively with congregations to respond to the need for adoptive homes for children. This faith-based initiative called "Saving a Generation" resulted in the adoption of more than 50 African American children.

Within communities, kin, informal networks, and natural support systems can be mobilized in much the same manner. For example, kinship care (e.g., the placement of children with kin) as a resource in child welfare is among the practices that organizations are encouraged to adopt as an alternative to foster care placement (Ayón, Aisenberg, & Cimino, 2013; Gibson, 1999; Haight, 1998; Jackson, 1998; Testa, 2002). Kinship studies found that this resource lasted longer and was more supportive of the child's stability, familial connections, and cultural, racial, or ethnic identity (Danzy & Jackson, 1997; Hegar, 1999; Testa, 2002).

Mobilizing resources can make use of natural support systems within communities. For example, training women in a community as nutritional counselors proved to be an effective means of teaching healthy eating habits to inner-city women who were at risk for type 2 diabetes. Because the women were connected through their community, they were more receptive when the information was provided by peers, neighbors, or friends (Mays, 2003). Using barbershops as natural gathering places, the Montgomery County, Maryland, Health and Human Services Department tapped into this resource to educate men about cancer and to address some of the barriers that prevented the men from seeking oncology screening (Mallory, 2004).

ENGAGING IN ADVOCACY AND SOCIAL ACTION

The social work profession has a long and proud tradition of engaging in advocacy and social action leading to social reform. Indeed, Stuart (1999) characterizes the "linking of clients and social policy as a

EP 8

distinctive contribution of the social work profession" (p. 335). Haynes and Mickelson (2000) and Reisch and Andrews (2008) trace the involvement of social workers in the development of some of the more enlightened, humane, and just social policies during both the 19th and 20th centuries. In some instances, in particular communities, practice with individuals involves advocacy and social action that focus on the "private troubles of individuals and the larger policy issues that affected them" (Carlton-LaNey, 1999). Diverse individuals and groups of social workers have been devoted activists and advocates, often acting in concert with grassroots or minority civic groups. For example, social workers supported the United Farm Workers, the Equal Rights Amendment, the National Welfare Rights Organization, and the Civil Rights Movement by either joining in the activities of these groups directly or providing expert testimony.

Case and Cause Advocacy

Perhaps you have acted as a case advocate, working on behalf of clients to ensure that they receive those benefits and services to which they are entitled and to ensure that as recipients their dignity is preserved. This aspect of advocacy closely corresponds to a dictionary definition of an *advocate* as one who acts on behalf of another person. But advocacy that involves action on a larger scale—for example, addressing the effects of legislation and policies—cannot rely on the efforts of a single social worker. Indeed, the profession has been and continues to be actively involved in addressing many of these causes (Marsh, 2005). The shift in policy making from the federal to the state level is also an opportunity for you to join in collaborative advocacy to influence policy at the state level on behalf of clients (Hoefer, 2005; Jackson-Elmore, 2005; Lens, 2005; Rice, 1998; Sherraden, Slosar, & Sherraden, 2002). Other opportunities for you to join advocacy efforts include the NASW collaboration with social work programs' "Social Work Day at the Capital" and the NASW nonpartisan Political Action for Candidate Election (PACE) Committee. PACE is committed to supporting and electing candidates who support policies that affect social work constituents, practice, and programs.

Advocacy and Social Action Defined

Proposing a new definition of advocacy, Schneider and Lester (2001) define social work advocacy as the "exclusive and mutual representation of a client(s) or cause in a forum, attempting to systematically influence decision making in an unfair and unresponsive system." Barker (1996) defined social action as "a coordinated effort to achieve institutional change to meet a need, solve a social problem, correct any injustices or enhance the quality of human life" (p. 350). Social action as described by Rothman (2007) brings pressure on those who hold power to correct a condition of inequality to the benefit of those for whom marginalized status and oppression are a way of life. Both advocacy and social action are inherently political. Hyde (1996), referring to a major principle of feminist organizing and advocacy, encourages the notion that there is a connection between the personal and the political.

Because there are often instances in which advocacy and social action are combined to achieve the desired results, we have adapted elements from each to form a unified definition. Together, advocacy and social action represent a process of initiating change either with or on behalf of client groups to:

- Obtain services or resources that would not otherwise be provided
- Modify or influence policies or practices that adversely affect groups or communities
- Promote legislation or policies that will result in the provision of requisite resources or services

Models of advocacy are defined and discussed by Haynes and Mickelson (2000) and Freddolino, Moxley, and Hyduk (2004). These authors stress that using particular models is important because they guide the intervention and the strategies used. We refer you to these informative resources as guides.

Indications for Advocacy or Social Action

Advocacy and social action may be appropriate when there are conditions or problems that affect a group or community, including the following:

1. When services or benefits to which people are entitled are denied to a group or community
2. When services or practices are dehumanizing, confrontational, or coercive
3. When discriminatory practices or policies occur because of race, gender, sexual orientation, religion, culture, family form, or other factors
4. When gaps in services or benefits cause undue hardship or contribute to dysfunction
5. When people lack representation or participation in decisions that affect their lives

6. When governmental or agency policies and procedures or community or workplace practices have a disparate impact that adversely affects or targets groups of people
7. When a significant group of people have common needs for which resources are unavailable
8. When clients are denied basic human, civil, or legal rights

Other circumstances for which advocacy or social action may be necessary include situations in which a group or community is unable to act effectively on its own behalf, such as persons who are institutionalized, people who have a need for immediate services or benefits because of a crisis situation, or people who cannot act as self-advocates because of their legal status.

Competence and Skills for Social Action

Skills that are used in direct practice easily translate to advocacy and social action (Breton, 2006). But Schneider and Lester (2001) emphasize that advocacy is not problem solving in the tradition of direct practice problem-solving models. In contrast to the problem-solving process, "advocacy requires particular actions, such as representation, influencing and the use of a forum" (p. 71) to bring about specific change for the benefit of a group or community. Specific skills required in advocacy or social action include the following:

- Policy analysis
- Group facilitation
- Oral and written communication skills
- Negotiation and mediation
- Analysis of multidimensional and systematic information

Let's say, for example, that you are the facilitator for a community-based parenting group. A common complaint among group members is the out-of-home placement of children in the community, which many perceived as unjust. Following a lengthy discussion on this topic, members of the group approach you to represent them and act on their behalf. The stories group members tell you of child placement are heart wrenching. It appears that the claim of injustice relates to policies that are disparate and have an adverse effect on communities of color. After hearing their stories, you decided that inaction on your part is not an option. Nonetheless, before acting, you are advised to document and determine the circumstances of each individual's

situation. For example, is there a pattern between individual and group stories? Are families with particular attributes and status more likely to experience child placement? Further, you would be advised to educate yourself about and analyze the relevant state and federal policies. Situations such as the stories of the parents, in which injustice—real or perceived—arouses emotions, can incite anger in those affected and in you the advocate. However, an assessment will help you and the groups that you intend to represent avoid making assumptions and premature or erroneous conclusions that may lead to undesired or embarrassing consequences. Methods for documenting and quantifying needs (discussed earlier in this chapter) are essential at this stage. For instance, gathering statistical data can help you determine the trends in the placement of children, by neighborhood, race, or economic status.

Assuming that an assessment of the situation indicates that advocacy or social action is necessary, a decision would be made as to how the group wishes to proceed. To gather support for a defined action, you would gather information that documents the problem, the population affected, and in what ways that population is affected. Then you would present this information to others who are interested in the problem. In essence, you are building a coalition of interested parties to support and mobilize a plan of action. In building a coalition, group facilitation, negotiation, consensus building, and interpersonal skills are critical.

Ethical Principles for Social Action and Advocacy

Both advocacy and social action assume a wide range of social work roles and skills, each of which observes the values and ethics of the profession, such as dignity and worth, self-determination, and giving a voice to the powerless, as guiding principles (Schneider & Lester, 2001). Advocacy and social action may, at times, constitute a delicate balance between self-determination and beneficence. Ezell (2001) calls attention to this dilemma, citing the conflict that can occur in deciding "whether to empower clients to advocate for themselves or to represent them" (p. 45). Schneider and Lester (2001) provide guidance with respect to ethical behavior in their definition of advocacy. They emphasize that the relationship between the social worker and the client group is mutual, which means observing their interdependence and reciprocity in collaborative decision making and planning. In other

EP 1

words, you are working with the group in your representation of their concerns. Furthermore, Schneider and Lester (2001) caution advocates to avoid dominating group or community decisions and the agenda. A potential dilemma that you might face with respect to self-determination and informed consent is that a group or community may not wish to assert this right if they believe they will face formidable opposition or backlash. Should a group make such a decision, you are ethically bound to respect their choice. In essence, the advocacy or social action effort should go no further than the client group wishes it to go.

Ethics are also indicated in informing groups about the inherent conflict, risks, and limitations associated with advocacy and social action. Rothman (1999) cautions community practitioners about the potential for opposition and obstacles to social action and organizing activities, including "institutions that block or oppose needed improvements in education, housing, employment and law enforcement." He further states that "change advocates have to keep in mind that elites will lash out when they perceive that their interests are challenged." To deal with this resistance, advocates should "calculate" their ability and that of their client group to maintain a sustained focus, as well as be able to defend themselves against counterattacks (p. 10). You have a responsibility to discuss potential barriers and the possible adversarial or negative consequences of advocacy and social action efforts with the client group. Implementing advocacy and social action typically creates a certain amount of strain and tension; moreover, a positive outcome cannot always be assured. For example, what if a landlord under pressure from a resident action group ignores building code violations that caused the complex to be condemned, resulting in the residents' being displaced? Discussing possible consequences or barriers not only allows for the planning of alternative strategies but also ensures that those with whom you work are informed about the pros and cons of an intended action, leaving the final decision in their hands.

Techniques and Steps of Advocacy and Social Action

Targets of advocacy or social action may be individuals (e.g., a landlord or public official), organizations, or divisions of government (e.g., on behalf of or with groups or communities). Approaches to situations vary considerably according to the target system, but all require a thorough understanding of how organizations or communities are structured and function, how

the legislative and rule-making processes work, and an appreciation of the influence of organizational politics (Alexander, 2003, 2010; Homan, 2008; Kirst-Ashman, 2014; Rothman, 1991).

Advocacy can involve different levels of assertive intensity, ranging from a discussion with or educating those who have power about a problem to a high level of social action such as organizing protests, boycotts, or social media campaigns. Sosin and Callum (1983) developed a useful typology of advocacy to assist practitioners in planning strategic advocacy actions. Along with the models discussed by Haynes and Mickelson (2000) and Freddolino, Moxley, and Hyduk (2004), Sosin and Callum's (1983) typology can help determine the opportunities that exist, the techniques or strategies to be used, and at what level these techniques and strategies should be implemented. As a general rule, you should rely on the techniques that have the greatest promise of achieving a given objective. Deciding which technique to use depends on the nature and analysis of the problem, the wishes of the group or community, the nature of the action, and the political climate. For instance, although militant action may be desirable, militancy should be utilized with great discretion because the short-term gains may not outweigh the long-term negative images, the public response, and the potential for fractured relationships. As you read the steps involved in social action and advocacy, consider how you would obtain the necessary information as an advocate to the previously discussed community parenting group in which out-of-home placement of children was a primary concern.

Effective social action and advocacy require a rational, planned approach incorporating the following steps:

1. Assess and document the problem or condition.
2. Systematically gather information and conduct an analysis of the people, structure, system, or policy to be changed.
3. Assess both the driving forces that may promote change and the forces that may conceivably inhibit change.
4. Identify specific goals, eliciting a broad range of viewpoints from within the client group.
5. Carefully match techniques or strategies to the desired outcome.
6. Make a feasible schedule for implementing the plan of action.
7. Incorporate in the plan a feedback process for evaluating the changes that the action stimulates.

In addition to the steps and skill competencies, other factors that are vital to effective social action and advocacy include a genuine concern for the cause, the ability to keep the cause in focus, tenacity, and stamina. Successful advocates have a thorough understanding of how the government and systems are organized and changed. Blind emotion may work a few times, but maintaining successful, sustained advocacy and action requires know-how. In many instances, class advocacy and social action are best described as a marathon rather than a race. Finally, the manner in which an issue is presented may make a substantial difference. The Frame-Works Institute suggests translating messages about what can be done to address social problems into language that engages ordinary people and advances their interest in policy and program solutions. Questions that facilitate formulating the institute's "strategic frame analysis" are illustrated in the following examples:

- What shapes public opinion about a particular social condition or problem—for example, issues that affect children, families, and poor people?
- What role do/can the media play?
- How do policy makers gauge public opinion?

Answers to these questions can facilitate the direction of advocacy or social action. Furthermore, the questions can help you sharpen your message to a specific group about a specific problem and effectively communicate about social conditions framed by the principles of social justice.

Improving the Organizational Environment

EP 5

There may be instances in which advocacy is indicated within an organization to improve the environment experienced by clients. Rothman (2007) uses the term **policy advocacy** to refer to an internal professional advocate who operates within a system to help an organization achieve its goals.

To function in this role, you should be aware that a change effort within an organization requires an understanding and analysis of organizational structure, function, culture, and resource environment. Martin and O'Connor (1989) analyzed the social welfare organization using systems theory as a conceptual framework. Using this framework helps you to assess and analyze the organization's relationship with its resource environment (funding sources, the organization's

internal structure and processes, and the social, cultural, and political-economic environment). Change efforts, according to Netting, Kettner, and McMurtry (2004), can occur in an organization on two levels:

- Improving resources provided to clients
- Enhancing the organization's working environment so that personnel can perform more efficiently and effectively, thus improving services to clients

Similarly, organizational change as conceptualized by Brager and Holloway (1978) can focus on three areas: people-focused change, technological change, and structural change, which may take the form of a new policy, modifications to an existing policy, the development of a program, or the initiation of a project in which the results can be used to inform service delivery. You should also consider whether the organization has positioned itself as a learning organization (Kettner, Daley, & Nichols, 1985; Senge, 1990, 1994).

Organizational Learning and Learning Organizations

In a **learning organization**, members of the organization periodically review performance and make adjustments to improve its services or achieve organizational goals. As defined by Daft (2010), Senge (1990, 1994), and Morgan (1997), a learning organization essentially speaks to the ecology of the organization. That is, it refers to a particular type of organization and its ability to scan, anticipate, and respond to environmental changes. The learning organization develops capacities that empower members to question and challenge operating norms and assumptions, thereby ensuring its stability and promoting its evolution through strategic responses and direction (Morgan, 1997). Further, a learning organization positions itself so that it can continuously review and revise its operations, purposes, and objectives so as to ensure the quality of the organizational experience for clients and staff. For example, a county human health and services administrator initiated a series of community dialogues among staff to position the organization as a learning organization and to develop a shared vision to facilitate organizational change to improve services to its clients. Interestingly, a learning organization is also considered a factor in the quality of staff work life with respect to job design and performance awards (Daft, 2010; Lewis et al., 2001; Morgan, 1997).

Staff as Agents of Change

Although social workers are generally adept in advocating for individual clients or causes, many may be reticent or feel unable to influence or propose changes within their own organizations. In some instances, they may identify organizational concerns in a hierarchical fashion and therefore conclude that the impetus for a change or resolution resides in the domain of management. In some instances, and with certain problems, this view may be valid. Nonetheless, because of the interactions between staff and clients, managers and administrators need to be able to rely on you and other staff at the street level of service delivery to alert them to the need for change in a program or policy or the development of a new resource. In initiating changes at the organizational level, you are acting as a diagnostician and facilitator/expediter. Assuming responsibility for and participating in change is the essence of staff empowerment, and participation in change efforts is consistent with the ethical obligation to your employment organization.

To be an effective organizational change advocate, you must be aware of the benefits and risks of a proposed change, including assessing the risk to you as a professional. In your benefit–risk analysis, it is essential that you document and clarify the need for change. If service delivery is a concern, for example, will your proposal improve the situation (Brager & Holloway, 1978; Netting, Kettner, & McMurtry, 2004)? In addition, what form should the proposed change take? For example, if service delivery is the target, would you recommend a change in a policy practice or program? Furthermore, what are the expected outcomes of the proposed change? Also consider: Are other staff also concerned? Who else should be involved? These questions position you to form a coalition to avoid the perception of your being a dilettante.

Risks, Benefits, and Opposition

Before initiating a change effort within your organization, it is important to describe and document the issue, including its context, a systems-level goal that is consistent with the organization's mission, a proposal to remedy the problem or condition, and the perceived benefits to the organization. Frey (1990) has developed a useful framework with which you can gauge the potential benefit of a change proposal to the organization and minimize potential risk or opposition. The process involves three key groups: (1) administrators, who must approve and allocate resources for the proposal; (2) supervisors and staff, who are responsible for

implementing the work involved; and (3) clients, the affected group. Client input is considered essential in determining the extent to which the proposed change offers direct benefits and will effectively alter and enhance the services they receive.

By considering the impact of the potential change on each group, you can weigh benefits against potential detrimental effects and plan strategies to counter reactions and resistance when the former (i.e., the benefits) clearly and substantially outweigh the latter.

Organizations are systems that seek to maintain equilibrium; therefore, you may encounter opposition to proposals for change. Opposition may arise in response to proposals that challenge or exceed the capacity of the organization due to resource constraints. Likewise, proposals that would significantly change the purpose, mission, and goals of the organization may spur resistance. Extending an agency's operating hours may be considered a peripheral change and have little or no effect on organizational goals or mission. In contrast, programmatic changes, which alter a program's objectives, have greater effects on organizational depth.

Culture and Environment of Organizations

Social welfare organizations are organized to provide a service, information, benefits, or goods. They are formal social systems with multiple constituents and dynamic arenas in which client eligibility for services is determined and the resources vital to the organization's existence are distributed. The culture of organizations includes core values and purposes as portrayed in mission statements, leadership styles, assumptions, and rituals (Daft, 2010; Schein, 1985).

An organization's environment—in particular, the culture of an organization—is influenced by its leadership, staff, resource environment, and public policy. The resource environment (e.g., the state of the economy and clients) and public policy can require changes or modifications to decisions with respect to how the organization functions, its leadership, the allocation of resources, and the strategies that are implemented to achieve the organization's goals or mission (Condrey, Facer, & Hamilton, 2005; Proehl, 2001).

Two examples of policies that had a significant impact on agencies' services and operations and staff are the Personal Responsibility and Work Opportunity Reconciliation Act of 1996 (welfare reform) and the Affordable Care Act (ACA) of 2010. Welfare reform, for example, influenced the internal operations of both public and private organizations, staff functions, job satisfaction, goals, and resources (Abramovitz, 2005; Condrey, Facer, & Hamilton, 2005; Proehl, 2001; Reisch & Sommerfeld, 2003). In effect, federal requirements set forth specific performance standards, which included monitoring and reporting the work-related activities of recipients. Many nonprofit organizations and staff struggled with the policy dictates and mandated goals of welfare reform, irrespective of whether staff agreed with them or perceived them to be unjust (Kirst-Ashman, 2014). At issue for social workers were the requirements that were counter to the ethics and values of the profession. A challenge for the leadership of the organization was to find ways to respond to the pressures of the policy that might be less disruptive and were beneficial to the organization (Condrey, Facer, & Hamilton, 2005; Reisch & Sommerfeld, 2003).

Passage of the ACA represented a culmination of efforts to reform health care and to provide access to quality health and mental health care to the previously uninsured (Bradley & Taylor, 2013). Although nonprofit organizations, including legal aid and community action programs, were routinely involved in helping clients access resources, the ACA and the Medicaid expansion presented an additional challenge to agency operations and resources. Nonprofit hospitals, for example, were required to conduct community needs assessments and to adopt strategies responsive to the identified needs (Doty, Blumenthal, & Collins, 2014). Organizations, many of which received state or federal funds for staff to act as navigators or assisters to help people during the open enrollment periods, were overwhelmed by client and programmatic demands, the least of which were enrollment deadlines in the face of technical malfunctions (Darnell, 2013).

EP 5

In highlighting these two examples, we hope that you understand and appreciate the challenges that social welfare organizations face as part of a larger social system, as well as how an organization's culture is a key factor in the organization's response to a change effort.

In the following sections, we highlight three areas in which the role of a policy advocate may be indicated:

- Organizational policies or practices and staff behavior that fail to promote client dignity and worth
- Institutionalized racism and discrimination
- Cultural competence at the organizational level

The aim of the discussion is consistent with Netting and colleagues' (2004) change strategy of "enhancing the organization's working environment so that personnel can perform more efficiently and effectively, thus improving services to clients." The quality of the organizational environment and the values of the organization, experienced by clients, are important aspects of service delivery.

Organizational Policies or Practices and Staff Behavior That Fail to Promote Client Dignity and Worth

Acting in the role of a policy advocate, a key part of your responsibility is to evaluate the impact of organizational policies, procedures, and practices on service delivery to clients. When certain organizational practices or policies impede service delivery or block the agency from fulfilling its mission in an optimal fashion, it is up to you to identify those barriers and propose a change. The policy advocate role involves functioning as an organizational diagnostician, facilitator, and mediator.

Focusing on the internal operations of the agency, you might examine the extent to which organizational policies and practices promote social justice, support client self-determination and dignity, and adhere to the principles of empowerment and strengths (G. D. Rooney, 2000). Policies or practices that lend themselves to a review include criteria for determining eligibility for services, rules that govern clients' behavior in residential or institutional settings, policies related to access to services, and procedures for developing treatment plans. The following are key points to consider when assessing organizational policies or practices:

1. What are the origins, ideology, and values that appear to have influenced the policy?
2. What are the intended and unintended consequences of the policy's application?
3. To what extent are the policy and its expectations of clients influenced by societal ideology (e.g., the worthy and unworthy poor), social control, or compliance?
4. What is the image of clients and practitioners portrayed by the policy?
5. What does the policy or practice demand of clients and practitioners?
6. How do clients react to the practice or policy?
7. To what extent do the policy and its procedures support or constrain social work values, ethics, and social justice?

Unfortunately, some organizations may have practices or policies that create barriers to delivering services fully and effectively. The implementation of such policies may deny people the resources to which they are entitled and result in others receiving services that are of lesser quality. In responding to the resource environment, organizational practice can be influenced by public policy rules and, in some instances, the language that communicates a certain ideology and image of people who are in need of services (Abramovitz, 2005; Lens, 2005; Reisch, 2002).

The series of questions for assessing organizational policies and practices are intended as guidelines to critique the effects of policy on clients and service delivery. Students who have completed this assessment in their organizations added the following critique questions:

- In working with involuntary clients, does the policy or practice require clients to be compliant, such that the social worker's role becomes that of an enforcer?
- How do you reconcile unintended consequences of the implementation of policies or rules?
- When clients have a strong reaction to a policy or practice, are there mechanisms in place so that the organization can respond humanely to their concerns?
- Do policies and practices provide an image of clients that promotes dignity and worth and acknowledges strengths as well as problems?
- How does the policy or practice ensure equal access to and equality of services? In particular, does the policy or practice provide differential treatment for one client group at the expense of another group?

Agency policies and practices are intended to help organizations manage limited resources and to ensure their distribution to those in need. For example, rules limiting the number of times people can access a food bank are critical to preserving resources, thereby ensuring that help is available to the greatest number possible. At the same time, from an individual's perspective, limits can convey the idea that they are taking advantage of this resource. Policies may be considered counterproductive when they intend to ensure compliance but unduly burden clients, and when procedures are implemented such that the potential for cheating takes precedence over service provision.

Because *staff* is the heart of the environment, they have an enormous influence on the organization's environment. The staffing mix of an organization includes professionals who have regular contact with clients, support personnel, and administrative personnel. Administrative personnel, specifically managers and supervisors, direct, monitor, coordinate, evaluate, and bear responsibility for the oversight of organizational operations. In the organization's highly interdependent environment, each position is critical to the organization's mission. To a large extent, staff behavior is governed by a mix of factors that are internal and external to the organization. Internal factors include things like organizational philosophy, goals, and mission. Professional orientations, ethical codes and standards, union contracts, funding sources, the media, public policy, and licensing or regulatory boards are external factors.

When an organization has staff who are dedicated, caring, and responsive to clients' needs, as well as congenial with one another, the climate in the organization's environment in effect is a **culture of caring** (Kirst-Ashman, 2014, p. 497) and is conducive to the growth and well-being of all concerned. To be optimally effective, an organization's culture (and hence its climate) should promote staff empowerment and a commitment to deliver high-quality client services. Characteristics of a healthy organizational culture and climate involve such factors as equality and trust, a sense of community in which staff care about each other, open communications, a willingness to deal with conflict, a balance between flexibility and risk taking, a sense of interdependence and cohesiveness, and respect for boundaries (e.g., they are learning organizations) (Daft, 2010).

Hackman and Oldham (1976, 1980) have conceptualized the most elaborate and widely accepted theories of job design and motivation as contributing to the overall psychological states of meaningfulness, staff responses, morale, and job satisfaction of staff. They have identified the following core characteristics as being instrumental in advancing toward an organizational environment in which staff is productive:

- Task identity
- Task significance
- Skill variety
- Job feedback
- Autonomy

Task identity, task significance, and skill variety add to the feeling that work is meaningful. Feedback with regard to one's job performance provides information about the results achieved, thereby acting as both a developmental and a motivating factor. Autonomy inspires a sense of responsibility for one's own work, the outcomes of this work, and the work of the team. Empowerment, which is implicit in autonomy, works in much the same way as self-determination does for clients. Just as clients may terminate social work contact when their interests and needs are ignored, a lack of staff empowerment can affect pride and job performance, reduce productivity, and contribute to rapid turnover. Lack of attention to these dynamics can have a spillover effect on staff–client interactions and create situations in which staff treat clients in ways that are counterproductive to the goals and purpose of the organization.

From this discussion, you can observe the contributions of staff to the overall environment of an organization. For instance, when staff behavior is guided by a lack of autonomy or significance in their work, the organization's environment may be perceived as a "psyche prison"—a construction of reality and conformity to a preferred way of thinking and doing (Morgan, 1997). The extent to which staff are empowered and able to participate in work-related decisions makes a significant difference in the extent to which they feel valued. Likewise, the five characteristics identified by Hackman and Oldham (1976, 1980) can influence the extent to which staff engage in prosocial or extra-role behavior within the organization—specifically, a willingness to go beyond what is generally required of an individual's position. Issues that may call for an advocate role are promoting client dignity and worth, institutional racism and discrimination, and the cultural competence of the organization.

Promoting Dignity and Worth

EP 1

Social welfare organizations have the best of intentions when it comes to serving clients. Areas to consider and assess include the extent to which routine service delivery, organizational policies and practices, and professional behavior retain clients' dignity. For example, is client dignity compromised by the image of those who are in need as presented by public policy, the media, funding resources, and the residual nature of assistance? Additional factors are organizational practices and the behavior of individual professionals. In some cases, organizations and staff may unintentionally strip service recipients of their dignity by requiring them to go to unreasonable lengths, for

example, to establish eligibility for concrete aid or services. A vignette titled "Four Pennies to My Name" is a powerful illustration of one client's perspective on this experience as she attempted to comply with the eligibility requirements for financial assistance (Compton & Galaway, 1994). In the vignette, a woman recounts her experience, which includes feeling humiliated and treated as just another number. Using social justice as an organizing perspective, Reisch (2002) proposes criteria for how people are to be treated, beginning with belonging, a notion articulated by Bertha Reynolds (1951), where people are "treated as human beings, not as problem to be solved" (p. 350). Further, Reisch (2002) states, the provision of services should observe people's humanity and be compassionate without regard to the ends sought by the profession or society.

In the highly charged and often emotional response to child abuse and neglect, for example, the dignity and worth of the parents involved can take a backseat to the demands of a rigid and legalized protocol inherent in the child welfare response system. In this system, contact with people begins with an assumption of guilt and that parents are not concerned about their children's well-being. Consequently, parents experience a less than empathetic system in which the focus is on punishment and compliance rather than understanding their situation; they therefore feel judged, fearful, and hopeless (Albert, 2000; Diorio, 1992; Dumbrill, 2003, 2006; Bundy-Fazioli, Briar-Lawson, & Hardiman, 2009; Holland, 2000; Maiter, Palmer, & Manji, 2006; Van Nanette, 2005).

Routine practices to which we may have become accustomed can compromise dignity—for example, inadequate privacy in the physical space where client interviews or calls take place within earshot of others. Concerns for safety and threats of violence have prompted both public and private organizations to install metal detectors to screen visitors. Another practice involves the use of private guards or off-duty police. While you as administrator or staff may regard these practices as essential for managing risks and ensuring a safe work environment, you should also be aware of the message such measures convey to clients and the power it affords to ancillary individuals (e.g., security guards, off-duty police) who are peripherally associated with the mission and goals of the organization. Safety measures, although responding to very real concerns, nonetheless convey an image to service recipients and influence how they experience the organization. It is important to recognize that some clients may view the practice as another form of oppression and social control. When practices such as this result in clients' being treated in an indiscriminate manner, without regard for their dignity, as a social worker you are obligated to call attention to these issues and advocate for change.

Positive staff behaviors and attitudes are essential to maintaining an organizational environment in which client dignity and worth are essential to operations and service delivery. In client–staff interactions, clients should be able to expect common courtesies, such as promptness of response, respect, and a nonjudgmental attitude, each of which is fundamental is to the organizational environment. It is unfortunate when staff are either openly or subtly judgmental of clients, making remarks about their morality, veracity, character, or worthiness. Also troubling are incidents when staff members are brusque or rude, act in a way that humiliates or demeans clients, breach confidentiality, or intrude unjustifiably into deeply personal aspects of clients' lives, needlessly subjecting them to embarrassment and humiliation.

You may encounter a situation that leads you to question a colleague's competence and to consider whether this behavior with clients is a result of his or her impairment. These ongoing behaviors or actions can evolve from bad professional behavior into an organizational issue when supervisors or managers and staff allow them to go unchallenged. Moreover, such behaviors are an inhumane and unethical practice (e.g., NASW Code, 2000, Standards, 2.09, 2.10, and 2.11). Speaking with the colleague is a first step, and further discussion may involve the organization's administration. If further action is indicated, you can pursue filing a complaint with the appropriate licensing board and professional organization. You may be thinking that these are dramatic or extreme measures. Further, you may question the benefits or risks associated with your becoming involved.

An equal consideration is the extent to which the colleague's behavior reflects a pattern of behavior among the organizational staff, in which case a more system-wide advocacy change effort is indicated. A lack of organizational response to the issue may lead to **whistle-blowing** as an option for the policy advocate (Rothman, 2007). As discussed by Greene and Latting (2004), whistle-blowing is a form of advocacy to be implemented when clients' rights are ignored or in situations that represent a serious threat to client well-being and dignity. A primary reason most people are reluctant to report wrongful acts or behaviors is that the act of whistle-blowing can have negative individual and organizational consequences. Of course, there are legitimate concerns that you may have. For example, you may question your perception of a situation or your motive. You may also fear losing status and relationships with colleagues and the organization (Greene & Latting, 2004). These authors have identified factors, with integrity at their core, that you can use to assess your potential action—for example, whether you are motivated by altruism and whether your actions are to the benefit of those being wronged; whether you are a utilitarian, with a high level of moral development, driven by a sense of integrity and the responsibility to speak out, even under symbolic or literal pressures to keep silent. Finally, you are encouraged to keep well-documented records.

Staff behavior is a critical facet of organizational culture. Further, the organization's stance on ethical behavior is vital to ensuring ethical conduct and, ultimately, the manner in which people are perceived and served. Practices that are instrumental in improving the organization's environment are those that diminish the role of staff as enforcers, which over time can have an adverse effect on their functioning and lead to burnout. Upholding standards that support their dignity, worth, and rights of clients are primary considerations for taking action.

Institutionalized Racism and Discrimination

Increasingly, the landscape of America is becoming more diverse, but it is still not a postracial society. Race, even hyphenated, is the way in which people are described and how people describe themselves. Despite the fact that race is a dominant

EP 3

social construct, racism and discrimination are embedded in the fabric of our society to such a pervasive extent that many people fail to understand or recognize the many manifestations. **Institutional racism** often affects service delivery and availability of resources and opportunities in subtle ways. Therefore, it is vital that you, irrespective of your role in the organization, are sensitized to its manifestations, especially in treatment, allocation of resources, and the client experience (Abramovitz, 2005; Anderson et al., 2004; Banerjee, 2002).

Racism and discrimination, whether direct, indirect, or subtle, are in reality facets of educational, legal, economic, and political institutions, all of which influence how people are perceived and treated and the services that they receive (Abramovitz, 2005;

Rodenborg, 2004; Savner, 2000; Williams, 1990). At times, discrimination can lead to organizational practices resulting in disparate treatment of clients and client outcomes (Blitz et al., 2014). At other times, discrimination can collude with a bias of theoretical perspectives and the personal bias of a professional. Ample evidence of professional bias shows that persons of color in their encounters with systems are much more likely to be perceived as pathological, without regard to their ecological circumstances or needs (Allen, 2007; Barnes, 2008; Feldman, 2008; Richman, Kohn-Woods, & Williams, 2007; Whaley, 1998; Wolf, 1991).

The NASW Code (4.02) speaks directly to the social worker's responsibility with regard to discrimination. Social workers have an ethical responsibility to work toward (1) obliterating institutional racism in organizational policies and practices and (2) enhancing cultural competence. These are worthy goals, but they also represent formidable challenges. The first step toward meeting these challenges is developing an awareness of possible traces of a racist attitude and bias within yourself and its influence on your practice. At the systems level, it is important for you to examine whether "organizational norm (or practices) privilege some and marginalized others" (Blitz et al., 2014, p. 347). The presence of discrimination and racism creates an opportunity for you as a policy advocate within the organization to address it and propose a change to the benefit of clients, thereby improving their experience in the organization's environment (Rothman, 2007).

Cultural Competence at the Organizational Level

Cultural competence has focused primarily on the interaction between the social worker and the client, in particular racial minority clients. More recently, cultural competence has included other differences, such as sexual orientation, religion, disability, and other statuses (Abrams & Moio, 2008). Although professionals are ethically obligated to engage in the process of becoming competent to work with diverse clients, achieving cultural competence and the commitment to competence is within the sphere of the organization's leadership's responsibilities (Sue, 2006; Yan, 2008).

Cultural competence is a three-pronged effort revolving around the competence of staff, committed leadership, and an analysis of public policy insofar as it acknowledges and respects diversity and the equality of service delivery. Achieving organizational cultural competence should not be limited to supporting the sensitivity and awareness of staff, assigning staff to work with their respective racial or cultural group, providing printed materials, or using interpreters. As worthy as these measures might be, they are only beginnings to an ongoing process of achieving competence.

Both public and private organizations have attempted to accommodate diverse populations by hiring professionals or community staff who represents a specific group. Public agencies have also developed purchase of service (POS) contracts with ethnic- or race-specific community-based agencies. Cultural or racial matching, in same-race or same-culture individuals and agencies, would more likely result in professionals' identifying with their respective clients and, as a result, having a greater understanding of the group experience. However, research about the effectiveness of racial or cultural matching and its benefits to clients is inconclusive (James, 2008; Karlsson, 2005; Malgady & Zayas, 2001; Neville, Spanierman, & Doan, 2006; Yan, 2008).

The practice of racial or cultural matching in organizations evolved out of a very real need to have a diversity of color, language, and understanding in organizations where the majority of staff members were white. Although this practice is useful on one level, it is a beginning rather than an end. In effect, it creates an agency within an agency and is, at best, an interim solution. As such, it is inadequate as a means to achieve organizational cultural competence. Although it can enhance the organization's standing within the affected communities, the practice of matching raises other concerns:

- In essence, the ethnic or racial representative is solely responsible for clients with whom they share demographic characteristics, and therefore may rarely have the opportunity to work with other clients.
- When representative staff provide services only to one client group, other staff may become limited in their exposure to clients who are different, further perpetuating racial inequality.
- The practice limits the organization's ability to expose all clients to diverse professionals.
- Representative staff assigned on the basis of their race, culture, or sexual orientation are often overwhelmed by the volume of work, which can include responding to the demands of representing their community.

The NASW Standard for Cultural Competence in Social Work Practice speaks to the issue of overload, asserting that the "special skills and knowledge that bicultural and bilingual staff bring to the profession" should be compensated rather than exploited (2001, p. 26). This issue should be addressed at the systems level because it has implications related to workload, morale, and unintentional forms of discrimination.

To be effective, an organization must embrace cultural sensitivity and competence and demonstrate its commitment through its policies and practices (Chesler, 1994a, 1994b; Fong & Gibbs, 1995; Nybell & Gray, 2004; Rodgers & Potocky, 1997; Sue, 2006). A key question is the extent to which the organization allows for, encourages, and demonstrates cultural competence in its policies, rules, practices, and organizational structure (Sue, 2006, p. 28). Nybell and Gray (2004) propose the following measures for assessing an organization's cultural competence:

- Reviewing organizational policies and practice
- Assessing the organization's standing in communities of color
- Evaluating the equity in resource allocation, in particular the programs or services that consist of a disproportionate number of poor clients and clients of color
- Assessing staffing patterns, with a specific focus on who is hired, what positions are held by whom, and who is promoted or terminated
- Examining the distribution of power, focusing on who benefits and who is excluded
- Examining the narrative structures that inform agency practices, public relations, fundraisers, and board members
- Analyzing the decision-making process—specifically, who is involved (including clients) in such matters as agency location and allocation of resources, and who has access to this process

Additional resources exist for organizations to analyze their competence. The Child Welfare League of America (1990), for example, has developed a Cultural Competence Self-Assessment Instrument, which provides guidance in assessing and developing cultural competence at all levels of an organization. In addition, Strom-Gottfried and Morrissey (2000) and Cross et al. (1989) have developed organizational audits for agency policies and practice and for assessing organizational strengths and effectiveness with respect to diversity.

Of course, a culturally competent social worker or organization cannot always ensure that clients are immune from direct or unintentional bias in public policy. In fact, in the face of public policy, organizations

and social workers are often at a disadvantage, irrespective of the level of cultural competence they have attained. To this end, we recommend analyzing the cultural competence of public policy. What is the basis for this recommendation? Bias is inherent in most policies, even though their intent is to be neutral with respect to race, class, culture, and gender. Public policy, for instance, has tended to have a narrow view of the culturally or racially determined dynamics that influence how people function. Further, seldom does public policy reflect recognition of how family networks and relationships are defined within diverse groups. For example, services for the elderly, mental health services, and child welfare services are structured around the Western concept of the nuclear family rather than broad informal or kinship networks. Informal kinship arrangements, such as those found in many diverse communities, tend to be unrecognized in public policy. In child welfare, for example, relatives as well as nonrelatives have often assumed responsibility for children; nevertheless, these individuals are unable to access resources unless they formally adopt the children. The concept of formally adopting a relative, while it has certain legal safeguards, is perceived differently in minority communities. In light of this discussion, you might conclude that the impact of public policy is not neutral.

Van Souest and Garcia (2003) suggest that cultural competence at the public policy level is an issue of social justice. As such, administrators and social workers, acting as advocates, are required to confront aspects of policies and practices that are inherently biased and that have disparate and oppressive effects on various segments of the population. As Weaver (2004) observes, "the social justice aspect of cultural competence is often obscured by cultural competence conceptualized and highly focused on individual interaction." Because of the emphasis on the cultural competence of practitioners, that is, the cultural relevance of public policy may be ignored. Voss et al. (1999), speaking to policies related to Native Americans, assert that when "social policies and interventions are not inclusive of cultural dynamics," these policies tend to "rigidly enforce a kind of clinical colonialism" (p. 233).

Given that laws and public policy influence service provisions, particularly who is served and how, a stronger focus on an analysis of public policy is crucial to the cultural competence of organizational practices and social worker–client interaction. This analysis should examine the effects of public policy as well as the extent to which public policies and laws are culturally relevant or incompetent, leading to different treatment of different groups or to discrimination.

As a policy advocate, you would encourage the organization to proactively examine the influence public policy has on constituent groups to ensure that the organization is not, in fact, acting as a party to social injustice. Finally, procedural justice demands that leaders of organizations position themselves with and/or on behalf of their constituents so that the needs of diverse groups are articulated to policy makers, thereby ensuring that public policy is indeed nondiscriminatory and is culturally relevant. Distributive justice, the aspect of justice in which agencies are most often engaged, is compromised without procedural justice. For example, ideally, procedural justice involves clients in the decision-making process related to the identification of needs and services. Policy advocacy, and hence your acting as a policy advocate, aims to improve the organization's environment and services as experienced by clients. By engaging in prosocial behavior, be aware that you are essentially involved in an extra-role activity, beyond what is included in your job description. In discussing a proposed change effort with your supervisor, it will be important for you to indicate whether your action will intrude upon your routine work expectations. Also be aware that the efficacy and power of a change effort is strengthened when others are involved. To this end, soliciting the point of view of colleagues and engaging them in becoming collaborative partners in the change effort through a concerned coalition can be crucial.

ENGAGING IN COMMUNITY ORGANIZATION

EP 8

Communities may be defined as (1) geographic, within a given boundary (for example, a shared physical space) and (2) nongeographic, including virtual communities in which people share a common bond, interests, beliefs, or values and communities in which people share certain attributes or physical characteristic (Alexander, 2010; Fellin, 2001). Notable individuals who were community organizers or organized communities include Saul Alinsky, Mohandas Ghandi, Dorothy Day, Cesar Chavez, Barack Obama, and the staff involved in the settlement house movement. David Plouffe, an adviser to the Obama for President campaign, in response to critiques about

community organizing, explained the essence of the strategy: Community organizing is "how ordinary people can respond to out-of-touch politicians and their failed policies." Plouffe identified community organizing as the foundation of historical movements such as the civil rights movement, women's suffrage, labor rights, and the 40-hour workweek (Benen, 2008).

Similar to advocacy and social action, community organizing is action oriented on a larger scale and intended to effect social change in which "neighborhood organizations, associations and faith communities join together to address social problems in their community" (Brueggemann, 2006, p. 204). Furthermore, it is an arena in which participants use the power of a coalition to assess and advance their needs, develop and own solutions, and build capacity in partnership with private or governmental organizations (Brueggemann, 2006; Minkler, 2012; Rothman, 2007; Weil & Gamble, 1995).

Acknowledging that community organizing is misunderstood and misrepresented, Barack Obama (1988) described the basics of organizing a change strategy as follows:

> In theory, community organizing provides a way to merge various strategies for neighborhood empowerment. Organizing begins with the premise that (1) the problems facing inner-city communities do not result from a lack of effective solutions, but from a lack of power to implement these solutions; (2) that the only way for communities to build long-term power is by organizing people and money around a common vision; and (3) that a viable organization can only be achieved if a broadly based indigenous leadership—and not one or two charismatic leaders—can knit together the diverse interests of their local institutions. (p. 41)

Obama's explanation is consistent with Hardina's (2004) notion that social transformation is a primary goal of community organizing.

Irrespective of how a community is defined, you should be aware that communities are social systems that have distinct characteristics, such as the way in which they are organized. As a system, communities have a collective sense of connectivity, identity and power, and the issues about which they have concerns. In some instances, these factors may be more or less pertinent to a specific geographic location or community.

Organizing communities requires that you have an understanding of what matters to the people involved,

EP 2

their needs and strengths, and the context of the person [community] in environment relationship. Kirst-Ashman (2014, pp. 395–398), summarizing the work of Sheafor and Horejsi (2012), Netting et al. (2012), and Rubin and Rubin (2008), offers a set of questions that are intended to provide an understanding of community dimensions and guide an assessment:

- What are the demographics of the community, including its boundaries and demographic characteristics?
- What is the area's history, specifically the age of the community, trends in its development, and the movement in or out of certain groups?
- What are the beliefs and attitudes, such as cultural, spiritual, and political values, of residents or factions, including traditional and cultural beliefs?
- What services are available in the community? Do residents feel connected or isolated?
- How does local politics inform how the government is structured? Who has decision-making power, and what are conflicting views of issues?
- What is the state of the local economy and businesses, especially with regard to employment opportunities for residents, the unemployment rate, business ownership, and services such as public transportation?
- How is income distributed (specifically, what is the income level of residents)? Is income derived from cash public assistance or noncash benefits such as food stamps or housing subsidies?
- What is the state of housing in the community, including the age, type, density, public or private ownership, and costs?
- What educational facilities and programs are available in the community, and to what extent are schools supported by the community? What educational opportunities exist (for example, early and adult education)? How are the needs of special students met?
- What health and welfare systems are available in the community, and how adequate are those systems? What gaps in services or unmet needs exist? How are resident interactions with the police and social justice system characterized?
- What are sources of information and public opinion in the community? How do residents obtain information (for example, through newspapers, from televised programs, or from community

leaders or groups who keep the community informed about issues that affect the community and who are engaged in promoting community interests)?

In addition to answering these questions, social workers provide a summary assessment of community issues, including questions related to the challenges faced by community residents and subgroups—for example, social problems such as poverty, community violence, the adequacy of housing, public transportation, jobs, educational opportunities, police and fire protection, and gaps in services. In addition to the earlier discussion about data collection methods, Kirst-Ashman (2014) recommends holding open public community forums, using social indicators and key informants to further guide the community assessment.

Models and Strategies of Community Intervention

EP 8

Models of community organizing and intervention and their basic means of influence have been described by Rothman, Erlich, and Tropman (2001) and Carter (2000). The most frequently mentioned methods or strategies for organizing communities are summarized in Table 14-1.

Locality development seeks to build relationships within the community and enhance community integration and capacity thorough broad participation. Locality development supports empowerment in that the community is actively involved in defining its problem and determining goals (Cnaan & Rothman, 1986). Rothman (2007) has reframed locality development as **community capacity development**, in which community cohesion, the creation of community, and community capability are integral to the community's becoming empowered to act on own behalf. In Quebec, Canada, for example, locality development utilized natural helping networks and lay citizens in analyzing

TABLE 14-1 Strategies and Methods of Community Intervention

Locality Development
Social Action
Social Planning
Capacity Building

problems and planning remedial measures (Gulati & Guest, 1990). Users of services were considered to be partners as opposed to client-consumers. They facilitated the integration and coordination of programs, services, and prevention efforts in their community. The flexibility in organizational structure and decentralized administration enabled the local communities to develop programs that responded to their unique needs.

Social action as a community organization strategy is similar to our discussion of advocacy in its approach. It is the action on the part of communities to advocate so that institutions and decision makers address unfairness in resource distribution (e.g., the relocation of bus routes that disadvantaged a specific population), remedy the imbalance of power through neighborhood associations or concerned citizens (e.g., the coordinated efforts of seniors, relatives, and senior citizen advocates), and solve problems or conditions identified by the community.

Social planning as a strategy tends to be expert driven, involving a reliance on consultants and technical assistance for solving problems (Rothman & Tropman, 1987). These professionals generally work with community leaders, and the focus of their work is to expand, develop, and coordinate social policies and social services (Carter, 2000). Unlike locality development, participation by the larger community may be, but is not always, limited.

Capacity building has as its main focus increasing the ability of a community to act on its own behalf, make decisions, and direct its own actions (Hannah, 2006). This approach takes exception to the assumption that expert or governmental interventions are a primary means to achieve a solution to a community problem. Instead, the community develops its own agenda, and the work to be completed is directed "from the inside out" (Rivera & Erlich, 1998, p. 68). Organizing efforts under the auspices of Communities United to Rebuild Neighborhoods (CURN) in Chicago is an example of residents working together to resolve their community concerns. They focused on their collective community strengths and individual talents at all age levels, believing that these attributes were central to the change effort, and therefore should be identified, energized, and deployed.

Within each of the first two methods, activities may support coalition building and evolve into political and social action or social movements capable of influencing social planning. In some instances, they may overlap or be employed simultaneously (Carter, 2000;

Hyde, 1996; Rothman, 1995, 2007). Carter (2000), for example, documents how a coalition evolved into organizing a community in effective political and social action in response to inaction on the part of the Department of Justice to incidents of arson at southern U.S. African American churches in isolated rural communities in 1996. By challenging the inaction of the agents and that of the United States Justice Department about the cause of the fires, communities realized their self-efficacy as a group, bolstering their coming together and taking action as an effective community organizing coalition. Hannah (2006) notes that community capacity initiatives must be able to gain and maintain involvement of the community, which is possible if the initiative has community support.

Relying on a specific model or strategy is useful for directing the organizing effort. Burghardt (2011), however, proposes three strategic development levels of community intervention that can facilitate decisions about which model would be most useful. **Entry**, the first strategic level, emphasizes capacity building and empowerment among community members, building their sense of their power, responsibilities, and skills. During this process, issues and long-term goals are identified. Burghardt refers to the second strategic level as **coalition strategy formation**. In this process, the organizer seeks to understand and make use of the various actors that may contribute to or distract from the problem to be addressed. For example, the extent to which there is a commonality of concerns should be identified among the various individuals, groups, or other organizations in the community that could form a unified issue coalition. The third level, **transformational strategy formation**, makes use of strategies from various models. At this level, building coalitions or individual and community capacity can be implemented to bring about a planned change.

Some advantages of the three strategic levels are that they provide a means to understand the position of a community relative to an issue, where development may be needed, and the fact that they build upon each other. For instance, in the entry strategic level, building capacity within a community can be a precursor to developing a coalition. Whether you begin with a specific model or make use of Burghardt's (2011) developmental strategies in advance of a model decision, maintaining focus is important. As Homan (1999) points out, you should keep in mind that organizing to promote change "involves more than just fixing a specific problem" (p. 160). Further, in advancing the empowering capacity of a community, productive organizing includes the goal of increasing people's capability to respond effectively in the face of future challenges. Empowerment is a basic principle for working with communities. Bush (2004) articulates five essential competencies for engagement and to facilitate empowerment:

- **Informational**, in which the social worker is knowledgeable about and understands the community with whom he or she is working, including worldview, communication, and behavioral patterns and lifestyles
- **Intellectual**, in which the social worker considers the way in which information is used to advance the work with the client system
- **Intrapersonal**, in which the social worker demonstrates authentic and genuine concern and care for individuals and the community
- **Interpersonal**, in which the social worker relates with genuineness, warmth, understanding, and appreciation for the ways in which people communicate and the language or expressions they use
- **Interventional**, in which the social worker makes use of the knowledge and various skills that promote empowerment (for example, in selecting the intervention plan for the work to be done, engaging the community network and resources in the change effort, and including community participation in the monitoring and evaluation of the outcome)

Steps and Skills of Community Intervention

Theorists conceptualize community organizing in different ways, outlining different stages that vary according to the level of elaboration of relevant tasks. Rothman, Erlich, and Tropman (1995) and Rothman (1999) use a six-phase process to prepare for and address community concerns:

1. Identification of need, condition, or problem as framed by the community
2. Definition and clarification of the need, condition, or problem
3. Systematic process of obtaining information
4. Analysis of the information
5. Development and implementation of a plan of action
6. Terminal actions and evaluation of outcome or effects

Of course, the process may not be entirely linear, because new information may require alternative action, including making a new start, reframing strategies and tactics, or using a mix of intervention models (Rothman, 2007; Rothman, Erlich, & Tropman, 1999).

Organizing Skills

When working with communities, implementing change strategies requires a set of behaviors and skills that are observable and measurable. For example, you should gauge your ability to establish rapport with and be sensitive to diversity, the extent to which you demonstrate genuineness and empathy, and the effectiveness of your communication skills. Because organizing involves groups or communities, skills in group facilitation, development of interpersonal relationships, and management of group dynamics are also critical. Homan (2008) adds to the skill base, emphasizing a balance between the objective and subjective, self-awareness, patience, focus, and timing. Other skills and competencies include those embodied in policy analysis, research methods, and the management of data.

Organizing and Planning with Diverse Groups

Rivera and Erlich (1998), in analyzing models of community development or organizing, challenge the assumption that prevailing models (i.e., locality development, social planning, and social action) are color-blind and therefore applicable in any community. They conclude that there are additional factors to be considered in working with communities of color:

- Racial, ethnic, and cultural aspects of the community
- Implications of this uniqueness in particular communities
- The empowerment process and the development of a critical consciousness

Rivera and Erlich's work is intended to guide our thinking in planning and organizing and, in fact, represents a significant contribution to organizing strategies. Heretofore, methods had an implicit assumption that good intentions sufficed in community interventions and that, unlike direct practice, considerations of race, ethnicity, and culture in this work were secondary. The three levels of contact for entry into communities, as conceptualized by Rivera and Erlich (1998), facilitate a greater understanding of work with diverse groups and of the roles beyond those traditionally considered in social work. Table 14-2 outlines the three levels.

TABLE 14-2 Levels of Community Contact

ENTRY LEVEL	CHARACTERISTICS
Primary	Requires that an individual have the same racial, cultural, and linguistic background as the community. The community is open to and respects this individual.
Secondary	The individual need not be a member of the same racial, ethnic, or cultural group but should be closely aligned and sensitive to community needs. He or she may serve as a liaison to the broader community and facilitate contact with institutions outside the community.
Tertiary	The individual is an "outsider" yet shares the community's concerns. The practitioner's skills and access to power—rather than his or her ethnic, racial, or cultural identity—are valued assets.

Source: Adapted from Rivera and Erlich (1998).

Ethical Issues in Community Organizing

EP 1

It is the groups or associations within communities that are best able to identify their needs and plan solutions. As social workers, we can become involved in their efforts as advocates, change agents, and planners, using our skills, knowledge, and values grounded in principles of social justice and empowerment to help groups and communities to achieve their goals. A question discussed earlier for advocates is equally applicable to organizers: When should organizers act on behalf of the community, and when is it advisable for representatives to speak for their community to represent themselves (Ezell, 2001)?

Hardina (2004) points out that community organizing and its methods address issues that are not directly covered in the social work Code of Ethics. For example, the Code does not address dual relationships (situations in which two or more distinct relationships involve the same person) between the organizer and community residents. Nor does the Code address the choice of tactics that an organizer might use. To the first point, specifically in regard to dual relationships, suppose you are a member of the community as well as an organizer at entry level 1 of the Rivera and Erlich (1998) schema. Because you are a part of the community, there may have been numerous occasions on which you have interacted with other residents socially and politically. In community practice, for instance, you may have relationships with people as friends, relatives, or members of a sports team. Your memberships in the community provide you with a familiarity to the community, the people, their values, and concerns. As a member, your involvement can lessen mistrust and, in effect, lessen the time needed to build relationships and bonds. However, in the strict sense of the Code, being

involved in boundary spanning relationships may be perceived as an ethical violation.

Ethical behavior requires that community organizers observe self-determination and that a community is informed of and consents to the tactics to be used and understands the risks and benefits. Hardina (2004) suggests that if the ethical principle and subsequent dilemma are not obvious, the organizer should use the Ethical Rule Screen proposed by Loewenberg, Dolgoff, and Harrington (2005). For example, "protection of life" or "privacy and confidentiality" must be weighed when considering a forceful tactic that may place people at risk. An ethical decision-making framework by Reisch and Lowe (2002), as discussed by Hardina (2004, p. 600), also provides a series of steps that are useful for community organizers:

- Identify the ethical principles that apply to the situation at hand.
- Collect additional information necessary to examine the ethical dilemma in question.
- Identify the relevant ethical values and/or rules that apply to the ethical problem.
- Identify any potential conflicts of interest and the people who are likely to benefit from such conflict.
- Identify ethical rules and rank them in terms of importance.
- Determine the consequences of applying different ethical rules or ranking these rules differently.

Although the Code may be limited with respect to specific macro-level strategies, in most instances the Code, along with the principal beliefs of the profession, guide ethical practice. For example, the Code and principal beliefs of the profession can be helpful in considering the primacy of clients' rights, the uniqueness and worth of people, and the social justice focus on economic and social equality.

Social Media as a Resource for Social Advocacy and Community Organizing

In today's world of text messaging, email, social media, online tools, and other forms of digital communication, the capacity to reach, engage, and organize a broad spectrum of people about a particular issue is infinite. Be aware, however, that social media can be combined with good old-fashioned face-to-face contact, such as door knocking. In any case, a focused message that has a direct appeal is essential to recruiting and engaging participants in the change effort. To sharpen the message in which you have identified a community issue, you might consider using the **SMART** goal framework along with the goal development process discussed in Chapter 12. Clearly defined goals promote interest and clarify the intent of the organizing effort.

Although the opportunities provided by social media are infinite, this means of communicating has limitations. For example, certain demographics may not have ready access to this form of communication. Social media may be generational in that their appeal can vary by age. Specifically, it may be easier for young people to access and respond to this form of communication than it is for some older people. Irrespective of age, certain other factors should be considered, such as whether individuals or communities have the capability to communicate using social media tools. Nonetheless, because these resources provide for connective relationship opportunities between people, you should evaluate their benefit.

MACRO PRACTICE EVALUATION

EP 9

Each of the macro-level strategies discussed in this chapter lends itself to a variety of procedures for which intermediate and final outcomes can be assessed. Evaluation seeks to assess the extent to which the change effort and the strategies employed were successful and can include collecting quantitative data, qualitative data, or a combination of the two. After completing an assessment that documented a need and the subsequent development of a resource, you would want to measure the extent to which the resource was responsive and the extent to which it was utilized, including the perceptions and opinions of individuals for whom the resource was developed.

Empowerment—whether in organizing, social action, or improving an organization's environment—is a consistent theme in macro-level practice. In keeping with the notion of empowerment, the evaluation process should include client groups. They should be involved in establishing success indicators and outcomes of the change effort, as well as their perceived level of empowerment (Gutierrez, Parsons, & Cox, 1998; Lum, 2004; Secret, Jordan, & Ford, 1999).

Because evaluation is a process, another facet involves examining how the outcome was achieved. For example, it is important to determine which of the strategies that were implemented to mobilize resources engaged the general public or public officials, organized a community, and resulted in the most effective response. Should your change effort enlist the help of volunteers and solicit feedback from them—for example, asking them to rate the appeal of specific recruitment literature or presentations? It may be necessary to target your evaluation to a specific group. For instance, did a group respond more favorably to an in-person presentation in comparison to other methods, such as a targeted social media message? Collecting this information helps to determine which strategies were the most effective, under what conditions, and for which populations.

Measures of success used by organizations tend to be reported in aggregated client statistical data; therefore, evaluating the effectiveness of macro-level practice can be a challenge. In evaluating the outcome of a program objective, for example, an organization's criterion might be the number of "homeless families with children that found affordable housing." Further analysis might involve examining a change in status of the families who obtained housing. Here, the evaluation focuses on the overall outcome.

A pre- and postintervention rating scale measuring the change may be applied in situations involving social action and advocacy (e.g., single subject design, scales). Change can be measured on an incremental basis, after a particular action technique, and at the end of the project. You may also decide to collect qualitative information along with statistical data. For example, in an interview format, groups and communities provide descriptive information regarding improved relationships between the police and a community. The evaluation may be implemented as a summative or formative process and include both qualitative and quantitative data (Weiss, 1998). For example, in conducting a needs assessment, you might question the extent to which needs were being met or whether new resources are required by using a survey and follow-up group interviews to help you better understand the statistical data collected from the survey.

Several innovative approaches hold promise for enhancing the effectiveness of developing and planning community programs. The first approach utilizes the methodology of developmental or intervention research (Comer, Meier, & Galinsky, 2004; Rothman & Thomas, 1994; Thomas, 1989). Developmental research is a rigorous, systematic, and distinctive methodology consisting of techniques and methods taken from other fields and disciplines. Its methodology relies on social research and model development and is sufficiently flexible to accommodate the unpredictable and uncontrolled conditions in most practice settings (Comer, Meier, & Galinsky, 2004). Using this approach allows for strategies and change efforts in the form of programs to be tested and then modified based on the results.

To see how this process works, let's say that your agency developed a program for youth who had repeated stays in the shelter system. The primary goal was to reunite them with their families, and a secondary goal was permanency. This approach was a significant departure from the way in which the shelter system functioned, so the system was the target of change. Home visits, while the youth were still in the residential phase of the program, were identified as critical factors in moving them toward reunification. After a period of time, you would collect both qualitative and quantitative data to determine the effectiveness of home visits and the resources required and whether a modification was indicated. Gathering this information would enable the agency to direct or redirect its resources toward achieving both the primary and secondary program goals.

Evaluation, irrespective of the method, requires clearly specified goals and clearly articulated objectives in measurable terms. In general, evaluation is an ongoing process for which it is important to establish indicators at the beginning of the intervention. The process involves continuous, systematic monitoring of the intervention's impact, and this requires development and implementation of techniques of data management. Systematic analysis of data allows you to determine, for example, if the program activity or intervention is being implemented as planned and whether it is accomplishing the stated program goals (Gardner, 2000; Lewis et al., 2001). Conducting an evaluation requires skills in selecting an appropriate research design, applying techniques of measurement, and analyzing data. The specific details of the various methods are beyond the scope of this book. The requisite knowledge needed to implement the evaluation process is commonly discussed in research courses. Keep in mind, however, that tracking the impact of a change effort with regard to the desired outcomes is essential.

SUMMARY

This chapter introduced you to macro-level intervention strategies for which the target of change is a system. Today's social, economic, demographic, and political trends present numerous opportunities for action and intervention at the macro practice level. In talking to social workers in preparation for writing this chapter, we were impressed with the breadth and depth of the macro practice strategies they used and the ease with which they understood the need to observe the bridge between micro and macro issues. The social workers saw their practice as holistic and were comfortable employing a range of strategies to help people resolve problems or change social conditions. As one social worker stated, "It would be difficult to ask people to change without also addressing the circumstances and conditions that contribute to their situations." The person and environment focus reflected in this statement, in essence, frames the fundamental tenets and foundation of macro practice.

COMPETENCY NOTES

EP 1 Demonstrate Ethical and Professional Behavior

- Make ethical decision by applying the standards of the NASW Code of Ethics, relevant laws and regulation, models for ethical decision making, ethical conduct of research, and additional codes of ethics as appropriate to context.

  Knowing the ethical behavior that is required for professional social work practice helps social workers to deal with situations and make sound decisions in working with clients and assessing organizational policies and practices. Knowledge of ethical standards is essential to maintain professional boundaries and to avoid dual relationships.

  In situations in which guidance in the CODE is unclear, or there are competing ethical obligations, social worker rely on an ethical decision-making framework to guide decisions.

- Demonstrate professional demeanor in behavior, appearance, and oral, written, and electronic communication.

Professional practice requires that social workers interact and problem solve with people in ways that demonstrate the values, principles and ethics of the social work profession.

Problem solving requires an understanding the group or community involved, considers diverse interests and needs and strengths and capacities.

EP 2 Engage Diversity and Difference in Practice

- Present oneself as a learner and engage clients and constituencies as experts in their own experiences.

Understanding diverse groups and communities is an ongoing process. Social workers view themselves as learners and engage those with whom they work as key informants.

EP 3 Advance Human Rights and Social, Economic, and Environmental Justice

- Apply an understanding of social, economic, and environmental justice to advocate for human rights at the individual and systems levels.

As advocates, social workers critique and analyze policies and practice to ensure that client's rights are observed and that clients are not disadvantaged by structural barriers that influence the ability of groups and communities to maximize their potential.

- Engage in practices that advance social, economic, and environmental justice.

Social workers are attuned to the continuous and changing needs of groups and communities, the mechanisms of oppression and discrimination, and where indicated advocate for policies that advance justice and wellbeing.

EP 4 Engage in Practice-Informed Research and Research-Informed Practice

- Use and translate research evidence to inform and improve practice, policy, and service delivery.

Social workers use research methods to collect data for assessment and to inform practice with groups and communities. For example, advocacy, social action or developing resource, and evaluating outcomes.

EP 5 Engage in Policy Practice

- Identify social policies at the state and federal level that affect well-being, service delivery, and access to resources.

As advocates, social workers provide leaderships for promoting change or improvement in the quality and services client's receive. Social worker acting as change agents in organizations, and as advocates for groups and communities by influencing policies and legislation.

- Apply critical thinking to analyze, formulate, and advocate for policies that advance human rights and social, economic, and environmental justice.

As advocates, social worker examine policies, including those in their organizations to ensure that client's rights are observed, and that policies are responsive to issues or justice.

EP 7 Assess Individuals, Families, Groups, Organizations, and Communities

- Collect and organize data, and apply critical thinking to interpret information from clients and constituencies.

Social workers use data from assessment questions to inform interventions with groups and communities so that focused goals are developed that respond to needs, and values of those involved and which in advances rights and justice.

EP 8 Intervene with Individuals, Families, Groups, Organizations, and Communities

- Critically choose and implement interventions to achieve practice goals and enhance the capacities of clients and constituencies.

Following the assessment of issues or concerns to be addressed, the intervention strategy selected shows evidence of being the best suited to achieved the results relative to identified needs, interests and the eventual goal outcome.

EP 9 Evaluate Practice with Individuals, Families, Groups, Organizations, and Communities

- Critically analyze, monitor, and evaluate interventions, programs, processes, and outcomes.

Social workers and clients engage in ongoing evaluation of an intervention and the outcome.

This process requires monitoring and measuring progress relative to effectiveness of the intervention in achieving stated goals.

SKILL DEVELOPMENT EXERCISES

in Developing Resources, Advocacy, and Organizing as Intervention Strategies

1. Assess the organizational policies or practices of your agency using the questions identified by Rooney.
2. Using Figure 14-1, think of the potential benefit of linking an individual client situation that you have worked with to a change effort at the macro level.
3. Choose a public policy or social problem. How would you describe your position on either one or both? Would you describe yourself as a liberal (conservative, moderate, or radical), a conservative (fiscal, religious, or social), or a centrist? Think about how your identified position influences your thinking about the policy or problem.
4. Describe how client dignity and worth are fostered in your agency.
5. Think about the potential ways in which social work practice is influenced by public policy.
6. Rate your current position on each of Hackman and Oldham's core characteristics of job design and motivation.
7. Identify a change that you would like to make in your agency. Identify the risks, benefits, and potential opposition to your change proposal.
8. Think about the range of client problems in your agency. Consider how you might conceptualize a micro-to-macro assessment and intervention.

CHAPTER 15

Enhancing Family Functioning and Relationships

with Craig Schwalbe

Chapter Overview

The purpose of this chapter is to introduce you to many of the intervention skills and strategies that social workers commonly employ with families. The chapter is designed to present social work practices across the multiple settings and ways in which families are engaged in interventions. Toward that end, the chapter provides an overview of selected skills that are used in family therapy settings, but also a range of skills and intervention strategies that can be employed when social workers seek to teach families new skills or to support families that are experiencing difficult problems related to a variety of psychosocial concerns, such as physical health diagnosis, disability, housing problems, mental health, justice system involvement, and substance abuse, among many others.

The chapter opens with a discussion of engagement strategies, what the family therapy literature often refers to as *joining*. The chapter proceeds with a discussion of *first-* and *second-order change strategies* and examples that are associated with each. In the end, this chapter will present intervention skills and strategies that underlie many of the contemporary evidence-based interventions to which family members can be referred.

In this chapter you will acquire knowledge that will enable you to:

- Engage and assess couples, families, and parents.
- Convene the initial session and engage families in the helping process.
- Understand the difference between first- and second-order change strategies.
- Utilize problem-solving strategies, skill training, and contingency contracting with families.
- Assist families in enhancing their interactions by increasing communication skills.
- Assist families in modifying their interactions.
- Assist families in understanding the influence of family roles and modifying them when needed.
- Assist family members in disengaging from conflict.
- Assist families in modifying misconceptions and distorted cognitions that impair their interactions.
- Assist families in modifying family alignments.

EPAS Competencies in Chapter 15

This chapter will give you the information needed to meet the following practice competencies:

- Competency 2: Engage Diversity and Difference in Practice
- Competency 6: Engage with Individuals, Families, Groups, Organizations, and Communities
- Competency 8: Intervene with Individuals, Families, Groups, Organizations, and Communities

INTERVENTION APPROACHES WITH FAMILIES

Throughout the history of the social work profession, social workers have engaged families as a routine part of their interventions. Mary Richmond urged family visitors to engage all family members, and particularly fathers, in intervention strategies designed to ameliorate poverty and protect children, and in their work with delinquent youths (Richmond, 1899, 1917). Similarly, advocates for social work practice in the juvenile justice system also wrote about the importance of engaging parents in the probation process, encouraging probation officers to partner with parents to lend strength to their leadership position and to assist them into bringing up their children (Flexnor & Baldwin, 1914). Both argued that enduring change and growth were not possible without involving family members in the intervention process.

These early texts bring to the fore two themes that have permeated social work with families to this day: families as a target of change, and families as a support system for individual clients. For instance, Functional Family Therapy, an evidence-based intervention for the treatment of adolescent delinquency, treats delinquency as a symptom of problematic family communication patterns and works to modify family system structure as its primary purpose (Alexander et al., 2013). Characteristic intervention strategies include reframing, diverting negativity, and on-the-spot interventions (described below), among others. Other evidence-based family interventions include multisystemic therapy (MST) for delinquency and adolescent mental health problems (Henggeler et al., 2009) and multidimensional family therapy (MDFT) for adolescent drug use (Liddle, 2009). When utilizing interventions such as these, the family is itself defined as the client.

On the other end of the spectrum are programs that treat family members as caregivers or as sources of social support. The Helping Carers to Care program is illustrative of interventions of this type (10/66 Dementia Research Group, 2009). In this intervention, family members who care for patients with Alzheimer's type dementia learn about the disease and develop caregiving skills and strategies for reducing caregiver burden. Other evidence-based family interventions of this type include parent education programs like The Incredible Years© (Webster-Stratton, 1984), parent management training (Kazdin, 2005), and family psychoeducation (SAMHSA, 2009). In these interventions, an individual family member may be defined as the identified client, whereas the family unit, or a subsystem within the family unit, may be described as the target system, or the focus of the change effort.

Whether working with families in familywide change processes or enlisting the support of family members on behalf of an individual client, social workers should implement interventions that are informed by a careful assessment of family system structure and that are adapted to the cultural milieu of families. Further, it is equally important to understand family interventions within the frameworks of human rights as well as the ethical standards of the profession that urge social workers to advance social justice. These themes will be addressed throughout the sections that follow.

FAMILY ENGAGEMENT

Social workers who work with families adopt a distinctive view of client engagement, in which the social worker establishes working relationships with each member of the family as well as with the family as a whole. Family therapists often use the word *joining* to describe this process. The term *joining* implies that, in some respects, the social worker enters into a family and becomes part of the family system. And just as individuals within a family have a distinctive relationship with other individual members as well as with the family as a whole, social workers who work with families strive to do the same.

In some respects, family engagement, or **joining**, is a matter of language and semantics. Social workers who adopt a family perspective often use collective language to emphasize the family unit. Whereas social workers may direct interventions to

EP 6

individual family members (e.g., "[name], I understand you to be saying that you feel extremely stressed by [something]. Is that correct?"), they may also direct interventions to the family as a whole (e.g., "It seems to me that your family is under a great deal of pressure and that in a way the family is trying to protect itself from [the source of stress]. Do you agree?") or to specific subsystems within the family unit (e.g., "I gather that the parents in this family are worried about the impact of [stress] on the family as a whole, and that the kids are trying to be helpful. Does this sound accurate?"). The discrete use of language can serve to separate individuals or to emphasize collective membership and a sense of togetherness and bonding.

Social workers who work with families employ collective language purposefully to establish simultaneous relationships with individuals within a family as well as with the family as a whole. In practical terms, successful family engagement happens when social workers establish working relationships with each member of the family and when social workers utilize family systems language that emphasizes boundaries, both around the family as a whole and boundaries that demarcate important family subsystems. To do this, it is recommended that social workers elicit the opinions and perspectives of each family member who participates in any meeting or intervention and to establish rapport with each member of a family early in an intervention. Indeed, clinical research in family therapy settings suggests that interventions are most successful when all members report strong relationships with their social worker, and that interventions are less successful when family members vary widely in the strength of their social worker–client relationships.

Throughout the engagement process, it is imperative that social workers avoid reductionist explanations based in blame, particularly as they relate to judgments about individual family members. As a practical matter, blame tends to aggravate family conflict and to erode family functioning (Patrika & Tseliou, 2015). Blame can also amplify emotional and behavioral problems in individual family members who shoulder ascribed responsibility for problematic family dynamics. Thus, blame is inconsistent with the goal of establishing rapport with each family member. Moreover, blaming individuals is inconsistent with a family systems approach to interventions, in that problematic behaviors of individual family members are seen as influenced by the family systems context in which they are embedded.

Who Should Participate?

There has been much debate over the years about which family members should be engaged in family interventions (Nichols, 2012). Some schools of family therapy argue that all members of a group that self-identifies as a "family" should be present. The argument favoring this perspective is grounded in a family systems view of family and individual functioning—that problems of individual family members are symptomatic of family system arrangements that involve all members. Thus, all family members, even the youngest, as well as family members who seem peripheral to a presenting problem, are responsible for participating in the change process. Such an argument is consistent with the family engagement perspective described above, which favors treating individuals as members of a collective, where the collective is treated as the client or as the unit of analysis. When implementing this approach, social workers emphasize collective language and maintain a strong focus on family system processes during all stages of the intervention, including active efforts to define presenting problems as manifestations of family system characteristics during the engagement phase.

Other family intervention models are less prescriptive and more flexible, and indeed this is the perspective that we are presenting here. In some settings, it will make sense to insist that all family members participate in an intervention. However, the diversity of settings in which social work is practiced, and the diversity of problem areas to which social work interventions are addressed, make a prescriptive rule unwieldy and inappropriate. Moreover, such a rule can itself become a barrier to social work interventions where family members refuse to participate or where their participation is not feasible. Therefore, the decision about who to engage in family interventions should be based in part on a clear understanding of the purpose of the intervention.

What should social workers do when the intervention purpose suggests that certain members of a family actively participate, but for some reason they either refuse or are unable to participate? Such can happen when children are encountering problems in school and when school social workers are seeking to enlist a partnership with parents to resolve school-based problems, or when adult children of parents who reside in nursing homes decline to visit their family member or to participate in critical decisions about end-of-life care. Often, though it is optimal to engage all caregivers in such situations, the ideal is simply not feasible. There is no magic formula, but there are options. In many contexts, social workers will be forced to accept limited family member engagement. When this happens, it may be important for social workers to inform family members who are present about the limitations of this approach, in the spirit of informed consent. Additionally, the limitation itself can become the topic of problem solving as part of the engagement process. Moreover, in rare occasions, social workers can take an assertive stance, utilizing the power of "no," and simply refuse to serve families when key members are unwilling to participate. This may be the ethical course of action when, in the social worker's judgment, a family cannot make progress without the active involvement of all key family members. Social workers can also attempt persuasion strategies, enlisting involved family members to try to convince reluctant family members to participate, even if only to try meeting with the social worker on one occasion.

Whether social workers adopt the position that all family members should participate or that only strategically selected family members should participate, they should strive to avoid the appearance of blaming family members who decline to participate. The spirit of family interventions generally avoids blame, as discussed above. When social workers attribute responsibility and blame to individual family members for choices about participation, or when social workers endorse blaming themes during meetings with family members, they inherently diminish their working relationship with the family as a whole even as they may gain short-term advantages by increasing rapport with individual members. Rather, social workers should consider family member choices about participation as information to consider in an assessment of family system structure. For example, the decision to participate or not can reflect how power dynamics and decision-making authority are wielded in a family. Or it could be emblematic of a level of subsystem strength or cohesiveness that either supports or erodes family adaptive capacity. These observations can be tested through a deeper assessment of family system structure, utilizing circular questioning as discussed in Chapter 10, for example.

Cultural Perspectives on Engagement

The engagement process with families is strongly influenced by sociocultural realities, which in turn demand culturally competent practices on the part of social workers. During engagement, social workers must also be aware of the potential intrusion of their own bias into the helping process. Different emphases on the quality of family life, marital relationships, or problem definition may be a function of cultural and class differences between you and the families with whom you are working. A study conducted by Lavee (1997), for example, showed noticeable differences between how social workers and families defined a healthy marriage. In the study, the professionals involved tended to focus more on such indicators as cooperation and communication, whereas families tended to place greater emphasis on cohesion, love, and understanding.

EP 2 and 6

Your sensitivity to culture and the acquisition of knowledge that will prepare you to be culturally competent are ongoing learning processes. Although certain factors may be germane to various cultural or racial groups, it is important that you clarify specific content and its relevance to a family's culture, subculture, or race. Goldenberg and Goldenberg (2000) suggest that learning about specific cultures requires social workers to assess the extent to which families identify with their ethnic or cultural background and to ascertain how much their background plays a role in the presenting family concern. Toward this end, "therapists must try to distinguish family patterns that are universal (common to a wide variety of families), culture-specific (common to a particular group) or idiosyncratic (unique to this particular family)" (p. 52). Patterns in family interactions vary, of course, and your understanding this fact essentially minimizes a tendency to formulate generalizations about family dynamics. Identification with a particular culture or race may be a peripheral issue for some families. In other instances, it may be useful to help families determine how culturally specific behavior affects the problem at hand (Flores & Carey, 2000; Sue, 2006).

Note that culture should not be used as an excuse to minimize or overlook family behavior or relationships that are damaging or harmful to the family or individuals. With these words of caution in mind, we highlight factors that may be considerations when initiating interventions with families who are diverse with respect to culture or race.

Differences in Communication Styles

Because there are differences in the speech patterns in nonnative English speakers, in many situations it may be more important to focus on process rather than content. For example, in some families, there may be a "pause time"—a period signaling when one person has finished and another can begin speaking. In other families, members may be comfortable when everyone talks at the same time. Your discomfort may result in your interrupting the speaker or speakers. In general, you will find a range of communication styles in which some are more demonstrative in both verbal and nonverbal language; others, unaccustomed to seeking outside help, may appear to be passive because of a sense of shame or suspicion in their encounter with professional helpers (Berg & Jaya, 1993; Boyd-Franklin, 1989; Fong, 1997; Pierce & Elisme, 1997).

Studies by Mackey and O'Brien (1998) and Choi (1997) that examined conflict resolution, emotional expression, and means of coping with stress revealed differences in communication styles based on gender and ethnicity. Emotions are complex experiences, expressing reactions to past, present, and future events. The person's worldview frames the emotional experience, as does his or her language. The range of words and language that many of us use daily to describe emotions may, in fact, be unfamiliar to or have a different connotation for diverse groups. Moreover, it is important that you examine your own communication style and assess how it is informed by your own cultural preferences.

In understanding communication styles and differences, techniques and strategies from postmodern family practice models may be used. For example, the narrative and social constructionist approaches emphasize a more conversational, collaborative approach, allowing for a dialogue that is more meaningful to the client, as well as facilitating communication between the family and social worker (Laird, 1993). Sue (2006) also draws attention to **high-** and **low-context communications**. In low-context cultures, such as the United States, there is a greater emphasis on verbal messages as well an orientation toward the individual. In contrast, high-context cultures rely on nonverbal expressions, group identity, and a shared understanding between the communicators. Of course, there are exceptions; for example, Sue (2006) notes that African Americans tend to be high-context communicators even though they live in the United States. Differences in meaning of words in other cultures may be subject to misinterpretation. For example, saying "no" may actually mean "yes" (e.g., Arab or Asian), although these are words that are taken for their literal meaning in Western societies.

Hierarchical Considerations

Depending on the age–sex hierarchies in some cultures, you are advised to address the father, then the mother, then other adults, and finally the older and younger children. Grandparents or other elders in the family may actually be held in greater esteem than parents and figure prominently in the family's hierarchical arrangement. Caution is particularly advised in working with immigrant families in which a child who has greater proficiency in the English language is used as an interpreter in interviews with parents. You should be sensitive to the fact that the child's role in this instance may undermine traditional roles in the family and result in tensions between parents and their children (Ho, 1987; Pierce & Elisme, 1997).

Beyond being sensitive, being empathetic and exploring the parents' feelings are means by which you reinforce your understanding of their role. In addition, when families come from cultures in which chronological age and familial hierarchy play a significant role (e.g., Asian Indian and African American families), open dialogue between parents and children may be viewed as insolent or disrespectful (Carter & McGoldrick, 1999; Segal, 1991). Also note that what may appear to you to be hierarchically defined roles in the family may instead be complementary. Flores and Carey (2000), in counteracting the popular notion of machismo dominance in Hispanic families, emphasized this point. Specifically, the father functions as the authoritarian, protective figure in the family; the mother's role is complementary to that of the father in that she is expected to be expressive, caring, and nurturing. As you join with the family, it is best to ask questions, seek their preferences, and explore their rules with respect to family order and hierarchy.

Authority of the Social Worker

The authority vested in the social worker can vary by culture and race. For some families, the helping practitioner is perceived as a knowledgeable expert who will guide them in the proper course of action. Therefore, they expect you to take a directive role when working with the family. An informal and egalitarian approach, which is second nature to many Americans, is actually considered improper in many cultures. Furthermore, your perceived authority, which is reflected by the use of first names, tends to emphasize social distance. In fact, addressing adult family members on a first name basis, unless you are invited to do so, can be disrespectful, magnifying the historical tradition of calling people by their first names in situations in which first names would not be permitted if both participants had the same social identity (Berg & Jaya, 1989; Flores & Corey, 2000; Robinson, 1989; Sue, 2006).

A passive response to authority from immigrants, migrants, or refugees, for example, may stem from their social and political status in the United States, a distrust of helpers, and a fear of expressing their true feelings to figures of authority (Janzen & Harris, 1997; Pierce & Elisme, 1997; Potocky-Tripodi, 2003; Sue, 2006). Eliciting information, for example, through direct questions about the needs and wants of each family member, can be problematic. Also, the informal use of language and expectations of full disclosure may diminish the family's trust. Devore and Schlesinger (1999) suggest using empathy instead, as a facilitative means to form an alliance.

Aponte (1982) perhaps summarizes these issues best by stating that power and authority are critical elements of the family–social worker relationship, especially for ethnic or racial minorities. Most diverse families perceive the social worker as acting in his or her professional role rather than fulfilling a social role; therefore, social workers are viewed as representatives of the majority society. Within this context, the social worker symbolizes the larger society's power, values, and standards. Because of the authority that is assigned to you as a professional, it is important to explicitly recognize families as decision makers and experts on their situations, and to ensure that you have their informed consent before proceeding further (Palmer & Kaufman, 2003).

As a social worker, you should not hesitate to discuss your professional background, because these families need assurance that you are capable of helping them resolve their difficulty. When writing notes, you should be aware that documenting in case notes—although necessary—may reinforce perceptions of the unequal power balance between you and the family (Boyd-Franklin, 1989; Flores & Carey, 2000). To alleviate clients' concerns, you will find it helpful to explain their purpose, standards of confidentiality, and requirements for information that may involve an identified third party.

The Dynamics of Minority Status and Culture in Exploring Reservations

Minority statuses, which encompass a range of social identities, are other factors that may cause a family or family member to have reservations about seeking help. Families may fear "what might happen" if their problems are brought out into the open (Nichols & Schwartz, 1998, p. 132). In truth, poor, minority, and gay or lesbian families have good reasons for their apprehensions and anxieties in encounters with helping professionals. Boyd-Franklin (1989) and Lum (2004) explain that the historical experience of minority families, in which they have often been perceived as unhealthy, may cause them to hide their problems until they have escalated to a point of crisis. Indeed, the communities in which these families live may reinforce the silence. Also, the unspoken rule of keeping family secrets can be more pronounced in minority families because of the value placed on privacy or a sense of shame about involving an outsider in family matters. Flores and Carey (2000) and Lum (2004) both emphasize that families are more likely to feel a level of comfort when they do not feel the need to defend who they are or their culture. Lum (2004) emphasizes the importance of the family's confidence in the helping relationship as well as the importance of mutual trust between the social worker and the family.

Reservations about attending family sessions may be a particular issue among ethnic minority families in which some members are undocumented or residing illegally in the United States (Falicov, 1996; Fong, 1997; Pierce & Elisme, 1997). In addition, immigrant or refugee families may be unfamiliar with formal helping systems, and their lack of familiarity can cause them to be hesitant about becoming involved (Potocky-Tripodi, 2002). Wright and Anderson (1998) suggest that in actively tuning into the family, you might pose a question such as "What is it like being with the client [family], in your preparation for the initial session?" The question has a twofold purpose. In effect, not only are you *tuning in* to the family, you are also evaluating whether you may have reactions to the family that have the potential to enter into the session. In your assessment, consider including two additional questions: "What is it like to be this family?" and "What does it mean to this family to seek professional help?" The answers to these questions will help you to show sensitivity in your initial interactions with the family and to understand their experience in seeking help. To lessen the family's concerns or reservations about the contact with you, it can be useful for you to affirm the protective function of reluctance, whether in a family member or the family system as a whole, as a measure of safety for the family.

ORCHESTRATING THE INITIAL FAMILY OR COUPLE SESSION

EP 6

The goal of bringing the family together is to identify the problem at hand by eliciting the viewpoints of the various family members. The initial session, whether it occurs in the office, home, or institution, is referred to as the **social** or **joining stage** (Boyd-Franklin, 1989; Nichols, 2012). In this stage, a central task is to establish rapport and build an alliance with the family.

VIDEO CASE EXAMPLE

In the video "Home for the Holidays 1," Kim, the social worker, is working with a lesbian couple, Jackie and Anna, who came to family treatment in conflict about how open to be about their relationship to their families, especially in light of the upcoming holiday. Jackie comes from a family in which there is open communication. She is frustrated with the reticence to deal openly with feelings that is reflected in Anna's family. Near the beginning of the session, Kim states, "Jackie contacted me because the two of you disagree about your holiday plans."

In facilitating the social or joining stage, the social worker's tasks are twofold:

1. Ensure that each family member can voice his or her opinion without interruptions from other family members.

2. Encourage family members to listen so that members feel understood and accepted.

You can further facilitate this stage by adopting an attitude of inquiry: What can I learn from and about this family that will help me work with them?

The initial session with families is crucial. The family members' experiences during this session determine in large measure whether they will join with you and contract to work toward specified goals or solutions. Moreover, they may perceive the initial session as a prototype of the helping process. Table 15-1 identifies the objectives to be accomplished that will further lay a solid foundation for future work with the family. All the objectives listed in the table will then be discussed, so that you understand their relevance and can use them in both planning for and evaluating initial sessions.

1. Establish a Personal Relationship with Individual Members and an Alliance with the Family as a Group

In working with couples or families (or groups), social workers have a twofold task of establishing a personal relationship with each individual while developing a "connectedness" with the family as a unit. To cultivate relationships with family members, you use **socializing**, a technique that involves brief social chitchat at the beginning of the session to reduce tension. Joining or coupling techniques to expedite entry into the family system must respect culture, family form, family rules, and the current level of functioning. You may also find that using the family's language and idioms—for example, "He's messing up in school"—facilitates your

TABLE 15-1 Orchestrating the Initial Family or Couple Session

1. Establish a personal relationship with individual members and an alliance with the family as a group.

2. Clarify expectations and explore reservations about the helping process, including potential dynamics of minority status and culture.

3. Clarify roles and the nature of the helping process.

4. Clarify choices about participation in the helping process.

5. Elicit the family's perception of the problem.

6. Identify wants and needs of family members.

7. Define the problem as a family problem.

8. Emphasize individual and family strengths.

9. Establish individual and family goals based on your earlier exploration of wants and needs.

connection to the family. You can further connect to the family by conveying your acceptance and by engaging them in identifying their strengths. Conveying acceptance and offering support may be especially critical to vulnerable members of the family.

In the initial session, empathic responding can be particularly useful in establishing rapport with a member who appears to be reserved or reluctant to be involved. For example, when a member does participate spontaneously, your task is to draw him or her into the session:

Social worker: Tamika, we haven't heard from you about how you felt when you learned you were coming to see a social worker.

Tamika: I thought that it would be a waste of time.

Social worker: My sense is that you are unsure about the reason that you are here. It is not unusual to feel that way. You said you thought that being here would be a waste of time. Would it be helpful if I explained the purpose of the session with you and your family?

The social worker's response included a reflection of Tamika's feelings and empathy as a facilitative skill. Empathic messages show genuine interest that can cause reserved family members to become more active. Conversely, if Tamika's lack of involvement is related to family dynamics rather than to her feelings, you will need to be mindful whether encouraging her to express an opinion has potential risks. In either case, you should endeavor to distribute time and attention somewhat equally among members, to highlight individual strengths, and to intervene when one member dominates the conversation or when the session involves members' communicating blaming, shaming, or put-down messages.

Finally, effectively connecting with families requires that you understand and have appreciation and empathy for the sociopolitical and cultural context of the family and for the family's collective strengths and competencies. Often, it is these attributes that have enabled the family to function in spite of their difficulties.

2. Clarify Expectations and Explore Reservations about the Helping Process

Family members have varying and often distorted perceptions of the helping process and may have misgivings about participating in sessions (e.g., a waste of time; talking won't help). To identify obstacles to full participation (which is a prerequisite to establishing a viable contract), you should elicit the responses of all family members to open-ended questions like the following:

- *What were your concerns about meeting with me?*
- *What did you hope might happen in our meetings together?*
- *What were your feelings about what might happen in this meeting today?*
- *Would you imagine for a moment how you would like things to be different in your family?*

Questions of a more specific nature, intended to help family members express their concerns, are illustrated in the following examples:

- *Are you concerned that your family might be judged?*
- *In your community, how would others deal with this problem?*
- *Does seeking help from someone outside of your family make you feel uncomfortable?*
- *In what way do you think that I can be of help to your family?*

As you explore reservations, concerns, and even hopes from each family member, you can broaden the focus to the family by asking: "I'm wondering if others share the same or similar concerns as . . .?" As members acknowledge similar feelings, they may begin to realize that, despite their feelings, as a unit they share certain concerns in common. For example, family members might disagree about the functionality of rigid family rules, but they all may have anxieties about less income due to job loss and the financial stability of the family.

In interpreting a family member who is reluctant, unwilling, or inactive in the family session, you should be sensitive to such factors as an individual's personality and cultural norms. Some individuals may prefer to observe processes before they engage or participate. Culture may influence such expressions as feelings, so a family member may be baffled by related questions. Personality or culture aside, certain family members will continue to have strong reservations. You can address their reluctance in the initial session by asking them one of the following questions and addressing their responses:

- *What, if anything, would make you feel better about participating?*
- *Having heard the concerns of other family members, on a scale of 1 to 10, which one would you rate as highest or lowest priority?*

- *Given your concerns, are you willing to stay for the remainder of the session and decide at the conclusion whether to continue?*

The intent of these questions shows willingness on your part to negotiate the terms under which a family member participates and also acknowledges his or her right of choice. If this type of question does not result in a change of heart, you might, for example, ask the member if he or she is willing to be physically present, but emphasize that he or she is not obligated to talk. This invitation diminishes the pressure on the person to contribute. As a caveat, however, it would be important to advise the individual that it is expected that he or she refrain from distracting nonverbal behavior. As a final note on the reluctant family member, be aware that his or her behavior may be self-protective because he or she has been identified as the source of the family's problem, especially if the person feels ganged up on by other family members.

3. Clarify Roles and the Nature of the Helping Process

In exploring misgivings and reservations, you should educate families about the nature of the helping process and clarify both your own and their roles. In educating families about the helping process, your objective is to create an atmosphere and structure in which problem solving can occur. Role clarification is also addressed toward the end of the initial session in which an initial contract is negotiated.

4. Clarify Choices about Participation in the Helping Process

In the instance of referred contact, you can reiterate that the family is free to decide whether further contact with you will meet their needs and, if so, what to work on, regardless of the concerns of the referring source. If contact is mandated, it is necessary to clarify what you are required to do (e.g., submit a report to the court) and the parameters of required contact. In addition to mandated concerns, you can advise families that they can choose to deal with other problems of concern to them.

5. Elicit the Family's Perception of the Problem

In initiating discussion of problems, social workers ask questions such as "Why did you decide to seek help?" (in the case of voluntary contact), "What changes do you want to achieve?," or "How could things be better in the family?" Eliciting the family's view of the

problem is equally important in involuntary or referred contacts. In such cases, the mandate or referral has been summarized, but time and space are provided so that the family members can tell their own story—for example, "Your family was required by the juvenile court judge to have contact with our agency because Juan was reported to the school truancy officer. This is the information that I have, but I still need to hear from you why you believe you are here." Juan and his parents both have a point of view, which may be similar or vastly different. As you elicit each person's viewpoint about the problem and its solution, you will, in some instances, hear different accounts. Your task, however, is to move the family toward reaching a consensus about the problem that they can all support.

In sessions with a family or a couple, you will want to be aware of differences in interpretation and the various family roles within the family with respect to issues of gender, power, and boundaries. In addition, Rosenblatt (1994) urges us to pay attention to the language and metaphors used by the family as they describe their concerns. In particular, how family members express their views reflects their culture, their realities, and the meaning assigned to the family experience. The family experience includes exploring spirituality or religion in the life of the family (Anderson & Worthen, 1997).

6. Identify Wants and Needs of Family Members

As you engage the family in a discussion of problems, listen for needs that are inherent in their messages, as illustrated in the family session with a foster mother and Twanna, an adolescent parent, in the following video case.

VIDEO CASE EXAMPLE

In the video "Adolescent Parent and Foster Mother, Part 1," Janet is the foster mother of Twanna, a parenting adolescent. Her child is 2 years old. The relationship between Janet and Twanna has generally been good. Janet cares for the child, which allows Twanna to attend school so that she can obtain a high school diploma. Janet called the social worker because she is frustrated, as lately Twanna has returned home after school later than expected. Janet has a strong bond with Twanna's 2-year-old; however, Janet stressed that it was important that Twanna spend time with her child as well.

She reported that the situation is "affecting the entire relationship" between the two of them.

Glenda, the social worker, began the initial session with a summary explanation of her understanding of the contact. Then she invited Janet, the foster mother who initiated the contact, and Twanna, the adolescent parent, to share their perceptions of the problem. During the initial discussions of needs and wants as expressed by Janet and Twanna, the social worker respected the rights of the foster mother while at the same time she created a safe place for the adolescent to express her views. Also, she summarized the situation and empathized with the potential developmental conflict that was occurring with Twanna. That is, even though she is a mother, as an adolescent her interest in being with friends is developmentally appropriate. In fact, her main reason for not coming home at the expected time is because she wants to "hang out with her friends." Further, she reasoned, "I know that Janet is here, it's not like I am leaving my baby alone."

At the same time, the social worker acknowledged Janet's unspoken need that her caring for the child not be taken for granted. Janet believed that Twanna should bond with the child, because she, Janet, "will not be there in the future." Attending to the different needs and wants as expressed by Janet and Twanna was a balancing act, as Glenda did not want to convey the perception that the needs of one person had priority and that she only supported that person's position. In summarizing the concerns identified by Janet and Twanna, Glenda asked them to identify what they would like to see changed. In preparation for problem solving, the objective was to pinpoint the conflict and to have the two of them explore options that would meet both of their needs. One option considered by Twanna, for example, was "I could call if I am going to be late." By identifying and highlighting common needs, the social worker focused the intervention on the similarities rather than the differences. In this way, Glenda helped Janet and Twanna to develop goals and tasks that they could mutually work toward to improve their relationship. The session concluded with the two of them having reached several critical agreements.

7. Define the Problem as a Family Problem

Earlier in the chapter, we highlighted the type of messages you can use in clarifying the systemic nature of problems. Continue to maintain this position stance throughout the family session, emphasizing that every member's perspective is important; that family members can do much to support the change efforts of other family members; that all members will need to make adjustments to alleviate the family's stress; and that the family can do much to increase the quality of relationships and the support that each member receives from others. Despite your efforts to define problems as belonging to the family, you will often encounter a persistent tendency of some members to blame others. In these situations, your tasks are to:

- Monitor your own performance to ensure that you do not collude with family members in labeling others as a problem, thus holding them responsible for the family's difficulties.
- Model the circular orientation to causality of behavior and emphasize that family members reciprocally influence one another in ways that perpetuate patterns of interaction.

In the discussion of wants and needs, you should take care to avoid a potential perception that you support one person's position over that of other family members. When one person is perceived as the source of the family's difficulties, your task is to challenge this linear thinking by asking others about their role in creating and maintaining the problem.

VIDEO CASE EXAMPLE

Returning to the case of Janet and Twanna, the patterned interaction between the two consisted of Janet's being frustrated because Twanna failed to return home at the agreed-upon time. In turn, Twanna reasoned that Janet was there to care for the child, so the fact that she delayed coming home was not neglectful behavior on her part. Neither had talked about what they really wanted, and their interactions ended up with both being dissatisfied because neither had recognized the ways in which their behaviors contributed to the problem.

Even though Janet attributed their strained relationship to Twanna's behavior, she was careful not to label it. In fact, she said, "I understand that she wants to be with her friends."

Unfortunately, this level of generosity is not always present in families, as there is a tendency to blame or label behavior, generally in negative terms. In these instances, you can move to counteract patterns of attributing blame by using the technique of delabeling. Rather than focusing on a member's perception of behavior, **delabeling** emphasizes the reciprocal nature of the problem. Use of the technique can also set the stage for each member to identify positive behaviors that each would like from the other. Consider the following case example in which the social worker poses a series of questions to a mother and son. The two individuals have a history of blaming messages that are counterproductive to their communicating with each other.

In this case, both mother and son were receptive, so the social worker helped them formulate reciprocal tasks that each could work on during the week to minimize the conflict in their relationship. Their reciprocal tasks were intended to change the dynamics of their interaction by changing their individual behavior and, therefore, their responses to each other. For example, the mother would refrain from labeling John's plan as stupid, and John, in turn, agreed to listen to her concerns.

8. Emphasize Individual and Family Strengths

In work with families, you can highlight family strengths and protective factors on two levels: the strengths of individual members and the strengths of the family as a whole. At the individual level, you may observe the strengths and resources of members during the session, drawing them to the attention of the family (e.g., Twanna is a good student). At the family level, you can report on the strengths you have observed in the way members operate as a group (Janet and Twanna have a good relationship). Protective factors and strengths include the presence of a supportive network as well as resources and characteristics of family members that contribute to and sustain the family unit. Examples of strengths-oriented statements follow:

- *It is my sense that even though there are problems in your family, you seem to be very loyal to each other.*
- *Anna, your family's getting together for the holidays seems to connect members to each other.*
- *Anna and Jackie, your relationship appears to be strong, despite the difficulties that Jackie has experienced with your family.*
- *Janet, taking care of Twanna's child while she goes to school shows that you are very supportive of her goal to obtain a high school diploma.*

Family strengths and protective factors may also be utilized to communicate a focus on the future. In particular, the hopes, dreams, talents, or capacities of individual members and the family as a whole are means to energize them to resolve current difficulties. While a goal in the initial session is to move the family toward reaching a consensus on their concerns, it is the

CASE EXAMPLE

John is a young man with mental illness. He has decided to move out of a group home and live independently with his girlfriend of several years. His mother, Mrs. G, is adamant that the move is a stupid decision, and she insists that John is incapable of living independently. Rather than focusing on John, the social worker utilized the following questions to focus on Mrs. G's participation in the problematic situation:

- *You've said that John doesn't listen to you about your concerns related to his plans. When you discuss your concerns with John, how do you approach him?*
- *When John says he doesn't want to talk to you about his decision, how do you respond?*

- *How does John's reluctance to talk to you affect you and your relationship with him?*

After posing questions to the mother, the social worker then divided questions between the mother and the son to explore the son's participation in the identified problem by asking the following questions:

- *John, how does your mother approach you when she wants to discuss her concerns?*
- *What is your reaction to her approach?*
- *What might she do differently that would make you want to talk to her about your plans?*

strength of the family—rather than the problem itself—that will ultimately enable them to resolve their difficulties. By exploring coping patterns with previous difficulties, experiences with positive episodes or past successes, and hopes and dreams for family life, you can activate family strengths and note their resilience in support of their capacity to change (Weick & Saleebey, 1995).

9. Establish Individual and Family Goals Based on Your Earlier Exploration of Wants and Needs

Goals that flow from this exploration include individual goals, family goals, and goals that pertain to subsystems (e.g., Anna and Jackie want to spend the holiday together). You might also help members to identify family goals by exploring answers to the "miracle question" (de Shazer, 1988, p. 5): "Janet and Twanna, imagine that one night while you are asleep, a miracle happens. When you awaken, how will the tension in your relationship have changed?" When asked this question, even the most troubled couples or families are able to describe a new miracle relationship. This vision and other desired conditions that they identify can then become goal statements, guiding efforts of both the family and the social worker.

FAMILY INTERVENTIONS

EP 8

Family interventions are here classified broadly according to two types: first-order and second-order change strategies (Nichols, 2012). The primary distinction between first- and second-order change strategies is that **first-order strategies** are aimed at solving a presenting problem without regard to modifying family system structure, whereas **second-order changes** involve modification to family system structures as the primary vehicle for problem solving. Or, said another way, first-order strategies attempt to solve problems within the current family structure; second-order strategies attempt to foster changes to family structure itself.

Both first- and second-order change strategies are consistent with a family systems perspective, and both rely on an assessment of family system functioning as discussed in Chapter 10. For the most part, first-order change strategies described below treat family system arrangements as resources or barriers to problem solving, and both types of intervention strategies rest on a thorough assessment of family resilience factors that can be leveraged in the support of change.

At times it can be tempting to dismiss or devalue first-order change strategies as less technical or less potent than second-order change strategies. To hold such a view is a cognitive distortion for several reasons, however. First, the challenges of implementing any family intervention are to be able to detect and assess family system characteristics, and to establish a strong working alliance with the entire family system. Both first- and second-order change strategies require careful assessment of family structure and successful joining. Second, devaluing first-order strategies carries with it the implicit assumption that family system structural changes are the better, more enduring kind of change. In fact, even "dysfunctional" family systems have adaptive capacity and strengths, and social workers should not assume that structural changes within families are always required. Lastly, in practice, first- and second-order strategies are usually blended. Indeed, an unintended consequence of a first-order strategy can be a second-order change, and at times it can be difficult to disentangle specific interventions in terms of their intended first-order and second-order change outcomes.

VIDEO CASE EXAMPLE

In the video "Adolescent Parent and Foster Mother," 17-year-old Twanna, a parenting adolescent, is single. Prior to coming to live with Janet, she had been in placement since the age of 8, with three other foster families. As she grew older, and especially after she became pregnant, she was no longer welcome as a member of the last family. Out-of-wedlock births, especially among adolescents and teens, remain taboo, and the young women are stigmatized. In fact, her previous foster parents were outraged and embarrassed by her pregnancy and requested that she be removed from their home. As Weinberg (2006) notes, young single mothers often "represent a number of marginalized categories": they are young, female, impoverished, racial or ethnic minorities, from lower- or working-class families, and most of all they have had children outside of the institution of marriage. Also, the young women have experienced a number of failures, from their families, the education system, and in some instances their community. In Twanna's case, she is also vulnerable because of an additional marginal category, that of being a ward of the state. Her biological mother had been judged inadequate, hence she became a ward, and her child now also has the same status. Until she came to live with Janet in her home, Twanna's support system consisted of a series of child welfare workers.

In working with Twanna, it would be important to be aware of the other challenges that she faces, specifically her developmental stage and that of her child. In many respects, her wants and needs and that of her child—related to their developmental journeys—have certain similarities, summarized in the comparisons below.

Twanna	Child
Identity and independence	Autonomy
Intimacy	Nurturing
Self-efficacy	Self-esteem
Attachment	Attachment
Relationships	Social interactions

Developmentally, however, they differ, as a young child needs consistency and the adolescent is in the process of exploration and experimentation. While adolescents search for their identity, separate and apart from their families and through their peers, the young child's sense of self is gained through interactions with his or her caretaker. In Twanna's case, she is attempting to meet her own needs and those of her child, which, without the support of Janet, could result in role strain and overload. The social worker noted this conflict in her summary statement to Twanna: "What you are saying is that you understand that you are responsible for your child, but that you also need to be with your friends."

In the broader scheme of things, changes in the bonds between an adolescent seeking greater autonomy and his or her adult caretakers may require changes in interactions and communication patterns (Baer, 1999). As a foster parent, Janet makes certain demands that are consistent with her role as a parent, aspects of which include her obligation to ensure the well-being of Twanna and her child. According to Weinberg (2006), interventions with minors who are also parents is a balancing act between being a disciplinarian and an emancipator. It is not uncommon for parents to establish protective boundaries, which may include anxieties about both peers and the neighborhood, and to undertake intense monitoring (Jarrett, 1995). For example, Janet wanted to meet Twanna's friends so she "could get to know them." This family unit is, however, different from the normative family structure, and the rules of the state that has custody of Twanna and her child set a certain tone for their interactions. For example, as a family unit, their interactions may be primarily with professionals; supportive family networks of kin and friends are not a given. In many respects, Janet and Twanna are attempting to establish functional family rules without the benefit of role models pertinent to their family form and structure.

FIRST-ORDER CHANGE STRATEGIES

The first-order change strategies reviewed below are all directed to helping families overcome challenges that disrupt their equilibrium, helping them to return to a state of homeostasis. They work with resources within families as currently structured to enable them to mitigate family system stress without focusing on such family system topics as boundary maintenance, decision-making power and authority, or implicit family rules. This chapter presents three first-order change strategies: problem solving, skills training, and contingency contracting.

Problem-Solving Approaches

Problem-solving models addressed in Chapter 13 can be extended directly to social work with families with positive effect. For instance, the application of the task-centered model, including the task implementation sequence, can be extended to social work with families with little to no modification (Tolson, Reid, & Garvin, 2003). Similarly, solution-focused therapy has a long history of direct application to family interventions

(Selekman, 2005). Both of these models utilize flexible procedures that, from a process standpoint, vary little whether the target system is an individual, a subset of family members, or all members of a family.

VIDEO CASE EXAMPLE

An example of the application of the task-centered model for families can be found in the case of Janet and Twanna. During the first session, the social worker, Glenda, helped Janet and Twanna identify the presenting problem (Twanna does not come home to care for her baby as agreed), to establish a common goal (that Twanna will be home to provide care for her baby), and to identify tasks (to call Janet when Twanna expects to be late, to be home every night to put the baby to bed at 6 p.m., to discuss plans on Sunday evenings, including plans to invite friends over). Further, the social worker asked Janet and Twanna to rehearse their conversation, and throughout the planning process, she prompted Janet and Twanna to be specific about their plans, including when tasks would be accomplished.

During the second session, completion of the first set of tasks revealed further conflict between Janet and Twanna about proper child care strategies (whether babies should be pampered with treats) and also about Janet's need for advice and help with managing tantrums. In the end, the social worker led Janet and Twanna into a conversation about how to problem-solve through these two emergent issues.

Although the steps or procedures of problem-solving models may not require modifications when working with families, the case of Janet and Twanna illustrates some of the ways in which family interventions vary from interventions with individuals. First, the case illustrates the importance of engaging family members simultaneously in the intervention process. Thus, social workers using problem-solving approaches with families will seek to obtain the perspectives of multiple family members on matters such as the definition of the problem, goals, exceptions (when using a solution-focused model), and tasks (when using a task-centered model). Often, social workers will need to mediate differences of opinion, all while striving to maintain strong relationships with each individual family member as well as with the family as a whole.

Second, although elements of the family system structure are usually not the target of an intervention when using a problem-solving approach as a first-order change strategy, this does not mean that social workers are inattentive to family system structure in their assessment. During the first session with Janet and Twanna, Janet revealed that she was in a dual role relationship, having the responsibility to assure the baby's care needs and also to help Twanna to take over the role of primary parent. Role conflict regarding the care of Twanna's baby became central during the second session. In this instance, role conflict represented an important source of conflict and thus a potential barrier to problem solving but also might be a source of strength as it afforded both Twanna and Janet of the secure knowledge that Twanna's baby would be well cared for. The social worker who adopts a family systems approach may discuss matters of family system structure such as role conflict directly with families during the task implementation sequence, for example, or search for exceptions to problematic family functioning when using a solution-focused approach.

Third, while problem-solving efforts can appear to be egalitarian processes, this is in fact not the case in most families. Power and decision-making authority, both formal and informal, vary across and within subsystems of a family. Social workers need to recognize power hierarchies and make decisions about how to lead the problem-solving process in light of this information. Rarely should a social worker act to negate a formal hierarchy, for example. Instead, interventions with families should reinforce an adaptive utilization of power and authority that maximizes human rights and social justice (Mcdowell, Libal, & Brown, 2012). At the same time, problem-solving efforts that are conducted without regard to the informal power of individual family members and subsystems may contribute to the failure of a problem-solving effort. Indeed, even young children have the power to derail a problem-solving effort through noncooperation and the exercise of personal agency.

Finally, the sociopolitical environment of the family can have important implications for problem-solving interventions as well. For example, in the Janet/Twanna case, Twanna's intersecting identities (teenager/parent/foster child) and the definition of the family (as a foster family) can have important social meaning among her friendship networks as well as for the internal functioning and roles within the family.

Social workers should be attentive to the meaning ascribed by family members to sociopolitical factors, and to the way in which the sociopolitical environment creates opportunities and barriers for achieving progress in problem-solving efforts.

Skills Training

Social workers are frequently called upon to teach skills either as a core intervention activity or as an ancillary intervention in support of a larger intervention effort with families. Examples of interventions with skill-training components include parenting skills programs, caregiver support programs, and communication skills training. Parenting skills programs teach child-rearing practices to minimize the use of harsh parenting practices and to increase the consistency of positive parenting practices such as the use of praise and strategic reinforcement of target behaviors in children (Kaminski et al., 2008). Caregiver support programs, often developed for family members who care for clients suffering from dementia, help caregivers to develop management strategies that meet client emotional and physical needs and de-escalation strategies for helping clients return to a baseline level of emotional functioning after becoming anxious, confused, or upset (Jensen et al., 2015). Communication skills training programs help families to maximize their problem-solving and listening skills and to decrease criticism and conflict (Hawkins et al., 2008).

For these and other problems, packaged evidence-based programs are available, and their use is recommended whenever possible. Indeed, in the skill-training categories presented above, large-scale synthesis of published and unpublished outcome research points strongly to the effectiveness of skill training when it is implemented consistently and in accordance with the intervention manuals that are frequently available (Henggeler, 2011). At the systems level, implementation of evidence-based skills training can make an important difference for families who are involved in child welfare, juvenile justice, and health care systems.

Often, however, social workers are called upon to teach skills for problems where manualized, evidence-based interventions do not exist. Moreover, skill training can be part of larger intervention efforts like task-centered social work and cognitive behavioral therapy where clients require specific skills in order to complete planned intervention activities. For these instances, research in the field of organizational psychology (Healy & Bourne, 2012), as well as research on skill-training programs in the human service fields, is directly relevant and is suggestive of a set of principles that can be built into any skill-training intervention. These principles are oriented toward skill mastery as well as transferability; that is, they help clients both to learn the skill and to implement the skill under real-world conditions.

The first principle is elementary for social workers: to conduct a careful assessment of clients' potential skill deficits. Care should be taken at this stage because a lack of skill expression does not necessarily indicate a skill deficit. Instead, environmental contingencies could suppress skillful behaviors or reinforce expression of behaviors that are opposite to a given skill. For example, Twanna may know specific soothing behaviors to use when her infant becomes upset or has tantrums, but employing these skills may require specific cues from Janet to act as reminders, or Twanna may need to employ other skills associated with emotion regulation to manage her own agitation. In such a case, an intervention may be needed to modify the environment to make skill expression more likely.

Second, once a skill deficit is ascertained, it is important for the social worker and client to define the skill as specifically as possible (McGinnis, Sprafkin, Gershaw, & Klein, 2011). Often, skills have cognitive as well as behavioral components. Both should be explicated. In conducting this step, it is important to incorporate as much as possible the contingencies and complications that clients will encounter when they transfer skill training to their day-to-day lives (Healy & Bourne, 2012). Research indicates that skill training that is divorced from the context in which clients will eventually utilize their new skills can impede skill transferability.

Third, teach skills through presentation and discussion. Often, skills taught by social workers include a series of mental and behavioral steps, so that skill implementation by clients initially requires effortful memory. To facilitate learning, research suggests that clients be engaged in a process of active learning (Healy & Bourne, 2012). Active learning can involve mental rehearsal, linking new knowledge to prior knowledge and experience, and developing their own definitions for key concepts and skill stages. The key is to help clients internalize and reinterpret knowledge, maximizing the depth of mental processing that they engage in on their way to learning.

Fourth, many skill-training programs include role models of successful skill expression. For example, The Incredible Years© program, an evidence-based intervention for the prevention and treatment of disruptive behavior problems in early childhood, utilizes video role modeling (Webster-Stratton, 1984; Webster-Stratton, Reid, & Marsenich, 2014). The videos present vignettes to model implementation of key intervention principles and to foster discussion among participants. Of course, video role models are not available, nor required, for most skill-training interventions. The social worker can provide role modeling through role-play exercises in which the social worker demonstrates positive use of skills. Here again, it is critical that the role model incorporate the complexity of the target environment in which clients will eventually use the skills.

Finally, clients should be afforded the opportunity for skill practice where direct feedback is possible (Healy & Bourne, 2012). Consideration should be given to the structure of practice, again ensuring that the practice context mirrors the contingencies that clients will face when implementing their skills in the real world. In a meta-analysis of parenting skills programs, among the most important components for parenting outcomes was the opportunity to practice skills under observation *with their own children* (Kaminski et al., 2008). Results of the meta-analysis revealed that such practice had a strong impact on outcomes. Contrariwise, role-play practice was not associated with skill gains. To be sure, the findings are specific to parenting skills programs, but the general principle is that the training strategy should mirror the complexity that clients will encounter when trying to generalize their newly learned skills.

Contingency Contracting

Social workers often broker reciprocal agreements among family members. In this kind of quid pro quo or **contingency contract**, a member agrees to disengage from conflict if the other party agrees to avoid using code words that always prompt a negative response. Individuals are receptive to making changes when other parties agree to make reciprocal changes for two reasons. First, people are more prone to give when they know they are getting something in return. Second, when all parties involved agree to make changes, no single person loses face by appearing to be the sole cause of an interactional problem.

Contracting for reciprocal changes can be a powerful means of inducing change. Contingency contracting counters the tendency to wait for others to initiate changes and encourages mutual engagement in the change process. This mutual involvement may spark collaboration in other dimensions of their relationships—an important gain where interactions have been largely dysfunctional rather than collaborative.

Family members are unlikely to be able to implement reciprocal contracts if they have not moved beyond competitive bickering and blaming one another for their problems. For this reason, we recommend deferring use of this technique (unless clients spontaneously begin to negotiate) until you have assisted them in listening attentively to one another and changing the tone of their interactions. It is also essential that participants demonstrate a commitment to improving their relationship. As Becvar and Becvar (2000a) point out, if family members view their own or others' changes as emanating primarily from meeting the stipulations of an agreement, rather than as a way to improve their relationship, they are likely to devalue the changes. Therefore, you will want to ask family members to explicitly clarify that improving their relationship is the primary factor motivating their willingness to make changes.

The following are examples of reciprocal agreements that could have been utilized with Jackie and Anna (see Video Case: "Home for the Holidays") and Twanna and Janet (see Video Case: "Adolescent Parent and Foster Mother"). You may use them as a guide in assisting families to develop their own agreements.

- Jackie agrees to talk with her family if Anna stops pushing and allows her to do so when she is ready.
- Jackie agrees to communicate her feelings if Anna agrees to accept that there are times when Jackie is too tired to talk.
- Janet will refrain from interfering with Twanna's parenting and agrees to help her strengthen her bonds with her child.

In developing reciprocal contracts, it is wise to encourage family members to make their own reciprocal behavioral agreement. By so doing, they become invested in the proposed changes. Moreover, they often generate innovative and constructive ideas, based on their knowledge of their particular family that might not occur to you. To facilitate families in making proposals, you can use a message such as the following: "It's clear that each of you is unhappy with the situation. Perhaps this is a good time for you to develop ideas about what you could do to improve the situation." You could then prompt them to think about reciprocal actions.

As you mutually consider proposals, it is important to explore potential barriers and guard against the tendency to undertake overly ambitious actions. Initial task exchanges in reciprocal agreements should be relatively simple and likely to succeed, especially when intense conflict has marked interactions. When a feasible reciprocal proposal has been agreed upon, you can assist family members to reach a further agreement that specifies the tasks each member will complete prior to the next session. In developing and planning to implement these tasks, follow the steps of the task implementation sequence (outlined in Chapter 13). As you plan task implementation with family members or couples, stress that each person must exercise *good faith* in carrying out his or her part of the contract, as illustrated in the following message:

Social worker: You have agreed to make the changes we've discussed in an effort to improve the situation for everyone. To make these changes successful, however, each of you will need to carry out your part—no matter what the other person does. Waiting for the other person to carry out his or her part first may result in neither of you making a move by the time of our next session. Remember, failure by the other person to honor the contract is no excuse for you to do likewise. If the other person doesn't keep to the agreement, you can take satisfaction in knowing that you did your part.

Stressing the individual responsibility of all family members to fulfill their respective commitments, as in the preceding message, counters the tendency of clients to justify their inaction in subsequent sessions by asserting, "He (or she) didn't carry out his part. I knew this would happen, so I didn't do my part either." If one or more family members have not fulfilled their parts of the agreement, you can focus on obstacles that prevented them from doing so. When the results have been favorable, you can focus on this experience to set the stage for exploring additional ways of achieving further positive interaction.

SECOND-ORDER CHANGE STRATEGIES

The second-order change strategies reviewed below aim to help families adopt family structural characteristics that are more adaptive than current modes of functioning. Whereas in first-order change strategies social workers help families solve presenting problems as the direct focus of their work together, second-order change strategies consider presenting problems as manifestations of the hidden taken-for-granted family characteristics that we described in Chapter 10 as family structure. Thus, the second-order change strategies presented here solve presenting problems indirectly through changes in family system structure characteristics. That is, these intervention strategies focus on such topics as family rules, boundaries, communication patterns, and hierarchy. This chapter presents four second-order change strategies: modifying misconceptions and distorted cognitions, modifying communication patterns, modifying family rules, and modifying family alignments and hierarchy.

Modifying Misconceptions and Distorted Cognitions

Cognitions are often the basis for erroneous beliefs that produce dissatisfaction in couple and family relationships. Left unresolved, resentment toward others can become fertile ground for repetitive dysfunctional interaction. Unrealistic expectations of others and myths are two other forms of misconceptions that contribute to relationship problems. As with rules, unrealistic expectations are not always obvious, so you may have to clarify them by asking family members about their expectations of one another. Myths are similar to rules in that they govern family operations by shaping beliefs and expectations that can profoundly influence interactions in couple and family relationships.

To diminish misconceptions and dispel myths, bring them out in the open, using empathy to help family members recognize their distorted cognitions. Misconceptions and myths generally protect people from having to face the reality of their cognitions and perceptions. Therefore, attempts to change them can be perceived as threatening. Seldom are they relinquished without a struggle because introducing an alternative perspective or new information that is contrary to a person's beliefs creates **cognitive dissonance**. In addition, making essential change entails resolving fears, not the least of which is risking the consequences of learning and implementing new behavior. In these instances, your empathetic response to fears and ambivalence and providing emotional support can be the impetus for people to change.

In this case example, observe that as the social worker addressed the family myth, he highlighted the adverse impact of the myths on Gary. This tactic

CASE EXAMPLE

Consider a family in which an adolescent, age 17, is experiencing extreme tension and anxiety as a result of parental expectations. During family sessions, it becomes apparent that the parents expect him to be a top student so that he can become a doctor. It is also obvious that the parents embrace the generalized myth "If you try hard enough, you can become anything you want." In an effort to reduce the pressure on the son, to dispel the myth as it applies to him, and to modify the parents' expectations, the social worker meets separately with the parents. The following excerpt is taken from that session:

Social worker: I've been very concerned that Gary has been making an almost superhuman effort to do well in chemistry and physics, but he is not doing well in these subjects. It is my impression that he feels pressured to become a doctor, and that one reason he's so anxious is that he doesn't believe that he can do better despite his best efforts. It's important to him to have you think well of him. But he is falling short even though he continues to drive himself.

Father: Poof! Of course he is working hard. Why shouldn't he? He can become a doctor if he really wants to and continues to apply himself.

You know, I could have been a doctor, but what did I do? I goofed off. I don't want Gary to repeat my mistake. He should recognize that he has opportunities that neither his mother nor I had.

Social worker: I sense your concern and care for Gary. Is it your perception that he is goofing off? I understand that both of you share the belief people can do anything they want. This message has been clear to Gary, and he's blaming himself because he's not making it, no matter how hard he tries.

Mother: Don't you think anyone can succeed in anything if they try hard enough?

Social worker: Actually, this belief is inconsistent with what I know about differences between people. Each of us has different aptitudes, talents, and learning styles. Some people are able to handle types of work that require dexterity. Others are able to visualize spatial relationships. Everyone has certain aptitudes, types of intelligence, and limitations. What's important in deciding a future career is discovering what our own aptitudes are and making choices that match them. I wonder if each of you can identify talents and limitations that you have.

switched the focus from the abstract to the concrete and provided the parents with an opportunity to review and evaluate their beliefs. The social worker then further attempted to invalidate the myth by asking them to apply it to themselves.

No doubt, you will frequently encounter families who have distorted perceptions of one another that contribute to repetitive dysfunctional interactions. Recall from Chapter 13 that labeling the behaviors of others is a common source of cognitive and perceptual distortions. Labeling is like wearing a blinder because it places people in a certain frame, thereby limiting their attributes and behaviors to fit the framed image. In effect, the frame effectively obscures other qualities, so that in dealing with an individual, a person simply has to rely on his or her preexisting cognitions or perceptions without having to think.

Myths that distort individual or family perceptions can extend beyond those that influence internal family dynamics. They can also be linked to discrimination, bigotry, and negative schemas ingrained in societal and institutional perceptions and in attitudes held about certain families. Distortions can be so embedded that for some individuals they do not warrant further critique. Instead, they become the generalized narrative that informs what people believe about others. For example, minority families are often criticized for their children's performance on standardized achievement tests; conclusions are drawn about youth based on their style of dress or music preferences; immigrant families are expected to act, dress, and speak in a certain way that is comfortable for mainstream society; and families who are

EP 2

different by virtue of their physical attributes, sexual orientation, language, or customs are mocked, shunned, or threatened. On a macro level, these perceptions and distortions can influence where families choose to live, how they perceive their safety, and with whom their children are allowed to interact.

When you observe myths and distortions about others operating in families, you have a responsibility to address them in the same manner as you would in intervening in family dynamics because they affect the families toward whom this behavior is directed. They are also a source of stress and strain for those who hold these beliefs, infusing negativity in their interactions. A word of caution is in order, however. In focusing on the impact of labeling, myths, and distorted perceptions, either in intrafamilial or extrafamilial interactions, take care to describe the specific behavior rather than using a label to characterize the behavior.

Modifying Communication Patterns

Communication approaches to families consist of teaching family members the rules of clear communication. The aim is to regulate and modify family communication patterns and alter communication styles to promote positive interactions and family relationships (Jackson & Weakland, 1961; Satir, 1967; Whitaker, 1958). It is believed that the patterns that family members use to communicate with one another are often interpreted in various ways and are often punctuated by faulty cognitions and perceptions. What the sender believes is the message is not necessarily what the receiver understands the message to be. A difficult relationship between sender and receiver can also strain or distort the message.

Giving and Receiving Feedback

Positive feedback from significant others (expressions of caring, approval, encouragement, affection, appreciation, and other forms of positive attention) nourish morale, emotional security, confidence, and the feeling of being valued by others. Thus, increasing positive feedback fosters the well-being of individuals and harmonious family relationships. To enable family members to increase positive feedback, social workers must have skills in the following areas:

- Engaging families in assessing the extent to which they give and receive positive feedback
- Educating families about positive feedback

In the following sections, each of these skills is discussed.

Assessing Positive and Negative Feedback

Destructive communication patterns often result from strained relationships, such that the family system eventually becomes unbalanced. Communication theorists view the family as a functional system that depends on two communication processes: negative and positive feedback. They also believe that all behavior is communication. Thus, they view the social worker's role as one of helping the family change the process of family interactions.

You can help families and individual members to directly explore dimensions of communication by assessing how often and in what manner they convey positive feedback to significant others. Questions you might ask in couple or family sessions to achieve this end include the following:

- *How do you send messages that let family members [or your partner] know that you care about them?*
- *How frequently do you send such messages?*
- *How often do you give feedback to others concerning their positive actions?*

In instances of severe couple or family breakdown, members may acknowledge that they send positive messages infrequently or not at all. In some cases, they may actually have tepid positive feelings, but they usually experience more than they express. Besides exploring how couples or family members convey positive feedback, you can explore their desires to receive increased feedback from one another. Discussing how family members send positive messages, or to what extent they desire increased positive feedback, can open up channels for positive communication and improve relationships that have been stuck in a cycle of repetitive arguments, criticisms, blaming, and put-down messages.

Teaching Positive Feedback

To assist families in conveying positive feedback, you can teach them to personalize their messages and guide them in giving positive feedback to others. Timely use of role-play as an educational intervention helps family members to form positive messages and to develop the skills needed to share their experiences in an authentic manner. When negative situations of some intensity have been part of the family's style for an extended period of time, you may also need to help family members learn how to accept and trust positive feedback.

The following are examples of messages that explicitly express a need for positive feedback:

Partner: When we were talking about plans for my mother, I didn't interrupt you. I wish you would notice when I do something different.

Adolescent: I felt discouraged when I showed you my grades yesterday. I really worked hard this term, and the only thing you seemed to notice was the one B. It didn't seem to matter that the rest were A's.

In each of these statements, the speaker used "I" to personalize his or her messages. Each message also clearly indicates what the speaker is seeking from the other person. When messages are less clear, they may lead to a further breakdown in communications. You can intervene in these situations by using the technique of **on-the-spot interventions**. When using this technique, you coach family members to formulate clear messages that express their feelings and needs, as illustrated in the following exchange. It begins with a message from a wife who is seeking positive feedback from her husband, but what she wants from him is unclear.

Ruth [to husband]: I worked really hard at picking up around the house before people arrived, but the only thing you noticed was what I had not done—like the comment you made about fingerprints on the bathroom door.

Carl [to Ruth]: Well, let's face it, the fingerprints were there, as you yourself admitted.

Social worker: Carl, Ruth was expressing what is important to her in the relationship, and I don't want her point to get lost in an argument. Ruth, think for a moment about what you said. What is it you are asking of Carl?

Ruth [after pausing]: Do you mean his not noticing what I do?

Social worker: In a way, yes. Would you like Carl to let you know you're appreciated for what you have done?

In this scenario, Ruth has shared important information—namely, the need to feel valued. People want to receive positive feedback for what they are and what they do. Interactions that continuously focus on negative results may leave an individual feeling discouraged and insecure, and, as a consequence, relationships suffer. In instructing Ruth and Carl about the importance of positive feedback, the social worker used this opportunity to allow them to practice communicating in a different manner:

Social worker: Ruth, I'd like you to start over and express that you want positive feedback from Carl. This time, however send an "I" message so that it is clear what you want from him.

Ruth [hesitating]: I hope that I can. Carl, I need to hear from you about the things that I do well and not only about what is wrong.

Initially, clients may feel timid about expressing their feelings clearly. The second part of helping family members to communicate is by assisting them in listening attentively. Asking Carl to repeat what he heard in Ruth's message is one way to emphasize listening for content. Because individuals may not always express their needs openly and clearly, family members may need to go beyond just listening. That is, they may need to become *attuned* to needs expressed in the form of complaints, questions, and the attitudes of others. *Tuning in* also involves alerting others to pay attention to nonverbal messages and what those messages communicate about feelings.

Because it is difficult for family members to be attuned to the needs inherent in the messages of others, you should take advantage of "teachable moments" to help them learn this skill, as illustrated in the preceding situation. Specifically, the social worker encouraged Ruth to express her need for positive feedback from Carl. Also, when the social worker focused on Ruth, she played a facilitative role in prompting her to express herself directly to Carl. The social worker likewise had Carl provide feedback to Ruth, thus performing a critical role in *facilitating positive interactions between the couple*. This is a crucial point. Serving as a catalyst, the social worker helped Carl and Ruth learn new communication skills by having them *actually engage in positive interaction*, which is an effective mode of learning.

After teaching the use of "I" statements during sessions with families, family members may be ready to work on the ultimate goal—increasing their rates of positive feedback. You can assist them by negotiating tasks that specify providing positive feedback at higher frequencies. Families, of course, must consent to tasks and determine the rate of positive feedback they seek to achieve. Family members can review their baseline information (gathered earlier through monitoring) and can be encouraged to set a daily rate that "stretches" them beyond their usual level. For example, an adolescent whose mean baseline daily rate in giving positive feedback to his father is a 1.0 might select an initial task of giving positive feedback twice daily. He would then gradually increase the number of positive messages until he reached a self-selected optimal rate of five times daily.

Modifying Family Rules

Family rules govern the range of behavior in the family system and the sequence of interactions or reactions to a particular event. Rules are a means by which the family system maintains its equilibrium. Dysfunctional family rules, however, can severely impair the functioning of family members. Because family rules are often covert, it follows that changes can occur only by bringing them into the open. You can assist family members to consider the effects of rules on family interactions.

VIDEO CASE EXAMPLE

To illustrate, we return to the video "Home for the Holidays," in which the focus of the conversation between Anna and Jackie is on family communication styles and family rules. Kim, the social worker, shares her observation about the differences between their families and makes the point that family rules and communication styles influence the interactions in relationships. To begin to resolve the conflict about these differences, Kim urges Anna and Jackie to consider ways to bring each other into a conversation in such a way that they are able to work out their differences. By encouraging them to openly discuss family-of-origin rules, they can begin to consider rules that might better serve their relationship needs.

It can be useful to have family members make a list of apparent and unspoken rules so that you and they can understand how the family operates. You can prepare families to consider rules by introducing them to the concept, as illustrated in the following message:

Social worker: As we begin to work on problems the family is experiencing, we need to know more about how your family operates. Every family has some rules or understandings about how members are to behave. Sometimes these rules are easy to spot. For example, each person is to clear his or her own plate after a meal is a rule that all members of a family might be expected to follow. This is an apparent rule because every member of the family could easily tell me what is expected of them at the end of the meal. But the family's behavior is also governed by other rules that are less easy to identify. Even though members follow these rules, they are often unaware that they exist. I'm going to ask you some questions that will help you to understand these two kinds of rules better and to identify some of the ones that operate in your family.

You can first ask family members to list some apparent rules, coaching them as needed, by asking questions such as "What are your rules about schoolwork (or watching television, household chores, friends)"? Once family members have identified some of their common and readily apparent rules, you can then lead them into a discussion of implicit rules. For example, you might ask them to identify family rules about showing anger or positive feelings or to explore decision-making or power (e.g., "Who do people go to in the family when they want something?"). The intent of these questions is not to engage in a lengthy exploration of rules but rather to illustrate how hidden rules can influence family behavior, stressing that certain rules may hamper their interactions.

Many avenues could be explored in this example, but the social worker chose to narrow the focus by helping the family to identify one of its major rules—the expectation to share. She also addressed the rule that specifies the father's role of mediator in disputes. Picture yourself as the social worker in this family situation. After further exploring specific patterned interactions of the family, you can use questions like the following to help them weigh whether they wish to continue relating under the old rules.

To the Father
- How effective are you in actually stopping the girls and their mother from fighting?
- What are your worst fears about what might occur in the family if you didn't play that role?
- Would you like to free yourself from the role of being the family mediator?

CASE EXAMPLE

Consider the social worker's role in the following excerpt from a third session with Mr. and Mrs. Johnson and their three daughters, in which the social worker assisted the family to identify how hidden rules influence their patterned interactions:

Martha [age 14]: You took the red jersey again, right out of my closet—and you didn't ask. That's really bogus.

Cynthia [age 15]: You took the Lady Gaga CD last week, and you still have it. What's up with that?

Mr. Johnson: In this family, we share, and you girls should know this.

Social worker: This seems to be a family rule. What does this rule mean in this family?

Mr. Johnson: It means that we have a limited amount of money to spend on extras, so we buy things for the girls to use together and no one person owns the things we buy. Besides, the girls are expected to share because they are so close in age and like similar things.

Social worker: So, what happens when there is a disagreement about a particular item?

Martha: I got mad at Cynthia, and I told her so.

Social worker [to Cynthia]: Then what did you do?

Cynthia: I told Martha she didn't have any right to complain because she wasn't sharing things either.

Social worker: Cynthia and Martha, the two of you were engaged in blaming messages; do you see it the same way? [Girls nod.] [To Mr. Johnson] I wonder if you remember what you did when Cynthia and Martha were arguing.

Mr. Johnson: I was trying to get them to stop arguing and yelling at each other and reminding them that they are expected to share.

Social worker [exploring hidden rule]: Is everyone in the family aware of the expectation of sharing? I'd like to begin by asking a few questions, to see if you can figure out what the rules are in

your family. Are you willing to explore this further?

Social worker [to Jennifer]: You weren't involved in this argument. Do you argue with anyone in the family?

Jennifer [age 12, laughs]: My mother and Martha, but mainly I argue with my mother.

Social worker: When you get in an argument with your mother, what happens?

Jennifer: If my dad is home, he tries to stop it. Sometimes he tells my mother to go upstairs, and he'll talk to me.

Social worker [to Mrs. Johnson]: When your husband stops an argument between the girls, or you and one of the girls, what do you do?

Mrs. Johnson: Sometimes I let him deal with the problem with Jennifer or one of the other girls. But when he gets involved like that, it makes me so furious that sometimes he and I end up in a fight ourselves.

Social worker: We need to do a lot more work to understand what happens in such situations, but for the moment, let's see, Mr. Johnson, if you can put your finger on the rule.

Mr. Johnson: I guess I'm always trying to stop everyone from fighting and arguing in the family. I expect the girls to share and get along with each other, and not cause their mother grief.

Social worker: It does seem as if you are the family's mediator. I would think that would be a very difficult role to play.

Mr. Johnson: Well, there are no rewards for it, I can tell you that!

Social worker: There's more to the rule. Who lets the father be the mediator?

Mrs. Johnson: We all do.

Social worker: That's right. It isn't the father's rule; it's the family's rule. It takes the rest of the family to argue and the father to break up the fights.

To Other Family Members

- Do you want the father to continue to be the third party in your arguments?
- What are the risks to your relationships if he discontinued playing the role of mediator?
- Do you want to work out your own disputes?

Questions such as these focus the attention of all members on their patterned interactions and encourage them to determine the *function* of the behavior in the system.

Next, you would have the major task of assisting the Johnson family to modify their rules by teaching them new skills for resolving disagreements. Also, you would coach the father in declining the role of mediator and the girls and their mother in requesting that he let them manage their own conflicts.

Modifying Family Alignments and Hierarchy

All families develop patterns of affiliation between members that either enhance or impair opportunities for individual growth or the family's ability to carry out survival functions. The functional structure—that is, the family's invisible or covert set of demands or code of behavior—reflects and regulates family functioning and determines transactional patterns (Minuchin, 1974). In this section, we draw upon structural approach techniques to guide intervention strategies when family functioning is impaired by dysfunctional alignments.

Structural family therapy is intended to strengthen current family relationships, interactions, and transactional patterns. The approach emphasizes the wholeness of the family—that is, its hierarchical organization and the interdependent functioning of subsystems (Goldenberg & Goldenberg, 2004; Minuchin, 1974). Because of its primary focus on improving family relationships, structural therapy pays attention to subsystems, boundaries, alignments in the family system, and power, using the resources and power inherent in families to effect change. Graphic symbols of the family structure and alignment include lines that show rigid, diffused, or clear boundaries, as well as conflict and coalitions (Nichols, 2006). Using the technique of **enactment**, family members are encouraged to interact with each other during a family session. This exercise is observed by the social worker, who subsequently intervenes to modify problematic interactions.

Interventions to modify alignments are generally indicated in the following circumstances:

- Bonds are weak between spouses, other individuals who form the parental subsystem, or other family members.
- Enmeshed alliances—that is, rigid or overly restrictive boundaries between members—limit appropriate bonds with other members (or outsiders).
- Two members of a family attempt to cope with dissatisfaction or conflict in their relationship by forming a coalition with a third family member, a phenomenon known as triangulation.
- Family members are disengaged or alienated from one another, tending to go their own ways, with little reliance on each other for emotional support.

- Members of the family have formed alliances with persons outside the immediate family (e.g., friends and relatives) that interfere with performing appropriate family roles or providing appropriate emotional support to other family members.

Structural Mapping

In intervening to modify alignments, **structural mapping** may be used to delineate family boundaries and to highlight and modify interactions and transactional patterns. Structural mapping identifies symptoms that may be exhibited by an individual family member as an expression of difficulties in the family system. The structure of the family is revealed by who talks to whom, and in what way—that is, in an unfavorable or favorable position—and how intense the family's transactions are. The goal of the structural approach is to change family structures by altering boundaries and by realigning subsystems to enhance family functioning. Interventions are thus devised to achieve the following goals:

- Develop alliances, cultivate new alliances, or strengthen underdeveloped relationships. For example, a social worker might help a new stepfather and stepson to explore ways that they can develop a relationship, or the social worker might help a parent who has been in prison to strengthen emotional bonds to his or her children.
- Reinforce an alliance by acting to maintain the alliance or to amplify its scope and/or strength. For instance, a social worker might assist a single parent in increasing his or her ability to operate as an effective executive subsystem (e.g., Twanna).
- Differentiate individuals and subsystems. For example, a social worker might help a mother who gives most of her attention to a newborn infant to understand the need for supervision of older children and to invest some of her emotional energy in them.
- Increase family interactions in disengaged families to make boundaries more permeable by changing the way in which members relate to one another.
- Help family members accommodate changing circumstances or transitions by decreasing rigid structures or rules that are no longer viable. For example, as a child reaches adolescence, the social worker might help the parents revise their expectations of the child's behavior or modify rules so as to accommodate this developmental change.

As can be surmised from these examples, structural problems may arise when the family structure is unable to adequately adjust to changing circumstances. Changing circumstances may be the result of external environmental forces, stressful transitions, or dynamics internal to the family system. Before you intervene to restructure the family system, it is important to understand the structural change as unique to the family's situation and make clear the nature of the structural dysfunction. Thus, the family should be involved in determining whether, and in what ways, such changes should take place.

Your first task in this respect is to assist family members in identifying the nature of their alignments. This may be accomplished by asking general questions that stimulate family members to consider their alignments:

- *If you had a difficult problem and needed help, whom would you seek out in the family (tribe or clan)?*
- *Sometimes members of a family feel closer to some members than to others and may pair up or group together. Which members of your family, if any, group together?*
- *In most families, members argue to some extent. With whom do you argue? With whom do other members argue?*
- *Is there one person in the family who is considered to be a favorite?*
- *[To parents] When you make a decision, do you feel that your decision is supported by the other parent? Are other people involved in your decisions?*

You can also bring alignments and coalitions to the family's attention as they are manifested in family sessions:

- *Martha, it seems that you're the center of the family. Most of the conversation seems to be directed through you, while other family members, with the exception of Joe, appear to be observers of the discussion.*
- *Janet, in your description of how you spend your day, it appears that the baby receives a great deal of your attention.*
- *[To Twanna] When you are upset, who do you talk to about how you feel?*
- *I noticed that each of you identified the same individual on your map. Can you tell me about this person and his (or her) role in your family?*

As family members become aware of their alignments, you can assist them in considering whether they wish to become closer to others and identifying obstacles that could prevent this movement from happening. Family alignments may, in fact, involve "complex extended patterns or configurations" (Boyd-Franklin, 1989, p. 124). Members of the various configurations may include clan or tribal members, extended kin, friends, or individuals from the family's religious or spiritual community, such as a minister, shaman, rabbi, monk, medicine person, or priest. Be mindful of the fact that any of these people (or a combination of them) may be involved in family structural arrangements. As a consequence, it may be necessary to explore relationships and alignments beyond the immediate family system.

Family Sculpting

Family sculpting is a technique used in experiential family practice models to assist family members in analyzing and observing their alliances and in making decisions concerning possible changes. This technique allows family members to communicate spatial family system relationships in a nonverbal tableau, to discern alignments, and to recognize the need to realign their relationships. A variation of this technique is to have family members portray historical and current family relationships using the genogram (see Chapter 10).

In family sculpting, family members are instructed to physically arrange other family members in a way that portrays their perceptions of members as well as their own place in the family system. Another aspect of family sculpting involves members expressing themselves by using drawings to disclose their perceptions of each other (Nichols, 2006). For example, you would instruct the family to draw a picture that shows how they see themselves as a family. After family members have completed their drawings, you would ask participants to draw family relationships as they would *like* them to be on the other side of the paper. In a subsequent discussion, you would ask members in turn to share their drawings of existing family relationships.

The benefit of the expressive exercise is that family members can observe the nature of their alignments and the emotional closeness and distance in their relationships with others. Invite family members to comment on their observations, based on hypothetical responses such as the following, from an earlier case in the chapter:

- *It looks like Martha and Cynthia are quite close to each other.*
- *Jennifer and Cynthia seem to have the least conflict with each other. Jennifer and Martha are in frequent conflict.*
- *All family members seem to be close to Grandmother Maggie.*

After all family members have an opportunity to make their observations, you can ask them to explain their second drawings, which show how they would like family relationships to be. During this discussion, you can highlight the desired changes, assist individuals to formulate goals that reflect changes they would like to make, and identify "exceptional" times—for example, when Jennifer and Martha are not in conflict with each other.

Elements of family sculpting or structural mapping include exercises that can be used with parents to portray family relationships, strengthen parental coalitions, and mark generational boundaries. For example, does one parent triangulate with a child or children or permit children to intrude into the parental subsystem? Does the father act as a mediator in family conflicts? Does one parent have the final say? Does one child have inordinate power in the family? The hazard associated with these alignments is that children may become adept at playing one parent against the other. In these instances, parental divisiveness is fostered, and in consequence, relationships between the children and the excluded parent are strained. In the case of the mother who expends a majority of her emotional energy on a newborn, emotional bonds and loyalty between her and her other children and family members may be lacking.

Joined Families

Developing cohesiveness, unity, and more effective alignments is a challenge that often confronts two families who have joined together—for example, in the development of a relationship between a new stepfather and stepson. Because these factors are apt to be present in foster or adoptive families, your attention to alliances and cohesiveness is equally important in such cases, especially when there are biological children in the home.

In situations where two families have joined together, you can assist parents to analyze whether differences or lack of agreement about their parenting styles are factors in parent–child alignments. Hare (1994) urges us to be mindful that in lesbian families, issues related to two families joining together and parenting styles are not dissimilar to those problems faced by heterosexual families. Strategies for strengthening parental coalitions may include negotiating "united front" agreements in parent–child transactions requiring decision making and/or disciplinary actions (unless, of course, the other partner is truly hurtful or abusive to the child). Finally, assisting families to realign themselves and forge new alliances is

particularly important in instances in which there has been a disruption in the family system. Examples include the reunification of a child who has been placed outside of the home, or when a parent or another key family member has been absent from the family's life for an extended period of time.

On-the-Spot Interventions

On-the-spot interventions are a potent way of modifying patterns of interaction by intervening immediately when problematic family patterns occur during a meeting with the social worker. On-the-spot interventions are appropriate when:

- A family member sends fuzzy or abrasive messages.
- The receiver of a message distorts its meaning.
- A receiver of a message fails to respond appropriately to important messages or feelings.
- A destructive interaction occurs as a result of a message.

In implementing on-the-spot interventions, you would focus on the destructive effects of the preceding communication, labeling the type of communication so that family members can subsequently identify their own dysfunctional behaviors. In using the intervention, you also need to teach and guide family members in how to engage in more effective ways of communicating.

Teaching and guiding family members toward more effective ways of communication is illustrated in the following example. The social worker intervened in a "blind alley" argument, one that cannot be resolved because neither party can be proved right or wrong.

Husband: I distinctly remember telling you to buy some deodorant when you went to the store.

Wife: You just think that you did, but you didn't. I'd have remembered if you said anything about it.

Husband: No, you just didn't remember. I told you for sure, and you're shifting the blame.

Wife [with obvious irritation]: Like hell you did! You're the one who forgot to tell me, and I don't appreciate your telling me I forgot.

Social worker: Can we stop for a moment and consider what's happening between you? Each of you has a different recollection of what happened, and there's no way of determining who's right and who's wrong. You are involved in what I call a *blind alley argument* because you can't resolve it.

You just end up arguing over who's right and feeling resentful because you're convinced the other person is wrong. That doesn't help you solve your problem; it just creates conflict in your relationship. Let's go back and start over. Are you willing to allow me to show you both a more effective way of dealing with this situation?

Alternatively, after describing and intervening in the interaction and guiding the couple to communicate constructively, you might challenge the couple (or family members) to identify their behavior and to modify it accordingly. For example, interrupt their interactions with a statement like this: "Wait a minute! Think about what you're doing just now and where it's going to lead you if you continue." In modifying patterns, the intermediate objective is for family members to recognize and decrease their counterproductive behavior, and to substitute newly gained communication skills for the harmful communication style. The ultimate goal, of course, is for family members to *eliminate* the counterproductive processes through concentrated efforts between sessions. The following are some guidelines for making on-the-spot interventions.

Focus on Process Rather Than Content. For you to be infinitely more helpful to family members, you must focus on their interaction processes rather than on the content of their conflicts. Conflicts typically are manifested over content issues, but *how* family members interact in dealing with the focal point of a conflict is far more important. As the blind alley argument example illustrated, the issue of who is right in a given dispute is usually trivial when compared to the destructive effects of the processes. Thus, you should usually deemphasize the topics of disputes and focus instead on helping family members to listen attentively and respectfully and to own their feelings and their responsibility in creating and maintaining the problem. Ultimately, you will want to teach them how to compromise, to disengage from competitive interaction, and to engage in conflict resolution.

Give Feedback That Is Descriptive and Neutral Rather Than General or Evaluative. As you intervene, it is important that you present feedback in a neutral manner that does not fault family members but rather allows them to pinpoint specific behaviors that produce difficulties. Feedback that evaluates their behavior produces defensiveness; overly general feedback fails to focus on behavior that needs to be changed.

To illustrate, consider a situation in which a man glares at his wife and says, "I've had it with going to your parents' house. You spend all the time while we are there talking with your mother, and I do not feel included or welcomed in the conversation. You can go by yourself in the future." A *general and evaluative message* would take the following form:

Social worker: "Garth, that message was an example of poor communication. Try again to send a better one."

The following message is neutral and behaviorally specific:

Social worker: "Garth, I noticed that when you just spoke to Barbara, you glared at her and sent a message that focused on what you thought she was doing wrong. I watched Barbara as you spoke, and noticed that she frowned and seemed to be angry. I'd like you to get some feedback from Barbara about how your message affected her. Barbara, would you share with Garth what you experienced as he talked?"

In summarizing what occurred, the social worker indicates that Garth's message to Barbara was problematic, but he or she avoids making an evaluative judgment. Moreover, by describing specific behavior and eliciting feedback about its impact, the social worker enhances the possibility that Garth will be receptive to examining and modifying his behavior. Note also that this message highlights the interaction of *both* participants, as specified in the next guideline.

Balance Interventions to Divide Responsibility. When more than one family member is involved in sessions, you must achieve a delicate balance while avoiding the appearance of singling out one person as being the sole cause of interpersonal difficulties. Otherwise, that person may feel that you and other family members are taking sides and blaming. By focusing on all relevant actors, you can distribute responsibility, model fairness, and avoid alienating one person. Moreover, although one person may contribute more to problems than others, all members of a system generally contribute to difficulties in some degree. The following example illustrates the technique of balancing in a situation in which the husband and wife are at odds with each other over caring for their baby and the amount of time the husband spends at work.

Social worker: Both of you seem to have some feelings and concerns that are legitimate, but for some reason you seem to be stuck and unable to work things out.

[To wife] You resent your husband when he does not do his part regarding child care. As a result, you feel that you can't trust him to take care of the children, even though you both agreed that you would return to work part-time.

[To husband] You feel that because you are on a new job, now is not the time to ask for time off for child care.

[To both] I'd like to explore what the two of you can do to make things better for each other.

In this example, the social worker responded empathically to the feelings of both husband and wife, thereby validating the feelings of each. In so doing, he remained neutral so as to avoid the appearance of siding with or against either of the participants. The empathic responses also soften the impact of the social worker's messages.

Redirect Hostile, Blaming Messages. When people are angry, they may express messages that are hostile, blaming, or critical, exacerbating an already difficult situation. Before redirecting messages, therefore, you must consider the likely consequences of the ensuing interaction. As you redirect such messages, you should actively intervene to facilitate positive interaction:

- Coach family members to own their feelings: "I am really angry with you for getting this family involved with the police."
- Translate complaints into requests for change: "I wish you would stay in school and stop hanging around with the neighborhood dropouts."
- Clarify positive intentions: "I want you to stay in school because I want your life to be better than mine."

Of course, these messages will be more effective when speakers' nonverbal behaviors are consistent with their verbal message. For example, unless there is a cultural imperative observed in the family, when family members are speaking they should face one another and maintain eye contact. You may need to interrupt and direct them as illustrated in the following message:

Social worker: Cassandra, please stop for just a moment. You were talking to me, not to Jamal. Will you please start again, but this time talk and look directly at him?

Assisting Families to Disengage from Conflict

One of the most common and harmful types of interaction within families involves arguments that quickly escalate, causing anger and resentment between the participants. Sustained over time, these interactions may eventually involve other family members and subsystems. More often than not, the family system becomes factionalized, and individual efforts to regain equilibrium may result in further conflict. The content of the conflict is generally secondary to the fact that on a process level each family member is struggling to avoid being one-down, losing face, or yielding power to the other member. To illustrate helping family members in disengaging from conflict, we return to the case of Twanna and Janet. Fortunately, the situation between Janet and Twanna has not reached a crisis point, but if left unresolved, it has all of the essential ingredients to escalate and affect the prior gains that the two of them have made.

Adolescent Parent and Foster Mother, Part 2

In the video, "Adolescent Parent and Foster Mother, Part 2," a call from Twanna has resulted in a second family session with the social worker. Twanna is frustrated because of the differences in parenting styles between herself and her foster mother, Janet. The primary issue is that Janet is much more permissive with the child, yet she expects Twanna to be more involved as the child's mother. Twanna has tended to rely on rules when interacting with the child—for example, no candy before meals. Although Janet wanted Twanna to be more involved, she is not ready to entirely give over parenting responsibility to Twanna. She also maintains that the child is not accustomed to her mother telling her what to do. When Twanna, for example, refused to allow the child to have candy, the child "throws a temper tantrum." Janet immediately responded to the child's distress and emphasized that "She's just a baby." During those times when Janet took over, Twanna retreated to her room, slamming the door, and listened to music using a headset to drown out the noise. When asked by the social worker how she felt about the situation, Twanna responded, "Janet made her this way, so she can deal with it." She also admitted that she does not know how to handle the tantrums and would like Janet to teach her.

Although the process of disengagement can be easy to learn, it is not simple to do, because many family members have nearly always responded in a reactive competitive pattern. In many ways, Janet is competing with Twanna as the child's parent. She reasoned that the child does not have tantrums with her because she is the more familiar caretaker. Janet is also sending a mixed message to Twanna—that Twanna should act as the child's parent, but if Janet does not approve, she intervenes in the situation. Glenda, the social worker, remarked that Janet wants Twanna to take a more active parenting role, but that she is not quite ready to play a secondary role. Glenda also asked Janet, "Does the baby throw tantrums with you?" as a means to highlight the conflict between the two parenting styles. Even so, the strength of their relationship had improved. For example, Janet began the session by praising Twanna for keeping her agreement about coming home and caring for her child.

To assist family members in avoiding competitive struggles, you can emphasize that everyone loses in competitive situations or arguments and that negative feelings or emotional estrangement is likely to be a result (e.g., Twanna's withdrawal, slamming the door). It is also vital to stress that safeguarding mutual respect is far more important than winning. The concept of disengaging from conflict simply means that family members avoid escalating arguments by declining to participate further. A graceful way in which people can disengage is by making a comment similar to the following: "Listen, it doesn't really matter who's right. If we argue, we just get mad at each other, and I don't want that to happen." Teaching family members to evaluate their behavior and its effects on others is another strategy: "How do the children react when the two of you are having an argument?" You can further assist family members to avoid conflict between sessions by teaching them to recognize code words that signal the need to disengage or reframe their message. Sentences or questions such as "When you do …," "How could you think …," "Did you think …," "I know that you won't …," "You never …," "Don't tell me what to do," and "Why did you …" are generally powerful prompts, along with labeling, that set the stage for conflict.

Negotiating tasks for disengaging from conflicted interactions between sessions can help family members transfer these skills to their daily lives. Of course, family members may be incapable of intervening to disengage conflict in some instances—for example, in domestic violence situations where there is a threat or the actuality of physical harm. In these situations, you can teach family members—especially children—to call for help as well as to develop a safety plan.

Conflict resolution strategies may vary based on differences in both gender and ethnicity (Berg & Jaya, 1993; Mackey & O'Brien, 1998). Being aware of these differences will assist you in choosing intervention strategies that recognize how these factors affect the family's behavior. Berg and Jaya (1993) note that in some Asian families, concerns are viewed as "our problems," emphasizing the interdependence between family members. This example suggests that you should explore the family narrative regarding how conflict is managed in the family's particular culture as well as the attached meanings or feelings. By doing so, you are able to engage members in formulating an effective intervention strategy.

In fact, understanding the family narrative with respect to conflict may yield benefits with all families, irrespective of their culture or ethnicity. Each family has its own style of communicating (e.g., Jackie, "We don't make a big deal of things"; Anna, "We talk about everything"). In some families, everyone talks simultaneously and makes outrageous statements; other members may remain passive during this display. Perhaps yelling or name-calling is a norm, as are demonstrative hand gestures, apparent threats, and a hostile or belligerent tone of voice. Be sensitive to the fact that these interactions in family communication styles are not necessarily evidence of destructive relational patterns, simply because they are not your own family's style. Observing the family and inquiring about their preferred patterns of relating will enable you to assess family members' communication styles and avoid drawing conclusions about their functional or dysfunctional status.

SUMMARY

This chapter has presented a set of skills that you can utilize to engage and intervene with families across a wide spectrum of social work practice settings. Indeed, these practice skills will generalize to most of the evidence-based family interventions currently in use today. They will also be useful for settings where social workers engage families in support of interventions with individual clients as well. When joining with families, bear in mind the need to use collective language purposefully to emphasize the relationship you have with the family as a whole in addition to the individual members within the family. When selecting interventions, consider the range of first- and second-order change strategies that are most appropriate for the nature of the presenting problem. Your interventions may involve helping families to solve problems within the framework of their existing family system structures, or helping families to adapt their family system structure toward improved family functioning. Often, you will be helping families to do both.

COMPETENCY NOTES

EP 2   Engage Diversity and Difference in Practice
- Apply self-awareness and self-regulation to manage the influence of personal biases and values in working with diverse clients and constituencies.

EP 6   Engage with Individuals, Families, Groups, Organizations, and Communities
- Apply knowledge of human behavior and the social environment, person-in-environment, and other multidisciplinary theoretical frameworks to engage with clients and constituencies.
- Use empathy, reflection, and interpersonal skills to effectively engage diverse clients and constituencies.

EP 8   Intervene with Individuals, Families, Groups, Organizations, and Communities
- Critically choose and implement interventions to achieve practice goals and enhance capacities of clients and constituencies.
- Apply knowledge of human behavior and the social environment, person-in-environment, and other multidisciplinary theoretical frameworks in interventions with clients and constituencies.

SKILL DEVELOPMENT EXERCISES
in Enhancing Family Functioning and Relationships

1. Identify some examples of verbal or nonverbal metacommunication that you have used.
2. Describe how an unspoken rule in your family governs the behavior of family members.
3. From your observation of the session with Anna and Jackie ("Home for the Holidays"), describe how the social worker uses the technique of on-the-spot intervention.
4. List three societal beliefs, and reflect upon how these beliefs may affect the families that you work with.
5. Choose several classmates to role-play a family situation. Acting as the social worker, facilitate the *joining* stage in the initial contact session.
6. Using the same family situation, identify the needs and wants expressed by each family member. What questions would you ask to help members identify their concerns?
7. In a family session in which one member is identified as being the problem, how would you proceed with the family?

CHAPTER 16

Intervening in Social Work Groups

Chapter Overview

In all social work groups, the leader's task is to intervene to help the group reach shared goals. In treatment groups, this role is particularly complex, requiring in-depth, balanced interventions to assist individuals and the group as a whole. To add to the complexity of this role, the leader must be astute in sorting through the maze of multilevel communication to bring meaning to the group's experience, shape the group's therapeutic character, and provide direction and focus to the group's processes at critical moments. Finally, when groups extend beyond a single session, the leader must formulate all interventions within the context of the stages of development. Leaders of task groups must play similar facilitative roles in assisting the group to meet its objectives.

This chapter builds on the skills introduced in Chapter 11 for forming and composing task, treatment, and support groups. This chapter addresses the stages of group development and skills needed to intervene effectively throughout group processes. Although this chapter focuses primarily on treatment groups, it provides specialized content on task groups in the final section. Because the leader's interventions are inextricably related to the group's stage of development, we begin at that point.

After reading this chapter, you will be able to:

- Describe the stages through which groups progress and the features of each stage.

- Explain the skills and knowledge needed to effectively intervene at each stage.

- Describe the ways that these concepts reveal themselves in the dialogue of the HEART group.

- Describe common worker errors at different stages of the group process.

- Describe variants on group work such as single-session and technology-mediated groups.

- Explain how concepts of group interventions apply to task groups.

EPAS Competencies in Chapter 16

This chapter will give you the information needed to meet the following practice competencies:

- Competency 4: Engage in Practice-Informed Research and Research-Informed Practice

- Competency 6: Engage with Individuals, Families, Groups, Organizations, and Communities

- Competency 7: Assess Individuals, Families, Groups, Organizations, and Communities

- Competency 8: Intervene with Individuals, Families, Groups, Organizations, and Communities

STAGES OF GROUP DEVELOPMENT

All ongoing groups go through natural stages of development, although the pace and complexity of each stage may vary. Your understanding of these stages is essential in anticipating and addressing the behaviors that characterize each phase so that the group's objectives can ultimately be met. You are also responsible for removing obstacles that threaten to derail the group's development and hinder the success of individual members. In doing so, you must make strategic, informed choices regarding your input and actions across the life span of the group.

Without knowledge of the group's stage of development, leaders may be prone to making errors, such as expecting group members to begin in-depth explorations in initial sessions or concluding that they have failed if the group exhibits the discord that is typical of early development. Leaders may also overlook positive behaviors that indicate that the group is approaching a more mature stage of development, or they may fail to intervene at critical periods to assist the group's evolution (for example, encouraging them to "stay on task," to "count in" all members in decision making, to foster free expression, or to adopt many other behaviors that are hallmarks of an experienced group).

Various models of group development offer frameworks for organizing your observations about the group and its characteristics, themes, and behaviors. All of these models identify progressive steps in group development, although they may organize these steps into four, five, or even six stages. Some theorists have noted variations in group stages based on the gender of group members. For example, Schiller (1997, 2007) has noted that groups composed of women may emphasize intimacy for a longer period and come to power and control later in the group's process. Berman-Rossi and Kelly (2000) suggest that stages of group development are influenced by variables such as worker skills, attendance patterns, group content, gender, and other member characteristics. Open-ended groups and those with turbulent changes in membership may not move through these stages in a linear fashion and may require more time at formative stages if cohesion is slow to develop (Galinsky & Schopler, 1989). In this chapter, we will use the classic model developed by Garland, Jones, and Kolodny (1965), which delineates five stages:

1. Preaffiliation
EP 6 and 7
2. Power and control
3. Intimacy
4. Differentiation
5. Separation

After discussing each stage, we present the interventions that are most relevant for each point in group development. Single-session groups and the variations in skills needed are addressed in a subsequent section.

Stage 1. Preaffiliation: Approach and Avoidance Behavior

As anyone who has ever experienced the first day of a new class can attest, the initial stage of group development is characterized by members' exhibiting **approach/avoidance behavior**. Apprehensions about becoming involved in the group are reflected in members' reluctance to volunteer answers to questions, to interact with others, and to support program activities and events. Hesitancy to participate is also shown by silence or tentative speech, as when members are occupied by the feelings of uneasiness and apprehension that emanate from their first encounter with the group. Fearful or suspicious members may be sensitive to the responses of others, fearing possible domination, aggression, isolation, rejection, and hostility.

At this **forming stage** (Tuckman, 1963), participant behavior is wary, sometimes even provocative, as members assess possible social threats and attempt to discern the kinds of behaviors the group wants and expects. Members also tend to identify one another in terms of each individual's status and roles and to engage in social rituals, stereotyped introductions, and detailed intellectual discussions rather than in-depth or highly revealing conversation (Berman-Rossi & Kelly, 2000). They may be uncertain about the group's purpose and the benefits it may bring to them.

At times during the **preaffiliation stage** members may employ testing behaviors to "size up" other members, to press the group's limits, to find out how competent the leader is, and to determine to what extent the leader will safeguard the rights of members and protect them from feared hurt and humiliation. Members may also move tentatively toward the group as they seek to find common ground with other members, search for viable roles, and seek approval, acceptance, and respect. Much of the initial communication in the group is directed toward the leader, and some members may openly demand that the social worker pursue a "take charge" approach, making decisions

CASE EXAMPLE

Preaffiliation in the HEART Group

Dave: Thank you to everyone for sharing your progress from last week. I would like to do this at the beginning of each session because I think it helps to bring us together and to create a space where you feel safe and energized to share and give each other support. I'm wondering if, based on how things went today, anybody has other ideas of how to make this opening ritual go better for them? Does anybody have any ideas about making improvements to what we're doing? Or can you tell me how it went for you today?

Amelia: Well, I think that check-in kinda depends on what your mood is. Like, I'm in a kind of okay mood today so my check-in is more positive, but like, Liz is kinda being bitchy, you know? And so maybe she's really had a bad day or whatever. So I think to have something that everybody does instead of just a check-in, I don't know, it's just really different for everybody, depending on how you're feeling.

Dave: How you're going to interact in group depends on how you're doing on that day.

Amelia: Yeah.

Dave: You know something I heard you say, Amelia, was that you felt that Liz was "bitchy," to use your word, and I want to check in with Liz to see how she received that, or how she heard that. So I'm wondering Liz, when Amelia said that, what came to mind?

Liz: It hurts my feelings because I thought people were talking about me all the time anyway, and then I come to this place, where everybody is supposed to be happy, and like me, and you call me bitchy. I think *that's* bitchy.

Amelia: Sorry.

Dave: Amelia, I think what you were saying was that during her introduction you heard that Liz was having a bad day. How does that sound?

Amelia: Yeah.

June: She didn't say you were a bitch, she said bitch-y, like kinda. I don't think she meant it in a mean way.

Liz: Well, that's how I took it, so I think that matters more than what you think you heard.

Dave: And June, I would actually agree with Liz on that point. How someone hears what you're saying matters as much as, or maybe more than, what you meant to say. One of the benefits of participating in group is having experiences like these to learn about how other people perceive you.

regarding group issues and structure and issuing prompt directives to control the behavior of members. The HEART group, introduced in Chapter 11, is designed to assist teen girls who have overweight. In this chapter, transcripts from the group are used to illustrate client statements and worker responses that are indicative of various phases of the group process, as in the above case example.

Stage 2. Power and Control: A Time of Transition

The first stage of group development merges imperceptibly into the second stage as members, having determined that the group experience is potentially safe and rewarding and worth the preliminary emotional investment, shift their concerns to matters related to autonomy, power, and control. The frame of reference for this **storming stage** (Tuckman, 1963) is transition—that is, members must endure the ambiguity and turmoil of change from a nonintimate to an intimate system of relationships.

After dealing with the struggle of whether they "belong" in the group, members now become occupied with how they "rank" in relation to other members. Turning to others like themselves for support and protection, members create subgroups and a hierarchy of statuses, or social "pecking order." Gradually, the processes of the group become stylized as various factions emerge and relationships solidify. Conflicts between opposing subgroups often occur in this stage, and members may team up to express anger toward the leader, other authority figures, or outsiders. Failed competition for favored status with the social worker

CASE EXAMPLE

Power and Control in the HEART Group

June: You know, Dave, I don't mean to be disrespectful, and I think this is a good discussion, but I just wonder, are we the first group you've done?

Dave: I've done a few others.

Maggie: With girls?

Dave: A few with girls.

Maggie: Like our age?

Dave: Some.

June: Like, fat?

Dave: Well, I've worked with adults and teenagers with overweight. I'm curious, June, why do you ask?

June: Because you're the only skinny person here. And you're the only boy.

Amelia: Mmhmm.

June: See, now nobody else dares to say anything.

Liz: Don't you think that maybe if he's skinny, maybe he can teach us some things?

Maggie: Yeah, but what does he know about what we're going through?

June: I mean, he knows boys.

Amelia: He's probably always been thin. He has no idea probably, you probably have no idea, what we've been through.

Dave: I'm hearing you say that you don't believe I can identify with you.

Amelia: Well, you're a boy, you're skinny, I'm a girl, and I'm fat.

June: And he's older.

Amelia: Yeah.

Amber: And he's probably always had girlfriends, I've never had a boyfriend.

Amelia: Do you have a girlfriend now?

Dave: I'd rather not answer that question.

Maggie: Why? We talk about our boyfriends and friends; I mean we're telling you stuff.

Dave: Actually, I think, you're also telling each other stuff, and the group is about you …

Amelia: And you.

Dave: My role here is to help the group along, and if I take up time with my relationships …

Amelia: So you have one.

Dave: As I said, I'd rather not address it, Amelia, but if I take up time with my business, then it robs the group …

June [to Amelia]**:** I mean, he can't be your boyfriend if he's your worker [taunting].

Dave: No, I can't date anyone in the group.

Amelia: I don't want to date you, oh my god!

Maggie: Sure …

Amelia: Don't even, you're so full of yourself! I like girls anyway.

Dave: The other thing I want to say is that I can learn from you and follow your concerns, solutions, and your strategies for dealing with some of the things that you're up against right now. I hope that in my role as facilitator I can help all of you to help yourselves, even though I'm neither overweight nor a girl.

may also produce hostility toward the group leader (Yalom, 2005).

Disenchantment with the group may reveal itself through hostility, withdrawal, or confusion about the group's purposes. Verbal abuse, attacks, and rejection of lower-status members may occur as well, and isolated members of the group who do not have the protection of a subgroup may stop attending. Attrition in membership may also occur if individuals find outside pursuits more attractive than the conflicted group experience. In fact, this depleted membership may put the group's very survival in jeopardy. The dynamics of the power and control stage must be managed sensitively and nondefensively, as we see in this example from the HEART group.

Stage 3. Intimacy: Developing a Familial Frame of Reference

Having clarified and resolved many of the issues related to personal autonomy, initiative, and power, the group moves from the "preintimate" power and control stage to that of **intimacy**. As the group enters this **norming stage** (Tuckman, 1963), conflicts fade, personal involvement between members intensifies, and members display a growing recognition of the significance of the group experience. Members also experience an increase in morale and "we-ness," a deepening commitment to the group's purpose, and heightened motivation to carry out plans and tasks that support the group's objectives. Mutual trust increases as members begin to acknowledge one another's uniqueness, spontaneously disclose feelings and problems, and seek the opinion of the group. To achieve this desired intimacy, however, group participants may suppress negative feelings that could produce conflict between themselves and others. In contrast to earlier sessions, they express genuine concern for absent members and may reach out to invite them to return to the group.

During this stage of development, a group "character" emerges as the group evolves its own culture, style, and values. Clear norms are established, based on personal interests, affection, and other positive forces. Roles also take shape as members find ways to contribute to the group and leadership patterns become firmly settled. The frame of reference for members is a familial one, as members liken their group experience to their experience with their own nuclear families, occasionally referring to other members as siblings or to the leader as the "mother" or "father" of the group.

How groups experience this stage depends on factors such as how regularly members attend group sessions, whether the group is open or closed, and how much member turnover occurs (Berman-Rossi & Kelly, 2000; Galinsky & Schopler, 1989). In groups that endure frequent transitions, it is important to develop rituals or a consistent format for meetings to help the members achieve cohesion and continuity. In the HEART group, the teens developed a culture of compassion and sensitivity when faced with the struggles of other members.

Stage 4. Differentiation: Developing Group Identity and an Internal Frame of Reference

The fourth stage of group development is marked by cohesion and harmony as members come to terms with intimacy and make choices to draw closer to others in the group. In this **performing stage** (Tuckman, 1963), group-centered operations are achieved and a dynamic balance between individual and group needs evolves. Members, who participate in different and complementary ways, experience greater freedom of personal expression and come to feel genuinely accepted and valued as their feelings and ideas are validated by

other members of the group. Gradually, the group becomes a mutual aid system in which members spontaneously give emotional support in proportion to the needs of each individual.

In experiencing this newfound freedom and intimacy, members begin to perceive the group experience as unique. Indeed, as the group creates its own mores and structure, in a sense it becomes its own frame of reference. Customs and traditional ways of operating emerge and the group may develop inside jokes or shared sayings, or adopt a "club" name or insignia that reflects its purpose. The group's energy is channeled into working toward purposes and carrying out tasks that are clearly understood and accepted. New roles—more flexible and functional than those originally envisioned—are developed to support the group's activity, and organizational structures (e.g., officers, dues, attendance expectations, rules) may evolve. Status hierarchies also tend to be less rigid and members may assume leadership roles spontaneously as the need for a particular expertise or ability arises.

By the time the group reaches the **differentiation stage**, members have accumulated experience in "working through problems" and have gained skill in analyzing their own feelings and the feelings of others, in communicating their needs and positions effectively, in offering support to others, and in grasping the complex interrelationships that have developed in the group. Having become conscious about the group's operations, members bring conflict out into the open and identify obstacles that impede their progress. All decisions are ultimately the unanimous response of the group and are strictly respected. Disagreements are not suppressed or overridden by premature group action; instead, the group carefully considers the positions of any dissenters and attempts to resolve differences and to achieve consensus among members. New entrants serve as catalysts and may express their amazement at the insight shared by veteran members, who in turn become increasingly convinced of the value of the group experience.

Members may now publicize their group meetings among peers, whereas previously membership in the group may have been linked with secret feelings of shame. Secure in their roles and relationships within the group, members may become interested in meeting with other groups or in bringing in outside culture. In the HEART group, the differentiation stage fostered the safety to talk about painful material and use insights gained from the group.

CASE EXAMPLE

Intimacy in the HEART Group

Amber: I was kind of down the other day. I went to the Fairmont Mall with my friends, and we were going to all the good stores like Abercrombie & Fitch, and Hollister, and American Eagle, that's one of my favorites …

June: And Bebe.

Amber: Yeah, and uh, all my friends were trying on the clothes, and I can't fit into any of the clothes there, but I really want to because they're really cute clothes. It makes me feel kind of out of the loop with my friends; do you guys have that problem too?

Amelia: Totally.

Amber: I can't shop at the same stores my friends shop at.

June: Yeah, I just mostly end up wearing sweats and T-shirts, you know, because … but you can't wear that everywhere.

Amber: Uh-huh.

Liz: Sometimes I feel like I lost my friends because they all wear those cute outfits and they all share clothes and I couldn't relate anymore, so we quit hanging out.

June: The peasant ones make you look pregnant if they come right under your boobs …

Dave: Amber, one of the things I want to ask you is what kind of feedback or what kind of support would you like right now?

Amber: I guess I just want to see if there are people in this group that felt that way sometimes, like if they didn't fit in with their friends sometimes that way.

Dave: Does anybody else have a similar experience as Amber does?

Amelia: I do. Yeah, like, I feel like when I go shopping with my mom I can try on the clothes that really fit me, but if I'm with my friends I have to stay on the rack that they're on. I'm

taller than most of them, and I'm fat, and they're like super skinny. So when they try on clothes, I feel like I need to choose clothes from that rack too. So then, I don't know, I can't believe I'm saying this, but like, I'll buy the clothes and, you know, pretend that they fit, and then make my mom take them back. So, I hear ya.

June: Like last summer when I lost 5 pounds I thought, "I can get into those jeans," and then my friends said I was muffin-top 'cuz like my fat was hanging over.

Maggie: Your friends said that to you?

June: Well, you know, other kids in the band and stuff. And, well, I don't think they're trying to be mean, they just, you know, maybe the jeans didn't look as good as I thought …

Dave: This is a difficulty and a concern for many of you. When you're at school or with your friends, you want to look your best, and you want to fit in.

Amber: I feel left out, um, before softball practice and games when we have to change in the locker rooms, sometimes I take my uniform into the bathroom stall; all the other girls change out in the locker room openly and I just don't feel that comfortable doing that.

June: Do they pick on you, like give you a flab grab or anything?

Amber: No, they're pretty nice, um, I just always feel like they're looking at me.

Amelia: Like you know you're different.

Amber: Yeah.

June: Are you the biggest person on the team?

Amber: Yeah.

Amelia: But you're pretty muscular.

Amber: Thanks.

Amelia: You're welcome.

Stage 5. Separation: Breaking Away

During the **adjourning phase** of group development, members begin to separate, loosening the intense bonds often established with other members and with the leader and searching for new resources and ties to satisfy their needs. Group members are likely to experience a broad range of feelings about leaving the group. Indeed, the approach of group termination may set off a number of reactions, the diversity of which is reminiscent of the approach/avoidance

CASE EXAMPLE

Differentiation in the HEART Group

Amber: So you gonna ask him?

Maggie: Ask him what?

June: Like is he just being a user. Using you.

Maggie: You know sometimes, I think he was just curious about stuff and that's sometimes why we maybe hooked up, you know? So maybe he was using me.

Jen: Well, what are you going to do the next time he tries to hook up with you?

Maggie: Smack him. I mean, not really! But I would say no. I'm not gonna … I don't know, maybe I will, 'cuz it's not all that bad. Awkward! Sorry, Dave. It's not all that bad when it happens.

June: I wouldn't know.

Liz: Nah, me neither.

Maggie: Maybe that's all I'm going to get, I don't know.

Dave: All you're going to get as far as the relationship with him, or …

Maggie: With him, or others; if all guys think like that, I should maybe just take what's there.

Amber: That's all I've gotten.

June: Like guys who only want to be with you in private and not in public?

Maggie: That's the guy, that's him!

June: Well, that sucks!

Maggie: It does.

Dave: So, does that sound like something that you want to have in your lives?

June: I don't think so. I mean I'm not in the situation, but if a guy's only going to want to be with me when no one else is around, then he doesn't really value me and he's just using me.

maneuvers displayed in Stage 1. Members may again feel anxiety, this time in relation to moving apart and breaking bonds that have been formed. There may be outbursts of anger against the leader and other members at the thought of the group's ending, the reappearance of quarrels that were previously settled, and increased dependence on the leader. Denial of the positive meaning of the group experience is not uncommon. These separation reactions may appear in flashes or clusters as members attempt to reconcile their positive feelings about the group with feelings of abandonment, rejection, or apprehension over termination.

EP 8

As we will discuss further in Chapter 19, termination is also a time of evaluation, contemplation of the work achieved, and consolidation of learning. It is a time of finishing unfinished business, getting and giving focused feedback, and savoring the good times and the close relationships gained in the group.[1] Members who have begun to pull back their group investments and to put more energy into outside interests speak of their fears, hopes, and concerns about the future and about one another. There is often discussion of how to apply what has been learned in the group to other situations and talk of reunions or follow-up meetings (Toseland & Rivas, 2009).

THE LEADER'S ROLE THROUGHOUT THE GROUP

EP 7

The leader's role shifts and changes with the evolution of the group. The leader's role is a primary one at the outset of the group in that he or she recruits members and determines the group's purpose, structure, location, and duration, brings structure to the group, plans its content and function, and negotiates reciprocal contracts with each prospective member. As the group gets started, the leader initiates and directs group discussion, encourages participation, and begins blending the individual contracts with members into a mutual group contract. In single-session groups, the social worker's role will continue in this fashion as each session is, in reality, a new group.

In ongoing groups, when the group evolves to new levels of connectedness, the leader intentionally steps back from the central location and primary role, and the members begin to supplant some of what the worker has been doing. In the vernacular of cinematography, the worker fades out as the group system comes up. However, because the group's internal and external systems are not yet stabilized at full functioning capacity, the worker needs to let the process run at its own speed and sometimes needs to move back in to help keep the system afloat. This is why the worker's role is referred to as variable, and the worker's location as pivotal (Henry, 1992, p. 34).

The leader's variable role and pivotal location continue in the group during the conflict/disequilibrium stage (Stage 2). When the group enters its maintenance or working phases (Stages 3 and 4), the leader assumes a facilitative role and occupies a peripheral location. Inasmuch as the group has achieved full capacity to govern itself, the leader fulfills a resource role instead of a central role. As the group moves into its separation or termination phase (Stage 5), the leader once again returns to a primary role and central location to support the divesting of members, who are launching their own independent journeys. The leader aids the group in working through any regression to earlier stages of development to assure the successful ending of the group.

INTERVENTIONS THROUGHOUT THE LIFE OF THE GROUP

EP 7

Although the leader's role ebbs and flows over the life span of the group, he or she must be prepared to employ interventions to deal with overarching issues whenever they occur. These include:

- Fostering cohesion
- Addressing group norms
- Intervening with members' roles
- Attending to subgroup structure
- Using the leadership role purposefully
- Attending to group and individual processes

Fostering Cohesion

Cohesion plays a central role in group success, and leadership is essential in developing this positive force. The leader forges connections among group members and tries to expand the interpersonal networks of subgroup members so that they relate to a broader range of people in the group. Further, the leader encourages cohesive behaviors by "pointing out who is present and who is absent, by making reference to 'we' and 'us' and 'our' and by including the group as a whole in his or her remarks in group sessions" (Henry, 1992, p. 167).

Leaders also encourage the development of cohesion by commenting on and reinforcing positive group-building behaviors as they occur—for example, when participants inquire about missing members, return to the group after absences or conflicts, take others' opinions into account in decision making, and seek increased responsibility for the group's operations.

Ironically, these efforts at developing cohesion must be restrained as groups wind down.

> For example, instead of increasing the frequency with which members have contact with one another, this may be reduced by having meetings less often and/or for a shorter time…. The worker may place less emphasis on resolving conflicts within the group and may not call attention to commonalities of experiences or attitudes except as those relate to ways of coping with termination. (Garvin, 1987, p. 222)

Addressing Group Norms

Chapter 11 introduced strategies to facilitate the development of constructive group norms. However, counterproductive norms may also emerge. For example, the group may split into several factions or subgroups that compete for control. Members may develop a habit of socializing rather than focusing on legitimate group tasks. Some participants may repeatedly cast others as scapegoats, harassing those members and blaming them for various group ills. In these and countless other ways, groups may develop negative behaviors that undermine their ability to coalesce and aid each other in reaching their goals.

As described in Chapter 11, leaders must observe evolving group behavior and determine whether these emerging patterns undermine or support the group's purposes. The facilitator sets the stage for a therapeutic atmosphere and a "working group" by establishing an explicit contract with members in initial sessions that includes normative guideposts for the group. Along the way, the leader helps the group identify and articulate norms they wish the group to follow. Once decided, the guidelines should be recorded and revisited regularly and the leader should take an active role in helping members consistently adhere to them. Some groups will even list them on a board that is posted in the meeting room, or on a laminated page for members' workbooks. Sample guidelines follow:

- Make group decisions by consensus.
- Personalize communications by using "I" statements (e.g., "I (think) (feel) (want) …").

EP 8

CASE EXAMPLE

Norm Setting in the HEART Group

Dave: June, to come back to a point that you mentioned before, there is a guideline that I like, which is to encourage people to participate. Because a good group is one where everyone contributes, and so I wonder the best way to say that—do the best you can, or …

June: Don't talk twice till everybody's talked once?

Dave: Well, I …

Liz: I disagree.

June: I'm just putting it out there. I don't know.

Dave: Liz, let's hear why you disagree.

Liz: Sometimes I'm just not in … I just don't want to contribute, I don't feel like talking.

Dave: And it might be too structured, then, June, to say to Liz, "We've all talked once and now you have to go." It might make the group unsafe for Liz, for the rule to be so measured out like that.

June: So I don't know what the rule should be.

Amelia: How about we all, like, try our best to actively participate.

Maggie: But don't call me out.

Jen: And actively participate doesn't necessarily mean talking, just paying attention.

Dave: That's a good point, Jen.

June: No sleeping in the group.

Maggie: Yeah, stay awake.

Amelia: If I'm talking about, like, pouring out my soul, and you're over there, like clearly thinking about something else or doodling or, you know, thinking about whatever, like, it shows on your face. You know what I mean, guys?

Dave: And that's probably covered by one of the rules we already mentioned, which is "Be respectful." So "no sleeping" June, I think, comes under "be respectful."

June: Okay.

Dave: And, Amelia, I like the idea of encouraging participation—what did you say? "Try as hard as we can … Do our best"?

Amelia: Do our best to participate actively.

Dave: How does everybody feel about that? [Agreement]

- Keep the group's focus on its task and mission.
- Put away cell phones and other devices.
- Keep discussions focused primarily on the present or future rather than the past.
- Avoid gossiping.
- Share the "airtime" so all members can participate.
- Take responsibility for concerns about how the group is going by bringing them to others' attention.

In the HEART group, Dave encouraged the generation of norms and reinforced constructive norms when offered by members.

In addition to generating structural guidelines that pave the way for the adoption of therapeutic norms, leaders may aid members in adopting personal guidelines, such as "I can decide what, how much, and when I share personal issues," "I will be an active participant in the group, not an observer," and "I will be open to feedback from others" (Corey & Corey, 2006). The leader often intervenes to remind people of these individual-level norms or to point out when they are being violated. In established groups, members will also speak up to hold one another accountable. Eventually, the locus of control for enforcing individual and group norms should reside with the members rather than with the leader (Carrell, 2000).

Intervening with Members' Roles

Roles are closely related to norms, as Toseland and Rivas (2009) explain:

> Whereas norms are shared expectations held, to some extent, by everyone in the group, roles are shared expectations about the functions of individuals in the group. Unlike norms, which define behavior in a wide range of situations, roles define behavior in relation to a specific function or task that the group member is expected to perform. (p. 68)

Leaders must be attuned to the development of roles and address them as they arise. Constructive roles or roles that are consistent with the members' goals for the group should be noted and reinforced.

Counterproductive roles also require the leader's attention. For example, a member who avoids conflict or intimacy might make jokes to keep discussion at a superficial level, or a member who struggles to be taken seriously may make distracting or ridiculous comments, thereby reinforcing this destructive role. Yalom discusses the effect of "the monopolist" (1995, p. 369), who, perhaps due to anxiety, talks excessively, taking up time and turning the group mood into one of frustration.

EP 8

The key, when facing counterproductive roles, is to encourage members to be self-observant, assure that they do not become locked into dysfunctional roles, and empower other participants to confront the member about the role and its impact. As Garvin notes:

The "clown" may wish to behave more seriously, the "mediator" to take sides, and passive people to function assertively. The worker, being cognizant of roles that are created out of group interactions, will attend to those that impede either the attainment of individual goals or the creation of an effective group. (1986, p. 112)

Dysfunctional role performance is a critical point for intervention. One means of intervening is to use a technique developed by Garvin (1986) to identify informal roles occupied by group participants. Leaders administer a questionnaire asking members to "vote" on who (if anyone) fulfills group roles such as referee, expert, humorist, nurturer, spokesperson, and "devil's advocate." The discussion that results from this exercise can powerfully influence both members' awareness and the group process. Another technique is to simply describe a specific role that a member seems to have assumed and to ask that member for observations regarding the accuracy of that assessment. Preface this observation by asking the member if he or she would like group feedback. Doing so reduces defensiveness and gives the member appropriate control over the situation.

Attending to Subgroup Structure

As introduced in Chapter 11, subgroups inevitably emerge and exist in groups, both hindering and enhancing group process. The leader can modify the impact of subgroups by taking these steps:

1. Initiating discussion of the reasons for the formation of dissident subgroups and their impact on the group as a whole. This discussion may reveal the difficulties that the cliques create for goal setting, communication, interaction, and decision making.

2. Neutralizing the effects of negative subgroups through programming or structuring. The leader, for example, might challenge dissident subgroups to work toward a common goal, change seating arrangements, use a "round robin" approach to get feedback from all members, assign members from different subgroups to work on common group tasks, or use programming materials or exercises to separate subgroup members (Carrell, 2000).

3. Helping powerful subgroups or individuals to relinquish power or to use it sparingly in the interest of other members (Garvin, 1987).

4. Appointing powerless members to roles that carry power, such as arranging for group activities, securing resources for the group, or fulfilling significant roles (e.g., observer, chairperson, or secretary).

5. Finding means to "connect" with dissident subgroups and to demonstrate a concern for their desires (Garvin, 1987).

6. Providing ways for subgroups to attain legitimate power by creating useful roles and tasks in the group.

Using the Leadership Role Purposefully

The leader's role in a group can be described as a set of behaviors that facilitate the attainment of group and individual goals and ensure maintenance of the group. Ultimately, the leader "puts him/herself out of business" by gradually distributing leadership functions to members as the group matures, while continuing to attend to the work of the group (Rose, 1989, p. 260).

Helping members to assume leadership behaviors is important for three reasons. First, members develop vital skills that they can transfer to other social groups, where leadership is usually highly valued. Second, the more that members exercise leadership, the more likely they are to become invested in the group. Third, performance of leadership activities enhances the perceived power or self-efficacy of members, who often experience powerlessness in a wide array of social situations (Rose, 1989).

Leaders may expedite the distribution of power by taking four steps (Shulman, 1984):

1. Encouraging member-to-member rather than member-to-leader communications

2. Asking for members' input into the agenda for the meeting and the direction the group should take in future meetings

3. Supporting indigenous leadership when members make their first tentative attempts at exerting their own influence on the group

4. Encouraging attempts at mutual sharing and mutual aid among group members during the first meeting

Group leadership problems occur when members or vying subgroups attempt to usurp the reins of power. Challenges to leadership are, in fact, an inherent part of the group's struggle over control, division of responsibility, and decision making (Corey & Corey, 2006). It is important not to interpret these efforts as negative because they may actually help the group succeed by calling attention to issues or roles that are important to individual members (Hurley, 1984). Examples of messages that illustrate control issues follow:

● *I don't want to talk just because you want me to talk. I learn just as much by listening and observing.*

● *There are several people in here who always get the attention. No matter what I do, I just don't seem to get recognized, especially by the leaders.*

● *You should pay more attention to Paul. He's been crying several times, and you haven't been taking care of him.*

EP 7

Group facilitators must respond authentically and purposefully, modeling the capacity to accept feedback and deal with conflict. To do so, leaders must be self-aware when challenged:

Typically, leaders have a range of feelings: being threatened by what they perceive as a challenge to their leadership role; anger over the members' lack of cooperation and enthusiasm; feelings of inadequacy to the point of wondering if they are qualified to lead groups; resentment toward several of the members, whom they label as some type of problem; and anxiety over the slow pace of the group, with a desire to stir things up so that there is some action (Corey & Corey, 1992, p. 155).

Facilitators can respond to such challenges by empathically exploring the statement, thanking the member for speaking up, eliciting feedback from other members regarding leadership style, and asking nondefensively for input (e.g., "Thanks for calling my attention to that. How could I handle it differently?").

Attending to Group and Individual Processes

Like interventions with families, group work requires the practitioner to attend to multiple sources of data in each meeting. While the content that is shared in group is important, so are the processes observed among members. As with families, leaders must attend to the messages demonstrated by each individual member and the process of the group as a whole. To do this, the worker reads body language, positioning in the room, who speaks, when, how much, and with what tone, the reactions of other participants when particular members are speaking, and the general tone, mood, or energy of the group. Is the group buoyant? Flat? Angry? Distractible? Is Hal unusually sullen? Does everyone "tune out" when Evelyn speaks? Does Crystal seem fidgety and eager to speak but unable to get the group's attention? Does Fred go on too long?

Once processes are observed, the worker will intervene in different ways depending on how these processes are enhancing achievement of group and individual goals and what phase of work the group is in. For instance, the worker might remark on collective impressions: "Today's group seems to have pretty low energy" or "It seems that you're having an especially hard time getting down to business today" or "I wonder what's happening; I'm sensing a lot of anger at this point." Comments may also reflect observations about individual behavior: "When Evelyn speaks, the rest of you seem to disengage," or the worker may invite comment or involvement: "Has anyone else noticed that?" "What might be going on with you when that happens?" "Crystal, I notice we haven't heard from you." In more developed groups, the members themselves may observe, comment on, and regulate process. In those cases, the facilitator can comment on those processes. "I like the way the group helped Evelyn give her input without getting impatient or checking out."

STAGE-SPECIFIC INTERVENTIONS

As previously mentioned, a leader's role must always be pursued within the framework of the group's stages of development. Thomas and Caplan (1999) suggest a wheel metaphor for leadership. That is, the leader takes a particularly active role in getting the "wheel spinning," then gradually provides a "lighter touch," and finally reduces that role as the group gathers its own momentum, while still standing by to assure that events or digressions do not throw the wheel off track.

EP 6 and 7

Table 16-1 illustrates the evolution of the leader's focus as a group advances through the various stages of development. Information contained in the table comes from a variety of sources, including Garland, Jones, and Kolodny (1965), Rose (1989), Henry (1992), and Corey and Corey (2006).

Interventions in the Preaffiliation Stage

Chapter 11 describes how pregroup individual interviews serve as orientation for potential members of the group. In initial sessions, the leader can prepare members for the experiences to come by explaining the basics of group process—for example, the stages of development through which the group will pass, ways to create a therapeutic working environment, behaviors and attitudes characteristic of an effective group, the importance of establishing and adhering to guidelines that lend structure and purpose to the group, and the importance of committing to "win-win" decisions regarding group matters. Research, in fact, suggests that direct instruction or teaching regarding group processes tends to facilitate a group's development during its early stages (Corey & Corey, 2006; Dies, 1983).

EP 8

Leaders must also intervene to address the initial concerns of members. In early sessions, members will probably be tentative about expressing what they hope to get from the group. Most also experience fear and apprehension regarding the group experience. They worry about many things: how they will be perceived by other members, whether they will be pressured to talk, whether they will be misunderstood or look foolish, whether they will be at risk of verbal attack, and whether they want to go through a change process at all. The leader may address and allay these anxieties by acknowledging the presence of mixed feelings or by asking all members to share their feelings about coming to the initial group session. For example, the leader might ask members to rate their feelings about being present in the group at that moment on a scale of 1 to 10, where 1 represents "I don't want to be here" and 10 represents "I'm completely at ease with being in the group." The leader could then invite discussion about reasons behind the various scores.

In focusing on members' fears, leaders need to draw out all members' feelings and reactions, validate the importance of fully disclosing feelings, and emphasize the need for the group to be a safe place in which such issues can be expressed openly. Finally, leaders should elicit suggestions for a group structure that will address member fears, out of which may flow the formulation of relevant group guidelines.

Leaders can measure the progress of a new group in addressing initial member concerns by administering a questionnaire developed by Rose (1989). This instrument contains items to which members can respond by circling a point on a scale. Examples of items include the following:

- How useful was today's session for you?
- Describe your involvement in today's session.
- Rate the extent of your self-disclosure of relevant information about yourself or your problem.
- How important to you were the problems or situations you discussed (or others discussed) in the group today?
- Circle all the words that best describe you at today's session (e.g., excited, bored, depressed, interested, comfortable).
- How satisfied were you with today's session?

In initial sessions, facilitators must repeatedly review basic information regarding the group's purpose, the manner in which the group will be conducted, and its ground rules. Although this information should be familiar to members, reiteration is necessary because initial anxiety may affect participants' ability to really digest the details. Assuring that all members are "on the same page" helps to prevent these issues from erupting later in the life of the group. In preliminary interviews, members contract with the leader for general goals they would like to achieve. In the initial group sessions, the leader must then blend these individual goals with the group's collective goals. Along the way, the binding contract expands from a reciprocal one between leader and individuals to a mutual contract between individuals and group. In the first meeting, the leader engages members in a discussion about the ways the group can help each person's initial objectives to be addressed. Henry (1992) utilizes a "Goal Questionnaire" to facilitate formulation of the mutual contract.

EP 8

TABLE 16-1 Stages, Dynamics, and Leader Focus

STAGE	DYNAMICS	LEADER FOCUS
Preaffiliation	Arm's-length exploration	Observe and assess
	Approach/avoidance	Clarify group objectives
	Issues of trust, preliminary commitment	Establish group guidelines
	Intellectualization of problems	Encourage development of personal goals
	Interaction based on superficial attributes or experiences	Clarify aspirations and expectations of members
	Protection of self; low-risk behavior	Encourage discussion of fears, ambivalence
	Milling around	Gently invite trust
	Sizing up of leader and other members	Give support; allow distance
	Formulation of individual and group goals	Facilitate exploration
	Leader viewed as responsible for group	Provide group structure
	Member evaluation as to whether group is safe and meets needs	Contract for help-seeking, help-giving roles
	Fear of self-disclosure, rejection	Facilitate linkages among members
	Uncertainty regarding group purpose	Model careful listening
	Little commitment to goals or group	Focus on resistance
		Assure opportunities for participation
Power and control	Rebellion; power struggles	Protect safety of individuals and property
	Political alignments forged to increase power	Clarify power struggles
	Issues of status, ranking, and influence	Turn issues back to group
	Complaints regarding group structure, process	Encourage expression and acceptance of differences
	Challenges to leader's roles	Facilitate clear, direct, nonabrasive communication
	Emergence of informal leadership, factional leaders	Examine nonproductive group processes
	Individual autonomy; everybody for himself/herself	Examine cognitive distortions
	Dysfunctional group roles	Facilitate member discussion of dissident subgroups
	Normative and membership crisis; dropout danger high	Hold group accountable for decision by consensus
	Testing of leader; other group members	Clarify that conflict, power struggles are normal
	Dependence on leader	Encourage norms consistent with therapeutic group
	Group experimentation in managing own affairs	Consistently acknowledge strengths, accomplishments
	Program breakdown at times; low planning	Nondefensively deal with challenges to leadership
	Feedback highly critical	Focus on the here and now
Intimacy	Intensified personal involvement	Encourage leadership
	Sharing of self, materials	Assume flexible role as group vacillates
	Striving to meet others' needs	Aid sharper focus on individual goals
	Awareness of significance of the group experience	Encourage deeper-level exploration, feedback
	Personality growth and change	Encourage acknowledgment, support of differences
	Mutual revelation, risk taking	Guide work of group
	Beginning commitment to decision by consensus	Encourage experimentation with different roles
	Beginning work on cognitive restructuring	Encourage use of new skills inside and outside group
	Importance of goals verbalized	
	Growing ability to govern group independently	

TABLE 16-1 Continued

STAGE	DYNAMICS	LEADER FOCUS
	Dissipation of emotional turmoil	Assist members to assume responsibility for change
	Member initiation of topics	
	Constructive feedback	Give consistent feedback regarding successes
		Reduce own activity
Differentiation	Here-and-now focus	Emphasize achievement of goals, exchange of skills
	High level of trust, cohesion	
	Free expression of feelings	Support group's self-governance
	Mutual aid	Promote behaviors that increase cohesion
	Full acceptance of differences	Provide balance between support, confrontation
	Group viewed as unique	
	Clarity of group purpose	Encourage conversion of insight into action
	Feelings of security, belonging, "we" spirit	Interpret; explore common themes
	Differentiated roles	Universalize themes
	Group self-directed	Encourage deeper-level exploration of problems
	Intensive work on cognitions	
	Goal-oriented behavior	Assure review of goals, task completion
	Work outside of group to achieve personal goals	Stimulate individual and group growth
	Members feel empowered	Support application of new behaviors outside group
	Communication open, spontaneous	
	Self-confrontation	
Separation	Review and evaluation	Prepare for letting go
	Development of outlets outside group	Facilitate evaluation and feelings about termination
	Stabilizing and generalizing	
	Projecting toward future	Review individual and group progress
	Recognition of personal, interpersonal growth	Redirect energy of individuals away from group and toward self-process
	Sadness and anxiety over reality of separation	
	Expression of fears, hopes, and others' anxiety for self	Enable individuals to disconnect
		Encourage resolution of unfinished business
	Some denial, regression	Reinforce changes made by individuals
	Moving apart, distancing	Administer evaluation instruments
	Less intense interaction	
	Plans as to how to continue progress outside group	
	Talk of reunions, follow-up	

On this questionnaire are two questions to which members respond in writing:

1. Why do you think all of you are here together?
2. What are you going to try to accomplish together?

Discussion of responses gives the group a beginning point from which to proceed.

In the contractual process of initial sessions, leaders also help members to refine their general goals. The next example from the HEART group illustrates the role of the leader in seeking concreteness to clarify global goals.

The leader also keeps accomplishment of goals at the forefront of the group's work. Through reading assignments (**bibliotherapy**), journaling, and mindfulness, members can read, write, and reflect on the themes they are addressing and the insights they have achieved during and between group sessions (Corey, 2006). Session time may be allocated for discussing these insights, thereby reinforcing the value of continuing work between sessions.

Paying attention to the way each session opens and concludes is important for maximizing member productivity and satisfaction. Corey and Corey (2006)

CASE EXAMPLE

Seeking Concreteness in the Forming Stage in the HEART Group

Dave: At our last session, I asked each of you to share what you'd like to get out of the group individually. I'd like to take some of our time today to think of group goals. What would you like to accomplish together?

Amelia: To lose weight.

Dave: I hope that happens for all of you, and that the group is a source of support to you in pursuing your weight loss goals; but losing weight is more of an individual goal.

Liz: Follow the group rules?

Dave: Tell us more …

Liz: Well, like, respect each other and actively participate.

Dave: Following the group guidelines will help you to reach your group goals, but …

Amber: I'd like to know how other people deal with the stuff I go through.

June: Yeah, like how to keep your mom off your back!

Dave: Okay, good. It sounds like a group goal is for you all to share experiences. Are there any others?

Amelia: Sometimes I just want somebody to listen, you know? I don't know, I know I shouldn't be eating so much, but then I do, and it makes me feel bad. I thought it would help to be around other people who, like, might know how I'm feeling.

Jen: Yeah, I thought that too.

Dave: So far, I've heard two suggestions for group goals. One is to share experiences and the other, which Amelia just mentioned, is to listen to each other and support one another, especially when it comes to feeling sad or worried.

encourage leaders to draw from the following procedures in opening meetings:

1. Give members a brief opportunity to say what they want from the upcoming session.
2. Invite members to share their accomplishments since the last session.
3. Elicit feedback regarding the group's last session and give any reflections you have of the session.

To bring meetings to a close, Corey and Corey (2006) emphasize the need to summarize and integrate the group experience by following these procedures:

1. Ask members what it was like for them to be in the group today.
2. Invite members to identify briefly what they are learning about themselves through their experience in the group. Are they getting what they want? If not, what would they be willing to do to get it?
3. Ask members whether there are any topics, questions, or problems they would like to explore in the next session.
4. Ask members to indicate what they would be willing to do outside of the session to practice new skills.

Incorporating group rituals into the structure of sessions increases the continuity that flows from meeting to meeting. Examples include check-in as a ritual to start each session, structured refreshment breaks, and closing meditations or readings (Subramanian, Hernandez, & Martinez, 1995). Such continuity heightens the transfer of insights and new behaviors from the group session into daily life.

Interventions in the Power and Control Stage

In Stage 2 of group development, the group enters a period in which its dynamics, tone, and atmosphere are often conflict ridden, and some groups may need encouragement to address underlying conflicts that threaten the health of the group (Schiller, 1997). Groups may be beset by problems in dealing with divisions among individuals and subgroups, complaints and unrest over group goals, processes, and structure, and challenges to leadership. At the same time, the group is trying out its capacity to manage its own affairs. The leader is responsible for guiding the group through this stormy period so that it remains intact and demonstrates an emerging capacity to cope with individual differences and to manage its own governance. Leaders can employ several strategies in carrying out this responsibility: minimize changes, encourage balanced feedback, increase effective communication, and create constructive norms.

Minimize Changes

During the "power and control" stage, groups with a closed format are particularly susceptible to inner and outer stressors such as a change of leader, a move to a new meeting place, the addition or loss of members, or a change in the meeting time. Traumatic events such as a runaway, a death, an incidence of physical violence in an institutional setting, or acutely disturbing political or natural events at the community or national level may also significantly affect a group at this stage.

Although such changes or events can be upsetting to a group at any stage of development, they are particularly difficult to manage in Stage 2. At this point, members have not yet become invested in the group to an appreciable extent and thus may become easily distracted or disenchanted. Adding new members or changing the group's leader is particularly stressful, causing members to raise their defenses because there are risks involved in revealing themselves when either the leader or a member is an unknown entity. The loss of a leader can also prove inordinately traumatic to members who have difficulty investing in relationships, affirming their stance that trusting others just brings disappointment.

In addition, making a significant change in the group structure without group involvement may cause members to conclude that the leader or agency disregards the impact of such decisions on the group and that the members' input is not important. Although changes are sometimes unavoidable, it behooves leaders to keep them to a minimum, to prepare members in advance whenever possible, and to aid them to "work through" their feelings when change is necessary.

Encourage Balanced Feedback

In Stage 2 of group development, leaders must ensure that feedback is balanced. As they observe that group members are tentatively moving into their first authentic encounters, leaders should intervene in negative interactions to draw the group's attention to the need to provide balanced feedback, reminding members to focus on positives as well as negatives. The following excerpt from an early group session with adult members illustrates this point.

Gary [to Wayne, in irritated voice]: Why do you keep grilling me with questions like that? I feel like I'm being interrogated.

Wayne: I just wanted to get to know you better!

Leader [to Wayne]: You said in the first session that you'd like to use the group as a way of getting feedback about how you come across to others. I'm wondering if this might be a time for that?

Wayne: Yeah. I don't know what's coming, but I really think I do need to know more about how you all see me. I was really surprised at what Gary said.

Leader [to Wayne]: Good. I can understand you may have reservations, but I'm also pleased that you're willing to take a risk this early in the group.

Leader [to group]: Because this is the group's first experience in giving feedback to members, I'd like to remind you of the contract not only to help members identify problems but also to share positive observations you may have. As you do so, I'd like you to personalize your statements. I'll help you do so.

Group members' first experiences in giving feedback to one another are crucial in setting the tone for all that follows in the group. By guiding members' first cautious efforts to drop their facades and to engage at an intimate level, the leader enables the group to experience success and incorporate attention to positives as a part of its character. As individuals come to trust that the group will attend to positives as well as negatives, they will often increase their level of participation and take the initiative in soliciting group feedback.

EP 7

In addition to encouraging positive feedback for individuals, leaders can reinforce behaviors observed during a session that have helped the group accomplish its tasks. Such behaviors may include being willing to participate in discussions, to answer questions, and to risk revealing oneself; showing support to others; speaking in turn; giving full attention to the task at hand; accepting differing values, beliefs, and opinions; and recognizing significant individual and group breakthroughs. The leader can also highlight the absence of destructive behaviors that might have occurred earlier (e.g., whispering, fidgeting, introducing tangential topics, dominating, or verbally and physically pestering other members). In addition, the leader must assist members to hear, acknowledge, and accept positive feedback, as illustrated in the following example.

Kim *[to Pat]:* I know you get discouraged sometimes, but I admire the fact you can manage four children by yourself and still work. I don't think I could ever do that in a million years.

Pat: I don't always manage it. Actually, I don't do near enough for my children.

Leader: I hear you saying, Pat, that you feel inadequate as a mother—and we can return to that in a moment—but right now would you reflect on what you just did?

Pat: I guess I blew off Kim's compliment. I didn't feel I deserved it.

Leader: I wonder if others of you have responded in a similar way when someone has told you something positive.

The last response broadens the focus to include the experience of other group members, which may lead into a discussion of the difficulties that others might encounter in accepting and internalizing positive feedback.

Increase Effective Communication

Achieving success during the "power and control" phase requires moment-by-moment interventions to increase the chances of effective communication. Facets of communication that enable members to relate effectively as a group include taking turns in talking, learning how to explore problems before offering solutions, speaking for themselves rather than for others, and speaking directly to the person for whom the message is intended. In addition, members can learn to distinguish between effective and ineffective ways of responding and can include improving their communication repertoire as one of their individual goals for work.

EP 8

Leaders increase the probability that members will adopt effective communication skills by heavily utilizing and modeling these skills themselves. In addition, leaders aid the acquisition of skills by assuming the role of "coach" and intervening to shape the display of communications in the group, as illustrated in the following examples:

- *[Eliminating negative communications]* "I'd like us to shy away from labeling, judging, sarcasm, and words like 'always' and 'never.' As we discussed in our group contract, try to give self-reports rather than indirect messages that put down or judge another person."

- *[Personalizing messages]* "That was an example of a 'you' message. I'd like you to try again, this time by starting out with the pronoun 'I.' Try to identify your feelings, or what you want or need."

- *[Talking in turn]* "Right now, several of you are speaking at the same time. Try to hold to the guideline that we all speak in turn. Your observations are too important to miss."

- *[Speaking directly to each other]* "Right now, you're speaking to the group, but I think your message is meant for Fred. If so, then it would be better to talk directly to him."

- *[Exploratory questions]* "Switching from closed- to open-ended questions right now could help Liz to tell her story in her own way." (The leader explains the difference between these two modes of questioning.)

- *[Listening]* "Try to really hear what she's saying. Help her to let out her feelings and to get to the source of the problem."

- *[Problem exploration versus problem solving]* "When the group offers advice too quickly, folks can't share their deeper-level feelings or reveal a problem in its entirety. We may need to allow Richard 5 to 10 minutes to share his concerns before the group offers any observations. The timing of advice is critical as we try to help members share and solve problems."

- *[Authenticity]* "Could you take a risk and tell the group what you're feeling at this very moment? I can see you choking up, and I think it would be good for the group to know what you're experiencing."

- *[Requesting]* "You've just made a complaint about the group. On the flip side of any complaint is a request. Tell the group what would help. Make a request."

Intervening moment by moment to shape the communications of members, as in the instances illustrated here, increases the therapeutic potential of a group.

Stage 2 of group development may also present a challenge when the group has co-leadership. The presence of two leaders may increase members' defensiveness as they seek to erect boundaries that protect them from the influence presented by two leaders. Members may also attempt to split the leaders by exploiting disagreements or differences between them or by affiliating with one leader and working against the other. Clarity of purpose, preparation for these maneuvers, and strong communication can help co-leaders resist these efforts when they emerge (Nosko & Wallace, 1997).

Create Constructive Norms

As mentioned earlier, leaders must be concerned about the nature of the norms that evolve in the group. Many of the group patterns form in the "power and control" stage. The leader can intervene then to shape the power structure, the stylistic communications of the group, and the ways in which the group chooses to negotiate and solve problems.

In shaping the group's norms, leaders need to intervene, for example, in the following instances:

- When socializing or distracting behavior substantially interferes with the group's task
- When one or more members monopolize the group's airtime
- When one or more members are "out of step" with the group process and/or experience strong feelings such as hurt, anger, disgust, disappointment, or disapproval
- When several members or the entire group begin to talk about one member
- When a member's behavior is incompatible with the governing guidelines set by the group
- When participants intellectualize about emotion-laden material
- When one or more members display hostility through jokes, sarcasm, or criticism, or when they interrogate, scapegoat, or gang up on a single member
- When the group offers advice or suggestions without first encouraging a member to fully explore a problem
- When there is silence or withdrawal by one or more members or the group itself seems to be "shut down"
- When a member adopts a "co-leader" role

EP 8

When problems such as these emerge, the leader must focus the group's attention on what is occurring in the here and now. Leaders may simply document what they see by describing specific behaviors or the progression of events that have occurred and then request group input. Once the group focuses on the problem, the leader should facilitate discussion and problem solving rather than take decisive action on his or her own. Ultimately, the responsibility for resolution needs to rest with the group.

Although leaders need to avoid prematurely closing heated issues in a group, they must intervene immediately to refocus the process when group members criticize, label, or insult others, or when they argue among themselves. Leaders may assume—incorrectly—that letting members verbally "fight it out" when they have conflicts is cathartic or helpful. In fact, ample research indicates that aggression begets aggression and that not intervening in conflict merely encourages members to continue venting their anger in the same fashion. A leader's passive stance could allow conflict to escalate to the point that it turns into harmful verbal or physical altercations. In instances of serious disruption, a leader's lack of intervention may "prove" to members who are scrutinizing the leader's behavior that it is dangerous to take risks in the group because the leader will not protect them (Smokowski, Rose, & Bacallao, 2001). Leaders must be willing to respond decisively when significant group disruption occurs, using physical and verbal measures as needed, such as clapping their hands loudly, standing up, speaking louder than group members, or putting themselves between members who are arguing.

Interventions should generally focus on group-related matters (rather than on individual attitudes or behaviors) because it is rare that the destructive or self-defeating behavior of an individual or subset will not affect the entire system. In fact, some problematic behaviors may be fostered or reinforced by the group as a whole. Focusing interventions on a pair, a trio, a foursome, or the group also avoids singling out one person or inadvertently "siding" with one segment of clients over others.

EP 7 and 8

A guideline for formulating interventions that confront dysfunctional behavior is that the behavior must be analyzed in the context of the group process, with the leader considering how such behavior affects and is affected by group members. This approach is illustrated by the following response to a situation in which two members are talking between themselves. Rather than asking the two to pay attention, the leader states the following:

EP 7

Leader: I'm concerned about what is happening right now. Several of you are not participating; some of you are whispering; one of you is writing notes; a few of you are involved in the discussion. As individuals, you appear to be at different places with the group, and I'd like to check out what each of you is experiencing right now.

This message focuses on all group members, neutrally describes behavior that is occurring, and encourages the group process. By not imposing a solution on the group, the leader assumes a facilitative rather than an authoritarian role and sets the stage for productive group discussion.

Interventions in the Intimacy and Differentiation Stages

Stage 3 (intimacy) and Stage 4 (differentiation) of group development constitute the group's working phases. In the initial stages of a group's evolution, the critical issues at stake focused on the struggle for power, trust versus mistrust, and self-focus versus focus on others. In the working phase, however, issues shift to those of disclosure versus anonymity, honesty versus game playing, spontaneity versus control, acceptance versus rejection, cohesion versus fragmentation, and responsibility versus blaming (Corey & Corey, 2006).

In the working phase, leaders continue to promote conditions that aid members to make healthy choices in resolving issues by straightforwardly addressing and resolving conflict, openly disclosing personal problems, taking responsibility for their problems, and making progroup choices. Thanks to the relaxed stance that characterizes this phase, leaders have more opportunities to intensify therapeutic group conditions. They may focus on refining feedback processes—for example, coaching members to give immediate feedback, to make such feedback specific rather than global, to render feedback in nonjudgmental ways, and to give feedback regarding strengths as well as problem behaviors (Corey & Corey, 2006).

Leaders can also enhance individual and group growth by focusing on the universality of underlying issues, feelings, and needs that members seem to share:

> The circumstances leading to hurt and disappointment may be very different from person to person or from culture to culture. But the resulting emotions have a universal quality. Although we may not speak the same language or come from the same society, we are connected through our feelings of joy and pain. It is when group members no longer get lost in the details of daily experiences and instead share their deeper struggles with these universal human themes that a group is most cohesive. (Corey & Corey, 1992, p. 209)

During these middle phases of group development, group members can participate in a number of activities to work on individual and commonly held goals. Such activities may reduce stress and encourage pleasure and creativity; assist the leader in assessment as members are observed while "doing" rather than "saying"; facilitate communication, problem solving, and rapport among members; and help members develop skills and competence in decision making (Northen & Kurland, 2001). Nevil, Beatty, and Moxley (1997) suggest a variety of structured activities and socialization games that can be employed to improve interpersonal skills, increase social awareness, and enhance prosocial competence. Although intended for use with persons with disabilities, many of these exercises can be adapted for use with a variety of populations. Other authors note their effectiveness with diverse populations, such as those of Hispanic heritage (Delgado, 1983) and Native Americans (Edwards et al., 1987).

EP 4

One element of a structured program targeting delinquency reduction consists of multifamily group meetings in which eight to 10 families meet for eight weekly sessions lasting two and one half hours each. In the meetings, family members sit together at designated tables, share a meal, and engage in "structured, fun, interactive" activities (McDonald, 2002, p. 719) that enhance communication skills, strengthen relationships, and facilitate networking among the families.

Although art therapy and other expressive techniques generally require specialized training, reviewing resources such as Coholic, Lougheed, and Cadell (2009), Cheung (2006), Ross (1997), and Rose (1998) can acquaint social workers with the principles for applying these techniques in groups to address issues related to aggressive behavior, trauma, self-esteem, body image, and awareness of emotions. With all groups, the leader must take the group's purpose, stage of development, and member characteristics into account when selecting and implementing an experiential exercise or activity (Wright, 1999).

In the working phase, leaders also support a continuing trend toward differentiation, in which members establish their uniqueness and separateness from others. Leaders do not create these expressions of differences but rather stimulate or advance them. For example, the leader may note when a member reveals "a heretofore hidden talent, or access to a resource that was previously believed inaccessible, or possession of a needed skill or perspective. A member may articulate a previously unspoken need, or offer an interpretation not thought of by the others, or pose a question that catalyzes or synthesizes a piece of the group's work" (Henry, 1992, p. 183).

The working phase is a time of intensive focus on achieving members' goals. Much of the group's work during this phase is devoted to carrying out contracts developed in the group's initial sessions. Members may have lost sight of their individual goals, so a major leadership role involves confirming goals periodically and promoting organized and systematic efforts to work on them. In one HEART group session, when the discussion of fitting in drifted to topics such as college, athletic teams, and peer groups, Dave brought the group back to focus by synthesizing the thread and saying, "I'd like to pose a question to the group. What would be one thing to change about your mindset? What thought could you change that might help you get through high school, or shopping, or gym?"

The leader assumes the ongoing responsibility of monitoring the time allocated to each member to work on goals. Toseland and Rivas (2009) suggest that the leader help each member to work in turn. If a group spends considerable time aiding one member to achieve his or her individual goals, the leader should generalize the concepts developed in this effort to other members so that everyone benefits. The leader should also encourage participants to share relevant personal experiences with the member receiving help, thus establishing a norm for mutual aid. In addition, he or she should check on the progress of members who did not receive due attention and encourage their participation in the next session.

EP 8

Finally, the leader should establish a systematic method of monitoring treatment goals and tasks in sessions. Without such procedures, monitoring may be haphazard and focus on only those members who are more assertive and highly involved; members who are less assertive or resistant will not receive the same attention. Without systematic monitoring, tasks to be completed between sessions may not receive the proper follow-up. Participants may become frustrated when they have completed "homework" between sessions and have no opportunity to report on the results. The expectation of a weekly progress report helps increase motivation to work toward goals between sessions, reduces the necessity of reminding members of their contract agreements, and aids them in gaining a sense of independence and accomplishment.

Interventions in the Termination Stage

EP 4

Termination is a difficult stage for members who have invested heavily in the group, have experienced intensive support, encouragement, and understanding, and have received effective aid for their problems. Leaders must be sensitive to the mixed feelings engendered by termination and carefully intervene to assist the group to come to an effective close. Chapter 19 identifies significant termination issues and change maintenance strategies. Here, we address aspects of the leader's role that are specific to facilitating planned endings in groups and evaluating group efficacy.

Leaders may assist group members in completing their "commencement" proceedings (Mahler, 1969) by adopting strategies such as the following:

- Ensure that the issues and concerns worked on by the group resemble those that members will encounter outside the group. Assure that the group is a place where members get honest feedback about how their behavior is likely to be received outside the group and a setting where they may obtain help in coping with those reactions (Toseland & Rivas, 2009).
- Refer to a variety of situations and settings throughout the group experience to help members practice and acquire skills, thereby better preparing them for the multifaceted situations they will inevitably encounter outside the group (Toseland & Rivas, 2009).
- Facilitate members' discussion of how they will respond to possible setbacks in an unsympathetic environment. Build member confidence in existing coping skills and abilities to solve problems independently. Also, teach therapeutic principles that underlie intervention methods, such as those inherent in assertiveness, effective communication, or problem solving (Toseland & Rivas, 2009). Share your reactions to endings as a way of helping members to identify their own conflicted feelings and any sense of abandonment, anger, sadness, or loss.
- Increase review and integration of learning by helping members to put into words what has transpired between themselves and the group from the first to the final session and what they have learned about themselves and others. Solicit information about what members were satisfied and unsatisfied with in the group and ways in which

sessions could have had greater impact. Ask members to spontaneously recall moments of conflict and pain as well as moments of closeness, warmth, humor, and joy in the group (Corey & Corey, 1992).

- Several sessions before termination suggest that members consider using the remaining time to complete their own agenda. For example, ask, "If this were the last session, how would you feel about what you have done, and what would you wish you had done differently?" (Corey & Corey, 2002, p. 261).

- Facilitate the completion of unfinished business between members. One technique involves an exercise in which each person, in turn, says in a few short phrases, "What I really liked was the way you … (supply a specific behavior exchanged between the persons, such as 'always gave me credit when I could finally say something that was hard for me to say')," and then, "But I wish we … (supplying a specific wish for a behavioral exchange between the two persons that did not occur, such as 'had made more opportunities to talk to each other more directly')" (Henry, 1992, p. 124). Note that this and other closure exercises should not be used to generate new issues but rather to bring resolution to the present situation.

- Encourage members to identify areas for future work once the group concludes. Consider asking members to formulate their own individual change contracts, which may be referred to once the group ends, and invite each member to review his or her contract with the group (Corey & Corey, 2006).

- Engage individual members in relating how they have perceived themselves in the group, what the group has meant to them, and how they have grown. Ask the other members to give feedback regarding how they have perceived and felt about each person, including measured feedback that helps members strengthen the perceptions that they gained during the course of the group (e.g., "One of the things I like best about you is …," "One way I see you blocking your strengths is …," or "A few things that I hope you'll remember are …") (Corey, 1990, p. 512).

- Use evaluative measures to determine the effectiveness of the group and the leader's interventions. Such measures have the following benefits: (1) they address the leader's professional concerns about the specific effects of interventions; (2) they help workers improve their leadership skills;

(3) they demonstrate the group's efficacy to agencies or funding sources; (4) they help leaders assess individual members' and the group's progress in accomplishing agreed-upon objectives; (5) they allow members to express their satisfactions and dissatisfactions with the group; and (6) they help leaders develop knowledge that can be generalized to future groups and other leaders (Reid, 1991; Toseland & Rivas, 2009).

EP 4

Like other areas of social work practice, group interventions face increased scrutiny to determine the efficacy of certain processes and the outcomes. Tolman and Molidor's (1994) review of research on social work with groups indicates that group work evaluation is growing ever more sophisticated and that multiple measures are being employed to determine group efficacy. For example, in addition to undertaking evaluation at the termination phase, more than one-third of the groups studied by Tolman and Molidor (1994) used follow-up measures to determine whether earlier gains had been maintained. These authors note, however, that although it is important to examine outcomes, the evaluative challenge lies in isolating those elements of group process that actually contributed to those outcomes.

Increasingly, curricula for group interventions include measurement instruments to assist in understanding both baseline and outcome measures. For example, in groups consisting of adolescents and preteens, Rose (1998) suggests using a variety of methods and sources of data, including standardized ratings by parents and teachers; self-monitoring or self-reports through checklists, logs, questionnaires, or sentence completion; observation of in-group behavior; performance during role-plays or simulations; sociometric evaluations; goal attainment scaling; and knowledge tests. Anderson-Butcher, Khairallah, and Race-Bigelow (2004) suggest that qualitative interviews may be used to ascertain client outcomes and to identify the characteristics of effective self-help groups. Magen's (2004) review of measurement issues in group evaluation offers guidance for effective selection of outcome and process measures.

At termination, members and the leader may all record their satisfaction with the group and their sense of its effectiveness. Members can respond to open-ended questions or a structured checklist, either of which may inquire about the changes the group brought about in each participant's life or relationships, the techniques used that had the greatest and least impact, perceptions of the leader, and so on (Corey et al., 2004). These authors also recommend that the leader keep a journal to evaluate group progress over time, note his or her reactions at various points, keep track of techniques or materials used and the perceived outcomes, and share self-insights that emerged during the life of the group.

Errors in Group Interventions

In addition to attending to recommended interventions across the life of the group, social workers must also take care to avoid errors that inhibit group development and process. Research on damaging experiences in therapeutic groups indicates that group leaders' behaviors (e.g., confrontation, monopolizing, criticizing) or inaction (e.g., lack of support, lack of structure) play a primary role in group casualties or dropouts (Smokowski, Rose, & Bacallao, 2001). Thomas and Caplan (1999) identify some of the most common mistakes, including:

- Doing one-on-one work in the context of the group. This practice inhibits the mutual aid that is the hallmark of group work.

- Having such a rigid agenda or adherence to a curriculum that members cannot pursue emerging themes or otherwise own the group process.
- Scapegoating or attacking individual members. This behavior inhibits others' involvement by sending a message that the group is not a safe place.
- Overemphasizing content and failing to universalize themes so that all members can benefit from and relate to the experience of other members.
- Ridiculing members or discounting some members' need to be heard.
- Lecturing the group. This practice disempowers members and inhibits group investment and momentum.
- Failing to address offensive comments or colluding with members around inappropriate, antiauthoritarian, racist, or sexist statements.

It may be helpful to think of the preceding list as behaviors that stop the evolution of the group or send it veering off course. In the next HEART group example, Dave demonstrates a common error in group work by focusing on content over process.

CASE EXAMPLE

Overemphasizing Content and Lecturing in the HEART Group

Dave: I want us to think about the word "fat" and to think about if that's an appropriate word to use to describe ourselves.

Liz: Not you, you're skinny.

Dave: When I speak to people who have been called fat, or who refer to themselves that way, I use the term "person with overweight." And that's the way I talk about it. None of us are guaranteed to keep the bodies we have. Whether we like them or not, our bodies can always change. So I say people have overweight because it's descriptive of a moment in time rather than an enduring quality that someone possesses.

Amelia: My psychiatrist calls, um, says that I have a disordered relationship with food. [The group laughs.]

Dave: What does that mean?

Amelia: Means I'm fat, I don't know! [more laughter]

Dave: Well, let's look at the words together then. What is disordered?

Amelia: Fat. I don't know, like not right, dysfunctional, not cool.

June: Out of order.

Amelia: Out of order. Yes, I'm out of order with food.

Dave: What do you think about that? Do you agree or disagree?

Amelia: I don't know; whatever, it makes sense to me.

Dave: What about it makes sense?

Amelia: Well, it's kind of a nice way of saying, I'm fat.

Dave: When I hear that phrase, it sounds to me as though your psychiatrist is telling you that you're using food for reasons other than nutrition.

Amelia: Yeah, maybe.

VARIATIONS IN SOCIAL WORK WITH GROUPS

The concepts for assessing and intervening with groups can be applied to a variety of settings, populations, and issues. However, two particular variations on group work deserve further discussion. Groups that occur in single sessions and those that take place online or through other electronic media require special attention and novel intervention strategies.

Single-Session Groups

As described in Chapter 11, attention is turning to the application of group work concepts to groups that meet only for a single session. For example, in interdisciplinary case meetings, the composition changes based on which professionals are involved with the particular case. In shelters, inpatient, and residential settings, group membership will shift depending on who is living in the facility at a given time. Fluctuations in the census from day to day will affect the attendance at required daily groups.

Some groups are simply designed to meet on only one occasion. For example, critical incident debriefing groups meet to assist people affected by a traumatic event—for example, after a workplace shooting (Reynolds & Jones, 1996). Other single-session groups include an abbreviated psychoeducational program for families of persons with mood disorders (Ruffalo, Nitzberg, & Schoof, 2011) or a program to educate college students about the risks of excessive alcohol use (Fried & Dunn, 2012).

As the name suggests, single-session groups come together in a particular configuration only once, and each group must negotiate its own purpose and contract (Block, 1985; Ebenstein, 1998). As identified in Chapter 11, some concepts used in the single-session groups—purpose, contracting, and worker roles—are variations on those used in groups of longer duration. Others—composition, member roles, norms, and group stages—may be less germane to single-session groups.

Research on single-session groups is limited, but existing literature suggests that they pose unique challenges for group facilitators, including how to handle recruitment, allow sufficient time for the beginning phase, deal with heterogeneous group membership, and set realistic goals (Ebenstein, 1998). Given these challenges, Kosoff (2003) argues that facilitators must possess comprehensive knowledge of the population to be served by the group, strong skills in planning and preparing for the sessions, the ability to exercise more active, direct, focused, and flexible leadership, and skill in structuring the session to encourage members to participate fully and move through the phases of development within the time allotted.

More specifically, Kosoff (2003) emphasizes the importance of developing a preliminary awareness of the issues and themes that preoccupy the population to be served in order to help focus the session on one or two concerns and limit goals to those that are achievable in one session (Ebenstein, 1998). This knowledge is also important in helping speed up the process whereby the group members develop rapport and sense of commonality in purpose and need (Block, 1985). Because of the condensed time frame, pacing is critical, as sufficient time must be allowed for a real beginning, middle, and end for the group session. Ebenstein (1998) suggests that crisis intervention theory can provide a helpful framework for this pacing in its here-and-now orientation, which focuses on strengthening existing defenses and developing new coping strategies.

Authors with expertise in single-session groups report that they proceed through the group stages described earlier in this chapter, but they do so in a condensed or concurrent fashion, and it is incumbent on the leaders to structure the group so that the tasks at each phase are met. To do so, leaders use the first 5 to 10 minutes of a session to facilitate interaction among the members and identify guidelines and feasible goals for the session. Facilitators may offer refreshments as members gather, use an innocuous ice breaker ("What is your favorite ice cream? How many of you are oldest children? Vegetarians? Like to watch football?") (Turner, 2001). Facilitators are prepared to share preliminary goals and ground rules, seek input on members' needs, and come to efficient agreement on the ground rules for the group.

To make effective use of the middle phases of group work, leaders should be prepared with various types of content to meet the needs of the particular configuration of individuals at a given session. This content may include educational material (on medications, symptoms, resources, diagnoses, phases of recovery) or activities to foster self-expression and problem solving (Keats & Sabharwal, 2008). Facilitators in single-session groups should be especially skilled at exploration and empathy to build trust and cohesion, and at linking, to help individual members understand and support each other (Keast, 2012; Kosoff, 2004). These skills foster self-reflection and sharing among members, both of which are essential for mutual aid (Steinberg, 2004). Leaders must also be comfortable with flexibly shifting roles and focus, based on the composition and needs of any given group. They must balance structure and independence, leaning in and being directive and leaning back and encouraging the members to take leadership. Leaders must also be attuned to timing and pacing. "Each session needs to be a complete experience and there cannot be any issues that are left unsettled. It is essential that enough time be left to ensure that members leave the space with an integral sense of experience" (Keast, 2012, p. 721).

Time must also be set aside for the closing phase of the group. Many groups utilize structured closing processes or rituals to bring the session to an end. This might involve giving the group a moment to reflect on the meaning of the session, then asking each member to share one insight or something learned in group that he or she might use in the future or identify their needs going forward (Galinsky & Schopler, 1985). Closings could include sharing an inspirational quote, a resource list, or a worksheet to expand on topics from the group. They may also include participant evaluations or posttest questionnaires for research or quality assurance purposes.

Whether the single-session group is analogous to open-ended/open-member groups or to educational sessions or workshops, some group concepts may be more germane and transferable than others. However, regardless of the type of single-session group, social workers must be attentive not only to the steps in planning but to the structure, dynamics, and worker roles when meetings take place.

Technology-Mediated Groups

Social workers are increasingly utilizing technological advances to enhance the delivery of services to clients individually and through groups. Persons who are homebound, are concerned about the stigma of receiving services, or find attendance at agency settings difficult may be able to experience the support and benefit of groups through texts, email, or the Internet (Harris, 1999; Hollander, 2001). The nature of typed, asynchronous communication means that members have more control and time for reflection as they craft their responses. In addition, they can participate in the virtual group at their convenience (Fingeld, 2000) and with a high degree of anonymity (Meier, 2002). However, participation may be stymied by Internet provider system problems and by trust issues, especially with

"lurkers" (those who read mail but do not post to the group) and with participants' actual level of engagement with the process. Online group facilitators must assure through informed consent that members understand the risks and benefits of such a model (ASWB, 2015).

Technological innovations have also brought significant changes to task groups. Such groups are no longer bound by geographic constraints; work teams, committees, coalitions, and classes can be conducted electronically. Webcasts, conference calls, and other technology-enhanced methods can save time and travel costs, provide access to expert consultation, and efficiently respond to crises and evolving circumstances in the practice environment.

Recent innovations in group work involve the use of web-based virtual reality experiences to bring group members together and foster interaction in a safe environment. In one example, rural elementary school students learned various social skills in a typical group setting, but then used a multiuser virtual environment (MUVE) to test and practice skills through avatars (Baker, Parks-Savage, & Rehfuss, 2009). In another example, social work students participated in peer-to-peer learning through a virtual community in which challenging situations could be posted and addressed by fellow students (Davis & Goodman, 2014). Rotondi and colleagues (2005) successfully utilized "telehealth" groups to assist individuals with schizophrenia and their family members. Technology-mediated groups are also well suited for people seeking support on a 24/7 basis, such as grieving parents who may log in to share feelings and seek help at any hour of the day or night (Edwards, 2007).

At this time, there is insufficient evidence to make claims about the ways that various technology-based or technology-enhanced group interventions parallel or diverge from face-to-face group practices. Clearly, social workers who employ these technologies must be aware of the technological and interpersonal capacities of prospective group participants and the pros and cons of various types of electronic interventions (Ramsey & Montgomery, 2014). Group facilitators must decide about the form of communication to be used and whether it will augment or replace face-to-face meetings. Social workers who lead electronic task or treatment groups must be active in guiding the process and drawing out implications for feelings and tone that are masked by the communication or interaction medium. They must also be wary of the potential for miscommunication and misuse of private data and take steps to educate group members and solicit their assistance in addressing problems as they arise (Bogo et al., 2012). Finally, advocacy is required to assure that all populations have proper access to electronic services.

INTERVENTIONS WITH TASK GROUPS

EP 6 and 7

As described earlier, a significant aspect of professional social work practice is performance in task and work groups. In contrast to treatment groups, task groups try to accomplish a purpose, create a product, or develop policies. You are likely to participate in task groups throughout your career, starting with group projects for class, continuing as a staff member, and eventually serving as a leader of such groups in your practice. As with treatment groups, task groups may have open or closed membership and they may be time-limited or open-ended. Task group membership may be voluntary (a neighborhood taskforce on crime), appointed (a coalition consisting of representatives of homeless shelters), elected (a board of directors), or determined by roles (an interdisciplinary team consisting of all professionals serving a particular family).

To the maximum extent possible, the membership should possess the skills and resources needed to accomplish the purpose for which the group was convened. For example, if a committee concerned about crime had no law enforcement personnel as members, it might seek out someone to fill that niche. As with therapeutic groups, those convening task groups should be alert to the characteristics of potential members and ensure that no member will be an isolate or an outlier. This consideration is particularly important when service consumers or their family members fill representative roles in a group consisting largely of professionals and service providers. Multiple representatives from consumer or family organizations should be included in committee membership, thereby ensuring that they are empowered and that their positions move beyond a token role.

The leadership of task groups is usually explicitly chosen and may be selected by the group itself or by an outside entity (voting for president of a professional organization or student government). For the purpose of discussing interventions with task groups, we will use the term "chair" to designate the group leader or facilitator, and we will focus on groups that are ongoing, such as a committee.

The stages of group development observed in treatment settings will also occur in task groups, though not necessarily in a linear fashion. As groups take on new issues and membership changes, the group may cycle back to revisit earlier stages. Further, the nature of task groups is such that the two middle phases (intimacy and differentiation) may not be distinguishable, and thus may be conceptualized as the "working phase" of the group.

Preaffiliation

A crucial part of successfully leading task groups involves getting the group off to a good start: identifying group purpose, helping to build connections among members, and identifying group guidelines. In this and other phases of the group, the chair must be attentive both to *group process* and *group content*. **Group process** refers to how the group is operating. Is there sufficient input and consideration of topics? Are all voices being heard? Is time being used wisely? **Group content** refers to the issues being discussed as opposed to *how* they are being discussed. In attending to content, the chair must be sure that the committee is addressing relevant issues, that they have proper background information to guide their discussion, and that they are clear on what is being asked of them (to give an opinion, explore options, make a decision, etc.). This is a delicate and challenging balance, as it can be tempting to rush through an agenda item and move on to another issue without assuring that all perspectives have been considered. On the other hand, too much attention to process and viewpoints can lead to "analysis paralysis," where one agenda item is discussed endlessly without progress toward action.

In the "forming" or preaffiliation stage, individuals enter with varying hopes and apprehensions about the group. Chairs can help diminish anxiety by clarifying the purpose of the group, asking members to introduce themselves, and using brainstorming or ice-breaking exercises to facilitate initial member interaction. Identifying the particular skills, experiences, and perspectives that different members bring can help members become more familiar with each other and more confident sharing their viewpoints. Please note, though, that early development in task groups will be affected by preexisting relationships among group members who already know or have worked with each other in other capacities. Depending on the quality of these past experiences, friction may be carried over into the new group or friendships may facilitate rapid movement into the work of the group. In either case, it is essential that individuals with existing relationships not form subgroups, as these splinter groups or voting blocs may diminish the comfort and cohesion of all members of the group.

At the preaffiliation stage, chairs solicit member input on how the group should function and begin to develop group guidelines. As discussed in Chapter 11, these typically include mutual expectations about attendance, communications, preparation for meetings, confidentiality, and decision making.

Power and Control

In Stage 2, the power and control or "storming" phase, task groups often display discord about the issues they will address and the guidelines they will use. The issues may vary from operational concerns ("Why didn't we receive the minutes from the last meeting before today?" "Why is X on the agenda?") to significant issues that question the group itself ("I don't see why we should be the hiring committee. The CEO will just pick who she wants anyway" "It is a waste of time to try to influence legislation this term. We should just focus on our own jobs and services.").

Conflict is to be expected as a sign of the members' investment in the group. Chairs must be prepared for this and respond nondefensively, putting complaints on the table for group discussion and decisions. In this, the process of debate is more important that the content of the issue being debated. All too often, task groups avoid conflict by evading thorny issues, sometimes even tabling an issue despite the availability of enough facts to make a decision. Establishing norms in which differing options are sought and evaluated on their own merits will aid the group in accomplishing its objectives. Leaders should attempt to stimulate idea-related conflict while managing and controlling personality-related conflict. Failure to achieve this balance may result in the marginalization of potential contributors and a less complete product. Without such healthy conflict, there is always the danger of **groupthink**, a condition in which members reach premature and superficial agreement and alternative views or options are not expressed or taken seriously. Leaders (and members) can assist others to express the rationale behind particular opinions, clarifying what information needs to be developed to answer questions raised in the course of the conflict.

Working Phase

Although task groups begin their "work" from the first time they meet, the middle phase of group process signals the internalization of group guidelines, the emergence of norms, and shared processes for addressing the group's responsibilities. At this stage, we observe shared responsibility for group progress and accepted strategies for preparing for meetings and making decisions.

EP 6 and 7

Task group leaders model and support the use of effective communication skills, as discussed earlier in this book regarding communications with clients. These important skills include listening, reframing, probing, seeking concreteness, and summarizing. Chairs contribute to the creation of a productive working atmosphere by conveying that each member has something to contribute and by maintaining civility so that no member—or his or her idea—is allowed to be degraded (Toseland & Rivas, 2009).

As groups develop procedures for examining and addressing issues, the chair should help them avoid responding prematurely—arriving at solutions before the problem is well defined. For example, if a board is discussing budgetary shortfalls, the chair would help the members look at the causes and long-term trends in the budget before focusing on cuts or revenue enhancement strategies. In specifying appropriate problems and goals, the group can employ techniques such as brainstorming and nominal group technique to consider an array of possibilities before selecting a focus. **Brainstorming** involves generating and expressing a variety of opinions without evaluating them. In the **nominal group technique**, members first privately list potential problems. The group then takes one potential problem from each member until all are listed. Finally, it evaluates and ranks those potential problems as a group in deciding which should take priority (Toseland & Rivas, 2009).

At this stage, groups also employ strategies for effective decision making. Some procedures may be prescribed. For example, the charter or bylaws of the group may require certain periods for commentary, use of clearly specified rules on who can vote, and adherence to Robert's Rules of Order. Other groups may determine their own norms, such as decision by consensus or majority rule. A challenge in consensus decision making is that members may feel compelled or coerced to agree when they do not, creating an aura of unanimity when dissent exists.

Termination Phase

EP 8

Termination in task groups may occur when individual members leave (unexpectedly or as anticipated at the end of a term of office) or when the group disbands. Evaluation and "commencement" are often overlooked in task groups, as members experience relief at the reduction of the demands on their time and their group-related responsibilities, and perhaps satisfaction in successfully achieving their goal. Nevertheless, it is important to evaluate what worked and what did not work well in the group process, to acknowledge the contributions of time and effort made by group members, and to share gratitude about the roles that facilitated group success.

SUMMARY

This chapter focused on the knowledge and skills you will need to effectively intervene in social work treatment and task groups. As new theories of change and new treatment modalities emerge, they will also be applied to work with groups. For example, evolving solution-focused interventions have been applied to groups in an array of situations, including recovery from sexual abuse, improving parenting skills, and resolving symptoms of anxiety and depression (Metcalf, 1998). Multifamily groups, composed of family members who share a common concern, are useful for addressing severe and persistent psychiatric disorders (McFarlane, 2002) and reducing the risk for child abuse and neglect (Burford & Pennell, 2004; Meezan & O'Keefe, 1998), among other issues (Vakalah & Khajak, 2000). Group interventions for PTSD have demonstrated effectiveness (van der Kolk, 1993). The innovations ahead will determine if these successes can be achieved with trauma from military service, disasters, and other emerging needs.

In this chapter, we addressed the stages of group development and the common member and group characteristics that arise with each phase, illustrating the leadership roles and skills necessary for an effective group experience. We examined unique areas of group work, including single-session groups and online groups. For groups to be successful, leaders must thoughtfully apply research on effective group practices and flexibly use their role and interventions to suit the needs of the individuals and the group as a whole, from inception to termination.

COMPETENCY NOTES

EP 4   Engage in Practice-Informed Research and Research-Informed Practice
- **Use and translate research evidence to inform and improve practice, policy, and service delivery.** It is especially difficult to control the variables in group work, making research in this area especially complex. Nevertheless, studies support the use of groups and specific techniques within group work.

EP 6   Engage with Individuals, Families, Groups, Organizations, and Communities
- **Apply knowledge of human behavior and the social environment, person-in-environment, and other multidisciplinary theoretical frameworks to engage with clients and constituencies.** Group workers employ a variety of novel frameworks in this intervention. For example, an understanding of the phases of group development guides the facilitator in understanding group process and employing different techniques at a given stage.

EP 7   Assess Individuals, Families, Groups, Organizations, and Communities
- **Apply knowledge of human behavior and the social environment, person-in-environment, and other multidisciplinary theoretical frameworks in the analysis of assessment data from clients and constituencies.** This chapter addresses the techniques social workers use to facilitate groups from beginning to end. Group workers must understand group process, individual needs and strengths, and the issues that may emerge at any stage of the group's development.
- **Select appropriate intervention strategies based on the assessment, research knowledge, and values and preferences of clients and constituencies.** Social workers call on a variety of skills during the life span of a group. In early stages, for example, reticent members would usually be allowed to "stand back" and participate when they are comfortable doing so. In later stages, group members themselves would be encouraged to reach out to the reticent member and seek his or her input and involvement.

EP 8 **Intervene with Individuals, Families, Groups, Organizations, and Communities**

- **Critically choose and implement interventions to achieve practice goals and enhance capacities of clients and constituencies.** Groups are often focused on mutual problem solving. Facilitators help members develop the capacities, norms, and processes to solve problems in group functioning and to solve the problems that are the focus of the group.

- **Facilitate effective transitions and endings that advance mutually agreed-on goals.** Termination in groups can be very powerful because the cohesion developed in the group process and the familiar routine of meetings are lost when the group ends. Social workers must be alert to reactions at termination that may detrimentally affect the success of the members and the group itself.

SKILLS DEVELOPMENT EXERCISES
in Group Interventions

To assist you in developing group work skills, we have provided a number of exercises with modeled social worker responses. Imagine that you are the facilitator and formulate a response that addresses the member's and group's needs, given the phase and type of group. We have drawn the statements from two types of groups. One is an interdisciplinary task group in a hospital working on policy and practice changes in response to confidentiality laws, undocumented immigrant admissions, indigent patients, and the avian flu threat. The other is the HEART therapy group for teen girls with obesity. The five statements contain modeled social worker responses so that you can compare your response with the one provided. (Bear in mind that the modeled response is only one of many possible acceptable responses.)

CLIENT STATEMENTS

1. *Task group member [in fifth meeting, having missed three]:* "Well, I think we should reconsider why we need to change the policy at all. After all, we've done it this way for years."

2. *Task group member [second meeting]:* "How are we going to make decisions—majority rule?"

3. *HEART group member [third meeting]:* "You're just here for the paycheck."

4. *HEART group member [first meeting]:* "I'm not sure why I'm even here except to make my mother happy."

5. *Task group member [first meeting]:* It looks like the legal department has this committee membership stacked. Is there any point in meeting if the decisions have already been made?

MODELED SOCIAL WORKER
Responses

1. "Gene, we talked about the reason we were convened in the first two meetings. I'm wondering why this is coming up at this point?"

2. *[to the group]* "What do you think are the pros and cons of different decision-making options?"

3. *[inquisitively]* "It is true that I'm paid for this work, but it sounds like there really is something more behind your statement."

4. *[to the group]* "I wonder if some other folks here share that feeling?"

5. It sounds like you have two concerns: who is here and why we are here. I assure you that the decisions have not been made, so the group's input is important and timely. I wonder, though, who is missing? What other perspectives do we need around the table?

NOTE

1. Reid (1997) has reviewed procedures for evaluating outcomes in groups, including group testimonials, content analysis of audiotapes or videotapes, sociometric analysis, self-rating instruments, and other subjective measures. We refer you to Corey and Corey (2006) and Macgowan (2008) for further discussion of evaluative measures.

Additive Empathy, Interpretation, and Confrontation

Chapter Overview

Chapter 17 builds on the skills introduced in Chapters 5 and 6 to assist clients in achieving a deeper understanding of their own behavior, the behavior of others, and their options in exploring change. Appropriate timing for and uses of confrontation are presented as means of clients' gaining greater self-knowledge. Such confrontation should assist clients in making informed decisions mindful of their potential consequences. As in earlier chapters, examples from videos linked to this chapter are featured.

As a result of reading this chapter and practicing with classmates, you will be able to:

- Employ additive empathy.
- Construct an interpretation.
- Construct a confrontation.

EPAS Competencies in Chapter 17

This chapter will give you the information needed to meet the following practice competencies:

- Competency 2: Engage Diversity and Difference in Practice
- Competency 6: Engage with Individuals, Families, Groups, Organizations, and Communities

- Competency 7: Assess Individuals, Families, Groups, Organizations, and Communities
- Competency 8: Intervene with Individuals, Families, Groups, Organizations, and Communities
- Competency 9: Evaluate Practice with Individuals, Families, Groups, Organizations, and Communities

THE MEANING AND SIGNIFICANCE OF CLIENT SELF-AWARENESS

Self-awareness refers largely to awareness of the various forces operating in the present. Social workers assist clients to expand their awareness of their needs or wants, motives, emotions, beliefs, and problematic behaviors, and their awareness of these items' impact on other people. We do *not* use self-awareness to refer to insight into the etiology of problems. As we noted in earlier chapters, people can and do change without achieving this type of insight. On occasion, brief explorations into the past may be productive and enlightening—for example, to determine which qualities attracted intimate partners to each other, to identify factors that have contributed to sexual dysfunction, to assess the chronicity of problems, or to highlight previous successes. When making such brief excursions, however, it is important to relate the information elicited along the way to current work and current problems, emphasizing to clients that they can change the present. In other words, they can alter the current effects of history but not history itself.

Social workers have numerous tools at their disposal to assist clients to gain expanded self-awareness. Of these tools, additive empathy, interpretation, and confrontation are probably employed most extensively. This chapter defines these techniques, specifies indications for their use, presents guidelines for employing them effectively, and provides skill development exercises related to these tools.

ADDITIVE EMPATHY AND INTERPRETATION

EP 8

Empathy has been defined as perceiving, understanding, experiencing, and responding to the emotional state of another person (Barker, 2003, p. 141).[1] Decety and Jackson (2004) describe **emotional empathy** as the ability to be affected by a client's emotions, whereas **expressed** or **cognitive empathy** is the translation of such feelings into words. Unfortunately, there is not an agreed-upon conceptualization or measurement of empathy. However, clients experiencing empathy have been shown to inhibit antisocial behavior (Eisenberg, Spinard, & Sadovsky, 2005). Meanwhile, a lack of empathy has been associated with bullying and aggressive behavior (Gini et al., 2008). In addition, Forrester et al. (2008) found empathy to be essential to effective communication in child protection.

The first component of empathy is **affective sharing**. The second component is self-awareness, so that the social worker recognizes himself or herself as different from the person with whom he or she has empathy. The third component is **mental flexibility**, requiring skills in both turning on receptivity and turning it off. Such skills are essential in regulating compassion fatigue by enabling the social worker to separate from the client's experience (Adams, Boscarinao, & Figley, 2006; Harr & Moore, 2011).

There have been debates about whether empathy is primarily a personal trait or a skill that can be learned (Fernandez-Olano, Montoya-Fernandez, & Salinas-Sanchez, 2008). Those who consider it to be a learnable trait often conceive it as requiring the practitioner to be in a special state of receptivity, learning to empty himself or herself of distractions and be open to the other person (Block-Lerner et al., 2007; Dimidjian &

Linehan, 2003; Lu, Dane, & Gellman, 2005; Segal, Williams, & Teasdale, 2002). Other social work educators have argued that it requires specific training and experience for social workers to be empathic to the social conditions and experiences of low-income clients (Segal, 2007; Smith, 2006). That is, it is not enough to be attentive to the internal experience of clients; one must also be sensitive to the conditions, struggles, and resources that emerge in their accounts. Further, some argue that it is insufficient for social workers to be "with" the client emotionally and cognitively. Rather, social workers strive to assist clients in taking empathic action to better the troubling personal or environmental conditions they have shared (Gerdes & Segal, 2009).

However conceived, empathy on the social worker's part is critical to the helping process. Earlier chapters examined uses of empathy in the initial phase of the helping process. During the action-oriented phase, additive levels of empathy serve to expand clients' self-awareness, to cushion the impact of confrontations, and to explore and resolve relational reactions and other obstacles to change. Of course, social workers also continue to use reciprocal levels of empathy during the goal attainment phase because the purposes for which empathy were employed in the initial phase persist throughout the helping process. The difference is that additive levels of empathy are employed sparingly in the initial phase but occupy a prominent position during the action-oriented phase. Consequently, there may be little place for additive empathy in kinds of contact that are time limited in nature, such as crisis intervention, discharge planning, and intake roles.

Additive empathic responses go somewhat beyond what clients have expressed and, therefore, require some degree of inference by social workers. Thus, these responses are moderately interpretive—that is, they interpret forces operating to produce feelings, cognitions, reactions, and behavioral patterns.

Such additive empathic responses lead us to **interpretation**, or the identification of patterns, goals, and wishes that clients imply but do not directly state (Cormier, Nurius, & Osborn, 2009). Insight through interpretation is the foremost therapeutic principle basic to psychoanalysis and closely related therapies. Proponents of several other theories (most notably, client-centered, Gestalt, and certain existential theories) have avoided the use of interpretation. For example, interpretation has little or no role in solution-focused treatment or motivational interviewing. In motivational interviewing, as we explored in Chapter 6, there can be a useful role for helping clients in examining discrepancies between values and behavior without imposing an external explanation for that discrepancy (Arkovitz Westra, Miller, & Rollnick, 2007).

Interpretation assists clients in viewing their problems from a different perspective, thereby opening up new possibilities for remedial courses of action. This generic view, which emphasizes a **discrepant viewpoint**, is sufficiently broad to encompass many change-oriented techniques identified in different theories, including reframing (Watzlawick, Weakland, & Fisch, 1974), relabeling (Barton & Alexander, 1981), positive connotation (Selvini-Palazzoli et al., 1974), positive reinterpretation (Hammond, Hepworth, & Smith, 1977), additive empathy, and traditional psychoanalytic interpretations.

Levy (1963) classifies interpretations into two categories: *semantic* and *propositional*. **Semantic interpretations** describe clients' experiences according to the social worker's conceptual vocabulary: "By 'frustrated,' I gather you mean you're feeling hurt and disillusioned." Semantic interpretations are closely related to additive empathic responses. **Propositional interpretations** involve the social worker's notions or explanations that assert causal relationships among factors involved in clients' problem situations: "When I hear you coming back to 'maybe I am not cut out for this' thinking, I hear that you are getting fearful once again about taking the licensing exam. Is that so? You have a tendency to worry about problems down the road and lose focus on dealing with your anxiety about taking the exam. Remember that you can choose not to take the exam. If you do choose to take it, we have planned together about how to control your anxiety about taking it."

Social workers should avoid making interpretations or additive empathic responses (we are using the terms interchangeably) that are far removed from the awareness of clients. Research (Speisman, 1959) has indicated that moderate interpretations (those that reflect feelings that lie at the margin of the client's experiences) facilitate self-exploration and self-awareness, whereas deep interpretations engender opposition. Because deep interpretations are remote from clients' experiences, they appear illogical and irrelevant to clients, who therefore tend to reject them despite the fact that such interpretations may be accurate. The following is an example of such an inept, deep interpretation.

Client: My boss is a real tyrant. He never gives anyone credit, except for Fran. She can do no wrong in his eyes. He just seems to have it in for me. Sometimes I'd like to punch his lights out.

Social worker: Your boss seems to activate the same feelings you had toward your father. You feel he favors Fran, who symbolizes your favored sister. It's your father who you feel was the real tyrant, and you're reliving your resentment toward him. Your boss is merely a symbol of him.

Understandably, the client would likely reject and perhaps resent this interpretation. Although the social worker may be accurate (the determination of which is purely speculative), the client is struggling with feelings toward his boss. To shift the focus to his feelings toward his father misses the mark entirely from the client's perspective.

The following interpretation, made in response to the same client message, would be less likely to create opposition because it is linked to recent experiences of the client.

Social worker: So you really resent your boss because he seems impossible to please and shows partiality toward Fran. *[Reciprocal empathy.]* Those feelings reminded me of similar ones you expressed about 2 weeks ago. You were talking about how, when your parents spent a week with you on their vacation, your father seemed to find fault with everything you did but raved about how well your sister was doing. You'd previously mentioned he'd always seemed to favor your sister and that nothing you did seemed to please him. I'm wondering if those feelings might be connected with the feelings you're experiencing at work.

In the preceding message, notice that the social worker carefully documented the rationale of the interpretation and offered it tentatively, a technique discussed later in the chapter. Because we discussed, illustrated, and provided exercises related to additive empathy in Chapter 5, we will not deal with these topics in this chapter. Instead, we limit our discussion here to the uses of interpretation and additive empathy in expanding clients' self-awareness of (1) deeper feelings; (2) underlying meanings of feelings, thoughts, and behavior; (3) wants and goals; (4) hidden purposes of behavior; and (5) unrealized strengths and potentialities.

VIDEO CASE EXAMPLE

Additive empathy or interpretation can provide a useful role in identifying and exploring patterns of couple behavior. In the video

"Home for the Holidays," the social worker, Kim, has heard discussions about different communication patterns in her clients', Jackie's and Anna's, families of origin. She asks Jackie about whether the way her family handled her coming out as a lesbian was symbolic of how other such issues were dealt with in her family. Rather than suggest that they are representative of other such issues, Kim asks a question. Similarly, Kim asks later whether the discussion about the wedding picture and Anna not being included in it is symbolic of challenges they have faced in making decisions or working out problems. Finally, Kim puts their difficulties in the context of becoming a new family: "Often when we are forming new families, new couples, we are torn between the family we come from and the new family we are creating; this plays out in logistical decisions about the holidays."

Deeper Feelings

Clients often have limited awareness of some emotions. Moreover, emotional reactions often involve multiple emotions, but clients may experience only the dominant or surface feelings. Further, some clients experience only negative emotions, such as anger, and are out of touch with more tender feelings, such as hurt and compassion. Additive empathic responses (semantic interpretations) may assist clients in becoming aware of the emotions that lie at the edge of their awareness, thereby enabling them to experience these feelings more sharply and fully, to become more aware of their humanness (including the full spectrum of emotions), and to integrate these emerging emotions into the totality of their experience.

Social workers frequently employ additive empathic responses directed at expanding clients' awareness of feelings for several purposes, which we identify and illustrate in the following examples.

1. To identify feelings that are only implied or hinted at in clients' verbal messages:

   Client *[in sixth session]:* I wonder if you feel we're making any progress. *[Clients frequently ask questions that embody feelings.]*

   Social worker: It sounds as though you're not satisfied with your progress. I wonder if you're feeling discouraged about how it's been going.

2. To identify feelings that underlie surface emotions:

   Client: I've just felt so bored in the evenings with so little to do. I text, tweet, go to chat rooms, and play video games, but that doesn't seem to help. Life's just a downer.

   Social worker: I'm getting the impression you're feeling empty and pretty depressed. I wonder if you're feeling lonely and wishing you could interact more with people in person to fill that emptiness?

3. To add intensity to feelings clients have minimized:

   Thirty-year-old socially isolated woman with mild intellectual disability: It was a little disappointing that Jana *[her childhood friend from another state]* couldn't come to visit. She lost her job and had to cancel her plane reservations.

   Social worker: I can see how very disappointed you were. In fact, you seem really down even now. You'd looked forward to her visit and made plans. It has been a real blow to you.

4. To clarify the nature of feelings clients express only vaguely:

   Gay male client: When Robert told me he didn't want to be with me anymore, I just turned numb. I've been walking around in a daze ever since, telling myself, "This can't be happening."

   Social worker: It has been a great shock to you. You were so unprepared. It hurts so much it's hard to admit it's really happening.

5. To identify feelings manifested only nonverbally:

   Client: My sister asked me to tend her kids while she's on vacation, and I will, of course. *[Frowns and sighs.]*

   Social worker: But your sigh tells me you don't feel good about it. Right now the message I get from you is that it seems an unfair and heavy burden to you and that you resent it.

6. Challenging beliefs stated as facts:

   Adolescent client: My mother will never understand what I have gone through, her life and experience are too different from mine.

   Social worker: So you doubt that your mother will ever understand your experience.

Underlying Meanings of Feelings, Thoughts, and Behavior

Used for this purpose, additive empathy or interpretation assists clients in conceptualizing and understanding feelings, thoughts, and behavior. Social workers assist clients in understanding what motivates them to feel, think, and behave as they do; to grasp how their behavior bears on their problems and goals; and to discern themes and patterns in their feelings, thoughts, and behavior. As clients discern similarities, parallels, and themes in their behavior and experiences, their self-awareness gradually expands in much the same way as single pieces of a puzzle fit together, gradually forming discrete entities and eventually coalescing into a coherent whole. The previous interpretation made to the client who resented his boss for favoring a coworker is an example of this type of additive empathic response and is a propositional interpretation.

In a more concrete sense, then, social workers may employ this type of interpretation or additive empathy to assist clients in realizing that they experience troublesome feelings in the presence of a certain type of person or in certain circumstances. For example, clients may feel depressed in the presence of critical people or feel extremely anxious in situations where they must perform (e.g., when expected to give a talk or take a test). Social workers may thus use additive empathy to identify negative perceptual sets and other dysfunctional cognitive patterns that can be modified by employing cognitive restructuring. Clients may attend exclusively to trivial indications of their imperfections and completely overlook abundant evidence of competent and successful performance.

Similarly, a social worker may assist a client in discerning a pattern of anticipating negative outcomes of relatively minor events and dreading (and avoiding) the events because of his or her perception of those outcomes as absolute disasters. One client dreaded visiting a lifelong friend who had recently sustained a severe fall, leaving her partially paralyzed. When the social worker explored possible negative events that the client feared might occur if she were to visit the friend, she identified the following:

- "What if I cry when I see her?"
- "What if I stare at her?"
- "What if I say the wrong thing?"

Using an additive empathic response, the social worker replied, "And if you did one of those things, how bad would that be?" The client readily agreed that it would not actually be a disaster. The social worker then employed cognitive restructuring to assist the client in viewing the situation in a more realistic perspective. The social worker discussed each feared reaction in turn, clarifying that anyone might react as the client feared reacting and that if she were to react in any of these ways it would be uncomfortable but certainly not a disaster. The social worker and client jointly concluded that the client had a certain amount of control over how she reacted rather than being totally at the mercy of circumstances. Following behavioral rehearsal, the client's fears of disaster gradually dwindled to manageable proportions.

Social workers may also employ this type of additive empathy to enhance clients' awareness of perceptual distortions that adversely affect their interpersonal relationships. For example, parents may reject children because they perceive characteristics in them that the parents abhor. Previous exploration, however, may have disclosed that parents identify the same qualities in themselves and project their self-hatred onto their children. By assisting clients to recognize how self-perceptions (which may also be distorted) warp their perceptions of their children, social workers enable such parents to make discriminations and to perceive and accept their children as unique individuals who are different from themselves.

Similar perceptual distortions may occur between couples. These problems may cause spouses to perceive and to respond inappropriately to each other as a result of unresolved and troublesome feelings that derive from past relationships.

VIDEO CASE EXAMPLE

In the video "Adolescent Mother and Foster Parent," the social worker, Glenda, observes behavioral patterns that are conflicting between a teen parent, Twanna, and her foster parent, Janet. Twanna is coming home late from school, leaving her 2-year-old child with the foster mother for extended periods. The foster mother is concerned that Twanna may not be around her child enough to bond with her. Meanwhile, the foster mother is at times pacifying the infant by giving her candy. When Twanna tries to stop this, her child has tantrums. Glenda hears the account of this interaction and suggests that when Twanna refuses to deal with the tantrums, going to her room and putting on her headphones, she may be thinking about Janet, "You made her this way … you deal with her."

Wants and Goals

Another important use of additive empathy is to assist clients to become aware of wants and goals that they imply in their messages but do not fully recognize. When beset by difficulties, people often tend to think in terms of problems and ways to obtain relief from them rather than in terms of growth and change—even though the latter two processes are often implied in the former. When they become more aware of the thrust toward growth implied in their messages, clients often welcome the prospect and may even experience enthusiasm about it. This type of additive empathy not only expands self-awareness but may also enhance motivation.

As is apparent in the following excerpt, additive empathic messages that highlight implied wants and goals often result in the formulation of explicit goals that pave the way to change-oriented actions. Moreover, such messages play a critical role in arousing hope in dispirited clients who feel overwhelmed by their problems and have been unable to discern any positive desires for growth manifested in their struggles. This type of message plays a key role both in the first phase of the helping process and in the change-oriented phase.

Client: I'm so sick of always being imposed upon. All of my family just take me for granted. You know: "Good old Marcie, you can always depend on her." I've taken about all of this that I can take.

Social worker: Just thinking about it stirs you up. Marcie, it seems to me that what you're saying adds up to an urgent desire on your part to be your own person—to feel in charge of yourself rather than being at the mercy of others' requests or demands.

Client: I hadn't thought of it that way, but you're right. That's exactly what I want. If I could just be my own person.

Social worker: Maybe that's a goal you'd like to set for yourself. It seems to fit, and accomplishing it would liberate you from the oppressive feelings you've described.

Client: Yes, yes! I'd like very much to set that goal. Do you really think I could accomplish it?

Hidden Purposes of Behavior

Social workers sometimes employ interpretation to help clients become more fully aware of the basic motivations that underlie their concerns. Other people may misinterpret clients' motives, and clients themselves may have only a limited awareness of them because of the obscuring effect of their problematic behaviors.

Prominent among these motives are the following: to protect tenuous self-esteem (e.g., by avoiding situations that involve any risk of failing), to avoid anxiety-producing situations, and to compensate for feelings of impotency or inadequacy. The following are typical examples of surface behaviors and the hidden purposes that may be served by those behaviors:

- Underachieving students may exert little effort in school (1) because they can justify failing on the basis of not having really tried (rather than having to face their fears of being inadequate), or (2) because they are seeking to punish parents who withhold approval and love when they fall short of their expectation, or (3) they don't want to be identified with the "smart kids" and betray their friends.
- Clients may present a facade of bravado to conceal from themselves and others underlying fears and feelings of inadequacy.
- Clients may set themselves up for physical or emotional pain to offset deep-seated feelings of guilt.
- Clients may engage in self-defeating behavior to validate myths that they are destined to be losers or to live out life scripts determined by circumstances beyond their control.
- Clients may avoid relating closely to others to protect against fears of being dominated or controlled.
- Clients may behave aggressively or abrasively to avoid risking rejection by keeping others at a distance.

Interpretations must be based on substantial supporting information that clients have disclosed previously. Without supporting information, interpretations are little more than speculations that clients are unlikely to accept. Indeed, such speculations may come from social workers' projections and are typically inaccurate. Clients may regard such interpretations as offensive or may question social workers' competence when they receive such responses.

The case example on the next page illustrates appropriate use of interpretation to expand awareness of the motives underlying a client's behavior.

Challenging Beliefs Stated as Facts

Sometimes clients have strongly held beliefs they consider to be facts. Those beliefs may serve a variety of

CASE EXAMPLE

Mr. R, age 33, and Mrs. R entered marital therapy largely at Mrs. R's instigation. Mrs. R complained about a lack of closeness in the relationship and felt rejected because her husband seldom sought affection from her. When she made overtures, he typically pulled back. Mr. R had revealed in the exploratory interviews that his mother had been (and still was) extremely dominating and controlling. He felt little warmth toward his mother and saw her no more than was absolutely necessary.

The following excerpt from a session with Mr. R focuses on an event that occurred during the week when the couple went to a movie. Mrs. R had reached over to hold her husband's hand. He abruptly withdrew it, and Mrs. R later expressed feelings of hurt and rejection. Their ensuing discussion was unproductive, and their communication became strained. Mr. R discussed the event that occurred in the theater.

Mr. R: I know Carol was hurt when I didn't hold her hand. I don't know why, but it really turned me off.

Social worker: So you're wondering why you turn off when she wants some affection. I wonder what was happening inside of you at that moment. What were you thinking and feeling?

Mr. R: Gee, let me think. I guess I was anticipating she'd do it, and I just wanted to be left alone to enjoy the movie. I guess I resented her taking my hand. That doesn't make sense when I think about it. Why should I resent holding hands with the woman I love?

Social worker: Jim, I think you're asking an awfully good question—one that's a key to some of the difficulties in your marriage. May I share an idea with you that might shed some light on why you respond as you do? *[They nod in affirmation.]* You mentioned that you felt resentful when Carol took your hand. Based on the feelings you just expressed, I'm wondering if perhaps you feel you're submitting to her if you respond positively when she takes the initiative and pull back to be sure you're not letting yourself be dominated by her *[the hidden purpose]*. Another reason for suggesting that is that as you were growing up you have said that you felt dominated by your mother and resented her for being that way. Even now you avoid seeing her any more than you have to. I'm wondering if, as a result of your relationship with her, you could have developed a supersensitivity to being controlled by a female so that you resent any behavior on Carol's part that even suggests her being in control. *[The latter part of the response provides the rationale for the interpretation.]*

purposes, such as to relieve anxiety or to avoid doubt, as illustrated in the following case example.

Unrealized Strengths and Potentialities

Another vital purpose served by interpretation and additive empathy is to expand clients' awareness of their strengths and undeveloped potentialities. Clients' strengths are demonstrated in a variety of ways, and social workers need to sensitize themselves to these often subtle manifestations by consciously cultivating a positive perceptual set. This objective is vital because clients are often preoccupied with their weaknesses. Moreover, becoming aware of strengths tends to arouse clients' hopes and to generate the courage they need to begin making changes.

Drawing clients' awareness to strengths tends to enhance self-esteem and to foster courage to undertake

tasks that involve risking new behaviors. With conscious effort, social workers can become increasingly aware of their clients' strengths. For example, when a client faces a child welfare investigation because his or her children were left alone, part of the assessment must necessarily focus on the circumstances of danger that occurred and alternatives that were available to the client. This investigation often provokes defensive behavior from the client. Clients are more likely to respond positively to explorations for other solutions if their own strengths are recognized (De Jong & Miller, 1995; McQuaide & Ehrenreich, 1997). For example, the following response identifies both strengths and problems:

Social worker: You have explained that you did not intend to leave your children alone for any extended period. Your daughter was cooking for her little brother when the grease fire broke out. She knew

CASE EXAMPLE

Marv had been unemployed for several months. However, recently he was accepted to interview for an attractive job. After a week of careful preparation for the interview, Marv shared in his next session: "I don't know why I am doing all this preparation for this job interview. I am not the kind of person they want for this job. I am afraid that I am setting myself up to fail." Following the social work value of self-determination, clients are entitled to their beliefs. However, social workers can help them examine the reasons for their beliefs (George, 2011). The social worker responded to Marv: "When you say you are not the kind of person they are looking for, Marv, what leads you to that conclusion? Did you see something in the job description that you did not see before?" Marv acknowledged that he did not. "Could it be that getting out there and performing in an interview is a little scary right now, that you are out of practice? When you prepared for an important interview in the past, how did you get yourself ready?

how to call 911 and get the fire department. We would all want this situation to never have happened. Still, your daughter knew what to do in case of an emergency. She was able to prepare a meal. You have done many things to prepare your children to cope. We will need to plan together so that they are not left alone without adult supervision.

In this case, the supporting of strengths is paired with identification of continuing concerns and the need to plan together to eliminate dangers.

VIDEO CASE EXAMPLE

In the video "Serving the Squeaky Wheel," the social worker, Ron Rooney, becomes aware of a pattern in many stories from Molly, the client, that concern grievances about being ill served by other social workers and the health system. When she mentions not wanting to be the "greasy wheel" (squeaky wheel), Rooney suggests the possibility that Molly has, in fact, been acting as a squeaky wheel by complaining when she feels underserved, and that pattern of assertiveness is sometimes rewarded by the system and sometimes punished: "You seem to be courageous in fighting battles and you have learned some skills in assertiveness—and, as you say, that can be a two-edged or three-edged sword. Sometimes your assertiveness gets you what you want, and sometimes your assertiveness causes some people to look at you as the squeaky wheel that has squeaked too much."

Guidelines for Employing Interpretation and Additive Empathy

Considerable finesse is required to effectively employ interpretation and additive empathy. The following guidelines will assist you in acquiring this skill.

EP 6

1. ***Use additive empathy sparingly until a sound working relationship has evolved.*** Because these responses go somewhat beyond clients' current level of self-awareness, clients may misinterpret the motives of a social worker and respond defensively. Hence, when clients have brief contact with a social worker, such as in discharge planning, they are unlikely to develop the kind of relationship in which additive empathy is appropriate. When clients demonstrate that they are confident of a social worker's goodwill, they are able to tolerate and often to benefit from additive empathic and interpretative responses.

   The exceptions to this guideline involve messages that identify (1) wants and goals and (2) strengths and potentialities, both of which are also appropriate in the initial phase of the helping process. Social workers must avoid identifying strengths excessively in the initial phase because some clients will interpret such messages as insincere flattery or as minimizing their distress.

2. ***Employ these responses only when clients are engaged in self-exploration or have shown that they are ready to do so.*** Clients or groups that are not ready to engage in self-exploration are likely to resist social workers' interpretive efforts and may perceive them as unwarranted attempts by social workers to impose their formulations on

them. Exceptions to this guideline are the same as those cited in the first guideline.

3. ***Pitch these responses to the edge of clients' self-awareness and avoid attempting to foster awareness that is remote from clients' current awareness or experiences.*** Clients generally are receptive to responses that closely relate to their experiences but resist those that emanate from social workers' unfounded conjectures. It is not good practice to push clients into rapidly acquiring new insights, because many of these deep interpretations will prove to be inaccurate and produce negative effects, including reducing clients' confidence in social workers, conveying lack of understanding, or engendering resistance. Social workers should not employ interpretive responses until they have enough information to be reasonably confident their responses are accurate. They should then take care to share the supportive information on which the interpretation is based.

4. ***Avoid making several additive empathic responses in succession.*** Because interpretation responses require time to think through, digest, and assimilate, a series of such responses tends to bewilder and overwhelm clients.

5. ***Phrase interpretive responses in tentative terms.*** Because these responses involve a certain degree of inference, there is always the possibility that the social worker might be wrong. Tentative phrasing openly acknowledges this possibility and invites clients to agree or disagree (Cormier, Nurius, & Osborn, 2009, p. 132). If social workers present interpretations in an authoritarian or dogmatic manner, however, clients may not feel free to offer candid feedback and may outwardly agree while covertly rejecting interpretations. Tentative phrases include "I wonder if …," "Could it be that your feelings may be related to …?," and "Perhaps you're feeling this way because… ." Using additive empathy to explore strengths is, of course, less threatening and can be done with less hesitation.

VIDEO CASE EXAMPLE

Note that in the video "Home for the Holidays," at several points, Kim, the social worker, suggests a tentative interpretation of what one or the other might be feeling and then says, "I don't want to put words into your mouth," giving them an opportunity to correct her interpretation.

6. ***To determine the accuracy of an interpretive response, carefully note clients' reactions after offering the interpretation.*** When responses are on target, clients affirm their validity, continue self-exploration by bringing up additional relevant material, or respond emotionally in a manner that matches the moment (e.g., ventilate relevant feelings). When interpretations are inaccurate or are premature, clients tend to disconfirm them (verbally or nonverbally), change the subject, withdraw emotionally, argue or become defensive, or simply ignore the interpretation.

EP 9

7. ***If the client responds negatively to an interpretative response, acknowledge your probable error, respond empathically to the client's reaction, and continue your discussion of the topic under consideration.*** Note that sometimes such interpretations are immediately rejected but a seed has been planted that clients may further reflect about.

EP 9

8. ***When providing an interpretation to a client who is culturally different from the social worker, recognize that the client may not readily understand the message the way it was intended.*** It has been argued that psychotherapeutic interventions have evolved from the experience of European Americans, with a monocultural bias that tends to misunderstand motives and behaviors occurring to persons whose cultural experiences and beliefs are different from the therapist's (Gone, 2015; Jackson, 2015). Indeed, it is best to consider the exchange to be a cultural transaction between the client and social worker, each with cultural identities (Jackson, 2015).

EP 2

To assist you in expanding your skill in formulating interpretive and additive empathic responses, a number of exercises, together with modeled responses, appear at the end of this chapter.

CONFRONTATION

Confrontation is similar to interpretation and additive empathy in that it is a tool to enhance clients' self-awareness and to promote change. Confrontation, however, involves facing clients with some aspect of their thoughts, feelings, or behavior that is

EP 8

contributing to or maintaining their difficulties. Social workers, perhaps more than members of other helping professions, must struggle to maintain a dual focus on both the individual's rights and social justice. Some claim that the ability to juggle these potentially conflicting demands is an essential strength of the profession (Regehr & Angle, 1997). Others argue that "there are some activities people can do that put them outside any entitlement to respect … some people called clients are not much respected" (Ryder & Tepley, 1993, p. 146). For example, individuals who act to harm or endanger others, such as the perpetrators of domestic violence or sexual abuse, challenge this dual commitment and social workers' ethical obligation to respect the inherent worth and dignity of all individuals regardless of the acts they may have committed. We take the position that it is not the professional role of social workers to morally judge perpetrators of harmful behavior. It is rather our role to assist such persons to learn and grow through gaining insight and taking appropriate responsibility. Judgment is not helpful in that pursuit.

In this context, when is confrontation appropriate? With whom? And under what conditions? Is confrontation a skill or a style of practice? In some settings, confrontation became a style of practice rather than a selective skill. That is, practitioners believed that some clients were so well defended with denial, rationalization, and refusal to accept responsibility that only repeated confrontations would succeed. For example, in work with batterers, some have claimed that "almost every word they [batterers] utter is either victim blaming or justification for their violence. So I have to start confronting all of that stuff right from the beginning and it gets very intense" (Pence & Paymar, 1993, p. 21). It was believed that only when the offender admitted responsibility for the behavior and accepted the label of offender could meaningful change occur. If the clients did not accept the label, and if they defended themselves, they were labeled as being in denial and resistant (Miller & Sovereign, 1989). Hence, confronting them in an authoritarian and aggressive style (Miller & Rollnick, 2013) was considered necessary to achieve an admission of guilt—that is, admission that they had a problem and were not in control of their behavior.

In short, clients were expected to give up their own views and to accept the views of those who had the power to confront them. It was assumed that disempowered persons who had no motivation and were incapable of making their own decisions and controlling their behavior—would then accept and cooperate with the formulation of the problem by the social workers and/or group (Kear-Colwell & Pollock, 1997). If they reacted by showing disagreement and resistance, they were seen as persisting in denial, as lacking motivation, and often as demonstrating pathological personality patterns.

This view too often leads to an interactive cycle of confrontation and denial in which the client acts to protect his or her self-esteem by denying charges (Miller & Sovereign, 1989). Social workers and theorists in fields such as treatment of domestic abuse perpetrators, persons with addictions, and sexual offenders have now questioned whether this style is effective or ethical (Fearing, 1996; Kear-Colwell & Pollock, 1997; Miller & Sovereign, 1989; Murphy & Baxter, 1997). These helping professionals contend that intense confrontation of defenses is not beneficial or it may unwittingly reinforce the belief that relationships are based on coercive influences (Murphy & Baxter, 1997). They suggest that a supportive and collaborative working alliance is more likely to increase motivation in clients. Motivational interviewing is more likely to create dissonance and encourage offenders to own the process. Even in work with addicted persons, new approaches acknowledge the importance of developing a positive, respectful approach toward the person who is the subject of the intervention (Fearing, 1996).

EP 7

Instead of all-purpose confrontation delivered at any time, it is more useful to acknowledge the stage of change the client is at regarding the problematic behavior. Prochaska, DiClemente, and Norcross (1992) proposed a six-stage process of change (see Table 17-1). Their model begins with precontemplation, in which the person has not considered the behavior to be a problem.

In the motivational interviewing approach, the social worker takes responsibility for pursuing a positive atmosphere for change based on accurate empathic understanding, mutual trust, acceptance, and understanding of the world from the offender's perspective (Kear-Colwell & Pollock, 1997; Miller, Rollnick, & Conforti, 2002). In this exploration, the focus is on the offending behavior and its effects and origins, not on the person (Kear-Colwell & Pollock, 1997). The effort seeks to be persuasive by creating an awareness that the person's problem behavior is dissonant with his or her personal goals. By engaging in a risk-benefit analysis, the social worker assists the client in deciding whether it makes sense to explore a change so as to better reach those goals. The social worker would then assist the client to make a decision.

TABLE 17-1 Stages of Change Model

STAGE	CHARACTERISTIC BEHAVIOR	SOCIAL WORKER'S TASK
Precontemplation	Client does not believe that he or she has a problem; is considered unmotivated by others	Raise awareness of concerns held by others: "What does your partner think about the effect of your drinking on your home life?" Stimulate dissonance with risk–benefit analysis: "What are the benefits to you from making your living by selling drugs? What are the costs to you from living by selling drugs?"
Contemplation	Becomes aware of the existence of the problem but is not moved to action Appears ambivalent—shows awareness, then discounts it	Attempt to tip decisional balance by exploring reasons to change: "As you add it up, what do you think the benefits are in relation to the costs? If you get a legal job, then what?"
Preparation	Recognizes problem; asks what can be done to change Appears motivated	Strengthen confidence in change as a possibility Help client plan appropriate course of action
Action	Implements plan of action	Develop plan to implement action Plan details to make it possible (e.g., transportation, child care)
Maintenance	Sustains change through consistent application of strategies	Identify strategies to prevent lapses and relapse: "What have been the triggers to expose you to a dangerous situation?"
Relapse	Slips into problematic behavior and may return to precontemplation stage	Attempt to return to contemplation without being stuck or demoralized Reinforce achievement; treat with respect: "This is a difficult time. You have been at this point before and you overcame it. What do you think about whether you want to overcome it again?"

Source: Adapted from Kear-Colwell and Pollock (1997) and Prochaska, DiClemente, and Norcross (1992).

Once a client has decided to act, then the form of influence can help him or her decide which action to pursue. For example, after he has decided to deal with a domestic violence problem, a male client can be helped to consider alternatives for how to go about it. When a decision has been made, efforts are aimed at planning useful action to reach the goal. When a change has occurred, efforts are aimed at exploring in detail the contingencies and triggers that have been associated with the behavior. Armed with such knowledge, alternatives can be planned and practiced to avoid a relapse into the offending behavior.

Constructive confrontation is most likely to be heard when it comes from a source liked and respected by the client. Consequently, confrontations that occur early in contact are often not accurately heard or heeded. Nevertheless, before a helping relationship has developed, social workers sometimes have responsibilities to confront clients who are in violation of the law and who are dangers to themselves or others. Such confrontations should occur sparingly, given the likelihood that they will not be heeded so early in contact (R. H. Rooney, 2009).

In the middle phase of work, social workers employ confrontation to assist clients to achieve awareness of the forces blocking their progress toward growth and goal attainment and to enhance their motivation to implement efforts toward change. Confrontation is particularly relevant when clients are blind to the discrepancies or inconsistencies in their thoughts, beliefs, emotions, and behavior, which produce or perpetuate dysfunctional behavior. Of course, blind spots in self-awareness are universal because all humans suffer from the limitation of being unable to step out of their perceptual fields and look at themselves objectively.

EP 8

VIDEO CASE EXAMPLE

In the video "How Can I Help?," the social worker, Peter Dimock, explores with the client, Julie, her efforts, or the lack of such efforts, to get involved in counseling for her depression. In the section that follows, he hears her explanation for what has occurred and does not blame her but rather notes that perhaps she was agreeing to work on this goal more to please him than because she owned it as her own goal. "You've been having some difficulty getting these appointments really set up or following through with making them and it sounds like you've been doing it more for me because I made it part of your case plan and you're really not sure whether this is something that you want, is that true?" In this way, Peter is matter of fact and not blaming in assessing her motivation for completing this task. Julie affirms, "I just want to get this stuff done on the case plan so I can just be done with it too, but I feel like I'm okay." She notes that she is doing it because it is on the plan, not because she agrees with it. Peter again does not judge her motivation but notes it: "so this is one that you'd like to be able to check off the list, but you don't think you really need it."

Peter asks what happened when Julie stopped taking her medication and seeing a counselor. Julie replies: "I don't know, I guess I was doing, you know, pretty good and they sent me home with you know, my meds, and the meds ran out and I know I had to like see somebody to get like a refill or something, but I don't know, I thought I was doing okay, I thought I was doing okay, so I just didn't take any more."

Peter notes his understanding of why she stopped taking the medication and then asks for permission to explore the depression topic. "Well, do you mind if we explore a little bit whether or not this depression, which you're not sure that you really have, is having some effect on you and on your kids, perhaps?" He then asks her if she knows the symptoms of depression. When she notes that she does not and is okay with hearing them, Peter responds:

"Among them are that you feel really kind of down, oftentimes tired, may be difficult getting out of bed, hard to look forward to doing a bunch of things, if anything, you don't feel things are all that important or you don't just feel the energy at times to do it. Sometimes you have difficulty sleeping or difficulty concentrating and you know, you just feel kind of blah. Is that ever true for you?" In this way, Peter is raising awareness in a tactful way about how the depression diagnosis may be relevant for her and the treatment and medication important for her and her baby. She admits that sometimes she is sleeping and the baby awakens her. He asks whether this is okay with her and she comments "Well, I guess I'd kind of like to do it different. I know, in my parenting classes, they talk about like you know, babies need routines and how that's really important and I just, I guess I shouldn't be staying in bed and I should, you know, maybe get baby more in a routine because, you know, he don't go to bed sometimes till 1, 2, 3 in the morning and you know, cause I'm up kind of like all night and I don't want to get out of bed when I am in bed or laying around." He comments, "So you know that in some ways a routine would be—and some consistency—would be a better way to parent, and that's important to you." In this way he elicits the insight from her rather than making a pronouncement about effective parenting. When she comments that keeping up with routines is difficult because of feeling tired, he notes "I'm just wondering and I don't know, but perhaps some of what you're describing has to do with being depressed. Do you think that's a possibility?" In this way, he has built toward a tactful interpretation and links it to her values: "It is important to you to provide good parenting, consistency for your son. He's important to you."

Peter moves on to make a suggestion: "I am wondering if seeing someone and trying to figure out whether or not there's some medication that might make a difference could be helpful." At this point, Julie offers to contact a clinic about another appointment to explore medication and counseling.

As the previous example with Julie shows, additive empathy and confrontation have much in common. Skillful confrontations incorporate consideration of clients' feelings that underlie obstacles to change. Because fears are often among these feelings, skill in relating with high levels of empathy is a prerequisite to using confrontation effectively. Indeed, effective confrontation is an extension of empathic communication because the focus on discrepancies and inconsistencies derives from a deep understanding of clients' feelings, experiences, and behavior.

Self-Confrontation

It is important for social workers to possess a range of confrontation skills and not to confront clients primarily to vent their own frustration with clients' lack of progress. Social workers would more appropriately consider confrontation to exist along a continuum that ranges from fostering **self-confrontation** at one extreme to **assertive confrontation** at the other extreme (R. H. Rooney, 2009). That is, clients can often be engaged quickly in self-confrontation by social workers' asking them questions that cause them to reflect on the relationship between their behaviors and their own values.

Skillfully designed intake forms can serve a similar function, asking potential clients to reflect on concerns and their perceptions of the causes. Such confrontations are subtle and respectful, and they rarely engender strong client opposition. As clients gain expanded awareness of themselves and their problems through self-exploration, they tend to recognize and to confront discrepancies and inconsistencies themselves. Self-confrontation is generally preferable to social worker–initiated confrontation because the former is less risky and because clients' resistance to integrating insights is not an obstacle when they initiate confrontations themselves.

Clients vary widely in the degree to which they engage in self-confrontation. Emotionally mature, introspective persons may engage in self-confrontations frequently. In contrast, individuals who are out of touch with their emotions, who lack awareness of their effects on others, and who blame others or circumstances for their difficulties are least likely to engage in self-confrontation.

Inductive questioning can be a form of confrontation that is more active on the social worker's part but is still conveyed in a respectful manner. The social worker asks questions that lead the client to consider potential discrepancies between thoughts, values, beliefs, and actions. Also, when the therapist asks a question that relates to facts rather than one that requires the client to label himself or herself, the question is more likely to be effective. For example, asking a client with a chemical dependency problem, "Are you powerless over alcohol?" would require the client to essentially label himself an alcoholic. On the other hand, "Do you ever have blackouts?," "Do you find it easier to bring up a problem with another person when you have had something to drink?," and "Do you ever find that once you begin drinking you can't easily stop?" are questions that, taken together, raise the possibility that drinking is a problem that might need attention (Citron, 1978). Such questions may be less intrusive on an intake assessment form than when presented in sequential interview questions. The latter can cause the client to feel that the social worker is trying to persuade him or her to immediately acknowledge the risks of his or her behavior.

Assertive Confrontation

When a danger is imminent, the social worker may not be able to rely on tactful self-confrontation facilitated by inductive questioning. Instead, he or she may have to engage in more assertive confrontation in which the connection between troubling thoughts, plans, values, and beliefs is stated in declarative form, connecting them explicitly for the client. Such assertive confrontation is a more high-risk technique because clients may interpret social workers' statements as criticisms, putdowns, or rejections. Paradoxically, the risk of these reactions is greatest among clients who must be confronted most often because they rarely engage in self-confrontation. These individuals tend to have weak self-concepts and are therefore prone to read criticism into messages when none is intended. Moreover, ill-timed and poorly executed confrontations may be perceived by clients as verbal assaults and may seriously damage helping relationships.

Therefore, using confrontation requires keen timing and finesse. Social workers must make special efforts to convey their helpful intent and goodwill as they employ this technique. Otherwise, they may engender hostility or offend and alienate clients.

Effective assertive confrontations embody four elements: (1) expression of concern; (2) a description of the client's purported goal, belief, or commitment; (3) the behavior (or absence of behavior) that is inconsistent or discrepant with the goal, belief, or commitment; and (4) the probable negative outcomes of the discrepant behavior. The format of a confrontive response may be depicted as follows:

$$
\text{I am concerned because you}
\begin{cases}
\text{(want)} \\
\text{(believe)} \\
\text{(are striving to)}
\end{cases}
$$

_____
(describe desired outcome)

but your _____
(describe discrepant action, behavior, or inaction)

is likely to produce _____
(describe probable negative consequences)

This format is purely illustrative. You may organize these elements in varying ways, and we encourage you to be innovative and to develop your own style. For example, you may challenge clients to analyze the effects of behaviors that are incongruous with their purported goals or values, as illustrated in the following excerpt:

Social worker *[to male on parole]:* Al, I know the last thing you want is to have to return to prison. I want you to stay out, too, and I think you sense that. But I have to level with you. You're starting to hang out with the same bunch you got in trouble with before you went to prison. You're heading in the same direction you were before, and we both know where that leads.

In this confrontation, the social worker begins by referring to the client's purported goal (remaining out of prison) and expresses a like commitment to the goal. The social worker next introduces concern about the client's behavior (hanging out with the same bunch the client got in trouble with before) that is discrepant with that goal. The social worker concludes the confrontation by focusing on the possible negative consequence of the discrepant behavior (getting into trouble and returning to prison).

Notice these same elements in the following examples of confrontive responses:

Social worker *[to father in family session]:* Mr. D, I'd like you to stop for a moment and examine what you're doing. I know you want the children not to be afraid of you and to talk with you more openly. Right? *[Father agrees.]* Okay, let's think about what you just did with Steve. He began to tell you about what he did after the school assembly, and you cut him off and criticized his behavior. Did you notice how he stopped talking and looked down?

Social worker *[to mother in child welfare system]:* I have a concern I need to share with you. You've expressed your goal of regaining custody of Pete, and we agreed that attending the parents' group was part of the plan to accomplish that goal. This week is the second time in a row you've missed the meeting because you overslept. I'm wondering about what missing the parents' group means for your goal of regaining custody of Pete.

Because employing assertive confrontation runs the risk of putting clients on the defensive or alienating them, expressing concern and helpful intent is a critical element because it reduces the possibility that clients will misconstrue the motive behind the confrontation. Tone of voice is also vital in highlighting helpful intent. If the social worker conveys the confrontation in a warm, concerned tone of voice, the client will be much less likely to feel attacked. If the social worker uses a critical tone of voice, any verbal reassurance that criticism was not intended is likely to fall on deaf ears. Keep in mind that people tend to attach more credence to nonverbal aspects of messages than to verbal aspects.

Guidelines for Employing Confrontation

To assist you in employing confrontation effectively, we offer the following guidelines.

EP 8

1. *When a violation of the law or imminent danger to self or others is involved, a confrontation must occur no matter how early in the working relationship.* Such confrontations may impede the development of the relationship, but the risk of harm to self and others is more important than the immediate effect on the relationship.

2. *Whenever possible, avoid confrontation until an effective working relationship has been established.* This can occur when a client is contemplating action (or inaction) that impedes his or her own goals but is not an imminent danger to self or others. Employing empathic responsiveness in early contacts conveys understanding, fosters rapport, and enhances confidence in the social worker's perceptiveness and expertise. When a foundation of trust and confidence has been established, clients are more receptive to confrontations and, in some instances, even welcome them.

3. *Use confrontation sparingly.* Confrontation is a potent technique that generally should be employed only when clients' blind spots are not responsive to other, less risky intervention methods. Poorly timed and excessive confrontations can inflict psychological damage on clients (Lieberman, Yalom, & Miles, 1973).

Another reason to employ confrontation judiciously is that some clients may yield to forceful confrontation for counterproductive reasons. Seeking to please social workers (or to avoid displeasing them), they may temporarily modify their behavior. But changing merely to comply with the expectations of a social worker may reinforce the idea that more powerful people can enforce their will on less powerful ones. This is not a model that social workers should want to reinforce with families (R. H. Rooney, 2009).

EP 6

4. *Deliver confrontations in an atmosphere of warmth, caring, and concern.* If social workers employ confrontations in a cold, impersonal, or critical way, clients are likely to feel that they are being attacked. By contrast, if social workers preface confrontations with genuine empathic concern, clients are more likely to perceive the helpfulness intended in the confrontation. In this regard, carrying out a confrontation when the social worker is tired, irritated, angry, disappointed, frustrated, or disillusioned—in a word, when the social worker is emotionally overwrought—is a bad idea. Carrying out a confrontation is about the client's needs, not the social worker's.

5. *Whenever possible, encourage self-confrontation.* Recall from the previous discussion that self-confrontation has decided advantages over social worker–initiated confrontation. Learning by self-discovery fosters independence and increases the likelihood that clients will act upon their newly gained self-awareness. Social workers can encourage self-confrontation by drawing clients' attention to issues, behaviors, or inconsistencies that they may have overlooked and by encouraging them to analyze the situation further.

For example, the social worker may directly intervene into dysfunctional interactions and challenge individuals, couples, families, or groups to identify what they are doing. Responses that encourage

self-confrontation in such a context include the following:

- "Let's stop and look at what you just did."
- "What just happened?"

Other inductive question responses that highlight inconsistencies and foster self-confrontation are as follows:

- "I'm having trouble seeing how what you just said (or did) fits with …"
- "I can understand how you felt, but how did [describe behavior] make it better for you?"
- "What you're saying seems inconsistent with what you want to achieve. How do you see it?"

Yet another technique is useful when clients overlook the dynamic significance of their own revealing expressions or when their expressed feelings fail to match their reported feelings. This technique involves asking them to repeat a message, to listen carefully to themselves, and to consider the meaning of the message. Examples of this technique follow:

- "I want to be sure you realize the significance of what you just said. Repeat it, but this time listen carefully to yourself, and tell me what it means to you."
- *[To marital partner in conjoint interview]:* "Joan just told you something terribly important, and I'm not sure you really grasped it. Could you repeat it, Joan, and I want you to listen very carefully, Bob, and check with Joan as to whether you grasped what she said."
- *[To group member]:* "You just told the group you're feeling better about yourself, but it didn't come through that way. Please say it again, but get in touch with your feelings and listen to yourself."

6. *Avoid using confrontation when clients are experiencing extreme emotional strain.* Confrontation tends to mobilize anxiety. When clients are under heavy strain, supportive techniques rather than confrontation are indicated. Clients who are overwhelmed with anxiety or guilt generally are not receptive to confrontation and will not benefit from it. In fact, confrontation may be detrimental, adding to their already excessive tension.

Conversely, confrontation is appropriate for clients who experience minimal inner conflict or anxiety when such conflict or anxiety would be appropriate in light of how his or her problematic behavior is experienced by others. Some persons are self-satisfied and relatively insensitive to the feelings and needs of others (whom they cause to be anxious); such clients often lack the anxiety needed to engender and maintain adequate motivation. Confrontation, when combined with the facilitative conditions, may mobilize the anxiety they need to examine their own behavior and to consider making constructive changes.

7. ***Follow confrontation with empathic responsiveness.*** Because clients may take offense to even skillful confrontation, it is vital to be sensitive to their reactions. Clients often do not express their reactions verbally, so social workers need to be especially attuned to nonverbal cues that suggest hurt, anger, confusion, discomfort, embarrassment, or resentment. If clients manifest these or other unfavorable reactions, it is important to explore their reactions and to respond empathically to their feelings. Discussing such reactions provides opportunities (1) for clients to vent their feelings and (2) for social workers to clarify their helpful intent and to assist clients to work through negative feelings. If social workers fail to sense negative feelings or clients withhold expressions of them, the feelings may fester and adversely affect the helping relationship.

8. ***Expect that clients will respond to confrontation with a certain degree of anxiety.*** Indeed, confrontation is employed to produce a temporary sense of disequilibrium that is essential to break an impasse. The anxiety or disequilibrium serves a therapeutic purpose in impelling the client to make constructive changes that eliminate the discrepancy that prompted the social worker's confrontation. Empathic responsiveness following confrontation is not aimed at diluting this anxiety but rather seeks to resolve untoward reactions that may derive from negative interpretations of the social worker's motives for making the confrontation.

9. ***Do not expect immediate change after confrontations.*** Although awareness paves the way to change, clients rarely succeed in making changes immediately following acquisition of insight. Even when clients fully accept confrontations, corresponding changes ordinarily occur by increments. Known as **working through**, this change process involves repeatedly reviewing the same conflicts and the client's typical reactions to them, gradually broadening the perspective to encompass increasingly more situations to which the changes are applicable. Pressing for immediate change can inflict psychological damage on clients.

Indications for Assertive Confrontation

EP 8

As noted previously, confrontation is appropriate in three circumstances: (1) when violations of the law or imminent threats to the welfare and safety of self or others are involved; (2) when discrepancies, inconsistencies, and dysfunctional behaviors (overt or covert) block progress or create difficulties; and (3) when efforts at self-confrontation and inductive questioning have been ineffective in fostering clients' awareness of these behaviors or attempts to make corresponding changes. Discrepancies may reside in cognitive/perceptual, emotional (affective), or behavioral functions or may involve interactions between these functions. A comprehensive analysis of types of discrepancies and inconsistencies has been presented elsewhere (Hammond, Hepworth, & Smith, 1977, pp. 286–318); therefore, we merely highlight some of the most commonly encountered.

Cognitive/Perceptual Discrepancies

Many clients have behavioral or perceptual difficulties that are a product of inaccurate, erroneous, or incomplete information, and confrontation may assist them in modifying their problematic behaviors. For example, clients may lack accurate information about indicators of alcoholism, normal sexual functioning, or reasonable expectations of children according to stages of development.

Even more common are misconceptions about the self. The most common of these, in the authors' experience, involve self-demeaning perceptions. Even talented and attractive persons may view themselves as inferior, worthless, inadequate, unattractive, or stupid. Such perceptions are often deeply embedded and do not yield to change without extensive working through. Nevertheless, confronting clients with their strengths or raising their awareness of other areas of competence can prove helpful in challenging such self-deprecating views.

Other cognitive/perceptual discrepancies include interpersonal perceptual distortions, irrational fears, dichotomous or stereotypical thinking, denial of problems, placing responsibility for one's difficulties outside of oneself, failing to discern available alternative solutions to difficulties, and failing to consider consequences of actions.

Affective Discrepancies

Discrepancies in the emotional realm are inextricably linked to cognitive/perceptual processes because emotions are shaped by the cognitive meanings that clients attribute to situations, events, and memories. For example, a client may experience intense anger that emerges from a conclusion that another person has intentionally insulted, slighted, or betrayed him or her. This conclusion is based on a meaning attribution that may involve a grossly distorted perception of the other person's intentions. In such instances, social workers can assist clients in exploring their feelings, providing relevant detailed factual information, considering alternative meanings, and realigning emotions with reality.

Affective discrepancies that social workers commonly encounter include denying or minimizing actual feelings, being out of touch with painful emotions, expressing feelings that are contrary to purported feelings (e.g., claiming to love a spouse or child but expressing only critical or otherwise negative feelings), and verbally expressing a feeling that contradicts feelings expressed nonverbally (e.g., "No, I'm not disappointed," said with a quivering voice and tears in the eyes). Gentle confrontations aimed at emotional discrepancies often pave the way to express troubling emotions, and many clients appreciate social workers' sensitivity in recognizing their suppressed or unexpressed emotions.

If a client appears unprepared to face painful emotions, the social worker should proceed cautiously. Indeed, it may be wise to defer further exploration of those hurtful emotions. Confronting the client vigorously may elicit overwhelming emotions and engender consequent resentment toward the social worker.

Behavioral Discrepancies

Clients may experience many behavioral concerns that create difficulties for themselves and for others. Even though these patterns may be conspicuous to others, clients may remain blind to their patterns or to the effects of their behaviors on others. Confrontation may be required to expand their awareness of these patterns and their pernicious effects.

Irresponsible behavior tends to spawn serious interpersonal difficulties for clients as well as problems with broader society. Neglect of children, weak efforts to secure and maintain employment, undependability in fulfilling assignments, failure to maintain property—these and similar behaviors often result in severe financial, legal, and interpersonal entanglements that may culminate in loss of employment; estrangement from others; and loss of property, child custody, self-respect, and even personal freedom.

Irresponsible behavior often pervades the helping process as well, sometimes indicated by clients' tardiness to sessions, unwillingness to acknowledge problems, and failure to keep appointments or pay fees. Effective confrontation with such clients requires employing a firm approach couched in expressions of goodwill and concern about wanting to assist them in avoiding the adverse consequences of not assuming responsibilities. Social workers do a disservice to their clients when they permit them to evade responsibility for their actions or inaction. Further, social workers must counter clients' tendency to blame others or circumstances for their difficulties by assisting them to recognize that *only they* can reduce the pressures that beset them.

Other common behavioral discrepancies involve repeated actions that are incongruous with purported goals or values. Adolescents may describe ambitious goals that require extensive training or education, but they may make little effort in school, are truant frequently, and otherwise behave in ways that are entirely inconsistent with their stated goals. Spouses or parents may similarly express goals of improving their marital or family life but persistently behave in abrasive ways that further erode their relationships.

Confrontation can be used to help clients desist from engaging in self-defeating behaviors. In some instances, therapeutic binds (a special form of confrontation discussed in Chapter 18) may be employed to supply needed leverage to motivate clients to relinquish destructive and unusually persistent patterns of behavior.

Three other common categories of discrepancies or dysfunctional behavior that warrant confrontation are manipulative behavior, dysfunctional communication, and resistance to change. In groups, certain members may attempt to dominate the group, bait group members, play one person against the other, undermine the leader, or engage in other destructive ploys. The price of permitting members to engage in such behaviors may be loss of certain group members, dilution of the group's effectiveness, or premature dissolution of the group. To avert such undesired consequences, the leader may elicit the reactions of other group members to this behavior and assist members to confront manipulators with their destructive tactics. Such confrontations should adhere to the guidelines delineated earlier, and the leader should encourage members to invite offending members to join with them in constructively seeking to accomplish the purposes for which the group was formed.

Because problematic communication frequently interpreted as resistance to change often occurs in individual, conjoint, and group sessions, social workers encounter abundant opportunities to employ confrontation to good effect. Intervening during or immediately following dysfunctional communication is a powerful means of enabling clients to experience firsthand the negative effects of their dysfunctional behaviors (e.g., interrupting, attacking, claiming, or criticizing). By shifting the focus to the negative reactions of recipients of problematic messages, social workers enable clients to receive direct feedback about how their behavior offends, alienates, or engenders defensiveness in others, thereby producing effects contrary to their purported goals.

SUMMARY

This chapter discussed three vital tools in working through clients' opposition to change and to relating openly in the helping relationship: additive empathy, interpretation, and confrontation. If individual clients are left to struggle alone with negative feelings about the helping process or the social worker, their feelings may mount to the extent that they resolve them by discontinuing their sessions. If family members or groups are permitted to oppose change by engaging in distracting, irrelevant, or otherwise dysfunctional behaviors, they may likewise lose both confidence in the social worker (for valid reasons) and motivation to continue. For these reasons, social workers must accord the highest priority to being helpful to clients who encounter obstacles or who may be opposed to change.

COMPETENCY NOTES

EP 2 Engage Diversity and Difference in Practice
- Apply and communicate understanding of the importance of diversity and difference in shaping life experiences in practice at the micro, mezzo, and macro levels.

EP 6 Engage with Individuals and Families (note that this competency includes groups, organizations, and communities, which were not addressed in this chapter)

- Apply knowledge of human behavior and the social environment and practice context to engage with clients.
- Use empathy, reflection, and interpersonal skills to effectively engage diverse clients.

EP 7 Assess Individuals (note that this competency includes families, groups, organizations, and communities, which were not addressed in this chapter)

- Collect and organize data, and apply critical thinking to interpret information from clients.
- Understand methods of assessment with diverse clients to advance practice effectiveness.
- Apply knowledge of human behavior and the social environment, person-in-environment, and other multidisciplinary theoretical frameworks in the analysis of assessment data from clients.

EP 8 Intervene with Individuals (note that this competency includes families, groups, organizations, and communities, which were not addressed in this chapter)

- Implement interventions to achieve practice goals and enhance capacities of clients.
- Apply knowledge of human behavior and the social environment, person-in-environment, and other multidisciplinary theoretical frameworks in interventions with clients.

EP 9 Evaluate Practice with Individuals (note that this competency includes families, groups, organizations, and communities, which were not addressed in this chapter)

- Select and use appropriate methods for evaluation of outcomes.
- Critically analyze, monitor, and evaluate intervention and program processes and outcomes.
- Apply evaluation findings to improve practice effectiveness at the micro level.

SKILL DEVELOPMENT EXERCISES
in Additive Empathy and Interpretation

To assist you in advancing your skills in responding with interpretation and additive empathy, we provide the following exercises. Read each client statement, determine the type of response required, and formulate a written response that you would employ if you were in an actual session with the client. Keep in mind the guidelines for employing interpretive and additive empathic responses. Compare your responses with the modeled social worker responses provided after the client statements.

Client Statements

1. *White female client [to African American male social worker]:* You seem to be accepting of white people—at least you have been of me. But somehow I still feel uneasy with you. I guess it's just me. I haven't really known many black people very well.

2. *Married woman, age 28:* I feel I don't have a life of my own. My life is controlled by *his* work, *his* hours, and *his* demands. It's like I don't have an identity of my own.

3. *Prison inmate, age 31 [1 week before the date of his scheduled parole, which was canceled the preceding week]:* Man, what the hell's going on with me? Here I've been on good behavior for 3 years and finally got a parole date. You'd think I'd be damned glad to get out of here. So I get all uptight and get in a brawl in the mess hall. I mean I really blew it, man. Who knows when they'll give me another date?

4. *Male, age 18:* What's the point in talking about going to Trade Tech? I didn't make it in high school, and I won't make it there either. You may as well give up on me—I'm just a dropout in life.

5. *Widow, age 54:* It was Mother's Day last Sunday, and neither of my kids did so much as send me a card. You'd think they could at least acknowledge I'm alive.

6. *Female secretary, age 21:* I don't have any trouble word processing when I'm working alone. But if the boss or anyone else is looking over my shoulder, I make a lot of mistakes and freeze up.

7. *Female, age 26, in a committed relationship; she is 5 pounds overweight:* When I make a batch of cookies or a cake on the weekend, Terri [her partner] looks at me with that condemning expression, as though I'm not really trying to keep my weight down. I don't think it's fair just because she doesn't like sweets. I like sweets, but the only time I eat any is on the weekend, and I don't eat much then. I feel I deserve to eat dessert on the weekend at least.

8. *Disabled male recipient of public assistance (with a back condition caused by a recent industrial accident):* This not being able to work is really getting to me. I see my kids needing things I can't afford to get them, and I just feel—I don't know—kind of useless. There's got to be a way of making a living.

9. *Depressed male, age 53:* Yeah, I know I do all right in my work. But that doesn't amount to much. Anyone could do that. That's how I feel about everything I've ever done. Nothing's really amounted to anything.

10. *Mother, age 29, who is alleged to have neglected her children:* I don't know. I'm just so confused. I look at my kids sometimes, and I want to be a better mother. But after they've been fighting, or throwing tantrums, or whining and I lose my cool, I feel like I'd just like to go somewhere—anywhere—and never come back. The kids deserve a better mother.

11. *Client with mental health diagnosis who is apprehensive about taking a licensing examination:* Sometimes I think I am just not cut out for this. I know I took exams as a student and did okay but I get really scared when I think of taking a licensing exam. I think that maybe this is too much for me. I am trying to get beyond myself.

Modeled Social Worker Responses for Interpretation and Additive Empathy

1. *[To clarify feelings experienced only vaguely]:* I gather that even though you can't put your finger on why, you're still a little uncomfortable with me. You haven't related closely to that many African Americans, and you're still not altogether sure how much you can trust me.

2. *[Implied wants and goals]:* Sounds like you feel you're just an extension of your husband and that part of you is wanting to find yourself and be a person in your own right.

3. *[Hidden purpose of behavior, underlying feelings]:* So you're pretty confused about what's happened. Fighting in the mess hall when you did just doesn't make sense to you. You know, Carl, about your getting uptight—I guess I'm wondering if you were worried about getting out—worried about whether you could make it outside. I'm wondering if you might have fouled up last week to avoid taking that risk.

4. *[Underlying belief about self]:* Sounds like you feel defeated before you give yourself a chance. Like it's hopeless to even try. Jay, that concerns me because when you think that way about yourself, you are defeated—not because you lack ability but because you think of yourself as destined to fail. That belief itself is a big challenge for you.

5. *[Deeper feelings]:* You must have felt terribly hurt and resentful that they didn't so much as call you. In fact, you seem to be experiencing those feelings now. It just hurts so much.

6. *[Underlying thoughts and feelings]:* I wonder if, in light of your tightening up, you get to feeling scared, as though you're afraid you won't measure up to their expectations.

7. *[Unrealized strengths]:* I'm impressed with what you just said. It strikes me that you're exercising a lot of control by limiting dessert to weekends and using moderation then. In fact, your self-control seems greater than that of most people. You and Terri have a legitimate difference concerning sweets. I wonder if Terri has a concern about sugar. Is that something you have looked into? Sugar can be very addictive, and most of us experience it. Is that something you would want to look into? There are ways to satisfy that craving for sweets that we all have that may not have some of the effects of sugar.

8. *[Unrealized strength and implied want]:* Steve, I can hear the frustration you're feeling, and I want you to know it reflects some real strength on your part. You want to be self-supporting and be able to provide better for your family. Given that desire, we can explore opportunities for learning new skills that won't require physical strength.

9. *[Underlying pattern of thought]:* Kent, I get the feeling that it wouldn't matter what you did. You could set a world record, and you wouldn't feel it amounted to much. I'm wondering if your difficulty lies more in long-time feelings you've had about yourself that you somehow just don't measure up. I'd be interested in hearing more about how you've viewed yourself.

10. *[Underlying feelings and implied wants]:* So your feelings tear you and pull you in different directions. You'd like to be a better mother, and you feel bad when you lose your cool. But sometimes you just feel so overwhelmed and inadequate in coping with the children. Part of you would like to learn to manage the children better, but another part would like to get away from your responsibilities.

11. *Anxiety about exam taking.* Barbara, it sounds as if preparing for the exam has rekindled some old fears about whether you are really up to this challenge. Part of you thinks that you have taken other examinations along the way and done alright. Another part of you is fearful that this is too much for you. When these kinds of fears have come to you earlier, such as when you took exams in school, how did you get over them?

SKILL DEVELOPMENT EXERCISES
in Confrontation

The following exercises involve discrepancies and dysfunctional behavior in all three experiential domains: cognitive/perceptual, emotional, and behavioral. After reading the brief summary of the situation involved and the verbatim exchanges between the client(s) and social worker, identify the type of discrepancy involved and formulate your response (observing the guidelines presented earlier) as though you were the social worker in a real-life situation. Next, compare your response with the modeled social worker response, keeping in mind that the model is only one of many possible appropriate responses. Carefully analyze how your response is similar to or differs from the modeled response and whether you adhered to the guidelines.

Situations and Dialogue

1. You have been working with Mr. Lyon for several weeks, following his referral by the court after being convicted for sexually molesting his teenage daughter. Mr. Lyon has been 15 minutes late for his last two appointments, and today he is 20 minutes late. During his sessions he has explored and worked on problems only superficially.

   Client: Sorry to be late today. Traffic was sure heavy. You know how that goes.

2. The clients are marital partners whom you have seen conjointly five times. One of their goals is to reduce marital conflict by avoiding getting into arguments that create mutual resentments.

   Mrs. J: This week has been just awful. I've tried to look nice and have his meals on time—like he said he wanted—and I've just felt so discouraged. He got on my back Tuesday and … *[Husband interrupts.]*

   Mr. J [angrily]: Just a minute. You're only telling half the story. You left out what you did Monday. *[She interrupts.]*

   Mrs. J: Oh, forget it. What's the use? He doesn't care about me. He couldn't, the way he treats me. *[Mr. J shakes head in disgust.]*

3. The client is a young adult who has a slight mental disability. He was referred by a rehabilitation agency because of social and emotional problems. The client has indicated a strong interest in dating young women and has been vigorously pursuing a clerk (Sue) in a local supermarket. She has registered no interest in him and obviously has attempted to discourage him from further efforts. The following excerpt occurs in the seventh session.

Client: I went through Sue's check stand this morning. I told her I'd like to take her to see a movie.
Social worker: Oh, and what did she say?
Client: She said she was too busy. I'll wait a couple of weeks and ask her again.

4. Tony, age 16, is a member of a therapy group in a youth correctional institution. In the preceding session, he appeared to gain a sense of power and satisfaction from provoking other members to react angrily and defensively, which disrupted the group process. Tony directs the following message to a group member early in the fourth session.

Tony: I noticed you trying to talk to Meg at the dance Wednesday. You think you're pretty cool, don't you?

5. The client is a mother, age 26, who keeps feelings inside until they mount out of control, at which time she discharges anger explosively.

Client: I can't believe my neighbor. She sends her kids over to play with Sandra at lunchtime and disappears. It's obvious her kids haven't had lunch, and I end up feeding them, even though she's better off financially than I am.
Social worker: It sounds as if you have some feelings about that. What do you feel when she does that?
Client: Oh, not much, I guess. But I think it's a rotten thing to do.

6. You have been working for several weeks with a family that includes the parents and four children ranging in age from 10 to 17. The mother is a domineering person who acts as spokesperson for the family, and the father is passive and soft-spoken. A teenage daughter, Tina, expresses herself in the following dialogue.

Tina: We always seem to have a hassle when we visit our grandparents. Grandma's so bossy. I don't like going there.

Mother: Tina, that's not true. You've always enjoyed going to her house. You and your grandmother have always been close.

7. Group members in their fifth session have been intently discussing members' social interaction difficulties. One of the members takes the group off on a tangent by describing humorous idiosyncrasies of a person she met while on vacation, and the other group members follow suit by sharing humorous anecdotes about "oddballs" they have encountered.

8. The client is an attractive, personable, and intelligent woman who has been married for 3 years to a self-centered, critical man. In the fourth session (an individual interview), she tearfully makes the following statements:

Client: I've done everything he's asked of me. I've lost 10 pounds. I support him in his work. I golf with him. I even changed my religion to please him. And he's still not happy with me. There's just something wrong with me.

9. The clients are a married couple in their early 30s. The following excerpt occurs in the initial interview:

Wife: We just seem to fight over the smallest things. When he gets really mad, he loses his temper and knocks me around.
Husband: The real problem is that she puts her parents ahead of me. She's the one who needs help, not me. If she'd get straightened out, I wouldn't lose my temper. Tell her where her first responsibility is. I've tried, and she won't listen to me.

10. The clients are a family consisting of the parents and two children. Taylor, age 15, has been truant from school and smoking marijuana. Angie, age 16, is a model student and is obviously her parents' favorite. The family was referred by the school when Taylor was expelled for several days. The father, a highly successful businessman, entered family therapy with obvious reluctance, which has continued to this, the fourth session.

Mother: Things haven't been much different this week. Everyone's been busy, and we really haven't seen much of each other.
Father: I think we'd better plan to skip the next 3 weeks. Things have been going pretty well, and I have an audit in process at the office that's going to put me in a time bind.

Modeled Social Worker Responses for Confrontation

1. *[Irresponsible behavior by the client]:* Ted, I'm concerned you're late today. This is the third time in a row you've been late, and it shortens the time available to us. But my concerns go beyond that. I know you don't like having to come here and that you'd like to be out from under the court's jurisdiction. But the way you're going about things won't accomplish that. I can't be helpful to you and can't write a favorable report to the court if you just go through the motions of coming here for help. Apparently it's uncomfortable for you to come. I'd be interested in hearing just what you're feeling about coming.

2. *[Discrepancy between purported goal and behavior, as well as dysfunctional communication]:* Let's stop and look at what you're doing right now. I'm concerned because each of you wants to feel closer to the other, but what you're both doing just makes each other defensive.

   [To husband]: Mr. J, she was sharing some important feelings with you, and you cut her off.
   [To wife]: And you did the same thing, Mrs. J, when he was talking.
   [To both]: I know you may not agree, but it's important to hear each other out and to try to understand. If you keep interrupting and trying to blame each other, as you've both been doing, you're going to stay at square one, and I don't want that to happen. Let's go back and start over, but this time put yourself in the shoes of the other and try to understand. Check out with the other if you really understood. Then you can express your own views.

3. *[Dysfunctional, self-defeating behavior]:* Pete, I know how much you think of Sue and how you'd like to date her. I'm concerned that you keep asking her out, though, because she never accepts and doesn't appear to want to go out with you. My concern is that you're setting yourself up for hurt and disappointment. I'd like to see you get a girlfriend, but your chances of getting a date are probably a lot better with persons other than Sue.

4. *[Abrasive, provocative behavior]:* Hold on a minute, guys. I'm feeling uncomfortable and concerned right now about what Tony just said. It comes across as a real put-down, and we agreed earlier that one of our rules was to support and help each other. Tony, would you accept some feedback from other members about how you're coming across to the group?

5. *[Discrepancy between expressed and actual feeling]:* I agree. But I'm concerned about your saying you don't feel much. I should think you'd feel taken advantage of and want to change the situation. Let's see if you can get in touch with your feelings. Picture yourself at home at noon and your neighbor's kids knock on the door while you're fixing lunch. Can you picture it? What are you feeling in your body and thinking just now?

6. *[Dysfunctional communication, disconfirming Tina's feelings and experiences]:* What did you just do, Mrs. Black? Stop and think for a moment about how you responded to Tina's message. It may help you to understand why she doesn't share more with you. *[or]* Tina, could you tell your mother what you're feeling right now about what she just said? I'd like her to get some feedback that could help her communicate better with you.

7. *[Discrepancy between goals and behavior, getting off topic]:* I'm concerned about what the group's doing right now. What do you think is happening?

8. *[Misconception about the self, cognitive/perceptual discrepancy]:* Jan, I'm concerned about what you just said because you're putting yourself down and leaving no room to feel good about yourself. You're assuming that you own the problem and that you're deficient in some way. I'm not at all sure that's the problem. You're married to a man who seems impossible to please. As we agreed earlier, you have tasks of feeling good about yourself, standing up for yourself, and letting your husband's problem be his problem. As long as your feelings about yourself depend on his approval, you're going to feel down on yourself.

9. *[Manipulative behavior]:* I don't know the two of you well enough to presume to know what's causing your problems.

   [To wife]: When you say "knock around," what are you referring to?
   [To husband]: If you're expecting me to tell your wife to shape up, you'll be disappointed. My job is to help each of you to see your part in the difficulties and to make appropriate changes so that you resolve such challenges in safe, non-violent ways. If I did what you asked, I'd be doing both of you a gross disservice. Things don't get better that way.

10. *[Discrepancy between behavior and purported goals]:* What you do, of course, is up to you. I am concerned, however, because you all agreed you wanted to relate more closely as family members and give one another more support. To accomplish that means you have to work at it steadily, or things aren't likely to change much.

[To father]: My impression is that you're backing off. I know your business is important, but I guess you have to decide whether you're really committed to the goals you set for yourselves.

NOTE

1. Much of this discussion of empathy is adapted from Gerdes, K., & Segal, E. (2013). Importance of empathy for social work practice: Integrating new science. *Social Work, 16*(1), 141–148.

CHAPTER 18

Managing Barriers to Change

Chapter Overview

This chapter considers potential barriers to change and ways of identifying and managing them so that they do not interrupt progress or cause unplanned termination by clients. Clients who have the best of intentions and who are highly motivated may nevertheless encounter obstacles that interfere with the helping process and goal attainment. These obstacles may occur within the client (e.g., interpersonal or intrapersonal dynamics or a mix of both) or be influenced by the client's social or physical environment. We also discuss the ways in which social workers' behaviors can either contribute to a resolution of barriers or unintentionally aggravate them. In the final portion of this chapter, we elaborate on the principles and techniques of motivational interviewing as a strategy to facilitate change.

After reading this chapter, you will gain skills to:

- Recognize and manage dynamics that can interfere with your relationship with clients and thereby interfere with their progress.

- Understand and manage dynamics in cross-cultural and cross-racial relationships.

- Use supportive and facilitative skills to promote change.

- Assess and gauge your behavior with clients and use of self.

EPAS Competencies in Chapter 18

This chapter provides the information that you will need to meet the following practice competencies:

- Competency 1: Demonstrate Ethical and Professional Behavior

- Competency 2: Engage Diversity and Difference in Practice

- Competency 6: Engage with Individuals, Families, Groups, Organizations, and Communities

- Competency 7: Assess Individuals, Families, Groups, Organizations, and Communities

- Competency 8: Intervene with Individuals, Families, Groups, Organizations, and Communities

BARRIERS TO CHANGE

In the best of circumstances, progress toward goal attainment is rarely smooth. Even getting started can be a formidable challenge with involuntary clients, when compliance is required; the help that is offered has not been solicited and may not be perceived as particularly useful. With all people, the change process is one in which there can be rapid spurts, plateaus, impasses, fears, and sometimes brief relapse periods.

Think about how often you have vowed to behave differently with a friend, coworker, spouse, or relative only to become involved in a situation that pushes your buttons, causing you to revert to old patterns of behaving. Eventually, you will accomplish your desired behavioral goal, but the fact that you had a setback does not mean that you are unable or unwilling to change. The same is true for clients. Barriers to change discussed in this chapter are:

● Relational dynamics that occur in the interactions between clients and practitioners
● Behaviors on the part of practitioners
● Dynamics that are challenging in cross-racial and cross-cultural relationships
● Sexual attraction toward clients and the ethical and legal implication of this behavior

RELATIONAL DYNAMICS

EP 1 and 6

Relational reactions are conscious and unconscious dynamics between people—for example, reactions of the social worker to the client or those of the client in response to the social worker. Your relationship with a client is the vehicle that animates the helping process. Indeed, the quality of the helping relationship can critically determine a client's moment-to-moment receptiveness to you. For better or worse, feelings and emotions that can influence the relationship constantly flow back and forth between you and the individuals with whom you are working. To maintain positive helping relationships, it is important that you be alert and manage relational dynamics so that they do not become threats.

The Importance of Reciprocal Positive Feelings

Because of the profound importance of the helping relationship, it is crucial that you be skilled in cultivating an alliance with clients that ensures that the relationship remains intact. Helping relationships that are characterized by reciprocal positive feelings between social workers and clients are conducive to personal growth and successful problem solving. Facilitative conditions, such as high levels of warmth, acceptance, unconditional caring, empathy, genuineness, and sensitivity to differences, promote the development of and sustain positive helping relationships.

Despite best efforts, however, some clients are unable to hear or respond positively to the helping relationship for a number of reasons, such as distrust, fear, or simply being overwhelmed. Social workers, too, may have difficulty building a productive alliance with some clients because of their subjective appraisal or bias, such as with clients who have certain personality traits, physical attributes, or a presenting problem and countertransference. For example, consider the following exchange between a social worker and a consultant during a case review session.

In this case, the client and social worker's relational dynamics prevented problem solving in that neither the social worker nor the client was engaged in this process. First, when we do not like clients for whatever reasons, they sense our feelings toward them, and therefore a psychological connection is unlikely to develop. Moreover, the nonverbal cues of the social worker communicated a lack of acceptance, warmth, and empathy. Note, for example, the social worker's description of the client as "sitting there like a big lump." What mental image of the mother is conveyed in this statement? Perhaps that she is overweight,

CASE EXAMPLE

Social worker [presenting a case]: How can you feel empathy for every client? I have this one client, and when I go to her house, she is just sitting there like a big lump. She doesn't seem to understand that she may lose her children, even though she says she does not want them to be removed from her care. She tells me that the man who abused her children is out of her life, but I don't believe her. She tells lies, she doesn't do anything to help herself,

and she sits there in the midst of a cluttered filthy apartment watching television. I'm just waiting to catch her in one of her lies. It's hard for me to feel anything for this client or to help her keep custody of her children.

Consultant: Wow, you really don't like this client and she knows it! Perhaps she feels, "Why bother to establish a relationship with you?" It is quite possible that she has feelings about your visits in the same way that you dread seeing her.

passive, lazy, and uncaring about her children. Further, the bias of the social worker appeared to be slanted toward Weinberg's (2006) assertion that single mothers are often judged by accepted standards of motherhood behavior, in which case, in the mind of the social worker, this mother was sorely lacking.

Sensing the social worker's reaction to her, you can be sure that the mother dreaded the visits. Moreover, the social worker's feelings about the mother set a tone that prevented an exploration of other contributing factors for the mother's behavior and the state of the apartment. For example, the possibility that the woman was depressed was overlooked. Subjective conclusions about clients also affect the way in which the assessment is conducted (for example, accrediting strengths) and decisions that are made with respect to a commitment to change. Clients who are perceived in a positive light—specifically, they are cooperative or compliant and readily accept the social worker's viewpoint—tend to be assessed in a positive manner. In contrast, if a client behaves in a passive way, like the mother in this case, or expresses anger or rejects the social worker's assessment, he or she is perceived more negatively and is assessed as being less willing to change (Dettlaff & Rycraft, 2010; Holland, 2000).

A second hindering factor in this case was the social worker's preoccupation with whether the client was telling the truth. There are times when you may feel that you are working harder than clients, and in consequence you become sidetracked by a certain behavior such as whether the client is telling the truth. Understandably, in the helping relationship, truth telling is a reciprocal expectation. Yet was it necessary for the social worker to determine whether the mother was lying, unless her dishonesty threatened the welfare of her children? Continuing to focus on catching her in a lie distracts the social worker from problem solving, in which case she relinquishes her role as a problem solver and instead acts as an investigator. The decisive assessment question is whether this mother could or is willing to (and under what circumstances) take steps to ensure that her children are safe.

Did the social worker come to like the client? Perhaps not, but after meeting with the consultant, she was able to understand and therefore manage her reactions to the mother that interfered with a working alliance and effectively stalled professional problem solving. We may not always like clients, but it is essential that we examine the basis of our emotions by examining our bias and behavior. Certainly, we do have emotional reactions to some clients, but acting on our feelings or taking it out on or judging a client is not the appropriate ethical and professional response. Instead, sharing your emotional reactions is a more constructive way for you to learn from the situation.

Steps to Take to Reduce the Risk of Negative Relational Dynamics

You may recall an experience that caused you to react to an individual in a similar manner. For the social worker in the case consultation scenario (and for you in your similar experience), self-understanding, self-awareness, and self-control would EP 1 have promoted ethical professional practice. Cournoyer (2011) has also identified preparatory self-reflection, centering, and planning as active steps that you can take to minimize or reduce the risk of relational dynamics that can interfere with establishing a working alliance with a client.

Self-exploration and self-reflection help you to clarify, and indeed understand, your bias, beliefs, values, and stereotypes. In essence, this process informs you of how you might judge people and subsequently draw positive or negative conclusions about them. The evaluation of self is instrumental in maintaining self-control. The process helps you manage personal factors, such as your emotional state (e.g. an argument with someone) or physical stressors (e.g. insufficient sleep), either of which can influence your readiness to interact with clients. **Self-awareness** also includes admitting and assessing your personal thoughts, feelings, and physical sensations, specifically centering, focusing, compartmentalizing, and, if needed, engaging in self-talk. Clearly, as noted above, it can be difficult to manage your feelings with some individuals and in some situations. **Self-control** is the ability to recognize and therefore manage your feelings, emotions, and behaviors. Actively taking steps to manage your potential reactions before and during a session can prevent you from becoming caught up in dynamics that can sidetrack a relationship. In fact, in preparing to meet with clients, you may find is useful to develop a mental checklist in which you focus on, for example, the reason and purpose of the contact and what is to be accomplished, taking into consideration your agenda as well the client's.

In your interactions with clients, especially those who may trigger a reaction in you, it is equally important to evaluate your performance relative to the essential elements of the helping relationship, specifically the extent to which you convey warmth, acceptance, and empathy. Even when a positive relationship evolves, various events and moment-by-moment transactions may pose risks to initiating and sustaining a workable relationship. As you work with clients, it is important that you be attentive to instances that indicate that something in the relationship between you and the client is off center. Failure to perceive that something has gone wrong and effectively manage the situation may result in a deadlock in which problem solving becomes stalled. The next section elaborates on the threats to the relationship that result from the social worker's actions or behaviors, those of the client, and a dynamic mix of both.

Under- and Overinvolvement of Social Workers with Clients

In your best effort to foster a positive relationship with clients and to be attuned to the interference of relational dynamics, there are times when something in the relationship can be off center. In some instances, you may become caught up with a client's situation to such an extent that your behavior and actions become an inhibiting force. Even though you may strive to maintain a balanced attitude, be appreciative of strengths and aware of obstacles, there are situations in which you may be inclined to emphasize one side of the story that is generally favorable or unfavorable to the client. Raines (1996) has classified such reactions as **overinvolvement** or **underinvolvement**. Levels of over- or underinvolvement can also be classified according to the practitioner's general viewpoint or attitude toward the client, which can be either positive or negative. Table 18-1 presents an adaptation of Raines's schema for classifying involvement.

EP 2

1. *When the social worker is underinvolved and has a negative attitude toward the client*, it can be reflected in his or her lack of attention or empathy, tuning out, biased or judgmental views, or dismissing or not recalling pertinent information. All social workers have had less than productive sessions with clients and days on which their level of attentiveness was less than desirable. The earlier case consultation scenario is an example of underinvolvement of the social worker because of her negative attitude toward the mother. Such behavior signals that the cause of the behavior must be examined.

Hence, part of professional behavior is the capacity for self-observation and correction when indicated. Noting one or more of the patterns highlighted in Table 18-1 is cause for supervision or consultation with peers so that you can develop a plan for rectifying the behavior.

2. *Underinvolvement when there is a positive social worker attitude* can occur when a social worker withholds assistance because of an overly optimistic assessment of an individual client's capacity and need for help. For example, a young woman who has made good progress toward her goals was praised by the social worker. Yet during a session, the young woman reported that she often wakes up feeling scared, angry, depressed, and overwhelmed by her responsibilities. In response to the client's complaint, however, the social worker encouraged her to focus on her strengths (e.g., "Look what you have accomplished so far!"), promising that her continued sessions would most likely resolve her concerns.

Two relational issues are at risk in this scenario. First, the social worker's level of empathy can be rated as low and as such is a potential barrier. In addition, she ignored the concerns and feelings expressed by the client. Challenging the client to focus on her strengths hampered the social worker's ability to address what the client had said, a signal that the social worker was tuned out and was underinvolved. Strengths notwithstanding, the young woman voiced some very real concerns, and it is sufficient to believe that future sessions with the social worker are unlikely to resolve her concerns. Would it surprise you to learn that the young woman showed up for future appointments only sporadically and when she had a concrete need? Underinvolvement can also take the form of settling on assignments or tasks that the client feels incapable of completing. In these cases, when clients fail, there is a tendency to question their commitment, rather than the influence of our own actions. Of course when faced with the pressure of a large caseload, a social worker may assign a client that he or she is underinvolved with to a lower level of contact than is actually warranted.

As in negative underinvolvement, positive decisions may happen with particular clients because of positive stereotyping of clients who possess what the social worker perceives to be positive attributes. Patterns of repeated positive underinvolvement, however, call for examination and correction. Again, self-reflection on these patterns and conversations

TABLE 18-1 Social Worker's Under- and Overinvolvement with Clients

	SOCIAL WORKER WITH UNFAVORABLE ATTITUDE TOWARD CLIENT	SOCIAL WORKER WITH FAVORABLE ATTITUDE TOWARD CLIENT
UNDERINVOLVEMENT	<ul><li>Finds it difficult to empathize with the client</li><li>Is inattentive to or "tunes out" the client</li><li>Has lapses of memory about important information previously revealed by the client</li><li>Is drowsy or preoccupied</li><li>Dreads sessions or comes late, cancels sessions inappropriately</li><li>Is off the mark with interpretations</li><li>Client perceives feedback as put-downs</li><li>Fails to acknowledge client growth</li><li>Never thinks about the client outside of sessions</li></ul>	<ul><li>Withholds empathy inappropriately due to belief in client's strengths</li><li>Refrains from interpretation to promote insight</li><li>Reflects or reframes excessively without answering</li><li>Never considers self-disclosure</li><li>Gives advice or assignments that the client feels incapable of carrying out</li></ul>
OVERINVOLVEMENT	<ul><li>Has an unreasonable dislike of the client</li><li>Is argumentative</li><li>Is provocative</li><li>Gives excessive advice</li><li>Employs inept or poorly timed confrontations</li><li>Disapproves of the client's planned course of action inappropriately</li><li>Appears to take sides against the client (or subgroup) or actually does so</li><li>Dominates discussions or frequently interrupts the client</li><li>Uses power with involuntary clients to interfere in lifestyle areas beyond the range of legal mandates</li><li>Competes intellectually</li><li>Has violent thoughts or dreams about the client</li></ul>	<ul><li>Is overly emotional or sympathetic</li><li>Provides extra time inappropriately</li><li>Fantasizes brilliant interpretations</li><li>Is unusually sensitive to criticisms</li><li>Has sexual thoughts or dreams about the client</li><li>Seeks nonprofessional contact with the client</li></ul>

Source: Adapted from Raines (1996).

with peers and supervisors can assist you in finding ways to adjust the involvement level. Hence, while focusing on client strengths and having a positive attitude toward clients is generally consistent with social work values, the possibility of positive under-involvement alerts us to ways that attention to perceived positives can be exaggerated and not completely helpful in all circumstances.

3. *Overinvolvement with a negative social worker attitude* refers to negative attention such that clients may feel punished or in combat with the social worker. Specific patterns such as arguing, acting provocatively, using confrontation inappropriately,

using power arbitrarily, and the like can signal negative overinvolvement as a result of counter-transference. This behavior is often observed in high-stress work settings in which social workers have close contact with clients who have been harmed and with individuals who have either harmed those clients or not acted fully to prevent the harm. Note that if the social worker is operating under a legal mandate to provide, for example, services to a parent who has mistreated a child, power and authority could be used appropriately in an ethical manner. Facilitative conditions—for example, empathy, genuineness, and unconditional caring for the client—are equally appropriate. In contrast, in cases of overinvolvement with a negative social worker attitude, the use of power becomes personal and punishing rather than applied in a manner that is appropriate to the circumstance. Negative attitudes can take the form of rigid rules of conduct in educational, residential, and corrections settings, in which clients are stereotyped and their strengths are ignored. This behavior is contrary to social work values, but as you are perhaps aware, it does occur.

An example of a social worker being overinvolved is illustrated in the following case example.

Overinvolvement can also lead to conflict between a social worker and members of his or her team or other professionals that can spill over into these relationships. The following two case examples have similar dynamics. The first example demonstrates how positive overinvolvement can cause negative interactions between professionals when one is invested in and advocates for a particular outcome. In consequence, other professionals are perceived as underinvolved, and their actions toward the client are seen as negative or unjust.

If you had been present at the team consultation meeting when the case was presented, how would you respond to the question "Am I too involved in this case?" Perhaps you would credit the social worker for asking the question. Is it clear what help the social worker is seeking? What is the social worker's level of involvement? Are you able to identify the relational dynamics between the social worker and the case manager that have spilled over into the work with the family?

The following case example illustration of overinvolvement describes a social worker who appears to have little insight into her behavior and its implications for her clients and the goals of the agency. The scenario also emphasizes how overinvolvement may arise as a result of a combination of positive and negative dynamics.

In this case example, you can observe levels of positive and negative overinvolvement. For example, Marta is passionate about her work, and she has a positive regard for the youth with whom she works. However, her use of self in the situation, particularly her reliance on her own parental and survival experience, has negative connotations and gets in the way of individual problem solving. Her behavior and lack of self-awareness exemplify a barrier to effective practice because of her own unresolved issues with her parents. In addition, this is a situation in which consulting with her supervisor would be important so that she becomes aware of the origin and influences of her behavior on her work with youth.

CASE EXAMPLE

Social worker [presenting a case]: Police were called to the home in response to a domestic violence incident. The husband was charged with interference in a 911 call because he had thrown the telephone into the pool while the wife was making the call. The court-ordered case plan identified improved communication between the couple and resolution of their domestic violence issues. In the initial session with the couple, they reported that they were attending conflict resolution sessions with their religious leader, and as a result they were now better able to communicate with each other. They also contended that "we don't have domestic violence issues." The couple's explanation for the incident was that the wife's pregnancy and hormonal changes caused her to experience mood swings that resulted in the conflict that prompted the call to the police. The social worker accepted the explanation but stated in her report that she did have one concern: "Unless encouraged to do so, the wife rarely spoke" during the session with the couple.

Based on the session with the couple, the social worker concluded that no further action was indicated and that the case should be closed. In her termination notes, the social worker noted that the couple "is involved in the community, both are professionals and are happy about the upcoming birth of their baby." Further, "they live in a spacious home, just off the golf course, in an outer-ring suburb." In this situation, the social worker's positive regard for the couple's attributes resulted in her becoming overinvolved with potentially negative consequences. For example, the social worker failed to further assess the meaning of the wife's behavior.

CASE EXAMPLE

Social worker [presenting a case]: Am I too mixed up in this case? Some of my colleagues believe that I am, and this is why I am presenting this case. First, there are many topics that I wish to discuss; for example, the county case manager's questioning of my professional boundaries, and the boundaries of our agency (here the social worker distributes copies of a dictionary definition of boundaries), and the lack of due process in the county's decisions about the clients. The case manager raised concerns about my boundaries after I submitted the first progress report on the family. In the report, I indicated the family's diligence in addressing the concerns outlined in the county's case plan. He indicated that I had not done a comprehensive report as the report was too positive. Further, he said that I was more involved than necessary with the family. This particular case manager has done this with other families that receive a positive report from us, as you all know …. The real issue here about boundaries must be dealt with first. If he means providing the family with resources, listening to them, and advocating on their behalf then, so be it. Who am I to judge the family's practice of witchcraft, or the mother's attending a witch's ball? I find these people different, but interesting, and hey, so are some of us! But I am concerned that my being an advocate for the family will have adverse consequences for them and for our agency. For example, what if the case manager reassigned the case or stopped making referrals to us, in which case my actions would affect all of us.

CASE EXAMPLE

Marta is a youth worker in a shelter for homeless youth. She is passionate about her work and believes that her relationship with her young clients will help them to become independent, productive adults. She sees herself as an example of a survivor. Her supervisor has approached her several times because she believes that Marta sometimes crosses professional boundaries with her clients. Marta's primary goal is to prepare homeless youth to become independent. Actually, youth gaining independence is a program goal, so her behavior is consistent with the intended program outcome. Another goal of the program, however, is to assist the youth to resolve conflicts with their parents whenever possible and achieve eventual reunification. Marta's work with youth is often in conflict with this goal.

Marta's own youth was marked by constant battles with her parents. At age 17, she left home, lived with friends for a period, and eventually became homeless. Her approach and her relationship with the youth in her caseload are generally as a "survivor of the streets," encouraging dependency by urging her clients to rely on her for support. Whenever a youth expressed an interest in reconnecting with his or her parents, Marta routinely rejected this idea as being unhealthy to the youth's progress and refused to help make contact. The supervisor considers Marta's work with youth to be generally exemplary, with the exception of her negative attitude toward parents. Marta points to the fact that many of her clients have in fact become independent; further, that they seek her out for ongoing support, which she finds frustrating at times, even though the contact is evidence of the importance of her work.

The preceding case examples illustrated the dynamics of over- and underinvolvement, both positive and negative and in some instances a combination of both. More important, they demonstrated how levels of involvement can obscure professional judgment, the results of which can have an adverse impact on client well-being.

4. *Overinvolvement with a positive social worker attitude* entails excessive preoccupation with a

particular client. The social worker tends to focus on a particular client in such a way that the client dominates the social worker's thoughts and dreams, and in some instances includes sexual fantasies. In the most extreme cases, positive overinvolvement can lead to more serious consequences—for example, boundary violations such as sexual contact with clients. Because of the seriousness of boundary violations, we discuss this issue later in greater detail.

Burnout, Compassion Fatigue, and Vicarious Trauma

EP 1

As social workers our work is often stressful as a result of workload demands and the issues presented by clients, many of whom have experienced or been exposed to trauma. Such conditions may cause becoming under- or overinvolved with clients and can have serious consequences for us on a personal and professional level. Constantly attending to the needs of and helping clients can result in *burnout*, *compassion fatigue*, or *vicarious trauma* (Bell, Kulkarni, & Dalton, 2003; James, 2008; Kanter, 2007).

James (2008) attributes **burnout** to identifying too closely with clients and their problems, as well as to being dedicated and idealistic. In the previous case example, Marta appears to be a candidate for burnout as she perceives herself as the primary vehicle for ensuring the success of the youth. Burnout occurs over a period of time. Initially, the social worker is enthusiastic and involved but starts to move into stagnation, which leads to frustration and, eventually, apathy. Over a prolonged period, these factors can also result in a "crisis state of disequilibrium" and chronic indifference (James, 2008, p. 537).

The following describe different circumstances of burnout resulting in over- or underinvolvement with clients:

- *Negative underinvolvement* can occur when you feel frustrated because you are unable to solve certain problems, you have a large caseload, and the outcomes of your work are unknown or uncertain (Dane, 2000; Dettlajf & Rycraft, 2010; James, 2008). In working with clients, you may become numb to demands that exceed your mental capacity. Thoughts such as "I have heard this story too many times" or "How can I change anything?" may occur to you, along with a feeling of helplessness.

- *Overinvolvement* is indicated when you have a strong need to be liked by a client or the urge to save, taking calls or texts at home, feeling responsible for clients' mistakes or relapses, and panicking when carefully detailed plans fail to produce the expected results. At the administrative level, overinvolvement leading to burnout may take the form of micromanaging or feeling that nothing will get done or done correctly unless you, the social worker, are involved (James, 2008). **Vicarious trauma** is also a concern because the social worker's response to the client is a concern, boundaries are less clear, and in some instances, the social worker behaves in a manner that distances himself or herself from or blames the client (Dunkley & Whelan, 2006).

- *Underinvolvement* can occur when a social worker has difficulty in bonding with and enlisting the cooperation of clients who are different (Dunkley & Whelan, 2006; Fontes, 2005).

- *Underinvolved* professionals often experience an organization in which the leadership is ineffective; there is a lack of rewards, recognition, or organizational support; decisions are perceived to be unfair or arbitrary; or the environment is unsupportive and the fit between organizational and individual beliefs at odds (Leiter & Maslach, 2005). Feeling a lack of control over a prolonged period of time can lead to apathy and ineffective service delivery to clients.

Compassion fatigue is different from burnout. Burnout is mainly associated with workload demands, uncertainty and stressors, and the urgency and size of caseloads. Compassion fatigue, in contrast, is a constant state of tension and preoccupation with the individual and collective trauma of clients (Figley, 1995, 2002). Social workers who are too deeply drawn into the trauma and emotions of clients and clients' situations are likely to become mentally exhausted (Figley, 1995, 2002). Conversely, the experience of **vicarious** or **secondary trauma** is recognized in situations in which knowledge of and exposure to others' trauma and wanting to help increase the susceptibility to indirect or direct trauma for the social worker (Badger, Royse, & Craig, 2008; Bride & Figley, 2007; Kanter, 2007). This form of trauma is most often evident in social workers who day after day listen to the disturbing narratives of clients in situations of family violence, child sexual abuse, and hospital oncology units. It may also be ignited by past experiences of the social worker—for example, a social worker's own adverse childhood experience—or provoked by the vulnerability of the client (Esaki & Larkin, 2013).

Research findings have shown that vicarious or secondary trauma has implications for the extent to which social workers become over- or underinvolved with clients. In a study of secondary trauma for family violence professionals, Bell (2003) found that constant "exposure to clients' stories negatively affects cognitions" of social workers, and therefore their professional judgment. Similar results were reported by Dane (2000) in a study of child welfare workers and by Cunningham (2003) in a study of group work with individuals with a history of trauma. Further, the response level of the social worker was related to whether the client's situation was similar to his or her own experience, which can be the basis of positive or negative transference by the client or a countertransference reaction on the part of the social worker.

Literature and research studies have recognized compassion fatigue, vicarious or secondary trauma, and the direct and indirect effects of stress on professionals in different settings (Badger, Royse, & Craig, 2008; Bell, 2003; Clemans, 2004; Dunkley & Whelan, 2006; Figley, 1995, 2002; Tehrani, 2007). These works have contributed to the growing awareness and understanding of the effects of vicarious or secondary trauma and compassion fatigue on social workers, as well as the need for organizations to recognize and take steps to remedy it and provide support. Irrespective of the organizational response, self-care is advanced as an action social workers can take (Bride & Figley, 2007; Kanter, 2007; Lee & Miller, 2013). Lee and Miller (2013), citing the National Association of Social Workers (NASW, 2009b) position on self-care as "a critical foundation for effective social work practice" (p. 98), emphasize the social worker's need for self-care and support in the workplace setting, which effectively counters burnout and secondary trauma. Resources for self-care assessment and strategies include Lee and Miller (2013), Bride and Figley (2007), Figley (2002), and O'Hollaran and Linton (2000).

REACTIONS OF CLIENTS: ASSESSING POTENTIAL BARRIERS AND INTERVENING

The preceding discussion emphasized social worker behaviors and circumstances that have the capacity to stimulate a professional reaction and thereby influence

EP 1 and 6

the helping relationship. The following discussion is focused on client reactions. In the interaction between social worker and client, there are times when the relationship can stall because of clients' reactions based on their perceptions or misperceptions of the social worker. Whatever the source, sensing and addressing clients' feelings and thoughts as they happen is crucial to preventing them from escalating. Clients may not always initiate a discussion of their negative reactions. The ability to do so may depend on their personality type, their age, cultural differences with regard to authority, their status (e.g., voluntary or involuntary), or their sense of power vis-à-vis the social worker's role or that of the organization (e.g., a residential treatment or correctional facility). Keep in mind that in view of a real or perceived power differential between the social worker and clients, sharing negative feelings and cognitions can be extremely difficult for some clients, and others may fear the implications when they do so.

You can reduce the threat that clients experience by being attentive and accepting, or by being an advocate, even though you may believe that their interpretation is off the mark or entirely unrealistic. If you are inattentive or insensitive to cues, either verbal or nonverbal, the associated feelings and cognitions will linger and remain unresolved. To prevent such a development, it is crucial to watch for indicators of negative reactions, which can present, for example, in changing the subject, frowning, fidgeting, sighing, appearing startled, becoming silent, or clearing the throat. Above all, because you have worked with the client over time, you are apt to be able to observe a change in how he or she reacts to you. When you observe a change, it is important to focus the session on the client's here-and-now feelings and cognitions. You should do this tentatively by checking out whether your perception is accurate. If it is accurate, proceed by expressing genuine concern for the client's discomfort and conveying your desire to understand what he or she is experiencing at the moment. Examples of responses that facilitate the discussion of troubling feelings and thoughts follow:

- **To a youth:** "I'm thinking, to use a phrase that I've heard from you, that what I said was a "flyover" *[not paying attention]* for you. What are you thinking and feeling at this moment?"
- **To a young minor:** "Are you feeling sad right now? Would it be helpful for you to draw a picture

of how you feel, and then you could explain the picture to me?"

- *To an adult client:* "You are quiet right now, looking away from me. I wonder if you have some feelings about my draft progress report to the court that I just shared with you."

Notice that in each of the situations, the verbalizations are specific to the moment that the individual reacted, but they rely on the person to express his or her own thoughts or feelings.

Eliciting a client's emotions, feelings, and thoughts provides you with an opportunity to correct misunderstandings, clarify your intentions, remedy any blunders, and identify adverse beliefs or thought patterns. Indeed, by observing you, some clients will benefit and be able to acknowledge their mistakes and perhaps apologize without feeling embarrassed. Moreover, clients may gain self-confidence by realizing that you value them and the relationship enough to be concerned about their thoughts and feelings and to rectify your errors of omission or commission. After productive discussions of here-and-now thoughts and feelings, most clients will regain their positive feelings about the relationship and be able to resume working on their problems.

On some occasions, a client may succeed in concealing negative thoughts and feelings, or you may overlook nonverbal cues. The feelings may escalate until it becomes obvious that the client is holding back, being overly formal, responding defensively, or engaging in other forms of reactance. Again, you should give priority to the relationship by shifting focus to what is bothering the client and responding to it. After you have worked through the negative reaction of the client, it is helpful to negotiate a **mini-contract** in which you and the client agree to discuss troublesome feelings and thoughts as they occur. The objective of this contract is to avert the recurrence of a negative reaction in the future. For those clients who may habitually withhold their reactions to the detriment of themselves and others, learning to express negative feelings and thoughts can be a milestone. The following is an example of a message aimed at negotiating an appropriate mini-contract:

Social worker: Okay, we got past the flyover, where you felt I was ignoring what you said. Thank you for telling me about how you don't like people to be telling you what you need to do. Because you told me how you felt, you helped me to understand and you gave me a chance to explain what I really meant last week. For us to work well together, it is important for both of us to put negative reactions on the table. Would you be willing for the two of us to agree that we will immediately alert each other to troubling thoughts and feelings that happen between us?

In developing the mini-contract, the social worker is conveying to the youth a willingness to be open to and respectful of his reactions. Almost all of us can recall a situation in which on occasion we committed an error or made a mistake in a particular case. Instilled in our memory is the reaction from the client involved and, most important, the steps that were taken to ensure that our behavior did not cause irreparable damage to the helping relationship.

Pathological or Inept Social Workers

Despite educational preparation, some social workers demonstrate behavior that lacks the values and basic tenets of a helping relationship—for example, a lack of empathy or being in tune with those seeking their help; a lack of genuine and authentic concern; and a lack of appreciation of different beliefs, lifestyles, and values. Their inept behavior may be attributed to anxiety, a lack of skill or experience, dealing with a problem beyond their scope of practice, or an inability to build collaborative relationships with clients. Ineptness and unethical practices on the part of social workers, such as being abrasive, egotistical, controlling, judgmental, demeaning, patronizing, or rigid, can cause an appropriate negative reaction from clients. In these interactions, clients' reactions can become a cycle of escalating conflict. For example, a social worker demeans a client, the client reacts, and so forth. Another disturbing pattern relates to a social worker's attempt to control by exerting his or her power and authority, which of course tends to escalate a client's reaction. Being habitually late or unprepared for appointments and appearing to be detached or disinterested and underinvolved are further indicators of troubling behavior. Most people will react to behavior that they view as disrespectful and unprofessional. In many cases, a social worker would not tolerate similar behaviors in a client.

Ineptness is a serious concern that calls for corrective behavior on the part of the social worker, through supervision, skill development, or self-reflection. Pathological behavior on the part of a social worker,

EP 1

in which there is a sustained pattern of repeated errors and insensitive behaviors, can cause psychological damage to clients. The social worker's behavior can be the result of his or her own personal unresolved issues for which he or she should seek help. Gottesfeld and Lieberman (1979) refer to social workers whose behavior harms a client, whether intentionally or unintentionally, as **pathological**, pointing out that "It is possible to have therapists who suffer from as many unresolved problems as do clients" (p. 388). Hence, these practitioners are incapable of providing help to clients because of their own troubles. Left unresolved, the relationship—in which helping is the hallmark—is severely diminished.

The majority of voluntary clients who experience the ineptitude of pathological practitioners have the good sense to vote with their feet by prematurely terminating their contact (Meyer, 2001). Mandated clients suffer greater consequences for deciding to terminate early. As a protective precaution, they may evade contact or attempt to be transferred to another social worker. Supervisors should be alert when there are several requests for transfer from the same social worker.

Pathological or inept social workers harm their clients, their agencies, and the profession as a whole. Often, social workers faced with a situation involving a colleague find that deciding what steps to take is easier said than done. Moreover, the privacy of the interaction between a client and a colleague may make it hard to conclude that behavior of a colleague is harmful. It is indeed a challenge to question the behavior or competence of another social worker. However, individuals who act in a manner that is harmful or demeaning to clients are often quite open about what they do—for example, telling stories about clients in which their own status is heightened, giving clients demeaning names as descriptors, breaching confidentiality, and talking down to clients, even when other clients or staff are present. You may also observe or hear a person's constant reactive behavior to the social worker. Unfortunately, when a client reacts, he or she may be ignored by the agency and other staff, who instead may tend to characterize his or her behavior as resistant or oppositional.

Both you and your agency have a responsibility to protect clients. By not acting, all involved become a party to a colleague's behavior that assaults the dignity and worth of clients. The primacy of clients' rights is clearly articulated in the NASW Code of Ethics. The Code also speaks directly to your obligation to peers and the employment organization. A caution by

Gottesfeld and Lieberman (1979) is timeless in this regard. They assert that, to protect clients' rights, "agencies organized to help clients should not accept employee pathology that defeats the system's purpose" (p. 392). Actions to rectify such situations, however, must safeguard the rights of both the social worker and the clients. Reports of pathological or inept behavior should be based on facts, not judgments or bias, and your motive and the outcome you are seeking should be clear. Involving your supervisor and reviewing information with this person or a consultant provide additional safeguards. You may also want to refer to the guidelines on whistle-blowing discussed in Chapter 14.

Ultimately, a referral to the local NASW state chapter and licensing board or certification authority may become necessary. NASW chapters and regulatory boards have committees that investigate complaints of unethical and unprofessional conduct. Information about misconduct is shared between NASW chapters and state boards of social work. Infractions that constitute egregious harm are routinely reported to the Association of Social Work Boards (ASWB) Public Protection Database (PPD), a system that is intended to protect the public. State social work regulatory boards can access the PPD system to verify the disciplinary background of individuals seeking licensure or renewal (ASWB Member Policy Manual).

Cross-Racial and Cross-Cultural Barriers

EP 2

Clients and social workers may experience adverse reactions in cross-racial or cross-cultural relationships for a variety of reasons. Tensions in social relations that are grounded in society may present as dynamics in the helping relationship—for instance, the nature of social work values that emphasize autonomy and self-direction are not shared by all societies (Al Krewani, 1999; Haj-Yahia, 1997; Lee, 2014; Yan, 2008). These tensions can become heightened in interactions with involuntary clients who are also members of a racial or ethnic minority. Issues of race, culture, and socioeconomic status are macro-level factors, but they nevertheless influence micro-level practice and relationships.

Cross-racial and cross-cultural relationships can be challenging on many levels. In their most basic form, barriers to a working relationship between a social worker and a client may stem from either a lack of knowledge of a client's culture, bias, or a lack of experience in working with members of a given racial, ethnic, or minority group. Diverse individuals may wonder whether you have sufficient knowledge of their world to help them. They may also enter the relationship with a set of preconceived notions about you. For example, believing that you are racially or culturally insensitive or biased, they may expect to be treated poorly because they are a member of a racial or cultural minority. They may also perceive that you are a representative of an oppressive system in which the goal is to alter who they are. Altering who they are may emphasize change or treatment goals that are bounded by assumptions of Western cultures that may have limited meaning or value to them (Hodge & Nadir, 2008; Lee, 2014; Sue, 2006; Yan, 2008). As such, values can become a barrier in the change process. In cross-cultural and cross-racial situations, it is important to understand clients' viewpoints, lifestyles, and the standards of well-being established by their reference group. To this end, Lee (2003) suggests that in cross-cultural relationships, social constructivism—specifically, a deliberate focus on clients' narratives and viewpoints in which they create solutions for themselves—allows the practitioner to understand the individual and thereby avoid potential relational tensions.

Yan (2008), based on research findings, has developed a typology of the tensions in cross-cultural relationships. The types of tensions are as follows:

- *Type 1* relates to the tensions between the cultures of social work clients, the dominant culture, and the culture of the organization in which the service is delivered. Specifically, there is a potential for three different cultures to be at odds with each other.
- *Type 2* pertains to differences between the culture of the social worker, the organization's culture, and the culture of clients. Examples include the social worker's professional culture and the dominant society as well as tensions that can arise between the organization's culture and those of the social worker. Yan also emphasizes that although differences can cause tensions, sameness (e.g., race or ethnicity) may be a complicating factor because social workers can have multiple personal and professional cultural identities.

Although we all seek to have a collective identity and to minimize differences, in reality, in U.S. society, social interactions and professional relationships remain configured around assumptions of sameness, including social class. Social workers who are members of ethnic, gender, or racial minority groups are perhaps more attuned than their nonminority counterparts to the values of minority group clients. For the most part, however, irrespective of racial or cultural demographics, **social distance** separates social workers from their clients. For example, there are power differences, differences in economic, social, or educational status, and the fact that few social workers may reside in the same communities as the people receiving services. These differences, each of which contributes to social distance, are made greater by diverse experiences and worldviews (Clifford & Burke, 2005; Davis & Gelsomino, 1994; Dettlaff & Rycraft, 2010; Green, Kiernan-Stern, & Baskind, 2005). Clifford and Burke (2005), emphasizing social distance, note the inherent challenge in balancing the ethical principle of being respectful of differences. Specifically, respect for another individual becomes much more difficult when the individual is of a very different social standing. Social distance, whatever the basis, can lead us to invalidate the cognitions and realities of those who are different (Sue et al., 2007).

Lacking familiarity and having limited contact with clients who are different may cause social workers to fill in their information void with stereotypes and preconceived notions and to be influenced by pervasive media images. Whaley (1998) asserts that racial and class bias is influenced by social and cognitive perceptions that fill in the blanks with general stereotypes; for example, black youth who are demonstrating the same traits as their white counterparts are four times more likely to be viewed as violent. Sufficient evidence exists pointing to professional and systems bias in which persons who are different are much more likely to have their behavior perceived as pathological in spite of their ecological circumstances or needs (Allen, 2007; Barnes, 2008; Feldman, 2008; Malgady & Zayas, 2001; Richman, Kohn-Woods, & Williams, 2007; Sue, 2006; Wolf, 1991). The conflict between the social worker's interpretation and assessment and clients' realities may become a form of racial or cultural micro-aggression (Sue et al., 2007). Specifically, social workers' automatic response to clients who are different is based on their cognition of what is or is not normal, and their perception is used to generalize and interpret behavior. Further, Sue et al. (2007) maintain that social workers may not recognize the resulting harm of their behavior.

In cross-cultural, cross-racial relationships, you may tend to become overly positive or negative about a particular racial or ethnic group in an effort to deal with your discomfort or lack of knowledge. Overidentification has both positive and negative features.

On the positive side, identification with a particular group and attempting to understand their reality is essential to becoming a more culturally competent professional. However, overidentification can obscure individuality as well as the subgroups that exist within a racial or ethnic culture. On the negative side, perceptions or stereotypes may lead you to erroneously generalize clients' problems to the group of which they are members, thereby influencing your capacity to be empathetic to the individual and his or her situation.

Given the potential obstacles that may emerge in cross-racial and cross-cultural relationships, you might wonder if the solution is to match clients with social workers of the same racial or ethnic group. Social workers who are members of ethnic or racial minority groups perhaps can be more attuned to the values of minority group clients. Desiring the best outcomes for clients, you might wonder if matching is a viable option. As a solution, matching is not always practical, nor is there sufficient evidence to suggest that it always works to clients' advantage (James, 2008; Karlsson, 2005; Malgady & Zayas, 2001). In addition, some minority individuals will react to and distrust any professional, even those who share their background or heritage. This distrust often arises at a systems level, specifically at the level of the organization that you represent, yet the dynamics emerge in your relationship.

In any of the situations previously described, it can be expected that dynamics in the client–social worker relationship will reflect a mutual strangeness. In some instances, social workers and agencies emphasize sameness rather than differences in an attempt to minimize potential barriers. Too often, differences of race and culture are ignored in the form of **color-blind practice** designed to avoid conflict and promote cultural competence (Davis & Gelsomino, 1994; Neville, Spanierman, & Doan, 2006; Proctor & Davis, 1994). Neville and colleagues (2006) suggest that color blindness has tended to minimize and further distort the existence of structural racism in the United States, the results of which have been newer and more subtle forms of discrimination and a lower level of cultural competence.

The notion of invisibility to differences can also be evident with regard to socioeconomic status. For example, Davis and Gelsomino (1994) caution both majority and minority social workers to be aware of their biases toward clients of a lower social class. In addition to the implications that class has for racial and ethnic minority groups, these authors suggest that class is equally relevant to the "social realities of low-income white clients." In particular, low-income nonminority individuals can be perceived as being responsible for their difficulties because they have failed to take advantage of life opportunities afforded to them because of race. Also, in cross-cultural, cross-racial interactions, they found that social workers tended to ignore environmental factors, such as racism and discrimination experienced by individuals who are different, and instead were more inclined to explore a client's internal functioning as the source of that individual's personal difficulties (Davis & Gelsomino, 1994).

Cultivating Positive Cross-Cultural Relationships

What can be done to minimize the dynamics of cultural or racial differences and their role as a potential relational barrier in the helping process? Self-disclosure, as discussed by Lee (2014), refers specifically to social workers sharing with the client their own culture, values, and beliefs as a means to minimize EP 2 and 6 power differences and create a working alliance. Citing O'Leary (2005), Lee (2014) further suggests talking openly about race and culture with the client as well as disclosing your culture, values, and beliefs. Both self-disclosure and the conversation may be strange and therefore unsettling to the client, yet Lee maintains that doing so can foster a trusting relationship.

Empathy and empathic communication are basic skills that facilitate engagement and bridge the gaps that may be present in cross-racial and cross-cultural client–social worker relationships. Dyche and Zayas (2001) and Parson (1993) emphasize that knowledge of culture is insufficient to evoke empathy. Instead, they refer to **cultural empathy** as an effective treatment tool. Cultural empathy is expressed at the affective level rather than solely at the cognitive level. Whereas the cognitive level references knowledge about different cultures, the affective level is where the social worker makes an effort to see and hear the world through the client's eyes and experiences and to grasp meaning from the client's perspective. Parson (1993) further characterizes cultural empathy as **ethnotherapuetic** in that it relies on the cross-cultural social worker's capacity for introspection and self-disclosure when the results are in support of the helping process.

Relational empathy, as described by Freedberg (2007), also facilitates helping in cross-cultural or racial relationships. As an interpersonal skill, relational empathy is an understanding of a person's cultural or racial background and the sociopolitics of the client's situation, even though as a social worker you may not be fully aware of each and every nuance. Grounded in relational culture theory, relational empathy may cross traditional boundaries in that the client–social worker relationship is based on a mutual sharing. Assessment skills in determining acculturation levels, including culturally derived behaviors or dysfunctions in the context of culture or race, are critical. Keep in mind, however, that the way in which a problem is perceived and framed by you as a professional can be either an inhibiting or a facilitative factor.

In addition to cultural and relational empathy and empathetic communications, **helper attractiveness** is an interpersonal factor to which diverse clients are reported to have responded favorably (Harper & Lantz, 1996). Essentially, it means that the clients perceive that you are interested in them and have compassion and a genuine desire to help, which results in their feeling hopeful about achieving goals (Guthrie et al., 2014). Further, helper attractiveness implies that diverse clients experience respectful, warm, genuine, committed, and ethical behavior on the part of the social worker. The following are representative comments from two separate focus group sessions, one with emancipated minority minors who had been wards of the state, the other with same and different race staff who believed that they had established successful relationships with racial minority adolescents.

Minors: Throughout your life in the system, you come in contact with a lot of indifferent professionals. They run in and tell you what to do; they are disinterested in you as a person and ignore your goals. They give you a case plan to follow and tell you to do this or that, and find a job so that you can support your child. I want to go to college, but no, I'm told to get a job. How is a minimum wage job going to sustain me and my baby in the long run? Having met with you because they are required to, then they move on to the next case. In all fairness, they do have large caseloads, but you never really feel that they are interested in you or really see you as an individual. When I get a worker who listens to me, tries to understand me, and is willing to treat me like a real person, I do better. Sometimes, they act like a parent, but this is okay if they treat me right and show that they care.

Staff: A large part of connecting with them is to remember that they are kids. They have been in the system so long, some almost all of their lives. They don't want to sit in an office and have you talk at them. Sometimes, just riding around with them or going to get a hamburger is when you really are able to connect with them. They talk and you listen. Sometimes you point out the contradictions in their words and behavior in a teasing way and they laugh. Even when they mess up, you have to respect them as individuals, do things with them. A lot of time, they say, "Miss X, I know that I let you down, and I felt bad, because you are real and you support me." A real turning point in even the most difficult cases often occurs when you support them unconditionally, are dependable, respond to them with compassion and in a caring and empathetic way. Above all, you need to include them in the decisions about their future. Some of their negative reactions to you are related to developmental stage, others are because they are scared or testing you to make sure you aren't going to leave them, and still others because the court or the foster home failed to respect them or treat them as individuals.

Despite what may appear to be the challenging trials and tribulations inherent in cross-cultural and cross-racial relationships, it is quite possible to have productive helping relationships with clients who are different from yourself. Key elements that foster positive cross-racial interactions were highlighted in the common themes of the minors and the staff: caring, empathy, and acceptance.

As a preventive measure, in your initial contact with diverse individuals, you might inquire about whether they have concerns on this front. Not all diverse individuals will have a negative reaction to you. Many may have resolved their feelings because they have had the normative experience of interacting with nonminority practitioners. When negative feelings do occur, either in verbal exchanges or discontent that is evident in nonverbal behaviors, you can neutralize the situation by empathically addressing and responding to their feelings.

Diverse clients need to be able to trust that you understand their situation or, at a minimum, that you are willing to learn. Earlier, in defining cultural competence, we put forth some general guidelines and conditions that can facilitate competence with diverse groups in an effort to lessen potential barriers in the helping relationship. In addition, a summary statement of the essence of cultural competence is discussed throughout this text. Building on this statement, we reinforced the evolutionary nature of achieving competence by highlighting parallel concepts such as adopting a posture of discovery (Green, 1999) and cultural humility (Tervalon & Murray-Garcia, 1998). In both, you assume the position of *not knowing* and a willingness to learn.

The notion that competent practice with people who are different evolves over time is consistent with the articulations of Dean (2001) and Williams (2006). They assert that competence is a continuous process of learning and growth. Striving for an arrival point, according to Dean, is based on the "belief that knowledge brings control and effectiveness which is to be achieved above all else" (p. 624). She suggests it is equally important for you to be aware of your lack of competence. In the spirit of Dean's (2001) evolving and changing competence, Williams has conceptualized cultural competence as a progression in which you have an initial anthropological awareness of culture, specifically learning about culture. Progressing to the highest level is embedded in critical theory in which social, political, and economic arrangements are considered and in which the outcomes sought are anti-oppression and social change. At this level, you seek to understand the extent to which macro-level conditions and marginalized status affect the lives of racial and cultural minority groups. Further, you are prepared to intervene at the micro, mezzo, or macro level because racial and ethnic minority persons' problems often involve all three levels.

It is equally important to be mindful of the fact that the helping relationship is between two human beings, albeit from different racial, cultural, or social classes, both of whom are attempting to work together to resolve a problem. Critical societal conditions, social distance, feelings of mistrust, fear, or resentment, and perceptions about you and your status can intrude. Even more daunting is the fact that your relationships with diverse clients may not resolve the oppressive forces that are evident in their lives. But you can control the interaction between you and your clients in a way that does not add to or recreate their negative experience. In general, developing cross-cultural and cross-racial relationships requires you to continually evaluate your knowledge of differences and to increase your level of cultural and oppression competence. In the process of learning, it also means that you are comfortable with differences, and when you are uncomfortable, you are willing to take steps to calm your vulnerabilities, anxieties, and fears about making mistakes.

Difficulties in Establishing Trust

Trust in the helping relationship evolves over time. Perlman (1957) described the climate as an essential element of the helping relationship in which a bond is created between the social worker and the client. Trust is integral to the climate in which the bonding between two people can occur. People can vary widely in their capacity to trust, and their ability to trust you may be a moment-to-moment transaction. For the most part, a majority of people function at an interpersonal level that enables them to enter into a relationship with you in a relatively short period of time after a few moments of checking you out. Others, no matter how much goodwill, warmth, and empathy you convey, will remain guarded or will test you to prove and demonstrate your worthiness. For racial or ethnically diverse persons, the basis for not readily trusting you or revealing feelings may be related to their experiences or systems paranoia, any one of which can be exaggerated when the individual is also involuntary. Involuntary clients, the majority of whom are minority and who have not sought a helping relationship, should not be expected to readily trust you. They can erect the barriers of social distance and their perceived or real powerlessness in their attitude and language—for example, addressing you formally or referring to others as "them" or "the system" (G. D. Rooney, 2009). As such, it is important that you understand that an individual's mistrust and rigid, reactive behavior may not be specific to you. In fact, attempting to persuade clients of your helpful intent is usually counterproductive. Indeed, they may trust your actions over your words. That is, they see trust as a process and product of the relationship that grows over time, reinforced by your helper attributes and action, such as your commitment to them, caring, and respect. These actions are the evidence that you are trustworthy.

Behavior such as showing respect, genuine interest, and caring, along with actions such as reaching out to these clients, can facilitate the perception of you as a trustworthy professional. For example, when they cancel or miss appointments, you can maintain contact by phoning them, making a home visit (if your agency permits), or writing a letter. Many involuntary clients urgently need and want help. In some instances, their failure to trust and engage or keep appointments may be caused by their fear or a pattern of avoidance rather than by a lack of motivation. Assisting such clients to come to terms with their fear or avoidance behavior is therapeutic, whereas allowing them to terminate by default can have grave consequences. Although the movies *Antoine Fisher, Good Will Hunting,* and, more recently, *Precious* are Hollywood productions, they are excellent examples of a developing bond between a professional helper and a client, and of reaching out to a client and building trust.

Transference Reactions

EP 1 and 6

Unrealistic perceptions of and reactions directed toward you or others are known as the **transference reaction** (Corey, 2009; Knight, 2006; Nichols, 2006). In such reactions, unresolved feelings, wishes, anxieties, and fears that are rooted in past relationships with others are ignited and applied to you. Transference reactions can be positive or negative. In whatever form, reactions lack objectivity and therefore can affect the development of a productive relationship between you and clients in much the same way that they create difficulties in other interpersonal relationships.

Treatment sessions with couples or in groups can be the place in which transference reactions are unfolded. Individual partners can react to each other. In groups, individual members can trigger a multiple transference reaction, including the social worker. In these situations, for example, a trauma survivor may assign motivations, thoughts, and feelings to other members, projecting the attributes of the individual who hurt them in hostile interactions (Knight, 2006).

Transference reactions tend to stall progress unless they are addressed. On a system-to-individual or system-to-group level, transference can involve responses to authority in any form. Besides preventing a person from making progress in resolving problems, transference reactions in therapeutic relationships can create opportunities for growth. The therapeutic relationship is, in effect, a social microcosm wherein clients' interpersonal behavior and conditioned patterns of perceiving and feeling are manifested. In this context, clients can recreate here-and-now interactions that are virtually identical to those that plague and defeat them in other relationships. The consequent challenge for the social worker is to assist individuals in recognizing their distorted perceptions. Instead of relying on projections, mental images, or beliefs, the client can eventually develop perceptual sets that help him or her differentiate between individuals and situations.

In group situations, your role as group facilitator is to assess the impact of this dynamic on the group and

intervene appropriately. You can then utilize group process and communication skills to refocus the attention of members on the group's purpose. You may also use this occasion as a teachable moment, emphasizing how distorted perceptions of others are based on other interpersonal relationships rather than on members of the group.

Not all negative transference reactions are based on an individual's unconscious unresolved conflicts or distorted perceptions. They can be the results of the social worker's behavior. Historical racial or cultural conflicts can also be the etiology of a negative reactive transference. Specifically, because of the reality of their experience in the larger society, past, present, or current, racial or cultural individuals bring dynamics such as mistrust and emotions and feelings about power into the helping relationship with social workers who are different (Lee, 2014). This type of transference can occur because of the collective psyche of a community. For example, reactions, subject to racial overtones, can happen in interactions with the police, teachers, or other figures of authority, and the experience of oppression can be automatically assigned to you. At the cognitive level, reactions are reinforced by the powerful messages of music about injustices and inequalities, which further shape the worldview of individuals and communities. Resolving transference based on the reality of an individual's experience may present a more difficult challenge.

Identifying Transference Reactions

Whatever the agency setting and the intervention, you will occasionally encounter transference reactions. To manage transference reactions, you must first be aware of their manifestations. Here are examples of some behaviors symptomatic of transference:

- Transference reactions involving interpersonal trauma are common (Knight, 2006). This includes fear, distrust, and hostile interactions or rages directed toward the social worker, group members, or projections of significant others in response to their grief, frustration, and fears (James, 2008; Knight, 2006).
- Behaving provocatively by arguing with or baiting the practitioner or becoming silent and hostile, avoiding making progress (Nichols, 2006).
- Questioning the interest of the social worker—in particular, whether he or she can understand the client's situation without having had a similar

experience (James, 2008). Also, feeling that the social worker couldn't possibly have a genuine interest because helping clients is his or her job.

- Misinterpreting a message as a result of feeling put down. Responding defensively, feeling rejected, or expecting criticism or punishment without realistic cause.
- Perceptions that their thoughts and feelings are extreme, and questioning whether others, even those with similar experiences, can understand (Knight, 2006).
- Trauma survivors seeing others' behaviors or reactions as signs of betrayal, abandonment, and rejection; assigning others the motivations, thoughts, and feelings of those who caused their trauma (Knight, 2006).
- Relating to the social worker in a clinging, dependent way or excessively seeking praise and reassurance. Attempting to please the social worker or group members by giving excessive compliments and praise or by ingratiating behavior.
- Attempting to engage the social worker socially, offering personal favors, presenting gifts, or seeking special considerations, and in some cases having dreams or fantasies about the social worker.
- Difficulty in discussing problems because the social worker or a group member reminds them of someone else in appearance (Nichols, 2006).

Although such reactions originate in an individual's past, the associated behaviors are manifest in the here and now. This raises an interesting question: Are transference reactions best resolved by focusing on the past so that an individual gains insight into their origins? In instances in which reactions driven by past experiences are played out in the present, they can be resolved by encouraging clients to engage in a deliberate examination of their current inaccurate and distorted perceptions. Of course, when clients bring up experiences and circumstances from their past, brief historical excursions often facilitate productive emotional catharsis and lead to an understanding of the origins of their patterns of thinking, feeling, and behaving. Moreover, in working with a client who has experienced ongoing traumatic stressors (e.g., physical or sexual abuse, sexual assault, war, injury, or other crisis events), probing and exploring these experiences may be vital to gaining an understanding of, and recovery from, the detrimental effects of those experiences (James, 2008; Knight, 2006; Rosenthal, 1988; Wartel, 1991).

Managing Transference Reactions

When a client's behavior is indicative of a possible transference reaction after any necessary examination of the past, it is important to shift the focus to his or her here-and-now feelings because such reactions generally cause the client to disengage from the relationship and from productive work, ultimately undermining the helping process. To assist you in managing transference reactions, we offer the following guidelines:

1. *Be open to the possibility that the client's reaction is not unrealistic and may be a product of your behavior.* If introspection indicates that the client's behavior is realistic, respond authentically by owning responsibility for your behavior.

2. *Be aware of the fact that a transference reaction can be triggered by a realistic appraisal of historical and current experiences of racial or cultural individuals*, in which feelings of anger, resentment, fear, social distance, and power are aroused. It is important that you acknowledge, rather than dismiss, minimize, or attempt to alter the client's perception, even though doing so may be uncomfortable.

3. *When a client appears to expect you to respond in an anti-therapeutic manner, as professionals or significant others have in the past, it is important to respond differently*, thereby disconfirming those expectations. Responses that contrast sharply with client expectations can result in an experience of temporary disequilibrium. Therefore, it is important that you assist the client to differentiate the experience from past figures or experiences. As a result, the client must deal with you and others as unique and real people rather than perpetuating expectations based on past experiences. Responding differently and authentically can be instrumental when reactions are based on historically oriented racial or cultural conflicts. In essence, the here and now is your behavior.

4. *Assist the client in determining the immediate source of distorted perceptions by exploring how and when the feelings emerged.* Carefully explore antecedents and meaning attributions associated with the feelings. Avoid attempting to correct distorted perceptions by immediately revealing your actual feelings. By first exploring how and when problematic feelings emerged, you can help clients expand their awareness of the schematic patterns in which they generalize and make faulty meaning

attributions and unwarranted assumptions based on past experience. The aim is to help an individual to recognize feelings that emanate from their conditioned perceptual sets and move toward reality-based feelings and reactions.

5. *After a client has recognized the unrealistic nature of his or her feelings and gains an awareness of the distortions that produced those feelings,* sharing your actual feelings can be reassuring.

6. *Examine problematic feelings and assist individuals to explore whether they have experienced similar reactions in other relationships.* Through exploration, clients may recognize patterns of distortions that create difficulties in other relationships.

Being aware of and managing transference reactions involves using a range of facilitative and communication skills. For example, it is important to acknowledge and be empathetic to clients' distorted or unrealistic feelings as you attempt to help them recognize their influence in their relationship with you or others. Seeking concreteness by specifically exploring the basis for a client's conclusions can assist the client in identifying the source of his or her perception or feelings and pinpoint when and how these feelings emerged. You can further draw out clients' reactions by using reflection to connect separate but related events to their patterned response in another relationship. For example:

Social worker: You know, when we were discussing your feelings toward your mother a few weeks ago, you said essentially the same thing.

Client: I'm not sure what you mean.

Social worker: You said your mother has always ignored or dismissed your feelings, when you tried to talk to her and she disapproves of the men you are dating.

As the exchange continues, notice how the social worker and the client further clarify transference reactions, in this case directed toward the social worker:

Client: Wow, the weeks sure did go by fast. *[Long pause]* I don't have much to talk about today. *[Ambivalence]*

Social worker [sensing the client is struggling with something]: I gather you didn't really feel ready for your appointment with me today *[empathic response]*. How did you feel about coming? *[Open-ended, probing]*

Client: I didn't want to come, but I thought I should. Actually, it has been an eventful week. But I didn't feel that I wanted to tell you about what has been happening. *[Possible transference reaction; seeking approval]*

Social worker: Sounds like you've had some misgivings about confiding certain things in me. *[Paraphrasing, responding to reaction]* Could you share with me some of your thoughts that you had about confiding in me? *[Focusing on the here and now]*

Client: I wanted you to think of me as a desirable person *[seeking approval, praise]*.

Social worker: First, let me tell you that I do not have thoughts about whether you are a desirable person. I'd like to explore where your doubts or fears that I don't see you as a desirable person came from. Have I done or said something that conveyed that to you? *[Probing, addressing perceptions and feelings]*

Client [thinks for a moment]: Well, no, nothing that I can think of.

Social worker: Yet I gather those feelings are very real to you. I wonder when you first became aware of those feelings.

Client [after a pause]: Well, I think it was when we began to talk about my feelings that guys are just interested in me for what they can get. I guess I wondered if you thought I was a real dud. I wanted you to know it wasn't so, that a desirable person could be attracted to me.

Social worker: So you haven't wanted to risk it turning out bad and worrying about how I would feel if it did. *[Additive empathy, interpretation, exploring basis of feelings]*

In this scenario, the social worker continues to explore the unrealistic nature of the woman's perceptions and how they influence her behavior in other relationships. When you have observed a potential transference reaction, it is important to focus on the here and now. For example, by sensitively exploring the woman's reluctance to attend the session, the social worker not only resolved an emerging obstacle to productive work, she also helped the client to further explore the reasons for her doubts about her attractiveness. By doing so, the social worker expanded her awareness of the way in which her doubts distorted her perceptions of how others, including the social worker, viewed her. Moreover, through the exploration, the social worker was able to identify a basic misconception that had influenced the client's relationships with others and help her to relate more comfortably to the social worker.

Countertransference Reactions

The counterpart of transference is **countertransference**. Just as clients can experience unrealistic, unresolved, or unconscious thoughts and feelings, so can certain client situations, attributes, or behaviors arouse feelings and unconscious defensive patterns on the part of the social worker. Unmet needs of the social worker, unresolved family conflicts, gender, and parenting roles can be the basis for countertransference reactions. Marta, for example, in one of the overinvolved case examples earlier in the chapter, based her work with youth on her own experience with her family. In addition, fears and anxieties or feelings at an unconscious level about clients who are different may also prompt a reaction in the social worker. In consequence, he or she may deny or in some instances overestimate or underestimate his or her reaction so as to minimize the conflict.

Irrespective of the source, the social worker's thoughts and feelings interfere with his or her objectivity, causing an emotional response that effectively blocks productive interactions with a client. For example, a social worker who leads a treatment group reported that he has to constantly check his reactions to men in the group when certain topics are discussed: "I say to myself, not this BS again, you know, because I've been there and I know when they are messing around, because I did the same thing when I was in treatment. Sometimes, I want to yell at them, 'Man, I know what you are playing at.' I do a lot of self-talk because if I challenged them, I know that my doing so would change the tone of the group, which would not be at all helpful. My behavior would also be unprofessional, but I admit to you that at times it is hard."

Countertransference in the traditional sense is grounded in psychoanalytic theory in which the social worker's past experiences and conscious and unconscious emotional reactions influence his or her relationship with a client (Hayes, 2004; McWilliams, 1999). A more contemporary view is that the social worker's reactions, real and unreal, to a client can occur irrespective of origin and can be based on the social worker's own past or present experiences or client characteristics (James, 2008; Knight, 2006; Nichols, 2006). Proposing a more transactional approach, specifically that of the person-in-the environment, Fauth (2006) maintains that such reactions and behaviors may be related to stressful interpersonal events and the social worker's appraisal as to whether the situation was harmful, was threatening, or taxed his or her coping resources.

Consistent with Fauth's (2006) transactional stress theory, Knight (2006) and James (2008) assert that countertransference, including vicarious trauma, is a common reaction among professionals who are involved in crisis work and with trauma survivors. Salston and Figley (2004) also point to the consequences of trauma for professionals working with criminal victims. Countertransference in high-stress situations may also signal a stage of burnout. James and Gilliland (2001) note that crisis professionals may experience "reawakened unresolved thoughts and feelings" as a result of working with clients who have had similar experiences (p. 419). Maintaining a professional distance may be difficult, especially when the countertransference reaction is related to the trauma experiences and "horror stories" of immigrants and refugees (Potocky-Tripodi, 2002). In instances when a social worker experiences compassion fatigue or secondary trauma, there is a tendency to become overinvolved with a client. Neither situation is productive in that either one can severely impair a social worker's ability to work effectively with clients.

Should you find that you are experiencing any one of the aforementioned behaviors, you should seek supervision or consultation. Also, you should consider whether taking time off will assist you to refocus and reenergize your professional work.

Countertransference reactions also contaminate the helping relationships by producing distorted perceptions, blind spots, and anti-therapeutic emotional reactions or behaviors (Kahn, 1997). Selected reactions that can result in counterproductive dynamics are:

- The social worker lacks the skills to integrate anger or conflict resolution into his or her coping repertoire or personality. For example, when confronted by a client who is angry, the tendency may be to become unduly uncomfortable and attempt to divert the expression of such feelings.
- The social worker has unresolved feelings about rejections by significant others and finds it difficult to relate to clients who exhibit similar behavior.
- The social worker fails to resolve resentful feelings toward authority, resulting in, for example, over-identification with a rebellious adolescent.
- The social worker is controlling and overidentifying with clients who have similar problems and is blind to reciprocal behavior between clients—for example, taking sides when working with a couple in marital counseling.
- The social worker has an excessive need to be loved and admired and may behave seductively

TABLE 18-2 Typical Professional Countertransference Reactions

- Being unduly concerned about or protective of a client, becoming his or her champion or rescuer
- Having persistent dreams or erotic fantasies about clients
- Dreading or anticipating sessions with clients
- Feeling uncomfortable when discussing certain problems with a client, including those who have anxieties, and fears about those who are different
- Hostility directed toward a client or inability to empathize with a client; underestimating the dynamics of differences
- Blaming others exclusively for a client's difficulties
- Feeling bored, being drowsy, or tuning out a client
- Regularly being late or forgetting appointments with certain clients
- Consistently ending sessions early or extending them beyond the designated time
- Trying to impress or being unduly impressed by clients
- Being overly concerned about losing a client
- Arguing with or feeling defensive or hurt by a client's criticisms or actions
- Being overly solicitous and performing tasks that clients are capable of performing
- Probing into a client's sex life
- Liking or disliking certain types of clients (may also be reality based)
- Identifying with the role of an abuser in a trauma situation or feeling responsible for his or her pain
- Attempting to manage feelings that include minimizing the stories of trauma clients, being disgusted with clients, or acting in a voyeuristic manner

or strive to impress clients by inappropriate disclosure of personal information. Of course, selective self-disclosure in the form of empathic responsiveness can be beneficial (Goldstein, 1997). Raines (1996) suggests that self-disclosure decisions may be considered within a range of over- and underinvolvement; therefore, personal sharing should be rational and related to the current relationship.

Before discussing how to manage countertransference reactions, it is first important to identify the typical manifestations in which they can occur. Table 18-2 lists some of the indicators based on the work of Knight (2006) and Etherington (2000). Also take note of the similarities between this table and behaviors of over- and underinvolvement described in Table 18-1. Both sources illustrate behaviors or reactions that prompt you to take immediate appropriate corrective measures. Otherwise, they can contribute to the client's problem and ultimately impair the helping relationship.

Managing Countertransference Reactions

Ordinarily, the first step in resolving countertransference (and often all that is needed) is to engage in introspection. **Introspection** involves an analytical dialogue with yourself aimed at discovering the sources of your feelings, reactions, cognitions, and behaviors. Examples of questions that facilitate introspection include the following:

- "Why am I feeling uncomfortable with this client? What is going on inside me that I am not able to relate in a professional manner?"
- "How well do I manage my own anxiety, anger, or discomfort with the client or the situation?"
- "Why do I dislike (or feel bored, impatient, or irritated about) this client? Are my feelings rational, or does this client remind me of someone else or my own experience?"
- "What is happening inside of me that I don't face certain problems with this client? Am I afraid of a negative reaction on the client's part?"
- "What purpose was served by arguing with this client? Am I feeling defensive or threatened?"
- "Why did I talk so much or give so much advice? Did I feel a need to give something to the client?"
- "What's happening with me that I'm fantasizing or dreaming about this client?"
- "Why am I constantly taking sides in my work with couples (parents, minors, authority), thereby overlooking one side. Am I over- or underidentifying with certain clients, and if so, why?"
- "Could my own experience, personality, or feelings block my objectivity?"

Managing countertransference reaction requires a social worker's conscious assessment of the dynamics that aroused and subsequently triggered his or her reaction. As discussed earlier in the social worker–consultation scenario, an assessment would involve preparatory planning, self-reflection and awareness, and centering and focusing on the purpose and content of a session. The self-aware professional understands his or her own history and manages the consequences of his or her interactions with individuals in which there is a potential for a reaction (Hayes, 2004).

Introspection and self-assessment, as well as the ability to maintain appropriate boundaries and distance, will assist you in achieving or regaining a realistic perspective on your relationships with clients. Discussion of such topics should also be part of consultation with colleagues and supervisors, in which you expose and explore your feelings and obtain their perspective and advice. Just as clients are sometimes too close to their problems to view them objectively and thus benefit from seeing them from the vantage point of a social worker, so you can likewise benefit from the unbiased perspective of an uninvolved colleague, consultant, or supervisor. However, professionals who repeatedly experience countertransference reactions need professional help beyond mere introspection or the input of a colleague. Specifically, ongoing reactions limit their effectiveness and create ethical and relational barriers to effective work with clients.

Realistic Practitioner Reactions

Not all of your negative feelings toward certain clients are indicative of a negative countertransference reaction to the individual or to situations. Some clients are abrasive, arrogant, or obnoxious, act tough, have irritating mannerisms, or are exploitative of and cruel toward others. Even the most accepting social worker may have difficulty developing positive feelings toward such clients. We are, after all, only human; thus, we are not immune from disliking someone or feeling irritated, indifferent, or impatient at times. When faced with this behavior from clients, the inclination is to attach a label to the clients, thereby giving us permission to ignore them. Despite their behavior, however, clients are entitled to service in which their uniqueness, dignity, and worth are respected. In fact, it may be the absence of such respect in their interactions that has caused them to act in such a way that alienates, offends, or irritates others, leaving them isolated and confused about relational difficulties.

When you look beyond the offending behavior or attitude of some clients, you will often discover that beneath their facade are desirable, even admirable qualities and vulnerabilities. A social worker noted in an interview with one of the authors that "during my contact with minors, in particular when race is a factor (the social worker is white), most will affect a negative posture with a big attitude. However, the key is to hang in there and gain their trust. In many instances, trust allows you to access the youth's private world. In asking the simple question 'What happened to you?,' you may find that they have endured severe emotional and environmental deprivation, and in some cases physical or sexual abuse or other traumatic experiences, that have exceeded their coping ability and capacity to trust. Once you get past the behavior, you often find a fragile kid who has been exposed to a life that you can hardly imagine!" Furthermore, the social worker emphasized that, in spite of the youths' behavior, connecting with them necessitated acceptance and empathy. She also shared that there are days when she is tired of their behavior, and "I tell them so. Oddly enough, most respond to me in a very caring, sometimes humorous way."

Abrasive or aggressive clients may, however, need far more than warmth and acceptance. Such individuals need feedback about how certain aspects of their behavior offend you and others. Feedback can be extremely helpful if it is conveyed sensitively and expressed in the context of goodwill. In providing such feedback, you must be careful to avoid evaluative or blaming comments that tend to elicit defensiveness—for example, "You boast too much and dominate conversations" or "You don't consider other people's feelings when and say hurtful things." An individual is apt to be far more likely to be receptive to a message that describes a specific behavior. The same is true when a response and the associated feeling are personalized. The following descriptive message embodies ownership of feelings: "When you sneered at me just now, I felt defensive and resentful. You've done that several times before, and I find myself backing away from you each time. I'm concerned because I suspect that this is how you interact with others." The message is authentic, nonjudgmental, and expresses a genuine concern. Be aware, however, that such a message will be more productive once a sound working relationship has been established. As you point out the specifics of clients' behavior, you can encourage them to risk new behaviors and give them opportunities to learn and practice altering ways of interacting with you and others.

Sexual Attraction toward Clients

EP 1

Romantic or sexual feelings toward clients can be especially hazardous to the helping relationship, although such feelings are by no means uncommon. Most social workers have at some point in their careers experienced this type of reaction toward a client. A majority of those who responded to a survey believed the attraction to be mutual; others assumed that the client was unaware of their attraction. When the latter was the case, they believed the attraction did not have any harmful effects on the helping process. By contrast, therapists who believed clients were aware of their attraction understood the detrimental impact on the helping process (Strom-Gottfried, 1999a).

Acting on the attraction has long-lasting grievous consequences for clients. No doubt you have heard about a social worker who justified engaging in sexual activities with clients on the basis of helping them to feel loved or to overcome sexual problems. Such explanations are often thinly disguised and feeble rationalizations for exploiting clients. In other instances, justifications are based on the client's behavior toward the social worker. Irrespective of circumstance, this behavior is unacceptable. Intimate involvement with a client, whether emotional or physical, is always unethical.

The consequences of sexual involvement are devastating for social workers as well. When such behaviors are discovered, the offending individuals can be sanctioned, sued for unethical practice, and have their professional license or certification revoked, essentially removing them from the profession. Ethical standards of conduct established by licensing boards and the NASW Code of Ethics are unequivocal about dual relationships with clients, especially those of a sexual nature. The NASW Code of Ethics states: "The social worker should under no circumstance engage in sexual activities or sexual contact with current clients, whether such contact is consensual or forced" (Section 1.09a).

Managing such attraction appropriately is critical. As Strom-Gottfried notes, "Even a small incidence warrants the attention of the professional, particularly supervisors and educators, to assure that any measures available to reduce the incidence further is fully pursued" (1999a, p. 448). Persistent erotic fantasies about clients who are particularly vulnerable signals an impaired professional, and a more serious remedy is indicated. Effectively managing sexual attraction requires engaging in the corrective measures identified

earlier for unrealistic feelings and reactions—namely, introspection and consulting with a supervisor. Introspections may also reveal whether you are over- and underinvolved with a client.

We cannot state too strongly that you must not allow your romantic feelings about a client or those of a client toward you to go unchecked. It is also important that in your interactions with clients you take precautions in the manner in which you dress, communicate, and behave in order to avoid problematic situations.

MOTIVATING CHANGE

Overcoming Resistance

EP 7

People who do not readily embrace a behavioral change are often considered resistant. The notion of resistance has been used in a fashion that holds clients responsible for their behavior, which, of course, tends to foster resistance and a reactive response. Without further exploration of the reason for resistance, the individual acquires a label that sticks, leading to the conclusion that he or she is opposed to change. Behaviors such as holding back, disengaging, or in some way subverting or sabotaging change efforts, whether knowingly or not, without open discussion, and any action or attitude that impedes the course of therapeutic work are thought to be general signs of resistance (Meyer, 2001; Nichols & Schwartz, 2004).

There are multiple factors to be considered in understanding behavior that may be assessed as resistance. In cross-cultural, cross-racial relationships, for example, Lum (2004) noted that resistance can be prominent in interactions with persons of color. Resistance may be recognized by the client's "minimal involvement, [being] reserved or being superficially pleasant" (pp. 152–153). The basis for resistance on the part of minority individuals and entire communities is rooted in a lack of trust or confidence in professionals. Establishing trust and reciprocity in relationships is a major thrust in overcoming the reluctance that people of color have about seeking help from agencies "that are controlled and dominated by whites" (Lum, 2004, p. 152).

Resistance as conceptualized by Freud is considered to be a normative, healthy, self-protective response, experienced by all human beings. In this light, ambivalence, anxiety, or opposition to change is a universal phenomenon, as anyone who has attempted to break long-established habits knows all too well. Indeed, the force of habit is relentless; hence, making a change often means foregoing gratifications or coping head-on with frightening or aversive situations or risking new behavior in the face of unknown consequences. Even though the status quo may cause pain, difficulty, or distress, there is a certain level of comfort in the familiar, and the consequences of habitual behaviors are predictable. Realistically, it is not uncommon for people to experience mixed feelings about change, both desiring it and being hesitant or ambivalent. Opposing feelings generally coexist—that is, part of them is motivated, even as another part strives to maintain the status quo.

An individual's hesitancy or reluctance to embrace change may be caused by his or her lack of understanding or misunderstanding about the nature of service to be provided or of a specific intervention. Should this occur, it is vital to explain fully the nature of the service or intervention (informed consent). This discussion should also clarify the roles of the individual and permit voluntary clients to feel free to decide whether to proceed with the therapy. With involuntary clients, the discussion would clarify what is required of them and where there is room for choice. In either case, a contract with the client in which roles are clarified, goals are made specific, and the rationale for specific interventions is clear can ease a client's apprehension. To further deal with feelings of uncertainty, clients should be given the opportunity to ask questions and discuss their misgivings.

It is possible that some clients become so caught up in a transference resistance that their behavior creates an obstacle to change (Nichols, 2006). Rather than focusing on change, they become preoccupied with their thoughts and perceptions, including unrealistic expectations of you. In this sense, they may not be resistant or opposed to change; however, their unresolved feelings get in the way. Unless you recognize and assist such individuals in resolving these feelings by discussing them in a realistic perspective, their progress is stalled and they may prematurely terminate the contact, convinced that their perceptions and feelings are accurate.

Have you ever been inclined to consider clients as resistant when they hesitated or were opposed to the direction that you wished them to take to resolve their situation? To understand resistance as a normative self-protective function, think about a situation in which you were told that you needed to make certain changes, whether at work (e.g. complete your case notes on

time), at home (e.g., be more helpful around the house), or a relationship (e.g., be more attentive). Reflect on:

- Your emotional response
- Your behavioral response
- Your reaction

Now transfer your responses to clients, especially those who are meeting with you for the first time. Did you perhaps use verbal ploys such as "I couldn't do that; it just wouldn't be me; I've tried that and it doesn't work; I understand what you're saying but" to justify your behavior? Recognizing your own feelings of ambivalence can help you to better understand and explore clients' ambivalent feelings and to assist them in weighing the advantages and disadvantages of making a change. Indeed, a first step in managing potential opposition to change is to focus on a client's underlying here-and-now feelings. As clients think through their feelings and reassess the implications of maintaining the status quo, the scales often tilt in favor of change.

Many of the verbal ploy statements that you or a client might use may not necessarily indicate opposition to change. Instead, careful exploration is needed when a client says that he or she cannot complete a particular action. Statements of this sort can be followed by rambling or dwelling on unimportant information as the client attempts to make some sense of the situation, to tell his or her story, to relieve anxiety and catharsis by venting frustration or airing grievances. If a client appears to have reached an impasse, however, and seems unable to move beyond this point, you can safely conclude that opposition is involved and shift the focus to exploring the factors that underlie this opposition. Other instances in which a client's hesitancy or ambivalence is not a sign of opposition and other factors should be considered are whether:

- The individual has the resources to change (e.g., developmental, social, cognitive)
- There are environmental barriers (e.g., economic, political, cultural) that can impede change
- Relational barriers may be present in the client–practitioner relationship

Reactance Theory

Reactance theory provides a more fruitful perspective for considering opposition to change with involuntary clients. Rather than blaming, dismissing, or concluding that an individual is opposed to change, this theory leads you to objectively anticipate the range of responses to be expected when valued freedoms and autonomy are threatened (Brehm, 1976; Markland, Ryan, Tobin, & Rollnick, 2005). First, some individuals may try to regain their freedom directly by attempting to take back what has been threatened (e.g., choice). Second, a frequent response is to restore freedom by implication or to "find the loophole" in which they engage in superficial compliance while violating the spirit of requirements (e.g., I will sit at my desk, but I won't do any work). Third, threatened behaviors and beliefs are apt to become more valued than ever before. Finally, they may perceive you as the person or source of the threat, in which case you are faced with hostile or aggressive behavior (R. H. Rooney, 1992).

Reactance theory also lends itself to proactive strategies designed to reduce this kind of behavior. For example, individuals who perceive global pressure to change their lifestyles are likely to experience reactance. Conversely, they are less likely to react if those pressures are narrowed in scope and the change effort emphasizes behaviors that remain free. Second, reactance is likely to be reduced if the client perceives that he or she has at least some constrained choices (R. H. Rooney, 1992). Understanding the client's perspective on the situation and avoiding labeling can also act to reduce reactance (p. 135).

Change Strategies

In the helping process, as you encounter behavior that can be characterized as resistant or reactive, it is advisable for you to assess the client's behavior in light of the stages of change model (Prochaska, DiClemente, & Norcross, 1992) discussed in Chapter 17. To refresh your memory, change is believed to progress through a sequence of stages, beginning with the *precontemplation stage* ("Leaving the children unsupervised for a short time was not a problem") and progression to *contemplation* ("I am willing to look at the harm that resulted from leaving the children unsupervised"). Self-evaluation can occur at this stage, leading to a goal. For example, a male who batters might deny that his behavior is abusive by saying, for example, "I had little choice; she was in my face," and progress to a point in which he might say, "I am willing to look at my behavior," at which point self-reflection and self-evaluation subsequently leads to a goal of examining "the effects of my behavior on self and significant others." Of course,

some individuals may argue for the status quo or discount, minimize, or excuse their behavior (Miller & Rollnick, 2013).

Similarly, you may believe that utilizing the stage change strategy shifts the focus away from clients' behavior. Research has shown, however, that a focus on a specific cognition or behavior can be a mediator between actions and change and ultimately increases the frequency of desired behaviors (Nichols, 2006). In addition, how you respond to the individual can create cognitive consonance or dissonance. For example, when a mother says, "This was the one time that I left the kids at home by themselves," your inductive open-ended question might be, "What would others say about leaving the kids at home alone?" or "When the children were home alone this one time, what happened?" In this way, you keep the change dialogue going, maintaining a focus on the specific problematic behavior. In addition to the change model, you will want to critique the appropriateness of the strategies discussed in Chapter 12 with involuntary individuals. Each of the strategies discussed is intended to appeal to the individual's self-interest and his or her involvement in the process of change. *Motivational congruence*, *agreeable mandate*, or *let's make a deal strategy*, for example, counter the notion that certain involuntary clients are opposed to change. Instead, both you and the client engage in exploring common ground in which mandated goals can be defined and achieved. With the agreeable mandate strategy, an involuntary client may transition through the stages of change, moving from being involuntary to a level of voluntary status. Keep in mind that when individuals feel free to make up their own minds, they are more likely to become engaged. Being able to do so is crucial because pressure often engenders an opposing force of reactance.

Motivational Interviewing

Let's now examine principles and techniques related to motivating change as a strategy for assisting clients to move forward in the change effort.

Change talk (Miller & Rollnick, 2002), an aspect of motivational interviewing, is an adaptation of the stages of change model. Motivational interviewing is defined as a "client-centered, directive method for enhancing motivation to change by exploring and resolving ambivalence" that can be integrated with other treatment approaches (Miller &

EP 8

Rollnick, 2002, p. 25). The "spirit" of the method is guided by the following:

- **Collaborative partnership** between the social worker and the client, developed in a climate that is conducive to change, in which the client's experience and perceptions are honored
- **Evocation**, the social worker's aim to elicit and draw out a client's intrinsic motivation, based on the belief that the resources and motivation for change are within the client relative to his or her goals, perceptions, and values
- **Autonomy** of clients and their capacity and right of self-direction, including the right to accept or not accept the counsel of the social worker, which facilitates clients' informed decision making

In essence, change becomes possible when the relationship between you and the client is collaborative rather than coercive, his or her self-determination is honored, and the aim of the interview is to explore and draw out what motivates the client. In the course of your interaction with clients, supportive and facilitative skills are instrumental for engaging them and for enhancing their motivation to change. In contrast, blaming, punishing, or arguing with clients to gain their acceptance of and compliance with change and using your authority to confront or coerce them are generally counterproductive. Markland, Ryan, Tobin, and Rollnick (2005), citing the compatibility of self-determination with motivational interviewing, emphasize that control rewards, or punishment intended to motivate, are external factors that are less likely to result in change.

Guiding Principles of Motivational Interviewing

Four key principles define motivational interviewing: *engaging*, *focusing*, *evoking*, and *planning*. **Engaging** refers to the process of creating a helpful connection and a strong working relationship between the social worker and the client. Once that is established, a **focused conversation** about change and the direction of the change can occur. **Evoking** is aimed at eliciting the client's motivation to change rather than imposing a change solution that is guided or thought to be appropriate by the social worker (Markland et al., 2005). Once this work is done, the social worker and the client develop a plan of action to achieve a change goal (Miller & Rollnick, 2013). The social worker–client

interactions are framed by OARS, an acronym for open-ended questions, affirmations supporting and encouraging the client's efforts to change, and reflections that echo what the client has said using different words (Miller & Rollnick, 2013). Also critical to the change process is an understanding that ambivalence or resistance is normal. Rather than challenging such behavior, the social worker highlights the discrepancy that exists between a current behavior and the change goal.

The spirit of motivational interviewing is consistent with the values and principles of social work practice, including empathy, acceptance, and supporting individual self-efficacy and self-direction. For example, consider the case of the mother who left her children unsupervised. Paraphrasing with empathy would include a statement such as "It must difficult to be a single parent, working all day and then coming home to…." This statement conveys to the mother that you are attempting to understand her situation, without judging or blaming her as a parent. In exploring a potential underlying issue related to leaving the children unsupervised, combined with an empathetic response, the mother's motivation to engage in developing problem-solving goals is strengthened.

VIDEO CASE EXAMPLE

The principles and the spirit of motivational interviewing are summarized in the video "How Can I Help?" In the beginning of the session, Judy, the client, recounts the numerous difficulties she has experienced during the past week. Responding with empathy, Peter, the social worker, asks her, "How can I help?" *[engaging]*. At this point, Judy responds, "Well, I guess I need a bus card." As Judy continues, she tells Peter how having a bus card will help her. In particular, a bus card would make it easier for her to attend her group sessions and leave a urine sample for analysis *[focusing]*. Supporting her self-efficacy, specifically her self-confidence, so that she is able to accomplish the necessary change tasks *[evoking]*, Peter reinforces her ability to do so. In general, a discussion of the content of a client's difficulties can yield cues as to the sources of his or her difficulties, which otherwise may be thought of as resistance (collaborative partnership).

Contrast Peter's behavior in this case with the social worker's views of the mother in the case consultation scenario discussed at the beginning of this chapter. Like the mother in that case, at first glance, Judy could have been perceived as less than committed to change. In this regard, instead of exploring the ways in which he could help, it would have been easy for Peter to ignore the numerous barriers that she detailed and thereby conclude that Judy lacked sufficient motivation to change. Additionally, Peter's authentic and empathetic responses conveyed his goodwill and concern that Judy's progress could become bogged down; it also reaffirmed the social worker's helpful intent and desire to work out whatever difficulties have arisen.

Motivational interviewing emphasizes that the client is responsible for change and that clients tend to be motivated to change when they are involved in the process. When clients appear to be resistant, which is not considered to be oppositional, the social worker avoids arguing for change. Arguing with clients has a limited effect on their behavior and simply invites resistance. Resistance signals the need for a different response.

VIDEO CASE EXAMPLE

Returning to the video "How Can I Help?," after discussing her inability to pay for a bus card and her concerns about her future housing situation, the client offers a solution *[autonomy]*. Specifically, the client asks Peter, the social worker, to write a letter that documents her progress so that she can be considered for a supportive housing program for women and their children. Here again, Peter affirms the client's self-efficacy. As the session progresses, Peter brings up the fact that the client has a diagnosis of depression. Clearly, the client is ambivalent about the diagnosis. Peter responds by exploring the source of the client's feelings and acknowledges her troubling thoughts about the diagnosis *[open-ended questions]*. In this instance, Peter opens up the client's feelings by asking her whether she knows the symptoms of depression. Rolling with her resistance, Peter continues, asking her, "Well, do you mind if we explore a little bit about whether or not this is depression?" With her permission, Peter summarizes moods or behaviors that are generally associated with depression. In effect, he is supporting her

autonomy by providing her with information, which she is free to accept or reject. As she describes her mood and behavior, in particular her sleeping patterns in which her child is mostly unsupervised, Peter queries that behavior. Rather than point to the consequence of unacceptable parenting, Peter asks, "Is it okay with you?"

As they continue, Peter uses the principle of discrepancy. Discrepancy (or confrontation, discussed in Chapter 17) focuses on an individual's expressed goal or value when his or her behavior indicates otherwise. A primary motivation for this client is keeping her child. She talks about the various steps that she has taken to prevent the reoccurrence of a child protection intervention. Peter praises her for wanting to be a good parent, but later he points out to her the discrepancy between her desire and her sleeping patterns and the potential risk to her child. Emphasizing the mismatch in the results of her perceived and actual behaviors relative to her goal of wanting to keep her child causes her to examine the situation. Confronting the client about the situation and then collaborating with her to sort through the pros and cons of her behavior places the responsibility on her as to whether she wants to seek help for her depression and prevent the intervention of child protective services. As you watch the interactions between Peter and the client, notice how the social worker continues to explore and draw out what motivates the client.

Motivational interviewing assumes that ambivalence is normal and further that ambivalent or resistant behavior is not in and of itself indicative of an individual's pathology or incapacity (Miller & Rollnick, 2002). As clients experience problems, they can, like Judy in the video, become stuck. The role of the social worker is to help them reach their own conclusions through the skillful use of communication skills like listening; open-ended questions intended to elicit information about their views, beliefs, and values; and facilitative skills, such as support, acceptance, and empathy. Acceptance is critical to the relationship in that it contributes to a relational climate in which an individual is free to openly discuss his or her feelings and misgivings about change without being judged, criticized, or blamed. When motivational interviewing is done well, it is the client's goals rather than those of the social worker that have center stage. By skillfully drawing out the intrinsic motivation, it is the client rather than the social worker who puts forth his or her own solution. "It is the client who gives voice to concerns, reasons for change, self-efficacy, and intentions to change" (Miller & Rollick, 2002, p. 39).

The essence of helping is to develop a relationship with individuals in which the essential elements of acceptance, expectation, support, and simulation are prominent (Perlman, 1957). Encouraging growth in clients depends on your critical assessment about how and when to utilize these elements in your interactions with them. Above all, what you do should facilitate problem solving in the context of a relationship that is intended to help a client to change. The following discussion highlights additional techniques that can be used to enhance a client's confidence and motivation.

Positive Connotation

Positive connotation is a technique that is useful in reducing the threat level associated with a client's thoughts and feelings in the face of change. In positive connotation, constructive intentions are attributed to what would otherwise be regarded as a client's undesirable or negative behavior. This allows clients to save face and protect their self-esteem when they risk talking about their feelings or perceptions. The goal of positive connotation is not to condone opposition or to reinforce the client's perceptions. Instead, consistent with the strengths perspective, the objective is to minimize clients' need to defend themselves and to safeguard a sense of self.

In using this technique, you recognize that the meaning ascribed to the behavior can be viewed in both positive and negative lights, depending on one's vantage point. For example, when a client's behavior or feelings appear to oppose change, thereby becoming an obstacle to progress, you are more than likely to view his or her behavior as negative. From the perspective of the client, however, the same behavior has a positive intent. For example, a client canceled an appointment. Even though she showed up the following week, during the session she was mostly silent, barely engaged, and her body language indicated that she was uncomfortable. Exploration of her behavior revealed that she resented the behavior of the social worker, whom she perceived as pressuring her to follow a certain course of action. In the eyes of the social worker, the client's

behavior was problematic. Conversely, the client saw her behavior as protecting her right to be self-directed. The usefulness of this technique is that it allows you to explore and understand clients' perceptions and subsequent reactions relative to your behavior as well as theirs.

Redefining Problems as Opportunities for Growth

The technique of **redefining problems as growth opportunities** is a close relative of positive connotation because it also involves **relabeling** or **reframing**. Both clients and social workers tend to view problems negatively. Moreover, clients often view remedial courses of action as "necessary evils," dwelling on the threat involved in risking new behaviors. Therefore, it is often helpful to reformulate problems and essential tasks as opportunities for growth. Relabeling or reframing emphasizes the positives—that is, the benefits of change rather than the discomfort, fear, and other costs of modifying one's behavior. At the same time, it is important that you not convey an unrealistically positive attitude. A client's fears and threats about the risk of change are very real to them. Thus, being unduly optimistic may simply convey a lack of understanding on your part.

Neither reframing nor relabeling minimizes clients' problems or ignores fears in risking new behaviors. Both do, however, enable clients to view their difficulties in a fuller perspective that embodies positive as well as negative factors. The following are examples of how problem situations might be relabeled as opportunities for growth:

- **Relabeling:** A teenager in a foster home continues to be on the run because the foster parents insist on adhering to a nighttime curfew. The teenager defends this behavior of refusing to return to the home because the foster parents "are unreasonable." The social worker acknowledges that returning to the foster home is a challenge; however, doing so deals with the problem head-on and is an opportunity to work out the difficulties with the foster parents rather than avoiding, which has been the youth's pattern.
- **Reframing:** A youth feels embarrassed about taking a battery of vocational tests and attending a vocational-technical school rather than attending college. The social worker acknowledges his discomfort but emphasizes that taking the tests offer

an opportunity to learn more about his aptitudes and to expand his choices in planning his future. In another example of reframing, a woman is apprehensive about leaving her abusive spouse. The social worker empathizes but points out that leaving her spouse will allow her to have the kind of life that she wants for herself and her children.

In some instances, clients fail to make progress toward their goals because of the persistence of pervasive particular patterns of behavior. Your effort to encourage or offer a different perspective by redefining, reframing, or relabeling can be met with a dismissal of your appraisal. For example, the clients may intellectualize, hold other people or circumstances responsible for their difficulties, or be reluctant to examine or acknowledge their part in creating the situation. Because such patterns of behavior often create an impasse, it is important that you recognize and handle them. Confronting clients with discrepancies between expressed goals and behaviors that prevent accomplishment of those goals is often needed to break an impasse. Because Chapter 17 discussed confrontation at length, the discussion here is limited to a specific type of confrontation: *therapeutic binds*.

Therapeutic Binds

This technique is used in those instances in which a client stubbornly clings to self-defeating behaviors that perpetuate his or her difficulties. In such instances, placing the client in a **therapeutic bind** may be the impetus needed to modify the problematic behaviors. The intent of the technique is to confront clients with their self-defeating behavior in such a way that they must either modify the behavior or own responsibility for choosing to perpetuate the difficulties despite their expressed intentions to the contrary (Goldenberg & Goldenberg, 2004; Nichols & Schwartz, 2004). The only way out of a therapeutic bind, unless one chooses to acknowledge no intention of changing, is to make constructive changes. In this regard, use of the therapeutic bind discrepancy is similar to motivational interviewing.

Following are some examples of situations in which therapeutic binds have been used successfully. Note that the social worker points out the specific inconsistent behavior relative to the client's stated goal:

- Despite efforts to resolve fears of being rejected in relationships with others, a client continued to decline social invitations and made no effort to reach out to others. The social worker asked her about her apparent choice to continue her social isolation. "You can either risk being with others or continue as you are, but you said that you wanted your life to be different."

- A supervisor complained to an Employee Assistance Program (EAP) social worker about conflict with other members on his team. In exploring the situation, the supervisor admitted that he consistently made unilateral decisions despite repeated feedback and negative reactions from team members. The social worker asked, "Is it your decision that it is more important for you to be in control rather than to improve your relationships with members of your team?"

- An adolescent persisted in being truant from school, violating family rules, and engaging in antisocial behaviors despite his assertion that he wanted to be independent. The social worker countered that he "seemed unprepared to use his freedom wisely," pointing out that if he continued to get in trouble, the juvenile court judge would further limit his choices unless his desire to be independent included setting limits on his behavior.

- In marital counseling, a wife constantly brought up her husband's previous infidelity despite expressing a desire to strengthen their marriage. When this occurred, the husband's response was to withdraw and disengage from the relationship. Presenting the wife with the contradiction in her behavior, the social worker stated, "Despite your claim of wanting to preserve the marriage, by your behavior it appears to be more important for you to continue to talk about your husband's previous behavior."

In using the therapeutic bind technique, it is vital to observe the guidelines for ethical confrontation, thereby avoiding clobbering or alienating the client. In this way, being empathetic as you ask a reflective question about the apparent contradiction or conclusion can be experienced by the client as a more respectful form of confrontation leading to self-reflection. Be aware, however, that a therapeutic bind is a potent but high-risk technique, and you should use it sparingly. In the best of circumstances, clients can experience an "aha" moment, which permits an opportunity for moving forward. When the technique is used, care should be taken to modify its upsetting effect with empathy, concern, and sensitive exploration of the dynamics behind the self-defeating patterns. Above all, the technique should be used to assist the client and not as a confrontational response to your frustrations about the client's contradictory behavior.

SUMMARY

This chapter described barriers to change with individuals, including relational dynamics that can occur in the social worker–client relationship and racial and cultural barriers. In this chapter we also described relational reactions that can occur as a result of your real or imagined perceptions of clients or that may derive from clients' perceptions of you. We emphasized assessing reactions and behaviors that are essential to creating a relational bond and a climate that is conducive to problem solving. Any bond that is created between you and the client in which you have and act on a sexual attraction is unacceptable and unethical and has severe consequences.

Relational reactions, including resistance, are normal manifestations of human behavior and, therefore, may not be indicative of opposition to change. In view of this reality, this chapter discussed at length techniques for recognizing and managing these reactions and increasing the likelihood of change. This chapter also emphasized that barriers to change can be the result of both micro and macro factors—for example, limited resources or environmental influences that are beyond the control of the client and therefore should be explored and addressed.

COMPETENCY NOTES

EP 1   Demonstrate Ethical and Professional Behavior
- Use self-reflection and self-regulation to manage personal values and maintain professionalism in practice situations.

In working with clients, social workers are required to act as professionals, and to understand their reactions to client. Understanding self and reflection are factors that aid managing behavior that can prevent developing a working alliance with clients that influence problem solving. In instances where the relationship has become fractured, it is important to take steps to minimize the risk to the relationship.

- Demonstrate professional demeanor in behavior, appearance, and oral, written, and electronic communication.

When the client reacts in a manner that is counterproductive to helping, social workers engage in self evaluation so that they understand their personal bias and values in order to maintain professional behavior in the interactions with clients. In developing and maintaining a working relationship with clients, social workers engage in behavior that is consistent with ethical codes of conduct.

EP 2   Engage Diversity and Difference in Practice
- Apply and communicate understanding of the importance of diversity and difference in shaping life experiences in practice at the micro, mezzo, and macro levels.

Social workers understand human behavior and this understanding guides interactions with clients. In some instances, the use of empathy as a facilitative skill can aid in understanding the client and to maintaining a relationship. Social workers strive to understand the relational dynamics that can occur as a result of differences between themselves and clients diverse backgrounds. It is equally important that social workers examine their behavior so they avoid contributing counterproductive relational interactions. Cultural competence includes self-awareness of biases and perceptions in engaging clients from diverse backgrounds. Working with clients also involves understanding how their behavior and client's experience with systems that of systems respond in that result in a sensitivity to biased judgments and discriminatory practices.

- Apply self-awareness and self-regulation to manage the influence of personal biases and values in working with diverse clients and constituencies.

Self-awareness and self regulation are important to maintaining professional behavior in client situations to avoid becoming over or under involved that may influence your professional response to client or situations.

EP 6   Engage with Individuals, Families, Groups, Organizations, and Communities
- Apply knowledge of human behavior and the social environment, person-in-environment, and other multidisciplinary theoretical frameworks to engage with clients and constituencies.

Social workers monitor their reactions to clients and to client situations to ensure that their conduct is ethical and professional.

- Use empathy, reflection, and interpersonal skills to effectively engage clients and constituencies.

When a social worker react to a client, self-reflection is advised. Understanding self can aid the social worker to respond, using facilitative skills in order to develop and maintain a productive relationship.

EP 7   Assess Individuals, Families, Groups, Organizations, and Communities
- Collect and organize data, and apply critical thinking to interpret information from clients and constituencies.

Assessment is a continuous process that includes assessing both client and social worker behavior in instances where progress toward a desired outcome becomes stalled. Identifying and responding to the factors that may contribute to client's reluctance or hesitation rather than labeling the behavior is critical to problem solving. It is also important to explore factors that bolster clients' motivation and confidence.

- Apply knowledge of human behavior and the social environment, person-in-environment, and other multidisciplinary theoretical frameworks in the analysis of assessment data from clients and constituencies.

Human behavior has a purpose. In working with clients, a nonjudgmental attitude and positive regard is critical understanding the reason for certain behavior that may present as clients attempt to move forward toward a preferred outcome. In doing so, you create an atmosphere of hope that can enhance motivation.

EP 8   Intervene with Individuals, Families, Groups, Organizations, and Communities
- Critically choose and implement interventions to achieve practice goals and enhance capacities of clients and constituencies.

In working with clients, it is important to use strategies that will help them to resolve problems. Client may initially engage in, or present behavior that without further exploration may be considered to be opposition to change. In understanding human behavior, social workers can engage and involve clients in a manner that can reduce their reactions and help them to move forward in achieving a desired outcome.

SKILL DEVELOPMENT EXERCISES
in Managing Relational Dynamics

1. Think about what your thoughts and reactions might be in the following situations. Then assess the nature of your reaction.
   - You are an only child. Your client has four children and the house is a mess. The oldest child, age 14, complains that her mother rarely pays attention to her.
   - Both of your parents were heavy drinkers, and at times they were difficult. Your client becomes abusive to his wife and children when he has been drinking.
   - You grew up in a middle-class family. A majority of the clients that you work with are poor, and many live in homes where there is evidence of rodents.
   - A coworker in the residential facility for minors where you work has posted pictures of former residents on his Facebook page, indicating that these clients are friends.

2. Review the case examples in this chapter in which the social worker was over- or underinvolved. As a colleague, what advice would you offer? What are the ethical and legal implications of the social worker's behavior in these cases?

3. After reading the section on cross-cultural barriers, what did you learn that could inform your practice with clients who are different?

4. Reflect on an occasion in which you had a strong reaction to a client. How would you handle the situation after reading this chapter?

5. Develop a checklist for yourself, using the barriers to change discussed in this chapter. Use the checklist as a self-assessment tool that you can apply in your work with clients.

6. Consider how you would integrate stages of change and motivational interviewing in your practice with clients.

SKILL DEVELOPMENT EXERCISES
in Managing Relational Reactions and Opposition

The following exercises are intended to assist you in expanding your skills in responding appropriately to relational reactions and opposition to change. Study each client statement and determine whether a relational reaction or opposition to change might be involved. Then write the response you would give if you were the social worker. Compare your response with the modeled social worker response provided at the end of the exercises. Bear in mind that the modeled response represents one of many possible appropriate responses.

Client Statements

1. *Male client [has been discussing feelings of rejection and self-doubt after his partner broke up with him; suddenly he looks down, sighs, then looks up]:* Say, did I tell you I got promoted at work?

2. *Female client, age 23 [to male social worker, age 25]:* I've been feeling very close to you these past weeks. I was wondering if you could hold me in your arms for just a moment.

3. *Male client, age 27 [agitated]:* I've been coming to see you for 8 weeks, and things haven't changed a bit. I'm beginning to question whether you are able to help me.

4. *Delinquent on probation, age 16:* I think it's crazy to have to come here every week. You don't have to worry about me. I'm not getting into any trouble.

5. *Female in welfare-to-work program:* Sure, you say you want to help me. All you social workers are just alike. You don't understand the pressure I have to get a good job in the time I have left on welfare. If you really want to help, you would increase the time I have left.

6. *Client, age 27 [to male social worker]:* I've just never been able to trust men. My old man was an alcoholic, and the only thing you could depend on with him was that he'd be drunk when you needed him most.

7. *Male client [to female mental health social worker]:* Sometimes I really felt I was cheated in life, you know, with parents who didn't give a damn about what happened to me. I think about you—how warm and caring you are, and—I know it sounds crazy but I wish I'd had you for a mother. Sometimes I even daydream about it.

8. *Client [after an emotional prior session, the client yawns, looks out the window, and comments]:* Not much to talk about today. Nothing much has happened this week.

9. *Male client, age 24 [in fifth session]:* I have this thing where people never measure up to my expectations. I know I expect too much, and I always end up feeling let down.

10. *Middle-aged minority male [challenging]:* I suppose you see me in the usual stereotype, you people have for [minority] males. I want you to know that I'm ambitious and want to do right by my family. I just need a job right now.

Modeled Social Worker Responses

1. "Congratulations! No, you didn't tell me about your promotion, but before you do, I'd like to know more about what you were feeling just a moment ago when you were discussing your breakup with your partner. I was sensing that that you don't want to talk about this. Let's focus on how you feel about this situation."

2. "I'm flattered that you would want me to hold you and pleased you could share those feelings with me. I feel close to you, too, but if I were to become romantically inclined toward you, I'd be letting you down and couldn't be helpful to you. I hope you can understand."

3. "I can see you're anxious to get things worked out, and that's a plus. *[Positive connotation]* But you're pretty unhappy with your progress and seem to feel that I am not doing my job. I'd like to better understand your feelings. What do you feel I should be doing differently?" *[Exploring feelings and expectations]*

4. "You sound pretty angry about having to report to me each week. I can't blame you for that. Still, the judge ordered it, and neither of us really has any choice. How do you suggest that we make the best of the situation?"

5. "I'm sorry you feel I'm not really interested in helping you. I gather you've had some bad experiences with other professionals, and I hope our relationship can be better. I sense your frustration at working under this time pressure and your anxiety about what will occur if you don't succeed in the time available. I will work with you to make the best use of the time to get a job you can feel good about. Sometimes as we come to the end of the time frame there are some possibilities for an extension, but that can't be guaranteed. I wonder if the best use of our time might be to do the best we can to get the kind of job you want in the time available."

6. "I can understand, then, that you might find it difficult to trust me—wondering if I'm really dependable."

7. *[Smiling]* "Thank you for the compliment. I gather you've been experiencing my care for you and find yourself longing for the love and care you didn't receive as a child. I can sense your feelings keenly and appreciate your sharing them."

8. "Somehow that doesn't fit with what we talked about last week. You expressed some very deep feelings about yourself and your marriage. I'd like to hear what you've been feeling about what we discussed last time."

9. "I wonder if that's what you're feeling just now in our relationship—that I haven't measured up to your expectations in some way. Could you share with me what you're feeling?"

10. "I appreciate your sharing those feelings with me. I understand how your life experiences would cause you to reach this conclusion about me. Because of this experience, I gather you've wondered how I see you. I won't say to you that I am not like that. I will tell you that I do see you are as responsible person, and that I appreciate this quality in you."

PART 4

The Termination Phase

19 The Final Phase: Evaluation and Termination

The third and final phase of the helping process encompasses the last evaluation of progress and the termination of the helping relationship. The final phase is important because the way in which social workers bring the helping relationship to a close strongly influences whether clients will maintain their progress and continue to grow following termination. Further, many people who receive social work services have previously been subject to difficult endings—those that involved ambiguity, abandonment, anger, abruptness, or failure. Properly handled, termination may itself be an intervention to model the ways in which relationships are concluded in a constructive and meaningful manner. Social workers must understand how to sensitively and skillfully conclude their work with clients, even if the end of the helping process is unplanned.

This chapter introduces you to strategies for evaluating case progress in work with individuals, groups, and families. The bulk of the chapter addresses the varieties of planned and unplanned terminations, with the remainder covering ethical considerations, common worker and client reactions to termination, strategies for maintaining case progress posttermination, and the use of rituals in effectively ending the helping relationship.

The Final Phase: Evaluation and Termination

....

Chapter Overview

Chapter 19 reviews methods for evaluating case progress, describes various factors that affect the termination process, identifies relevant tasks for both social workers and clients, and discusses skills essential to effectively managing termination.

After reading this chapter, you will be able to:

- Describe how evaluation builds on the assessment measures and goal-setting procedures employed earlier in the helping process.
- Distinguish between outcome, process, and satisfaction forms of evaluation.
- Appreciate the dynamics associated with various forms of planned and unplanned endings.
- Assist clients in solidifying gains made in treatment.
- Describe common termination reactions and how to address them.
- Describe how to use rituals to achieve closure.

EPAS Competencies in Chapter 19

This chapter provides the information that you will need to meet the following practice competencies:

- Competency 1: Demonstrate Ethical and Professional Behavior

- Competency 2: Engage Diversity and Difference in Practice
- Competency 4: Engage in Practice-Informed Research and Research-Informed Practice
- Competency 8: Intervene with Individuals, Families, Groups, Organizations, and Communities
- Competency 9: Evaluate Practice with Individuals, Families, Groups, Organizations, and Communities

EVALUATION

Evaluation has assumed ever-increasing significance in direct practice to measure client change and satisfaction, assure worker accountability, monitor the effectiveness of services, and evaluate the impact of the interventions themselves.

EP 9

Chapter 12 introduced you to the ways in which goals and objectives, client self-monitoring, and other measures can be used to create clear directions for service and benchmarks against which progress can be measured. The conclusion of service is thus the final point at which goal attainment and other aspects of change can be assessed prior to termination. If you have systematically obtained baseline measures and tracked progress, clients will be prepared for evaluation at termination. You can further enhance their cooperation by again reviewing the rationale and actively involving them in the process. For example, you can introduce this topic by making any of the following statements:

EP 2

- *"An important part of termination is to assess the results we have achieved and to identify what helped you most and least during our work together."*
- *"As an agency, we're committed to improving the quality of our services. Your honest feedback will help us to know how we're doing."*
- *"Our evaluation measures will help you and me see how your symptoms have changed since you were admitted."*
- *"One way we determine success on the case plan is to evaluate how your situation has changed since we began working together."*
- *"Our agency regularly evaluates the effectiveness of treatment groups. You'll all be sent a survey link each week so that you can give us anonymous feedback about the session."*

Several different evaluation methods can be used to determine client progress throughout the helping process and at its conclusion—for example, standardized tests, direct observation, goal attainment scaling, and client self-reports though logs, journals, and surveys. The power of evaluation is strengthened when multiple sources of information are used. Whatever method is used, evaluations focus on three dimensions of service: (1) outcomes, (2) process, and (3) satisfaction.

Outcomes

EP 9

Outcome evaluation involves assessing the results achieved against the goals that were formulated during the contracting phase of work. As described in Chapters 8 and 12, the methods utilized during the assessment and goal-setting phases will, in part, determine which outcomes you measure. For example, you may measure changes in the *frequency of difficulties* (e.g., being late for work, getting detention, bingeing, over-spending, experiencing negative cognitions, forgetting to take medications). You may also measure the *frequency of target behaviors*, such as exercising, using "I" statements, engaging in safe sex practices, or taking family outings. You may also assess outcomes by looking at changes in the *severity of problems* (e.g.,

self-esteem scores on rapid assessment instruments, anxiety as measured by a self-anchored rating scale, sleep disturbance as measured by a client's journal, or distractibility as measured by observations from a child's classroom teacher and caregivers). A fourth measure of outcomes involves the *achievement of goals or tasks* (e.g., applying for and getting a job, completing homework, improving parenting and disciplinary practices, maintaining sobriety, developing a safety plan, completing assignments between task group sessions). These items, when compared with the baseline measures taken when the client first entered service, will help determine the extent of progress and the client's readiness for termination (Epstein & Brown, 2002).

A specific type of success measure is **goal attainment scaling (GAS)**. In this process, the social worker and client identify a handful of problem behaviors or targeted changes and the related goals. Then, together, they assign each item a number corresponding to the likelihood of achievement or success on a scale from –2 to +2. A –2 would be an unfavorable outcome or a task or goal the client is highly unlikely to meet. A rating of 0 would indicate no expected outcome and +2 would indicate the most favorable outcome or the task with the greatest likelihood of completion (Yegidis & Weinbach, 2002). Ratings of –1 or +1 would be used to indicate more moderate expectations. For example, if the client's goal in a weight loss group is to keep a record of all food and exercise for a week, the scale might be as follows:

–2 = Keep inconsistent or incomplete records for the majority of days of the week.

–1 = Keep the log for 2 days, marking all food and exercise, along with related calories.

 0 = Keep the log for 4 days, marking all food and exercise, along with related calories.

+1 = Keep the log for 5 or 6 days, marking all food and exercise, along with related calories.

+2 = Keep the log for 7 days, marking all food and exercise, along with related calories.

The client's goal attainment, then, is evaluated in light of the likelihood that he or she will achieve the goal, with better outcomes associated with the ideal or "stretch" goals. Clearly, GAS is best suited for clients who are motivated to complete tasks and are reliable in reporting the results. The consistent use of GAS will help the social worker and client track incremental steps toward service outcomes and can ultimately serve as one indicator of readiness for termination.

Other models for measuring outcomes link empirically supported interventions with evaluation. Keenan and Grady (2014) suggest and demonstrate an integrated model that links evidence-based frameworks for use in demanding practice environments. In another model, Managing and Adapting Practices (MAP) creates a "treatment selection, design, implementation, and evaluation kit" that facilitates the search for recommended treatments and a clinical dashboard that organizes data on client progress (Chorpita, Daleiden, & Collins, 2014).

Manualized (guided by a manual) or evidence-based interventions often contain measures as part of the work. Typically, these instruments would have been used as part of the assessment and treatment- or service-planning to determine areas of difficulty and strength and to establish baseline scores against which progress can be measured. Numerous texts offer standardized scales and information on selecting and administering them in practice to target outcomes (Bloom, Fischer, & Orme, 2009; Fischer & Corcoran, 2006a, 2006b; Unrau, Gabor, & Grinnell, 2007). Some of these instruments lend themselves to repeated use, enabling social workers and clients to track progress over time. Through such **single-subject designs** (also referred to as single-system research, single-case time series, or $n = 1$ designs), the client is compared to himself or herself on baseline scores from earlier administrations. If the initial goals for work were vague or immeasurable or if no baseline measures were taken, social workers and clients could still evaluate the current status of the client's difficulties, goal attainment, symptoms, or achievements to develop an approximate sense of progress and readiness for termination; however, comparative analyses would be impossible.

In addition to comparative measures, you can use interviews or questionnaires to determine clients' views in order to evaluate their sense of progress against your own observations.

- *"To what extent did you learn skills to help your family get along better?"*
- *"How have your anxiety symptoms changed since you began treatment?"*
- *"How has your grief changed since you have been in the support group?"*

The difficulty with these recollections and other forms of self-report are, of course, that they may be highly selective and may be affected by numerous factors, such as the client's desire to please (or punish) the social worker, the client's interest in concluding service, or the hope that problems are resolved and that further services are not necessary. Although it is unwise to challenge clients' perceptions, you can reduce biases by asking them to provide actual examples of recent events ("critical incidents") that illustrate their attainment of goals, a decline in difficulties, or an increase in capacities. This discussion also provides an opportunity for you to reaffirm the accomplishments, which tends to heighten the client's confidence and satisfaction. In initiating these discussions, the social worker might say, for example, to members of the HEART group discussed in Chapters 11 and 16, "From what you are saying, it sounds like the group has been helpful to each of you. Can you identify some recent experiences that you handled differently because of your experiences in the group?"

As noted, clients' perceptions of their progress can be supplemented by other data or sources where feasible. For example, feedback from collateral contacts, such as family members, teachers, other helpers, or fellow clients (in family, group, or residential settings), may provide perspectives on an individual's progress that can be compared with self-reports.

Process

Another dimension of evaluation involves identifying the aspects of the helping process that were useful or detrimental. Feedback about techniques and incidents that enhanced or blocked progress will help you to hone certain skills, eliminate others, and use techniques with greater discrimination. Such **formative evaluation methods** also help organizations to determine which elements of their programs were effective in bringing about the desired change or whether the techniques used were consistent with standardized agency protocols and delivered as efficiently as possible (Royse et al., 2006). These evaluations capture the nuances of client–social worker interactions that contribute to treatment effectiveness. A technique that is useful with an assertive client, for example, may produce the opposite effect with a depressed client. Likewise, a family intervention may be effective only if it is carried out in a particular way. A social worker may have attributed a positive outcome to a masterfully executed technique, only to find that the client was helped far more by the practitioner's willingness to reach out and maintain hope when the client had almost given up (McCollum & Beer, 1995).

Clearly, clients' feedback can be used to identify beneficial aspects of the helping process, though self-reports about process are subject to the same biases as self-reports about outcomes described above. Evaluation instruments can also be used to more precisely measure the aspects of the helping process that were instrumental in achieving change.

With manualized or other evidence-based interventions, **fidelity assessments** can address how closely the process and skills used by the program or the individual social worker match the design of the intervention (Substance Abuse and Mental Health Services Administration [SAMHSA], 2003a). These can include qualitative case study reviews in which supervisory meetings, observation of sessions, audit interviews with clinicians, or focus groups with colleagues are used to examine a particular social worker's actions (O'Hare, 2005). Quantitative fidelity measures include statistics on the type, frequency, duration, and pattern of services, chart reviews and other administrative or quality assurance data, the level of congruence with the intervention model, and inventories that capture the degree to which the worker employed particular skills. One such instrument, the Practice Skills Inventory (PSI), documents the number of client contacts, the frequency with which particular skills were used (e.g., "Provided emotional support for my client," "Taught specific skills to deal with a certain problem") (O'Hare, 2005, pp. 555–556), and examples of those skills for the case (e.g., "Acknowledged how painful it is to move from home into assisted living," "Role-played ways of meeting other residents").

Published measures are also available for social workers who wish to evaluate outcomes and processes in their work with groups and families. Toseland and Rivas (2009) describe six self-reported measures that can capture feedback on the therapeutic elements of treatment groups. For example, Yalom's Curative Factors Scale (Stone, Lewis, & Beck, 1994) might identify the different dimensions of treatment groups and their relative therapeutic effectiveness. You can also construct valid measures of practice effectiveness by combining measures (e.g., records about sessions, client self-reports, observations) to provide an approximate measure of the effectiveness of the intervention processes used.

With children and other clients who lack high written or verbal ability, the use of expressive techniques, such as collages or paintings, may help to tap into evaluative content. For example, the client may be asked to draw or display something to illustrate "what I liked best/least about our work together" or "what helped me during my time here." Feedback from caregivers and other observers can be sought on a periodic basis, and their appraisals can be linked to the interventions being used at a given point in time.

Satisfaction

The outcomes achieved and the means used to achieve them are important measures of client progress. Another measure in the increasingly competitive and consumer-conscious practice environment seeks information about client satisfaction. You may gauge this level of satisfaction in your evaluative discussions with the client. Some settings facilitate the gathering of formal feedback by sending out written evaluation surveys at the termination of service or after a specified follow-up period. Some payers, such as managed care companies, will also evaluate providers by directly seeking client input.

These instruments address satisfaction with the social worker's service by asking questions such as "Would you refer a friend or family member to us for services in the future?," "Were you and the clinician able to meet your goal?," and "Do you believe you needed additional services that were not provided?" (Corcoran & Vandiver, 1996, p. 57). Satisfaction surveys also evaluate structural or operational issues such as appropriateness of the waiting room, convenience of parking, time elapsed between the client's request for service and first appointment, the worker's promptness in making a home visit, and friendliness of reception staff (Ackley, 1997; Corcoran & Vandiver, 1996). Satisfaction measures may specifically evaluate particular elements of an agency's services or progress on particular initiatives. For example, they may inquire about the cultural competence of the staff, the openness of the facility to diverse populations, or the turnaround time in responding to client calls and requests.

The Kansas Consumer Satisfaction Survey uses a 26-item, Likert-type scale with ratings 1 to 5 (strongly agree to strongly disagree, or does not apply) in which clients respond to statements such as "If I have an emergency at night or on the weekend, I am able to get help from the program," "I can choose where I live," and "My opinions and ideas are included in my treatment plan" (SAMHSA, 2003a). A related instrument, the Quality of Life Self-Assessment, asks consumers to tell the agency "how things are going … these days" (SAMHSA, 2003b) by rating such issues as social life, level of independence, physical health, and access to transportation on a four-point scale (poor-fair-good-excellent); it also measures mental health symptoms and the effects of alcohol and other drug use on a four-point scale (severe-moderate-minimal-none). The instrument also invites the client to indicate whether any of the items should be reflected on his or her service plan. Both the satisfaction and self-assessment surveys offer open-ended items to which clients can respond with other thoughts or questions. Clearly, the utility of these or any evaluation instrument depends on professionals' and agencies' willingness and ability to incorporate them into standard practices and procedures (Rzepnicki, 2004).

Hybrid Models

Consistent and relevant evaluation can be difficult to achieve in many service settings. A fourth option incorporates measures of outcome, satisfaction, and progress, and can be administered in 2 to 3 minutes. These client-oriented, outcome-informed tools, such as the Partners for Change Outcome Management System (PCOMS; Duncan, 2012), capture feedback through brief questions at the outset and conclusion of each session. The PCOMS has been scientifically validated and is well endorsed for practical utility in a variety of service settings (Duncan, 2012).

The Outcome Rating Scale (ORS) is administered at the beginning of each session. Clients are instructed to indicate with a mark on a line how well they have been doing over the previous week in regard to personal well-being, family and social relationships, and overall well-being. On the Session Rating Scale (SRS), at the end of each session, clients mark their responses on a continuum between two statements such as "I did not feel heard, understood, and respected" and "I did feel heard, understood and respected" or "The therapist's approach is not a good fit for me" and "The therapist's approach is a good fit for me." The full instruments are available online, in children's versions, and in more than a dozen languages (Heart and Soul of Change Project, 2015). The findings can be incorporated into the work of the session and can also be tracked over time to measure client progress and encourage retention in services.

The notion of practice evaluation may be conflated with research and thus seem like a cumbersome and irrelevant task, requiring special expertise. Although practice research is important for the development of knowledge, all social workers owe it to themselves, their clients, and funding bodies to assure that services are appropriate and effective. A core competence for social work students involves recognizing the importance of evaluation, selecting proper evaluation measures, critically evaluating findings, and using those findings to improve practice effectiveness (CSWE, 2015). A robust array of resources exists to help in this effort, regardless of the setting or population served. Evaluation is also intricately tied to termination, as clients may cease services because of concerns about the quality of care or lack of progress. Evaluations also indicate whether goals are met and thus lead to planned termination or transfer.

TERMINATION

Termination refers to the process of formally ending the individual social worker–client relationship. It is a feature of practice with all client systems, from individuals and families to support groups, coalitions, and communities, and it occurs regardless of the duration of the helping relationship.[1] Terminations can occur when goals are met, when clients make a transition to other services, when time-limited services are concluded, and when social workers or clients leave the helping relationship. Even if clients are likely to "come and go" from service over a period of time as their concerns and needs change, it is important to draw closure to each unique episode of care.

The notion of ending is often introduced at the beginning of service, when the social worker discusses the likely duration of care, the number of sessions allotted, or the goals that will guide the helping process. In some time-limited treatment models, the fixed length of care is part of informed consent discussions at the outset. For example, the social worker might explain, "We believe that brief treatment is effective and helps both you and me make efficient use of our time together. So we'll begin today by getting an idea of the goals you want to work on and the best way to use our time over the next 6 to 8 weeks to achieve those goals."

Whether in short- or long-term therapy models, successful termination involves preparing clients adequately for separation from the social worker and/or group and accomplishing other tasks that facilitate the transition from being a client to being "on one's own." The four primary tasks of termination are:

1. Evaluating the service provided and the extent to which goals were accomplished
2. Determining when to implement termination
3. Mutually resolving emotional reactions experienced during the process of ending
4. Planning to maintain gains achieved and to achieve continued growth

EP 4

The significance of these tasks and the extent to which they can be successfully accomplished are governed in large measure by the context in which the helping relationship takes place.[2] The intensity of the termination process is affected by factors such as the type of contact (voluntary or involuntary), the size and characteristics of the client system, and the nature of the intervention used. In crisis or single-session services, the focus of termination will be narrower—determining the effectiveness of the encounter in meeting the clients' needs and clarifying next steps (tasks, referrals, subsequent contact). In crisis work, this would also include an evaluation of the client's safety and stability before the contact is terminated.

Emotional reactions will also vary depending on the nature and length of the helping relationship and the characteristics and past experiences of the individuals involved. That is, involuntary clients and those with more structured or time-limited services will be less likely to experience a sense of loss at termination than those who have engaged in longer and more voluntary relationships with the social worker. For example, termination of a time-limited educational group may be less intense and require less preparation of members than would the ending of an ongoing interpersonal support group or discharge from a residential treatment setting. Clients who have experienced difficult losses in the past may require more time and sensitivity in bringing the helping relationship to a close. Terminations from brief crisis intervention, case management, or discharge planning relationships may differ in intensity depending on the nature of the needs met and the length of service. Termination from family sessions may be less difficult than those from individual work because most of the client system will continue to work and be together, albeit without the social worker's involvement.

Types of Termination

Terminations generally fall into one of two categories: unplanned and planned. **Unplanned terminations**, or early terminations, occur when clients withdraw prematurely from services or when social workers leave helping relationships due to illness, job change, or other circumstances. **Planned terminations** occur when clients' goals are achieved, when transfer or referral is anticipated and necessary, or when service is concluded due to the time-limited nature of the setting (such as hospitals or schools) or the treatment modality

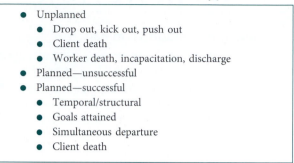

TABLE 19-1 Termination Subtypes

- Unplanned
  - Drop out, kick out, push out
  - Client death
  - Worker death, incapacitation, discharge
- Planned—unsuccessful
- Planned—successful
  - Temporal/structural
  - Goals attained
  - Simultaneous departure
  - Client death

used (such as brief treatment or fixed-length groups). Examples of both types of termination, along with their subtypes, are included in Table 19-1 and explained further below.

Unplanned Terminations

Unplanned terminations occur when the working relationship is halted suddenly or prematurely. Client-initiated unplanned terminations can be triggered by dropping out of treatment, by an adverse event that renders the client unavailable for service, or by the client behaving in such a way that services are withdrawn or he or she is ejected from the setting. Examples of adverse events include being arrested, running away, committing suicide, or otherwise dying unexpectedly. The category of "dropouts" from service is similarly broad, including clients who are seeking services involuntarily or are otherwise unmotivated, clients who are dissatisfied with the social worker, clients who feel they have made satisfactory progress and thus "are done" whether the social worker thinks so or not, and clients who decide to quit for pragmatic reasons like a lack of funds or the inconvenience of the service setting.[3] A mixed form of unplanned termination can be characterized as a "push-out," where the social worker and the client have failed to "click" and the client's discontinuation is prompted or reinforced by the practitioner's disinterest, incompetence, or lack of commitment (Hunsley et al., 1999).

A common theme of all these client-initiated endings is that they are unanticipated and thus allow no opportunity for discussion, processing, or closure, yet the residue of feelings and unfinished business remains. The tasks of termination (reflection on the work together, planning for the future, marking the end of treatment) remain undone, and both parties may experience feelings of abandonment, anger, rejection, failure, relief, and shame.

IDEAS IN ACTION

Avoiding Premature Termination

It is important for social workers to understand cases in which the client drops out of service prematurely. A meta-analysis of studies (Swift & Greenberg, 2012) found a weighted average dropout rate of 19.7% among adult voluntary clients. The attrition of one in five clients has significant implications for clients and their loved ones, as well as for wasted resources. It is easy to blame early termination on resistance or another client attribute rather than explore the role that the social worker or the services themselves played in the decision to leave care. By understanding the predictors of early termination, social workers are better able to prevent unnecessary endings. Swift et al. (2013) conceptualize clients' decisions to drop out of care as a cost–benefit analysis wherein the benefits or progress in treatment are weighed against the expense, time, stigma, discomfort, and inconvenience of care. Several interlocking practice strategies may help social workers prevent premature termination (Swift et al., 2012). The recommendations include:

- Educate clients about what to expect in regard to the duration and process of change so that expectations are realistic from the outset of service.

- Explain the roles that each participant will play in the process of care to dispel inaccurate or stereotyped beliefs about counseling. This "role induction" can be done by video, brochure, or discussion, and should educate the client about what to expect in sessions, how meetings will be structured, what the social worker will do, and so on.

- Incorporate client preferences about the timing, structure, and form of treatment.

- Instill hope through a focus on strengths, a clear problem formulation and rationale for services, expressions of confidence in the client, and professional compassion, competence, and credibility. Paying attention to pacing and progress, especially early in the helping process, can also encourage hope.

- Foster the therapeutic alliance by creating a safe environment, expressing empathy, and collaborating with the client in setting goals and tasks for service.

- Consistently assess and discuss treatment progress. Does the client's progress deviate from his or her expectations or from typical change trajectories? Social workers who employ outcome monitoring and feedback systems can get timely input and make changes in service if indicated (Lambert & Shimokowa, 2011).

Unplanned terminations can also be worker initiated—for example, when the social worker dies, becomes incapacitated, or is dismissed. The suddenness and finality of these endings can result in feelings of abandonment, self-blame, and shock. Other practitioner-initiated unplanned endings, such as those due to layoffs or job transfers, may elicit strong reactions from the client but generally allow time for processing and closure. We will discuss managing those feelings and endings in a later section. All unplanned endings require special measures so that the tasks of termination can be approximated to the extent possible.

Managing Unplanned Terminations

Some estimates suggest that 50% of the overall client population will drop out of service (Kazdin & Wassell,

1998; Sweet & Noones, 1989) and that this figure may be even higher for certain subgroups. Some settings may have their own protocols for dealing with "no shows," and a different mechanism may be needed for the client who fails to reappear after a first session (see Meyer, 2001) compared to one who ceases to appear for service midway through the course of treatment.

A common response to unplanned termination by the client is for the social worker to reach out to him or her by phone, email, or letter. The goals in doing so may be to acknowledge the decision to conclude services, to encourage the client to come in for a closing session, or to achieve the purposes of such a session through the communication itself. For example, one client who was arrested could not receive phone calls or return for services. Nevertheless, the social worker was able to write him a letter in which she reviewed the goals he had achieved and the issues with which he continued to struggle. She conveyed her regard for him and informed him of the availability of other services during his incarceration and following his release. A similar technique can be used when a social worker must leave abruptly, when a client quits service, or when a client leaves an institution against medical advice. Such endings are not ideal because they do not allow the client the opportunity to express his or her views or participate in evaluation, but they do help to mark the ending and "clear the air" regarding future services.

When a social worker dies or otherwise becomes incapacitated, it is incumbent upon his or her colleagues to intervene for the care or transfer of the clients involved. They must also recognize that these clients' needs and reactions will be shaped by the abruptness and nature of the loss, their personal loss histories, and the particular issues for which they were seeking help (Philip, 1994; Philip & Stevens, 1992). Thus, grieving the lost relationship may become a primary task alongside continued work on their treatment goals identified earlier.

Likewise, when a client dies unexpectedly, whether through an accident or a traumatic act such as homicide or suicide, the loss has significant implications for the helping professionals left behind. Out of respect for the client's continuing right to privacy, the social worker is ethically bound to keep known details about those individuals confidential, even after death. This being the case, the social worker's family members and friends are unable to help address the grief and may not even be aware of the loss. Supervisory and collegial support should be the primary resource for the mourner, with coworkers offering empathy, permission to grieve, and encouragement to talk about and integrate the feelings that emerge (Chemtob et al., 1988; Kruger et al., 1979; Strom-Gottfried & Mowbray, 2006).

Formal processes for reviewing the case—referred to as "postvention" by Shneidman (1971)—can take the form of individual or group processing of the case (Pilsecker, 1987), a psychological autopsy (Chemtob et al., 1988; Kleepsies, Penk, & Forsyth, 1993), or critical incident stress debriefing (Farrington, 1995). Each of these mechanisms has a slightly different intent and focus, but each offers the opportunity for the social worker to acknowledge the loss, contemplate the experience with the client, have a supportive review, and deepen understanding of what took place.

Unplanned terminations of a member from a group may occur for a number of reasons. Sometimes,

EP 1

departure is due to the group itself, such as poor fit, discomfort with the leader or other members, or a distressing incident. At other times, members terminate because of transportation difficulties or time conflicts (Toseland & Rivas, 2009). In any case, the unplanned departure presents challenges for achieving termination-related tasks. Because cohesion is central to the success of a group, the loss of a member can threaten that bond, make members question their own achievements or appropriateness for the group, and make them reluctant to continue building trusting relationships with the remaining group members. The social worker should try to encourage closure in some form, both for the departing member and for the rest of the group. Even if it derails the group's preexisting agenda or timeline, this effort is time well spent because it supports the future health and success of the group process and the individual members.

Planned Terminations with Unsuccessful Outcomes

Sometimes termination occurs in a planned manner, but the endings are not marked by successful achievement of service goals. This may occur when:

- The social worker or the client is dissatisfied with the helping relationship.
- The client is hopelessly stalemated despite vigorous and persistent efforts to overcome his or her difficulties.
- The social worker is not competent to address the client's needs.
- The client fails to comply with appropriate treatment requirements.

Unlike unplanned terminations, these endings are not accompanied by abrupt disappearance from service and thus afford the social worker and client a chance to achieve the goals of closure. Groups also occasionally end with unsuccessful results, and members may be frustrated, disappointed, or angry with the leader or with other members (Smokowski, Rose, & Bacallao, 2001).

When the helping process ends unsuccessfully, termination should include discussion of (1) factors that prevented achieving more favorable results and (2) clients' feelings about seeking additional help in the future. This effort requires you to create as safe an atmosphere as possible so that both parties can honestly air concerns with the intention of both achieving closure and keeping open possibilities for future service.

It also requires the ability to hear and share feedback in a nondefensive manner. As a result of this termination conversation, you and a client may come to agreement on the conditions under which you would reconnect and develop a new contract for future services. At this final session, social workers should be prepared to offer referrals to other services if the issue for termination has been a poor fit with the individual practitioner or agency.

Planned Terminations with Successful Outcomes

As noted earlier, planned terminations can take many forms. The nature of the setting, intervention method, or funding source can all impose external pressures to terminate within a specific period of time. Other planned endings emerge from the helping relationship itself as clients achieve their goals and move on to independence from the social worker. This step may not signal that the client has completed all of his or her desired goals or tasks (or that they are "done" in the social worker's eyes) but means only that the client has experienced "at least enough relief so that he no longer wants help *at that point*" (Reid, 1972, p. 199). Related to this development is what Cummings (1991) calls "brief intermittent therapy throughout the life cycle" (p. 35). That is, individuals who need social work services may come to use them as they do medical and other services—seeking them out in times of need to address acute problems rather than pursuing single episodes of extended treatment. In these termination situations, the social worker and client may therefore establish contingencies under which they will resume services in the future.

Termination Due to Temporal or Structural Limits

In organizations or agencies whose function involves providing service according to fixed time intervals, termination must be planned accordingly. In school settings, for example, services are generally discontinued at the conclusion of an academic year. In hospitals and other institutional settings, the duration of service is determined by the length of hospitalization, confinement, or insurance coverage.

Some service models such as time-limited groups or fixed-length residential programs are clearly designed to pace and conclude services within a specific time frame. For example, some treatment programs are organized such that clients progress from one program (and one set of workers) to another as their needs change. In residential programs or other settings with finite lengths of stay, the course of treatment will involve a relatively predictable process whereby the client progresses through steps or phases leading to termination. Depending on the context of treatment, services may extend from several days to several months. Temporal factors are also central in termination for social work students, who leave a given practicum setting at the completion of an academic year. These can be emotional experiences for social work interns, given the intensity of the practicum experience, especially if they are terminating with the entire caseload simultaneously. For clients who have been assigned to a series of social work interns, the endings may be predictable but also aggravating if it is difficult to repeatedly establish trust and continuity of care with a series of time-limited workers-in-training.

Terminations that are prompted by program structure or preexisting time constraints involve certain peculiar factors. First, the ending of a school year or of a training period for students is a predetermined time for termination, which reduces the possibility of clients interpreting time limits as being arbitrarily imposed or a sign of desertion or abandonment. Knowing the termination date well in advance also provides ample time to resolve feelings about separation. Conversely, it also means that in school settings student clients may lose many supports all at one time.

Another factor common to terminations that are determined by temporal constraints or agency function rather than by individual factors is that the client's problems may not have been adequately resolved by the time termination occurs. The predetermined, untimely ending may lead to intense reactions from the client who is losing service and end the helping relationship in what feels like midstream (Weiner, 1984). Social workers are therefore confronted with the dual tasks of working through feelings associated with untimely separation and referring clients for additional services when indicated.

Predetermined endings imposed by the close of a school year or a fixed length of service do not necessarily convey the same expectations of a positive outcome as do time limits that are determined by individual client progress. In other words, to say "I will see you until May because that is sufficient time to achieve your goals" conveys a far more positive expectation than "I will see you until May because that is all the time I will have available before leaving the placement." Time-limited treatment can lead to satisfactory outcomes as clients benefit from the focused nature of this work and may develop a fruitful relationship with the social worker even if termination results in referral for other services.

For example, one of the authors of this book worked with a client with serious, long-term mental health problems. During the time allotted for her field placement, she was able to help the client through a crisis and assist him to build his social supports so that future crises would not inevitably result in rehospitalization. In the termination process, they reviewed the accomplishments made during the year and the client met his new social worker, who would meet with him on a less intensive basis for support and maintenance of the gains made previously.

Other Determinants of Planned Termination

When terminations are not predetermined by agency setting, client circumstance, or form of service, how do the social worker and client know when to end? When services are highly goal directed, the termination point may be clear: it occurs when goals are reached and changes are sustained. When goals are amorphous or ongoing, however, determining a proper ending point can be more difficult. Theoretically, humans can grow indefinitely, and determining when clients have achieved optimal growth is no simple task. Ordinarily, it is appropriate to introduce the idea of termination when the client has reached the point of diminishing returns—that is, when the gains from sessions taper off to the point of being minor in significance. The client may indicate through words or actions that he or she is ready to discontinue services, or the social worker may initiate such discussion.

Two other variants on planned termination warrant discussion. **Simultaneous termination** occurs when the client and the social worker leave the service or agency at the same time, as when the end of services aligns with the practitioner's departure from the agency. It offers the advantage of powerful, mutually shared experiences of ending, and it often focuses the time and attention devoted to termination tasks (Joyce et al., 1996). Simultaneous termination also requires a good deal of self-awareness on the part of the social worker to ensure that his or her personal reactions to leaving are not projected onto the client. As with other endings involving the social worker's departure from the organization, termination must address the conditions and resources for the client if he or she should need future service.

The second type of planned termination occurs when the client dies but the death is anticipated and lanned for. Some settings, such as hospice care, nursing homes, or hospitals, expose social workers and other caregivers to death on a regular basis.

The orientation and supervision offered in such settings must address this crucial aspect of practice, as particular skills are needed to assist individuals in such circumstances and effectively manage professionals' responses. For example, when the helping relationship is expected to end in conjunction with the patient's death, it may involve life review and reminiscences, plans to address end-of-life concerns, and attention to spiritual matters (Arnold, 2002).[4]

Understanding and Responding to Clients' Termination Reactions

Inherent in termination is separation from the social worker (and other clients, in the case of groups, inpatient, or residential settings). Separation typically involves mixed feelings for both the social worker and the client, which vary in intensity according to the degree of success achieved, the strength of the attachment, the type of termination, the cultural orientation of the client, and his or her previous experiences with separations from significant others (Bembry & Ericson, 1999; Dorfman, 1996). When individuals successfully accomplish their goals, they experience a certain degree of pride and satisfaction as the helping process draws to a close. If they have grown in strength and self-confidence, they view the future optimistically as an opportunity for continued growth.

Most people in individual, conjoint, family, and group therapy experience positive emotions in termination. The benefits from the gains achieved usually far outweigh the impact of the loss of the helping relationship. Clients may reflect on the experience by saying things like "I was such a wreck when I first came to see you—I'm surprised I didn't scare you away," "You helped me get my thinking straight, so I could see the options I had before me," or "Even if things didn't change that much with my son, it helped me a lot to be in the group and know I'm not alone."

As noted earlier, clients and social workers alike commonly experience a sense of loss during the termination process. Indeed, sadness is a common element of many of the endings that are a part of life itself (even positive ones), such as leaving parents to attend school, advancing from one grade to another, graduating, moving into a new community, or changing jobs. The loss in termination may be a deeply moving experience involving the "sweet sorrow" generally associated with parting from a person whom one has grown to value. Adept social workers help clients to give voice to these ambivalent feelings, acknowledging that transitions can be difficult but that successfully handling both good times and difficult ones is a necessary part of growth.

For the social worker, the nature of termination and the comfort with which it occurs appear to be linked to the overall health of the organization in which it takes place and the social worker's level of job satisfaction (Resnick & Dziegielewski, 1996). In work sites where workloads are high, where there is a rapid turnover in cases, or where staff support and effective supervision are lacking, sufficient attention may not be paid to the tasks and emotions that accompany clinical endings. Of course, like other elements of practice, the impact of termination on the social worker is also shaped by his or her overall well-being, including the ability to maintain a proper balance between his or her personal and professional lives. This balance is particularly important when the social worker has an illness that might imperil the continuation of services. He or she must weigh the benefits of honesty and transparency with the risks that self-disclosure about a serious illness might prove distressing to the client and disruptive to the focus of treatment (Farber, 2006).

VIDEO CASE EXAMPLE

The video "Serving the Squeaky Wheel" illustrates the challenges for professionals who take over case responsibility after the unanticipated departure of a former worker. The client, Molly, is forthright about her mistrust of professionals following the abrupt and poorly managed ending with Nancy, her previous worker. As a result of the ending, Molly experienced confusion, anger, and abandonment, which further complicated her current treatment. Too often, new social workers observe client resistance without knowing the source of the client's distrust. In the video, Molly's ability to identify her feelings helps Ron, the new social worker, address them. In the video, he attempts to help Molly address the loss by asking, "What would you say to Nancy?" What other strategies can social workers use to get at the feelings created by unplanned, abrupt, or poorly managed endings?

Because termination can evoke feelings associated with past losses and endings, clients (and social workers) may respond to it in a variety of ways (and in any of these ways to varying degrees), which we discuss here.

Anger   EP 1 and 8

Clients may experience anger at termination, especially when termination occurs because the social worker leaves the agency. Because the termination is not goal related and occurs with little forewarning, reactions are sometimes similar to those that involve other types of sudden crises. The social worker may need to reach for the feelings evoked by his or her departure, as clients may have difficulty expressing negative emotions while they are simultaneously experiencing sadness or anxiety about the impending loss. It is important to encourage the verbal expression of emotions and respond empathically to them. It is vital, however, not to empathize to the extent of overidentification, thereby losing the capacity to assist the client with negative feelings and to engage in constructive planning.

When the social worker's departure is caused by circumstances outside his or her control (such as layoffs or firing), it is important that the practitioner not fuel the client's anger to satisfy his or her own indignation or desire for vindication. Not only is this clinically unhelpful to the client, but it is at odds with the NASW Code of Ethics. The Code of Ethics cautions us not to "exploit clients in disputes with colleagues or engage clients in any inappropriate discussion of conflicts between social workers and their colleagues" (NASW, 2008a, 2.04b).

Denial

Clients may contend that they were unaware of the impending termination or time limits on service and behave as if termination is not imminent. They may deny having feelings about the termination or refuse to acknowledge that it affects them. Others may avoid endings by failing to appear for concluding sessions with the social worker (Dorfman, 1996). It is a mistake to interpret this "business as usual" demeanor as an indication that he or she is unaffected by the termination or is taking it in stride, because the unruffled exterior may represent "the calm before the storm."

To assist clients in getting in touch with their emotions, it is helpful to reintroduce the topic of termination and to express your desire to assist them in formulating plans to continue working toward their goals after your departure. As you bring up the topic of termination, be sensitive to nonverbal cues to clients' emotional reactions. We also recommend employing empathic communication that conveys understanding of and elicits the hurt, resentment, and rejection experienced when a valued person leaves. The following responses demonstrate this type of communication:

- "I know that being discharged is scary and that makes you wish you didn't have to leave, but not talking about it won't keep it from happening. I want very much to use the time remaining to reflect on our work together so you are prepared to carry all that you've achieved here out into the world."
- "You've worked really hard here, and I know a lot of it wasn't easy for you. It's hard for me to believe you now when you shrug your shoulders and say it means nothing. I think it means a lot."

Avoidance

Occasionally, clients may express their anger and hurt over a social worker's leaving by rejecting the social worker before the social worker can reject them. Some people may silently protest by failing to appear for sessions as termination approaches. Others may ignore the social worker or profess that they no longer need him or her—in effect, employing the strategy that "the best defense is a good offense." When clients act in this fashion, it is critical to reach out to them. Otherwise, they may interpret the failure to do so as evidence that the social worker never really cared about them at all. In reaching out, a personal contact by phone, text, email, letter, or home visit is essential because it creates an opportunity for interaction in which the social worker can reaffirm his or her concern and care and convey empathy and understanding of the client's emotional reaction.

Reporting Recurrence of Old Problems or Generating New Ones

Some people tend to panic as treatment reaches an end and they experience a return of difficulties that have been under control for some time (Levinson, 1977). In an effort to continue the helping relationship, some may introduce new stresses and problems during the terminal sessions and even during the final scheduled session. Clients who normally communicate minimally may suddenly open up, and other clients may reveal confidential information they have previously withheld. Still other people may display more severe reactions by engaging in self-destructive or suicidal acts. The severity of the client's revelation, regression, or return of symptoms will dictate how you respond.

It is important to acknowledge the anxiety and apprehension that accompany termination. Some people will benefit from a preemptive discussion of these issues as termination nears. The social worker might say, "Sometimes people worry that problems will reemerge once services end, but I'm confident about how far you've come. I trust that even if there are setbacks, they won't affect our ending." Some theoretical models suggest that the social worker engage the client in an explicit discussion about what it would take to return to the former level of functioning that necessitated treatment. The underlying idea here is that such a discussion creates significant discomfort and therefore, paradoxically, inoculates the individual against future setbacks (Walsh, 2007).

On some occasions, it may make sense for you and the client to reconsider a planned ending. Limited "extensions by plan" (Epstein & Brown, 2002, p. 232) can be made to accomplish agreed-upon tasks if it appears that additional time would enable the client to achieve decisive progress. There may be legitimate reasons for recontracting for additional sessions—for example, identifying key problems only late in the helping process, returning to problems that were identified earlier but had to be set aside in favor of work on more pressing issues, or anticipating transitional events that bear on the client's problems (e.g., getting married, "aging out" of foster care, regaining custody of a child). In these instances, continuing the working relationship may be warranted, if supported by the agency, especially if the client has achieved substantial progress on other problems during the initial contract period.

Determining whether the emergence of new issues (or the reemergence of old ones) is a ploy to avoid termination or a legitimate cause for developing a new contract can be tricky, but the decision should be based on your sense of the client's progress to date, the degree of dependency, and the significance of the issues being raised (Reid, 1972). Supervisory discussions can help workers look critically at these variables. If you believe that the problem is worthy of intervention but worry that continuing treatment may foster harmful dependence, you might consider referring the client to another clinician or continuing work with the person yourself but in a less intensive format—through groups or through less frequent sessions, for example.

Attempting to Prolong Contact

Sometimes, rather than reveal new or renewed problems, a person may seek continued contact with the social worker more directly by suggesting a social or business relationship following termination.

For example, the client may suggest meeting for coffee on occasion or exchanging cards or letters, may try to connect with the worker through online social networking, or may propose joining a training program that will put him or her in regular contact with the social worker. This phenomenon is also evident when groups decide to continue meeting after the agency's involvement has concluded.

EP 1

Any security brought by such plans is only fleeting, and the negative effects of continued contact can be serious. Some requests for continued contact would be inappropriate given the profession's ethical proscriptions against dual relationships. Other forms of contact, while not prohibited, may still be unwise in that they may undo the work done in the helping relationship and may undermine the client's confidence in his or her ability to function without the social worker. Further, continued informal involvement may constrain the client from becoming invested in other rewarding relationships (Bostic, Shadid, & Blotcky, 1996).

In the case of groups, it is not usually the social worker's role to discourage the group from continuing to meet, although he or she should be clear about his or her own stance and may share the wisdom of past experience. For example, at the conclusion of one bereavement group, the group members planned a cookout at one member's home. In response to the invitation to join them, the group leader simply said, "I'll be ending with you after our session next week, but I appreciate your offer to include me." In another group with a particularly fragile and more easily disappointed membership, the social worker said, "I'm glad you feel close enough to one another to try to continue meeting after the group has formally ended. It's been my experience that sometimes it's hard to keep that going outside the group. If that happens to you, I hope you won't be discouraged or take it as a reflection on all you've accomplished in your time together."

This is not to say that planned follow-up phone calls, appointments, and "booster sessions" are always inappropriate. To the contrary, such plans are made within the goals of the helping process and have a clear therapeutic purpose rather than being an attempt to evade the inevitability of ending.

Social Workers' Reactions to Termination

Clients are not the only ones who have reactions to termination. Social workers' responses may include guilt (at letting the client down or failing to sufficiently help him or her), avoidance (delaying announcement of termination to avoid the feelings or reactions evoked), relief (at ending involvement with a difficult or challenging client), sadness (at the end of a positive relationship), anxiety (about the client's future or well-being), and difficulty letting go (because of financial or emotional fulfillment experienced by the clinician) (Dorfman, 1996; Joyce et al., 1996; Murphy & Dillon, 2008). In settings where premature terminations are the norm, workers may experience burnout and decreased sensitivity to clients after repeatedly working on cases where closure is not possible and treatment ends before interventions are carried out (Resnick & Dziegielewski, 1996). Self-understanding and good supervision are the essential elements by which even veteran social workers can recognize the reactions involved in terminations. These reactions negatively affect clients, so identifying and managing them is crucial.

EP 1

CONSOLIDATING GAINS AND PLANNING MAINTENANCE STRATEGIES

In addition to managing the emotional and behavioral reactions to ending, another task of termination involves summarizing and stabilizing the changes achieved and developing a plan to sustain those changes. A similar aim of group work is to assist members to not only interact successfully within the group context but also transfer their newly developed interpersonal skills to the broad arena of social relationships.

The failure to maintain gains has been attributed to a variety of factors:

1. A natural tendency to revert to habitual response patterns (e.g., use of alcohol or drugs, aggressive or withdrawn behavior, poor communication patterns)
2. Personal and environmental stressors (e.g., family conflicts, financial pressures, personal rejection, loss of job, health problems, deaths of loved ones)
3. Lack of opportunities in the environment for social and leisure activities
4. Absence of positive support systems (peer or family networks may not have changed in the same way the client has)

5. Inadequate social skills
6. Lack of reinforcement for functional behaviors
7. Inadequate preparation for environmental changes
8. Inability to resist peer pressures
9. Return to dysfunctional or destructive environments
10. Inadequately established new behaviors[5]

In planning maintenance strategies, you must anticipate such forces and prepare clients for coping with them. A monitoring phase may be useful for some people. In this phase, the number and frequency of sessions decrease while support systems are called on to assist the client with new concerns. This technique, in effect, "weans" the individual from the social worker's support yet allows a transitional period in which he or she can try out new skills and supports while gradually concluding the helping relationship. The ascendance of electronic communications mechanisms (text messaging, Twitter, email, social networks) has led to an array of promising innovations for aftercare and relapse prevention. These models send reminders about medication or treatment adherence, encouragement and wellness tips, and feedback on symptoms or questions recorded by clients (Aguilera, Gerza, & Munoz, 2010; Shapiro et al., 2009).

When working with individuals and families, you may actively encourage people to consider means for coping with setbacks. One model suggests asking what "would be required of each person to contribute to a resurgence of the problem" and organizing role-plays in which the members engage in old behavioral patterns and describe afterward what thoughts and feelings they experienced in doing so (Walsh, 2007). Similar forms of anticipation and practice may help inoculate clients against future relapses.

Social workers may encourage clients to return for additional help if problems appear to be mounting out of control. Although it is important to express confidence in people's ability to cope independently with their problems, it is equally important to convey your continued interest in them and to invite them to return if they need to do so.

Follow-Up Sessions

Posttermination follow-up sessions are another important technique in ensuring successful termination and change maintenance. These sessions benefit both clients and social workers. Many people continue to progress after termination, and follow-up sessions provide an opportunity for the social worker to acknowledge such gains and encourage them to continue their efforts.

These sessions also provide the social worker with an opportunity to provide brief additional assistance for residual difficulties. Social workers may assess the durability of changes in these sessions—that is, determine whether clients have maintained gains beyond the immediate influence of the helping relationship. Additional benefits of planned follow-up sessions are that they may soften the blow of termination and they allow opportunities for longitudinal evaluation of practice effectiveness.

By introducing the notion of the follow-up session as an integral part of the helping process, social workers can avoid the risk that clients will later view these sessions as failure, an intrusion into their private lives, or as an attempt to satisfy the social worker's curiosity. Wells (1994) recommends that in arranging for the follow-up session, social workers not set a specific date but rather explain that they will contact the client after a designated interval. This period of time offers the individual an opportunity to test out and further consolidate the learning and changes achieved during the formal helping period.

In the follow-up session, the social worker generally relates more informally than during the period of intervention. After observing the appropriate social courtesies, you should guide the discussion to the client's progress and administer postintervention measures when appropriate. The follow-up session also provides an excellent opportunity for further evaluation of your efforts during the period of intervention. In retrospect, what was most helpful? What was least helpful? Further efforts can be made to consolidate gains at this point as well. What was gained from treatment that the client can continue to use in coping with life? Finally, at this point you can contract for more formalized help if this step appears necessary. Follow-up sessions thus enable social workers to arrange for timely assistance that may arrest deterioration in functioning.

One caution related to follow-up sessions is warranted: They may not allow the client to make a "clean break" from services. Individuals who had difficulty separating during termination may use follow-up sessions as an excuse to prolong contact with the social worker. This continued attachment is detrimental to the change process and inhibits the person from establishing appropriate attachments with social networks and with other helping professionals. Social workers should be alert to this possibility in proposing follow-up sessions and ensure that clients understand the specific purpose and focus of these sessions.

Ending Rituals

In many settings, termination may be concluded by a form of celebration or ritual that symbolically marks the goals achieved and the relationship's conclusion (Murphy & Dillon, 2003). For example, in residential programs and some treatment groups, termination may be acknowledged in "graduation" or "status elevation" ceremonies, during which other residents or members comment on the departing member's growth and offer good wishes for the future. Certificates, cards, or "memory books"

(Elbow, 1987) are but a few of the symbolic gifts that terminating clients may receive from staff and/or fellow clients. In individual and family work, social workers may choose to mark termination with small gifts such as a book, a plant, a framed inspirational quote, a bookmark, or some other token that is representative of the working relationship or the achievements while in service. Groups may conclude by creating a lasting product that is symbolic of the group, such as a collage or mural; in the process of creating this item, participants can reflect on the meaning the group had for them as members (Northen & Kurland, 2001).

The decision to use rituals to mark termination should be based on an understanding of the client, the

CASE EXAMPLE

Horizons is a halfway house for youth whose behavioral problems have resulted in hospitalization or incarceration. The program is intended to help teenagers readjust to community life and establish social supports so that they can return to their homes or move successfully into independent living. Given this focus, the length of stay for any individual resident varies considerably. Some youth encounter difficulties or reoffend; they are then returned to jail or to inpatient settings or simply "drop out of sight." These endings can be difficult for staff as they deal with disappointment in the client's failure to "make it" this time around and perhaps question what they might have done to prevent this outcome. It is also disturbing for other clients as they worry about their own challenges and their ability to successfully move on to the next step.

When residents terminate prematurely from the program, they are asked to attend a community meeting where they can process with the group their experiences in the program and the things they learned that can be of use in the future. Staff and other residents are also invited to share their observations and feelings with the intention of giving supportive and constructive feedback from a caring community—one to which the resident might someday return. When clients quit the program and drop out of sight, such sessions are still held. In these sessions, the residents and staff who remain process their feelings about the departure and discern lessons they can take away from it.

When residents have met their goals and are ready to move on to a more permanent living situation, staff discuss the plan and timeline for departure and stay alert to the difficulties that can arise at termination. The staff members make a point of discussing, in groups and individual sessions, the fears that can arise in moving from some place "comfortable" to the unknown. Sometimes, alumni of the program will visit to talk about their experiences and offer advice and encouragement. At this time, goals are reviewed, progress is charted, and the client's views are sought on which aspects of the program facilitated change. Clients and staff work together to anticipate the challenges ahead and to put in place the strategies necessary to address them.

During a resident's final days, the Horizons staff and residents create a "graduation" ceremony, and each resident offers the one who is leaving symbolic gifts to take on "the journey." These gifts may consist of inspirational quotes, reminders of inside jokes or shared experiences, and more tangible items, such as towels or pots and pans from the local secondhand store to help get established in the new setting.

Family members, teachers, and workers from other agencies are encouraged to attend the graduation and at the ceremony are asked to support the client in the next steps ahead. These ceremonies are often tearful and moving events, where the emphasis is on achievement and on hope for the future.

appropriateness of such actions for the agency or setting, and the meaning that the client may attribute to such actions. For example, giving a personal greeting card may be misinterpreted as a gesture of intimate friendship by some clients; for other clients, such as a child leaving foster care for a permanent placement, it may be a source of comfort and continuity. A gift that is too lavish may cause discomfort if the client feels the need to reciprocate in some way. "Goodbye parties" may reinforce feelings of accomplishment and confidence or they may obviate the feelings of sadness or ambivalence that must also be addressed as part of closure (Shulman, 1992). Graduation ceremonies may recreate past disappointments and lead to further setbacks if, for example, family members refuse to attend and acknowledge the changes the client has achieved (Jones, 1996).

Dorfman (1996) suggests asking the client how he or she would like to mark the final session and offering options if the person seems unsure what to suggest. Useful and meaningful ending rituals are numerous. For example, at the final session of the "Banana Splits" group for children of families undergoing divorce or separation, participants make and eat banana splits (McGonagle, 1986). A social worker may create a card depicting the "gift" or wish that he or she has for the client's continued success; participants in groups may write poems or rewrite lyrics to popular song melodies to mark the ending of a class or group (Walsh, 2007). Some clients may ask the social worker to create a "diploma" indicating what they have achieved and ask to have a photo taken together (Dorfman, 1996). Events to mark group terminations can facilitate the tasks of termination and model meaningful rituals in a way that clients might not have experienced previously (Jones, 1996). These endings can be linked symbolically to the goals for work and may help motivate other clients to strive toward the achievements being celebrated by fellow group or residence members.

SUMMARY

Social workers are well aware of the importance of engaging with clients and the skills and attitudes needed to build an effective working relationship. Unfortunately, when this relationship concludes, social workers may not be equally astute about "taking the relationship apart." Effective evaluation and termination leave both the practitioner and the client with a shared sense of the accomplishments achieved in their work together. This process affords the opportunity to model ending a relationship in a way that is not hurtful or damaging to the client. Effective termination equips the client with the skills and knowledge necessary to sustain gains or to seek further help as needed in the future.

COMPETENCY NOTES

EP 1   Demonstrate Ethical and Professional Behavior
- **Make ethical decisions by applying the standards of the NASW Code of Ethics, relevant laws and regulations, models for ethical decision making, ethical conduct of research, and additional codes of ethics as appropriate to context.** Clear boundaries are vital to the helping relationship. Social workers should handle the elements of termination (feelings, follow-up contact, closing rituals) carefully so that conflicts of interest and dual relationships are not created.
- **Use reflection and self-regulation to manage personal values and maintain professionalism in practice situations.** Social workers must be attuned to the feelings that they experience at termination and assure that they do not detrimentally affect the helping relationship.
- **Use supervision and consultation to guide professional judgment and behavior.** Supervision is an appropriate arena in which to address countertransference and other feelings and experiences that arise during termination. Supervisors can also help the worker manage questions of self-disclosure and confidentiality that might arise in unplanned endings. Consultation can be effective in designing and interpreting the results of practice evaluation.

EP 2   Engage Diversity and Difference in Practice
- **Present oneself as a learner and engage clients and constituencies as experts of their own experiences.** Evaluation requires that professionals open themselves up to client feedback.

EP 4   Engage in Practice-Informed Research and Research-Informed Practice
- **Apply critical thinking to engage in analysis of quantitative and qualitative research methods and research findings.** Social workers utilize critical thinking and existing literature

to create and evaluate plans and consider the factors that will affect termination.

EP 8 **Intervene with Individuals, Families, Groups, Organizations, and Communities**

- **Facilitate effective transitions and endings that advance mutually agreed-on goals.** In this chapter, readers learn about the factors that determine when termination takes place, the different kinds of endings, and the worker and client reactions that accompany them. Workers learn skills for helping clients with termination and sustaining the gains made in treatment.

EP 9 **Evaluate Practice with Individuals, Families, Groups, Organizations, and Communities**

- **Critically analyze, monitor, and evaluate intervention and program processes and outcomes.** The termination phase provides the opportunity to look with the client at his or her satisfaction with service, the elements of service that were effective, and the outcomes or goals attained. Social workers can use interviewing skills, standardized measures, goal attainment scaling, and other tools to evaluate their practice.

SKILLS DEVELOPMENT EXERCISES

in Evaluation and Termination

In the video "Problem Solving with the Corning Family," in her last session with Angela and Irwin Corning, the social worker, Ali, engages the couple in reflecting on the aspects of the helping process that were helpful and unhelpful to them. Based on your knowledge of evaluation and termination, address the following questions:

1. What goals were reached during the course of the Cornings' work with Ali?

2. What goals were not achieved?
3. How could the worker evaluate the efficacy of the helping process beyond asking for the clients' general feedback?
4. Based on the feedback Irwin and Angela provided, what further questions might Ali have asked to evaluate her intervention?
5. What risks do the Cornings face that might lead to a recurrence of problems?
6. What might Ali do in the final session to address those risks?
7. What feelings do Ali and her clients have about termination?
8. What steps might Ali take to strengthen her termination session with the Comings?

NOTES

1. For information on the concepts and steps of termination as they apply to macro practice, we suggest an article by Fauri, Harrigan, and Netting (1998).
2. For an excellent source on the considerations and strategies in termination across settings or using various theoretical orientations, see Walsh (2007).
3. See Meyer (2001) for a discussion of the dynamics of "no shows" and an effective clinical response.
4. For information on services in end-of-life care, see NASW's Standards of Social Work Practice in Palliative and End of Life Care (www.naswdc.org, 2011).
5. Baker, Piper, McCarthy, Majeskie, and Fiore (2004), Feltenstein (2008), Koob and Le Moal (2008), Matto (2005), Smyth (2005), and others have authored articles and books that describe the neurobiology of relapse, identify various factors that contribute to relapse, discuss beliefs and myths associated with addictions, and delineate models for relapse education and treatment with addicted and impulse-disordered clients.

Bibliography

10/66 Dementia Research Group (2009). *Helping carers to care: Trainers manual*. London: Alzheimer's Disease International.

A

Abbott, A. A., & Wood, K. M. (2000). Assessment: Techniques and instruments for data collection. In A. Abbott (Ed.), *Alcohol, tobacco, and other drugs: Challenging myths, assessing theories, individualizing interventions* (pp. 159–186). Washington, DC: NASW Press.

Abramovitz, M. (2005). The largely untold story of welfare reform and the human services. *Social Work, 50*, 174–186.

Abrams, L., & Moio, J. A. (2008). Critical race theory and the cultural competence dilemma in social work education. *Journal of Social Work Education, 45*(2), 254–261.

Abramson, M. (1985). The autonomy-paternalism dilemma in social work. *Social Work, 27*, 422–427.

Ackley, D. C. (1997). *Breaking free of managed care*. Orlando, FL: Guilford Press.

Adams, J., & Drake, R. (2006). Shared decision-making and evidence-based practice. *Community Mental Health Journal, 42*, 87–105.

Adams, K., Matto, H., & Le Croy, C. (2009). Limitations of evidence-based practice for social work education: Unpacking the complexity. *Journal of Social Work Education, 45*, 165–186.

Adams, R., Boscarinao, J., & Figley, C. (2006). Compassion fatigue and psychological distress among social workers: A validation study. *American Journal of Orthopsychiatry, 76*(1), 103–108.

Agbayani-Siewart, P. (2004). Assumptions of Asian-American similarity: The case of Filipino and Chinese American students. *Social Work, 49*, 39–51.

Aguilar, I. (1972). Initial contact with Mexican-American families. *Social Work, 20*, 379–382.

Aguilera, A., Gerza, M. J., & Munoz, R. F. (2010). Group cognitive-behavioral therapy for depression in Spanish: Culture-sensitive manualized treatment in practice. *Journal of Clinical Psychology: In Session, 66*, 857–867.

Ahijevych, K., & Wewers, M. (1993). Factors associated with nicotine dependence among African American women cigarette smokers. *Research in Nursing and Health, 16*, 292–293.

Aisenberg, E. (2008). Evidence-based practice in mental health care to ethnic minority communities: Has its practice fallen short of its evidence? *Social Work, 53*, 297–306.

Albert, S. M., Im, A., Brenner, L., Smith, M., & Waxman, R. (2002). Effect of a social work liaison program on family caregivers to people with brain injury. *Journal of Head Trauma Rehabilitation, 17*, 175–189.

Albert, V. (2000). Redefining welfare benefits: Consequences for adequacy and eligibility benefits. *Social Work, 45*, 300–310.

Alexander, J. F., Waldron, H. B., Robbins, M. S., & Neeb, A. A. (2013). *Functional family therapy for adolescent behavior problems*. Washington, DC: American Psychological Association.

Alexander, R., Jr. (2003). *Understanding legal concepts that influence social welfare policy and practice*. Pacific Grove, CA: Brooks/Cole.

Alexander, R., Jr. (2010). *Human behavior in the social environment: A macro, national, and international perspective*. Newbury Park, CA: Sage.

Al-Krenawi, A. (1998). Reconciling Western treatment and traditional healing: A social worker walks with the wind. *Reflections, 4*(3), 6–21.

Al-Krenawi, A. (1999) Social workers' practices in their non-Western home communities: Overcoming conflicts between professional and cultural values. *Families in Society: The Journal of Contemporary Social Services, 80*(5), 488–495.

Al-Krenawi, A., & Graham, J. (2000). Culturally sensitive social practice with Arab clients in mental health settings. *Health and Social Work, 25*, 9–22.

Allen, D. (2007). Black people have been let down by mental health services. *Nursing Standard, 22*(4), 28–31.

Allen, S., & Tracy, E. (Eds.). (2009). *Delivering home-based services: A social work perspective*. New York: Columbia University Press.

Allen-Meares, P., & Garvin, C. (Eds.). (2000). *The handbook of social work direct practice*. Thousand Oaks, CA: Sage.

Alley, G. R., & Brown, L. B. (2002). A diabetes problem-solving support group: Issues, process, and preliminary outcomes. *Social Work in Health Care, 36*, 1–9.

Altman, J., & Gohagen, D. (2009). Work with involuntary clients in child welfare settings. In R. H. Rooney (Ed.), *Strategies for work with involuntary clients* (2nd ed., pp. 334–347). New York: Columbia University Press.

American Association of Suicidology. (2004). *How do you recognize the warning signs of suicide?* Retrieved from http://www.suicidology.org/associations/1045/files/Mnemonic.pdf

American Psychiatric Association (APA). (2003). Practice guideline for the assessment and treatment of patients with suicidal behaviors. *American Journal of Psychiatry, 160,* 1–50.

American Psychiatric Association. (2013a). *Diagnostic and statistical manual of mental disorders* (5th ed.). Washington, DC: Author.

American Psychiatric Association. (2013b). *Highlights of changes from DSM-IV-TR to DSM-5.* Retrieved from http://www.dsm5.org/Documents/changes%20from%20dsm-iv-tr%20to%20dsm-5.pdf

Anderson, D. (2007). Multicultural group work: A force for developing and healing. *Journal for Specialists in Group Work, 32*(3), 224–244.

Anderson, D. A., & Worthen, D. (1997). Exploring a fourth dimension: Spirituality as a resource for the couple therapist. *Journal of Marital and Family Therapy, 23,* 3–12.

Anderson, S. G., Halter, A. P., & Gryzlak, B. M. (2004). Difficulties after leaving TANF: Inner-city women talk about reasons for returning to welfare. *Social Work, 49,* 185–194.

Anderson-Butcher, D., Khairallah, A. O., & Race-Bigelow, J. (2004). Mutual support groups for long-term recipients of TANF. *Social Work, 49,* 131–140.

Andrade, J. T. (2009). *Handbook of violence risk assessment and treatment: New approaches for forensic mental health professionals.* New York: Springer.

Andrews, A. B., & Ben-Arieh, A. (1999). Measuring and monitoring children's well-being across the world. *Social Work, 44,* 105–115.

Andrews, C. M., Darnell, J. S., McBride, T. D., & Gehbert, S. (2013). Social work and the implementation of the Affordable Care Act. *Health & Social Work, 38*(2), 67–71.

Anetzberger, G. J., Ishler, K. J., Mostade, J., & Blair, M. (2004). Gray and gay: A community dialogue on issues and concerns of older gays and lesbians. *Journal of Gay and Lesbian Social Services, 17,* 23–45.

Aponte, H. (1982). The person of the therapist: The cornerstone of therapy. *Family Therapy Networker, 21*(46), 19–21.

Applegate, J. S. (1992). The impact of subjective measures on nonbehavioral practice research: Outcome vs. process. *Families in Society, 73,* 100–108.

Appoh, L. Y., & Kekling, S. (2004). Effects of early childhood malnutrition on cognitive performance of Ghanaian children. *Journal of Psychology in Africa, 14*(1), 1–7.

Arean, P. A., Alexopoulos, G., & Chu, J. P. (2008). Cognitive behavioral case management for depressed low-income older adults. In D. Gallagher-Thompson, A. M. Steffen, L. W. Thompson, D. Gallagher-Thompson, A. M. Steffen, & L. W. Thompson (Eds.), *Handbook of behavioral and cognitive therapies with older adults* (pp. 219–232). New York: Springer Science + Business Media.

Arnold, E. M. (2002). End-of-life counseling and care: Assessment, interventions and clinical issues. In A. R. Roberts & G. J. Greene (Eds.), *Social workers' desk reference* (pp. 452–457). New York: Oxford University Press.

Association of Social Work Boards (ASWB). *Public protection database.* Culpeper, VA. Retrieved from http://www.aswb.org/members/public-protection-database

Association of Social Work Boards (ASWB). (2015). *Model regulatory standards for technology and social work practice.* Retrieved from https://www.aswb.org/wp-content/uploads/2015/03/ASWB-Model-Regulatory-Standards-for-Technology-and-Social-Work-Practice.pdf

Austin, K. M., Moline, M. E., & Williams, G. T. (1990). *Confronting malpractice: Legal and ethical dilemmas in psychotherapy.* Newbury Park, CA: Sage.

Austin, M. J., Coombs, M., & Barr, B. (2005). Community-centered clinical practice: Is the integration of micro and macro social work practice possible? *Journal of Community Practice, 13*(4), 9–30.

Ayón, C. (2014). Service needs among Latino immigrant families: Implications for social work practice. *Social Work, 59*(1), 13–48.

Ayón, C., Aisenberg, E., & Cimino, A. (2013). Latino families in the nexus of child welfare, welfare reform, and immigration policies: Is kinship care a lost opportunity? *Social Work, 58*(1), 91–94.

B

Badger, K., Royse, D., & Craig, C. (2008). Hospital social worker and indirect trauma exposure: An exploratory study of contributing factors. *Health and Social Work, 33*(1), 63–71.

Baer, J. (1999). Family relationships, parenting behavior, and adolescent deviance in three ethnic groups. *Families in Society, 80,* 279–285.

Bailey, M. J., & Danziger, S. (Eds.). (2013). *Legacies of the war on poverty.* New York: Russell Sage Foundation.

Bailey, V. (2001). Cognitive-behavioral therapies for children and adolescents. *Advances in Psychiatric Treatment, 7,* 224–232.

Bailey-Dempsey, C., & Reid, W. J. (1996). Intervention design and development: A case study. *Research on Social Work Practice, 6,* 208–228.

Baker, J., Parks-Savage, A., & Rehfuss, M. (2009). Teaching social skills in a virtual environment: An exploratory study. *Journal for Specialists in Group Work, 34,* 209–226.

Baker, T. B., Piper, M. E., McCarthy, D. E., Majeskie, M. R., & Fiore, M. C. (2004). Addiction motivation reformulated: An affective processing model of negative reinforcement. *Psychological Review, 11,* 33–51.

Bakker, L., Ward, T., Oyer, M., & Hudson, S. M. (1997). Out of the rut. A cognitive-behavioral treatment program for driving-while-disqualified offenders. *Behavioral Change, 14*, 29–38.

Balgopal, P., & Vassil, T. (1983). *Groups in social work: An ecological perspective*. New York: Macmillan.

Bandura, A. (1977). Self-efficacy: Toward a unifying theory of behavioral change. *Psychological Review, 84*, 191–215.

Bandura, A. (1986). *Social foundations of thought and action*. Englewood Cliffs, NJ: Prentice-Hall.

Bandura, A. (1988). Social cognitive theory. In R. Vasta (Ed.), *Annals of child development: Six theories of child development: Revised formulations and current issues* (pp. 1–60). Greenwich, CT: JAI Press.

Bandura, A. (1997). *Self-efficacy: The exercise of control*. New York: Freeman.

Bandura, A., & Locke, E. (2003). Negative self-efficacy and goal effects revisited. *Journal of Applied Psychology, 88*, 87–99.

Banerjee, M. M. (2002). Voicing realities and recommending reform in PRWORA. *Social Work, 47*, 315–328.

Barber, J. G. (1995). Working with resistant drug abusers. *Social Work, 40*, 17–23.

Bargal, D. (2004). Groups for reducing intergroup conflicts. In C. D. Garvin, L. M. Gutierrez, & M. J. Galinsky (Eds.), *Handbook of social work with groups* (pp. 292–306). New York: Guilford Press.

Barker, R. L. (1996). *The social work dictionary* (3rd ed.). Washington, DC: NASW Press.

Barker, R. L. (2003). *The social work dictionary* (5th ed.). Washington, DC: NASW Press.

Barkley, R. A. (2014). History of ADHD. In R. A. Barkley (Ed.), *Attention deficit hyperactivity disorder: A book for diagnosis & treatment* (pp. 1–122). New York: Guilford Press.

Barnes, A. (2008). Race and hospital diagnoses of schizophrenia and mood disorders. *Social Work, 53*, 77–83.

Barnhill, J. W. (Ed.). (2014). *DSM-5 clinical cases*. Arlington, VA: American Psychiatric Publishing.

Barsky, A., & Gould, J. (2002). *Clinicians in court: A guide to subpoenas, depositions, testifying, and everything else you need to know*. New York: Guilford Press.

Barth, R. P., Wildfire, J., & Green, R. L. (2006). Placement into foster care and the interplay of urbanicity, child behavior problems, and poverty. *American Journal of Orthopsychiatry, 76*, 358–366.

Barth, R. P., Lee, B. R., Lindsey, M. A., Collins, K. S., Strieder, F., Chorpita, B. F., et al. (2012). Evidence-based practice at a crossroads: The timely emergence of common elements and common factors. *Research on social work practice, 22*(1), 108–119.

Bartlett, H. M. (1970). *The common base of social work practice*. New York: National Association of Social Workers.

Bartlett, H. M. (1964). The place and use of knowledge in social work practice. *Social Work, 9*(3), 36–46.

Barton, C., & Alexander, J. (1981). Functional family therapy. In A. Gurman & D. Kniskern (Eds.), *Handbook of family therapy* (pp. 403–443). New York: Brunner/Mazel.

Barusch, A. S. (2002). *Foundations of social policy, social justice, public programs, and the social work profession*. Itasca, IL: Peacock.

Beck, A. (1974). Phases in the development of structure in therapy and encounter groups. In D. Wexler & L. Rice (Eds.), *Innovations in client-centered therapy*. New York: Wiley.

Beck, A. T. (1967). *Depression*. New York: Harper.

Beck, A. T. (1976). *Cognitive therapy and the emotional disorders*. New York: International Universities Press.

Beck, A. T., Rush, A. J., Shaw, B. F., & Emery, G. (1979). *Cognitive therapy of depression*. New York: Guilford Press.

Beck, A. T., Steer, R. A., & Brown, G. K. (1996). *BDI-II, Beck depression inventory: Manual*. Boston: Harcourt Brace.

Beck, J. S. (1995). *Cognitive therapy: Basics and beyond*. New York: Guilford Press.

Becvar, D. S., & Becvar, R. J. (2000a). *Family therapy: A systemic integration* (4th ed.). Boston: Allyn & Bacon.

Becvar, D. S., & Becvar, R. J. (2000b). Family relationships, parenting behavior, and adolescent deviance in three ethnic groups. *Families in Society, 80*, 279–285.

Bedell, S. E., Jabbour, S., Boldberg, R., Glaser, H., Gobble, S., Young-Xu, Y., et al. (2000). Discrepancies in the use of medications: Their extent and predictors in an outpatient practice. *Archives of Internal Medicine, 160*(14), 2129–2134.

Behnke, A. O., Plunkett, S. W., Sands, T., & Bamaca-Colber, M. Y. (2011). The relationship between adolescents' perceptions of discrimination, neighborhood risk, and parenting on self-esteem and depressive symptoms. *Journal of Cross Cultural Psychology, 42*(7), 1179–1197.

Behroozi, C. S. (1992). A model for work with involuntary applicants in groups. *Social Work with Groups, 15*, 223–238.

Bell, H., Kulkarni, S., & Dalton, L. (2003). Organizational prevention of vicarious trauma. *Families in Society: The Journal of Contemporary Social Services, 84*(4), 463–470.

Bell, J. L. (1995). Traumatic event debriefing: Service delivery designs and the role of social work. *Social Work, 40*, 36–43.

Bell, L. (2001). Patterns of interaction in multidisciplinary child protection teams in New Jersey. *Child Abuse and Neglect, 25*, 65–80.

Bell-Tolliver, L., Burgess, R., & Brock, L. J. (2009). African American therapists working with African American families: An exploration of the strengths perspective in treatment. *Journal of Marital & Family Therapy, 35*, 293–307.

Bembry, J. X., & Ericson, C. (1999). Therapeutic termination with the early adolescent who has experienced multiple losses. *Child and Adolescent Social Work Journal, 16,* 177–189.

Benen, S. (2008, September 4). In defense of community organizers. *Washington Monthly.* Retrieved from http://www.washingtonmonthly.com/archives/individual/2008_09/014559.php

Bengtson, V. L. (2001). Beyond the nuclear family: The increasing importance of multigenerational bonds. *Journal of Marriage and Family, 63,* 1–16.

Bennett, C. J., Legon, J., & Zilberfein, F. (1989). The significance of empathy in current hospital based practice. *Social Work in Health Care, 14*(2), 27–41.

Benson, M. J., Schindler-Zimmerman, T., & Martin, D. (1991). Accessing children's perceptions of their family: Circular questioning revisited. *Journal of Marital and Family Therapy, 17,* 363–372.

Berg, I. K., & Jaya, A. (1993). Different and same: Family therapy with Asian-American families. *Journal of Marital and Family Therapy, 19,* 31–38.

Berg, I. K., & Kelly, S. (2000). *Building solutions in child protection.* New York: Norton.

Bergeron, L. R., & Gray, B. (2003). Ethical dilemmas of reporting suspected elder abuse. *Social Work, 48,* 96–105.

Bergold, J., & Thomas, S. (2012). Participatory research methods: A methodological approach in motion. *Forum: Qualitative Social Research, 13*(1). Retrieved from http://www.qualitative-research.net

Berlin, S. B. (2001). *Clinical social work: A cognitive-integrative perspective.* New York: Oxford University Press.

Berlin, S. B., & Marsh, J. C. (1993). *Informing practice decisions.* New York: Macmillan.

Berman-Rossi, T., & Kelly, T. B. (2000, February). *Teaching students to understand and utilize the changing paradigm of stage of group development theory.* Paper presented at the 46th annual program meeting of the Council on Social Work Education, New York.

Berman-Rossi, T., & Rossi, P. (1990). Confidentiality and informed consent in school social work. *Social Work in Education, 12,* 195–207.

Bernard, H., Burlingame, G., Flores, P., Greene, L., Joyce, A., Kobos, J. C., & Feirman, D. (2007). *Practice guidelines for group psychotherapy.* Retrieved from http://www.agpa.org/guidelines/index.html

Bernstein, B. (1977). Privileged social work practice. *Social Casework, 66,* 387–393.

Bernstein, B. E., & Hartsell, T. L. (2005). *The portable guide to testifying in court for mental health professionals: An A–Z guide to being an effective witness.* Hoboken, NJ: Wiley.

Bertcher, H., & Maple, F. (1985). Elements and issues in group composition. In P. Glasser, R. Sarri, & R. Vinter (Eds.), *Individual change through small groups* (pp. 180–202). New York: Free Press.

Bertolino, B., & O'Hanlon, B. (2002). *Collaborative, competency-based counseling and therapy.* Boston: Allyn & Bacon.

Beyer, J. A., & Balster, T. C. (2001). Assessment and classification in institutional corrections. In A. Walsh (Ed.), *Correctional assessment, casework, and counseling* (3rd ed., pp. 137–159). Lanham, MD: American Correctional Association.

Biddle, B. J. (1986). Recent developments in role theory. *Annual Review of Sociology, 12,* 67–92.

Bidgood, B., Holosko, M., & Taylor, L. (2003). A new working definition of social work practice: A turtle's view. *Research on Social Work Practice, 13,* 400–408.

Biestek, F. (1957). *The casework relationship.* Chicago: Loyola University Press.

Binder, C. (2008). *Medicaid targeted case management (TCM). Benefits.* Congressional Research Service Report for Congress. Retrieved September 29, 2010 from www.pascenter.org/document/RL34426.pdf

Birmaher, B., Williamson, D. E., Dahl, R. E., Axelson, D. A., Kaufman, J., Dorn, L. D., & Ryan, N. D. (2004). Clinical presentation and course of depression in youth: Does onset in childhood differ from onset in adolescence? *Journal of the American Academy of Child and Adolescent Psychiatry, 43*(1), 63–70.

Blitz, L. V., Pender Greene, M., Bernabei, S., & Shah, V. P. (2014). Think creatively and act decisively: Creating antiracist alliance for social work. *Social Work, 59*(4), 1–4.

Block, L. R. (1985). On the potentiality and limits of time: The single-session group and the cancer patient. *Social Work with Groups, 8,* 81–99.

Block-Lerner, J., Adair, C., Plumb, J., Rhatigan, D., & Orsillo, S. (2007). The case for mindfulness-based approaches in the cultivation of empathy: Does non-judgmental present moment awareness increase capacity for perspective-taking and empathic concern? *Journal of Marital and Family Therapy, 33,* 501–516.

Blome, W., & Steib, S. (2004). Whatever the problem, the answer is "evidence-based practice"—or is it? *Child Welfare, 83,* 611–615.

Bloom, M., Fischer, J., & Orme, J. G. (2003). *Evaluating practice: Guidelines for the accountable professional* (4th ed.). Boston: Allyn & Bacon.

Bloom, M., Fischer, J., & Orme, J. G. (2006). *Evaluating practice: Guidelines for the accountable professional* (5th ed.). Boston: Allyn & Bacon.

Bloom, M., Fischer, J., & Orme, J. G. (2009). *Evaluating practice: Guidelines for the accountable professional* (6th ed.). Boston: Allyn & Bacon.

Boehm, A., & Staples, L. H. (2004). Empowerment: The point of view of consumers. *Families in Society, 85,* 270–280.

Bohart, A., & Greenburg, L. (1997). Empathy and psychotherapy: An introductory overview. In A. Bohart & L. Greenburg (Eds.), *Empathy reconsidered: New directions in psychotherapy* (pp. 3–31). Washington, DC: American Psychological Association.

Borum, R., Bartel, P., & Forth, A. (2003). *Manual for the Structured Assessment for Violence Risk in Youth (SAVRY): Version 1.1.* Tampa, FL: Louis de la Parte Florida Mental Health Institute, University of South Florida.

Borum, R., & Verhaagen, D. (2006). *Assessing and managing violence risk in juveniles.* New York: Guilford Press.

Borys, D. S., & Pope, K. S. (1989). Dual relationships between therapist and client: A national study of psychologists, psychiatrists, and social workers. *Professional Psychology: Research and Practice, 20,* 283–293.

Bostic, J. Q., Shadid, L. G., & Blotcky, M. J. (1996). Our time is up: Forced terminations during psychotherapy. *American Journal of Psychotherapy, 50,* 347–359.

Bowman, E. S., & Chu, J. A. (2000). Trauma–A fourth paradigm for the third millennium. *Journal of Trauma and Disassociation, 1*(2), 1–12.

Boyd, R. (2014). African American disproportionality and disparity in child welfare: Toward a comprehensive conceptual framework. *Child and Youth Services Review, 37,* 12–27.

Boyd-Franklin, N. (1989). *Black families in therapy: A multisystems approach.* New York: Guilford Press.

Boyd-Franklin, N., & Bry, B. H. (2000). *Reaching out in family therapy: Home-based school and community interventions.* New York: Guilford Press.

Bradley, E. H., & Taylor, L. A. (2013). *The American health care paradox: Why spending more is getting us less.* New York: United States Public Affairs/Perseus Book Group.

Bradshaw, W. (1996). Structured group work for individuals with schizophrenia: A coping skills approach. *Research on Social Work Practice, 6,* 139–154.

Brady, J. (2006). The association between alcohol misuse and suicidal behaviour. *Alcohol and Alcoholism, 4*(5), 473–478.

Brager, G., & Holloway, S. (1978). *Changing human service organizations: Politics and practice.* New York: Free Press.

Brager, G., & Holloway, S. (1983). A process model for changing organizations from within. In R. M. Kramer & H. Specht (Eds.), *Readings in community organization practice* (pp. 198–208). Englewood Cliffs, NJ: Prentice-Hall.

Brehm, S. S. (1976). *The application of social psychology to clinical practice.* New York: Wiley.

Brehm, S. S., & Brehm, J. W. (1981). *Psychological reactance: A theory of freedom and control.* New York: Academic Press.

Brekke, J. (2012). Shaping a science of social work. *Research on Social Work Practice, 22*(5), 455–464.

Brent, D. A., Johnson, B., Bartle, S., Bridge, J., Rather, C., Matta, J., et al. (1993). Personality disorder tendency to impulsive violence, and suicidal behavior in adolescents. *Journal of the American Academy of Child and Adolescent Psychiatry, 32,* 69–75.

Breton, M. (1985). Reaching and engaging people: Issues and practice principles. *Social Work with Groups, 8*(3), 7–21.

Breton, M. (2006). Path dependence and the place of social action in social work. *Social Work with Groups, 29,* 25–44.

Bride, B., & Figley, C. (2007). The fatigue compassionate social workers: An introduction to the Special Issue on Compassion Fatigue. *Clinical Social Work Journal, 35*(3), 151–153.

Briggs, H. E., & Rzepnicki, T. L. (Eds.). (2004). *Using evidence in social work practice: Behavioral perspectives.* Chicago: Lyceum Books.

Bronfenbrenner, U. (1989). Ecological systems theory. In R. Vasta (Ed.), *Annals of child development: Six theories of child development: Revised formulations and current issues* (pp. 187–247). Greenwich, CT: JAI Press.

Brown, J. L., & Pollitt, E. (1996). Malnutrition, poverty, and intellectual development. *Scientific American, 274*(2), 38–43.

Brown, L. S. (1994). *Subjective dialogues: Theory in feminist therapy.* New York: Basic Books.

Brownlee, K. (1996). Ethics in community mental health care: The ethics of nonsexual relationships: A dilemma for the rural mental health professionals. *Community Mental Health Journal, 32,* 497–503.

Brueggemann, W. G. (2006). *The practice of macro social work* (3rd ed.). Belmont, CA: Brooks/Cole.

Brun, C., & Rapp, C. (2001). Strengths-based case management: Individuals' perspectives on strengths and the case manager relationship. *Social Work, 46,* 278–288.

Bundy-Fazioli, K., Briar-Lawson, K., & Hardiman, E. R. (2009). A qualitative examination of power between child welfare workers and parents. *British Journal of Social Work, 39,* 1447–1464.

Burford, G., & Hudson, J. (2009). *Family group conferencing: New directions in community-centered child and family practice.* Piscataway, NJ: Aldine-Transactions.

Burford, G., & Pennell, J. (2004). From agency client to community-based consumer: The family group conference as a consumer-led group in child welfare. In C. D. Garvin, L. M. Gutierrez, & M. J. Galinsky (Eds.), *Handbook of social work with groups* (pp. 415–431). New York: Guilford Press.

Burghardt, S. (2011). *Macro practice in social work for the 21st century.* Los Angeles: Sage.

Burghardt, S. (2013). *Macro practice for the 21st century* (2nd ed.). Thousand Oaks, CA: Sage.

Burlingame, G. M., Fuhriman, A., & Mosier, J. (2003). The differential effectiveness of group psychotherapy: A meta-analytic perspective. *Group Dynamics: Theory, Research, and Practice, 7*(1), 3–12.

Burlingame, G. M., MacKenzie, K. R., & Strauss, B. (2004). Small group treatment: Evidence for effectiveness and mechanisms of change. In M. Lambert (Ed.), *Bergin and Garfield's handbook of psychotherapy and behavior change* (5th ed., pp. 647–696). New York: Wiley.

Burlingame, G. M., Strauss, B., Joyce, A., MacNair-Semands, R., MacKenzie, K. R., Ogrodniczuk, J., & Taylor, S. (2006). *CORE Battery-Revised: An assessment tool kit for promoting optimal group selection, process, and outcome.* New York: American Group Psychotherapy Association.

Burnette, D. (1999). Custodial grandparents in Latino families: Patterns of service use and predictors of unmet needs. *Social Work, 44,* 22–34.

Burns, A., Lawlor, B., & Craig, S. (2004). *Assessment scales in old age psychiatry* (2nd ed.). London: Martin Dunitz.

Bush, I. R. (2004). An examination of five essential competencies for empowerment practice. *Journal of Baccalaureate Social Work, 9*(2), 47–62.

Butler, S. S., & Hope, B. (1999). Health and well-being for late middle-aged and old lesbians in a rural area. *Journal of Gay and Lesbian Social Services, 9*(4), 27–46.

C

Cain, R. (1991a). Relational contexts and information management among gay men. *Families in Society, 72,* 344–352.

Cain, R. (1991b). Stigma management and gay identity development. *Social Work, 36,* 67–71.

Cameron, E., Fox, J., Anderson, M., & Cameron, C. (2010). Resilient youths use humor to enhance socioemotional functioning during a day in the life. *Journal of Adolescent Research, 25*(5), 716–742.

Cameron, M., & Keenan, E. (2010). The common factors model: Implications for transtheoretical clinical social work practice. *Social Work, 55,* 63–73.

Cameron, S., & Turtle-Song, I. (2002). Learning to write case notes using the SOAP format. *Journal of Counselling and Development, 80,* 286–292.

Campbell, J. A. (1988). Client acceptance of single-subject evaluation procedures. *Social Work Research Abstracts, 24,* 21–22.

Campbell, J. A. (1990). Ability of practitioners to estimate client acceptance of single-subject evaluation procedures. *Social Work, 35,* 9–14.

Campbell Collaboration. (n.d.). *The Campbell Collaboration Library of Systematic Reviews.* Retrieved from http://www.campbellcollaboration.org/library.php

Canda, E. R. (1983). General implications of shamanism for clinical social work. *International Social Work, 26,* 14–22.

Canda, E. R. (1997). Spirituality. In R. L. Edwards (Ed.), *Encyclopedia of social work 1997 supplement* (19th ed., pp. 299–309). Washington, DC: NASW Press.

Caplan, G. (1964). *Principles of preventive psychiatry.* New York: Basic Books.

Caplan, T. (1995). Safety and comfort, content and process: Facilitating open group work with men who batter. *Social Work with Groups, 18*(2/3), 33–51.

Carkhuff, R. (1969). *Helping and human relations: Practice and research.* New York: Holt, Rinehart & Winston.

Carlton-LaNey, I. (1999). African American social work pioneers' response to need. *Social Work, 44,* 311–321.

Carniol, B. (1992). Structural social work: Maurice Moreau's challenge to social work practice. *Journal of Progressive Human Services, 3*(1), 1–19.

Caro, R. (2012). *Passage of power: The years of Lyndon Johnson.* New York: Knopf.

Carr, E. S. (2004). Accessing resources, transforming systems: Group work with poor and homeless people. In C. D. Garvin, L. M. Gutierrez, & M. J. Galinsky (Eds.), *Handbook of social work with groups* (pp. 360–383). New York: Guilford Press.

Carrell, S. (2000). *Group exercises for adolescents: A manual for therapists* (2nd ed.). Thousand Oaks, CA: Sage.

Carter, B., & McGoldrick, M. (1999). Coaching at various stages of the life cycle. In B. Carter & M. McGoldrick (Eds.), *The expanded family life cycle: Individual, family, and social perspectives* (2nd ed., pp. 436–454). Boston: Allyn & Bacon.

Carter, B., & McGoldrick, M. (Eds.). (1988). *The changing life cycle: A framework for family therapy* (2nd ed.). New York: Gardener Press.

Carter, B., & McGoldrick, M. (Eds.). (2005). *The expanded life cycle. Individual, family and social perspectives* (3rd ed.). Boston: Allyn & Bacon.

Carter, C. S. (2000). Church burning: Using a contemporary issue to teach community organization. *Journal of Social Work Education, 36,* 79–88.

Case Management Society of America (CMSA). (2010). *Standards of practice for case management.* Little Rock, AR: Author. Retrieved from www.cmsa.org.

Caspi, J. (2008). Building a sibling aggression treatment model: Design and development research in action. *Research on Social Work Practice, 18,* 575–585.

Caspi, J., & Reid, W. J. (2002). *Educational supervision in social work. A task-centered model for field instruction and staff development.* New York: Columbia University Press.

Center for Economic and Social Justice. (n.d.). *Defining economic and social justice.* Retrieved from http://www.cesj.org/thirdway/economicjustice-defined.htm

Centers for Disease Control and Prevention. (2009). *Depression is not a normal part of growing old.* Retrieved from http://www.cdc.gov/aging/mentalhealth/depression.htm

Centers for Disease Control and Prevention. (2015). *Suicide prevention.* Injury Prevention and Control, Division of Violence Prevention. Retrieved from http://www.cdc.gov/violenceprevention/pub/youth_suicide.html

Chandler, S. (1985). Mediation: Conjoint problem solving. *Social Work, 30,* 346–349.

Charnley, H., & Langley, J. (2007). Developing cultural competence as a framework for anti-heterosexist social work practice: Reflections from the UK. *Journal of Social Work, 7*, 307–321.

Chau, K. L. (1993). Needs assessment for group work with people of color: A conceptual formulation. *Social Work with Groups, 15*(2/3), 53–66.

Chazin, R., Kaplan, S., & Terio, S. (2000). The strengths perspective in brief treatment with culturally diverse clients. *Crisis Intervention, 6*, 41–50.

Chemtob, C. M., Hamada, R. S., Bauer, G., Torigoe, R. Y., & Kinney, B. (1988). Patient suicide: Frequency and impact on psychologists. *Professional Psychology Research and Practice, 19*, 416–420.

Chen, E. C., Kakkad, D., & Balzano, J. (2008). Multicultural competence and evidence-based practice in group therapy. *Journal of Clinical Psychology: In Session, 64*(11), 1261–1278. Doi:10.1002/jclp.20533

Chen, S. W., & Davenport, D. (2005). Cognitive behavioral therapy with Chinese American clients: Cautions and modifications. *Psychotherapy Theory Research, Practice and Training, 42*(1), 101–110.

Chesler, M. (1994a). Organizational development is not the same as multicultural organizational development. In E. Y. Cross, J. H. Katz, F. A. Miller, & E. H. Seashore (Eds.), *The promise of diversity* (pp. 240–351). Burr Ridge, IL: Irwin.

Chesler, M. (1994b). Strategies for multicultural organizational development. *Diversity Factors, 2*(2), 12–18.

Cheung, M. (2006). *Therapeutic games and guided imagery: Tools for mental health and school professionals working with children, adolescents, and their families.* Chicago: Lyceum Books.

Child Welfare League of America. (1990). *Agency self-improvement checklist.* Washington, DC: Author.

Chinman, M. J., Rosenheck, R. A., & Lam, J. A. (2000). Client–case manager racial matching in a program for homeless persons with serious mental illness. *Psychiatric Services, 51*, 1265–1272.

Choi, G. (1997). Acculturative stress, social support, and depression in Korean American families. *Journal of Family Social Work, 2*, 79–81.

Chorpita, B. F., Daleiden, E. L., & Weisz, J. R. (2005). Identifying and selecting the common elements of evidence based interventions: A distillation and matching model. *Mental Health Services, 7*(5), 20.

Chorpita, B. F., Daleiden, E. L., & Collins, K. S. (2014). Managing and adapting practice: A system for applying evidence in clinical care with youth and families. *Clinical Social Work Journal, 42*, 134–142.

Cingolani, J. (1984). Social conflict perspective on work with involuntary clients. *Social Work, 29*, 442–446.

Citron, P. (1978). Group work with alcoholic poly-drug involved adolescents with deviant behavior syndrome. *Social Work with Groups, 1*, 39–52.

Cleaveland, C. (2010). "We are not criminals." Social work advocacy and unauthorized migrants. *Social Work, 55*(1), 74–81.

Clemans, S. E. (2004). Recognizing vicarious traumatization: A single session group model for trauma workers. *Social Work with Groups, 27*(2/3), 55–74.

Clifford, D., & Burke, B. (2005). Developing anti-oppression ethics in the new curriculum. *Social Work Education, 87*, 677–692.

Clinical Social Work Federation. (1997). *Definition of clinical social work* (revised). Retrieved from: http://www.cswf.org/www/info/html

Cnaan, R. A., & Rothman, J. (1986). Conceptualizing community intervention: An empirical test of three models of community organization. *Administration in Social Work, 10*(3), 41–55.

Coady, N., & Lehmann, P. (Eds.). (2008). *Theoretical perspectives for direct social work practice: A generalist-eclectic approach* (2nd ed.). New York: Springer.

Coady, N., & Marziali, E. (1994). The association between global and specific measures of the therapeutic relationship. *Psychotherapy, 31*, 17–27.

Cobb, N. H. (2008). Cognitive-behavioral theory and treatment. In N. Coady & P. Lehmann (Eds.), *Theoretical perspectives for direct social work practice: A generalist-eclectic approach* (2nd ed., pp. 221–248). New York: Springer.

Cohen, E. D., & Cohen, G. S. (1999). *The virtuous therapist: Ethical practice of counseling and psychotherapy.* Belmont, CA: Brooks/Cole.

Coholic, D., Lougheed, S., & Cadell, S. (2009). Exploring the helpfulness of arts-based methods with children living in foster care. *Traumatology, 15*(3), 64–71.

Colvin, J., Lee, M., Maganano, J., & Smith, V. (2008). The partners in prevention program: The evaluation and evolution of the task-centered case management model. *Research on Social Work Practice, 18*, 607–615.

Comer, E., Meier, A., & Galinsky, M. J. (2004). Development of innovative group work practice using the intervention research paradigm. *Social Work, 49*, 250–260.

Comey, J. (2015). Speech on race. February 13, 2015. Retrieved from http://www.washingtonpost.com/blogs/on-leadership/wp/2015/02/13/fbi-director-james-comeys-unprecedented-speech-on-race/

Compton, B. R., & Galaway, B. (1994). *Social work processes* (6th ed.). Pacific Grove, CA: Brooks/Cole.

Compton, B. R., Galaway, B., & Cournoyer, B. (2005). *Social work processes* (7th ed.). Pacific Grove, CA: Brooks/Cole.

Condrey, S. E., Facer, R. L., & Hamilton, J. P. (2005). Employees amidst welfare reform: TANF employees overall and organizational job satisfaction. *Journal of Human Behavior in the Social Environment, 12*, 221–242.

Congress, E. P. (1994). The use of culturegrams to assess and empower culturally diverse families. *Families in Society, 75,* 531–540.

Congress, E. P. (2000). Crisis intervention with diverse families. In A. R. Roberts (Ed.), *Crisis intervention handbook: Assessment, treatment and research* (2nd ed., pp. 430–448). New York: Oxford University Press.

Congress, E. P. (2002). Using the culturegram with diverse families. In A. R. Roberts & G. J. Green (Eds.), *Social workers' desk reference* (pp. 57–61). New York: Oxford University Press.

Congress, E. P., & Kung, W. W. (2005). *Using the culturagram to assess and empower culturally diverse families.* In E. P. Congress & M. Gonzalez (Eds.), *Multicultural perspectives in working with families* (pp. 3–21). New York: Springer.

Congress, E. P., & Lynn, M. (1994). Group work programs in public schools: Ethical dilemmas and cultural diversity. *Social Work in Education, 15,* 107–114.

Congress, E. P., & Lynn, M. (1997). Group work practice in the community: Navigating the slippery slope of ethical dilemmas. *Social Work with Groups, 20*(3), 61–74.

Conner, K., & Grote, N. K. (2008). Enhancing the cultural relevance of empirically-supported mental health interventions. *Families in Society, 89,* 587–595.

Connolly, C. M. (2006). A feminist perspective of resilience in lesbian couples. *Journal of Feminist Family Therapy, 18*(1/2), 137–162.

Conrad, D., & Kellar-Guenther, Y. (2006). Compassion fatigue, burnout and compassion satisfaction among Colorado child protection workers. *Child Abuse and Neglect, 30*(10), 1071–1080.

Constable, R., & Lee, D. B. (2004). *Social work with families: Content and process.* Chicago: Lyceum Books.

Cook, J. B., & Kaffenberger, C. J. (2003). Solution shop: A solution-focused counseling and study skills program for middle school. *Professional Counseling Journal, 7*(12), 116–124.

Copeland, R., & Ashley, D. (2005). *Adolescent and child urgent threat evaluation: Professional manual.* Lutz, FL: Psychological Assessment Resources.

Corcoran, J. (1997). A solution-oriented approach to working with juvenile offenders. *Child and Adolescent Social Work Journal, 14,* 227–288.

Corcoran, J. (1998). Solution-focused practice with middle and high school at-risk youth. *Social Work in Education, 20,* 232–243.

Corcoran, J. (2000). *Evidence-based social work practice with families: A lifespan approach.* New York: Springer.

Corcoran, J. (2002). Evidence-based treatment of adolescents with externalizing disorders. In A. R. Roberts & G. J. Greene (Eds.), *Social workers' desk reference* (pp. 793–796). New York: Oxford University Press.

Corcoran, J. (2008). Solution-focused therapy. In N. Coady & P. Lehmann (Eds.), *Theoretical perspectives for direct social work practice: A generalist-eclectic approach* (2nd ed., pp. 429–446). New York: Springer.

Corcoran, J., & Franklin, C. (1998). A solution-focused approach to physical abuse. *Journal of Family Psychotherapy, 9,* 69–73.

Corcoran, J., & Pillai, V. (2009). A review of the research on solution-focused therapy. *British Journal of Social Work, 39,* 234–242.

Corcoran, J., & Stephenson, M. (2000). The effectiveness of solution-focused therapy with child behavior problems: A preliminary report. *Families in Society, 81,* 468–474.

Corcoran, J., & Walsh, J. (2010). *Clinical assessment and diagnosis in social work practice* (2nd ed.). New York: Oxford University Press.

Corcoran, K., & Vandiver, V. (1996). *Maneuvering the maze of managed care: Skills for mental health practitioners.* New York: Free Press.

Corey, G. (1990). *Theory and practice of group counseling.* Pacific Grove, CA: Brooks/Cole.

Corey, G. (2009). *Theory and practice of counseling and psychotherapy* (8th ed.). Belmont, CA: Brooks/Cole.

Corey, G., Corey, M. S., & Callanan, P. (2007). *Issues and ethics in the helping professions* (7th ed.). Pacific Grove, CA: Brooks/Cole.

Corey, G., Corey, M. S., Callanan, P. J., & Russell, J. M. (2004). *Group techniques* (3rd ed.). Pacific Grove, CA: Brooks/Cole.

Corey, G., Corey, M. S., Corey, C., & Callanan, P. (2014). *Issues and ethics in the helping professions* (9th ed.). Belmont, CA: Brooks/Cole.

Corey, G., Haynes, R. H., Moulton, P., & Muratori, M. (2014). *Clinical supervision in the helping professions: A practical guide* (2nd ed.). Alexandria, VA: Wiley, American Counseling Association.

Corey, M. S., & Corey, G. (1992). *Groups: Process and practice* (4th ed.). Pacific Grove, CA: Brooks/Cole.

Corey, M. S., & Corey, G. (2002). *Groups: Process and practice* (6th ed.). Pacific Grove, CA: Brooks/Cole.

Corey, M. S., & Corey, G. (2006). *Groups: Process and practice* (7th ed.). Pacific Grove, CA: Brooks/Cole.

Cormier, S., & Nurius, P. S. (2003). *Interviewing and change strategies for helpers: Fundamental skills and cognitive behavioral interventions.* Pacific Grove, CA: Brooks/Cole.

Cormier, S., Nurius, P. S., & Osborn, C. J. (2009). *Interviewing and change strategies for helpers: Fundamental skills in cognitive behavioral interventions* (6th ed.). Belmont, CA: Brooks/Cole.

Cornelius, L. J., Simpson, G. M., Ting, L., Wiggins, E., & Lipford, S. (2003). Reach out and I'll be there: Mental health crisis intervention and mobile outreach services to urban African Americans. *Health and Social Work, 28,* 74–78.

Corwin, M. (2002). *Brief treatment in clinical social work practice*. Pacific Grove, CA: Brooks/Cole.

Council on Social Work Education (CSWE). (2015). *Educational policy and accreditation standards*. Alexandria, VA: Council on Social Work Education. Retrieved from http://www.cswe.org/File.aspx?id=13780

Cournoyer, B. R. (2004). *Evidence-based social work practice skills book*. Boston: Allyn & Bacon.

Cournoyer, B. R. (1991). *Selected techniques for eclectic practice: Clinically speaking*. Indianapolis, IN: Author.

Cournoyer, B. R. (2011). *The social work skills workbook* (6th ed.). Belmont, CA: Brooks/Cole.

Cowger, C. D. (1992). Assessment of client strengths. In D. Saleebey (Ed.), *The strengths perspective in social work practice* (pp. 139–147). New York: Longman.

Cowger, C. D. (1994). Assessing client strengths: Clinical assessment for client empowerment. *Social Work, 39*, 262–267.

Cowger, C. D., & Snively, C. A. (2002). Assessing client strengths: Individual, family and community empowerment. In D. Saleebey & A. R. Roberts (Eds.), *The strengths perspective in social work practice* (3rd ed., pp. 106–123). Boston: Allyn & Bacon.

Cox, E. O. (1991). The critical role of social action in empowerment oriented groups. *Social Work with Groups, 14*(3/4), 77–90.

Crabtree, B. F., & Miller, W. L. (1992). *Doing qualitative research*. Newbury Park, CA: Sage.

Cross, T. L., Bazron, B. J., Dennis, K., & Isaacs, M. R. (1989). *Towards a culturally competent system of care*. Washington, DC: Georgetown University Child Development Center.

Crosson-Tower, C. (2004). *Exploring child welfare: A practice perspective*. Boston: Allyn & Bacon.

Cummings, N. A. (1991). Brief intermittent therapy throughout the life cycle. In C. S. Austad & W. H. Berman (Eds.), *Psychotherapy in managed health care: The optimal use of time and resources* (pp. 35–45). Washington, DC: American Psychological Association.

Cunningham, M. (2003). Impact of trauma social work clinicians: Empirical findings. *Social Work, 48*, 451–459.

Curry, R. (2007, November/December). Surviving professional stress. *Social Work Today*, pp. 25–28.

D

Daft, R. L. (2010). *Organization theory and design* (10th ed.). Marion, OH: Southwestern.

Dahlen, E. R., & Deffenbacher, J. L. (2000). A partial component analysis of Beck's cognitive therapy for anger control. *Journal of Cognitive Psychotherapy, 14*, 77–95.

Dane, B. O. (2000). Child welfare workers: An innovative approach for interacting with secondary trauma. *Journal of Social Work Education, 36*, 27–38.

Dane, B. O., & Simon, B. L. (1991). Resident guests: Social workers in host settings. *Social Work, 36*, 208–213.

Danzy, J., & Jackson, S. M. (1997). Family preservation and support services: A missed opportunity. *Child Welfare, 76*, 31.

Darnell, J. S. (2013). Navigators and assisters: Two case management roles for social workers in the Affordable Care Act. *Health & Social Work, 38*(2), 123–126.

Davis, B. (2005). Ms. Palmer on second street. *Social Work, 50*, 89–92.

Davis, C., & Goodman, H. (2014). Virtual communities of practice in social group work education. *Social Work with Groups, 37*(1), 85–95.

Davis, I. P., & Reid, W. J. (1988). Event analysis in clinical practice and process research. *Social Casework, 69*, 298–306.

Davis, L. E., Galinsky, M. J., & Schopler, J. H. (1995). RAP: A framework for leadership of multiracial groups. *Social Work, 40*, 155–165.

Davis, L. E., & Gelsomino, J. (1994). An assessment of practitioner cross-racial treatment experiences. *Social Work, 39*, 116–123.

Dawes, R. M. (1999). A message from psychologists to economists: Mere predictability doesn't matter like it should (without a good story appended to it). *Journal of Economic Behavior & Organization, 39*, 29–40.

De Anda, D. (1984). Bicultural socialization: Factors affecting the minority experience. *Social Work, 29*, 172–181.

De Jong, P. (2001). Solution-focused therapy. In A. R. Roberts & G. J. Greene (Eds.), *Social workers' desk reference* (pp. 112–115). New York: Oxford University Press.

De Jong, P., & Berg, I. K. (1998). *Interviewing for solutions*. Pacific Grove, CA: Brooks/Cole.

De Jong, P., & Berg, I. K. (2001). Co-constructing cooperation with mandated clients. *Social Work, 46*, 361–374.

De Jong, P., & Berg, I. K. (2002). *Learner's workbook for interviewing for solutions* (2nd ed.). Pacific Grove, CA: Brooks/Cole.

De Jong, P., & Berg, I. K. (2003). *Interviewing for solutions* (2nd ed.). Pacific Grove, CA: Brooks/Cole.

De Jong, P., & Berg, I. K. (2008) *Interviewing for solutions* (3rd ed.). Pacific Grove, CA: Brooks/Cole.

De Jong, P., & Miller, S. D. (1995). How to interview for client strengths. *Social Work, 40*, 729–736.

de Shazer, S. (1988). *Clues: Investigating solutions in brief therapy*. New York: Norton.

de Shazer, S., & Berg, I. K. (1993). Constructing solutions. *Family Therapy Networker, 12*, 42–43.

Deal, K. H. (1999). Clinical social work students' use of self-disclosure: A case for formal training. *Arete, 23*(3), 33–45.

Deal, K. H., & Brintzenhofeszok, K. M. (2004). A study of MSW students' interviewing skills over time. *Journal of Teaching in Social Work, 24*, 181–197.

Dean, R. G. (2001). The myth of cross-cultural competence. *Families in Society, 82,* 623–630.

Decety, J., & Jackson, P. L. (2004). The functional architecture of human empathy. *Behavioral and Cognitive Neuroscience Reviews, 3,* 71–100.

Delgado, M. (1983). Activities and Hispanic groups: Issues and suggestions. *Social Work with Groups, 6*(1), 85–96.

DeLine, C. (2000). *The back door: An experiment or an alternative.* Alberta, Canada: The Back Door.

Demby, G. (2013). *A battle for fair housing still raging, but mostly forgotten.* Retrieved from http://www.npr.org/sections/codeswitch/2013/12/01/248039354/a-battle-for-fair-housing-still-raging-but-mostly-forgotten

Demer, S., Hemesath, C., & Russell, C. (1998). A feminist critique of solution-focused therapy. *The America Journal of Family Therapy, 26,* 239–250.

Denison, M. (2003). The PDR for mental health professionals. *Psychotherapy: Theory, Research, Practice, and Training, 40,* 317–318.

DePalma, J. A. (2001). Evidence-based case management. *Home Health Case Management & Practice, 13,* 330–331.

DePoy, E., Hartman, A., & Haslett, D. (1999). Critical Action Research: A model for social work knowing. *Social Work, 44,* 560–569.

Dettlaff, A. J., & Rycraft, J. R. (2010). Factors contributing to disproportionality in the child welfare system: Views for the legal community. *Social Work, 55,* 213–224.

Devore, W., & Schlesinger, E. G. (1999). *Ethnic-sensitive social work practice* (5th ed.). Boston: Allyn & Bacon.

Dewayne, C. (1978). Humor in therapy. *Social Work, 23,* 508–510.

Di Clemente, C. C., & Prochaska, J. O. (1998). Toward a comprehensive transtheoretical model of change: Stages of change and addictive behaviors. In W. R. Miller & N. Heather (Eds.), *Treating addictive behaviors* (2nd ed., pp. 3–24). New York: Plenum Press.

Dickson, D. T. (1998). *Confidentiality and privacy in social work.* New York: Free Press.

Dies, R. R. (1983). Clinical implications of research on leadership in short-term group psychotherapy. In R. R. Dies & R. McKenzie (Eds.), *Advances in group psychotherapy: Integrating research and practice* (pp. 27–28). New York: International Universities Press.

Dietz, C. (2000). Reshaping clinical practice for the new millennium. *Journal of Social Work Education, 36,* 503–520.

Dietz, C., & Thompson, J. (2004). Rethinking boundaries: Ethical dilemmas in the social worker–client relationship. *Journal of Progressive Human Services, 15*(2), 2–22.

Dimidjian, S., & Linehan, M. M. (2003). Defining an agenda for future research on the clinical application of mindfulness practice. *Clinical Psychology: Science and Practice, 10,* 166–171.

Diorio, W. D. (1992). Parental perceptions of the authority of public child welfare caseworkers. *Families in Society: Journal of Contemporary Human Services, 73*(4), 222–235.

Dobbie, D., & Richards-Schuster, K. (2008). Building solidarity through difference: A practice model for critical multicultural organizing. *Journal of Community Practice, 16*(3), 317–337.

Dobson, K. S., & Dozios, D. J. (2001). Historical and philosophical basis of cognitive behavioral therapies. In K. S. Dobson (Ed.), *Handbook of cognitive therapies* (pp. 3–39). New York: Guildford Press.

Doherty, W. J. (1995). *Soul-searching: When psychotherapy must promote moral responsibility.* New York: Basic Books.

Dolan, S., Martin, R., & Rosenow, D. (2008). Self-efficacy for cocaine abstinence: Pretreatment correlates and relationship to outcomes. *Addictive Behaviors, 33,* 675–688.

Dombo, E. A., Kays, L., & Weller, K. (2014). Clinical social work practice and technology: Personal, practical, regulatory, and ethical considerations for the twenty-first century. *Social Work in Healthcare, 53*(9), 900–919.

Donovan, K., & Regehr, C. (2010). Elder abuse: Clinical, ethical, and legal considerations in social work practice. *Clinical Social Work Journal, 38,* 174–182.

Dore, M. M. (1993). The practice-teaching parallel in educating the micropractitioner. *Journal of Social Work Education, 29,* 181–190.

Dorfman, R. A. (1996). *Clinical social work: Definition, practice, and vision.* New York: Brunner/Mazel.

Dossick, J., & Shea, E. (1995). *Creative therapy III: 52 more exercises for groups.* Sarasota, FL: Professional Resource Press.

Doster, J., & Nesbitt, J. (1979). Psychotherapy and self-disclosure. In G. Chelune & Associates (Eds.), *Self-disclosure: Origins, patterns, and implications of openness in interpersonal relationships* (pp. 177–224). San Francisco: Jossey-Bass.

Doty, M. M., Blumenthal, D. J., & Collins, S. R. (2014). The Affordable Care Act and health insurance for Latinos. *Journal of the American Medical Association, 312,* 1735–1736.

Drankus, D. (2010). Indicators of acculturation: A bilinear, multidimensional model. *Advocates' Forum,* pp. 35–49.

Drisko, J. W. (2014). Research evidence and social work practice: The place of evidence-based practice. *Clinical Social Work Journal, 42,* 123–133.

Drisko, J. W. (2004). Common factors in psychotherapy outcome: Meta-analytic findings and their implications for practice and research. *Families in Society, 85*(1), 81–90.

Duan, C., & Hill, C. E. (1996). The current state of empathy research. *Journal of Counseling Psychology, 43*(3), 261–274.

Dubowitz, H., & DePanitilis, D. (2000). *Handbook for child protection practice*. Thousand Oaks, CA: Sage.

Dudley, J. R., Smith, C., & Millison, M. B. (1995). Unfinished business: Assessing the spiritual needs of hospice clients. *American Journal of Hospice and Palliative Care, 12*(2), 30–37.

Duehn, W., & Proctor, E. (1977). Initial clinical interactions and premature discontinuance in treatment. *American Journal of Orthopsychiatry, 47*, 284–290.

Dulcan, M. K. (2009). *Dulcan's textbook of child adolescent psychiatry*. Arlington, VA: American Psychiatric Publishing.

Dumbrill, G. C. (2006). Parental experience of child protection intervention: A qualitative study. *Child Abuse & Neglect, 30*, 17–37.

Dumbrill, G. C. (2003). Child welfare: AOP's nemesis? In W. Shera (Ed.), *Emerging perspectives on anti-oppressive practice*. Toronto: Canadian Scholars' Press.

Duncan, B. L. (2012). The partners for change outcome management system (PCOMS): The heart and soul of change project. *Canadian Psychology, 53*(2), 93–104.

Duncan, B. L., & Miller, S. D. (2000). *The heroic client*. San Francisco: Jossey-Bass.

Duncan, B. L., Miller, S. D., & Sparks, J. A. (2011). *The heroic client: A revolutionary way to improve effectiveness through client-directed, outcome-informed therapy*. San Francisco: Wiley.

Duncan, B. L., Miller, S. D., Wampold, B. E., & Hubble, M. A. (Eds.). (2010). *The heart and soul of change: Delivering what works in therapy* (2nd ed.). Washington, DC: American Psychological Association.

Dunkley, J., & Whelan, T. S. (2006). Vicarious traumatization in telephone counselors: Internal and external influences. *British Journal of Guidance & Counseling, 34*(4), 451–469.

Dunlap, E., Golub, A., & Johnson, B. D. (2006). The severely-distressed African American family in the crack era: Empowerment is not enough. *Journal of Sociology and Social Welfare, 53*(1), 115–139.

Durlak, J. A., Weissberg, R. P., Dymnicki, A. B., Taylor, R. D., & Schellinger, K. B. (2011). The impact of enhancing students' social and emotional learning: A meta-analysis of school-based universal interventions. *Child Development, 82*(1), 405–432.

Duvall, E. M. (1977). *Marriage and family development* (5th ed.). Philadelphia: Lippincott.

Dyche, L., & Zayas, L. H. (2001). Cross-cultural empathy and training the contemporary psychotherapist. *Clinical Social Work Journal, 29*, 245–258.

E

Eamon, M. K., & Zhang, S.-J. (2006). Do social work students assess and address economic barriers to clients implementing agreed task? *Journal of Social Work Education, 42*, 525–542.

Eaton, T. T., Abeles, N., & Gutfreund, M. J. (1993). Negative indicators, therapeutic alliance, and therapy outcome. *Psychotherapy Research, 3*, 115–123.

Ebenstein, H. (1998). Single-session groups: Issues for social workers. *Social Work with Groups, 21*, 49–60.

Edin, K., & Kafalas, M. (2005). *Promises I can keep: Why poor women put motherhood before marriage*. Berkeley: University of California Press.

Edwards, A. (1982). The consequences of error in selecting treatment for blacks. *Social Casework, 63*, 429–433.

Edwards, E. (2007). *Saving graces*. New York: Broadway.

Edwards, E. D., Edwards, M. E., Davies, G. M., & Eddy, F. (1987). Enhancing self-concept and identification of American Indian girls. *Social Work with Groups, 1*, 309–318.

Efran, J., & Schenker, M. (1993). A potpourri of solutions: How new and different is solution-focused therapy? *Family Therapy Networker, 17*(3), 71–74.

Eisenberg, E. (2008). Evidence-based practice in mental health care to ethnic minority communities: Has its practice fallen short of its evidence? *Social Work, 53*(4): 297–306.

Eisenberg, N., Spinard, T. L., & Sadovsky, A. (2005). Empathy-related responding in children. In M. Killen & J. G. Smetna (Eds.), *Handbook of moral development* (pp. 517–549). Mahwah, NJ: Erlbaum.

Elbow, M. (1987). The memory books: Facilitating termination with children. *Social Casework, 68*, 180–183.

Ell, K. (1995). Crisis intervention: Research needs. In E. L. Edwards (Ed.), *Encyclopedia of social work* (19th ed., pp. 660–667). Washington, DC: NASW Press.

Ellis, A. (1962). *Reason and emotion in psychotherapy*. New York: Lyle Stuart.

Ellis, A. (2001). *Overcoming destructive beliefs, feelings, and behaviors: New directions for rational emotive behavior therapy*. Amherst, NY: Prometheus.

Ellis, R. A., & Sowers, K. M. (2001). *Juvenile justice practice: A cross-disciplinary approach to intervention*. Belmont, CA: Brooks/Cole.

Ellor, J. W., Netting, F. E., & Thibault, J. M. (1999). *Religious and spiritual aspects of human service practice*. Columbia: University of South Carolina Press.

Ephross, P. H., & Vassil, T. V. (1988). *Groups that work: Structure and process*. New York: Columbia University Press.

Epstein, L. (1992). *Brief treatment and a new look at the task-centered approach* (3rd ed.). Boston: Allyn & Bacon.

Epstein, L., & Brown, L. B. (2002). *Brief treatment and a new look at the task-centered approach* (4th ed.). Boston: Allyn & Bacon.

Epstein, R. S., Simon, R. I., & Kay, G. G. (1992). Assessing boundary violations in psychotherapy: Survey results with the Exploitation Index. *Bulletin of the Menninger Foundation, 56*(2), 150–166.

Erford, B. T. (2003). *Transforming the school counseling profession*. Upper Saddle River, NJ: Prentice-Hall.

Erickson, S. H. (2001). Multiple relationships in rural counseling. *The Family Journal: Counseling and Therapy for Couples and Families, 9,* 302–304.

Esaki, N., & Larkin, H. (2013). Prevalence of adverse childhood experiences (ACE) among child services providers. *Families in Society: The Journal of Contemporary Social Services, 94*(1), 31–37.

Etherington, K. (2000). Supervising counselors who work with survivors of childhood sexual abuse. *Counseling Psychology Quarterly, 13,* 377–389.

Evans, T. (2004). A multidimensional assessment of children with chronic physical conditions. *Health and Social Work, 29,* 245–248.

Ezell, M. (2001). *Advocacy in the human services.* Pacific Grove, CA: Brooks/Cole.

F

Falicov, C. (1996). Mexican families. In M. McGoldrick, J. Giordano, & J. Pearce (Eds.), *Ethnicity and family therapy* (2nd ed., pp. 169–182). New York: Guilford Press.

Fallot, R. D., & Harris, M. (2002). The Trauma Recovery and Empowerment Model (TREM): Conceptual and practical issues in a group intervention for women. *Community Mental Health Journal, 38,* 475–485.

Farber, B. A. (2006). *Self disclosure in psychotherapy.* New York: Guilford Press.

Farrington, A. (1995). Suicide and psychological debriefing. *British Journal of Nursing, 4*(4), 209–211.

Fast, J. D. (2003). After Columbine: How people mourn sudden death. *Social Work, 48,* 484–491.

Fauri, D. P., Harrigan, M. P., & Netting, F. E. (1998). Termination: Extending the concept for macro social work practice. *Journal of Sociology and Social Welfare, 25*(4), 61–80.

Fauth, J. (2006). Counselors' stress appraisals as predictors of countertransference behavior with male clients. *Journal of Counseling and Development, 84,* 430–439.

Fearing, J. (1996). The changing face of intervention. *Behavioral Health Management, 16,* 35–37.

Feeny, S. L. (2004). The cognitive behavioral treatment of social phobia. *Clinical Case Studies, 3,* 124–146.

Feldman, N. (2008). Exercising power from the bottom up: Co-creating the conditions for the development with youth at an urban high school. *Families in Society, 89,* 438–445.

Fellin, P. (2001). Understanding American communities. In J. Rothman, J. L. Erlich, & J. E. Tropman (Eds.), *Strategies of community organization* (3rd ed.). Itasca, IL: Peacock.

Feltenstein, M. W. (2008). The neurocircuitry of addiction: An overview. *British Journal of Pharmacology, 154,* 261–274.

Ferguson, K. M. (2007). Implementing a social enterprise intervention with homeless, street-living youth in Los Angeles. *Social Work, 52,* 103–112.

Fernandez-Olano, C., Montoya-Fernandez, J., & Salinas-Sanchez, A. (2008). Impact of clinical interview training on the empathy level of medical students and medical residents. *Medical Teacher, 30,* 322–324.

Figley, C. R. (2002). Compassion fatigue: Psychotherapists' chronic lack of self-care. *Journal of Clinical Psychology, 58*(11), 1433–1441.

Figley, C. R. (Ed.). (1995). *Compassion fatigue: Dealing with secondary traumatic stress disorder in those who treat the traumatized.* New York: Brunner/Mazel.

Figley, C. R. (Ed.). (2002). *Treating compassion fatigue.* New York: Brunner-Routledge.

Fingeld, D. (2000). Therapeutic groups online: The good, the bad, and the unknown. *Issues in Mental Health Nursing, 21,* 241–255.

Finn, J. L., & Jacobson, M. (2003). Just practice: Steps toward a new social work paradigm. *Journal of Social Work Education, 39,* 57–78.

Fischer, J. (1973). Is casework effective? A review. *Social Work, 18,* 5–20.

Fischer, J., & Corcoran, K. (2006). *Measures for clinical practice and research: Couples, families, and children, A sourcebook, Vol. 1* (4th ed.). New York: Oxford University Press.

Fischer, J., & Corcoran, K. (2007). *Measures for clinical practice and research: Adults, A sourcebook, Vol. 2* (4th ed.). New York: Oxford University Press.

Fiske, A., Wetherell, J. L., & Gatz, M. (2009). Depression in older adults. *Annual Review of Clinical Psychology, 5,* 363–389.

Flexnor, B., & Baldwin, R. N. (1914). *Juvenile courts and probation.* New York: Century.

Flores, M. T., & Carey, G. (2000). *Family therapy with Hispanics: Toward appreciating diversity.* Boston: Allyn & Bacon.

Fluhr, T. (2004). Transcending differences: Using concrete subject matter in heterogeneous groups. *Social Work with Groups, 27*(2/3).

Fong, L. G. W., & Gibbs, J. T. (1995). Facilitating service to multicultural communities in a dominant culture setting: An organizational perspective. *Administration in Social Work, 19*(2), 1–24.

Fong, R. (1997). Child welfare practice with Chinese families: Assessment issues for immigrants from the People's Republic China. *Journal of Family Social Work, 2*(1), 33–47.

Fong, R. (2007). Cultural competence with Asian Americans. In D. Lum, *Culturally competent practice: A framework for understanding diverse groups and justice issues.* Pacific Grove, CA: Brooks/Cole.

Fong, R., Armour, M., Busch-Armendariz, N. B., & Heffron, L. (2008). *Case management intervention with immigrant and refugee students and families.* In A. R. Roberts (Ed.), *Social workers' desk reference* (2nd ed., pp. 1031–1038). New York: Oxford University Press.

Font, S. A., Berger, L. M., & Slack, K. S. (2012). Examining racial disproportionality in child protective services case decisions. *Child Services Review, 34,* 2188–2200.

Fontes, L. A. (2005). *Child abuse and culture: Working with diverse families.* New York: Guilford Press.

Forrester, D., Kershaw, S., Moss, H., & Hughes, L. (2008). Communication skills in child protection: How do social workers talk to parents? *Child and Family Social Work, 13,* 41–51.

Fortune, A. E. (1985). Treatment groups. In A. E. Fortune (Ed.), *Task-centered practice with families and groups* (pp. 33–44). New York: Springer.

Fortune, A. E., McCallion, P., & Briar-Lawson, K. (Eds.). (2010). *Social work practice research for the twenty-first century: Building on the legacy of William J. Reid.* New York: Columbia University Press.

Fortune, A. E., Pearlingi, B., & Rochelle, C. D. (1992). Reactions to termination of individual treatment. *Social Work, 37,* 171–178.

Frager, S. (2000). *Managing managed care: Secrets from a former case manager.* New York: Wiley.

Frankenburg, W. K., Dodds, J., Archer, P., Shapiro, H., & Bresnick, B. (1992). The Denver II: A major revision and restandardization of the Denver Developmental Screening Test. *Pediatrics, 89,* 91–97.

Franklin, C. (2002). Developing effective practice competencies in managed behavioral health care. In A. R. Roberts & G. J. Greene (Eds.), *Social workers' desk reference* (pp. 3–10). New York: Oxford University Press.

Franklin, C., Moore, K., & Hopson, L. (2008). Effectiveness of brief treatment in a school setting. *Children and Schools, 30*(1), 15–26.

Franklin, C., & Streeter, C. L. (2004). *Solution-focused alternatives for education: An outcome evaluation of Garza High School.* Retrieved from http://www.utexas.edu. libproxy.lib.unc.edu/courses/franklin/safed_report_final .doc

Fraser, M. W. (Ed.). (2004). *Risk and resilience in childhood: An ecological perspective* (2nd ed.). Washington DC: NASW Press.

Freddolino, P., Moxley, D., & Hyduk, C. (2004). A differential model of advocacy in social work practice. *Families in Society, 85,* 119–128.

Fredriksen-Goldsen, K. I., & Scharlach, A. E. (2001). *Families and work: New directions in the twenty-first century.* New York: Oxford University Press.

Freed, A. (1988). Interviewing through an interpreter. *Social Work, 33,* 315–319.

Freedberg, S. (2007). Re-examining empathy: A relational-feminist point of view. *Social Work, 52,* 251–259.

Freud, S. (1999). The social construction of normality. *Families in Society, 80,* 333–339.

Frey, A. J., & Dupper, D. R. (2005). A broader conceptual approach to clinical practice for the 21st century. *Children and Schools, 29*(1), 33–44.

Frey, G. A. (1990). Framework for promoting organizational change. *Families in Society, 7,* 142–147.

Fried, A. E., & Dunn, M. (2012). The Expectancy Challenge Alcohol Literacy Curriculum (ECALC): A single session group intervention to reduce alcohol use. *The Psychology of Addictive Behaviors, 26*(3), 615–620.

Froeschle, J. G., Smith, R. L., & Ricard, R. (2007). The efficacy of a systematic substance abuse program for adolescent females. *Professional School Counseling, 10,* 498–505.

Fullerton, C. D., & Ursano, R. J. (2005). Psychological and psychopathological consequences of disasters. In J. J. Lopez-Ibor, G. Christodoulou, M. Maj, N. Sartorius, & A. Okasha (Eds.), *Disaster and mental health* (pp. 25–49). New York: Wiley.

Furman, R. (2009). Ethical considerations of evidence-based practice. *Social Work, 54,* 57–59.

G

Gabbard, G. O. (1996). Lessons to be learned from the study of sexual boundary violations. *American Journal of Psychotherapy, 50,* 311–322.

Galinsky, M. J., & Schopler, J. H. (1989). Developmental patterns in open-ended groups. *Social Work with Groups, 12,* 99–114.

Galinsky, M. J., Terzian, M. A., & Fraser, M. W. (2006). The art of group work practice with manualized curricula. *Social Work with Groups, 29,* 11–26.

Gallo, J. J. (2005). Activities of daily living and instrumental activities of daily living assessment. In J. J. Gallo, H. R. Bogner, T. Fulmer, & G. Paveza (Eds.), *Handbook of geriatric assessment* (4th ed., 193–240). Sudbury, MA: Jones and Bartlett.

Gallo, J. J., Bogner, H. R., Fulmer, T., & Paveza, J. (Eds.). (2005). *Handbook of geriatric assessment* (4th ed.). Sudbury, MA: Jones and Bartlett.

Gallo, J. J., Fulmer, T., Paveza, G. J., & Reichel, W. (Eds.). (2000). *Handbook of geriatric assessment* (3rd ed.). Gaithersburg, MD: Aspen.

Gambrill, E. (1995). Behavioral social work: Past, present and future. *Research on Social Work Practice, 5,* 466–484.

Gambrill, E. (2004). Contributions of critical thinking and evidence-based practice to the fulfillment of the ethical obligation of professions. In H. Briggs & T. Rzepnicki (Eds.), *Using evidence in social work practice* (pp. 3–19). Chicago: Lyceum Books.

Gambrill, E. (2007). Views of evidence-based practice: Social workers' code of ethics and accreditation standards as guides for choice. *Journal of Social Work Education, 43,* 447–462.

Garcia Coll, C., Akerman, A., & Cicchetti, D. (2000). Cultural influences on developmental processes and outcomes: Implications for the study of development and psychopathology. *Development and Psychopathology, 12,* 333–356.

Garcia Coll, C., Lamberty, G., Jenkins, R., McAdoo, H. P., Crinic, K., Wasik, B. H., & Vasquez Garcia, H. (1996). An integrative model for the study of developmental competencies in minority children. *Child Development, 67,* 1891–1914.

Gardner, F. (2000). Design evaluation: Illuminating social work practice for better outcomes. *Social Work, 45,* 176–182.

Gardner, L. I., Metsch, L. R., Andrson-Mahoney, P., Loughlin, A. M., del Rio, C., Strathdee, S., et al. (2005). Efficacy of brief case management intervention to link recently diagnosed HIV-infected persons to care. *AIDS, 19,* 423–431.

Garland, J., Jones, H., & Kolodny, R. (1965). A model for stages in the development of social work groups. In S. Bernstein (Ed.), *Explorations in group work.* Boston: Milford House.

Gartrell, N. K. (1992). Boundaries in lesbian therapy relationships. *Women & Therapy, 12*(3), 29–50.

Garvin, C. D. (1986). Family therapy and group work: "Kissing cousins or distant relatives" in social work practice. In M. Parnes (Ed.), *Innovations in social group work: Feedback from practice to theory: Proceedings of the annual group work symposium* (pp. 1–16). New York: Haworth Press.

Garvin, C. D. (1987). *Contemporary group work* (2nd ed.). Englewood Cliffs, NJ: Prentice-Hall.

Garvin, C. D. (2011). Group treatment with adults. In J. R. Brandell (Ed.), *Theory & practice in clinical social work* (323–346). Los Angeles: Sage.

Garvin, C. D., & Galinsky, M. J. (2008). Groups. In T. Mizrahi & L. E. Davis (Eds.), *Encyclopedia of social work.* New York: Oxford University Press.

Gasker, J. A., & Fischer, A. C. (2014). Toward a context-specific definition of social justice for social work: In search of overlapping consensus. *Journal of Social Work Values and Ethics, 11*(1), 42–53.

Gavin, D. R., Ross, H. E., & Skinner, H. A. (1989). Diagnostic validity of the Drug Abuse Screening Test in the assessment of DSM-III drug disorders. *British Journal of Addiction, 84,* 301–307.

Gelman, C. R., & Mirabito, D. M. (2005). Practicing what we teach: Using case studies from 911 to teach crisis intervention from a generalist perspective. *Journal of Social Work Education, 4,* 479–494.

Gelman, S. R., Pollack, D., & Weiner, A. (1999). Confidentiality of social work records in the computer age. *Social Work, 44*(3), 243–252.

Gendlin, E. (1974). Client-centered and experiential psychotherapy. In D. Wexler & L. Rice (Eds.), *Innovations in client-centered therapy.* New York: Wiley.

Gendolla, G. H. E. (2004). The intensity of motivation when the self is involved: An application of Brehm's theory of motivation to effort-related cardiovascular response. In R. Wright, J. Greenberg, & S. S. Brehm (Eds.), *Motivational analysis of social behavior* (pp. 205–224). Mahwah, NJ: Erlbaum.

Gendron, C., Poitras, L., Dastoor, D. P., & Perodeau, G. (1996). Cognitive-behavioral group intervention for spousal caregivers: Findings and clinical observations. *Clinical Gerontologist, 17*(1), 3–19.

George, L. (2011). Working in the transference and promoting self-determination: Treating beliefs as opinions rather than certainties. *Psychoanalytic Social Work, 18*(2), 93–106.

George, L., & Fillenbaum, G. (1990). OARS methodology: A decade of experience in geriatric assessment. *Journal of the American Geriatrics Society, 33,* 607–615.

Gerdes, K., & Segal, E. (2009). A social work model of empathy. *Advances in Social Work, 10*(2), 114–127.

Gerdes, K., & Segal, E. (2013). Importance of empathy for social work practice: Integrating new science. *Social Work, 16*(1), 141–148.

Geriatric Mental Health Foundation. (n.d.). *Late life depression: A fact sheet.* Retrieved from http://www.gmhfonline.org/gmhf/consumer/factsheets/depression_factsheet.html

Getzel, G. S. (1998). Group work practice with gay men and lesbians. In G. P. Mallon (Ed.), *Foundations of social work practice with lesbian and gay persons* (pp. 131–144). Binghamton, NY: Haworth Press.

Giacola, P. R., Mezzich, A. C., Clark, D. B., & Tarter, R. E. (1999). Cognitive distortions, aggressive behaviors and drug use in adolescent boys with and without prior family history. *Psychology of Addictive Behavior, 13,* 22–32.

Gibbs, J. (1995). *Tribes: A new way of learning and being together.* Sausalito, CA: Center Source Systems.

Gibson, P. A. (1999). African American grandmothers: New mothers again. *Affilia, 14*(3), 329–343.

Gilbert, D. J. (2003). Multicultural assessment. In C. Jordan & C. Franklin (Eds.), *Clinical assessment for social workers: Quantitative and qualitative methods* (2nd ed., pp. 351–383). Chicago: Lyceum Books.

Gilbert, N. (1977). The search for professional identity. *Social Work, 22,* 401–406.

Gilgun, J. F. (1994). Hand to glove: The grounded theory approach and social work practice research. In L. Sherman & W. J. Reid (Eds.), *Qualitative research in social work* (pp. 115–125). New York: Columbia University Press.

Gilgun, J. F. (2001). CASPARS: New tools for assessing client risks and strengths. *Families in Society, 82,* 450–459.

Gilliland, B. (1982) The six-stage model of crisis intervention. In R. K. James, *Crisis intervention strategies* (4th ed., p. 38). Pacific Grove, CA: Brooks/Cole.

Gingerich, W. J., & Eisengard, S. (2000). Solution-focused brief treatment: A review of outcome research. *Family Process, 39*, 477–498.

Gingerich, W. J., & Wabeke, T. (2001). A solution-focused approach to mental health interventions in school settings. *Children in Schools, 23*(1), 33–47.

Gini, G., Albiero, P., Benelli, B., & Altoe, G. (2008). Determinants of adolescents' active defending and passive bystanding behavior in bullying. *Journal of Adolescence, 31*, 93–105.

Gitterman, A. (1996). Ecological perspectives: Response to Professor Jerry Wakefield. *Social Service Review, 70*, 472–476.

Gitterman, A., & Knight, C. (2013). Evidence-guided practice: Integrating the science and art of social work. *Families in Society, 94*(2), 70–78.

Glancy, G., & Saini, M. (2005). An evidence-based review of psychological treatment of anger and aggression. *Brief Treatment and Crisis Intervention, 5*, 229–248.

Golan, N. (1981). *Passing through transitions: A guide for the practitioners.* New York: Free Press.

Gold, M. (1986, November). Is that child bad or depressed? *Parade Magazine, 2*, 10.

Gold, N. (1990). Motivation: The crucial but unexplored component of social work practice. *Social Work, 35*, 49–56.

Goldenberg, I., & Goldenberg, H. (1991). *Family therapy: An overview* (3rd ed.). Pacific Grove, CA: Brooks/Cole.

Goldenberg, I., & Goldenberg, H. (2000). *Family therapy: An overview* (5th ed.). Pacific Grove, CA: Brooks/Cole.

Goldenberg, I., & Goldenberg, H. (2004). *Family therapy: An overview* (6th ed.). Pacific Grove, CA: Brooks/Cole.

Goldfried, M. (1977). The use of relaxation and cognitive re-labeling as coping skills. In R. Stuart (Ed.), *Behavioral self-management* (pp. 82–116). New York: Brunner/Mazel.

Goldner, V. (1985). Feminism and family therapy. *Family Process, 24*, 31–47.

Goldstein, E. G. (1997). To tell or not to tell: The disclosure of events in the therapist's life to the patient. *Clinical Social Work Journal, 25*, 41–58.

Gone, J. (2015). Reconciling evidence-based practice and cultural competence in mental health services: Introduction to a special issue. *Transcultural Psychiatry, 52*(2), 139–149.

González, M. J. (2012). Evidence-based practice with ethnically diverse clients. In E. P. Congress & M. J. González (Eds.), *Multicultural perspectives in social work practice with families* (3rd ed., pp. 31–40). New York: Springer.

González, M. J., & Acevedo, G. (2012). Clinical practice with Hispanic individuals and families. In E. P. Congress & M. J. González, *Multicultural perspectives in working with families* (3rd ed., pp. 141–156). New York: Springer.

Goodman, H. (1997). Social group work in community corrections. *Social Work with Groups, 20*(1), 51–64.

Goodman, H., Getzel, G. S., & Ford, W. (1996). Group work with high-risk urban youths on probation. *Social Work, 41*, 375–381.

Goodwin, D. W., & Gabrielli, W. F. (1997). Alcohol: Clinical aspects. In J. H. Lowinson, P. Ruiz, R. B. Millman, & J. G. Langrod (Eds.), *Substance abuse: A comparative textbook* (3rd ed., pp. 142–148). Baltimore, MD: Williams & Wilkins.

Gordon, W. (1965). Toward a social work frame of reference. *Journal of Education for Social Work, 1*, 19–26.

Gottesfeld, M., & Lieberman, F. (1979). The pathological therapist. *Social Casework, 60*, 387–393.

Goyer, A. (2006). *Intergenerational relationships: Grandparents raising grandchildren.* Policy and Research Report, American Association of Retired Persons.

Graham, P. (1998). *Cognitive behavior therapy for children and families.* Cambridge, UK: Cambridge University Press.

Grame, C., Tortorici, J., Healey, B., Dillingham, J., & Wilklebaur, P. (1999). Addressing spiritual and religious issues of clients with a history of psychological trauma. *Bulletin of the Menninger Clinic, 63*, 223–239.

Green, J. P., Duncan, R. E., Barnes, G. L., & Oberklaid, F. (2003). Putting informed into consent: A matter of plain language. *Journal of Pediatric Child Health, 39*, 700–703.

Green, J. W. (1999). *Cultural awareness in the human services: A multi-ethnic approach.* Boston: Allyn & Bacon.

Green, R. G., Kiernan-Stern, M., & Baskind, F. R. (2005). White social workers' attitudes about people of color. *Journal of Ethnic and Cultural Diversity in Social Work, 14*(1/2), 47–68.

Greenberg, J., & Tyler, T. R. (1987). Why procedural justice in organizations. *Social Justice Research, 1*, 127–143.

Greene, A. D., & Latting, J. K. (2004). Whistle-blowing as a form of advocacy: Guidelines for the practitioner and the organization. *Social Work, 49*, 219–230.

Greene, G. J., Kondrat, D. C., Lee, M. Y., Clement, J., Siebert, H., Mentzer, R. A., & Pinnell, S. R. (2006). A solution-focused approach to case management and recovery with consumers who have a severe mental disability. *Families in Society, 87*, 339–350.

Greene, G. J., Lee, M. Y., & Hoffpauir, S. (2005). The language of empowerment and strengths in clinical social work: A constructivist perspective. *Families in Society, 86*, 267–277.

Greenfield, S. F., Brooks, A. J., Gordon, S. M., Green, C. A., Kropp, F., McHugh, R. K., et al. (2007). Substance abuse treatment entry, retention, and outcome in women: A review of the literature. *Drug and Alcohol Dependence, 86*(1), 1–21.

Greif, G. L., & Ephross, P. H. (Eds.). (2011). *Group work with populations at risk* (3rd ed.). New York: Oxford University Press.

Gross, E. (1995). Deconstructing politically correct practice literature: The American Indian case. *Social Work, 40*, 206–213.

Grote, N. K., Zuckoff, A., Swartz, H., Bledsoe, S. E., & Geibel, S. (2007). Engaging women who are depressed and economically disadvantaged in mental health treatment. *Social Work, 52*(4), 295–308.

Guadalupe, K. L., & Lum, D. (2005). *Multidimensional contextual practice: Diversity and transcendence.* Belmont, CA: Brooks/Cole.

Gulati, P., & Guest, G. (1990). The community-centered model: A garden variety approach or a radical transformation of community practice? *Social Work, 35*, 63–68.

Gumpert, J., & Saltman, J. E. (1998). Social group work practice in rural areas: The practitioners speak. *Social Work with Groups, 21*(3), 19–34.

Gurman, A. (1977). The patientss perception of the therapeutic relationship. In A. Gutman & A. Razin (Eds.), *Effective psychotherapy: A handbook of research.* New York: Pergamon Press.

Guthrie, D. D., Ellison, V. S., King, S., & McCrea, K. T. (2014). Clients' hope arising from social workers' compassion: African American youth's perspectives on surmounting the obstacles of disadvantage. *Families in Society: The Journal of Contemporary Social Services, 95*(2), 131–139.

Gutierrez, L. M. (1994). Beyond coping: An empowerment perspective on stressful life events. *Journal of Sociology and Social Welfare, 21*, 201–219.

Gutierrez, L. M. (2001). Working with women of color: An empowerment perspective. In J. Rothman, J. L. Erhlich, & J. E. Tropman (Eds.), *Strategies for community intervention* (6th ed., pp. 208–217). Itasca, IL: Peacock.

Gutierrez, L. M., GlenMaye, L., & Delois, K. (1995). The organizational context of empowerment practice: Implications for social work in administration. *Social Work, 40*, 249–258.

Gutierrez, L. M., & Lewis, E. A. (1999). Strengthening communities through groups: A multicultural perspective. In H. Bertcher, L. F. Kurtz, & A. Lamont (Eds.), *Rebuilding communities: Challenges for group work* (pp. 5–16). New York: Haworth Press.

Gutierrez, L. M., & Ortega, R. (1991). Developing methods to empower Latinos: The importance of groups. *Social Work with Groups, 14*(2), 23–43.

Gutierrez, L. M., Parsons, R. J., & Cox, E. O. (Eds.). (1998). *Empowerment in social work practice: A sourcebook.* Pacific Grove, CA: Brooks/Cole.

H

Hackman, J. R., & Oldham, G. R. (1976). Motivation through the design of work: Test of a theory. *Organizational Behavior and Human Performance, 16*, 250–279.

Hackman, J. R., & Oldham, G. R. (1980). Work design. Reading, MA: Addison-Wesley.

Hackney, H., & Cormier, S. (2005). *The professional counselor: A professional guide to helping* (5th ed.). Boston: Pearson.

Hage, D. (2004). *Reforming welfare by rewarding work.* Minneapolis: University of Minnesota Press.

Hagen, B. F., & Mitchell, D. L. (2001). Might within the madness: Solution-focused therapy and thought-disordered clients. *Archives of Psychiatric Nursing, 15*(2), 86–93.

Haight, W. L. (1998). Gathering the spirit at First Baptist Church: Spirituality as a protective factor in the lives of African American children. *Social Work, 43*, 213–221.

Haj-Yahia, M. M. (1997). Culturally sensitive supervision of Arab social work students in Western universities. *Social Work, 42*(2), 167–174.

Hall, J. A., Carswell, C., Walsh, E., Huber, D. L., & Jampoler, J. S. (2002). Iowa case management: Innovative social casework. *Social Work, 47*, 132–141.

Hallfors, D. D., Waller, M. W., Ford, C. A., Halpern, C. T., Brodish, P. H., & Iritani, B. (2004). Adolescent depression and suicide risk: Associations with sex and drug behavior. *American Journal of Preventative Medicine, 27*(3), 224–231.

Halpern, J., & Tramontin, M. (2007). *Disaster: Mental health theory and practice.* Belmont, CA: Brooks/Cole.

Hamama, L., & Ronen, T. (2009). Children's drawing as a self-report measure. *Child and Family Social Work, 14*, 99–102.

Hammond, D., Hepworth, D., & Smith, V. (1977). *Improving therapeutic communication.* San Francisco: Jossey-Bass.

Hankin, B. L., Abramson, L. Y., Moffitt, T. E., Silva, P. A., McGee, R., & Angell, K. E. (1998). Development of depression from preadolescence to young adulthood: Emerging gender differences in a 10-year longitudinal study. *Journal of Abnormal Psychology, 107*, 128–140.

Hannah, G. (2006). Maintaining product: Process balance in community anti-poverty initiatives. *Social Work, 51*, 9–17.

Hardina, D. (2004). Guidelines for ethical practice in community organization. *Social Work, 49*, 595–604.

Hare, J. (1994). Concerns and issues faced by families headed by a lesbian couple. *Families in Society, 75*, 27–35.

Harper, K. V., & Lantz, I. (1996). *Cross-cultural practice.* Chicago: Lyceum Books.

Harr, C., & Moore, B. (2011). Compassion fatigue among social work students in field placements. *Journal of Teaching in Social Work, 31*(3), 350–363.

Harris, I. (1999). First steps in telecollaboration. *Learning and Leading with Technology, 27*, 54–57.

Harris, M., & Franklin, C. (2003). Effects of cognitive-behavioral, school-based group intervention with Mexican American pregnant and parenting adolescents. *Social Work Research, 27,* 74–84.

Hartford, M. (1971). *Groups in social work.* New York: Columbia University Press.

Hartman, A. (1981). The family: A central focus for practice. *Social Work, 26,* 7–13.

Hartman, A. (1993). The professional is political. *Social Work, 38,* 365, 366, 504.

Hartman, A. (1994). Diagrammatic assessment of family relationships. In B. R. Compton & B. Galaway (Eds.), *Social work processes* (5th ed., pp. 153–165). Pacific Grove, CA: Brooks/Cole.

Hartman, A., & Laird, I. (1983). *Family-centered social work practice.* New York: Free Press.

Hasenfeld, Y., & Garrow, E. E. (2012). Nonprofit service organizations, social rights and advocacy in a neoliberal welfare state. *Social Service Review, 86,* 295–322.

Haugebrook, S., Zgoba, K., Maschi, T., Morgen, K., & Brown, D. (2010). Trauma, stress, health and mental health issues among ethnically diverse older prisoners: A correctional health care concern. *Journal of Correctional Healthcare, 16*(3), 220–229.

Havens, J. R., Cornelius, L. J., Ricketts, E. P., Latkin, C. A., Bishai, D., Lloyd, I. I., et al. (2007). The effect of case management intervention on drug treatment entry among treatment-seeking injection drug users with and without comorbid antisocial personality disorder. *Journal of Urban Health, 84,* 267–271.

Hawkins, A. J., Blanchard, V. L., Baldwin, S. A., & Fawcett, E. B. (2008). Does marriage and relationship education work? A meta-analytic study. *Journal of Consulting and Clinical Psychology, 76,* 723–734.

Haynes, K. S., & Mickelson, I. S. (2000). *Affecting change: Social workers in the political arena* (4th ed.). Boston: Allyn & Bacon.

Haynes, R., Corey, G., & Moulton, P. (2003). *Clinical supervision in the helping professions: A practical guide.* Pacific Grove, CA: Brooks/Cole.

Hays, P. A. (1995). Multicultural applications of cognitive behavioral therapy. *Professional Psychology, 26,* 309–315.

Hays, P. A. (2009). Integrating culturally competent based practice and evidence-based practice in cognitive behavioral therapy. *Professional Psychology Research and Practice and Multicultural Therapy, 40,* 354–360.

Healy, A. F., & Bourne, Jr., L. E. (Eds.). (2012). *Training cognition: Optimizing efficiency, durability, and generalizability.* New York: Psychology Press.

Healy, L. M. (2007). Universalism and cultural relativism in social work ethics. *International Social Work, 50,* 11–26.

Heart and Soul of Change Project. (2015). See www.heartandsoulofchange.com

Hegar, R. (1999). The cultural roots of kinship care. In R. Hegar & M. Scannapieco (Eds.), *Kinship foster care, policy, practice, and research* (pp. 17–27). New York: Oxford University Press.

Heisel, M. J., & Flett, G. L. (2006). The development and initial validation of the Geriatric Suicide Ideation Scale. *American Journal of Geriatric Psychiatry, 14,* 742–751.

Heisel, M. J., Flett, G. L., Duberstein, P. R., & Lyness, I. M. (2005). Does the geriatric depression scale (GDS) distinguish between older adults with high versus low levels of suicidal ideation? *American Journal of Geriatric Psychiatry, 13,* 876–883.

Helvic, C. O., & Alexey, B. B. (1992). Using after shelter case management to improve outcomes for families with children. *Public Health Report, 107,* 585–588.

Henggeler, S. W. (2011). Efficacy studies to large-scale transport: The development and validation of multisystemic therapy programs. *Annual Review of Clinical Psychology, 7,* 351–381.

Henggeler, S. W., Schoenwald, S. K., Borduin, C. M., Rowland, M. D., & Cunningham, P. B. (2009). *Multisystemic therapy for antisocial behavior in children and adolescents* (2nd ed.). New York: Guilford Press.

Henry, M. (1988). Revisiting open groups. *Group Work, 1,* 215–228.

Henry, S. (1992). *Group skills in social work: A four-dimensional approach* (2nd ed.). Pacific Grove, CA: Brooks/Cole.

Herman, D., Conover, S., Felix, A., Nakagawa, K., & Mills, D. (2007). Critical time intervention: An empirically supported model for preventing homelessness in high risk groups. *Journal of Primary Prevention, 28,* 296–312.

Hersen, M., & Thomas, I. (Eds). (2007). *Handbook of clinical interviewing with children.* Thousand Oaks, CA: Sage.

Hill, C. E., & Nakayama, E. Y. (2000). Rogerian therapy: Where has it been and where is it going? A comment on Hathaway (1948). *Journal of Clinical Psychology, 56,* 861–875.

Hillier, A. (2007). Why social work needs mapping. *Journal of Social Work Education, 43,* 205–221.

Hinton, D. E., Hofman, S. G., Rivera, E., Otto, M. W., & Pollack, M. H. (2011). Culturally adapted CBT (CA-CBT) for Latino women with treatment-resistant PTSD: A pilot study comparing CA-CBT applied to muscle relaxation. *Journal of Behavior Research and Therapy, 49*(4), 275–280.

HIPAA Medical Privacy Rule. (2003). Retrieved May 1, 2004, from http://www.socialworkers.org/hipaa/medical.asp

Hirayama, K. K., Hirayama, H., & Cetingok, M. (1993). Mental health promotion for South East Asian refugees in the USA. *International Social Work, 36,* 119–129.

Ho, M. (1987). *Family therapy with ethnic minorities.* Newbury Park, CA: Sage.

Hoagwood, K. E., Burns, B. J., Kiser, L., Ringeisen, H., & Schoenwald, S. K. (2001). Evidence-based practice in child and adolescent mental health services. *Psychiatric Services, 52,* 1179–1189.

Hoagwood, K. E., Kelleher, K., Murray, L. K., Jensen, P. S., & Integrated Services Program Task Force. (2006). Implementation of evidence-based practices for children in four countries: A project of the World Psychiatric Association. *Revista Brasileira de Psiquiatria, 28,* 59–66.

Hodge, D. R. (2005). Spiritual lifemaps: A client-centered pictorial instrument for spiritual assessment, planning and intervention. *Social Work, 50,* 77–87.

Hodge, D. R. (2007). Social justice and people of faith: A transnational perspective. *Social Work, 52*(2), 139–148.

Hodge, D. R., & Nadir, A. (2008). Moving toward culturally competent practice with Muslims: Modifying cognitive therapy with Islamic tenets. *Social Work, 53,* 31–41.

Hoefer, R. (2005). Altering state policy: Interest group effectiveness among state-level advocacy groups. *Social Work, 50,* 219–225.

Holbrook, T. L. (1995). Finding subjugated knowledge: Personal document research. *Social Work, 40,* 746–750.

Holland, S. (2000). The assessment relationship: Interaction between social workers and parents in child protection assessment. *British Journal of Social Work, 30,* 149–163.

Hollander, E. M. (2001). Cyber community in the valley of the shadow of death. *Journal of Loss and Trauma, 6,* 136–146.

Hollis, F., & Woods, M. (1981). *Casework: A psychosocial therapy* (3rd ed.). New York: Random House.

Holloway, M., & Moss, B. (2010). *Spirituality and social work.* New York: Palgrave Macmillan.

Holt, B. J. (2002). *The practice of generalist case management.* Needham Heights, MA: Allyn & Bacon.

Homan, M. S. (1999). *Promoting community change: Making it happen in the real world* (2nd ed.). Belmont, CA: Brooks/Cole.

Homan, M. S. (2008). *Promoting community change: Making it happen in the real world* (4th ed.). Pacific Grove, CA: Brooks/Cole.

Hopson, L. M., & Kim, J. S. (2005). Solution-focused brief treatment approach to crisis intervention with adolescents. *Journal of Evidence-Based Social Work, 1*(2/3), 93–110.

Houston-Vega, M. K., Nuehring, E. M., & Daguio, E. R. (1997). *Prudent practice: A guide for managing malpractice risk.* Washington, DC: NASW Press.

Howard, M., Allen-Meares, P., & Ruffolo, M. (2007). Teaching evidence-based practice: Strategic and pedagogical recommendations for schools of social work. *Research on Social Work Practice, 17,* 561–568.

Hoyt, M. F. (2000). *Some stories are better than others: Doing what works in brief therapy and managed care.* Philadelphia: Brunner/Mazel.

Hsu, W. S. (2009). The components of the solution-focused supervision. *Bulletin of Education Psychology, 41,* 475–496.

Hubble, M. A., Duncan, B. L., & Miller, S. D. (1999). Introduction. In M. A. Hubble, B. L. Duncan, & S. D. Miller (Eds.), *The heart and soul of change: What works in therapy.* Washington, DC: American Psychological Association.

Hudson, W. W. (1992). *The WALMYR assessment scales scoring manual.* Tempe, AZ: WALMYR.

Hudson, W. W., & McMurtry, S. L. (1997). Comprehensive assessment in social work practice: The Multi-Problem Screening Inventory. *Research on Social Work Practice, 7*(1), 79–98.

Huffine, C. (Summer, 2006). Bad conduct, defiance, and mental health. *Focal Point, 20*(2), 13–16.

Hulewat, P. (1996). Resettlement: A cultural and psychological crisis. *Social Work, 41,* 129–135.

Hull, G. H., Jr. (1982). Child welfare services to Native Americans. *Social Casework, 63,* 340–347.

Hunsley, J., Aubrey, T., Vestervelt, C. M., & Vito, D. (1999). Comparing therapist and client perspectives on reasons for psychotherapy termination. *Psychotherapy, 36,* 380–388.

Hunt, L. M. (2001). Beyond cultural competence: Applying humility to clinical settings. *The Park Ridge Center Bulletin, 24,* 3–4.

Hurley, D. J. (1984). Resistance and work in adolescent groups. *Social Work with Groups, 1,* 71–81.

Hurvitz, N. (1975). Interactions hypothesis in marriage counseling. In A. Gutman & D. Rice (Eds.), *Couples in conflict* (pp. 225–240). New York: Jason Aronson.

Huxtable, M. (January, 2004). *Defining measurable behavioral goals and objectives.* School Social Work Association of America, Northlake, IL.

Hyde, C. (1996). A feminist's response to Rothman's "The interweaving of community intervention approaches." *Journal of Community Practice, 3*(3/4), 127–145.

I

Ingersoll-Dayton, B., Schroepfer, T., & Pryce, J. (1999). The effectiveness of a solution-focused approach for problem behaviors among nursing home residents. *Journal of Gerontological Social Work, 32,* 49–64.

International Federation of Social Workers (IFSW). (2000). *New definition of social work.* Berne: International Federation of Social Workers.

Ivanoff, A. M., Blythe, B. J., & Tripodi, T. (1994). *Involuntary clients in social work practice: A research-based approach.* New York: Aldine de Gruyter.

J

Jackson, A. P. (1998). The role of social support in parenting for low-income, single, black mothers. *Social Service Review, 72*, 365–378.

Jackson, D. D., & Weakland, J. H. (1961). Conjoint family therapy: Some considerations on theory, technique, and results. *Psychiatry, 24*, 3–45.

Jackson, V. (2015). Practitioner characteristics and organizational contexts as essential elements in the evidence-based practice versus cultural competence debate. *Transcultural Psychiatry, 52*(2), 150–173.

Jackson-Elmore, C. (2005). Informing state policymakers: Opportunities for social workers. *Social Work, 50*, 251–261.

Jacobs, E. E., Masson, R. L., & Harvill, R. L. (1998). *Group counseling strategies and skills*. Pacific Grove, CA: Brooks/Cole.

James, R. K. (2008). *Crisis intervention strategies* (6th ed.). Pacific Grove, CA: Brooks/Cole.

James, R. K., & Gilliland, B. E. (2001). *Crisis intervention strategies*. Pacific Grove, CA: Brooks/Cole.

James, R. K., & Gilliland, B. E. (2005). *Crisis intervention strategies* (5th ed.). Pacific Grove, CA: Brooks/Cole.

Janzen, C., & Harris, O. (1997). *Family treatment in social work practice* (3rd ed.). Itasca, IL: Peacock.

Jarrett, R. L. (1995). Growing up poor: The family experience of socially mobile youth in low-income African American neighborhoods. *Journal of Adolescent Research, 10*, 111–135.

Jayaratne, S. (1994). Should systematic assessment, monitoring and evaluation tools be used as empowerment aids for clients? In W. W. Hudson & P. S. Nurius (Eds.), *Controversial issues in social work research* (pp. 88–92). Needham Heights, MA: Allyn & Bacon.

Jaycox, L. H., Zoellner, L., & Foa, E. B. (2002). Cognitive-behavior therapy for PTSD in rape survivors. *Journal of Clinical Psychology, 58*(8), 891–907.

Jennings, H. (1950). *Leadership and isolation*. New York: Longmans Green.

Jensen, M., Agbata, I. N., Canavan, M., & McCarthy, G. (2015). Effectiveness of educational interventions for informal caregivers of individuals with dementia residing in the community: Systematic review and meta-analysis of randomized controlled trials. *International Journal of Geriatric Psychiatry, 30*, 130–143.

Jessop, D. (1998, February 1). Caribbean norms vs. European ethics. *The Sunday Observer* (Jamaica), p. 13.

Jimenez, J. (2002). The history of grandmothers in the African American community. *Social Services Review, 76*, 524–551.

Johnson, Y. M., & Munch, S. (2009). Fundamental contradictions in cultural competence. *Social Work, 54*, 222–231.

Jones, D. M. (1996). Termination from drug treatment: Dangers and opportunities for clients of the graduation ceremony. *Social Work with Groups, 19*(3/4), 105–115.

Jordan, C., & Franklin, C. (1995). *Clinical assessment for social workers: Quantitative and qualitative methods*. Chicago: Lyceum Books.

Jordan, C., & Franklin, C. (2003). *Clinical assessment for social workers: Quantitative and qualitative methods* (2nd ed.). Chicago: Lyceum Books.

Jordan, C., & Hickerson, J. (2003). Children and adolescents. In C. Jordan & C. Franklin (Eds.), *Clinical assessment for social workers: Quantitative and qualitative methods* (2nd ed., pp. 179–213). Chicago, IL: Lyceum Books.

Joseph, S., Williams, R., & Yule, W. (1993). Changes in outlook following disaster: Preliminary development of measures to assess positive and negative responses. *Journal of Traumatic Stress, 6*, 271–279.

Joyce, A. S., Duncan, S. C., Duncan, A., Kipnes, D., & Piper, W. E. (1996). Limiting time-unlimited group therapy. *International Journal of Group Psychotherapy, 46*(6), 61–79.

Juhnke, G. A. (1996). The adapted-SAD PERSONS: A suicide assessment scale designed for use with children. *Elementary School Guidance & Counseling, 30*, 252–258.

Julia, M. C. (1996). *Multicultural awareness in the health care professions*. Needham Heights, MA: Allyn & Bacon.

K

Kaboli, P. J., McClimon, B. J., Hoth, A. B., & Barnett, M. J. (2004). Assessing the accuracy of computerized medication histories. *American Journal of Managed Care, 10*, 872–877.

Kadushin, A. (1977). *Consultation in social work*. New York: Columbia University Press.

Kadushin, A., & Kadushin, G. (1997). *The social work interview: A guide for human service professionals* (4th ed.). New York: Columbia University Press.

Kadushin, G., & Kulys, R. (1993). Discharge planning revisited: What do social workers actually do in discharge planning? *Social Work, 38*, 713–726.

Kagle, J. D. (1994). Should systematic assessment, monitoring and evaluation tools be used as empowerment aids for clients? Rejoinder to Dr. Jayaratne. In W. W. Hudson & P. S. Nurius (Eds.), *Controversial issues in social work research* (pp. 88–92). Needham Heights, MA: Allyn & Bacon.

Kagle, J. D., & Kopels, S. (2008). *Social work records* (3rd ed.). Long Grove, IL: Waveland Press.

Kahn, M. (1997). *Between therapist and client: The new relationship*. New York: W. H. Freeman.

Kaminski, J. W., Valle, L. A., Filene, J. H., & Boyle, C. L. (2008). A meta-analytic review of components associated with parent training effectiveness. *Journal of Abnormal Child Psychology, 36,* 567–589.

Kane, N. (1995). Looking at the lite side. "I feed more cats, than I have T-cells." *Reflections, 1*(2), 26–36.

Kanter, J. (2007). Compassion fatigue and secondary trauma: A second look. *Clinical Social Work Journal, 30*(4), 289–293.

Karlsson, R. (2005). Ethnic matching between therapist and patient in psychotherapy: An overview of findings, together with methodological and contextual issues. *Cultural Diversity and Ethnic Minority Psychology, 11,* 113–129.

Kasprow, W. J., & Rosenheck, R. A. (2007). Outcomes of critical time intervention case management for homeless veterans after psychiatric hospitalization. *Psychiatric Services, 58,* 929–935.

Katiuzhinsky, A., & Okech, D. (2014). Human rights, cultural practices, and state policies: Implications for global social work practice and policy. *International Journal of Social Welfare, 23,* 80–88.

Katz, S., Ford, A. B., Moskowitz, R. W., Jackson, B. A., & Jaffe, M. W. (1963). Studies of illness in the aged: The Index of ADL: A standardized measure of biological and psychosocial function. *Journal of the American Medical Association, 185,* 914–919.

Kazdin, A. E. (2005). *Parent management training: Treatment for oppositional, aggressive, and antisocial behavior in children and adolescents.* New York: Oxford University Press.

Kazdin, A. E., & Wassell, G. (1998). Treatment completion and therapeutic change among children referred for outpatient therapy. *Professional Psychology: Research and Practice, 29,* 332–340.

Kear-Colwell, J., & Pollock, P. (1997). Motivation or confrontation: Which approach to the child sex offender? *Criminal Justice and Behavior, 24,* 20–33.

Keast, K. (2012). A toolkit for single-session groups in acute care settings. *Social Work in Health Care, 51*(8), 710–724.

Keats, P. A., & Sabharwal, V. V. (2008). Time-limited service alternatives: Using therapeutic enactment in open group therapy. *Journal for Specialists in Group Work, 33*(4), 297–316.

Keehner Engelke, M., Guttu, M., Warren, M. B., & Swanson, M. B. (2008). School nurse case management for children with chronic illness: Health, academic, and quality of life outcomes. *Journal of Nursing, 24*(4), 205–214.

Keenan, E. K., & Grady, M. D. (2014). From silos to scaffolding: Engaging and effective social work practice. *Clinical Social Work Journal, 42*(2), 193–204.

Kelly, M. S. (2008). Task-centered practice. In T. Mizrahi & L. Davis (Eds.), *Encyclopedia of social work* (20th ed., pp. 197–199). Washington, DC: NASW Press–Oxford University Press.

Kelly, M. S., Kim, J. S., & Franklin, C. (2008). *Solution-focused brief therapy in schools: A 360-degree review of practice and research.* New York: Oxford University Press.

Kerig, P. K., Ward, R. M., Vanderzee, K. L., & Moeddel, M. A. (2009). Posttraumatic stress as a mediator of the relationship between trauma and mental health problems among juvenile delinquents. *Journal of Youth and Adolescence, 38*(9), 1214–1225.

Kessler, D., Lewis, G., Kaur, S., Wiles, N., King, M., Weich, S., & Peters, T. J. (2009). Therapist-delivered internet psychotherapy for depression in primary care: A randomised controlled trial. *Lancet, 374,* 628–634. Retrieved from http://www.nationalstress clinic.com/wp-content/uploads/lancet-study.pdf

Kessler, M., Gira, E., & Poertner, J. (2005). Moving best practice to evidence-based practice in child welfare. *Families in Society, 86,* 244–250.

Kettenbach, G. (2003). *Writing SOAP notes: With patient/client management formats* (3rd ed.). Philadephia: Davis.

Kettner, P. M., Daley, J. M., & Nichols, A. W. (1985). *Initiating change in organizations and communities.* Monterey, CA: Brooks/Cole.

Kilpatrick, A. C., & Cleveland, P. H. (1993). Level of needs: Issues and relevant interventions. In A. C. Kilpatrick & T. P. Holland (Eds.), *Working with families: An integrative model by level of need* (p. 4). Boston: Allyn & Bacon.

Kilpatrick, A. C., & Holland, T. P. (2006). *Working with families. An integrative model by level of need* (4th ed.). Boston: Allyn & Bacon.

Kim, J. S. (2008). Examining the effectiveness of solution-focused brief therapy: A meta-analysis. *Research on Social Work Practice, 18,* 107–116.

Kim, J. S., & Franklin, C. (2009). Solution-focused brief therapy in schools: A review of the outcome literature. *Children and Youth Services Review, 31*(4), 464–470.

Kirk, S. A., & Kutchins, H. (1992). *The selling of DSM: The rhetoric of science in psychiatry.* New York: Aldine De Gruyter.

Kirst-Ashman, K. K. (2014). *Human behavior in the macro social environment: An empowerment approach to understanding communities, organizations and groups.* Belmont, CA: Brooks/Cole.

Kirst-Ashman, K. K., & Hull, G. H., Jr. (2012). *Generalist practice with organizations and communities* (5th ed.). Belmont, CA: Brooks/Cole.

Kleespies, P. M., Penk, W. E., & Forsyth, J. P. (1993). The stress of patient suicidal behavior during clinical training: Incidence, impact, and recovery. *Professional Psychology: Research and Practice, 24,* 293–303.

Klein, A. (1970). *Social work through group process*. Albany: State University of New York at Albany, School of Social Welfare.

Knight, C. (2006). Groups for individuals with traumatic histories: Practice considerations for social workers. *Social Work, 51*, 20–30.

Knight, J. R., Sherritt, L., Shrier, L. A., Harris, S. K., & Chang, G. (2002). Validity of the CRAFFT substance abuse screening test among adolescent clinic patients. *Archives of Pediatrics and Adolescent Medicine, 156*, 607–614.

Knox, K. S., & Roberts, A. R. (2008). The crisis intervention model. In N. Coady & P. Lehmann (Eds.), *Theoretical perspectives for direct social work practice. A generalist-eclectic approach* (2nd ed., pp. 249–274). New York: Springer.

Ko, S. J., Ford, J. D., Kassam-Adams, N., Berkowitz, S. J., Wilson, C., Wong, M., et al. (2008). Creating trauma-informed systems: Child welfare, education, first responders, health care and juvenile justice. *Professional Psychology: Research and Practice, 39*(4), 396–404.

Kohn, L. P., Oden, T. M., Munoz, R. F., Robinson, A., & Leavitt, D. (2002). Adapted cognitive-behavioral group therapy for depressed low-income, African American women. *Community Mental Health Journal, 38*, 497–504.

Komar, A. A. (1994). Adolescent school crises: Structures, issues and techniques for postventions. *International Journal of Adolescence and Youth, 5*(1/2), 35–46.

Konrad, S. C. (2013). *Child and family practice: A relational perspective*. Chicago: Lyceum Books.

Koob, G. F., & Le Moal, M. (2008). Addiction and the brain antireward system. *Annual Review of Psychology, 59*(1), 29–53.

Koob, J. J. (2003). Solution-focused family interventions. In A. C. Kilpatrick & T. P. Holland, *Working with families: An integrative model by level of need* (3rd ed., pp. 131–150). Boston: Allyn & Bacon.

Kopp, J. (1989). Self-observation: An empowerment strategy in assessment. *Social Casework, 70*, 276–284.

Korol, M. S., Green, B. L., & Grace, M. (1999). Developmental analysis of the psychosocial impact of disaster on children: A review. *Journal of the American Academy of Child and Adolescent Psychiatry, 38*, 368–375.

Kosoff, S. (2003) Single session groups: Applications and areas of expertise. *Social Work with Groups, 26*(1), 29–45.

Koss, M. P., & Shiang, J. (1994). Research on brief psychotherapy. In A. E. Bergin & S. L. Garfield (Eds.), *Handbook of psychotherapy and behavioral change* (3rd ed., pp. 664–700). New York: Wiley.

Krahenbuhl, S., & Blades, M. (2006). The effect of interviewing techniques on young children's responses to questions. *Child Care Health and Development, 32*, 321–333.

Kroenke, K., Spitzer, R. L., & Williams, J. B. W. (2001). The PHQ-9: Validity of a brief depression severity measure. *Journal of General Internal Medicine, 16*, 606–613.

Krogsrud Miley, K., O'Melia, M., & Dubois, B. (2013). *Generalist social work practice: An empowering approach*. New York: Pearson.

Kruger, L., Moore, D., Schmidt, P., & Wiens, R. (1979). Group work with abusive parents. *Social Work, 24*, 337–338.

Kuehlwein, K. T. (1992). Working with gay men. In A. Freeman & F. M. Dattilio (Eds.), *Comprehensive casebook of cognitive therapy* (pp. 249–252). New York: Plenum Press.

Kumabe, K., Nishada, C., & Hepworth, D. (1985). *Bridging ethnocultural diversity in social work and health*. Honolulu: University of Hawaii Press.

Kung, W. W. (2003). Chinese Americans' help seeking behavior for emotional distress. *Social Service Review, 77*(1), 110–134.

Kurland, R., & Salmon, R. (1998). Purpose: A misunderstood and misused keystone of group work practice. *Social Work with Groups, 21*(3), 5–17.

Kutchins, H. (1991). The fiduciary relationship. The legal basis for social workers' responsibilities to clients. *Social Work, 36*, 103–106.

L

Laing, R. (1965). Mystification, confusion and conflict. In I. Boszormenyi-Nagy & J. Framo (Eds.), *Intensive family therapy: Theoretical and practical aspects*. New York: Harper & Row.

Laird, J. (1993). Family-centered practice: Cultural and constructionist reflections. *Journal of Teaching in Social Work, 8*(1/2), 77–109.

Lamb, M., & Brown, D. (2006). Conversational apprentices: Helping children become competent informants about their own experiences. *British Journal of Developmental Psychology, 24*, 215–234.

Lambert, M. J., & Shimokawa, K. (2011). Collecting client feedback. In J. C. Norcross (Ed.), *Psychotherapy relationships that work* (2nd ed., pp. 203–223). New York: Oxford University Press.

Lane, E. J., Daugherty, T. K., & Nyman, S. J. (1998). Feedback on ability in counseling, self-efficacy, and persistence on task. *Psychological Reports, 83*, 1113–1114.

Lantz, J., & Walsh, J. (2007). *Short-term existential interventions in clinical practice*. Chicago, IL: Lyceum.

Larsen, J. (1980). Accelerating group development and productivity: An effective leader approach. *Social Work with Groups, 3*, 25–39.

Larsen, J., & Mitchell, C. (1980). Task-centered, strength-oriented group work with delinquents. *Social Casework, 61*, 154–163.

Lau, A. S. (2006). Making the case for selective and directed evidence culturally addressed evidence-based-treatment:

Examples from parent training. *Clinical Psychology*, *12*(4), 295–310.

Lavee, Y. (1997). The components of healthy marriages: Perceptions of Israeli social workers and their clients. *Journal of Family Social Work, 2*(1), 1–14.

Lavitt, M. R. (2009). What is advanced in generalist practice? A conceptual discussion. *Journal of Teaching in Social Work, 29*(4), 461–473.

Lazarus, A. A. (1994). How certain boundaries and ethics diminish therapeutic effectiveness. *Ethics and Behavior, 4*, 255–261.

Leadbeater, B. J., Kuperminc, G. P., Blatt, S. J., & Hertzog, C. (1999). A multivariate model of gender differences in adolescents' internalizing and externalizing problems. *Developmental Psychology, 35*, 1268–1282.

Leahy, R. H., & Holland, S. J. (2000). *Treatment plans and interventions for depression and anxiety disorders*. New York: Guildford Press.

Lee, E. (2014). A therapist's self disclosure and its impact on the therapy process in cross-cultural encounters: Disclosure of personal self, professional self, and/or cultural self? *Families in Society: The Journal of Contemporary Social Services, 95*(1), 15–23.

Lee, J. J., & Miller, S. E. (2013). A self-care framework for social workers: Building a strong foundation for practice. *Families in Society: The Journal of Contemporary Social Services, 94*(2), 96–103.

Lee, M. Y. (2003). A solution-focused approach to cross-cultural clinical social work practice: Utilizing cultural strengths. *Families in Society, 84*, 385–395.

Lee, M. Y., Greene, G. J., & Rheinscheld, J. (1999). A model for short-term solution-focused group treatment of male domestic violence offenders. *Journal of Family Social Work, 3*(2), 39–57.

Lee, M. Y., Uken, A., & Sebold, J. (2004). Accountability for change: Solution-focused treatment with domestic violence offenders. *Families in Society, 85*, 463–476.

Lee, S. J. (2005). Facilitating the welfare-to-work transition for women with a mental health work barrier. *Journal of Human Behavior in the Social Environment, 12*, 127–143.

Lehman, A. F. (1996). Heterogeneity of person and place: Assessing co-occurring addictive and mental disorders. *American Journal of Orthopsychiatry, 66*(1), 32–41.

Leiter, M. P., & Maslach, C. (2005). *Banishing burnout: Six involving feelings, attitudes, motives and strategies for improving your relationship expectations with work*. San Francisco: Jossey-Bass.

Lens, V. (2005). Advocacy and argumentation in the public arena: A guide for social workers. *Social Work, 50*, 231–238.

Lesure-Lester, E. G. (2002). An application of cognitive behavioral principles in the reduction of aggression among abused African American adolescents. *Journal of Interpersonal Violence, 17*, 394–403.

Levi, D. (2007). *Group dynamics for teams* (2nd ed.). Thousand Oaks, CA: Sage.

Levick, K. (1981). Privileged communication: Does it really exist? *Social Casework, 62*, 235–239.

Levine, C. O., & Dang, J. (1979). The group within the group: The dilemma of cotherapy. *International Journal of Group Psychotherapy, 29*(2), 175–184.

Levinson, H. (1977). Termination of psychotherapy: Some salient issues. *Social Casework, 58*, 480–489.

Levy, A. J., & Frank, M. G. (2011). Clinical practice with children. In J. Brandell (Ed.), *Theory and practice in clinical social work* (2nd ed., pp. 101–121). Thousand Oaks, CA: Sage.

Levy, C. (1973). The value base of social work. *Journal of Education for Social Work, 9*, 34–42.

Levy, L. (1963). *Psychological interpretation*. New York: Holt, Rinehart & Winston.

Lewis, E. (1991). Social change and citizen action: A philosophical exploration for modern social group work. *Social Work with Groups, 14*(3/4), 23–34.

Lewis, J. A., Lewis, M. D., Packard, T., & Souflee, F. (2001). *Management of human service programs* (3rd ed.). Pacific Grove, CA: Brooks/Cole.

Lewis, T., & Osborn, C. (2004). Solution-focused counseling and motivational interviewing: A consideration of confluence. *Journal of Counseling and Development, 82*, 38–48.

Liau, A. K., Barriga, A. Q., & Gibbs, J. C. (1998). Relations between self-serving cognitive distortions and overt versus covert antisocial behaviors in adolescents. *Aggressive Behavior, 24*, 335–346.

Liddle, H. A. (2009). *Adolescent drug abuse: A family-based multidimensional approach, clinician's manual*. Center City, MN: Hazelden.

Lieberman, M., Yalom, I., & Miles, M. (1973). *Encounter groups: First facts*. New York: Basic Books.

Lietz, C. A. (2006). Uncovering stories of family resilience: A mixed methods study of resilient families: Part 1. *Families in Society, 87*, 575–582.

Lietz, C. A. (2007). Uncovering stories of family resilience: A mixed methods study of resilient families: Part 2. *Families in Society, 88*, 147–155.

Ligon, J. (1997). Brief crisis stabilization of an African American woman: Integrating cultural and ecological approaches. *Journal of Multicultural Social Work, 6*(3/4), 111–123.

Lindemann, E. (1944). Symptomatology and management of acute grief. *American Journal of Psychiatry, 101*, 141–148.

Lindemann, E. (1956). The meaning of crisis in individual and family. *Teachers College Record, 57*, 310.

Lindsey, M. A., Korr, W. S., Broitman, M., Bone, L., Green, A., & Leaf, P. J. (2006). Help-seeking behaviors and depression among African American adolescent boys. *Social Work, 51*, 49–58.

Linhorst, D. M. (2002). Federalism and social justice: Implications for social work. *Social Work, 47*, 201–208.

Linzer, N. (1999). *Resolving ethical dilemmas in social work practice.* Boston: Allyn & Bacon.

Lipchik, E. (1997). My story about solution-focused brief therapist/client relationships. *Journal of Systemic Therapies, 16,* 159–172.

Lipchik, E. (2002). *Beyond technique in solution-focused therapy: Working with emotions and the therapeutic relationship.* New York: Guilford Press.

Lister, L. (1987). Contemporary direct practice roles. *Social Work, 32,* 384–391.

Littell, J., & Girvin, H. (2004). Ready or not: Uses of the stages of change model in child welfare. *Child Welfare, 83,* 341–366.

Lo, T. W. (2005). Task-centered group work: Reflections on practice. *International Social Work, 48,* 455–456.

Loewenberg, F. M., Dolgoff, R., & Harrington, D. (2005). *Ethical decisions for social work practice* (7th ed.). Itasca, IL: Peacock.

Logan, S. M. L., Freeman, E. M., & McRoy, R. G. (1990). *Social work practice with black families: A culturally specific perspective.* New York: Longman.

Long, D. L., Tice, C. J., & Morrison, J. D. (2006). *Macro social work practice: A strengths perspective.* Pacific Grove, CA: Brooks/Cole.

Longres, J. F. (1991). Toward a status model of ethnic sensitive practice. *Journal of Multicultural Social Work, 1*(1), 41–56.

Longres, J. F. (1995). *Human behavior in the social environment.* Itasca, IL: Peacock.

Loo, C. M., Ueda, S. S., & Morton, R. K. (2007). Group treatment for race-related stresses among Vietnam veterans. *Transcultural Psychiatry, 44*(1), 115–135.

Louis, W. R., Lalonde, R. N., & Esses, V. M. (2010). Bias against foreign-born or foreign-trained doctors: Experimental evidence. *Medical Education, 44*(12), 1241–1247.

Lowenstein, D. A., Amigo, E., Duara, R., Guterman, A., Kurwitz, D., Berkowitz, N., et al. (1989). A new scale for the assessment of functional status in Alzheimer's disease and related disorders. *Journal of Gerontology: Psychological Sciences, 44,* 114–121.

Lu, Y., Dane, B., & Gellman, A. (2005). An experiential model: Teaching empathy and cultural sensitivity. *Journal of Teaching Social Work, 25*(3/4), 89–103.

Lucas, C. P., Zhang, H., Fisher, P. W., Shaffer, D., Regier, D. A., Narrow, W. E., & Friman, P. (2001). The DISC Predictive Scales (DPS): Efficiently screening for diagnoses. *Journal of the American Academy of Child & Adolescent Psychiatry, 40,* 443–449.

Lukas, S. (1993). *Where to start and what to ask: An assessment handbook.* New York: Norton.

Lukton, R. (1982). Myths and realities of crisis intervention. *Social Casework, 63,* 275–285.

Lum, D. (1996). *Social work practice and people of color: A process-stage approach* (3rd ed.). Pacific Grove, CA: Brooks/Cole.

Lum, D. (2004). *Social work practice and people of color: A process-stage approach* (5th ed.). Pacific Grove, CA: Brooks/Cole.

Lum, D. (2007). *Culturally competent practice: A framework for understanding diverse groups and justice issues.* Pacific Grove, CA: Brooks/Cole.

M

Macgowan, M. J. (1997). A measure of engagement for social group work: The group work engagement measure (GEM). *Journal of Social Service Research, 23*(2), 17–37.

Macgowan, M. J. (2004). Prevention and intervention in youth suicide. In P. Allen-Mears & M. W. Fraser (Eds.), *Intervention with children and adolescents: An interdisciplinary perspective* (pp. 282–310). Boston: Pearson.

Macgowan, M. J. (2008). *A guide to evidence-based group work.* New York: Oxford University Press.

Mackey, R. A., & O'Brien, B. A. (1998). Marital conflict management: Gender and ethnic differences. *Social Work, 43,* 128–141.

Magen, R. H. (2004). Measurement issues. In C. D. Garvin, L. M. Gutierrez, & M. J. Galinsky (Eds.), *Handbook of social work with groups.* New York: Guilford Press.

Magen, R. H., & Glajchen, M. (1999). Cancer support groups: Client outcome and the context of group process. *Research on Social Work Practice, 9,* 541–554.

Maguire, L. (2002). *Clinical social work: Beyond generalist practice with individuals, groups and families.* Pacific Grove, CA: Brooks/Cole.

Mahler, C. (1969). *Group counseling in the schools.* Boston: Houghton Mifflin.

Mailick, M. D., & Vigilante, F. W. (1997). The family assessment wheel: A social constructionist perspective. *Families in Society, 80,* 361–369.

Maiter, S., Palmer, S., & Manji, S. (2006). Strengthening social worker–client relationship in child protective services. *Qualitative Social Work, 5,* 167–186.

Major, S. (2004). Evidence weak for case management for frail elderly. *British Medical Journal, 329,* 1306.

Malekoff, A. (2006). Strengths-based group work with children and adolescents. In C. D. Garvin, L. M. Gutierrez, & M. J. Galinsky (Eds.), *Handbook of social work with groups* (pp. 227–244). New York: Guilford Press.

Malgady, R. G., & Zayas, L. H. (2001). Cultural and linguistic considerations in psychodiagnosis with Hispanics: The need for an empirically informed process model. *Social Work, 46,* 39–49.

Mallory, K. (2004, May 8). Barbers cutting cancer out in Montgomery County. *The Washington Afro American, 112,* 39.

Manhal-Baugus, M. (2001). E-therapy: Practical, ethical, and legal issues. *CyberPsychology and Behavior, 4,* 551–563.

Markland, C., Ryan, R. M., Tobin, V. J., & Rollnick, R. (2005). Motivational interviewing and self-determination theory. *Journal of Social and Clinical Psychology, 24*(6), 811–831.

Marsh, J. C. (2002). Learning from clients. *Social Work, 47,* 341–342.

Marsh, J. C. (2003). Arguments for family strengths. *Social Work, 42,* 147–148.

Marsh, J. C. (2004). Theory-driven versus theory-free research in empirical social work practice. In H. Briggs & T. Rzepnicki (Eds), *Using evidence in social work practice* (pp. 20–35). Chicago: Lyceum Books.

Marsh, J. C. (2005). Social justice: Social work's organizing value. *Social Work, 50,* 345–346.

Marshall, J. M., & Haight, W. L. (2014). Understanding racial disproportionality affecting African American youth who cross over from the child welfare to the juvenile justice system: Communication, power, race, and social class. *Children & Youth Services Review, 42,* 82–90.

Martin, P. Y., & O'Connor, G. G. (1989). *The social environment: Open systems applications.* Upper Saddle River, NJ: Longman.

Maschi, T. (2006). Unraveling the link between trauma and male delinquency: The cumulative versus differential risk perspective. *Social Work, 11,* 59–70.

Maschi, T., Bradley, C., & Ward, K. (Eds.). (2009). *Forensic social work: Psychosocial and legal issues in diverse practice settings.* New York: Springer

Mason, J. L., Benjamin, M. P., & Lewis, S. A. (1996). The cultural competence model: Implications for child and family mental health services. In C. A. Heflinger & C. T. Nixon (Eds.), *Families and the mental health system for children and adolescents: Policy, services, and research* (pp. 165–190). Thousand Oaks, CA: Sage.

Mason, M. (2009). Rogers redux: Relevance and outcomes of motivational interviewing across behavioral problems. *Journal of Counseling & Development, 87,* 357–362.

Mattaini, M. (1995). Visualizing practice with children and families. *Early Child Development and Care, 106,* 59–74.

Matto, H. C. (2005). A bio-behavioral model of addiction treatment: Applying dual representation theory to craving management and relapse prevention. *Substance Use & Misuse, 40,* 529–541.

Mau, W., & Jepsen, D. A. (1990). Help seeking perceptions behaviors: A comparison of Chinese and American graduate students. *Journal of Multicultural Counseling and Development, 18*(2), 95–104.

Mayadas, N. S., Ramanathan, C. S., & Suarez, Z. (1998–1999). Mental health, social context, refugees, and immigrants: A cultural interface. *Journal of Intergroup Relations, 25*(4), 3–14.

Mayo Clinic. (2007, January 12). *Elder abuse: Signs to look for, action to take.* Retrieved from http://www.mayoclinic.com/health/elder-abuse/HA00041

Mays, N. (2003, Fall). Investigating how culture impacts health. *Washington University in Saint Louis Magazine.*

McCarter, S. A. (2008). Adolescence. In E. D. Hutchison (Ed.), *Dimensions of human behavior: The changing life cycle* (3rd ed., pp. 227–281). Thousand Oaks, CA: Sage.

McCollum, E. E., & Beer, J. (1995). The view from the other chair. *Family Therapy Networker, 19*(2), 59–62.

McCollum, E. E., & Trepper, T. S. (2001). *Creating family solutions for substance abuse.* New York: Haworth Press.

McConaughy, S. H., & Auchenbach, T. M. (1994). *Manual for the semistructured clinical interview for children and adolescents.* Burlington: University of Vermont, Department of Psychiatry.

McDonald, L. (2002). Evidence-based, family-strengthening strategies to reduce delinquency: FAST: Families and Schools Together. In A. R. Roberts & G. J. Greene (Eds.), *Social workers' desk reference* (pp. 717–722). New York: Oxford University Press.

McDowell, T., Libal, K., & Brown, A. L. (2012). Human rights in the practice of family therapy: Domestic violence, a case in point. *Journal of Feminist Family Therapy, 24,* 1–23.

McFarlane, W. R. (2002). *Multifamily groups in the treatment of severe psychiatric disorders.* New York: Guilford Press.

McGinnis, E., Sprafkin, R. P., Gershaw, N. J., & Klein, P. (2011). *Skillstreaming the adolescent: A guide for teaching prosocial skills* (3rd ed.). Chicago: Research Press.

McGoldrick, M. (Ed.). (1998). *Re-visioning family therapy: Race, culture and gender in clinical practice.* New York: Guilford Press.

McGoldrick, M., Gerson, R., & Petry, S. (2008). *Genograms: Assessment and intervention* (3rd ed.). New York: Norton.

McGonagle, E. (1986). *Banana splits: A peer support group for children of transitional families.* Ballston Spa, NY: Author.

McGovern, J. (2015). Living better with dementia: Strengths-based social work practice and dementia care. *Social Work in Health Care, 54,* 408–421.

McKenry, P. C., & Price, S. J. (Eds.). (2000). *Families and change: Coping with stressful events and transitions* (2nd ed.). Thousand Oaks, CA: Sage.

McKenzie, A. (2005). Narrative-oriented therapy with children who have experienced sexual abuse. *Envision: The Manitoba Journal of Child Welfare, 4*(2), 1–29.

McKinnon, J. (2008). Exploring the nexus between social work and the environment. *Australian Social Work, 61,* 256–268.

McLaughlin, A. M. (2002). Social work's legacy: Irreconcilable differences? *Clinical Social Work Journal, 30*(2), 187–198.

McMillen, J. C., & Fisher, R. (1998). The perceived benefit scales: Measuring perceived positive life changes after negative events. *Social Work Research, 22*(3), 173–187.

McMillen, J. C., Morris, L., & Sherraden, M. (2004). Ending social work's grudge match: Problems versus strengths. *Families in Society, 85*, 317–325.

McMillen, J. C., Smith, E. M., & Fisher, R. (1997). Perceived benefit and mental health after three types of disaster. *Journal of Consulting and Clinical Psychology, 63*, 1037–1043.

McMillen, J. C., Zuravin, S., & Rideout, G. B. (1995). Perceptions of benefits from child sexual abuse. *Journal of Consulting and Clinical Psychology, 63*, 1037–1043.

McNeely, R., & Badami, M. (1984). Interracial communication in school social work. *Social Work, 29*, 22–25.

McQuaide, S. (1999). Using psychodynamic, cognitive behavioral and solution-focused questioning to construct a new narrative. *Clinical Social Work, 27*, 339–353.

McQuaide, S., & Ehrenreich, J. H. (1997). Assessing client strengths. *Families in Society, 78*, 201–212.

McRoy, R. G. (2003, June 6). *Impact of systems on adoption in the African American community.* Keynote address presented at the meeting of the Institute on Domestic Violence in the African American Community, Minneapolis, MN.

McWilliams, N. (1999). *Psychoanalytic formulation.* New York: Guilford Press.

Meenaghan, T. M. (1987). Macro practice: Current trends and issues. In A. Minehan (Ed.), *Encyclopedia of social work* (18th ed., pp. 82–89). Silver Spring, MD: National Association of Social Workers.

Meezan, W., & O'Keefe, M. (1998). Evaluating the effectiveness of multifamily group therapy in child abuse and neglect. *Research on Social Work Practice, 8*, 330–353.

Meier, A. (2002). An online stress management support group for social workers. *Journal of Technology in Human Services, 20*(1/2), 107–132.

Meier, A. (2006). Technology-mediated groups. In C. D. Garvin, L. M. Gutierrez, & M. J. Galinsky (Eds.), *Handbook of social work with groups* (pp. 13–31). New York: Guilford Press.

Mercier, C., & Racine, G. (2005). A follow-up study of homeless women. *Journal of Social Distress and Homeless, 2*, 207–222.

Metcalf, L. (1998). *Solution focused group therapy: Ideas for groups in private practice, schools, agencies, and treatment programs.* New York: Free Press.

Metcalf, L., Thomas, R., Duncan, B., Miller, S., & Hubble, M. (1996). What works in solution-focused brief therapy: A qualitative analysis of client and therapist's perceptions. In S. Miller, M. Hubble, & B. Duncan (Eds.), *Handbook of solution-focused brief therapy.* San Francisco: Jossey-Bass.

Meyer, C. (1990, April 1). *Can social work keep up with the changing family!* [Monograph]. The fifth annual Robert J. O'Leary Memorial Lecture. Columbus: The Ohio State University College of Social Work.

Meyer, R. A., Williams, R. C., Ottens, A. J., & Schmidt, A. E. (1991). Triage assessment system: Crisis intervention. In R. K. James (Ed.), *Crisis intervention strategies* (6th ed.). Pacific Grove, CA: Brooks/Cole.

Meyer, W. (2001). Why they don't come back: A clinical perspective on the no-show client. *Clinical Social Work, 29*, 325–339.

Meystedt, D. M. (1984). Religion and the rural population: Implications for social work. *Social Casework, 65*(4), 219–226.

Milgram, D., & Rubin, J. S. (1992). Resisting resistance: Involuntary substance abuse group therapy. *Social Work with Groups, 15*(1), 95–110.

Miller, J., & Garran, A. M. (2008). *Racism in the United States: Implications for the helping professions.* Belmont, CA: Brooks/Cole.

Miller, R., & Mason, S. E. (2001). Using group therapy to enhance treatment compliance in first episode schizophrenia. *Social Work with Groups, 24*(1), 37–52.

Miller, S., Hubble, M., Chow, D., & Seidel, J. (2013). The outcome of psychotherapy: Yesterday, today and tomorrow. *Psychotherapy, 50*(1), 88–97.

Miller, W. R., & Rollnick, S. (2002). *Motivational interviewing: Preparing people for change* (2nd ed.). New York: Guilford Press.

Miller, W. R., & Rollnick, S. (2013). *Motivational interviewing: Helping people change* (3rd ed.). New York: Guilford Press.

Miller, W. R., & Sovereign, R. G. (1989). The check-up: A model for early intervention in addictive behaviors. In T. Loberg, W. R. Miller, P. E. Nathan, & G. A. Marlatt (Eds.), *Addictive behaviors: Prevention and early intervention* (pp. 219–231). Amsterdam: Swets and Zeitlinger.

Minahan, A., & Pincus, A. (1977). Conceptual framework for social work practice. *Social Work, 22*(5), 347–352.

Minkler, M. (Ed.). (2012). *Community organizing and community building for health and welfare* (3rd ed.). New Brunswick, NJ: Rutgers University Press.

Minkler, M., & Wallerstein, N. (Eds.). (2008). *Community-based participation for research: From process to outcomes.* New York: Wiley.

Minuchin, S. (1974). *Families and family therapy.* Cambridge, MA: Harvard University Press.

Mishna, F., Bogo, M., Root, J., Sawyer, J., & Khoury-Kassabri, M. (2012). "It just crept in": The digital age and implications for social work practice. *Clinical Social Work Journal, 40*(3), 277–286.

Mokuau, N., & Fong, R. (1994). Assessing the responsiveness of health services to ethnic minorities of color. *Social Work in Health Care, 28*(1), 23–34.

Moline, M. E., Williams, G. T., & Austin, K. M. (1998). *Documenting psychotherapy: Essentials for mental health practitioners.* Thousand Oaks, CA: Sage.

Montross, C. (2014). *Falling into the fire.* New York: Penguin Books.

Morgan, A. (2000). *What is narrative therapy?* Adelaide, Australia: Dulwich Centre.

Morgan, G. (1997). *Images of organizations.* Thousand Oaks, CA: Sage.

Morrison, J. (1995). *The first interview: Revised for DSM-IV.* New York: Guilford Press.

Moyers, T. B., Martin, T., Manuel, J. K., & Miller, W. R. (2003). *The Motivational Interviewing Treatment Integrity (MITI) Code, Version 2.0.* Retrieved January 7, 2011, from http://casaa.unm.edu/download/miti.pdf

Moyers, T. B., & Rollnick, S. (2002). A motivational interviewing perspective on resistance in psychotherapy. *Journal of Clinical Psychology, 58,* 185–193.

Munson, C. E. (2002). The techniques and process of supervisory practice. In A. R. Roberts & G. J. Greene (Eds.), *Social workers' desk reference* (pp. 38–44). New York: Oxford University Press.

Murdach, A. D. (1996). Beneficence re-examined: Protective intervention in mental health. *Social Work, 41,* 26–32.

Murphy, B. C., & Dillon, C. (2003). *Interviewing in action: Relationship, process, and change* (2nd ed.). Pacific Grove, CA: Brooks/Cole.

Murphy, B. C., & Dillon, C. (2008). *Interviewing in action in a multicultural world* (3rd ed.). Pacific Grove, CA: Brooks/Cole.

Murphy, B. C., & Dillon, C. (2010). *Interviewing in action in a multicultural world* (4th ed.). Belmont, CA: Brooks/Cole.

Murphy, C. M., & Baxter, V. A. (1997). Motivating batterers to change in the treatment context. *Journal of Interpersonal Violence, 12,* 607–619.

Murray, C. E., & Murray, T. L. (2004). Solution-focused premarital counseling: Helping couples build a vision for their marriage. *Journal of Marital and Family Therapy, 30,* 349–358.

Murray-Swank, N. A., & Pargament, K. I. (2011). Seeking the sacred: The assessment of spirituality in the therapy process. In J. D. Aten, M. R. McMinn, & E. L. Worthington, Jr. (Eds.), *Spiritually oriented interventions for counseling and psychotherapy* (pp. 107–135). Washington, DC: American Psychological Association.

Mwanza. (1990). *Afrikan naturalism.* Columbus, OH: Pan Afrikan Publications.

N

Nader, K., & Mello, C. (2008). Interactive trauma/grief-focused therapy with children. In N. Coady & P. Lehmann (Eds.), *Theoretical perspectives for direct social work practice: A generalist-eclectic approach* (2nd ed., pp. 493–519). New York: Springer.

Nadler, A. (1996). Help-seeking behavior as a coping resource. In M. Rosenbaum (Ed.), *Learned resourcefulness: On coping skills, self-control, and adaptive behavior* (pp. 127–162). New York: Springer.

Naleppa, M. J., & Reid, W. J. (2000). Integrating case management and brief-treatment strategies: A hospital-based geriatric program. *Social Work in Health Care, 31*(4), 1–23.

Naleppa, M. J., & Reid, W. J. (2003). *Gerontological social work: A task-centered approach.* New York: Columbia University Press.

National Alliance on Mental Illness. (2009). *Depression in older persons fact sheet.* Retrieved from http://www .nami.org/Template.cfm?Section=By_Illness&template=/ ContentManagement/ContentDisplay.cfm& ContentID=7515

National Association of Social Workers (NASW). (1992). *NASW standards for social work case management.* Retrieved from http://www.NASWDC.org/practice/ standards/sw-case-management.asp

National Association of Social Workers (NASW). (2001). *NASW standard for cultural competence for social work practice.* Washington, DC: NASW Press.

National Association of Social Workers (NASW). (2006). *Immigration policy toolkit.* Washington, DC: NASW Press.

National Association of Social Workers (NASW). (2007). *Indicators for the achievement of the NASW standards for cultural competence in social work practice.* Washington, DC: NASW Press.

National Association of Social Workers (NASW). (2008a). *Code of ethics.* Washington, DC: NASW Press.

National Association of Social Workers (NASW). (2008b). *Law note series.* Retrieved from http://www. socialworkers.org/ldf/lawnotes/Default.asp

National Association of Social Workers (NASW). (2009a). Cultural and linguistic competence in the social work profession. In *Social work speaks: National Association of Social Workers policy statements, 2009–2012* (8th ed., pp. 70–76). Washington, DC: NASW Press.

National Association of Social Workers (NASW). (2009b). Professional self-care and social work. In *Social work speaks: National Association of Social Worker policy statements, 2009–2012* (8th ed., pp. 268–272). Washington, DC: NASW Press.

National Association of Social Workers (NASW) & Association of Social Work Boards (ASWB). (2013). *Best practice standards for social work supervision.* Washington, DC: National Association of Social Workers.

National Council on Alcoholism and Drug Dependence. (n.d.). *Alcohol and crime.* Retrieved from https://ncadd .org/learn-about-alcohol/alcohol-and-crime

Negriff, S., & Susman, E. J. (2011). Pubertal timing, depression, and externalizing problems: A framework, review, and examination of gender differences. *Journal of Research on Adolescence, 21*(3), 717–746.

Nelson, T. D., & Kelley, L. (2001). Solution-focused couples groups. *Journal of Systemic Therapies, 20*, 47–66.

Nelson-Becker, H., Nakashima, M., & Canda, E. R. (2007). Spiritual assessment in aging: A framework for clinicians. *Journal of Gerontological Social Work, 48*, 331–347.

Nelson-Zlupko, L., Kauffman, E., & Dore, M. M. (1995). Gender differences in drug addiction and treatment: Implications for social work intervention with substance abusing women. *Social Work, 40*, 45–54.

Netting, F. E., Kettner, P. M., & McMurtry, S. L. (2004). *Social work macro practice* (3rd ed.). Boston: Allyn & Bacon.

Netting, F. E., Kettner, P. M., McMurty, S. L., & Thomas, M. L. (2012). *Social work macro practice* (5th ed.). Boston: Pearson.

Nevil, N., Beatty, M. L., & Moxley, D. P. (1997). *Socialization games for persons with disabilities: Structured group activities for social and interpersonal development.* Springfield, IL: C. C. Thomas.

Neville, H. A., Spanierman, L., & Doan, B. T. (2006). Exploring the association between color-blind racial ideology and multicultural counseling competencies. *Cultural Diversity and Ethnic Minority Psychology, 12*, 275–290.

Newsome, S. (2004). Solution-focused brief treatment (SFBT) group work with at-risk junior high school students: Enhancing the bottom line. *Research on Social Work Practice, 14*, 336–343.

Nichols, M. P. (2012). *Family therapy: Concepts and methods* (10th ed.). Boston: Pearson.

Nichols, M. P., & Schwartz, R. C. (1998). *Family therapy: Concepts and methods* (4th ed.). Boston: Allyn & Bacon.

Nichols, M. P., & Schwartz, R. C. (2004). *Family therapy: Concepts and methods* (6th ed.). Boston: Allyn & Bacon.

Nichols, M. P., & Schwartz, R. C. (2006). *Family therapy: Concepts and methods* (7th ed.). Boston: Allyn & Bacon.

Norcross, J. C., & Lambert, M. J. (2006). The therapy relationship. In J. C. Norcross, L. E. Beutler, & R. F. Levant (Eds.), *Evidence-based practices in mental health: Debate and dialogue on the fundamental questions* (pp. 208–217). Washington, DC: American Psychological Association.

Norrick, N., & Spitz, A. (2008). Humor as a resource for mitigating conflict in interaction. *Journal of Pragmatics, 40*, 1661–1686.

Norris, J. (1999). *Mastering documentation* (2nd ed.). Springhouse, PA: Springhouse.

Northen, H. (2006). Ethics and values in group work. In C. D. Garvin, L. M. Gutierrez, & M. J. Galinsky (Eds.), *Handbook of social work with groups* (pp. 76–89). New York: Guilford Press.

Northen, H., & Kurland, R. (2001). The use of activity. In H. Northen (Ed.), *Social work with groups* (3rd ed., pp. 258–287). New York: Columbia University Press.

Nosko, A., & Wallace, R. (1997). Female/male co-leadership in groups. *Social Work with Groups, 20*(2), 3–16.

Nugent, W. R. (1992). The affective impact of a clinical social worker's interviewing style: A series of single-case experiments. *Research on Social Work Practice, 2*, 6–27.

Nugent, W. R., & Halvorson, H. (1995). Testing the effects of active listening. *Research on Social Work Practice, 5*, 152–175.

Nugent, W. R., Umbriet, M. S., Wilnamaki, L., & Paddock, J. (2001). Participation in victim-offender mediation and reoffense: Successful replications? *Research on Social Work Practice, 11*, 5–23.

Nybell, L. M., & Gray, S. S. (2004). Race, place, space: Meaning of cultural competence in three child welfare agencies. *Social Work, 49*, 17–26.

O

Obama, B. (1988, August & September). Why organize? Problems and promise in the inner city. *Illinois Issues*, pp. 40–42.

Oettingen, G., Bulgarella, C., Henderson, M., & Collwitzer, P. M. (2004). The self-regulation of goal pursuit. In R. Wright, J. Greenberg, & S. S. Brehm (Eds.), *Motivational analysis of social behavior* (pp. 225–244). Mahwah, NJ: Erlbaum.

Ogbu, J. U. (1994). From cultural differences to differences in cultural frame of reference. In P. M. Greenfield & R. R. Cocking (Eds.), *Cross-cultural roots of minority child development* (pp. 365–392). Hillsdale, NJ: Erlbaum.

Ogbu, J. U. (1997). Understanding the school performances of urban blacks: Some essential knowledge. In H. J. Walbery, O. Reyes, & P. R. Weissberg (Eds.), *Children and youth: Interdisciplinary perspectives.* Thousand Oaks, CA: Sage.

O'Hanlon, W. (1996, January/February). Case commentary. *Family Therapy Networker*, pp. 84–85.

O'Hare, T. (2005). *Evidence-based practices for social workers: An interdisciplinary approach.* Chicago: Lyceum Books.

O'Hare, T. (2009). *Essential skills of social work practice: Assessment, intervention and evaluation.* Chicago: Lyceum Books.

O'Hollaran, T. M., & Linton, J. M. (2000). Stress on the job: Self-care resources for counselors. *Journal of Mental Health Counseling, 22*, 254–265.

Okun, B. F. (2002). *Effective helping: Interviewing and counseling techniques.* Pacific Grove, CA: Brooks/Cole.

Okun, B. F. (1996). *Understanding diverse families: What practitioners need to know.* New York: Guilford Press.

Okun, B. F., Fried, J., & Okun, M. L. (1999). *Understanding diversity. A learning-as-practice primer.* Pacific Grove, CA: Brooks/Cole.

Organista, K., Dwyer, E. V., & Azocar, F. (1993). Cognitive behavioral therapy with Latino clients. *The Behavior Therapist, 16*, 229–228.

Orme, J. (2002). Social work: Gender, care and justice. *British Journal of Social Work, 32*, 799–814.

Orwin, R. G., Sonnefeld, J., Garrison-Mogren, R., & Gray Smith, N. (1994). Pitfalls in evaluating the effectiveness of case management programs for homeless persons: Lessons from the NIAAA Community Demonstration Program. *Evaluation Review, 18*, 153–207.

Ozawa, M. N., & Yoon, H. (2005). Leavers of TANF and AFDC: How do they fare economically? *Social Work, 50*, 239–248.

P

Pack-Brown, J. P., Whittington-Clark, L. E., & Parker, W. M. (1998). *Images of me: A guide to group work with African-American women.* Boston: Allyn & Bacon.

Padgett, D. K. (Ed.). (2004). *The qualitative research experience.* Pacific Grove, CA: Brooks/Cole.

Padilla, Y., Shapiro, E., Fernandez-Castro, M., & Faulkner, M. (2008). Our nation's immigrants in peril: An urgent call to social workers. *Social Work, 53*, 5–8.

Palmer, B., & Pablo, S. (1978). Community development possibilities for effective Indian reservation child abuse and neglect efforts. In M. Lauderdale, R. Anderson, & S. Cramer (Eds.), *Child abuse and neglect: Issues on innovation and implementation.* Austin: University of Texas.

Palmer, N., & Kaufman, M. (2003). The ethics of informed consent: Implications for multicultural practice. *Journal of Ethnic and Cultural Diversity in Social Work, 12*(1), 1–26.

Panos, P. T., Panos, A., Cox, S., Roby, J. L., & Matheson, K. W. (2004). Ethical issues concerning the use of videoconferencing to supervise the placement of international social work field practicum students. *Journal of Social Work Education, 40*, 467–478.

Parad, H. J. (1965). *Crisis intervention: Selected readings.* New York: Family Service Association of America.

Parad, H. J., & Caplan, G. (1960). A framework for studying families in crisis. *Social Work, 5*(3), 3–15.

Parad, H. J., & Parad, L. G. (Eds.). (1990). *Crisis intervention book 2: The practitioner's sourcebook for brief therapy.* Milwaukee, WI: Family Service America.

Parad, H. J., & Parad, L. G. (Eds.). (2006). *Crisis intervention book 2: The practitioner's sourcebook for brief therapy* (2nd ed.). Tucson, AZ: Fenestra Books.

Parihar, B. (1984). *Task-centered management in human service organizations.* Springfield, IL: Thomas.

Parks, S., & Novielli, K. (2000). A practical guide for caring for caregivers. *American Family Physician, 62*(12).

Parloff, M., Waskow, I., & Wolfe, B. (1978). Research on therapist variables in relation to process and outcome. In S. Garfield & A. Bergin (Eds.), *Handbook of psychotherapy and behavior change* (pp. 233–282). New York: Wiley.

Parson, E. R. (1993). Ethnotherapeutic empathy (ETE): Part 1. Definition, theory and process. *Journal of Contemporary Psychology, 33*(1), 5–12.

Parsons, R. J. (2002). Guidelines for empowerment-based social work practice. In A. R. Roberts & G. J. Greene (Eds.), *Social workers' desk reference* (pp. 396–401). New York: Oxford University Press.

Parsons, R. J., Jorgenson, J. D., & Hernandez, S. H. (1988). Integrative practice approach: A framework for problem solving. *Social Work, 35*, 417–421.

Parsons, R. J., Jorgensen, J. D., & Hernandez, S. H. (1994). *The integration of social work practice.* Pacific Grove, CA: Brooks/Cole.

Patrika, P., & Tseliou, E. (2015). Blame, responsibility and systematic neutrality: A discourse analysis methodology to the study of family therapy problem talk. *Journal of Family Therapy,* doi:10.1111/1467-6427.12076

Paveza, G. J., Prohaska, T., Hagopian, M., & Cohen, D. (1989). *Determination of need—Revision: Final report, Volume I.* Chicago: University of Illinois at Chicago.

Pavlov, I. P. (1927). *Conditioned reflexes.* Oxford, UK: Oxford University Press.

Payne, M. (2005). *Modern social work theory* (3rd ed.). Chicago: Lyceum Books.

Pazaratz, D. (2000). Task-centered child and youth care in residential treatment. *Residential Treatment for Children and Youth, 17*(4), 1–16.

Pelton, L. H. (2001). Social justice and social work. *Journal of Social Work Education, 37*(3), 433–439.

Pence, E., & Paymar, M. (1993). *Education groups for men who batter: The Duluth model.* New York: Springer.

Perlman, H. (1957). *Social casework: A problem-solving process.* Chicago: University of Chicago Press.

Peterson, A. L., Goodie, J. L., & Andrasik, F. (2015). Introduction to biopsychosocial assessment in clinical health psychology. In F. Andrasik, J. L. Goodie, & A. L. Peterson (Eds.), *Biopsychosocial assessment in clinical health psychology* (pp. 3–8). New York: Guilford Press.

Petr, C., & Walter, U. (2005). Best practices inquiry: A multidimensional, value-critical framework. *Journal of Social Work Education, 41*, 251–267.

Pew Partnership for Civic Change. (2001). *Ready, willing and able: Citizens working for change.* Retrieved from http://www.pew-partnership.org/pubs/rwa/printable/full_report.html

Philip, C. E. (1994). Letting go: Problems with termination when a therapist is seriously ill or dying. *Smith College Studies in Social Work, 64*, 169–179.

Philip, C. E., & Stevens, E. V. (1992). Countertransference issues for the consultant when a colleague is critically ill (or dying). *Clinical Social Work Journal, 20*, 411–419.

Pichot, T., & Dolan, Y. (2003). *Solution-focused brief therapy: Its effective use in agency settings.* New York: Haworth Press.

Pierce, W. J., & Elisme, E. (1997). Understanding and working with Haitian immigrant families. *Journal of Family Social Work, 2*(1), 49–65.

Pilsecker, C. (1987). A patient dies—A social worker reviews his work. *Social Work in Health Care, 13*(2), 35–45.

Pincus, A., & Minahan, A. (1973). *Social work practice: Model and method*. Itasca, IL: Peacock.

Poindexter, C. C. (1997). In the aftermath: Serial crisis intervention for people with HIV. *Health and Social Work, 22*, 125–132.

Pokorny, A. D., Miller, B. A., & Kaplan, H. B. (1972). The Brief MAST: A shortened version of the Michigan Alcoholism Screening Test. *American Journal of Psychiatry, 129*, 342–345.

Pollack, S. (2004). Anti-oppressive social work practice with women in prison: Discursive reconstructions and alternative practices. *British Journal of Social Work, 34*, 693–707.

Pollio, D. E. (1995). Use of humor in crisis intervention. *Families in Society, 76*, 376–384.

Pollio, D. E. (2006). The art of evidence-based practice. *Research on Social Work Practice, 16*, 224–232.

Polowy, C. I., & Gilbertson, J. (1997). *Social workers and subpoenas: Office of General Counsel Law Notes*. Washington, DC: NASW Press.

Pomeroy, E. C., Rubin, A., & Walker, R. J. (1995). Effectiveness of a psychoeducational and task-centered group intervention of family members of people with AIDS. *Social Work Research, 19*, 129–152.

Pomeroy, E. C., & Steiker, L. H. (2012). Prevention and intervention on the care continuum. *Social Work, 57*(2), 102–105.

Pooler, D., Wolfer, T., & Freeman, M. (2014). Finding joy in social work: II. Intrapersonal sources. *Social Work, 59*(3), 213–221.

Pope, K. S., Sonne, J. L., & Greene, B. (1993). *What therapists don't talk about and why: Understanding taboos that hurt us and our clients*. Washington, DC: American Psychological Association.

Potocky-Tripodi, M. (2002). *Best practices for social work with refugees and immigrants*. New York: Columbia University Press.

Potocky-Tripodi, M. (2003). Refugee economic adaptation: Theory, evidence and implications for policy and practice. *Journal of Social Service Research, 30*, 63–91.

Potter-Efron, R., & Potter-Efron, P. (1992). *Anger, alcoholism and addiction: Treating anger in a chemical dependency setting*. New York: Norton.

Powell, M., Thomson, D., & Dietze, P. (1997). Memories of separate occurrences of an event: Implications for interviewing children. *Families in Society, 78*, 600–608.

Prochaska, J. O., & DiClemente, C. C. (1986). Towards a comprehensive model of change. In W. R. Miller & N. Heather (Eds.), *Treating addictive behaviors: Processes of change* (pp. 3–28). New York: Pergamon Press.

Prochaska, J. O., DiClemente, C. C., & Norcross, J. C. (1992). Transtheoretical therapy: Toward a more integrative model of change. *Psychotherapy: Theory, Research, and Practice, 19*, 276–288.

Proctor, E. K. (2007). Implementing evidence-based practice in social work education: Principles, strategies, and partnerships. *Research on Social Work Practice, 17*, 583–591.

Proctor, E. K., & Davis, L. E. (1994). The challenge of racial difference: Skills for clinical practice. *Social Work, 39*, 314–323.

Proehl, R. A. (2001). *Organizational change in human services*. Thousand Oaks, CA: Sage.

Project Cork, (n.d.) *CAGE*. Retrieved from http://www.projectcork.org/clinical_tools/html/CAGE.html

Protecting the privacy of patients' health information. (2003). Retrieved from http://www.hhs.gov/news/facts/privacy.html

Q

Quan, H., Sundararajan, V., Halfron, P., Fong, A., Burnand, B., Luthi, J.-C., et al. (2005). Coding algorithms for defining comorbidities in ICD-9-CM and ICD-10 administrative data. *Medical Care, 43*(11), 1130–1139.

Quinsey, V. L., Harris, G. T., Rice, M. E., & Cormier, C. (2006). *Violent offenders: Appraising and managing risk* (2nd ed.). Washington, DC: American Psychological Association.

R

Ragg, D., Okagbue-Reaves, J., & Piers, J. (2007, October 28). *Shaping student interactive habits: A critical function of practice education*. Presentation at Council of Social Work Education Annual Program Meeting #74a.

Raines, J. C. (1996). Self-disclosure in clinical social work. *Clinical Social Work Journal, 24*, 357–375.

Ramakrishnan, K. R., Balgopal, P. R., & Pettys, G. L. (1994). Task-centered work with communities. In E. R. Tolson, W. J. Reid, & C. D. Garvin (Eds.), *Generalist practice: A task-centered approach*. New York: Columbia University Press.

Ramos, B. M., & Garvin, C. (2003). Task-centered treatment with culturally diverse populations, In E. R. Tolson, W. J. Reid, & C. D. Garvin (Eds.), *Generalist practice: A task-centered approach* (2nd ed., pp. 441–463). New York: Columbia University Press.

Ramos, B. M., & Tolson, E. R. (2008). The task-centered model. In N. Coady & P. Lehmann (Eds.), *Theoretical perspectives for direct social work practice. A generalist-eclectic approach* (2nd ed., pp. 275–295). New York: Springer.

Ramsey, A. T., & Montgomery, K. (2014). Technology-based interventions in social work practice: A systematic review of mental health interventions. *Social Work in Health Care, 53*(9), 883–899.

Rapoport, L. (1967). Crisis-oriented short-term casework. *Social Service Review, 41*(1), 31–43.

Rapp, C. A. (1993). Theory, principles and methods of the strengths model of case management. In M. Harris & H. C. Bergman (Eds.), *Case management for mentally ill patients: Theory and practice*. Langhorne, PA: Harwood.

Rapp, C. A. (2002). A strengths approach to case management with clients with severe mental disability. In A. R. Roberts & G. J. Greene (Eds.), *Social workers' desk reference* (pp. 486–491). New York: Oxford University Press.

Rathbone-McCuan, E. (2008). Elder abuse. In T. Mizrahi & L. E. Davis (Eds.), *Encyclopedia of social work*. Washington, DC: National Association of Social Workers and Oxford University Press.

Rauch, J. B. (1993). *Assessment: A sourcebook for social work practice*. Milwaukee, WI: Families International.

Ravid, S. (2000). Discrepancies in the use of medications: Their extent and predictors in an outpatient practice. *Archives of Internal Medicine, 160*(14), 2129–2134.

Raymond, G. T., Teare, R. J., & Atherton, C. R. (1996). Is "field of practice" a relevant organizing principle for the MSW curriculum? *Journal of Social Work Education, 32*(1), 19–30.

Reamer, F. G. (1989). *Ethical dilemmas in social service* (2nd ed.). New York: Columbia University Press.

Reamer, F. G. (1994). *Social work malpractice and liability: Strategies for prevention*. New York: Columbia University Press.

Reamer, F. G. (1995). Malpractice claims against social workers: First facts. *Social Work, 40*, 595–601.

Reamer, F. G. (1998). *Ethical standards in social work*. Washington, DC: NASW Press.

Reamer, F. G. (1999). *Social work values and ethics* (2nd ed.). New York: Columbia University Press.

Reamer, F. G. (2001). *Tangled relationships: Managing boundary issues in the human services*. New York: Columbia University Press.

Reamer, F. G. (2005). Ethical and legal standards in social work: Consistency and conflicts. *Families in Society, 86*, 163–169.

Reamer, F. G. (2006). *Social work values and ethics* (3rd ed.). New York: Columbia University Press.

Red Horse, J. G., Martinz, C., Day, P., Day, D., Poupart, J., & Scharnberg, D. (2000). *Family preservation concepts in American Indian communities*. National Indian Child Welfare Association. Retrieved from http://www.nicwa.org/research/01.FamilyPreservation.pdf

Reese, D. J., Ahern, R. E., Nair, S., O'Faire, J. D., & Warren, C. (1999). Hospice access and use by African Americans: Addressing cultural and institutional barriers through participatory action research. *Social Work, 44*, 549–559.

Regehr, C., & Angle, B. (1997). Coercive influences: Informed consent in court-mandated social work practice. *Social Work, 42*, 300–306.

Reid, K. E. (1991). *Social work practice with groups: A clinical perspective*. Pacific Grove, CA: Brooks/Cole.

Reid, K. E. (2002). Clinical social work with groups. In A. R. Roberts & G. J. Greene (Eds.), *Social workers' desk reference* (pp. 432–436). New York: Oxford University Press.

Reid, W. J. (1972). *Task-centered casework*. New York: Columbia University Press.

Reid, W. J. (1975). A test of the task-centered approach. *Social Work, 22*, 3–9.

Reid, W. J. (1977). Process and outcome in the treatment of family problems. In W. Reid & L. Epstein (Eds.), *Task-centered practice. Self-help groups and human service agencies: How they work together*. Milwaukee, WI: Family Service of America.

Reid, W. J. (1978). *The task-centered system*. New York: Columbia University Press.

Reid, W. J. (1987). Task-centered research. In *Encyclopedia of social work* (Vol. 2, pp. 757–764). Silver Spring, MD: NASW Press.

Reid, W. J. (1992). *Task strategies*. New York: Columbia University Press.

Reid, W. J. (1994). The empirical practice movement. *Social Service Review, 68*(2), 165–184.

Reid, W. J. (1996). *Task-centered social work*. In F. J. Turner (Ed.), *Social work treatment: Interlocking theoretical approaches* (4th ed., pp. 617–640). New York: Free Press.

Reid, W. J. (1997). Research on task-centered practice. *Social Work, 21*, 131–137.

Reid, W. J. (2000). *The task planner*. New York: Columbia University Press.

Reid, W. J., & Bailey-Dempsey, C. (1995). The effects of monetary incentives on school performance. *Families in Society, 76*, 331–340.

Reid, W. J., & Epstein, L. (Eds.). (1972). *Task-centered casework*. New York: Columbia University Press.

Reid, W. J., Epstein, L., Brown, L., Tolson, E. R., & Rooney, R. H. (1980). Task-centered school social work. *Social Work in Education, 2*, 7–24.

Reid, W. J., & Fortune, A. E. (2002). The task-centered model. In A. R. Roberts & G. J. Greene (Eds.), *Social workers' desk reference* (pp. 101–104). New York: Oxford University Press.

Reid, W., & Hanrahan, P. (1982). Recent evaluations of social work: Grounds for optimism. *Social Work, 27*, 328–340.

Reid, W., & Shyne, A. (1969). *Brief and extended casework*. New York: Columbia University Press.

Reisch, M., & Andrews, J. (2002). *The road not taken: A history of radical social work in the United States*. Philadelphia: Brunner-Routledge.

Reisch, M., & Sommerfeld, D. (2003). The "Other America" after welfare reform: A view from the nonprofit sector. *Journal of Poverty, 7*(1/2), 69–95.

Rempel, G. R., Neufeld, A., & Kushner, K. E. (2007). Interactive use of genograms and ecomaps in family caregiving research. *Journal of Family Nursing, 13*(4), 403–419.

Renfrey, G. S. (1992). Cognitive-behavior therapy and the Native American client. *Behavior Therapy, 23*, 321–340.

Resnick, C., & Dziegielewski, S. F. (1996). The relationship between therapeutic termination and job satisfaction among medical social workers. *Social Work in Health Care, 23*(3), 17–33.

Reuben, D. B., & Siu, A. L. (1990). An objective measure of physical function of elderly outpatients: The Physical Performance Test. *Journal of the American Geriatrics Society, 38*, 1105–1112.

Reynolds, B. C. (1951). *Social work and social living.* New York: Citadel Press.

Reynolds, T., & Jones, G. (1996). Trauma debriefings: A one-session group model. In B. L. Stempler, M. Glass, & C. M. Savinelli (Eds.), *Social group work today and tomorrow: Moving to advanced training and practice* (pp. 129–139). Binghamton, NY: Haworth Press.

Reynolds, W. M. (1987). *Suicidal Ideation Questionnaire— Junior.* Odessa, FL: Psychological Assessment Resources.

Reynolds, W. M. (1988). *Suicidal Ideation Questionnaire professional manual.* Odessa FL: Psychological Assessment Resources.

Rheingold, A. A., Herbert, J. D., & Franklin, M. E. (2003). Cognitive bias in adolescents with social anxiety disorder. *Cognitive Therapy and Research, 27*, 639–655.

Ribner, D. S., & Knei-Paz, C. (2002). Client's view of a successful helping relationship. *Social Work, 47*, 379–387.

Rice, A. H. (1998). *Focusing on strengths: Focus group research on the impact of welfare reform.* A paper presented for the XX Symposium Association for the Advancement of Social Work with Groups, October 1998, Miami, FL.

Richardson, V. E., & Barusch, A. S. (2006). *Gerontological practice for the twenty-first century: A social work perspective.* New York: Columbia University Press.

Richey, C. A., & Roffman, R. A. (1999). One the sidelines of guidelines: Further thoughts on the fit between clinical guidelines and social work practice. *Research on Social Work Practice, 9*, 311–321.

Richman, L. S., Kohn-Woods, L., & Williams, D. R. (2007). Discrimination and racial identity for mental health service utilization. *Journal of Social and Clinical Psychology, 26*, 960–980.

Richmond, M. E. (1899). *Friendly visiting among the poor: A handbook for charity workers.* New York: Macmillan.

Richmond, M. E. (1917). *Social diagnosis.* New York: Russell Sage Foundation.

Rittenhouse, J. (1997). Feminist principles in survivor's groups: Out-of-group contact. *Journal for Specialists in Group Work, 22*, 111–119.

Ritter, B., & Dozier, C. D. (2000). Effects of court-ordered substance abuse treatment on child protective services cases. *Social Work, 45*, 131–140.

Rivera, F. G., & Erlich, J. L. (1998). *Community organizing in a diverse society* (3rd ed.). Boston: Allyn & Bacon.

Roberts, A. R. (1990). *Crisis intervention handbook: Assessment, treatment, and research.* Belmont, CA: Wadsworth.

Roberts, A. R. (2005). *Crisis intervention handbook: Assessment, treatment and research* (3rd ed.). New York: Oxford University Press.

Roberts, A. R., Monferrari, I., & Yeager, K. R. (2008). Avoiding malpractice lawsuits by following standards of care guidelines and preventing suicide: A guide for mental health professionals. In A. R. Roberts (Ed.), *Social workers' desk reference* (pp. 128–135). New York: Oxford University Press.

Roberts, A. R., & Yeager, K. R. (2006). *Foundations of evidence-based social work practice.* New York: Oxford University Press.

Roberts, D. (2002). *Shattered bonds: The color of child welfare.* New York: Basic Books.

Robinson, J. B. (1989). Clinical treatment of black families: Issues and strategies. *Social Work, 34*, 323–329.

Robinson, V. (1930). *A changing psychology in social work.* Chapel Hill: University of North Carolina Press.

Robles, R. R., Reyes, J. C., Colon, H. M., Sahai, H., Marrero, C. A., Matos, T. M., et al. (2004). Effects of combined counseling and case management to reduce HIV risk behavior among hip drug injectors in Puerto, Rico: A randomized correlated study. *Journal of Substance Abuse Treatment, 27*(2), 145–153.

Rodenborg, N. (2004, November). Services to African American children in poverty: Institutional discrimination in child welfare. *Journal of Poverty: Innovations on Social, Political and Economic Inequalities, 3*(3).

Rodgers, A. Y., & Potocky, M. (1997). Evaluating culturally sensitive practice through single-system design: Methodological issues and strategies. *Research on Social Work Practice, 7*, 391–401.

Rogers, C. (1957). The necessary and sufficient conditions of therapeutic personality change. *Journal of Consulting Psychology, 22*, 95–103.

Rooney, G. D. (1997). Concerns of employed women: Issues for employee assistance programs. In A. Daly (Ed.), *Workforce diversity: Issues and perspectives in the world of work* (pp. 314–330). Washington, DC: NASW Press.

Rooney, G. D. (2000). Examining the values and ethics reflected in policy decisions. In K. Strom-Gottfried (Ed.), *Social work practice: Cases, activities and exercises* (pp. 50–54). Thousand Oaks, CA: Pine Forge Press.

Rooney, G. D. (2009). Oppression and involuntary status. In R. H. Rooney (Ed.), *Strategies for work with involuntary clients* (2nd ed.). New York: Columbia University Press.

Rooney, R. H. (1981). A task-centered reunification model for foster care. In A. A. Maluccio & P. Sinanoglu (Eds.), *The challenge of partnership: Working with biological parents of children in foster care* (pp. 135–159). New York: Child Welfare League of America.

Rooney, R. H. (1992). *Strategies for work with involuntary clients*. New York: Columbia University Press.

Rooney, R. H. (2010). The task-centered approach in the United States. In A. Fortune, P. McCallion, & K. Briar-Larsen (Eds.), *Social work practice research for the twenty-first century*. New York: Columbia University Press.

Rooney, R. H. (Ed.). (2009). *Strategies for work with involuntary clients* (2nd ed.). New York: Columbia University Press.

Rooney, R. H., & Bibus, A. A. (1996). Multiple lenses: Ethnically sensitive practice with involuntary clients who are having difficulties with drugs or alcohol. *Journal of Multicultural Social Work, 4*(2), 59–73.

Rooney, R. H., & Chovanec, M. (2004). Involuntary groups. In C. Garvin, L. Gutierrez, & M. Galinsky (Eds.), *Handbook of social work with groups*. New York: Guilford Press.

Rose, S. D. (1989). *Working with adults in groups: Integrating cognitive-behavioral and small group strategies*. San Francisco: Jossey-Bass.

Rose, S. D. (1998). *Group therapy with troubled youth: A cognitive behavioral interactive approach*. Thousand Oaks, CA: Sage.

Rosen, A. (1972). The treatment relationship: A conceptualization. *Journal of Clinical Psychology, 38*, 329–337.

Rosenblatt, E. (1994). *Metaphor of family systems theory*. New York: Guilford Press.

Rosenthal, K. (1988). The inanimate self in adult victims of child abuse and neglect. *Social Casework, 69*, 505–510.

Rosenthal-Gelman, C. (2004). Empirically-based principles for culturally competent practice with Latinos. *Journal of Ethnic and Cultural Diversity in Social Work, 13*(1), 83–108.

"Rosa's Law." Public Law 111-156 (October 5, 2010). S. 2781. Retrieved March 12, 2015, from http://www.gpo.gov/fdsys/pkg/PLAW-111publ256/pdf/PLAW-111publ256.pdf

Ross, C. (1997). *Something to draw on: Activities and interventions using an art therapy approach*. London: Jessica Kingsley.

Ross, D. E. (2000). A method for developing a biopsychosocial formulation. *Journal of Child and Family Studies, 9*(1), 1–6.

Roth, W. (1987). Disabilities: Physical. In A. Minehan (Ed.), *Encyclopedia of social work* (Vol. 1, pp. 434–438). Silver Spring, MD: NASW Press.

Rothman, J. (1991). A model of case management: Toward empirically based practice. *Social Work, 36*, 521–528.

Rothman, J. (1995). Approaches to community intervention. In F. M. Cox, J. L. Erlich, J. J. Rothman, & J. Tropman (Eds.), *Strategies of community intervention*. Itasca, IL: Peacock.

Rothman, J. (1999). Intent and consent. In J. Rothman (Ed.), *Reflections on community organizations: Enduring themes and critical issues* (pp. 3–26). Itasca, IL: Peacock.

Rothman, J. (2002). *An overview of case management*. In A. R. Roberts & G. J. Greene (Eds.), *Social workers' desk reference* (pp. 467–472). New York: Oxford University Press.

Rothman, J. (2007). Multi modes of intervention at the macro level. *Journal of Community Practice, 15*(4), 11–40.

Rothman, J., Erlich, J. L., & Tropman, J. E. (1999). *Strategies of community interventions* (5th ed.). Itasca, IL: Peacock.

Rothman, J., Erlich, J. L., & Tropman, J. E. (2001). *Strategies of community interventions* (6th ed.). Itasca, IL: Peacock.

Rothman, J., & Mizrahi, T. (2014). Balancing micro and macro practice: A challenge for social work. *Social Work, 59*(1), 91–93.

Rothman, J., & Thomas, E. J. (1994). *Intervention research: Design and development of human services*. Binghamton, NY: Haworth Press.

Rothman, J., & Tropman, J. (1987). Models of community organization and development and macro practice perspectives: Their mixing and phasing. In F. M. Cox, J. L. Erlich, J. J. Rothman, & J. Tropman (Eds.), *Strategies of community organizing* (pp. 3–26). Itasca, IL: Peacock.

Rotondi, A. J., Haas, G. L., Anderson, C. M., Newhill, C. E., Spring, M. B., Ganguli, R., et al. (2005). A clinical trial to test the feasibility of a telehealth psychoeducational intervention for persons with schizophrenia and their families: Intervention and 3-month findings. *Rehabilitation Psychology, 50*(4), 325–336.

Rowan, A. B. (2001). Adolescent substance abuse and suicide. *Depression and Anxiety, 14*, 186–191.

Royse, D., Thyer, B. A., Padgett, D. K., & Logan, T. K. (2006). *Program evaluation: An introduction* (4th ed.). Belmont, CA: Brooks-Cole.

Rozzini, R., Frisoni, G. B., Bianchetti, A., Zanetti, O., & Trabucchi, M. (1993). Physical Performance Test and Activities of Daily Living scales in the assessment of health status in elderly people. *Journal of the American Geriatrics Society, 41*, 1109–1113.

Rubin, A. (2007). Improving the teaching of evidence-based practice: Introduction to the special issue. *Research on Social Work Practice, 17*, 541–547.

Rubin, H. J., & Rubin, I. S. (2008). *Community organizing and development* (4th ed.). Boston: Allyn & Bacon.

Rubin, R., & Babbie, E. R. (2005). *Essential research methods for social work*. Belmont, CA: Brooks-Cole.

Rudolph, K. D., & Clark, A. G. (2001). Conceptions of relationship in children with depression and aggressive symptoms: Social-cognitive distortions or reality. *Journal of Abnormal Child Psychology, 29*(1), 41–56.

Ruffolo, M., Nitzberg, L., & Schoof, K. (2011). One-session family workshops for bipolar disorder and depression. *Psychiatric Services, 62*(3), 323.

Ryder, R., & Tepley, R. (1993). No more Mr. Nice Guy: Informed consent and benevolence in marital family therapy. *Family Relations, 42*, 145–147.

Rzepnicki, T. L. (1991). Enhancing the durability of intervention gains: A challenge for the 1990s. *Social Service Review, 65*(1), 92–111.

Rzepnicki, T. L. (2004). Informed consent and practice evaluation: Making the decision to participate meaningful. In H. E. Briggs & T. L. Rzepnicki (Eds.), *Using evidence in social work practice: Behavioral perspectives* (pp. 273–290). Chicago: Lyceum Books.

S

Sadock, B. J., Sadock, V. A., & Ruiz, P. (2014). *Kaplan and Sadock's synopsis of psychiatry* (11th ed.). Philadelphia: Wolters Kluwer.

Safran, J. D., & Muran, J. C. (2000). Resolving therapeutic alliance ruptures: Diversity and integration. *In Session: Psychotherapy in Practice, 56*, 597–605.

Saleebey, D. (2004). The power of place: Another look at the environment. *Families in Society, 85*, 7–16.

Saleebey, D. (2013). *The strengths perspective in social work practice.* Boston: Pearson/Allyn & Bacon.

Saleebey, D. (Ed.). (1997). *The strengths perspective in social work practice* (2nd ed.). Needham Heights, MA: Allyn & Bacon.

Salmon, R., & Graziano, R. (Eds.). (2004). *Group work and aging: Issues in practice research and education.* New York: Haworth Press.

Salston, M., & Figley, C. R. (2004). Secondary traumatic stress effects of working with survivors of criminal victimization. *Journal of Traumatic Stress, 16*, 167–174.

Sands, R. G. (1989). The social worker joins the team: A look at the socialization process. *Social Work in Health Care, 14*(2), 1–14.

Sands, R. G., Stafford, J., & McClelland, M. (1990). "I beg to differ": Conflict in the interdisciplinary team. *Social Work in Health Care, 14*(3), 55–72.

Santhiveeran, J. (2009). Compliance of social work e-therapy websites to the NASW code of ethics. *Social Work in Health Care, 48*, 1–13.

Sarkisian, N., & Gerstel, N. (2004). Kinship support among blacks and whites: Race and family organization. *American Sociological Review, 69*, 812–836.

Sarnoff, J. D. (2004). Abolishing the doctrine of equivalents and claiming the future after *Festo. Berkeley Technical Law Journal, 19*, 1157–1225.

Sarri, R. (1987). Administration in social welfare. In *Encyclopedia of social work* (Vol. 1, pp. 27–40). Silver Spring, MD: NASW Press.

Satir, V. (1967). *Conjoint family therapy.* Palo Alto, CA: Science & Behavior Books.

Saulnier, C. F. (1997). Alcohol problems and marginalization: Social group work with lesbians. *Social Work with Groups, 20*(3), 37–59.

Saulnier, C. F. (2002). Deciding who to see: Lesbians discuss their preferences in health and mental health care providers. *Social Work, 47*, 355–365.

Savner, S. (2000, July/August). Welfare reform and racial/ethnic minorities: The questions to ask. *Poverty & Race, 9*(4), 3–5.

Schaffer, D. (1992). *NIHM diagnostic interview schedule for children, version 2.3.* New York: Columbia University, Division of Child and Adolescent Psychiatry.

Schein, E. H. (1985). *Organizational culture and leadership.* San Francisco: Jossey-Bass.

Scheyett, A. (2006). Danger and opportunity in teaching evidence-based practice in the social work curriculum. *Journal of Teaching in Social Work, 26*, 19–29.

Schiller, L. Y. (1997). Rethinking stages of development in women's groups: Implications for practice. *Social Work with Groups, 20*(3), 3–19.

Schiller, L. Y. (2007). Not for women only: Applying the relational model of group development with vulnerable populations. *Social Work with Groups, 30*(2), 11–26.

Schneider, R. L., & Lester, L. (2001). *Social work advocacy: A new framework for action.* Belmont, CA: Brooks/Cole.

Schopler, J. H., & Galinsky, M. J. (1974). Goals in social group work practice: Formulation, implementation and evaluation. In P. Glasser, R. Sarri, & R. Vinter (Eds.), *Individual change through small groups.* New York: Free Press.

Schopler, J. H., & Galinsky, M. J. (1981). Meeting practice needs: Conceptualizing the open-ended group. *Social Work with Groups, 7*(2), 3–21.

Schopler, J. H., Galinsky, M. J., & Abell, M. (1997). Creating community through telephone and computer groups: Theoretical and practice perspectives. *Social Work with Groups, 20*(4), 19–34.

Schopler, J. H., Galinsky, M. J., Davis, L. E., & Despard, M. (1996). The RAP model: Assessing a framework for leading multicultural groups. *Social Work with Groups, 19*(3/4), 21–39.

Schwartz, G. (1989). Confidentiality revisited. *Social Work, 34*, 223–226.

Seay, H. A., Fee, V. E., Holloway, K. S., & Giesen, J. M. (2003). A multi component treatment package to increase anger control in teacher referred boys. *Child and Family Behavior Therapy, 25*(1), 1–18.

Secret, M., Jordan, A., & Ford, J. (1999). Empowerment evaluation as a social work strategy. *Social Work, 24*, 120–127.

Segal, E. A. (2007). Social empathy: A tool to address the contradictions of working but still poor. *Families in Society, 88*, 333–337.

Segal, E. A. (2010). *Social welfare policy and social programs: A values perspective.* Belmont, CA: Brooks/Cole.

Segal, U. A. (1991). Cultural variables in Asian Indian families. *Families in Society, 72,* 233–244.

Segal, Z. V., Williams, J. M., & Teasdale, J. D. (2002). *Mindfulness-based cognitive therapy for depression: A new approach to preventing relapse.* New York: Guilford Press.

Selekman, M. D. (2005). *Pathways to change: Brief therapy with difficult children* (2nd ed.). New York: Guilford Press.

Selvini-Palazzoli, M., Boscolo, L., Cecchin, G., & Prata, G. (1974). The treatment of children through brief therapy of their parents. *Family Process, 13,* 429–442.

Selzer, M. L. (1971). The Michigan Alcoholism Screening Test: The quest for a new diagnostic instrument. *American Journal of Psychiatry, 27,* 1653–1658.

Senge, P. M. (1990). *The fifth discipline: The art and practice of learning organization.* New York: Doubleday Currency.

Senge, P. M. (1994). *The fifth discipline field book: Strategies and tools for building a learning organization.* New York: Bantam, Doubleday, Dell.

Shaffer, Q., Scott, M., Wilcox, H., Maslow, C., Hicks, R., Lucas, C. P., et al. (2004). The Columbia Suicide Screen: Validity and reliability of a screen for youth suicide and depression. *Journal of the American Academy of Child & Adolescent Psychiatry, 43,* 71–79.

Shamai, M. (2003). Therapeutic effects of qualitative research: Reconstructing the experience of treatment as a by-product of qualitative evaluation. *Social Service Review, 77,* 454–467.

Shapiro, J. R., Bauer, S., Andrews, E., Pisetsky, E., Bulik-Sullivan, B., Hamer, R. M., & Bulik, C. M. (2009). Mobile therapy: Use of text-messaging in the treatment of bulimia nervosa. *International Journal of Eating Disorders, 43,* 513–519.

Sharpe, L., & Tarrier, M. (1992). A cognitive-behavioral treatment approach for problem gambling. *Journal of Cognitive Psychotherapy, 5,* 119–127.

Sheafor, B. W., & Horejsi, C. R. (2012). *Techniques and guidelines for social work practice* (9th ed.). Boston: Allyn & Bacon.

Sheafor, B. W., Horejsi, C. R., & Horejsi, G. A. (1994). *Techniques and guidelines for social work practice* (3rd ed.). Boston: Allyn & Bacon.

Sherraden, B., Slosar, B., & Sherraden, M. (2002). Innovation in social policy: Collaborative policy advocacy. *Social Work, 47,* 209–211.

Sherrer, M., & O'Hare, T. (2008). Clinical case management. In K. Mueser & D. Jeste (Eds.), *Clinical handbook of schizophrenia* (pp. 309–318). New York: Guilford Press.

Sherwood, D. A. (1998). Spiritual assessment as a normal part of social work practice: Power to help and power to harm. *Social Work and Christianity, 25*(2), 80–90.

Shih, M., & Sanchez, D. (2005). Perspectives and research on the positive and negative implications of having multiple racial identities. *Psychology Bulletin, 131,* 569–591.

Shneidman, E. S. (1971). The management of the presuicidal, suicidal, and postsuicidal patient. *Annals of Internal Medicine, 75,* 441–458.

Shoham, V., Rohrbaugh, M., & Patterson, J. (1995). Problem and solution-focused couples therapies: The MRI and Milwaukee modes. In N. S. Jacobson & A. S. Gurman (Eds.), *Clinical handbook for couple therapy* (pp. 142–163). New York: Guildford Press.

Shulman, L. (1984). *The skills of helping individuals and groups* (2nd ed.). Itasca, IL: Peacock.

Shulman, L. (1992). *The skills of helping individuals and groups* (3rd ed.). Itasca, IL: Peacock.

Shulman, L. (2009). *The skills of helping individuals, families, groups, and communities* (6th ed.). Belmont, CA: Brooks/Cole.

Siegal, H. A., Fisher, J. A., Rapp, R. C., Kelliher, C. W., Wagner, J. H., O'Brien, W. F., & Cole, P. A. (1996). Enhancing substance abuse treatment with case management: Its impact on employment. *Journal of Substance Abuse Treatment, 13,* 93–98.

Siegal, H. A., Rapp, C. A., Kelliher, C. W., Fisher, J., Wagner, J. H., & Cole, P. A. (1995). The strengths perspective of case management: A promising inpatient substance abuse treatment enhancement. *Journal of Psychoactive Drugs, 27,* 67–72.

Silove, D. (2000). A conceptual framework for mass trauma: Indications for adaptation, intervention and debriefing. In B. Raphael & J. P. Wilson (Eds.), *Psychology, debriefing, theory, practice and evidence* (pp. 337–350). New York: Cambridge University Press.

Silvawe, G. W. (1995). The need for a new social work perspective in an African setting: The case of social casework in Zambia. *British Journal of Social Work, 25,* 71–84.

Simmons, C., & Rycraft, J. (2010). Ethical challenges of military social workers serving in a combat zone. *Social Work, 55*(1), 9–18.

Simons, K., Shepherd, N., & Murro, J. (2008). Advancing the evidence-base for social work in long-term care: The disconnect between practice and research. *Social Work in Health Care, 47,* 392–415.

Singer, G. H. S., Biegel, D. E., & Conway, P. (Eds.). (2012). *Family support and family caregiving across disabilities.* New York: Routledge/Taylor & Francis Group.

Siporin, M. (1980). Ecological systems theory in social work. *Journal of Sociology and Social Welfare, 7,* 507–532.

Skinner, B. F. (1974). *About behaviorism.* New York: Knopf.

Sluzki, C. E. (2008). Migration and the disruption of the social network. In M. McGoldrick & K. V. Hardy (Eds.), *Re-visioning family therapy* (2nd ed., 39–47). New York: Guilford Press.

Smith, B. D., & Marsh, J. C. (2002). Client-service matching in substance abuse treatment for women with children. *Journal of Substance Abuse Treatment, 22*, 161–168.

Smith, C., & Nylund, D. (1997). *Narrative therapies with children and adolescents.* New York: Guilford Press.

Smith, J. C., & Medalia, C. (2014). *Health insurance coverage in the United States: 2013.* Washington, DC: United States Census Bureau, U.S. Government Printing Office.

Smith, N. A. (2006). "Unfit" mother: Increasing empathy, redefining the label. *Affilia, 21*, 448–457.

Smith, T. B. (2004). *Practicing multiculturalism: Affirming diversity in counseling and psychology.* Boston: Pearson.

Smokowski, P. R., & Bacallao, M. (2011). *Becoming bicultural: Risk, resilience, and Latino youth.* New York: New York University Press.

Smokowski, P. R., Rose, S. D., & Bacallao, M. L. (2001). Damaging therapeutic groups: How vulnerable consumers become group casualties. *Small Group Research, 32*, 223–251.

Smyth, N. J. (2005). Drug use, self-efficacy, and coping skills among people with concurrent substance abuse and personality disorders: Implications for relapse prevention. *Journal of Social Work Practice in the Addictions, 5*(4), 63–79.

Social Workers and Psychotherapist-Patient Privilege: Jaffee v. Redmond *revisited.* (2005). Retrieved from http://www.socialworkers.org/ldf/legalrissue/200503

Sommers-Flanagan, R. (2007). Ethical considerations in crisis and humanitarian interventions. *Ethics and Behavior, 17*, 187–202.

Sosin, M., & Callum, S. (1983). Advocacy: A conceptualization for social work practice. *Social Work, 28*, 12–17.

Sotomayor, M. (1991). Introduction. In M. Sotomayor (Ed.), *Empowering Hispanic families: A critical issue for the 90s* (pp. xi–xxiii). Milwaukee, WI: Family Service America.

Sousa, L., Ribeiro, C., & Rodrigues, S. (2006). Intervention with multiproblem poor clients: Toward a strengths-focused perspective. *Journal of Social Work Practice, 20*, 189–204.

Specht, H., & Courtney, M. E. (1994). *Unfaithful angels: How social work abandoned its mission.* Toronto: Maxwell Macmillan Canada.

Speisman, J. (1959). Depth of interpretation and verbal resistance in psychotherapy. *Journal of Consulting Psychology, 23*, 93–99.

Spoth, R., Guyll, M., Chao, W., & Molgaard, V. (2003). Exploratory study of a preventive intervention with general population African American families. *Journal of Early Adolescence, 23*, 435–468.

Spriggs, W. E. (2007). *The changing face of poverty in America: Why are so many women, children, racial and cultural minorities still poor?* Ending Poverty in America, Special Report of The American Prospect, The Annie E. Casey Foundation & The Northwest Area Foundation. A5–A7.

Springer, D. W., Lynch, C., & Rubin, A. (2000). Effects of solution-focused mutual aid group for Hispanic children or incarcerated parents. *Child and Adolescent Social Work, 17*, 431–442.

Srebnik, D. S., & Saltzberg, E. A. (1994). Feminist cognitive-behavioral therapy for negative body image. *Women and Therapy, 15*, 117–133.

St. Lawrence, J. S., Brasfield, T. L., Jefferson, K. W., O'Bannon, R. E., & Shirley, A. (1995). Cognitive-behavioral intervention to reduce African adolescents' risk for HIV infection. *Journal of Counseling Psychology, 63*, 221–237.

Steigerwald, F., & Stone, D. (1999). Cognitive restructuring and the 12-step program of Alcoholics Anonymous. *Journal of Substance Abuse, 16*, 321–327.

Steinberg, D. M. (2004). *The mutual aid approach to working with groups: Helping people help one another* (2nd ed.). Binghamton, NY: Haworth Press.

Steinman, M. A., & Hanlon, J. T. (2010). Managing medications in clinically complex elders: "There's got to be a happy medium." *Journal of American Medical Association, 304*(14), 1592–1601.

Stokes, J. P. (1983). Components of group cohesion: Inter-member attraction, instrumental value, and risk taking. *Small Group Behavior, 14*, 163–173.

Stone, M., Lewis, C., & Beck, A. (1994). The structure of Yalom's Curative Factors Scale. *International Journal of Group Psychotherapy, 23*, 155–168.

Storm, C. (1991). The remaining thread: Matching change and stability signals. *Journal of Strategic and Systemic Therapies, 10*, 114–117.

Strom-Gottfried, K. J. (1998a). Applying a conflict resolution framework in managed care. *Social Work, 43*, 393–401.

Strom-Gottfried, K. J. (1998b). Informed consent meets managed care. *Health and Social Work, 23*, 25–33.

Strom-Gottfried, K. J. (1999a). Professional boundaries: An analysis of violations by social workers. *Families in Society, 80*, 439–448.

Strom-Gottfried, K. J. (1999b). *Social work practice: Cases, activities and exercises.* Thousand Oaks, CA: Pine Forge Press.

Strom-Gottfried, K. J. (2005). Ethical practice in rural environments. In L. Ginsberg (Ed.), *Social work in rural communities* (4th ed., pp. 141–155). Alexandria, VA: Council on Social Work Education.

Strom-Gottfried, K. J. (2007). *Straight talk about professional ethics.* Chicago: Lyceum Books.

Strom-Gottfried, K. J. (2008). *The ethics of practice with minors: High stakes, hard choices.* Chicago: Lyceum Books.

Strom-Gottfried, K. J. (2009). Ethical issues and guidelines. In S. Allen & E. Tracy (Eds.), *Delivering home-based services: A social work perspective* (pp. 14–33). New York: Columbia University Press.

Strom-Gottfried, K. J. (2015). *Straight talk about professional ethics* (2nd ed.). Chicago: Lyceum Books.

Strom-Gottfried, K. J., & Morrissey, M. (2000). The organizational diversity audit. In K. Strom-Gottfried (Ed.), *Social work practice: Cases, activities, and exercises* (pp. 168–172). Thousand Oaks, CA: Pine Forge Press.

Strom-Gottfried, K. J., & Mowbray, N. D. (2006). Who heals the helper? Facilitating the social worker's grief. *Families in Society, 87*, 9–15.

Strom-Gottfried, K. J., Thomas, M. S., & Anderson, H. (2014). Social work and social media: Reconciling ethical standards and emerging technologies. *Journal of Social Work Values and Ethics, 11*(1), 54–65.

Stuart, P. H. (1999). Linking clients and policy: Social work's distinctive contribution. *Social Work, 44*, 335–347.

Studt, E. (1968). Social work theory and implications for the practice methods. *Social Work Education Reporter, 16*, 22–46.

Subramanian, K., Hernandez, S., & Martinez, A. (1995). Psychoeducational group work for low-income Latina mothers with HIV infection. *Social Work with Groups, 18*(2/3), 53–64.

Substance Abuse and Mental Health Services Administration (SAMHSA). (2003a). *Family Psychoeducation Fidelity Scale*. Retrieved from http://download.ncadi.samhsa.gov/ken/pdf/toolkits/family/ 12.FamPsy_Fidelity.pdf

Substance Abuse and Mental Health Services Administration (SAMHSA). (2003b). *Assertive community treatment: Monitoring client outcomes*. Retrieved from http://download.ncadi.samhsa.gov/ken/pdf/toolkits/community/19.ACT_Client_Outcomes.pdf

Substance Abuse and Mental Health Services Administration (SAMHSA). (2005). *Substance abuse treatment: Group therapy* (Treatment Improvement Protocol (TIP) Series 41, DHHS Publication No. (SMA) 05-3991.) Retrieved from http://www.ncbi. nlm.nih.gov/books/NBK 14531/

Substance Abuse and Mental Health Services Administration (SAMHSA). (2013). *2013 National Survey on Drug Use and Health (NSDUH)*. Retrieved from http://www.samhsa.gov/data/sites/default/files/NSDUH-DetTabs PDFWHTML2013/Web/HTML/NSDUH-DetTabs Sect5peTabs1to56-2013.htm#tab5.5a

Substance Abuse and Mental Health Services Administration (SAMSHA). (2014). *Results from the 2013 National Survey on Drug Use and Health: Summary of national findings*. NSDUH Series H-48, HHS Publication No. (SMA) 14-4863. Rockville, MD: Author.

Sue, D. W. (2006). *Multicultural social work practice*. Hoboken, NJ: Wiley.

Sue, D. W., Capodilupo, C. M., Torino, G. C., Bucceri, J. M., Holder, A. M. B., Nadal, K. L., & Esquilin, M. (2007). Racial microaggressions in everyday life: Implications for clinical practice. *American Psychologist, 62*(4), 271–286.

Sue, D. W., & Sue, S. (1990). *Counseling the culturally different: Theory and practice* (2nd ed.). New York: Wiley.

Sukhodolsky, D. G., Kassinore, H., & Gorman, B. S. (2004). Cognitive behavioral therapy for anger in children and adolescents: A meta-analysis. *Aggression and Violent Behavior, 9*, 247–269.

Sunley, R. (1997). Advocacy in the new world of managed care. *Families in Society, 78*, 84–94.

Susser, E., Valencia, E., Conover, S., Felix, A., Tsai, W. Y., & Wyatt, W. J. (1997). Preventing recurrent homelessness among mentally ill men: A "critical time" intervention after discharge from a shelter. *American Journal of Public Health, 87*, 258–262.

Sweet, C., & Noones, J. (1989). Factors associated with premature termination from outpatient treatment. *Hospital and Community Psychiatry, 40*, 947–951.

Swenson, C. (1998). Clinical social work's contribution to a social justice perspective. *Social Work, 43*, 527–537.

Swift, J. K., & Greenberg, R. P. (2012). Premature discontinuation in adult psychotherapy: A meta-analysis. *Journal of Consulting and Clinical Psychology, 80*(4), 547–559.

Swift, J. K., Greenberg, R. P., Whipple, J. L., & Kominiak, N. (2012). Practice recommendations for reducing premature termination in therapy. *Professional Psychology: Research and Practice, 43*(4), 379–387.

T

Taft, J. (1937). The relation of function to process in social casework. *Journal of Social Work Process, 1*(1), 1–18.

Tate, T. (2001). Peer influencing positive cognitive relationship. *Reclaiming Children & Youth, 9*, 215–218.

Taylor, R. J., Chatters, L. M., Woodward, A. T., & Brown, E. (2013). Racial and ethnic differences in extended family, friendship, fictive kin, and congregational informal support networks. *Family Relations, 62*, 609–624.

Teall, B. (2000). Using solution-oriented intervention in an ecological frame: A case illustration. *Social Work in Education, 22*(1), 54–61.

Tehrani, N. (2007). The cost of caring: The impact of secondary trauma on assumptions, values and beliefs. *Counseling Psychology Quarterly, 20*(4), 325–339.

Terr, L. C. (1991). Childhood traumas: An outline and overview. *American Journal of Psychiatry, 148*, 10–20.

Terr, L. C. (1995). Childhood trauma: An outline and overview. In G. S. Everly, Jr., & J. M. Lating (Eds.), *Psychotraumatology* (pp. 301–320). New York: Plenum Press.

Tervalon, M., & Murray-Garcia, J. (1998). Cultural humility versus cultural competence: A critical distinction in defining physician training outcomes in multicultural education. *Journal of Healthcare for the Poor and Underserved, 9*, 117–125.

Testa, M. (2002). Subsidized guardianship: Testing an idea whose time has finally come. *Social Work Research*, *26*, 145–158.

Teyber, E. (2006). *Interpersonal processes in therapy: An integrative model* (5th ed.). Pacific Grove, CA: Brooks/Cole.

Thibault, J., Ellor, J., & Netting, F. (1991). A conceptual framework for assessing the spiritual functioning and fulfillment of older adults in long-term care settings. *Journal of Religious Gerontology*, *7*(4), 29–46.

Thomas, E. J. (1989). Advances in developmental research. *Social Service Review*, *14*, 20–31.

Thomas, H., & Caplan, T. (1997). Client, therapist and context: Addressing resistance in group work. *The Social Worker*, *65*(3), 27–36.

Thomas, H., & Caplan, T. (1999). Spinning the group process wheel: Effective facilitation techniques for motivating involuntary clients. *Social Work with Groups*, *21*(4), 3–21.

Thomas, M., & Strom-Gottfried, K. J. (2011). *The best of boards: Sound governance and leadership for nonprofit organizations*. New York: AICPA.

Thomlison, B. (2005). Using evidence-based knowledge in child welfare to improve policies and practices: Current thinking and continuing challenges. *Research on Social Work Practice*, *15*, 321–322.

Thomlison, B., & Corcoran, K. (2008). *The evidence-based internship: A field manual*. New York: Oxford University Press.

Thyer, B. A. (2001a). Evidence-based approaches to community practice. In H. Briggs & K. Corcoran (Eds.), *Social work practice: Treating common client problems* (pp. 54–65). Chicago: Lyceum Books.

Thyer, B. A. (2001b). Single case designs. In B. A. Thyer (Ed.), *Handbook of social work research methods* (pp. 239–235). Thousand Oaks, CA: Sage.

Thyer, B. A. (2002). Principles of evidence-based practice and treatment development. In A. R. Roberts & G. J. Greene (Eds.), *Social workers' desk reference* (pp. 739–742). New York: Oxford University Press.

Thyer, B. A. (2013). Evidence-based practice or evidence-guided practice: A rose by any other name would smell as sweet. Invited response to Gitterman and Knight's Evidence Guided Practice. *Families in Society*, *94*(20), 79–84.

Tishler, C. L., Reiss, N. S., & Rhodes, A. R. (2007). Suicidal behavior in children younger than twelve: A diagnostic challenge for emergency department personnel. *Academic Emergency Medicine*, *14*(9), 810–818.

Tohn, S. L., & Oshlag, J. A. (1996). Solution-focused therapy with mandated clients: Cooperating with the uncooperative. In S. D. Miller, M. A. Hubble, & B. L. Duncan (Eds.), *Handbook of solution-focused brief therapy* (pp. 152–183). San Francisco: Jossey-Bass.

Tolman, R. M., & Molidor, C. E. (1994). A decade of social group work research: Trends in methodology, theory and program development. *Research on Social Work Practice*, *4*, 142–159.

Tolson, E. R., Reid, W. J., & Garvin, C. D. (1994). *Generalist practice. A task-centered approach*. New York: Columbia University Press.

Tolson, E. R., Reid, W. J., & Garvin, C. D. (2003). *Generalist practice: A task-centered approach* (2nd ed.). New York: Columbia University Press.

Toseland, R. W., Jones, L. V., & Gellis, Z. D. (2006). Group dynamics. In C. D. Garvin, L. M. Gutierrez, & M. J. Galinsky (Eds.), *Handbook of social work with groups* (pp. 13–31). New York: Guilford Press.

Toseland, R. W., & Rivas, R. F. (2009). *An introduction to group work practice* (6th ed.). Boston: Allyn & Bacon.

Tracy, E. M., & Whittaker, J. K. (1990). The social network map: Assessing social support in clinical practice. *Families in Society*, *71*, 461–470.

Trepper, T. S., Dolan, Y., McCollum, E. E., & Nelson, T. (2006). Steve De Shazer and the future of solution-focused therapy. *Journal of Marital and Family Therapy*, *32*, 133–139.

Trotter, C. (1999). *Working with involuntary clients*. London: Sage.

Trotter, C. (2006). *Working with involuntary clients: A guide to practice* (2nd ed.). London: Sage.

Truax, C., & Carkhuff, R. (1964). For better or for worse: The process of psychotherapeutic personality change. In B. T. Wigdor (Ed.), *Recent advances in the study of behavior change* (pp. 118–163). Montreal: McGill University Press.

Truax, C., & Carkhuff, R. (1967). *Toward effective counseling and psychotherapy: Training and practice*. Chicago: Aldine-Atherton.

Tsui, P., & Schultz, G. L. (1988). Ethnic factors in group process: Cultural dynamics in multi-ethnic therapy groups. *American Journal of Orthopsychiatry*, *58*, 136–142.

Tuckman, B. (1963). Developmental sequence in small groups. *Psychological Bulletin*, *63*, 384–399.

Turner, H. (2011). Concepts for effective facilitation of open groups. *Social Work with Groups*, *34*(3–4), 246–256.

U

U.S. Department of Health and Human Services. (2003). *Office for Civil Rights: HIPAA*. Retrieved from http://www.hhs.gov/ocr/hipaa/

U.S. Department of Health and Human Services. (2007). Summary of the HIPAA Privacy Rule. Retrieved November 16, 2007, from http://www.hhs.gov/ocr/privacy/hipaa/administrative/privacyrule/index.html

U.S. Department of Health and Human Services, Office of Minority Health. (2001). *Standards of culturally and linguistically appropriate services in health care: Final report*. Retrieved from http://www.OMHRC.govtassetts/pdf/checkerd/finalreport.pdf

U.S. Department of the Interior, Bureau of Indian Affairs. (2015). *Frequently asked questions*. Retrieved from http://www.bia.gov/FAQs/

Ussher, J. (1990). Cognitive behavioral couples therapy with gay men referred for counseling in an AIDS setting: A pilot study. *AIDS Care, 2*, 43–51.

V

Vakalah, H. F., & Khajak, K. (2000). Parent to parent and family to family: Innovative self-help and mutual support. In A. Sallee, H. Lawson, & K. Briar-Lawson (Eds.), *Innovative practices with children and families* (pp. 271–290). Dubuque, IA: Eddie Bowers.

Valencia, R. R., & Black, M. S. (2002). Mexican Americans don't value education! *Journal of Latinos and Education, 1*(2), 81–103.

van der Kolk, B. A. (1993). Group for patients with histories of catastrophic trauma. In A. Alonso & H. I. Swiller (Eds.), *Group therapy in clinical practice* (pp. 289–305). Washington, DC: American Psychological Association.

Van Hook, M. P., Berkman, B., & Dunkle, R. (1996). Assessment tools for general health care settings: PRIME-MD, OARS and SF-36. *Health and Social Work, 21*, 230–235.

Van Souest, D., & Garcia, B. (2003). *Diversity education for social justice*. Alexandria, VA: Council on Social Work Education.

Van Voorhis, R. M., & Hostetter, C. (2006). The impact of MSW education on the social worker empowerment and commitment to client empowerment through social justice advocacy. *Journal of Social Work Education, 47*(1), 105–121.

Van Wormer, K. (2002). Our social work imagination: How social work has not abandoned its mission. *Journal of Teaching in Social Work, 22*(3/4), 21–37.

Van Wormer, K., & Boes, M. (1997). Humor in the emergency room: A social work perspective. *Health and Social Work, 22*(2), 87–92.

VandeCreek, L., Knapp, S., & Herzog, C. (1988). Privileged communication for social workers. *Social Casework, 69*, 28–34.

Varlas, L (2005). Bridging the widest gap: Raising the achievement of black boys. *Education Update, 47*(8), 1, 2, 8.

Vera, E. M., & Speight, S. L. (2003). Multicultural competencies, social justice and counseling psychology: Expanding our roles. *The Counseling Psychologist, 31*, 253–272.

Vodde, R., & Gallant, J. P. (2002). Bridging the gap between micro and macro practice: Larger scale change and a unified model of narrative-deconstructive practice. *Journal of Social Work Education, 38*, 439–458.

Voisin, D. R. (2007). The effects of family and community violence exposure among youth. Recommendations for practice and policy. *Journal of Social Work Education, 43*, 51–64.

Vosler, N. R. (1990). Assessing family access to basic resources: An essential component of social work practice. *Social Work, 35*, 434–441.

Voss, R. W., Douville, V., Little Soldier, A., & Twiss, G. (1999). Tribal and shamanic-based social work practice: A Lakota perspective. *Social Work, 44*, 228–241.

W–X

Wagner, C. C., & Conners, W. (2008, June). Motivational interviewing: Resources for clinicians, researchers, and trainers. Retrieved from http://www.motivationalinterview.org/

Waites, G., MacGowan, J. P., Pennell, J., Carlton-LaNey, I., & Weil, M. (2004). Increasing the cultural responsiveness of family group conferencing. *Social Work, 49*(2), 291–300.

Wakefield, J. C. (1996a). Does social work need the ecosystems perspective? Part 1. Is the perspective clinically useful? *Social Service Review, 70*, 1–32.

Wakefield, J. C. (1996b). Does social work need the ecosystems perspective? Part 2. Does the perspective save social work from incoherence? *Social Service Review, 70*, 183–213.

Walsh, J. (2006). *Theories for direct social work practice*. Belmont, CA: Brooks/Cole.

Walsh, J. (2007). *Endings in clinical practice: Effective closure in diverse settings* (2nd ed.). Chicago: Lyceum Books.

Waltman, G. H. (1996). Amish health care beliefs and practices. In M. C. Julia, *Multicultural awareness in the health care professions*. Needham Heights, MA: Allyn & Bacon.

Warren, K., Franklin, C., & Streeter, C. L. (1998). New directions in systems theory: Chaos and complexity. *Social Work, 43*, 357–372.

Wartel, S. (1991). Clinical considerations for adults abused as children. *Families in Society, 72*, 157–163.

Washington, O., & Moxley, D. (2003). Promising group practices to empower low income minority women coping with chemical dependency. *American Journal of Orthopsychiatry, 73*, 109–116.

Watzlawick, P., Weakland, J., & Fisch, R. (1974). *Change: Principles of problem formulation*. New York: Norton.

Weaver, H. N. (2004). The elements of cultural competence: Application with Native American clients. *Journal of Ethics & Cultural Diversity in Social Work, 13*(1), 19–35.

Webb, N. (2003). *Social work practice with children*. New York: Guilford Press.

Webster-Stratton, C. H. (1984). Randomized trial of two parent-training programs for families with conduct-disordered children. *Journal of Consulting and Clinical Psychology, 52*, 666–678.

Webster-Stratton, C. H., Reid, M. J., & Marsenich, L. (2014). Improving therapist fidelity during implementation of evidence-based practices: Incredible years program. *Psychiatric Services, 65,* 789–795.

Weick, A., & Saleebey, D. (1995). Supporting family strengths: Orienting policy and practice in the 21st century. *Families in Society, 76,* 141–149.

Weil, M. O. (1996). Community building: Building community practice. *Social Work, 41,* 481–499.

Weil, M. O., & Gamble, D. N. (1995). Community practice models. In R. L. Edwards (Ed.), *Encyclopedia of social work* (19th ed., pp. 577–593). Washington, DC: NASW Press.

Weinberg, M. (2006). Pregnant with possibility: The paradoxes of "help" as anti-oppression and discipline with a young single mother. *Families in Society, 67,* 161–169.

Weiner, M. F. (1984). *Techniques of group psychotherapy.* Washington, DC: American Psychiatric Press.

Weiss, C. H. (1998*). Evaluation: Methods for studying programs and policies* (2nd ed.). Upper Saddle River, NJ: Prentice-Hall.

Weiss-Ogden, K. R. (2014). *The relationship between trauma and spiritual well-being of women with substance use disorders* (Doctoral dissertation). Retrieved from ProQuest. (UMI 3624922).

Wells, R. A. (1994). *Planned short-term treatment* (2nd ed.). New York: Free Press.

Wells, R. A., & Gianetti, V. J. (Eds.). (1990). *Handbook of the brief psychotherapies.* New York: Plenum Press.

Wells, S. (2008). Child abuse and neglect. In T. Mizrahi & L. E. Davis (Eds.), *Encyclopedia of social work.* Retrieved from http://www.oxford-naswsocialwork.com/entry?entry=t203.e47

Wenar, C. (1994). *Developmental psychopathology from infancy through adolescence* (3rd ed.). New York: McGraw-Hill.

West, L., Mercer, S. O., & Altheimer, E. (1993). Operation Desert Storm: The response of a social work outreach team. *Social Work in Health Care, 19*(2), 81–98.

Westermeyer, J. J. (1993). Cross-cultural psychiatric assessment. In A. C. Gaw (Ed.), *Culture, ethnicity and mental illness* (pp. 125–146). Washington, DC: American Psychiatric Press.

Whaley, A. L. (1998). Racism in the provision of mental health services: A social cognitive analysis. *American Journal of Orthopsychiatry, 88,* 48–57.

Whaley, A. L., & Davis, K. E. (2007). Cultural competence and evidence-based practice in mental health services: A complementary perspective. *American Psychologist, 62,* 563–574.

Whitaker, C. (1958). Psychotherapy with couples. *American Journal of Psychotherapy, 12,* 18–23.

White, M., & Epston, D. (1990). *Narrative means to therapeutic ends.* New York: Norton.

White, M., & Morgan, A. (2006). *Narrative therapy with families and children.* Adelaide, Australia: Dulwich Centre.

Whittaker, J. K., & Tracy, E. M. (1989). *Social treatment: An introduction to interpersonal helping in social work practice.* New York: Aldine de Gruyter.

Widom, C. S., & Hiller-Sturmhofel, S. (2001). Alcohol abuse as a risk factor for and consequence of child abuse. *Alcohol Research & Health, 25*(1), 52–57.

Wiger, D. E. (2009). *The clinical documentation sourcebook: The complete paperwork resource for your mental health practice* (4th ed.). Hoboken, NJ: Wiley.

Will, G. F. (2007, October 14). Code of coercion. *Washington Post,* p. B7.

Williams, C. C. (2006). The epistemology of cultural competence. *Families in Society, 87,* 209–220.

Williams, J. A., & Stockton, R. (1973). Black family structures and functions: An empirical examination of some suggestions made by Billingsley. *Journal of Marriage and the Family, 35,* 39–49.

Williams, L. F. (1990). The challenge of education to social work: The case for minority children. *Social Work, 35,* 236–242.

Wilper, A. P., Woolhandler, S., Lasser, K. E., McCormick, D., Bor, D. H., & Himmelstein, D. U. (2009). Health insurance and mortality in U.S. adults. *American Journal of Public Health, 99*(12), 2289–2295.

Windle, K., Francis, J., & Coomber, C. (2011). *Preventing loneliness and social isolation: Interventions and outcomes.* Social Care Institute for Excellence, *Research Briefing 39.* Retrieved from http://www.scie.org.uk/publications/briefings/files/briefing39.pdf

Witkin, S. (1993). A human rights approach to social work research and evaluation. In J. Laird (Ed.), *Revisioning social work education: A social constructionist approach.* Binghamton, NY: Haworth Press.

Wodarski, J. S., Holosko, M. J., & Feit, M. D. (Eds.). (2015). *Evidence-informed assessment and practice in child welfare.* New York: Springer.

Wolf, K. T. (1991). The diagnostic and statistical manual and the misdiagnosis of African-Americans: An historical perspective. *Social Work Perspectives, 10*(1), 33–38.

Wolfe, J. L. (1992). Working with gay women. In A. Freeman & F. M. Dattilio (Eds.), *Comprehensive casebook of cognitive therapy* (pp. 249–255). New York: Springer Science + Business Media.

Wong, D. K. (2007). Crucial individuals in the help-seeking pathway of Chinese caregivers of relatives in early psychosis in Hong Kong. *Social Work, 52,* 127–135.

Wood, S. A. (2007). The analysis of an innovative HIV-positive women's support group. *Social Work with Groups, 30,* 9–28.

World Health Organization. (2008). *Suicide prevention (SUPRE).* Retrieved July, 2, 2008, from http://www.who.int/mental_health/prevention/suicide/ suicideprevent/en/index.html

World Health Organization. (2014). *Suicide fact sheet.* Retrieved from http://www.who.int/mediacentre/ factsheets/fs398/en/

World Health Organization. (n.d.). *World Health Organization intimate partner violence and alcohol fact sheet.* Retrieved from http://www.who.int/violence_injury_ prevention/violence/world_report/factsheets/ft_intimate .pdf

Wright, J. H., Basco, M. R., & Thase, M. E. (2006). *Learning cognitive-behavioral therapy: An illustrated guide.* Washington, DC: American Psychiatric Publishing.

Wright, O. L., Jr., & Anderson, J. P. (1998). Clinical social work practice with urban African American families. *Families in Society, 79,* 197–205.

Wright, R. A., Greenberg, J., & Brehm, S. S. (2004). *Motivational analyses of social behavior.* Mahwah, NJ: Erlbaum.

Wright, W. (1999). The use of purpose in ongoing activity groups: A framework for maximizing the therapeutic impact. *Social Work with Groups, 22*(2/3), 33–57.

Wylie, M. S. (1990). Brief therapy on the couch. *Family Therapy Networker, 14,* 26–34, 66.

Xenakis, N., & Primack, S. (2013). Clinical aspects of case management and its role in graduate field education. *Social Work Education, 32*(5), 685–691.

Y

Yaffe, J., Jenson, J. M., & Howard, M. O. (1995). Women and substance abuse: Implications for treatment. *Alcoholism-Treatment Quarterly, 13*(2), 1–15.

Yalom, I. D. (2005). *The theory and practice of group psychotherapy* (5th ed.). New York: Basic Books.

Yamamoto, J., Silva, J. A., Justice, L. R., Chang, C. Y., & Leong, G. B. (1993). *Cross-cultural psychotherapy.* In A. C. Gaw (Ed.), *Culture, ethnicity and mental illness* (pp. 101–124). Washington, DC: American Psychiatric Press.

Yan, M. C. (2008). Exploring cultural tensions in cross-cultural social work practice. *Social Work, 53*(4), 317–327.

Yegidis, B. L., & Weinbach, R. W. (2002). *Research methods for social workers.* Boston: Allyn & Bacon.

Yesavage, J. A., Brink, T. L., Rose, T. L., Lum, O., Huang, V., Adey, M., et al. (1983). Development and validation of a geriatric depression screening scale: A preliminary report. *Journal of Psychiatric Research, 17,* 37–49.

Young, N. K., & Grella, C. E. (1998). Mental health and substance abuse treatment services for dually diagnosed clients: Results of a statewide survey of county administrators. *Journal of Behavioral Health Services and Research, 25*(1), 83–92.

Z

Zastrow, C. H. (2011). *Social work with groups: A comprehensive workbook* (8th ed.). Belmont, CA: Brooks/ Cole.

Zastrow, C. H., & Kirst-Ashman, K. (1990). *Understanding human behavior and the social environment* (2nd ed.). Chicago: Nelson-Hall.

Zeira, A., Astor, R. A., & Benbenishty, R. (2003). School violence in Israel: Findings of a national survey. *Social Work, 48,* 471–483.

Zivin, K., & Kales, H. C. (2008). Adherence to depression treatment in older adults: A narrative review. *Drugs and Aging, 25*(7), 559–571.

Zuckerman, E. L. (2008). *The paper office: The tools to make your psychotherapy practice work ethically, legally and profitably: Forms, guidelines, and resources* (4th ed.). New York: Guilford Press.

Zung, W. (1965). A self-rating depression scale. *Archives of General Psychiatry, 12,* 63–70.

Author Index

Subject Index